HUMAN SEXUALITY
Diversity in Contemporary America

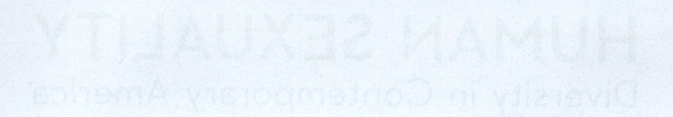

NINTH EDITION

HUMAN SEXUALITY
Diversity in Contemporary America

William L. Yarber

INDIANA UNIVERSITY

Barbara W. Sayad

CALIFORNIA STATE UNIVERSITY, MONTEREY BAY

Mc
Graw
Hill
Education

HUMAN SEXUALITY: DIVERSITY IN CONTEMPORARY AMERICA, NINTH EDITION

Published by McGraw-Hill Education, 2 Penn Plaza, New York, NY 10121. Copyright © 2016 by McGraw-Hill Education. All rights reserved. Printed in the United States of America. Previous editions © 2013, 2010, and 2008. No part of this publication may be reproduced or distributed in any form or by any means, or stored in a database or retrieval system, without the prior written consent of McGraw-Hill Education, including, but not limited to, in any network or other electronic storage or transmission, or broadcast for distance learning.

Some ancillaries, including electronic and print components, may not be available to customers outside the United States.

This book is printed on acid-free paper.

2 3 4 5 6 7 8 9 10 DOW 21 20 19 18 17 16

Student Edition
ISBN 978-0-07-786194-0
MHID 0-07-786194-9

Instructor Review Edition
978-1-259-68062-5
1-259-68062-2

Senior Vice President, Products & Markets:
  Kurt L. Strand
Vice President, General Manager, Products &
  Markets: *Michael Ryan*
Vice President, Content Design & Delivery:
  Kimberly Meriwether David
Managing Director: *William Glass*
Executive Director: *Krista Bettino*
Senior Brand Manager: *Nancy Welcher*
Director, Product Development: *Meghan Campbell*
Lead Product Developer: *Dawn Groundwater*
Senior Product Developer: *Sarah Colwell*
Marketing Managers: *Ann Helgerson, Christina Yu*
Digital Product Analyst: *Neil Kahn*
Editorial Coordinator: *Elisa Odoardi*

Director, Content Design & Delivery: *Terri Schiesl*
Program Manager: *Debra Hash*
Content Project Managers: *Sandy Wille;*
  Amber Bettcher
Buyer: *Jennifer Pickel*
Design: *Matt Diamond*
Content Licensing Specialists: (photo)
  Melissa Homer; (text) *Beth Thole*
Cover Image: (small photos left to right) © *Zhang*
  Bo/Getty Images; © *Thomas Barwick/Getty*
  Images; © *Tony Garcia/Corbis;* © *John Shepherd/*
  Getty Images; © *Alamy Images;* © *Matt Dutile/*
  Corbis. (large photo) © *Getty Images*
Compositor: *Lumina Datamatics, Inc.*
Printer: *LSC Communications*

All credits appearing on page or at the end of the book are considered to be an extension of the copyright page.

Library of Congress Cataloging-in-Publication Data
Yarber, William L. (William Lee), 1943-
  Human sexuality: diversity in contemporary America / William L. Yarber, Indiana University,
Barbara W. Sayad, California State University, Monterey Bay.—Ninth edition.
    p. cm.
Includes bibliographical references and index.
  ISBN 978-0-07-786194-0 (alk. paper)
  1. Sex.   2. Sex customs.   3. Sexual health.   I. Sayad, Barbara Werner.   II. Title.

HQ21.S8126 2016
306.7—dc23

2015015172

The Internet addresses listed in the text were accurate at the time of publication. The inclusion of a website does not indicate an endorsement by the authors or McGraw-Hill Education, and McGraw-Hill Education does not guarantee the accuracy of the information presented at these sites.

mheducation.com/highered

Dedication

This book is dedicated to Ryan White, an Indiana native-son who died from AIDS on April 8, 1990.

During his illness Ryan experienced public scorn, harassment, and rejection, yet faced these difficulties with courage, dignity, and grace. He became the poster boy for the AIDS crisis, speaking out against the misconceptions about the disease and calling for persons with AIDS to be treated with compassion.

Ryan died at age 18, the spring before he planned to attend Indiana University (IU), Bloomington. To honor the legacy of Ryan, the Rural Center for AIDS/STD Prevention at IU established the Ryan White Distinguished Leadership Award for recognition of significant national/international leadership in HIV/AIDS prevention and the Ryan White Legacy Scholarship for IU Masters of Public Health students.

Sir Elton John said, "I have met a lot of people who were brave and courageous. . . . Ryan White gave a new meaning to these words. . . . He was a miracle of humanity."

—W. L. Y.

This book is dedicated to the students of human sexuality who quest for knowledge and understanding, to the instructors who diligently and compassionately support and inspire them, and to a system of governing that advocates for the sexual rights of all people.

I want my family to know that I cannot do this work without their love and support.

—B. W. S.

Brief Contents

Contents

2 Studying Human Sexuality 27

3 Female Sexual Anatomy, Physiology, and Response 65

4 Male Sexual Anatomy, Physiology, and Response 102

5 Gender and Gender Roles   122

6 Sexuality in Childhood and Adolescence 155

7 Sexuality in Adulthood 184

8 Love and Communication in Intimate Relationships 214

11 Contraception and Abortion 322

14 Sexual Function Difficulties, Dissatisfaction, Enhancement, and Therapy 429

15 Sexually Transmitted Infections 479

16 HIV and AIDS   516

17 Sexual Coercion   557

18 Sexually Explicit Materials, Prostitution, and Sex Laws   601

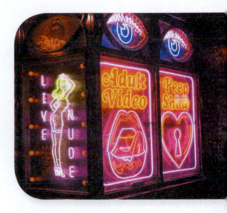

connect McGraw-Hill Education Psychology's APA Documentation Style Guide

Celebrating Sexual Diversity in Contemporary America

Since the first edition, *Human Sexuality: Diversity in Contemporary America* has presented students with a nonjudgmental view of human sexuality while encouraging them to become proactive about their own sexual well-being and identity. This sex-positive approach, combined with an integrated exploration of cultural diversity and contemporary research, continues today and includes an emphasis on the importance of affirming and supporting intimacy, pleasuring, and mutual satisfaction in sexual expression. Yarber and Sayad encourage students to critically assess their own values and modes of sexual expression while connecting them to research.

The new edition integrates SmartBook, a personalized learning program, offering students the insight they need to study smarter and improve classroom results.

Better Data, Smarter Revision, Improved Results

Students helped inform the revision strategy:

STEP 1. Over the course of three years, data points showing concepts that caused students the most difficulty were anonymously collected from McGraw-Hill Education Connect for Human Sexuality's LearnSmart® adaptive learning system.

STEP 2. The authors were provided with data from LearnSmart that graphically illustrated "hot spots" in the text impacting student learning (see following image).

STEP 3. The authors used the heat map data to refine content and reinforce student comprehension in the new edition. Additional quiz questions and assignable activities were created for use in Connect for Human Sexuality to further support student success.

RESULT: With empirically based feedback at the paragraph and even sentence level, the authors developed the new edition using precise student data to pinpoint concepts that caused students to struggle.

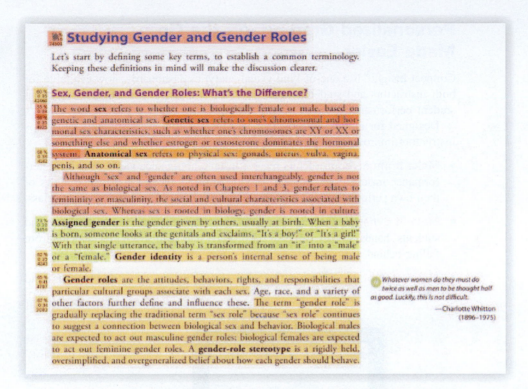

Studying Gender and Gender Roles

Let's start by defining some key terms, to establish a common terminology. Keeping these definitions in mind will make the discussion clearer.

Sex, Gender, and Gender Roles: What's the Difference?

The word **sex** refers to whether one is biologically female or male, based on genetic and anatomical sex. **Genetic sex** refers to one's chromosomal and hormonal sex characteristics, such as whether one's chromosomes are XY or XX or something else and whether estrogen or testosterone dominates the hormonal system. **Anatomical sex** refers to physical sex: gonads, uterus, vulva, vagina, penis, and so on.

Although "sex" and "gender" are often used interchangeably, gender is not the same as biological sex. As noted in Chapters 1 and 3, gender relates to femininity or masculinity, the social and cultural characteristics associated with biological sex. Whereas sex is rooted in biology, gender is rooted in culture. **Assigned gender** is the gender given by others, usually at birth. When a baby is born, someone looks at the genitals and exclaims, "It's a boy!" or "It's a girl!" With that single utterance, the baby is transformed from an "it" into a "male" or a "female." **Gender identity** is a person's internal sense of being male or female.

Gender roles are the attitudes, behaviors, rights, and responsibilities that particular cultural groups associate with each sex. Age, race, and a variety of other factors further define and influence these. The term "gender role" is gradually replacing the traditional term "sex role" because "sex role" continues to suggest a connection between biological sex and behavior. Biological males are expected to act out masculine gender roles; biological females are expected to act out feminine gender roles. A **gender-role stereotype** is a rigidly held, oversimplified, and overgeneralized belief about how each gender should behave.

> Whatever women do they must do twice as well as men to be thought half as good. Luckily, this is not difficult.
> —Charlotte Whitton (1896–1975)

LEARNSMART®

LearnSmart is an adaptive learning program designed to help students learn faster, study smarter, and retain more knowledge for greater success. Distinguishing what students know from what they don't, and focusing on concepts they are most likely to forget, LearnSmart continuously adapts to each student's needs by building an individual learning path. Millions of students have answered over a billion questions in LearnSmart since 2009, making it the most widely used and intelligent adaptive study tool that's proven to strengthen memory recall, keep students in class, and boost grades.

SMARTBOOK®

Fueled by LearnSmart, SmartBook is the first and only adaptive reading experience currently available.

Make It Effective.   SmartBook creates a personalized reading experience by highlighting the most impactful concepts a student needs to learn at that moment in time. This ensures that every minute spent with SmartBook is returned to the student as the most value-added minute possible.

Make It Informed.   Real-time reports quickly identify the concepts that require more attention from individual students—or the entire class.

Personalized Grading, on the Go, Made Easier

Connect Insight® is a one-of-kind visual analytics dashboard—now available for both instructors and students—that provides at-a-glance information regarding student performance.

Designed for mobile devices, Connect Insight empowers students and helps instructors improve class performance.

- **Make it intuitive.** Instructors receive instant, at-a-glance views of student performance matched with student activity. Students receive at-a-glance views of their own performance and how they are doing compared to the rest of the class.

- **Make it dynamic.** Connect Insight puts real-time analytics in instructors' and students' hands, so they can take action early and keep struggling students from falling behind.

- **Make it mobile.** Connect Insight is available on-demand wherever, and whenever, it's needed.

Experience the Course You Want to Teach

The **Instructor Resources** have been updated to reflect changes to the new edition; these can be accessed by faculty through Connect Psychology. Resources include the test bank, instructor's manual, PowerPoint presentation, and image gallery.

Easily rearrange chapters, combine material, and quickly upload content you have written, such as your course syllabus or teaching notes, using **McGraw-Hill Education Create**. Find the content you need by searching through thousands of leading McGraw-Hill Education textbooks. Arrange your book to fit your teaching style. Create even allows you to personalize your book's appearance by selecting the cover and adding your name, school, and course information. Order a Create book, and you will receive a complimentary print review copy in three to five business days or a complimentary electronic review copy via e-mail in about an hour. Experience how McGraw-Hill Education empowers you to teach your students your way: http://create.mheducation.com

Capture lessons and lectures in a searchable format for use in traditional, hybrid, "flipped classes" and online courses by using **Tegrity** (http://www.tegrity.com). Its personalized learning features make study time efficient, and its affordability brings this benefit to every student on campus. Patented search technology and real-time Learning Management System (LMS) integrations make Tegrity the market-leading solution and service.

McGraw-Hill Education Campus (www.mhcampus.com) provides faculty with true single sign-on access to all of McGraw-Hill Education's course content, digital tools, and other high-quality learning resources from any LMS. This innovative offering allows for secure and deep integration, enabling seamless access for faculty and students to any of McGraw-Hill Education's course solutions, such as McGraw-Hill Education Connect® (all-digital teaching and learning platform), McGraw-Hill Education Create (state-of-the-art custom-publishing platform), McGraw-Hill Education LearnSmart (online adaptive study tool), and Tegrity (fully searchable lecture-capture service).

McGraw-Hill Education Campus includes access to McGraw-Hill Education's entire content library, including ebooks, assessment tools, presentation slides, multimedia content, and other resources. McGraw-Hill Education Campus provides instructors with open, unlimited access to prepare for class, create tests/quizzes, develop lecture material, integrate interactive content, and more.

Annual Editions: Human Sexualities

This volume offers diverse topics on sex and sexuality with regard to the human experience. *Learning Outcomes, Critical Thinking* questions, and *Internet References* accompany each article to further enhance learning. Customize this title via **McGraw-Hill Create** at http://create.mheducation.com.

Taking Sides: Clashing Views in Human Sexuality

This debate-style reader both reinforces and challenges students' viewpoints on the most crucial issues in human sexuality today. Each topic offers current and lively pro and con essays that represent the arguments of leading scholars and commentators in their fields. *Learning Outcomes,* an *Issue Summary,* and an *Issue Introduction* set the stage for each debate topic. Following each issue is the *Exploring the Issue* section with *Critical Thinking and Reflection* questions, *Is There Common Ground?* commentary, *Additional Resources,* and *Internet References* all designed to stimulate and challenge the student's thinking and to further explore the topic. Customize this title via **McGraw-Hill Create** at http://create.mheducation.com.

Chapter-by-Chapter Changes

The research on sexuality is ever increasing, thereby providing the material to allow this new edition to be current and relevant. This new edition is based on the trends, data, and laws from 2012–2015, including the U.S. Supreme Court's ruling that legalized same-sex marriage in all 50 states, the role of media in singlehood, dating, and partnerships, expanding definitions and meanings of gender and gender identity; increased focus on sexual desire, pleasure, and satisfaction; and how the *DSM-5* has reframed paraphilic behavior and sexual function difficulties. *Human Sexuality: Diversity in Contemporary America* addresses these and many other important changes in the field.

Chapter 1: Perspectives on Human Sexuality

- Updated and expanded material on media use and its impact on teens
- New data on social networking
- New *Think About It* box: "Before Pressing 'Send': Trends and Concerns About Texting, Sexting, and Dating"
- New data on online dating sites
- Updated language used to describe gender and gender identity
- Updated Declaration of Sexual Rights

Chapter 2: Studying Human Sexuality

- New *Think About It* box: "Does Sex Have an Inherent Meaning?"
- Expanded discussion of computer-based technology and the Internet for the collection of sexuality-related research data
- Expanded presentation of the Kinsey Heterosexual-Homosexual Rating Scale
- Findings of the latest Centers for Disease Control Youth Risk Behavior Survey
- Findings of the latest American College Health Association research on college student sexual behavior
- Expanded discussion of African American sexuality

Chapter 3: Female Sexual Anatomy, Physiology, and Response

- Continued discussion and research on the G-spot
- New research on sexual fluidity

- Expanded discussion about the role of female desire
- New *Think About It* box: "'Did You Come?' What College Students Think About Women's Orgasms During Heterosexual Sex"

Chapter 4: Male Sexual Anatomy, Physiology, and Response

- Increased discussion about men's hormone cycles
- Updated and new to Chapter 4 *Think About It* box: "'Oh to Be Bigger': Breast and Penis Enhancement" with added discussion on the significance of a man's penis size
- Discussion of the biological differences between men's and women's orgasms
- Update on the sexual health of men

Chapter 5: Gender and Gender Roles

- Changing terminology and laws related to gender
- New steps that college campuses can take to address sexual violence
- Added emphasis about the ways in which contemporary sexual scripts can influence attitudes and behaviors
- New "Tips for Allies of Transgender People"
- New *DSM-5* diagnosis and explanation of gender dysphoria
- New material on disorders of sex development
- Updated and re-titled *Think About It* box: "A Cautious Approach to Addressing Disorders of Sexual Development (DSD) in Children"
- Expanded discussion of transgender
- Updated and re-titled *Think About It* box: "Psychological and Medical Treatment of Gender Dysphoria"

Chapter 6: Sexuality in Childhood and Adolescence

- Review of literature on early adolescence and precocious puberty and its impact on boys and girls
- Expanded discussion on the harassment of GLBT adolescents and its impact on behavior
- Updated data on teen sexuality and research about what predisposes teens to sexual behavior
- New discussion about first intercourse and the varied cultural and personal meanings young people give to it
- Introduction to the President's Teen Pregnancy Prevention Initiative, which replaces abstinence-only programs
- New *Think About It* box: "Healthy Teen Sexuality"

Chapter 7: Sexuality in Adulthood

- New discussion of Centers for Disease Control's data related to sexual orientation and its impact on government funding and research decisions
- Expanded discussion about bisexuality
- Updated discussion on the motivations for college students to have sex

- New material on men having sex with men and racial and ethnic identity
- New data on rates of cohabitation, same-sex marriage, and parenthood

Chapter 8: Love and Communication in Intimate Relationships

- New *Think About It* box: "Let's (Not) Talk About Sex: Avoiding the Discussion About Past Lovers"
- Expanded discussion on the health of children raised by gay and lesbian parents
- Updates in the *Think About It* box: "The Science of Love"
- New data on extradyadic relationships and the motivations for nonexclusiveness
- Added discussion about and motivations for "rebound sex"
- Expanded scale in the *Practically Speaking* box: "Communication Patterns and Partner Satisfaction"
- New discussion on argumentation and the resolution of conflicts

Chapter 9: Sexual Expression

- Expanded discussion on factors that influence sexual attractiveness
- New material on the similarities and differences in sexual desire and desired traits of a potential sexual partner of same-sex and mixed-sex individuals
- New summary of the results of studies related to the Sexual Strategies Theory
- Expanded discussion and new research on the prevalence, sexual behaviors, and outcomes of hooking up among college students
- Updated and re-titled *Think About It* box: "Hooking Up Among College Students: As Simple As One Might Think?"
- New research on sexual scripts among college students
- Expanded discussion of the sexual repertoires of same-sex and opposite-sex couples
- New research on the meaning of the first kiss with a possible new romantic partner and the role of kissing in exclusive relationships
- New data on college women's attitudes toward and experiences with cunnilingus

Chapter 10: Variations in Sexual Behavior

- Updated discussion of sexual paraphilias based on the American Psychiatric Association (APA) *Diagnostic and Statistical Manual of Mental Disorders—5th Edition* (DSM-5)
- New discussion of the distinction between APA paraphilias (relatively harmless variant sexual behavior) and APA paraphilic disorders (relatively harmful variant sexual behavior)

- Discussion of the changes in the *DSM-5* description of paraphilias compared to *DSM-IV-TR* description
- New *Think About It* box: "Classifying Variant Sexual Behaviors as Paraphilia: The Changing Medical Views of Psychology"
- Expanded and updated discussion of sex addiction in the *Think About It* box: "'Sexual Addiction': Repressive Morality in a New Guise?"

Chapter 11: Contraception and Abortion

- Updated material about navigating reproductive health, including a brief history of contraception, Title X, and Affordable Health Care
- Added discussion on long-acting reversible contraceptive methods (LARCs)
- Complete review and update of contraceptive methods
- New information about breastfeeding and hormonal methods of birth control
- New data on the rates of abortion

Chapter 12: Conception, Pregnancy, and Childbirth

- Updated data on pregnancies, by race and ethnicity, and marital status
- Increased focus on preconception and prenatal care
- Expanded discussion on maternal obesity
- Updates on male and female infertility and assisted reproductive technologies
- Revised *Think About It* box: "The Question of Male Circumcision"
- Updated and expanded discussion on breastfeeding

Chapter 13: The Sexual Body in Health and Illness

- New *Think About It* box: "Body Image and Sexuality: Are They One and the Same?"
- New focus on myths about disability and sexuality
- Thorough revision of statistics, research, and new and controversial guidelines for the detection of breast cancer
- Discussion of sexual adjustment following breast cancer treatment
- New screening recommendations for cervical cancer and prostate cancer
- New material on sexual orientation and health, especially as they relate to disparities and discrimination

Chapter 14: Sexual Function Difficulties, Dissatisfaction, Enhancement, and Therapy

- Updated *Think About It* box: "Is Intercourse Enough? The Big 'O' and Sexual Behaviors"
- Updated discussion of sexual function difficulties based on the American Psychiatric Association (APA) *Diagnostic and Statistical Manual of Mental Disorders—5th Edition (DSM-5)*
- Discussion of the changes in the *DSM-5* description of sexual dysfunctions compared to the *DSM-IV-TR* description

- New data on sexual function difficulties among men and women with same-sex or opposite-sex partners and lesbian and heterosexual women
- Discussion of a new *DSM-5* category: substance/medication-induced sexual dysfunction
- New discussion of the hierarchy of sexual behaviors
- New *Think About It* box: "My Partner Could Be a Better Lover If . . . : What Men and Women Want From Their Sexual Partners"
- New material on strategies to cope with sexual difficulties
- Updated *Think About It* box: "The Medicalization of Sexual Function Problems"

Chapter 15: Sexually Transmitted Infections

- Updated information on the prevalence and incidence of major STIs
- Updated medical information on the major STIs
- Expanded discussion on the role of male and female condoms in STI prevention
- New stances of the Centers for Disease Control and Prevention American Academy of Pediatrics on the impact of male circumcision in stopping the spread of HIV infection and other STIs
- Information on a new HPV vaccination
- Expanded discussion of the impact of HPV vaccination on sexual behavior
- Added discussion of the role of STI testing in preventing STIs

Chapter 16: HIV and AIDS

- Updated information on the prevalence and incidence of HIV/AIDS in the United States and worldwide
- New discussion on the worldwide progress in reducing new HIV infections, the recent decrease in annual HIV diagnoses, and stability of new HIV infections in the United States
- Updated biological information on HIV/AIDS
- Expanded discussion on the impact of HIV stigma
- Expanded discussion of myths and modes of HIV transmission and estimated lifetime risk for HIV diagnosis
- Updated and expanded discussion of HIV/AIDS among minority races/ethnicities and sexual minorities
- New and expanded discussion of pre-exposure prophylaxis and new material on post-exposure prophylaxis
- Updated information on HIV testing and treatment

Chapter 17: Sexual Coercion

- New and expanded information on stalking and sexual harassment in the military and public places
- Updated information on sexual harassment, discrimination, legal equality, and rejection of GLBT persons

- New material on the lifetime prevalence of men and women who have experienced sexual violence
- Updated and expanded information on preventing sexual assault
- New material on campus sexual violence, including sexual coercion strategies of both men and women
- New *Think About It* box: "Can Men and Women Accurately Judge a Partner's Willingness to Have Casual Sex?"
- New *Think About It* box: "How College Students Indicate and Interpret Consent to Have Sex"
- New material on strategies men and women employ to obtain sexual contact with unwilling partners
- New information on the mental health and sexual functioning of persons who experience sexual violence

Chapter 18: Sexually Explicit Materials, Prostitution, and Sex Laws

- New material on the 2015 U.S. Supreme Court's ruling that legalized same-sex marriage in all 50 states
- New material on the consumption of sexually explicit materials, including men's and women's preferences for various types of visual sexual stimuli
- New research on the content of sexually explicit videos and the characteristics of "porn stars"
- New *Think About It* box: "Sexually Explicit Material Use in Romantic Couples: Beneficial or Harmful?"
- Expanded discussion on viewing sexually explicit videos and college students, including its relationship with hooking up
- New material on whether the label "porn addiction" is accepted among mental health professionals
- Expanded and updated discussion on research to determine any influence of pornography consumption on sexual aggression
- Expanded and updated information on female and male prostitution, why individuals become prostitutes, and the characteristics of clients who pay for sex with male escorts
- Updated and re-titled *Think About It* box: "Sex Trafficking: A Modern-Day Slavery"

• Acknowledgments

In addition to student user feedback through McGraw-Hill Education's Learn-Smart, feedback from instructor reviews were instrumental in guiding this revision. Special thanks to the following:

Daria A. Bakina, *SUNY Oswego*

Coreen Haym, *University of Nevada at Las Vegas*

Nancy King, *Western Michigan University*

Jennifer Mewes, *Pima Community College*

Elizabeth Morgan, *Springfield College*

Jonathan Moss, *William Paterson University*

Helen J. Powell, *Wayne State University*

Mary E. Ramey, *University of Illinois at Urbana-Champaign*

Marie Wallace, *Pima Community College, Northwest Campus*

Anthony D. Yankowski, *Bergen Community College*

We would also like to thank our team at McGraw-Hill Education: Nancy Welcher, Senior Brand Manager, Lead Product Developer Dawn Groundwater, Senior Product Developer Sarah Colwell, Product Developer Joni Fraser, Senior Marketing Managers AJ Laferrera, Ann Helgerson, and Christina Yu, Content Production Manager Sandy Wille, Content Licensing Specialists Beth Thole (text), Keri Johnson and Melissa Homer (photo), and Matt Diamond Designer. Additional thanks go out to: Alijah Marquez personal assistant and input editor, Angie Sigwarth and Christopher Greene, freelance proofreaders, and David Tietz, freelance photo researcher.

Letter From the Authors

"Sex is like dynamite. . . . It can be the cement of a relationship, but it can be the level that breaks people apart."

—Joseph Fletcher
(1905–1991)

When students first enter a human sexuality class, they may feel excited, nervous, and uncomfortable, all at the same time. These feelings are common. This is because the more an area of life is judged "off limits" to public and private discussion the less likely it is to be understood and embraced. Yet, sex surrounds us and impacts our lives every day from the provocative billboard ad on the highway, to the steamy social media images of the body, to men's and women's fashions, and to prime-time television dramas. People *want* to learn about the role and meaning of human sexuality in their lives and how to live healthy psychologically and physically, yet they often do not know whom to ask or what sources to trust. In our quest for knowledge and understanding, we *need* to maintain an intellectual curiosity. Author William Arthur Ward observes, "Curiosity is the wick in the candle of learning."

Students begin studying sexuality for many reasons: to gain insights into their sexuality and relationships, to become more comfortable with their sexuality, to learn how to enhance sexual pleasure for themselves and their partners, to explore personal sexual issues, to dispel anxieties and doubts, to validate their sexual identity, to avoid and resolve traumatic sexual experiences, and to learn how to avoid STIs and unintended pregnancies. Many students find the study of human sexuality empowering; they develop the ability to make intelligent sexual choices based on reputable information and their own needs, desires, and values rather than on stereotypical, haphazard, unreliable, incomplete, or unrealistic information; oppressive cultural dictums; or guilt, fear, or conformity. They learn to differentiate between what they have been told about their own sexuality and what they truly believe; that is, they begin to own their sexuality. Those studying this subject often report that they feel more appreciative and less apologetic, defensive, or shameful about their sexual feelings, attractions, and desires.

Particularly in a country as diverse as the United States, the study of human sexuality calls for us to be open-minded: to be receptive to new ideas and to various perspectives; to respect those with different experiences, values, orientations, ages, abilities, and ethnicities; to seek to understand what we have not understood before; to reexamine old assumptions, ideas, and beliefs; and to embrace and accept the humanness and uniqueness in each of us.

Sexuality can be a source of great pleasure and, yes, the "cement" of a relationship. Through it, we can reveal ourselves, connect with others on the most intimate levels, create strong bonds, and bring new life into the world. Paradoxically, though, sexuality can also be a source of guilt and confusion, anger and disappointment, a pathway to infection, and a means of exploitation and aggression. We hope that by examining the multiple aspects of human sexuality presented in this book, you will come to understand, embrace, and appreciate your own sexuality and the unique individuality of sexuality among others, to learn how to make healthy sexual choices for yourself, to integrate and balance your sexuality into your life as a natural health-enhancing component, and to express your sexuality with partners in sharing, nonexploitive, and nurturing ways.

William L. Yarber
Barbara W. Sayad

About the Authors

William L. Yarber

WILLIAM L. YARBER is professor of applied health science and affiliated faculty member in gender studies at Indiana University, Bloomington. He is also a senior research fellow at The Kinsey Institute for Research in Sex, Gender, and Reproduction and the senior director of the Rural Center for AIDS/STD Prevention at Indiana University.

Dr. Yarber, who received his doctorate from Indiana University, has authored or co-authored numerous scientific reports on sexual risk behavior and AIDS/STI prevention in professional journals and has received federal and state grants to support his research and prevention activities. He is a member of The Kinsey Institute Condom Use Research Team (CURT), comprised of researchers from Indiana University, University of Kentucky, University of Guelph (Canada), and University of Southampton (United Kingdom). For over 15 years, with federal and institutional research support, CURT has investigated male condom use errors and problems and has developed behavioral interventions designed to improve correct and consistent condom use.

At the request of the U.S. federal government, Dr. Yarber authored the country's first secondary school AIDS prevention education curriculum, *AIDS: What Young People Should Know* (1987). He also co-edited the *Handbook of Sexuality-Related Measures,* third edition (2011). Dr. Yarber and Dr. Sayad's textbook *Human Sexuality: Diversity in Contemporary America* (McGraw-Hill), which is used in colleges and universities throughout the United States, was published in 2012 by the Beijing World Publishing Company as the most up-to-date text on human sexuality published in China in the past half century. Also in 2012, the text was published in Korea.

Dr. Yarber chaired the National Guidelines Task Force, which developed the *Guidelines for Comprehensive Sexuality Education: Kindergarten–12th Grade* (1991, 1996, 2004), published by the Sexuality Information and Education Council of the United States (SIECUS) and adapted in six countries worldwide. Dr. Yarber is past president of The Society for the Scientific Study of Sexuality (SSSS) and a past chair of the SIECUS board of directors. His awards include the SSSS Distinguished Scientific Achievement Award; the Professional Standard of Excellence Award from the American Association of Sex Educators, Counselors, and Therapists; the Indiana University President's Award for Distinguished Teaching; and the inaugural Graduate Student Outstanding Faculty Mentor Award at Indiana University.

Dr. Yarber has been a consultant to the World Health Organization Global Program on AIDS as well as sexuality-related organizations in Brazil, China, Jamaica, Poland, Portugal, and Taiwan. He regularly teaches undergraduate and graduate courses in human sexuality. He was previously a faculty member at Purdue University and the University of Minnesota, as well as a public high school health science and biology teacher. Dr. Yarber endowed at Indiana University, for perpetuity, the world's first professorship in sexual health, the William L. Yarber Professorship in Sexual Health.

Barbara Werner Sayad

BARBARA WERNER SAYAD is a consummate teacher, trainer, writer, and consultant. As a recently retired faculty member from California State University, Monterey Bay, Dr. Sayad has taught a wide variety of courses, including human sexuality, women's health, community health education, multi-cultural health education and promotion, and senior capstone. Her work in the classroom has earned her several nominations for outstanding faculty member and she has and continues to serve as a McNair Scholars mentor. Additionally, she has chaired a number of university committees, spoken at dozens of university-related events, and trained and collaborated with other faculty members in areas related to public health and personal well-being.

Dr. Sayad has presented her work at a variety of institutions, most significant of which is focused on comprehensive sexuality education programming. One that she is most proud of is her alliance with Aibai, the largest GLBT organization in China, where she traveled with her co-author, Dr. Yarber, to present to the Asian Conference on Sexual Education. There she also provided training for American delegates and Chinese scholars at the U.S. Embassy, U.S. State Department, and UNESCO and was invited to speak at Xixi, the equivalent of a TED Talk, in Shanghai.

The vast majority of Dr. Sayad's 34-year career has been connected to issues of social justice: women's reproductive rights, GLBT education and advocacy, and health access. As a result of this focus coupled with her global travels, she has contributed to a variety of health-related texts, curricular guides, and publications and has facilitated a wide array of training programs, presented at professional conferences, and worked as a trainer and curriculum specialist.

Dr. Sayad holds a Bachelor of Science degree in Foods and Nutrition, a Masters degree in Public Health, and a PhD in health services.

Dr. Sayad is most proud of her three children, new grandchild, and extended family and is eternally grateful to be married for 33 years to Dr. Robert Sayad.

Perspectives on Human Sexuality

CHAPTER OUTLINE

"The media, especially magazines and television, has had an influence on shaping my sexual identity. Ever since I was a little girl, I have watched the women on TV and hoped I would grow up to look sexy and beautiful like them. I feel that because of the constant barrage of images of beautiful women on TV and in magazines young girls like me grow up with unrealistic expectations of what beauty is and are doomed to feel they have not met this exaggerated standard."

—21-year-old female

"The phone, television, and Internet became my best friends. I never missed an episode of any of the latest shows, and I knew all the words to every new song. And when Facebook entered my life, I finally felt connected. At school, we would talk about status updates: whom we thought was cute, relationship status, and outrageous photos. All of the things we saw were all of the things we fantasized about. These are the things we would talk about."

—23-year-old female

"Though I firmly believe that we are our own harshest critics, I also believe that the media have a large role in influencing how we think of ourselves. I felt like ripping my hair out every time I saw a skinny model whose stomach was as hard and flat as a board, with their flawless skin and perfectly coifed hair. I cringed when I realized that my legs seemed to have an extra 'wiggle-jiggle' when I walked. All I could do was watch the television and feel abashed at the differences in their bodies compared to mine. When magazines and films tell me that for my age I should weigh no more than a hundred pounds, I feel like saying, 'Well, gee, it's no wonder I finally turned to laxatives with all these pressures to be thin surrounding me.' I ached to be model-thin and pretty. This fixation to be as beautiful and coveted as these models so preoccupied me that I had no time to even think about anyone or anything else."

—18-year-old female

"I am aware that I may be lacking in certain areas of my sexual self-esteem, but I am cognizant of my shortcomings and am willing to work on them. A person's sexual self-esteem isn't something that is detached from his or her daily life. It is intertwined in every aspect of life and how one views his or her self: emotionally, physically, and mentally. For my own sake, as well as my daughter's, I feel it is important for me to develop and model a healthy sexual self-esteem."

—28-year-old male

> *Nature is to be reverenced, not blushed at.*
>
> —Tertullian
> (c. 155 CE–c. 220 CE)

Sexuality was once hidden from view in our culture: Fig leaves covered the "private parts" of nudes; poultry breasts were renamed "white meat"; censors prohibited the publication of the works of D. H. Lawrence, James Joyce, and Henry Miller; and homosexuality was called "the love that dares not speak its name." But over the past few generations, sexuality has become more open. In recent years, popular culture and the media have transformed what we "know" about sexuality. Not only is sexuality *not* hidden from view; it often seems to surround and embed itself into all aspects of our lives.

In this chapter, we discuss why we study human sexuality and examine popular culture and the media to see how they shape our ideas about sexuality. Then we look at how sexuality has been conceptualized in different cultures and at different times in history. Finally, we examine how society defines various aspects of our sexuality as natural or normal.

● Studying Human Sexuality

The study of human sexuality differs from the study of accounting, plant biology, and medieval history, for example, because human sexuality is surrounded by a vast array of taboos, fears, prejudices, and hypocrisy. For many, sexuality creates ambivalent feelings. It is linked not only with intimacy and pleasure but also with shame, guilt, and discomfort. As a result, you may find yourself confronted with society's mixed feelings about sexuality as you study it. You may find, for example, that others perceive you as somehow "unique" or "different" for taking this course. Some may feel threatened in a vague, undefined way. Parents, partners, or spouses (or your own children, if you are a parent) may wonder why you want to take a "sex class"; they may want to know why you don't take something more "serious"—as if sexuality were not one of the most important issues we face as individuals and as a society. Sometimes this uneasiness manifests itself in humor, one of the ways in which we deal with ambivalent feelings: "You mean you have to take a *class* on sex?" "Are there labs?" "Why don't you let me show you?"

Ironically, despite societal ambivalence, you may quickly find that your human sexuality text or ebook becomes the most popular book in your dormitory or apartment. "I can never find my textbook when I need it," one of our students complained. "My roommates are always reading it. And they're not even taking the course!" Another student observed: "My friends used to kid me about taking the class, but now the first thing they ask when they see me is what we discussed in class." "People borrow my book so often without asking," writes one student, "that I hide it now."

As you study human sexuality, you will find yourself exploring topics not ordinarily discussed in other classes. Sometimes they are rarely talked about even among friends. They may be prohibited by family, religious, or cultural teaching. For this reason, behaviors such as masturbation and sexual fantasizing are often the source of considerable guilt and shame. But in your human sexuality course, these topics will be examined objectively. You may be surprised to discover, in fact, that part of your learning involves *unlearning* myths, factual errors, distortions, biases, and prejudices you learned previously.

Sexuality may be the most taboo subject you study as an undergraduate, but your comfort level in class will probably increase as you recognize that you and your fellow students have a common purpose in learning about sexuality. Your sense of ease may also increase as you and your classmates get to know one another and discuss sexuality, both inside and outside the class. You may find that, as you become accustomed to using the accepted sexual vocabulary, you are more comfortable discussing various topics. For example, your communication with a partner may improve, which will strengthen your relationship and increase sexual satisfaction for both of you. You may never before have used the word *masturbation, clitoris*, or *penis* in a class setting or any kind of setting, for that matter. But after a while, using these and other terms may become second nature to you. You may discover that discussing sexuality academically becomes as easy as discussing computer science, astronomy, or literature. You may even find yourself, as many students do, discussing with your friends what you learned in class while on a bus or in a restaurant, as other passengers or diners gasp in surprise or lean toward you to hear better!

Studying sexuality requires respect for your fellow students. You'll discover that the experiences and values of your classmates vary greatly. Some have little sexual experience, while others have a lot of experience; some students hold progressive sexual values, while others hold conservative ones. Some students are gay, lesbian, queer, bisexual, or asexual individuals, while the majority are heterosexual people. Most students are young, others middle-aged, some

Educating the mind without educating the heart is no education at all.

—Aristotle
(384 B.C.–322 B.C.)

Taking a course in human sexuality is like no other college experience. It requires that students examine their sexual beliefs and behaviors in the context of a wide variety of social and cultural factors and incorporate this new perspective into their sexual lives and well-being.

© Andersen Ross/Getty Images

older—each in a different stage of life and with different developmental tasks before them. Furthermore, the presence of students from any of the numerous ethnic groups in the United States reminds us that there is no single behavior, attitude, value, or sexual norm that encompasses sexuality in contemporary America. Finally, as your sexuality evolves you will find that you will become more accepting of yourself as a sexual human being. From this, you will truly "own" your sexuality.

• Sexuality, Popular Culture, and the Media

Much of sexuality is influenced and shaped by popular culture, especially the mass media. Popular culture presents us with myriad images of what it means to be sexual. But what kinds of sexuality do the media portray for our consumption?

Media Portrayals of Sexuality

> One picture is worth more than a thousand words.
>
> —Chinese proverb

What messages do the media send about sexuality to children, adolescents, adults, and older people? To men and women and to those of varied races, ethnicities, and sexual orientations? Perhaps as important as what the media portray sexually is what is not portrayed—masturbation, condom use, and older adults' sexuality, for example.

The media are among the most powerful forces in people's lives today. Adults ages 18 and over spend more time engaging with the media than in any other activity—an average of 12 hours per day, 7 days per week (see Figure 1). Watching TV, playing video games, texting, listening to music, and searching the Internet provide a constant stream of messages, images, expectations, and values about which few (if any) of us can resist. Whether and how this exposure is related to sexual outcomes is complex and debatable, depending on the population studied. However, the data that are available may provide an impetus for policymakers who are forming media policies, parents who are trying to support their children's identity and learning, and educators and advocates who are concerned about the impact of media on youth and who wish to underscore the

Images of sexuality permeate our society, sexualizing our environment. Think about the sexual images you see or hear in a 24-hour period. What messages do they communicate about sexuality?

© Robert Landau/Alamy

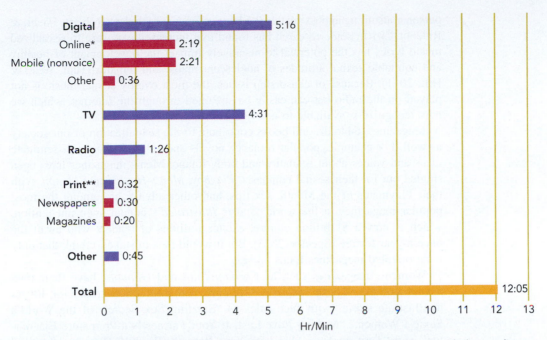

Note: Ages 18+; time spent with each medium includes all time spent with that medium, regardless of multitasking; for example, 1 hour of multitasking online while watching TV is counted as 1 hour for TV and 1 hour for online; *includes all Internet activities on desktop and laptop computers; **offline reading only.

● **FIGURE** 1

Average Time Spent per Day in the United States with Media, Aged 18+ and Over, 2013. Includes all time spent with medium, regardless of multitasking.

(*Source*: www.eMarketer.com [July 2013].)

potential impact of media in individuals' lives. For those concerned about promoting sexual health and well-being, understanding media's prominence and role in people's lives is essential.

Mass-media depictions of sexuality are meant to entertain and exploit, not to inform. As a result, the media do not present us with "real" depictions of sexuality. Sexual activities, for example, are usually not explicitly acted out or described in mainstream media, nor is interracial dating often portrayed. The social and cultural taboos that are still part of mainstream U.S. culture remain embedded in the media. Thus, the various media present the social *context* of sexuality; that is, the programs, plots, movies, stories, articles, newscasts, and vignettes tell us *what* behaviors are appropriate (e.g., kissing, sexual intercourse), *with whom* they are appropriate (e.g., girlfriend/boyfriend, partner, heterosexual), and *why* they are appropriate (e.g., attraction, love, to avoid loneliness).

Probably nothing has revolutionized sexuality the way that access to the Internet has. A click on a website link provides sex on demand. The Internet's contributions to the availability and commercialization of sex include live images and chats, personalized pages and ads, and links to potential or virtual sex partners. The spread of the web has made it easy to obtain information, solidify social ties, and provide sexual gratification.

The music industry is awash with sexual images too. Contemporary pop music, from rock 'n' roll to rap, is filled with lyrics about sexuality mixed with messages about love, rejection, violence, and loneliness. With the average young

Would you like to come back to my place and do what I'm going to tell my friends we did anyway?

—Spanky

person consuming approximately 2.5 hours of music each day (Roberts, Foehr, & Rideout, 2010), some research has found that increased exposure to sexualized music lyrics has the potential to negatively impact the development of healthy and equitable sexual attitudes of adolescent males and females (Hall, West, & Hill, 2011). Because of censorship issues, the most overtly sexual music is not played on the radio but can easily be streamed through the Internet, which we now recognize is available to nearly everyone.

Magazines, tabloids, and books contribute to the sexualization of our society as well. For example, popular romance novels and self-help books disseminate ideas and values about sexuality and body image. Men's magazines have been singled out for their sexual emphasis. *Playboy, Men's Health,* and *Maxim,* with their Playmates of the Month, sex tips, and other advice, are among the most popular magazines in the world. *Sports Illustrated*'s annual swimsuit edition, which is now a $1 billion empire, excites millions of readers who await the once-a-year feature (Spector, 2013). But it would be a mistake to think that only male-oriented magazines focus on sex.

Women's magazines such as *Cosmopolitan* and *Glamour* have their own sexual content. These magazines feature romantic photographs of lovers to illustrate stories with such titles as "Sizzling Sex Secrets of the World's Sexiest Women," "Making Love Last: If Your Partner Is a Premature Ejaculator," and "Turn on Your Man with Your Breasts (Even If They Are Small)." Preadolescents and young teens are not exempt from sexual images and articles in magazines such as *Seventeen* and *YM*. In fact, of the top four teen magazines aimed at girls, 44% of the articles focused on dating and 37% on appearance (American Academy of Pediatrics, 2014.1a). Given this heavy emphasis on looks, it's not surprising that for those who read a lot of women-focused magazines, they are more likely to have internalized the thin ideal, have negative views of their appearance, and engage in restricted eating and bulimic behaviors (Northrup, 2013). Some of the men's health magazines have followed the lead of women's magazines, featuring sexuality-related issues as a way to sell more copies.

Advertising in all media uses the sexual sell, promising sex, romance, popularity, and fulfillment if the consumer will only purchase the right soap, perfume, cigarettes, alcohol, toothpaste, jeans, or automobile. In reality, not only does one *not* become "sexy" or popular by consuming a certain product, but the product may actually be detrimental to one's sexual well-being, as in the case of cigarettes or alcohol.

Media images of sexuality permeate a variety of areas in people's lives. They can produce sexual arousal and emotional reactions, provide social connection, entertain, increase sexual behaviors, and be a source of sex information. On the other hand, unmonitored Internet access among youth raises significant concerns about its risks (Federal Bureau of Investigation, 2014). Given the fact that 91% of 12- to 13-year-old girls have Internet access and 72% have mobile access via smartphones, tablets, and other devices, it's clear that media consumption and exposure explode between the early and later tween years (Jones, 2014).

Studies examining the impact of exposure to sexual content in media have found a modest but significant association between adolescents' sexual beliefs and early sexual initiation. When studies collectively examine adolescents' online exposure to pornography, they suggest that youth may develop unrealistic sexual values and beliefs (Owens, Behun, Manning, & Reid, 2012).

Women's magazines such as *Cosmopolitan, Women's Health,* and *Glamour* use sex to sell their publications. How do these magazines differ from men's magazines such as *Men's Health, Playboy,* and *Maxim* in their treatment of sexuality?

© Consumer Trends/Alamy

Gender differences in self-concept have also been noted in adolescents' use of pornography, with girls reporting feelings of physical inferiority, while boys fear they may not be as virile or able to perform compared to those in these media (Lofgren-Martenson & Mansson, 2010). As such, it isn't surprising that self-objectification, choosing to evaluate ourselves based on appearance, has received some scrutiny from the American Psychological Association (2007), which warns that young people "may internalize an observer's perspective on their physical selves and learn to treat themselves as objects to be looked at and evaluated for their appearance" (p. 18).

Television and Digital Media

Among all types of media, television and digital (online and mobile) have been the most prevalent, pervasive, and vexing icons, saturating every corner of public and private space, shaping consciousness, defining reality, and entertaining the masses. Between ages 12 and 17, the average youth spends over 100 hours a month watching TV and online videos (see Figure 2). By the time an American teenager finishes high school, he or she will have spent more time in front of a television or mobile device screen than in the classroom or sleeping. At the same time, most of the consumption of media leaves the majority of young people outside the purview of adult comment and with few messages or images that demonstrate the risks and responsibilities that accompany sexuality.

While the frequency of TV and digital viewing has been increasing, so has been the number of sexual references in programs. Television and digital video viewing are major sources of information about sex for teenagers, contributing to many aspects of young people's sexual knowledge, beliefs, and behavior. Reporting on the health effects of media on children and adolescents, Strasburger and colleagues (2010) state that "virtually every Western country makes birth control available to adolescents, including allowing birth control advertisements in the media, but the major U.S. television networks balk at airing ads for contraception" (p. 760).

In the accumulated volume of media research, media content does not reflect the realities of the social world; rather, the media images of women and men reflect and reproduce a set of stereotypical and unequal but changing gender roles. For example, women wearing skimpy clothing and expressing their sexuality to attract attention underscores the objectification of women seen in

Reality shows, such as *The Bachelorette,* frequently highlight idealized and sexual themes. What are some of the most popular reality shows? Do they differ according to ethnicity?

© Raymond Hall/GC Images/Getty Images

● **FIGURE 2**

Adolescents' and Young Adults' Monthly Video Viewing Time by Type of Device, 2012.

Source: The teen transition: Adolescents of today, adults of tomorrow (2013). New York: The Nielsen Company.

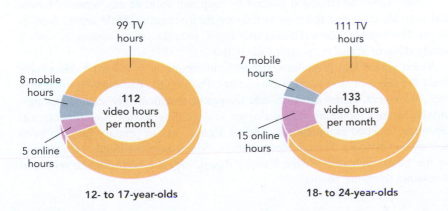

99 TV hours
8 mobile hours
5 online hours
112 video hours per month

12- to 17-year-olds

111 TV hours
7 mobile hours
15 online hours
133 video hours per month

18- to 24-year-olds

136 TV hours
5 mobile hours
11 online hours
152 video hours per month

25- to 34-year-olds

many genres of media. And men's messages are equally unilateral, which is that they should accumulate sexual experience with women by any means possible. Sexist advertising and stereotypical roles in comedy series and dramas may take subtle (or not so subtle) forms that, over time, may have an effect on the way some women and men view themselves. For example, studies examining the effects of television have shown a positive connection between television viewing and poor self-image and self-esteem, particularly among girls and young women (Tiggemann, 2005). Girls who regularly watch reality television, for example, are significantly more likely to believe that a girl's looks are the most important thing about her and are more likely to say they would rather people recognize them for their outer beauty than what's inside (Girl Scout Research Institute, 2011). While it is apparent that exposure to television does not affect all people in the same way, it is clear that the sexual double standard that does exist taps into our national ambivalence about sex, equality, morality, and violence. In spite of this, television is making strides to educate teens and young adults about sexuality and parenting. Programs such as *Teen Mom 2 and 3, Parenthood, East Los High, The Mindy Project,* and *The Fosters* have consulted with organizations such as The National Campaign to Prevent Teen and Unplanned Pregnancy to help educate viewers. This type of alliance is good for all of us.

Unlike the film industry, which uses a single ratings board to regulate all American releases, television has been governed by an informal consensus. In 1997, networks began to rely on watchdog standards and practices departments to rate their shows; however, these divisions have few, if any, hard-and-fast rules. While the Federal Communication Commission (FCC) does not offer clear guidelines about what is and is not permissible on the airwaves, the agency does permit looser interpretations of its decency standards for broadcasts between 10 P.M. and 6 A.M. Additionally, in 2006, the television industry launched a large campaign to educate parents about TV ratings and the V-chip, technology that allows the blocking of programs based on their rating category.

Watching female icons such as Miley Cyrus *twerk,* or dance in a provocative manner, has become mainstream in most music videos.

© Andrew H. Walker/WireImage/Getty Images

Music and Game Videos   MTV, MTV2, VH1, BET, and music Internet programs are very popular among adolescents and young adults. Unlike audio-recorded music, music videos play to the ear and the eye. At the same time, young female artists such as Alicia Keys and Rihanna have brought energy, sexuality, and individualism to the young music audience. Music videos have also objectified and degraded women by stripping them of any sense of power and individualism and focusing strictly on their sexuality. Male artists such as Justin Timberlake, Robin Thicke, and Jay-Z provide young audiences with a steady dose of sexuality, power, and rhythm.

Video games that promote sexist and violent attitudes toward women have filled the aisles of stores across the country. Pushing the line between obscenity and amusement, games often provide images of unrealistically shaped and submissive women mouthing sexy dialogues in degrading scenes. Men, in contrast, are often revealed as unrealistic, violent figures whose primary purpose is to destroy and conquer. Though many of these video games are rated "M" (mature) by the Entertainment Software Ratings Board, they are both popular with and accessible to young people.

Feature-Length Films

From their very inception, motion pictures have dealt with sexuality. In 1896, a film titled *The Kiss* outraged moral guardians when it showed a couple stealing a quick kiss. "Absolutely disgusting," complained one critic. "The performance comes near being indecent in its emphasized indecency. Such things call for police action" (quoted in Webb, 1983). Today, in contrast, film critics use "sexy," a word independent of artistic value, to praise a film. "Sexy" films are movies in which the requisite "sex scenes" are sufficiently titillating to overcome their lack of aesthetic merit. What is clear is that movies are not that dissimilar from television in their portrayal of the consequences of unprotected sex, such as unplanned pregnancies or sexually transmitted infections (STIs), including HIV/AIDS.

While one might argue that it is unwise to confuse entertainment with education, media use is not without its consequences on health. Studies find that high levels of media use are associated with academic problems, sleep deprivation, unhealthy eating, and more (Office of Adolescent Health, 2013). The American Academy of Pediatrics (AAP) (2010) recommends that adolescents have less than 2 hours of screen time per day in part because of its increasing association with childhood obesity. While health professionals can use media to promote people's health, it's going to take a lot more commitment and resources to achieve this goal.

Gay Men, Lesbian Women, and Bisexual and Transgender People in Film and Television

Gay men, lesbian women, and bisexual and transgender individuals are slowly being integrated into mainstream films and television. However, when gay men and lesbian women do appear, they are frequently defined in terms of their sexual orientation, as if there were nothing more to their lives than sexuality. Though the situation is changing, gay men are generally stereotyped as effeminate, flighty, or "arty," or they may be closeted. Lesbian women are often stereotyped as either super-feminine or supermasculine.

Writers in television and film are finally giving gay characters prominence beyond their sexuality. These include Cameron Monaghan ("Shameless"), Andrew Rannells ("Girls"), Naya Rivera ("Glee"), and Sarah Paulson ("American Horror Story: Asylum").
© Matteo Prandoni/BFAnyc/Sipa USA/Newscom

"Coming out" stories are now the standard for television programs that deal with gay characters. However, what has recently changed is that the age of these characters has become younger. Teen coming-out stories seem relevant in that they reflect the identity issues of being **gay**, transsexual, **queer**, questioning, or unsure about their sexual identity and expose the vulnerability most young people in junior high and high school feel about being bullied. Different from stories in which gay people are marginalized and stereotyped, the messages in many of the shows for younger audiences are quite consistent: that you will be accepted for who you are. Still, television and mainstream media have a long way to go in terms of normalizing healthy sexual relationships between gay and queer people. The biggest hurdle remains in showing adults, particularly two males, kissing on screen as their heterosexual counterparts would. While teen shows may have somewhat overcome this barrier, most "adult" programs have not.

Online Social Networks

Surfing the web is a major recreational activity that has altered the ways in which individuals communicate and carry on interpersonal relationships. Though social theorists have long been concerned with the alienating effects of technology, the Internet appears quite different from other communication technologies. Its efficacy, power, and influence, along with the anonymity and depersonalization that accompany its use, have made it possible for users to more easily obtain and distribute sexual materials and information, as well as to interact sexually in different ways.

It is apparent that social networking sites, like Facebook, Instagram, and Twitter, are well integrated into the daily lives of most people in the United

For anyone with a computer, social networks provide readily accessible friends and potential partners, help to maintain friendships, and shape sexual culture.
© Dean Mitchell/Getty Images

States. Their popularity cannot be underestimated: Facebook alone reports to have over 1 billion global users (Social, Digital and Mobile Around the World, 2014). Add this to the additional 2 billion users with other or supplemental platforms and it's obvious that the digital landscape is highly populated.

Social networking sites provide an opportunity for many to display their identities: religious, political, ideological, work-related, and sexual orientation. While doing so, individuals can also gain feedback from peers and strengthen their bonds of friendship. At the same time, social networking can be a place of "relationship drama" (Pew Research Internet Project, 2013). By posting details or pictures from a date on a social networking site, younger adults in particular are more likely to live out their relationships through these sites. While many who acknowledge that they use the Internet to flirt with others have largely positive opinions and experiences, significant numbers of others have negative ones. Over 25% of social networking users report having unfriended or blocked someone who was flirting in a way that made them feel uncomfortable, and 22% have unfriended or blocked someone they are no longer dating. Many have also used these sites to check up on someone they dated in the past or to research potential romantic partners. Not surprising, many realize that these sites can serve as an unwanted reminder that relationships have ended and, maybe even worse, that their previous beloved one is now dating someone else.

Like other forms of media, the Internet does not simply provide sexual culture; it also shapes sexual culture. With the widespread use of online dating sites, the medium has become an accepted means by which numerous individuals meet new partners for dating, matchmaking, and/or sex (see the "Think About It" box "Before Pressing 'Send'"). For the isolated, underrepresented, and disenfranchised whose sexual identities up until now have been hidden, Internet communications may be a lifeline. The use of the Internet also provides a means of avoiding the pitfalls inherent in relying solely on real-world meetings and experiences. Thus, it's probably not surprising that someone you know has found a long-term partner or spouse via an online dating site. With more positive attitudes toward online dating and social network sites playing a prominent role in navigating romantic relationships, it has been reported that 1 in 10 Americans have used an online dating site or mobile dating app (Pew Research Internet Project, 2013). Though people in nearly every major demographic group—old and young, straight and gay, urbanites and rural dwellers, and college graduates—are likely to know someone who uses online dating, the most common users are those in their mid-20s through mid-40s.

Even as online daters themselves give the experience high marks, many have had negative experiences. Half (54%) of online daters have felt that someone seriously misrepresented him- or herself, while over 28% have been contacted by someone in a way that made them feel harassed or uncomfortable (Pew Research Internet Project, 2013). Women are much more likely than men to have experienced this.

With thousands of sexual health sites maintained online, new forms of media are also powerful tools for learning. When credible sources are located, these media have become convenient avenues by which people can get important sexual health information. There are, however, two significant concerns associated with using new media to learn about sexuality and sexual health: the possibility that the information is inaccurate or misleading and that those who turn to the media may turn away from real people in their lives. Given that only a small number of new media interventions have been systematically evaluated, it is still unclear about their impact on health and well-being.

think
about it

Before Pressing "Send": Trends and Concerns About Texting, Sexting, and Dating

The popularity and accessibility of digital media and technology, including Internet social networking sites (SNS), have allowed individuals to present themselves publically in ways and means that were previously never possible. In fact, they have become what the Pew Research Internet Project (2014) describes as "key actors" in the lives of most Americans. Social media facilitate communication and support, play a prominent role in navigating and documenting romantic relationships, and, for many, provide an outlet for sexual exploration and expression. Individuals use technology throughout the day; they negotiate over when, with whom, and how to use it. What has drastically changed the culture of interpersonal communication is what is now commonly called **sexting**—the creating, sharing, and forwarding of sexually suggestive images. It's what others have referred to in the past as "phone sex." Unlike phone sex, however, sexting leaves little to the imagination. For many, sexting may be a means for those who are curious about sex and sexuality. The wide array of media available provides the opportunity for choosing different purposes for sending and receiving sexts, including sexual self-expression, experimentation, self-definition, and education. At the same time, it can have serious consequences, including shame and guilt. In most states, teens caught with sexting photos can be charged with possession of child porn, even if they are under 18 and if the images are of themselves.

As can be seen in Figure 3, sexting is not reserved to teens and young adults. When looking at the relationship status of those who send and receive sexts, the landscape becomes more varied than one may imagine. For example, it's clear that relationship status does not necessarily play a significant role in who sends and receives sexts. Three common scenarios for sexting are to make congruent with the rest of the book: (1) the exchange of images solely between two romantic partners, (2) exchanges between a partner and someone outside the relationship, and (3) exchanges between people who are not yet in a relationship but at least one person hopes to be.

All of this invites concern, especially for tweens, those between the ages 8 and 14, who share provocative or sexual imagery of themselves. A recent survey of 12- to 13-year-olds found that 93% had access to the Internet, 71% had mobile access to the Internet (e.g., cell phone and tablet), and 16% had

● **FIGURE 3**

Percentage of Those Who Sext Monthly, By Age

Source: Adapted from Pew Research Internet Project, 2013.

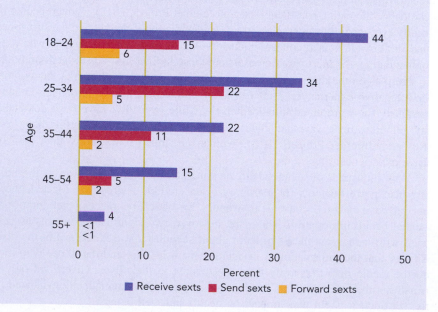

access to the Internet mostly on a cell phone (Lenhart, 2014). Additionally, texting is the most common form of daily communication used by teenagers (more than phones or face-to-face), with a median of 60 texts sent per day (Lenhart, 2012). What's concerning about this is that even though young people may be technologically savvy, many lack the maturity to be aware of the consequences that can accompany unrestricted access to the media. This may be particularly true for those who are considered emotionally or behaviorally at-risk. Recent evidence underscored this concern when, among a group of at-risk seventh graders, it was found that sexting was associated with higher rates of engaging in a variety of sexual behaviors, including touching genitals over clothes and oral and vaginal sex (Rice et al., 2014). This study also found that those who sexted were more likely to perceive approval of sexual behavior from others, including peers, parents, and the media; demonstrated higher intensions to engage in sexual behavior; and exhibited lower emotional awareness and self-esteem. The authors reported: "Sexual text messaging behavior of any kind, with or without pictures, was associated with a greater likelihood of engaging in sexual behaviors, including touching genitals, having a 'friend with benefits,' oral sex, or vaginal sex" (p. 279). This higher prevalence of sexual behaviors and lower personal insight underscore the concern that many parents, teachers, and others have about the awareness and emotional competence of many youth who have unrestricted access to the media.

The altered social environment of today's youth can no longer be left to chance. It's clear that young users need to be taught how to resist the temptation and pressure to engage in sexting and to find and assess media sources that promote healthy sexual behavior. Parents need to monitor cell phone and computer use, limit unrestricted access, and use electronic communication as opportunities to discuss relationship health.

The National Campaign to Prevent Teen and Unplanned Pregnancy (2009) suggests "Five Things to Think About Before Pressing 'Send'":

1. *Don't assume anything you send or post is going to remain private.*
2. *There is no changing your mind in cyberspace— anything you send or post will never truly go away.*
3. *Don't give in to the pressure to do something that makes you uncomfortable, even in cyberspace.*
4. *Consider the recipient's reaction.* Just because the message is meant to be fun doesn't mean the person who gets it will see it that way. Whatever you write, post, or send does contribute to the real-life impression you're making.
5. *Nothing is truly anonymous.* It is important to remember that even if individuals know you only by screen name, online profile, phone number, or e-mail address, they can probably find you if they try hard enough.

Think Critically

1. Would you consider participating in or have you participated in sexting? If so, what kind of image did you or might you send? Under what circumstances? If you would not consider participating in this activity, what prevents you from doing so?
2. Do you believe that Internet sites and their use should be censored? Why or why not?
3. Which of the "Five Things to Think About Before Pressing 'Send'" is most concerning to you? Why? How does this influence your thoughts around sexting?

For most users, the Internet provides a fascinating venue for experiencing sex. For some users, however, porn consumption gets them in trouble: maxed-out credit cards, neglected responsibility, and overlooked loved ones. There are both online and community resources for those who desire counseling. While searching for such sources, however, consumers and professionals must be aware of the differences between therapy, consultation, and entertainment. Additionally, because entrepreneurs can make more money from hype and misinformation than from high-quality therapy and education, consumers must remain vigilant in assessing the background of the therapist and the source of the information.

Because of the high volume of sexual discussions and material available on the Internet, there is an increasing demand for government regulation. In 1996, Congress passed the Communications Decency Act, which made it illegal to use computer networks to transmit "obscene" materials or place "indecent" words or images where children might read or see them. However, courts have declared this legislation a violation of freedom of speech.

● Sexuality Across Cultures and Times

What we see as "natural" in our culture may be viewed as unnatural in other cultures. Few Americans would disagree about the erotic potential of kissing. But other cultures perceive kissing as merely the exchange of saliva. To the Mehinaku of the Amazon rain forest, for example, kissing is a disgusting sexual abnormality; no Mehinaku engages in it (Gregor, 1985). The fact that others press their lips against each other, salivate, *and* become sexually excited merely confirms their "strangeness" to the Mehinaku.

Culture takes our **sexual interests**—our incitements or inclinations to act sexually—and molds and shapes them, sometimes celebrating sexuality and other times condemning it. Sexuality can be viewed as a means of spiritual enlightenment, as in the Hindu tradition, in which the gods themselves engage in sexual activities; it can also be at war with the divine, as in the Judeo-Christian tradition, in which the flesh is the snare of the devil (Parrinder, 1980).

Among the variety of factors that shape how we feel and behave sexually, culture is possibly the most powerful. A brief exploration of sexual themes across cultures and times will give you a sense of the diverse shapes and meanings humans have given to sexuality.

Sexual Interests

All cultures assume that adults have the *potential* for becoming sexually aroused and for engaging in sexual intercourse for the purpose of reproduction. But cultures differ considerably in terms of how strong they believe sexual interests are. These beliefs, in turn, affect the level of desire expressed in each culture.

The Mangaia Among the Mangaia of Polynesia, both sexes, beginning in early adolescence, experience high levels of sexual desire (Marshall, 1971). Around age 13 or 14, following a circumcision ritual, boys are given instruction in the ways of pleasing a girl: erotic kissing, cunnilingus, breast fondling and sucking, and techniques for bringing her to multiple orgasms. After 2 weeks, an older, sexually experienced woman has sexual intercourse with the boy to instruct him further on how to sexually satisfy a woman. Girls the same age are instructed by older women on how to be orgasmic: how to thrust their hips and rhythmically tighten their vagina in order to experience repeated orgasms. A girl finally learns to be orgasmic through the efforts of a "good man." If the woman's partner fails to satisfy her, she is likely to leave him; she may also ruin his reputation with other women by denouncing his lack of skill. Young men and women are expected to have many sexual experiences prior to marriage.

This adolescent paradise, however, does not last forever. The Mangaia believe that sexuality is strongest during adolescence. As a result, when the Mangaia leave young adulthood, they experience a rapid decline in sexual desire and activity, and they cease to be aroused as passionately as they once were. They attribute this swift decline to the workings of nature and settle into a sexually contented adulthood.

The Dani In contrast to the Mangaia, the New Guinean Dani show little interest in sexuality (Schwimmer, 1997). To them, sex is a relatively unimportant aspect of life. The Dani express no concern about improving sexual techniques or enhancing erotic pleasure. Extrarelational sex and jealousy are rare. As their only sexual concern is reproduction, sexual intercourse is performed quickly,

The sensual movements of Latin American dancing have become mainstream in American culture, as can be seen in the popularity of *Dancing With the Stars*.

© Ethan Miller/AEG Live/Getty Images

ending with male ejaculation. Female orgasm appears to be unknown to them. Following childbirth, both mothers and fathers go through 5 years of sexual abstinence. The Dani are an extreme example of a case in which culture, rather than biology, shapes sexual attractions.

Victorian Americans In the nineteenth century, White middle-class Americans believed that women had little sexual desire. If they experienced desire at all, it was "reproductive desire," the wish to have children. Reproduction entailed the unfortunate "necessity" of engaging in sexual intercourse. A leading reformer wrote that in her "natural state" a woman never makes advances based on sexual desires, for the "very plain reason that she does not feel them" (Alcott, 1868). Those women who did feel desire were "a few exceptions amounting in all probability to diseased cases." Such women were classified by a prominent physician as suffering from "Nymphomania, or Furor Uterinus" (Bostwick, 1860).

Whereas women were viewed as asexual, men were believed to have raging sexual appetites. Men, driven by lust, sought to satisfy their desires by ravaging innocent women. Both men and women believed that male sexuality was dangerous, uncontrolled, and animal-like. It was part of a woman's duty to tame unruly male sexual impulses.

The polar beliefs about the nature of male and female sexuality created destructive antagonisms between "angelic" women and "demonic" men. These beliefs provided the rationale for a "war between the sexes." They also led to the separation of sex from love. Intimacy and love had nothing to do with male sexuality. In fact, male lust always lingered in the background of married life, threatening to destroy love by its overbearing demands.

The Sexual Revolution Between the 1960s and the mid-1970s, significant challenges to the ways that society viewed traditional codes of behavior took place in the United States. Dubbed the "sexual revolution," or "sexual liberation,"

> *Sex is hardly ever just about sex.*
> —Shirley MacLaine
> (1934–)

Similar to beliefs about sexuality, ideals about body image and what women are willing to do to achieve it change over time.

(first) © History Archives/Alamy; (second) © Mirrorpix/Newscom

this period of rapid and complex changes invited individuals and society to confront the sexually repressive Victorian era and begin to recognize a separation and autonomy in what was thought to be unexamined decisions and regulations. This counterculture movement questioned previously established rules, regulations, and decisions in these areas:

- *Individual self-expression and autonomy.* Previously structured around the collective good of the family and community, the counterculture found meaning and purpose in supporting the individual rights of men and women, including the right to sexual expression.

- *Women's rights.* The traditional, stereotypical role of the man being breadwinner and of the woman being the homemaker were challenged by roles whereby individuals could choose according to their needs. It became acceptable for women to express their inherent sexuality and for men to be their emotional and authentic selves. It was during this period that abortion became legal and widespread accessibility and dissemination of birth control became available.

- *Relationship status.* No longer was marriage the only context within which couples could express their sexuality, love, and commitment for one another. A new philosophy of sex, referred to as "free love," allowed individuals to broaden and act on their sexual desires without marriage, judgment, or contempt.

- *Sexual orientation.* Overriding previous dogma from church and state, there has been a broader acceptance of homosexuality. This was reinforced in 1973 when the American Psychiatric Association removed homosexuality from its list of diagnosable mental disorders. More recently in 2015, the U.S. Supreme Court ruled same-sex marriage legal in all states.

- *Sexuality education.* Though a handful of sexuality education programs had been introduced prior to the 1960s, few were uniformly embraced or included in school curriculums until the Sexuality Information and Education Council of the United States (SIECUS) became a vocal force in educational and policy circles.

Although a significant amount of time has passed since the end of the Victorian era and the counterculture's attempt to shift values and attitudes about sexuality, many traditional sexual beliefs and attitudes continue to influence us. These include the belief that men are "naturally" sexually aggressive and women sexually passive, the sexual double standard, and the value placed on women being sexually inexperienced. While the media continue to push boundaries about what is acceptable and desirable in sexual expression, so do most Americans continue to adapt their thinking about what is acceptable, desirable, normal, and tolerable.

Sexual Orientation

Sexual orientation is the pattern of sexual and emotional attraction based on the gender of one's partner. **Heterosexuality** refers to emotional and sexual attraction between men and women; **homosexuality**, more commonly referred to as **gay**, refers to emotional and sexual attraction between persons of the same sex; **bisexuality** is an emotional and sexual attraction to both males and females. There is significant debate about whether **asexuality**, a state of having no sexual attraction to anyone or low or absent interest in sexual activity, is a sexual ori-entation. Now that same-sex marriage has been legalized in all states, full social legitimacy and dignity have been granted to all people. This view of marriage is currently shared by 21 other countries.

Ancient Greece   In ancient Greece, the birthplace of European culture, the Greeks accepted same-sex relationships as naturally as Americans today accept heterosexuality. For the Greeks, same-sex relationships between men represented the highest form of love.

The male-male relationship was based on love and reciprocity; sexuality was only one component of it. In this relationship, the code of conduct called for the older man to initiate the relationship. The youth initially resisted; only after the older man courted the young man with gifts and words of love would he reciprocate. The two men formed a close emotional bond. The older man was the youth's mentor as well as his lover. He introduced the youth to men who would be useful for his advancement later; he assisted him in learning his duties as a citizen. As the youth entered adulthood, the erotic bond between the two evolved into a deep friendship. After the youth became an adult, he married a woman and later initiated a relationship with an adolescent boy.

Greek male-male relationships, however, were not substitutes for male-female marriage. The Greeks discouraged exclusive male-male relationships because marriage and children were required to continue the family and society. Men regarded their wives primarily as domestics and as bearers of children (Keuls, 1985). (The Greek word for woman, *gyne,* translates literally as "child-bearer.") Husbands turned for sexual pleasure not to their wives but to *hetaerae* (hi-TIR-ee), highly regarded courtesans who were usually educated slaves.

In ancient Greece, the highest form of love was that expressed between males.

Digital image courtesy of the Getty's Open Content Program

The Sambians   Among Sambian males of New Guinea, sexual orientation is very malleable (Herdt & McClintock, 2000). Young boys begin with sexual activities with older boys, move to sexual activities with both sexes during adolescence, and engage in exclusively male-female activities in adulthood. Sambians believe that a boy can grow into a man only by the ingestion of semen, which is, they say, like mother's milk. At age 7 or 8, boys begin their sexual activities with older boys; as they get older, they seek multiple partners to accelerate their growth into manhood. At adolescence, their role changes, and they must provide semen to boys to enable them to develop. At first, they worry about their own loss of semen, but they are taught to drink tree sap, which they believe magically replenishes their supply. During adolescence, boys are betrothed to preadolescent girls, with whom they engage in sexual activities. When the girls mature, the boys give up their sexual involvement with other males. They become fully involved with adult women, losing their desire for men.

Gender

Although sexual interests and orientation may be influenced by culture, it may be difficult for some people to imagine that culture has anything to do with **gender,** the socially constructed roles, behaviors, activities, and attributes that a society considers appropriate for men and women. Other terms used to describe gender are **gender normative** and **cisgender,** people whose sex assignment at birth corresponds to their gender identity and expression.

For those who do not ascribe to gender normative behaviors or expression, the umbrella term of **transgender** is used. This broad term describes those whose gender expression or identity is not congruent with the sex assigned at birth and whose gender is not validated by the dominant culture. Transgender is inclusive of **transsexuality,** a phenomenon in which a person is intent to live through actions, dress, hormone therapy, and/or surgery as a gender other than that which he or she was assigned at birth, and **transvestism**, the wearing of clothes of or passing as a member of the other sex.

Our sex appears solidly rooted in our biological nature. But is being male or female *really* biological? The answer is yes *and* no. Having male or female genitals is anatomical. But the possession of a penis does not *always* make a person a man, nor does the possession of a clitoris and vagina *always* make a person a woman. Men who consider themselves women, "women with penises," are accepted or honored in many cultures throughout the world (Bullough, 1991). Thus, culture and a host of other factors help to shape masculinity and femininity, while biology defines men and women. But this is not the case in all regions of the world.

Transgendered people reside in many cultures, crossing age, religion, and social status.

© Maciej Dakowicz/Alamy

Two-Spirited People   A Native American tradition involving the existence of cross-gender roles, the male-female, the female-male is what is called the **two-spirit** person (Laframboise & Anhorn, 2008). These individuals often expressed their gender through dress and work roles; however, they were celibate and so did not convey it through their sexual practices. Two-spirit people were often visionaries, healers, medicine people, nannies of orphans, and caregivers. They were respected as fundamental components of the Native American culture and societies. However, since European colonization and persecution by the church to eradicate these individuals, the two-spirit community is now often viewed as perverted, untraditional, or untrustworthy. As such, two-spirit people have lost their place in society and their dignity.

In South Asian society, the third gender is known as the *hijra*. Regarded as sacred, they perform as dancers or musicians at weddings and religious ceremonies, as well as providing blessings for health, prosperity, and fertility (Nanda, 1990). It is almost always men who become two-spirits, although there are a few cases of women assuming male roles in a similar fashion (Blackwood, 1984). Two-spirits are often considered shamans, individuals who possess great spiritual power.

Among the Zuni of New Mexico, two-spirits are considered a third gender (Roscoe, 1991). Despite the existence of transsexual people and those born with disorders of sexual development (e.g., two testes or two ovaries but an ambiguous genital appearance), Westerners tend to view gender as biological, an incorrect assumption. The Zuni, in contrast, believe that gender is socially acquired.

American Indian two-spirits were suppressed by missionaries and the U.S. government and were considered "unnatural" or "perverted." As a result of cultural genocide and other factors, some of Native American communities now regard homophobia and sexism as common. This relatively new and unfortunate set of beliefs makes some who identify as Native American and queer feel both isolated and unsupported (Laframboise & Anhorn, 2008).

● Societal Norms and Sexuality

The immense diversity of sexual behaviors across cultures and times immediately calls into question the appropriateness of labeling these behaviors as *inherently* natural or unnatural, normal or abnormal. Too often, we give such labels to sexual behaviors without thinking about the basis on which we make those judgments. Such categories discourage knowledge and understanding because they are value judgments, evaluations of right and wrong. As such, they are not objective descriptions about behaviors but statements of how we feel about those behaviors.

Natural Sexual Behavior

How do we decide if a sexual behavior is natural or unnatural? To make this decision, we must have some standard of nature against which to compare the behavior. But what is "nature"? On the abstract level, nature is the essence of all things in the universe. Or, personified as nature, it is the force regulating the universe. These definitions, however, do not help us much in trying to establish what is natural or unnatural.

When we asked our students to identify their criteria for determining which sexual behaviors they considered "natural" or "unnatural," we received a variety of responses, including the following:

- "If a person feels something instinctive, I believe it is a natural feeling."
- "Natural and unnatural have to do with the laws of nature. What these parts were intended for."
- "I decide by my gut instincts."
- "I think all sexual activity is natural as long as it doesn't hurt you or anyone else."
- "Everything possible is natural. Everything natural is normal. If it is natural and normal, it is moral."

In some cultures, men who dress or identify as women are considered shamans. We'wha was a Zuni two-spirit who lived in the nineteenth century.

© History Archives/Alamy

Am I Normal?

The question "Am I normal?" seems to haunt many people. For some, it causes a great deal of unnecessary fear, guilt, and anxiety. For others, it provides the motivation to study the literature, consult with a trusted friend or therapist, or take a course in sexuality.

What is normal? We commonly use several criteria in deciding whether to label different sexual behavior "normal" or "abnormal." According to professor and psychologist Leonore Tiefer (2004), these criteria are subjective, statistical, idealistic, cultural, and clinical. Regardless of what criteria we use, they ultimately reflect societal norms.

- *Subjectively "normal" behavior.* According to this definition, normalcy is any behavior that is similar to one's own. Though most of us use this definition, few of us will acknowledge it.

- *Statistically "normal" behavior.* According to this definition, whatever behaviors are more common are normal; less common ones are abnormal. However, the fact that a behavior is not widely practiced does not make it abnormal except in a statistical sense. Fellatio (fel-AY-she-o) (oral stimulation of the penis) and cunnilingus (cun-i-LIN-gus) (oral stimulation of the female genitals), for example, are widely practiced today because they have become "acceptable" behaviors. But years ago, oral sex was tabooed as something "dirty" or "shameful."

- *Idealistically "normal" behavior.* Taking an ideal for a norm, individuals who use this approach measure all deviations against perfection. They may try to model their behavior after Christ or Gandhi, for example. Using idealized behavior as a norm can easily lead to feelings of guilt, shame, and anxiety.

- *Culturally "normal" behavior.* This is probably the standard most of us use most of the time: We accept as normal what our culture defines as normal. This measure explains why our notions of normalcy do not always agree with those of people from other countries, religions, communities, and historical periods. Men who kiss in public may be considered normal in one place but abnormal in another. It is common for deviant behavior to be perceived as dangerous and frightening in a culture that rejects it.

- *Clinically "normal" behavior.* The clinical standard uses scientific data about health and illness to make judgments. For example, the presence of the syphilis bacterium in body tissues or blood is considered abnormal because it indicates that a person has a sexually transmitted infection. Regardless of time or place, clinical definitions should stand the test of time. The four criteria mentioned previously are all somewhat arbitrary—that is, they depend on individual or group opinion—but the clinical criterion has more objectivity.

These five criteria form the basis of what we usually consider normal behavior. Often, the different definitions and interpretations of "normal" conflict with one another. How does a person determine whether he or she is normal if subjectively "normal" behavior—what that person actually does—is inconsistent with his or her ideals? How could our ideas about what we consider to be "normal" sexual functioning be altered if we knew that diversity, not homogeneity, was more characteristic of real-life sexual behavior (van Lankveld, 2013)? Such dilemmas are commonplace and lead many people to question their normalcy. However, they should not question their normalcy as much as their *concept* of normalcy.

Think Critically

1. How do you define normal sexual behavior? What criteria did you use to create this definition?

2. How do your sexual attitudes, values, and behaviors compare to what you believe are "normal" sexual behaviors? If they are different, how do you reconcile these? If they are similar, how do you feel about others who may not share them?

3. In Nepal, young women are isolated for one week during their first menses, whereas in Brazil, it is common to see men embrace or kiss in public. What are your thoughts about how other cultures define normality?

SOURCE: Tiefer, L. (2004). *Sex is not a natural act and other essays* (2nd ed.). Boulder, CO: Westview Press.

When we label sexual behavior as "natural" or "unnatural," we are typically indicating whether the behavior conforms to our culture's sexual norms. Our sexual norms appear natural because we have internalized them since infancy. These norms are part of the cultural air we breathe, and, like the air, they are invisible. We have learned our culture's rules so well that they have become a "natural" part of our personality, a "second nature" to us. They seem "instinctive."

Normal Sexual Behavior

Closely related to the idea that sexual behavior is natural or unnatural is the belief that sexuality is either normal or abnormal. More often than not, describing behavior as "normal" or "abnormal" is merely another way of making value judgments in the ways in which people perceive and appraise sexuality. Psychologist Sandra Pertot (2007) quips, "Normal today means that a person should have a regular and persistent physical sex drive, easy arousal, strong erections and good control over ejaculation for males, powerful orgasms, and a desire for a variety and experimentation [for women]" (p. 13). Normal has often been used to imply "healthy" or "moral" behavior. **Normal sexual behavior** is behavior that conforms to a group's average, or median, patterns of behavior. Normality has nothing to do with moral or psychological deviance. Rather, the term is often used when one is critical of one's partner and wants to "wheel in the heavy artillery of 'you're not normal. I'm normal'" (Klein, 2012).

Ironically, although we may feel pressure to behave like the average person (the statistical norm), most of us don't actually know how others behave sexually. People don't ordinarily reveal much about their sexual activities. If they do, they generally reveal only their most conformist sexual behaviors, such as sexual intercourse. They rarely disclose their masturbatory activities, sexual fantasies, or anxieties or feelings of guilt. All that most people present of themselves—unless we know them well—is the conventional self that masks their actual sexual feelings, attitudes, and behaviors.

The guidelines most of us have for determining our normality are given to us by our friends, partners, and parents (who usually present conventional sexual images of themselves) through stereotypes, media images, religious teachings, customs, and cultural norms. None of these, however, tell us much about how people *actually* behave. Because we don't know how people really behave, it is easy for us to imagine that we are abnormal if we differ from our cultural norms and stereotypes. We wonder if our desires, fantasies, and activities are normal: Is it normal to fantasize? To masturbate? To enjoy erotica? To be attracted to someone of the same sex? Some of us believe that everyone else is "normal" and that only we are "sick" or "abnormal" (or vice-versa). The challenge, of course, is to put aside our cultural indoctrination and try to understand sexual behaviors objectively.

Because culture determines what is normal, there is a vast range of normal behaviors across different cultures. What is considered the normal sexual urge for the Dani would send most of us into therapy for treatment of low sexual desire. And the idea of teaching sexual skills to early adolescents, as the Mangaia do, would horrify most American parents.

Are there behaviors, however, that are considered essential to sexual functioning and consequently universally labeled as normal? Not surprisingly, **reproduction**, or the biological process by which individuals are produced, is probably one shared view of normal sexual behavior that most cultures would agree upon. All other beliefs about sexual expression and behavior develop from social context.

> *The greatest pleasure in life is doing what people say you cannot do.*
>
> —Walter Bagehot
> (1826–1877)

Kissing is "natural" and "normal" in our culture. It is an expression of intimacy, love, and passion for young and old, and persons of all sexual orientations.

Sexual Behavior and Variations

Sex researchers have generally rejected the traditional sexual dichotomies of natural/unnatural, normal/abnormal, moral/immoral, and good/bad. Regarding the word "abnormal," sociologist Ira Reiss (1989) writes:

> We need to be aware that people will use those labels to put distance between themselves and others they dislike. In doing so, these people are not making a scientific diagnosis but are simply affirming their support of certain shared concepts of proper sexuality.

Instead of classifying behavior into what are essentially moralistic normal/abnormal and natural/unnatural categories, researchers view human sexuality as characterized by **sexual variation**—that is, sexual variety and diversity. As humans, we vary enormously in terms of our sexual orientation, our desires, our fantasies, our attitudes, and our behaviors. Alfred Kinsey and his colleagues (1948) succinctly stated the matter: "The world is not to be divided into sheep and goats."

Researchers believe that the best way to understand our sexual diversity is to view our activities as existing on a continuum. On this continuum, the frequency with which individuals engage in different sexual activities (e.g., sexual intercourse, masturbation, and oral sex) ranges from never to always. Significantly, there is no point on the continuum that marks normal or abnormal behavior. In fact, the difference between one individual and the next on the continuum is minimal (Kinsey,

Declaration of Sexual Rights

Sexuality is an integral part of the personality of **every human being.** Since health is a fundamental human right, so must sexual health be recognized, promoted, respected, and defended by all societies and through all means. Sexual health is the result of an environment that recognizes, respects, and exercises these rights.

1. **The right to equality and nondiscrimination.** Everyone is entitled to enjoy all sexual rights set forth in this Declaration without distinction of any kind.

2. **The right to life, liberty, and security of the person.** This right cannot be arbitrarily threatened, limited, or taken away for reasons related to sexuality. These include: sexual orientation, consensual sexual behavior and practices, gender identity and expression, or because of accessing or providing services related to sexual and reproductive health.

3. **The right to autonomy and bodily integrity.** Everyone has the right to control and decide freely on matters related to their sexuality and their body. This includes the choice of sexual behaviors, practices, partners, and relationships with due regard to the rights of others.

4. **The right to be free from torture and cruel, inhumane, or degrading treatment or punishment.** This right includes traditional practices, forced sterilization, contraception, or abortion; and other forms of torture, cruel, inhumane, or degrading treatment perpetrated for any reason.

5. **The right to be free from all forms of violence and coercion.** This right includes rape, sexual abuse, sexual harassment, bullying, sexual exploitation and slavery, trafficking for purposes of sexual exploitation, virginity testing, and violence.

6. **The right to privacy.** Everyone has the right to privacy related to sexuality, sexual life, and choices regarding their own body and consensual sexual relations and practices without arbitrary interference and intrusion.

7. **The right to the highest attainable standard of health, including sexual health; with the possibility of pleasurable, satisfying, and safe sexual experiences.** This requires the accessibility to quality health services and access to the conditions that influence health including sexual health.

8. **The right to enjoy the benefits of scientific progress and its application.** This right is inclusive of sexuality and sexual health.

9. **The right to information.** Everyone shall have access to scientifically accurate and understandable information related to sexuality, sexual health, and sexual rights through diverse sources.

10. **The right to education and the right to comprehensive sexuality education.** Comprehensive sexuality education must be age appropriate, scientifically accurate, culturally competent, and grounded in human rights, gender equality, and a positive approach to sexuality and pleasure.

11. **The right to enter, form, and dissolve marriage and other similar types of relationships based on equality and full and free consent.** All persons are entitled to equal rights entering into, during, and at dissolution of marriage, partnership, and other similar relationships without discrimination or exclusion of any kind.

12. **The right to decide whether to have children, the number and spacing of children, and to have the information and means to do so.** To exercise this right requires access to the conditions that influence and determine health and wellbeing.

13. **The right to freedom of thought, opinion, and expression.** Everyone has the right to express their own sexuality with due respect to the rights of others.

14. **The right to freedom of association and peaceful assembly.** Everyone has the right to peacefully demonstrate and advocate including about sexuality, sexual health, and sexual rights.

15. **The right to participation in public and political life.** Everyone is entitled to an environment that enables active, free, and meaningful participation in all aspects of human life.

16. **The right to access to justice, remedies, and redress.** This right requires effective, adequate, accessible, and appropriate educative, legislative, judicial, and other measures.

Think Critically

1. What are your reactions to the "Declaration of Sexual Rights"? For whom should these rights, be promoted? Would you delete, edit, or add rights to this list?

2. Why do you suppose such a declaration is necessary and important?

3. What (if any) consequences should there be for governments, cultures, or individuals who do not follow these rights?

Pomeroy, & Martin, 1948; Kinsey, Pomeroy, Martin, & Gebhard, 1953). The most that can be said of a person is that his or her behaviors are more or less typical or atypical of the group average, whatever that group may be. Furthermore, nothing can be inferred about an individual whose behavior differs significantly from the group average other than his or her behavior is atypical. Except for engaging in sexually atypical behavior, one person may be indistinguishable from any other.

Many activities that are usually thought of as "deviant" or "abnormal" sexual behavior—activities diverging from the norm, such as exhibitionism, voyeurism, and fetishism—are engaged in by most of us to some degree. We may delight in displaying our bodies on the beach (exhibitionism) or in "twerking" in crowded clubs. We may like watching ourselves having sex, viewing erotic scenes, or seeing our partner undress (voyeurism). Or we may enjoy kissing our lover's photograph, keeping a lock of his or her hair, or sleeping with an article of his or her clothing (fetishism). Most of the time, these feelings or activities are only one aspect of our sexual selves; they are not especially significant in our overall sexuality. Such atypical behaviors represent nothing more than sexual nonconformity when they occur between mutually consenting adults and do not cause distress.

The rejection of natural/unnatural, normal/abnormal, and moral/immoral categories by sex researchers does not mean that standards for evaluating sexual behavior do not exist. There are many sexual behaviors that are harmful to oneself (e.g., masturbatory asphyxia—suffocating or hanging oneself during masturbation to increase sexual arousal) and to others (e.g., rape, child molestation, and obscene phone calls). Current psychological standards for determining the harmfulness of sexual behaviors center around the issues of coercion, potential harm to oneself or others, and personal distress.

We, the authors, believe that the basic standard for judging various sexual activities is whether they are between consenting adults and are expressed in sharing, enhancing, and nonexploitive ways. Understanding diverse sexual attitudes, motives, behaviors, and values will help deepen our own value systems and help us understand, accept, and appreciate our own sexuality and that of others.

Imagination is more important than knowledge.

—Albert Einstein
(1879–1955)

Final Thoughts

Sexuality can be a source of great pleasure and profound satisfaction as well as a source of guilt and means of exploitation. Popular culture both encourages and discourages sexuality. It promotes stereotypical sexual interactions but fails to touch on the deeper significance sexuality holds for us or the risks and responsibilities that accompany it. Love and sexuality in a committed relationship are infrequently depicted, in contrast to casual sex. The media often ignore or disparage the wide array of sexual behaviors and choices—from masturbation to gay, lesbian, bisexual, and transgender relationships—that are significant in many people's lives. They discourage the linking of sex and intimacy, contraceptive responsibility and the acknowledgment of the risk of contracting sexually transmitted infections.

What is clear from examining other cultures is that sexual behaviors and norms vary from culture to culture and, within our own society, from one time to another. The variety of sexual behaviors even within our own culture testifies to diversity not only between cultures but within cultures as well. Understanding diversity allows us to acknowledge that there is no such thing as inherently "normal" or "natural" sexual behavior. Rather, sexual behavior is strongly influenced by culture—including our own.

Summary

Studying Human Sexuality

- Students study sexuality for a variety of reasons. Examining the multiple aspects of this fascinating topic can help students understand, accept, and appreciate their own sexuality and that of others.

Sexuality, Popular Culture, and the Media

- The media are among the most powerful forces in people's lives today. Mass-media depictions of sexuality are meant primarily to entertain and exploit, not to inform.

- The Internet's contributions to the availability and commercialization of sex and sexuality information have made it easy for individuals to obtain information, strengthen social ties, and provide sexual gratification.

- Television and digital media are the most prevalent and pervasive media. At the same time, the risks and responsibilities that accompany this programming remain disproportionate to the sexual images that are portrayed.

Sexuality Across Cultures and Times

- One of the most powerful forces shaping human sexuality is culture. Culture molds and shapes our *sexual interests.*

- The Mangaia of Polynesia and the Dani of New Guinea represent cultures at the opposite ends of a continuum, with the Mangaia having an elaborate social and cultural framework for instructing adolescents in sexual technique and the Dani downplaying the importance of sex.

- Middle-class Americans in the nineteenth century believed that men had strong sexual drives but that women had little sexual desire. Because sexuality was considered animalistic, the Victorians separated sex and love. The sexual revolution brought significant changes to previous assumptions about sexuality.

- *Sexual orientation* is the pattern of sexual and emotional attraction based on the sex of one's partner. In contemporary America, *heterosexuality,* or attraction between men and women, is the only sexual orientation that receives full societal and legal legitimacy. *Homosexuality* refers to same-sex attractions, *bisexuality* involves attraction to both males and females, and *asexuality* is a state of having no sexual attraction to anyone, or low or absent sexual activity.

- In ancient Greece, same-sex relationships between men represented the highest form of love. Among the Sambians of New Guinea, boys have sexual contact with older boys, believing that the ingestion of semen is required for growth. When the girls to whom they are betrothed reach puberty, adolescent boys cease these same-sex sexual relations.

- The socially constructed roles, behaviors, activities, and attributes that a society considers appropriate for men and women are otherwise called *gender.* While culture helps to shape masculinity or femininity, biology defines men and women.

- A *two-spirit* is a person of one sex who identifies with the other sex; in some communities, such as the Zuni, a two-spirit is considered a third gender and is believed to possess great spiritual power.

Societal Norms and Sexuality

- Sexuality tends to be evaluated according to categories of natural/unnatural, normal/abnormal, and moral/immoral. These terms are value judgments, reflecting social norms rather than any quality inherent in the behavior itself.

- There is no commonly accepted definition of natural sexual behavior. *Normal sexual behavior* is what a culture defines as normal. We commonly use five criteria to categorize sexual behavior as normal or abnormal: subjectively normal, statistically normal, idealistically normal, culturally normal, and clinically normal.

- Human sexuality is characterized by *sexual variation.* Researchers believe that the best way to examine sexual behavior is on a continuum. Many activities that are considered deviant sexual behavior exist in most of us to some degree. These include exhibitionism, voyeurism, and fetishism.

- Behaviors are not abnormal or unnatural; rather, they are more or less typical or atypical of the group average. Many of those whose behaviors are atypical may be regarded as sexual nonconformists rather than as abnormal or perverse.

Questions for Discussion

- At what age do you believe a young person should be given a smartphone? What, if any, type of education should accompany it?

- To what extent do you think your peers are influenced by the media? How does it affect you?

- While growing up, what sexual behaviors did you consider to be normal? Abnormal? How have these views changed now that you are older?

Sex and the Internet

Sex and the Media

With hundreds of millions of sexuality-related websites available, you might wonder about the issues and laws associated with access to cyberspace. Though the following sites each deal primarily with intellectual freedom, they also contain information and links to other sites that address issues of sex and the media. Select one of the following:

- Electronic Frontier Foundation
  http://www.eff.org
- Entertainment Software Rating Board
  http://www.esrb.org/index-js.jsp
- National Coalition for Sexual Freedom
  http://www.ncsfreedom.org
- Pew Research Internet Project
  http://www.pewinternet.org

Go to the site and answer the following questions:

- What is the mission of the site—if any?
- Who are its supporters and advocates?
- Who is its target audience?
- What is its predominant message?
- What current issue is it highlighting?

Given what you have learned about this site, how do your feelings about sex and the Internet compare with those of the creators of this website?

Suggested Websites

National Gay and Lesbian Task Force

http://thetaskforce.org

Helps to build the grassroots power of the LGBT community by training activists, organizing campaigns, and providing research and policy analysis to support equality.

Sexuality Information and Education Council of the United States (SIECUS)

www.siecus.org

Educates, advocates, and informs about sexuality and sexual and reproductive health.

World Association for Sexual Health

http://www.worldsexology.org/

Promotes sexual health throughout the world by developing and supporting the field of human sexuality and sexual rights for all.

Suggested Reading

Castaneda, L., & Campbell, S. B. (Eds.). (2005). *News and sexuality: Media portrayals of diversity.* Thousand Oaks, CA: Sage. Provides an understanding of issues and perspectives on gender, race, ethnicity, and sexual orientation as addressed in the media.

Dines, G., & McMahon, J. M. (Eds.). (2015). *Gender, race and class in media: A critical reader* (4th ed.). Thousand Oaks, CA: Sage. An analysis of media entertainment culture.

Francoeur, R. T., & Noonan, R. (Eds.). (2004). *The continuum complete international encyclopedia of sexuality.* New York: Continuum. The foremost reference work on sexual behavior throughout the world.

Middleton, D. R. (2001). *Exotics and erotics: Human culture and sexual diversity.* Prospect Heights, IL: Waveland Press. Explores universal human sexuality in conjunction with its local manifestations in specific cultural contexts; topics include the body, patterns of sexuality, sexual behavior, romantic passion, marriage, and kinship.

Strasburger, V. C., Wilson, B. J., & Jordan, A. B. (2014). *Children, adolescents, and the media* (3rd ed.). Thousand Oaks, CA: Sage. Explores mass media, including the sexual messages the media convey and their impact on adolescents.

Tiefer, L. (2004). *Sex is not a natural act and other essays* (2nd ed.). Boulder, CO: Westview Press. A revised collection of provocative essays on sex and its many meanings in our culture.

Studying Human Sexuality

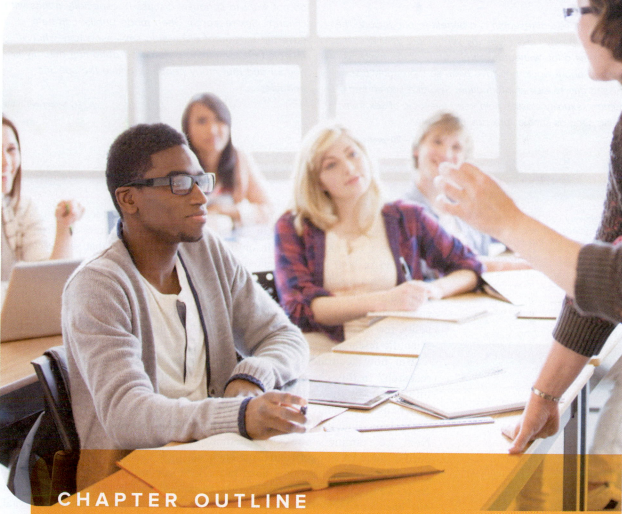

© Hero/Corbis/Glow Images

"I've heard about those sex surveys, and I wonder how truthful they are. I mean, don't you think that people who volunteer for those studies only report behaviors which they deem socially acceptable? I just don't think people who lose their virginity, for instance at age 12 or age 30, would actually report it. Besides, no sex study is going to tell me what I should do or whether I am normal."

—21-year-old male

"I feel that sexual research is a benefit to our society. The human sexuality class I took my sophomore year in college taught me a lot. Without research, many of the topics we learned about would not have been so thoroughly discussed due to lack of information. Sexual research and human sexuality classes help keep the topic of sex from being seen as such a faux pas by society."

—20-year-old female

"I took a sex survey once, during my undergraduate years. I found that the survey was easy to take, and the process of answering the questions actually led me to ask myself more questions about my sexual self. The survey was detailed, and I was encouraged to answer truthfully. Ultimately, every answer I gave was accurate because I knew that the research would benefit science (and it was completely anonymous)."

—22-year-old female

"I think sex research is great because it helps remove the taboo from the topic. Sex, in this country, is on TV, on the Internet, and in movies all the time, but people do not want to seriously discuss it, especially adults with children. Sex research, when made public, can help ease the tension of discussing sex—especially when it reveals that something considered abnormal actually is normal and that many people practice the specific behavior."

—24-year-old male

Discovery consists of seeing what everybody has seen and thinking what nobody has thought.

—Albert Szent-Györgyi
(1893–1986)

"**A** NEW UNIVERSITY STUDY finds that many college students lie to a new sexual partner about their sexual past . . . but first, a message from . . ." So begins a commercial lead-in on the news, reminding us that sex research is often part of both news and entertainment. In fact, most of us learn about the results of sex research from television, newspapers, the Internet, and magazines rather than from scholarly journals and books. After all, the mass media are more entertaining than most scholarly works. And unless we are studying human sexuality, few of us have the time or interest to read the scholarly journals in which scientific research is regularly published.

But how accurate is what the mass media tell us about sex and sex research? In this chapter, we discuss the dissemination of sexuality-related information by the various media. Then we look at the critical-thinking skills that help us evaluate how we discuss and think about sexuality. When are we making objective statements? When are we reflecting biases or opinions? Next, we examine sex research methods because they are critical to the scientific study of human sexuality. Then we look at some of the leading sex researchers to see how they have influenced our understanding of sexuality. Next, we discuss five national studies as examples of important research that has been conducted. Finally, we examine feminist, gay, lesbian, bisexual, transgender, and ethnic sex research to see how they enrich our knowledge of sexuality.

● Sex, Advice Columnists, and Pop Psychology

As we've seen, the mass media convey seemingly endless sexual images. Besides various television, film, Internet, and advertising genres, there is another genre, which we might call the **sex information/advice genre,** which transmits information and norms, rather than images, about sexuality to a mass audience to both inform and entertain in a simplified manner. For many college students, as well as others, the sex information/advice genre is a major source of their knowledge about sex. This genre is ostensibly concerned with transmitting information that is factual and accurate. In addition, on an increasing number of college campuses, sex columns in student-run newspapers have become popular and sometimes controversial, as some college administrators have been concerned that the information provided is too explicit.

Information and Advice as Entertainment

Newspaper columns, Internet sites, syndicated radio shows, magazine articles, and TV programs share several features. First, their primary purpose is financial profit. This goal is in marked contrast to the primary purpose of scholarly research, which is to increase knowledge. Even the inclusion of survey questionnaires in magazines asking readers about their sexual attitudes or behaviors is ultimately designed to promote sales. We fill out the questionnaires for fun, much as we would crossword puzzles or anagrams. Then we buy the subsequent issue or watch a later program to see how we compare to other respondents.

Second, the success of media personalities rests not so much on their expertise as on their ability to present information as entertainment. Because the genre seeks to entertain, sex information and advice must be simplified. Complex explanations and analyses must be avoided because they would interfere with the entertainment purpose. Furthermore, the genre relies on high-interest or bizarre material to attract readers, viewers, and listeners. Consequently, we are more likely to read, view, or hear stories about unusual sexual behaviors or ways to increase sexual attractiveness than stories about new research methods or the negative outcomes of sexual stereotyping.

If you believe everything you read, don't read.

—Chinese proverb

Third, the genre focuses on how-to information or on morality. Sometimes it mixes information and normative judgments. How-to material tells us how to improve our sex lives. Advice columnists often give advice on issues of sexual morality: "Is it all right to have sex without commitment?" "Yes, if you love him/her" or "No, casual sex is empty" and so on. These columnists act as moral arbiters, much as ministers, priests, and rabbis do.

Fourth, the genre uses the trappings of social science and psychiatry without their substance. Writers and columnists interview social scientists and therapists to give an aura of scientific authority to their material. They rely especially heavily on therapists, whose background is clinical rather than academic. Because clinicians tend to deal with people with problems, they often see the problematic aspects of sexuality.

The line between media sex experts and advice columnists is often blurred. This line is especially obscure on the Internet, where websites dealing with sexuality have proliferated. Most of these sites are purely for entertainment rather than education, and it can be difficult to determine a site's credibility. One way to assess the educational value of a website is to investigate its sponsor. Reputable national organizations like the American Psychological

Does Sex Have an Inherent Meaning?

Some people are afraid that if sex has no inherent meaning and they do not salute it, they won't behave ethically.

—Marty Klein (2012, p. 158)

Renowned sex therapist and author Marty Klein **addresses a commonly believed idea that sex has inherent meaning by provocatively stating that "sex has no inherent meaning" (Klein, 2012).** He states that individuals can make their sexual experiences meaningful but that sex is meaningless until and unless they give it meaning. Klein continues by noting that many people give sex too much meaning and often the wrong type of meaning. When sex has too much meaning, too much is riding on each sexual encounter, producing both pressure and anxiety that interferes with pleasurable and rewarding sexual expression.

The meanings of sexuality are derived from the religious, political, ethical, and legal interpretations of sexuality, reflecting how culture describes why we have sex. Some meanings or distinctive purposes of human sexual expression commonly held include:

■ What individuals do when they love each other
■ The ultimate expression of love
■ A divine gift to humans
■ A validation of our identities as a man or woman
■ A supreme gift to another person
■ A method of strengthening a relationship
■ A way of fulfilling desire

Historically, the naming and categorization of sexual behaviors have reflected efforts to "normalize" specific sexual behavior and to label unsanctioned behavior as abnormal, resulting in many persons being stigmatized. The variation of sexual expression was not recognized or endorsed. An example of efforts to attach meaning to sexuality is the "invention of heterosexuality" and heterosexual-homosexual dichotomization of sexual orientation.

In her book *Straight: The Surprisingly Short History of Heterosexuality,* author Hanne Blank (2012) states that the term "heterosexuality" first appeared in the medical literature in 1869, offering a way to validate and support the religious priorities of heterosexual marriage and to be a synonym of "sexually normal." Blank contends that normal is not a mode of eternal truth but a mechanism to describe commonness and conformity to expectations. She continues by noting:

The original creation of "heterosexual" and "homosexual" had nothing to do with scientists or science at all. Nor did it have anything to do with biology or medicine. There is, biomedically speaking, nothing about what human beings do sexually that requires that something like what we now think of as "sexual orientation" exists. Virtually everyone alive today, especially in the developed world, has lived their entire lives in a culture of sexuality that assumes that "heterosexual" and "homosexual" are objectively real elements of nature (pp. xiv–xvi).

As described in this chapter, Alfred C. Kinsey ordered individuals on a 0–6 scale instead of the binary heterosexual-homosexual model or triad model of homosexual, bisexual, and heterosexual. His scale shifted the perspective and conversation about the classification of sexual behavior toward a focus on multiple varieties and combinations of sexual desire, behavior, and fantasy, resulting in variation being more culturally, scientifically, and politically determined to be normal (Drucker, 2014). In speaking about the diversity of sexual orientation, Kinsey (Kinsey, Pomeroy, & Martin, 1948) said:

Males [similarly for females] do not represent two discrete populations, heterosexual and homosexual. The world is not to be divided into sheep and goats. Not all things are black and white. It is a fundamental of taxonomy that nature rarely deals with discrete categories. Only the human mind invents categories and tries to force facts into separated pigeon-holes. The living world is a continuum in each and every one of its aspects. The sooner we learn this concerning human sexual behavior the sooner we shall reach a sound understanding of the realities of sex (p. 639).

Klein contends that when people believe that sex has inherent meaning they want to experience sex that fulfills the meaning, and if they don't, they assume there is something wrong with them or their partner. Some worry that they are not fulfilling some duty to "honor" sex, such as avoiding having sex "like animals." He purports that we should not be serving sex but sex should be serving us: this perspective enables one to experience a huge range of sexual feelings and meanings. Klein states:

> If we think that sex has inherent meaning and that it's our job to both find and conform to that meaning, we won't be able to see sex freshly, we won't be motivated to perceive or act counterintuitively, and we'll accept arbitrary, outside limits on our erotic activities. If you want to give sex meaning, go ahead. At the same time, remember to enjoy the freedom of playful, amoral (not immoral, *amoral*) sex (p. 157).

SOURCES: Blank, H. (2012). *Straight: The Surprisingly Short History of Heterosexuality.* Boston: Beacon Press; Drucker, D. J. (2014). *The Classification of Sex: Alfred Kinsey and the Organization of Knowledge.* Pittsburgh: University of Pittsburgh Press; Kinsey, A., Pomeroy, W., & Martin, C. *Sexual Behavior in the Human Male.* Philadelphia: Saunders; Klein, M. (2012). *Sexual Intelligence: What We Really Want from Sex—and How to Get It.* New York: Harper One.

Association (http://www.apa.org) and the Sexuality Information and Education Council of the United States (http://www.siecus.org) provide reliable information and links to other, equally reputable, sites.

The Use and Abuse of Research Findings

To reinforce their authority, the media often incorporate statistics from a study's findings, which are key features of social science research. Further, the media may report the results of a study that are contradicted by subsequent research. It is common, particularly in the medical field, for the original results not to be replicated when continued research is conducted (Tanner, 2005). For example, a review of major studies published in three influential medical journals from 1990 to 2003 found that one third of the results do not hold up (Ionannidis, 2005). But, of course, changes in "current knowledge" also happen in behavioral research. For example, an assertion that is often presented in the media as definitive is that the consumption of alcohol always leads to risky sexual behaviors. However, studies have found that among young people the relationship between alcohol use and risky sexual behaviors is complex and often the research findings are inconsistent or inconclusive (Cooper, 2006). An alternative explanation is that possibly a high proportion of young people take more risks than other young people in several areas such as cigarette use, drug use, alcohol use, driving, and sex. That is, there is a clustering of risk behaviors representing high sensation seeking, and alcohol use alone does not cause risky sex but both are part of the total risk behavior pattern (Coleman, 2001; Coleman & Cater, 2005).

The media frequently quote or describe social science research, but they may do so in an oversimplified or distorted manner. An excellent example of distorted representation of sex-related research was some of the media coverage of the research on ram sheep by Charles Roselli, a researcher at the Oregon Health and Science University. Roselli searched for physiological explanations of why 8% of rams exclusively seek sex with other rams instead of ewes. His research was funded by the National Institutes of Health and published in major scientific journals. Following media coverage of his research, animal-rights activists, gay advocates, and others criticized the studies. A *New York Times* article in January 2007 noted that his research drew outrage based on, according to Roselli and his colleagues, "bizarre misinterpretation of what the work is about." The researchers contended that discussion of possible human implications of their findings in their reports differed from intentions of carrying the work over to humans. Critics claimed that the research could lead to altering or controlling sexual orientation. According to the *Times* article, *The Sunday Times* in London asserted, incorrectly, that Dr. Roselli found a way to "cure" homosexual rams with hormone treatment, adding that critics feared the research "could pave the way for breeding out homosexuality in humans." John Schwartz, author of the *Times* article, concluded that "the story of the gay sheep became a textbook example of the distortion and vituperation that can result when science meets the global news cycle" (Schwartz, 2007). As this example illustrates, scholars tend to qualify their findings as tentative or limited to a certain group, and they are very cautious about making generalizations. In contrast, the media tend to make results sound generalizable.

● Thinking Objectively About Sexuality

He who knows nothing doubts nothing.

—French proverb

Although each of us has our own perspective, values, and beliefs regarding sexuality, as students, instructors, and researchers, we are committed to the scientific study of sexuality. Basic to any scientific study is a fundamental commitment to **objectivity,** or the observation of things as they exist in reality as opposed to our feelings or beliefs about them. Objectivity calls for us to suspend the beliefs, biases, or prejudices we have about a subject in order to understand it.

Objectivity in the study of sexuality is not always easy to achieve, for sexuality can be the focal point of powerful emotions and moral ambivalence. We experience sex very subjectively. But whether we find it easy or difficult to be objective, objectivity is the foundation for studying sexuality.

Most of us think about sex, but thinking about it critically requires us to be logical and objective. It also requires that we avoid making value judgments; put aside our opinions, biases, and stereotypes; and not fall prey to common fallacies such as egocentric and ethnocentric thinking.

Value Judgments Versus Objectivity

Morality is simply the attitude we adopt towards people we personally dislike.

—Oscar Wilde
(1854–1900)

For many of us, objectivity about sex is difficult because our culture has traditionally viewed sexuality in moral terms: Sex is moral or immoral, right or wrong, good or bad, normal or abnormal. When examining sexuality, we tend, therefore, to make **value judgments,** evaluations based on moral or ethical standards rather than objective ones. Unfortunately, value judgments are often blinders to understanding. They do not tell us about what motivates people, how frequently they behave in a given way, or how they feel. Value judgments do not tell us anything about sexuality except how we ourselves feel. In studying human sexuality, then, we need to put aside value judgments as incompatible with the pursuit of knowledge.

How can we tell the difference between a value judgment and an objective statement? Examine the following two statements and determine which is a value judgment and which is an objective statement:

- College students should be in a committed relationship before they have sex.
- The majority of students have sexual intercourse sometime during their college careers.

The first statement is a value judgment; the second is an objective statement. There is a simple rule of thumb for telling the difference between the two: Value judgments imply how a person *ought* to behave, whereas objective statements describe how people *actually* behave.

There is a second difference between value judgments and objective statements: Value judgments cannot be empirically validated, whereas objective statements can be. That is, the truth or accuracy of an objective statement can be measured and tested.

Opinions, Biases, and Stereotypes

Value judgments obscure our search for understanding. Opinions, biases, and stereotypes also interfere with the pursuit of knowledge.

Opinions   An **opinion** is an unsubstantiated belief or conclusion about what seems to be true according to our thoughts. Opinions are not based on accurate knowledge or concrete evidence. Because opinions are unsubstantiated, they often reflect our personal values or biases and rarely change unless we are open to verifiable facts.

> The human understanding when it has once adopted an opinion . . . draws all things else to support and agree with it.
>
> —Francis Bacon
> (1561–1626)

Biases   A **bias** is a personal leaning or inclination that reflects a prejudice in favor of or against a person, group, or thing in contrast to another. Biases lead us to select information that supports our views or beliefs while ignoring information that does not. We need not be victims, however, of our biases. We can make a concerted effort to discover what they are and overcome them. To avoid personal bias, scholars apply the objective methods of social science research.

> Facts do not cease to exist because they are ignored.
>
> —Aldous Huxley
> (1894–1963)

Stereotypes   A **stereotype** is a set of simplistic, rigidly held, overgeneralized beliefs about a particular type of individual or group of people, an idea, and so on. Stereotypical beliefs are resistant to change. Furthermore, stereotypes—especially sexual ones—are often negative.

Common sexual stereotypes include the following:

- Men are always ready for sex.
- "Nice" women are not interested in sex.
- Women need a reason for sex; men need a place.
- Virgins are uptight and asexual.
- The relationships of gay men never last.
- Lesbian women hate men.
- African American men lust after White women.
- Latino men are promiscuous.

Psychologists believe that stereotypes structure knowledge. They affect the ways in which we process information: what we see, what we notice, what we remember, and how we explain things. Or as humorist Ashleigh Brilliant said, "Seeing is believing. I wouldn't have seen it if I hadn't believed it." A stereotype is a type of **schema,** a way in which we organize knowledge in our thought processes. Schemas help us channel or filter the mass of information we receive so that we can make sense of it. They determine what we will regard as important. Although these mental plans are useful, they can also create blind spots. With stereotypes, we see what we expect to see and ignore what we don't expect or want to see.

Sociologists point out that sexual stereotyping is often used to justify discrimination. Targets of stereotypes are usually members of subordinate social groups or individuals with limited economic resources. As we will see, sexual stereotyping is especially powerful in stigmatizing African Americans, Latinos, Asian Americans, gay men, lesbian women, and bisexual and transgender individuals.

We all have opinions and biases, and most of us to varying degrees think stereotypically. But the commitment to objectivity requires us to become aware of our opinions, biases, and stereotypes and to put them aside in the pursuit of knowledge.

Common Fallacies: Egocentric and Ethnocentric Thinking

A **fallacy** is an error in reasoning that affects our understanding of a subject. Fallacies distort our thinking, leading us to false or erroneous conclusions. In the field of sexuality, egocentric and ethnocentric fallacies are common.

The Egocentric Fallacy   The **egocentric fallacy** is the mistaken belief that our own personal experience and values generally are held by others. On the basis of our belief in this false consensus, we use our own beliefs and values to explain the attitudes, motivations, and behaviors of others. Of course, our own experiences and values are important; they are the source of personal strength and knowledge, and they can give us insight into the experiences and values of others. But we cannot necessarily generalize from our own experience to that of others. Our own personal experiences are limited and may be unrepresentative. Sometimes, our generalizations are merely opinions or disguised value judgments.

The Ethnocentric Fallacy   The **ethnocentric fallacy,** also known as ethnocentrism, is the belief that our own ethnic group, nation, or culture is innately superior to others. **Ethnocentrism** is reinforced by opinions, biases, and stereotypes about other groups and cultures. As members of a group, we tend to share similar values and attitudes with other group members. But the mere fact that we share these beliefs is not sufficient proof of their truth.

Ethnocentrism has been increasingly evident as a reaction to the increased awareness of ethnicity, or ethnic affiliation or identity. For many Americans, a significant part of their sense of self comes from identification with their ethnic group. An ethnic group is a group of people distinct from other groups because of cultural characteristics, such as language, religion, and customs, that are transmitted from one generation to the next.

Although there was little research on ethnicity and sexuality until the 1980s, evidence suggests that there are significant ethnic variations in terms of sexual attitudes and behavior. When data are available, the variations by ethnicity will be presented throughout this book.

Ethnocentrism is the belief that one's own culture or ethnic group is superior to others. Although child marriage is prohibited in our society, it is acceptable in many cultures throughout the world, including India.

© STRDEL/AFP/Getty Images

Ethnocentrism results when we stereotype other cultures as "primitive," "innocent," "inferior," or "not as advanced." We may view the behavior of other peoples as strange, exotic, unusual, or bizarre, but to them it is normal. Their attitudes, behaviors, values, and beliefs form a unified sexual system that makes sense within their culture. In fact, we engage in many activities that appear peculiar to those outside our culture.

● Sex Research Methods

One of the key factors that distinguish the findings of social science from beliefs, prejudice, bias, and pop psychology is the field's commitment to the scientific method. The **scientific method** is the method by which a hypothesis is formed from impartially gathered data and tested empirically. The scientific method relies on **induction**—that is, drawing a general conclusion from specific facts. The scientific method seeks to describe the world rather than evaluate or judge it.

Although sex researchers, sometimes called **sexologists,** use the same methodology as other social scientists, they are constrained by ethical concerns and taboos that those in many other fields do not experience. Because of the taboos surrounding sexuality, some traditional research methods are inappropriate (Schick, Calabrese, & Herbenick, 2014).

Sex research, like most social science research, uses varied methodological approaches. These include clinical research, survey research (questionnaires and interviews), observational research, and experimental research. And as in many fields, no single research approach has emerged in sexual science (Weis, 2002).

Research Concerns

Researchers face two general concerns in conducting their work: (1) ethical concerns centering on the use of human beings as subjects and (2) methodological concerns regarding sampling techniques and their accuracy. Without a representative sample, the conclusions that can be drawn using these methodologies are limited.

Ethical Issues   A fundamental principle of research is informed consent. **Informed consent** means that people are free to decide, without coercion, whether to participate in a research study. This occurs following the full disclosure to an individual of the study purpose and the potential risks and the benefits of being a participant in the research project. Studies involving children and other minors typically require parental consent. Once a study begins, participants have the right to withdraw at any time without penalty.

Each research participant is entitled to **protection from harm.** Some sex research, such as the viewing of explicit films to measure physiological responses, may cause some people emotional distress. The identity of research subjects should be kept confidential. Because of the highly charged nature of sexuality, participants also need to be guaranteed anonymity.

All colleges and universities have review boards or human-subject committees to make sure that researchers follow ethical guidelines. Proposed research is submitted to the committee for approval before the project begins.

A couple is being interviewed by a sex researcher. The face-to-face interview, one method of gathering data about sexuality, has both advantages and disadvantages.

© sturti/iStock/Getty Images

Sampling In each research approach, the choice of a sample—a portion of a larger group of people or population—is critical. To be most useful, a sample should be a **random sample**—that is, a sample collected in an unbiased way, with the selection of each member of the sample based solely on chance. Furthermore, the sample should be a **representative sample,** with a small group representing the larger group in terms of age, sex, ethnicity, socioeconomic status, sexual orientation, and so on. With a random sample, information gathered from a small group can be used to make inferences about the larger group. Samples that are not representative of the larger group are known as **biased samples** (Crosby, DiClemente, & Salazar, 2006).

Using samples is important. It would be impossible, for example, to study the sexual behaviors of all college students in the United States. But we could select a representative sample of college students from various schools and infer from their behavior how other college students behave. Using the same sample to infer the sexual behavior of Americans in general, however, would mean using a biased sample. We cannot generalize the sexual activities of American college students to the larger population.

Most samples in sex research are limited for several reasons:

- They depend on volunteers or clients. Because these samples are generally self-selected, we cannot assume that they are representative of the population as a whole. Volunteers for sex research are often more likely to be male, sexually experienced, liberal, and less religious and to have more positive attitudes toward sexuality and less sex guilt and anxiety than those who do not choose to participate (Strassberg & Lowe, 1995; Wiederman, 1999).

- Most sex research takes place in a university or college setting with student volunteers. Their sex-related attitudes, values, and behaviors may be very different from those of other adults.

- Some ethnic groups are generally underrepresented. Representative samples of African Americans, Latinos, American Indians, Middle Eastern Americans, and some Asian Americans, for example, are not easily found because these groups are underrepresented at the colleges and universities where subjects are generally recruited.

- The study of gay men, lesbian women, and bisexual and transgender individuals presents unique sampling issues. Are gay men, lesbian women, and bisexual individuals who have **come out**—publicly identified themselves as gay, lesbian, or bisexual—different from those who have not? How do researchers find and recruit subjects who have not come out?

Because these factors limit most studies, we must be careful in making generalizations from studies.

Clinical Research

Clinical research is the in-depth examination of an individual or group that goes to a psychiatrist, psychologist, or social worker for assistance with psychological or medical problems or disorders. Clinical research is descriptive; inferences of cause and effect cannot be drawn from it. The individual is interviewed and treated for a specific problem. At the same time the person is being treated, he or she is being studied. In their evaluations, clinicians attempt to determine what caused the disorder and how it may be treated. They may also try to infer from dysfunctional people how healthy people develop. Clinical research often focuses on atypical, unhealthy behaviors, problems related to sexuality (e.g., feeling trapped in the body of the wrong gender), and sexual function problems (e.g., lack of desire, early ejaculation, erectile difficulties, or lack of orgasm).

A major limitation of clinical research is its emphasis on **pathological behavior,** or unhealthy or diseased behavior. Such an emphasis makes clinical research dependent on cultural definitions of what is "unhealthy" or "pathological." These definitions, however, change over time and in the context of the culture being studied. In the nineteenth century, for example, masturbation was considered pathological. Physicians and clinicians went to great lengths to root it out. In the case of women, surgeons sometimes removed the clitoris. Today, masturbation is viewed more positively.

Survey Research

Survey research is a method that uses questionnaires or **interviews** to gather information. Questionnaires offer anonymity, can be completed fairly quickly, and are relatively inexpensive to administer; however, they usually do not allow an in-depth response. A person must respond with a short answer or select from a limited number of options. The limited-choices format provides a more objective assessment than the short-answer format and results in a total score. Interview techniques avoid some of the shortcomings of questionnaires, as interviewers are able to probe in greater depth and follow paths suggested by the participant.

Although surveys are important sources of information, the method has several limitations, as people may be poor reporters of their own sexual behavior:

- Some people may exaggerate their number of sexual partners; others may minimize their casual encounters.

- Respondents generally underreport experiences that might be culturally considered deviant or immoral, such as bondage and same-sex experiences.

- Some respondents may feel uncomfortable about revealing information—such as about masturbation or fetishes—in a face-to-face interview.

- The accuracy of one's memory may fade as time passes, and providing an accurate estimation, such as how long sex lasted, may be difficult.

- Some ethnic groups, because of their cultural values, may be reluctant to reveal sexual information about themselves.

- Interviewers may allow their own preconceptions to influence the way in which they frame questions and to bias their interpretations of responses.

- The interviewer's sex, race, religion, or sexual orientation may also influence how comfortable respondents are in disclosing information about themselves.

One of the great tragedies of life is the murder of a beautiful theory by a gang of brutal facts.

—Benjamin Franklin
(1705–1790)

Interestingly, despite these limitations of self-reporting of sexual behavior, a recent review of seven population-based surveys of adults in the United States concluded that self-reported data may not be as unreliable as generally assumed. The study examined the consistency in the number of sexual partners reported in these seven national studies and found a remarkable level of consistency among the studies. The researchers concluded that the findings show promise for research that relies on self-reported number of sexual partners (Hamilton & Morris, 2010).

Some researchers use computers to improve interviewing techniques for sensitive topics. With the audio computer-assisted self-interviewing (audio-CASI) method, the respondent hears the questions over headphones or reads them on a computer screen and then enters his or her responses into the computer. Audio-CASI, an increasingly popular method of data collection, apparently increases feelings of confidentiality and accuracy of responses on sensitive topics such as sexual risk behaviors (Cooley et al., 2001; Des Jarlais et al., 1999; Potdar & Koenig, 2005). Even though the use of audio-CASI has advantages, research has found that the use of the audio part by respondents was limited and that gains in more candid responses from the audio component are modest relative to text-only CASI (Couper, Tourangeau, & Marvin, 2009).

Other types of computer-based technology being used for data collection include: (1) computer-assisted telephone interviewing, involving a telephone interviewer administering a scripted questionnaire and then entering the participant's responses directly into the computer and (2) computer-assisted personal interviewing, during which a face-to-face interviewer administers a scripted questionnaire and enters the responses of the participant directly into the computer. Such technologies, including smart phones, have several advantages including convenient data entry and the ability to enter information about sexual-related variables (e.g., attitudes and behaviors) at a specified time such as soon after a sexual episode with a partner (McCallum & Peterson, 2012; Schick, Calabrese, & Herbenick, 2014).

Another technology technique is the use of the Internet to administer questionnaires and conduct interviews. Since the mid-1990s, the use of the Internet has become a popular method of survey research, largely because of its ability to collect data quickly and to eliminate the costs of other methods such as travel expenses for interviews, office space for interviews, printing and mailing of written questionnaires, and the software for audio-CASI. The use of the Internet can also result in larger samples. For example, a British Internet study on sexuality and gender had about 255,000 participants (Reimers, 2007). Because of the large number of Internet websites, social networks, and chat rooms that serve particular populations such as sexual minorities, the Internet facilitates access to hard-to-reach groups as well as geographically isolated persons. For example, stigmatized groups such as bisexual individuals may feel more comfortable participating via the Internet. While an advantage of the Internet is the perceived anonymity by the participant, it can be a disadvantage in that a researcher is not present to clarify survey instructions or questions or to verify that the participant is the person he or she claims to be (Schick et al., 2014).

Daily data collection, using a **sexual diary,** or personal notes of one's sexual activity, can increase the accuracy of self-reported data and make possible the analysis of any specific sexual-related event (Crosby et al., 2006). Often, research participants make daily diary entries online or by phone, for example, about sexual variables such as interest, fantasies, and behavior. Or they may be requested to make entries only after a certain sexual activity has occurred, such

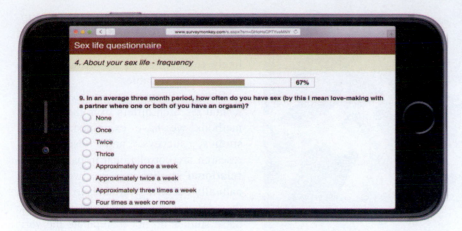

as intercourse. Research suggests that event-specific behaviors such as condom use during sex will be more accurately recalled in diaries than by retrospective methods such as self-report questionnaires and interviews (Fortenberry, Cecil, Zimet, & Orr, 1997; Gilmore et al., 2001; Graham & Bancroft, 1997; McAuliffe, DiFranceisco, & Reed, 2007).

Observational Research

Observational research is a method by which a researcher unobtrusively observes and makes systematic notes about people's behavior without trying to manipulate it. The observer does not want his or her presence to affect the subject's behavior, although this is rarely possible. Because sexual behavior is regarded as significantly different from other behaviors, there are serious ethical issues involved in observing people's sexual behavior without their knowledge and consent. Researchers cannot observe sexual behavior as they might observe, say, flirting at a party, dance, or bar, so such observations usually take place in a laboratory setting. In such instances, the setting is not a natural environment, and participants are aware that their behavior is under observation.

Ignorance is like a delicate exotic fruit; touch it and the bloom is gone.

—Oscar Wilde
(1854–1900)

    Participant observation, in which the researcher participates in the behaviors he or she is studying, is an important method of observational research. For example, a researcher may study prostitution by becoming a customer or may study anonymous sex between men in public restrooms by posing as a lookout (Humphreys, 1975). There are several questions raised by such participant observation: How does the observer's participation affect the interactions being studied? For example, does a prostitute respond differently to a researcher if he or she tries to obtain information? If the observer participates, how does this affect his or her objectivity? And what are the researcher's ethical responsibilities regarding informing those he or she is studying?

Experimental Research

Experimental research is the systematic manipulation of individuals or the environment to learn the effects of such manipulation on behavior. It enables researchers to isolate a single factor under controlled circumstances to determine its influence. Researchers are able to control their experiments by using **variables,** or aspects or factors that can be manipulated in experiments. There are two types of variables: independent and dependent. **Independent**

Participant observation is an important means by which anthropologists gain information about other cultures.

© Pascale Beroujon/Getty Images

variables are factors that can be manipulated or changed by the experimenter; **dependent variables** are factors that are likely to be affected by changes in the independent variable.

Because it controls variables, experimental research differs from the previous methods we have examined. Clinical studies, surveys, and observational research are correlational in nature. **Correlational studies** measure two or more naturally occurring variables to determine their relationship to each other. Because these studies do not manipulate the variables, they cannot tell us which variable *causes* the other to change. But experimental studies manipulate the independent variables, so researchers *can* reasonably determine what variables cause the other variables to change.

Much experimental research on sexuality depends on measuring physiological responses. These responses are usually measured by **plethysmographs** (pluh-THIZ-muh-grafs)—devices attached to the genitals to measure physiological response. Two of the most frequently used methods of penile plethysmograph assessment is the measurement of the penis circumference using a **strain gauge** (a device resembling a rubber band that fits around the penis) and the measurement of the volume of the penis using an airtight cylinder and cuff placed on the base of the penis. The device measures penile engorgement but not necessarily sexual desire or sexual arousal as we know that men can experience erections (e.g. awaken from sleep with an erection). The vaginal plethysmograph is about the size of a menstrual tampon and is inserted into the vagina like a tampon. The device measures the amount of blood within the vaginal walls, which increases as a woman becomes sexually aroused (Chivers, Suschinsky, Timmers, & Bossio, 2014). The device may not be a good indicator of female sexual arousal as studies have shown poor correlations between women's self-reported sexual desire and device readings (Chivers, Seto, Lalumière, Laan, & Grimbos, 2010).

Suppose researchers want to study the influence of alcohol on sexual response. They can use a plethysmograph to measure sexual response, the dependent variable. In this study, the independent variable is the level of alcohol consumption: no alcohol consumption, moderate alcohol consumption (1–3 drinks), and high alcohol consumption (3+ drinks). In such an experiment, subjects may view an erotic video. To get a baseline measurement, researchers measure the genitals' physiological patterns in an unaroused state, before participants view the video or take a drink. Then they measure sexual arousal (dependent variable) in response to erotica as they increase the level of alcohol consumption (independent variable).

● The Sex Researchers

Judge a man by his questions rather than by his answers.

—Voltaire (1694–1778)

It was not until the nineteenth century that Western sexuality began to be studied using a scientific framework. Prior to that time, sexuality was the domain of religion rather than science; sex was the subject of moral rather than scientific scrutiny. From the earliest Christian era, treatises, canon law, and papal bulls, as well as sermons and confessions, catalogued the sins of the flesh. Reflecting this Christian tradition, the early researchers of sexuality were concerned with the supposed excesses and deviances of sexuality rather than its healthy functioning. They were fascinated by what they considered the pathologies of sex, such as fetishism, sadism, masturbation, and homosexuality—the very behaviors that religion condemned as sinful. Alfred Kinsey ironically noted that nineteenth-century researchers created "scientific classifications . . . nearly identical with theological classifications and with moral pronouncements . . . of the fifteenth century" (Kinsey, Pomeroy, & Martin, 1948).

As we will see, however, there has been a liberalizing trend in our thinking about sexuality. Both Richard von Krafft-Ebing and Sigmund Freud viewed sexuality as inherently dangerous and needing repression. But Havelock Ellis, Alfred Kinsey, William Masters and Virginia Johnson, and many other more recent researchers have viewed sexuality more positively; in fact, historian Paul Robinson (1976) regards these later researchers as modernists, or "sexual enthusiasts." Three themes are evident in the work of modernists: (1) They believe that sexual expression is essential to an individual's well-being, (2) they seek to broaden the range of legitimate sexual activity, including homosexuality, and (3) they believe that female sexuality is the equal of male sexuality.

As much as possible, sex researchers attempt to examine sexuality objectively. But, as with all of us, many of their views are intertwined with the beliefs and values of their times. This is especially apparent among the early sex researchers, some of the most important of whom are described here.

Richard von Krafft-Ebing

Richard von Krafft-Ebing (1840–1902), a Viennese professor of psychiatry, was probably the most influential of the early researchers. In 1886 he published his most famous work, *Psychopathia Sexualis,* a collection of case histories of fetishists, sadists, masochists, and homosexuals. (He invented the words "sadomasochism" and "transvestite.")

Krafft-Ebing traced variations in Victorian sexuality to "hereditary taint," to "moral degeneracy," and, in particular, to masturbation. He intermingled descriptions of fetishists who became sexually excited by certain items of clothing with those of sadists who disemboweled their victims. For Krafft-Ebing, the origins of fetishism and murderous sadism, as well as most variations, lay in masturbation, the prime sexual sin of the nineteenth century. Despite his misguided focus on masturbation, Krafft-Ebing's *Psychopathia Sexualis* brought to public attention and discussion an immense range of sexual behaviors that had never before been documented in a dispassionate, if erroneous, manner. A darkened region of sexual behavior was brought into the open for public examination.

Sigmund Freud

Few people have had as dramatic an impact on the way we think about the world as the Viennese physician Sigmund Freud (1856–1939). In his attempt to understand the **neuroses,** or psychological disorders characterized by anxiety or tension, plaguing his patients, Freud explored the unknown territory of the unconscious. If unconscious motives were brought to consciousness, Freud believed, a person could change his or her behavior. But, he suggested, **repression,** a psychological mechanism that kept people from becoming aware of hidden memories and motives because they aroused guilt, prevents such knowledge.

Richard von Krafft-Ebing (1840–1902) viewed most sexual behavior other than marital coitus as a sign of pathology.

© Imagno/Getty Images

Sigmund Freud (1856–1939) was the founder of psychoanalysis and one of the most influential European thinkers of the first half of the twentieth century. Freud viewed sexuality with suspicion.

© Ingram Publishing

To explore the unconscious, Freud used various techniques; in particular, he analyzed dreams to discover their meaning. His journeys into the mind led to the development of **psychoanalysis,** a psychological system that ascribes behavior to unconscious desires. He fled Vienna when Hitler annexed Austria in 1938 and died a year later in England.

Freud believed that sexuality begins at birth, a belief that set him apart from other researchers. Freud described five stages in psychosexual development. The first stage is the **oral stage,** lasting from birth to age 1. During this time, the infant's eroticism is focused on the mouth; thumb sucking produces an erotic pleasure. Freud believed that the "most striking character of this sexual activity . . . is that the child gratifies himself on his own body; . . . he is autoerotic" (Freud, 1938). The second stage, between ages 1 and 3, is the **anal stage.** Children's sexual activities continue to be autoerotic, but the region of pleasure shifts to the anus. From age 3 through 5, children are in the **phallic stage,** in which they exhibit interest in the genitals. At age 6, children enter a **latency stage,** in which their sexual impulses are no longer active. At puberty, they enter the **genital stage,** at which point they become interested in genital sexual activities, especially sexual intercourse.

The phallic stage is the critical stage in both male and female development. The boy develops sexual desires for his mother, leading to an **Oedipal complex.** He simultaneously desires his mother and fears his father. This fear leads to **castration anxiety,** the boy's belief that his penis will be cut off by his father because of jealousy. Girls follow a more complex developmental path, according to Freud. A girl develops an **Electra complex,** desiring her father while fearing her mother. Upon discovering that she does not have a penis, she feels deprived and develops **penis envy.** By age 6, boys and girls have resolved their Oedipal and Electra complexes by relinquishing their desires for the parent of the other sex and identifying with their same-sex parent. In this manner, they develop their masculine and feminine identities. But because girls never acquire their "lost penis," Freud believed, they fail to develop an independent character like that of boys.

In many ways, such as in his commitment to science and his explorations of the unconscious, Freud seems the embodiment of twentieth-century thought. But in recent times, his influence among American sex researchers has dwindled. Two of the most important reasons are his lack of empiricism and his inadequate description of female development.

Because of its limitations, Freud's work has become mostly of historical interest to mainstream sex researchers. It continues to exert influence in some fields of psychology but has been greatly modified by other fields. Even among contemporary psychoanalysts, Freud's work has been radically revised.

Havelock Ellis

English physician and psychologist Havelock Ellis (1859–1939) was the earliest important modern sexual theorist and scholar. His *Studies in the Psychology of Sex* (the first six volumes of which were published between 1897 and 1910) consisted of case studies, autobiographies, and personal letters. One of his most important contributions was pointing out the relativity of sexual values. In the nineteenth century, Americans and Europeans alike believed that their society's dominant sexual beliefs were the only morally and naturally correct standards. But Ellis demonstrated not only that Western sexual standards were hardly the only moral standards but also that they were not necessarily rooted in nature. In doing so, he was among the first researchers to appeal to studies in animal behavior, anthropology, and history.

Havelock Ellis (1859–1939) argued that many behaviors previously labeled as abnormal were actually normal, including masturbation and female sexuality. For example, he found no evidence that masturbation leads to mental disorders, and he documented that women have sexual drives no less intense than those of men.

© Hulton-Deutsch Collection/Corbis

Ellis also challenged the view that masturbation was abnormal. He argued that masturbation was widespread and that there was no evidence linking it with any serious mental or physical problems. He recorded countless men and women who masturbated without ill effect. In fact, he argued, masturbation had a positive function: It relieved tension.

In the nineteenth century, women were viewed as essentially "pure beings" who possessed reproductive rather than sexual desires. Men, in contrast, were driven by such strong sexual passions that their sexuality had to be severely controlled and repressed. In countless case studies, Ellis documented that women possessed sexual desires no less intense than those of men.

Ellis asserted that a wide range of behaviors was normal, including much behavior that the Victorians considered abnormal. He argued that both masturbation and female sexuality were normal behaviors and that even the so-called abnormal elements of sexual behavior were simply exaggerations of the normal.

He also reevaluated homosexuality. In the nineteenth century, homosexuality was viewed as the essence of sin and perversion. It was dangerous, lurid, and criminal. Ellis insisted that it was not a disease or a vice but a congenital condition: A person was *born* homosexual; one did not *become* homosexual. By insisting that homosexuality was congenital, Ellis denied that it could be considered a vice or a form of moral degeneracy, because a person did not *choose* it. If homosexuality were both congenital and harmless, then, Ellis reasoned, it should not be considered immoral or criminal.

Alfred Kinsey

Alfred C. Kinsey (1894–1956), a biologist at Indiana University and America's leading authority on gall wasps, destroyed forever the belief in American sexual innocence and virtue. He accomplished this through two books, *Sexual Behavior in the Human Male* (Kinsey, Pomeroy, & Martin, 1948) and *Sexual Behavior in the Human Female* (Kinsey, Pomeroy, Martin, & Gebhard, 1953). These two volumes statistically documented the actual sexual behavior of Americans. In massive detail, they demonstrated the great discrepancy between *public* standards of sexual behavior and *actual* sexual behavior. Kinsey believed that sex was as legitimate a subject for study as any other and that the study of sex should be treated as a scientific discipline involving compiling and examining data and drawing conclusions without moralizing. He challenged the traditional medical field's dominance of sexual research, leading to the field becoming open to many more disciplines (Bullough, 1994).

In the firestorm that accompanied the publication of Kinsey's books (popularly known as the *Kinsey Reports*), many Americans protested the destruction of their cherished ideals and illusions. Kinsey was highly criticized for his work—and that criticism continues even today. Many people believed that his findings were responsible for a moral breakdown in the United States. Eminent sex researcher Vern Bullough (2004) stated that

few scholars or scientists have lived under the intense firestorm of publicity and criticism that he did but even as the attacks on him increased and as his health failed, he continued to gather his data, and fight for what he believed. He changed sex for all of us.

Sexual Diversity and Variation What Kinsey discovered in his research was an extraordinary diversity in sexual behaviors. He declared that all types of sexual behavior—even those that occur infrequently—are simply variants on the complex

We are the recorders and reporters of facts—not judges of the behavior we describe.

—Alfred C. Kinsey
(1894–1956)

Alfred C. Kinsey (1894–1956) photographed by William Dellenback, 1953. Kinsey shocked Americans by revealing how they actually behaved sexually. His scientific efforts led to the termination of his research funding because of political pressure.

© Arthur Siegel/The LIFE Images Collection/ Getty Images

continuum of human behavior. A fundamental tenet of Kinsey was his commitment to be objective in research, refraining from traditional and religious judgments and from suggesting that persons participating in variant behavior should change their behavior (Drucker, 2014). Among men, he found individuals who had orgasms daily and others who went months without orgasms. Among women, he found individuals who had never had orgasms and others who had them several times a day. He discovered one male who had ejaculated only once in 30 years and another who ejaculated 30 times a week on average. "This is the order of variation," he commented dryly, "which may occur between two individuals who live in the same town and who are neighbors, meeting in the same place of business and coming together in common social activities" (Kinsey, Pomeroy, & Martin, 1948).

> *You shall know the truth and the truth shall make you mad.*
>
> —Aldous Huxley
> (1894–1963)

A Reevaluation of Masturbation   Kinsey's work aimed at a reevaluation of the role of masturbation in a person's sexual adjustment. Kinsey made three points about masturbation: (1) It is harmless, (2) it is not a substitute for sexual intercourse but a distinct form of sexual behavior that provides sexual pleasure, and (3) it plays an important role in women's sexuality because it is a more reliable source of orgasm than heterosexual intercourse and because its practice seems to facilitate women's ability to become orgasmic during intercourse. Indeed, Kinsey believed that masturbation is the best way to measure a woman's inherent sexual responsiveness because it does not rely on another person.

Sexual Orientation   Prior to Kinsey's work, an individual was identified as homosexual if he or she had ever engaged in any sexual behavior with a person of the same sex. Kinsey found, however, that many people had sexual experiences with persons of both sexes. He reported that 50% of the men and 28% of the women in his studies had had same-sex experiences and that 38% of the men and 13% of the women had had orgasms during these experiences (Kinsey, Pomeroy, & Martin, 1948; Kinsey, Pomeroy, Martin, & Gebhard, 1953). Furthermore, he discovered that sexual attractions could change over the course of a person's lifetime. Kinsey's research led him to conclude that it was erroneous to classify people as either heterosexual or homosexual. A person's sexuality was significantly more complex and fluid.

Kinsey wanted to eliminate the concept of heterosexual and homosexual *identities*. He did not believe that homosexuality, any more than heterosexuality, existed as a fixed psychological identity. Instead, he argued, there were only sexual behaviors, and behaviors alone did not make a person gay, lesbian, bisexual, or heterosexual. It was more important to determine what proportion of behaviors were same-sex and other-sex than to label a person as gay, lesbian, or heterosexual.

He devised the Kinsey Heterosexual-Homosexual Rating Scale to represent the proportion of an individual's sexual behaviors and psychosexual reactions with the same or other sex (see Figure 1). The scale charts sexual behavior and psychosexual reactions exclusively directed toward either persons of the same or the other sex and along a continuum of both sexes. Kinsey's scale radicalized the categorization of human sexual expression and represents his signature theoretical model of human sexuality (Drucker, 2014; McWhirter, 1990).

> *I don't see much of Alfred anymore since he got so interested in sex.*
>
> —Clara Kinsey
> (1898–1982)

Rejection of Normal/Abnormal Dichotomy   As a result of his research, Kinsey insisted that the distinction between normal and abnormal was meaningless. Like Ellis, he argued that sexual differences were a matter of degree, not kind. Almost any sexual behavior could be placed alongside another that differed

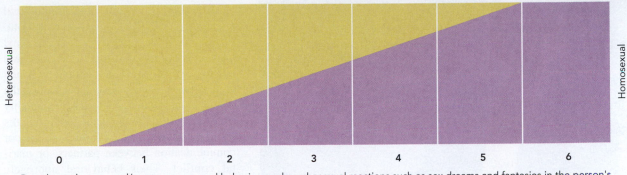

Based on other-sex and/or same-sex sexual behaviors and psychosexual reactions such as sex dreams and fantasies in the person's sexual history, individuals rate as follows:

| Exclusively heterosexual with no homosexual | Predominately heterosexual, only incidentally homosexual | Predominately heterosexual, but more than incidentally homosexual | Equally heterosexual and homosexual | Predominately homosexual, but more than incidentally heterosexual | Predominately homosexual, but incidentally heterosexual | Exclusively homosexual |

● **FIGURE 1**

The Kinsey Heterosexual-Homosexual Rating Scale. This scale illustrates the continuum of sexual expression.

from it only slightly. His observations led him to be a leading advocate of the acceptance of sexual diversity.

William Masters and Virginia Johnson

In the 1950s, William Masters (1915–2001), a St. Louis physician, became interested in treating sexual function difficulties—such problems as early ejaculation and erection difficulties in men and lack of orgasm in women. As a physician, he felt that a systematic study of the human sexual response was necessary, but none existed. To fill this void, he decided to conduct his own research. Masters was joined several years later by Virginia Johnson (1925–2013).

Masters and Johnson detailed the sexual response cycles of 382 men and 312 women during more than 10,000 episodes of sexual behavior, including masturbation and sexual intercourse. The researchers combined observation with direct measurement of changes in male and female genitals using electronic devices. (Their four-phase sexual response cycle will be discussed in chapters 3 and 4.)

Human Sexual Response (1966), their first book, became an immediate success among both researchers and the public. What made their work significant was not only their detailed descriptions of physiological responses but also the articulation of several key ideas. First, Masters and Johnson discovered that, physiologically, male and female sexual responses are very similar. Second, they demonstrated that women experience orgasm primarily through clitoral stimulation. Penetration of the vagina is not needed for orgasm to occur. By demonstrating the primacy of the clitoris, Masters and Johnson destroyed once and for all the Freudian distinction between vaginal and clitoral orgasm. (Freud believed that an orgasm a woman experienced through masturbation was somehow physically and psychologically inferior to one experienced through sexual intercourse. He made no such distinction for men.) By destroying the myth of the vaginal orgasm, Masters and Johnson legitimized female masturbation.

William Masters (1915–2001) and Virginia Johnson (1925–2013) detailed the sexual response cycle in the 1960s and revolutionized sex therapy in the 1970s.

© Bettmann/Corbis

The profoundest of all our sensualities is the sense of truth.

—D. H. Lawrence
(1885–1930)

In 1970, Masters and Johnson published *Human Sexual Inadequacy,* which revolutionized sex therapy by treating sexual problems simply as difficulties that could be treated using behavioral therapy. They argued that sexual problems were not the result of underlying neuroses or personality disorders. More often than not, problems resulted from a lack of information, poor communication between partners, or marital conflict. Their behavioral approach, which included "homework" exercises such as clitoral or penile stimulation, led to an astounding increase in the rate of successful treatment of sexual problems. Their work made them pioneers in modern sex therapy.

● Contemporary Research Studies

Several large, national sexuality-related studies have been conducted in recent years. We briefly describe five national surveys here to illustrate research on the general population of men and women, adolescents, and college students. These studies, largely directed to determine the prevalence of certain behaviors, give little or no attention to factors that help explain the findings. Further, they represent only the tip of the sexuality-related research pertinent to the topics covered in this textbook. Sex research continues to be an emerging field of study. Most studies are not national projects but are smaller ones dealing with special populations or issues and focus on examining factors that are related to or influence sexual behavior. Even though these studies may be smaller in scope, they provide valuable information for furthering our understanding of human sexual expression. Throughout the book, we cite numerous studies to provide empirical information about the topic.

Before describing these studies, it is important to note that, just as in the days of Alfred Kinsey, these are difficult times in which to conduct sex research. For example, members of Congress and some conservative groups are attacking the value of certain sex research topics, even those related to HIV prevention. The result has been a chilling effect on sex research. Funding for sex research has become more limited, and sexuality-related grant applications to the National Institutes of Health that have been approved by peer review have been questioned. Sex research is a relatively young area of study when compared to longer and better-established fields such as psychology, and the number of researchers specializing in sexuality-related study is small. Hopefully, these efforts to limit and discredit sex research will not discourage the next generation of researchers from becoming sex researchers. (To read a brief discussion about the controversy surrounding sex research, see the "Think About It" box "Sex Research: A Benefit to Individuals and Society or a Threat to Morality?")

The National Health and Social Life Survey

In 1994, new figures from the first nationally representative survey of Americans' sexual behavior were released, showing us to be in a different place than when Kinsey did his research a half century earlier. Researchers from the University of Chicago published two titles—the popular trade book *Sex in America: A Definitive Survey* (Michael, Gagnon, Laumann, & Kolata, 1994) and a more detailed and scholarly version, *The Social Organization of Sexuality* (Laumann, Gagnon, Michael, & Michaels, 1994). The survey contradicted many previous findings and beliefs about sex in America.

The study, titled the National Health and Social Life Survey (NHSLS), involved 3,432 randomly selected Americans aged 18–59, interviewed face-to-face. Even though this study was conducted over two decades ago (1992) and had some sampling limitations, sexual scientists regard it as one of the most methodologically sound studies; hence, we highlight major findings here and in subsequent chapters of this text.

Released as the first study to explore the social context of sexuality, the NHSLS revealed the following:

- *Americans are largely exclusive.* The median number of sexual partners since age 18 for men was six and for women two.

- *On average, Americans have sex about once a week.* Nearly 30% had sex with a partner only a few times a year or not at all, 35% had sex once or several times a month, and about 35% had sex two or more times a week.

- *Extramarital sex is the exception, not the rule.* Among those who were married, 75% of men and 85% of women said they had been sexually exclusive with their spouse.

- *Most Americans have fairly traditional sexual behaviors.* When respondents were asked to name their preferences from a long list of sexual behaviors, vaginal intercourse was considered "very appealing" by most of those interviewed. Ranking second, but far behind, was watching a partner undress. Oral sex ranked third.

- *Homosexuality is not as prevalent as originally believed.* Among men, 2.8% described themselves as homosexual or bisexual; among women, 1.4% did so.

- *Orgasms appear to be the rule for men and the exception for women.* Seventy-five percent of men claimed to have orgasms consistently with their partners, whereas only 29% of women did. Married women were most likely to report that they always or usually had orgasms.

- *Forced sex and the misperception of it remain critical problems.* Twenty-two percent of women said they had been forced to do sexual things they didn't want to do, usually by a loved one. Only 3% of men reported ever forcing themselves on women.

- *Three percent of adult Americans claim never to have had sex.*

The National Survey of Family Growth

Periodically, the National Center for Health Statistics (NCHS) conducts the National Survey of Family Growth (NSFG) to collect data on marriage, divorce, contraception, infertility, and the health of women and infants in the United States. In 2011, the NCHS published *Sexual Behavior, Sexual Attraction, and Sexual Identity in the United States: Data from the 2006–2008 National Survey of Family Growth*, which presents national estimates of several measures of sexual behavior, sexual attraction, and sexual identity among males and females 15–44 years of age in the United States. In-person, face-to-face interviews and

think
about it

Sex Research: A Benefit to Individuals and Society or a Threat to Morality?

Socrates said, **"There is only one good, knowledge, and one evil, ignorance."** This philosophy has been a core tenet in the growth of humankind and cultures since it was first written sometime between 469 BCE and 399 BCE. But in one area of life, human sexuality, some espouse that there is one good, ignorance, and one evil, knowledge. In our culture, the value of sexual knowledge is debated. One way this ambivalence manifests itself is through criticism and barriers to research on human sexuality (Yarber, 1992; Yarber & Sayad, 2010).

Sex research faces many issues that other areas of scientific inquiry do not, largely because human sexuality in our culture is too often surrounded by fear and denial, and its expression is often accompanied by shame, guilt, and embarrassment. These discomforts, particularly the fear of sexual knowledge, have fueled efforts to refute sex research. Some opposed to sex research believe that it has little value, and the research may be discredited. As such, the researchers may face public scorn, as Alfred Kinsey did. In fact, because of public outcry, Alfred Kinsey lost foundation funding for his research following the publication of his first book on male sexuality. The National Health and Social Life Survey (Laumann, Gagnon, Michael, & Michaels, 1994) conducted in the 1990s had to seek funding from foundations and private donors after a large federal grant was withdrawn following political pressure. Even today, federal government funding of sexuality-related areas is limited primarily to the study of HIV/STI risk behavior and prevention, which means researchers must search for nongovernment funding sources for topics outside this area. For example, a study of relationships between masturbation and mental health among older adults who no longer have a partner would most likely not be federally funded. The National Survey of Sexual Health and Behavior (Herbenick et al., 2010.2a), a national study of Americans' sexual behavior conducted in 2010, was funded by a condom manufacturer.

A major test of academic freedom within the university occurred over 60 years ago when Alfred Kinsey's research was heavily criticized and outside pressure was exerted upon Indiana University to end Kinsey's work (Capshew, 2012). Herman B. Wells, president of IU then, defended Alfred Kinsey by declaring that the search for truth is an important function of a university and that a fundamental university tenet and core value is that a faculty member is free to conduct research on any subject in which the person has competence. Wells (1980)

unequivocally articulated the tenet that ". . . a university that bows to the wishes of a person, group, or segment of society is not free." Wells's support of Alfred Kinsey's research is considered a landmark victory for academic freedom and helped pave the way for sex research at other universities (Clark, 1977). William Masters stated that without Kinsey's work and the support it received from IU, he and Virginia Johnson would not have been able to conduct their observational research on sexual response and dysfunction (Maier, 2009).

In the face of criticism, sex research has shown value—many individuals and society have benefited in so many ways from the deeper understanding of human sexual expression that research brings. But not all persons agree. Here are just three examples of the cultural ambiguity surrounding sex research and sexual knowledge:

- Some persons believed that Kinsey's research was destructive, leading to the sexual revolution of the 1960s and the breakdown of traditional mores. However, renowned sexologists consider Kinsey's scientific findings profound, making it possible for individuals, couples, and the public to talk about sex as well as freeing many persons from the stigma of abnormality (Bullough, 2004; Gagnon, 1975).

- Some persons were outraged upon learning that Masters and Johnson actually observed persons having sex, believing that such research had gone too far. However, Masters and Johnson's laboratory observation and measurement of the sexual responses of men and women led to the development of effective behavioral therapy for sexual function problems that have benefited many individuals and couples (Masters & Johnson, 1970).

- Some individuals and evangelical religious groups support abstinence-only education and contend that sexuality education that discusses methods of preventing HIV/STIs and pregnancy other than abstinence leads to sexual behavior among young persons outside of marriage. However, research has shown that abstinence-only sexuality education is largely ineffective in delaying the onset of sex and that comprehensive approaches, which included information about HIV/STIs and pregnancy prevention methods, postponed the initiation of first vaginal intercourse and increased condom and contraception use (Grossman, Tracy, Charmaraman, Ceder, & Erkut, 2014; Kirby, 2007, 2008; Stanger-Hall & Hall, 2011).

Supporters of sex research contend that we all suffer and the public loses when sex research is hampered. They believe that a fundamental principle of a democracy is at stake: the individual right to know. One way of making it possible for people to learn more about sexuality is through sex research's goals to increase people's knowledge about sexuality and its various components and to show them the positive impact that a rewarding and health-enhancing sexuality can have. But many opponents believe that sex research is harmful to society and should be limited or even eliminated. So, what do you think? For human sexuality, was Socrates right or wrong when he said, "There is one good, knowledge, and one evil, ignorance"?

Think Critically

1. Do you believe that sex research benefits individuals and society or that it leads to moral decay? Explain.

2. Should researchers at colleges and universities have the academic freedom to conduct any type of sex research? Defend your answer.

3. Given that the vast majority of federal government–funded sexuality-related research deals with HIV/STI risk behavior, do you think that other areas of human sexuality should be funded? If so, what areas? If not, why?

audio-CASI were used with a nationally representative sample of 13,495 males and females in the household population of the United States. Important findings for this sample include the following:

- Sexual behaviors among males and females aged 15–44, based on the 2006–2008 NSFG, were generally the same as those reported in a similar report of 2002.

- Among adults aged 25–44, about 98% of females and 97% of males ever had sexual intercourse, 89% of females and 90% of males ever had oral sex with an other-sex partner, and 36% of females and 44% of males ever had anal sex with an other-sex partner.

- For men aged 15–44, the mean number of lifetime female partners was 5.1 and for women 3.2 lifetime male partners.

- For ages 15–44, 21% of men and 8% of women reported 15 or more lifetime sexual partners.

- For ages 15–44, 12.5% of women and 5.2% of men reported any same-sex contact in their lifetimes, and 9.3% of women and 5% of men reported oral sex with a same-sex partner.

- For ages 15–44, for sexual identity, 92.8%, 1.0%, and 3.5% of women self-identified as heterosexual (straight), homosexual (gay or lesbian), and bisexual, respectively. For men, 95.0%, 1.6%, and 1.1% self-identified as heterosexual (straight), homosexual (gay or lesbian), and bisexual, respectively.

- Of sexually active people aged 15–24, 63% of females and 64% of males had oral sex, down from 69% in 2002.

- Among teenagers aged 15–19, 7% of females and 9% of males had oral sex with an other-sex partner, but no vaginal intercourse.

For a full copy of the report, see the National Center for Health Statistics website: http://www.cdc.gov/nchs/data/nhsr/nhsr036.pdf.

The Youth Risk Behavior Survey

The Youth Risk Behavior Survey (YRBS), conducted biannually by the Centers for Disease Control and Prevention (CDC), measures the prevalence of six categories of health risk behaviors among youths through representative national, state, and local surveys using a self-report questionnaire. Sexual behaviors that contribute to unintended pregnancy and sexually transmitted infections, including HIV, are among those assessed. The 2013 YRBS includes a national school-based survey of 13,583 students in grades 9–12, from 148 public and private schools in 42 states, and 21 local surveys, revealing the following (CDC, 2014.2b):

- Forty-seven percent of students (46% of females and 48% of males) reported ever having had sexual intercourse.

- Fifteen percent of students (13% of females and 17% of males) reported having had sexual intercourse with four or more partners during their life.

- Six percent of students (3% of females and 8% of males) reported having had sexual intercourse for the first time before age 13.

- Thirty-four percent of students (35% of females and 33% of males) reported having had sexual intercourse with at least one person during the 3 months before the survey.

- Sixty percent of students (53% of females and 66% of males) who reported being currently sexually active (34%) also reported using a condom during their most recent sexual intercourse.

- Nineteen percent of students (23% of females and 15% of males) who reported being currently sexually active (34%) also reported that either they or their partner had used birth control pills before their most recent sexual intercourse.

- Fourteen percent of students (16% of females and 12% of males) did not use any method of contraception to prevent pregnancy during their last intercourse.

- Twenty-two percent of students (19% of females and 26% of males) who reported being currently sexually active (34%) also reported using alcohol or drugs prior to their most recent sexual intercourse.

- Seven percent of students (11% of females and 4% of males) reported ever being forced to have sexual intercourse.

- Among the 74% of students who dated or went out with someone during the 12 months prior the survey, 10% of students (14% of females and 6% of males) had been kissed, touched, or physically forced to have sexual intercourse when they did not want to by someone they were dating or going out with one or more times during the 12 months before the survey.

- Thirteen percent of students (17% of females and 11% of males) reported having been tested for HIV (not counting being done while donating blood).

See http://www.cdc.gov/mmwr/pdf/ss/ss6304.pdf for more information on the 2013 YRBS.

The National College Health Assessment

Since year 2000, every fall and spring term the American College Health Association has conducted research at colleges and universities throughout the United States to assess students' health behaviors and their perceptions of the prevalence of these behaviors among their peers. Areas covered are general health; disease and injury prevention; academic impacts; violence, abusive relationships, and personal safety; alcohol, tobacco, and other drug use; sexual behavior; nutrition and exercise; mental health; and sleep. The data reported below is for the 66,887

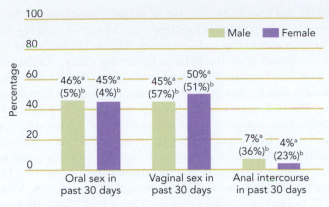

FIGURE 2

Percentage of Undergraduate College Students Who Reported Having Oral Sex, Vaginal Sex, and Anal Intercourse in the Past 30 Days and the Percentage Reporting Using a Condom or Other Protective Barrier, Spring 2014.

(*Source*: American College Health Association National College Health Assessment II: Undergraduate Students Reference Group Executive Summary, Spring 2014.)

[a]Percentage reporting the behavior.

[b]Percentage of sexually active students reporting using a condom or other protective barrier during the specific sexual behavior within the past 30 days.

undergraduate students at 140 U.S. campuses (American College Health Association, 2014). Findings from the sexual health questions include

- Within the last school year, 70% of college men and 69% of college women had at least one sexual partner. Most had one sexual partner—39% of men and 43% of women—although 14% of men and 9% of women had four or more partners. (See Figure 2 for the percentage reporting having oral, vaginal, and anal intercourse in the past 30 days and the percentage who used protection during these behaviors.)

- Among sexually active students, birth control pills and male condoms were the most common (between 6 and 7 of 10 students for each method) birth control methods used to prevent pregnancy by the students or their partner the last time they had vaginal intercourse.

- Sixty-seven percent and 51% reported receiving the vaccination against hepatitis B and against human papillomavirus, respectively.

- Within the last 12 months, students reported sexual touch without their consent (10% of females and 4% of males), sexual penetration attempt without their consent (4% of females and 1% of males), and sexual penetration without their consent (3% of females and 1% of males).

- Among sexually active students, 16% reported using (or reported their partner used) emergency contraception ("morning-after pill") within the last school year.

A copy of the report can be found at the American College Health Association website: http://www.acha-ncha.org/docs/ACHA-NCHA-II_ReferenceGroup_DataReport_Spring2014.pdf.

The National Survey of Sexual Health and Behavior

The most expansive nationally representative study of sexual and sexual-health behaviors, the National Survey of Sexual Health and Behavior (NSSHB), was published in 2010, 16 years following the first nationally representative study, the 1994 National Health and Social Life Survey, described earlier. The NSSHB, a study based on Internet reports from 5,865 American adolescents and adults aged 14–94, provides a needed and valuable updated overview of Americans'

The good thing about science is that it's true whether you believe it or not.

—Neil deGrasse Tyson (1958–)

sexual behavior and reveals an increase in sexual diversity since the NHSLS. A major strength of the NSSHB is its larger range of ages—spanning 80 years—in contrast to other studies that had narrow age ranges. The study was conducted and led by researchers from the Indiana University Center for Sexual Health Promotion with collaboration from researchers from The Kinsey Institute for Research in Sex, Gender, and Reproduction and the Indiana University School of Medicine. The first reports of the NSSHB findings were published in 2010 in nine articles as a special issue of the *Journal of Sexual Medicine.* (The NSSHB was funded by Church & Dwight, makers of Trojan condoms.)

The NSSHB provides data on masturbation (solo and partnered), oral sex (given and received), vaginal intercourse, and anal intercourse, categorized by 10 age ranges. These new data will be highlighted throughout the textbook. Major generalized NSSHB findings include the following (Dodge et al., 2010; Herbenick et al., 2010.2a, 2010.2b, 2010.2c; Reece et al., 2010.2a, 2010.2b; Sanders et al., 2010):

- A large variability of sexual repertoires of adults was found, with numerous combinations of sexual behaviors described at adults' most recent sexual event.

- Men and women participated in diverse solo and partnered behaviors throughout their life course, yet in spite of lower frequency of these behaviors among older adults, many reported active, pleasurable sex lives.

- Masturbation was more common among all age groups but more common among men than women and individuals aged 25–29.

- Vaginal intercourse occurred more frequently than other sexual behaviors from early to late adulthood.

- Partnered noncoital behaviors—oral sex and anal intercourse—were well-established components of couple sexual behavior and were reported in greater numbers than in the NHSLS.

- Among adults, many sexual episodes included partnered masturbation and oral sex, but not intercourse.

- Fewer than 1 in 10 men and women self-identified as a gay man, lesbian woman, or bisexual person, but the proportion of study participants having same-gender interactions sometime in their lives was higher.

- Masturbation, oral sex, and vaginal intercourse were prevalent among all ethnic groups and among men and women throughout the life course.

- During a single sexual event, orgasm among men was facilitated by vaginal intercourse with a relationship partner, whereas women's orgasm was facilitated by varied sexual behaviors.

- Higher rates of condom use during most recent vaginal intercourse were found compared to other recent studies, and condoms were used more frequently with casual partners than relationship partners.

● Emerging Research Perspectives

Although sex research continues to explore diverse aspects of human sexuality, some scholars feel that their particular interests have been given insufficient attention. Feminist, gay, lesbian, bisexual, and transgender research has focused on issues that mainstream research has largely ignored. And ethnic research, only recently undertaken, points to the lack of knowledge about the sexuality of some ethnic groups, such as African Americans, Latinos, Asian

Americans, Middle Eastern Americans, and American Indians. These emerging research perspectives enrich our knowledge of sexuality.

Feminist Scholarship

The initial feminist research generated an immense amount of groundbreaking work on women in almost every field of the social sciences and humanities. Feminists made gender and gender-related issues significant research questions in a multitude of academic disciplines, with the goal of producing useful knowledge that can be valuable to individual and societal change (Harding and Norberg, 2005; Letherby, 2003). In the field of sexuality, feminists expanded the scope of research to include the subjective experience and meaning of sexuality for women; sexual pleasure; sex and power; erotic material; risky sexual behavior; and issues of female victimization, such as rape, the sexual abuse of children, and sexual harassment.

There is no single feminist perspective; instead, there are several. For our purposes, **feminism** is "a movement that involves women and men working together for equality" (McCormick, 1996). Feminism centers on understanding female experience in cultural and historical context—that is, the social construction of gender asymmetry. **Social construction** is the development of social categories, such as masculinity, femininity, heterosexuality, and homosexuality, by society.

Feminists believe in these basic principles:

- *Gender is significant in all aspects of social life.* Like socioeconomic status and ethnicity, gender influences a person's position in society.

- *The female experience of sex has been devalued.* By emphasizing genital sex, frequency of sexual intercourse, and number of orgasms, both researchers and society ignore other important aspects of sexuality, such as kissing, caressing, love, commitment, and communication. Sexuality in lesbian women's relationships is even more devalued. Until the 1980s, most research on homosexuality centered on gay men, making lesbian women invisible.

- *Power is a critical element in male-female relationships.* Because women are often subordinated to men as a result of our society's beliefs about gender, women generally have less power than men. As a result, feminists believe that men have defined female sexuality to benefit themselves. Not only do men typically decide when to initiate sex, but the man's orgasm often takes precedence over the woman's. The most brutal form of the male expression of sexual power is rape.

- *Ethnic diversity must be addressed.* Women of color, feminists point out, face a double stigma: being female *and* being from a minority group. Although an inadequate number of studies exist on ethnicity and sexuality, feminists are committed to examining the role of ethnicity in female sexuality (Amaro, Raj, & Reed, 2001).

Despite its contributions, feminist research and the feminist approach have often been marginalized. However, the feminist perspective in sex research has expanded in recent years, and many more women are making important contributions to the advancement of sexual science. As one consequence, the research literature has increased, resulting in an expansion of our understanding of female as well as male sexuality. For example, renowned sex researcher Charlene

> *It is better to debate a question without settling it than to settle a question without debating it.*
> —Joseph Joubert
> (1754–1824)

> *One of the greatest pains to human nature is the pain of a new idea.*
> —Walter Bagehot
> (1826–1877)

Muehlenhard of the University of Kansas has developed a body of research that has defined the field of women's experiences with sexual coercion. She has addressed controversial issues such as token sexual resistance and has challenged researchers to clarify their conceptualizations of wanted and unwanted sex, particularly among young women (Muehlenhard & Peterson, 2005; Peterson & Muehlenhard, 2007; Muehlenhard, 2011).

Gay, Lesbian, Bisexual, and Transgender Research

During the nineteenth century, sexuality became increasingly perceived as the domain of science, especially medicine. Physicians competed with ministers, priests, and rabbis in defining what was "correct" sexual behavior. However, as noted previously, medicine's so-called scientific conclusions were not scientific; rather, they were morality disguised as science. "Scientific" definitions of healthy sex closely resembled religious definitions of moral sex. In studying sexual activities between men, medical researchers "invented" and popularized the distinction between heterosexuality and homosexuality (Blank, 2012; Gay, 1986; Gray & Garcia, 2013; Weeks, 1986).

Early Researchers and Reformers   Although most physician-moralists condemned same-sex relationships as not only immoral but also pathological, a few individuals stand out in their attempt to understand same-sex sexuality.

Karl Heinrich Ulrichs   Karl Ulrichs (1825–1895) was a German poet and political activist who in the 1860s developed the first scientific theory about homosexuality (Kennedy, 1988). As a rationalist, he believed reason was superior to religious belief and therefore rejected religion as superstition. He argued from logic and inference and collected case studies from numerous men to reinforce his beliefs. Ulrichs maintained that men who were attracted to other men represented a third sex, whom he called "Urnings." Urnings were born as Urnings; their sexuality was not the result of immorality or pathology. Ulrichs believed that Urnings had a distinctive feminine quality about them that distinguished them from men who desired women. He fought for Urning rights and the liberalization of sex laws.

Magnus Hirschfeld (1868–1935) was a leading European sex reformer who championed homosexual rights. He founded the first institute for the study of sexuality, which was burned when the Nazis took power in Germany. Hirschfeld fled for his life.

© Keystone-France/Gamma-Keystone via Getty Images

Karl Maria Kertbeny   Karl Kertbeny (1824–1882), a Hungarian physician, created the terms "heterosexuality" and "homosexuality" in his attempt to understand same-sex relationships (Feray & Herzer, 1990). Kertbeny believed that "homosexualists" were as "manly" as "heterosexualists." For this reason, he broke with Ulrichs's conceptualization of Urnings as inherently "feminine" (Herzer, 1985). Kertbeny argued that homosexuality was inborn and thus not immoral. He also maintained "the rights of man" (quoted in Herzer, 1985):

> The rights of man begin . . . with man himself. And that which is most immediate to man is his own body, with which he can undertake fully and freely, to his advantage or disadvantage, that which he pleases, insofar as in so doing he does not disturb the rights of others.

Magnus Hirschfeld   In the first few decades of the twentieth century, there was a great ferment of reform in England and other parts of Europe. While Havelock Ellis was the leading reformer in England, Magnus Hirschfeld (1868–1935) was the leading crusader in Germany, especially for homosexual rights.

Hirschfeld was a gay man and possibly a transvestite (a person who wears clothing of the other sex). He eloquently presented the case for the humanity of transvestites (Hirschfeld, 1991). And in defense of homosexual rights, he argued that homosexuality was not a perversion but rather the result of the hormonal development of inborn traits. His defense of homosexuality led to the popularization of the word "homosexual." Hirschfeld's importance, however, lies not so much in his theory of homosexuality as in his sexual reform efforts. In Berlin in 1897, he helped found the first organization for homosexual rights. In addition, he founded the first journal devoted to the study of sexuality and the first Institute of Sexual Science, where he gathered a library of more than 20,000 volumes.

Evelyn Hooker   As a result of Kinsey's research, Americans learned that same-sex sexual relationships were widespread among both men and women. A few years later, psychologist Evelyn Hooker (1907–1996) startled her colleagues by demonstrating that homosexuality in itself was not a psychological disorder. She found that "typical" gay men did not differ significantly in personality characteristics from "typical" heterosexual men (Hooker, 1957). The reverberations of her work continue to this day.

Earlier studies had erroneously reported psychopathology among gay men and lesbian women for two reasons. First, because most researchers were clinicians, their samples consisted mainly of gay men and lesbian women who were seeking treatment. The researchers failed to compare their results against a control group of similar heterosexual individuals. (A **control group** is a group that is not being treated or experimented on; it controls for any variables that are introduced from outside the experiment, such as a major media report related to the topic of the experiment.) Second, researchers were predisposed to believe that homosexuality was in itself a sickness, reflecting traditional beliefs about homosexuality. Consequently, emotional problems were automatically attributed to the client's homosexuality rather than to other sources.

Later Contributions: Michel Foucault
One of the most influential social theorists in the twentieth century was the French thinker Michel Foucault (1926–1984). A cultural historian and philosopher, Foucault explored how society creates social ideas and how these ideas operate to further the established order. His most important work on sexuality was *The History of Sexuality, Volume I* (1978), a book that gave fresh impetus to scholars interested in the social construction of sex, especially those involved in gender and gay and lesbian studies.

Foucault challenged the belief that our sexuality is rooted in nature. Instead, he argued, it is rooted in society. Society "constructs" sexuality, including homosexuality and heterosexuality. Foucault's critics contend, however, that he underestimated the biological basis of sexual impulses and the role individuals play in creating their own sexuality.

Contemporary Gay, Lesbian, Bisexual, and Transgender Research
In 1973, the American Psychiatric Association (APA) removed homosexuality from its list of psychological disorders in its *Diagnostic and Statistical Manual of Mental Disorders (DSM-II)*. The APA decision was reinforced by similar resolutions by the American Psychological Association and the American Sociological Association. In 1997 at its annual meeting, the American Psychological Association overwhelmingly passed a resolution stating that there is no sound scientific evidence on the efficacy of reparative therapies for gay

Never underestimate the difficulty of changing false beliefs by fact.
—Henry Rosovsky
(1927–)

Michel Foucault (1926–1984) of France was one of the most important thinkers who influenced our understanding of how society "constructs" human sexuality.

© AFP/Getty Images

men and lesbian women. This statement reinforced the association's earlier stand that, because there is nothing "wrong" with homosexuality, there is no reason to try to change sexual orientation through therapy. In 1998, the APA issued a statement opposing reparative therapy, thus joining the American Psychological Association, the American Academy of Pediatrics, the American Medical Association, the American Counseling Association, and the National Association of Social Workers.

As a result of the rejection of the psychopathological model, social and behavioral research on gay men, lesbian women, and bisexual individuals has moved in a new direction. Research no longer focuses primarily on the causes and cures of homosexuality, and most of the contemporary research approaches homosexuality in a neutral manner.

Directions for Future Research

Historically, sex research has focused on preventive health, which "prioritizes sexuality as a social problem and behavioral risk" (di Mauro, 1995). In light of the HIV/AIDS pandemic and other social problems, this emphasis is important, but it fails to examine the full spectrum of individuals' behaviors or the social and cultural factors that drive those behaviors. If sex research is to expand our understanding of human sexual expression, it should examine the numerous components of a broader definition of sexuality.

Sex research, globally, faces several challenges. Few sex researchers and sex research centers exist worldwide, particularly in developing countries. Only a few Western countries have comprehensive statistics, and most of them are about fertility or sexually transmitted infections rather than sexual behaviors of various groups. There is no international depository for sex data.

● Ethnicity and Sexuality

Researchers have begun to recognize the significance of ethnicity in various aspects of American life, including sexuality. Although there have been modest increases in ethnic diversity of research samples, important questions must still be addressed (CDC, 2011.2a). These include the differences that socioeconomic status and environment play in sexual behaviors, the way in which questions are posed in research studies, the research methods that are used, and researchers' preconceived notions regarding ethnic differences. Diversity-related bias can be so ingrained in the way research is conducted that it is difficult to detect. Although limited research is available, this section attempts to provide some background to enhance an understanding of sexuality and ethnicity.

African Americans

Several factors must be considered when studying African American sexuality, including sexual stereotypes, racism, socioeconomic status, and Black subculture.

Sexual stereotypes greatly distort our understanding of Black sexuality. One of the most common stereotypes, strongly rooted in American history, culture, and religion, is the image of Blacks as hypersexual beings (Scott, 2010; Staples, 2006). This stereotype, which dates back to the fifteenth century, continues to hold considerable strength among non-Blacks. Family sociologist Robert Staples (1991) writes: "Black men are saddled with a number of stereotypes that label

In the rich cultural history of African Americans, family life is very important.
© BananaStock/PunchStock

them as irresponsible, criminalistic, hypersexual, and lacking in masculine traits." Evelyn Higginbotham (1992), a leading authority on the African American experience, discusses the racialized constructions of African American women's sexuality as primitive, animal-like and promiscuous, and nonvirtuous. During the days of slavery, this representation of Black sexuality rationalized sexual exploitation of Black women by White masters (Nagel, 2003). The belief that Black women were "promiscuous" by nature was perpetuated by a variety of media, such as theater, art, the press, and literature. From this, historian Darlene Hine (1989) notes that silence arose among women: a "culture of dissemblance." To protect the sanctity of inner aspects of their lives and to combat pervasive negative images and stereotypes about them, Black women (particularly the middle class) began to represent their sexuality through silence, secrecy, and invisibility. For example, they would dress very modestly to remain invisible— hence, not drawing attention that might lead to being sexually assaulted. Efforts to adhere to Victorian ideology and represent pure morality were deemed by Black women to be necessary for protection and upward mobility and to attain respect and justice. These representations continue today for many older African American women (Rose, 2004). For some younger, African American women, however, the opposite is happening: being more visible and less reserved about their sexuality. These younger women feel more self-assured about themselves and their sexuality. The emphasis on sexuality of the younger African American woman is often depicted, for example, in advertising and rap music videos, particularly Gangsta rap. Unfortunately, much Gangsta rap is explicit about both sex and violence and rarely illustrates the long-term consequences of sexual risk behaviors; research has shown that these videos lead to increased sexual risk behavior among African American adolescents (Wingood et al., 2002).

Socioeconomic status is a person's ranking in society based on a combination of occupational, educational, and income levels. It is an important element in African American sexual values and behaviors (CDC, 2014.2a; Staples, 2006; Staples & Johnson, 1993). For example, a study of White and African American women and Latinas who voluntarily sought HIV counseling and testing found that socioeconomic status, not race, was directly related to HIV risk behavior. Women with lower incomes had riskier (e.g., drug-injecting) sexual partners and higher levels of stress, factors related to risky sexual behaviors (Ickovics et al., 2002). Values and behaviors are shaped by culture and social class. The subculture of Blacks of low socioeconomic status is deeply influenced by poverty, discrimination, and structural subordination.

Although there has been a significant increase in African American research, much still needs to be done. For example, researchers need to (1) explore the sexual attitudes and behaviors of the general African American population, not merely adolescents, (2) examine Black sexuality from an African American cultural viewpoint, (3) utilize a cultural equivalency perspective that rejects differences between Blacks and Whites as signs of inherent deviance, and (4) assess confusion about race-based stereotypes and historical health disparities and mistrust. The **cultural equivalency perspective** is the view that the attitudes, values, and behaviors of one ethnic group are similar to those of another ethnic group. Research focused on furthering our understanding of Black sexuality will facilitate the development of effective behavioral interventions that address sexual health within the context of African American life (Wyatt, Williams, & Myers, 2008).

Latinos

Latinos are the fastest-growing ethnic group in the United States. There is very little research, however, about Latino sexuality.

Two common stereotypes depict Latinos as sexually permissive and Latino males as pathologically macho. Like African Americans, Latino males are often stereotyped as being "promiscuous," engaging in excessive and indiscriminate sexual activities. No research, however, validates this stereotype.

The macho stereotype paints Latino males as hypermasculine—swaggering and domineering. But the stereotype of machismo distorts its cultural meaning among Latinos. (The Spanish word "machismo" was originally incorporated into English in the 1960s as a slang term to describe any male who was sexist.) Within its cultural context, however, **machismo** is a positive concept, celebrating the values of courage, strength, generosity, politeness, and respect for others. This is particularly true for the younger generation of Latino males who are acculturated into American life. And in day-to-day functioning, relations between Latino men and women are significantly more egalitarian than the macho stereotype suggests. This is especially true among Latinos who are more acculturated (Sanchez, 1997). **Acculturation** is the process of adaptation of an ethnic group to the values, attitudes, and behaviors of the dominant culture.

Another trait of Latino life is **familismo,** a commitment to family and family members.

In studying Latino sexuality, it is important to remember that Latinos come from diverse ethnic groups, including Mexican American, Cuban American, and Puerto Rican, each with its own unique background and set of cultural values.

© JGI/Blend Images LLC

Researcher Rafael Diaz (1998) notes that familismo can be a strong factor in helping heterosexual Latinos reduce rates of unprotected sex with casual partners outside of primary relationships. He warns, however, that for many Latino men who have sex with men, familismo and homophobia can create conflict because families may perceive homosexuality as wrong.

Rebellion against the native culture may be expressed through sexual behavior (Gonzalez-Lopez & Vival-Ortiz, 2008; Sanchez, 1997). Traditional Latinos tend to place a high value on female virginity while encouraging males, beginning in adolescence, to be sexually active. Females are viewed according to a virgin/whore dichotomy—"good" girls are virgins and "bad" girls are sexual. Females are taught to put the needs of others, especially males, before their own. Among traditional Latinos, fears about American "sexual immorality" produce their own stereotypes of Anglos. Adolescent boys learn about masturbation from peers; girls rarely learn about it because of its tabooed nature. There is little acceptance of gay men and lesbian women, whose relationships are often regarded as "unnatural" or sinful (Bonilla & Porter, 1990; Raffaelli & Ontai, 2004). In traditional Latino culture, Catholicism plays an important role, especially in the realm of sexuality. The Church advocates premarital virginity and prohibits both contraception and abortion.

Three important factors must be considered when Latino sexuality is studied: (1) diversity of ethnic groups, (2) significance of socioeconomic status, and (3) acculturation. Latinos comprise numerous ethnic subgroups, such as Mexican American, Cuban American, and Puerto Rican. Each group has its own unique background and set of cultural traditions that affect sexual attitudes and behaviors.

Given the high rate of immigration of Latinos into the United States, particular research attention has been given to examining the impact of acculturation. For example, studies have addressed the relationship between acculturation and sexual risk behavior. Research has examined the personal and family conflict caused by the traditional Latino values and the progressive sexual values in the United States, and whether acculturation results in liberality among Latinos. For example, one study of college students found that Latinos who had greater identification with mainstream culture had more liberal sexual attitudes than those who had less identification with mainstream culture (Ahrold & Meston, 2010).

Asian Americans and Pacific Islanders

Asian Americans and Pacific Islanders represent one of the fastest-growing and most diverse populations in the United States. Significant differences in attitudes, values, and practices in this population make it difficult to generalize about these groups without stereotyping and oversimplifying. Given this caveat, we can say that many Asian Americans are less individualistic and more relationship oriented than members of other cultures. Individuals are seen as the products of their relationships to nature and other people. Asian Americans are less verbal and expressive in their interactions and often rely on indirection and nonverbal communication, such as silence and avoidance of eye contact as signs of respect.

In traditional Chinese culture, the in-laws of a married woman were responsible for safeguarding her chastity and keeping her under the ultimate control of her spouse. Where extended families worked and lived in close quarters for extended periods, many spouses found it difficult to experience intimacy with each other. As in other Asian American populations, the rate of cross-cultural marriage

Among Asian Americans (as with other ethnic groups), attitudes toward relationships, family, and sexuality are related to the degree of acculturation.

© Dex Image/PunchStock

among younger Chinese Americans is higher than in their parents' and grandparents' generations. Still, Confucian principles, which teach women to be obedient to their spouse's wishes and attentive to their needs and to be sexually loyal, play a part in maintaining exclusivity and holding down the divorce rate among traditional Chinese families (Ishii-Kuntz, 1997). In contrast, men are expected to be sexually experienced, and their engagement in nonmarital sex is frequently accepted.

For more than a century, Japanese Americans have maintained a significant presence in the United States. Japanese cultural values of loyalty and harmony are strongly embedded in Confucianism and feudalism (loyalty to the ruler), yet Japanese lives are not strongly influenced by religion (Ishii-Kuntz, 1997). Like Chinese Americans born in the United States, Japanese Americans born in the United States base partner selection more on love and individual compatibility than on family concerns (Nakano, 1990).

Traditional Japanese values allowed sexual freedom for men but not for women. Japanese women were expected to remain pure; sexual permissiveness or nonexclusiveness on the part of women was considered socially disruptive and threatening (Ishii-Kuntz, 1997). Over time, attitudes and conditions related to sexuality have changed so that sexual activity is no longer considered solely procreational, and there is increased use of contraceptives.

As with other groups, the degree of acculturation may be the most important factor affecting sexual attitudes and behaviors of Asian Americans. Compared with those who were raised in the United States, those who were born and raised in their original homeland tend to adhere more closely to their culture's norms, customs, and values. Further, a research study of Asian women attending a large Canadian university found that those who maintained affiliation with traditional Asian heritage became less acculturated with the more liberal, Western sexuality–related attitudes (Brotto, Chik, Ryder, Gorzalka, & Seal, 2005). This finding was verified in a study at a southern U.S. university in which students with less identification with their heritage culture had sexual attitudes similar to those of Euro-Americans (Ahrold & Meston, 2010).

Researcher and psychologist Sumie Okazaki (2002) reviewed the scientific literature concerning several aspects of Asian Americans' sexuality: sexual knowledge, attitudes, norms, and behavior. Okazaki reports that she found notable differences in several sexuality-related areas between Asian Americans and other ethnic groups:

> For example, relative to other U.S. ethnic group cohorts, Asian American adolescents and young adults tend to show more sexually conservative attitudes and behavior and initiate intercourse at a later age. There are indications that as Asian Americans become more acculturated to the mainstream American culture, their attitudes and behavior become more consistent with the White American norm. Consistent with their more sexually conservative tendencies in normative sexual behavior, Asian American women also appear more reluctant to obtain sexual and reproductive health care, which in turn places them at greater risk for delay in treatment for breast and cervical cancer as well as other gynecological problems.

As in other areas of social science, there are gaps in the research concerning the sexuality of Asian Americans and other racial and ethnic groups. Obviously, more empirical work is needed.

❝ Men do not seek truth. It is the truth that pursues men who run away and will not look around.

—Lincoln Steffens
(1866–1936)

Middle Eastern Americans

There is a scarcity of research on the sexuality of Middle Eastern Americans, especially as it concerns women who have migrated from parts of the Middle East (Rashidian, 2010). Furthermore, other than in the context of heterosexual relationships, research is almost nonexistent in the areas of sexual expression and sexual orientation. Wide historical contexts—cultural and ideological—of gender and gender bias suggest that the patriarchal system in place helps perpetuate some of the struggles that many Middle Eastern women face when they arrive here (Ebadi & Moaveni, 2006). At the same time, it is known that many Middle Eastern immigrants have a poor understanding about sexuality-related topics (Khan & Khanum, 2000). For example, given that traditional beliefs dictate that women should not learn about sexual relationships until marriage, more often than not their primary source of sexuality information, besides the media, is married friends.

In the case of Iranian American women, culture has been a major factor in the construction of their sexual self, gender role, gender identity, and knowledge about sex. However, many of the messages received regarding their roles as women have been confusing and have resulted in a sense of self-worthlessness (Rashidian, 2010). Gender, birth order, family honor, religion, and traditional cultural values are all highly regarded and are often associated with lower status of women, male dominance, and discrimination against women. Obedience and fear of reprisal often help sustain many of the related practices.

With increasing numbers of immigrants moving from other countries to the United States, it is important that American professionals be knowledgeable about the significance of culture and gender role in the immigrant community. Research, sexuality education, and counseling need to take into consideration an awareness of individuals' sexual beliefs; attempt to understand their current view of themselves as individuals, their values, and the presence and types of interpersonal relationships that exist in their lives; and ascertain their level of communication skills related to sexual topics (Rashidian, 2010).

Final Thoughts

Popular culture surrounds us with sexual images, disseminated through advertising, music, television, film, video games, and the Internet, that form a backdrop to our daily living. Much of what is conveyed is simplified, overgeneralized, stereotypical, shallow, sometimes misinterpreted—and entertaining. Studying sexuality enables us to understand how research is conducted and to be aware of its strengths and its limitations. Traditional sex research has been expanded in recent years by feminist, gay, lesbian, bisexual, and transgender research, which provides fresh insights and perspectives. Although the study of sexuality and ethnicity has yet to reach its full potential, it promises to enlarge our understanding of the diversity of attitudes, behaviors, and values in contemporary America.

Summary

Sex, Advice Columnists, and Pop Psychology

- The *sex information/advice genre* transmits information to both entertain and inform; the information is generally oversimplified and sometimes distorted so that it does not interfere with the genre's primary purpose, entertainment. Much of the information or advice conveys dominant social norms.

Thinking Objectively About Sexuality

- *Objective statements* are based on observations of things as they exist in themselves. *Value judgments* are evaluations based on moral or ethical standards. *Opinions* are unsubstantiated beliefs based on an individual's personal thoughts. *Biases* are personal leanings or inclinations. *Stereotypes*—rigidly held beliefs about the personal characteristics of a group of people—are a type of *schema*, which is the organization of knowledge in our thought processes.

- *Fallacies* are errors in reasoning. The *egocentric fallacy* is the belief that others necessarily share one's own values, beliefs, and attitudes. The *ethnocentric fallacy* is the belief that one's own ethnic group, nation, or culture is inherently superior to any other.

Sex Research Methods

- Ethical issues are important concerns in sex research. The most important issues are *informed consent, protection from harm,* and confidentiality.

- In sex research, *sampling* is a particularly acute problem. To be meaningful, samples should be representative of the larger group from which they are drawn. But most samples are limited by volunteer bias and dependence on college students.

- The most important methods in sex research are clinical, survey, observational, and experimental. *Clinical research* relies on in-depth examinations of individuals or groups who go to the clinician seeking treatment for psychological or medical problems. *Survey research* uses questionnaires, interviews, or diaries, for example, to gather information from a representative sample of people. *Observational research* requires the researcher to observe interactions carefully in as unobtrusive a

manner as possible. *Experimental research* presents subjects with various stimuli under controlled conditions in which their responses can be measured.

- Experiments are controlled through the use of *independent variables* (which can be changed by the experimenter) and *dependent variables* (which change in relation to changes in the independent variable). Clinical, survey, and observational research efforts, in contrast, are *correlational studies* that reveal relationships between variables without manipulating them. In experimental research, physiological responses are often measured by a *plethysmograph,* often measured by a *plethysmograph.*

The Sex Researchers

- Richard von Krafft-Ebing was one of the earliest sex researchers. His work emphasized the pathological aspects of sexuality.

- Sigmund Freud was one of the most influential thinkers in Western civilization. Freud believed there were five stages in psychosexual development: the *oral stage, anal stage, phallic stage, latency stage,* and *genital stage.*

- Havelock Ellis was the first modern sexual theorist and scholar. His ideas included the relativity of sexual values, the normality of masturbation, a belief in the sexual equality of men and women, the redefinition of "normal," and a reevaluation of homosexuality.

- Alfred Kinsey's work documented enormous diversity in sexual behavior, emphasized the role of masturbation in sexual development, and argued that the distinction between normal and abnormal behavior was meaningless. The Kinsey scale charts sexual behaviors and psychosexual reactions along a continuum ranging from exclusively other-sex behaviors to exclusively same-sex behaviors.

- William Masters and Virginia Johnson detailed the physiology of the human sexual response cycle. Their physiological studies revealed the similarity between male and female sexual responses and demonstrated that women experience orgasm through clitoral stimulation. Their work on sexual inadequacy revolutionized sex therapy through the use of behavioral techniques.

Contemporary Research Studies

- The National Health and Social Life Survey (NHSLS) in 1994 was the first nationally representative survey of Americans' sexual behavior, and its findings contradicted many prior findings and beliefs about sex in America.

- The National Survey of Family Growth (NSFG) is a periodic survey that collects data related to marriage, divorce, contraception, infertility, and the health of women and infants in the United States. A 2011 NSFG is one of the most recent comprehensive surveys of the prevalence of certain sexual behaviors in the general population.

- The Youth Risk Behavior Study (YRBS), conducted biennially since 1991, is a large, national, school-based study of the health behaviors of adolescents. Behaviors related to sexuality and risk taking are assessed.

- The American College Health Association's National College Health Assessment has conducted research on campuses throughout the United States since 2000 to determine students' health and sexual behaviors.

- The National Survey of Sexual Health and Behavior (NSSHB), conducted in 2010, was a nationally representative Internet study of adolescents and adults aged 14–95, an age range much greater than in other studies. The NSSHB provided an update on Americans' sexual behavior, showing an increase in sexual diversity since the NHSLS.

Emerging Research Perspectives

- There is no single feminist perspective in sex research.

- Most feminist research focuses on gender issues, assumes that the female experience of sex has been devalued, believes that power is a critical element in female-male relationships, and explores ethnic diversity.

- Research on homosexuality has rejected the moralistic-pathological approach. Researchers in gay and lesbian issues include Karl Ulrichs, Karl Kertbeny, Magnus Hirschfeld, Evelyn Hooker, and Michel Foucault.

- Contemporary gay, lesbian, bisexual, and transgender research focuses on the psychological and social experience of being other than heterosexual.

Ethnicity and Sexuality

- The role of ethnicity in human sexuality has been largely overlooked until recently.

- *Socioeconomic status* is important in the study of African American sexuality. Other factors to consider include the stereotype of Blacks as hypersexual and "promiscuous" and racism.

- Two common stereotypes about Latinos are that they are sexually permissive and that Latino males are pathologically macho. Factors to consider in studying Latino sexuality include the diversity of national groups, the role of socioeconomic status, and the degree of *acculturation*.

- Significant differences in attitudes, values, and practices make it difficult to generalize about Asian Americans and Pacific Islanders. Degree of acculturation and adherence to traditional Asian heritage are important factors affecting sexual attitudes and behaviors. Religious and cultural values still play an important role in the lives of many Asian Americans and Pacific Islanders. Little research has been conducted on the sexuality of Middle Eastern Americans, yet it is known that many immigrants from the Middle East have a poor understanding of sexuality-related topics.

Questions for Discussion

- Is sex research valuable or necessary? If you feel that it is, what areas of sexuality do you think need special attention? Which, if any, areas of sexuality should be prohibited from being researched?

- Alfred Kinsey was, and continues to be, criticized for his research. Some people even believe that he was responsible for eroding sexual morality. Do you think his research was valuable, or that it led to the sexual revolution in the United States, as many people claim?

- Would you volunteer for a sex research study? Why or why not? If so, what kind of study?

Sex and the Internet

The Kinsey Institute for Research in Sex, Gender, and Reproduction

Few centers that conduct research exclusively on sexuality exist in the world. One of the most respected and well-known centers is The Kinsey Institute for Research in Sex, Gender, and Reproduction (KI) at Indiana University, Bloomington. The institute bears the name of its founder, Alfred C. Kinsey, whose research was described earlier in this chapter. Visit the institute's website (http://www.kinseyinstitute.org) and find out information about the following:

- The mission and history of KI
- A chronology of events and landmark publications
- The KI research staff and their publications
- KI's current research projects
- KI's exhibitions, services, and events
- KI's library and special collections
- Graduate education in human sexuality at KI and Indiana University
- Links to related sites in sexuality research

Suggested Websites

Advocates for Youth
http://www.advocatesforyouth.org
Focuses on teen sexual health; provides valuable data on issues related to teen sexual health.

Centers for Disease Control and Prevention
http://www.cdc.gov
A valuable source of research information about sexual behavior and related health issues in the United States.

Gallup Poll
http://www.gallup.com
Provides results of current surveys, including those dealing with sexuality-related issues.

International Academy of Sex Research
http://www.iasr.org
A scientific society that promotes research in sexual behavior; provides announcements of IASR conferences and abstracts of its journal's recent articles.

Kinsey Confidential
http://kinseyconfidential.org
A sexuality information service designed by The Kinsey Institute for Research in Sex, Gender, and Reproduction to meet the sexual health information needs of college-age adults.

Society for the Scientific Study of Sexuality
http://www.sexscience.org
A nonprofit organization dedicated to the advancement of knowledge about sexuality; provides announcements of the SSSS conferences and other meetings.

Suggested Reading

Bancroft, J. (Ed.). (1997). *Researching sexual behavior.* Bloomington: Indiana University Press. A discussion of the methodological issues of large-scale survey research in studying human sexuality.

Bullough, V. L. (1994). *Science in the bedroom: A history of sex research.* New York: Basic Books. A comprehensive history of sex research of the twentieth century.

Drucker, D. J. (2014). *The classification of sex: Alfred Kinsey and the organization of knowledge.* Pittsburgh: University of Pittsburgh Press. A detailed description of Alfred Kinsey's early research of the gall wasp, which provided the scientific foundation for this assembling, analysis, and publication of the research of over 18,000 personal sexual behavior histories.

Garton, S. (2004). *Histories of sexuality: Antiquity to sexual revolution.* New York: Routledge. A comprehensive historical review of major figures, from Havelock Ellis to Alfred Kinsey, and an exploration of such topics as the "invention" of homosexuality in the nineteenth century and the rise of sexual sciences in the twentieth century.

Maier, T. (2009). *Masters of sex.* New York: Basic Books. An unprecedented look at Masters and Johnson and their pioneering work together that highlights interviews with both.

Meezen, W., & Martin, J. I. (Eds.). (2006). *Research methods with gay, lesbian, bisexual and transgendered populations.* New York: Harrington Park Press. Discusses the unique issues in sexuality-related research among gay, lesbian, bisexual, and transgender populations and provides suggestions for doing this research.

Staples, R. (2006). *Exploring Black sexuality.* Boulder, CO: Rowman & Littlefield. A distinguished Black sexologist explores the sexual mores, folkways, and values among African Americans.

Wiederman, M., & Whitley, B., Jr. (2002). *Handbook for conducting research on human sexuality.* Mahwah, NJ: Erlbaum. A reference tool for researchers and students interested in research in human sexuality from a variety of disciplines; examines the specific methodological issues inherent in conducting human sexuality research.

Wyatt, G. (1997). *Stolen women: Reclaiming our sexuality and taking back our lives.* New York: Wiley. Discusses sociocultural influences, such as slavery and institutionalized racism, on the expression of sexuality among African American women.

Female Sexual Anatomy, Physiology, and Response

CHAPTER OUTLINE

"I identify with the passion [of women], the strength, the calmness, and the flexibility of being a woman. To me being a woman is like being the ocean. The ocean is a powerful thing, even at its calmest moments. It is a beauty that commands respect. It can challenge even the strongest men, and it gives birth to the smallest creatures. It is a provider, and an inspiration; this is a woman and this is what I am."

—20-year-old female

"The more I think about things that annoy me about being a woman, the more I realize that those annoyances are what make it so special. When I get my period, it isn't just a 'monthly curse'; it is a reminder that I can have children."

—19-year-old female

"When I started my period, my father kept a bit of a distance. How could I forget [that day]? The entire family was at my aunt's house, and no one had pads. You would think among 67 or so people one female would have a pad. I remember crying and my grandmother asking me what was wrong. After I told her, she began to laugh and said it was a natural cycle. I knew this from sixth-grade sexuality education class, but I still didn't want it. I was finally a woman."

—19-year-old female

"I think I am a good sexual partner and enjoy pleasing a woman. I especially love the foreplay that occurs between two people because it gets the body more excited than just going at it. I can go on forever with foreplay because I get to explore my partner's body, whether it is with my hands, lips, or tongue."

—25-year-old male

ALTHOUGH WOMEN AND MEN are similar in many more ways than they are different, we tend to focus on the differences rather than the similarities. Various cultures hold diverse ideas about exactly what it means to be female or male, but virtually the only differences that are consistent are actual physical differences, most of which relate to sexual structure and function. In this chapter and the following one, we discuss both the similarities and the differences in the anatomy (body structures), physiology (body functions), and sexual response of females and males. This chapter introduces the sexual structures and functions of women's bodies, including hormones and the menstrual cycle. We also look at models of sexual arousal and response, the relationship of these to women's experiences of sex, and the role of orgasm.

● Female Sex Organs: What Are They For?

Anatomically speaking, all embryos are female when their reproductive structures begin to develop (see Figure 1). If it does not receive certain genetic and hormonal signals, the fetus will continue to develop as a female. In humans and most other mammals, the female, in addition to providing half the genetic instructions for the offspring, provides the environment in which it can develop until it becomes capable of surviving as a separate entity. She also nourishes the offspring, both during gestation (the period of carrying the young in the uterus) via the placenta and following birth via the breasts through lactation (milk production).

In spite of what we do know, we haven't yet mapped all of the basic body parts of women, especially as they relate to the microprocesses of sexual response. Such issues as the function of the G-spot, the role of orgasm, and the placement of the many nerves that spider through the pelvic cavity still are not completely understood. Add to these puzzles the types, causes, and treatments of sexual function problems and one can quickly see that the science of sexual response is still emerging.

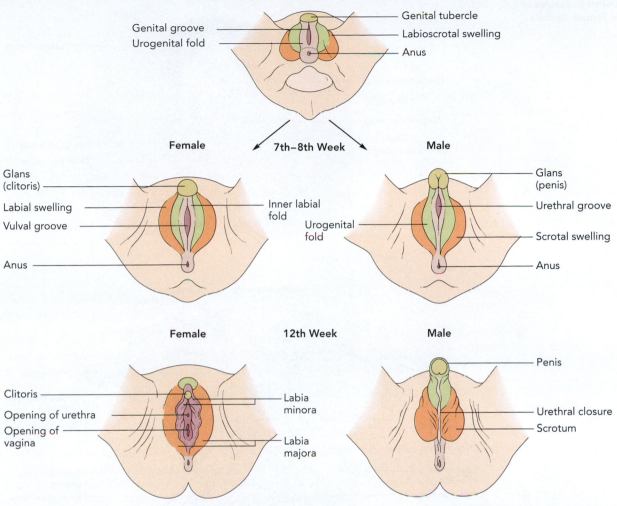

Undifferentiated Stage Prior to 6th Week

Genital groove
Urogenital fold

Genital tubercle
Labioscrotal swelling
Anus

Female — **7th–8th Week** — **Male**

Glans (clitoris)
Labial swelling
Vulval groove
Anus

Inner labial fold
Urogenital fold

Glans (penis)
Urethral groove
Scrotal swelling
Anus

Female — **12th Week** — **Male**

Clitoris
Opening of urethra
Opening of vagina

Labia minora
Labia majora

Penis
Urethral closure
Scrotum

- **FIGURE 1**

Embryonic-Fetal Differentiation of the External Reproductive Organs. Female and male reproductive organs are formed from the same embryonic tissues. An embryo's external genitals are female in appearance until certain genetic and hormonal instructions signal the development of male organs. Without such instructions, the genitals continue to develop as female.

Clearly, the female sex organs serve a reproductive function. But they perform other functions as well. Significant to nearly all women are the sexual parts that bring them pleasure; they may also attract potential sexual partners. Because of the mutual pleasure partners give each other, we can see that sexual structures also serve an important role in human relationships. People demonstrate their affection for one another by sharing sexual pleasure and form enduring partnerships at least partially on the basis of mutual sexual sharing. Let's look at the features of human female anatomy and physiology that provide pleasure to women and their partners and that enable women to conceive and give birth.

External Structures (the Vulva)

The sexual and reproductive organs of both men and women are usually called **genitals,** or genitalia, from the Latin *genere,* "to beget." The external female genitals are the mons pubis, the clitoris, the labia majora, and the labia minora, collectively known as the **vulva** (see Figures 2 and 3). (People often use the word "vagina" when they are actually referring to the vulva. The vagina is an internal structure.)

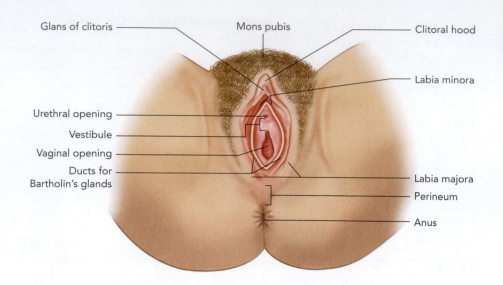

Glans of clitoris — Mons pubis — Clitoral hood

Labia minora

Urethral opening

Vestibule

Vaginal opening

Ducts for
Bartholin's glands

Labia majora

Perineum

Anus

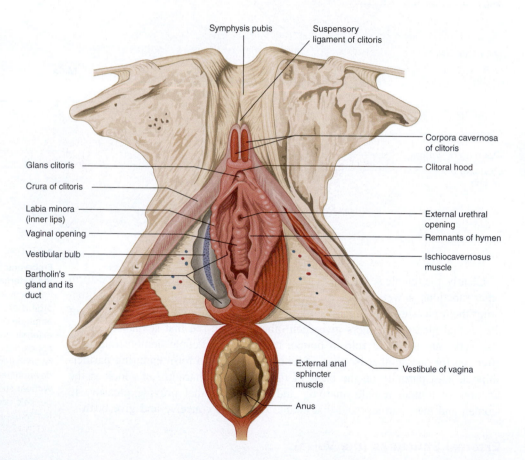

Symphysis pubis — Suspensory
ligament of clitoris

Corpora cavernosa
of clitoris

Glans clitoris — Clitoral hood

Crura of clitoris

Labia minora
(inner lips)

External urethral
opening

Vaginal opening — Remnants of hymen

Vestibular bulb

Ischiocavernosus
muscle

Bartholin's
gland and its
duct

External anal
sphincter
muscle — Vestibule of vagina

Anus

● **FIGURE 3**

**Internal Structures of
the Female Genitalia**

❞ *People will insist on treating the
mons veneris as though it were
Mount Everest.*

—Aldous Huxley
(1894–1963)

The Mons Pubis   The **mons pubis** (pubic mound), or **mons veneris** (mound
of Venus), is a pad of fatty tissue that covers the area of the pubic bone about
6 inches below the navel. Beginning in puberty, the mons is covered with pubic
hair. Because there is a rich supply of nerve endings in the mons, caressing it
can produce pleasure in most women.

The current practice of trimming and shaving pubic hair has become one barometer of fashion. Over the past few years, it has become commonplace in both sexes and for similar reasons: aesthetic and psychosexual. Its acceptance and practice among women expresses itself in a diverse range of pubic hair–grooming practices that have become an important component of sexual expression and participation in sexual activity (Herbenick, Schick, Reece, Sanders, & Fortenberry, 2010.3a). Findings revealed that pubic hair styles are diverse and that it is more common than not for women to have at least some pubic hair on their genitals. The study found that women's total removal of their pubic hair was associated with being young, being partnered, having looked closely at one's own genitals, cunnilingus, positive genital self-image, and sexual function. At the same time, the growing trend of male pubic hair removal, or what some call "manscaping," also contributes to the male's feelings of sexiness and cleanliness (Gale & Pettypiece, 2013).

Implicated in the shift in cultural attitudes regarding pubic hair is Internet-based pornography, where hair removal has become the "norm." In fact, more than 80% of male and female college students in the United States remove all or some of their pubic hair (Smolak & Murnen, 2011). This practice, however, is not new; many societies have for centuries decorated and sculpted their pubic hair, while others have removed the hair to avoid body lice. Many anecdotal reports on the removal of pubic hair highlight increased genital sensitivity and increased partner satisfaction. From a public health perspective, body hair removal may be a risk factor for folliculitis (infection in the hair follicle). On the other hand, a significant drop has been found in the number of cases of pubic lice (Armstrong & Wilson, 2006). If people choose to shave, wax, or tweeze, they should use only clean tools and exercise caution, since this is obviously a sensitive area.

The Clitoris

The **clitoris** (KLIH-tuh-rus) is considered the center of sexual arousal. It contains a high concentration of sensory nerve endings and is exquisitely sensitive to stimulation, especially at the tip of its shaft, the **glans clitoris.** A fold of skin called the **clitoral hood** covers the glans when the clitoris is not engorged. Although the clitoris is structurally analogous to the penis (it is formed from the same embryonic tissue), its sole function is sexual arousal. (The penis serves the additional functions of urine excretion and semen ejaculation.) The clitoris is a far more extensive structure than its visible part, the glans, would suggest (Bancroft, 2009). The shaft of the clitoris is both an external and an internal structure. The external portion is about 1 inch long and a quarter inch wide. Internally, the shaft is divided into two branches called **crura** (KROO-ra; singular, *crus*), each of which is about 3.5 inches long, which are the tips of erectile tissue that attach to the pelvic bones. The crura contain two **corpora cavernosa** (KOR-por-a kav-er-NO-sa), hollow chambers that fill with blood and swell during arousal. The hidden erectile tissue of the clitoris plus the surrounding muscle tissue all contribute to muscle spasms associated with orgasm. When stimulated, the clitoris enlarges initially and then retracts beneath the hood just before and during orgasm. With repeated orgasms, it follows the same pattern of engorgement and retraction, although its swellings may not be as pronounced after the initial orgasm. The role of the clitoris in producing an orgasm is discussed later in the chapter.

The Labia Majora and Labia Minora

The **labia majora** (LAY-be-a maJOR-a) (outer lips) are two folds of spongy flesh extending from the mons pubis and enclosing the labia minora, clitoris, urethral opening, and vaginal entrance. The **labia minora** (inner lips) are smaller folds within the labia majora that meet above the clitoris to form the clitoral hood. The labia minora also enclose the

> *Really that little dealybob is too far away from the hole. It should be built right in.*
>
> —Loretta Lynn
> (1935–)

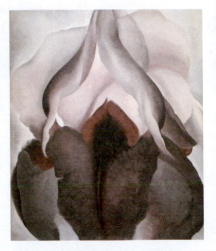

Artwork often imitates anatomy, as can be seen in this painting titled *Black Iris* (Georgia O'Keeffe, 1887–1986).

© Tomas Abad/AGE Fotostock

urethral and vaginal openings. They are smooth and hairless and vary quite a bit in appearance from woman to woman. Another rich source of sexual sensation, the labia are sensitive to the touch and swell during sexual arousal, doubling or tripling in size and changing in color from flesh-toned to a deep wine-red hue. The area enclosed by the labia minora is referred to as the **vestibule.** During sexual arousal, the clitoris becomes erect, the labia minora widen, and the vestibule (vaginal opening) becomes visible. Within the vestibule, on either side of the vaginal opening, are two small ducts from the **Bartholin's glands,** which secrete a small amount of moisture during sexual arousal.

Internal Structures

The internal female sexual anatomy and reproductive organs include the vagina; the uterus and its lower opening, the cervix; the ovaries; and the fallopian tubes. (Figure 4 provides illustrations of the front and side views of the female internal sexual anatomy.)

• **FIGURE 4**

Internal Female Sexual Structures

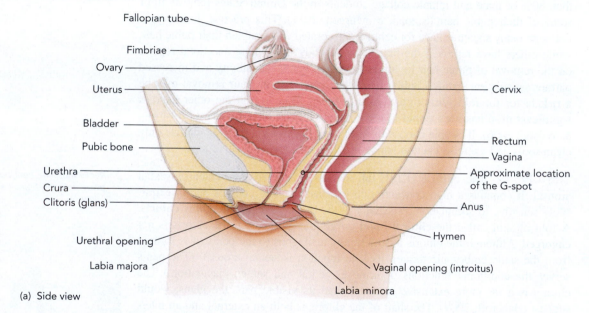

(a) Side view

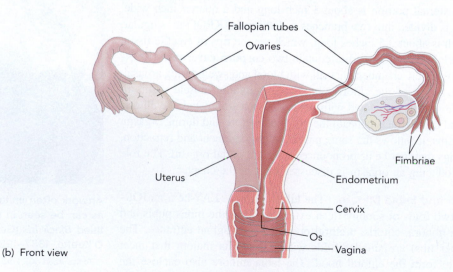

(b) Front view

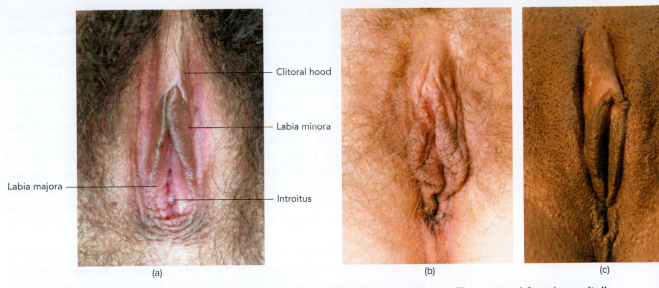

Clitoral hood

Labia minora

Labia majora

Introitus

(a)

(b)

(c)

The external female genitalia (vulva) can assume many different colors, shapes, and structures.

(a) © Daniel Sambraus/Science Source;
(b) © H.S. Photos/Alamy;
(c) © Custom Medical Stock Photo

The Vagina   The **vagina** (va-JI-na), from the Latin word for "sheath," is a flexible, muscular structure that extends 3–5 inches back and upward from the vaginal opening. It is the **birth canal** through which an infant is born, allows menstrual flow to pass from the uterus, and encompasses the penis or other object during sexual expression. In the unaroused state, the walls of the vagina are relaxed and collapsed together, but during sexual arousal, the inner two thirds of the vagina expand while pressure from engorgement causes the many small blood vessels that lie in the vaginal wall to produce lubrication. In response to sexual stimulation, lubrication can occur within 10–30 seconds. The majority of sensory nerve endings are concentrated in the **introitus** (in-TROY-tus), or vaginal opening. This part of the vagina is the most sensitive to erotic pressure and touch. In contrast, the inner two thirds of the vagina has virtually no nerve endings, which make it likely that a woman cannot feel a tampon when it is inserted deep in the vagina. Although the vaginal walls are generally moist, the wetness of a woman's vagina can vary by woman, by the stage of her menstrual cycle, and after childbirth or at menopause. Lubrication also increases substantially with sexual excitement. This lubrication serves several purposes. First, it increases the possibility of conception by alkalinizing the normally acidic chemical balance in the vagina, thus making it more hospitable to sperm, which die faster in acid environments. Second, it can make penetration more pleasurable by reducing friction in the vaginal walls. Third, the lubrication helps prevent small tears in the vagina, which, if they occur, can make the vagina more vulnerable to contracting HIV (the virus that causes AIDS) and some other STIs.

Prior to first intercourse or other form of penetration, the introitus is partially covered by a thin membrane containing a relatively large number of blood vessels, the **hymen** (named for the Roman god of marriage). The hymen typically has one or several perforations, allowing menstrual blood and mucous secretions to flow out of the vagina (and generally allowing for tampon insertion). In many cultures, it is (or was) important for a woman's hymen to be intact on her wedding day. Blood on the nuptial bedsheets is taken as proof of her virginity. The stretching or tearing of the hymen may produce some pain or discomfort and possibly some bleeding. Usually, the partner has little trouble inserting the penis or other object through the hymen if he or she is gentle and there is adequate lubrication. Prior to first intercourse, the hymen may be stretched or ruptured by tampon insertion, by the woman's self-manipulation, by a partner during noncoital sexual activity, by accident, or by a health care provider conducting a routine pelvic examination. Hymenoplasty, a controversial procedure that re-attaches the hymen to the vagina, is now sought by some women, particularly in Muslim countries where traditionalists place a high value on a woman's virginity, to create the illusion that they are still virgins. Hymen repair, also referred to as "revirgination," may also be performed for women who have been abused or those from cultures who risk a violent reaction from their partners. In spite of its availability, the American College of Obstetricians and Gynecologists has issued strong warnings to women that there is no evidence cosmetic genital surgery is safe or effective (ACOG, 2007).

An area inside the body, surrounding the urethra, is what many women report to be an erotically sensitive area, the **Grafenberg spot,** or **G-spot.** The name is derived from Ernest Grafenberg, a gynecologist, who first discussed its erotic significance. Located on the front wall of the vagina midway between the pubic bone and the cervix on the vaginal side of the urethra (see Figure 5), this area varies in size from a small bean to a half walnut. It can be located by pressing one or two fingers and about two knuckles deep into the front wall of a woman's vagina. Coital positions such as rear entry, in which the penis makes contact with the spot, may also produce intense erotic pleasure (Ladas, Whipple, & Perry, 1982; Whipple & Komisaruk, 1999). A variety of responses have been reported by women who first locate this spot. Initially, a woman may experience a slight feeling of discomfort or the need to urinate, but shortly thereafter, the tissue may swell and a pleasurable feeling may occur. Women who report orgasms as a result of stimulation of the G-spot describe them as intense and

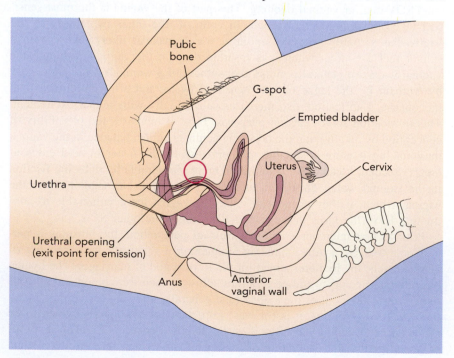

• **FIGURE 5**

The Grafenberg Spot (G-Spot). To locate the Grafenberg spot, insert two fingers into the vagina and press deeply into its anterior wall.

extremely pleasurable (Perry & Whipple, 1981; Whipple, 2002). Though an exact gland or site has not been found in all women, nor do all women experience pleasure when the area is massaged (Kilchevsky, Vardi, Lowenstein, Gruenwald, 2012), it has been suggested that the orgasm occurring in the area called the G-spot could be caused by the contact and connection of the richly innervated internal clitoris and the anterior vaginal wall (Foldes & Buisson, 2009). More specifically, by using special instruments and photography that measure changes in the vagina, it was found that the displacement of the anterior vaginal wall that occurs with pressure of the finger on this site, along with movement of the engorged and enlarged clitoris that occurs during sexual arousal, could provide close contact between the internal root of the clitoris and the anterior vaginal wall and thereby lead to what is known as a G-spot orgasm, sometimes with accompanying emission of fluid, which spurts out of the urethra (not vagina). This fluid, referred to as the "female ejaculate," has the appearance of skim milk and is chemically similar to seminal fluid, but different from urine (Komisaruk, Whipple, Nasserzadeh, & Beyer-Flores, 2010). It has been suggested that the emitted fluid comes from the para-urethral glands, also called the Skene's glands, better known as the "female prostate gland."

Despite the controversy that still exists around the presence of the G-spot, most women would agree that having more than one area of erotic arousal is sexually liberating and, as such, expands sexual enjoyment beyond the clitoris. In fact, some women who are concerned about their lack of ability to experience orgasm during vaginal intercourse have sought out G-spot amplification, in which collagen is injected into the vicinity of the G-spot to increase its size and sensitivity (Lehmiller, 2014). Still, reliable reports and anecdotal testimonials of the existence of this highly sensitive area will continue to raise the question about whether sufficient research has been done to verify the existence of the G-spot and, even more so, whether it is safe and effective to enhance it.

The Uterus and Cervix   The **uterus** (YU-te-rus), or womb, is a hollow, thick-walled, muscular organ held in the pelvic cavity by a number of flexible ligaments and supported by several muscles. It is pear-shaped, with the tapered end, the **cervix,** extending down and opening into the vagina. If a woman has not given birth, the uterus is about 3 inches long and 3 inches wide at the top; it is somewhat larger in women who have given birth. The uterus expands during pregnancy to the size of a volleyball or larger, to accommodate the developing fetus. The inner lining of the uterine walls, the **endometrium** (en-doe-MEE-tree-um), is filled with tiny blood vessels. As hormonal changes occur during the monthly menstrual cycle, this tissue is built up and then shed and expelled through the cervical **os** (opening), unless fertilization has occurred. In the event of pregnancy, the pre-embryo is embedded in the nourishing endometrium.

In addition to the more or less monthly menstrual discharge, mucous secretions from the cervix also flow out through the vagina. These secretions tend to be somewhat white, thick, and sticky following menstruation, becoming thinner as ovulation approaches. At ovulation, the mucous flow tends to increase and to be clear, slippery, and stretchy, somewhat like egg white.

The Ovaries   On each side of the uterus, held in place by several ligaments, is one of a pair of ovaries. The **ovary** is a **gonad,** an organ that produces **gametes** (GA-meets), the sex cells containing the genetic material necessary for

practically speaking

Performing a Gynecological Self-Examination

While reading this material, some females may wish to examine their own genitals and discover their unique features. In a space that is comfortable for you, take time to look at your vulva, or outer genitals, using a mirror and a good light. The large, soft folds of skin with hair on them are the outer lips, or labia majora. The color, texture, and pattern of this hair vary widely among women. Inside the outer lips are the inner lips, or labia minora. These have no hair and vary in size from small to large and protruding. They extend from below the vagina up toward the pubic bone, where they form a hood over the clitoris. The glans may not be visible under the clitoral hood, but it can be seen if a woman separates the labia minora and retracts the hood. The size and shape of the clitoris, as well as the hood, also vary widely among women. These variations have nothing to do with a woman's ability to respond sexually. You may also find some cheesy white matter under the hood. This is called smegma and is normal.

Below the clitoris is a smooth area and then a small hole. This is the urethral opening. Below the urethral opening is the vaginal opening, which is surrounded by rings of tissue. One of these, which you may or may not be able to see, is the hymen. Just inside the vagina, on both sides, are the Bartholin's glands. These may secrete a small amount of mucus during sexual excitement, but little else of their function is known. If they are infected, they will be swollen, but otherwise you won't notice them. The smooth area between your vagina and anus is called the perineum.

You can also examine your inner genitals, using a speculum, flashlight, and mirror. A speculum is an instrument used to hold the vaginal walls apart, allowing a clear view of the vagina and cervix. You should be able to obtain a speculum and information about doing an internal exam from a clinic that specializes in women's health or family planning.

It is a good idea to observe and become aware of what your normal vaginal discharges look and feel like. Colors vary from white to gray, and secretions change in

Examining your genitals can be an enlightening and useful practice that can provide you with information about the health of your body.

© H.S. Photos/Alamy

consistency from thick to thin and clear (similar to egg white that can be stretched between the fingers) over the course of the menstrual cycle. Distinct changes or odors, along with burning, bleeding between menstrual cycles, pain in the pelvic region, itching, or rashes, should be reported to a health care provider.

By inserting one or two fingers into the vagina and reaching deep into the canal, it is possible to feel the cervix, or tip of the uterus. In contrast to the soft vaginal walls, the cervix feels like the end of a nose: firm and round.

In doing a vaginal self-exam, you may initially experience some fear or uneasiness about touching your body. In the long run, however, your patience and persistence will pay off in increased body awareness and a heightened sense of personal health.

Once you're familiar with the normal appearance of your outer genitals, you can check for any changes, especially unusual rashes, soreness, warts, or parasites, such as pubic lice, or "crabs."

reproduction. Female gametes are called **oocytes** (OH-uh-sites), from the Greek words for "egg" and "cell." Oocytes are commonly referred to as eggs or **ova** [singular, **ovum**]. Technically, however, the cell does not become an egg until it completes its final stages of division following fertilization. The ovaries are the size and shape of large almonds. In addition to producing oocytes, they serve the important function of producing hormones such as estrogen, progesterone, and testosterone. (These hormones are discussed later in this chapter.)

At birth, the female's ovaries contain about half a million oocytes. During childhood, many of these degenerate; then, beginning in puberty and ending after menopause, a total of about 400 oocytes mature and are released during a woman's reproductive years. The release of an oocyte is called **ovulation.** The immature oocytes are embedded in saclike structures called **ovarian follicles.** The fully ripened follicle is called a vesicular or Graffian follicle. At maturation, the follicle ruptures, releasing the oocyte. After the oocyte emerges, the ruptured follicle becomes the **corpus luteum** (KOR-pus LOO-tee-um) (from the Latin for "yellow body"), a producer of important hormones; it eventually degenerates. The egg is viable for about 24 hours.

The Fallopian Tubes   At the top of the uterus are two tubes, one on each side, known as **fallopian tubes,** uterine tubes, or oviducts. The tubes are about 4 inches long. They extend toward the ovaries but are not attached to them. Instead, the funnel-shaped end of each tube (the **infundibulum**) fans out into fingerlike **fimbriae** (fim-BREE-ah), which drape over the ovary but may not actually touch it. Tiny, hairlike **cilia** on the fimbriae become active during ovulation. Their waving motion, along with contractions of the walls of the tube, transports the oocyte that has been released from the ovary into the fallopian tube. (The process of ovulation and the events leading to fertilization are discussed later in this chapter.)

Other Structures

There are several other important anatomical structures in the genital areas of both men and women. Although they may not serve reproductive functions, they may be involved in sexual activities. Some of these areas may also be affected by sexually transmitted infections. In women, these structures include the urethra, anus, and perineum. The **urethra** (yu-REE-thra) is the tube through which urine passes; the **urethral opening** is located between the clitoris and the vaginal opening. Between the vagina and the **anus**—the opening of the rectum, through which excrement passes—is a diamond-shaped region called the **perineum** (per-e-NEE-um). This area of soft tissue covers the muscles and ligaments of the **pelvic floor,** the underside of the pelvic area extending from the top of the pubic bone (above the clitoris) to the anus.

The anus consists of two sphincters, which are circular muscles that open and close like valves. The anus contains a dense supply of nerve endings that, along with the tender rings at the opening, can respond erotically. In sex play or intercourse involving the anus or rectum, care must be taken not to rupture the delicate tissues. This may occur because of the lack of adequate lubrication or very rough anal sex play. Anal sex, which involves insertion of the penis or other object into the rectum, is potentially unsafe, as is vaginal sex, because abrasions of the tissue provide easy passage for pathogens, such as HIV, to the

Girls got balls. They're just a little higher up, that's all.

Joan Jett
(1960–)

• **FIGURE 6**

The Female Breast. Front and cross-sectional views.

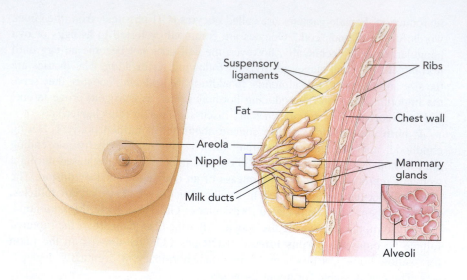

bloodstream. To practice safer sex, partners who engage in anal intercourse should use a latex condom with a water-based lubricant.

The Breasts

Uncorsetted, her friendly bust gives promise of pneumatic bliss.

—T. S. Eliot
(1888–1965)

With the surge of sex hormones that occurs during adolescence, the female breasts begin to develop and enlarge (see Figure 6). The reproductive function of the breasts is to nourish offspring through **lactation,** or milk production. A mature female breast, also known as a **mammary gland,** is composed of fatty tissue and 15–25 lobes that radiate around a central protruding nipple. Around the nipple is a ring of darkened skin called the **areola** (a-REE-o-la). Tiny muscles at the base of the nipple cause it to become erect in response to touch, cold, or sexual arousal.

Western culture tends to be ambivalent about breasts and nudity. Most people, however, are comfortable with artistic portrayals of the nude female body.

© Anthony Saint James/Getty Images

When a woman is pregnant, the structures within the breast undergo further development. Directly following childbirth, in response to hormonal signals, small glands within the lobes called **alveoli** (al-VEE-a-lee) begin producing milk. The milk passes into ducts, each of which has a dilated region for storage; the ducts open to the outside at the nipple. During lactation, a woman's breasts increase in size from enlarged glandular tissues and stored milk. Because there is little variation in the amount of glandular tissue among women, the amount of milk produced does not vary with breast size. In women who are not lactating, breast size depends mainly on fat content, which is determined by hereditary factors.

In the Western culture, women's breasts capture a significant amount of attention and serve an erotic function. Many, but not all, women find breast stimulation intensely pleasurable, whether it occurs during breastfeeding or sexual contact. Partners tend to be aroused by both the sight and the touch of women's breasts. Although there is no basis in reality, some believe that large breasts denote greater sexual responsiveness than small breasts. (Table 1 provides a summary of female sexual anatomy.)

TABLE 1 • Summary Table of Female Sexual Anatomy

External Structures

Mons pubis (mons veneris)	Fatty tissue that covers the area of the pubic bone
Clitoris	Center of sexual arousal
Clitoral hood	Covers the glans clitoris when the clitoris is not engorged
Crura (singular, crus)	Tips of erectile tissue that attach to the pelvic bones
Corpora cavernosa	Hollow chambers that fill with blood and swell during sexual arousal
Labia majora (outer lips)	Two folds of spongy flesh that extend from the mons pubis and run downward along the sides of the vulva
Labia minora (inner lips)	Smaller, hairless folds within the labia majora that meet above the clitoris to form the clitoral hood
Vestibule (vaginal opening)	Area enclosed by the labia minora
Bartholin's glands	Glands that secrete a small amount of moisture during sexual arousal

Internal Structures

Vagina (birth canal)	Flexible, muscular structure in which menstrual flow and babies pass
Introitus	Vaginal opening
Hymen	Thin membrane that partially covers the introitus and contains a relatively large number of blood vessels
Grafenberg spot (G-spot)	Located on the upper front wall of the vagina, an erotically sensitive area that may produce intense erotic pleasure and a fluid emission in some women
Uterus (womb)	Hollow, thick-walled muscular organ in which a fertilized ovum implants and develops until birth
Cervix	Lower end of the uterus that extends down and opens to the vagina
Endometrium	Inner lining of the uterine wall to which the fertilized egg attaches; partly discharged (if pregnancy does not occur) with the menstrual flow
Os	Opening to the cervix
Ovary (gonad)	Organ that produces gametes (see below)
Gametes	Sex cells containing the genetic material necessary for reproduction; also referred to as oocytes, eggs, ova (singular, ovum)
Ovarian follicles	Saclike structures that contain the immature oocytes
Corpus luteum	Tissue formed from a ruptured ovarian follicle that produces important hormones after the oocyte emerges
Fallopian tubes (oviducts)	Uterine tubes that transport the oocyte from the ovary to the uterus
Infundibulum	Funnel-shaped end of each fallopian tube
Fimbriae	Fingerlike projections that drape over the ovary and help transport the oocyte from the ovary into the fallopian tube
Cilia	Tiny, hairlike structures that provide waving motion to help transport the oocyte within the fallopian tube to the ovary
Ampulla	Widened part of the fallopian tube in which fertilization normally occurs

Other Structures

Urethra	Tube through which urine passes
Urethral opening	Opening in the urethra, through which urine is expelled
Anus	Opening in the rectum, through which excrement passes
Perineum	Area that lies between the vaginal opening and the anus
Pelvic floor	Underside of the pelvic area, extending from the top of the pubic bone (above the clitoris) to the anus

During ovulation, the ovarian follicle swells and ruptures, releasing the mature oocyte to begin its journey through the fallopian tube.

© Petit Format/Science Source

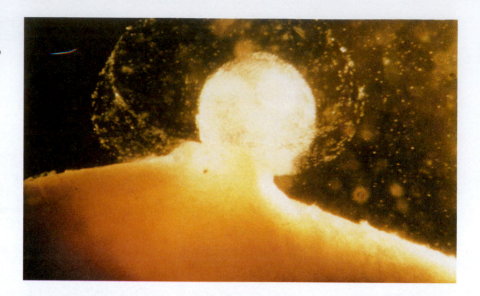

● Female Sexual Physiology

Just how do the various structures of the female anatomy function to produce the menstrual cycle? The female reproductive cycle can be viewed as having two components (although, of course, multiple biological processes are involved): (1) the ovarian cycle, in which eggs develop, and (2) the menstrual, or uterine cycle, in which the womb is prepared for pregnancy. These cycles repeat approximately every month for about 35 or 40 years. The task of directing these processes belongs to a class of chemicals called hormones.

TABLE 2 ● Female Sex Hormones

Hormone	Where Produced	Functions
Estrogen (including estradiol, estrone, estriol)	Ovaries, adrenal glands, placenta (during pregnancy)	Promotes maturation of reproductive organs, development of secondary sex characteristics, and growth spurt at puberty; regulates menstrual cycle; sustains pregnancy; maintains libido
Progesterone	Ovaries, adrenal glands, placenta	Promotes breast development, maintains uterine lining, regulates menstrual cycle, sustains pregnancy
Gonadotropin-releasing hormone (GnRH)	Hypothalamus	Promotes maturation of gonads, regulates menstrual cycle
Follicle-stimulating hormone (FSH)	Pituitary	Regulates ovarian function and maturation of ovarian follicles
Luteinizing hormone (LH)	Pituitary	Assists in production of estrogen and progesterone, regulates maturation of ovarian follicles, triggers ovulation
Human chorionic gonadotropin (HCG)	Embryo and placenta	Helps sustain pregnancy
Testosterone	Adrenal glands and ovaries	Helps stimulate sexual desire
Oxytocin	Hypothalamus	Stimulates uterine contractions during childbirth and possibly during orgasm, promotes milk let-down
Prolactin	Pituitary	Stimulates milk production
Prostaglandins	All body cells	Mediates hormone response, stimulates muscle contractions

Reproductive Hormones

Hormones are chemical substances that serve as messengers, traveling within the body through the bloodstream. Most hormones are composed of either amino acids (building blocks of proteins) or steroids (derived from cholesterol). They are produced by the ovaries and the endocrine glands—the adrenals, pituitary, and hypothalamus. Hormones assist in a variety of tasks, including development of the reproductive organs and secondary sex characteristics during puberty, regulation of the menstrual cycle, maintenance of pregnancy, initiation and regulation of childbirth, initiation of lactation, and, to some degree, the regulation of **libido** (li-BEE-doh; sex drive or interest). Hormones that act directly on the gonads are known as **gonadotropins** (go-nad-a-TRO-pins). Among the most important of the female hormones are the **estrogens,** which affect the maturation of the reproductive organs, menstruation, and pregnancy, and **progesterone,** which helps maintain the uterine lining until menstruation occurs. (The principal hormones involved in a woman's reproductive and sexual life and their functions are described in Table 2.) (Testosterone is discussed later in this chapter.)

The Ovarian Cycle

The development of female gametes is a complex process that begins even before a woman is born. In infancy and childhood, the cells develop into ova (eggs). During puberty, hormones trigger the completion of the process of **oogenesis** (oh-uh-JEN-uh-sis), literally, "egg beginning" (see Figure 7). The oocyte, otherwise referred to as germ cell or immature ovum, marks the start of mitosis, the process by which a cell divides, creating two daughter cells. Oogenesis results in the formation of both primary oocytes, before birth, and

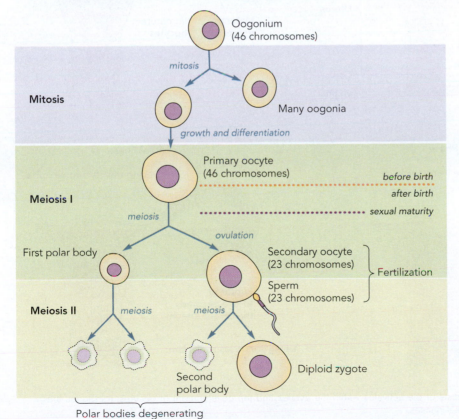

● **FIGURE 7**

Oogenesis. This diagram charts the development of an ovum, beginning with embryonic development of the oogonium and ending with fertilization of the secondary oocyte, which then becomes the diploid zygote. Primary oocytes are present in a female at birth; at puberty, hormones stimulate the oocyte to undergo meiosis.

as secondary oocytes after it and as part of ovulation. This process, called the **ovarian cycle**, continues until a woman reaches menopause.

The ovarian cycle averages 28 days in length, although there is considerable variation among women, ranging from 21 to 40 days. In their own particular cycle length after puberty, however, most women experience little variation. Generally, ovulation occurs in only one ovary each month, with only a 50-50 chance of releasing an egg from the opposite ovary as the month before. If a single ovary is removed, the remaining one begins to ovulate every month. The ovarian cycle has four phases: menstrual, follicular (fo-LIK-u-lar), ovulatory (ov-UL-a-toree), and luteal (LOO-tee-ul) (see Figure 8). As an ovary undergoes its changes, corresponding shifts occur in the uterus. Menstruation marks the end of this sequence of hormonal and physical changes in the ovaries and uterus.

The Follicular Phase   On the first day of the cycle, **gonadotropin-releasing hormone (GnRH)** is released from the hypothalamus. GnRH begins to

Menstrual Phase

(Menstruation)

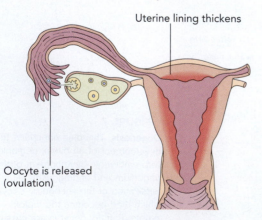

Follicular Phase

(Follicle development)

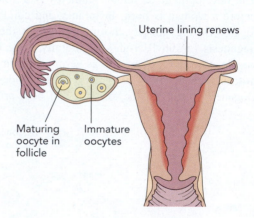

Ovulatory Phase

Luteal Phase

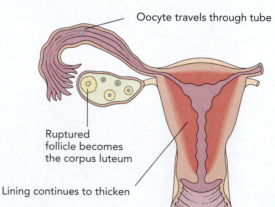

• **FIGURE 8**

Ovarian Cycle. The ovarian cycle consists of the activities within the ovaries and the development of oocytes; it includes the menstrual, follicular, ovulatory, and luteal phases.

stimulate the pituitary to release **follicle-stimulating hormone (FSH)** and **luteinizing hormone (LH),** initiating the **follicular phase.** During the first 10 days, 10–20 ovarian follicles begin to grow, stimulated by FSH and LH. In 98–99% of cases, only one of the follicles will mature completely during this period. (The maturation of more than one oocyte is one factor in multiple births.) All the developing follicles begin secreting estrogen. Under the influence of FSH and estrogen, the oocyte matures, bulging from the surface of the ovary. This may also be referred to as the proliferative phase.

Ovulatory Phase   The **ovulatory phase** begins at about day 11 of the cycle and culminates with ovulation at about day 14. An exact day of ovulation cannot be predicted. Stimulated by an increase of LH from the pituitary, the primary oocyte undergoes cell division and becomes ready for ovulation. The ballooning follicle wall thins and ruptures, and the oocyte enters the abdominal cavity near the beckoning fimbriae. Ovulation is now complete. Some women experience a sharp twinge, called **Mittelschmerz,** on one side of the lower abdomen during ovulation. A very slight bloody discharge from the vagina may also occur. Occasionally, more than one ovum is released. If two ova are fertilized, nonidentical twins will result. If one egg is fertilized and divides into two separate zygotes, identical twins will develop.

The Luteal Phase   Following ovulation, estrogen levels drop rapidly, and the ruptured follicle, still under the influence of increased LH, becomes a corpus luteum, which secretes progesterone and small amounts of estrogen. Increasing levels of these hormones inhibit pituitary release of FSH and LH. Unless fertilization has occurred, the corpus luteum deteriorates. In the event of pregnancy, the corpus luteum maintains its hormonal output, helping sustain the pregnancy. The hormone human chorionic gonadotropin (HCG)—similar to LH—is secreted by the embryo and signals the corpus luteum to continue until the placenta has developed sufficiently to take over hormone production.

The **luteal phase** starts on ovulation day and can occur anytime from day 7 to 22, depending on the length of the menstrual cycle. Even when cycles are more or less than 28 days, the duration of the luteal phase remains the same; the time between ovulation and the beginning of menstruation, an average 14 days. At this point, the ovarian hormone levels are at their lowest, GnRH is released, and FSH and LH levels begin to rise.

Menstrual Phase   As hormone levels decrease following the degeneration of the corpus luteum, the uterine lining (endometrium) is shed because it will not be needed to help sustain the fertilized ovum. The shedding of endometrial tissue and the bleeding that accompanies it are known as the **menstrual phase,** a monthly event in the lives of women from puberty through menopause. Cultural and religious attitudes, as well as personal experience, influence our feelings about this phenomenon.

The Menstrual Cycle

Most American women who menstruate use sanitary pads, panty liners, or tampons to help absorb the flow of menstrual blood. While pads and panty liners are used outside the body, tampons are placed inside the vagina. For a wide variety of reasons, including environmental concerns, comfort, chemical residues, and **toxic shock syndrome (TSS)** (a bacterial infection that can occur in menstruating women and cause a person to go into shock), women are turning to alternative means for catching menstrual flow.

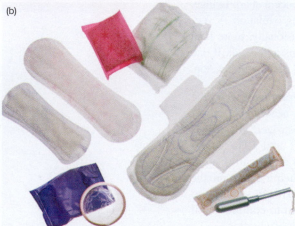

An array of choices that collect and absorb menstrual flow are now available to women.

(a) © Editorial Image, LLC/Alamy;
(b) © Editorial Image, LLC/Alamy

While some Americans may question the use of alternative products, across time and cultures a wide variety of methods have been used to absorb the flow of blood. Cloth menstrual pads, for example, are reusable, washable, and quite comfortable.

For those desiring to wear something internally, reusable, or disposable, menstrual cups are another alternative to tampons. The cup is inserted inside the vagina a few inches below the cervix and is held in place by the muscles of the lower vagina. If put into place properly, the cup should not be felt. About 10 brands of menstrual cups are available on the market today, including The Keeper, The Keeper Mooncup, and The DivaCup. These cups are made of rubber or medical-grade silicon, making them easy to fold and insert. The cups come in two sizes; the larger size is recommended for women who have delivered a baby vaginally. Reusable menstrual cups can be worn about 6–12 hours, depending on the amount of blood flow. When it's time to change the cup, it is removed, emptied into a drain, rinsed, and reinserted (this can be awkward in public restrooms). Menstrual cups are not linked to TSS because they only collect the blood, rather than absorb it. They also do not protect against pregnancy or sexually transmitted infections ("Ins and Outs of Menstrual Cups," 2012). Some women have used the diaphragm or cervical cap in a similar manner.

Reusable sea sponges can work like tampons in absorbing blood. Boiling the sponge before use and between uses can help to rid it of possible ocean pollutants and help to keep it sanitary. Sewing or tying a piece of cotton string on the sponge for easy retrieval is suggested. Most likely, the majority of American women will continue to rely on more widely available and advertised commercial tampons or sanitary pads; however, alternatives provide women with an opportunity to take charge of how they respond to their menstrual flow and the environmental impacts of that decision.

The **menstrual cycle** (uterine cycle), is divided into three phases: menstrual, proliferative, and secretory. What occurs within the uterus is inextricably related to what is happening in the ovaries, but only in their final phases do the two cycles actually coincide (see Figure 9).

Menstruation   With hormone levels low because of the degeneration of the corpus luteum, the outer layer of the endometrium becomes detached from the uterine wall. The shedding of the endometrium marks the beginning of the menstrual phase. This endometrial tissue, along with mucus, other cervical and vaginal secretions, and a small amount of blood (2–5 ounces per cycle), is expelled through the vagina. The menstrual flow, or **menses** (MEN-seez), generally occurs over a period of 3–5 days. FSH and LH begin increasing around day 5, marking the end of this phase. A girl's first menstruation is known as **menarche** (MEH-nar-kee).

The Proliferative Phase   The **proliferative phase** lasts about 9 days. During this time, the endometrium thickens in response to increased estrogen. The mucous membranes of the cervix secrete a clear, thin mucus with a crystalline structure that facilitates the passage of sperm. The proliferative phase ends with ovulation.

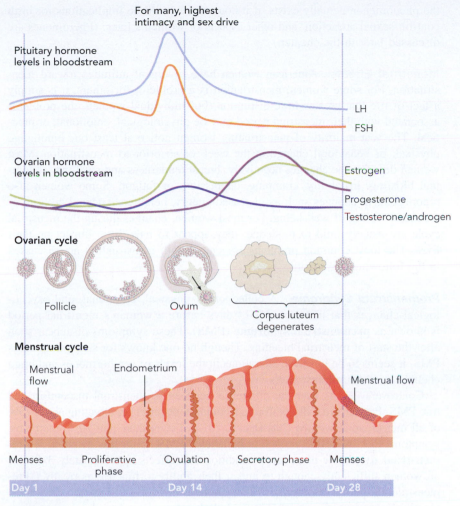

For many, highest
intimacy and sex drive

Pituitary hormone
levels in bloodstream

LH

FSH

Ovarian hormone
levels in bloodstream

Estrogen

Progesterone

Testosterone/androgen

Ovarian cycle

Follicle

Ovum

Corpus luteum
degenerates

Menstrual cycle

Menstrual
flow

Endometrium

Menstrual flow

Menses

Proliferative
phase

Ovulation

Secretory phase

Menses

Day 1

Day 14

Day 28

● **FIGURE 9**

The Menstrual Cycle, Ovarian Cycle, and Hormone Levels. This chart compares the
activities of the ovaries and uterus and shows the relationship of blood hormone levels to
these activities.

The Secretory Phase   During the first part of the **secretory phase,** with the
help of progesterone, the endometrium begins to prepare for the arrival of a
fertilized ovum. Glands within the uterus enlarge and begin secreting glycogen,
a cell nutrient. The cervical mucus thickens and starts forming a plug to seal
off the uterus in the event of pregnancy. If fertilization does not occur, the corpus luteum begins to degenerate, as LH levels decline. Progesterone levels then
fall, and the endometrial cells begin to die. The secretory phase lasts approximately 14 days, corresponding with the luteal phase of the ovarian cycle. It ends
with the shedding of the endometrium.

Menstrual Synchrony   Women who live or work together sometimes report
developing similarly timed menstrual cycles (Cutler, 1999). Termed **menstrual
synchrony,** this phenomenon appears to be related to the sense of smell—more
specifically, a response to **pheromones,** chemical substances secreted into the
air. Though there is considerable controversy among researchers as to whether

the phenomenon actually exists, if it does, there could be implications for birth control, sexual attraction, and other aspects of women's lives. (Pheromones are discussed later in the chapter.)

Menstrual Effects   American women have divergent attitudes toward menstruation. For some women, menstruation is a problem; for others, it is simply a fact of life that creates little disruption. For individual women, the problems associated with their menstrual period may be physiological, emotional, or practical. The vast majority of menstruating women notice at least one emotional, physical, or behavioral change in the week or so prior to menstruation. Most women describe the changes negatively: breast tenderness and swelling, abdominal bloating, irritability, cramping, depression, or fatigue. Some women also report positive changes such as increased energy, heightened sexual arousal, or a general feeling of well-being. For most women, changes during the menstrual cycle are usually mild to moderate; they appear to have little impact on their lives. The most common problems associated with menstruation are discussed in the following paragraphs.

Premenstrual Syndrome   A collection of physical, emotional, and psychological changes that may occur 7–14 days before a woman's menstrual period is known as **premenstrual syndrome (PMS).** These symptoms disappear soon after the start of menstrual bleeding. Though no one knows for sure what causes PMS, it seems to be linked to alterations in the levels of sex hormones and brain chemicals, or neurotransmitters.

Controversy exists over the difference between premenstrual discomfort and true PMS. Premenstrual discomfort is a common occurrence, affecting about 75% of all menstruating women (IntelHealth, 2013). Fewer than 1 in 10 women have symptoms that are severe enough to be labeled PMS. Even less common is **premenstrual dysphoric disorder,** a condition that affects approximately 3–8% of all women sufficiently enough to impair their ability to function normally ("Premenstrual dysphoric disorder," 2012). Symptoms of PMS fall into two categories: (1) physical symptoms, which may include bloating, breast tenderness, swelling and weight gain, headaches, cramping, migraine headaches, and food cravings and (2) psychological and emotional symptoms, which include fatigue, depression, irritability, crying, and decrease in libido. For many, symptoms may be worse some months and better other ones. It may also be comforting to know that in most women, PMS symptoms begin to subside after the age of 35 and at menopause.

Menorrhagia   At some point in her menstrual life, nearly every woman experiences heavy or prolonged bleeding during her menstrual cycle, also known as **menorrhagia.** Although heavy menstrual bleeding is common among most women, only a few experience blood loss severe enough for it to be defined as menorrhagia. Signs and symptoms may include a menstrual flow that soaks through one or more sanitary pads or tampons every hour for several consecutive hours, the need to use double sanitary protection throughout the menstrual flow, menstrual flow that includes large blood clots, and/or heavy menstrual flow that interferes with the regular lifestyle. Though the cause of heavy menstrual bleeding is unknown, a number of conditions may cause menorrhagia, including hormonal imbalances, uterine fibroids, having an IUD, cancer, or certain medications. The combined effect of hormonal imbalances and uterine fibroids accounts for 80% of all cases of menorrhagia. Excessive or prolonged menstrual bleeding can lead to iron deficiency anemia and other medical conditions; thus, it is advisable for women with this problem to seek medical care and treatment.

Dysmenorrhea While menstrual cramps are experienced by some women before or during their periods, a more persistent, aching, and serious pain sufficient to limit a woman's activities is called **dysmenorrhea.** There are two types of dysmenorrhea. Primary dysmenorrhea is not associated with any diagnosable pelvic condition. It is characterized by pain that begins with (or just before) uterine bleeding when there is an absence of pain at other times in the cycle. It can be very severe and may be accompanied by nausea, weakness, or other physical symptoms. In secondary dysmenorrhea, the symptoms may be the same, but there is an underlying condition or disease causing them; pain may not be limited to the menstrual phase alone. Secondary dysmenorrhea may be caused by pelvic inflammatory disease (PID), endometriosis, endometrial cancer, or other conditions that should be treated.

The effects of dysmenorrhea can totally incapacitate a woman for several hours or even days. Once believed to be a psychological condition, primary dysmenorrhea is now known to be caused by high levels of **prostaglandins** (pros-ta-GLAN-dins), natural substances made by cells in the endometrium and other parts of the body. When excessive amounts are produced, the woman may have extreme pain with her menstrual cycle along with headaches, nausea, vomiting, and diarrhea. Prostaglandin production can be decreased with over-the-counter drugs such as aspirin or ibuprofen. Birth control pills or Depo-Provera can also be used to prevent ovulation and thus decrease the thickness of the endometrium, where the prostaglandins are produced.

Amenorrhea When women do not menstruate for reasons other than aging, the condition is called **amenorrhea** (ay-meh-neh-REE-a). Principal causes of amenorrhea are pregnancy and breastfeeding. Lack of menstruation, if not a result of pregnancy or nursing, is categorized as either primary or secondary amenorrhea. Women who have passed the age of 16 and never menstruated are diagnosed as having primary amenorrhea. It may be that they have not yet reached their critical weight, when an increased ratio of body fat triggers menstrual cycle–inducing hormones, or that they are hereditarily late maturers. But it can also signal hormonal deficiencies, abnormal body structure, or an intersex condition or other genital anomaly that makes menstruation impossible. Most primary amenorrhea can be treated with hormone therapy.

Secondary amenorrhea exists when a previously menstruating woman stops menstruating for several months. If it is not due to pregnancy, breastfeeding, or the use of hormonal contraceptives, the source of secondary amenorrhea may be found in stress, lowered body fat, heavy physical training, cysts or tumors, disease, or hormonal irregularities. Anorexia is a frequent cause of amenorrhea. If a woman is not pregnant, is not breastfeeding, and can rule out hormonal contraceptives as a cause, she should see her health care practitioner if she has gone 3 months without menstruating.

Lifestyle changes or treatment of the underlying condition can almost always correct amenorrhea, unless it is caused by a congenital anomaly. Because there is no known harm associated with amenorrhea, the condition is corrected when an underlying problem presents itself or it causes a woman psychological distress.

Sexuality and the Menstrual Cycle Although studies have tried to determine whether there is a biologically based cycle of sexual interest and activity

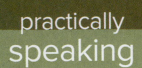

Vaginal and Menstrual Health Care

Many factors can influence the way we experience the changes that occur over the course of the menstrual cycle. While the vast majority of women feel few and minor changes, others experience changes that are uncomfortable and debilitating. The variations can be significant in any one woman and from month to month. For women, recognizing their menstrual patterns, learning about their bodies, and recognizing and dealing with existing difficulties can be useful in heading off or easing potential problems. Different remedies work for different women. We suggest that you try varying combinations of them and keep a record of your response to each. Following are some common changes that occur during the menstrual cycle and self-help means to address them.

For Vaginal Changes

The mucous membranes lining the walls of the vagina normally produce clear, white, or pale yellow secretions. These secretions pass from the cervix through the vagina and vary in color, consistency, odor, and quantity, depending on the phase of the menstrual cycle, the woman's health, and her unique physical characteristics. It is important for you to observe your secretions periodically and note any changes, especially if symptoms accompany them. Because self-diagnosis of unusual discharges is inaccurate over half the time, it is wise to go ahead with self-treatment only after a diagnosis is made by a health care practitioner. Call a health professional if you feel uncertain or suspicious and/or think you may have been exposed to a sexually transmitted infection.

Here are some simple guidelines that may help a woman avoid getting vaginal infections (vaginitis):

1. Avoid douching and vaginal deodorants, especially deodorant suppositories or deodorant tampons. The vagina is a clean environment and does not need to be washed. Douching upsets the natural chemical balance of the vagina.
2. Maintain good genital hygiene by washing the labia and clitoris regularly (about once a day) with mild soap.
3. After a bowel movement, wipe the anus from front to back, away from the vagina, to prevent contamination with fecal bacteria.
4. Wear cotton underpants with a cotton crotch. Nylon does not "breathe," and it allows heat and moisture to build up, creating an ideal environment for infectious organisms to reproduce.
5. If you use a vaginal lubricant, be sure it is water-soluble. Oil-based lubricants such as Vaseline encourage bacterial growth.
6. Socialize with others or go to a support group to help reduce the stress that may cause or exacerbate the infection.

For Premenstrual Changes

1. Consume a well-balanced diet, with plenty of whole-grain cereals, fruits, and vegetables.
2. Moderate your intake of alcohol, avoid tobacco, and get sufficient sleep.
3. Exercise at least 30–45 minutes a day. Aerobic exercise brings oxygen to body tissues and stimulates the production of endorphins, chemical substances that help promote feelings of well-being.

For Cramps

1. Relax and apply heat by using a heating pad or hot-water bottle (or, in a pinch, a cat) applied to the abdominal area may help relieve cramps; a warm bath may also help.
2. Get a lower-back or other form of massage, such as acupressure, or Shiatsu.
3. Take prostaglandin inhibitors, such as aspirin and ibuprofen, to reduce cramping of the uterine and abdominal muscles. Aspirin increases menstrual flow slightly, whereas ibuprofen reduces it. Stronger anti-prostaglandins may be prescribed by your health care practitioner.
4. Having an orgasm (with or without a partner) is reported by some women to relieve menstrual congestion and cramping.

When symptoms are severe, further medical evaluation is needed.

in women that correlates with the menstrual cycle (such as higher interest around ovulation), the results have been varied. There is also variation in how people feel about sexual activity during different phases of the menstrual cycle.

There has been a general taboo in our culture, as in many others, against sexual intercourse during menstruation. This taboo may be based on religious or cultural beliefs. Among Orthodox Jews, for example, women are required to refrain from intercourse for 7 days following the end of menstruation. They may then resume sexual activity after a ritual bath, the *mikvah*. Contact with blood may make some people squeamish. Some women, especially at the beginning of their period, feel bloated or uncomfortable; they may experience breast tenderness or a general feeling of not wanting to be touched. Others may find that sexual activity helps relieve menstrual discomfort.

For some couples, merely having to deal with the logistics of bloodstains, bathing, and laundry may be enough to discourage them from intercourse at this time. For many people, however, menstrual blood holds no special connotation. In a study of 108 women aged 18–23, females described their experiences with sexuality during menstruation. Nearly one half, most of whom were in committed relationships, stated they had sexual activity during their menstrual cycle (Allen & Goldberg, 2009). Young adults who were comfortable with menstrual sex saw it as just another part of a committed intimate relationship. It is important to note that although it is unusual, conception *can* occur during menstruation. Some women find that a diaphragm or menstrual cup can collect the menstrual flow. Menstrual cups, however, are not a contraceptive. It is not recommended that women engage in intercourse while a tampon is inserted because of possible injury to the cervix. And inventive lovers can, of course, find many ways to give each other pleasure that do not require putting the penis into the vagina.

● Human Sexual Response

The ways in which individuals respond to sexual arousal are highly varied. Women's sexuality, though typically thought of as personal and individual, is significantly influenced by the social groups to which women belong. Sociocultural variables include gender, religious preference, class, educational attainment, age, marital status, race, and ethnicity. For many women, gender—the social and cultural characteristics associated with being male or female—is probably the most influential variable in shaping their sexual desires, behaviors, and partnerships. Because gender is largely defined by cultural expectations, women's sexual experiences must be understood in terms of cultural, political, and relational forces. Research into the anatomy and physiology of sexuality has helped us increase our understanding of **orgasm,** the climax of sexual sensation that involves rhythmic contractions in the genital area and intensely pleasurable sensations. By looking beyond the genitals to the central nervous system, where electrical impulses travel from the brain to the spinal cord, researchers are examining nerves and pathways to better understand the biology of the orgasm. What is probably most critical to all of these functions are the ways we interpret sexual cues.

Though scientific research has contributed much to our understanding of sexual arousal and response, there is still much to be learned. One way in which researchers investigate and describe phenomena is through the creation of

think
about it

Sexual Fluidity: Women's Variable Sexual Attractions

When the media report stories about same-sex lovers, such as actress Anne Heche leaving Ellen DeGeneres for a man, Cynthia Nixon (from *Sex and the City*) leaving her male partner of 15 years for a woman, and Julie Cypher leaving a heterosexual marriage for Melissa Etheridge then later leaving her for a man, what are your responses? Are these incidents simply flukes? Are the women confused? Bisexual? None of these, according to Lisa Diamond, professor of psychology and gender studies at the University of Utah. Rather, she has coined the term "sexual fluidity" to describe sexual desires and attractions as situation-dependent in sexual responsiveness (Diamond, 2008).

Based on her own research and analysis of animal mating and women's sexuality coupled with reviews of others', Diamond suggests that female desire may be dictated by both intimacy and emotional connection. She came to this conclusion after 10 years following the erotic attractions of nearly 100 young women who, at the start of her work, identified themselves as lesbian or bisexual or refused a label. From her analysis of their shifts between sexual identities and descriptions of their erotic lives, Diamond suggests that for her participants and possibly for women on the whole, desire is malleable, embedded in the nature of female desire, and cannot be captured by asking women to categorize their attractions. Among the women in her study who called themselves lesbian, one third reported attraction solely to women, while the other two thirds revealed periodic and genuine desire and attraction to men. When discussing sexual orientation, Diamond sees significance in the fact that many of her subjects agreed with the statement "I am the kind of person who becomes physically attracted to the person rather than their gender."

Thus it is, in the cases of Diamond's subjects, that emotional closeness overrode predominant orientation, resulting in attraction and desire. This concept seems to violate the core underlying assumption of our model of sexuality: that sexual orientation is defined by sexual behavior. Not long ago, the sexualities—heterosexuality, homosexuality, and even bisexuality—were categorical. Sexual attraction and desire, sexual behavior, and sexual identity were assumed to be congruent; same-gender sexual attraction/behavior assumed a gay, lesbian, or bisexual identity; and other sexual attraction/behavior assumed a heterosexual identity (Schecter, 2009). Now, Diamond's work, along with others', reveals this may be true for some women but not true for all. In fact, desire/behavior and orientation/identity do not always match up.

The more scholars learn about sexual desire, the more it becomes apparent that it involves a complex interplay among biological, environmental, psychological, cultural, and interpersonal factors. Evidence points to three characteristics about desire: (1) It is both hormonally and situationally driven, (2) individuals are often unaware of the full range of their desires, and (3) women's sexual desires show more variability than do men's. Probably the largest review of all the published data on the subject around the variability of women's sexual desires was published by Roy Baumeister (2000), professor of psychology at Florida State University. The study found that women show greater variability than men in a wide range of sexual behaviors, including desired frequency of sex, preferred contexts for sexual behavior, types and frequency of fantasy, and desirable partner characteristics. Baumeister cited this phenomenon as "erotic plasticity." Newer research concerning the connection between sexual orientation and fluidity has shown that though heterosexuality was the most stable identity for men and women, among women, sexual fluidity was a pattern that applied more to bisexual and homosexual women than those who identified as heterosexual. Among men, those who identified as bisexual were more sexually fluid (Mock & Eiback, 2012). Nevertheless, sex researchers still do not understand the mechanisms that underlie sexual fluidity (Diamond, 2013).

While tremendous strides have been made to foster greater acceptance of a diversity of sexual expression, sexual minorities as a whole still remain isolated and unsupported. Textbooks, media, and culture continue to assume that there is a fixed model of same-sex sexuality, in spite of the fact that many individuals know differently. Although the notion of sexual fluidity may be confusing, frightening, or threatening to some, it does offer one more variable to the broad spectrum of sexual expression of which humans are capable and can celebrate.

Think Critically

1. Is sexual orientation innate and/or fixed? As a result of the research described, is your understanding of sexual orientation changing?

2. Have you experienced sexual fluidity? If so, what were your reactions?

3. What would you do if your same-sex or other-sex best friend told you that he or she was romantically interested in you?

models, hypothetical descriptions used to study or explain something. Although models are useful for promoting general understanding or for assisting in the treatment of specific clinical problems, we should remember that they are only models. It may be helpful to think of sexual functioning as interconnected, linking desire, arousal, orgasm, and satisfaction. Turbulence or distraction at any one point affects the functioning of the others.

Sexual Response Models

A number of sexologists have attempted to outline the various physiological changes that both men and women undergo when they are sexually stimulated and aroused. Three important models are described here. The sequence of changes and patterns that take place in the body during sexual arousal is referred to as the **sexual response cycle. Masters and Johnson's four-phase model of sexual response** identifies the significant stages of response as excitement, plateau, orgasm, and resolution (see Figure 10). Helen Singer Kaplan (1979) collapses the excitement and plateau phases into one, eliminates the resolution phase, and adds a phase to the beginning of the process. **Kaplan's tri-phasic model of sexual response** consists of desire, excitement, and orgasm phases. Though Masters and Johnson's and Kaplan's are the most widely cited models used to describe the phases of the sexual response cycle, they do little to acknowledge the affective parts of human response. A third but much less known pattern is **Loulan's sexual response model,** which incorporates both the biological and affective components into a six-stage cycle. Beyond any questions of similarities and differences in the female and male sexual response cycle is the more significant issue of variation in how individuals experience each phase. The diversity of experiences can be described only by the individual. (These models are described and compared in Table 3.)

To help organize our thinking about the complexities of human behavior, the **dual control model** provides a theoretical perspective of sexual response that is based on brain function and the interaction between sexual excitation (responding with arousal to sexual stimuli) and sexual inhibition (inhibiting sexual arousal) (Bancroft, Graham, Janssen, & Sanders, 2009). The authors of this model argue that though much research has been dedicated to understanding sexual excitation, little research has been conducted on the inhibitory brain mechanisms that provide an equally significant role in sexual arousal and response. They purport that the adaptive role the inhibitory mechanism produces is relevant to our understanding of "normal" sexuality, individual variability, and problematic sexuality. The functions of the inhibitory response can be found in the following circumstances: (1) When sexual activity in a specific situation is potentially risky (as when you or your partner suspects an unintended pregnancy could result); (2) when a nonsexual challenge occurs and sex needs to be suppressed (as when a child calls out for help); (3) when excessive involvement in the pursuit of sexual pleasure distracts from other important functions (as when someone is late for work because he or she is distracted by viewing sexually explicit materials); (4) when social or environmental pressure results in suppression of reproductive behavior (as when someone is so stressed during finals week he or she doesn't feel like having sex); and (5) when the consequences of continued excessive sexual behavior potentially reduces possible conception (as when repeated ejaculations can result in lower sperm count).

Passion, though a bad regulator, is a powerful spring.

—Ralph Waldo Emerson
(1803–1882)

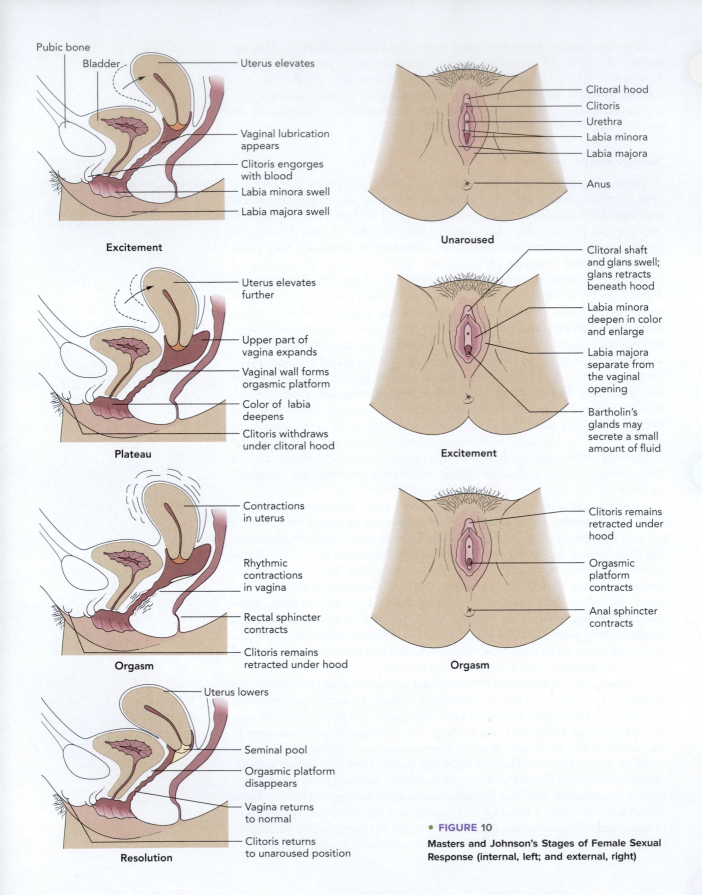

Pubic bone

Bladder

Uterus elevates

Vaginal lubrication appears

Clitoris engorges with blood

Labia minora swell

Labia majora swell

Excitement

Uterus elevates further

Upper part of vagina expands

Vaginal wall forms orgasmic platform

Color of labia deepens

Clitoris withdraws under clitoral hood

Plateau

Contractions in uterus

Rhythmic contractions in vagina

Rectal sphincter contracts

Clitoris remains retracted under hood

Orgasm

Uterus lowers

Seminal pool

Orgasmic platform disappears

Vagina returns to normal

Clitoris returns to unaroused position

Resolution

Clitoral hood

Clitoris

Urethra

Labia minora

Labia majora

Anus

Unaroused

Clitoral shaft and glans swell; glans retracts beneath hood

Labia minora deepen in color and enlarge

Labia majora separate from the vaginal opening

Bartholin's glands may secrete a small amount of fluid

Excitement

Clitoris remains retracted under hood

Orgasmic platform contracts

Anal sphincter contracts

Orgasm

● **FIGURE** 10

Masters and Johnson's Stages of Female Sexual Response (internal, left; and external, right)

TABLE 3 • Models of the Sexual Response Cycle

Psychological/Physiological Process	Name of Phase		
People make a conscious decision to have sex even if there might not be emotional or physical desire.	Willingness (Loulan)		
Some form of thought, fantasy, or erotic feeling causes individuals to seek sexual gratification. (An inability to become sexually aroused may be due to a lack of desire, although some people have reported that they acquire sexual desire after being sexually aroused.)	Desire (Kaplan, Loulan)		
Physical and/or psychological stimulation produces characteristic physical changes. In men, increased amounts of blood flow to the genitals produce erection of the penis; the scrotal skin begins to smooth out, and the testicles draw up toward the body. Later in this phase, the testes increase slightly in size. In women, vaginal lubrication begins, the upper vagina expands, the uterus is pulled upward, and the clitoris becomes engorged. In both women and men, the breasts enlarge slightly, and the nipples may become erect. Both men and women experience increasing muscular contractions.	Excitement (Masters/Johnson, Loulan)	Excitement (Kaplan)	Engorgement (Loulan)
Sexual tension levels off. In men, the testes swell and continue to elevate. The head of the penis swells slightly and may deepen in color. In women, the outer third of the vagina swells, lubrication may slow down, and the clitoris pulls back. Coloring and swelling of the labia increase. In both men and women, muscular tension, breathing, and heart rate increase.	Plateau (Masters/Johnson)		
Increased tension peaks and discharges, affecting the whole body. Rhythmic muscular contractions affect the uterus and outer vagina in women. In men, there are contractions of the glands and tubes that produce and carry semen, the prostate gland, and the urethral bulb, resulting in the expulsion of semen (ejaculation).	Orgasm (Masters/Johnson, Kaplan, Loulan)		
The body returns to its unaroused state. In some women, this does not occur until after repeated orgasms.	Resolution (Masters/Johnson)		Pleasure (Loulan)
Pleasure is one purpose of sexuality and can be defined only by the individual. One can experience pleasure during all or only some of the above stages, or one can leave out any of the stages and still have pleasure.			

A major finding of the dual control model is that it views excitation and sexual inhibition as separate systems, as opposed to other models that view these as two ends of a single dimension. Additional findings from this model include the following:

- Though most people fall in the moderate range on propensities toward sexual excitation and sexual inhibition, there is great variability from one person to the next.

- Men, on average, score higher on excitation and lower on inhibition than women.

- Gay men, on average, score higher on excitation and lower on inhibition than straight men.

- Bisexual women, on average, score higher on excitation than lesbian and straight women.

- Excitation lessens with age for men and women; however, inhibition is not age-related in women but is somewhat age-related in men.
- The relation between negative mood and sexuality is best predicted by inhibition scores in men, but by excitation scores in women.

The dual control model suggests that individuals who have a low propensity for sexual excitation or a high propensity for sexual inhibition are more likely to experience difficulties related to sexual response or sexual interest. Furthermore, those who have a high propensity for sexual excitation or low propensity for sexual inhibition are more likely to engage in problematic sexuality such as high-risk sexual behaviors, for example, not using a condom. Because the focus is on sexual arousal, there remain questions about if and how this model might apply to orgasm.

Desire and Arousal: Mind or Matter?

Desire is the psychological component of sexual arousal. Although we can experience desire without becoming aroused, and in some cases become aroused without feeling desire, some form of erotic thought or feeling is usually involved in our sexual behavior.

The physical manifestations of sexual arousal involve a complex interaction of thoughts and feelings, sensory organs, neural responses, and hormonal reactions. These involve various parts of the body, including the nucleus accumbens, cerebellum, and hypothalamus of the brain, the nervous system, the circulatory system, and the endocrine glands—as well as the genitals.

In a comprehensive review of women's sexual desire, it was clear how little is understood about what women desire (Meana, 2010). The author pointed to the distinction between "desire to be desired," which does not necessarily lead to sexual interaction (as being desired may be rewarding in itself) and "desire to have sex." Qualitative data indicated that many women report that feeling desired enhances their arousal. It's these kinds of issues that contribute to our still limited understanding of the fundamental aspects of women's sexuality (Bancroft & Graham, 2011).

A meta-study, which combined the results of several studies, of men's and women's sexual arousal patterns found that in women, lubrication was only one of the physiological changes that occurred when they were sexually aroused, and not a necessary condition for women to report that they were sexually aroused (Chivers, Seto, Lalumière, & Grimbos, 2010). Much of the science behind sexuality was designed around a very linear model: First, there's desire; then there's arousal, followed by orgasms, then snuggling. For most women, this process is more circular, whereby sexuality is about intimacy, relationships, and wanting to cuddle first and feel close to someone. It's also about how women feel about themselves. If they do not feel desirable or comfortable with their bodies, it's likely that they will not be able to relax and enjoy the sexual interchange (Wortman & van den Brink, 2012).

Among men who have trouble getting erect, genital engorgement is aided by drugs such as Viagra because the pills target genital capillaries. Thus, the medications may enhance male desire by granting men a feeling of power and control, but not medically increasing desire or want. For some men, desire is not an issue. However, for women, there still are uncertainties about what is common female sexuality in its various forms (Bancroft & Graham, 2011). The roles of androgens and estrogens are unclear, though we know that there is a testosterone-dependent component of women's sexuality that is more important for some than

Some desire is necessary to keep life in motion.

—Samuel Johnson
(1709–1784)

others. Until we learn more about women's sexuality, our ability to effectively treat women's sexual difficulties remains somewhat elusive.

The Neural System and Sexual Stimuli

The brain is crucial to sexual response and is currently a focus of research to understanding how we respond to sexual stimulation. Through the neural system, the brain receives stimuli from the five senses plus one: sight, smell, touch, hearing, taste, *and* the imagination.

The Brain   The brain, of course, plays a major role in all of our body's functions. Nowhere is its role more apparent than in our sexual functioning. The relationship between our thoughts and feelings and our actual behavior is not well understood (and what is known would require a course in neurophysiology to satisfactorily explain it). Relational factors and cultural influences, as well as expectations, fantasies, hopes, and fears, combine with sensory inputs and neurotransmitters (chemicals that transmit messages in the nervous system) to bring us to where we are ready, willing, and able to be sexual. Even then, potentially erotic messages may be short-circuited by the brain itself, which can inhibit as well as incite sexual responses. It is not known how the inhibitory mechanism works, but negative conditioning and emotions will prevent the brain from sending messages to the genitals. In fact, the reason moderate amounts of alcohol and marijuana appear to enhance sexuality is that they reduce the control mechanisms of the brain that act as inhibitors. Conversely, women who feel persistent sexual arousal and no relief from orgasm reveal unusually high activation in regions of the brain that respond to genital stimulation (Komisaruk et al., 2010).

Anatomically speaking, the part of the body that appears to be involved most in sexual behaviors of both men and women is the vast highway of nerves called the vagus nerve network, which stretches to all the major organs, including the brain. Using MRI scans to map the brain, researchers have found increases in brain activity during sexual arousal (Holstege et al., 2003; Komisaruk et al., 2010). Since specific parts of the brain send their sensory signals via specific nerves, the different quality of orgasms that result from clitoral or anal stimulation, for example, is divided among the different genital sensory nerves.

As many of us know, the early stages of a new romantic relationship are characterized by intense feelings of euphoria, well-being, and preoccupation with the romantic partner. This was observed in one study in which college students were shown photos of their beloved intermixed with photos of an equally attractive acquaintance (Younger, Aron, Parke, Chatterjee, & Mackey, 2010). Induced with pain during the experiment, students reported their pain was less severe when they were looking at photos of their new love. The test results suggest the chemicals the body releases in the early stages of love—otherwise referred to as endogenous opioids—work on the spinal cord to block the pain message from getting to the brain. MRI scans showed that, indeed, the areas of the brain activated by intense love are the same areas targeted by pain-relieving drugs.

The Senses   An attractive person (sight), a body fragrance or odor (smell), a lick or kiss (taste), a loving caress (touch), and erotic whispers (hearing) are all capable of sending sexual signals to the brain. Preferences for each of these sensory inputs are both biological and learned and are very individualized. Many of the connections we experience between sensory data and emotional responses are probably products of the **limbic system,** or those structures of the brain that are associated with emotions and feelings and involved in sexual arousal. Some sensory inputs may evoke sexual arousal without a lot of conscious thought or

Women might be able to fake orgasms. But men can fake whole relationships.

—Sharon Stone
(1958–)

emotion. Certain areas of the skin, called **erogenous zones,** are highly sensitive to touch. These areas may include the genitals, breasts, mouth, ears, neck, inner thighs, and buttocks; erotic associations with these areas vary from culture to culture and from individual to individual. Our olfactory sense (smell) may bring us sexual messages below the level of our conscious awareness. Scientists have isolated chemical substances, called pheromones, that are secreted into the air by many kinds of animals, including humans, ants, moths, pigs, deer, dogs, and monkeys. One function of pheromones, in animals at least, appears to be to arouse the libido.

Hormones   The libido in both men and women is biologically influenced by the hormone **testosterone.** In men, testosterone is produced mainly in the testes; in women, it is produced in the adrenal glands and the ovaries. Growing evidence suggests that testosterone may play an important role in the maintenance of women's bodies (Davis, Davison, Donath, & Bell, 2005). Although it does not play a large part in a woman's hormonal makeup, it is present in the blood vessels, brain, skin, bone, and vagina. Testosterone is believed to contribute to bone density, blood flow, hair growth, energy and strength, and libido.

Although women produce much less testosterone than men, this does not mean that they have less sexual interest; apparently, women are much more sensitive than men to testosterone's effects. Though testosterone decreases in women as they age, the ovaries manufacture it throughout life. Symptoms produced by the decrease of testosterone can be similar to those related to estrogen loss, including fatigue, vaginal dryness, and bone loss. Signs specific to testosterone deficiency are associated with reduced sexual interest and responsiveness in men. It is believed that for some women, very low levels may contribute to reduced libido and weaker orgasmic responses (North American Menopause Society, 2014). In spite of widespread claims of testosterone's effect in treating low sex desire in women, in December 2004, the Food and Drug Administration voted against approval of a testosterone patch, citing concerns about the safety of long-term use of the patch and use by groups that have not been adequately studied. Though research has shown that testosterone delivered via a skin patch increases sexual desire and frequency of satisfying sex among some menopausal women with low desire, common side effects of supplemental testosterone range from acne and increased facial and body hair to rare but sometimes seen liver problems and declines in good cholesterol (North American Menopause Society, 2014). Until long-term safety data are submitted, prescribed use of testosterone to treat difficulties in sexual functioning among women remains illegal in the United States and Canada.

It's important to remember that although sexual problems, including low libido and/or sexual dissatisfaction, may have a physiological link, they can also be caused, for example, by relationship issues, work fatigue, past experiences, or financial problems. Thus, it is necessary to look beyond medical solutions when assisting women who have the desire to confront their sexual dissatisfaction.

Estrogen also plays a role in sexual functioning, though its effects on sexual desire are not completely understood. In addition to protecting the bones and heart, in women estrogen helps maintain the vaginal lining and lubrication, which can make sex more pleasurable. Men also produce small amounts of estrogen, which facilitates the maturation of sperm and maintains bone density. Too much estrogen, however, can cause erection difficulties. Like testosterone replacement, some doctors are also promoting estrogens and bioidentical, or natural, estrogen supplements to treat conditions caused by estrogen deficiency. The most significant push is aimed at menopausal women. Because no risk-free hormone has ever been identified,

Sensory inputs, such as the sight, touch, or smell of someone we love or the sound of his or her voice, may evoke desire and sexual arousal.

© Design Pics/Darren Greenwood

The age of a woman doesn't mean a thing. The best tunes are played on the oldest fiddles.

—Ralph Waldo Emerson
(1803–1882)

claims that human estrogens will protect against cardiovascular effects and other maladies are misleading. While a number of estrogens are effective treatments for hot flashes and vaginal dryness, any health-promotion claims for these drugs are clearly misguided. Nevertheless, over-the-counter lubricants and/or long-acting vaginal moisturizers may be helpful for women who have insufficient lubrication.

Oxytocin is a hormone more commonly associated with contractions during labor and with breastfeeding. It is also increased by nipple stimulation in men and women. This neurotransmitter, which has also been linked to bonding, is released in variable amounts in men and women during orgasm and remains raised for at least 5 minutes after orgasm. This is why oxytocin is sometimes referred to as the "cuddle hormone" (Gray & Garcia, 2013). It helps us feel connected and promotes touch, affection, and relaxation. Interestingly, oxytocin is important in stimulating the release of all the other sex hormones and, since it peaks during orgasm, it may be responsible for the desire to touch or cuddle after orgasm occurs (Chia & Abrams, 2005).

In spite of what we do know about the importance of biological influences on sexual desire and performance, when biological determinants or evolutionary accounts are given undue weight and psychosocial forces are ignored or minimized, a medical model that negates the significance of culture, relationships, and equality can emerge.

Experiencing Sexual Arousal

For both males and females, physiological changes during sexual excitement depend on two processes: vasocongestion and myotonia. **Vasocongestion** is the concentration of blood in body tissues. For example, blood fills the genital regions of both males and females, causing the penis to become erect and the clitoris to swell. **Myotonia** is increased muscle tension accompanying the approach of orgasm; upon orgasm, the body undergoes involuntary muscle contractions and then relaxes. The sexual response pattern remains the same for all forms of sexual behavior, whether autoerotic or sex with a partner, heterosexual or homosexual. Nevertheless, approximately 30% of women report problems related to arousal (Chivers et al., 2010).

Those who restrain desire do so because theirs is weak enough to be restrained.

—William Blake
(1757–1827)

● Female Sexual Response

Sexual Excitement

Many women do not separate sexual desire from arousal (Tiefer, 2004). Additionally, many seem to care less about physical arousal but rather place more emphasis on the relational and emotional aspects of intimacy. In any case, for women, one of the first signs of sexual excitement is the seeping of moisture through the vaginal walls through a process called vaginal transudation or **sweating.** Some women also report "tingling" in the genital area. Blood causes lymphatic fluids to push by the vaginal walls, engorging them, lubricating the vagina, and enabling it to encompass the penis or other object. The upper two thirds of the vagina expands in a process called **tenting;** the vagina expands about an inch in length and doubles its width. The labia minora begin to protrude outside the labia majora during sexual excitement, and breathing and heart rate increase. These signs do not occur on a specific timetable; each woman has her own pattern of arousal, which may vary under different conditions, with different partners, and so on.

Contractions raise the uterus, but the clitoris remains virtually unchanged during this early phase. Although the clitoris responds more slowly than the penis to

The reason so many women fake orgasms is that so many men fake foreplay.

—Graffito

think
about it

"Did You Come?" What College Students Think About Women's Orgasms During Heterosexual Sex

la petite mort (French) *"The little death"*

—the human orgasm

While nearly all men report that they usually or always experience orgasm during heterosexual intercourse, the majority of women report that they do not always orgasm (Dawood et al., 2005; Lloyd, 2005; Wade, Kremer, & Brown, 2005). Given this major gap, psychologists Claire Salisbury and William Fisher (2014) at Western University in Ontario, Canada, conducted a study focusing on gender differences in the experiences, beliefs, and concerns surrounding the lack of female orgasm during penile-vaginal intercourse.

A total of 24 female and 21 male undergraduates (mean age = 19) from an Ontario university participated in focus group discussions. One female reported never having had sexual intercourse, and one female reported never having had an orgasm. All of the men had experienced both sexual intercourse and orgasm. From the analysis of the focus group discussions, six themes emerged from the females, and seven themes emerged from the males. Following are the themes and a summary the major concerns.

Female Discussion Group Themes

Males are responsible for the physical stimulation of females to orgasm.
The women viewed men as responsible for giving them orgasms and themselves as responsible for being psychologically ready to receive the orgasm.

Female orgasm is not necessary for women's sexual satisfaction during partnered interactions.
Female sexual satisfaction was viewed as not being dependent on having an orgasm. Instead, the women viewed female orgasm as a "bonus" and not the goal of sexual interaction.

Female orgasm is more important for the male partner than the female partner.
The importance of female orgasm rested not with increasing the female's sexual satisfaction and pleasure but centered around the male partner's ego and sense of himself as a competent lover capable of "giving" her an orgasm. Some women faked orgasms to avoid negative partner reaction.

Reliance on working assumptions and lack of communication.
The women assumed that men highly valued them having an orgasm and judged themselves harshly if she did not experience one. However, there was little direct communication between partners about the absence of female orgasm or the woman's assumption about its importance.

Superiority of male concerns over female physical pleasure.
Concern for the male partner's feelings, ego, and judgments inhibited the women from acting on their own desires. Even if desired, women tended to avoid requesting for clitoral stimulation or engaging in clitoral stimulation during intercourse or other sexual activity, fearing the male partner would feel incompetent or would judge them.

Orgasm beliefs and concerns differ by relationship status.
In a casual sexual encounter, the women thought that female orgasm was not very important to men and that faking orgasm was more acceptable. However, for committed romantic relationships, the women thought that female orgasm was very important to the male partner and that faking was not acceptable. Communication was considered easier but still difficult in the committed relationship.

Male Discussion Group Themes

Male coital orgasm is very important for men.
For men, the occurrence of their own orgasm during sexual intercourse is very important and expected to be a common occurrence.

Females are perceived to have a strong desire for orgasm during intercourse.

Given the sexual pleasure from experiencing orgasm, the men assumed that orgasm during intercourse was also very important to women, particularly when they were in casual encounters.

Female orgasm is extremely satisfying and important to men.

The occurrence of female orgasm was viewed by men as extremely satisfying and extremely important. Most men listed the occurrence of female orgasm as one of the most satisfying sexual experiences a man could have. The men concurred with the women, believing that it was their physical responsibility to "give" their female partner orgasms and that is was the psychological responsibility of the women to be prepared to receive the orgasm.

Lack of female orgasm is very distressing for men.

The female partner not experiencing an orgasm during sexual interactions brought negative reactions to the men, especially within a relationship context. The most common concern was self-focused in worrying about his skills as a sexual partner. Secondly, they worried that the female partner would not experience the pleasure she could have had if she had an orgasm. Men indicated that they were highly motivated to make their partner orgasm in the future and that a repeated lack of female orgasm has a negative impact on the relationship.

Positive and encouraging view of (manual) clitoral stimulation:

The men were highly motivated to increase the female partner's sexual pleasure, expressing positive reactions to: (1) stimulating their female partner's clitoris during intercourse, (2) the female stimulating her clitoris during intercourse, and (3) the female partner asking for additional clitoral stimulation. These views were most positive from manual clitoral stimulation, however these extremely positive reactions disappeared when a vibrator was used as the source of stimulation.

Importance of female communication on lack of orgasm occurrence:

Men reported the need for communication about female orgasm so they could employ different techniques to give their partners orgasm. However, they generally preferred their partner to directly bring up this topic herself. Men in relationships preferred that the woman not fake an orgasm but directly communicate the truth about the lack of an orgasm.

Orgasm beliefs and concerns differ between casual versus relationship sexual interactions.

The men reported that in casual relationships their focus was on themselves; however of great importance was the attainment of orgasm by both partners. In committed relationships, the men's goals of both his and his female partner's experiencing orgasm were very important.

As you see, the men and women in the focus groups agreed on two main things: the man's responsibility to physically produce female orgasm and the importance of the male ego relative to female orgasm. The most frequent concern of both sexes was on the male partner's judgment of himself as a lover and the impact on his self-esteem if the female did or did not attain orgasm. Salisbury and Fisher concluded by stating that:

> By not actively engaging in clitoral self-stimulation during sexual interactions (particularly intercourse), those women who desire more frequent orgasms during partnered sex are limiting the extent of sexual pleasure they can obtain. Perceived male responsibility for producing female orgasms may therefore be an obstacle to sexual gratification for both partners, and perceived female responsibility for protecting the male ego may be a burden for women (pp. 12–13).

While these results cannot be extended to all college students, they can provide a barometer and (hopefully) an impetus for increased communication about sexual behaviors between college students of both sexes.

Think Critically

1. Which of the findings of this study surprise you and/or confirm the norms at your college or university? Explain.
2. What does the study imply about female orgasms during sexual intercourse? In your opinion, are intercourse orgasms inherently more important than orgasms from other sexual behaviors such as oral sex or masturbation?
3. What do the findings suggest about gender roles of men and women related to female orgasm during heterosexual sexual activities? What, if anything, should change?

SOURCES: Dawood, K., Kirk, K. M., Bailey, J. M., Andrews, P. W., & Martin, N. G. (2005). Genetic and environmental influences on the frequency of female orgasm. *Twin Research and Human Genetics, 8*, 27–33; Lloyd, E. A. (2005). *The case of female orgasm: The bias in the science of evolution.* Cambridge, MA: Harvard University Press; Salisbury, C.M.A., & Fisher, W. A. (2014). "Did you come?" A qualitative exploration of gender differences in beliefs, experiences, and concerns regarding female orgasm occurrence during heterosexual sexual interactions. *Journal of Sex Research, 51*(6), 616–631.

Most women experience orgasm through clitoral stimulation rather than through vaginal penetration. Masturbation can be an important step in learning how to be orgasmic.
© Chris Rout/Alamy

❝ *What is the earth? What are the body and soul without satisfaction?*

—Walt Whitman
(1819–1892)

vasocongestion, it is still affected. The initial changes, however, are minor. Clitoral tumescence (swelling) occurs simultaneously with engorgement of the labia minora. During masturbation and oral sex, the clitoris is generally stimulated directly. During intercourse, clitoral stimulation is mostly indirect, caused by the clitoral hood being pulled over the clitoris or by pressure in the general clitoral area. At the same time that these changes are occurring in the genitals, the breasts are also responding. The nipples become erect, and the breasts may enlarge somewhat because of the engorgement of blood vessels; the areolae may also enlarge. Many women (and men) experience a **sex flush,** a darkening of the skin or rash that temporarily appears as a result of blood rushing to the skin's surface during sexual excitement.

As excitement increases, the clitoris retracts beneath the clitoral hood and virtually disappears. The labia minora become progressively larger until they double or triple in size. They deepen in color, becoming pink, bright red, or a deep wine-red color, depending on the woman's skin color. This intense coloring is sometimes referred to as the "sex skin." When it appears, orgasm is imminent. Meanwhile, the vaginal opening and lower third of the vagina decrease in size as they become more congested with blood. This thickening of the walls, which occurs in the plateau stage of the sexual response cycle, is known as the **orgasmic platform.** The upper two thirds of the vagina continues to expand, but lubrication decreases or may even stop. The uterus becomes fully elevated through muscular contractions.

Changes in the breasts continue. The areolae become larger even as the nipples decrease in relative size. If the woman has not breastfed, her breasts may increase by up to 25% of their unaroused size; women who have breastfed may have little change in size.

Orgasm

Continued stimulation brings orgasm, a peak sensation of intense pleasure that creates an altered state of consciousness and is accompanied by involuntary, rhythmic uterine and anal contractions, myotonia, and a state of well-being and contentment. The upper two thirds of the vagina does not contract; instead, it continues its tenting effect. The labia do not change during orgasm, nor do the breasts. Heart and respiratory rates and blood pressure reach their peak during orgasm.

After orgasm, the orgasmic platform rapidly subsides. The clitoris reemerges from beneath the clitoral hood. Orgasm helps the blood flow out of the genital tissue quickly. If a woman does not have an orgasm once she is sexually aroused, the clitoris may remain engorged for up to an hour. This unresolved vasocongestion sometimes leads to a feeling of frustration, analogous to what men call "blue balls." The labia slowly return to their unaroused state, and the sex flush gradually disappears. About 30–40% of women perspire as the body begins to cool.

Interestingly, when women and men are asked to use adjectives to describe their experience of orgasm, data suggest that beyond the awareness of ejaculation that men report, their sensations bear more similarities than differences (Mah & Binik, 2002).

Prolactin levels double immediately following orgasm and remain elevated for about 1 hour (Meston & Buss, 2009). This prolactin is thought to be responsible for the refractory period, in which men are unable to ejaculate again. In contrast, women are often physiologically able to be orgasmic immediately following the previous orgasm. As a result, women can have repeated orgasms, also called multiple orgasms, if they continue to be stimulated. Though findings vary on the percentage of women who experience multiple orgasms (estimates range from 14% to 40%), what is clear is that wide variability exists among women and within any one woman from one time to another.

Another chapter will discuss the anatomical features and physiological functions that characterize men's sexuality and sexual response. The information in these two chapters should serve as a comprehensive basis for understanding the material that follows.

Summary

Female Sex Organs: What Are They For?

- All embryos appear as female at first. Genetic and hormonal signals trigger the development of male organs in those embryos destined to be male.

- Sex organs serve a reproductive purpose, but they perform other functions also: giving pleasure, attracting sex partners, and bonding in relationships.

- The external female *genitals* are known collectively as the *vulva.* The *mons pubis* is a pad of fatty tissue that covers the area of the pubic bone. The *clitoris* is the center of sexual arousal. The *labia majora* are two folds of spongy flesh extending from the mons pubis and enclosing the other external genitals. The *labia minora* are smooth, hairless folds within the labia majora that meet above the clitoris.

- The internal female sexual structures and reproductive organs include the *vagina,* the *uterus,* the *cervix,* the *ovaries,* and the *fallopian tubes.* The vagina is a flexible, muscular organ that encompasses the penis or other object during sexual expression and is the *birth canal* through which an infant is born. The opening of the vagina, the *introitus,* is partially covered by a thin, perforated membrane, the *hymen,* prior to first intercourse or other intrusion.

- Many women report the existence of an erotically sensitive area, the *Grafenberg spot (G-spot),* on the upper front wall of the vagina midway between the introitus and the cervix.

- The *uterus,* or womb, is a hollow, thick-walled, muscular organ; the tapered end, the *cervix,* extends downward and opens into the vagina. The lining of the uterine walls, the *endometrium,* is built up and then shed and expelled through the cervical *os* (opening) during menstruation. In the event of pregnancy, the pre-embryo is embedded in the nourishing endometrium. On each side of the uterus is one of a pair of *ovaries,* the female *gonads* (organs that produce *gametes,* sex cells containing the genetic material necessary for reproduction). At the top of the uterus are the *fallopian tubes,* or uterine tubes. They extend toward the ovaries but are not attached to them. The funnel-shaped end of each tube (the *infundibulum*) fans out into fingerlike *fimbriae,* which drape over the ovary. Hairlike *cilia* on the fimbriae transport the ovulated *oocyte* (egg) into the fallopian tube. The *ampulla* is the widened part of the tube in which fertilization normally occurs. Other important structures in the area of the genitals include the *urethra, anus,* and *perineum.*

- The reproductive function of the female breasts, or *mammary glands,* is to nourish the offspring through *lactation,* or milk production. A breast is composed of fatty tissue and 15–25 lobes that radiate around a central protruding nipple. *Alveoli* within the lobes produce milk. Around the nipple is a ring of darkened skin called the *areola.*

Female Sexual Physiology

- *Hormones* are chemical substances that serve as messengers, traveling through the bloodstream. Important hormones that act directly on the gonads (*gonadotropins*) are *follicle-stimulating hormone (FSH)* and *luteinizing hormone (LH).* Hormones produced in the ovaries are *estrogen,* which helps regulate the menstrual cycle, and *progesterone,* which helps maintain the uterine lining, until menstruation occurs.

- At birth, the human female's ovaries contain approximately half a million *oocytes,* or female gametes. During childhood, many of these degenerate. In a woman's lifetime, about 400 oocytes will mature and be released, beginning in puberty when hormones trigger the completion of *oogenesis,* the production of oocytes, commonly called eggs or ova.

- The activities of the ovaries and the development of oocytes for ovulation, the expulsion of the oocyte, are described as the four-phase *ovarian cycle,* which is on average about 28 days long. The phases are *menstrual, follicular* (maturation of the oocyte), *ovulatory* (expulsion of the oocyte), and *luteal* (hormone production by the corpus luteum).

- The *menstrual cycle* (uterine cycle), like the ovarian cycle, is divided into four phases. The shedding of the endometrium marks the beginning of the *menstrual phase.* The menstrual flow, or *menses,* generally occurs over a period of 3–5 days. Endometrial tissue builds up during the *proliferative phase;* it produces nutrients to sustain an embryo in the *secretory phase.*

- Women who live or work together may develop similarly timed menstrual cycles, called *menstrual synchrony.*

- The most severe menstrual problems have been attributed to *premenstrual syndrome (PMS),* a cluster of physical, psychological, and emotional symptoms that may occur 7–14 days before the menstrual period. Some women experience very heavy bleeding (*menorrhagia*), while others have pelvic cramping and pain during the menstrual cycle (*dysmenorrhea*). When women do not menstruate for reasons other than aging, the condition is called *amenorrhea.* Principal causes of amenorrhea are pregnancy and nursing.

Human Sexual Response

- *Masters and Johnson's four-phase model of sexual response* identifies the significant stages of response as excitement, plateau, *orgasm*, and resolution. *Kaplan's tri-phasic model of sexual response* consists of three phases: desire, excitement, and orgasm. *Loulan's sexual response model* includes both biological and affective components in a six-stage cycle. The *dual control model* helps explain the interaction between sexual excitation and sexual inhibition.

- The physical manifestations of sexual arousal involve a complex interaction of thoughts and feelings, sensory perceptions, neural responses, and hormonal reactions occurring in many parts of the body. For both males and females, physiological changes during sexual excitement depend on two processes: *vasocongestion,* the concentration of blood in body tissues, and *myotonia,* increased muscle tension with approaching orgasm.

Female Sexual Response

- For women, an early sign of sexual excitement is the moistening, or vaginal transudation or *sweating,* of the vaginal walls. The upper two thirds of the vagina expands in a process called *tenting;* the labia may enlarge or flatten and separate; the clitoris swells. Breathing and heart rate increase. The nipples become erect, and the breasts may enlarge somewhat. The uterus elevates. As excitement increases, the clitoris retracts beneath the clitoral hood. The vaginal opening decreases by about one third, and its outer third becomes more congested, forming the *orgasmic platform.*

- Continued stimulation brings orgasm, a peak sensation of intense pleasure that creates an altered state of consciousness and is accompanied by contractions, myotonia, and a state of well-being and contentment. Women are often able to be orgasmic following a previous orgasm if they continue to enjoy giving and receiving sexual pleasure.

Questions for Discussion

- Are changes in mood that may occur during a woman's menstrual cycle caused by biological factors, or are they learned? What evidence supports your response?

- Given the choice between the environmentally friendly menstruation products and commercial products, which would you choose for yourself (or recommend to a woman), and why?

- If another adult were to ask you "What is an orgasm?" how would you reply? If the person were to proceed to ask you how to induce one in a woman, what would you say?

- What are your thoughts and reactions to learning about the Grafenberg spot? Do you believe it is an invented erotic spot for some women or a genuine gland or erogenous zone?

- How important is it to you that *both* you and your partner enjoy sexual pleasuring and pleasure?

- For women only: What is your response to looking at your genitals? For men only: What is your response to viewing photos of women's genitals? Why is it that women are discouraged from touching or looking at their genitals?

- How do you feel about the idea of having sex during a woman's menstrual period? Why do you feel this way?

Sex and the Internet

Sexuality and Ethnicity

Of the 317 million people living in the United States, over 161 million are women. Many of these women are in poor health, use fewer reproductive health services, and continue to suffer disproportionately from premature death, disease, and disabilities. In addition, there are tremendous economic, cultural, and social barriers to achieving optimal health. To find out more about the reproductive health risks of special concern to women of color, go to the National Women's Health Information Center website: womenshealth.gov/minority-health/index.html. From the menu, select one minority group of women and report on the following:

- One reproductive health concern

- Obstacles women may encounter that would prevent them from obtaining services

- Potential solutions to this problem

Suggested Websites

American College of Obstetricians and Gynecologists
http://www.acog.org
A professional association with information about women's reproductive health, including pregnancy and childbirth.

Centers for Disease Control and Prevention
http://www.cdc.gov/women/
Provides a wide variety of specific information and links related to all aspects of women's health and well-being.

Guttmacher Institute
http://www.guttmacher.org
A global research institute that explores aspects of sexuality and relationships.

National Organization for Women (NOW)
http://www.now.org
An organization of women and men who support full equality for women in truly equal partnerships.

National Women's Health Information Center (NWHIC)
http://www.4woman.org/
Information, health, and topics for the woman of today.

National Women's Health Network
http://www.nwhn.org
Provides clear and well-researched information about a variety of women's health- and sexuality-related issues.

North American Menopause Society
http://www.menopause.org
Promotes women's health during midlife and beyond through an understanding of menopause.

Our Bodies, Ourselves
http://www.ourbodiesourselves.org
Provides a multicultural and up-to-date perspective on women's physical and sexual health.

The Women's Sexual Health Foundation
http://www.twshf.org
Focuses on medical treatment and provides a multidisciplinary approach to sexual problems and health.

Suggested Reading

Bergner, D. (2013). *What do women want? Adventures in the science of female desire.* New York: HarperCollins. Recaps studies and gives a fresh perspective to this lifelong question.

Boston Women's Health Book Collective and Norsigian, J. (2011). *Our bodies, ourselves.* New York: Touchstone. A thorough, accurate, and proactive women's text covering a broad range of health- and sexuality-related issues.

Brizendine, L. (2006). *The female brain.* New York: Broadway Books. An enlightening guide to the biological foundations of human behavior.

Diamond, L. M. (2008). *Sexual fluidity: Understanding women's love and desire.* Cambridge, MA: Harvard University Press. Offers insight into the context-dependent nature of female sexuality.

Komisaruk, B. R., Whipple, B., Nasserzadeh, S., & Beyer-Flores, C. (2010). *The orgasm answer guide.* Baltimore: Johns Hopkins University Press. Provides a broad overview of women's orgasm and men's orgasm, their anatomy and physiology, and their connection to relationships and health.

Meston, C. M., & Buss, D. M. (2009). *Why women have sex.* New York: Henry Holt. Combines psychology and biology to help uncover women's sexual motivations.

chapter

4

Male Sexual Anatomy, Physiology, and Response

© Cultura RM/Moof/Getty Images

CHAPTER OUTLINE

Male Sex Organs: What Are They For?

Male Sexual Physiology

Male Sexual Response

CLEARLY, MALE SEXUAL STRUCTURES and functions differ in many ways from those of females. What may not be as apparent, however, is that there are also a number of similarities in the functions of the sex organs and the sexual response patterns of men and women. In the previous chapter, we learned that the sexual structures of both females and males derive from the same embryonic tissue (see Figure 1 in the chapter titled Female Sexual Anatomy, Physiology, and Response). But when this tissue receives the signals to begin differentiation into a male, the embryonic reproductive organs begin to change their appearance dramatically.

> Behold—the penis mightier than the sword.
>
> —Mark Twain
> (1835–1910)

Male Sex Organs: What Are They For?

Like female sex organs, male sex organs serve several functions. In their reproductive role, a man's sex organs manufacture and store gametes and can deliver them to a woman's reproductive tract. Some of the organs, especially the penis, provide a source of physical pleasure for both the man and his partner.

External Structures

The external male sexual structures are the penis and the scrotum.

The Penis The **penis** (from the Latin word for "tail") is the organ through which both semen and urine pass. It is attached to the male perineum, the diamond-shaped region extending from the base of the scrotum to the anus.

The penis consists of three main sections: the root, the shaft, and the head (see Figure 1). The **root** attaches the penis within the pelvic cavity; the body of the penis, the **shaft,** hangs free. At the end of the shaft is the head of the penis, the **glans penis,** and at its tip is the **urethral opening,** for semen ejaculation or urine excretion. The rim at the base of the glans is known as the **corona** (Spanish for crown). On the underside of the penis is a triangular area of sensitive skin called the **frenulum** (FREN-you-lem), which attaches the glans

• FIGURE 1

External Male Sexual Structures

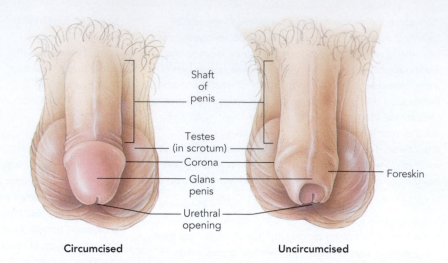

Circumcised   Uncircumcised

to the foreskin (see Figure 2). The glans penis is particularly important in sexual arousal because it contains a relatively high concentration of nerve endings, making it especially responsive to stimulation.

A loose skin covers the shaft of the penis and extends to cover the glans penis; this sleevelike covering is known as the **foreskin** or *prepuce* (PREE-pews). It can be pulled back easily to expose the glans. The foreskin of a male infant can sometimes be surgically removed by a procedure called **circumcision.** As a result of this procedure, the glans penis is left exposed. The reasons for circumcision seem to be rooted more in tradition and religious beliefs (it is an important ritual in Judaism and Islam) than in any firmly established health principles, although some recent scientific evidence has shown that circumcision can help prevent HIV and other sexually transmitted infections. Beneath the foreskin are several small glands that produce a cheesy substance called **smegma.** If smegma accumulates, it thickens, produces a foul odor, and can become granular and irritate the penis, causing discomfort and infection. It is important for uncircumcised adult males to observe good hygiene by periodically retracting the skin and washing the glans and penile shaft to remove the smegma.

The shaft of the penis contains three parallel columns of erectile tissue (see Figure 3). The two that extend along the front surface are known as the **corpora cavernosa** (KOR-por-a kav-er-NO-sa; cavernous bodies), and the third, which runs beneath them, is called the **corpus spongiosum** (KOR-pus spun-gee-OH-sum; spongy body), which also forms the glans. At the root of the penis, the tips of the corpora cavernosa form the **crura** (KROO-ra), which are anchored by muscle to the pubic bone. The **urethra,** a tube that transports both urine and semen, runs from the bladder through the prostate and corpus spongiosum, to the tip of the penis, where it opens to the outside. Inside the three chambers are a large number of blood vessels through which blood freely circulates when the penis is flaccid (relaxed). During sexual arousal, these vessels fill with blood and expand, causing the penis to become erect. (Sexual arousal, including erection, is discussed in greater detail later in the chapter.)

In men, the urethra serves as the passageway for both urine and semen. Because the urethral opening is at the tip of the penis, it is vulnerable to injury and infection. During sexual activity, the sensitive mucous membranes around

> *There is nothing about which men lie so much as about their sexual powers. In this at least every man is, what in his heart he would like to be, a Casanova.*
>
> —W. Somerset Maugham
> (1874–1965)

• FIGURE 2

Underside of the Penis

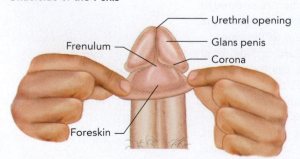

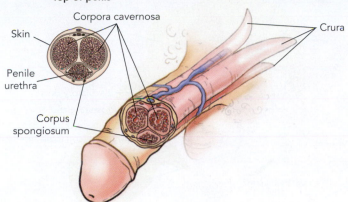

Top of penis

Corpora cavernosa

Skin

Penile
urethra

Corpus
spongiosum

Crura

• **FIGURE 3**

**Interior Structure of the Penis with
Cross-Section**

the opening may be subject to abrasion and can provide an entrance into the body for infectious organisms. Condoms, properly used, can provide an effective barrier between this vulnerable area and potentially infectious organisms.

In an unaroused state, the *average* penis is slightly under 3 inches long, although there is a great deal of individual variation. When erect, penises become more uniform in size, as the percentage of volume increase is greater with smaller penises than with larger ones. The mean erect penis length is about 5 1/2 inches, while the mean erect penis circumference is 4.8 inches (Herbenick, Reece, Schick, & Sanders, 2013). Cold air or water, fear, and anxiety, for example, often cause the penis to temporarily be pulled closer to the body and to decrease in size. When the penis is erect, the urinary duct is temporarily blocked, allowing for the ejaculation of semen. But erection does not necessarily mean sexual excitement. A man may have erections at night during REM sleep, the phase of the sleep cycle when dreaming occurs, or when he is anxious.

Myths and misconceptions about the penis abound, especially among men. Many people believe that the size of a man's penis is directly related to his masculinity, aggressiveness, sexual ability, or sexual attractiveness. Others believe that there is a relationship between the size of a man's penis and the size of his hands, feet, thumbs, or nose. In fact, the size of the penis is not specifically related to body size or weight, muscular structure, race or ethnicity,

There is great variation in the appearance, size, and shape of the male genitalia. Note that the penis on the left is not circumcised, whereas the other two are.

(a) © John Henderson/Alamy;
(b) © Medicimage Ltd/AGE Fotostock;
(c) © H.S. Photos/Alamy

(a)

(b)

(c)

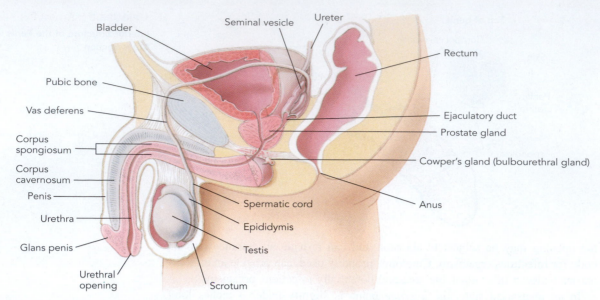

Bladder

Seminal vesicle

Ureter

Rectum

Pubic bone

Vas deferens

Corpus spongiosum

Corpus cavernosum

Penis

Urethra

Glans penis

Urethral opening

Scrotum

Testis

Epididymis

Spermatic cord

Ejaculatory duct

Prostate gland

Cowper's gland (bulbourethral gland)

Anus

• **FIGURE 4**

Internal Side View of the Male Sex Organs

or sexual orientation; it is determined by individual hereditary factors. Except in very rare and extreme cases, there is no relationship between penis size and a man's ability to have sexual intercourse or to satisfy his partner.

The Scrotum Hanging loosely at the root of the penis is the **scrotum,** or scrotal sac, a pouch of skin that holds the two testes. The skin of the scrotum is more heavily pigmented than the skin elsewhere on the body; it is sparsely covered with hair and divided in the middle by a ridge of skin. The skin of the scrotum varies in appearance under different conditions. When a man is sexually aroused, for example, or when he is cold, the testes are pulled close to the body, causing the skin to wrinkle and become more compact. The changes in the surface of the scrotum help maintain a fairly constant temperature within the testes (about 93°F). Two sets of muscles control these changes: (1) the dartos muscle, a smooth muscle under the skin that contracts and causes the surface to wrinkle, and (2) the fibrous cremaster muscle within the scrotal sac that causes the testes to elevate.

Internal Structures

Male internal reproductive organs and structures include the testes (testicles), seminiferous tubules, epididymis, vas deferens, ejaculatory ducts, seminal vesicles, prostate gland, and Cowper's (bulbourethral) glands (see Figure 4).

❝ Nowhere does one read of a penis that quietly moseyed out for a look at what was going on before springing and crashing into action.

—Bernie Zilbergeld (1939–2002)

The Testes Inside the scrotum are the male reproductive glands, or gonads, which are called **testes** (singular, *testis*), or **testicles.** The testes have two major functions: sperm production and hormone production. Each olive-shaped testis is about 1.5 inches long and 1 inch in diameter and weighs about 1 ounce; in adulthood and as a male ages, the testes decrease in size and weight. The testes are usually not symmetrical; the left testis generally hangs slightly lower than the right one. Within the scrotal sac, each testis is suspended by a **spermatic cord** containing nerves, blood vessels, and a tube called the vas deferens (see Figure 5). Within each testis are around 1,000 **seminiferous tubules,** tiny, tightly compressed tubes 1–3 feet long (they would extend several hundred yards if laid end to end). Within these tubes, spermatogenesis—the production of sperm—takes place. (Spermatogenesis is discussed in greater detail later in the chapter.)

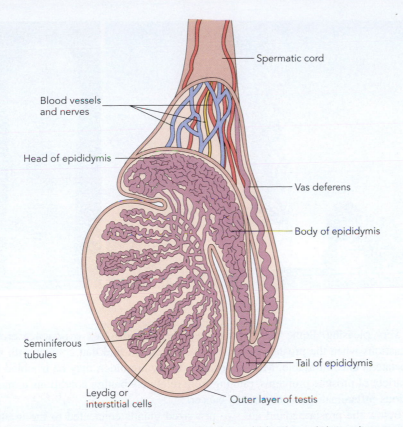

Spermatic cord

Blood vessels
and nerves

Head of epididymis

Vas deferens

Body of epididymis

Seminiferous
tubules

Tail of epididymis

Leydig or
interstitial cells

Outer layer of testis

As a male fetus grows, the testes develop within the pelvic cavity; toward the end of the gestation period, the testes usually descend into the scrotum. In about 3–4% of full-term infants and more commonly in premature infants, one or both of the testes fail to descend, a condition known as **cryptorchidism,** or undescended testis. In most cases, the testes will descend by the time a child is 9 months old. If they do not, surgery is often recommended because bringing the testes into the scrotum maximizes sperm production and increases the odds of fertility. It also allows examination for early detection of testicular cancer.

The Epididymis and Vas Deferens   The epididymis and vas deferens carry sperm from the testes to the urethra for ejaculation. The seminiferous tubules merge to form the **epididymis** (ep-e-DID-i-mes), a comma-shaped structure consisting of a coiled tube about 20 feet long, where the sperm mature. Each epididymis drains into a **vas deferens,** a tube about 18 inches long, extending into the abdominal cavity, over the bladder, and then downward. The vas deferens joins the seminal vesicle to form the **ejaculatory duct.** The vas deferens can be felt easily in the scrotal sac. Because it is easily accessible and is crucial for sperm transport, it is usually the point of sterilization for men. The operation is called a vasectomy.

The Seminal Vesicles, Prostate Gland, and Cowper's Glands   At the back of the bladder lie two glands, each about the size and shape of a finger. These **seminal vesicles** secrete a fluid that makes up about 60% of the seminal fluid. Encircling the urethra just below the bladder is a small, muscular gland about the size and shape of a chestnut called the **prostate gland,** which produces about 30–35% of the seminal fluid in the ejaculated semen. These secretions flow into the urethra through a system of tiny ducts. The prostate gland is located in front of the rectum, and stimulation of this and nearby structures can

My brain. It's my second favorite organ.

—Woody Allen
(1935–)

The penis is a prominent symbol in both ancient and modern art. Here we see a contemporary phallic sculpture in Frogner Park, Oslo, Norway, and a stone *lingam* from Thailand.

(a) © DeAgostini/Getty Images;
(b) © Luca I. Tettoni/Corbis

(a)   (b)

Male breasts, which are usually referred to euphemistically as "the chest" or "pecs," may or may not be considered erotic areas. Men are allowed to display their breasts in certain public settings. Whether the sight is sexually arousing depends on the viewer and the context.

© Purestock/Getty Images

be very pleasing. Some men who enjoy receiving anal sex experience erotic sensations when the prostate is gently stroked; others find that contact with the prostate is uncomfortable. Men, especially if they are older, may be troubled by a variety of prostate problems, ranging from relatively benign conditions to more serious inflammations and prostate cancer.

Below the prostate gland are two pea-sized glands connected to the urethra by tiny ducts. These are **Cowper's glands,** or **bulbourethral** (bul-bo-you-REE-thrul) *glands,* which secrete a thick, clear mucus prior to **ejaculation,** the process by which semen is forcefully expelled from the penis. This fluid may appear at the tip of the erect penis; its alkaline content helps buffer the acidity within the urethra and provides a more hospitable environment for sperm. Fluid from the Cowper's glands may contain sperm that have remained in the urethra since a previous ejaculation or that have leaked in from the ejaculatory duct. Consequently, it is possible for a pregnancy to occur from residual sperm even if the penis is withdrawn before ejaculation.

Other Structures

Male anatomical structures that do not serve a reproductive function but that may be involved in or affected by sexual activities include the breasts, buttocks, rectum, and anus.

Although the male breast contains the same basic structures as the female breast—nipple, areola, fat, and glandular tissue—the amounts of underlying fatty and glandular tissues are much smaller in men. Our culture appears to be ambivalent about the erotic function of men's breasts, but it does appear to place emphasis on their appearance. We usually do not even call them breasts, but refer to the general area as the chest or "pecs." Some men find stimulation of their nipples to be sexually arousing; others do not. **Gynecomastia** (gine-a-ko-MAS-tee-a), the swelling or enlargement of the male breast, is triggered by a decrease in the amount of testosterone compared with estrogen. This condition can occur during adolescence or adulthood. In puberty, gynecomastia is a normal response to hormonal changes. In adulthood, its prevalence peaks again between the ages of 50 and 80 and affects at least one in four men. Its causes may include the use of certain medications, alcoholism, liver or thyroid disease, and cancer. Probably not surprising in this perfection-driven society is the rise in pectoral implants among men who wish to have sculpted chests. Though still a niche market, some men are finding these semisolid silicon implants to be a confidence booster. The risks of the procedure are similar to those of female implant procedures (migration, infection, loss of feelings around the nipple).

An organ used primarily for excretion, the anus can be stimulated by both men and women during sexual activity. Because the anus is kept tightly closed by the external and internal anal sphincters, most of the erotic sensation that occurs during anal sex is derived from the penetration of the anal opening. Beyond the sphincters lies a larger space, the rectum. Because the anus and rectum do not provide significant amounts of lubrication, most people use some sort of water-based lubricant for penetrative sexual activity. Both men and women may enjoy oral stimulation of the anus ("rimming"); the insertion of fingers, a hand ("fisting"), a dildo, or a penis into the rectum may bring erotic pleasure to both the receiver and the giver. (Table 1 provides a summary of male sexual anatomy.)

TABLE 1 • Summary Table of Male Sexual Anatomy

External Structures

Penis	Organ through which both semen and urine pass
Root of penis	Attaches the penis within the pelvic cavity
Shaft	Body of the penis that hangs free
Glans penis	Head of the penis
Corona	Rim at the base of the glans
Frenulum	Triangular area of sensitive skin that attaches the glans to the foreskin
Foreskin (prepuce)	Loose skin or sleevelike covering of the glans; the removal of the foreskin in male infants is called circumcision
Corpora cavernosa	Two parallel columns of erectile tissue that extend along the front surface of the penis
Corpus spongiosum	One of three parallel columns of erectile tissue that run beneath the corpora cavernosa, surround the urethra, and form the glans
Crura	Root of the penis that is anchored by muscle to the pubic bone
Urethra	Tube that transports both urine and semen and runs from the bladder
Scrotum	Pouch of loose skin that holds the two testes

Internal Structures

Testes (testicles)	Male reproductive glands, or gonads, whose major functions are sperm and hormone production
Spermatic cord	Located within the scrotal sac; suspends each testis and contains nerves, blood vessels, and a vas deferens
Seminiferous tubules	Tiny, highly compressed tubes where the production of sperm takes place
Epididymis	Merged from the seminiferous tubules, a comma-shaped structure where the sperm mature
Vas deferens	Tube that extends into the abdominal cavity and carries the sperm from the testes to the urethra for ejaculation
Ejaculatory duct	One of two structures within the prostate gland connecting to the vas deferens
Seminal vesicle	One of two glands at the back of the bladder that together secrete about 70% of the seminal fluid
Prostate gland	Produces about 30% of the seminal fluid in the ejaculated semen
Cowper's glands	Also called bulbourethral glands; secrete a clear, thick, alkaline mucus prior to ejaculation

Other Structures

Urethral opening	Opening in the urethra, through which urine and semen are expelled
Anus	Opening in the rectum, through which excrement passes
Perineum	Area that lies between the scrotum and anus
Pelvic floor	Underside of the pelvic area, extending from the top of the pubic bone to the anus

• Male Sexual Physiology

The reproductive processes of the male body include the manufacture of hormones and the production and delivery of sperm. Although men do not have a monthly reproductive cycle comparable to that of women, they do experience regular fluctuations of hormone levels; there is also some evidence that men's moods follow a cyclical pattern (American Psychological Association, 2011).

Sex Hormones

Within the connective tissues of a man's testes are **Leydig cells** (also called interstitial cells), which secrete **androgens** (male hormones). The most important of these is testosterone, which triggers sperm production and regulates the sex drive. Other important hormones in male reproductive physiology are gonadotropin-releasing hormone (GnRH), follicle-stimulating hormone (FSH), and luteinizing hormone (LH). In addition, men produce the protein hormone inhibin, oxytocin, and small amounts of estrogen. (Table 2 describes the principal hormones involved in sperm production and their functions.)

Testosterone   Testosterone is a steroid hormone synthesized from cholesterol. Testosterone is made by both sexes—by women mostly in the adrenal glands (located above the kidneys) and ovaries and by men primarily in the testes. Furthermore, the brain converts testosterone to estradiol (a female hormone). This flexibility of the hormone makes the link between testosterone and behavior precarious.

During puberty in males, besides acting on the seminiferous tubules to produce sperm, testosterone targets other areas of the body. It causes the penis, testes, and other reproductive organs to grow and is responsible for the development of **secondary sex characteristics,** those changes to parts of the body other than the genitals that indicate sexual maturity. In men, these changes include

> *Women say it's not how much men have, but what we do with it. How many things can we do with it? What is it, a Cuisinart? It's got two speeds: forward and reverse.*
>
> —Richard Jeni
> (1957–2007)

TABLE 2 • Male Reproductive Hormones		
Hormone	**Where Produced**	**Functions**
Testosterone	Testes, adrenal glands	Stimulates sperm production in testes, triggers development of secondary sex characteristics, regulates sex drive
Gonadotropin-releasing hormone (GnRH)	Hypothalamus	Stimulates pituitary during sperm production
Follicle-stimulating hormone (FSH)	Pituitary	Stimulates sperm production in testes
Luteinizing hormone (LH)	Pituitary	Stimulates testosterone production in interstitial cells within testes
Inhibin	Testes	Regulates sperm production by inhibiting release of FSH
Oxytocin	Hypothalamus, testes	Stimulates contractions in the internal reproductive organs to move the contents of the tubules forward; promotes touch, affection, and relaxation
Relaxin	Prostate	Increases sperm motility

practically speaking

Sexual Health Care: What Do Men Need?

Men's sexual health is directly related to their general health. However, because men do not get pregnant or bear children, and because condoms are available without a prescription, men's sexual and reproductive health needs are not as obvious as women's and often are ignored. In recent years, however, such issues as the high incidence of HIV and other sexually transmitted infections (STIs), prevalence of sexual function problems, and concerns regarding the role of males in teenage pregnancies and births have begun to alter this trend. Clearly, a movement toward a holistic and broad-based approach to sexual and reproductive health care for men is needed, one that embraces the full range of men's physical and emotional capacities and needs.

Here are some facts you may not know about the sexual health of men (Guttmacher Institute, 2008.4a; Lindau & Gavrilova, 2010; Planned Parenthood, 2014.4a):

- Men have five birth control options: abstinence, condoms, outercourse (sex play without penile penetration into a vagina or an anus), vasectomy, and withdrawal.

- Testicular cancer is the most common cancer among men aged 20–34. If treated early, it is usually curable.

- Only 5% of those who receive services by the Title X Family Planning Program are men.

- Men (and women) can prevent sexual problems by having a healthy lifestyle that includes regular exercise, good nutrition, limited alcohol use, and avoiding or stopping smoking.

From adolescence on, most men need information and referrals for their sexual and reproductive concerns. Fortunately, preventive health and most reproductive services are now provided to those who are insured under the Affordable Care Act or other insurers. However, few health professionals are specifically trained to provide men with sexual and reproductive health education and services. Men's reproductive health involves both their own well-being and their ability to engage in healthy, fulfilling relationships. To achieve this, men need the following:

1. Information and education about contraceptive use, pregnancy, and childbearing

2. Education about prevention and access to routine screening and treatment for STIs

3. Information about where to obtain and how to use condoms correctly

4. Counseling and support regarding how to talk about these and other sexuality-related issues with partners

5. Surgical services for vasectomies, screening and treatment for reproductive cancers (particularly prostate and testicular cancer), sexual function difficulty counseling and treatment, and infertility treatment

Additionally, skills development related to self-advocacy, risk assessment and avoidance, resistance to peer pressure, communication with partners, fatherhood skills, and role expectations are both needed and desired.

The complex relationships between poverty, high-risk behaviors, and poor health outcomes are undeniable for both men and women. Helping men lead healthier sexual and reproductive lives is a goal that is garnering attention and legitimacy. What is increasingly seen as good for men in their own right should turn out to be just as good for their partners—to the ultimate benefit of society as a whole.

the growth of pubic, facial, underarm, and other body hair and the deepening of the voice. (In women, estrogen and progesterone combine to develop secondary sex characteristics such as breast development, the growth of pubic and underarm hair, and the onset of vaginal mucous secretions.) Testosterone also influences the growth of bones and increase of muscle mass and causes the skin to thicken and become oilier, leading to acne in many teenage boys.

Though numerous studies have attempted to understand the impact of testosterone on personality, findings are mixed. What complicates the research is that testosterone levels vary according to what specific components of the hormone testosterone were measured and the fact that levels are rarely stable; they appear to respond positively or negatively to almost every challenge, and not necessarily in a way we might predict. Consequently, if a man suspects he has a testosterone deficiency, he would be wise to have his testosterone level assessed in the morning when it is at its peak (Brambilla, Matsumoto, Araujo, & McKinlay, 2013). New research is also emerging about the role of estrogen in men's bodies, demonstrating that, with age, declining levels of estrogen contribute to increased waistline sizes (Snyder, 2014).

The increasing literature about testosterone and its derivatives, the anabolic-androgenic steroids, has fueled a market for those seeking anti-aging therapies, desiring athletic bodies and performance, and feeling entitled to unfailing and lifelong sexual prowess and fulfillment. The complex interaction of hormonal, psychological, situational, and physical factors that men experience with age can result in erectile problems, decreased bone density, heart disease, changes in moods, difficulty in thinking, and weakness (National Institute on Aging, 2014). Some of these symptoms can be reversed with **testosterone replacement therapy;** however, a cautious approach to testosterone therapy should be taken because there is still mixed evidence about its role in cardiovascular problems and prostate cancer (Harvard Men's Health Watch, 2014). To underscore this concern, the Food and Drug Administration (FDA) now requires warning labels about the general risk of blood clots associated with testosterone products. Because of lack of solid evidence, testosterone replacement therapy is recommended only for those who prove to have a deficiency of testosterone, with a blood level confirmed by medical tests as the cause of the symptoms.

Male Cycles Studies comparing men and women have found that both sexes are subject to hormonal cycles resulting in changes in mood, behavior, and sexual desire (Law, 2011). Whereas such changes in women are often attributed (rightly or

> *The sex organ has a poetic power, like a comet.*
>
> —Joan Miró
> (1893–1983)

> *Men always want to be a woman's first love—women like to be a man's last romance.*
>
> —Oscar Wilde
> (1854–1900)

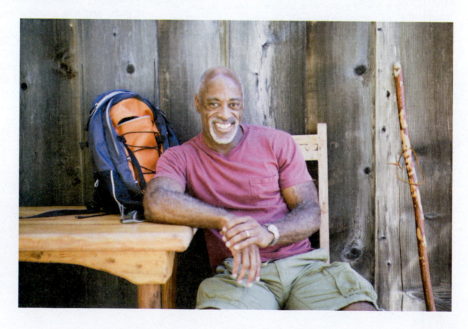

Though changes in sexual functioning are a common occurrence, men (and women) can, as they age, maintain their physical and psychological vitality through a healthy lifestyle.

© Picturenet/Blend Images LLC

wrongly) to monthly menstrual cycle fluctuations, men's testosterone appears to cycle throughout the day, month, and possibly season. On a daily basis, men's testosterone levels appear to be lowest in the evening and highest in the morning. They also decline with age. Though much is still unclear about the role of hormone levels in men and women, what is known is that neither sex has much awareness of how much hormonal fluctuations in their bodies impact what they do (van Anders, 2012).

Throughout the night, specifically during REM sleep, men experience spontaneous penile erections. (Women experience labial, vaginal, and clitoral engorgement.) These erections are sometimes referred to as "battery-recharging mechanisms" for the penis, because they increase blood flow and bring fresh oxygen to the penis. Typically, men have penile engorgement during 95% of REM sleep stages (Komisaruk, Whipple, Nasserzadeh, & Beyer-Flores, 2010). If a man has erectile difficulties while he is awake, it is important to determine whether he has normal erections during sleep. If so, his problems may have to do with something other than the physiology of erection. Approximately 90% of men and nearly 40% of women have ever experienced **nocturnal orgasms;** for men, these are often referred to as "wet dreams" (Kinsey, Pomeroy, & Martin, 1948; Wells, 1986).

Spermatogenesis

Within the testes, from puberty on, **spermatogenesis,** the production of the male gametes, or **sperm,** is an ongoing process. Every day, a healthy, fertile man produces several hundred million sperm within the seminiferous tubules of his testes (see Figure 6). After they are formed in the seminiferous tubules, which takes 64–72 days, immature sperm are stored in the epididymis. It then takes about 20 days for the sperm to travel the length of the epididymis, during which time they become fertile and motile (able to move). Upon ejaculation, sperm in the tail section of the epididymis are expelled by muscular contractions of its walls into the vas deferens; similar contractions within the vas deferens propel the sperm into the urethra, where they are mixed with semen, also called seminal fluid, and then expelled, or ejaculated, through the urethral opening.

The sex of the zygote, the one-celled organism produced by the union of egg and sperm, is determined by the chromosomes of the sperm. The ovum always contributes a female sex chromosome (X), whereas the sperm may contribute either a female or a male sex chromosome (Y). The combination of two X chromosomes (XX) means that the zygote will develop as a female; with an X and a Y chromosome (XY), it will develop as a male. In some cases, combinations of sex chromosomes other than XX or XY occur, causing sexual development to proceed differently.

Semen Production

Semen, or **seminal fluid,** is the ejaculated liquid that contains sperm. The function of semen is to nourish sperm and provide them with a hospitable environment and means of transport if they are deposited within the vagina. Semen is mainly made up of secretions from the seminal vesicles and prostate gland, which mix together with sperm and are ejaculated through the urethra. Immediately after ejaculation, the semen is somewhat thick and sticky from clotting factors in the fluid. This consistency keeps the sperm together initially;

Between 100 million and 600 million sperm are present in the semen from a single ejaculation. Typically, following ejaculation during intercourse, fewer than 1,000 sperm will get as far as a fallopian tube, where an ovulated oocyte may be present. Though many sperm assist in helping dissolve the egg cell membrane, typically only one sperm ultimately achieves fertilization.

© CNRI/Science Source

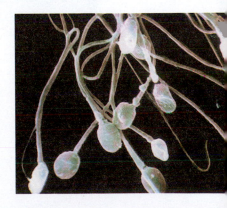

Spermatogenesis. This diagram shows the development of spermatozoa, beginning with a single spermatogonium and ending with four complete sperm cells. Spermatogenesis is an ongoing process that begins in puberty. Several hundred million sperm are produced every day within the seminiferous tubules of a healthy man.

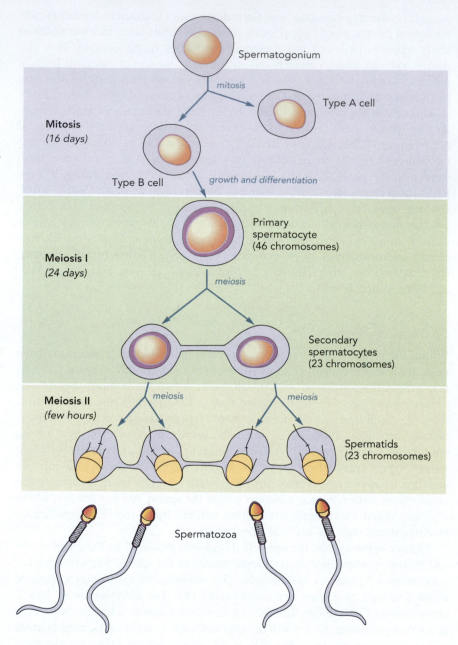

then the semen becomes liquefied, allowing the sperm to swim out. Semen ranges in color from opalescent or milky white to yellowish or grayish upon ejaculation, but it becomes clearer as it liquefies. Normally, about 2–6 milliliters (about 1 teaspoonful) of semen is ejaculated at one time; this amount of semen generally contains between 100 million and 600 million sperm. In spite of their significance, sperm occupy only about 1% of the total volume of semen; the remainder comes primarily from the seminal vesicles (70%) and the prostate gland (30%). Fewer than 1,000 sperm will reach the fallopian tubes. Most causes of male infertility are related to low sperm count and/or low motility.

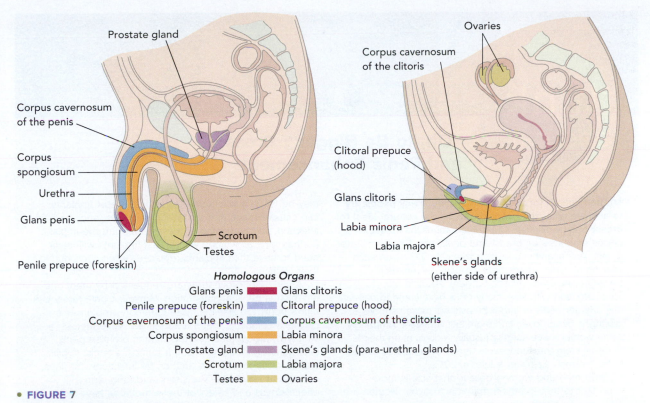

Homologous Organs

Glans penis		Glans clitoris
Penile prepuce (foreskin)		Clitoral prepuce (hood)
Corpus cavernosum of the penis		Corpus cavernosum of the clitoris
Corpus spongiosum		Labia minora
Prostate gland		Skene's glands (para-urethral glands)
Scrotum		Labia majora
Testes		Ovaries

● **FIGURE 7**

Homologous Structures of Male and Female Genitalia. Note that males and females share many of the same structures since they developed from the same cells during fetal development.

Homologous Organs

Interestingly, each of the male sexual structures has a **homologous structure,** or similar characteristic, that is developed from the same cells in the developing female fetus. The presence of a Y chromosome in a male produces testosterone in greater amounts. Without this Y chromosome, the fetus would become a female. (See Figure 7 for the homologous structures of males and females.)

● Male Sexual Response

At this point, it might be useful to review the material on sexual arousal and response, including the models of Masters and Johnson, Kaplan, and Loulan. Even though their sexual anatomy is quite different, women and men follow roughly the same pattern of excitement and orgasm, with two exceptions: (1) Generally (but certainly not always), men become fully aroused and ready for penetration in a shorter amount of time than women do; and (2) once men experience ejaculation, they usually cannot do so again for some time, whereas women may experience repeated orgasms.

Probably one of the most controversial topics in the field of sexuality theory is whether sexual desire is shaped more by nature or culture. Societal expectations, health, education, class, politics, and relational factors are thought to influence both men's and women's sexual desire and functioning. Combined, these influence sexual desire and response in profound ways.

Bring me my bow of burning gold.
Bring me my arrow of desire.

—William Blake
(1757–1827)

think
about it

"Oh, to Be Bigger": Breast and Penis Enhancement

In their search for the "perfect" body, many people try to achieve what they consider to be the cultural ideal for breast and penis size. Our culture, more than most, places emphasis on breast and penis size: Bigger is better. In fact, Americans spend approximately $10 billion each year on all types of cosmetic procedures (American Society of Aesthetic Plastic Surgery, 2013). In our preoccupation with size, many of us have come to believe that a larger penis or larger breasts will make us more alluring, a better lover, and more self-confident. Amazingly, some women have surgery (usually reduction) on their labia to make them the supposedly "ideal" or what they consider to be "normal" size (Kim & Iglesia, 2013).

Both men and women believe that size is more important to their partners than it actually is. Women are often more unhappy than their partner about their own breasts. In fact, when men were surveyed about the size of women's breasts that they found most physically attractive, results showed that medium breasts were rated most frequently as attractive (32.7%) (Swami & Tovee, 2013). Similarly, while some men worry that their penis is too small, a study of 52,031 heterosexual men and women found that 85% of women were satisfied with their partner's penis size (only 55% of men were satisfied with their penis size and 45% wanted it larger) (Lever, Frederick, & Peplau, 2006). The reality is that most individuals prefer a caring, skilled, and warm lover instead of a partner who focuses on his or her anatomical size.

The desire to have longer penises or bigger breasts, for example, has led to ads that try to make people feel inadequate or embarrassed if they are not "large." The ads promote methods such as drugs to increase size and promise quick and easy results. What they may not address, however, are questions of safety, functioning, erotic pleasure, and necessity. Rarely, if ever, have the products been approved by the U.S. Food and Drug Administration (FDA) or been shown to be effective in clinical tests.

In 2013, the American Society of Plastic Surgeons (2014) reported a "silicon surge" with 290,000 breast augmentation procedures, an increase of 36% since 2000, making breast implantation the most popular cosmetic surgery performed in this country. Though they may be warranted in some occasions, breast implants can cause serious and costly complications, such as pain, infection, and hardening of the area around the implant. Furthermore, all women with breast implants will likely need to have their implants replaced or removed during their lifetime.

A variety of procedures are requested by men, one of which is penis augmentation. However, only rarely is a man's penis too small; a more common problem is a partner's complaint that it is too large. Nevertheless, a variety of procedures and techniques promise penis enlargement, including vacuum pumps, exercises, pills, and surgical procedures such as fat injections, fat flaps, and silicon injections. The short- and long-term effectiveness and safety of these methods have not been well established, and the degree of patient satisfaction varies. Given that size has been found to play a significant role in the sexual positions that individuals may enjoy (Grov, Parsons, & Bimbi, 2010), it is imperative that we learn more about the consequences for all men and women of living in a "penis-driven" society.

If you are unhappy with your breast or penis size, talk to a professional health care provider such as a physician or mental health counselor. If you are in a relationship, talk to your partner. In most cases, you will learn that size is usually not an important issue. However, intimacy, communication, mutual respect, and acceptance of your own body and sexuality are.

Think Critically

1. How do you feel about the size of your penis, breasts, or genitals? If you are uncomfortable, what might help you feel satisfied?

2. Have you ever been rejected by a sexual partner because he or she was dissatisfied with your breast or penis size? Have you ever rejected a sexual partner for the same reason?

3. What could you do to help a sexual partner feel more comfortable about accepting his or her body?

Sexual arousal in men includes the processes of myotonia (increased muscle tension) and vasocongestion (engorgement of the tissues with blood). Vasocongestion in men is most apparent in the erection of the penis.

Erection

When a male becomes aroused, the blood circulation within the penis changes dramatically (see Figure 8). During the process of **erection,** the blood vessels expand, increasing the volume of blood, especially within the corpora cavernosa. At the same time, expansion of the penis compresses the veins that normally carry blood out, so the penis becomes further engorged. (There are no muscles in the penis that make it erect, nor is there a bone in it.) Secretions from the Cowper's glands appear at the tip of the penis during erection.

An erection at will is the moral equivalent of a valid credit card.

—Alex Comfort, MD
(1920–2000)

• **FIGURE 8**

Masters and Johnson's Stages in Male Sexual Response

(1) Excitement

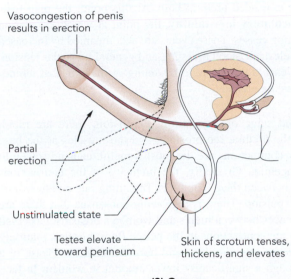

Vasocongestion of penis results in erection

Partial erection

Unstimulated state

Testes elevate toward perineum

Skin of scrotum tenses, thickens, and elevates

(2) Late Excitement or Plateau

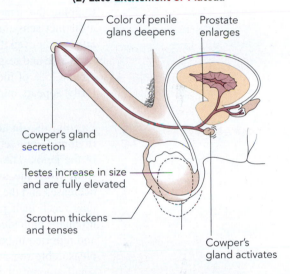

Color of penile glans deepens

Prostate enlarges

Cowper's gland secretion

Testes increase in size and are fully elevated

Scrotum thickens and tenses

Cowper's gland activates

(3) Orgasm

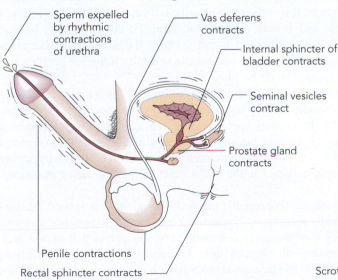

Sperm expelled by rhythmic contractions of urethra

Vas deferens contracts

Internal sphincter of bladder contracts

Seminal vesicles contract

Prostate gland contracts

Penile contractions

Rectal sphincter contracts

(4) Resolution

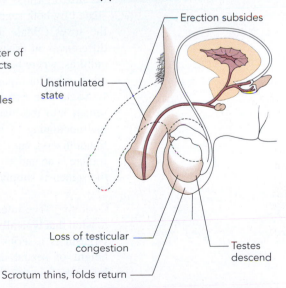

Erection subsides

Unstimulated state

Loss of testicular congestion

Scrotum thins, folds return

Testes descend

Ejaculation and Orgasm

What triggers the events that lead to ejaculation are undetermined, but it appears that it may be the result of a critical level of excitation in the brain or spinal cord (Komisaruk et al., 2010). Regardless, increasing stimulation of the penis generally leads to ejaculation. Orgasm occurs when the impulses that cause erection reach a critical point and a spinal reflex sets off a massive discharge of nerve impulses to the ducts, glands, and muscles of the reproductive system. Ejaculation then occurs in two stages: emission and expulsion.

Emission In the first stage, **emission,** contractions of the walls of the tail portion of the epididymis send sperm into the vasa deferentia (plural for *vas deferens*). Rhythmic contractions also occur in the prostate, seminal vesicles, and vasa deferentia, which spill their contents into the urethra. The bladder's sphincter muscle closes to prevent urine from mixing with the semen and semen from entering the bladder, and another sphincter below the prostate also closes, trapping the semen in the expanded urethral bulb. At this point, the man feels a distinct sensation of **ejaculatory inevitability,** the point at which ejaculation *must* occur even if stimulation ceases. These events are accompanied by increased heart rate and respiration, elevated blood pressure, and general muscular tension. About 25% of men experience a sex flush, a darkening of the skin that temporarily appears during sexual excitement.

Expulsion In the second stage of ejaculation, **expulsion,** there are rapid, rhythmic contractions of the urethra, the prostate, and the muscles at the base of the penis. The first few contractions are the most forceful, causing semen to spurt from the urethral opening. Gradually, the intensity of the contractions decreases and the interval between them lengthens. Breathing rate and heart rate may reach their peak at expulsion. There is a growing consensus that there are no major biological differences between men's and women's orgasms. Observed and reported in both sexes are contractions in the pelvic floor muscles, intensely pleasurable sensations, release of endorphins and hormones, and a release of a small amount of fluid, though a significantly lower amount in women. In fact, because orgasm is a very individual and subjective experience with commonalities shared by both sexes, it is difficult to identify self-reported differences between the sexes ("Male and female orgasm – different?", 2013). Where, however, differences in orgasm are noticed is not between the sexes but rather among cultures, where beliefs about male and female sexuality influence people's ideas about what an orgasm should be like.

Some men experience **retrograde ejaculation,** the "backward" expulsion of semen into the bladder rather than out of the urethral opening. This unusual malfunctioning of the urethral sphincters may be temporary (e.g., induced by tranquilizers), but if it persists, the man should seek medical counsel to determine if there is an underlying problem. Retrograde ejaculation is not normally harmful; the semen is simply collected in the bladder and eliminated during urination.

Orgasm The intensely pleasurable physical sensations and general release of tension that typically accompany ejaculation constitute the experience of orgasm. Orgasm is a series of muscular contractions of the pelvis that occurs at the height of sexual arousal. Orgasm does not always occur with ejaculation, however. It is possible to ejaculate without having an orgasm and to experience

Can an Erection Be Willed?

The erection reflex can be triggered by various sexual and nonsexual stimuli, including tactile stimulation (touching) of the penis or other erogenous areas; sights, smells, or sounds (usually words or sexual vocalizations); and emotions or thoughts. Even negative emotions such as fear can produce an erection. Conversely, emotions and thoughts can also inhibit erections, as can unpleasant or painful physical sensations. The erectile response is controlled by the parasympathetic nervous system, a component of the involuntary, or "autonomic," nervous system and therefore cannot be consciously willed. What can be regulated in some men is their sexual arousal (Winters, Christoff, & Gorzalka, 2009). This knowledge can provide some men with a sense of comfort and reduce their vulnerability in precarious situations.

The length of time an erection lasts varies greatly from individual to individual and from situation to situation. With experience, most men are able to gauge the amount of stimulation that will either maintain the erection without causing ejaculation or cause ejaculation to occur too soon. Not attaining an erection when one is desired is something most men experience at one time or another.

There are, however, some things you can do to maximize your chances of producing viable erections. Because you need a steady flow of blood to your penis, you should get enough aerobic exercise and refrain from smoking to maintain your circulation. A diet low in fat and cholesterol and high in fiber and complex carbohydrates may also prevent hardening of the arteries, which restricts blood flow. Also, learning to relax during sexual activity with a partner can help with erections.

Some conditions, including diabetes, stress, depression, and abnormalities in blood pressure, and some medications that treat these conditions may have an adverse effect on blood flow and erectile capacity. If any of these conditions are present, or if the failure to attain an erection is persistent, see your physician.

What can you do about unwanted erections at inappropriate times? Distract yourself or stop your thoughts or images. Remember, the brain is the most erotic (and unerotic) organ of the body.

---

orgasm without ejaculating. Additionally, ejaculation and orgasm don't necessarily require an erection. Some men have reported having more than one orgasm without ejaculation ("dry orgasm") prior to a final, ejaculatory orgasm. Following ejaculation, men experience a **refractory period,** during which they are not capable of having an ejaculation again. This is the time in which nerves cannot respond to additional stimulation. Refractory periods vary greatly in length, ranging from a few minutes to many hours (or even days, in some older men). Other changes occur immediately following ejaculation. The erection diminishes as blood flow returns to normal, the sex flush (if there was one) disappears, and fairly heavy perspiration may occur. Men who experience intense sexual arousal without ejaculation may feel some heaviness or discomfort in the testes; this is generally not as painful as the common term "blue balls" implies. If discomfort persists, however, it may be relieved by a period of rest or by ejaculation. When the seminal vesicles are full, feedback mechanisms diminish the quantity of sperm produced. Excess sperm die and are absorbed by the body. For some men, the benefits of strengthening the muscles that surround the penis by doing what are called **Kegel exercises** can produce more intense orgasms and ejaculations.

> *When the appetite arises in the liver, the heart generates a spirit which descends through the arteries, fills the hollow of the penis and makes it hard and stiff. The delightful movements of intercourse give warmth to all the members, and hence to the humor which is in the brain; this liquid is drawn through the veins which lead from behind the ears to the testicles and from them it is squirted by the penis into the vulva.*
>
> —Constantinus Africanus (c. 1070)

In this chapter, we have looked primarily at the *physical* characteristics that designate us as female or male. But as we discover, there's more to gender than mere chromosomes or reproductive organs. How we feel about our physical selves (our male or female anatomy) and how we act (our gender roles) also determine our identities as men or women.

Summary

Male Sex Organs: What Are They For?

- In their reproductive role, a man's sex organs produce and store gametes and can deliver them to a woman's reproductive tract. The *penis* is the organ through which both sperm and urine pass. The *shaft* of the penis contains two *corpora cavernosa* and a *corpus spongiosum,* which fill with blood during arousal, causing an erection. The head is called the *glans penis;* in uncircumcised men, it is covered by the *foreskin.* Myths about the penis equate its size with masculinity and sexual prowess. The *scrotum* is a pouch of skin that hangs at the root of the penis. It holds the *testes.*

- The paired testes, or testicles, have two major functions: sperm production and hormone production. Within each testis are about 1,000 *seminiferous tubules,* where the production of sperm takes place. The seminiferous tubules merge to form the *epididymis,* a coiled tube where the sperm finally mature, and each epididymis merges into a *vas deferens,* which joins the *ejaculatory duct* within the *prostate gland.* The *seminal vesicles* and prostate gland produce *semen,* or *seminal fluid,* which nourishes and transports the sperm. Two tiny glands called *Cowper's glands* or *bulbourethral glands* secrete a thick, clear mucus prior to *ejaculation,* whereby semen is forcefully expelled from the penis.

- Male anatomical structures that do not serve a reproductive function but that may be involved in or affected by sexual activities include the breasts, *urethra,* buttocks, rectum, and anus.

Male Sexual Physiology

- The reproductive processes of the male body include the manufacture of hormones and the production and delivery of *sperm,* the male gametes. Although men do not have a monthly reproductive cycle comparable to that of women, they do experience regular fluctuations of hormone levels; there is also some evidence that men's moods follow a cyclical pattern. The most important male hormone is *testosterone,* which triggers sperm production and regulates the sex drive. Other important hormones in male reproductive physiology are GnRH, FSH, LH, inhibin, and oxytocin.

- Sperm carry either an X chromosome, which will produce a female zygote, or a Y chromosome, which will produce a male.

- Semen is the ejaculated liquid that contains sperm. The function of semen is to nourish sperm and provide them with a hospitable environment and means of transport if they are deposited within the vagina. It is mainly made up of secretions from the seminal vesicles and prostate gland. The semen from a single ejaculation generally contains between 100 million and 600 million sperm, yet only about 1,000 make it to the fallopian tubes.

Male Sexual Response

- Male sexual response, like that of females, involves the processes of vasocongestion and myotonia. *Erection* of the penis occurs when sexual or tactile stimuli cause its chambers to become engorged with blood. Continuing stimulation leads to ejaculation, which occurs in two stages. In the first stage, *emission,* semen mixes with sperm in the urethral bulb. In the second stage, *expulsion,* semen is forcibly expelled from the penis. Ejaculation and orgasm, a series of contractions of the pelvic muscles occurring at the height of sexual arousal, typically happen simultaneously. However, they can also occur separately. Following orgasm is a *refractory period,* during which ejaculation is not possible.

Questions for Discussion

- Make a list of anything you have heard about men's sexuality. Identify the myths and compare them with information from the text.

- How do you feel about penis or breast enhancement? Is it something that you might consider? Why or why not?

- Do you believe that men have cycles, similar to women's menstrual cycles? If so, what might contribute to this phenomenon? If not, why not?

Sex and the Internet

Men's Sexuality

Try to locate Internet sites about men's sexuality. You'll find that, apart from those relating to erectile dysfunction, AIDS, and sexually explicit materials, few sites address this topic. What does this say about men? About the topic of men and sexuality? Because of this absence of content-specific sites, it is necessary to search a broader topic: men's health. Go to the Men's Health Network (http://www.menshealthnetwork .org) and, in the Library section, either select one of the more popular topics on the website or conduct your own search. When you find a topic that interests you, see if you can find the following:

- Background information about the topic
- The incidence or prevalence of the issue/problem
- Whom it impacts or affects
- The causes and potential solutions
- A related link that might broaden your understanding of this topic

Last, what recommendation might you make to someone who identified with this issue?

Suggested Websites

American Urological Association

http://auanet.org

Provides a variety of information on adult sexual functioning and infertility.

eHealth Forum

http://ehealthforum.com/health/mens_sexual_health.html

Member and doctor discussions ranging from a specific symptom to related conditions, treatment options, and emotional issues surrounding sexuality.

Male Health Center

http://www.malehealthcenter.com

Provides information on a wide variety of issues related to male genital health, birth control, and sexual functioning, from the male perspective.

WebMD

http://www.webmd.com/men/

Focuses on a variety of health topics, including men's sexuality.

Suggested Reading

Bering, J. (2012). *Why is the penis shaped like that?: And other reflections on being human.* New York City, NY: Scientific American/Farrar, Straus and Giroux. A captivating journey through some of the most taboo issues related to evolutionary and human sexual behavior.

Danoff, D. S. (2011). *Penis power: The ultimate guide to male sexual health.* Beverly Hills, CA: Del Monaco Press. Educational and informative book on male sexual health.

McLaren, A. (2007). *Impotence: A cultural history.* Chicago: University of Chicago Press. The history of impotence along with the pains that a society and culture take in goading men in the pursuit of what is normal and natural.

Thompson, E. H., & Kaye, L. W. (2013). *A man's guide to healthy aging.* Baltimore, MD: Johns Hopkins Press. A guide to a wide variety of health-related topics from a man's perspective.

Zilbergeld, B. (1999). *The new male sexuality* (Rev. Ed.). New York: Bantam Books. A classic in the field of male sexuality; the author provides an explanation of both male and female anatomy and sexual response, plus communication, sexual problem solving and much more.

5

Gender and Gender Roles

© Jared C. Tilton/NASCAR via Getty Images

CHAPTER OUTLINE

Studying Gender and Gender Roles

Gender-Role Learning

Contemporary Gender Roles and Scripts

Gender Variations

"As early as preschool I learned the difference between boy and girl toys, games, and colors. The boys played with trucks while the girls played with dolls. If a boy were to play with a doll, he would be laughed at and even teased. In the make-believe area, once again, you have limitations of your dreams. Girls could not be police, truck drivers, firefighters, or construction workers. We had to be people that were cute, such as models, housewives, dancers, or nurses. We would sometimes model ourselves after our parents or family members."

—23-year-old female

"I grew up with the question of 'why?' dangling from the tip of my tongue. Why am I supposed to marry a certain person? Why do I have to learn how to cook meat for my husband when I am a vegetarian? Why can't I go out on dates or to school formals? The answer was the same every time: 'Because you're a girl.' Being that she is such a strong woman, I know it tore a bit of my grandmother's heart every time she had to say it."

—19-year-old female

"My stepfather and I did not get along. I viewed him as an outsider, and I did not want a replacement father. Looking back, I feel like I overcompensated for the lack of a male figure in my life. I enlisted in the Navy at 18, have a huge firearm collection, and play ice hockey on the weekends. All of these activities seem to be macho, even to me. I guess it's to prove that even though a woman raised me I'm still a man's man."

—27-year-old male

"I was in fifth grade, and my parents put me on restriction. My mom inquired where I got the [Playboy] magazine. I told her we found it on the way home from school. She wanted to know where. I lied and said it was just sitting in somebody's trashcan and I happened to see it. She wanted to know where. I said I forgot. My sexual identity was being founded on concealment, repression, and lies. Within my family, my sexual identity was repressed."

—27-year-old male

How can we tell the difference between a man and a woman? Everyone knows that women and men, at a basic level, are distinguished by their genitals. However, as accurate as this answer may be academically, it is not particularly useful in social situations. In most social situations—except in nudist colonies or while sunbathing au naturel—our genitals are not visible to the casual observer. We do not expose ourselves (or ask another person to do so) for gender verification. We are more likely to rely on secondary sex characteristics, such as breasts and body hair, or on bone structure, musculature, and height. But even these characteristics are not always reliable, given the great variety of shapes and sizes we come in as human beings. And from farther away than a few yards, we cannot always distinguish these characteristics. Instead of relying entirely on physical characteristics to identify individuals as male and female, we often look for other clues.

Culture provides us with an important clue for recognizing whether a person is female or male in most situations: dress. In almost all cultures, male and female clothing differs to varying degrees so that we can easily identify a person's gender. Some cultures, such as our own, may accentuate secondary sex characteristics, especially for females. Traditional feminine clothing, for example, emphasizes a woman's gender: dress or skirt, a form-fitting or low-cut top revealing cleavage, high heels, and so on. Most clothing, in fact, that emphasizes or exaggerates secondary sex characteristics is female. Makeup (lipstick, mascara, eyeliner) and hairstyles also mark or exaggerate the differences between females and males. Even smells (perfume for women, cologne for men) and colors (blue for boys, pink for girls) help distinguish females and males.

There is no essential sexuality. Maleness and femaleness are something we are dressed in.

—Naomi Wallace
(1960–)

Clothing and other aspects of appearance further exaggerate the physical differences between women and men. And culture encourages us to accentuate (or invent) psychological, emotional, mental, and behavioral differences. But what happens when these lines are blurred, especially in young children who defy gender norms? Should parents and their doctors be permitted to block puberty medically in order to buy time and figure out who these children are? Should the United States follow Germany to allow "undetermined" as a gender type for newborn babies? Legislation enacted in 2013 in Germany specifies that babies born without gender-defining physical characteristics can be registered as having an "undetermined" gender on their birth certificate. While a biological understanding of gender identity remains somewhat of a mystery, medical, ethical, and parental maps are being created to respond to the growing number of individuals who see gender variance an alternative to psychiatric diagnoses and a normal part on the wide continuum of gender expression.

In this chapter, we look at the connection between our genitals; our identity as female, male, or intersex; and our feelings of being feminine, masculine, or a mixture of these qualities. We also examine the relationship between femininity, masculinity, and sexual orientation. Then we discuss how masculine and feminine traits result from both biological and social influences. Next, we focus on theories of socialization and how we learn to act masculine and feminine in our culture. Then we look at traditional, contemporary, and androgynous gender roles. We then examine gender variation—gender dysphoria and transsexuality—along with disorders of sex development. Finally, we address coming to terms with gender differences.

● Studying Gender and Gender Roles

Let's start by defining some key terms, to establish a common terminology. Keeping these definitions in mind will make the discussion clearer.

Sex, Gender, and Gender Roles: What's the Difference?

The word **sex** refers to whether one is biologically female or male, based on genetic and anatomical sex. **Genetic sex** refers to one's chromosomal and hormonal sex characteristics, such as whether one's chromosomes are XY or XX and whether estrogen or testosterone dominates the hormonal system. **Anatomical sex** refers to physical sex: gonads, uterus, vulva, vagina, penis, and so on.

Although "sex" and "gender" are often used interchangeably, gender is not the same as biological sex. Gender relates to femininity or masculinity, the social and cultural characteristics associated with biological sex. Whereas sex is rooted in biology, gender is rooted in culture. **Assigned gender** is the gender given by others, usually at birth. When a baby is born, someone looks at the genitals and exclaims, "It's a boy!" or "It's a girl!" With that single utterance, the baby is transformed from an "it" into a "male" or a "female." **Gender identity** is a person's internal sense of being male or female.

Gender roles are the attitudes, behaviors, rights, and responsibilities that particular cultural groups associate with our assumed or assigned sex. Age, race, and a variety of other factors further define and influence these. A **gender-role stereotype** is a rigidly held, oversimplified, and overgeneralized belief about how each gender should behave. Stereotypes tend to be false or misleading, not only for the group as a whole (e.g., women are more interested in relationships than sex) but also for any individual in the group (e.g., Eric may be more interested in sex than

Whatever women do they must do twice as well as men to be thought half as good. Luckily, this is not difficult.

—Charlotte Whitton
(1896–1975)

relationships). Even if a generalization is statistically valid in describing a group average (e.g., males are generally taller than females), such generalizations do not necessarily predict the facts (e.g., whether Roberto will be taller than Andrea).

Sex and Gender Identity

We develop our gender through the interaction of its biological, cultural, and psychosocial components. The biological component includes genetic and anatomical sex; the cultural component creates gender distinctions; the psychosocial component includes assigned gender and gender identity. Because these dimensions are learned together, they may seem to be natural. For example, if a person looks like a girl (biological), believes she should be feminine (cultural), feels as if she is a girl (psychological), and acts like a girl (social), then her gender identity and role are congruent with her anatomical sex. Our culture emphasizes that there are only two genders and that there should be coherence among the biological, social, cultural, and psychological dimensions of each gender. Deviations, still often stigmatized, are now being reexamined, evaluated, and viewed as **gender variations.** Those individuals who cannot or choose not to conform to societal gender norms associated with their biological sex are **gender variant.** Other terms for this variation include *gender atypical behavior, gender identity disorder*, and *gender dysphoria*. Many experts are now finding that molding children's gender identity is not as important as allowing them to be who they are, regardless of what their genitals may tell them.

The nuances and controversies inherent in gender studies force many of us to think about our assumptions and biases about those whom we regard as different or variant. When trying to make sense of gender, Jack Drescher (2014), psychiatrist and outspoken expert in the field of gender variations, cuts across lives and cultures when he reflects:

> The closest I have come to an overview of the subject is the image of six blindfold scientists in white coats trying to describe an elephant. Each of them, touching only one of six parts (trunk, horn, tail, ear, leg, flank), understandably mistakes the part for the whole. I have come to appreciate that any understanding of this subject requires a capacity to hold complexity and tolerate the anxiety of uncertainty.

It will become clear in the following pages that though little is known about the causes of gender, gender identity, and gender variations, many of us will often

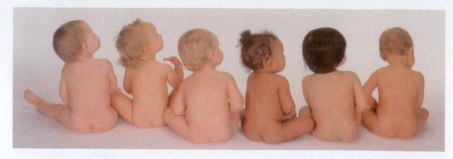

Roles come with costumes and speeches and stage directions. In a role, we don't have to think.

—Ellen Goodman
(1941–)

fall back on our opinions and biases about this subject. Instead, the goal of this discussion is to help raise awareness about those who are gender variant.

Assigned Gender   When we are born, we are assigned a gender based on anatomical appearance. Assigned gender is significant because it tells *others* how to respond to us. As youngsters, we have no sense of ourselves as female or male. We *learn* that we are a girl or a boy from the verbal responses of others. "What a pretty *girl*" or "What a good *boy*," our parents and others say. We are constantly given signals about our gender. Our birth certificate states our sex; our name, such as Jarrod or Felicia, is most likely gender-coded. Our clothes, even in infancy, reveal our gender.

By the time we are 2 years old, we are probably able to identify ourselves as a girl or a boy based on what we have internalized from what others have told us coupled with factors not yet understood. We might also be able to identify strangers as "mommies" or "daddies." But we don't really know *why* we are a girl or a boy. We don't associate our gender with our genitals. In fact, until the age of 3 or so, most children identify girls or boys by hairstyles, clothing, or other nonanatomical signs. At around age 3, we begin to learn that the genitals are what make a person male or female.

By age 4 or 5, children have learned a wide array of social stereotypes about how boys and girls should behave. Consequently, they tend to react approvingly or disapprovingly toward each other according to their choice of sex-appropriate play patterns and toys. Fixed ideas about adult roles and careers are also established by this time.

Gender Identity   By about age 2, we internalize and identify with our gender. We *think* we are a girl or a boy. This feeling of our femaleness or maleness is our gender identity. For most people, gender identity is permanent and is congruent with their sexual anatomy and assigned gender.

Some cultures recognize that sex and gender are not always divided along binary lines, such as male and female or homosexual and heterosexual (World Health Organization [WHO], 2011). In some East African societies, for example, a male child is referred to as a "woman-child"; there are few social differences between young boys and girls. Around age 7, the boy undergoes male initiation rites, such as circumcision, whose avowed purpose is to "make" him into a man. Such ceremonies may serve as a kind of "brainwashing," helping the young male make the transition to a new gender identity with new role expectations. Other cultures allow older males to act out a latent female identity with such practices as the couvade, in which husbands mimic their wives giving birth. And in our own society, into the early twentieth century, boys were dressed in gowns and wore their hair in long curls until age 2. At age 2 or 3, their dresses were replaced by pants, their hair was cut, and they were socialized to conform to their anatomical sex. Children who deviated from this expected conformity were referred to as sissies (boys) or tomboys (girls) and ridiculed to conform to gender stereotypes. More recently, a new brand of thinking supported by advocates of gender-identity rights has sparked debate among professionals over how to best counsel families whose child does not conform to gender norms in either clothing or behavior and has identified intensely with the other sex. **Transgender** is currently the umbrella term for those whose gender expression or identity is not congruent with the sex assigned at birth and whose gender is not validated by the dominant culture.

Masculinity and Femininity: Opposites, Similar, or Blended?

Each culture determines the content of gender roles in its own way; however, cultural norms fluctuate and change with time and across cultures. Among the Arapesh of New Guinea, for example, members of both sexes possess what we consider feminine traits. Both men and women tend to be passive, cooperative, peaceful, and nurturing. The father as well as the mother is said to "bear a child"; only the father's continual care can make the child grow healthily, both in the womb and in childhood. Eighty miles away, the Mundugumor live in remarkable contrast to the peaceful Arapesh. "Both men and women," Margaret Mead (1975) observed, "are expected to be violent, competitive, aggressively sexed, jealous, and ready to see and avenge insult, delighting in display, in action, in fighting." Biology creates males and females, but it is culture that creates our concepts of masculinity and femininity and its inherent fluidity and complexity.

In the traditional Western view of masculinity and femininity, men and women have been seen as polar opposites. Our terminology, in fact, reflects this view. Women and men refer to each other as the "opposite sex." But this implies that women and men are indeed opposites, that they have little in common. (We use "other sex" in this book.) Our gender stereotypes have fit this pattern of polar differences: Men are aggressive, whereas women are passive; men embody **instrumentality** and are task-oriented, whereas women embody **expressiveness** and are emotion-oriented; men are rational, whereas women are irrational; men want sex, whereas women want love; and so on.

Changes in gender stereotypes and related expectations have been occurring over the past decades such that as women have moved into the workforce and taken on occupations previously ascribed to men, their self-views and perceptions have also evolved and expanded. While the male stereotype in recent decades has not significantly changed, one might argue that the female stereotype has become more fluid. These changes in gender stereotypes are most likely linked to global shifts in culture, politics, and economics (Lips, 2014).

It is important to recognize that gender-role stereotypes, despite their depiction of men and women as opposites, are usually not all-or-nothing notions. Most of us do not think that only men are assertive or only women are nurturing. Stereotypes merely reflect *probabilities* that a woman or a man will have a certain characteristic based on her or his gender. When we say that men are more independent than women, we simply mean that there is a greater probability that a man will be more independent than a woman.

Recently, many individuals have been rejecting the traditional binary model of male versus female gender identity. Once again, this may be suggestive of greater acknowledgment of gender fluidity, which needs to be understood if we are to embrace the complex nature of gender and sexual expression.

Men are taught to apologize for their weaknesses, women for their strength.

—Lois Wyse
(1926–2007)

The main difference between men and women is that men are lunatics and women are idiots.

—Rebecca West
(1892–1983)

Same-sex marriage has been on the political radar as legislation and legal action change around the world.

© Aristide Economopoulos/Star Ledger/Corbis

Stereotypes fall in the face of humanity . . . this is how the world will change for gay men and lesbians.

—Anna Quindlen
(1953–)

Sexism, discrimination against people based on their sex rather than their individual merits, is often associated with gender stereotypes and may prevent individuals from expressing their full range of emotions or seeking certain vocations. A different and more hostile form of prejudice is **misogyny,** or the hatred of or disdain for women. Sexism may discourage a woman from pursuing a career in math or inhibit a man from choosing nursing as a profession. Children may develop stereotypes about differences between men and women and carry these into their adult lives.

As technology becomes more advanced, we learn more about what contributes to making the sexes different. We are recognizing that our identities as men and women are a combination of nature and nurture. It is through new technology that researchers can observe brains in the act of cogitating, feeling, or remembering. In fact, many differences and similarities that were once attributed to learning or culture have been found to be biologically based. Add to this our individual choices, sense of identities, environmental factors, and life experiences, and we can begin to get a picture of what contributes to making each person unique.

Gender and Sexual Orientation

Gender, gender identity, and gender role are conceptually independent of sexual orientation. But in many people's minds, these concepts are closely related to sexual orientation. Our traditional notion of gender roles assumes that heterosexuality is a critical component of masculinity and femininity. That is, a "masculine" man is attracted to women and a "feminine" woman is attracted to men. From this assumption follow two beliefs about homosexuality: (1) If a man is gay, he cannot be masculine, and if a woman is lesbian, she cannot be feminine; and (2) if a man is gay, he must have some feminine characteristics, and if a woman is lesbian, she must have some masculine characteristics. What these beliefs imply is that homosexuality is somehow associated with a failure to fill traditional gender roles. A "real" man is not gay; therefore, gay men are not "real" men. Similarly, a "real" woman is not a lesbian; therefore, lesbian women are not "real" women. These negative stereotypes, which hold that people fall into distinct genders, with natural roles, and are presumed to be heterosexual, are referred to as **heteronormativity.**

● Gender-Role Learning

As we have seen, gender roles are socially constructed and rooted in culture. So how do individuals learn what their society expects of them as males or females?

Theories of Socialization

It is important to recognize that definitions and concepts of how gender emerges come from a wide variety of theoretical perspectives. Theories influence how we approach sexuality research, practice, education, and policy. Two of the most prominent theories are cognitive social learning theory and cognitive development theory. In the study of sexuality, a growing body of literature uses a social constructionist theory on gender, including queer theory.

Cognitive social learning theory is derived from behavioral psychology. In explaining our actions, behaviorists emphasize observable events and their consequences, rather than internal feelings and drives. According to behaviorists, we learn attitudes and behaviors as a result of social interactions with others—hence the term "social learning" (Bandura, 1977).

The cornerstone of cognitive social learning theory is the belief that consequences control behavior. Behaviors that are regularly followed by a reward are likely to occur again; behaviors that are regularly followed by a punishment are less likely to recur. Thus, girls are rewarded for playing with dolls ("What a nice mommy!"), but boys are not ("What a sissy!").

This behaviorist approach has been modified to include cognition—mental processes that intervene between stimulus and response, such as evaluation and reflection. The cognitive processes involved in social learning include our ability to: (1) use language, (2) anticipate consequences, and (3) make observations. By using language, we can tell our daughter that we like it when she does well in school and that we don't like it when she hits someone. A person's ability to anticipate consequences affects behavior. A boy doesn't need to wear lace stockings in public to know that such dressing will lead to negative consequences. Finally, children observe what others do. A girl may learn that she "shouldn't" play video games by seeing that the players in video arcades are mostly boys.

We also learn gender roles by imitation, through a process called modeling. Most of us are not even aware of the many subtle behaviors that make up gender roles—the ways in which men and women use different mannerisms and gestures, speak differently, use different body language, and so on. Initially, the most powerful models that children have are their parents. As children grow older and their social world expands, so does the number of people who may act as their role models, including siblings, friends, teachers, athletes, and media figures. Children sift through the various demands and expectations associated with the different models to create their own unique selves.

In contrast to cognitive social learning theory, **cognitive development theory** (Kohlberg, 1966) focuses on children's active interpretation of the messages they receive from the environment. Whereas cognitive social learning theory assumes that children and adults learn in fundamentally the same way, cognitive development theory stresses that we learn differently depending on our age. At age 2, children can correctly identify themselves and others as boys or girls, but they tend to base this identification on superficial features such as hair and clothing: Girls have long hair and wear dresses; boys have short hair and wear pants. Some children even believe they can change their gender by changing their clothes or hair length. When children are 6 or 7, they begin to understand that gender is permanent; it is not something they can alter in the same way they can change their clothes. Children not only understand the permanence of gender but also tend to insist on rigid adherence to gender-role stereotypes.

Social construction theory views gender as a set of practices and performances that occur through language and a political system (Bartky, 1990; Butler, 1993; Connell, 1995; Gergen, 1985). Social constructionists suggest that gendered meanings are only one vehicle through which sexuality is constituted. Another way of viewing gender is through the lens of **queer theory,** which identifies gender and sexuality as systems that are not gender neutral and cannot be understood by the actions of heterosexual males and females (Parker & Gagnon, 1995). Queer theory views the meaning and realities associated with sexuality as socially constructed to serve political systems. They furthermore underscore the role of institutional power in shaping the ideas of what is normal, deviant, natural, or essential. Thus, a social constructionist approach to gender would inquire about ways in which males and females make meaning out of their experiences with their bodies, their relationships, and their sexual choices, while queer theorists would challenge the notion of gender as fixed and seek to reframe it as being socially constructed and hence varying with context.

The war between the sexes is the only one in which both sides regularly sleep with the enemy.

—Quentin Crisp
(1908–1999)

If men knew all that women think, they'd be twenty times more audacious.

—Alphonse Kerr
(1808–1890)

Gender-Role Learning in Childhood and Adolescence

It is difficult to analyze the relationship between biology and personality because learning begins at birth. In our culture, infant girls are usually held more gently and treated more tenderly than boys, who are ordinarily subjected to rougher forms of play. The first day after birth, parents may characterize their daughters as soft, fine-featured, and small and their sons as strong, large-featured, big, and bold. When children do not measure up to these expectations, they may stop trying to express their authentic feelings and emotions.

Parents as Socializing Agents During infancy and early childhood, children's most important source of learning is the primary caregiver, whether the mother, father, grandmother, or someone else. Many parents are not aware that their words and actions contribute to their children's gender-role socialization. Nor are they aware that they treat their daughters and sons differently because of their gender. Although parents may recognize that they respond differently to sons than to daughters, they usually have a ready explanation: the "natural" differences in the temperament and behavior of girls and boys.

Children are socialized in gender roles through several very subtle processes (Oakley, 1985):

- *Manipulation.* Parents manipulate their children from infancy onward. They treat a daughter gently, tell her she is pretty, and advise her that nice girls do not fight. They treat a son roughly, tell him he is strong, and advise him that big boys do not cry. Eventually, most children incorporate their parents' views in such matters as integral parts of their personalities.

  - *Channeling.* Children are channeled by directing their attention to specific objects. Toys, for example, are differentiated by sex. Dolls are considered appropriate for girls, and cars for boys.

  - *Verbal appellation.* Parents use different words with boys and girls to describe the same behavior. A boy who pushes others may be described as "active," whereas a girl who does the same is usually called "aggressive."

  - *Activity exposure.* The activity exposure of girls and boys differs markedly. Although both are usually exposed to a variety of activities early in life, boys are discouraged from imitating their mothers, whereas girls are encouraged to be "mother's little helper."

Although numerous studies have examined gender roles and their importance, most have focused primarily on the traditional mainstream of White, middle-class, heterosexual people, many of whom underscore the idea that women's primary roles should be centered around the home and family. Social roles, cultural traditions, economic realities, acculturation, and individual self-determination, however, have changed the landscape of gender roles in this country and worldwide.

As a result of their heritage of slavery, which meant among other things that women could not depend economically on men, African American women have represented the symbol of strength in their communities. This may account in part for more egalitarian roles and assignment of household chores as not seen in other

> *What are little girls made of? Sugar and spice And everything nice. That's what little girls are made of. What are little boys made of? Snips and snails And puppy dogs' tails. That's what little boys are made of.*
>
> —Nursery rhyme

Parents' influence on children is fundamental to their healthy development.

© trbfoto/Brand X Pictures/Jupiterimages

ethnic or cultural groups (Glauber, 2008). There is also some evidence that African American families socialize their daughters to be more self-reliant and assertive than White families do (Hill, 2002). The African American female role model in which the woman is both wage-earner and homemaker is more common and more accurately reflects the African American experience than does the traditional female role model. As for African American boys, those who had the same relationship with their mothers as the girls tended to be just as engaged, happy, and relaxed as the girls (Mandara, Murray, Telesford, Varner, & Richman, 2012).

The Hispanic cultural stereotypes of *marianismo* and *machismo,* derived from the Roman Catholic belief that women should be pure and self-giving, has created a double standard that encourages boys to be sexually adventurous and girls to be virtuous and virginal (Bourdeau, Thomas, & Long, 2008). Assimilation, urbanization, and upward mobility of Hispanic Americans, however, have challenged and reduced gender-role inequities, especially among young Hispanic Americans (Cespedes & Huey, 2008).

Asian Americans represent a diverse number of cultures and beliefs. Traditionally, the woman is expected to adhere to family obligations over individual aspirations. Many attitudes and practices, however, often change with increased exposure to American culture (Okazaki, 2002). Though no typical pattern exists, young Asian Americans are less likely to embrace culturally based gender-role stereotypes than are older Asian Americans (Ying & Han, 2008).

As children grow older, their social world expands, and so do their sources of learning. Around the time children enter day care or kindergarten, teachers and peers become important influences.

The beautiful bird gets caged.
—Chinese proverb

Teachers as Socializing Agents Day-care centers, nursery schools, and kindergartens are often children's first experience in the world outside the family. Teachers become important role models for their students. Because most day-care workers and kindergarten and elementary school teachers are women, children tend to think of child-adult interactions as primarily the province of women. In this sense, schools reinforce the idea that women are concerned with children and men are not. Teachers may also tend to be conventional in the gender-role

Among African Americans, the traditional female gender role includes strength and independence.

© Brendan Smialowski/Getty Images

messages they convey to children (Sadker & Zittleman, 2005). They may encourage different activities and abilities in boys and girls such as contact sports for boys and gymnastics or dance for girls. Academically, teachers tend to rate females higher than males in both math and science (Robinson & Lubienski, 2011). Nevertheless, beginning in fifth grade, females lose some ground in math, but they regain test scores in middle school. Gaps favoring females widen among low-achieving students. It has also been observed that teachers and parents may shame males into conforming to the traditional image of masculinity. For example, males are taught to hide their emotions, act brave, and demonstrate independence. Even though males may get good grades and be considered normal, healthy, and well-adjusted by peers, parents, and teachers, they may also report feeling deeply troubled about the roles and goals of their gender.

Gender bias often follows students into the college arena and can be witnessed both in and outside the classroom. This environment coupled with high rates of sexual violence has resulted in impediments to academic success, lower graduation rates, health problems, and mental health issues (American College Health Association [ACHA], 2011). In recognition of this campus and public health concern, the ACHA has suggested policy and programming that reflect intolerance for sexual bias and violence across its continuum—from sexist statements to sexual harassment to sexual assault.

Peers as Socializing Agents   Children's age-mates, or peers, become especially important when they enter school. By granting or withholding approval, friends and playmates influence what games children play, what they wear, what music they listen to, what TV programs they watch, and even what cereal they eat. Peers provide standards for gender-role behavior in several ways:

- Peers provide information about gender-role norms through play activities and toys. Girls often play with dolls that cry and wet themselves or with glamorous dolls with well-developed figures and expensive tastes. Boys often play with video games in which they kill and maim in order to dominate and win.

- Peers influence the adoption of gender-role norms through verbal approval or disapproval. "That's for boys!" or "Only girls do that!" is a strong negative message to the girl playing with a football or the boy playing with dolls.

When boys and girls participate in sports together, they develop comparable athletic skills. Segregation of boys and girls encourages the development of differences that otherwise might not occur.

© Fuse/Getty Images

- Children's perceptions of their friends' gender-role attitudes, behaviors, and beliefs encourage them to adopt similar ones to be accepted. If a girl's same-sex friends play soccer, she is more likely to play soccer. If a boy's same-sex friends display feelings, he is more likely to display feelings.

Even though parents tend to fear the worst in general from peers, peers can provide important positive influences. It is within their peer groups, for example, that adolescents learn to develop intimate relationships.

Media Influences   Media and the public benefit when a broad range of voices are included; however, much of television and video programming promotes or condones negative stereotypes about gender, ethnicity, age, ability, and sexual orientation. Female characters on television typically are under age 30, well groomed, thin, and attractive. In contrast, male characters are aggressive and constructive; they solve problems and rescue others from danger. Indeed, all forms of media glorify stereotypical gender norms. With 24/7 access to media, beginning as early as 5 years of age or younger, the influence of media cannot be understated or ignored.

That's not me you're in love with. That's my image. You don't even know me.

—Kelly McGillis
(1957–)

Gender Schemas: Exaggerating Differences

Actual differences between females and males are minimal or nonexistent, except in levels of aggressiveness and visual/spatial skills, yet culture exaggerates these differences or creates differences where none otherwise exist. One way that culture does this is by creating a schema: a set of interrelated ideas that helps us process information by categorizing it in a variety of ways. We often categorize people by age, ethnicity, nationality, physical characteristics, and so on. Gender is one such way of categorizing.

Psychologist Sandra Bem (1983) observed that although gender is not inherent in inanimate objects or in behaviors, we treat many objects and behaviors as if they were masculine or feminine. These gender divisions form a complex structure of associations that affects our perceptions of reality. Bem referred to this cognitive organization of the world according to gender as a **gender schema.** We use gender schemas in many dimensions of life, including activities (nurturing, fighting), emotions (compassion, anger), behavior (playing with dolls or action figures), clothing (dresses or pants), and even colors (pink or blue), considering some appropriate for one gender and some appropriate for the other.

Processing information by gender is important in cultures such as ours, for several reasons. First, gender-schema cultures make multiple associations between gender and other non-sex-linked qualities such as affection and strength. Our culture regards affection as a feminine trait and strength as a masculine one. Second, such cultures make gender distinctions important, using them as a basis for norms, status, taboos, and privileges. These associations, however, often undermine and undervalue the uniqueness of individuals.

● Contemporary Gender Roles and Scripts

In the past several decades, there has been a significant shift toward more egalitarian gender roles. Although women's roles have changed more than men's, men's are also changing, and these changes seem to affect all socioeconomic classes. Members of conservative religious groups still tend to adhere most strongly to traditional gender roles. Despite the ongoing disagreement, it is likely that the egalitarian trend will continue.

Traditional Gender Roles and Scripts

As has been previously discussed, much of what we believe about men and women come from stereotypes and the popular media. Cartoons that depict the male brain as filled with nothing other than fantasies of sex and that depict women as obsessing and conniving to obtain love are so prevalent that they are barely entertaining. What purpose, if any, do these roles serve?

The Traditional Male Gender Role

What does it take to be a man? What is a real man? One can simply go online to find stereotypical jokes, images, and lyrics to demonstrate what this looks like. The real answer to this question, however, is complex, multifaceted, dynamic, and dependent on a variety of factors (Bowleg, Teti, Massie, et al., 2011).

Central personality traits associated with the traditional male role—no matter the race or ethnicity—may include aggressiveness, emotional toughness, independence, feelings of superiority, and decisiveness. Males are generally regarded as being more power-oriented than females, and they exhibit higher levels of aggression, especially violent aggression, dominance, and competitiveness. Although these tough, aggressive traits may be useful in the corporate world, politics, and the military (or in hunting saber-toothed tigers), they are rarely helpful to a man in his intimate relationships, which require understanding, cooperation, communication, and nurturing.

What perpetuates the image of the dominance of men, and what role does it serve in a society that no longer needs or respects such an image? It may be that a human's task is not to define gender roles but rather to redefine what it means to be human.

Male Sexual Scripts

Different from a role, which is a more generalized behavior, a **script** consists of the behaviors, rules, and expectations associated with a particular role. It is like the script handed out to an actor. Unlike most dramatic scripts, however, social scripts allow for considerable improvisation within their general boundaries. We are given many scripts in life according to the various roles we play. Among them are sexual scripts that outline how we are to behave sexually when acting out our gender roles. Sexual scripts and gender roles for heterosexuals may be different from those for gay, lesbian, bisexual, or transgender people. Perceptions and patterns in sexual behavior are shaped by sexual scripts.

Psychologist Bernie Zilbergeld (1992) suggested that the male sexual script includes the following elements:

- *Men should not have (or at least should not express) certain feelings.* Men should not express doubts; they should be assertive, confident, and aggressive. Tenderness and compassion are not masculine emotions.

- *Performance is the thing that counts.* Sex is something to be achieved, to win at. Feelings only get in the way of the job to be done. Sex is not for intimacy but for orgasm.

- *The man is in charge.* As in other realms, the man is the leader, the person who knows what is best. The man initiates sex and gives the woman her orgasm. A real man doesn't need a woman to tell him what women like; he already knows.

- *A man always wants sex and is ready for it.* No matter what else is going on, a man wants sex; he is always able to become erect. He is a machine.

- *All physical contact leads to sex.* Because men are basically sexual machines, any physical contact is a sign for sex. Touching is seen as the

A man is by nature a sexual animal. I've always had my share of pets.

—Mae West
(1893–1980)

Men ought to be more conscious of their bodies as an object of delight.

—Germaine Greer
(1939–)

first step toward sexual intercourse, not an end in itself. There is no physical pleasure other than sexual pleasure.

- *Sex equals intercourse.* All erotic contact leads to sexual intercourse. Foreplay is just that: warming up, getting one's partner ready for penetration. Kissing, hugging, erotic touching, and oral sex are only preliminaries to intercourse.

- *Sexual intercourse leads to orgasm.* The orgasm is the "proof in the pudding." The more orgasms, the better the sex. If a woman does not have an orgasm, she is not sexual. The male feels that he is a failure because he was not good enough to give her an orgasm. If she requires clitoral stimulation to have an orgasm, she has a problem.

Common to all these myths is a separation of sex from love and attachment. Sex is seen as performance.

The Traditional Female Gender Role   Though there are striking ethnic and individual differences, traditional female roles are expressive, or assume emotional or supportive characteristics. They emphasize passivity, compliance, physical attractiveness, and being a partner or wife and mother.

In recent years, the traditional role has been modified to include work and marriage. Work roles, however, are clearly subordinated to marital and family roles. Upon the birth of the first child, the woman is expected to both work and parent or, if economically feasible, to become a full-time mother.

Female Sexual Scripts   Whereas the traditional male sexual script focuses on sex over feelings, the traditional female sexual script focuses on feelings over sex, on love over passion. The traditional female sexual script cited by psychologist and sex therapist Lonnie Barbach (2001) includes the following ideas:

- *Sex is good and bad.* Women are taught that sex is both good and bad. What makes sex good? Sex in marriage or a committed relationship. What makes sex bad? Sex in a casual or uncommitted relationship. Sex is "so good" that a woman needs to save it for her husband (or for someone with whom she is deeply in love). Sex is bad—if it is not sanctioned by love or marriage, a woman will get a bad reputation.

- *It's not OK to touch themselves "down there."* Girls are taught not to look at their genitals, not to touch them, and especially not to explore them. As a result, some women know very little about their genitals. They are often concerned about vaginal odors and labia size, making them uncomfortable about oral sex.

- *Sex is for men.* Men want sex; women want love. Women are sexually passive, waiting to be aroused. Sex is not a pleasurable activity as an end in itself; it is something performed *by* women *for* men.

- *Men should know what women want.* This script tells women that men know what they want even if women don't tell them. The woman is supposed to remain pure and sexually innocent. It is up to the man to arouse the woman even if he doesn't know what she finds arousing. To keep her image of sexual innocence, she does not tell him what she wants.

- *Women shouldn't talk about sex.* Many women are uncomfortable talking about sex because they are expected not to have strong sexual feelings. Some women (and men) may know their partners well

A man can sleep around, no questions asked, but if a woman makes nineteen or twenty mistakes, she's a tramp.

—Joan Rivers
(1933–2014)

Women are made, not born.

—Simone de Beauvoir
(1908–1986)

think
about it

The Purity Standard: Defining Women by Their Sexuality

So what is this thing called virginity and what does it have to say about women and men? Feminist writer and scholar Jessica Valenti, in her book *The Purity Myth: How America's Obsession With Virginity Is Hurting Young Women* (2009), takes a sharp and uncompromising look at purity, virginity, and abstinence education and provides solid evidence to reveal how the myth of "saving one-self" especially is hurting girls and women. Valenti states: "The message that the virginity movement is working so hard to send to women [is that] sex makes us less whole and a whole lot dirtier."

Outside of the occasional reference to the male virgin, the term "virgin" is almost always synonymous with "woman." Even the dictionary definitions of virgin cite an "unmarried girl or woman" or a "religious woman, especially a saint." No such characterization exists for men or boys. The relationship between sexual purity and women makes the concept of virginity, normalcy, and acceptance a dangerous mix, yet one that few are willing to challenge.

In fact, normalcy itself is hard to define, but there is a lot of evidence to purport that it is no longer defined by women or men. Rather, the media seem to be gaining an upper hand on what is viewed as acceptable and "normal," in terms of both gender and gender roles. Center stage is sexuality whereby, among girls, virginity is seemingly the only truly valued personal characteristic. Women's identities are seemingly tied up with whether or not they've had sex, or how sexual or abstinent they are.

Some of these purity efforts can be seen in the use of "V-cards," where, for example, abstinence commitment cards are distributed to students or sold on a website, along with a note that the card can be kept in their wallet to remind them of their decision to remain abstinent. In this case, not only is being sexual discouraged, virginity is commodified. Or consider the gold rose pin with an attached small card that reads, "You are like a beautiful rose. Each time you engage in premarital sex, a precious petal is stripped away.

Don't leave your future husband holding a bare stem. Abstain." The message is clear: Without virginity, you're secondhand goods.

Society's current version of sexuality also makes it difficult for young women to have a healthy sexual outlook that centers on their desires. In fact, it appears that most desirable women are not women at all—they're girls. No one embodies the "perfect" young American woman like beauty queens. They're pretty, thin, anxious to please, and supposedly virgin-like. Contrary to these models of women are those of "girls-gone-wild" and "raunch culture" seen in the media where young women are connected to disturbing narratives with some degree of pathologized sexuality. All of these images can lead to the emotional, moral, and spiritual erosion of women's sexuality.

Creating new media, critiquing online sources, launching more nationwide campaigns, taking action when abstinence education is up for refunding, and educating the people in our lives about sexuality-related issues we care about are significant initiatives that can help change the way we regard women and sexuality. Continuing to tell the truth about how young women are suffering under an unrealistic model of sexuality is a risky act, but one that can be accomplished.

Think Critically

1. How do you define virginity? Where did this definition come from (parents, friends, society)? To whom does it most apply? Why?

2. What are your thoughts about female sexuality? Male sexuality? How do these views affect you?

3. What are some ways of creating a more positive perception of women's sexuality?

SOURCE: Adapted from Valenti, J. (2009). *The purity myth: How America's obsession with virginity is hurting young women.* Berkeley, CA: Seal Press.

enough to have sex with them but not well enough to communicate their needs to them.

- *Women should look like models.* The media present ideally attractive women as beautiful models with slender hips, supple breasts, and no fat or cellulite; they are always young, with never a pimple, wrinkle, or gray hair in sight. As a result of these cultural images, many women are self-conscious about their physical appearance. They worry that they are too fat, too plain, or too old. Because of their imagined flaws, they often feel awkward without clothes on.

- *Women are nurturers.* Women give; men receive. Women give themselves, their bodies, their pleasures to men. Everyone else's needs come first: his desire over hers, his orgasm over hers.

- *There is only one right way to have an orgasm.* Women often "learn" that there is only one "right" way to have an orgasm: during sexual inter-course as a result of penile stimulation.

Changing Gender Roles and Scripts

Contemporary gender roles are evolving from traditional hierarchical gender roles (in which one sex is subordinate to the other) to egalitarian roles (in which both sexes are treated equally) and to androgynous roles (in which both sexes display the traits of instrumentality and expressiveness previously associated with only one sex). Thus, contemporary gender roles often display traditional elements along with egalitarian and androgynous ones. Furthermore, they operate on cultural, intrapersonal, and interpersonal levels, each one influencing the other to impact the individual's sexual beliefs and behaviors (Masters, Casey, Wells, & Morrison, 2013).

Contemporary Sexual Scripts The role of culture in guiding gender scripts tends to be remarkably similar to that seen in traditional, mainstream, dominant literature; both influence and mold attitudes and behaviors (Masters et al., 2013). At the individual level, however, many desire or enact very different scripts than those they cite as cultural norms. For example, one might conform ideologically to stereotypical beliefs about men, women, and sex yet might demonstrate very different attitudes or behaviors. This may be the case with a woman who believes in marriage yet tends to be more sexually open and unwilling to play by the rules. Another person might seek to transform the sexual scripts he or she learned so that they are distinctly different from mainstream cultural scripts. A man might acknowledge being part of a sexual subculture where verbal consent is very, very important, where no means no and yes may need elaboration or clarification. A woman might initiate a no-strings-attached sexual relationship even while acknowledging that it is more typical for a man to seek this type of partnership. Such shifts suggest progress in transforming sexual scripts to those that are more congruent, authentic, and reflective of one's individual needs and values.

Contemporary sexual scripts include the following elements for both sexes:

- Sexual expression is positive and healthy.

- Sexual activities involve a mutual exchange of erotic pleasure.

- Sexuality is equally involving, and both partners are equally responsible.

- Legitimate sexual activities are not limited to sexual intercourse but include a wide variety of sexual expression.

> " *I don't know why people are afraid of new ideas. I am terrified of the old ones.*
>
> —John Cage
> (1912–1992)

Men have traditionally coached women's and men's sports teams without ever being questioned or challenged. Becky Hammon made history when she became the first woman in the U.S. to hold a full-time coaching position in the NBA ever.

© Matt York/AP Images

- Sexual activities may be initiated by either partner.
- Both partners have the freedom to accept sexual pleasure and experience orgasm, no matter from what type of stimulation.

These contemporary scripts can support intimacy and satisfaction by allowing individuals to better understand gender-related issues and their impact on relationships. This deepened understanding along with the celebration of the uniqueness of each individual can assist couples in recognizing and freeing themselves from ineffectual and limiting stereotypes.

Androgyny   Some scholars have challenged the traditional masculine/feminine gender-role dichotomy, arguing that such models are unhealthy and fail to reflect the real world. Instead of looking at gender roles in terms of polar opposites, they suggest examining them in terms of androgyny. **Androgyny** refers to the combination of both traditional masculine and feminine qualities. (The term "androgyny" is derived from the Greek *andros,* "man," and *gyne,* "woman.") An androgynous person combines the trait of instrumentality traditionally associated with masculinity with the trait of expressiveness traditionally associated with femininity. An androgynous lifestyle allows men and women to choose from the full range of emotions and behaviors, according to their temperament, situation, and common humanity, rather than their gender.

Flexibility and adaptability are important aspects of androgyny. Individuals who rigidly express instrumentality or expressiveness, despite the situation, are not considered androgynous. A woman who is always aggressive at work and passive at home, for example, would not be considered androgynous, as work may call for compassion and home life for assertion.

Filling an androgynous gender role, however, may be just as stultifying to an individual as trying to be traditionally feminine or masculine. In advocating the expression of both feminine and masculine traits, perhaps we are imposing a new form of gender-role rigidity on ourselves.

● Gender Variations

For most of us, there is no question about our gender: We *know* we are female or male. We may question our femininity or masculinity, but rarely do we question being female or male. For gender-variant individuals, or those who see themselves as part of a normal phenomenon with a right to self-definition and actualization in regard to sexual identity, "What sex am I?" is a dilemma. Their answer to this question reinforces the fact that little is known about the origins of a gender identity, whether cisgender or transgender (Dresher, 2014). What is reported reinforces the fact that psychosexual development is influenced by multiple factors, including exposure to androgens, sex chromosome genes, and brain structure, as well as social circumstances and family dynamics (Hughes, Houk, Ahmed, Lee, et al., 2006). The American Psychiatric Association Task Force report acknowledged:

> Opinions vary widely among experts and are influenced by theoretical orientation as well as assumptions and beliefs (including religious) regarding the origins, meanings and perceived fixity or malleability of gender identity (Byne et al., 2012, p. 76).

Over time, more individuals have been rejecting the traditional binary model of male versus female gender identity (Singh et al., 2010). This may be suggestive

Gender variance is behavior or expression that does not match masculine or feminine gender norms.

© Francisco Romero/iStock/Getty Images

Once made equal to man, woman becomes his superior.

—Socrates
(c. 469–399 BCE)

Throughout history the more complex activities have been defined and redefined, now as male, now as female—sometimes as drawing equally on the gifts of both sexes. When an activity to which each sex could have contributed is limited to one sex, a rich, differentiated quality is lost from the activity itself.

—Margaret Mead
(1901–1978)

of greater acknowledgment of gender fluidity, which needs to be understood if we are to embrace the complex nature of gender and sexual expression. The global third-gender movement is gaining momentum, with laws and language trying to keep pace. This category, sometimes referred to as "nonspecific," is "broad, mind-boggling and potentially subversive" in terms of the ways we think about the sexes and our habit of dividing people into two distinct groups (Baird, 2014). For example, in order to keep up with the third-gender movement, Facebook recently announced that it would offer users 50 different possibilities of gender identification (Ball, 2014). Under "Basic Information," the drop-down box includes identities such as non-binary, intersex, neutrois, androgyne, agender, gender questioning, and gender fluid. Though some of the terms are not yet found in dictionaries, they are part of a language that is still evolving. What many know is that the terms "male" and "female" are too confining.

Because our culture views sexual anatomy as a male/female dichotomy, it is difficult for many people to accept another view of gender variation, that of a gender continuum (see Figure 1). Note that the gender continuum includes a multitude of gender-variant identities, all of which reflect the diversity of human expression. Most people still think of genetic sex—XX or XY—as a person's "true sex." Because gender is related to biological sex for most people, one of the primary challenges facing the public is to place the transgender experience into a context by which it can be understood and accepted. Transgender people are some of the most vulnerable members of American society (Human Rights Campaign, 2014.5a). While transgender people are most familiar with gender-variant expressions and cross-gender identities, there are many other forms of gender variance exhibited by all kinds of people. Revealing these other forms of gender variance can provide an important context to understand transgender people. At the same time, it is important to recognize that none of the forms of gender variance necessarily makes anyone a transgender, gay, lesbian, or bisexual individual.

The Transgender Phenomenon

In recent years, there has been a major shift in the gender world. Upsetting old definitions and classification systems, a new transgender community, one that embraces the possibility of numerous genders and multiple social identities, has emerged. Though the transgender population makes up only about 0.3% of the U.S. adult population, it has slowly become a visible and proactive group in mainstream media and politics (Chalabi, 2014).

Transgender is an inclusive category. The term "transgenderist" was first coined by Virginia Prince, the founder of the U.S. contemporary cross-dressing community, to describe someone who lives full-time in a gender role different from the gender role presumed by society to match the person's genetic sex (Richards, 1997).

• **FIGURE** 1

Gender Variations: The Gender Continuum. In contrast to the traditional binary view, the concept of gender is on a continuum with a multitude of gender-variant identities.

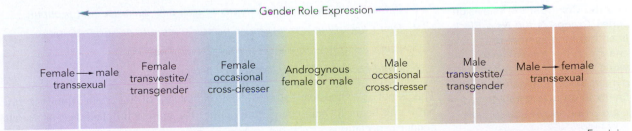

Gender Role Expression

Female → male transsexual

Female transvestite/ transgender

Female occasional cross-dresser

Androgynous female or male

Male occasional cross-dresser

Male transvestite/ transgender

Male → female transsexual

Masculine

Feminine

Caitlyn Jenner poses for Annie Leib the cover of Vanity Fair #CallMeCait vnty.fr/1AFTXXc

Caitlyn Jenner stunned the world when she make it clear that her self-identity allows her to finally be her own person: a free woman.

© Mladen Antonov/AFP/Getty Images

> *Treat people as if they were what they ought to be and you help them become what they are capable of being.*
>
> —Johann Goethe (1749–1832)

Laverne Cox from the television series *Orange Is the New Black* is an inspiring symbol of change in the transgender world and the first transgender person to be nominated for an Emmy in an acting category.

© Rabbani and Solimene Photography/ Getty Images

In past decades, those who were transgender could escape from the traditional male and female categories only if they were "diagnosed" as transvestite or transsexual (Denny, 1997). This resulted in a larger number of "heterosexual" cross-dressers who were actually gay or bisexual or who had transsexual issues. It also involved diagnosis on the part of the psychiatric community and subsequent labeling and stigma. In North America, a paradigm shift has occurred that challenges the male/female dichotomy of gender, thereby making it more acceptable to live without the threat of "cure."

Transgenderist Sky Renfro describes his gender identity (quoted in Feinberg, 1996):

> My identity, like everything else in my life, is a journey. It is a process and an adventure that in some ways brings me back to myself, back into the grand circle of living. . . . My sense of who I am at any given time is somewhere on that wheel and the place that I occupy there can change depending on the season and life events as well as a number of other influences. Trying to envision masculine at one end of a line and feminine on the other, with the rest of us somewhere on that line, is a difficult concept for me to grasp. Male and female—they're so close to each other, they sit next to each other on that wheel. They are not at opposite ends as far as I can tell. In fact, they are so close that they're sometimes not distinguishable.

Transgender people are defined according to their gender identity and presentation (Institute of Medicine, 2011). This group encompasses individuals whose gender identity differs from the sex originally assigned to them at birth or whose gender expression varies significantly from what is traditionally associated with that sex, as well as others who vary from or reject traditional cultural views of gender. Transgender people can be heterosexual, homosexual, or bisexual in their sexual orientation and may represent their sexual orientation in non-binary ways, such as queer or **pansexual,** being sexually interested in and open to other people regardless of gender (Kuper, Nussbaum, & Mustanski, 2012). In fact, many individuals may wish to represent their attractions in ways that do not specifically reference their own sex or gender, which may be in transition, fluid, or not fully captured by a label.

Support and treatment are no longer aimed at identifying the "true transsexual" but is open instead to the possibility of affirming a unique transgender identity and role. To help in understanding and respecting transgender people, the Gay & Lesbian Alliance Against Defamation (GLAAD) (2014) has developed "Tips for Allies of Transgender People," which include the following:

1. *Respect the terminology transgender persons use to describe their identity.*
2. *Don't make assumptions about a person's sexual orientation.*
3. *If you don't know what pronouns to use, ask; then use that pronoun.*
4. *Don't ask about a transgender person's genitals or surgical status.*
5. *Don't ask a person what his or her "real name" is.*
6. *Avoid backhanded compliments or "helpful" tips.*

This is not an exhaustive list nor does it include all of the "right" things to say, but it can begin to help change the culture for those who challenge or violate gender expectations.

think
about it

Psychological and Medical Treatment of Gender Dysphoria

For those seeking care for gender dysphoria, a person's sense of 'incongruence' or intense discomfort with their natural or birth gender, a variety of therapeutic options are available. These treatments are focused on helping maximize overall psychological well-being and fulfillment among transsexual, transgender, and gender nonconforming individuals and those who care about them. In fact, most medical groups, including the American Medical Association and the American Psychological Association, consider sex reassignment surgery (also known as gender reassignment surgery or gender affirmation) to be a safe option for those experiencing gender dysphoria. In 2014, the Obama administration ended a 33-year ban on Medicare coverage for sex reassignment surgery—a decision that is likely to put pressure on more insurers to provide coverage for such services.

Changes in Gender Expression and Role

Living part-time or full-time as a member in another gender role, consistent with one's gender identity, is essential. This is not an easy task, for such subtle gender clues as mannerisms, voice inflections, and body movement, learned in childhood, must be altered.

Psychotherapy

Many individuals, couples, families, or groups find that psychotherapy, either in-person or online support, can be helpful for purposes such as exploring gender identity, role, and expression; addressing the negative impact of gender dysphoria and stigmas; alleviating internalized transphobia, a negative attitude toward transsexual people; enhancing social and peer support; improving body image; and promoting resilience. Though effective for many, psychotherapy is not an absolute requirement for other types of treatments. If, on the other hand, a person seeks sex reassignment surgery, Standards of Care (SOC) (World Professional Association, 2012) recommend that one referral from a qualified mental health professional be required for breast/chest surgery, while two referrals from qualified mental health professionals be required for genital surgery.

Hormone Therapy

Feminizing/masculinizing hormone treatment is a medically necessary intervention for many transsexual, trans-gender, and gender nonconforming individuals. When physicians administer androgens (testosterone) to female-to-male patients and estrogens, progesterone, and testosterone-blocking agents to male-to-female patients, physical changes that are more congruent with a patient's gender identity will occur over the course of 2 years. Hormone therapy can provide an intervention to patients who do not wish to make a social gender role transition or are unable or do not choose to undergo surgery.

Sex Reassignment Surgery

While many transsexual, transgender, and gender nonconforming individuals find comfort with their gender identity, role, and expression without surgery, many others say surgery is essential and medically necessary to establish congruence with their gender identity. Surgery to change the primary and/or secondary sex characteristics, including the breasts/chest, external and/or internal genitalia, facial features, and body contouring, is a treatment that has proven to have a beneficial effect on selective individuals' sense of well-being, body image, and sexual functioning.

For male-to-female (MtF) individuals, genital surgery involves a penile inversion technique in which doctors create a vaginal cavity with inverted penile skin; a rectosigmoid transplant, in which tissue is cut from the sigmoid section of the colon and used to create a vaginal cavity; or a free-skin graft to line the neovagina. A clitoris is formed from penile corpus spongiosum, and inner and outer lips are crafted from scrotal tissue. Other cosmetic procedures such as nose surgery, tracheal shave, and electrolysis, may be performed.

For female-to-male (FtM) individuals, also known as transmen, the ovaries, uterus, and breasts can be removed and the uterus lengthened to allow the patient to void while standing. The clitoris, which has been enlarged by testosterone therapy, can be refashioned into a penis, and the labia are formed into a scrotum, where skin is usually grafted from the forearm. Several techniques may be used to simulate penile erection, ranging from the insertion of a semi-erect rod to the surgical implantation of an inflatable device, any of which are performed some time after 6 months of the original surgery. In one study, more than 80% of the patients with an erection prosthesis were able to have were able to have normal sexual intercourse with penetration (Hoebeke, Selvaggi, Ceulemans, et al., 2005). In one long-term study on postoperative sexual and physical health, more than 80% of the patients reported sexual satisfaction and greater ease in reaching orgasm (De Cuypere, T'Sjoen, Beerten, et al., 2005).

Reproductive Health

Many transgender, transsexual, and gender nonconforming people want to have children. Consequently, before hormone therapy or surgery is initiated, individuals need to make decisions about fertility. If a person has not completed a sex reassignment surgery, it may be possible to stop hormones long enough for natal hormones to recover in order to allow for the production of mature gametes.

Follow-up and Prognosis

From both a physical and a psychological perspective, long-term follow-up is needed and encouraged. The majority of people who have undergone sex reassignment surgery report that it was the most appropriate treatment to alleviate the suffering that accompanies incongruent anatomy.

When transgender people get the care they need:

- Overall mental health improves: 78% of trans people had improved psychological function after receiving gender confirming treatment.

- Suicide rates drop (from a range of 29% to 19% before gender confirming treatment, to a range of 6% to .8% after treatment).

- Medicaid money is saved: transgender individuals who receive gender confirming treatment have fewer mental health and substance abuse costs along with higher rates of employment.

Think Critically

1. What would you say to another person who confided in you that he or she was experiencing gender dysphoria?

2. What are your thoughts about psychotherapy as a requirement prior to sex reassignment surgery?

3. How might you feel or react if it was revealed to you that your good friend, fellow student, or co-worker had undergone sex reassignment surgery and hormone therapy? Would it make any difference if this were a close or distant relative? Lover?

SOURCES: Coleman, E., et al. (2011). Standards of care for the health of transsexual, transgender, and gender-nonconforming people, Version 7. *International Journal of Transgenderism, 13,* 165–232; Monstrey, S., Ceulemans, P., & Hoebeke, P. (2011). Sex reassignment surgery in the female-to-male transsexual. *Seminars in Plastic Surgery, 25*(3), 229–244; GLADD (2014). Everyone needs access to safe, reliable healthcare. Available: http://www.glaad.org/healthcare

The fact that we are all human beings is infinitely more important than all the peculiarities that distinguish humans from one another.

—Simone de Beauvoir
(1908–1986)

Gender Dysphoria

Gender dysphoria is a new diagnosis in *The Diagnostic and Statistical Manual-5 (DSM-5)*, the American Psychiatric Association's (APA's) classification and diagnostic tool, whereby the emphasis for the diagnosis is on the individual's felt sense of "incongruence" with natal gender, rather than cross-gender behavior (American Psychiatric Association, 2013). It is a category that describes a condition in which someone is intensely uncomfortable and distressed with his or her biological gender and strongly identifies with, and wants to be, the other gender. Gender dysphoria is not the same as transgender. Transgender refers to those who identify with a gender different from the one they were assigned at birth and are not distressed by their cross-gender identification.

Gender dysphoria has replaced the psychiatric diagnosis termed gender identity disorder and is meant to be a more inclusive category (Moran, 2013). The category consists of one overarching diagnosis with separate developmentally appropriate criteria for children and adolescents. Additionally, it is separate from *DSM-5* chapters on sexual dysfunction and paraphilia disorders. Mental health care providers make the diagnosis of this unique condition, although a large proportion of the treatment is endocrinological and surgical. Many live as their desired gender and may seek gender reassignment surgery also known as **sex reassignment surgery (SRS),** also referred to as **gender reassignment surgery** or more recently, **gender affirmation** can allow them to replace, for example, a penis for a clitoris and a scrotum for a vagina. Separate criteria are provided for gender dysphoria in children and in adolescents, as in the case of a disorder of sex development or intersex. Furthermore, in the wording of the criteria, "the other sex" is replaced by "some alternative gender" because the concept of sex is inadequate when referring to individuals with a disorder of sex development (DSD). While there is some objection that the gender diagnosis is still included as a pathology that arguably might be considered a normal variation of sexual expression, the diagnosis of a marked incongruence and strong desire to live as the other sex allows access to care for children, adolescents, and adults. Furthermore, APA (2012a, 2012b) has issued two position statements, one opposing any form of discrimination against transgender individuals and one to ensure access to care and coverage by third-party payers for individuals seeking medically necessary treatment. In spite of this, 19% of transgender people report lacking any form of health insurance, including Medicaid, making treatment difficult, if not impossible (GLADD, 2014).

Transsexuality

In transsexuality, a person's gender identity and sexual anatomy are not compatible. Transsexual individuals believe and acknowledge that they have been given the body of the wrong sex. They generally want to change their sex, not their personality.

Transsexuality revolves around issues of gender identity; it is a distinctly different phenomenon from homosexuality. Being a lesbian or gay person reflects sexual orientation rather than gender questioning. Furthermore, following surgery, transsexual individuals may or may not change their sexual orientation, whether it is toward members of the same, the other, or both sexes.

Transitioning does not always involve medical or surgical treatment. By dressing in preferred-gender clothing, modifying their bodies through exercise, adjusting mannerisms and speech patterns, and/or requesting that friends and family address them with preferred names and pronouns, transgender people can use nonmedical options to comfortably live their gender identities or expressions. These individuals may identify as transsexual, transgender, or gender variant. Others may opt not to

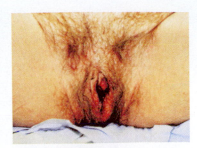

(a)

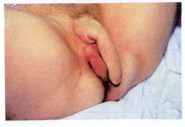

(b)

The genitals of a postoperative male-to-female transsexual (a), and the genitals of a postoperative female-to-male transsexual (b).

(a) © Dr. Daniel Greenwald;
(b) © Dr. Daniel Greenwald

Following hormone treatment and surgery, most transsexual individuals cannot be identified or differentiated from others.

(first) © Steve Nesius/AP Images;
(second) © China Photos/Getty Images

identify as men or women but rather to live completely outside the gender binary. Still others seek SRS to bring their genitals in line with their gender identity and to help diminish the suffering they experience. Hormone treatment often accompanies surgery and, combined, they help align these individuals' bodies with the gender they know themselves to be.

The prevalence of transsexuality is unknown, though it is estimated that worldwide there may be 1 transsexual in 11,900 males and 1 transsexual in 30,400 females (World Professional Association for Transgender Health, 2012).

Disorders of Sex Development (DSD)

Disorders of sex development (DSD) include a range of conditions that lead to abnormal development of the sex organs and ambiguous genitalia—genitals that are not clearly male or female ("Disorders of Sex Development," 2014). When a child is born with DSD, it may be difficult to determine the gender of the child. In other cases, signs are subtle and may not be diagnosed until the child reaches puberty.

Previously identified as intersex, DSD is a medical term used to describe a variety of conditions in which there is a discrepancy between the external genitals and the internal genitals (i.e., testes and ovaries) ("Intersex," 2014). DSD is biological and involves chromosomal, genital, and gonadal variations. Though some individuals with a DSD may be considered gender dysphoric, they may have a subtype of gender dysphoria. For example, a person who was born with ambiguous genitalia and is extremely distressed about the incongruity between his or her existing genitals and gender identity may be diagnosed with gender dysphoria, whereas another person also experiencing this condition may feel quite comfortable and desire no intervention. The latter person would not receive a diagnosis, other than the disorder of sex development. These differences exist because individuals with DSD vary in the presentation of symptoms, epidemiology, life trajectories, and etiology (Meyer-Bahlburg, 2009).

A variety of conditions are included under the DSD umbrella. Several dozen biological variations and conditions are included; some have their basis in genetic variations, some result from nongenetically caused prenatal development anomalies, and a few involve ambiguous genitalia. Still others involve more subtle blends of male and female characteristics.

As you may recall, humans are born with 46 chromosomes in 23 pairs. The X and Y chromosomes determine a person's sex, with most women born with 46,XX and most men 46,XY. The chromosome that carries the gene responsible for sexual differentiation will, by week 7 or 8, usually dictate the sex of the child at birth. Research suggests that in a few births per thousand, some individuals will be born with a single sex chromosome (45,X or 45,Y) and some with three or more sex chromosomes (47,XXX, 47,XYY, or 47,XXY, etc.). In addition, some males are born with 46,XX; similarly, some females are born with 46,XY. Clearly, there are not only females who are XX and males who are XY; rather, there is a range of chromosome complements, hormone balances, and phenotypic variations that determine sex (WHO, 2011b). When the genetic or hormonal process that causes this fetal tissue to become male or female is disrupted, ambiguous genitalia can develop. Thus, a person is born with sex chromosomes, external genitalia, or an internal reproductive system that is not considered standard for either male or female, thereby making the person's sex ambiguous (Accord Alliance, 2011). (The most common anomalies of sex development are summarized in Table 1.)

> ❚ *Each time a person stands up for an ideal, or acts to improve the lot of others, or strikes out against injustice, he sends forth a tiny ripple of hope.*
>
> *That ripple builds others.*
>
> *Those ripples—crossing each other from a million different centers of energy—build a current that can sweep down the mightiest walls of oppression and injustice.*
>
> —Senator Robert F. Kennedy (1925–1968)

The genitals of a fetally androgenized female may resemble those of a male.

© 2009 Michael English, M.D./Custom Medical Stock Photo

TABLE 1 • Disorders of Sex Development/Intersex

	Chromosomal Sex[a]	Gonads	Internal Reproductive Structures	External Reproductive Structures	Secondary Sex Characteristics	Fertility	Gender Identity
Turner syndrome	Female (45,XO)	Nonfunctioning or absent ovaries	Normal female except for ovaries	Underdeveloped genitals	Undeveloped/ no breast development	Infertile	Usually female
Klinefelter syndrome	Male (47,XXY)	Testes	Normal male	Small penis and testes, gynecomastia (breast development)	Some female secondary sex characteristics	Infertile	Usually male, but there may be gender identity confusion at puberty
Androgen insensitivity syndrome	Male (46,XY)	Undescended testes	Lacks normal male or female structures	Labia, shallow vagina	Female secondary sex characteristics develop at puberty; no menstruation	Infertile	Usually female
Congenital adrenal hyperplasia	Female (46,XX)	Ovaries	Normal female	Ambiguous tending toward male appearance; fused vagina and enlarged clitoris may be mistaken for empty scrotal sac and micropenis	Female secondary sex characteristics develop at puberty; abnormal growth for both sexes	Fertile	Usually female unless condition discovered at birth and altered by hormonal therapy
5-alpha reductase deficiency	Male (46,XY)	Testes undescended until puberty	Partially formed internal structures but no prostate	Ambiguous; clitoral appearing micropenis; phallus enlarges and testes descend at puberty	Male secondary sex characteristics develop at puberty	Infertile	Female identity until puberty; majority assume male identity later
Hypospadias	Male (46,XY)	Normal	Normal	Opening of penis located on underside rather than tip of penis; penis may also be twisted and small	Male secondary sex characteristics develop at puberty	Fertile	Male

[a]*Chromosomal sex* refers to 46,XX (female) or 46,XY (male). Sometimes a chromosome will be missing, as in 45,X, or there will be an extra chromosome, as in 47,XXY. In these notations, the number refers to the number of chromosomes (46, in 23 pairs, is normal); the letters *X* and *Y* refer to chromosomes.

Sex Chromosome Anomalies Two syndromes resulting from erroneous chromosomal patterns may result in gender confusion: Turner syndrome and Klinefelter syndrome. In both of these, the body develops with some marked physical characteristics of the other sex.

Turner Syndrome (45,XO) **Turner syndrome,** otherwise referred to as **45,XO,** is a chromosomal condition in which a female does not have the usual pair of two X chromosomes in her cells: one normal X chromosome is present and the other X chromosome is missing (hence the O). It is one of the most common chromosomal DSDs among females, occurring in an estimated 1 in 2,500 live female births worldwide ("Turner syndrome," 2014). Infants and young girls with Turner syndrome appear normal externally, but they have no ovaries. At puberty, changes initiated by ovarian hormones cannot take place. The body does not gain a mature look or height, and menstruation cannot occur. The adolescent girl may question her femaleness because she does not menstruate or develop breasts or pubic hair like her peers (see Figure 2) Girls with Turner syndrome are usually of normal intelligence; however, some may have problems in math, poor memory, and difficulty with fine finger movement. Hormonal therapy, including estrogen replacement therapy and human growth hormone therapy, replaces the hormones necessary to produce normal adolescent changes, such as growth and secondary sex characteristics. Even with ongoing hormonal therapy, women with Turner syndrome will likely remain infertile, although they may successfully give birth through embryo transfer following in vitro fertilization with donated ova. Having appropriate medical

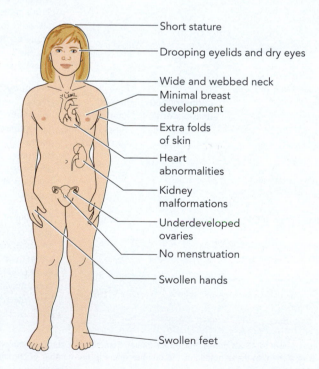

Short stature

Drooping eyelids and dry eyes

Wide and webbed neck

Minimal breast development

Extra folds of skin

Heart abnormalities

Kidney malformations

Underdeveloped ovaries

No menstruation

Swollen hands

Swollen feet

● **FIGURE 2**

Characteristics of Turner Syndrome

treatment and support allows a woman with Turner syndrome to lead a healthy and happy life.

Klinefelter Syndrome   Males with **Klinefelter syndrome** have one or more extra X chromosomes (47,XXY) ("Klinefelter syndrome," 2014a). Klinefelter syndrome is fairly common, occurring in 1 in 500 to 1,000 newborn males. The effects of Klinefelter syndrome are variable, and many men with the syndrome are never diagnosed because the condition may not be identified when there are only mild signs and no symptoms. The presence of the Y chromosome designates a person as male. It causes the formation of small, firm testes and ensures a masculine physical appearance. However, the presence of a double X chromosome pattern, which is a female trait, interferes with male sexual development, often preventing the testes from functioning normally and reducing the production of testosterone. At puberty, traits may vary: tallness, gynecomastia (breast development in men), sparse body hair, and/or small penis and testes (see Figure 3). XXY boys also tend to exhibit some degree of intellectual disability, developing attention deficit hyperactivity disorder, depression, and some autoimmune disorders ("Klinefelter syndrome," 2014b). Because of low testosterone levels, there may be a low sex drive, an inability to experience erections, and infertility. Consequently, individuals may need testosterone therapy to prevent osteoporosis and maintain physical energy, sexual functioning, and well-being. In vitro techniques can allow some men to become biological fathers.

Hormonal Disorders   Prenatal hormonal imbalances may cause males or females to develop physical characteristics associated with the other sex.

Androgen Insensitivity Syndrome   When a person who is genetically male (has XY chromosomes) is unable to respond to male hormones or androgens, he is said to have **androgen insensitivity syndrome (AIS)** ("Androgen insensitivity syndrome," 2014). As a result, the person has some or all of the female sex characteristics despite having the genetic makeup of a male. At birth the child appears to be a girl. This syndrome is divided into three categories: complete, partial, and mild, with 2 to 5 per 100,000 infants born with complete androgen insensitivity. Complete AIS prevents the development of the penis and other male body parts. Thus, a person with complete AIS appears to be female but has no uterus. At puberty, female secondary sex characteristics (such as breasts) develop, but menstruation and fertility do not occur, nor does the person have armpit or pubic hair. They are usually raised as females and have a female gender identity. Persons with partial or mild forms of AIS have a broader range of symptoms, including infertility, breast development in men, failure of one or both testes to descend into the scrotum after birth, and hypospadias, a condition in which the opening of the urethra is on the underside rather than at the tip of the penis. Those with partial androgen insensitivity may be raised as males or females and may have a male or female gender identity.

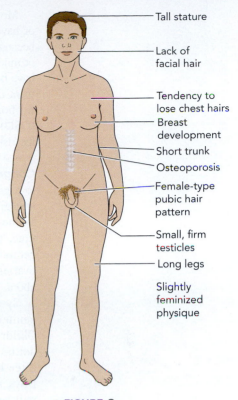

Tall stature

Lack of facial hair

Tendency to lose chest hairs

Breast development

Short trunk

Osteoporosis

Female-type pubic hair pattern

Small, firm testicles

Long legs

Slightly feminized physique

● **FIGURE 3**

Characteristics of Klinefelter Syndrome

Most people with complete AIS are not diagnosed until they fail to menstruate or have difficulties becoming pregnant. If it is discovered in childhood, it may be because the recognition of a mass that turns out to be a testicle. Those with partial or mild AIS, however, are often diagnosed during childhood because the person may have both male and female physical characteristics. Treatment and gender reassignment can be a very complex issue and must be individualized (see "Think About It" box "A Cautious Approach to Addressing Disorders of Sex Development (DSD) in Children"). This may involve removal of the undescended testes (to reduce the risk of cancer) and estrogen replacement therapy (to prevent osteoporosis).

Congenital Adrenal Hyperplasia **Congenital adrenal hyperplasia** refers to a group of inherited disorders of the adrenal gland and can affect both boys and girls. People with congenital adrenal hyperplasia lack an enzyme needed by the adrenal gland to make the hormones cortisol and aldosterone. At the same time, the body produces more androgen, a type of male sex hormone ("Congenital adrenal hyperplasia," 2014). Thus, a genetic female (XX) is born with ovaries and a vagina but develops externally as male. This condition occurs in about 1 in 10,000–18,000 children.

Symptoms in both boys and girls vary, depending on the type of congenital adrenal hyperplasia and the age in which the disorder was diagnosed. Children with milder forms may not have signs or symptoms and thus may not be diagnosed until adolescence. Girls with more severe forms at birth will often have abnormal genitals and may be diagnosed before symptoms appear. Boys with a more severe type at birth will appear normal. Both, however, will soon experience poor feeding ability, vomiting, dehydration, and abnormal heart rhythm. Girls with the milder form will usually have normal female reproductive organs, but as they mature they may experience abnormal menstrual periods or failure to menstruate, experience an early appearance and/or excessive amount of pubic or facial hair growth, and notice some enlargement of the clitoris. As boys with the milder form enter puberty, symptoms may include a deepening voice, early appearance of pubic or armpit hair, enlarged penis but normal testes, and well-developed muscles. Both boys and girls will be taller as children but as they mature will be much shorter than average adults.

Treatment for congenital adrenal hyperplasia is aimed at returning the hormone levels to normal by taking a form of cortisol. Additionally, the health care provider will check the chromosomes to help determine the genetic sex of the baby. Girls with male-appearing genitals may, during infancy, have surgery to correct the abnormal appearance.

5-Alpha Reductase Deficiency **5-Alpha reductase deficiency** is a condition whereby a genetic male (XY) does not produce enough of a hormone called dihydrotestosterone (DHT) ("5-alpha reductase deficiency," 2014). Given DHT's significant role in male sexual development, a shortage of this hormone in utero disrupts the formation of the external sex organs before birth, causing individuals to be born with external genitalia that appear female. In other cases, the external genitalia do not look clearly male or clearly female (sometimes called ambiguous genitalia). Still other affected infants have genitalia that appear primarily male, often with an extremely small penis (micropenis) and the urethra opening on the underside of the penis (hypospadias). Because of the rarity of this condition, there is no available estimate about how often it occurs. Children with 5-alpha reduc-

A Cautious Approach to Addressing Disorders of Sex Development (DSD) in Children

Researchers estimate that Disorders of Sex Development (DSD) conditions affect 1 in 2,000 children (Blackless et al., 2000). Sexually ambiguous infants have historically been given a gender assignment (usually female) along with treatment to support the assignment, including surgery and, later, hormones and psychotherapy. Some physicians have defended the practice of "correcting" ambiguous genitals, citing the success of current technology. For more than a decade, however, this practice has undergone scrutiny by some researchers, physicians, and patients who point to the lack of evidence supporting its unintended consequences, including the risk of assigning the wrong gender, along with other potentially negative outcomes associated with surgery.

Endocrinologists, physicians, ethicists, and gender activists began in the 1990s to seriously challenge the traditional pediatric postulates for sex assignment/reassignment (Diamond, 1996; Diamond & Sigmundson, 1997). Their research and that of others suggest that one's sexual identity is not fixed by the gender one is reared in, that atypical as well as typical individuals undergo psychosexual development, and that sexual orientation develops independent of rearing (Accord Alliance, 2011; Hughes et al., 2006).

Many individuals consider whether or not to have surgery a decision best delayed unless medically urgent, for example when a genetic anomaly interferes with urination or creates a risk of infection, or requested by the individual. They believe that letting well enough alone is the better course and that the individualized, erotic, and reproductive needs of the adult should take precedence over the cosmetic needs of the child. Pointing to their own dissatisfaction, as well as to the lack of research supporting the long-term success of surgical treatment, those affected recommend that the professional community offer support and information to parents and families and empower the individual with DSD to understand his or her status and choose (or reject) medical intervention (Diamond & Sigmundson, 1997; Intersex, 2014). In cases where puberty may be psychologically traumatic, hormones may be used to delay its onset.

Following an evidence-based review of the literature, 50 international experts in the field of pediatric endocrinology prepared a framework for the management of DSD. As a result, a consensus document, agreed on and published by the American Academy of Pediatrics, suggested the following (Lee, Houk, Ahmed, Ieuan, & Hughes, 2006):

- Avoid gender assignment before expert evaluation of newborns.
- Carry out evaluation and long-term management at a center with an experienced multidisciplinary team.
- Assign all individuals a gender.
- Encourage patients and families to communicate openly and participate in decision making.
- Address and respect patient and family concerns in strict confidence.

Since this document was first published, there has been progress in diagnosis, surgical techniques, understanding psychosocial issues, and recognizing and accepting the place of patient advocacy. According to Edgardo Menvielle, a child-adolescent psychiatrist, "We know that sexually marginalized children have a higher rate of depression and suicide attempts. The goal is for the child to be well-adjusted, healthy, and have good self-esteem. What's not important is molding their gender" (quoted in Brown, 2006). Such thinking, though still controversial, will no doubt continue to alter the gender-identity landscape. In the meantime, a team of health care professionals with expertise in DSD should work together to understand and treat the child as well as provide counseling and support to the whole family.

Think Critically

1. Imagine you are the parent of a newborn and the doctor approaches you with the diagnosis that your child's sex is ambiguous. What, if anything, would you do? Whom might you consult? What might you tell your family and others?

2. What do you believe are the pros and cons to early versus late gender assignment? Which would you choose if your child were diagnosed with DSD?

3. What are your thoughts about cosmetic genital surgeries performed on DSD infants being compared to the practice of female genital cutting performed in some African and Asian countries? Which, if either, is more acceptable?

tase deficiency are often raised as girls, about half of whom adopt a male gender role in adolescence or early adulthood. Most affected males are infertile.

Unclassified Form of Abnormal Sexual Development

Of unknown origin, but in some cases passed down through families, is a condition called **hypospadias** (hi-puh-SPAY-dee-as), in which the opening of the penis in boys, rather than being at the tip, is located somewhere on the underside, glans, or shaft, or at the junction of the scrotum. In addition, the foreskin may form a hood over the top of the glans, and there may be a twist in the shaft. In most cases, the condition will form a slit in the underside of the glans. In severe cases, the urethra may be open from midshaft out to the glans, or the urethra may be absent so that the urine exits the bladder behind the penis ("Facts about hypospadias," 2013). Hypospadias affects about 5 in 1,000 boys born in the United States. Infants with hypospadias should not be circumcised. Surgery, which consists of straightening the penis and correcting the hypospadias, is usually done before the child is 18 months old.

Coming to Terms With Differences

Everyone wishes and deserves to be loved, accepted, and supported. At the same time, most societies have a difficult time with differences. Western society is not exempt, especially when these differences are complex, are not understood, and/or may challenge the traditional or religious notions of "normal." Because rejection and loss are common concerns for individuals facing gender transition, some may feel their only choice is transition or suicide. When the real or perceived risk of loss and rejection is too great a price to pay, many will choose suicide. This may result when families and communities avoid discussing children's gender differences or sharing their own gender identity history. Most professionals, however, acknowledge that the more one educates oneself and talks about these issues, the easier it gets.

Self-acceptance, beginning with an understanding and appreciation of our physical appearance and the expectations that come with our preferred gender, can be a gateway to building intimacy in personal relationships. Pleasure and satisfaction can be strengthened when individuals have a better understanding of gender issues and differences. Because people sometimes react negatively to variations simply because they are fearful or ignorant, educating others about gender nonconforming individuals, or those who don't conform to society's expectations of masculinity and femininity, may help reduce their fear and ignorance and the stigmatization that accompanies both. While societies, laws, and some individuals may remain closed to accepting and supporting the wide variability in sexuality differentiation, gender, and expression, progress can be seen when education, advocacy, and open communication occur. It's this kind of work that will help all of us embrace our full humanity.

How does the law address people who are considered gender nonconforming? Australia had to address this after its High Court ruled that a person could register on official certificates as "nonspecific" (Baird, 2014). The implications in this decision are considerable in that the ruling can be used for interpretation of any laws that refer to a person's sex. More specifically, people in Australia can now mark X for "indeterminate" in the gender category of their passports without having had surgery. In 2013, Nepal also started to issue citizenship papers with a category for a "third gender," and Germany now allows parents of intersex children to mark their birth certificates with an X. Some members of the intersex community argue that the intersex labeling should apply only to those who are technically born so; however, the existing laws have not yet addressed this.

An important function among schools and campuses across the country is to provide a safe space for all students. This includes lesbian, gay, bisexual, transgender, and questioning (GLBTQ) and ally students who wish to share their thoughts and experiences in a social environment that is supportive, fun, and friendly. Such a student group can be the first point of contact for individuals during the coming-out process, a time when many feel doubt, fear, and shame. Often a GLBTQ and ally group works to educate and advocate on behalf of equal rights. As such, the goals and purposes of the organization need to be communicated to potential members and to the administration, and partnerships need to be built with departments and services, including that of the counseling offices to address the mental health needs of the group.

In addition to supporting advocacy groups, universities and schools across the country are slowly responding to gender equity mandates articulated in **Title IX,** an education amendment that protects people from discrimination based on sex in education programs or activities that receive federal financial assistance. On April 29, 2014, the United States Department of Education (DOE) released guidance aimed at protecting transgender and gender nonconforming students. It focused specifically on schools' obligations to combat sexual assault on campus and provided much-needed clarity around the rights of those who identify as gender nonconforming. The guidance states, "Title IX's sex discrimination prohibition extends to claims of discrimination based on gender identity or failure to conform to stereotypical notions of masculinity or femininity. Title IX requires schools to address sexual assault and other forms of sex discrimination because failing to do so limits or denies a student's ability to participate in or benefit from the school's educational program" (Orr, 2014). Though much of the attention around this anti–gender discrimination law is centered on combating sexual assault, there are a number of best practices to support transgender and other gender nonconforming students, including the following (Beemyn, 2015):

Chaz Bono is a female-to-male transgender man who has documented his life in order to help educate others who might be questioning their own gender identity.

© Beck Starr/FilmMagic/Getty Images

1. *Add the phrase "gender identity or expression" to the institution's non-discrimination policy.*

2. *Ask "gender identity" on college forms and surveys. This would mean changing options from male and female to woman, man, trans woman, trans man, and a range of non-binary gender identities.*

3. *Enable students to change their gender and use a chosen name on campus records and documents. This can prevent a student from being 'outed' as transgender when an instructor takes attendance or when someone sees a student's identification card.*

4. *Offer gender-inclusive bathrooms and adopt a policy that enables students to use the campus restrooms that are in keeping with their gender identity and expression.*

5. *Offer gender-inclusive housing, which enables two or more students to share a multiple-occupancy room, suite, or apartment, in mutual agreement, regardless of the students' gender assignment or gender identity.*

6. *Enable insurance coverage for transsexual-related psychotherapy, hormone replacement therapy, and gender-affirming surgeries.*

Final Thoughts

We ordinarily take our gender as female or male for granted. The making of gender, however, is a complex process involving biological, cultural, and psychological elements. Biologically, we are male or female in terms of genetic and anatomical makeup. Psychologically, we are male or female in terms of our assigned gender and our gender identity. Only in rare cases, as with chromosomal and hormonal anomalies or gender dysphoria, can our gender identity be problematic. For most of us, gender identity is rarely a source of concern. More often, what concerns us is related to our gender roles: Am I sufficiently masculine? Feminine? What it means to be feminine or masculine differs from culture to culture. Although femininity and masculinity are generally regarded as opposites in our culture, there are relatively few significant inherent differences between the sexes aside from males impregnating and females giving birth and lactating. The majority of social and psychological differences are exaggerated or culturally encouraged. All in all, women and men are more similar than different. The more that we as individuals and as a society do to educate ourselves, the more likely the shame and stigmatization that accompany sexual and gender variations will be reduced.

Summary

Studying Gender and Gender Roles

- *Sex* is the biological aspect of being female or male. Gender encompasses the social and cultural characteristics associated with biological sex. Normal gender development depends on biological, cultural, and psychological factors. Psychological factors include *assigned gender* and *gender identity*. *Gender roles* tell us how we are to act with our assumed or assigned sex in a particular culture. *Gender variations* occur among those who cannot or choose not to conform to societal gender norms.
- Although our culture encourages us to think that men and women are "opposite" sexes, they are more similar than dissimilar. Innate gender differences are generally minimal; differences are primarily encouraged by socialization.
- Masculine and feminine stereotypes assume heterosexuality. *Heteronormativity* refers to the belief that if men or women do not fit gender or sexual stereotypes, they are likely to be considered gay or lesbian. Gay men and lesbian women, however, are as likely as heterosexuals to be masculine or feminine.

Gender-Role Learning

- *Cognitive social learning theory* emphasizes learning behaviors from others through cognition and modeling. *Cognitive development theory* asserts that once children learn gender is permanent they independently strive to act like "proper" girls and boys because of an internal need for congruence.
- *Social construction theory* views gender as a set of practices and performances that occur through language and a political system. *Queer theory* views gender and sexuality as systems that cannot be understood as gender neutral or by the actions of heterosexuals.
- Though the stereotypes are somewhat outmoded, children still learn their gender roles from parents through manipulation, channeling, verbal appellation, and activity exposure. Parents, teachers, peers, and the media are the most important agents of socialization during childhood and adolescence.
- A *gender schema* is a set of interrelated ideas used to organize information about the world on the basis of gender. We use our gender schemas to classify many non-gender-related objects, behaviors, and activities as male or female.

Contemporary Gender Roles and Scripts

- The trait most associated with the traditional male gender role is *instrumentality*. Traditional male roles emphasize aggression, emotional toughness, and independence. Traditional male sexual *scripts* include the denial of the expression of feelings, an emphasis on performance and being in charge, and the belief that men always want sex and that all physical contact leads to sex.

- The trait most associated with the traditional female gender role is *expressiveness*. Traditional female roles emphasize passivity, compliance, physical attractiveness, and being a wife and mother. Female sexual scripts suggest that sex is good and bad (depending on the context); genitals should not be touched; sex is for men; women shouldn't talk about sex; women should look like models; and there is only one "right" way to experience an orgasm.

- Important changes affecting today's gender roles and sexual scripts include increasing questioning of values and expectations around parenting, dating, and careers.

- Contemporary sexual scripts are more egalitarian than traditional ones and include the belief that sex is positive, that it involves a mutual exchange, and that it may be initiated by either partner.

- *Androgyny* combines traditional female and male characteristics into a more flexible pattern of behavior, rather than seeing them as opposites.

Gender Variations

- For most of us, there is no question about our gender. However, for many others, gender variant expressions and cross-gender identities are an important means of identity.

- A transgender community, one that embraces the possibility of numerous genders and multiple social identities, has emerged. A *transgender* individual is one who lives full-time in a gender role different from the gender role presumed by society to match that person's genetic sex.

- *Gender dysphoria* emphasizes the individual's felt sense of incongruence with natal gender. People who plan to or do transition to the "other" gender are known as transsexuals. The procedure to correct this is referred to as *sex reassignment surgery, gender reassignment surgery, or gender affirmation*. The causes of transsexuality are not known.

- Variations in congenital sex anatomy that are considered atypical for females or males are referred to as *disorders of sex development*. Disorders of gonadal differentiation include *Turner syndrome* and *Klinefelter syndrome, androgen insensitivity syndrome, congenital adrenal hyperplasia*, and *5-alpha reductase deficiency*. An unclassified form of abnormal development is *hypospadias*.

Questions for Discussion

- How have gender stereotypes and roles influenced your views of your sexuality and the ways in which you relate to others?

- If you had an infant born with ambiguous genitalia, would you opt for surgery? Inhibit the onset of puberty with drugs? What gender would you raise the child? If surgery were chosen, when the child was old enough, would you inform him or her about this treatment? Or would you not choose surgery and instead leave the decision to the individual at a later time?

- Do you believe that your gender identity was biologically or socially determined? Who or what most influenced your gender identity? In what ways?

Sex and the Internet

Working for LGBT Equal Rights

The number of education and advocacy groups working around sexual orientation and gender has increased tremendously in recent years. Go to the Human Rights Campaign (http://www.hrc.org). From there, click "Topics," identify two topics of interest, and read what they have to offer. Once you have read about two issues, answer the following questions:

- How does the new information you have gathered influence the way you think about gender and/or sexual orientation?

- What was one specific aspect of this subject that most interested you?

- What is one point you still have questions about?

- What have you learned as a result of this research?

Suggested Websites

About Kids Health

http://www.aboutkidshealth.ca/En/HowTheBodyWorks/
SexDevelopmentAnOverview/Pages/default.aspx
An interactive website that provides pediatric health care information in multiple languages.

Accord Alliance

http://www.accordalliance.org
Information, referrals, and support for those who are seeking information and advice about disorders of sex development (formerly the Intersex Society of North America).

Disorders of Sex Development

www.dsdguidelines.org
Handbooks for clinicians and patients about the diagnosis, treatment, education, and support of children with disorders of sex development.

Gender Spectrum

https://www.genderspectrum.org
Provides education, training, and support to help create a gender-sensitive and inclusive environment for children and adults.

National Center for Transgender Equality

http://www.transquality.org
Dedicated to advancing the equality of transgender people through advocacy, collaboration, and empowerment.

Trans Awareness Project

http://www.transawareness.org/index.html
A poster and digital media campaign that attempts to challenge stereotypes and cultivate an environment that celebrates and respects people of all genders.

United Nations Inter-Agency Network on Women and Gender

http://www.un.org/womenwatch
Gateway to information and resources on the promotion of gender equality.

World Professional Association for Transgender Health (WPATH)

http://www.path.org
A professional organization that provides evidence-based care, education, research, and advocacy in transgender and transsexual health.

Suggested Reading

Dreger, A. D. (2004). *One of us: Conjoined twins and the future of normal.* Cambridge, MA: Harvard University Press. An analysis of children born with anatomical anomalies and the lives they lead.

Eliot, L. (2009). *Pink brain, blue brain: How small differences grow into troublesome gaps—and what we can do about it.* New York: Houghton. Blends culture and biology to provide insights into parenting, educating, and raising children in a way that refutes an overemphasis on sex differences.

Erickson-Schroth, L. (2014). *Trans bodies, trans selves: A resource for the transgender community.* New York: Oxford University Press. Varied viewpoints that express the diversity of trans communities.

Fausto-Sterling A. (2012). *Sex/gender: Biology in a social world.* New York: Routledge. Provides an explanation of the biological and cultural underpinnings of gender.

Feder, E. K. (2014). *Making sense of intersex: Changing ethical perspectives in biomedicine.* Bloomington: Indiana University Press. An engaging argument about a new approach for doctors and parents caring for children with atypical sex anatomy.

Lips, H. (2014). *Gender: The basics.* New York: Routledge. An examination of gender theories, research, and issues, highlighting the fact that there is more to gender than biological sex.

Meyer, I. H., & Northridge, M. E. (Eds.). (2010). *The health of sexual minorities. Public health perspectives on lesbian, gay, bisexual and transgender populations.* New York: Springer. Challenges assumptions about how people manage their identities at various stages of their lives.

Teich, N. M. (2012). *Transgender 101: A simple guide to a complex issue.* New York: Columbia University Press. A look below the surface to see that gender variance and the social systems that have led to and exacerbate the condition cannot help but be moved.

6

Sexuality in Childhood and Adolescence

© Axel Bernstorff/cultura/Corbis

CHAPTER OUTLINE

Sexuality in Infancy and Childhood (Ages 0 to 11)

Sexuality in Adolescence (Ages 12 to 19)

"I cannot say that I am sexually attracted to females, but I get lost in their looks and their angelic energy. I love to kiss girls and have close relationships with them. There is a liberating and beautiful trust that I find between certain women and myself that I have not shared with a man. I am, however, sexually attracted to men and love to be affectionate and have relationships with them."

—22-year-old female

"I discovered that White and Latino men find me attractive, but I'm still hurt that I don't fit in completely with my own people. I'm sure most of it has to do with my baggage and me. I sometimes see Black men's heads turn, and some speak to me. But it's when that one or two don't; it's like a stab in the heart again. I believe that I reject those who show interest because of what Black guys in my past have put me through. Perhaps I think if I'm myself around them they may think I talk White and I'm stuck up. Because they have never wanted me, my preference is now Latino men."

—19-year-old Black female

"For most of college, I dated several women, but I never found the right one. Sex is special to me, and although at times I feel like just doing it with anyone, like all my friends, I don't. However, the first time that I did have actual intercourse was in my sophomore year with a random person. I was almost 20 years old and living in my fraternity house. Constantly, I was bombarded with stories of the conquests of my fraternity brothers. Why was I different? I had remained a virgin for so long, and up until then I was pretty secure about it. But during that time, not only did I give up my virginity, but I also slipped in life. This represented a major down time for me."

—25-year-old male

As we consider the human life cycle from birth to death, we cannot help but be struck by how profoundly sexuality weaves its way through our lives. From the moment we are born, we are rich in sexual and erotic potential, which begins to take shape in our sexual curiosity and experimentations in childhood. As children, we are only partly formed, but the world around us helps shape our sexuality. In adolescence, our education continues as a random mixture of learning, yearning, and experimenting with new behaviors.

In this chapter, we discuss both the innate and the learned aspects of sexuality, from infancy through adolescence. We examine both physical development and **psychosexual development,** which involve the psychological aspects of sexuality. We see how culture, family, media, and other factors affect children's feelings about their bodies and influence their sexual feelings and activities. We look at how the physical changes experienced by teenagers affect their sexual awareness and sexual identity. And we discuss adolescent sexual behaviors, teenage pregnancy, teenage parenthood, and sexuality education.

● Sexuality in Infancy and Childhood (Ages 0 to 11)

Our understanding of infant sexuality is based on observation and inference. It is obvious that babies derive sensual pleasure from stroking, cuddling, bathing, and other tactile stimulation. Ernest Borneman, a researcher of children's sexuality in the 1950s, suggested that the first phase of sexual development be called the cutaneous phase (from the Greek *kytos,* "skin"). During this period, an infant's skin can be considered a "single erogenous zone" (Borneman, 1983).

The young child's healthy psychosexual development lays the foundation for further stages of growth. Psychosexual maturity, including the ability to love, begins to develop in infancy, when babies are lovingly touched all over their bodies (which appear to be designed to attract the caresses of their elders).

Infants and young children communicate by smiling, gesturing, crying, and so on. Before they understand the language, they learn to interpret movements, facial expressions, body language, and tone of voice. Humans' earliest lessons are conveyed in these ways. Infants begin to learn how they "should" feel about their bodies. If a parent frowns, speaks sharply, or slaps an exploring hand, the infant quickly learns that a particular activity—touching the genitals, for example—is wrong. The infant may or may not continue the activity, but if he or she does, it will be in secret, probably accompanied by feelings of guilt and shame.

Infants also learn about the gender role they are expected to fulfill (Bussey & Bandura, 1999). While there is evidence of inborn influences on sex-typed toy preferences (Jadva, Hines, & Golombok, 2008), much of what children experience is reinforced by parental and societal upbringing. In our culture, baby girls are often handled more gently than baby boys, are dressed up more, and are given soft toys and dolls to play with. Baby boys, in contrast, are often expected to be "tough." Their dads may roughhouse with them and speak more loudly to them than to baby girls. They are given "boy toys"—blocks, cars, and action figures. This gender-role learning is reinforced as the child grows older.

Infancy and Sexual Response (Ages 0 to 2)

Infants can be observed discovering the pleasure of genital stimulation soon after they are born. However, the body actually begins its first sexual response even earlier, in utero, when sonograms have shown that boys have erections. This begins a pattern of erections that will occur throughout their lives. Signs of sexual arousal in girls, though less easily detected, begin soon after birth and include vaginal lubrication and genital swelling. In some cases, both male and female infants have been observed experiencing what appears to be an orgasm. Obviously, an infant is unable to differentiate sexual pleasure from other types of enjoyment, so viewing these as sexual responses are adult interpretations of these normal reflexes and do not necessarily signify the infant's desire or interest. What it does reveal is that the capacity for sexual response is present soon after conception (DeLamater & Friedrich, 2002). Following birth, the accumulation of a wide range of physical, emotional, and intellectual experiences begins (Carpenter & DeLamater, 2012).

Childhood Sexuality (Ages 3 to 11)

Children become aware of sex and sexuality much earlier than many people realize. They generally learn to disguise their interest rather than risk the disapproval of their elders, but they continue as small scientists—collecting data, performing experiments, and attending conferences with their colleagues. In fact, as part of normative childhood sexual behavior, children engage in self-stimulatory behavior, demonstrate interest in sexual topics, reveal their bodies and sexual parts to adults and children, and show interest in viewing the bodies of others (Friedrich, Fisher, Broughton, Houston, & Shafran, 1998; Thigpen, 2009, 2012).

Curiosity and Sex Play
Starting as early as age 3, when they begin interacting with their peers, children begin to explore their bodies together. They may masturbate or play "mommy and daddy" and hug and kiss and lie on top of each other; they may play "doctor" so that they can look at each other's genitals. Author and social justice activist Letty Cottin Pogrebin (1983) suggests that we

Conscience is the inner voice which warns us that someone may be looking.

—H. L. Mencken
(1880–1956)

I do not think that there is even one good reason for denying children the information which their thirst for knowledge demands.

—Sigmund Freud
(1856–1939)

Kissing and cuddling are essential to an infant's healthy psychosexual development.
© Jose Luis Pelaez Inc./Blend Images LLC

think of children as "students" rather than "voyeurs." It is important for them to know what others look like in order to feel comfortable about themselves.

Physician and noted sexuality educator Mary Calderone (1983) stressed that children's sexual interest should never be labeled "bad" but that it may be deemed inappropriate for certain times, places, or persons. According to Calderone, "The attitude of the parents should be to socialize for privacy rather than to punish or forbid." If children's natural curiosity about their sexuality is satisfied, they are likely to feel comfortable with their own bodies as adults.

Children who participate in sex play generally do so with children of their own sex. In fact, same-sex activity is probably more common during the childhood years when the separation of the sexes is particularly strong (DeLamater & Friedrich, 2002). Most go on to develop heterosexual orientations; some do not. But whatever a person's sexual orientation, childhood sex play clearly does not *create* the orientation. The origins of sexual orientation are not well understood; in some cases, there may indeed be a biological basis. Many gay men and lesbian women say that they first became aware of their attraction to the same sex during childhood, but many heterosexual people also report attraction to the same sex during this time. These feelings and behaviors appear to be quite common and congruent with healthy psychological development in heterosexual, lesbian, and gay individuals (DeLamater & Friedrich, 2002). (See Table 1 for common childhood sexual behaviors.)

Masturbation and Permission to Feel Pleasure Most of us masturbate; most of us also were raised to feel guilty about it. In fact, by the end of adolescence, nearly all males and many females have masturbated (Friedrich et al., 1998; Laumann, Gagnon, Michael, & Michaels, 1994). Virtually all health professionals consider masturbation a normal, harmless, and common childhood behavior. But the message "If it feels good, it's bad" is often internalized at an early age, which sometimes leads to psychological and sexual difficulties in later life. Virtually all psychologists, physicians, child development specialists, and other professionals agree that masturbation is healthy. Negative responses from adults only magnify the guilt and anxiety that a child is taught to associate with this behavior.

A good thing about masturbation is that you don't have to dress up for it.

—Truman Capote
(1924–1984)

Children are naturally curious about bodies. It is important that these kinds of explorations are seen as normal and not be labeled "bad."

© Christine DeVault Mendes/Buena Vista Photography

Children often accidentally discover that playing with their genitals is pleasurable and continue this activity until reprimanded by an adult. Male infants have been observed with erect penises a few hours after birth. A baby boy may laugh in his crib while playing with his erect penis. Baby girls sometimes move their bodies rhythmically, almost violently, appearing to experience orgasm. By the time they are 4 or 5, children have usually learned that adults consider this form of behavior "nasty." Parents generally react negatively to masturbation,

TABLE 1 • Childhood Sexual Behaviors Witnessed by at Least 20% of Parents, by Age Group and Gender			
Age Group	**Behavior**	**% of Boys**	**% of Girls**
2–5 Years	Stands too close to people	29	16
	Touches own sex parts when in public places	27	44
	Touches/tries to touch mother's or other woman's breast	42	44
	Touches sex parts at home	60	44
	Tries to look at people when they are nude or undressing	27	27
6–9 Years	Touches own sex parts at home	40	21
	Tries to look at people when they are nude or undressing	20	21
10–12 Years	Is very interested in the other sex	24	29

SOURCE: Adapted from Table 3, Friedrick, W. N. (2003). Studies of sexuality of nonabused children. In Bancroft, J. (Ed.), *Sexual development in childhood*. Bloomington: Indiana University Press. Reprinted by permission.

regardless of the age and sex of the child. Later, this negative attitude becomes generalized to include the sexual pleasure that accompanies the behavior. Children thus learn to conceal their masturbatory play. Although children vary in the age at which they begin to conceal their sexuality, it appears to occur between the ages of 6 and 10 (Bancroft, 2009).

Children need to understand that pleasure from masturbation is normal and acceptable. But they also need to know that masturbation is something that we do in private.

When Children "Act Out": Red Flags for Problematic Sexual Behavior

Distinguishing between normal and problematic childhood sexual behaviors is a matter of degree and context of the behavior and may be difficult for many parents and adults to recognize. When sexual behaviors are persistently intrusive, coercive, developmentally abnormal, or abusive, there may be broader issues that need to be addressed (Kellogg, 2009). For example, if a child appears preoccupied with touching himself or herself or others in public or appears to know "too much" about sexual behaviors, there may be cause for concern for parents or caregivers. It is important, at the same time, to know that the expression of sexuality is only one component of many factors to consider before designating a behavior as a sexual problem (Kellogg, 2009). If, however, sexual abuse or an emotional problem is suspected, professional help should be sought.

The Family Context

Family styles of physical expression and feelings about modesty, privacy, and nudity vary considerably.

> Learning about sex in our society is learning about guilt.
>
> —John Gagnon (1931–) and William Simon (1927–2000)

Family Nudity Some families are comfortable with nudity in a variety of contexts: bathing, swimming, sunbathing, dressing, or undressing. Others are comfortable with partial nudity from time to time, for example when sharing the bathroom or changing clothes. Still others are more modest and carefully guard their privacy. Most researchers and therapists would agree that styles of modesty can be compatible with the formation of sexually well-adjusted children, as long as some basic guidelines are observed:

- *Accept and respect a child's body and nudity.* If 4-year-old Chantel runs naked into her parents' dinner party, she should be greeted with friendliness, not horror or harsh words. If her parents are truly uncomfortable, they can help her get dressed matter-of-factly, without recrimination.

- *Do not punish or humiliate a child for seeing his or her parents naked, going to the bathroom, or being sexual with each other.* If the parent screams or lunges for a towel, young Antonio will think he has witnessed something wicked or frightening. He can be gently reminded that mommy or daddy wants privacy at the moment.

- *Respect a child's need for privacy.* Many children, especially as they approach puberty, become quite modest. It is a violation of the child's developing sense of self not to respect his or her need for privacy. If 9-year-old Jeremy starts routinely locking the bathroom door or 11-year-old Sarah covers her chest when a parent interrupts her while she is dressing, it is most likely a sign of normal development. Children whose privacy and modesty are respected will learn to respect that of others.

Expressing Affection   Families also vary in the amount and type of physical contact in which they engage. Some families hug and kiss, give back rubs, sit and lean on each other, and generally maintain a high degree of physical closeness. Some parents extend this closeness to their sleeping habits, allowing their infants and small children in their beds each night. (In many cultures, this is the rule rather than the exception.) Other families limit their contact to hugs and tickles. Variations of this kind are normal. Concerning children's needs for physical contact, we can make the following generalizations:

- *All children (and adults) need freely given physical affection from those they love.* Although there is no prescription for the right amount or form of such expression, its quantity and quality affect both children's emotional well-being and the emotional and sexual health of the adults they will become.

- *Children should be told, in a nonthreatening way, what kind of touching by adults is "acceptable" and what is "not acceptable."* Children need to feel that they are in charge of their own bodies, that parts of their bodies are "private property," and that no one has the right to touch them with sexual intent.

- *It is not necessary to frighten a child by going into great detail about the kinds of bad things that others might do to them sexually.* A better strategy is to instill a sense of self-worth and confidence in children so that they will not allow themselves to be victimized.

- *We should listen to children and trust them.* Children need to know that if they are sexually abused it is not their fault. They need to feel that they can tell about it and still be worthy of love.

● Sexuality in Adolescence (Ages 12 to 19)

Puberty is the stage of human development when the body becomes capable of reproduction. For legal purposes (e.g., laws relating to child abuse), puberty is considered to begin at age 12 for girls and age 14 for boys. As will be discussed later, the actual age of puberty in girls and boys varies, depending on a wide host of factors. **Adolescence** is the social and psychological state that occurs between the beginning of puberty and acceptance into full adulthood.

Psychosexual Development

Adolescents are sexually mature (or close to it) in a physical sense, but they are still learning about their gender and social roles, and they still have much to learn about their sexual scripts. They may also be struggling to understand the meaning of their sexual feelings for others and their sexual orientation.

Physical Changes During Puberty   Though the mechanisms that activate the chain of development that occurs during puberty are not fully understood, researchers have observed that as the child approaches puberty, typically beginning between the ages of 8 and 13 for girls and 9 and 14 for boys, the levels of hormones begin to increase. This period of rapid physical changes is triggered by the hypothalamus, which plays a central role in increasing secretions that cause the pituitary gland to release large amounts of hormones into the bloodstream. The hormones, called gonadotropins, stimulate activity in the gonads

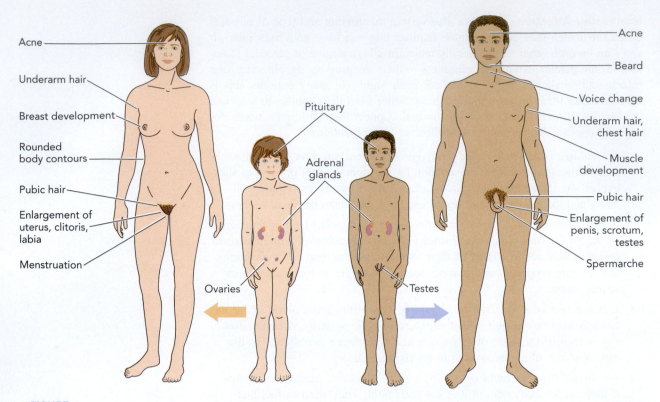

**Physical and Hormonal Changes
During Puberty**

and are chemically identical in boys and girls. In girls, they act on the ovaries to produce estrogen; in boys, they cause the testes to increase testosterone production. These higher levels of male and female hormones result in the development of specific external signs of male and female sexual maturation, known as secondary sex characteristics, including the onset of menstruation (in girls), and **spermarche** (in boys), the development of sperm in the testicles (see Figure 1).

The first sign of puberty in girls, which occurs at about 10.5 years of age in the United States, is breast development. This is also the beginning of a girl's growth spurt, which is followed by the growth of pubic and underarm hair and the onset of vaginal mucus secretion. Menarche, the onset of menstruation, follows within 1 or 2 years. The average age for menstruation in the United States is 12.2 for Black girls and 12.9 for White girls, although this can vary, depending on the sequence and time frame of events that occur (Sarpolis, 2011). Data over the past several decades regarding timing of puberty have shown that girls are experiencing earlier breast development, associating it with an elevated body mass index (BMI) (Biro, Greenspan, & Galvez, 2012). Although the literature is consistent regarding the relationship of body mass index and timing of puberty in girls, it is not consistent about this relationship in boys (Biro et al., 2013).

Precocious puberty refers to the appearance of physical and hormonal signs of pubertal development at an earlier age than is considered typical: before age 7 in girls and before age 9 in boys ("Early puberty," 2014). About 1 in 5,000 children, most of whom are girls, are affected. Sometimes, precocious puberty stems from a structural problem in the brain or a brain injury, an infection, or a problem in the ovaries or thyroid gland. However, for the majority of girls there is no underlying medical problem; they simply start puberty earlier than what is considered typical (Downshen, 2012). In boys, the condition is less common and more likely to be associated with an underlying medical problem or, for a small percentage, inherited from father to son.

When puberty ends, growth in height stops. Because their skeletons mature and bone growth stops at an earlier age than normal, children with precocious puberty usually don't achieve their full adult height potential. The goal of treating precocious puberty is to halt or even reverse sexual development and stop the rapid growth and bone maturation that can result in short stature.

Perhaps as troubling as the early physical changes that are occurring are the potential psychological effects of premature sexual development. The concern, of course, is that young girls who *look* older than they are might be pressured by others to *act* older. Unfortunately, when children are bombarded by sexual images and their bodies push them toward adulthood before they are ready psychologically, they lose the freedom to be a child. The cultural pressure to short-circuit the time when a young girl is developing her sense of self and her place in the world can set a dangerous precedent for later behavior. Additionally, society's relentless pressure to **sexualize** girls, defined as "when a person's value comes only from her or his sexual appeal or behavior, to the exclusion of other characteristics, and when a person is sexually objectified, e.g., made into a thing for another's sexual use" (American Psychological Association, 2010), can be found in all forms of media. Because hormonal changes often stoke the fires of sexual curiosity and behavior in young people, early dating and possible progression toward sexual intercourse may begin at a young age. Given the many psychological motives that are involved in sexual activity, if a young person is not prepared for the outcomes and responsibilities that accompany sexual behavior, social, psychological, and emotional problems may result.

In response to some young girls' earlier maturation coupled with the many examples of the sexualization of girls and girlhood in U.S. culture, the American Psychological Association published the *Report of the APA Task Force on the Sexualization of Girls* (2010), which reviewed the evidence linking sexualization to a variety of damaging consequences. These included harm to the sexualized individuals themselves, to their relationships, and to society. It is not uncommon to see, for example, impaired cognitive performance, body dissatisfaction, low self-esteem, depression, and physical health problems among adolescent girls and women (and some men).

As previously stated, puberty generally begins later in boys, at an average age of 9 to 14 years, though the age at which puberty is construed legally is 14. It usually takes 3 to 4 years for a boy's body to experience the hormonal changes that transition his body into that of a man's; this process may continue until he is 20 years old. The first sign is an increase in the size of the testicles, followed by the growth of pubic hair. Physical changes continue, including a growth spurt; hand and foot growth; muscle-mass growth; voice deepening; and hair growth on the face, underarms, and sometimes other parts of the body. The penis also grows larger. Some boys reach puberty around age 12; others, not until their later teens. Generally, however, they lag about 2–3 years behind girls in pubertal development.

The scarcity of research on early orgasm is apparent in contemporary sexology. However, we do know that at puberty boys begin to ejaculate semen, which accompanies the experience of orgasm they may have been having for some time. Just as girls often do not know what is happening when they begin to menstruate, many boys are unnerved by the first appearance of semen as a result of masturbation or **nocturnal emissions** during sleep ("wet dreams"). Like menstruation for girls, the onset of ejaculation is a sexual milestone for boys: It is the beginning of their fertility. Alfred Kinsey called first ejaculation the most important psychosexual event in male adolescence (Kinsey, Pomeroy, & Martin, 1948).

Influences on Psychosexual Development Besides biological forces, numerous factors are known to increase or decrease teen sexual behavior. Though teens' behaviors cannot necessarily be controlled, parents and other concerned adults can attempt to affect the factors that influence teens' sexual decisions in order to facilitate the development of a healthy sexuality.

Parental Influence Children learn a great deal about sexuality from their parents. For the most part, however, they learn not because their parents set out to teach them but because they are avid observers of their parents' behavior and family dynamics and characteristics. Much of what they learn involves the connection (or lack of) they have with their parents.

As they enter adolescence, young people are especially concerned about their own sexuality, but they are often too embarrassed to ask their parents directly about these "secret" matters. And many parents are ambivalent about their children's developing sexual nature. Parents often underestimate their children's involvement in sexual activities, even as their children progress through adolescence, and so perceive less need to discuss sexuality with them. They are often fearful that their children (daughters especially) will become sexually active if they have "too much" information. They tend to indulge in wishful thinking: "I'm sure Jenny's not really interested in boys yet"; "I know Jose would never do anything like that." Parents may put off talking seriously with their children about sex, waiting for the "right time." Or they may bring up the subject once, make their points, breathe a sigh of relief, and never mention it again. Still, teens continue to say that parents most influence their decisions about sex (38%)—more than peers, popular culture, teachers, and others (Albert, 2012). Even more teens (87%) say that it would be much easier for them to delay sexual activity and avoid teen pregnancy if they were able to have more open,

> *Most mothers think that to keep young people from love making it is enough not to speak of it in their presence.*
>
> —Marie Madeline de la Fayette
> (1634–1693)

Rites of passage are built into the traditions of most cultures. Among them are the Jewish Bar and Bat Mitzvahs, Indian Navjote ritual, and South African Xhosa initiation rite.

(a) © Rob Melnychuk/Getty Images;
(b) © Lindsay Hebberd/Corbis;
(c) © Inge Yspeert/Corbis

(a)

(b)

(c)

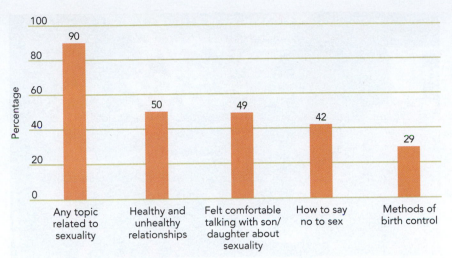

● FIGURE 2

Percentage of Parents Who Talked About Sexuality With Their Adolescent, Aged 15–18, United States, 2012.

(*Source:* Planned Parenthood, 2012.)

honest conversations about sexuality with their parents (see Figure 2). Not talking about sex-related issues can have serious consequences, leaving adolescents vulnerable to other sources of information and opinions that flow from media and peers.

Family characteristics and dynamics exhibit a strong influence on teens' sexual attitudes and behaviors, most notably living with and experiencing close relationships with both parents, having parents who are more educated and have adequate family income, feeling parental support and connection, having no family abuse of alcohol or drugs, and having parents who identify sexual risk taking and early childbearing as inconsistent with their own values (Kirby, 2007). When parents have early and consistent conversations in an open and comfortable manner with their children, many of the risk factors associated with teen sexuality can be reduced. In fact, it is critical to explore not only the negative consequences associated with risky sexual behaviors but also the positive outcomes that adolescents experience during and following sexual activity with another person (Halpern-Felsher & Reznik, 2009).

Peer Influence   No doubt, adolescents receive a lot of information about sex from peers (especially same-sex peers). With this, they may put pressure on each other to carry out traditional gender roles. Boys encourage other boys to be sexually active even if they are unprepared or uninterested. They must camouflage their inexperience with bravado, which increases misinformation; they cannot reveal sexual ignorance.

Even though many teenagers find their early sexual experiences less than satisfying, they still seem to feel a great deal of pressure to conform, which means becoming or continuing to be sexually active. The social effects on teen sexuality are strong. Teens are more likely to be sexually active if their best friends and peers are sexually active and are older, use alcohol or drugs, or engage in other risky behaviors (Kirby, 2007). Similarly, simply having a romantic partner increases the chances of sexual activity, especially if that partner is older.

The Media   As discussed previously, erotic portrayals—nudity, sexually provocative language, and displays of sexual passion—are of great interest to the American viewing public. This public includes many curious and malleable children and adolescents who don't just absorb mass media representations but respond to them in various ways. Given that teens ages 12–17 watch about

In addition to biological factors, social forces strongly influence young teenagers. Because certain types of violence and aggression are considered "manly" in our culture, the boy in this photograph (top) takes great pleasure in a video game featuring simulated violence. For adolescent girls, the physical and social changes of puberty often result in a great deal of interest (some would say obsession) with personal appearance, including the selection of makeup, clothing, and shoes.

3.3 hours of television and spend almost 4 hours online each day, they are likely to encounter sexually explicit material (Hinkley, 2014; "Teen health and the media," 2014). In an era in which we are bombarded with sexual images, the challenge of making healthy choices about sex is substantial.

Although some people would protect young viewers by censoring what is shown on television or the Internet, or played on the radio or CDs, a more viable solution to sexual hype in the media is to balance it with information about real life. It's also important to remember that the media also offer positive and informative sexual messages and outcomes that can be instrumental in educating young people about sex.

Religiosity Among emerging adults, religion is an important factor to consider in the development of sexual attitudes. Though most research examines the extent to which religion shapes adolescent sexual behaviors, little is known about its impact on attitudes about sexuality. College students who indicate stronger religious beliefs and practices are more likely to reveal more

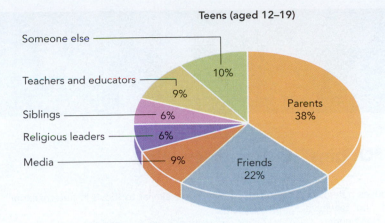

Teens (aged 12–19)

- Someone else
- Teachers and educators — 9%
- Siblings — 6%
- Religious leaders — 6%
- Media — 9%
- 10%
- Parents 38%
- Friends 22%

• **FIGURE 3**

When it comes to your/teens' decisions about sex, who is most influential?

(*Source:* From Albert, B. (2012). *With one voice, America's adults and teens sound off about teen pregnancy.* Washington, DC: The National Campaign to Prevent Teen and Unplanned Pregnancy. Reprinted by permission.)

conservative sexual attitudes and fewer sexual partners (Brelsford, Luquis, & Murray-Swank, 2011). They are also less likely to use contraception effectively (Lefkowitz, Gillen, Shearer, & Boone, 2004) (see Figure 3).

Gay, Lesbian, and Questioning Adolescents

During adolescence and early adulthood, sexual orientation becomes a very salient issue. In fact, few adolescents experience this as a trouble- or anxiety-free time. Many young people experience sexual fantasies involving others of their own sex; some engage in same-sex play. For many, these feelings of sexual attraction are a normal stage of sexual development, but for 2–10% of the population, the realization of a romantic attraction to members of their own sex will begin to grow (Chandra, Mosher, Copen, & Sionean, 2011; Laumann et al., 1994). Some gay men and lesbian women report that they began to be aware of their "difference" in middle or late childhood. Thus, the term "questioning" is used to describe those individuals who are examining their sexual orientation during this time of life. Gay and lesbian adolescents usually have heterosexual dating experiences, and some engage in intercourse during their teens, but they often report ambivalent feelings about them.

Society in general has difficulty dealing with adolescent sexuality. Accepting the fact of gay and lesbian (or bisexual) adolescent sexuality has been especially problematic. Although there is more understanding and acceptance of homosexuality now than in decades past, a better awareness that "reforming" gay people is ineffective, and more counseling and support services available in some areas, lesbian, gay, bisexual, and transgender (LGBT) individuals are still subject to ridicule and rejection. The assumed heterosexuality, or what some refer to as heteronormativity, of society has resulted in a collective **homophobia,** the irrational or phobic fear of gay men and lesbian women, such that the phrase "That's so gay" (used as a derogatory statement) is part of mainstream and youth vernacular. Teachers, parents, and administrators also perpetuate homophobia by ignoring and/or contributing to the harassment of sexual minorities. Though there has been a continued decline in anti-LGBT language over the years, middle and high school students who identify themselves as LGBT still report hearing biased language, experiencing harassment and assault, being victims of discriminatory school policies and practices, and lacking supportive school resources (2011 National School Climate Survey, 2012; Mustanski & Liu, 2013). A safer school climate directly relates to the availability of LGBT school-based resources and support, including Gay-Straight Alliances, an inclusive curriculum, supportive school staff, and comprehensive and enforced anti-bullying policies.

Nowadays the polite form of homophobia is expressed in safeguarding the family, as if homosexuals somehow came into existence independent of families and without family ties.

—Dennis Altman (1943–)

The "Origins" of Homosexuality

What causes homosexuality? What causes heterosexuality? Many have asked the first question, but few have asked the second. Although researchers don't understand the origins of sexual orientation in general, they have nevertheless focused almost exclusively on homosexuality, and their explanations generally fall into either biological or psychological categories.

Biological Factors

In genetic studies of homosexuality, researchers found a strong link between both gay men and lesbian women and their identical twins (Bailey, Dunne, & Martin, 2000; Bailey, Pillard, Neale, & Agyei, 1993; Langstrom, Rahman, Carlstrom, & Lichtenstein, 2010). (Identical twins are genetic clones, having developed from a single egg that split after fertilization; fraternal twins develop simultaneously from two separate eggs and two sperm.) The researchers matched identical and fraternal twins and adopted siblings of the same age to determine if there was a genetic component in homosexuality. The results from the studies were similar in that, among both gay men and lesbian women, a genetic marker for homosexuality was identified in identical twins (depending on the study, there was between a 20% and 50% chance that the identical sibling would also be homosexual), less prevalent among fraternal twins (2–22%) and only to a small degree among genetically unrelated (adopted) siblings (10%).

Researchers have found a statistically significant association in the number of older brothers a man has and his likelihood of being gay, regardless of the brothers' sexual orientation; this is known as the "big brother effect" (Motluk, 2003; Savin-Williams & Ream, 2007). It has been found across cultures that each additional older brother increases the odds of a gay sexual orientation by one third (Cantor, Blanchard, Paterson, & Bogaert, 2002).

In another study, Swedish researchers used brain scanning technology to examine brain areas related to emotional expression and verbal skills (Savic & Lindstrom, 2008). When comparing the brains of homosexual and heterosexual subjects, researchers found that the brain structures related to language and emotional expression were similar for gay men and heterosexual women. To a lesser extent, these areas in lesbian

women's brains were similar to those in heterosexual men's brains.

Other researchers have explored the possibility that sexual orientation could have a hormonal basis. Because hormonal levels are sensitive to such factors as general health, diet, smoking, and stress, it is very difficult to control studies measuring sexual orientation. There are some relevant studies, however. It has been found that women who took the synthetic estrogen DES when pregnant were more likely to have daughters with bisexual or same-sex attraction (Fagin, 1995). No such increase was found in males. Suggesting biological influences in the development of some homosexual people, additional research has found a correlation between same-sex attraction and handedness in that same-sex participants had a 39% greater chance of being left-handed than heterosexuals (Lalumière, Blanchard, & Zucker, 2000). Additional findings have shown that lesbian women and gay men are more likely to be left-handed than are heterosexual people (Blanchard, Cantor, Bogaert, Breedlove, & Ellis, 2006). Other indicators of prenatal influences on the brain come as a result of studying age of onset of puberty (Bogaert, Friesen, & Klentrou, 2002), birth order of siblings (Blanchard & Bogaert, 2004), and finger-length patterns (Williams, Pepitone, Christensen, & Cooke, 2000). Collectively, these studies suggest a linkage but not necessarily a causation between biology and sexual orientation.

Social Construction and Psychological Theories

A different school of thought, known as social construction theory, regards sexual orientation as a malleable concept that varies from one culture to another. Daryl Bem, a social psychologist from Cornell University, states in a theory he refers to as "exotic becomes erotic" that children who infrequently view members of the other sex (and in a minority of the cases, members of the same sex) see them as exotic. Exotic peers elicit physiological tingles and jolts that seem offensive at first but that fire up sexual desire later in life (Bem, 1996, 2000).

In spite of what these and many other studies report on the "origins" of homosexuality or any sexual orientation, much still remains unsettled or unknown. Thus, it is important to examine any study in the context of biological, sociological, and psychological factors, any or all of which might influence sexual orientation. Additionally, because research on the origins of sexual orientation focuses on homosexuality and not heterosexuality, there tends to be an underlying bias that homosexuality is not an acceptable or normal sexual variation. This bias has skewed research studies, especially psychoanalytic studies. Research should examine the origins of sexual orientation in general, not the origins of one type of orientation. As same-sex attraction has become increasingly accepted as one type of sexual orientation, scholars have shifted their research from determining the "causes" of homosexuality to understanding the nature of gay men and lesbian women as individuals and in relationships.

Think Critically

1. What, in your opinion, causes a person to have an other-sex attraction? A same-sex one? How do your thoughts about this compare and contrast with those presented in this box?

2. How important is it to understand the causes or factors that lead to same-sex attraction?

3. Who in your family would be most accepting and most rejecting of homosexuality? Why? How do these attitudes impact you and your feelings about sexual orientation?

Very few gay and lesbian teens feel that they can talk to their parents about their sexual orientation. Many (especially boys) leave home or are kicked out because their parents cannot accept their sexuality. It is sobering to think that a significant number of our children are forced into lives of secrecy, suffering, and shame because of parents' and society's reluctance to openly acknowledge the existence of same-sex attractions.

Along with feeling isolated from one's parents, there may be other issues, including absenteeism from school and lower grades, self-mutilation, sexual abuse, drug and alcohol problems, and suicide ideation, to name a few (2011 National School Climate Survey, 2012). It's extremely important that those who are feeling alone connect with others and with resources that will support them around the reality that what they are feeling is probably normal and that self-acceptance is paramount to their well-being.

Evidence suggests a positive association between coming out to oneself and feelings of self-worth. Those who are "out" to themselves and have integrated

The "It Gets Better" Project was created to show lesbian, gay, bisexual, and transgender (LGBT) youth the levels of happiness and potential they can achieve with support during their teen years.

© Stacy Walsh Rosenstock/Alamy

a sexual identity with their overall personal identity are usually more psychologically well adjusted than individuals who have not moved through this process (Savin-Williams, 2005). Support groups such as the Gay/Straight Alliance network and the "It Gets Better" Project can help adolescents attracted to their own sex deal with the discrimination and other difficulties they face. For those who do not want their sexuality to define them, an option is to shun their gay label.

Developing a mature identity is a more formidable task for LGBT individuals who also face issues of color. The racial or ethnic background of a youth may be both an impediment and an advantage in forming a sexual identity. Though racial, ethnic, and cultural communities can provide identification, support, and affirmation, all too often families and peer groups within the community present youths with biases and prejudices that undermine the process of self-acceptance as a lesbian, gay, bisexual, or transgendered person. The individual may have to struggle with the question of whether sexual orientation or ethnic identification is more important; in some instances, he or she may even have to choose one identity over the other.

Sex is a holy thing, and one of the most marvelous revelations of the divine.

—Alan Watts
(1915–1973)

Adolescent Sexual Behavior

Hormonal changes during puberty bring about a dramatic increase in sexual interest. Whether this results in sexual activity is individually determined (see Table 2).

Masturbation   If children have not begun masturbating before adolescence, they likely will begin this normal activity once the hormonal and physical changes of puberty start. Among 14- to 17-year-olds, it has been found that 74% of males and 48% of females have ever masturbated either alone or with a partner (Robbins et al., 2011). Rates of masturbation appear to be affected by a wide range of factors. In addition to providing release from sexual tension,

TABLE 2 • Trends Among 9th–12th Graders in the Prevalence of Sexual Behaviors (%): 1991–2013			
Sexual Behaviors	**1991**	**2013**	**Long term change (1991–2013)**
Ever had sexual intercourse	54	47	Decrease
Had sexual intercourse before age 13 (for the first time)	10	6	Decrease
Were sexually active (sex in the past 3 months)	38	34	Decrease
Have had four or more partners (during their life)	19	15	No change 2002–2013
Used alcohol or drugs at last sexual intercourse	22	22	Increase '91–'01 Decrease '01–'13
Contraceptive Behaviors			
Used a condom at last sexual intercourse	46	59	Increase '91–'03 No change '03–'13
Used the birth control pill at last sexual intercourse	21	19	Decrease
Did not use any method to prevent pregnancy	17	14	Mixed

SOURCE: Youth Risk Behavior Survey, 2013 (2014).

masturbation gives us the opportunity to learn about our sexual functioning, knowledge that can also be shared with a sex partner.

When boys reach adolescence, they no longer regard masturbation as ambiguous play; they know that it is sexual. Data reveal that many males begin masturbating between ages 13 and 15, whereas among females it occurs later (Bancroft, 2009). Additionally, among those adolescents who do masturbate, prevalence is higher in males than females in all age groups (Robbins et al., 2011).

Gender differences may be the result of social conditioning, culture, and communication. Though both boys and girls may feel guilt and shame for engaging in a behavior that their parents and other adults indicate is wrong or bad, most boys discuss masturbatory experiences openly with one another, whereas girls seldom talk about their own sexuality, including masturbatory activities.

Though most parents generally support comprehensive sexuality education, that is, education that helps youth remain healthy and avoid negative sexual health outcomes, they may draw the line when that discussion includes masturbation as well as sexual orientation, oral and anal sex, and other topics that move beyond penile-vaginal intercourse. It probably is also not surprising to note that parents themselves report having difficulty discussing masturbation with their adolescent children, hoping perhaps that they will not engage in this behavior. Additionally, health care providers almost always omit discussion of masturbation. For example, while 64% of parents with children aged 12 and older recalled discussions with their health care provider about sexuality, only 6% reported discussions about masturbation (Thomas, Flaherty, & Binns, 2004).

Motivations for Sexual Activity   As most of us know, the motivations for sexual experimentation and activity are numerous and complex: curiosity, pleasure, and desire, to name a few. In spite of these strong drives and feelings, why teens are indeed waiting longer to have sex for the first time is not clear. What we do know is that teens seem to be slightly less sexually experienced and if currently sexually active seem to be using birth control (Centers for Disease Control and Prevention, 2014.6a). Additionally, some suggest that this generation may be more cautious, more aware of STIs, more interested in postponing sexual activity for a quality sexual experience, or simply too busy.

Sexuality researchers have been able to target and cluster several important factors that predispose teenagers to sexual behavior: social/environmental factors (which include community, family structure, peers, and romantic partners) and individual characteristics. Being in a relationship appears to be important among those who have had sexual experience in their teens, with 70% of females and 56% of males reporting that their first sexual experience was with a steady partner. This compares with 16% of females and 28% of males who reported first having sex with someone they had just met or who was just a friend. In recent years, the most common reason that teens have given for not having had sex was that it was "against my religion or morals" followed by "I don't want to get pregnant" (females) and "I haven't found the right person yet" (males and females) (Martinez et al., 2011).

First Intercourse   With the advent of the "sexual revolution" in the 1960s, adolescent sexual behavior began to change. The revolution, otherwise called sexual liberation, challenged traditional sexual behaviors, including acceptance of sex outside of heterosexual, monogamous relationships; the use of contraception, public nudity, and legalization of abortion. Between that time and now, the

For most teens, increased commitment is accompanied by increased likelihood of sexual intimacy.
© Masterfile

explosion of media has both altered and sharpened the attention given to sexuality, resulting in vast changes in the ways in which we view ourselves and others. One notable change is the average age for first intercourse—which, although it has vacillated over time, is currently age 17 (Guttmacher, 2014). Even with some important differences, though, both men and women experience similar events.

Just what constitutes having "had sex" is debatable and context-specific. For example, age group, gender, and factors such as orgasm and giving/receiving stimulation may affect whether a person recognizes a behavior as "having had sex." Researchers from The Kinsey Institute and the Rural Center for AIDS/STD Prevention at Indiana University conducted a telephone survey of nearly 500 Indiana residents, ranging in age from 18 to 96 years. Here's what they found. There was no universal consensus on which behaviors constituted having "had sex" (Sanders et al., 2010). This was true even though 90% indicated that having penile-vaginal intercourse was "having sex," and about 80% believed that penile-anal intercourse was "having sex." Though responses did not differ significantly overall between men and women, what did vary significantly were the responses of the oldest and youngest men. For example, when participants were asked whether they agreed with the statement, "If two people had oral sex, but not intercourse, you would still consider that they had sex together," three quarters of those aged 50–59 agreed, but only half of those aged 16–19 did. These findings not only provide insight into how people of varying ages define sex but also highlight the need to use behavior-specific terminology when discussing, teaching, and researching sexual health promotion.

Given the strong memories and different meanings that young people give to the first time they have sex, it's not surprising that they also have a lot to say about this subject. In 2014, the National Campaign to Prevent Teen and Unplanned Pregnancy in partnership with MTV's "It's Your (Sex) Life" campaign conducted online interviews with 1,001 high school graduates, ages 18–24, to assess what they thought, what they remembered, and how they

Before she said, "I do . . ." she did.
—Bill Margold
(1943–)

felt about the first time they had sexual intercourse and how they feel about it now. Major findings include (Kramer, 2014):

- There is tremendous support among young adults for waiting longer to have sex.

- Pressure to have sex is common, but the pressure comes more from within than from others; many young adults want the media to show more and varied portrayals of those not having sex and they want the media to improve the way they portray young adults' sex lives.

- There are differences between men and women about how they recall their first time, what they think young teenagers need to know, what kinds of pressure exist, and where pressure comes from.

- Most young adults—men and women—place a much higher value on romance and relationships than they do on sex alone.

The experience of first sexual intercourse, sometimes also referred to as **sexual debut,** often carries enormous personal and social meaning, often symbolizing an important milestone of adolescent development. (See Figure 4 for percentages of adolescents and young adults who have had sexual intercourse by each age.) While public health organizations and researchers have devoted considerable attention to the implications of first intercourse, few studies have explored how young people view and experience their sexual debut.

It's clear that the cultural significance of sexual debut is substantial, including a transition into adulthood, loss of "sexual innocence," and for some an association with marital status (Humphreys, 2013). This subjective meaning and interpretation of sexual debut is associated with differences in the ways in which individuals go about their first experience. Researcher Laura Carpenter (2001, 2002, 2005), in conducting qualitative interviews among a sample of 61 respondents, ages 18–35, about the varied meanings of virginity and virginity loss, identified three frameworks around the meaning of virginity: the gift frame ("virginity is something special"); the stigma frame ("virginity is unwanted and something to get rid of"); and the process frame ("virginity is a rite of passage and the starting of a process of sexuality"). Extending and applying these frames, another scholar found that of 226 students from an undergraduate psychology class in Canada, 54% identified their attitudes about virginity to be as

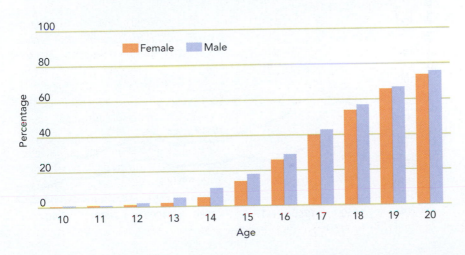

● **FIGURE 4**

Percentage of Adolescents and Young Adults Who Have Had Sexual Intercourse, by Age.

(*Source:* Guttmacher.org, 2014.)

a process, almost 38% as a gift, and 8% as a stigma (Humphreys, 2013). Individuals who viewed virginity as a stigma tended to initiate sexual activity at relatively early ages, thereby increasing the chances of contracting STIs or having an unintended pregnancy. Not surprisingly, people who valued virginity typically delayed sexual activity and had relatively few partners outside of marriage or committed relationships. Given the traditional sexual scripts for women and men in North American culture, it's probably also not surprising to learn that these frameworks tend to be gendered, with women more likely to self-classify as gift-oriented and men more likely to self-classify as stigma-oriented. In terms of affective reactions to first intercourse, men appear to have more positive feelings and attitudes about their sexual experience than do women (Humphreys, 2013).

Teenage Pregnancy

After a steady rise between the years 1990 and 2005, the overall teen birth rate fell 9% from 2009 to 2010, to 34%, and then another 10% from 2012 to 2013, to 29%, a historic low for the nation (Hamilton, Martin, Osterman, & Curtin, 2014) (see Figure 5). These trends generally held true for both older teens and younger teens. Still, almost 615,000 teens, aged 15–19, in this country get pregnant each year.

It's not surprising that the vast majority of these pregnancies are unplanned. Teen pregnancies trap most of the young mothers and fathers and their children in a downward spiral of lowered expectations, economic hardship, and poverty. Only 38% of teen girls who have had a baby by age 18 earn a high school diploma (The National Campaign, 2014). Because of poor nutrition and inadequate medical care during pregnancy, babies born to teenagers are twice as likely to lack prenatal care and have higher rates of pre-term birth and low birth weight, which are responsible for numerous physical and developmental problems. Also, many of these children will have disrupted family lives, absent fathers, and the attendant problems of poverty, such as poor diet, violent neighborhoods, limited health care, and limited access to education. They are also at higher risk for being abused than children born to older parents. Monetary costs are also high (The National Campaign, 2014).

• **FIGURE 5**

Birth Rates for Women, Aged 15–19: United States, 1980–Preliminary 2013.

(*Source:* Hamilton, B. E., Martin, J. A., Osterman, M. J. K., & Curtin, S. C. (2014, May 29). Births: Preliminary data for 2013. *CDC/NCHS, National Vital Statistics Reports, 63*(2). Available: http://www.cdc.gov/nchs/data/nvsr/nvsr63/nvsr63_02.pdf (Last accessed 8/13/14).

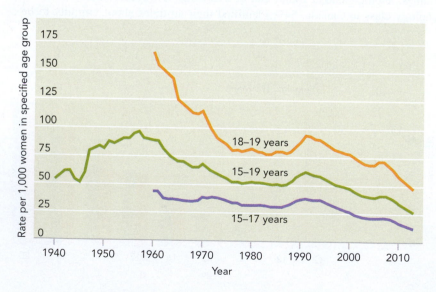

practically speaking

First Sexual Intercourse Reaction Scale

When individuals recall or anticipate their first sexual experience, they can and often do experience a myriad of feelings. In fact, no sexual milestone carries as much cultural or personal significance as what is sometimes referred to as "virginity loss." Have you ever really identified and broken down those feelings into subcomponents and asked whether or how they might affect the way you see yourself? Such an assessment can significantly help in facilitating a better understanding of the relationship between these feelings and sexual behaviors, attitudes, and norms. The First Sexual Intercourse Reaction Scale consists of 13 items designed to indicate the degree to which you have experienced various feelings in reaction to your first sexual intercourse at the time that it occurred. If you have not yet had sexual intercourse, you can still complete the scale by following the directions.

Directions

The following items deal with your feelings about your first sexual intercourse, defined as penile-vaginal or anal penetration. Please answer *all items* "a" through "m" by using a 7-point scale, 1 representing not experiencing the feeling at all, 7 representing strongly experiencing the feeling, and the numbers in between representing gradations between these extremes. *Please circle the number in each item that most closely represents the way you feel or the way you anticipate you may feel towards your first sexual intercourse.*

What were your reactions to your first sexual intercourse at the time that it occurred? I felt:

a.	Not at all confused	1	2	3	4	5	6	7	Very confused
b.	Not at all satisfied	1	2	3	4	5	6	7	Very satisfied
c.	Not at all anxious	1	2	3	4	5	6	7	Very anxious
d.	Not at all guilty	1	2	3	4	5	6	7	Very guilty

e.	Not at all romantic	1	2	3	4	5	6	7	Very romantic
f.	No pleasure at all	1	2	3	4	5	6	7	Much pleasure
g.	Not at all sorry	1	2	3	4	5	6	7	Very sorry
h.	Not at all relieved	1	2	3	4	5	6	7	Very relieved
i.	Not at all exploited	1	2	3	4	5	6	7	Very exploited
j.	Not at all happy	1	2	3	4	5	6	7	Very happy
k.	Not at all embarrassed	1	2	3	4	5	6	7	Very embarrassed
l.	Not at all excited	1	2	3	4	5	6	7	Very excited
m.	Not at all fearful	1	2	3	4	5	6	7	Very fearful

Scoring

Greater positive feelings are represented by a lower total score, while a higher total score represents more negative feelings. Items 2 (satisfied), 5 (romantic), 6 (pleasure), 8 (relieved), 10 (happy), and 12 (excited) are reversed in scoring, with 1 being very satisfied and 7 being not at all satisfied, so that on all items a 1 represents a positive response and a 7 signifies a negative response. Items can also be looked at separately to assess the degree to which a specific reaction was experienced (e.g., guilt, exploitation, pleasure).

SOURCE: From Schwartz, I. M. (1993). First Coital Affective Reaction Scale. In T. D. Fisher, C. M. Davis, W. L. Yarber, & S. L. Davis (Eds.), *Handbook of sexuality related measures* (3rd ed., pp. 640–642). Copyright © 2011 by Routledge. Reprinted by permission of the publisher (Taylor & Francis Group, http://www.informaworld.com).

According to the website of The National Campaign to Prevent Teen and Unplanned Pregnancy (2014):

Simply put, if more children in this country were born to parents who are ready and able to care for them, we would see a significant reduction in a host of social problems afflicting children in the United States.

Teenage Mothers   In 2013, nearly 275,000 women younger than 20 gave birth (Hamilton, Martin, Osterman, & Curtin, 2014). Among unmarried women in their 20s, 75% of births resulting from unplanned pregnancies are to women who have already had at least one pregnancy. Almost 20% of teen mothers have a second birth before turning 20 (The National Campaign, 2014). Most of these young mothers feel that they are "good" girls and that they became pregnant in a moment of unguarded passion. The reality of the *boy + girl = baby* equation often doesn't sink in until pregnancy is well advanced. This lack of awareness makes it difficult (emotionally and physically), if not impossible, for those who might otherwise choose to do so to have an abortion.

Not only are African American, Hispanic, and American Indian teens more likely to be sexually active than Whites, but their birth rates are also higher (see Figure 6). This is partly explained by the way in which the forces of racism and poverty combine to limit the options of young people of color. (Whites living in poverty also have disproportionately high teenage birth rates.) But additional factors contribute to pregnancy and childbirth among Black and Hispanic teens. For one thing, African American communities are far more accepting of births to unmarried women than their White counterparts; among Hispanics and African Americans, three-generation families are much more common, with the result that grandparents often play an active role in child rearing.

Teenage mothers have special needs, the most pressing of which are health care and education. Improving preconception health and regular prenatal care are essential to monitor fetal growth and the mother's health, including diet, possible STIs, and possible alcohol or drug use. Babies born to young mothers are more likely to have childhood health problems and to be hospitalized than those born to older mothers. After the birth, both mother and child need

● **FIGURE 6**

Birth Rates for Women Aged 15–19, by Race and Hispanic Origin: United States, 1991–2013.

(*Source:* CDC/Morbidity and Mortality Weekly Report, 2014.6b July 18).

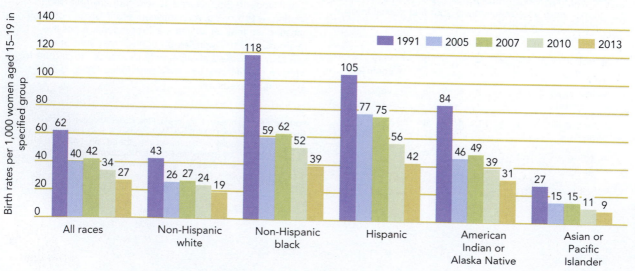

continuing care. The mother may need contraceptive counseling and services, and the child needs regular physical checkups and immunizations. Graduation from high school is an important goal of education programs for teenage mothers because it directly influences their employability and ability to support (or help support) themselves and their children. Some teenage mothers need financial assistance, at least until they complete their education. Government programs such as food stamps, Medicaid, and WIC (Women, Infants, and Children, which provides coupons for essential foods) are often crucial to the survival of young parents and their children. Even with programs such as these in place, most families need additional income to survive.

Coordination of health, educational, and social services is important because it reduces costs and provides the most comprehensive support for both mothers and fathers, who, as a result of an unplanned pregnancy, are at greater risk for depression and family turmoil (The National Campaign, 2014). Such programs may be costly, but the costs of *not* providing them are far greater.

Teenage Fathers   The rate of teenage fatherhood has also significantly declined over the past decade. Most teen males report that they would be very upset (37%) or a little upset (34%) if they got someone pregnant. The remaining 18% say they would be pleased or a little pleased (Guttmacher Institute, 2014.6a). Teen fatherhood is not a function of any single risk factor. Living in poverty, having certain expectations and values about early childbearing, having poor school achievement, and engaging in delinquent behavior seem to be pathways leading to adolescent fatherhood. Such circumstances may prompt some men to react by avoiding marriage or rejecting the responsibilities of fatherhood.

Adolescent fathers typically remain physically or psychologically involved throughout the pregnancy and for at least some time after the birth (see Figure 7). It is usually difficult for teenage fathers to contribute much to the support of their children, although most express the intention of doing so during the pregnancy. Most have a lower income, less education, and more children than men who postpone having children until age 20 or older. They may feel overwhelmed by the responsibility and may doubt their ability to be good providers. Though many teenage fathers are the sons of absent fathers, most do want to learn to be fathers. Teen fathers are a seriously neglected group who face many hardships. Policies and interventions directed at reducing teen fatherhood will have to take into consideration the many factors that influence it and focus efforts throughout the life cycle.

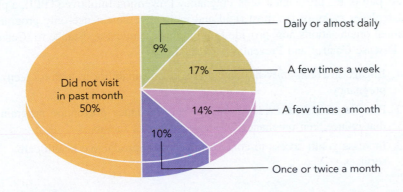

Daily or almost daily

9%

A few times a week

17%

Did not visit in past month 50%

A few times a month

14%

10%

Once or twice a month

● **FIGURE 7**

Frequency of Visits from Nonresident Fathers with Children Born to Teen Mothers.

(*Source*: The National Campaign, 2012.)

MTV's *16 and Pregnant* focuses on the often challenging terrain of adolescence, navigating relationships, and coming of age, all while dealing with a pregnancy.
© David J. Green - Lifestyle/Alamy

Sexuality Education

For over 30 years, abstinence-only sexuality education has been a focal point in school sexuality education policy and curriculum in the United States. This approach began in 1981 when, during the Reagan administration, federal policymakers began pouring taxpayer money into a form of sexuality education that excluded all types of sexual and reproductive health education and focused exclusively on abstinence from sexual behaviors until marriage. During the administration of George W. Bush, the federal government spent $1.5 billion on programs that encouraged teens to delay sex until marriage. Critics cited that it was grounded in conservative and religious doctrine, was ineffective, and failed to educate teens about condoms in the age of sexually transmitted infections (STIs). The Obama administration reversed this trend when it reduced federal funding for abstinence-only programming and launched a teen pregnancy prevention program focusing on age-appropriate, evidence-based education primarily emphasizing teenage pregnancy prevention and STI prevention. These programs are also required to address life skills that help teens make responsible decisions that lead to safe and healthy lives.

As part of the president's Teen Pregnancy Prevention Initiative (TPPI), a plan that replaces many of the most rigid and ineffective abstinence-only programs, national organizations now provide training and technical assistance to (Centers for Disease Control and Prevention, 2013.6a):

1. Engage in community mobilization and sustainability to address teen pregnancy

2. Provide teens with evidence-based teen pregnancy prevention programs that reduce teen pregnancy and associated risk factors

3. Increase youth access to contraceptive and reproductive health care services

4. Educate civic leaders, parents, and other community members about evidence-based strategies to reduce teen pregnancy and improve adolescent reproductive health

5. Work with diverse communities about the link between teen pregnancy and the social determinants of health to ensure culturally and linguistically appropriate programs and reproductive health care services to youth

While critics continue to argue the merits of this approach, many scholars make a case for a more holistic developmental view, one that includes the possibility of a positive framework for understanding adolescent sexuality (Russell, Van Campen, & Muraco, 2012; Yarber & Sayad, 2010).

Most teens and adults wish young people would get information about both abstinence and contraception rather than one or the other and believe religious leaders and groups should be doing more to help support young people's ability to develop a healthy and positive sexuality. (Rodriguez, 2012).

Expanding National and Worldwide Views   The Sexuality Information and Education Council of the United States (SIECUS) developed the *Guidelines for Comprehensive Sexuality Education* (SIECUS, 2004), the first national model for comprehensive sexuality education. The guidelines, the most widely recognized and implemented framework for comprehensive sexuality education in the United States and several countries worldwide, along with the National Sexuality Education Standards published by the *Journal of School Health* ("National sexuality education standards," 2012), have used evidence-based research to suggest age-appropriate topics and means to teach them.

Sexuality education is a lifelong process. From the time that we are born, we learn about love, touch, affection, and our bodies. As we grow, the messages continue from both our families and the social environment, with school-based programs complementing and augmenting these primary sources of information.

Just what is comprehensive sexuality education? According to SIECUS (2009), comprehensive sexuality education:

> . . . is a lifelong process of acquiring information and forming attitudes, beliefs, and values about such important topics as identity, relationships and intimacy. . . . The primary goal of sexuality education is to promote adult sexual health. It should assist young people in the developing a positive view of sexuality, provide them with information they need to take care of their sexual health, and help them acquire skills to make decisions now and in the future.

In response to the increased attention that sexuality education has received, 35 organizations, including the American Psychological Association, American College of Obstetricians and Gynecologists, and Planned Parenthood Federation of America, have joined together to urge the federal government to support funding for comprehensive sexuality education.

In 2010, the World Health Organization (WHO) released guidelines to help public health decision makers develop a new approach to sexuality education (WHO, 2010.6a). These guidelines, though similar to those proposed by SIECUS, offer a global perspective. The recommendations place facts in the broader context of values, knowledge, and life skills. These guidelines are based on a positive interpretation of sexuality as part of physical and mental health. Such

think
about it

Healthy Teen Sexuality

We need a new vision for sexual health in America.

—John Santelli, professor and chair,
Columbia University

Programs are useless unless they are linked to all the things that make young people whole.

—Michael Carrera, professor emeritus
at Hunt College of Public Health

Adolescence is a crucial time in one's life for the development of sexuality, which involves not only body changes, sexual behaviors, and new health care needs but also "building emotional maturity, relationship skills, and healthy body image" (ACT for Youth, 2014). At the same time, adolescence is a time when individuals and society swing between viewing teens as innocent and uninterested in sexuality on the one hand and pathologized and acting out in ways that are physically and mentally harmful on the other. In light of this, can teens and young adults ever become sexually healthy adults? What does it even mean to be a sexually healthy teenager?

There are no easy answers to these questions, just as there is no specific program that provides a complete solution to helping young people delay having sex, use protection against pregnancy and STIs, and become healthy sexual beings. However, when we begin to provide a positive interpretation of sexuality as part of physical and mental health, as the World Health Organization (2010.6a) has suggested, we can begin to challenge negative stereotypes of young people and create a new dialogue about what it means to be sexually healthy individuals.

This transition in thinking about what it means to be a sexually healthy young person does not occur in a vacuum. Nor should it be left to young people and their peers, who, with 24/7 access to the Internet, are susceptible to what they see and hear. Adults have many significant roles to play in supporting positive sexual health for young people, including being positive parents, supporting sexual health programming, and becoming involved in communities that engage in youth development (ACT for Youth, 2014). Furthermore, communities should underscore these views by maximizing the use of information and communication through technology; taking a multilevel approach, including family-inclusive programming and the incorporation of youth voices that meet their developmental needs; utilizing a positive, holistic

approach to education that is beyond a problem focus; and addressing funding issues such as easier access to health insurance (ACT for Youth, 2009). A positive, holistic approach might include discussion of such concepts as sexual pleasure, the process of becoming more accepting and comfortable with one's sexuality, sexual communication, a sexual code of behavior, and sexual response and functioning at an age-appropriate level.

In order to reverse our thinking about young people's sexuality, creative and dynamic changes will have to occur in families, schools, communities, and policy. Definitions and discussions about sexual health will need to be broadened so that someday a sexually healthy adolescent (or adult) might say (ACT for Youth, 2014):

- I am comfortable with my body and my sexuality.
- I can talk effectively with my peers, family, and partners.
- I know my body and how it functions.
- I understand the risks, responsibilities, and consequences of sexual behavior.
- I am able to recognize risks and ways to reduce risks.
- I know how to access and use health care services and information.
- I am able to set boundaries when it comes to sex and sexual relationships.
- I act responsibly according to my personal values.
- I am able to form and maintain healthy relationships.

Until we use every opportunity to champion adolescent sexual health, we will continue to perpetuate ineffective and inaccurate views of youth that impede their potential to develop a healthy sexuality.

Think Critically

1. How would you define a sexually healthy teen? How did you arrive at this?
2. What is the role of parents in communicating and modeling a definition of sexual health? What topics should be included in this discussion? What (if anything) should be omitted?
3. How do you think a sexually healthy adolescent would respond to each of the statements in the box? What might a person do to become a sexually healthy person?

topics as HIV/AIDS and sexual violence are embedded in a curriculum that focuses on the individual's self-determination and responsibility for themselves and others. It is intended that the guidelines will continue to challenge the one-sided emphasis of abstinence-only sexuality education programs and create the conditions for a sexually healthy society.

Although more research needs to be done on sexuality education and its impact on young people, most professionals agree that it is one of the most important means we have to help young people to become sexually healthy adults. Young people, guided by their parents and armed with knowledge and self-confidence, can make informed decisions and direct their own sexual destinies.

Final Thoughts

From birth, humans are rich in sexual and erotic potential. As children, the world around us begins to shape our sexuality and the ways that we ultimately express it. As adolescents, our education continues as a random mixture of learning and yearning. With sexual maturity, the gap between physiological development and psychological development begins to narrow and emotional and intellectual capabilities begin to expand. Responses to and decisions about sexuality education, sexual activity, sexual orientation, and pregnancy begin to emerge. Each of these presents a challenge and an opportunity to more fully evolve into the sexual beings that we are.

Summary

Sexuality in Infancy and Childhood (Ages 0 to 11)

- *Psychosexual development* begins in infancy, when we begin to learn how we "should" feel about our bodies and our gender roles. Infants need stroking and cuddling to ensure healthy psychosexual development.
- Children learn about their bodies through various forms of sex play. Their sexual interest should not be labeled "bad" but may be deemed inappropriate for certain times, places, or persons. Children need to experience acts of physical affection and to be told nonthreateningly about "good" and "bad" touching by adults.

Sexuality in Adolescence (Ages 12 to 19)

- *Puberty* is the biological stage when reproduction becomes possible. The psychological state of

puberty is *adolescence,* a time of growth and often confusion as the body matures faster than the emotional and intellectual abilities. The traits of adolescence are culturally determined.

- Pubertal changes that result in secondary sex characteristics in girls begin between ages 8 and 13. They include a growth spurt, breast development, pubic and underarm hair, vaginal secretions, and menarche (first menstruation). Pubertal changes in boys generally begin between 9 and 14. They include a growth spurt, a deepening voice, hair growth, development of external genitals, and spermarche. *Precocious puberty* refers to the appearance of pubertal signs at an earlier age than is considered typical. Preparing young people for these changes is helpful.
- Children and adolescents often learn a great deal about sexuality from their family dynamics and characteristics. A strong bond between parent and

child reduces the risk of early sexual involvement and pregnancy.

- Peers provide a strong influence on the values, attitudes, and behavior of adolescents. They are also a source of much misinformation regarding sex.
- The media present highly charged images of sexuality that are often out of context. Parents can counteract media distortions by discussing the context of sexuality with their children and balancing it with information about real life.
- Young gay and lesbian individuals are largely invisible because of society's assumption of heterosexuality. They may begin to come to terms with their sexual orientation during their teenage years. Because of society's reluctance to acknowledge homosexuality openly, most gay, lesbian, and bisexual teens suffer a great deal of emotional pain.
- Most adolescents engage in masturbation. Gender differences in rates of masturbation may be the result of social conditioning and communication.
- The birth rate among teens aged 15–19 has declined to 26.6 births per 1,000 women, an historic low for the nation.
- Most teenagers have pressing concerns about sexuality, and most parents and the public favor comprehensive sexuality education for children. National and international organizations have designed and are using evidence-based comprehensive sexuality education programs.

Sex and the Internet

Sexual Activity and Teens

Data on teen STI rates and unintended pregnancy have recently appeared in the headlines of our newspapers, not to remind us of the dismal figures but to inform us that the rates are unacceptably high. One of the most helpful and thorough sites that report on this and other adolescent sexuality issues is The National Campaign to Prevent Teen and Unplanned Pregnancy: http://www.thenationalcampaign.org. Access this site and see if you can find each of the following:

- The age of first intercourse among teens
- The most common type of contraceptive used
- The risk of acquiring a specific STI with one act of intercourse
- The percentage of teen mothers who complete high school
- The number of pregnancies that are terminated by abortion

Now answer the following questions:

- Which fact was the most surprising to you?
- Which fact was the least surprising?
- If you had unlimited resources, how might you go about solving the problem of teen pregnancy?

Questions for Discussion

- Who or what taught you the most about sexuality when you were a child and teenager? What lessons did you learn? What would have made the transition from childhood to adolescence easier?

- Should masturbation in young children be ignored, discouraged, or encouraged? What effect might each of these responses have on a child who is just beginning to learn about herself or himself?

- To what do you attribute the decline in teen pregnancy rates? What are some ways to reduce the rates of unintended teenage pregnancy?

Suggested Websites

Advocates for Youth
www.advocatesforyouth.org
Champions efforts to help young people make informed and responsible decisions about their reproductive and sexual health.

American Academy of Pediatrics
http://www.aap.org
A wealth of information about the physical, mental, and social health and well-being of infants, children, adolescents, and young adults.

Bedsider
Bedsider.org
Especially for teens, provides information about birth control and a birth control reminder.

Gay, Lesbian & Straight Education Network (GLSEN)

http://www.glsen.org/

Mission is to ensure that every member of every school community is valued and respected regardless of sexual orientation, gender identity, or gender expression.

Guttmacher Institute

http://www.guttmacher.org/

Seeks to advance sexual and reproductive health and rights through research, policy analysis, and public education.

Healthy Children

www.healthychildren.org

Endorsed by the American Academy of Pediatrics, a parenting website offering a wide range of topics around mental, physical, and social health and well-being for infants, children, adolescents, and young adults.

"It Gets Better" Project

http://www.itgetsbetter.org

Spreads the message that everyone deserves to be respected and denounces hate and intolerance.

Midwest Teen Sex Show

http://wwwwestteensexshow.com

Uses broadcast media to provide sex information to teens.

National Federation of Parents and Friends of Lesbians and Gays (PFLAG)

http://www.pflag.org

Provides information and support for those who care about gay, lesbian, bisexual, and transgender persons.

Scarleteen

http://www.scarleteen.com

Staffed by volunteers, some of whom are young adults; provides sexuality education for a young adult population.

Suggested Reading

Bancroft, J. (2003). *Sexual development in childhood.* Bloomington: Indiana University Press. Scholarly and well-researched edited text by one of the leaders in the field; also, one of the few books available on this subject.

Bromberg, D., & O'Donohue, W. T. (Eds.). (2013). *Handbook of child and adolescent sexuality: Developmental and forensic psychology.* New York: Elsevier. Aimed at a broad audience, this edited reference book addresses sexuality across development, sexual victimization, and sexual behavior problems.

Haffner, D. W. (2008). *What every 21st-century parent needs to know: Facing today's challenges with wisdom and heart.* New York: New Market Press. A practical and reassuring book for parents.

Levokoff, L., & Widner, J. (2014). *Got teens? The doctor moms' guide to sexuality, social media and other adolescent realities.* Berkeley, CA: Seal Press. Combining their medical and psychological backgrounds, these two authors answer the often sensitive sexuality-related questions that kids ask their parents.

Savage, D. (2013). *American Savage.* New York: Dutton. A personal and deeply felt book about marriage, religion, and being gay.

Steinberg, L. D. (2013). *Adolescence* (10th ed.). New York: McGraw-Hill. A comprehensive, research-based examination of adolescent development within the context of environmental and social relationships.

Sexuality in Adulthood

© Jose Luis Pelaez Inc./Getty Images

CHAPTER OUTLINE

Sexuality in Early Adulthood

Sexuality in Middle Adulthood

Sexuality in Late Adulthood

As we enter adulthood, with greater experience and understanding, we develop a potentially mature sexuality. We establish our sexual orientation; we integrate love and sexuality; we forge intimate connections and make commitments; we make decisions regarding our fertility; and we develop a coherent sexual philosophy. Then, in our middle years, we redefine the role of sex in our intimate relationships, accept our aging, and reevaluate our sexual philosophy. Finally, in later adulthood we reinterpret the meaning of sexuality in accordance with the erotic capabilities of our bodies. We come to terms with the possible loss of our partner and our own eventual decline. In all these stages, sexuality weaves its bright and dark threads through our lives.

In this chapter, we continue the exploration and discussion of sexuality over the human life cycle. We begin with an examination of the developmental concerns of young adults, further explore the establishment of sexual orientations, turn to singlehood and cohabitation, then to middle adulthood, continuing to focus on developmental concerns, relational and nonrelational sexuality, and separation and divorce. Next, we look at sexuality in late adulthood, examining developmental issues, stereotypes, and differences and similarities in aging and sex between men and women and among gay couples. Finally, we examine the role of the partner in sustaining health.

> *The good life is one inspired by love and guided by knowledge.*
>
> —Bertrand Russell
> (1872–1970)

● Sexuality in Early Adulthood

Like other life passages, the one from adolescence to early adulthood offers potential for growth if one is aware of and remains open to the opportunities this period brings (see Figure 1).

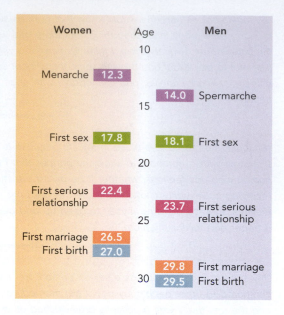

● **FIGURE** 1

Sexual and Reproductive Time Line: Mean Age of Major Events.

(*Source:* Finer, L. B., & Philbin, J. M. (2014). Trends in ages at key reproductive transitions in the United States, 1951–2010. *Women's Health Issues, 23*(3), e1–e9.

Developmental Concerns

Several tasks challenge young adults as they develop their sexuality (Gagnon & Simon, 1973):

- *Establishing sexual orientation.* Children and adolescents may engage in sexual experimentation, such as playing doctor, kissing, and fondling, with members of both sexes, but they do not necessarily associate these activities with sexual orientation. Instead, their orientation as heterosexual, gay, lesbian, bisexual, or transgender is in the process of emerging.

- *Integrating love and sex.* Traditional gender roles call for men to be sex-oriented and women to be love-oriented. In adulthood, this sex-versus-love dichotomy should be addressed. Instead of polarizing love and sex, people need to develop ways of uniting them.

- *Forging intimacy and making commitments.* Young adulthood is characterized by increasing sexual experience. Through dating, courtship, and cohabitation, individuals gain knowledge of themselves and others as potential partners. As relationships become more meaningful, the degree of intimacy and interdependence increases. Sexuality can be a means of enhancing intimacy and self-disclosure, as well as a source of physical pleasure. As adults become more intimate, most desire to develop their ability to make commitments.

- *Making fertility/childbearing decisions.* Becoming a parent is socially discouraged during adolescence, but it becomes increasingly legitimate when people reach their 20s, especially if they are married or partnered. Fertility issues are often critical but sometimes unacknowledged, especially for single young adults.

- *Practicing safer sex to protect against sexually transmitted infections (STIs).* An awareness of the various STIs and ways to best protect against them must be integrated into the communication, values, and behaviors of all people.

Let's face it, a date is like a job interview that lasts all night.

—Jerry Seinfeld
(1954–)

think
about it

Life Behaviors of a Sexually Healthy Adult

In 1996, the Sexuality Information and Education Council of the United States (SIECUS) published the first national guidelines for comprehensive sexuality education in kindergarten through 12th grade. These guidelines covered the life behaviors of a sexually healthy adult in six areas and were updated in 2004.

Behaviors of the Sexually Healthy Adult

1. Human development:
   a. Appreciate one's own body.
   b. Seek further information about reproduction as needed.
   c. Affirm that human development includes sexual development, which may or may not include reproduction or sexual experience.
   d. Interact with all genders in respectful and appropriate ways.
   e. Affirm one's own sexual orientation and respect the sexual orientation of others.
   f. Affirm one's own gender identities and respect the gender identities of others.

2. Relationships:
   a. Express love and intimacy in appropriate ways.
   b. Develop and maintain meaningful relationships.
   c. Avoid exploitative or manipulative relationships.
   d. Make informed choices about family options and relationships.
   e. Exhibit skills that enhance personal relationships.

3. Personal skills:
   a. Identify and live according to one's own values.
   b. Take responsibility for one's own behavior.
   c. Practice effective decision making.
   d. Develop critical thinking skills.
   e. Communicate effectively with family, peers, and romantic partners.

4. Sexual behavior:
   a. Enjoy and express one's sexuality throughout life.
   b. Express one's sexuality in ways congruent with one's values.
   c. Enjoy sexual feelings without necessarily acting on them.
   d. Discriminate between life-enhancing sexual behaviors and those that are harmful to oneself and/or others.
   e. Express one's sexuality while respecting the rights of others.
   f. Seek new information to enhance one's sexuality.
   g. Engage in sexual relationships that are consensual, nonexploitative, honest, pleasurable, and protected.

5. Sexual health:
   a. Practice health-promoting behaviors, such as regular checkups, breast and testicular self-exams, and early identification of potential problems.
   b. Use contraception effectively to avoid unintended pregnancy.
   c. Avoid contracting or transmitting an STI, including HIV.
   d. Act consistent with one's values in dealing with an unintended pregnancy.
   e. Seek early prenatal care.
   f. Help prevent sexual abuse.

6. Society and culture:
   a. Demonstrate respect for people with different sexual values.
   b. Exercise democratic responsibility to influence legislation dealing with sexual issues.
   c. Assess the impact of family, cultural, religious, media, and societal messages on one's thoughts, feelings, values, and behaviors related to sexuality.
   d. Critically examine the world around them for biases based on gender, sexual orientation, culture, ethnicity, and race.
   e. Promote the rights of all people to have access to accurate sexuality information.
   f. Avoid behaviors that exhibit prejudice and bigotry.
   g. Reject stereotypes about the sexuality of different populations.
   h. Educate others about sexuality.

Think Critically

1. Is it possible for young people to enact or achieve all of the behaviors? If so, how? If not, why not?
2. Which of the behaviors would seem to be the most difficult to achieve? Why?
3. Which of the behaviors change over the life span?
4. What life behaviors related to sexuality are missing from the list?

SOURCE: National Guidelines Task Force. (2004). *Guidelines for comprehensive sexuality education: Kindergarten–12th grade* (3rd ed.). New York: Sexuality Information and Education Council of the United States. 130 W. 42nd St., Suite 350, New York, NY 10036. Reprinted with permission.

Critical life questions, such as those involving relationships, personal skills, sexual behavior, and health, often arise during the college-age years when young people begin to live independently and away from their parents.

© Stockbyte/Punchstock

Somewhere in the mounting and mating, rutting and butting is the very secret of nature itself.

—Graham Swift
(1949–)

Sex lies at the root of life, and we can never learn to revere life until we know how to understand sex.

—Havelock Ellis
(1859–1939)

■ *Evolving a sexual philosophy.* As individuals move from adolescence to adulthood, they reevaluate their moral standards, moving from decision making based on authority to standards based on their personal principles of right and wrong, caring, and responsibility. They become responsible for developing their own moral code, which includes sexual issues. They also need to differentiate between what they have been taught about sexuality and what they truly believe about themselves. This is an important step in "owning one's own sexuality." In doing so, they need to evolve a personal philosophical perspective to give coherence to sexual attitudes, behaviors, beliefs, and values. They need to place sexuality within the larger framework of their lives and relationships. They need to integrate their personal, religious, spiritual, and humanistic values with their sexuality.

Establishing Sexual Orientation

A critical task of adulthood is establishing one's sexual orientation as heterosexual, gay, lesbian, bisexual, or transgender. As mentioned previously, in childhood and early adolescence, there is often sex play or sexual experimentation with members of the other sex and same sex. These exploratory experiences are tentative in terms of sexual orientation. But in late adolescence and young adulthood, men and women are confronted with the important developmental task of establishing intimacy. And part of the task of establishing intimate relationships is exploring and solidifying one's sexual orientation.

Most people develop a heterosexual identity by adolescence or young adulthood. Their task is simplified because their development as heterosexuals is approved by society. But for those who are attracted to the same or both sexes or are unsure, their development features more doubt and anxiety. Because those who are attracted to the same sex are aware that they are questioning deep societal taboos, it can take them longer to confirm and accept their sexual orientation. It may also be difficult and dangerous for them to establish a relationship.

Models of Sexual Orientation   Sexual orientation is an area of human sexuality that has been clouded by misunderstanding, myth, and confusion. To help explain the complex nature of sexual orientation, psychologists and researchers in sexuality have developed various models (see Figure 2). Much as our views of gender, masculinity, and femininity have changed, so have conceptualizations of sexual orientation, although these are different phenomena. It is important to note that sexual orientation labels do not constitute the entirety of sexual orientations (Savin-Williams, 2014). Though discrete categories are more easily understood and conveyed, this labeling disguises variability and complexity within a sexual orientation. According to Cornell University researcher and gender specialist Ritch C. Savin-Williams (2014), "sexual orientation is a continuously distributed characteristic of individuals, and all decisions to categorize it into discrete units, regardless of how many, are ultimately external impositions placed on individuals' experiences."

Until the research of Alfred C. Kinsey and his colleagues, sexual orientation was dichotomized into "heterosexual" and "homosexual"—that is, a person

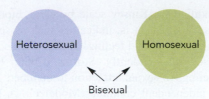

Model A: Dichotomous—psychoanalytic

Model B: Unidimensional—bipolar (Kinsey)

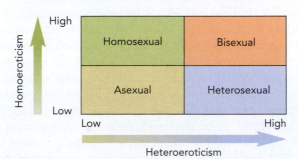

Model C: Two-dimensional—orthogonal (Storms)

could be one or the other. As shown in Model A in Figure 2, some researchers considered a third category, bisexuality, although others believed that a bisexual individual was a homosexual person trying to be heterosexual. One of Kinsey's most significant contributions was his challenge to this traditional model. Research by Kinsey and others showed that same-sex sexual behavior was not uncommon and did not necessarily indicate a person's sexual orientation. They also found that participation in both same- and other-sex behavior was not uncommon. This led them to conclude that sexual orientation is a continuum from exclusively heterosexual to exclusively homosexual, as depicted in Model B, and that a person's sexual behavior pattern can change across a lifetime. Since that time, this continuum has been widely utilized in sexuality research, education, and therapy.

Kinsey rejected the traditional explanation of sexual orientation and sexuality by saying:

> The world is not divided into sheep and goats. Not all things are black nor all things white. . . . Nature rarely deals with discrete categories. Only the human mind invents categories and tries to force facts into separated pigeonholes. The living world is a continuum in each and every one of its aspects. The sooner we learn this concerning human sexual behavior the sooner we shall reach a sound understanding of the realities of sex (Kinsey, Pomeroy, & Martin, 1948).

The Kinsey continuum has been criticized for its implication that the more heterosexual a person is the less homosexual he or she must be, and vice versa. Sex researchers Sanders, Reinisch, and McWhirter (1990) note that some researchers have modified the Kinsey scale by using bipolar ratings of hetero-sexuality and homosexuality; that is, indicators such as sexual behavior, sexual fantasies, the person one loves, and feelings about which sex is more "attractive" can each be assessed independently. Storms (1980, 1981) suggested that **homoeroticism**—feelings of sexual attraction to members of the same sex—and heteroeroticism are independent continua (Model C). A bisexual individual is high on both homoeroticism and heteroeroticism dimensions, a heterosexual per-son is high on heteroeroticism and low on homoeroticism, and a homosexual individual is high on homoeroticism and low on heteroeroticism. A person low on both dimensions would be considered asexual.

Prevalence of Varied Sexual Orientations   We do not know the exact num-bers of men and women who identify as heterosexual, gay, lesbian, bisexual, or transgender people. In large part, this is because homosexuality is stigmatized. Gay men, lesbian women, and bisexual individuals are often reluctant to reveal their identities in research surveys for reasons of personal hesitancy as well as conceptual problems surrounding what constitutes sexual orientation.

The majority of studies on the prevalence of people's variations in sexual orientation suggest that about 1–4% of males and females consider themselves to be something other than heterosexual (either homosexual, bisexual, or something else) (Ellis, 1996; Herbenick et al., 2010; Laumann et al., 1994; Ward, Dahlhamer, Galinsky, & Joestl, 2014). For the first time in its 57-year history, the 2013 National Health Interview Survey collected data on sexual orientation. Among adults aged 18 and over, 96.6% identified as straight, 1.6% identified as gay or lesbian, and 0.7% identified as bisexual. The remaining 1.1% identified as "something else," stated, "I don't know the answer," or did not provide an answer (Ward et al., 2014). In an earlier study, 10–15% report at least occasional sexual attraction to or sexual fantasy about their same sex (Smith et al., 2003).

What are we to make of these findings? In part, the variances that exist in the literature regarding prevalence of varied sexual orientation may be explained by different methodologies, interviewing techniques, sampling procedures, definitions of sexual orientation, random response errors, and differences in the way questions are framed. Furthermore, sexuality is more than simply sexual behaviors; it also includes attraction and desire. One can be a virgin or celibate and still identify as gay, lesbian, bisexual, transgender, or heterosexual. One can also participate in sexual behavior with a person of the other or same sex but not label oneself as heterosexual or homosexual. Stigma and discrimination may also prevent some from disclosing their sexual orientation, particularly if they feel judged. Finally, because sexuality is varied and changes over time, its expression at any one time is not necessarily the same as at another time or for all time (Diamond, 2008).

The Gay/Lesbian/Bisexual Identity Process   Identifying oneself as a lesbian, gay, or bisexual person takes considerable time and, for some, may involve multiple paths (Rosario, Scrimshaw, & Hunter, 2011). The most intense phase in the development of one's sexual identity is during late adolescence and early adulthood. Researchers have found that college graduates are more likely to identify themselves as gay, lesbian, or bisexual while they are attending college because postsecondary education tends to engage students with issues of pluralism, diversity, and self-evaluation. Homoeroticism almost always precedes lesbian or gay activity by several years (Bell, Weinberg, & Hammersmith, 1981).

Love is sacred, and sex is sacred too. The two things are not a part; they belong together.

—Lame Deer, Lakota Indian holy man (1903–1976)

think
about it

Bisexuality: The Nature of Dual Attraction

"**Heterosexuality**" and "**homosexuality**" are terms used to categorize people according to the sexuality of their sex partners. But as noted in the previous discussion of Kinsey's work, such categories do not always adequately reflect the complexity of sexual orientation or of human sexuality in general. In fact, bisexuality could be considered an "invisible" minority, mentioned in passing or viewed as indistinguishable from the gay and lesbian community (Kaestle & Ivory, 2012). Still, between 0.7% and 4.5% of men and women over the age of 18 identify themselves as bisexual (Herbenick et al., 2010; Ward et al., 2014). In the 2013 National Health Interview Survey noted previously, 11% of those who identified as bisexual experienced serious psychological distress in the past 30 days compared with 3.9% of those who identified as straight (Ward et al., 2014). While it is unclear about why this may be true, stigmas against bisexual people, including the belief that bisexuality is not a real sexual orientation, and the stereotype that bisexual men in particular are less inclined toward monogamous relationships and not able to maintain a long-term partnership could be factors (Friedman et al., 2014; Zivony & Lobel, 2014).

Most individuals view bisexuality as a pattern of erotic responsiveness to both sexes. This broad thinking leaves some questions unanswered: Do short-term sexual experiences with both sexes qualify one to be labeled bisexual? Does everyone have the potential to be bisexual? Does attraction to the same or both sexes mean one is bisexual? Though some may suggest that love has no sexual orientation, others may desire a category for the feelings they experience. Regardless, researchers still wonder whether bisexuality is: (1) a temporary stage of transition or experimentation; (2) a third type of sexual orientation, characterized by fixed patterns of attraction to both sexes; or (3) a strong form of all individuals' capacity for sexual fluidity (Diamond, 2008).

Bisexual Identity Formation

In contrast to homosexuality, there is little research on bisexuality. The process of bisexual identity formation appears to be complex, requiring the rejection of the two recognized categories of sexual orientation. Consequently, bisexual people often find themselves stigmatized by gay men and lesbian women, as well as by heterosexual individuals, a kind of discrimination called biphobia.

Those people who do identify as bisexual have partners of both sexes. Sometimes, they have had only one or two same-sex experiences; nevertheless, they identify themselves as bisexual. They believe they can love and enjoy sex with both women and men. In other instances, those with predominately same-sex experience and only limited other-sex experience consider themselves bisexual. In most cases, bisexual people do not have sex with men one week and women the next. Rather, their bisexuality is sequential. That is, they are involved in other-sex relationships for certain periods, ranging from a few weeks to years; later, they are involved in same-sex relations for another period of time.

The Nature of Bisexuality

As discussed previously, sexuality runs along a continuum, with bisexuality falling midway between exclusive heterosexuality and exclusive homosexuality. Given this, one might ask whether bisexual people are merely in transition toward one or the other end of the continuum or whether bisexuality is a sexual orientation in its own right. Research among women reveals some interesting findings that are inconsistent with the long-debated belief that bisexuality is a transitional stage or "phase" (Diamond, 2008). Longitudinal data collected from 79 lesbian, bisexual, and "unlabeled" women reveal that there are, in fact, boundaries between the long-term development stages of lesbian, bisexual, and unlabeled women, but these boundaries are rather fluid. More specifically, over time, it was found that more women appeared to have adopted bisexual/unlabeled identities rather than relinquish them. Hence, bisexuality is seen as a third type of sexual orientation and, as such, has a capacity for flexibility in erotic response. Whether this finding is applicable to men remains unknown. Ultimately, accepting bisexuality as a healthy and legitimate orientation reflects acknowledging our diversity.

Think Critically

1. What are your thoughts about bisexuality: a legitimate sexual identity or one that is uncertain or temporary?

2. Would you agree to completing a questionnaire on sexual orientation? If so, how might you feel if the results were different from what you expected?

3. What might your reaction be if a dating partner revealed that he or she was bisexual?

Gay pride commemorates the LGBT rights movement both in the U.S. and abroad.

© Justin Sullivan/Getty Images

Bisexuality immediately doubles your chances for a date on a Saturday night.

—Rodney Dangerfield
(1921–2004)

How does one arrive at one's sexual orientation? Does it really matter if one is born heterosexual or homosexual, whether it comes later, or whether one chooses? For some, the awareness of being or feeling something other than heterosexual occurs in phases. This first phase is marked by the initiation of a process of self-discovery and exploration, including becoming aware of one's sexual orientations; questioning whether one may be a lesbian, gay, or bisexual (LGB) person; and having sex with members of the same sex. The second phase, identity integration, is a continuation of sexual identity development as individuals integrate and incorporate the identity into their sense of self. Engaging in LGB-related social activities, addressing society's negative attitudes, and feeling more comfortable about disclosing one's identity to others are part of this process (Rosario et al., 2011). Difficulties in developing an integrated LGB identity often cause distress and may have particularly negative implications for the psychological adjustment of LGB youth. At the same time, the categorization of individuals as gay, straight, or bisexual does not allow for the fact that some may move back and forth among sexual identities, and it is this fluidity that is a crucial variable in sexual development (Diamond, 2008).

New to the U.S. Department of Health and Human Services' *Healthy People 2020* goals (2012.7a) is the goal to improve the health, safety, and well-being of lesbian, gay, bisexual, and transgender (LGBT) individuals. Now that there is inclusion of sexual orientation in the National Health Interview Survey data, government funding and research decisions about special health needs of LGBT individuals can be guided by data (Ward et al., 2014). Though data did not reveal one sexual orientation group was less physically healthy than another, it found that, compared with straight people, those who self-identified as gay or lesbian were more likely to smoke and to have consumed five or more drinks in 1 day at least once in the past year. Eliminating disparities and enhancing efforts to improve gay, lesbian, bisexual, and transgender individuals' mental and physical health are necessary to ensure that they, like everyone else, can lead long, healthy lives.

For many, being a lesbian or gay person is associated with a total lifestyle and way of thinking. Publicly acknowledging one's same-sex attraction (coming out) has become especially important. Coming out is a major decision because it may jeopardize many relationships, but it is also an important means of self-validation and self-affirmation. By publicly acknowledging a lesbian, gay, or bisexual orientation, a person begins to reject the stigma and condemnation associated with it. Generally, coming out to heterosexual people occurs in stages involving friends and family members.

Lesbian women, gay men, and bisexual individuals are often "out" to varying degrees. Some are out to no one, not even themselves, while others are out only to selected individuals and lovers, and others to close friends and lovers but not to their families and employers. Because of fear of reprisal, dismissal, or public reaction, many gay, lesbian, and bisexual professionals are not out to their employers, their co-workers, or the public.

Contradicting many assumptions about sexual orientation as being early developing and unstable, sexual fluidity is situation-dependent flexibility in the gender of a woman's sexual attraction (Diamond, 2008). Regardless of their sexual orientation, this flexibility makes it possible for some women under unique circumstances to experience same-sex or other-sex desires. While men appear more likely to regard their sexual orientation as fixed and innate, women are more likely to acknowledge choice and change, depending on the circumstances.

Many gay men and lesbian women experience some of the same negative attitudes toward homosexuality as their heterosexual counterparts. **Internalized homophobia** is a set of negative attitudes and affects toward homosexuality in other persons and toward same-sex attraction in oneself. Growing up in a heterosexual world that condones only one way of sexual expression and reproduction, many gay men and lesbian women learn to believe that heterosexuality is the only option and that homosexuality is a perversion. Such self-hatred can significantly impede the self-acceptance process that many gay men and lesbian women go through in order to come out and embrace their sexuality.

Being Single

In recent decades, there has been a staggering increase in the numbers of unmarried adults (never married, divorced, or widowed), such that singles now form the majority of adults aged 16 and over in America (Haverluck, 2014). Most of this increase has been the result of men and women, especially young adults, marrying later.

The New Social Context of Singlehood The outcomes of this dramatic increase in unmarried young adults include the following:

- *Greater sexual experience.* Men and women who marry later are more likely to have had more sexual experience and sex partners than earlier generations. Nonmarital sex has become the norm among many adults.

- *Increased number of singles, or those who have never married, are divorced, or are widowed.* Of all Americans, 44% of those over the age of 18 are single (U.S. Census Bureau, 2014.7a). Many factors may contribute to this, including financial instability, societal acceptance, and personal preference.

- *Widespread acceptance of cohabitation.* As young adults are deferring marriage longer and cohabitation is seen as a viable living arrangement, it has also become an integral part of adult life for approximately 7 million Americans (American Community Survey, 2013.) Now that same-sex marriage has been legalized in all states, it is anticipated that marriage will replace domestic partnerships among many gay men and lesbian women.

- *Unintended pregnancies.* Because greater numbers of women are single and sexually active, they are more likely to become unintentionally pregnant as a result of unprotected sexual intercourse or contraceptive failure.

- *Increased numbers of abortions and births to single women.* The significant number of unintended pregnancies has led to more abortions and births to single mothers. Birth among unmarried couples now rivals birth to married ones as a pathway by which children enter family structures.

- *Greater numbers of separated and divorced men and women.* Approximately 12% of individuals in the United States who got married in the previous year are now separated or divorced (U.S. Census Bureau, 2014.7a). Because of their previous marital experience, separated and divorced men and women tend to have different expectations about relationships than never-married young adults. Nearly half of all marriages are now remarriages for at least one partner.

The college social setting provides opportunities for students to meet others and establish relationships.
© Digital Vision/Getty Images

- *A rise in the number of single-parent families.* Approximately 28% of all single parents—mostly mothers—are living with their children (U.S. Census Bureau, 2012.7a).

The world that unmarried young adults inhabit is one in which greater opportunities than ever before exist for exploring intimate relationships.

The College Environment   The college environment is important not only for intellectual development but also for social development. The social aspects of the college setting—classes, dormitories, fraternities and sororities, parties, clubs, and athletic events—provide opportunities for meeting others. For many, college is a place to search for or find mates.

Dating in college is similar to high school dating in many ways. It may be formal or informal ("getting together" or "hooking up"); it may be for recreation or for finding a mate. Features that distinguish college dating from high school dating, however, include the more independent setting (away from home, with diminished parental influence), the increased maturity of partners, more role flexibility, and the increased legitimacy of sexual interactions. For most college students, love and dating become qualitatively different during emerging adulthood, with more focus on sexuality as it relates to developing one's own identity.

Although acceptance of sex outside of marriage is widespread among college students, there are more boundaries placed on women. If a woman has sexual intercourse, most people still believe it should take place in the context of a committed relationship. Women who "sleep around" or "hook up" are often morally censured. Reflecting the continuing sexual double standard, men are not usually condemned as harshly as women for having sex without commitment.

For those who identify as nonheterosexual or transgender, the college environment is often liberating because campuses tend to be more accepting of sexual diversity than society at large is. College campuses often have lesbian, gay, bisexual, and transgender organizations that sponsor social events and get-togethers. There, individuals can freely meet others in open circumstances that

I must paint you.

—Paul Gauguin, pick-up line (1848–1903)

Why College Students Have Sex

Sex and death are the only things that can interest a serious mind.

—William Butler Yeats
(1885–1939)

The reasons people have sex may appear obvious and simple when, in fact, they are actually quite complex and diverse. Add gender differences to this mix, and the reasons for having sex begin to mount. Researchers Cindy Meston and David Buss (2007), in a 5-year study, sought to identify an array of potential reasons that motivate people to engage in sexual intercourse and to classify reasons by gender. Meston suggests these findings have "refuted a lot of gender stereotypes that men only want sex for the physical pleasure and women want love." What they found is that college-age men and women seek sex for mostly the same reason: lust in the body more than a love connection in the heart. In fact, both sexes agree that their primary reason for having sex was attraction; they wanted to experience physical pleasure. Men and women were not found to be very different on many counts: 20 of the top 25 reasons given for having sex were the same for men and women. Though expressing love and showing affection were in the top 10 for both men and women, the clear number-one reason was "I was attracted to the person."

The researchers began with 444 men and women—ranging in age from 17 to 52—and a list of 237 reasons people have sex (Meston & Buss, 2007). Among the top 10 reasons that all ages and both genders are having sex were to experience physical pleasure, to express love, and to show affection. From the same list of reasons, the researchers asked 1,549 college students to rank the reasons and collected some interesting data. What motived college-age students most of the time were primarily:

- *Physical reasons* ("I was stressed"), pleasure ("I felt horny"), improve or expand experiences ("I was curious about anal sex"), and the physical desirability of their partner ("The person was hot")

- *Goal-based reasons, practical considerations* ("I wanted to have a baby"), social status ("I wanted to be popular"), and revenge ("I wanted to give someone else a sexually transmitted disease")

- *Emotional reasons* such as love and commitment ("I wanted to feel connected") and expression ("I wanted to show how much I loved her")

- *Insecurity-based reasons,* including self-esteem ("I wanted the attention"), pressure ("My partner insisted"), and to maintain a relationship ("I wanted to keep my partner to myself")

Men, significantly more than women, cited reasons for having sex centered on physical appearance and desirability of a partner. Additionally, they indicated experience-seeking and mere opportunity as factors. Women exceeded men in endorsing certain emotional motivations for sex, such as wanting to express love and realizing they were in love. Interestingly, among both the college students and older individuals, none of the gender differences for why humans had sex were significantly different.

When examining the psychological motivations for having sex, the researchers noted that what constituted a rare reason for the population as a whole might constitute a major motivation for some individuals. For example, though most people are not motivated by the desire to humiliate another or to feel humiliated through sex, for others, who practice sadism or masochism, this is their principal sexual motivation.

Think Critically

1. Can you relate to any of these data? What are the reasons you have or do not have sex?
2. Do you feel the data found in this study can be replicated across cultures? Across age groups?
3. To what extent do the reasons for having sex change across the life span?

permit meaningful relationships to develop and mature. Although prejudice against those who are different continues to exist in some colleges and universities, college life has been an important haven for many.

The Singles World Men and women involved in the singles world tend to be older than college students, typically ranging in age from 25 to 40. They have never been married, or, if they are divorced, they usually do not have primary responsibility for children. Single adults are generally working (or looking for a job) rather than attending school.

Although dating in the singles world is somewhat different from dating in high school and college, there are similarities. Singles, like their counterparts in school, emphasize recreation and entertainment, sociability, and physical attractiveness.

The isolation many single people feel can be quite overwhelming. In college, students meet each other in classes or dormitories, at school events, or through friends. There are many meeting places and large numbers of eligibles. Singles who are working may have less opportunity than college students to meet available people. For single adults, the most frequent means of meeting others are introductions by friends, the Internet, parties, and social or religious groups.

Sexual experimentation and activity are important for many singles. Although individuals may derive personal satisfaction from sexual activity, they must also manage the stress of conflicting commitments, loneliness, and a lack of connectedness. To fill the demand for meeting others, the singles world has spawned a multibillion-dollar industry—bars, resorts, clubs, housing, and Internet sites dedicated solely to them. Of the 40 million U.S. adult singles, nearly 40% rely on online dating sites such as eHarmony.com or Match.com (Broussard, 2014), in which men tend to emphasize their financial or employment status, while women frequently focus on their physical attributes and personality characteristics. Additionally, many utilize social networking sites such as Facebook to advertise their "status" and to solicit interest from potential partners.

In the late nineteenth century, as a result of the stigmatization of homosexuality, groups of gay men and lesbian women began congregating in their own clubs and bars. There, in relative safety, they could find acceptance and support, meet others, and socialize. Today, there are neighborhoods in most large cities that are identified with gay, lesbian, bisexual, and transgender people. These communities feature not only openly gay and/or lesbian bookstores, restaurants, coffeehouses, and bars but also places of worship, clothing stores, medical and legal offices, hair salons, and so on.

A growing body of evidence indicates that sexual minorities in the United States exhibit higher levels of psychiatric distress than their heterosexual counterparts (Chae & Ayala, 2010). For example, lesbian, gay, and bisexual individuals had a higher prevalence of psychiatric disorders, met criteria for having a psychiatric disorder, or were more likely to report a recent suicide attempt. These elevated levels of psychiatric distress may, in part, be explained by the experience of social hazards associated with sexual minority status, including institutional and interpersonal forms of discrimination and prejudice and instances of physical and verbal bullying, violence, and harassment.

Overall it appears that men who have sex with men (MSM) of color attempt to conceal their sexuality for different reasons, depending on their racial/ethnic groups (Choi, Han, Paul, & Ayala, 2011). Black MSM are more likely to report the need for self-preservation within the larger Black community, whereas among Latino MSM, concealment is aimed at being seen as an individual rather

Wherever there are rich men trying not to feel old, there will be young girls trying not to feel poor.

—Julie Burchill
(1959–)

than as a sexual orientation. Choi et al. (2011) also found that many Asian men tried to actively pass as straight. Most participants indicated that they often avoided situations where they might experience racism. One way in which many MSM draw strength and comfort from the impact of racism and homophobia is from external sources, including finding role models within their community and online resources.

African American gay men and lesbian women often experience a conflict between their Black and gay identities. African Americans are less likely to disclose their gay identity because the Black community is less accepting of homosexuality than is the White community (Edozien, 2003). Several factors contribute to this phenomenon. Although there is some support for gay civil rights among Black leaders, strong fundamentalist Christian beliefs influence some African Americans to be unaccepting of lesbian women and gay men. Additionally, because homosexuality is sometimes thought of as having originated from slavery or imprisonment, these beliefs result in openly gay Black individuals being considered traitors to their own race. The internalization of the dominant culture's stereotyping of African Americans as highly sexual beings may also prompt many African Americans to feel a need to assert and express their sexuality in ways that are considered "normal."

While many gay men and lesbian women choose to have or adopt children, states across the country continue to argue about what constitutes "family."

© Consumer Trends/Alamy

For gay Latinos and lesbian Latinas living in cities with large Latino populations, there is usually at least one gay bar. Such places specialize in dancing or female impersonation. The extent to which a gay Latino or lesbian Latina participates in the Anglo or Latino gay world depends on the individual's degree of acculturation, with those who are U.S.-born more likely to identify as gay, lesbian, or bisexual persons (Chae & Ayala, 2010). While traditional standards of Latino and Latina culture expect men to support and defend the family and women to be submissive to men and maintain their virginity until married, it is not uncommon for some Latinos and Latinas to engage in same-sex behavior without declaring any particular sexual identity (Chandra, Mosher, Copen, & Sionean, 2011). Additionally, lesbian Latinas are doubly stigmatized because they may be seen as defying expectations of women's roles and challenging the traditional male dominance of the culture (Trujillo, 1997).

Traditional Asian cultures place significance on respecting elders, conforming to one's family's expectations, and assuming distinct gender roles with less regard for individual needs and desires. As in strict traditional Latino cultures, traditional Asian American culture de-emphasizes the importance of sex to women. Open acknowledgment of lesbian or gay identity is seen by mainstream Asian society as a rejection of traditional cultural roles and a threat to the continuity of family life. If, however, family expectations can be met, then secretly engaging in same-sex behavior may not cause the individual to feel guilty or bring embarrassment to the family.

An exception to the negativity experienced by many gay and lesbian people of color is experienced among Native American cultures, whose traditions place high value on individual differences. Based on the belief of the Great Spirit, who acknowledges the sacredness of each person's sexual orientation and gender role, tolerance of individual differences has persisted despite long-standing assaults on the Native American culture (Epstein, 1997).

• FIGURE 3

Type of First Relationship Among Women Aged 15–44; United States, 1995, 2002, and 2006–2010.

Source: Copen, C., Daniels, K., & Mosher, W. D. (2013). First premarital cohabitation in the United States: 2006–2010. National Survey of Family Growth. *National Health Statistics Reports, 64.* Available: http://www.cdc.gov/nchs/data/nhsr/nhsr064.pdf

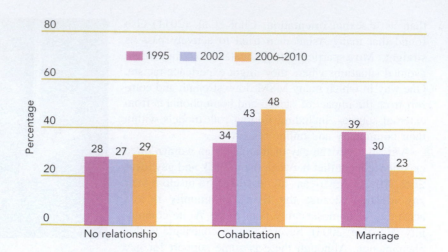

With the increased acceptance of cohabitation, many couples are postponing decisions about marriage and children until their 30s.

© Purestock/SuperStock

Cohabitation

In recent years, women ages 15–44 in first relationships are increasingly cohabitating (Copen, Daniels, & Mosher, 2013) (see Figure 3). This increase was seen across all race and Hispanic origin groups, except Asian women. Though marriage remains an ideal, albeit a more elusive one, cohabitation is the lifestyle choice for a vast number of adults in this country.

An Accepted Norm **Cohabitation,** or the practice of living together and having a sexual relationship, is increasingly accepted at almost every level of society. In fact, by age 20, one in four women aged 15–44 has cohabited, and by 30, that ratio climbs to three in four women (Copen et al., 2013). At the same time, the length of first cohabitation has also increased, regardless of whether the relationship remains intact, transitions to marriage, or dissolves. The length of first cohabitation for women aged 15–44 is 22 months, with higher rates among White women and those with higher education (bachelor's degree or higher) and among women with less than a high school diploma. Also increasing among those who are cohabiting is the probability of a pregnancy within the first 2 years of a woman's first cohabitation.

The concept of **domestic partnership,** which refers to the rights of unmarried adults who choose to live together in the same manner as a married couple, has led to laws granting some of the protections of marriage to men and women, including gay men and lesbian women, who cohabit in committed relationships.

Cohabitation has become more widespread and accepted in recent years for several reasons. First, the general climate regarding sexuality is more open-minded than it was a generation ago. Sexuality is more widely considered to be an important part of people's lives, whether or not they are married. The moral criterion for judging sexual intercourse has shifted; a committed relationship or love rather than marriage is now widely regarded as making sex with another person moral. Second, divorce is seen now as more preferable than an unhappy marriage. Because of the dramatic increase in divorce rates in recent decades, marriage is no longer thought of as necessarily a permanent commitment. In fact, the average marriage now lasts approximately 7 years. Permanence is increasingly replaced by **serial monogamy,** a succession of relationships or marriages. Third, young adults are continuing to defer marriage. At the same time, they want the companionship found in living intimately with another person.

In a landmark opinion, the Supreme Court ruled in 2015 that states cannot ban same-sex marriage. Now, married same-sex couples will enjoy the same legal rights and benefits as married heterosexual couples and will be recognized on official documents such as birth and death certificates. In 2013, nearly 727,000 households in the United States Consisted of same-sex couples, 34% of whom were same-sex spouses (U.S. Census Bureau, 1014.7b.). It is expected that this statistic will quickly change now that same-sex marriage is legal. Regardless of the negative stereotypes about the relationships of gay men and lesbian women, including lack of sexual exclusiveness, and less 'real' love between them, the fact is most people want a close, loving relationship with another person.

For gay men, lesbian women, and heterosexual individuals, intimate relationships provide love, romance, satisfaction, and security. There is one important difference, however: Many lesbian and gay relationships resist the traditional heterosexual provider/homemaker roles. Among heterosexual couples, these divisions are often gender-linked as male or female. In same-sex couples, however, tasks are often divided pragmatically, according to considerations such as who likes cooking more (or dislikes it less) and who works when. Most gay couples are dual-worker couples; neither partner supports or depends on the other economically. And because partners in gay and lesbian couples are the same sex, the economic discrepancies based on greater male earning power are often absent. Although gay couples emphasize egalitarianism, if there are differences in power, they are attributed to personality; if there is an age difference, the older partner is usually more powerful.

The American Academy of Pediatrics recognizes the literature that suggests those children who grow up in same-sex households will develop emotionally, cognitively, socially, and sexually as well as children whose parents are heterosexual ("Where we stand," 2014). In fact, the group states, parents' sexual orientation is much less important than having loving and nurturing parents. One large Australian study found that children with same-sex parents score higher than population samples on a number of parent-reported measures of child health. What may not be surprising is to also note that the stigma that often occurs against these family units is negatively associated with mental health (Crouch, Waters, McNair, Power, & Davis, 2014).

Lesbian women, including celebrities such as Ellen DeGeneres and her wife, Portia de Rossi, are increasingly accepted into mainstream media.

© Valerie Macon/Getty Images

The censor believes that he can hold back the mighty traffic of life with a tin whistle and a raised hand. For after all, it is life with which he quarrels.

—Heywood Broun
(1888–1939)

● Sexuality in Middle Adulthood

In the middle-adulthood years, family and work become especially important. Personal time is spent increasingly on marital and family matters, especially if a couple has children. Sexual expression often decreases in frequency, intensity, and significance, to be replaced by family and work concerns. Sometimes, the change reflects a higher value placed on family intimacy; other times, it may reflect habit, boredom, or conflict.

Developmental Concerns

In the middle-adulthood years, some of the psychosexual developmental tasks begun in young adulthood may be continuing. These tasks, such as ones related to intimacy issues or parenting decisions, may have been deferred or only partly completed in young adulthood. Because of separation or divorce, people may find themselves facing the same intimacy and commitment tasks at age 40 that they thought they had completed 15 years earlier (Cate & Lloyd, 1992). But life does not stand still; it moves steadily forward, and other developmental issues appear, including the following:

- *Redefining sex in marital or other long-term relationships.* In new relationships, sex is often passionate and intense; it may be the central focus. But in long-term marital or cohabiting relationships, habit, competing family and work obligations, fatigue, and unresolved conflicts often erode the passionate intensity associated with sexuality. Sex may need to be redefined as more of an expression of intimacy and caring. Individuals may also need to decide how to deal with the possibility, reality, and meaning of extramarital or extrarelational sex.

- *Reevaluating one's sexuality.* Single women and single men may need to weigh the costs and benefits of sex in casual or lightly committed relationships. In long-term relationships, sexuality may become less than central to relationship satisfaction, as nonsexual elements such as communication, intimacy, and shared interests and activities become increasingly important. Women who desire children and who have deferred their childbearing begin to reappraise their decision: Should they remain child-free, race against their biological clock, or adopt a child? Some people may redefine their sexual orientation. One's sexual philosophy continues to evolve.

- *Accepting the biological aging process.* As people age, their skin wrinkles, their waistline increases, their flesh sags, their hair turns gray (or falls out), their vision blurs—and they become, in the eyes of society, less attractive and less sexual. By their 40s, their physiological responses have begun to slow. By their 50s, society begins to "neuter" them, especially women who have gone through menopause. The challenge of aging is to come to terms with its biological changes and challenges.

Sexuality in Marriage and Established Relationships

When people marry, they may discover that their sex lives are very different from what they were before marriage. Sex is now more morally and socially sanctioned. It is in marriage that the great majority of heterosexual interactions take place, yet as a culture, we feel ambivalent about marital sex. On the one hand, marriage is traditionally the only relationship in which sexuality is legitimized. On the other, marital sex is an endless source of humor and ridicule.

Frequency of Sexual Interactions   Ask any long-term couple about their patterns of lust over time, and you'll no doubt find wide variations, from no lust to large fluctuations in desire and activity from day to day. Sexual intercourse tends to diminish in frequency the longer a couple is partnered or married. For newly partnered couples, the average frequency of sexual intercourse is about three times a week. As couples get older, the frequency drops. In early middle age, married couples have sexual intercourse an average of one to two times a week. After age 50, the rate is about once a week or less (American Association of Retired Persons [AARP], 2010). Decreased frequency, however, does not necessarily mean that sex is no longer important or that the partnership is unsatisfactory. It may be the result of biological aging and declining sexual drive, or it could be the way our brains adapt, from the initial surge of dopamine that prompts romance and desire to the relative quiet of an oxytocin-induced attachment. Oxytocin is a hormone that produces a feeling of connectedness and bonding. Decreasing frequency of sexual interaction may, for example, simply mean that one or both partners are too tired. For dual-worker families and families with children, stress, financial worries, fatigue, and lack of private time may be the most significant factors in the decline of frequency. One survey conducted by Trojan and YourTango.com found that 78% of parents report that their sex lives have significantly diminished ("Infographic," 2014).

Many married couples don't seem to feel that declining frequency in sexual intercourse is a major problem if their overall relationship is good (Cupach & Comstock, 1990; Sprecher & McKinney, 1993). Sexual intercourse is only one erotic bond among many in committed relationships. There are also kisses, caresses, nibbles, massages, candlelight dinners, hand-in-hand walks, intimate words, and so on.

The demands of parenting may diminish a couple's ability to be sexually spontaneous.

© Noel Hendrickson/Digital Vision/Getty Images

Sexual Satisfaction and Pleasure   Higher levels of sexual satisfaction and pleasure seem to be found in marriage than in singlehood or extramarital relationships (Laumann et al., 1994). More than 50% of married men report that they are extremely satisfied physically and emotionally with their partner, while 40–45% of married women report similar levels of satisfaction (Laumann et al., 1994; Lindau & Gavrilova, 2010; Smith et al., 2003). The lowest rates of satisfaction were among those who were neither married nor living with someone, a group thought to have sex most frequently.

Adult love relationships often have complex expectations: emotional stabilization, shared time and values, personal enrichment, security, and support, to name a few (see Figure 4).

Married partners have a commitment to learning each other's likes and dislikes and being sensitive to the other's needs. The longer the partnership lasts,

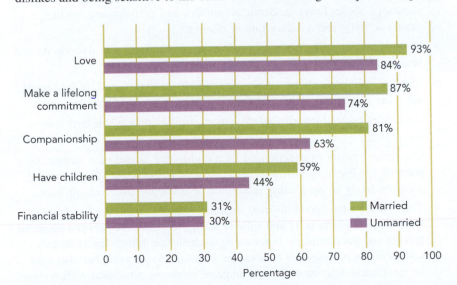

• **FIGURE 4**

Why Get Married? Percentage of American Adults Saying Each Reason Is a Very Important Consideration to Marry, by Marital Status, 2010.

Source: Cohn, D. (2013). Love and marriage. Pew Research Social and Demographic Trends. Available: http://www.pewsocialtrends.org/2013/02/13/love-and-marriage/

the greater the commitment is likely to be to making its various aspects—including the sexual component—work.

Divorce and After

Divorce has become a fact of life for many American families. A quick observation of demographics in this country points to a growing way of life: postdivorce singlehood. Contrary to divorce trends in the twentieth century, in recent decades, the divorce rate has actually dropped. In 1990, the divorce rate was 7.2 per 1,000; in 2000, it was 6.2; and in 2011, the rate dropped to 3.6 (U.S. Census Bureau, 2013.7b). And since more couples now live together without marrying, the divorce rate is down, especially among those who are college-educated (Aughinbaugh, Robles, & Sun, 2013). Many reasons for the declining divorce rate have been noted, including later marriages, birth control, and the increase in what are referred to as "love marriages" or those based on love rather than duty (Miller, 2014).

Scholars suggest that divorce represents not a devaluation of marriage but, oddly enough, an idealization of it. We would not divorce if we did not have such high expectations for marriage's ability to fulfill various needs. Our divorce rate further tells us that we may no longer believe in the permanence of marriage. Instead, we remain married only as long as the marriage is rewarding or until a potentially better partner comes along.

Consequences of Divorce Because divorce is so prevalent, many studies have focused on its effects on partners and children. From these, a number of possible outcomes of divorce have been identified (Amato, 2000, 2010; Amato, Kane, & James, 2011; Hymowitz, 2014; Thables, 1997; Whitehead & Holland, 2003):

- There is often stigmatization by family, friends, and co-workers.
- There is a change of income (usually a substantial decline for women and their children).
- There is a higher incidence of physical, emotional, behavioral, and social problems among both men and women, including depression, injury, and illness.
- There are significantly more problems with children, including criminality, substance abuse, lower academic attainment and performance, earlier sexual activity, and a higher rate of divorce.
- Children are more likely than those in two-parent families to develop mental health problems and addictions later in life.
- Many individuals report being less close to their parents and, if they marry, are more likely to get divorced than persons from two-parent families.
- Poverty rates are higher in single-parent families than when both parents are present.
- The more transitions experienced by a child—the arrival of a stepparent, a parental boyfriend or girlfriend, or a step- or half-sibling—the more children are likely to have either emotional or academic problems or both.
- The notion of the "good divorce," in which therapists and the family court system seek help to build and solidify strong relationships between divorced parents and their children, is for many, a challenge. Improving children's well-being in post-divorce families are undoubtedly of value but also may be insufficient to counter the full range of problems associated with divorce.

Slightly over half of all divorces involve children. It should be noted that differences between children with divorced parents and those with continuously married parents are modest and individual; thus, one should not assume that children of divorced parents have or will develop adjustment problems (Kuehnle & Drozd, 2012). In fact, encouraging views emerge from studies (see Ahrons, 2004; Amato, 2003, 2010) that demonstrate the majority of children whose parents have divorced do not suffer long-term consequences simply because of the divorce. Rather, the consequences of divorce for children and adults are contingent on the quality of family relationships prior to marital dissolution. In most cases, the way the children think and feel about the important relationships in their families are not significantly altered. In fact, most of these children grow up to be well-adjusted adults who sustain family connections and commitments.

Single Parenting

In 2012, 28% of all families were headed by single parents, the vast majority of whom were single mothers (U.S. Census Bureau, 2013.7a). Several demographic trends have affected the shift from two-parent to one-parent families, including a larger proportion of births to unmarried women, the delay of marriage, and the increase in divorce among couples with children.

Single parents are not often a part of the singles world, which involves more than simply not being married. It generally requires leisure and money, both of which single parents, especially women, generally lack because of their family responsibilities.

Dating Again

A first date after years of marriage and subsequent months of singlehood evokes some of the same emotions felt by inexperienced adolescents. Separated or divorced men and women who are beginning to date again may be excited and nervous; worry about how they look; and wonder whether it's OK to hold hands, kiss, or be sexual. They may believe that dating is incongruous with their former selves, or they may be annoyed with themselves for feeling excited and awkward. Furthermore, they may know little about the norms of postmarital dating.

No longer confined to one's small network of friends and family, newly single people can now reach out to countless others to find another who shares their interests. A 2013 survey shows that 11% of American adults—and 38% of those who are currently "single and looking" for a partner—have used online

You have to accept the fact that part of the sizzle of sex comes from the danger of sex.

—Camille Paglia
(1947–)

Because of their child-rearing responsibilities, single parents are often not part of the singles world.

© PNC/Digital Vision/Getty Images

dating sites (Smith & Dugga, 2013). There are pros and cons to online dating. The advantages of using online dating sites are that: (1) the technology enables one to overcome many geographical limitations, and (2) one may have a better chance of meeting people with similar beliefs and values, which are often listed in people's profiles. On the other hand, one must: (1) be wary of any distinct, special, or "scientific" claims for matching people and (2) acknowledge that the sites are moneymaking endeavors. Despite online dating site claims, no one has mastered the science of matchmaking, and though they usually allow a person to register and browse for free, once you confirm, fees average $75–$130 a month or more depending on the level of service.

Sexual activity is an important component in the lives of separated and divorced men and women. Engaging in sexual behavior with someone for the first time following separation may help some people accept their newly acquired single status.

The bed: A place where marriages are decided.

—Anonymous

Sexuality in Late Adulthood

Sexual feelings and desires continue throughout the life cycle. Though many of the standards of activity or attraction are constant, it may be necessary for each of us to overcome the taboos and stereotypes associated with sex and aging in order to create a place for its expression in our lives.

Developmental Concerns

Many of the psychosexual tasks older Americans must undertake are directly related to the aging process, including the following (Das, Waite, & Laumann, 2012; DeLamater & Sill, 2005):

- *Biological changes.* As older men's and women's physical abilities change with age, their sexual responses change as well. A 70-year-old person, though still sexual, is not sexual in the same manner as an 18-year-old individual. As men and women continue to age, their sexuality tends to be more diffuse, less genitally oriented, and less insistent. Chronic illness, hormonal changes, vascular changes, and increasing frailty understandably result in diminished sexual activity. These considerations contribute to the ongoing evolution of the individual's sexual philosophy.

- *Death of a partner.* One of the most critical life events is the loss of a partner. After age 60, there is a significant increase in spousal deaths. Because having a partner is the single most important factor determining an older person's sexual interactions, the absence of a sexual partner signals a dramatic change in the survivor's sexual interactions.

- *Psychological influences.* Given America's obsession with youth and sexuality, it is not surprising that many people consider it inappropriate for older men and women to continue to be sexually active. Such factors as lack of sexual information, negative attitudes toward sexual expression, and mental health problems, including depression (along with the treatments that remedy it), may interfere with older individuals' ability or willingness to see themselves as sexual beings.

Older adults negotiate these issues within the context of continuing aging. Resolving them as we age helps us accept the eventuality of our death.

Stereotypes of Aging

Our society stereotypes aging as a lonely and depressing time, but most studies of older adults find that, relative to younger people, they express high levels of satisfaction and well-being. Poverty, loneliness, and poor health can make old age difficult. Even so, older people have a lower poverty rate than young adults, middle-aged women, and children. More importantly, until their mid-70s, most older people report few, if any, restrictions on their activities because of health.

The sexuality of older Americans tends to be invisible, as society discounts their sexuality. Several factors account for this in our culture. First, we associate sexuality with young people, assuming that sexual attraction exists only between those with youthful bodies. Interest in sex is considered normal in 25-year-old men, but in 75-year-old men, it is considered lecherous. Second, we associate the idea of romance and love with the young; many of us find it difficult to believe that older adults can fall in love or love intensely. Third, we continue to associate sex with procreation, measuring a woman's femininity by her childbearing and maternal role and a man's masculinity by the children he has. Finally, many older people do not have sexual desires as strong as those of younger people, and they do not express them as openly.

Aging gay men and lesbian women face a double stigma: stigmas related to their sexual orientation and to their age, which paint them as undesirable and target them for ostracism. But, like other stigmas of aging Americans, these reflect myths rather than realities. Targeted educational programs can help reduce fears and discomfort related to both aging and sexual orientation.

Stereotypes and myths about aging are not the only factors that affect the sexuality of older Americans. The narrow definition of sexuality, which focuses almost exclusively on intercourse, contributes to the problem. Sexual behavior is viewed by researchers and the general population as varied and unpredictable. The continued focus on physical and hormonal changes highlights the general trend toward the medicalization of sexual functioning and the pathology that accompanies it rather than the emotional, sensual, and relationship aspects that are enjoyed by all people, regardless of age (Tiefer, 2004).

Sexuality and Aging

Sexuality remains an essential element in the lives of individuals 55 and over. In particular, cultural attitudes toward sexuality and aging appear to influence whether sex among older individuals is encouraged or discouraged. Sexual expression has historically been viewed in the United States as an activity reserved for young and newly partnered people. However, this viewpoint is not universally accepted. Cross-cultural studies show that in many countries sexual activity is not only accepted but also expected among older adults.

Despite conventional wisdom, recent studies conducted in the United States have revealed that older Americans continue to be sexual. Not surprisingly, one of the major factors associated with the likelihood of being sexually active is the availability of a partner. Findings from the American Association of Retired Persons (AARP) 2010 survey of nearly 1,700 Americans aged 45 and over found that opposition to sex among those who are not married has, over time, been significantly reduced, as has the belief that there is too much emphasis on sex in our culture. Between 2004 and 2010, the frequency of sexual intercourse and

One of the most famous twentieth-century sculptures is Auguste Rodin's *The Kiss,* which depicts young lovers embracing. Here, the aging model Antoni Nordone sits before the statue that immortalized his youth.

© Jean Mounicq/Roger-Viollet/The Image Works

You only possess what will not be lost in a shipwreck.

—Al Ghazali
(1058–1111)

overall sexual satisfaction declined. However, the frequency of masturbation and sexual thoughts and fantasies did not. Other findings include the qualities that comprise a happy sexual relationship:

- A sexual partner but not necessarily a spouse
- Frequent sexual intercourse (more than once a week, but not necessarily daily)
- Good health (self and partner)
- Low levels of stress
- Absence of financial worries

For a few highlights from this study, see Figure 5.

• **FIGURE 5**

Sexual Frequency, Gender Gaps, and Sexual Satisfaction among Older Adults.

(Adapted from American Association of Retired Persons. (2010). *Sex, romance, and relationships.* Reprinted by permission.)

During the past 6 months, how often, on average, have you engaged in sexual Intercourse?	Frequency of Sexual Intercourse by Gender and Age			
	At least once a week %	Once or twice a month %	Less than once a month %	Never in last 6 months %
Total: Males and Females 45+	28	12	12	48
Male Age 45–49	50	9	10	31
Age 50–59	41	22	9	28
Age 60–69	24	18	18	40
Age 70+	15	7	18	60
Total: Males	33	16	13	37
Female Age 45–49	26	12	20	42
Age 50–59	32	10	9	49
Age 60–69	24	8	13	55
Age 70+	5	6	3	87
Total: Females	23	9	10	58

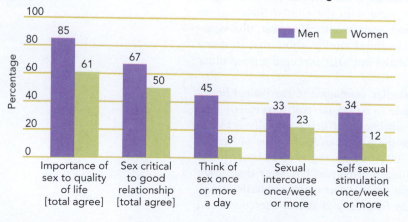

Gender Gap in Sexual Attitudes, Thoughts, and Behaviors, Aged 45 and Over

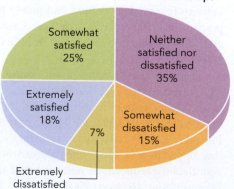

Satisfaction With Sex and Relationships

Marital satisfaction and emotional health foster the desire for emotional intimacy. The greatest determinants of an older person's sexual activity are the availability of a partner and health.

© Lisette Le Bon/Purestock/SuperStock

Among older lesbian and gay couples, as well as heterosexual ones, the happiest are those with a strong commitment to the relationship. The need for intimacy, companionship, and purpose transcends issues of sexual orientation.

Because our society tends to desexualize the old, aging people may interpret their slower responses as signaling the end of their sexuality. In fact, when exploring the link between sexual touching and difficulties with sexual arousal and orgasm among a group of men and women aged 57–84, it was infrequent sexual touching, and not age, that was associated with arousal and orgasm difficulties (Galinsky, 2012). Sexuality education programs for older people, in which they learn about anatomy, physiology, STIs, and sexual response, have been shown to be helpful in dispelling myths, building confidence, and giving permission to be sexual (Davila, 2008).

Women's Issues Beginning sometime in their 40s, most women start to experience a normal biological process resulting in a decline in fertility. This period of gradual change and adjustment is referred to as **perimenopause.** During this time, the ovaries produce less and less estrogen and progesterone, and ovulation becomes less regular. Many women are relieved when they no longer have to worry about getting pregnant and pleased when they no longer have to deal with a monthly menstrual flow. Over a few years' time, menstrual periods become irregular and eventually stop, usually between the ages of 45 and 55, but it can happen anytime from the 30s to mid-50s or later. The average age of **menopause,** the complete cessation of menstruation for at least 1 year, is 51 (National Institute on Aging, 2012). A woman can also undergo menopause as a result of a hysterectomy, the surgical removal of the uterus, if both ovaries are also removed. In postmenopausal women, estrogen levels are about one tenth those in premenopausal women, and progesterone is nearly absent. Most women experience some physiological or psychological symptoms during menopause, but for only about 5–15% of women are the effects severe enough to cause them to seek medical assistance.

> *Old age has its pleasures, which, though different, are not less than the pleasures of youth.*
>
> —W. Somerset Maugham
> (1874–1965)

Physical Effects of Menopause

Whether a woman goes through menopause naturally or surgically, symptoms can appear as the woman's body attempts to adjust to the drop in estrogen levels. The symptoms vary from one woman to the next: Some may breeze through menopause with few symptoms, whereas others may experience many discomforting symptoms for several months or even years. The most common symptoms of menopause are hot flashes, vaginal dryness, and sleeping disturbances (National Institute on Aging, 2012). Another symptom, thinning of the vaginal walls, can result in the length and width of the vagina decreasing and the vagina not being able to expand during penile-vaginal intercourse as it once could. Intercourse can be painful, bleeding can occur, and the vagina can be more susceptible to infection. These effects may begin while a woman is still menstruating and may continue after menstruation has ceased. As many as 85% of women experience some degree of **hot flashes,** periods of intense warmth, flushing, and (often) perspiration, typically lasting for a minute or two but ranging anywhere from 15 seconds to 1 hour in length. While hot flashes usually diminish within 2 years of the menopausal transition, more than half of women continue to experience them for more than seven years, and they may last even longer for African American women. (Avis, Crawford, Greendale, et al., 2015). A hot flash occurs when falling estrogen levels cause the body's "thermostat" in the brain to trigger dilation (expansion) of blood vessels near the skin's surface, producing a sensation of heat. Hot flashes that occur with severe sweating during sleep are called night sweats. Some women who are going through menopause experience insomnia, which can be related to hot flashes, changes in sexual interest (more commonly a decrease), urinary incontinence, weakening of pelvic floor muscles, headaches, or weight gain. Some women also report depression, irritability, and other emotions.

Long-term effects related to lowered estrogen levels may be experienced by some women. Osteoporosis, the loss of bone mass, leads to problems such as wrist and hip fractures. Lowered estrogen can also contribute to diseases of the heart and arteries related to rising levels of LDL (low-density lipoprotein, or "bad" cholesterol) and falling levels of HDL (high-density lipoprotein, or "good" cholesterol). Hereditary factors also play a part in cardiovascular disease.

The physical effects of menopause may be reduced by a diet low in saturated fat and high in fiber; calcium and vitamin D to reduce risk of osteoporosis; weight-bearing exercise; maintenance of a healthy weight; topical lubricants to counteract vaginal dryness; and Kegel exercises to strengthen pelvic floor muscles. Frequent masturbation by oneself or partner may help maintain vaginal moistness and well-being. For women who smoke, quitting provides benefits in many areas, including postponing the onset of menopause, reducing the risk of osteoporosis, diminishing the intensity of hot flashes, and establishing an improved sense of well-being (North American Menopause Society, 2012).

Menopausal Hormone Therapy

To relieve the symptoms of menopause, a physician may prescribe **menopausal hormone therapy (MHT),** also called hormone replacement therapy (HRT). The National Institutes of Health (NIH) has begun using the term "menopausal hormone therapy," believing that it is a more current, umbrella term that describes several different hormone combinations available in a variety of forms and doses. This therapy involves the use of the hormone estrogen or a combination of estrogen with another hormone, progesterone, or progestin in its synthetic form.

Estrogen and progestin normally help regulate a woman's menstrual cycle. In MHT, progestin is added to estrogen to prevent the overgrowth of cells in the lining of the uterus, which can lead to uterine cancer. If a woman is going through menopause and is experiencing symptoms that are interfering with her quality of life, she might be prescribed estrogen-plus-progestin therapy; a woman who has had a hysterectomy, a medical procedure in which the uterus is removed, would receive estrogen-only therapy. The hormones can be taken daily or only on certain days of the month. Depending on their purpose, the hormones can be taken orally, applied as a patch on the skin, used as a spray or gel, given as a shot, or absorbed via an intrauterine device (IUD), implant, or vaginal ring. A vaginal estrogen ring or cream can minimize vaginal dryness, urinary leakage, and vaginal or urinary infection, but it does not ease hot flashes. MHT may cause side effects such as bloating, breast tenderness or enlargement, bleeding, headaches, irritability, depression, nausea, and sometimes spotting or a return of monthly periods for a few months or years (National Institute on Aging, 2012).

Menopause is a normal part of life, not a disease that must be treated. Still, some women may be bothered enough by symptoms to seek medical advice or assistance. Some women may be concerned about the possibility of future problems such as osteoporosis. Others may be concerned about changes in their sexual feelings or patterns or about the implications of fertility loss, aging, and changing standards of attractiveness. Because some physicians may treat menopause as a medical "problem," women may find themselves subjected to treatments they don't understand or would not choose if they were better informed. It's important that women seek out health care practitioners who will work with them to meet their needs.

Though there are benefits associated with taking MHT, a clear understanding of the benefits versus the more significant risks should be considered by any woman considering treatment (see Table 1). As a result of these risks, since 1999 there has been a dramatic decline in the use of MHT. Between 2009–2010, approximately 5% of women aged 40 and over reported using HRT (National Health & Nutrition Exam Survey, 2011). In a follow-up report on the results of a 3-year study conducted by the Women's Health Initiative, a study of 15,730 postmenopausal women aged 50–79 with an intact uterus, researchers concluded that the health risks of long-term use of combination (estrogen plus progestin) MHT to healthy, postmenopausal women persist even a few years after stopping the drugs and outweigh the benefits (Heiss et al., 2008). About 3 years after women stopped taking combination MHT, many of the health effects of the hormones, such as increased risk of heart disease, were diminished; however, overall risks, including risk of stroke, blood clots, and cancer, remained high. Additionally, the study found an increased risk of dementia in women who started MHT after age 65. The U.S. Food and Drug Administration (FDA) now recommends that women with moderate to severe menopausal symptoms who wish to try MHT for relief use it for the shortest time needed and at the lowest effective dose (National Institute on Aging, 2012).

Men's Issues Changes in male sexual responsiveness begin to become apparent when men are in their 40s and 50s, a period of change referred to as the male climacteric, andropause, or sometimes manopause. For a minority of men, these physical changes of aging may be accompanied by experiences such as fatigue, an inability to concentrate, depression, loss of appetite, and a decreased interest in sex. As a man ages, his frequency of sexual activity declines, achieving erection requires more stimulation and time, and the erection may not be as firm. Ejaculation takes longer and may not occur every time the penis is stimulated;

Generally by the time you become real, most of your hair has been loved off and your eyes drop out and you get loose in the joints and very shabby. But these things don't matter at all, because once you are real you can't be ugly, except to people who don't understand.

—The Velveteen Rabbit
by Margery Williams
(1881–1944)

TABLE 1 • Benefits and Risks of Menopausal Hormone Therapy

	Women With a Uterus: Estrogen + Progestin	Women Without a Uterus[a]: Estrogen Only
Benefits		
Relieves hot flashes/night sweats	Yes	Yes
Relieves vaginal dryness	Yes	Yes
Reduces risk of bone fractures	Yes	Maybe
Improves cholesterol levels	Yes	Yes
Reduces risk of colorectal cancer	Yes	Don't know
Risks		
Increases risk of stroke	Yes	Yes
Increases risk of serious blood clots	Yes	Yes
Increases risk of heart disease	Yes	No
Increases risk of gallbladder disease	Yes	Yes
Increases risk of breast cancer	Yes	No
Increases risk of urinary incontinence	Yes	Yes
Increases risk of dementia, when begun by women age 65 and older	Yes	Yes
Unpleasant side effects, such as bloating, tender breasts, spotting or return of monthly periods, cramping	Yes	Yes

[a]Women who have had a hysterectomy have had their uterus but not their ovaries removed.

SOURCES: National Institute on Aging. (2012). Hormones and menopause: Tips from the National Institute on Aging; Nelson, Walker, Zakher, & Mitchell (2012). Menopausal hormone therapy for the primary prevention of chronic conditions: A systematic review to update the U.S. Preventive Services Task Force recommendations.

also, the force of the ejaculation is less than before, as is the amount of ejaculate; and the refractory period is extended up to 24 hours or longer in older men. However, sexual interest and enjoyment generally do not decrease, as witnessed by the frequency and variety of sexual activity reported by older men. Although some of the changes are related directly to age and a normal decrease in testosterone production, others may be the result of diseases and conditions associated with aging. Poor general health, diabetes, atherosclerosis, urinary incontinence, and some medications can contribute to sexual function problems.

It is important for older men to understand that slower responses are a normal function of aging and are unrelated to the ability to give or receive sexual pleasure. "The senior penis," wrote Bernie Zilbergeld (1999), "can still give and take pleasure, even though it's not the same as it was decades ago." Prescription drugs have become available to aid men in getting erections. However, these drugs have known side effects, including headaches, body aches and pains, dizziness, and vision changes. Though erectile dysfunction medications can provide a boost in the bedroom, men should be aware of their side effects before asking a doctor for a prescription.

About half of men over age 50 are affected to some degree by **benign prostatic hyperplasia (BPH),** an enlargement of the prostate gland. The prostate starts out about the size of a walnut. By age 40, it may have grown slightly larger, to the size of an apricot. By age 60, it may be the size of a lemon in men with BPH. By age 70, almost all men have some prostate enlargement. BPH is not linked to cancer and does not raise a man's chance of getting prostate cancer, yet the symptoms of BPH and prostate cancer can be similar. The enlarged prostate may put pressure on the urethra, resulting in difficulty urinating and the frequent and urgent need to urinate. It does not affect sexual functioning. BPH symptoms do not always get worse. At the same time, BPH cannot be cured, but drugs can often relieve its symptoms. If the blockage of the urethra is too severe, surgery can correct the problem.

Testosterone Supplementation   As you may recall, testosterone plays an important role in puberty and throughout a man's life. Although it is the main sex hormone of men, women produce small amounts of it as well. Testosterone production is the highest in adolescence and early adulthood and declines as a man ages. But the chance that a man will ever experience a major shutdown of hormone production similar to a woman's menopause is remote. Most older men maintain a sufficient amount for normal functioning.

As men age, changes such as less energy and strength, decreased bone density, and erectile difficulties may occur; these changes are often erroneously blamed on decreasing testosterone levels. Because of changes like these—particularly sexual declines—a rapidly growing number of older men are considering taking supplemental testosterone. Testosterone is currently available in deep muscle injections, patches, and topical gels. However, despite the fact that some older men who have tried these supplements report feeling more energetic, experts are inconclusive about whether testosterone supplements should be prescribed and encourage men to discuss this matter with their health care practitioner. The National Institute on Aging (2010) states that supplemental testosterone remains a scientifically unproven method for preventing or relieving any physical or psychological changes that men with normal testosterone levels may experience as they age. Until more rigorous scientific studies are conducted, it is not known if the possible benefits of testosterone therapy outweigh its potential risks.

Final Thoughts

As this chapter has shown, psychosexual development occurs on a continuum rather than as a series of discrete stages. Each person develops in his or her own way, according to personal and social circumstances and the dictates of biology. In early adulthood, tasks that define adult sexuality include establishing sexual orientation, making commitments, entering long-term intimate relationships, and deciding whether or not to have children. None of these challenges is accomplished overnight. Nor does a task necessarily end as a person moves into a new stage of life.

In middle adulthood, individuals face new tasks involving the nature of their long-term relationships. Often, these tasks involve reevaluating these relationships. As people enter late adulthood, they need to adjust to the aging process—to changed sexual responses and needs, declining physical health, the loss of a partner, and their own eventual death. Each stage is filled with its own unique meaning, which gives shape and significance to life and to sexuality.

Summary

Sexuality in Early Adulthood

- Several tasks challenge young adults as they develop their sexuality, including establishing a sexual orientation, integrating love and sex, and making fertility/childbearing decisions.

- As our views of gender, masculinity, and femininity have changed, so have the ways that we conceptualize sexual orientation.

- The increase in the number of single adults in the United States has resulted in more sexual experience and sex partners, a widespread acceptance of cohabitation, and among single women, increased birth and abortion rates.

- For gay men, lesbian women, and bisexual and transgendered individuals, the college environment is often liberating because of greater acceptance and tolerance.

- Among single men and women not or no longer attending college, meeting others can be a problem. Singles often meet via the Internet and at work, clubs, resorts, housing complexes, and churches.

- Internalization of a culture's stereotyping about homosexuality may be among the issues that prevent gay men and lesbian women of color from coming out.

- *Cohabitation* has become more widespread and accepted in recent years. *Domestic partnerships* provide some legal protection for cohabiting couples in committed relationships.

Sexuality in Middle Adulthood

- Developmental issues of sexuality in middle adulthood include redefining sex in long-term relationships, reevaluating one's sexuality, and accepting the biological aging process.

- In marriage, sexual activity tends to diminish in frequency the longer a couple is partnered or married. Most partnered couples don't feel that declining frequency is a major problem if their overall relationship is good.

- Divorce has become a major force in American life. Single parents are usually not a part of the singles world because the presence of children constrains their freedom.

Sexuality in Late Adulthood

- Many of the psychosexual tasks older Americans must undertake are directly related to the aging process, including changing sexuality and the loss of a partner. Most studies of older adults find that they express relatively high levels of satisfaction and well-being. Older adults' sexuality tends to be invisible because society associates sexuality and romance with youthfulness and procreation.

- Although some physical functions may be slowed by aging, sexual interest and activity remain high for many older people. Diminished sexual activity for both men and women is primarily due to health issues and/or loss of a partner.

- In their 40s, women's fertility begins to decline. Generally, between ages 45 and 55, *menopause*, cessation of menstrual periods, occurs. Other physical changes occur, which may or may not present problems. *Menopausal hormone therapy (MHT)* may be used to treat these symptoms, ideally for the shortest time needed and at the lowest effective dose.

- Men need to understand that slower responses are a normal part of aging and are not related to the ability to give or receive sexual pleasure.

Questions for Discussion

- The text describes some of the challenges faced by people who choose to live together without marrying. Should society support cohabitation regardless of sexual orientation by providing tax benefits or acknowledging domestic partnerships? If so, how? If not, why not?

- Many changes have taken place in marriage policies, and there has been liberalization of divorce laws. Has it become too easy to get divorced? What factors do you feel contribute to long-term partnerships?

- Given the three models of sexual orientation (see Figure 2), which model do you think is most accurate? Can you find a place for yourself within each model?

Suggested Websites

American College Health Association

http://www.acha.org

Provides advocacy, education, and research for and about college-age students.

American Institute of Bisexuality

http://www.bisexual.org

Encourages, supports, and assists research and education about bisexuality.

Bedsider

http://www.bedsider.org

An online, honest and unbiased birth control support network operated by The National Campaign to Prevent Teen and Unplanned Pregnancy.

National Institutes of Health—Menopausal Hormone Therapy Information

http://www.nih.gov/PHTindex.htm

New findings from large studies offering important information about the risks and benefits of long-term menopausal hormone therapy.

National Institute on Aging

http://www.nia.nih.gov

Leads the federal government's efforts on aging research.

Singles in America

http://www.singlesinamerica.com/

A comprehensive study produced by match.com that focuses on relationships, desires, love, and other topics related to single Americans.

The Williams Institute

http://williamsinstitute.law.ucla.edu

Advances sexual orientation law and public policy through research.

Suggested Reading

Boies, D., & Olson, T. B. (2014). *Redeeming the dream: The case for marriage equality.* New York: Viking Press. Written by two attorneys, this accessible text follows the legal battle over gays' and lesbians' right to marry.

Savage, D. (2013). *American Savage: Insights, slights, and fights over faith, sex, love and politics.* New York: Plume. The advice columnist and talk show personality provides a thought-provoking collection of essays about sexuality and life.

Sheehy, G. (2007). *Sex and the seasoned woman.* New York: Random House. For women (and their partners) who are willing to embrace their "second adulthood" as a period of reawakening.

Sprecher, S., Wenzel, A., & Harvey, J. H. (Eds.). (2008). *Handbook of relationship initiation.* New York: Taylor & Francis. Focuses on beginning stages of first relationships: how people meet, communicate for the first time, and begin to define themselves as being in a relationship.

Wallerstein, J. S., Lewis, J., & Blakeslee, S. (2008). *The unexpected legacy of divorce: A 25-year landmark study.* New York: Hyperion. A long-term study assessing the effects of divorce on children as they grow into adulthood and pursue relationships of their own.

Zilbergeld, B., & Zilbergeld, G. (2010). *Sex and love at midlife: It's better than ever.* New York: Crown. A guide for couples who wish to maintain a passionate relationship.

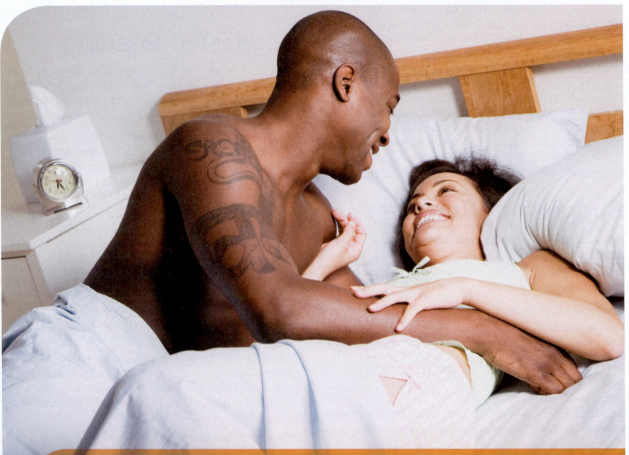

© Andersen Ross/Getty Images

chapter

8

Love and Communication in Intimate Relationships

CHAPTER OUTLINE

Friendship and Love

Love and Sexuality

How Do I Love Thee? Approaches and Attitudes Related to Love

Jealousy

Making Love Last: From Passion to Intimacy

The Nature of Communication

Sexual Communication

Developing Communication Skills

Conflict and Intimacy

only stable and robust gender difference that emerged was a desire for relationship support, expressed more by women than by men (Perrin et al., 2011).

Traditionally, women were labeled "good" or "bad" based on their sexual experiences and values. "Good" women were virginal, sexually naïve, and passive, whereas "bad" women were sexually experienced, independent, and passionate. This perception is sometimes altered as women and men age, and when societies come to terms with women's and men's sexuality. In spite of changing gender norms, however, our society remains ambivalent about sexually active and experienced women.

Researchers suggest that heterosexual men are not as different from gay men in terms of their acceptance of casual sex. Heterosexual men, they maintain, would be as likely as gay men to engage in casual sex if women were equally interested. Women, however, are generally not as interested in casual sex; as a result, heterosexual men do not have as many willing partners as gay men do (Blum, 1997).

Gay men are especially likely to separate love and sex. Although gay men value love, many also value sex as an end in itself. Furthermore, some place less emphasis on sexual exclusiveness in their relationships (Gomez et al., 2012). Many gay men appear to successfully negotiate sexually open relationships. Keeping the sexual agreements they make seems to matter most to these men.

Lesbian women tend to engage in sex less often than gay male couples or heterosexual couples. Studies have revealed that gay men have sex more frequently and lesbians less frequently than heterosexual married couples (Peplau, Fingerhut, & Beals, 2004; Solomon, Rothblum, & Balsam, 2005). For many lesbian women, caresses, nongenital stimulation, and affectionate foreplay are the preferred expressions of sexuality and love.

Love is equally important for heterosexuals, gay men, lesbian women, and bisexual individuals. With the Supreme Court declaring in 2015 same-sex marriage legal in all states, communities can be strengthened by offering dignity and equal status to all couples and their families.

For gay men, lesbian women, and bisexual individuals, love is an important component in the formation and acceptance of their sexual orientation. The public declaration of love and commitment is a milestone in the lives of many couples.

© Creatas/PunchStock

Love Without Sex: Celibacy and Asexuality

In a society that often seems obsessed with sexuality, it may be surprising to find individuals who choose to be celibate as a lifestyle. **Celibacy**—abstention from sexual activity—is not necessarily a symptom of a problem or disorder. It is important to note that though some researchers may blur the definitions of celibacy with **asexuality,** the absence of a traditional sexual orientation in which there is little or no sexual attraction to males or females, differences do exist. Implicit in this discussion is consideration about what constitutes a "normal" level of sexual desire.

While most people consider celibacy to be a choice of refraining from sexual activity with a partner, a diverse set of understandings about what constitutes asexuality exists. Is an asexual person one who does not engage in sexual behavior, one who experiences no sexual desire, one who calls him- or herself an asexual, or some combination of these (Poston & Baumle, 2010)? Asexuality has been classified according to three features: one's behavior, one's desire, and one's self-identification. When only asexual behavior is used as the criterion—that is, never having sex in one's lifetime—the prevalence rates among U.S. adults aged 15–44 are 5% of females and slightly more than 6% of males. On the other hand, if lack of sexual desire (rarely or never thinking about sex) is used as the criterion, the rates are 14% of women and 4% of men (Laumann et al., 1994).

There is hardly any activity, any enterprise, which is started with such tremendous hopes and expectations and yet fails so regularly as love.

—Erich Fromm
(1900–1980)

Familiar acts are beautiful through love.

—Percy Bysshe Shelley
(1792–1822)

think
about it

Are Gay/Lesbian Couples and Families Any Different From Heterosexual Ones?

Meeting you was fate, becoming your friend was a choice, but falling in love with you was beyond my control.

—Leo Buscaglia
(1924–1998)

What impact does sexual orientation have on the longevity and quality of relationships? Are those qualities that help sustain heterosexual couples and families any different for same-sex ones? Though there is not much research yet on the impact that commitment and various other factors have on the quality of same-sex relationships and families, what researchers have found may have implications for all of us who desire healthy relationships and longevity with those we love.

The lack of social support has been among the many challenges facing same-sex couples and their families, even though same-sex marriage is now legal in most states and domestic partnerships or civil unions acknowledged in others. We know that in 2014, 58% of Americans supported same-sex marriage, also called marriage equality (Human Rights Campaign, 2014.8a). The legal recognition of same-sex households varies by state. Regardless, approximately 40% of same-sex households contain children.

The notion that committed same-sex relationships are atypical or psychologically immature is not supported by research. Nor are gay or lesbian individuals less satisfied with their relationships (Roisman, Clausell, Holland, Fortuna, & Elieff, 2008). In fact, it appears that same-sex relationships are similar to those of other-sex couples in many ways. In one study, though both groups indicated positive views of their relationships, those in committed relationships (gay and straight) resolved conflict better than heterosexual dating couples. And lesbian couples worked together especially harmoniously to resolve their conflicts (Roisman et al., 2008). It is the level and type of communication that partners share that underscores much of the success or lack of success in the relationship. Same-sex couples are significantly less belligerent, domineering, and fearful, use more humor, and show greater affection than heterosexual married couples (Gottman et al., 2003). However, when gay men initiate difficult discussions with their partners, they are less likely to make up afterward.

Assessing the influence that stability has in partnerships by comparing same-sex couples in civil unions (same-sex cohabiting couples), researchers have found that same-sex couples were also similar to heterosexual couples on most relationship variables (e.g., frequency of sexual behavior,

contact with parents) and that the legalized status of a relationship did not seem to be the overriding factor affecting same-sex relationships (Roisman et al., 2008).

When, in 2002, the American Academy of Pediatrics endorsed same-sex adoptions, saying gay couples can provide the loving, stable, and emotionally healthy family life that children need, concerns among heterosexuals about the quality of parenting among gay and lesbian parents were somewhat diminished. In fact, among households with only adopted children or only stepchildren, same-sex couples do not differ significantly from married heterosexual couples in terms of education, employment, home ownership, and residential stability (Krivickas & Lofquist, 2010). At the same time, gay men and lesbian women still fight for the legal rights and protections they deserve. Because in some states they cannot legally marry and because of pervasive anti-gay prejudices, such issues as custody, visitation, and adoption remain legal dilemmas or obstacles for many who are contemplating becoming parents or trying to become parents.

Many studies have demonstrated that children's well-being is significantly affected by their relationships with their parents, their parents' sense of competence and security, and the presence of social and economic security more than the gender or sexual orientation of their parents (Perrin et al., 2013). The American Academy of Pediatrics claims that, "it is in the best interests of children that: they be able to partake in the security of permanent nurturing and care that comes with the civil marriage of their parents, without regard to their parents' gender or sexual orientation" (Perrin et al., 2013, p. 1381). In fact, gay and lesbian couples and families are not that different from heterosexual ones in their desire to achieve healthy and long-term involvement. Both groups have a lot to learn from each other.

Think Critically

1. What characteristics are important for you in maintaining a committed relationship with another person? Do you feel that sexual orientation can alter these characteristics? If so, how?

2. Why does society perpetuate concerns about gay men and lesbian women as parents?

3. How might the presence or absence of children influence the longevity of a same-sex relationship?

Celibacy may be a choice for some, such as those who have taken religious vows or are in relationships in which nonsexual affection and respect provide adequate fulfillment. For others, it is a result of life circumstances, such as the absence of a partner or imprisonment. Still others report very low interest in sex or express concern over the spread of HIV or other sexually transmitted infections.

Individuals who choose celibacy may report a better appreciation of the nature of friendship. In giving up their sexual pursuits, celibate individuals may learn to relate to others without sexual tension. Although these traits may also be developed within a sexual relationship, those who choose celibacy as a lifestyle may feel that it frees up energy for personal growth or other kinds of relationships.

● How Do I Love Thee? Approaches and Attitudes Related to Love

For most people, love and sex are closely linked in the ideal intimate relationship. Love reflects the positive factors—such as caring—that draw people together and sustain them in a relationship. Sex reflects both emotional and physical elements, such as closeness and sexual excitement, and differentiates romantic love from other forms of love, such as parental love. Although love and sex are related, they are not necessarily connected. One can exist without the other; that is, it is possible to love someone without being sexually involved, and it is possible to be sexually involved without love.

Styles of Love

Sociologist John Lee describes six basic styles of love (Borrello & Thompson, 1990; Lee, 1973, 1988). These styles of love, he cautions, reflect relationship styles, not individual styles. The style of love may change as the relationship changes or when individuals enter different relationships.

Eros was the ancient Greek god of love, the son of Aphrodite, the goddess of love and fertility. (The Romans called him Cupid.) As a style of love, **eros** is the love of beauty. Erotic lovers are passionate and delight in the tactile, the sensual, the immediate; they are attracted to beauty (though beauty is in the eye of the beholder). They love the lines of the body, its feel and touch. They are fascinated by every physical detail of their beloved. Their love burns brightly and is idealized but soon flickers and dies.

Mania, from the Greek word for madness, is obsessive and possessive love. For manic lovers, nights are marked by sleeplessness and days by pain and anxiety. The slightest sign of affection brings ecstasy for a short while, only to disappear. Satisfactions last for but a moment before they must be renewed. Manic love is roller-coaster love.

Ludus, from the Latin word for play, is playful love. For ludic lovers, love is a game, something to play at rather than to become deeply involved in. Love is ultimately "*ludicrous*"; encounters are casual, carefree, and often careless. "Nothing serious" is the motto of ludic lovers. Those with a ludus style thrive on attention and are often willing to take risks (Paul, McManus, & Hayes, 2000).

Storge (STOR-gay), from the Greek word for natural affection, is the love between companions. It is, wrote Lee, "love without fever, tumult, or folly, a peaceful and enchanting affection." It usually begins as friendship and gradually deepens into love. If the love ends, that also occurs gradually, and the people often become friends once again.

" Love is the irresistible desire to be irresistibly desired.

—Robert Frost
(1874–1963)

" Love and you shall be loved. All love is mathematically just, as much as two sides of an algebraic equation.

—Ralph Waldo Emerson
(1803–1882)

" If you love somebody, let them go. If they return, they were always yours. If they don't, they never were.

—Anonymous

According to sociologist John Lee, there are six styles of love: eros, mania, ludus, storge, agape, and pragma. What style do you believe this couple illustrates? Why?

© John Rowley/Digital Vision/Getty Images

❞ *Love never dies a natural death. It dies because we don't know how to replenish its source.*

—Anaïs Nin
(1903–1977)

❞ *When you are courting a nice girl an hour seems like a second. When you sit on a red-hot cinder a second seems like an hour. That's relativity.*

—Albert Einstein
(1879–1955)

Agape (AH-ga-pay), from the Greek word for brotherly love, is the traditional Christian love that is chaste, patient, undemanding, and altruistic; there is no expectation of reciprocation. It is the love of saints and martyrs. Agape is more abstract and ideal than concrete and real. It is easier to love all of humankind than an individual in this way.

Pragma, from the Greek word for business, is practical love. Pragmatic lovers are, first and foremost, businesslike in their approach to looking for someone who meets their needs. They use logic in their search for a partner, seeking background, education, personality, religion, and interests that are compatible with their own. If they meet a person who satisfies their criteria, erotic, manic, or other feelings may develop.

In addition to these pure forms, there are mixtures of the basic types, for example: storge-eros, ludus-eros, and storge-ludus. Lee believes that, to have a mutually satisfying relationship, people have to find a partner who shares the same style and definition of love. The more different two people are in their styles of love, the less likely they are to understand each other's love.

One could expect there to be some consistency between love styles and sexual attitudes, since beliefs about sexuality could help determine the choice and maintenance of a romantic relationship. But are there gender differences in the ways men and women express their love style? Research reports the presence of significant gender differences in love styles and attraction criteria among college students (Grello, Welsh, & Harper, 2006; Lacey, Reifman, Scott, Harris, & Fitzpatrick, 2004). Surveying the love styles of college students, researchers have found that men were more likely to have a ludus style, while others who endorsed an eros style were more likely to either be virgins or engage in sexual activity with only a romantic partner (Grello et al., 2006).

The Triangular Theory of Love

The **triangular theory of love,** developed by psychologist and educator Robert Sternberg (1986), emphasizes the dynamic quality of love relationships. According to this theory, love is composed of three elements, as in the points of a triangle: intimacy, passion, and commitment (see Figure 1). Each can be enlarged or diminished in the course of a love relationship, which will affect the quality of the relationship. They can also be combined in different ways. Each combination produces a different type of love, such as romantic love, infatuation, empty love, and liking. Partners may combine the components differently at different times in the same love relationship.

The Components of Love   Intimacy refers to the warm, close, bonding feelings we get when we love someone. According to Sternberg and Grajek (1984), there are 10 signs of intimacy:

1. Wanting to promote your partner's welfare
2. Feeling happiness with your partner

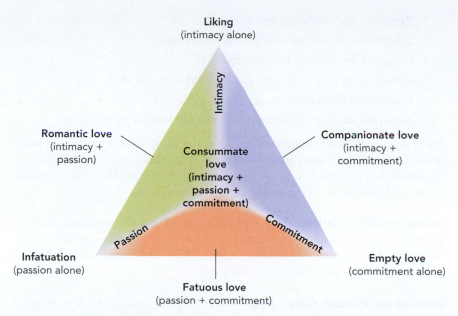

• **FIGURE 1**

Sternberg's Triangular Theory of Love. The three elements of love are intimacy, passion, and commitment.

(*Source:* From Sternberg, R. J. (1988). *The triangle of love: Intimacy, passion, commitment.* New York: Basic Books, 1988. Used by permission of Robert J. Sternberg.)

3. Holding your partner in high regard

4. Being able to count on your partner in times of need

5. Being able to understand your partner

6. Sharing yourself and your possessions with your partner

7. Receiving emotional support from your partner

8. Giving emotional support to your partner

9. Being able to communicate with your partner about intimate things

10. Valuing your partner's presence in your life

The passion component refers to the elements of romance, attraction, and sexuality in the relationship. These may be fueled by a desire to increase self-esteem, to be sexually active or fulfilled, to affiliate with others, to dominate, or to subordinate.

The commitment component consists of two separate parts—a short-term part and a long-term part. The short-term part refers to an individual's decision that he or she loves someone. People may or may not make the decision consciously. But it usually occurs before they decide to make a commitment to the other person. The long-term part refers to commitment, or the maintenance of love. But a decision to love someone does not necessarily entail a commitment to maintaining that love.

Kinds of Love   The intimacy, passion, and commitment components can be combined in eight basic ways, according to Sternberg:

1. Liking (intimacy only)

2. Infatuation (passion only)

> *You know you're in love when you can't fall asleep because reality is finally better than your dreams.*
>
> —Dr. Seuss

> *Don't threaten me with love, baby.*
>
> —Billie Holiday
> (1915–1959)

3. Romantic love (intimacy and passion)

4. Companionate love (intimacy and commitment)

5. Fatuous love (passion and commitment)

6. Consummate love (intimacy, passion, and commitment)

7. Empty love (commitment only)

8. Nonlove (absence of intimacy, passion, and commitment)

These types represent extremes that few of us are likely to experience. Not many of us, for example, experience infatuation in its purest form, in which there is absolutely *no* intimacy. And empty love is not really love at all. These categories are nevertheless useful for examining the nature of love.

Liking: Intimacy Only   Liking represents the intimacy component alone. It forms the basis for close friendships but is neither passionate nor committed. As such, liking is often an enduring kind of love. Boyfriends and girlfriends may come and go, but good friends remain.

Infatuation: Passion Only   Infatuation is "love at first sight." It is the kind of love that idealizes its object; the infatuated individual rarely sees the other as a "real" person with normal human foibles. Infatuation is marked by sudden passion and a high degree of physical and emotional arousal. It tends to be obsessive and all-consuming; one has no time, energy, or desire for anything or anyone but the beloved (or thoughts of him or her). To the dismay of the infatuated individual, infatuations are usually asymmetrical: The passion (or obsession) is rarely returned equally. And the greater the asymmetry, the greater the distress in the relationship.

Romantic Love: Intimacy and Passion   Romantic love combines intimacy and passion. It is similar to liking except that it is more intense as a result of physical or emotional attraction. It may begin with an immediate union of the two components, with friendship that intensifies into passion, or with passion that also develops intimacy. Although commitment is not an essential element of romantic love, it may develop.

Companionate Love: Intimacy and Commitment   Companionate love is essential to a committed friendship. It often begins as romantic love, but as the passion diminishes and the intimacy increases, it is transformed into companionate love. Some couples are satisfied with such love; others are not. Those who are dissatisfied in companionate love relationships may seek extrarelational partners to maintain passion in their lives. They may also end the relationship to seek a new romantic relationship that they hope will remain romantic.

Fatuous Love: Passion and Commitment   Fatuous, or deceptive, love is whirlwind love; it begins the day two people meet and quickly results in cohabitation or engagement, and possibly marriage. It develops so quickly that they hardly know what happened. Often, nothing much really did happen that will permit the relationship to endure. As Sternberg and Barnes (1989) observe, "It is fatuous in the sense that a commitment is made on the basis of passion without the stabilizing element of intimate involvement—which takes time to develop." Passion fades soon enough, and all that remains is commitment. But commitment that has had relatively little time to deepen is a poor foundation

Being deeply loved by someone gives you strength; loving someone deeply gives you courage.

—Lao Tzu
(sixth century BCE)

We are never so defenseless against suffering as when we love.

—Sigmund Freud
(1856–1939)

on which to build an enduring relationship. With neither passion nor intimacy, the commitment wanes.

Consummate Love: Intimacy, Passion, and Commitment Consummate love results when intimacy, passion, and commitment combine to form their unique constellation. It is the kind of love we dream about but do not expect in all our love relationships. Many of us can achieve it, but it is difficult to sustain over time. To sustain it, we must nourish its different components, for each is subject to the stress of time.

Empty Love: Commitment Only This is love that lacks intimacy or passion. Empty love involves staying together solely for the sake of appearances or the children, for example.

Nonlove: Absence of Intimacy, Passion, and Commitment Nonlove can take many forms, such as attachment for financial reasons, fear, or the fulfillment of neurotic needs.

Though all three components of Sternberg's love triangle are important in a loving relationship, each often manifests in varying degrees over time and in different patterns. Regardless of these shifts and variations, evidence shows that when both partners experience similar levels of passion, commitment, and intimacy, there is greater compatibility (Drigotas, Rusbult, & Verette, 1999).

The Geometry of Love The shape of the love triangle depends on the intensity of the love and the balance of the parts. By varying both the area and the shape of the triangles, it becomes possible to represent a wide variety of kinds of relationships. Intense love relationships lead to triangles with greater area; such triangles occupy more of one's life. Just as love relationships can be balanced or unbalanced, so can love triangles. The balance determines the shape of the triangle (see Figure 2). A relationship in which the intimacy, passion, and commitment components are equal results in an equilateral triangle. But if the components are not equal, differences in amounts of love are experienced and unbalanced triangles form. The size and shape of a person's triangle give a good pictorial sense of how that person feels about another. The greater the match between the triangles of the two partners in a relationship, the more likely each is to experience satisfaction in the relationship.

Love as Attachment

Humans desire to bond with other people. At the same time, many people fear bonding. Where do these contradictory impulses and emotions come from? Can they ever be resolved?

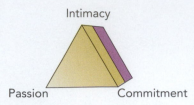

Intimacy

Passion   Commitment

Perfectly matched relationship
(Amount of love and balance
of love are matched.)

Closely matched relationship

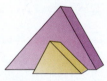

Moderately mismatched
relationship

Severely mismatched
relationship

 Self   Other

● **FIGURE 2**

The Geometry of Love. According to
the triangular theory of love, the
shape and size of each person's
triangle indicate how well each is
matched to the other.

(*Source:* From Sternberg, R. J. [1988]. *The
triangle of love: Intimacy, passion, commitment.* New York: Basic Books, 1988, p. 79.
Used by permission of Robert J. Sternberg.)

Attachment theory, the most prominent approach to the study of love, helps us understand how adult relationships develop, what can go wrong in them, and what to do when things do go wrong. In this theory, love is seen as a form of **attachment,** a close, enduring emotional bond that finds its roots in infancy (Hazan & Shaver, 1987; Shaver, 1984; Shaver, Hazan, & Bradshaw, 1988). Research suggests that romantic love and infant-caregiver attachment have similar emotional dynamics.

Infant-Caregiver Attachment

- The attachment bond's formation and quality depend on the attachment object's (AO) responsiveness and sensitivity.
- When the AO is present, the infant is happier.
- The infant shares toys, discoveries, and objects with the AO.
- The infant coos, talks baby talk, and "sings."
- The infant shares feelings of oneness with the AO.

Romantic Love

- Feelings of love are related to the lover's interest and reciprocation.
- When the lover is present, the person feels happier.
- Lovers share experiences and goods and give gifts.
- Lovers coo, sing, and talk baby talk.
- Lovers share feelings of oneness.

The implications of attachment theory are far-reaching. Attachment affects the way we process information, interact with others, and view the world. Basically, it influences our ability to love and to see ourselves as lovable (Fisher, 2004).

The core elements of love appear to be the same for children as for adults: the need to feel emotionally safe and secure. When a partner responds to a need, for instance, adults view the world as a safe place. In this respect, we don't differ greatly from children.

The most basic concept of attachment theory is that to be whole adults we need to accept the fact that we are also vulnerable children. In a secure, intimate adult relationship, it is neither demeaning nor diminishing nor pathological to share honest emotions. It is the capacity to be vulnerable and open and accepting of others' giving that makes us lovable and human.

Based on observations made by Mary Ainsworth and colleagues (1978, cited in Shaver et al., 1988), Phillip Shaver and colleagues (1988) hypothesized that the styles of attachment developed in childhood—secure, anxious/ambivalent, and avoidant—continue through adulthood. Their surveys revealed similar styles in adult relationships.

Adults with **secure attachments** found it relatively easy to get close to other people. They felt comfortable depending on others and having others depend on them. They didn't frequently worry about being abandoned or having someone get too close to them. More than anxious/ambivalent and avoidant adults, they felt that others usually liked them; they believed that people were generally well intentioned and good-hearted. Their love experiences tended to be happy, friendly, and trusting. They accepted and supported their partners. On average, their relationships lasted 10 years. About 56% of the adults in the study were secure.

Adults with **anxious/ambivalent attachments** believed that other people did not get as close as they themselves wanted. They worried that their partners didn't really love them or would leave them. They also wanted to merge completely with another person, which sometimes caused others to withdraw. More than others, they felt that it was easy to fall in love. Their experiences in love were often obsessive and marked by desire for union, high degrees of sexual attraction, and jealousy. Their love relationships lasted an average of 5 years. Approximately 19–20% of the adults were identified as anxious/ambivalent.

Adults with **avoidant attachments** felt discomfort in being close to other people; they were distrustful and fearful of being dependent. More than others, they believed that romance seldom lasts but that at times it can be as intense as it was at the beginning. Their partners wanted more closeness than they did. Avoidant partners were not likely to focus on their partners' needs, which explains why partners were often sexually dissatisfied (Peloquin, Brassard, Lafontaine, & Shaver, 2014). Avoidant lovers feared intimacy and experienced emotional highs and lows and jealousy. Their relationships lasted an average of 6 years. Approximately 23–25% of the adults in the study were avoidant.

In adulthood, the attachment style developed in infancy combines with sexual desire and caring behaviors to give rise to romantic love. However, it is also important to know that an individual's past does not necessarily determine the future course of his or her relationships. Rather, as individuals and couples mature and evolve, so can their capacity to foster physical proximity, to be attuned to each other's needs and distress cues, and work together to help solve problems. Not only are these qualities satisfying to the relationship, but they nurture sexual satisfaction as well (Peloquin et al., 2014).

According to attachment theory, the holding and cuddling behaviors between parents and babies resemble those of adult lovers.

© PBNJ Productions/Blend Images LLC

Unrequited Love

As most of us know from painful experience, love is not always returned. People may suffer tremendous anguish when they feel they have been rejected or ignored, even if the relationship was imagined. **Unrequited love**—love that is one-sided or not openly reciprocated or understood—is distressing for both the would-be lover and the rejecting person. Would-be lovers may have both positive and intensely negative feelings about their failed relationship. The rejectors, however, often feel uniformly negative about the experience. Unlike the rejectors, the would-be lovers feel that the attraction is mutual, that they have been led on, and that the rejection was never clearly communicated. Rejectors, in contrast, feel that they have not led the other person on; moreover, they feel guilty about hurting him or her. Nevertheless, many find the other person's persistence intrusive and annoying; they wish the would-be lover would simply get the hint and go away. Rejectors view would-be lovers as self-deceiving and unreasonable; would-be lovers see their rejectors as inconsistent and mysterious.

Adults with secure attachments may find it easy to get close to others.

© Asia Images Group/Getty Images

The Science of Love

Any man who can drive safely while kissing a pretty girl is simply not giving the kiss the attention it deserves.

—Albert Einstein
(1879–1955)

Throughout history there have been poems and stories, plays and pictures that have attempted to explain love. Each has provided some insight into the ways that passion grabs us and, almost as quickly, leaves us. More recently, science has explored the complexities involved in love by examining the parts of the brain linked to reward and pleasure and providing us with particulars of its chemical components.

The scientific tale of love begins with the reward and pleasure part of the brain: the ventral tegmental area, the part of the midbrain that is rich in the chemicals dopamine and serotonin, and the caudate nucleus (located deep within the brain and involved with the control of involuntary movement). Dopamine and serotonin are powerful chemical messengers that regulate numerous physical and emotional responses, including sexual arousal and response. Anthropologist Helen Fisher, professor emeritus at Rutgers University, has studied the biochemical pathways of love with the aid of an MRI machine. Fisher found that love lights up the caudate nucleus—home to a dense spread of receptors for dopamine, the chemical in the brain that stimulates feelings of attraction and accompanies passion. This is the same chemical that is produced in response to the ingestion of cocaine. Following the flooding of dopamine, the caudate then sends signals for more dopamine. "The more dopamine you get, the more high you feel," says Lucy Brown, neurologist at the Albert Einstein College of Medicine in New York. In the right proportions, dopamine creates intense energy, focused attention, exhilaration, and desire. It is why a newly-in-love person can live passionately without sleep, feel bold and bright, and take risks. At the same time, a breakup can cause withdrawal symptoms such as depression and poor sleep. A broken-hearted lover can relapse, for example, when he or she hears a favorite song, which can trigger the craving once again.

The simple act of kissing triggers and sends a flood of chemicals, including testosterone, and neural messages that transmit tactile sensations, sexual excitement, feelings of closeness, and euphoria (Brizendine, 2010;

Walter, 2008). Since lips are densely populated with sensory neurons, when we kiss, these neurons, along with those in the tongue and mouth, send messages to the brain and body that intensify emotions and physical reactions. Kissing also unleashes a cocktail of chemicals that govern stress, motivation, social bonding, and sexual stimulation. While enjoyable for both, kissing has different meanings for some men and women. For men, it may be an indicator of sexual readiness while for women, it may be a key to the significance of the relationship (Kirshenbaum, 2011). As the relationship continues, those who kiss for affection rather than as part of a sexual expression report being more sexually satisfied (Northrup, Schwartz, & Witte, 2014). Regardless of when it first occurred, the first kiss is said to provide some of our strongest romantic memories.

Interestingly, the brains of love-struck men and women seem to differ: More activity exists for men in the brain region that integrates visual stimuli, whereas for women the areas of the brain that govern memories are more active. Women's brain activity is different than men's, but it may be that when a woman really studies a man, she can remember things about his behavior in order to determine whether he'd make a reliable mate and father. Though differences appear in the male and female brain while they are being stimulated, there are few differences that occur during orgasm itself (Linden, 2011).

Aside from the intense and short-lived pleasure of orgasm, there is also a warm, post-orgasmic afterglow caused by the release of the hormone oxytocin, which is thought to be crucial for sexual pair-bond formation. Oxytocin has also been found to play a role in trust, mother-infant bonding, and perception of emotional state. Though many have speculated that those with "cheating hearts" might have more differences in brain chemistry than their more exclusive counterparts, there are some initial findings in support of this (Linden, 2011). While there is a great deal of interest in understanding what enhances or undermines long-term human attachment, there is still much research to be done before we can finally understand the role of orgasm in human bonding.

In studying romance and passion historically and globally, scientists now believe that romance is universal and has been embedded in our brains since prehistoric times.

It has been observed that, in all societies, passion usually diminishes over time. From a physiological perspective, this makes sense. The dopamine-drenched state of romantic love adapts and changes into a relatively quiet one that is explained by the presence of oxytocin, a hormone that promotes feelings of connectedness and bonding. For most, these changes are anticipated and welcomed. However, for some who experience the novelty of new love replaced with a more companionate love composed of deep affection and liking, the change may be both unwelcomed and unacceptable. Thus, couples would be wise to slow down the habituation that can lead to boredom and do what may seem obvious, which is to build companionship, continue touching and hugging, and fill the relationship with words and actions that elicit more positive emotion (Lyubomirsky, 2013).

What researchers have learned from lovers' brains is that romantic love isn't really an emotion—it's a drive that is based deep within our brains that results in a flood of hormones and helps explain why we might do crazy things for love.

Think Critically

1. How important is it that science investigates the "brain in love"? What impact might this information have on you or others?

2. How accurate do you feel the various chemical changes that the brain undergoes actually occurs in response to love? Have you experienced these variations?

3. What gender differences do you see, if any, between how men and women respond to love?

SOURCES: Brizendine, L. (2010). *The male brain.* New York: Crown; Cohen, E. (2007, February 15). Loving with all your . . . brain. Available: http://www.cnn.com/2007/HEALTH/02/14/love.science/index.html; Linden, D. J. (2011). *The compass of pleasure.* New York: Penguin; Slater, L. (2006, Feb.). Love: The chemical reaction. *National Geographic,* pp. 34–49; Kirshenbaum, S. (2011). *The science of kissing.* New York: Grand Central; Lyubomirsky, S. (2013). *The myths of happiness.* New York: Penguin; Northrup, C., Schwartz, P., & Witte, J. (2014). *The normal bar.* New York: Crown.

Jealousy

Jealousy is an aversive response that occurs because of a partner's real, imagined, or likely involvement with a third person. Jealousy sets boundaries for the behaviors that are acceptable in relationships; the boundaries cannot be crossed without evoking jealousy. Though a certain amount of jealousy can be expected in any loving relationship, it is important that partners communicate openly about their fears and boundaries. A strong connection or closeness to a significant other can create the potential for jealousy when the relationship is threatened. Jealousy can also occur when partners are not spending enough time together, creating for some suspicious thoughts about the exclusiveness of one's partner (Attridge, 2013). Jealousy is a paradox; it doesn't necessarily signal difficulty between partners, nor does it have to threaten the relationship.

Many of us think that the existence of jealousy proves the existence of love. We may try to test someone's interest or affection by attempting to make him or her jealous by flirting with another person. If our date or partner becomes jealous, the jealousy is taken as a sign of love. But provoking jealousy proves only that the other person can be made jealous. Making jealousy a litmus test of love is dangerous, for jealousy and love are not necessarily companions. Jealousy may be a more accurate yardstick for measuring insecurity or immaturity than for measuring love (Pistole, 1995).

It is important to understand jealousy for several reasons. First, jealousy is a painful emotion associated with anger, hurt, and loss. If we can understand jealousy, especially when it is irrational, then we can eliminate some of its pain. Second, jealousy can help cement or destroy a relationship. Jealousy helps maintain a relationship by guarding its exclusiveness. But in its irrational or extreme forms, it can destroy a relationship by its insistent demands and attempts at control. We need to understand when and how jealousy is functional and when it is not. Third, jealousy is often linked to violence in marriages and dating

> *Jealousy is not a barometer by which the depth of love can be read. It merely records the depth of the lover's insecurity.*
>
> —Margaret Mead
> (1901–1978)

> *Beware, my lord, of jealousy. It is the green-eyed monster that mocks the meat it feeds on.*
>
> —William Shakespeare
> (1564–1616)

relationships (Buss, 1999; Easton & Shackelford, 2009). Furthermore, marital violence and rape are often provoked by jealousy. Rather than being directed at a rival, jealous aggression is often used against the partner.

The Psychological Dimension

As most of us know, jealousy is a painful emotion. It is an agonizing compound of hurt, anger, depression, fear, and doubt. When we are jealous, we may feel less attractive and acceptable to our partner. Jealousy can also enrich relationships and spark passion by increasing the attention individuals pay to their partner. According to David Buss (2000), professor of psychology at the University of Texas at Austin, the total absence of jealousy is a more ominous sign than its presence for romantic partners because it signals indifference. Though both sexes may elicit jealousy intentionally as an assessment tool to gauge the strength of a partner's commitment, they seem to use it unequally. Buss (2000) found that 31% of women and 17% of men had intentionally elicited jealousy in their relationship.

Sex differences in the context and expression of jealousy have been documented. For example, men more than women are upset by a partner's sexual nonexclusiveness, whereas women more than men are upset by a partner's emotional nonexclusiveness (Buss, Larsen, Westen, & Semmelroth, 1992; Cann, Mangum, & Wells, 2001). These results are consistent with findings reported across many cultures (Buss, 1999). Gender differences can partly be explained using an evolutionary model, which proposes that men, because they cannot be completely confident about the paternity of any offspring from a relationship, will be more upset by sexual nonexclusiveness. Women, in contrast, are more often upset by emotional nonexclusiveness, which might signal the man's lack of commitment to the long-term success of the relationship and any offspring.

Comparing cohabiting couples and noncohabiting couples did not reveal lower emotional or physical satisfaction in either group when jealous conflict occurred (Gatzeva & Paik, 2011). Rather, jealous responses are most intense in marital relationships, as compared to cohabiting or noncohabiting couples. An expectation occurs because our intimate partner is different from everyone else. With him or her, we are our most confiding, revealing, vulnerable, caring, and trusting. There is a sense of exclusiveness. Being intimate outside the relationship violates that sense of exclusiveness because intimacy (especially sexual intimacy) symbolizes specialness. Words such as "disloyalty," "cheating," and "infidelity" reflect the sense that an unspoken pledge has been broken. This unspoken pledge is the normative expectation that serious relationships will be sexually exclusive.

When jealousy is excessive or morbid, research has demonstrated that a greater percentage of men than women use physical violence, attempt to kill or actually kill their partners, and use their hands rather than an object as the instrument of violence. Women, on the other hand, are less likely to use violence against partners, even when they are threatened with partner infidelity. However, they do sometimes use violence in self-defense (Easton & Shackelford, 2009).

Managing Jealousy

Jealousy can be unreasonable, based on fears and fantasies, or realistic, in reaction to genuine threats or events. Unreasonable jealousy can become a problem when it interferes with an individual's well-being or that of the relationship. Dealing with irrational suspicions can often be very difficult, for such feelings

Love is like quicksilver in the hand. Leave the fingers open and it stays. Clutch it, and it darts away.

—Dorothy Parker
(1893–1967)

think
about it

The Passionate Love Scale

Are you in love with someone right now? Have you ever been in love? How intense are your feelings compared to those of other lovers? Researchers have suggested that almost everyone is capable of loving passionately. Social psychologists Hatfield and Walster (1978) described a kind of love, passionate love, as "a state of intense longing for union with another. Reciprocated love (union with the other) is associated with fulfillment and ecstasy while unrequited love (separation) is associated with emptiness, anxiety, or despair. Both involve a state of profound physiological arousal" (p. 9).

Sometimes labeled "puppy love," "infatuation," or "lovesickness," passionate love often includes sexual desire. The Passionate Love Scale (PLS), which follows, is a measure of these emotions (Hatfield, 2010).

Directions

For each of the 15 sentences below, choose a number from 1 (not at all true) to 9 (definitely true) that most accurately describes your feelings toward the person you love or have loved in a romantic relationship. Indicate your answer by circling the number in the corresponding row.

	Not at all true				Moderately true				Definitely true
1. I would feel deep despair if _____ left me.	1	2	3	4	5	6	7	8	9
2. Sometimes I feel I can't control my thoughts; they are obsessively about _____.	1	2	3	4	5	6	7	8	9
3. I feel happy when I am doing something to make _____ happy.	1	2	3	4	5	6	7	8	9
4. I would rather be with _____ than anyone else.	1	2	3	4	5	6	7	8	9
5. I'd get jealous if I thought _____ were falling in love with someone else.	1	2	3	4	5	6	7	8	9
6. I yearn to know all about _____.	1	2	3	4	5	6	7	8	9
7. I want _____ physically, emotionally, mentally.	1	2	3	4	5	6	7	8	9
8. I have an endless appetite for affection from _____.	1	2	3	4	5	6	7	8	9
9. For me, _____ is the perfect romantic partner.	1	2	3	4	5	6	7	8	9
10. I sense my body responding when _____ touches me.	1	2	3	4	5	6	7	8	9
11. _____ always seems to be on my mind.	1	2	3	4	5	6	7	8	9
12. I want _____ to know me—my thoughts, fears, and hopes.	1	2	3	4	5	6	7	8	9
13. I eagerly look for signs indicating _____'s desire for me.	1	2	3	4	5	6	7	8	9
14. I possess a powerful attraction for _____.	1	2	3	4	5	6	7	8	9
15. I get extremely depressed when things don't go right in my relationship with _____.	1	2	3	4	5	6	7	8	9

Passionate Love Scale Scores

Extremely passionate = 106–135 (wildly, recklessly in love)
Passionate = 86–105 (passionate, but less intense)
Average = 66–85 (occasional bursts of passion)
Cool = 45–65 (tepid, infrequent passion)
Extremely cool = 15–44 (the thrill is gone)

Think Critically

1. How does your score compare to the PLS scores with any other persons you have loved passionately? How reliable do you believe this instrument to be?

2. Do you believe that love changes over time? If so, in a long-term relationship, can passionate love be maintained? If it can, how?

3. What steps might you consider if you felt that the passion in your relationship was waning?

SOURCE: The Passionate Love Scale (shorter version) reprinted by permission of Elaine Hatfield. From Hatfield, E. (2010). The Passionate Love Scale. In Fisher, T. D., Davis, C. M., Yarber, W. L., & Davis, S. L., *Handbook of sexuality-related measures* (3rd ed). New York: Routledge.

touch deep recesses in ourselves. As noted previously, jealousy is often related to personal feelings of insecurity and inadequacy. The source of such jealousy lies within ourselves, not within the relationship.

If we can work on the underlying causes of our insecurity, then we can deal effectively with our irrational jealousy. Excessively jealous people may need considerable reassurance, but at some point they must also confront their own irrationality and insecurity. If they do not, they emotionally imprison their partner. Their jealousy may destroy the very relationship they have been desperately trying to preserve.

But jealousy is not always irrational. Sometimes, there are valid reasons, such as the relationship boundaries being violated. In this case, the cause lies not within ourselves but within the relationship. If the jealousy is well founded, the partner may need to modify or end the relationship with the third party whose presence initiated the jealousy. Modifying the third-party relationship reduces the jealous response and, more importantly, symbolizes the partner's commitment to the primary relationship. If the partner is unwilling to do this, because of a lack of commitment, unsatisfied personal needs, or problems in the primary relationship, the relationship is likely to reach a crisis point. In such cases, jealousy may be the agent for profound change.

There are no set rules for dealing with jealousy. Each person must deal with it using his or her own understanding and insights. As with many of life's problems, jealousy is a complex emotion that has no simple answers.

Extradyadic Involvement

A fundamental assumption in our culture is that committed relationships are sexually exclusive. Each person remains the other's exclusive intimate partner, in terms of both emotional and sexual intimacy. **Extradyadic involvement,** sexual or romantic relationships outside of a primary or dating couple, alters that assumption.

It is difficult to determine accurately how many people have extradyadic involvements, because those involved may be reluctant to admit engaging in this behavior. Accurately determining the percentage of extradyadic relationships is also difficult because of terminology (e.g., monogamous by agreement or not) and the nature of the nonexclusiveness (e.g., one-time fling, long-term relationship or both) (Mark, Janssen, & Milhausen, 2011). Additionally, because of the negative terms and connotations associated with this behavior ("affairs," "cheating," "sleeping around"), extradyadic relationships are often underreported or undetected. Nevertheless, extradyadic involvement—also called extramarital sex—is common in supposedly monogamous relationships. According to nationally representative data, approximately 11% of Americans have had at least one concurrent or extradyadic sexual relationship in the previous 12 months (Adimora, Schoenbach, & Doherty, 2007; Laumann et al., 1994). In a more recent study of couples (average age of men = 33; average age of women = 28), nearly one-quarter of the men (23%) and one-fifth of the women (19%) indicated that they had "cheated" during their current relationship (Mark et al., 2011). Looking at motivations for nonexclusiveness, the same authors found that for both men and women, sexual personality characteristics such as the need for sexual excitement or performance concerns and, specifically for women, relationship factors were most relevant to predicting sexual exclusiveness. Furthermore, individuals who had engaged in nonexclusive behavior reported more one-night stands—this in spite of the fact that they also reported they were having regular sex with their primary partner. What both of these men and women shared was lower relationship happiness.

Love withers under constraints: its very essence is liberty: it is compatible neither with obedience, jealousy, nor fear: it is there most pure, perfect, and unlimited where its votaries live in confidence, equality and unreserve.

—Percy Bysshe Shelley
(1792–1822)

What I have seen of the love affairs of other people has not led me to regret that deficiency in my experience.

—George Bernard Shaw
(1856–1950)

Of course heaven forbids certain pleasures, but one finds means of compromise.

—Molière, Tartuffe
(1622–1673)

When extradyadic sex occurs, a crisis in the primary relationship usually results.
© Image Source

Extradyadic Involvement in Dating and Cohabiting Relationships Both cohabiting couples and those in committed relationships usually have expectations of sexual exclusiveness. But like some married men and women who take vows of exclusivity, these couples do not always remain sexually and/or emotionally exclusive. Research has revealed that cohabitors are more likely to have relationships outside their primary one, suggesting that perhaps they have lower investments in their unions (Treas & Giesen, 2000) or concerns about their sexual well-being (Allen et al., 2005). Gay men have more partners than cohabiting and married men, while lesbian women have fewer partners than any other group.

Extradyadic Involvement in Exclusive Marriages and Partnerships In marriages and committed partnerships that assume emotional and sexual exclusivity, mutuality and sharing are emphasized. Extradyadic sexual relationships are assumed to be destructive of marriage and committed partnerships; nonsexual heterosexual relationships may also be judged threatening.

As a result of assumptions, both sexual and nonsexual extradyadic relationships take place without the knowledge or permission of the other partner. If the extradyadic sex is discovered, a crisis often ensues. Many people feel that the partner who is not exclusive has violated a basic trust. Sexual accessibility implies emotional accessibility. When a person learns that his or her partner is having another relationship, the emotional commitment of that spouse is brought into question. How can the person prove that he or she still has a commitment? He or she cannot—commitment is assumed; it can never be proved. Furthermore, the extradyadic sex may imply to the partner (rightly or wrongly) that he or she is sexually inadequate or uninteresting.

Extradyadic Involvement in Nonexclusive Marriages and Partnerships There are several types of nonexclusive partnerships: (1) open in which intimate but nonsexual friendships with others are encouraged, (2) open in which outside sexual relationships are allowed, and (3) group marriage/multiple relationships. In **open marriage**, partners may mutually agree to allow sexual contact with others. Other terms used to describe these individuals are swingers and polyamorists, though these have slightly different connotations. **Swinging**

> There is one thing I would break up over, and that is if she caught me with another woman. I won't stand for that.
>
> —Steve Martin
> (1945–)

> To be faithful to one is to be cruel to all the others.
>
> —Wolfgang Amadeus Mozart
> (1756–1791)

involves engaging in a wide range of sexual activities that may or may not involve commitment with another couple, multiple couples, or a single individual. *Polyamory* literally means "multiple loves." **Polyamory** involves a lifestyle of being open to having more than one loving intimate relationship at a time, with the full knowledge and consent of all partners involved. The committed relationship is considered the primary relationship in both nonsexual extradyadic relationships and open marriages. Only the group marriage/multiple relationships model rejects the primacy of the relationship. Group marriage is the equal sharing of partners, as in polygamy; it may consist of one man and two women, one woman and two men, or two couples. Open marriages are more common than group marriages.

Rebound Sex

Sexual experiences in the aftermath of a romantic relationship breakup are sometimes referred to as **rebound sex.** Also called revenge sex, or being on the rebound, many who engage in this behavior report having been in a committed relationship followed by a loss that some otherwise regard as "being dumped." Negative reactions that occur among both men and women following a breakup include sadness, distress, and anger (Sprecher, 1994; Tashiro & Frazier, 2003). Using a longitudinal, online diary method to explore beliefs about recovery from the loss of a romantic relationship and whether people use sex as a way to get over it or get back at their ex-partners, recent research among 170 undergraduate students, most of whom were in their first semester of college, has found that having sex to cope and to get back at the ex-partner increased immediately following the split-up. It was, however, shown to decline over time, as did the probability of having sex with a new partner (Barber & Cooper, 2014). This was particularly true for those who considered themselves "dumped" by their ex-partner. The motivations for rebound sex included a need to boost self-esteem, to ease pain and loneliness, and to get over the breakup. Anger and distress might have also played a role in the desire to get back at the ex-partner.

● Making Love Last: From Passion to Intimacy

Ultimately, passionate love may be transformed or replaced by a quieter, more lasting love. Otherwise, the relationship will likely end, and each person will search for another who will once again ignite her or his passion.

Although love is one of the most important elements of our humanity, it seems to come and go. The kind of love that lasts is what we might call **intimate love.** In intimate love, each person knows he or she can count on the other. The excitement comes from the achievement of other goals—from creativity, from work, from child rearing, from friendships—as well as from the relationship. The key to making love endure seems to be not maintaining love's passionate intensity but transforming it into intimate love. Intimate love is based on commitment, caring, and self-disclosure.

Commitment is an important component of intimate love. It reflects a determination to continue a relationship or marriage in the face of bad times as well as good. It is based on conscious choices rather than on feelings, which, by their very nature, are transitory. Commitment involves a promise of a shared future, a promise to be together, come what may. We seem to be as much in search of commitment as we are in search of love or marriage. We speak of making a commitment

Thou shalt not commit adultery . . . unless in the mood.

—W. C. Fields
(1879–1946)

Tis better to have loved and lost Than never to have loved at all.

—Alfred, Lord Tennyson
(1809–1892)

to someone or to a relationship. A committed relationship has become almost a stage of courtship, somewhere between dating and being engaged or living together.

Caring involves the making of another person's needs as important as your own. It requires what the philosopher Martin Buber called an "I-Thou" relationship. Buber described two fundamental ways of relating to people: I-Thou and I-It. In an I-Thou relationship, each person is treated as a Thou—that is, as a person whose life is valued as an end in itself. In an I-It relationship, each person is treated as an It; the person has worth only as someone who can be used. When a person is treated as a Thou, his or her humanity and uniqueness are paramount.

Self-disclosure is the revelation of personal information that others would not ordinarily know because of its riskiness. When we self-disclose, we reveal ourselves—our hopes, our fears, our everyday thoughts—to others. Self-disclosure deepens others' understanding of us. It also deepens our own understanding, for we discover unknown aspects as we open up to others. Without self-disclosure, we remain opaque and hidden. If others love us, such love makes us anxious: Are we loved for ourselves or for the image we present to the world?

Together, these principles help transform love. But in the final analysis, perhaps the most important means of sustaining love are our words and actions; caring words and deeds provide the setting for maintaining and expanding love.

Being able to sustain love in the day-to-day world involves commitment, compassion, and most importantly communication. Clear communication can take the guesswork out of relationships, subdue jealousy, increase general satisfaction, and possibly put couple therapists out of business.

Everyone has experienced that truth: that love, like a running brook, is disregarded, taken for granted; but when the brook freezes over, then people begin to remember how it was when it ran, and they want it to run again.

—Kahlil Gibran
(1883–1931)

The Nature of Communication

Communication is a transactional process by which we use symbols, such as words, gestures, and movements, to establish human contact, exchange information, and reinforce or change our own attitudes and behaviors and those of others. Communication takes place simultaneously within cultural, social, and psychological contexts. These contexts affect our ability to communicate clearly by prescribing rules (usually unwritten or unconscious) for communicating about various subjects, including sexuality.

The Cultural Context

The cultural context of communication consists of the language that is used and the values, beliefs, and customs associated with it. Traditionally, reflecting a Judeo-Christian heritage, our culture has viewed sexuality negatively. Thus, sexual topics are often taboo. Children and adolescents are discouraged from obtaining sexual knowledge; they learn that they are not supposed to talk about sex. Censorship abounds in the media, with the ever-present "bleep" on television, though on the Internet there appears to be virtually no filtering. Our language has a variety of words for describing sex, including scientific or impersonal ones ("sexual intercourse," "coitus," "copulation"), moralistic ones ("fornication"), euphemistic ones ("doing it," "hooking up," "sleeping with"), and taboo ones ("fucking," "screwing," "banging"). A few terms place sexual interactions in a relational category, such as "making love." But love is not always involved, and the term does not capture the erotic quality of sex. Furthermore, the gay, lesbian, bisexual, and transgender subcultures have developed their own sexual slang, because society suppresses the open discussion or expression of same-sex behavior.

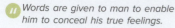

Words are given to man to enable him to conceal his true feelings.

—Voltaire
(1694–1778)

The greatest science in the world, in heaven and on earth, is love.

—Mother Teresa
(1910–1997)

Different ethnic groups within our culture also have different language patterns that affect the way they communicate about sex and sexuality. African American culture, for example, creates distinct communication patterns. Among African Americans, language and expressive patterns are characterized by, among other things, emotional vitality, realness, confrontation, and a focus on direct experience (Mackey & O'Brien, 1999). Emotional vitality is communicated through the animated, expressive use of words. *Realness* refers to "telling it like it is," using concrete, nonabstract language.

Among Latinos, especially traditional Latinos, there may be power imbalances that are potentially more significant for women than men. This may be due to the cultural values of a traditionally *machista* society in which men are defined by their ability to maintain control and to assert dominance by being the active sexual partner. Among traditional Latinos, the type and frequency of sexual behaviors are most often determined by men (Wood & Price, 1997). Although most Latinos agree that men tend to be the initiators of sexual activity and women are more likely to suggest condom use, they report that couples share responsibility for decisions regarding sexual activities and contraceptive use.

Asian Americans constitute a population group that defies simple characterizations; it includes a variety of demographic, historical, and cultural factors and traditions. At the same time, Asian Americans share many cultural characteristics, such as the primacy of the family and of collective goals over individual wishes, an emphasis on propriety and social roles, the appropriateness of sex only within the context of marriage, and sexual restraint and modesty (Okazaki, 2002). Because harmonious relationships are highly valued, Asian Americans have a greater tendency to avoid direct confrontation if possible. Despite significant steps in modernization and sexual liberation in recent decades, many Asian Americans' views of sexuality are still rooted in cultural heritage and traditional beliefs (So & Cheung, 2005). In one study, most women reported that their parents did not speak to them about sexuality, yet they perceived clear and consistent messages about their parents' values and expectations for their sexual behavior through nonverbal and indirect cues (Kim, 2009). To avoid conflict, their verbal communication is often indirect or ambiguous; it skirts issues rather than confronts them. As a consequence, Asian Americans rely on each other to interpret the meaning of conversations or nonverbal cues.

Among those from the Middle East, partnered sexual behaviors are often rooted in power and based on dominant and subordinate positions (Rathus, Nevid, & Fichner-Rathus, 2005). Islam is the dominant religion in the Middle East; the family is the backbone of Islamic society. Because Muhammad decreed that marriage represents the only road to virtue, celibacy is frowned on, while homosexuality is condemned.

The Social Context

The social context of communication consists of the roles we play in society as members of different groups. For instance, as men and women, we play out masculine and feminine roles. As members of marital units, we act out roles of husband and wife. As members of cohabiting units, we perform heterosexual, gay, or lesbian cohabiting roles.

Roles exist in relation to other people; thus, **status**—a person's position or ranking in a group—is important. In traditional gender roles, men are accorded higher status than women; in traditional marital roles, husbands are superior in status to wives. And in terms of sexual orientation, society awards higher status to heterosexual people than to gay men, lesbian women, or bisexual or transgender individuals. Because of this male/female disparity, heterosexual couples tend to have a greater power imbalance than do gay and lesbian couples (Lips, 2007).

The Psychological Context

Although the cultural and social contexts are important factors in communication, they do not *determine* how people communicate. The psychological context of communication does that. We are not prisoners of culture and society; we are unique individuals. We may accept some cultural or social aspects, such as language taboos, but reject, ignore, or modify others, such as traditional gender roles. Because we have distinct personalities, we express our uniqueness by the way we communicate: We may be assertive or submissive, rigid or flexible, and sensitive or insensitive; we may exhibit high or low self-esteem.

Our personality characteristics affect our ability to communicate, change, or manage conflict. Rigid people, for example, are less likely to change than are flexible ones, regardless of the quality of communication. People with high self-esteem may be more open to change because they do not necessarily interpret conflict as an attack on themselves. Personality characteristics such as negative or positive feelings about sexuality affect our sexual communication more directly.

Nonverbal Communication

There is no such thing as not communicating. Even when we are not talking, we are communicating by our silence (an awkward silence, a hostile silence, a tender silence). We are communicating by our body movements, our head positions, our facial expressions, our physical distance from another person, and so on. We can make sounds that aren't words to communicate nonverbally; screams, moans, grunts, sighs, and so on communicate a range of feelings and reactions. Look around you: How are the people in your presence communicating nonverbally?

Most of our communication of feeling is nonverbal. We radiate our moods: A happy mood invites companionship; a solemn mood pushes people away. Joy infects; depression distances—all without a word being said. Nonverbal expressions of love are particularly effective—a gentle touch, a loving glance, or the gift of a flower.

One of the problems with nonverbal communication, however, is the imprecision of its messages. Is a person frowning or squinting? Does the smile indicate friendliness or nervousness? Is the silence reflective, or does it express disapproval or remoteness?

Three of the most important forms of nonverbal communication are proximity, eye contact, and touching.

Proximity Nearness in physical space and time is called **proximity.** Where we sit or stand in relation to another person signifies a level of intimacy. Many of our words that convey emotion relate to proximity, such as feeling "distant" or "close" or being "moved" by someone. We also "make the first move," "move in" on someone else's partner, or "move in together."

In a social gathering, the distances between individuals when they start a conversation are clues to how they wish to

The cruelest lies are often told in silence.

—Robert Louis Stevenson (1850–1894)

Proximity, eye contact, and touching are important components of nonverbal communication. What do you think this man and woman are "saying" to each other?

© Sonda Dawes/The Image Works

define the relationship. All cultures have an intermediate distance in face-to-face interactions that is neutral. In most cultures, decreasing the distance signifies either an invitation to greater intimacy or a threat. Moving away denotes the desire to terminate the interaction. When we stand at an intermediate distance from someone at a party, we send the message "Intimacy is not encouraged." If we move closer, however, we invite closeness and risk rejection.

From a partner's perspective, physical proximity, along with a touch or a hug when needing comfort, may set the stage for both psychological intimacy and sexual closeness and affection. It may also increase the frequency and level of satisfaction in sexual interactions by underscoring greater ease and comfort for both partners (Peloquin et al., 2014).

Eye Contact   Much can be discovered about a relationship by watching how the two people look at each other. Making eye contact with another person, if only for a split second longer than usual, is a signal of interest. Brief and extended glances, in fact, play a significant role in women's expression of initial interest. When we can't take our eyes off another person, we probably have a strong attraction to him or her. In addition to eye contact, dilated pupils may be an indication of sexual interest. (They may also indicate fear, anger, and other strong emotions.)

The amount of eye contact between partners in conversation can reveal couples who have high levels of conflict and those who don't. Those with the greatest degree of agreement have the most eye contact with each other. Those in conflict tend to avoid eye contact unless it is a daggerlike stare. As with proximity, however, the level of eye contact may differ by culture.

> Touch is a language that can communicate more love in five seconds than words can in five minutes.
>
> —Ashley Montagu
> (1905–1999)

Touching   It is difficult to overestimate the significance of touch and its relevance to human development, health, and sexuality. Touch is the most basic of all senses. The skin contains receptors for pleasure and pain, heat and cold, roughness and smoothness. "Touch is the mother sense and out of it, all the other senses have been derived," writes anthropologist Ashley Montagu (1986). Touch is a life-giving force for infants. If babies are not touched, they can fail to thrive and even die. We hold hands and cuddle with small children and with people we love. Levels of touching differ among cultures and ethnic groups. Although the value placed on nonverbal expression may vary across groups and cultures, the ability to communicate and understand nonverbally remains important in all cultures.

But touch can also be a violation. Strangers or acquaintances may touch inappropriately, presuming a level of familiarity that does not actually exist. A date or partner may touch the other person in a manner he or she doesn't like or want. And sexual harassment includes unwelcome touching.

> Married couples who love each other tell each other a thousand things without talking.
>
> —Chinese proverb

Touch often signals intimacy, immediacy, and emotional closeness. In fact, touch may very well be the *closest* form of nonverbal communication. One researcher writes: "If intimacy is proximity, then nothing comes closer than touch, the most intimate knowledge of another" (Thayer, 1986). And touching seems to go hand in hand with self-disclosure. Those who touch appear to self-disclose more; in fact, touch seems to be an important factor in prompting others to talk more about themselves.

If touching is an issue in your relationship, discussing what it means to each of you can begin to unravel and expose existing patterns of behavior. Also, experiment with nonsexual touching. Learn to enjoy giving and receiving touch. Give and accept feedback nondefensively. Give feedback, especially verbal cues, about what does and does not feel good. Initiate touch when it is appropriate, even though it may be awkward at first. Don't be afraid to be adventurous in learning and utilizing methods that are pleasing to both you and your partner.

At the same time, be prepared to accept individual differences. In spite of forthright and ongoing communication, people still have unique comfort levels. Again, honest feedback will help you and your partner find a mutually acceptable level. If you are both able to understand and enjoy the rich and powerful messages that touch sends, then your relationship can be enriched by yet another dimension.

" Healing touch belongs to all of us.
—Dolores Krieger
(1935–)

● Sexual Communication

Communication is important in developing and maintaining sexual relationships. In childhood and adolescence, communication is critical for transmitting sexual knowledge and values and forming our sexual identities. As we establish our relationships, communication enables us to signal sexual interest and initiate sexual interactions. In developed relationships, communication allows us to explore and maintain our sexuality as couples.

Sexual Communication in Beginning Relationships

Our interpersonal sexual scripts provide us with "instructions" on how to behave sexually, including the initiation of potentially sexual relationships. Because as a culture we share our interpersonal sexual scripts, we know how we are supposed to act at the beginning of a relationship. These scripts are changing, however, as individuals rely more on social media to communicate and share their personal and sexual desires and needs. Using the anonymity feature that various social media platforms allow, an individual is free to become anyone he or she wishes, without consequences, until a face-to-face meeting occurs. Still, the questions remain: How do we begin a relationship? What is it that attracts and allows us to bond with certain individuals?

The Halo Effect   Imagine yourself unattached at a party. You notice someone standing next to you as you reach for some chips. In a split second, you decide whether you are interested in him or her. On what basis do you make that decision? Is it looks, personality, style, sensitivity, intelligence, smell, or what?

If you're like most people, you base this decision, consciously or unconsciously, on appearance. Physical attractiveness is particularly important during the initial meeting and early stages of a relationship. If you don't know anything else about a person, you tend to judge on appearance.

Most people would deny that they are attracted to others simply because of their looks. We like to think we are deeper than that. But looks are important, in part because we tend to infer qualities based on looks. This inference is based on what is known as the **halo effect,** the assumption that attractive or charismatic people also possess more desirable social characteristics than are actually present.

One of the most primal means of assessment is smell. Humans, like all animals, assign values to scents, recognizing those that affect them in powerful ways (Fisher, 2004). Scent lets both sexes narrow their choices of potential partners by identifying those unspoken characteristics, such as level of testosterone and ovulation, that may lead toward mating.

Interest and Opening Lines   After sizing someone up based on his or her appearance, what happens next in interactions between men and women? (Gay

Nontraditional roles are changing the ways in which couples make contact and initiate conversation. What appear to be the roles of each person in this photograph?

© Neil Marriott/Digital Vision/Getty Images

Whereas a lot of men used to ask for conversation when they really wanted sex, nowadays they often feel obliged to ask for sex even when they really want conversation.

—Katharine Whitehorn (1928–)

men's and lesbian women's beginning relationships are discussed later.) Does the man initiate the encounter? On the surface, yes, but in reality, the woman often covertly sends nonverbal signals of interest and availability. The woman may "glance" at the man once or twice and "catch" his eye; she may smile or flip her hair. If the man moves into her physical space, the woman then communicates interest by nodding, leaning close, smiling, or laughing.

If the man believes the woman is interested, he then initiates a conversation with an opening line, which tests the woman's interest and availability. Men use an array of opening lines. According to women, the most effective ones are innocuous, such as "I feel a little embarrassed, but I'd like to get to know you" or "Are you a student here?" The least effective lines are sexually blunt ones, such as "You really turn me on."

In the digital world of dating, words or a single photo can capture or repel the potential love object. Since this method of communication can occur without having to make eye contact or interpret facial cues, it is safer, bolder, and uncensored. Consequently, individuals may be inclined to misrepresent or reveal themselves more quickly and intimately on social networking sites, which can result in relationships that escalate more quickly than those that begin face-to-face.

The First Move and Beyond   When we first meet someone, we weigh his or her attitudes, values, and philosophy to see if we are compatible. We evaluate his or her sense of humor, intelligence, "partner" potential, ability to function in a relationship, sex appeal, and so on. Based on our overall assessment, we may decide to pursue a friendship or relationship. If the relationship continues on a romantic level, we may decide to move into one that includes some kind of physical intimacy. To signal this transition from nonphysical to physical intimacy, one of us must "make the first move." Making the first move marks the transition from a potentially sexual relationship to one that is actually sexual.

If the relationship develops along traditional gender-role lines, one of the partners, usually the man, will make the first move to initiate sexual intimacy, whether it is kissing, fondling, or engaging in sexual intercourse. The point at which this occurs generally depends on two factors: the level of intimacy and the length of the relationship. The more emotionally involved the two people are, the more likely they will be sexually involved as well. Similarly, the longer the relationship, the more likely there is sexual involvement (Christopher & Sprecher, 2000). Those who perceive that they are in more-committed relationships tend to enjoy their partnered sexual expression more, on average, than those in less-committed relationships (Galinsky & Sonenstein, 2013).

In new relationships, we communicate *indirectly* about sex because, although we may want to become sexually involved with the other person, we also want to avoid rejection. By using indirect strategies, such as turning down the lights, moving closer, and touching the other person's face or hair, we can test his or her interest in sexual involvement. If he or she responds positively to our cues, we can initiate a sexual encounter. Because so much of our sexual communication is indirect, ambiguous, or nonverbal, there is a high risk of misinterpretation.

Gay men and lesbian women, like heterosexual men and women, rely on both nonverbal and verbal communication in expressing sexual interest in others. Unlike heterosexual people, however, they cannot necessarily assume that the person in whom they are interested is of the same sexual orientation. Instead, they must rely on specific identifying factors, such as meeting at a gay or lesbian bar, wearing a gay/lesbian pride button, participating in gay/lesbian events, or being introduced by friends to others identified as lesbian or gay. In situations in which sexual orientation is not clear, some gay men and lesbian women use "gaydar" (gay radar), in which they look for clues as to orientation. They give ambiguous cues regarding their own orientation while looking for cues from the other person. These cues can include mannerisms, speech patterns, slang, and lingering glances. They may also include the mention of specific places for entertainment or recreation that are frequented mainly by lesbian women or gay men, songs that can be interpreted as having "gay" meanings, or movies with gay or lesbian themes. Once a like orientation is established, lesbian women and gay men often use nonverbal communication to express interest.

Regardless of our sexual orientation, age, gender, or ethnicity, much of our sexual communication is nonverbal.

© Thinkstock

Directing Sexual Activity   As we begin a sexual involvement, we have several tasks to accomplish. First and foremost, we must practice safer sex. We should gather information about our partner's sexual history, determine whether he or she knows how to practice safer sex, and use condoms. Unlike much of our sexual communication, which is nonverbal or ambiguous, practicing safer sex requires direct verbal communication. Second, heterosexual couples must discuss birth control (unless both partners have agreed to try for pregnancy, or one is sterile). Contraceptive responsibility, like safer sex, requires verbal communication.

In addition to communicating about safer sex and contraception, we need to communicate about what we like. What kind of touching do we like? For example, do we like to be orally or manually stimulated? If so, how? What stimulation does each partner need to be orgasmic? Many of our needs and desires can be communicated nonverbally by movements or physical cues. But if our partner does not pick up our nonverbal signals or cues, we need to discuss them directly and clearly to avoid ambiguity.

> *If you don't risk anything, you risk even more.*
>
> —Erica Jong
> (1942–)

Sexual Communication in Established Relationships

In developing relationships, partners begin modifying their individual sexual scripts as they interact with each other. The scripts become less rigid and conventional as each partner adapts to the uniqueness of the other. Partners ultimately develop a shared sexual script. Through their sexual interactions, they learn what each other likes, dislikes, wants, and needs. Much of this learning takes place nonverbally: Partners in established relationships, like those in emerging relationships, tend to be indirect and ambiguous in their sexual communication. Like partners in new relationships, they want to avoid rejection. Indirection allows them to express sexual interest and, at the same time, protect themselves from embarrassment or loss of face.

> *When in doubt, tell the truth.*
>
> —Mark Twain
> (1835–1910)

Let's (Not) Talk About Sex: Avoiding the Discussion About Past Lovers

Seal up your lips and give no words but mum.

—William Shakespeare
Henry IV, Part 2, 1592

Revealing one's past sexual experiences early in a new relationship—as difficult and as threatening as it may seem—can both enhance trust in a new relationship as well as protect the other by, for example, providing information about sexually transmitted infections (STIs). Still, many refrain from honest conversations about past sexual experiences. In effect, they "seal up their lips," as Shakespeare stated. Deciding what to reveal and conceal in any close relationship is often difficult to navigate because it represents a tension between self-disclosure and privacy. Self-disclosure is a fundamental component for the development of relationship intimacy; however, too much can hinder relationship growth (Anderson, Kunkel, & Dennis, 2011; Dindia, 1992, 1994; Ijams & Miller, 2000; Pawlowski, 1998).

One-hundred and two students (49 men and 53 women) from a large midwestern university who were currently in a romantic relationship and who had prior sex experience with a partner were assessed about disclosure of past romantic relationships (Anderson et al., 2011). They were asked to: (1) list all the topics they avoided discussing in their current romantic relationship (i.e., taboo topics) and (2) describe reasons for avoiding discussing one's sexual history if they or their current partner were reluctant to have that discussion. Here are the major study findings:

- Past romantic relationships, and in particular past sexual experiences, was the most frequently cited taboo topic. Men and women were similar in the frequency with which they indicated particular reasons for avoidance.

- Four reasons for avoiding discussion of prior sexual experiences were given: (1) belief that the past should be kept in the past, (2) identity issues, (3) perceived threats to their current relationship, and (4) emotionally upsetting feelings.

- Relative to "the past should be the past," participants commonly cited the lack of its relevance to the current relationship. Some stated that they did not want to know, think about, or visualize the details of a partner's prior sexual activities.

- The identity theme captured the respondents' desire to not be subjected to evaluation, especially not being compared to prior partners. Many worried about whether their level of sexual experience differed from their partner's level—that is, having had "too much" or

"too little" past experiences. However, the greatest concern was being perceived as too inexperienced.

- Participants expressed concern that revealing past sexual experiences would be a threat to current relational soundness, as individuals or the relationship might be judged to be less close or special.

- The possibility of jealousy and embarrassment for oneself or by the partner was another somewhat commonly cited reason for avoiding discussion of sexual past.

The researchers stressed the importance of keeping any damage to the current relationship to a minimum by assuring one's partner that nothing from the past can make the current relationship less special. They noted that identifying how individuals become comfortable with self-disclosure "may provide further insights into why and how past sexual experience in romantic relationships may be beneficially discussed" (p. 390).

Think Critically

1. If you have had sexual experiences with another person(s), what topics about past relationships did you find to be the most "taboo topics" to be discussed in a new relationship?

2. Do you believe that there are gender differences between what men and women share about past lovers? If so, why do these exist? If not, why not?

3. If you were starting a new relationship with a person who has had prior sexual relationships, what would you want to know and not want to know about the sexual relationship?

4. If you or a new partner has had prior sexual relationships, what can be done to help both of you feel secure in the new relationship?

SOURCES: Anderson, M., Kunkel, A., & Dennis, M. R. (2011). "Let's (not) talk about that": Bridging the past sexual experiences taboo to build healthy romantic relationships. *Journal of Sex Research, 48,* 381–391; Dindia, K. (1992). Sex differences in self-disclosure: A meta-analysis. *Psychological Bulletin, 112,* 106–124; Dindia, K. (1994). The intrapersonal-interpersonal dialectical process of self-disclosure. In S. Duck (Ed.), *Understanding relationship processes IV: The dynamics of relationships* (pp. 27–57). Mahwah, NJ: Erlbaum; Ijam, K., & Miller, L. D. (2000). Perceptions of dream-disclosure: An exploratory study. *Communication Studies, 51,* 135–148; Pawlowski, D. R. (1998). Dialectical tensions in marital partners' accounts of their relationships. *Communication Quarterly, 46,* 369–412.

Not surprisingly, achieving desired sexual outcomes requires both coordination and communication between the partners, such as planning sexual events, enticing one another, or developing shared meaning about their sex life (Hess & Coffelt, 2012). While one may believe that married couples would be more adept at this than nonmarried ones, experts believe that married individuals are often less than fully effective in their communication. While there are many factors that contribute to this observation, it is clear that increased and direct communication about sexuality help improve marital bliss.

Initiating Sexual Activity

Within established heterosexual relationships, men continue to overtly initiate sexual encounters more frequently than women. But women continue to signal their willingness. They show their interest in sexual activity with nonverbal cues, such as giving a "certain look" or lighting candles by the bed. (They may also overtly suggest "making love.") Their partners pick up on the cues and "initiate" sexual interactions. In established relationships, many women feel more comfortable with overtly initiating sex. In part, this may be related to the decreasing significance of the double standard as relationships develop. In a new relationship, the woman's initiation of intercourse may be viewed negatively, as a sign of a "loose" sexual standard. But in an established relationship, the woman's initiation may be viewed positively, as an expression of love. This shift may also be the result of couples becoming more egalitarian in their gender-role attitudes. Not surprisingly, sexual initiations are more often successful in long-term relationships than in new or dating relationships.

In both lesbian and gay relationships, the more emotionally expressive partner is likely to initiate sexual interaction. The gay or lesbian individual who talks more about feelings and who spontaneously gives his or her partner hugs or kisses is generally the one who most often begins sexual activity.

Gender Differences in Partner Communication   Though men and women speak about the same number of words each day, gender differences lie in the topics they discuss and the terms they use. Traditionally, men often talk about technology, sports, and money, while women often talk about social events, fashion, and relationships. Specific gender differences in communication between sexual partners also seem to occur such that some men may avoid talking about feelings and personal issues, while some women may be inclined to show more interest and seek agreement and acceptance in the context of the sexual relationship (Gottman & Carrere, 2000). Though the use of a wide variety of terms about sex is associated with higher satisfaction with sexual communication and greater overall relationship quality among both men and women, men's use of erotic terms is also related to their feelings of closeness. In particular, men use more crude slang and equate the use of erotic terms with feelings of closeness. For women, use of everyday and slang terms is associated with communication satisfaction and relational satisfaction, and the use of all terms is related to closeness (Hess & Coffelt, 2012).

• Developing Communication Skills

Generally, poor communication skills precede the onset of relationship problems. The material that follows will help you understand and develop your skills in communicating about sexual matters.

Charm is a way of getting the answer without having asked any question.

—Albert Camus
(1913–1960)

Men and women use the same words but speak a different language.

—Deborah Tannen
(1945–)

To say what we think to our superiors would be inexpedient; to say what we think to our equals would be ill-mannered; to say what we think to our inferiors is unkind. Good manners occupy the terrain between fear and pity.

—Quentin Crisp
(1908–1999)

Talking About Sex

Good communication is central to a healthy intimate relationship. Unfortunately, it is not always easy to establish or maintain.

Obstacles to Sexual Discussions   The process of articulating our feelings about sex can be very difficult, for several reasons. First, we rarely have models for talking openly and honestly about sexuality. As children and adolescents, we probably never discussed sex with our parents, let alone heard them talking about sex. Second, talking about sexual matters defines us as being interested in sex, and interest in sex is often identified with being sexually obsessive, immoral, prurient, or "bad." If the topic of sex is tabooed, we further risk being labeled "bad." Third, we may believe that talking about sex will threaten our relationships. We don't talk about tabooed sexual feelings, fantasies, or desires because we fear that our partners may be repelled or disgusted. We also are reluctant to discuss sexual difficulties or problems because doing so may bring attention to our own role in them.

Keys to Good Communication   Being aware of communication skills and actually using them are two separate matters. Furthermore, even though we may be comfortable sharing our feelings with another, we may find it more difficult to discuss our sexual preferences and needs. Self-disclosure, trust, and feedback are three keys to good communication.

Self-Disclosure   Self-disclosure creates the environment for mutual understanding. Most people know us only through the conventional roles we play as female/male, wife/husband, parent/child, and so on. These roles, however, do not necessarily reflect our deepest selves. If we act as if we are nothing more than our roles, we may reach a point at which we no longer know who we are.

Through the process of self-disclosure, we not only reveal ourselves to others but also find out who we are. We discover feelings we have hidden, repressed, or ignored. We nurture forgotten aspects of ourselves by bringing them to the surface. Moreover, self-disclosure is reciprocal: In the process of our sharing, others share themselves with us. The ability to disclose or reveal private thoughts and feelings, especially positive ones, can contribute to enhancing relationships (MacNeil & Byers, 2009). Men are less likely than women, however, to disclose intimate aspects of themselves (Lips, 2007). Because they have been taught to be "strong and silent," they are more reluctant to express feelings of tenderness or vulnerability. Women generally find it easier to disclose their feelings because they have been conditioned from childhood to express themselves (Tannen, 2001). These differences can drive wedges between men and women. Even when people cohabit or are married, they can feel lonely because there is little or no interpersonal contact. And the worst kind of loneliness is feeling alone when we are with someone to whom we want to feel close.

Trust   When we talk about intimate relationships, the two words that most frequently pop up are "love" and "trust." Trust is the primary characteristic we associate with love. But what, exactly, is trust? **Trust** is a belief in the reliability and integrity of a person. When someone says, "Trust me," he or she is asking for something that does not easily occur.

Trust is critical in close relationships for two reasons. First, self-disclosure requires trust because it makes us vulnerable. A person will not self-disclose if he or she believes the information may be misused—by mocking or revealing a

A little sincerity is a dangerous thing, and a great deal of it is absolutely fatal.

—Oscar Wilde (1854–1900)

The other night I said to my wife, Ruth: "Do you feel that the sex and excitement has gone out of our marriage?" Ruth said: "I'll discuss it with you during the next commercial."

—Milton Berle (1908–2002)

Ninety-nine lies may save you, but the hundredth will give you away.

—West African proverb

Communication Patterns and Partner Satisfaction

Give me the gift of a listening heart.

—King Solomon
(circa 970–931 BC)

Researchers studying relationship satisfaction have found a number of communication patterns that offer clues to enhancing our intimate relationships (Byers, 2005; Gottman & Carrere, 2000; Hess & Coffelt, 2012). They found that men and women in satisfying heterosexual relationships tend to have the following common characteristics regarding communication:

■ *The ability to disclose or reveal private thoughts and feelings, especially positive ones.* Dissatisfied partners tend to disclose mostly negative thoughts. Satisfied partners say such things as "I love you," "You're sexy," or "I feel vulnerable; please hold me." Unhappy partners may also say that they love each other, but more often they say things like "Don't touch me; I can't stand you," "You turn me off," or "This relationship makes me miserable and frustrated."

■ *The expression of more or less equal levels of affective disclosures.* Both partners in satisfied couples are likely to say things like "You make me feel happy," "I love you more than I can ever say," or "I love the way you touch me."

■ *More time spent talking, discussing personal topics, and expressing feelings in positive ways.* Satisfied couples talk about their sexual feelings and the fun they have in bed together.

■ *Ability to talk explicitly about sex using a variety of terms.* Talking explicitly with one's partner about desired specific behaviors or using erotic words can enhance sexual experiences and result in more satisfying sexual interactions.

■ *A willingness to accept and engage in conflict in nondestructive ways.* Satisfied couples view conflict as a natural part of intimate relationships. When partners have sexual disagreements, they do not accuse or blame; instead, they exchange viewpoints, seek common ground, and, when appropriate, compromise.

■ *Less frequent conflict and less time spent in conflict.* Both satisfied and unsatisfied couples, however, experience perpetual problems surrounding the same issues, especially communication, sex, and personality characteristics.

■ *The ability to accurately encode (send) verbal and nonverbal messages and accurately decode (understand) such messages.* This ability to send and understand nonverbal messages is especially important for couples who seek satisfying sexual interactions.

How good are your sexual communication skills? Take the following Dyadic Sexual Communication Scale to find out.

Instructions

Below is a list of statements people have made about discussing sex with their primary partner. Thinking about your current partner, indicate how much you agree or disagree with each statement.

1 = Strongly disagree
2 = Slightly disagree
3 = Neutral—neither agree nor disagree
4 = Slightly agree
5 = Strongly agree

1. My partner rarely responds when I want to talk about our sex life.
2. Some sexual matters are too upsetting to discuss with my sexual partner.
3. There are sexual issues or problems in our sexual relationship that we have never discussed.
4. My partner and I never seem to resolve our disagreements about sexual issues.
5. Whenever my partner and I talk about sex, I feel like he or she is lecturing me.
6. My partner often complains that I am not very clear about what I want sexually.
7. My partner and I have never had a heart-to-heart talk about our sex life together.
8. My partner has no difficulty in talking to me about his or her sexual feelings and desires.
9. Even when angry with me, my partner is able to appreciate my views on sexuality.
10. Talking about sex is a satisfying experience for both of us.
11. My partner and I can usually talk calmly about our sex life.
12. I have little difficulty in telling my partner what I do or don't do sexually.
13. I seldom feel embarrassed when talking about the details of our sex life with my partner.

Scoring

Add up the scores for each question, *reversing your scores for questions 1 through 7* (so that 5 = 1; 4 = 2; 3 = 3, and so on). A higher total score indicates better sexual communication skills.

SOURCE: Catina, J. A. (2010). Dyadic sexual communication scale. In T. D. Fisher, C. M. Davis, & W. L. Yarber (Eds.), *Handbook of sexuality-related measures* (3rd ed.). New York: Routledge.

secret, for example. Second, the degree to which we trust a person influences how we interpret ambiguous or unexpected messages from him or her. If our partner says that he or she wants to study alone tonight, we are likely to take the statement at face value if we have a high level of trust. But if we have a low level of trust, we may believe that he or she actually will be meeting someone else.

Self-disclosure is reciprocal. If we self-disclose, we expect our partner to self-disclose as well. As we self-disclose, we build trust; as we withhold self-disclosure, we erode trust. To withhold ourselves is to imply that we don't trust the other person, and if we don't, that person will not trust us.

Feedback A third critical element in communication is **feedback,** the ongoing process of restating, checking the accuracy of, questioning, and clarifying messages. Feedback often begins with active listening, a technique in which the listener paraphrases or restates what he or she has heard. If someone self-discloses to a partner, his or her response to that self-disclosure is feedback, and the partner's response is feedback to that feedback. It is a continuous process, or loop (see Figure 3). The most important form of feedback for improving relationships is constructive feedback. Constructive feedback focuses on self-disclosing information that will help partners understand the consequences of their actions—for each other and for the relationship. For example, if your partner discloses his or her doubts about the relationship, you can respond in a number of ways. Among these are remaining silent, venting anger, expressing indifference, and giving constructive feedback. Of these responses, constructive feedback is the most likely to encourage positive change.

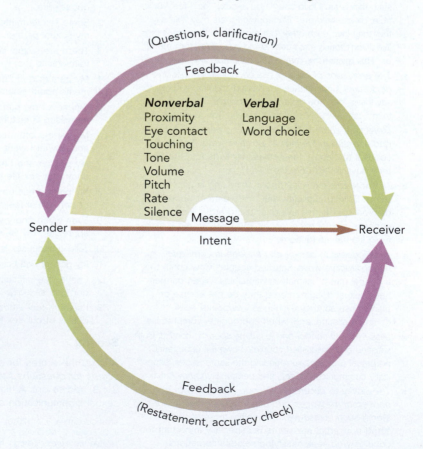

● **FIGURE** 3

Communication Loop. In successful communication, feedback between the sender and the receiver ensures that both understand or are trying to understand what is being communicated. For communication to be clear, the message and the intent behind the message must be congruent. Nonverbal and verbal components must also support the intended message. Communication includes not just language and word choice but also nonverbal characteristics such as tone, volume, pitch, rate, and silence.

● Conflict and Intimacy

Conflict is the process in which people perceive that incompatible goals and interference from others is hindering them from achieving their goals.

We expect love to unify us, but sometimes it doesn't. Two people do not become one when they love each other, although at first they may have this feeling or expectation. Their love may not be an illusion, but their sense of ultimate oneness is. In reality, we retain our individual identities, needs, wants, and pasts—even while loving each other. It is a paradox that, the more intimate two people become, the more likely they are to experience conflict. The sharing of space, time, resources, and investments creates arenas for both support and conflict in relationships (Robles, Slatcher, Trombello, & McGinn, 2013). In fact, a lack of arguing can signal trouble in a relationship because it may mean that issues are not being resolved or that there is indifference. Conflict itself is not dangerous to intimate relationships; it is the manner in which the conflict is handled that is more significant. The presence of conflict does not necessarily indicate that love is waning or has disappeared. It may mean that love is *growing*. A willingness to accept and engage in conflict in nondestructive ways can assist couples in enhancing their relationship.

Conflict is natural in intimate relationships because each person has his or her unique identity, values, needs, and history.

© Image Source/Getty Images

How one quarrels is far more important than what one quarrels about, whether it be finances, careers, sex, communication, or a wet towel on the floor. The key to a satisfying relationship is how the couple approaches and discusses the issues. In reviewing 100 middle-income couples, married for an average of 12 years and with an average of two to three children, the most frequent source of conflict were children, by a wide margin (nearly 40%) (Papp, Cummings, & Goeke-Morey, 2009). Of these, most issues were around what the children were doing and why, how to respond to a certain behavior, and child care. Moderately frequent sources of conflict included annoying habits, money and spending, demands of work and jobs, leisure and recreation, communication and listening, and chores (16–25%). Least frequent sources were annoying personality styles, friends, intimacy and sex, commitment and expectations, and relatives (6–12%). It's important to note that this sample involved only couples who had been successful in negotiating 12 years of marriage, which suggests that many of these issues had been managed pretty well.

Resolving conflicts requires many tactics, including maintaining an open dialogue and managing the feelings each partner has about the issue, as well as embracing the knowledge that each partner may never have as much time, money, or patience as he or she desires (Bradbury, n.d.). Partners who understand and accept the unique demands and issues that will inevitably complicate and enrich their relationship will be in a better position to address conflict when it arises.

Sexual Conflicts

Common practices such as using sex as a scapegoat for nonsexual problems and using arguments as a cover-up for other problems frequently lead to additional disagreements and misunderstandings. Clinging to these patterns can interfere with problem solving and inhibit conflict resolution.

Lessons from the Love Lab

Perhaps love is the process of my leading you gently back to yourself.

—Antoine de Saint-Exupery
(1900–1944)

For many people, forming a new relationship appears to be a lot easier (and a lot more fun) than maintaining one. If this were not the case, then marital therapy and how-to articles and books on keeping love alive would not be so prevalent. One person who has spent a significant part of his career investigating the quandaries of partnerships is John M. Gottman, professor emeritus of psychology at the University of Washington–Seattle's Family Research Lab, better known as the "Love Lab." Over the past 35 years, Gottman and his wife, Julie, and colleagues have videotaped thousands of conversations between couples, scoring words and sentences based on facial expressions such as disgust, affection, and contempt. Though most of their work has involved married couples, applications can be made to any couple interested in improving their relationship.

The Gottmans believe that in order to keep love going strong or to rescue a relationship that has deteriorated, partners, regardless of their sexual orientation, need to follow seven principles:

1. *Enhance your love map.* Emotionally intelligent couples are intimately familiar with each other's world. They have a richly detailed love map—they learn the major events in each other's history, and they keep updating their information as their partner's world changes.

2. *Nurture fondness and admiration.* Without the belief that your partner is worthy of honor and respect, there is no basis for a rewarding relationship. By reminding yourself of your partner's positive qualities—even as you grapple with each other's flaws—and verbally expressing your fondness and admiration, you can prevent a happy partnership from deteriorating.

3. *Turn toward each other.* In long-term commitments, people periodically make "bids" for their partner's attention, affection, humor, or support. Turning toward

one another is the basis of emotional connection, romance, passion, and a good sex life.

4. *Let your partner influence you.* The happiest, most stable partnerships are those in which each individual treats the other with respect and does not resist power sharing and decision making. When the couple disagree, individuals actively search for common ground rather than insisting on getting their way.

5. *Solve your solvable problems.* Start with good manners when tackling your solvable problems by (1) using a softened startup, such as stating your feelings without blame, expressing a positive need, and using "I" statements; (2) learning to make and receive repair attempts, such as de-escalating the tension and sharing what you feel; (3) soothing yourself and each other; and (4) when appropriate, compromising.

6. *Overcome gridlock.* Many ongoing conflicts have a sustained base of unexpressed dreams behind each person's stubborn position. In happy relationships, partners incorporate each other's goals into their concept of what their partnership is about. The bottom line in getting past gridlock is not necessarily to become a part of each other's dreams but to honor these dreams.

7. *Create shared meaning.* Long-term partnerships can have an intentional sense of shared purpose, meaning, family values, and cultural legacy that forms a shared inner life. This culture incorporates both of their dreams, and it is flexible enough to change as both partners grow and develop. When a marriage or partnership has this shared sense of meaning, conflict is less intense and perpetual problems are unlikely to lead to gridlock.

SOURCE: This article is reprinted with permission from Bainbridge Island-based *YES! Magazine's* Winter 2011 issue, "What Happy Families Know." It was adapted from *Seven Principles for Making Marriage Work,* by John M. Gottman, Ph.D., and Nan Silver, Three Rivers Press, 1999.

Disagreement About Sex   Conflict about sex can be intertwined in several ways. A couple may have a disagreement about sex that leads to conflict. For example, if one person wants to be sexual and the other does not, they may argue.

Sex can also be used as a scapegoat for nonsexual problems. If a person is angry because a partner has called him or her a lousy communicator, that person may take it out on the partner sexually by calling him or her a lousy lover. They argue about their lovemaking rather than about the real issue, their lack of honest communication.

Finally, an argument can be a cover-up. If a person feels sexually inadequate and does not want to have sex as often as his or her partner, they may argue and make the other feel so angry that the last thing the partner would want to do is to be sexual with him or her.

For couples with children, relationships tend to follow a predictable pattern of satisfaction in the early years, a decrease in satisfaction during the child-rearing years, and a return to a higher level after the children are grown. An awareness of this pattern can be helpful to couples whose levels of conflict are escalating. Acknowledging a relationship's changing nature and focusing on strengths that each person brings to the relationship are ways to adapt to the inevitable changes that occur over time.

Conflict Resolution

The ways in which couples deal with conflict reflect and perhaps contribute to their relationship happiness. Partners who communicate with affection and interest and who integrate humor when appropriate can use such positive affect to defuse conflict (Gottman & Carrere, 2000).

Sometimes, differences can't be resolved, but they can be lived with. If a relationship is sound, differences can be absorbed without undermining the basic ties. All too often, we regard differences as threatening rather than as the unique expression of two personalities. If one person likes to masturbate, the partner can accept it as an expression of his or her unique sexuality. Coexistence focuses on the people over whom we have the most power—ourselves.

> For a marriage to be peaceful, the husband should be deaf and the wife blind.
>
> —Spanish proverb

> Hatred does not cease by hatred at any time. Hatred ceases by love. This is an unalterable law.
>
> —Siddhartha Gautama, the Buddha (c. 563–483 BCE)

Final Thoughts

The study of love, while still evolving, is helping us understand the various components that make up this complex emotion. Although there is something to be said for the mystery of love, understanding how it works in the day-to-day world may help us keep our love vital and growing.

If we can't talk about what we like and what we want, there is a good chance we won't get either one. Communication is the basis for good sex and good relationships. Communication and intimacy are reciprocal: Communication creates intimacy, and intimacy, in turn, creates good communication. But communication is learned behavior. If we have learned *not* to communicate, we can learn *how* to communicate. Communication allows us to expand ourselves and to feel more connected to and intimate with another person.

Summary

Friendship and Love

- Close friend relationships are similar to spouse/lover relationships in many ways. But lovers/spouses have more fascination and a greater sense of exclusiveness with their partners.

Love and Sexuality

- Sexuality and love are intimately related in our culture. Sex is most highly valued in loving relationships. A loving relationship rivals marriage as an acceptable moral standard for intercourse.

- Nonmarital sex among young adults, but not adolescents, in a relational context has become the norm. An important factor in this shift is the surge in the numbers of unmarried men and women.

- Men and women tend to have different ideas about how they view love, sex, and attraction. Love, however, is equally important for heterosexual people, gay men, lesbian women, and bisexual individuals.

- For a variety of reasons, some people choose *celibacy* as a lifestyle. These individuals may have a better appreciation of the nature of friendship and an increased respect for the bonds of long-term partnerships. Fewer people may be *asexual,* or not attracted to either sex.

How Do I Love Thee? Approaches and Attitudes Related to Love

- According to sociologist John Lee, there are six basic styles of love: *eros, mania, ludus, storge, agape,* and *pragma.*

- The *triangular theory of love* views love as consisting of three components: intimacy, passion, and commitment.

- The *attachment* theory of love views love as being similar in nature to the attachments we form as infants. The attachment (love) styles of both infants and adults are *secure, anxious/ambivalent,* and *avoidant.*

- *Unrequited love*—love that is not returned—is distressing for both the would-be lover and the rejecting partner.

Jealousy

- *Jealousy* is an aversive response to a partner's real, imagined, or likely involvement with a third person. Jealous responses are most likely in committed or marital relationships because of the presumed "specialness" of the relationship, symbolized by sexual exclusiveness.

- As individuals become more interdependent, there is a greater fear of loss. There is some evidence that jealousy may ignite the passion in a relationship.

- *Extradyadic involvement* exists in dating, cohabiting, and marital relationships. In exclusive partnerships, extradyadic involvement is assumed to be destructive and is kept secret. In nonexclusive partnerships, extradyadic involvement is permitted. In *open marriage,* partners mutually agree to allow sexual relationships with others.

- Extradyadic involvement appears to be related to three factors: values, opportunities, and the quality of the relationship.

- Sexual experiences in the aftermath of a romantic relationship breakup are sometimes referred to as *rebound sex.*

Making Love Last: From Passion to Intimacy

- Time affects romantic relationships, potentially transforming it, with words and actions, into something that sustains and expands. *Intimate love* is based on *commitment, caring,* and *self-disclosure,* the revelation of information not normally known by others.

The Nature of Communication

- The ability to communicate is important in developing and maintaining relationships. Partners satisfied with their sexual communication tend to be satisfied with their relationship as a whole.

- *Communication* is a transactional process by which we use symbols, such as words, gestures, and movements, to establish human contact, exchange information, and reinforce or change the attitudes and behaviors of ourselves and others.

- Communication takes place within cultural, social, and psychological contexts. The cultural context consists of the language that is used and the values, beliefs, and customs associated with it. Ethnic groups communicate about sex differently, depending on their language patterns and values. The social context consists of the roles we play in society that influence our communication. The most important roles affecting sexuality are those relating to gender and sexual orientation. The psychological context consists of our personality characteristics, such as having positive or negative feelings about sex.

- Communication is both verbal and nonverbal. The ability to correctly interpret nonverbal messages is important in successful relationships. *Proximity,* eye contact, and touching are especially important forms of nonverbal communication.

Sexual Communication

- In initial encounters, physical appearance is especially important. Because of the *halo effect,* we infer positive qualities about people based on their appearance. Women typically send nonverbal cues to men indicating interest; men often begin a conversation with an opening line.

- The "first move" marks the transition to physical intimacy. In initiating the first sexual interaction, people generally keep their communication nonverbal, ambiguous, and indirect. Sexual disinterest is usually communicated nonverbally. With sexual involvement, the couple must communicate verbally about contraception, STI prevention, and sexual likes and dislikes.

- Unless there are definite clues as to sexual orientation, gay men and lesbian women try to determine through nonverbal cues whether others are appropriate partners.

- In established heterosexual relationships, many women feel more comfortable in initiating sexual interactions than in newer relationships. Sexual initiations are more likely to be accepted in established relationships; sexual disinterest is communicated verbally. Women do not restrict sexual activities any more than do men.

Developing Communication Skills

- The keys to effective communication are self-disclosure, trust, and feedback. *Self-disclosure* is the revelation of intimate information about ourselves. *Trust* is the belief in the reliability and integrity of another person. *Feedback* is a constructive response to another's self-disclosure.

Conflict and Intimacy

- *Conflict* is natural in intimate relationships. Conflicts about sex can be specific disagreements about sex, arguments that are ostensibly about sex but that are really about nonsexual issues, or disagreements about the wrong sexual issue.

- Conflict resolution both reflects and contributes to relationship happiness.

Questions for Discussion

- Using Sternberg's triangular theory of love, identify one significant past or a current relationship and draw triangles for yourself and your partner. Compare the components of each. Have you coupled with someone who shares the same view of love as you? Why or why not is/was this person your "ideal match"? What characteristics in a relationship are important to you?

- What has been your experience when friends ask, "Are you two attracted to each other?" Can individuals be "just friends"? What are the meanings and implications of engaging in sex with a friend? What are the reasons underlying the decision to have sex?

- Do you think sexual activity implies sexual exclusiveness? Do you feel that it is important for you and your partner to agree on this? If not, how might you address this?

- How comfortable are you about sharing your sexual history with your partner? Do you feel that individuals should be selective in what they share, or do you find it beneficial to discuss your likes, dislikes, and past partners? How does this type of disclosure influence the nature of a relationship (dating, cohabiting, or married)?

Sex and the Internet

Sexual Intelligence

Sex therapist and licensed marriage and family therapist Marty Klein has established an online newsletter of sexuality-related information, updates, and political commentaries available at http://www .sexualintelligence.org. Go to the site and select and read one recent article; then answer these questions:

- Why did you select this article?

- What was the main point?

- How was your thinking influenced by the viewpoint of the author?

Suggested Websites

Advocate

http://www.advocate.com

A comprehensive lesbian, gay, bisexual, and transgender news and resource site.

American Association for Marriage and Family Therapy

http://aamft.org

Provides referrals to therapists, books, and articles that address family and relationship problems and issues.

Asexual Visibility and Education Network

http://www.asexuality.org/home/

Strives to create open, honest discussion about asexuality.

Intercultural Communication Institute

http://www.intercultural.org/

Fosters awareness and appreciation of cultural difference, including those around sexuality and gender, in both the international and domestic arenas.

My Beautiful Sex Life

http://mybeautifulsexlife.com/

An honest, realistic, and reassuring daily dose of sexuality education.

Psychology Today Relationship Center

http://psychologytoday.com/topics/relationships.html

Articles on friendship, relationship stages, sex, moods, and behavior, to name a few.

Your Tango

www.yourtango.com

A media company that is dedicated to love and relationships and helps to connect people in matters of the heart.

Suggested Reading

Ackerman, D. (2004). *An alchemy of mind: The marvel and mystery of the brain.* New York: Scribner. Reports on discoveries in neuroscience and addresses such controversial subjects as the effects of trauma, nature versus nurture, and male versus female brains.

Buss, D. M. (2003). *Evolution of desire.* New York: Basic Books. A study encompassing more than 10,000 people, which resulted in a unified theory of human mating behavior.

Diamond, L. (Ed.). (2010). *Psychology of love.* San Diego, CA: Cognella. Research on the psychology of love and relationships, including the neurobiology of bonding, long-term predictors of marital satisfaction and stability, and same-sex relationships.

Fisher, H. (2015). *Anatomy of love: A natural history of mating, marriage, and why we stray.* New York: Owl Books. By examining the brain in love, love addictions, and why we are biologically drawn to specific partners, the author suggests we are returning to patterns of sex, romance, love, and attachment that echo our ancient past.

Fredrickson, B. L. (2013). *Love 2.0: Creating happiness and health in moments of connection.* New York: Hudson Street Press. Suggests and substantiates why a flourishing relationship needs three times as many positive emotions as negative ones.

Gottman, J., & Silver, N. (2012). *What makes love last: How to build trust and avoid betrayal.* New York: Simon & Schuster. Based on laboratory findings, this book shows readers how to identify signs, behaviors, and attitudes that indicate a fraying relationship and provides strategies for repairing what may seem lost or broken.

Jones, D. (2014). *Love illuminated.* New York: HarperCollins. Drawing from 50,000 stories about love from his column in the *New York Times,* the author explores 10 aspects of love in a funny and lively book.

Lyubomirsky, S. (2013). *The myths of happiness: What should make you happy, but doesn't. What shouldn't make you happy, but does.* New York: Penguin Books. Covers 10 adult crisis points, beginning with relationships and ending with problems inherent to middle age and beyond.

Northrup, C., Schwartz, P., & Witte, J. (2013). *The normal bar: The surprising secrets of happy couples and what they reveal about creating a new normal in your relationship.* New York: Crown. An empirical look at marriages across continents and cultures.

Tannen, D. (2011). *That's not what I meant!: How conversational style makes or breaks relationships.* New York: Harper. Combines a novelist's ear for the way people speak with a rare power of original analysis.

chapter

9

Sexual Expression

© Tom Merton/Getty Images

CHAPTER OUTLINE

Sexual Attractiveness

Sexual Scripts

Autoeroticism

Sexual Behavior With Others

"I grew up thinking that I would wait until I got married before having sex. It was not just a religious or moral issue—it was more about being a 'good' girl. When I went away to college, some of my new friends were sexually active and had more open thoughts about having sex. I did have sex with someone during my first year in college, but afterwards I felt really embarrassed about it. When some of my friends at home found out, they were really shocked as well. Even though my first sexual relationship was one full of love and commitment, these feelings of shame and embarrassment and shock kept me from sleeping with my boyfriend for the next four months. I really struggled with the 'good girl' versus 'slut' extreme images I had grown up with."

—29-year-old female

"I remember the first time one of my girlfriends told me she went down on a guy. I was seventeen and she was eighteen. We were still in high school. I thought it

was the grossest thing and couldn't imagine doing it. I'm embarrassed to admit that I kind of thought she was a slut. Then, a few months later, I tried it with my boyfriend. Then I began to feel like a slut."

—20-year-old female

"It's funny now how easy it is to talk about masturbation. When you get to college, some of the taboo is lifted from the subject, at least between the guys, I think. When someone brings up masturbating, we all kind of have that uncomfortable moment, but then we get into talking about when our last time was, how often, how we administer clean-up, techniques. It has become a normal subject with us. Considering how many males I have spoken to about masturbation, I think it is less taboo than they thought."

—20-year-old male

"It bothers me as a woman that other women, or at least several I have come in contact with, feel that it is nasty for their partners to please them orally but have no problem pleasing their partners that way. That's crazy!"

—21-year-old female

> *Sex is as important as eating or drinking and we ought to allow one appetite to be satisfied with as little restraint or false modesty as the other.*
>
> —Marquis de Sade
> (1740–1814)

Sexual expression is a complex process through which we reveal our sexual selves. Sexual expression involves more than simply sexual behaviors; it involves our feelings as well. "Behavior can never be unemotional," one scholar observes (Blechman, 1990). As human beings, we do not separate feelings from behavior, including sexual behavior. Our sexual behaviors are rich with emotions, ranging from love to anxiety and from desire to antipathy.

To fully understand our sexuality, we need to examine our sexual behaviors *and* the emotions we experience along with them. If we studied sexual activities apart from our emotions, we would distort the meaning of human sexuality. It would make our sexual behaviors appear mechanistic, nothing more than genitals rubbing against each other.

In this chapter, we first discuss sexual attractiveness. Next, we turn to sexual scripts that give form to our sexual drives. Finally, we examine the most common sexual behaviors, both autoerotic, such as fantasies and masturbation, and interpersonal, such as oral-genital sex, sexual intercourse, and anal eroticism. When we discuss sexual behaviors, we cite results from numerous studies to illustrate the prevalence of those behaviors in our society. These results most often represent self-reports of a certain group of people. As discussed previously, self-reporting of sexual behavior is not always exact or unbiased. The research data provide only a general idea of what behaviors actually occur and do not indicate how people should express their sexuality or what "normal" behavior is. Sexuality is one of the most individualistic aspects of life; each of us has our own sexual values, needs, and preferences.

Sexual Attractiveness

Sexual attractiveness is an important component in sexual expression. As we will see, however, there are few universals in what people from different cultures consider attractive.

A Cross-Cultural Analysis

In a landmark cross-cultural survey, anthropologists Clelland Ford and Frank Beach (1951) discovered that there appear to be only two characteristics that women and men universally consider important in terms of sexual attractiveness: youthfulness and good health. All other aspects may vary significantly from culture to culture. Even though this large survey was conducted over a half century ago, subsequent smaller and more-local studies support the importance of youthfulness and good health in sexual attraction, as well as the significance of culture in determining sexual attractiveness. One might ask why youthfulness and health were the only universals identified by Ford and Beach. Why not other body traits, such as a certain facial feature or body type?

Although we may never find an answer, sociobiologists offer a possible, but untestable, explanation. They theorize that all animals instinctively want to reproduce their own genes. Consequently, humans and other animals adopt certain reproductive strategies. One of these strategies is choosing a mate capable of reproducing one's offspring. Men prefer women who are young because young women are the most likely to be fertile. Good health is also related to reproductive potential, because healthy women are more likely to be both fertile and capable of rearing their children. Evolutionary psychologist David Buss (1994.9a, 2003.9a) notes that our ancestors looked for certain physical characteristics that indicated a woman's health and youthfulness. Buss identifies certain physical features that are cross-culturally associated with beauty: good muscle tone; full lips; clear, smooth skin; lustrous hair; and clear eyes. Our ancestors also looked for behavioral cues such as animated facial expressions; a bouncy, youthful gait; and a high energy level. These observable physical cues to youthfulness and health, and hence to reproductive capacity, constitute the standards of beauty in many cultures.

Vitality and health are important to human females as well. Women prefer men who are slightly older than they are, because an older man is likely to be more stable and mature and to have greater resources to invest in children. Similarly, in the animal kingdom, females choose mates who provide resources, such as food and protection. Among American women, Buss (1994.9a, 2003.9a) points out, countless studies indicate that economic security and employment are much more important for women than for men. If you look in the personal ads on online dating sites, you'll find this gender difference readily confirmed. A woman's ad typically reads: "Lively, intelligent woman seeks professional, responsible gentleman for committed relationship." A man's ad typically reads: "Financially secure, fit man looking for attractive woman interested in having a good time. Send photo."

Women also prefer men who are in good health and physically fit so as to be good providers. If a woman chooses someone with hereditary health problems, she risks passing on his poor genes to her children. Furthermore, an unhealthy partner is more likely to die sooner, decreasing the resources available to the woman and her children. Ford and Beach (1951) found that signs of ill health are universally considered unattractive.

What constitutes physical attractiveness may vary among cultures.

(first) © Gabriela Medina/Getty Images; (second) © Ichiro/Taxi Japan/Getty Images; (third) © Bigshots/The Image Bank/Getty Images; (fourth) © Jose Luis Pelaez, Inc./Getty Images; (fifth) © Vladimir Pcholkin/Photographer's Choice/Getty Images; (sixth) © Marcy Maloy/Digital Vision/Getty Images; (seventh) © Yukmin/Asia Images/Getty Images; (eighth) © Dan Hallman/Photodisc/Getty Images

Aside from youthfulness and good health, however, Ford and Beach found no universal standards of physical sexual attractiveness. In fact, they noted considerable variation from culture to culture in what parts of the body are considered erotic. In some cultures, the eyes are the key to sexual attractiveness; in others, it is height and weight; and in still others, the size and shape of the genitals matter most. In our culture, female breasts, for example, are considered erotic; in other cultures, they are not.

Since the classic study by Ford and Beach (1951), researchers have continued to attempt to identify other factors that influence sexual attractiveness, such as physical characteristics, personality traits, and fertility factors. Through research involving various cultures, it has been discovered that one of the most important physical traits of attractiveness is symmetry. That is, both sides of the person—the right and left sides—are the same. For example, both eyes are the same shape, the ears are similar, the hands are the same size, and the arms are the same length. Throughout the animal kingdom, which includes humans, males and females rate persons whose right and left sides are symmetrical as more attractive. One very noticeable physical feature is the face, and studies have shown that the more symmetrical a face, the more attractive persons of the other sex find it (Fisher, 2009; Jasienska, Lipson, Thune, & Ziomkiewicz, 2006; Little,

Apicella, & Marlowe, 2007; Quist et al., 2012; Tovee, Tasker, & Benson, 2000). Studies of face preferences have largely focused on the views of heterosexual individuals and have generally excluded homosexual participants, although one inclusive study is presented here. To test for similarity and differences among heterosexual and homosexual males and females in preference for face shape, researchers showed participants 10 pairs of faces sequentially (each pair consisting of a masculinized and a feminized version of the same face) and asked which face was considered most attractive. Of the four groups, homosexual men demonstrated stronger preferences for masculinity in male faces. Homosexual women had stronger preference for masculinity in female faces than did heterosexual women. The researchers stated that "these results suggest attractiveness judgments of same-sex faces made by homosexual individuals are not a mirror image of those made by heterosexual individuals of the opposite sex" (Glassenberg, Feinberg, Jones, Little, & DeBruine, 2010). Another study assessed not only face preference but also the combined effect of both facial and voice attractiveness cues. Female and male students from a United Kingdom university rated attractiveness of other-sex faces and voices in a computer-based experiment. The findings showed that despite being unrelated, face and voice traits positively influenced the attractiveness of both females and males. However, the influence of the voice was much smaller than that of facial attractiveness. Possibly the assessment of both facial and voice attractiveness provides a better estimate of overall mate quality (Wells, Baguley, Sergeant, & Dunn, 2013).

Another significant factor in sexual attraction is scent. The other person's smell—that is, his or her natural body scent mixed with the lingering smells of the day—plays a major role in drawing people together and finding optimal partners. Some people report that they know right away from his or her smell that a person is the one for them, and, of course, conversely some conclude that his or her body odor is a "deal-breaker." Psychologist Rachel Herz, author of the book *The Scent of Desire: Discovering Our Enigmatic Sense of Smell* (2007), states that "body odor is an external manifestation of the immune system and smells we think are attractive come from people who are most genetically compatible with us" (quoted in Svoboda, 2008). Interestingly, men and women whose body odors are judged to be sexy by others are also more likely to have symmetrical faces. For partners to find out each other's true scent, they can go fragrance-free for a few days. People may worry about their own scent, and some people may indeed not like it, but there will always be persons who will be attracted to their natural body odor (Fisher, 2009; Herz, 2007; Martins et al., 2005; Moalem, 2009; Svoboda, 2008).

Cultures that agree on which body parts are erotic may still disagree on what constitutes attractiveness. In terms of female beauty, American culture considers a slim body attractive. But worldwide, Americans are in the minority, for the type of female body most desired cross-culturally is plump. Similarly, Americans prefer slim hips, but in the majority of cultures in Ford and Beach's study, wide hips were most attractive. In our culture, large breasts are ideal, but other cultures prefer small breasts or long and pendulous breasts.

Male preference for female breast size varies within any given culture. For example, a study of British White men from London, England, required participants to view rotating (360 degrees) figures of women with varied breast sizes. Findings revealed that medium breasts were rated the most attractive (33%), followed by large (24%), very large (19%), small (16%), and very small (8%) breasts (Swami & Tovée, 2013).

Ken, my husband, just smelled like he belonged to me. I'm talking about when you hug him, he either feels like a member of your tribe or not. It's their scent.

—Eric Jong
(1942–)

In recent years, well-defined pectoral, arm, and abdominal muscles have become part of the ideal male body. Interestingly, a study of college undergraduate women rated muscular men as sexier than nonmuscular and very muscular men, but men with moderate muscularity were considered most attractive and more desirable for long-term relationships. Participants thought that the more brawny men would be more domineering, volatile, and less committed to their partners, whereas the moderately muscular man would be more sexually exclusive and romantic (Frederick & Haselton, 2007; Jayson, 2007).

In other sections of this text, we discuss men's and women's views about ideal erect penis length, largely relative to sexual satisfaction of the female partner, and whether they are satisfied with their own or their partner's penis size. However, the attractiveness of the flaccid person, per se, is understudied. In the flaccid state the human penis is displayed prominently and it has been suggested that penile traits have influenced sexual selection in human evolution (Potts & Short, 1999). Women living in California and New Zealand assessed the attractiveness of front-posed male figures that varied only in nonerect penis length (five lengths were presented). The smallest penis was rated the least attractive of the three intermediate sizes. The largest penis was not rated the most attractive but received higher scores than the smallest penis. The researchers state that "such preferences reflect female judgments of what is healthy and normal in a male, while the smallest and the greatest penile lengths may be perceived as aesthetically abnormal." Relative to another male body trait, images of men lacking chest and abdominal hair were rated as most attractive (Dixson, Dixson, Bishop, & Parish, 2010).

We have discussed various studies that examined desirable traits in potential sexual partners and mates. Although these studies report findings by sex, little research has been conducted around sexual orientation. Behavioral scientists from Radboud University Nijmegen in The Netherlands examined partner preferences of heterosexual and homosexual men and women, focusing on the importance of attractiveness and another variable, status (ambition, finished education, and high salary). From photographs and status-related profiles, heterosexual men valued attractiveness as the most important trait. Heterosexual women rated social status as most important. The mate preferences of homosexual men and women were remarkably similar to those of heterosexual men and women. Compared to attractiveness, status generally played a smaller role in an individual's desire to date someone (Ha, van den Berg, Engels, & Lichtwarck-Aschoff, 2012).

Evolutionary Mating Perspectives

One prominent theoretical explanation for human mating is the **sexual strategies theory** (Buss, 2003.9b; Buss & Schmitt, 1993). An important component of this theory addresses gender differences in short-term and long-term heterosexual relationships from an evolutionary mating perspective. This theory posits that males and females face different adaptive problems in "casual," or short-term, mating and long-term, reproductive mating, leading to different strategies or behaviors for solving these problems. A woman may select a partner who offers immediate resources, such as food or money, for short-term mating, whereas for long-term mating, more substantial resources are important. For males, a sexually available female may be chosen for a short-term liaison, but this type of woman would be avoided when selecting a long-term mate (Hyde & DeLamater, 2008).

A promiscuous person is someone who is getting more sex than you are.

—Victor Lownes
(1928–)

David Geary and colleagues (Geary, Vigil, & Byrd-Craven, 2004) reviewed the evolutionary theory and empirical research on mating and identified the potential costs and benefits of short-term and long-term sexual relationships in both men and women. The most fundamental difference is that women are predicted to be most selective in mate choices for both short-term and long-term relationships, given the costs of reproduction. Even in selecting a short-term mate, a woman may be more choosy than a man because she is evaluating him as a potential long-term mate. But in general, women are predicted to avoid short-term relationships, given that the possible costs outweigh the possible benefits. In contrast, the opposite is evident for men, given that the potential benefits outweigh the potential costs. In choosing a short-term partner, the man may want to minimize commitment. Once a man commits to a long-term relationship, the costs increase and the level of choosiness is predicted to increase. In their research on short-term sexual relationships, Todd Shackelford and colleagues (2004) found that women preferred short-term partners who are not involved in other relationships to present a greater potential as a long-term partner and that men were more likely than women to pursue short-term, or casual, sexual relationships.

Evolutionary biologists have hypothesized that men's short-term mating strategy is rooted in the desire for sexual variety, and a massive cross-cultural study of 16,288 people across 10 major world regions seems to demonstrate this (Schmitt, 2003). This study on whether the sexes differ in the desire for sexual variety found strong and conclusive differences that appear to be universal across the world regions: Men possess more desire than women for a variety of sexual partners and are more likely than women to seek short-term relationships. This was true regardless of the participant's relationship status or sexual orientation. The researchers concluded that these findings confirm that men's short-term sexual strategy is based on the desire for numerous partners. This behavior, from an evolutionary perspective, would maximize reproductive success. Interestingly, the study also found that men required less time to elapse than women before consenting to intercourse.

Continuing through the lens of an evolutionary perspective, a study of undergraduate college students examined gender differences in a imagined desired number of sex partners during the next year (Fenigstein & Preston, 2007). In this imaginary scenario, the sex would be either safe from STIs and pregnancy or dangerous and relatively unavailable. The study found that over the next year, the majority of women desired one sex partner. In contrast, the men indicated a desire for numerous partners, especially when they imagined less negative sexual concerns. The researchers concluded that the results can be explained by the sexual strategies theory, discussed earlier in this section, and social role theory (Eagly, 1987), which contends that men are socialized toward the pleasurable components of sexual interaction and that women are more concerned with the relational components of sex.

Various preferences and behaviors that occur both immediately before and after sexual intercourse that may reflect adaptive reproductive strategies from an evolutionary perspective were examined among 170 undergraduate females and male students (Hughes & Kruger, 2011). Behaviors related to pair-bonding with long-term mates and short- and long-term mating contexts were assessed. The study hypothesis that females would be more likely than males to value and initiate post-coital activities that reflect pair-bonding with a long-term partner was strongly supported. Females expressed greater importance than did males of five pre- and post-coital behaviors: intimate talking, kissing, cuddling and caressing, professing their love for their partner, and talking about their

The degree and kind of a person's sexuality reaches up into the ultimate pinnacle of his spirit.

—Friedrich Nietzsche
(1844–1900)

relationship. Females were also more likely to engage in post-intercourse behaviors with both short-term and long-term partners. The researchers stated that these findings "further support the idea that females tend to have a greater need than males to pair-bond in order to secure provisioning and care for themselves and their offspring from their mate." The study also found that males were more likely to participate in behaviors that were extrinsically rewarding or that increased the likelihood of further sexual behavior. For example, males were more likely to initiate kissing prior to sex, possibly to increase the likelihood of their partner being sexually aroused, and females were more likely to initiate kissing after sex, possibly to help secure a bond with their long-term partner. Lastly, intimate talk and kissing were rated by both females and males as more important than intercourse with a long-term partner, and cuddling and professing one's love was rated more important after having intercourse than before.

One mating strategy is **mate poaching,** the behavior designed to lure a person who is already in a romantic relationship into either a temporary, brief sexual liaison or a long-term relationship. Buss (2006) states that mate poaching evolved as a mating strategy because desirable mates attract many suitors and usually end up in relationships. Hence, to find a desirable mate, it is often necessary to attempt to seek (mate poach) persons already in relationships. Table 1 presents the frequency of romantic attraction and mate-poaching experiences of 173 college

TABLE 1 • Frequency of Romantic Attraction and Mate-Poaching Experiences of Undergraduates		
	Have You Ever?	
Mate Attraction Experience	**% of Men**	**% of Women**
Attempted to attract someone		
as a long-term mate	87	86
as a short-term mate	91	74
Attempted to poach someone		
as a long-term mate	52	63
as a short-term mate	64	49
Experienced someone try to poach you		
as a long-term mate	83	81
as a short-term mate	95	91
Been successfully poached away from a past partner[a]		
as a long-term mate	43	49
as a short-term mate	50	35
Experienced someone try to poach your partner		
as a long-term mate	70	79
as a short-term mate	86	85
Had a past partner successfully poached from you[a]		
as a long-term mate	35	30
as a short-term mate	27	25

[a]"Have you ever?" was defined as scoring greater than 1 on a 1 (not at all successful) to 7 (very successful) scale for the success experiences.

SOURCE: Adapted from Schmitt & Buss, 2001.

undergraduates (45 men and 128 women) (Schmitt & Buss, 2001). As shown, mate poaching is a common practice, with nearly equal frequencies for men and women undergraduates but occurs less often than just trying to attract someone. The vast majority had experienced someone trying to poach them or their partner, but many attempts were not successful. Mate-poaching tactics were also assessed, and these included trying to drive a wedge in the relationship, enhancing one's physical appearance, providing easy sexual access, developing an emotional connection, and demonstrating that one has resources. Like mate poaching, sexual nonexclusiveness in relationships poses significant adaptive threats (Buss, 2006).

Recently, a group of scientists have been critical of the perspective that gender differences in human sexual behavior are rooted in evolutionary grounds. These scientists question whether there is adequate empirical evidence to justify the claimed differences. Some contend that gender differences are more the effect of cultural norms than biology (Slater, 2013). Evolutionary biologists David Buss and David Schmitt, developers of the sexual strategies theory, acknowledge that the research support for the theory model was limited in scope when it was developed in the early 1990s (Buss & Schmitt, 1993) but that a large body of research worldwide has been and continues to be generated in support of the theory, as shown in Table 2 (Buss & Schmitt, 2011).

TABLE 2 • **Results of Research Studies Related to the Sexual Strategies Theory**

Men are more likely than women to engage in extradyadic sex (sex outside of a committed relationship).

Men are more likely than women to be sexually nonexclusive multiple times with different sexual partners.

Men are more likely than women to seek short-term partners who are already married.

Men are more likely than women to have fantasies involving short-term sex and multiple other-sex partners.

Men are more likely than women to pay for short-term sex with male or female prostitutes.

Men are more likely than women to enjoy sexual magazines and videos containing themes of short-term sex and sex with multiple partners.

Men are more likely than women to desire, have, and reproductively benefit from multiple mates and spouses.

Men desire larger numbers of sex partners than women do over brief periods of time.

Men are more likely than women to seek "one-night stands."

Men are quicker than women to consent to having sex after a brief period of time.

Men are more likely than women to consent to sex with a stranger.

Men are more likely than women to want, initiate, and enjoy a variety of sex behaviors.

Men have more positive attitudes than women toward casual sex and short-term mating.

Men are less likely than women to regret short-term sex or hookups.

Men have more unrestricted sociosexual attitudes and behaviors than women.

Men are less selective of mates in short-term contexts whereas women increase selectivity for physical attractiveness.

Men perceive more sexual interest from strangers than women do.

SOURCE: Adapted from Buss & Schmitt, 2011.

This list shows consistent differences in sexual behaviors between men and women. However, we need to remind ourselves that there are individual differences within each sex and group variation among populations and cultures for all of the behaviors that may not reflect these findings. Even with the research showing these behaviors, the debate will continue on whether they are the effects of evolution or culture, or a combination of both.

Hooking Up and College Students

Today, college students and other young adults have their own form of casual sex, commonly called **hooking up** or **friends with benefits.** This type of casual sex, analogous to the "one-night stands" of prior generations, consists of sexual interactions between two people who do not necessarily expect a subsequent sexual encounter or a romantic commitment. For hooking up, the two people may or may not already be friends, but both friendship and intimacy are blended and the sex may be recurring. Sex researchers Justin Garcia and colleagues (2012) state that "a review of the literature suggests that these encounters [hooking up] are becoming increasingly normative among adolescents and young adults in North America, representing a marked shift in openness and acceptance of uncommitted sex." One study of undergraduate students found that both men and women had almost twice the number of hookup experiences compared to first dates (Bradshaw, Kahn, & Saville, 2010). However, most college-age young adults state that they prefer to be in a romantic relationship: One study showed that 63% of college-age men and 83% of college-age women would rather, at this stage of life, to be in a traditional romantic relationship rather than in an uncommitted sexual relationship (Garcia, Reiber, Merriwether, Heywood, & Fisher, 2010). Another study revealed that 65% of college-age women and 45% of college-age men had hoped their hookup encounter would develop into a committed relationship, and 51% of women and 42% of men had tried to discuss with their hookup the possibility of starting a relationship (Owen & Fincham, 2011). About one third of both college men and women have reported that their hookup turned into a long-term relationship (Garcia & Fisher, in press).

Almost all hookups involving college students involve kissing and slightly greater than one half include sexual touching above and below the waist; however, only about one third of hookups include oral and/or vaginal sex (Figure 1) (Reiber & Garcia, 2010), which are behaviors experienced more commonly in romantic relationships than in hookups (Fielder, Carey, & Carey, 2013). Likewise, orgasm for both sexes, particularly females, occurs less frequently in

> *Sex is one of the nine reasons for reincarnation. . . . The other eight are unimportant.*
>
> —Henry Miller
> (1891–1980)

● **FIGURE 1**

Percentage of College Women and Men Reporting Participation in Hookup Behaviors.

(*Source:* Adapted from Reiber & Garcia, 2010.)

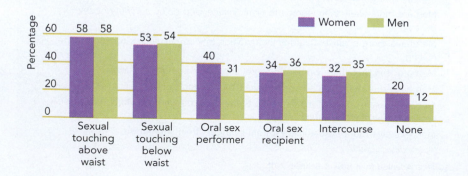

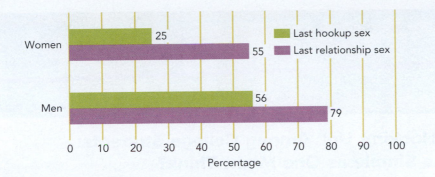

• **FIGURE 2**

Percentage of College Women and Men Experiencing Orgasm During Last Hookup Sex and Last Relationship Sex.

(*Source*: Adapted from Garcia, Massey, Merriwether, & Seibold-Simpson, 2013.)

hookup sex in contrast to relationship sex (Figure 2). As hookup behavior is increasing on college campuses, so is research on the antecedents, and positive and negative outcomes of hooking up. A brief discussion of important studies of hooking up is presented in the "Think About It" box "Hooking Up Among College Students: As Simple as One Might Think?"

Certainly, hooking up has the potential for adverse emotional and physical health outcomes because of the context in which it most occurs (e.g., alcohol use), but romantic relationships also have risks. Further, a romantic relationship experience is neither the only nor the most important sexual milestone of young adult development. Many college students prefer experiencing sexual pleasure and intimacy in hookups, which do not have the more consuming components of a romantic relationship (Calzo, 2013). Nevertheless, individual and couple efforts to enhance both sexual fulfillment and risk reduction are important for hooking up and romantic relationships.

Sexual Desire

Desire can exist separately from overtly physical sexual expression. Recall that desire is the psychobiological component that motivates sexual behavior. But little scientific research exists on sexual desire. One of the most important reasons researchers have avoided studying it is that desire is difficult to define and quantify. An online survey of 423 adults (mean age = 30 years) assessed the subjective reports of four groups—men and women in same-sex relationships, and men and women in mixed-sex relationships—relative to their sexual desire for both solitary (e.g., masturbation) and couple sexual behavior (Holmberg & Blair, 2009). This research showed that heterosexual men clearly report desiring sex more than heterosexual women, but whether these differences were also reflected in same-sex relationships was not clear. As anticipated, men in both same-sex and mixed-sex relationships expressed higher, but only moderately, levels of sexual desire than women in same-sex and mixed-sex relationships. Men and women in same-sex relationships reported greater sexual desire than men and women in mixed-sex relationships. Persons in same-sex relationships expressed slightly stronger sexual desire for solitary sexual behaviors and for attractive dating partners than individuals in mixed-sex relationships, and individuals in same-sex relationships tended to place greater value on the more sensual or erotic

think
about it

"Hooking Up" Among College Students: As Simple as One Might Think?

"**H**ooking up," a term used by college students to describe sexual interactions between persons who are not in a romantic relationship, has replaced traditional dating rituals—in fact, many have never gone out on a date—and is as ambiguous as the term "having sex." For many college-age students, marriage no longer comes on the heels of graduation. Hooking up for "casual sex" allows them to put off serious romance yet be sexual with another person and free to pursue personal and career goals. A similar mating strategy among college students is having "friends with benefits" or making "booty calls," which involve explicit or implicit solicitation of a non-long-term sex partner (Jonason, Li, & Cason, 2009). Recent studies have shown that between 60% and 80% of North American college students have experienced some type of hookup (Garcia, Reiber, Massey, & Merriwether, 2012).

Although hooking up is prevalent among college students, casual sex may not be as simple as it sounds. Hooking up can have both positive and negative emotional, physical, and health outcomes, which may be different for females and males. Research on factors related to hooking up has revealed some conflicting findings. Here are the results from a few of the important studies:

- A study involving 30 colleges across the United States found, from a multiethnic sample, that casual sex was negatively associated with well-being and positively associated with psychological distress. This leads the researchers to conclude that, for college students, engaging in casual sex may increase the risk for negative psychological outcomes, such as depression and low self-esteem (Bersamin et al., 2014).

- A study of 832 college students found that while similar percentages of men and women had hooked up, students of color were less likely to hook up than Caucasian students. Women study participants were less likely than men to report that hooking up was a positive emotional experience for them (Owen, Rhoades, Stanley, & Fincham, 2010).

- Hookups that involved penetrative sex increased psychological distress for female first-year college students but not for first-year male college students (Fielder & Carey, 2010).

- Among first-year female college students, sexual hookup behavior was associated with experiencing depression, sexual victimization, and STIs (Fielder, Walsh, Carey, & Carey, 2014).

- For their most recent hookup, students reported more positive feelings than negative feelings about it, but

Comfort Levels of College Men and Women with Various Hookup Behaviors.

(*Source:* Adapted from Reiber & Garcia, 2010.)

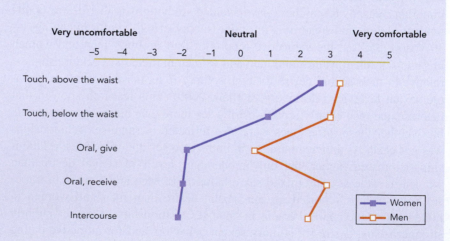

men reported more positive feelings and lower negative feelings than women did (Lewis, Granato, Blayney, Lostutter, & Kilmer, 2012).

- Both men and women university students reported being comfortable with touching above and below the waist during hookups, but only men were comfortable with oral sex and intercourse behaviors (see the accompanying figure) (Garcia, Massey, Merriwether, & Seibold-Simpson, 2013).

- Female Canadian university students reported more regret following uncommitted sexual encounters than male students, although high-quality sex (that is, psychologically and physically arousing sex) rarely led to regret (Fisher, Worth, Garcia, & Meredith, 2012).

- Both female and male college students did not experience orgasm as frequently as desired during hookups, but the gap between desiring and experiencing orgasms was greater for female students than for male students (Garcia, Massey, Merriwether, & Seibold-Simpson, 2013).

A study of 642 urban adults found that sexual involvements in nonromantic and casual dating contexts were related to reporting less rewarding and less satisfying relationships in contrast to more serious involvements (Paik, 2010). However, the study also found that people who hook up can have as rewarding long-term relationships, should they pursue them, as those students who establish a meaningful connection before becoming sexual. Those who had sex as friends or acquaintances and who were interested in a serious relationship were as happy as those who dated but delayed having couple sex (Paik, 2010).

These studies highlight the need for both female and male college students to understand the newer sexual norms and culture of hooking up on college campuses. Particularly important to know is that hooking up has both positive and negative outcomes and that females and males often have different experiences that have implications for individuals and couples.

Think Critically

1. If you know people who have hooked up, have they talked about it positively or negatively?

2. Have you ever hooked up? If so, did you have experiences that were similar to those found in the research studies reported here?

3. Why do you think that the female students, in general, from the reported students had more negative and less positive experiences with hooking up than the male students? What implications do these findings have for college-age students?

4. Do you think that hooking up behavior has increased on your college campus? If so, what impact do you think it has on men and women?

SOURCES: Bersamin, M. M., Zamboango, B. L., Schwartz, S. J., Donellan, M. B., Hudson, M., Weisskirch, R. S., et al. (2014). Risky business: Is there an association between casual sex and mental health among emerging adults? *Journal of Sex Research, 51,* 43–51; Fielder, R. L., & Carey, M. P. (2010). Predictors and consequences of sexual "hookups" among college students: A short-term prospective study. *Archives of Sexual Behavior, 39,* 1105–1119; Fielder, R. L., Walsh, J. L., Carey, K. B., & Carey, M. P. (2014). Sexual hookups and adverse health outcomes: A longitudinal study of first-year college women. *Journal of Sex Research, 51,* 131–144; Garcia, J. R., Reiber, C., Massey, S. G., & Merriwether, A. M. (2012). Sexual hookup culture: A review. *Review of General Psychology, 16,* 161–176; Garcia, J. R., Massey, S. G., Merriwether, A. M., & Seibold-Simpson, S. M. (2013, Aug.). *Orgasm experiences among emerging adult men and women: Gender, relationship context, and attitudes toward casual sex.* Poster presented at the annual meeting of the International Academy of Sex Research, Chicago, Illinois; Jonason, P. K., Li, N. P., & Cason, M. J. (2009). The "booty call": A comparison between men's and women's ideal dating strategies. *Journal of Sex Research, 46,* 460–470; Lewis, M. A., Granato, H., Blayney, J. A., Lostutter, T. W., & Kilmer, J. R. (2012). Predictors of hooking up sexual behaviors and emotional reactions among U.S. college students. *Archives of Sexual Behavior, 41,* 1219–1229; Paik, A. (2010). "Hookups," dating, and relationship quality: Does the type of sexual involvement matter? *Sexual Science Research, 39,* 739–753; Reiber, C., & Garcia, J. R. (2010). Hooking up: Gender differences, evolution, and pluralistic ignorance. *Evolutionary Psychology, 8,* 390–404.

aspects of sexuality. In interpreting these findings, the researchers (Holmberg & Blair, 2009) stated:

> Possibly, those in same-sex relationships, having already broken one major sexual taboo, also tend to be slightly more permissive regarding other sexual matters than heterosexuals, viewing masturbation or harmless fantasizing about attractive others as natural outlets for sexual desire. (p. 64)

Sexual desire is affected by physical, emotional, and sexual relationship issues, as discussed throughout this book. Life events can have both positive and negative impacts on sexual desire.

Two factors affecting sexual desire are erotophilia and erotophobia. **Erotophilia** is a positive emotional response to sexuality, and **erotophobia** is a negative emotional response to sexuality. Researchers have hypothesized that where someone falls on the erotophilic/erotophobic continuum strongly influences his or her overt sexual behavior (Fisher, 1986, 1998). In contrast to erotophobic individuals, for example, erotophilic men and women accept and enjoy their sexuality, experience less guilt about engaging in sex, seek out sexual situations, engage in more autoerotic and interpersonal sexual activities, enjoy talking about sex, and are more likely to engage in certain sexual health practices, such as obtaining and using contraception. Furthermore, erotophilic people are more likely to have positive sexual attitudes, to engage in more involved sexual fantasies, to be less homophobic, and to have seen more erotica than erotophobic people. A person's emotional response to sex is also linked to how he or she evaluates other aspects of sex. Erotophilic individuals, for example, tend to evaluate sexually explicit material more positively.

Erotophilic and erotophobic traits are not fixed. Positive experiences can alter erotophobic responses over time. In fact, some therapy programs work on the assumption that consistent positive behaviors, such as loving, affirming, caring, touching, and communicating, can do much to diminish sexual fears and anxieties. Positive sexual experiences can help dissolve much of the anxiety that underlies erotophobia.

> I am never troubled by sexual desires. In fact I rather enjoy them.
> —Tommy Cooper
> (1921–1984)

● Sexual Scripts

As discussed previously, gender roles have a significant impact on how we behave sexually, for sexual behaviors and feelings depend more on learning than on biological drives. Our sexual drives can be molded into almost any form. What is "natural" is what society says is natural; there is very little spontaneous, unlearned behavior. Sexual behavior, like all other forms of social behavior (such as courtship, classroom behavior, and sports), relies on scripts.

As you will also recall, scripts are like plans that organize and give direction to our behavior. The **sexual scripts** in our culture are highly gendered, meaning that they strongly influence our sexuality as men and women (Mahay, Laumann, & Michaels, 2001; Wiederman, 2005). Our sexual scripts have several distinct components (Simon & Gagnon, 1987):

- *Cultural.* The cultural component provides the general pattern that sexual behaviors are expected to take. Our cultural script, for example, emphasizes heterosexuality, gives primacy to sexual intercourse, and discourages masturbation.

- *Intrapersonal.* The intrapersonal component deals with the internal and physiological states that lead to, accompany, or identify sexual arousal, such as a pounding heart and an erection or vaginal lubrication.

- *Interpersonal.* The interpersonal component involves the shared conventions and signals that enable two people to engage in sexual behaviors, such as body language, words, and erotic touching.

Cultural Scripting

> Many are saved from sin by being inept at it.
> —Mignon McLaughlin
> (1913–1983)

Our culture sets the general contours of our sexual scripts. It tells us which behaviors are acceptable ("moral" or "normal") and which are unacceptable ("immoral" or "abnormal"). For example, a norm may have a sequence of sexual events consisting of kissing, genital caressing, and sexual intercourse. Imagine a scenario in which two people from different cultures try to initiate a sexual encounter. One person follows the script of kissing, genital caressing, and sexual intercourse, while the one from a different culture follows a sequence beginning with sexual intercourse, moving to genital caressing, and ending with passionate kissing. At least initially, such a couple might experience frustration and confusion as one partner tries to initiate the sexual encounter with kissing and the other with sexual intercourse.

However, this kind of confusion occurs fairly often because there is not necessarily a direct correlation between what our culture calls erotic and what any particular individual calls erotic. Culture sets the general pattern, but there is too much diversity in terms of individual personality, socioeconomic status, and ethnicity for everybody to have exactly the same erotic script. Thus, sexual scripts can be highly ambiguous and varied.

We may believe that everyone shares our own particular script, projecting our experiences onto others and assuming that they share our erotic definitions of objects, gestures, and situations. But often, they initially do not. Our partner may have come from a different socioeconomic or ethnic group or religious background and may have had different learning experiences regarding sexuality (Mahay et al., 2001). Each of us has to learn the other's sexual script and be able to complement and adjust to it. If our scripts are to be integrated, we must make our needs known through open and honest communication involving words, gestures, and movements. This is the reason many people view their first intercourse as something of a comedy or tragedy—or perhaps a little of both.

In our society, passionate kissing is part of the cultural script for sexual interactions.

© Leland Bobbe/Taxi/Getty Images

Intrapersonal Scripting

On the intrapersonal level, sexual scripts enable people to give meaning to their physiological responses. The meaning depends largely on the situation. An erection, for example, does not always mean sexual excitement. Young boys sometimes have erections when they are frightened, anxious, or worried. Upon awakening in the morning, adolescent boys and men may experience erections that are unaccompanied by arousal. Adolescent girls sometimes experience sexual arousal without knowing what these sensations mean. They report them as funny, weird kinds of feelings or as anxiety, fear, or an upset stomach. The sensations are not linked to a sexual script until the girl becomes older and her physiological states acquire a definite erotic meaning.

Intrapersonal scripts provide a sequence of body movements by acting as mechanisms that activate biological events and release tension. We learn, for example, that we may create an orgasm by manipulating the penis or clitoris and other body parts during masturbation.

Interpersonal Scripting

The interpersonal level is the area of shared conventions, which make sexual activities possible. Very little of our public life is sexual, yet there are signs and gestures—verbal and nonverbal—that define encounters as sexual. We make our sexual motives clear by the looks we exchange, the tone of our voices, the movements of our bodies, and other culturally shared phenomena. A bedroom or a hotel room, for example, is a potentially erotic location; a classroom or an office may not be. The movements we use in arousing ourselves or others are erotic activators. Within a culture, there are normative scripts leading to intimate sexual behavior.

People with little sexual experience, especially young adolescents, are often unfamiliar with sexual scripts. What do they do after kissing? Do they embrace? Caress above the waist? Below? Eventually, they learn a comfortable sequence based on cultural inputs and personal and partner preferences. For gay men and lesbian women, learning the sexual script is more difficult because it is socially stigmatized. The sexual script is also related to age. Older children and young adolescents often limit their scripts to kissing, holding hands, and embracing, and they may feel completely satisfied. Kissing for them may be as exciting as intercourse for more experienced people. When the range of their scripts increases, they lose some of the sexual intensity of the earlier stages.

The concept of sexual scripts has been used often in research to further explain sexual expression among individuals and couples. To illustrate with a study pertinent to college students, Columbia University researchers Sheri Dworkin and Lucia O'Sullivan (2005) note that research on men's sexuality has tended to disregard looking at sexual scripts (e.g., aggressive initiators and orchestrators of sexual activity) or culturally dominant scripts. By interviewing 32 college-age men, they found that indeed these men wished to share initiation of sex, enjoyed being a desired sex object, and wanted egalitarian scripts. Dworkin and O'Sullivan conclude that these findings may "mean shifts in broader gender relations towards more companionate norms, a stretching of traditional scripts, a desire for egalitarian relationships, or social structural shifts in women's or men's power that may make sexual scripts more flexible." These results appear to counter the findings from college "hooking-up" studies. Possibly, college men who hook up desire a more egalitarian relationship with women but are influenced by the dominant script on the college campus, which is hooking up.

A study of 39 undergraduate heterosexual men and women from an Ontario, Canada, university assessed adherence to gendered sexual scripts (Sakaluk, Todd, Milhausen, Lachowsky, & Undergraduate Research Group in Sexuality, 2014). The study indicated that there are numerous distinct, and often related, sexual scripts that exert influence on establishing appropriate and expected sexual behavior among emerging heterosexual adults. Findings from focus groups pertaining to traditional sexual scripts were strongly congruent with the results of prior studies of the gendered aspects of sexual scripts. For example, (1) men have a strong physical orientation to sex, whereas women have an emotional orientation to sex; (2) men initiate sexual encounters, whereas women serve as the "gatekeeper"; (3) men are expected to be sexually skilled and knowledgeable; and (4) men should be ready for sex. The study also found some scripts that deviated from the more traditional scripts, such as respect for men who turned down opportunities to have sex. The researchers contend that the scripts that varied from the more traditional ones suggest that "sexual experimentation may not be evaluated positively, especially for women who choose to be sexual outside of the context of a committed relationship and for men who are seen to lie and manipulate to have sex with women (i.e., players)"; hence, a movement toward conservative sexual scripts may be occurring among today's emerging young adults. Like the Dworkin and O'Sullivan (2005) study above, the results of this research seem to reveal sexual scripts that contradict the current hooking-up culture on college campuses and show that some of the more traditional scripts are maintaining their dominance.

● Autoeroticism

Autoeroticism consists of sexual activities that involve only the self. Autoeroticism is an *intrapersonal* activity rather than an *interpersonal* one. It includes sexual fantasies, erotic dreams, viewing sexually explicit material by oneself, using vibrators and other sex toys by oneself, and **masturbation** (stimulating one's genitals for pleasure). A universal phenomenon in one form or another (Ford & Beach, 1951), autoeroticism is one of our earliest and most common expressions of sexual stirrings.

It is also one that traditionally has been condemned in our society. Figure 3 shows devices created to curb masturbation. By condemning it, however, our culture set the stage for the development of deeply negative and inhibitory attitudes toward sexuality.

Do people participate in autoerotic activities because they do not have a sex partner? The National Health and Social Life Survey (Laumann, Gagnon, Michael, & Michaels, 1994) found the opposite to be true:

> Those who engage in relatively little autoerotic activity are less likely to prefer a wider range of sexual techniques, are less likely to have a partner, and if they have a partner, are less likely to have sex frequently or engage in oral or anal sex. Similarly, individuals who engage in different kinds of autoerotic activity more often find a wider range of practices appealing and are more likely to have had at least one partner with whom they have sex frequently. Individuals who frequently think about sex, masturbate, and have used some type of pornography/erotica within the last year are much more likely to report enacting more elaborate interpersonal sexual scripts.

● **FIGURE 3**

Devices Designed to Curb Masturbation. Because of the widespread belief in the nineteenth century that masturbation was harmful, various devices were introduced to prevent the behavior.

(*Sources:* Crooks & Baur, 2005; Rathus, Nevid, & Fichner-Rathus, 2002.)

Sexual Fantasies and Dreams

Men and women, but especially men, think about sex often. According to sex researchers Harold Leitenberg and Kris Henning (1995), about 95% of men and women say that they have had sexual fantasies in one context or another. And a *Details* magazine study of more than 1,700 college students reported that 94% of men and 76% of women think about sex at least once a day (Elliott & Brantley, 1997).

Erotic fantasy is probably the most universal of all sexual activities. Nearly everyone has experienced such fantasies, but because they touch on feelings or desires considered personally or socially unacceptable, they are not widely discussed. Furthermore, many people have "forbidden" sexual fantasies that they never act on.

Whether occurring spontaneously or resulting from outside stimuli, fantasies are part of the body's regular, healthy functioning. Research indicates that sexual fantasies are related to sexual drives: the higher the sexual drive, the higher the frequency of sexual fantasies and level of satisfaction in one's sex life (Leitenberg & Henning, 1995). Fantasies help create an equilibrium between our environment and our inner selves, as we seek a balance between the two. We use them to enhance our masturbatory experiences, as well as oral-genital sex, sexual intercourse, and other interpersonal experiences.

A study of the sexual fantasies of 85 men and 77 women aged 21–45, from a midsized midwestern city in the United States, found gender differences in fantasies, many of which reflect common sexual scripts that both sexes learn from their culture (Zurbriggen & Yost, 2004):

 *Grant yourself and your lover freedom of fantasy. Sexual fantasies are normal, healthy and sex enhancing.*

—Michael Castleman (1950–)

- Men's fantasies, in contrast to women's, were more sexually explicit and more likely involved multiple partners. Women's fantasies were more emotional-romantic and more likely involved a single partner.

- Men more often fantasized about dominance, and women fantasized more about submission. Men's fantasies of dominance were associated with greater acceptance of rape myths, whereas women's greater acceptance of rape myths was associated with emotional-romantic fantasy themes.

- Women tended to mention fantasies related only to their own desire and pleasure, not to the desire and pleasure of their partners. In contrast, men mentioned the sexual desire and sexual pleasure of their partners as well as their own.

Relative to the fantasy about sexual desire and pleasure, the researchers note that the traditional cultural heterosexual script has encouraged women to put their partner's sexual desire and pleasure ahead of their own. They conclude that "it makes sense, then, that in the realm of fantasy women might choose to emphasize their own needs rather than those of their male partners."

In regard to types of fantasies based on sexual orientation, Leitenberg and Henning (1995) found that the content of sexual fantasies for gay men and lesbian women tends to be the same as for their heterosexual counterparts, except that homosexuals imagine same-sex partners and heterosexuals imagine other-sex partners.

In another study, Thomas Hicks and Harold Leitenberg (2001) found gender differences in the proportion of sexual fantasies that involved someone other than a current partner (extradyadic fantasies). In a sample of 349 university students and employees in heterosexual relationships, 98% of men and 80% of women reported having extradyadic fantasies in the past 2 months.

> The only way to get rid of temptation is to yield to it.
>
> —Oscar Wilde (1854–1900)

The Function of Sexual Fantasies Sexual fantasies have a number of important functions. First, they help direct and define our erotic goals. They take our generalized sexual drives and give them concrete images and specific content. We fantasize about certain types of men or women and reinforce our attraction through fantasy involvement. Unfortunately, our fantasy model may be unreasonable or unattainable, which is one of the pitfalls of fantasy; we can imagine perfection, but we rarely find it in real life.

Second, sexual fantasies allow us to plan for or anticipate situations that may arise. They provide a form of rehearsal, allowing us to practice in our minds how to act in various situations. Our fantasies of what *might* take place on a date, after a party, or in bed with our partner serve as a form of preparation.

Third, sexual fantasies provide escape from a dull or oppressive environment. Routine or repetitive behavior often gives rise to fantasies as a way of coping with boredom.

Fourth, even if our sex lives are satisfactory, we may indulge in sexual fantasies to bring novelty and excitement into the relationship. Fantasy offers a safe outlet for sexual curiosity. One study found that some women are capable of experiencing orgasm solely through fantasy (Whipple, Ogden, & Komisaruk, 1992).

Fifth, sexual fantasies have an expressive function in somewhat the same manner that dreams do. Our sexual fantasies may offer a clue to our current interests, pleasures, anxieties, fears, or problems. Repeated fantasies of extradyadic relationships, for example, may signify deep dissatisfaction with a marriage or steady relationship, whereas mental images centering around erectile difficulties may represent fears about sexuality or a particular relationship.

> When two people make love, there are at least four people present—the two who are actually there and the two they are thinking about.
>
> —Sigmund Freud (1856–1939)

Fantasies During Sexual Expression A sizable number of people fantasize during sex. The fantasies are usually a continuation of daydreams or masturbatory fantasies, transforming one's partner into a famous, attractive Hollywood star, for example. Couples often believe that they should be totally focused on each other during sex and not have any thoughts about others, particularly sexual thoughts. However, during the passion of sex, many people have thoughts not only about their partner but also about others such as past lovers, acquaintances, and movie stars. Many people feel guilty about such thoughts, feeling that they are being "mentally unfaithful" to their partner. However, sex therapists consider fantasies of other lovers to be quite normal and certainly typical.

Women who fantasize about being forced into sexual activity or about being victimized do not necessarily want this to actually occur. Rather, these women tend to be more interested in a variety of sexual activities and to be more sexually experienced than women who don't have these fantasies.

Erotic Dreams   Almost all of the men and two thirds of the women in Alfred Kinsey's studies reported having had overtly erotic or sexual dreams (Kinsey, Pomeroy, & Martin, 1948; Kinsey, Pomeroy, Martin, & Gebhard, 1953). Sexual images in dreams are frequently very intense. Although people tend to feel responsible for their fantasies, which occur when they are awake, they are usually less troubled by sexual dreams.

Overtly sexual dreams are not necessarily exciting, although dreams that are apparently nonsexual may cause arousal. It is not unusual for individuals to awaken in the middle of the night and notice an erection or vaginal lubrication or to find their bodies moving as if they were making love. They may also experience nocturnal orgasm (or emission). About 2–3% of women's total orgasms may be nocturnal, whereas for men the number may be around 8% (Kinsey et al., 1948, 1953).

Dreams almost always accompany nocturnal orgasm. The dreamer may awaken, and men usually ejaculate. Although the dream content may not be overtly sexual, it is always accompanied by sensual sensations. Erotic dreams run the gamut of sexual possibilities: Women seem to feel less guilty or fearful about nocturnal orgasms than men do, accepting them more easily as pleasurable experiences.

Masturbation

People report that they masturbate for many reasons, including for relaxation, for relief of sexual tension, because a partner is not available or does not want sex, for physical pleasure, as an aid to falling asleep, and as a means to avoid STIs. They may masturbate during particular periods or throughout their entire lives (see Table 3). For older adults, often after the loss of their partners, masturbation regains much of the primacy of their earlier years and is often the most common sexual activity.

Masturbation is an important means of learning about our bodies. Through masturbation, individuals learn what is sexually pleasing, how to move their bodies,

Masturbation is an intrinsically and seriously disordered act.
—Vatican Declaration on Sexual Ethics, 1976

MASTURBATION, n. An extremely disgusting act performed on a regular basis by everyone else.
—Robert Tefton

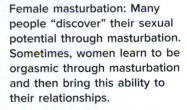

Female masturbation: Many people "discover" their sexual potential through masturbation. Sometimes, women learn to be orgasmic through masturbation and then bring this ability to their relationships.

© Jochen Schoenfeld/AGE Fotostock

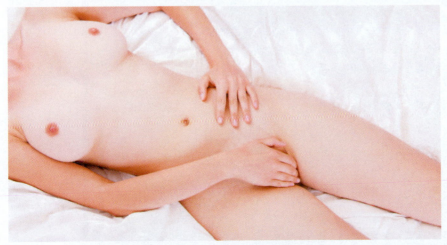

TABLE 3 ● Percentage of Americans, Aged 14 to 70+, Who Participated in Selected Sexual Behaviors in the Past Year

Sexual Behavior	14–15 % of Men	14–15 % of Women	16–17 % of Men	16–17 % of Women	18–19 % of Men	18–19 % of Women	20–24 % of Men	20–24 % of Women	25–29 % of Men	25–29 % of Women	30–39 % of Men	30–39 % of Women	40–49 % of Men	40–49 % of Women	50–59 % of Men	50–59 % of Women	60–69 % of Men	60–69 % of Women	70+ % of Men	70+ % of Women
Masturbated alone	62	40	75	45	81	60	83	64	84	72	80	63	76	65	72	54	61	47	46	33
Masturbated with partner	5	8	16	19	42	36	44	36	49	48	45	43	38	35	28	18	17	13	13	5
Received oral from women	12	1	31	5	54	4	63	9	77	3	78	5	62	2	49	1	38	1	19	2
Received oral from men	1	10	3	24	6	58	6	70	5	72	6	59	6	52	8	34	3	25	2	8
Gave oral to women	8	2	18	7	51	2	55	9	74	3	69	4	57	3	44	1	34	1	24	2
Gave oral to men	1	12	2	22	4	59	7	74	5	76	5	59	7	53	8	36	3	23	3	7
Vaginal intercourse	9	11	30	30	53	62	63	80	86	87	85	74	74	70	58	51	54	42	43	22
Received penis in anus	1	4	1	5	4	18	5	23	4	21	3	22	4	12	5	6	6	4	2	1
Inserted penis into anus	3		6		6		11		27		24		21		11		6		2	

Note: Data based on 5,865 Americans.

SOURCE: Herbenick, D., et al. (2010). Sexual behavior in the United States: Results from a national probability sample of men and women aged 14–94. *Journal of Sexual Medicine, 7,* 255–265.

and what their natural rhythms are. The activity has no harmful physical effects. Although masturbation often decreases when individuals are regularly sexual with another person, it is not necessarily a temporary substitute for sexual intercourse but rather is a legitimate form of sexual activity in its own right. Sex therapists may encourage clients to masturbate as a means of overcoming specific sexual problems and discovering their personal sexual potential. Masturbation, whether practiced alone or mutually with a partner (see Figure 4), is also a form of safer sex.

Prevalence of Masturbation As shown in Table 3, all 10 of the National Survey of Sexual Health and Behavior (NSSHB) age groups incorporating men and women aged 14–70+ reported solo masturbation and masturbation with partners in the past year. Figures 5 and 6 show the percentages of NSSHB men and women aged 18–39, by racial/ethnic group, who reported ever participating in solo masturbation or partnered masturbation. Both the table and figures indicate that masturbation is a common behavior that can be practiced alone or in a partnered relationship; occurs among all ages, sexual orientations, and ethnicities; and can be considered a typical and pleasurable part of an individual's and a couple's sexuality.

A study of college undergraduates (78 men, 145 women) found that almost all of the men (98%) and the majority of women (64%) reported that they had masturbated in the past. Both indicated frequent masturbation: men averaging 36 times and women 14 times in the past 3 months. The study also examined factors that would predict frequent masturbation. For the college men, higher frequency of masturbation occurred in men who believed that their peers masturbated frequently. And men who believed that masturbation was pleasurable also reported more frequent masturbation. For women, masturbation frequency was most associated with perceived pleasure and somewhat with the frequency of intercourse. The researchers concluded that, for this sample, perceived social norms, perceived pleasure, and sexual behaviors helped explain masturbation among college students (Pinkerton, Bogart, Cecil, & Abramson, 2002).

Masturbatory behavior is influenced by education, ethnicity, religion, and age, with education a particularly strong factor. The more educated one becomes, the more frequently one masturbates. A nationally representative British study of masturbation among the general population (aged 16–44) found that masturbation frequency was greater for both men and women with higher levels of education, in higher social classes, and at younger ages (Gerressu, Mercer, Graham, Wellings, & Johnson, 2008).

Masturbation in Adulthood Masturbation is common among youth, peaks in young adulthood, and tends to decrease in later years (see Table 3).

Women and Masturbation One way in which women become familiar with their own sexual responsiveness is through masturbation. The NSSHB found that the percentage of women who had masturbated in the preceding year ranged from 72% for the 25–29 age group to 33% for the 70+ age group (see Table 3) (Herbenick et al., 2010.9a). For women aged 18–39, 86%, 73%, and 68% of White, Black, and Hispanic women, respectively, reported ever masturbating alone and 63%, 56%, and 45% of White, Hispanic,

Male masturbation: Masturbation is an important form of sexual behavior in which individuals explore their erotic capacities and bring pleasure to themselves.

© H.S. Photos/Alamy

"Masturbation! The amazing availability of it!

—James Joyce
(1882–1941)

● **FIGURE** 4

Mutual Masturbation. Many couples enjoy mutual masturbation, one form of safer sex.

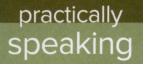

Assessing Your Attitude Toward Masturbation

Masturbation guilt is a learned script in which the negative affects of guilt, disgust, shame, and fear are related to masturbation (Abramson & Mosher, 1975). As discussed in this chapter, feelings of shame and guilt have long been associated with masturbation, and a positive attitude has emerged only recently. Still, many people continue to feel guilty about their own masturbatory activity. Take this inventory to determine how much you have been affected by negative messages about masturbation.

Directions

Indicate how true each of the following statements is for you, on a scale from "Not at all true" to "Very true," by circling the appropriate number.

	Not at all true				Very true
1. People masturbate to escape feelings of tension and anxiety.	1	2	3	4	5
2. People who masturbate will not enjoy sexual intercourse as much as those who refrain from masturbation.	1	2	3	4	5
3. Masturbation is a private matter that neither harms nor concerns anyone else.	1	2	3	4	5
4. Masturbation is a sin against yourself.	1	2	3	4	5
5. Masturbation in childhood can help a person develop a natural, healthy attitude toward sex.	1	2	3	4	5
6. Masturbation in an adult is juvenile and immature.	1	2	3	4	5
7. Masturbation can lead to deviant sexual behavior.	1	2	3	4	5
8. Excessive masturbation is physically impossible, so it is needless to worry.	1	2	3	4	5
9. If you enjoy masturbating too much, you may never learn to relate to a sex partner.	1	2	3	4	5
10. After masturbating, a person feels degraded.	1	2	3	4	5
11. Experience with masturbation can potentially help a woman become orgasmic for sexual intercourse.	1	2	3	4	5
12. I feel guilt about masturbating.	1	2	3	4	5
13. Masturbation can be a "friend in need" when there is no "friend indeed."	1	2	3	4	5
14. Masturbation can provide an outlet for sex fantasies without harming anyone else or endangering oneself.	1	2	3	4	5
15. Excessive masturbation can lead to problems with erections in men and women not being able to have an orgasm.	1	2	3	4	5

	Not at all true				Very true
16. Masturbation is an escape mechanism that prevents a person from developing a mature sexual outlook.	1	2	3	4	5
17. Masturbation can provide harmless relief from sexual tension.	1	2	3	4	5
18. Playing with your own genitals is disgusting.	1	2	3	4	5
19. Excessive masturbation is associated with neurosis, depression, and behavioral problems.	1	2	3	4	5
20. Any masturbation is too much.	1	2	3	4	5
21. Masturbation is a compulsive, addictive habit that once begun is almost impossible to stop.	1	2	3	4	5
22. Masturbation is fun.	1	2	3	4	5
23. When I masturbate, I am disgusted with myself.	1	2	3	4	5
24. A pattern of frequent masturbation is associated with introversion and withdrawal from social contacts.	1	2	3	4	5
25. I would be ashamed to admit publicly that I have masturbated.	1	2	3	4	5
26. Excessive masturbation leads to mental dullness and fatigue.	1	2	3	4	5
27. Masturbation is a normal sexual outlet.	1	2	3	4	5
28. Masturbation is caused by an excessive preoccupation with thoughts about sex.	1	2	3	4	5
29. Masturbation can teach you to enjoy the sensuousness of your own body.	1	2	3	4	5
30. After I masturbate, I am disgusted with myself for losing control of my body.	1	2	3	4	5

Scoring

To obtain an index of masturbation guilt, sum the circled numbers to yield a score from 30 to 150. Before summing, reverse the scoring for these 10 items: 3, 5, 8, 11, 13, 14, 17, 22, 27. That is, a 1 would be converted to a 5, a 2 to a 4, a 4 to a 2, and 5 to a 1. The lower your score, the lower your guilt about and negative attitude toward masturbation.

SOURCE: Adapted from Abramson, P. R., & Mosher, D. L. (1975). The development of a measure of negative attitudes toward masturbation. *Journal of Consulting and Clinical Psychology, 43,* 485–490. (Table 1, p. 487). Copyright © 1975 by the American Psychological Association. Adapted with permission. No further reproduction or distribution is permitted without written permission from the American Psychological Association.

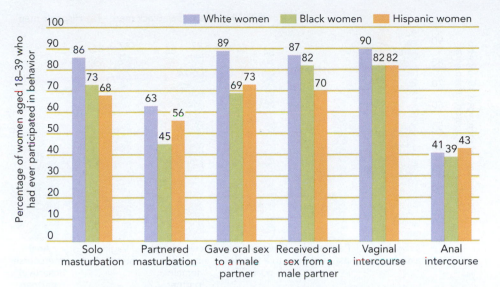

• **FIGURE 5**

Percentage of American Women Aged 18–39 Who Had Ever Participated in Selected Sexual Behaviors.

(*Source:* Reece et al., 2010.9a.)

and Black women reported ever experiencing partnered masturbation (see Figure 5) (Reece et al., 2010.9a). The British study of masturbation among the general population found that masturbation was more common among those who reported more frequent vaginal intercourse in the past 4 weeks, who had the greater repertoire of sexual behaviors such as oral and anal sex, who had the most sexual partners in the past year, who reported same-sex partners, and who were less religiously devout (Gerressu et al., 2008). Women who masturbate appear to hold more positive sexual attitudes and are more likely to be orgasmic than those who don't (Kelly, Strassberg, & Kircher, 1990; Schnarch, 2002). Although the majority of women believe that orgasms experienced through masturbation differ from those experienced in sexual intercourse, they feel the same levels of sexual satisfaction (Davidson & Darling, 1986).

Though no two women masturbate in exactly the same manner, a number of common methods are used to experience orgasm. Most involve some type of clitoral stimulation, by using the fingers, rubbing against an object, or using a vibrator. The rubbing or stimulation tends to increase just prior to orgasm and continues during orgasm.

Because the glans clitoris is often too sensitive for prolonged direct stimulation, women tend to stroke gently on the shaft of the clitoris. Another common method, which exerts less direct pressure on the clitoris, is to stroke the mons areas or the minor lips. Individual preferences play a key role in what method is chosen, how rigorous the stimulation is, how often masturbation occurs, and whether it is accompanied by erotic aids such as a vibrator or sensual oils. One study found that water- and silicon-based lubricants were associated with significantly higher reports of sexual pleasure and satisfaction and rarely associated with genital symptoms (Herbenick et al., 2011). Some women find that running a stream of warm water over the vulva or sitting near the jet stream in a hot tub is sexually arousing. Stimulation of the breasts and nipples is also very common, as is stroking the anal region. Some women enjoy inserting a finger or other object into their vagina; however, this is less common than clitoral stimulation. Some women apply deep pressure in the region of the G-spot to give themselves a different type of orgasm. Using common sense in relation to cleanliness, such

What I like about masturbation is that you don't have to talk afterwards.

—Milos Forman
(1932–)

• FIGURE 6

Percentage of American Men Aged 18–39 Who Had Ever Participated in Selected Sexual Behaviors.

(*Source:* Reece et al., 2010.9a.)

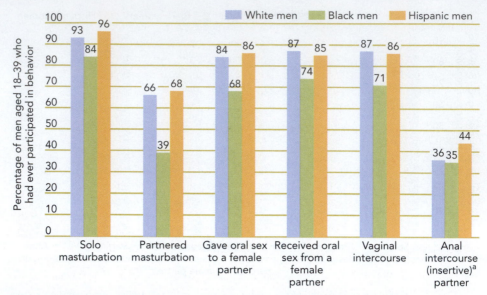

[a]The insertion of the penis into the rectum of either a female or male partner.

> *Masturbation is the primary sexual activity of [human] kind. In the nineteenth century it was a disease; in the twentieth, it's a cure.*
>
> —Thomas Szasz
> (1920–2012)

as not inserting an object or a finger from the anus into the vagina and keeping vibrators and other objects used for insertion clean, helps prevent infection.

Men and Masturbation   According to the NSSHB, the percentage of men reporting masturbation in the preceding year ranged from 84% in the 25–29 age group to 40% in the 70+ age group (see Table 3) (Herbenick et al., 2010.9a). For men aged 18–39, 96%, 93%, and 84% of Hispanic, White, and Black men, respectively, reported ever masturbating alone and 68%, 66%, and 39% of Hispanic, White, and Black men reported ever experiencing partnered masturbation (see Figure 6) (Reece et al., 2010.9a). The study of masturbation of the British general population found that the prevalence of masturbation was higher among men reporting less frequent vaginal intercourse and among those reporting same-sex partners (Gerressu et al., 2008).

Like women, men have individual preferences and patterns in masturbating. Nearly all methods involve some type of direct stimulation of the penis with the hand. Typically, the penis is grasped and stroked at the shaft, with up-and-down or circular movements of the hand, so that the edge of the corona around the glans and the frenulum on the underside are stimulated. How much pressure is applied, how rapid the strokes are, how many fingers are used, where the fingers are placed, and how far up and down the hands move vary from one man to another. Whether the breasts, testicles, anus, or other parts of the body are stimulated also depends on the individual, but it appears to be the up-and-down stroking or rubbing of the penis that triggers orgasm. The stroking tends to increase just prior to ejaculation and then to slow or stop during ejaculation.

To add variety or stimulation, some men may elect to use lubricants, visual or written erotic materials, artificial vaginas, inflatable dolls, or rubber pouches in which to insert their penis. Regardless of the aid or technique, it is important to pay attention to cleanliness to prevent bacterial infections.

Masturbation in Sexual Relationships   Most people continue to masturbate after they marry or are in a steady relationship, although the rate is significantly lower. Actually, the National Health and Social Life Survey (NHSLS) found that married people are less likely to have masturbated during the preceding 12 months than those never married or formerly married. About 57% and 37% of married men and women, respectively, reported having masturbated in the preceding year, as opposed to about 48% and 69% of formerly married and never-married men and women, respectively (Laumann et al., 1994).

There are many reasons for continuing the activity during marriage or other sexual relationships; for example, masturbation is pleasurable, a partner is away or unwilling, sexual intercourse or other intimate sexual behavior is not satisfying, the partner(s) fear(s) sexual inadequacy, the individual acts out fantasies, or he or she seeks to release tension. During times of relationship conflict, masturbation may act as a distancing device, with the masturbating partner choosing masturbation over sexual interaction as a means of emotional protection.

● Sexual Behavior With Others

We often think that sex is sexual intercourse, but sex is not limited to sexual intercourse. Heterosexuals engage in a wide variety of sexual activities, which may include erotic touching, kissing, and oral and anal sex. A study of four groups—men and women (mean age = 30) in both same-sex and mixed-sex relationships—found that they were strikingly identical in their sexual repertoires. The study measured solitary behaviors such as masturbation, orgasm alone and with partner, and couple behavior such as kissing your partner, watching your partner undress, and oral sex (Holmberg & Blair, 2009). Which of these "sexual" activities actually constitute sex? This topic has been publicly debated, largely fueled by former president Clinton's declaration that he did not have sex with Monica Lewinsky despite the fact that she performed oral sex on him. (To find out what a representative sample of young adults believed constituted having "had sex," see the "Think About It" box "You Would Say You 'Had Sex' If You. . . .")

Most Recent Partnered Sex

Like many national sex surveys, the NSSHB assessed the frequency of numerous sexual behaviors of which the major findings are cited throughout this book. However, the NSSHB went beyond the typical sexual behavior statistics to assess other contextual factors during the last, single event of couple or partnered sex (Herbenick et al., 2010.9a). The contextual findings from a nationally representative sample of 3,990 adults, aged 18–59, provide greater understanding of the circumstances and experiences of couple sex, such as where people have sex, with whom they have sex, and sexual function during sex (e.g., pleasure, arousal, orgasm). Some of the more intriguing findings give us a brief "snapshot" of the sexual repertoire of Americans' reported last-partnered sexual event:

- Most participants reported that their most recent sexual event occurred in their or their partner's home.

- The majority of the most recent sexual events occurred within a relationship or with a dating partner, although a sizable minority reported their most recent sexual event occurred with a friend. However, most of the participants aged 18–24 reported that their partner was a casual or dating partner.

> Love is the self-delusion we manufacture to justify the trouble we take to have sex.
>
> —Dan Greenberg

You Would Say You "Had Sex" If You . . .

When people say they "had sex," "hooked up," or "did some things" but did not have sex, what do they mean? Many people have different ideas about what it means to have sex; it all depends on the behavioral criteria they use. Social and legal definitions of "sex" and crimes related to "having sex" vary and are sometimes vague, depending on the source. Some definitions may be used by couples or individuals to justify a wide range of intimate behaviors other than penile-vaginal intercourse or penile-anal intercourse in order to, for example, preserve or lose their virginity, not to "have cheated" on another person, or to believe they had sex. Without a universal definition of "having sex," confusion or false assumptions can result (Sanders & Reinisch, 1999).

Researchers at The Kinsey Institute for Research in Sex, Gender, and Reproduction and the Rural Center for AIDS/STD Prevention at Indiana University conducted a public opinion study of a representative sample of adults to determine if certain sexual behaviors, as well as whether male ejaculation, female orgasm, condom use, or brevity during penile-vaginal intercourse or penile-anal intercourse, are considered "having sex." The opinions of 482 adult Indiana residents of varying ages were obtained by telephone, using random digital dialing.

Results of the participants, aged 18–29, are shown in the accompanying table.

Not surprisingly, nearly all of the participants considered penile-vaginal intercourse—even under the specific circumstances listed—as having "had sex." This was basically true for penile-anal intercourse, although the percentage indicating "yes" was not quite as high. As expected, the percentage indicating "yes" to oral sex and manual stimulation of the genitals was less than intercourse; interestingly, the responses varied considerably by gender, with a much greater percentage of women than men indicating "yes" to these two behaviors.

Two additional studies of college students further our understanding of young adults' definition of "having sex." A study of 164 heterosexual Canadian university students not only asked their views of what constitutes "having sex" but also examined what constitutes a sexual partner and what they consider to be "unfaithful" in a sexual partner. The results showed discrepancies in the students' opinions on these three issues. For example, although 25% of the students considered oral-genital behaviors as having sex, more than 60% thought that the giver or receiver of oral sex was a sex partner, and more than 97% considered a sex partner who had oral sex

Percentages of 18- to 29-year-old Indiana residents (31 females, 31 males) answering "yes" to the question "Would you say you 'had sex' with someone if the most intimate behavior you engaged in was . . . ?"

Behavior	% of Women	% of Men
You touched, fondled, or manually stimulated a partner's genitals	29	10
A partner touched, fondled, or manually stimulated your genitals	32	17
You had oral (mouth) contact with a partner's genitals	61	33
A partner had oral (mouth) contact with your genitals	67	40
Penile-vaginal intercourse	94	97
Penile-vaginal intercourse with no ejaculation; that is, the man did not "come"	94	90
Penile-vaginal intercourse with no female orgasm; that is, the woman did not "come"	90	97
Penile-vaginal intercourse, but very brief	97	97
Penile-vaginal intercourse with a condom	94	100
Penile-anal intercourse	84	77
Penile-anal intercourse with no male ejaculation	84	77
Penile-anal intercourse with no female orgasm	84	77
Penile-anal intercourse, but very brief	84	76
Penile-anal intercourse with a condom	84	83

SOURCES: Sanders, S. A., Hill, B. J., Yarber, W. L., Graham, C. A., Crosby, R. A., & Milhausen, R. R. (2010). Misclassification bias: Diversity in conceptualizations about having "had sex." *Sexual Health, 7* (Suppl. 5), 31–34; Yarber, W. L., Sanders, S. A., Graham, C. A., Crosby, R. A., & Milhausen, R. R. (2007, Nov.). *Public opinion about what behaviors constitute "having sex": A state-wide telephone survey in Indiana.* Paper presented at the annual meeting of The Society for the Scientific Study of Sexuality, Indianapolis, Indiana.

with someone else to have been unfaithful (Randall & Byers, 2003). Further, while masturbating to orgasm in the presence of another person was considered as having sex by less than 4% of the students, 34% reported that this behavior would make that person a sexual partner and 95% considered it to be unfaithful if done with someone else.

Lastly, another study of 298 heterosexual Canadian university students asked about their definitions of the terms "abstinence" and "having sex," with some intriguing results. For example, the researchers found a clear consensus that deep kissing was considered abstinence, with a majority viewing nongenital behaviors such as showering together and breast play as abstinence. As other studies have found, there was a consensus that penile-vaginal and penile-anal activities did not constitute sexual abstinence (Byers, Henderson, & Hobson, 2009).

Think Critically

1. Do any of the results of the research studies on the definition of "having sex" surprise you? Do you agree or disagree with the findings?
2. Does it make any difference how "having sex" is defined?
3. How do you define "having sex"? Has your definition changed over time?

SOURCES: Byers, F. S., Henderson, J., & Hobson, K. M. (2009). University students' definitions of sexual abstinence and having sex. *Archives of Sexual Behavior, 38,* 665–674; Randall, H. E., & Byers, E. S. (2003). What is sex? Students' definitions of having sex, sexual partner, and unfaithful sexual behavior. *Canadian Journal of Human Sexuality, 12,* 87–96; Sanders, S., & Reinisch, J. (1999). Would you say you "had sex" if . . . ? *Journal of the American Medical Association, 281,* 275–277.

- The vast majority, but not all, reported that their most recent sexual event was with an other-sex partner.

- An enormous variability in the sexual repertoire of the participants was found, with a diverse range of sexual behaviors in a given sexual episode.

- Penile-vaginal intercourse was the most commonly reported sexual behavior of both men and women during the most recent sexual event, although oral sex (given and received) occurred frequently.

- The largest proportion of men and women reported engaging solely in penile-vaginal intercourse during their most recent sexual event, although some indicated participating solely in noncoital behaviors such as partnered oral sex and masturbation.

- Most men and women reported that neither they nor their partner used alcohol or marijuana around the time of their most recent sexual event.

Findings related to the participants' evaluation of their most recent partnered sexual event—such as arousal, pleasure, orgasm, and sexual function difficulties—will be reported in the chapter on sexual function problems.

Sex is like money—only too much is enough.

—John Updike
(1932–2009)

Couple Sexual Styles

Barry McCarthy, a psychologist and renowned sex therapist, and his wife, Emily McCarthy, in their book *Discovering Your Couple Sexual Style* (2009), challenge couples, married or not, to develop a mature sexuality rather than adhering to unrealistic expectations of sexuality. The McCarthys contend that each couple develops their own sexual style. The challenge is for each partner to maintain individuality as well as experience being part of an intimate, erotic sexual couple. They state, in talking to couples, that "it takes most couples six months or longer to transition from the romantic love/passionate sex/idealized phase to develop a mature, intimate couple sexual style" (p. 33). They continue by telling couples that they can develop a mutually comfortable level of intimacy that promotes sexual desire and eroticism and provides energy for their relationship.

The McCarthys identify four couple sexual styles and state that there is no "right" style that is best for all couples. They state that most couples maintain their core sexual style because it is comfortable and satisfying, but the McCarthys also encourage couples to make adjustments and modifications as the relationship continues.

Complementary Style   This is the most common sexual style and it allows each partner to have a positive sexual voice yet share in an intimate relationship. The couples who choose this style realize that the best aphrodisiac is an involved, aroused partner. Each partner is responsible for his or her sexual desire and response and feels free to initiate sex, say no to sex, and request a different sexual scenario. In this style, it is not the partner's role to give the partner an orgasm but rather to be an intimate friend receptive and responsive to the partner's sexual feelings and preferences. The strength of this style is its variability, its flexibility, and the value each person places on intimacy and eroticism. A possible vulnerability is that sex can become routine and, if the couple takes sex and each other for granted, they may become disappointed and frustrated in their sexual relationship.

Traditional Style   This is the most predictable and stable style and is often called "acceptance and security," as it places high value on keeping the peace, commitment, and stability. In this conflict-minimizing relationship, traditional gender scripts of sex being the man's domain and affection and intimacy being the woman's domain are paramount. Since emotional and erotic expression is discouraged, this is the least intimate and erotic couple sexual style, with sex being a lower priority than it is in the other couple sexual styles. The male initiates sex and the female is less erotically active but is open to the male preferences. The strength of this style is predictability, security, and clearly defined roles, with sex rarely becoming an explosive issue. The vulnerability is that this style does not have enough mutual and sexual intimacy and, of all the couple sexual styles, it is most resistant to change.

Soulmate Style   Being soulmates means experiencing the highest level of intimacy and closeness, a sexual couple style that has been considered the "perfect" style. These couples share feelings, spend a lot of time together, enjoy shared experiences, and place a high priority on meeting each other's needs. The fundamental tenet of this style is that the greater the intimacy, the better the couple sex. The advantages of this style are a feeling of being accepted for who one truly is; feeling loved, desired, and desirable; and not having a fear of judgment or rejection. When working well, this style really meets the partners' needs for intimacy and security. A major danger of this style is that too much closeness and predictability can subvert sexuality and partners can "de-eroticize" each other. That is, people can become so close to their partner that they lose erotic feelings for him or her. In this style, the couple is hesitant to face the problems that come up in their relationship. Persons in this style need to be autonomous enough to maintain their own sexual voice, and partners should be committed to integrating intimacy and eroticism.

Emotionally Expressive Style   This is the most erotic style and is dominated with strong emotion and drama. Each partner is free to share positive and negative passions in word and deed. Of the four couple sexual styles, this one is the most engaging, exciting, fun, and unpredictable. It focuses on external stimuli to enhance eroticism while downplaying intimacy. The openness to emotional and sexual expression and spontaneity are major strengths of this style. This style is the most resilient and engaging of the four styles, and couples often use sex to reconnect after a conflict. The major drawback of this style is that it is the highest in relational instability. These couples "wear each other out" with all of their emotional upheavals. Partners in this sexual style should honor personal boundaries and not be hurtful when the issue involves sexuality.

Touching

Whether sex begins with the heart or the genitals, touch is the fire that melds the two into one. Touching is both a sign of caring and a signal for arousal.

Touching does not need to be directed solely toward the genitals or erogenous zones. The entire body is responsive to a touch or a caress. Even hand-holding can be sensual for two people sexually attracted to each other. Women appear to be especially responsive to touch, but traditional male gender roles give little significance to touching. Some men regard touching as simply a prelude to intercourse. When this occurs, touch is transformed into a demand for intercourse rather than an expression of intimacy or erotic play. The man's partner may become reluctant to touch or show affection for fear her gestures will be misinterpreted as a sexual invitation.

William Masters and Virginia Johnson (1970) suggest a form of touching they call "pleasuring." **Pleasuring** is nongenital touching and caressing. Neither partner tries to sexually stimulate the other; they simply explore, discovering how their bodies respond to touching. One partner guides the other partner's hand over his or her body, telling the partner what feels good; the roles are then reversed. Such sharing gives each a sense of his or her own responses; it also allows each to discover what the other likes and dislikes. We can't assume we know what a particular person likes, for there is too much variation among people: Watching a partner masturbate can provide clues on how he or she likes to be stimulated. Pleasuring opens the door to communication; couples discover that the entire body, not just the genitals, is erogenous. Actually, Masters and Johnson (1970) noted that women tend to prefer genital touching after general body contact, whereas many men prefer stroking of their genitals early.

Some forms of touching are directly sexual, such as caressing, fondling, or rubbing our own or our partner's genitals or breasts. Sucking or licking earlobes, the neck, toes, or the insides of thighs, palms, or arms can be highly stimulating. Oral stimulation of a woman's or man's breasts or nipples is often exciting. Moving one's genitals or breasts over a partner's face, chest, breasts, or genitals is very erotic for some people. The pressing together of bodies with genital thrusting is called **tribidism,** "dry humping," or "scissoring." Many lesbian women enjoy the overall body contact and eroticism of this form of genital stimulation; sometimes, the partners place their pelvic areas together to provide mutual clitoral stimulation (see Figure 7).

> I scarcely seem to be able to keep my hands off you.
>
> —Ovid
> (43 BCE–17 CE)

> Sex, indeed, has been called the highest form of touch. In the profoundest sense, touch is the true language of sex.
>
> —Ashley Montagu
> (1905–1999)

• FIGURE 7

Tribidism.

Touching can increase relaxation and enhance intimacy.

© Tom & Dee Ann McCarthy/Corbis

Rubbing the penis between the thighs of a partner is a type of touching called **interfemoral intercourse.** Heterosexual couples who do not use contraception must be sure the man does not ejaculate near the vaginal opening so as to avoid conception, however unlikely it may seem.

Stimulating a partner's clitoris or penis with the hand or fingers can increase excitement and lead to orgasm. A word of caution: Direct stimulation of the clitoral glans may be painful for some women at specific stages of arousal, so stimulation of either side of the clitoris may work better. Certainly, the clitoris and surrounding areas should be moist before much touching is done. Inserting a finger or fingers into a partner's wet vagina and rhythmically moving it at the pace she likes can also be pleasing. Some women like to have their clitoris licked or stimulated with one hand while their vagina is being penetrated with the other. Men like having their penises lubricated so that their partner's hand glides smoothly over the shaft and glans penis. Be sure to use a water-based lubricant if you plan to use a condom later, because oil-based lubricants may cause the condom to deteriorate. Masturbating while one partner is holding the other can be highly erotic for both people. Mutual masturbation can also be intensely sexual. Some people use sex toys such as dildos, vibrators, or ben-wah balls to enhance sexual touching.

The Advocate, a magazine focusing on gay and lesbian issues, conducted a survey of its readers concerning relationships and sexuality. A strong majority of the lesbian women said they loved many nongenital, touching activities: 91% loved hugging, caressing, and cuddling; 82% loved French kissing; 74% loved simply holding hands. Three quarters loved both touching a woman's genitals and having their own touched. About 80% enjoyed caressing another woman's breasts or sucking her nipples; 68% enjoyed receiving such attention (Lever, 1995). For 85% of gay men, hugging, kissing, and snuggling were also the favorite activities (Lever, 1995).

Sex therapist and psychologist Barry McCarthy and his wife, Emily McCarthy, have conceptualized five dimensions of touch from affection to intercourse. In a novel way, they frame the five touches as gears of a stick-shift automobile. See "Think About It" box "Giving and Receiving Pleasurable Touch" to learn more about the five gears of touch.

Kissing

Kissing is usually our earliest interpersonal sexual experience, and its primal intensity may be traced back to our suckling as infants. The kiss is magic: Fairy tales keep alive the ancient belief that a kiss can undo spells and bring a prince or princess back to life. Parental kisses show love and often remedy the small hurts and injuries of childhood.

Kissing is probably the most acceptable of all sexual activities. The tender lover's kiss symbolizes love, and the erotic lover's kiss, of course, simultaneously represents and *is* passion. Both men and women regard kissing as a romantic expression, a symbol of affection as well as desire. A study of both men and women, aged 18–63, found that kissing frequency was related to relationship quality: For couples in an exclusive relationship, the couples who reported the most frequent kissing also reported the greater relationship

The kiss originated when the first male reptile licked the first female reptile, implying in a subtle, complimentary way that she was as succulent as the small reptile he had for dinner the night before.

—F. Scott Fitzgerald (1896–1940)

think about it

Giving and Receiving Pleasurable Touch: "Gears of Connection"

The essence of sexuality is giving and receiving pleasure-oriented touching.

—McCarthy & McCarthy
(2009, p. 31)

Sex therapist and psychologist Barry McCarthy and his wife, Emily McCarthy, in their book *Discovering Your Couple Sexual Style* (2009), state that healthy sexual couples learn to value a range of ways to connect and reconnect physically and emotionally as a way to maintain a vital, satisfying sexuality. One important way this is done is through pleasure-oriented, nondemanding touch ranging from affectionate touch to intercourse touch. Sexual expression often does not include intercourse and nondemand pleasuring affirms the value of nonintercourse touch. The McCarthys state that "touch counts, whether it eventually proceeds to intercourse or not." Actually, sex often does not include intercourse.

The concept of pleasure-oriented touch options helps negate the traditional male-female sexual script and power struggle about sex. Typically, the man pushes for intercourse and perceives touch only as "foreplay"; this often results in the woman feeling pressured rather than invited and conflicted about initiating touch unless she wants to have intercourse. With an "intercourse or nothing" perspective, other pleasure-oriented touch is devalued and often left out. The McCarthys use a metaphor, the "gears of connection," as a way to conceptualize five touch dimensions: affection, sensuality, playfulness, erotic nonintercourse, and intercourse. Imagine the five touch dimensions as the five gears of a stick-shift car where one starts with the first gear and shifts through the gears, all the way to fifth. A 10-point scale of sexual arousal is used: 0 is neutral, 5 is the beginning of sexual touch, and 10 is orgasm.

First gear: Affectionate touch. This type of touch involves enjoying the same warm, romantic experiences as when a couple first meets. It is a genuine "reaching out" to the other person, feeling safe and connected, which facilitates receptivity to sensual and sexual connection. Examples of affectionate touch are clothes-on interactions such as holding hands, hugging, kissing, and walking arm-in-arm. This gear is a 1 on the 10-point scale and is not sexual, but it is an important part of an intimate relationship. Knowing that gear 1 is as far as the interaction may get can enhance the joy of the moment.

Second gear: The sensual gear. Being in the 2–4 range of the 10-point arousal continuum, this gear can be engaged in with clothes on, semiclothed, or nude and includes touching the body, except the genitals. This nongenital touching gear is labeled nondemand pleasuring by sex therapists, meaning that the person enjoys giving touch and pleasure but does not expect anything in return except the good feelings of the touch. Neither partner demands moving beyond gear 2. Examples are cuddling while watching television or a DVD,

kissing and cuddling before going to sleep, giving and receiving a back rub, and cradling each other with arms intertwined.

Third gear: The playful gear. This gear involves playful nongenital and genital touching, while either nude or seminude. Playful touch can be fun, inviting, and unpredictable and is 4–6 on the 10-point arousal scale. Called genital pleasuring by sex therapists, examples of playful touch are full-body massages, showering or bathing together, and playing with the other's body. Playful touch, like the other gears, has value in itself, but it can also be a bridge to sexual desire and intercourse.

Fourth gear: The erotic gear. Being 7–10 on the 10-point arousal scale, this gear involves erotic, nonintercourse touch and includes manual and oral genital touch, rubbing, and vibrator stimulation leading to high arousal and orgasm for one or both partners. Hence, this is the most challenging gear for couples to enjoy without feeling pressure to transition to intercourse. This gear often leads to intercourse but has value in itself as an erotic alternative to intercourse. Numerous erotic scenarios and techniques are possible in fourth gear that can be rewarding in themselves.

Fifth gear: Intercourse. Fifth gear involves intercourse but is conceptualized differently than the "sex equals intercourse" perspective in that it is considered merely as one dimension of pleasure-oriented touch. Some couples hurry through the first four gears in a race to intercourse (called "sexual drag racing"). Some couples transition to intercourse soon after reaching a high enough level that they can have intercourse, usually at level 5 on the 10-point arousal scale, though couples can learn to savor the pleasure-oriented touch of various types and not transition to intercourse until they are highly aroused, at 7 or 8 on the 10-point scale. Intercourse then occurs as part of a continuing erotic flow. Further, couples who enjoy multiple stimulation techniques during pleasuring can incorporate these behaviors during intercourse to enhance sexual function and satisfaction.

Touch is an invitation to share pleasure. Learning about each other's touch will help a couple nurture and develop their sexual style. The McCarthys state that "in celebrating the everyday joys of loving each other and incorporating all five dimensions of touch into your relationship, you can learn to value a variable, flexible sexuality, which maintains couple vitality and satisfaction" (p. 31).

Think Critically

1. What message does the "intercourse or nothing" stance convey to men and women? And what would be the benefits of dismissing this concept?

2. Why do many couples fall into the "sexual drag racing" trap?

3. What can be done to help couples accept and value all of the "gears of connection"?

satisfaction. Actually, the higher frequency of kissing was more strongly related to greater relationship quality than higher occurrence of sexual intercourse, although both predicted relationship quality to greater relationship quality. Interestingly, the study also found that although kissing did cause sexual arousal, it was not the primary driver for kissing (Wlodarski & Dunbar, 2013).

The lips and mouth are highly sensitive to touch and are exquisitely erotic parts of our bodies. Kisses discover, explore, and excite the body. They also involve the senses of taste and smell, which are especially important because they activate unconscious memories and associations. Often, we are aroused by familiar smells associated with particular sexual memories, such as a person's body scent or a perfume or fragrance. In some languages—among the Borneans, for example—the word "kiss" literally translates as "smell." In fact, among the Eskimos and the Maoris of New Zealand, there is no mouth kissing, only the touching of noses to facilitate smelling.

If it's uplift you're after, if it's that thrust, stop talking, put lips and tongue to other use.

—Horace
(65–8 BCE)

Although kissing may appear innocent, it is in many ways the height of intimacy. The adolescent's first kiss is often regarded as a milestone, a rite of passage, the beginning of adult sexuality. It is an important developmental step, marking the beginning of a young person's sexuality. (To find out the meanings of kissing, including their first kiss, among a sample of college students, see the "Think About It" box "The First Kiss: A Deal Breaker?")

Ordinary kissing is considered safer sex. French kissing is probably safe, unless the kiss is hard and draws blood or either partner has open sores or cuts in or around the mouth.

Oral-Genital Sex

As for the topsy turvy tangle known as soixante-neuf, personally I have always felt it to be madly confusing, like trying to pat your head and rub your stomach at the same time.

—Helen Lawrenson
(1904–1982)

In recent years, oral sex has become a part of many people's sexual scripts. The two types of **oral-genital sex** are cunnilingus and fellatio, which may be performed singly or simultaneously. Recall that cunnilingus is the erotic stimulation of a woman's vulva and/or clitoris by her partner's mouth and tongue. Recall, too, that fellatio is the oral stimulation of a man's penis by his partner's sucking and licking. When two people orally stimulate each other simultaneously, their activity is sometimes called "sixty-nine." The term comes from the configuration "69," which visually suggests the activity.

For people of every orientation (high school and college students), oral sex is an increasingly important aspect of their sexual selves. The percentages of American men and women who received oral sex in the past year from either a man or a woman and gave oral sex to either a man or a woman, by the 10 NSSHB age groups, are shown in Table 3. Also, the percentages of men and women aged 18–39 who had ever given oral sex to a partner or received oral sex from a partner are shown in Figures 5 and 6.

According to a study of nearly 2,000 college students, almost all of the students who had ever had sexual intercourse had also engaged in oral sex, in contrast to only about one in four virgins having had oral sex (Chambers, 2007). In comparing both sexes, men reported more pleasure in receiving and giving oral sex than women. Nearly all of the sample cited the pleasure of their partner as the most important reason they gave or received oral sex. The study also found that the students, particularly the women, perceived oral sex as less intimate than intercourse. Most study participants noted that they felt comfortable engaging in oral sex in a committed relationship.

think
about it

The First Kiss: A Deal-Breaker?

The decision to kiss for the first time is the most critical in any love story. It changes the relationship of two people more strongly than even the final surrender, because this kiss already has in it that surrender.

—Emil Ludwin
(1881–1948)

Is there more to kissing than just lips touching? Surprisingly, there has been little scientific research on this topic, although philosophers have written about "the kiss" for centuries. However, a seminal study on college students and kissing published in the scientific journal *Evolutionary Psychology* revealed that a lot of information is exchanged during kissing (Hughes, Harrison, & Gallup, 2007). The study, involving in-depth interviews, provided a descriptive account of kissing behavior in a sample of 1,041 undergraduate students (limited to those indicating kissing preference only or mostly with the other sex) at a large university in the eastern United States. About 70% of the students reported kissing 6 or more people, and 20% estimated to have kissed more than 20 people; no differences were found between men and women in the number of kissing partners or the age of first romantic kiss.

An intriguing finding of the study was that the majority of both men and women noted that a bad kiss is a "deal-breaker," often leading to the ending of a potential new relationship. Slightly more women than men—66% versus 59%—said they were attracted to someone until they kissed the person, then they were no longer interested. One of the study's researchers, Gordon Gallup, stated that while a kiss may not make a relationship, it can kill one and that "there may be unconscious mechanisms that would make people make an assessment of genetic compatibility through a kiss" (Gordon, quoted in Best, 2007). Another study of 904 men and women, aged 18–63 years (mean = 25 years), showed similar results: Women were more likely than men to restate that a first kiss would affect their attraction to a potential mate (Wlodarski & Dunbar, 2013).

The research by Hughes and colleagues (2007) suggests that the meanings associated with kissing vary considerably between men and women. In this study, women placed more significance on kissing as a way of assessing the person as a potential mating partner and as a means of initiating, bonding, maintaining, and monitoring the current status of a long-term relationship. Men, on the other hand, placed less emphasis on kissing, especially with short-term partners, and appeared to use kissing as a means to an end—that is, to gain sexual access. About one half of the men, in contrast to one third of the women, assumed that kissing would lead to sex whether they were in a short-term or long-term relationship. Gallup notes that kissing for males is one way of keeping their partners physically interested, stating that "as a consequence of male saliva exchange extending over a long period of time, it's conceivable that the testosterone in male saliva can stimulate female sex hormones and make females more receptive to sex" (Gordon, quoted in Best, 2007).

Other notable gender differences found in the study were the following:

- Taste and smell of the person were more important to women.
- Women were more likely to rebuff sex with a partner unless they kissed first.
- More women indicated that they would refuse to have sex with a bad kisser.
- Men were more likely to desire exchanging saliva during a kiss, showing greater preference for tongue contact and open-mouth kissing.
- Men were more likely to believe that kissing could stop a fight.
- More men felt that it was OK to kiss on the first date and it was OK for the female partner to make the move for the first kiss.

The first kiss is a memorable, once-in-a-lifetime experience. A study of 356 heterosexual students at a large university in the western United States examined the emotional responses that commonly accompany the first kiss (Regan, Shen, De La Pena, & Gosset, 2007). The researchers found that most reported an array of emotions—dread, nervousness, fright, awkwardness, and confusion—as they approached their first kiss. They found that emotions shifted during the kiss. For men, their anxiety and fear were replaced with elation, happiness, sexual arousal, enjoyment, and other positive feelings. Women experienced a mixed reaction: disgust, uncertainty, boredom, enjoyment, tenderness, and excitement. Following the first kiss, most men continued to feel positive responses, but some experienced embarrassment and other negative feelings. For women, although many reported positive feelings, negative responses such as disappointment, regret, and distress were more commonly experienced.

Think Critically

1. Do you agree that a bad first kiss can be a potentially new relationship "deal-breaker"? Has this happened to you?
2. How important is kissing to you in a relationship?
3. What is a good kiss? Should a kiss lead to sexual intercourse?
4. What were your experiences with your first kiss?

SOURCES: Best, K. (2007, December 17). Kiss and tell: Smooches make or break a relationship. *Indianapolis Star*, p. E1; Hughes, S. M., Harrison, M. A., & Gallup, G. G. (2007). Sex differences in romantic kissing among college students: An evolutionary perspective. *Evolutionary Psychology, 5*, 612–631; Regan, P. C., Shen, W., De La Pena, E., & Gosset, E. (2007). "Fireworks exploded in my mouth": Affective responses before, during, and after the very first kiss. *International Journal of Sexual Health, 19*(2), 1–16; Wlodarski, R., & Dubar, R. I. M. (2013). Examining the possible function of kissing in romantic relationships. *Archive of Sexual Behavior.* doi: 10.1007/s10508-013-0190-1.

● FIGURE 8

Cunnilingus.

Cunnilingus In **cunnilingus,** a woman's genitals are stimulated by her partner's tongue and mouth, which gently and rhythmically caress and lick her clitoris and the surrounding area (see Figure 8). During arousal, the mouth and lips can nibble, lick, and kiss the inner thighs, stomach, and mons pubis and then move to the sensitive labia minora clitoral area. Orgasm may be brought on by rhythmically stimulating the clitoris. During cunnilingus, some women also enjoy insertion of a finger into the vagina or anus for extra stimulation. Many women find cunnilingus to be the easiest way to reach orgasm because it provides such intense stimulation.

Some women, however, have concerns regarding cunnilingus. The most common worries revolve around whether the other person is enjoying it and, especially, whether the vulva has an unpleasant odor. Concerns about vaginal odors may be eased by washing. Undeodorized white soap will wash away unpleasant smells without disturbing the vagina's natural, erotic scent. If an unpleasant odor arises from the genitals, it may be because the woman has a vaginal infection.

A woman may also worry that her partner is not enjoying the experience because he or she is giving pleasure rather than receiving it. What she may not recognize is that such sexual excitement is often mutual. Because our mouths and tongues are erotically sensitive, the giver finds erotic excitement in arousing his or her partner.

An interview study of 43 college women explored women's attitudes toward and experiences with cunnilingus (Backstrom, Armstrong, & Puentes, 2012). The authors note that contemporary sexual scripts of college students assume cunnilingus will occur in relationships but not in hookups, where this behavior is more frequently contested. The interviews found that tension occurred when the desire for cunnilingus contradicted the relationship's sexual script. Major study findings included the following:

- The taken-for-granted assumption of cunnilingus in relationships was a source of pleasure for women who enjoyed it but a source of difficulty for those who wished to not participate in the behavior.

- In relationships, some women's reluctance for cunnilingus was negated by men's enthusiasm for the behavior.

- Women who wanted cunnilingus in hookups had to be assertive to receive it, whereas those not desiring cunnilingus were relieved that the partner did not expect this behavior.

Fellatio In **fellatio,** a man's penis is taken into his partner's mouth. The partner licks the glans penis and gently stimulates the shaft (see Figure 9). Also, the scrotum may be gently licked. If the penis is not erect, it usually will become erect within a short time. The partner sucks more vigorously as excitement increases, down toward the base of the penis and then back up, in a rhythmical motion, being careful not to bite hard or scrape the penis with the teeth. While the man is being stimulated by mouth, his partner can also stroke the shaft of the penis by hand. Gently playing with the testicles is also arousing as long as they are not held too tightly. As in cunnilingus, the couple should experiment to discover what is most stimulating and exciting. The man should be careful not to thrust his penis too deeply into his partner's throat, for that may cause a gag reflex. He should let his partner control how deeply the penis goes into the mouth. The partner can do this by grasping the penis below his or her lips so that the depth of insertion can be controlled. Furthermore, gagging is less likely when the one performing fellatio is on top. The gag reflex can also be reconditioned by slowly inserting the penis into the mouth at increasing depth over time. Some women feel that fellatio is more intimate than sexual intercourse; others feel that it is less intimate. It is the most common form of sexual activity performed on men by prostitutes (Monto, 2001). Most men find fellatio to be highly arousing.

● **FIGURE 9**
Fellatio.

For gay men, fellatio is an important component of their sexuality. As with sexual intercourse for heterosexual men, however, fellatio is only one activity in their sexual repertoire. Generally, the more often gay couples engage in giving and receiving oral sex, the more satisfied they are. Because oral sex often involves power symbolism, reciprocity is important. If one partner always performs oral sex, he may feel he is subordinate to the other. The most satisfied gay couples alternate between giving and receiving oral sex.

A common concern about fellatio centers around ejaculation. Should a man ejaculate into his partner's mouth? Some people find semen to be slightly bitter, but others like it. Some find it exciting to suck even harder on the penis during or following ejaculation; others do not like the idea of semen in the mouth. For many, a key issue is whether to swallow the semen. Some swallow it; others spit it out. It is simply a matter of personal preference, and the man who is receiving fellatio should accept his partner's feelings about it and avoid equating a dislike for swallowing semen with a personal rejection.

Some men try to provide oral stimulation to their own penis, a practice called **autofellatio.** Kinsey and his colleagues (1948) found that many males try this behavior, but less than 1% of their sample were actually able to achieve it.

Sexual Intercourse

Sexual intercourse is another name for vaginal intercourse, penile-vaginal intercourse, or **coitus**. Sometimes, "sexual intercourse" is also used to describe penile-anal sex. But for our discussion here, we mean penile-vaginal intercourse when we use the term "sexual intercourse." Sexual intercourse has intense personal meaning; it is a source of pleasure, communication, connection, and love. If forced, however, it becomes an instrument of aggression and pain. Its meaning changes depending on the context in which we engage in it. How we feel about sexual intercourse may depend as much on the feelings and motives we bring to it as on the techniques we use or the orgasms we experience. As sexual intercourse is the most valued and sought-after sexual behavior among persons desiring sex with the other sex, the prevalence of sexual intercourse is very high, as shown in Table 3 and Figures 5 and 6.

> Sex is the great amateur art.
>
> —David Cort

The Significance of Sexual Intercourse Although sexual intercourse is important for most sexually involved couples, the significance of it often differs between men and women. For many men, "sex equals intercourse" and its occurrence is the pass-fail performance test. Most men have one orgasm that occurs during the intercourse part of a sexual episode. For many heterosexual women, however, intercourse is the most central but not the only component of their sexual satisfaction. More than any other heterosexual sexual activity, sexual intercourse can involve equal participation by both partners. Both partners equally and simultaneously give and receive. As a result, a woman may feel greater shared intimacy than she does in other sexual activities. McCarthy and McCarthy (2009) state that it is most important to view intercourse as a natural extension of the pleasuring and eroticism process.

> The sexual embrace can only be compared with music and prayer.
>
> —Havelock Ellis
> (1859–1939)

The Positions The playfulness of the couple, their movement from one bodily configuration to another, and their ingenuity can provide an infinite variety of sexual intercourse positions. The same positions played out in different settings can cause an intensity that transforms the ordinary into the extraordinary.

The most common position is face-to-face with the man on top (see Figure 10). Many people prefer this position, for several reasons. First, it is the traditional, correct, or "official" position in our culture, which many people find reassuring and validating in terms of their sexuality. The man-on-top position is commonly

● **FIGURE** 10

Face-to-Face, Man on Top.

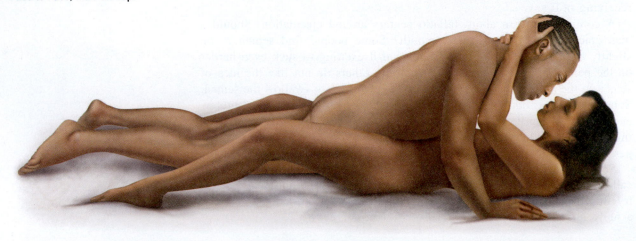

known as the missionary position because it was the position missionaries traditionally encouraged people to use. Second, it can allow the man maximum activity, movement, and control of coitus. Third, it allows the woman freedom to stimulate her clitoris to assist in her orgasm. The primary disadvantages are that it makes it difficult for the man to caress his partner or to stimulate her clitoris while supporting himself with his hands and for the woman to control the angle, rate, and depth of penetration. Furthermore, some men have difficulty controlling ejaculation in this position, because the penis is highly stimulated.

Another common position is face-to-face with the woman on top (see Figure 11). The woman either lies on top of her partner or sits astride him. This position allows the woman maximum activity, movement, and control. She can control the depth to which the penis penetrates. Additionally, when the woman sits astride her partner, either of them can caress or stimulate her labia and clitoris, thus facilitating orgasm in the woman. As with the man-on-top position, kissing is easy. A disadvantage is that some men or women may feel uneasy about the woman assuming a position that signifies an active role in coitus. This position tends to be less stimulating for the man, thus making it easier for him to control ejaculation.

Intercourse can also be performed with the man positioned behind the woman. There are several variations on the rear-entry position. The woman may kneel supported on her arms and receive the penis in her vagina from behind. The couple may lie on their sides, with the woman's back to her partner (see Figure 12). This position offers variety and may be particularly suitable during pregnancy because it minimizes pressure on the woman's abdomen.

" When I said I had sex for seven hours, that included dinner and a movie.

—Phil Collins
(1951–)

● **FIGURE 11**
Face-to-Face, Woman on Top.

• **FIGURE 12**
Rear Entry.

This position facilitates clitoral stimulation by the woman. Generally, it is also possible for the man to stimulate her during intercourse.

In the face-to-face side position, both partners lie on their sides, facing each other (see Figure 13). Each partner has greater freedom to caress and stimulate the other. As with the rear-entry position, a major drawback is that keeping the penis in the vagina may be difficult.

Tantric sex is a type of sexual intimacy based on Eastern religious beliefs beginning in India around 5000 BCE. The tantric sex technique involves the couple sharing their "energies" by initially thrusting minimally, generating energy via subtle, inner sexual movements. They visualize the energy of the genitals moving upward in their bodies (see Figure 14). The couple may harmonize their breathing and achieve intimacy (often looking into each other's eyes), ecstasy, and abandon. Many books have been written on tantric sex, and numerous websites are devoted to it.

● **FIGURE** 14
Tantric Sex.

Anal Eroticism

Anal eroticism refers to sexual activities involving the anus, whose delicate membranes, as well as taboo nature, make it erotically arousing for many people. These activities include **analingus,** the licking of the anal region colloquially known as "rimming" or "tossing salad." Anal-manual contact consists of stimulating the anal region with the fingers; sometimes, an entire fist may be inserted (known as "fisting" among gay White males and "fingering" among gay African American males). Many couples engage in this activity along with fellatio or sexual intercourse. Though little is known about the prevalence of this activity, many report it to be highly arousing because of the sensitivity of the skin around the anus. Keeping this area clean is extremely important because the intestinal tract, which extends to the anus, carries a variety of microorganisms.

Anal intercourse refers to the male's inserting his erect penis into his partner's anus (see Figure 15). Both heterosexual people and gay men participate

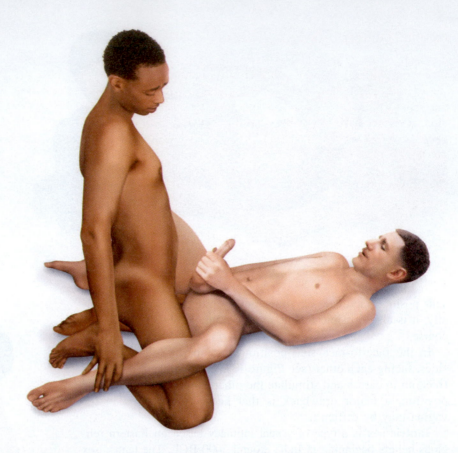

in anal intercourse. The prevalence of anal intercourse in the 10 NSSHB age groups in the past year is shown in Table 3. For the 18–39 NSSHB age groups (Figures 5 and 6), about 4 in 10 men reported ever having been the insertive partner during anal intercourse with a male or female partner. Likewise, about 4 in 10 women reported ever having experienced anal intercourse (Reece et al., 2010.9a).

Anal intercourse is prevalent among gay men, although studies have shown it is less common than oral sex. For example, a British study found that, for the past year, slightly more than half of men who have sex with men reported having anal sex (57% of insertive partners, 54% of receptive partners) and about 7 in 10 reported engaging in oral sex (71% of insertive partners, 71% of receptive partners) (Mercer et al., 2004). An Australian study of the most recent same-sex behavior among men who have sex with men found that about one third of encounters involved anal intercourse (38% of insertive partners, 30% of receptive partners) with about three quarters involving oral sex (76% of insertive partners, 76% of receptive partners) (Grulich, de Visser, Smith, Rissel, & Richters, 2003). Although heterosexual imagery portrays the person who penetrates as "masculine" and the penetrated person as "feminine," this imagery does not generally reflect gay reality. For both partners, anal intercourse is regarded as masculine.

Although anal sex may heighten eroticism for those who engage in it, from a health perspective, it is riskier than most other forms of sexual interaction. The rectum is particularly susceptible to STI.

Health Benefits of Sexual Activity

Throughout this chapter and others in this textbook, we have emphasized ways to enhance sexual pleasure. And, certainly, experiencing sexual pleasure is a powerful motive itself to participate in sexual activity. When sex is fun, it brings a unique joy and satisfaction. But beyond the pleasure reward of sexual expression, does sex have health benefits? Physician Eric Braverman, author of the book *Younger (Sexier) You* (2011), states that "sex is like an electric charge, and an orgasm is like rebooting your entire computer, powering up your health in multiple ways." Braverman contends that being sexually active can help keep one younger by decreasing stress, enhancing intimacy in relationships, and keeping hormone levels up, including testosterone, estrogen, and oxytocin, the "love hormone."

Persons who frequently engage in sexual activity are reported to experience numerous benefits, such as a longer life, a healthier heart, a better defense against illnesses, pain relief, lower blood pressure, a healthier body weight, lower risk of prostate cancer, better cognitive skills, better hormone levels, lower risk of breast cancer, and more satisfying relationships (Braverman, 2011; Brody, 2010; Cohen, 2010; Jannini, Fisher, Bitzer, & McMahon, 2009; Whipple, Knowles, & Davis, 2007). But does good sex enhance health or does good health make sex more frequent and pleasurable? Sex researcher Beverly Whipple states that "it is not entirely clear whether sex makes people healthier, or whether healthy people tend to have more sex" (Whipple et al., 2007). Nearly all of the studies on the health benefits of sex are correlational; that is, they show a relationship but not cause and effect (Jannini et al., 2009). Nevertheless, what we can say with some certainly is that good sex and good health reinforce each other (Braverman, 2011).

Final Thoughts

As we have seen, sexual behaviors cannot be separated from attraction and desire. Our autoerotic activities are as important to our sexuality as are our interpersonal ones. Although the sexual behaviors we have examined in this chapter are the most common ones in our society, many people engage in other, less typical activities. We discuss these atypical behaviors subsequently.

Summary

Sexual Attractiveness

- The characteristics that constitute sexual attractiveness vary across cultures. Youthfulness and good health appear to be the only universals. Body symmetry and smell are important to sexual attraction. Our culture prefers slender women with large breasts and men who are muscular but not too brawny. A study on the importance of attractiveness and status found that heterosexual men valued attractiveness the most, followed by homosexual men, heterosexual women, and homosexual women.

- *Hooking up* and *friends with benefits* relationships are increasingly becoming common on college campuses and have numerous advantages and disadvantages.
- Sexual desire is affected by *erotophilia,* a positive emotional response to sex, and by *erotophobia,* a negative response to sex.

Sexual Scripts

- *Sexual scripts* organize our sexual expression. They have three major components: cultural, intrapersonal, and interpersonal. The cultural script provides the general forms sexual behaviors are expected to take in a particular society. The intrapersonal script interprets our physiological responses as sexual or not. The interpersonal script is the shared conventions and signals that make sexual activities between two people possible.

Autoeroticism

- *Autoeroticism* refers to sexual activities that involve only oneself. These activities include sexual fantasies, erotic dreams and *nocturnal orgasm,* and *masturbation,* or stimulation of the genitals for pleasure. Persons practicing various types of autoerotic activity are also more likely to report enacting more elaborate interpersonal sexual scripts.
- Sexual fantasies and dreams are probably the most universal of all sexual behaviors; they are normal aspects of our sexuality. Erotic fantasies have several functions: They take our generalized sexual drives and help define and direct them, they allow us to plan or anticipate erotic situations, they provide pleasurable escape from routine, they introduce novelty, and they offer clues to our unconscious.
- Most men and women masturbate. Masturbation may begin as early as infancy and continue throughout old age and can be practiced alone or in a partnered relationship.

Sexual Behavior With Others

- Each couple develops their own sexual style, although it may take several months for that to occur. Four common couple styles are complimentary, traditional, soulmate, and emotionally expressive.
- Sexual intercourse is the most appealing sexual activity for both female and male heterosexuals, although there are several dimensions of pleasure-oriented touching.
- The erotic potential of touching has been undervalued, especially among males, because our culture tends to be orgasm-oriented.
- Erotic kissing is usually our earliest interpersonal sexual experience and is regarded as a rite of passage into adult sexuality. Higher frequency of kissing is related to greater relationship quality.
- *Oral-genital sex* is becoming increasingly accepted, especially among young adults. Cunnilingus is the stimulation of the vulva with the tongue and mouth. It is engaged in by both men and women. Fellatio is the stimulation of the penis with the mouth; it is engaged in by both men and women.
- *Sexual intercourse* can be an intimate and rewarding interaction between two people. It is both a means of reproduction and a pleasurable form of communication.
- *Anal eroticism* refers to sexual activities involving the anus. It is engaged in by heterosexuals, gay men, and lesbian women.
- Good health and good sex are highly associated with each other.

Questions for Discussion

- What is your sexual script relative to initiating sexual behavior with another person? Do you always want to take the lead, or are you comfortable with the other person doing that or sharing in initiating the sexual behavior?

- How often do you fantasize about sex? Are you comfortable about your fantasies? Have you ever shared them with anyone?

- What can be done to help persons become more accepting of pleasure-oriented touching that does not include intercourse?

Sex and the Internet

WebMD Sexual and Relationships Center

A well-done and comprehensive website, the WebMD Sex and Relationship Center offers the latest information on several topics such as health benefits of sex, relationship savers, getting in the mood, dating after divorce, emotional infidelity, and dating deal-breakers. A top story section features recent research studies. The site also has the WebMD Sex and Relationship Community, with two parts: Second Opinion (e.g., When Is a Relationship Worth Saving?) and Communities (e.g., Relationships and Coping Community, Sexual Health Community). Visit this website (http://www.webmd.com/sex-relationships) and find out the following:

- What is the featured news story?
- What are the recent Top Stories?
- Which Top 12 Concerns topic interests you the most?
- Which WebMD Sex and Relationships Community interests you the most?

Suggested Websites

Hooking Up Smart

http://www.hookingupsmart.com
Supports women and men in their search for meaningful relationships by providing strategic insight and perspective as they manage their social and sexual interactions.

JackinWorld

http://www.jackinworld.com
Provides articles, forums, questions and answers, and surveys related to masturbation.

iVillage Love and Sex

http://www.ivillage.com/love-sex
Provides information on a broad range of sexuality and relationship issues, top stories on love and sex, and suggestions for enhancing sexual pleasure. Click on the "Love" section.

Tantra.com

http://tantra.com
An online resource for tantric sex, tantra, and the Kama Sutra as well as numerous commercial products for enhancing sexual expression.

Suggested Reading

Braverman, E. R. (2011). *Younger (sexier) you.* New York: Rodale. A physician offers a plan for restoring and invigorating one's sexual life.

Corwin, G. (2010). *Sexual intimacy for women: A guide for same-sex couples.* Berkeley, CA: Seal. Written by a clinical psychologist, this book includes exercises and client-based anecdotes to help women in same-sex relationships increase intimacy.

Giles, J. (2008). *The nature of sexual desire.* Lanham, MD: University Press of America. Sexual desire is explored from a psychological, philosophical, and anthropological perspective and in relation to sexual interaction, erotic pleasure, the experience of gender, and romantic love.

Groy, P. B., & Garcia, J. R. (2013). *Evolution and human sexual behavior.* Cambridge, MA: Harvard University Press. Provides an interdisciplinary synthesis of the latest discoveries in evolutionary theory, genetics, neuroscience, comparative primate research, and cross-cultural sexuality studies.

Joannides, P. (2015). *Guide to getting it on* (7th ed.). Waldport, OR: Goofy Foot Press. A very popular and thorough sex manual that has been translated into over 10 languages; has superb anatomical and sexual behavior drawings.

Kirshenbaum, S. (2011). *The science of kissing: What our lips are telling us.* New York: Grand Central. A noted science journalist presents a wonderful, witty, and fascinating exploration of how and why we kiss.

McCarthy, B. W., & McCarthy, E. (2009). *Discovering your couple sexual style.* New York: Routledge. The goal of this book is to assist persons to discover and enjoy their couple sexual style.

Moalem, S. (2009). *How sex works.* New York: HarperCollins. Discusses, in a popular writing style, the psychological, relationship, biological, and historical aspects of numerous sex topics while blending in anecdotes.

Northrup, C., Schwartz, P., & Witte, J. (2012). *The Normal Bar: The Surprising Secrets of Happy Couples and What They Reveal About Creating a New Normal in Your Relationship.* New York: Harmony. This book answers what constitutes "normal" behavior among happy couples. Based on data from nearly 100,000 respondents, the book offers readers an array of perspective tools that will help them establish a "new normal."

10

Variations in Sexual Behavior

© Mark Wragg/Getty Images

CHAPTER OUTLINE

"I do like sex a lot, but I wouldn't call myself addicted. I think an addiction to sex would only be a bad thing in the event that it's interfering with other parts of a person's life."

—27-year-old male

"I think that some fetishes are good and healthy. I really don't think that someone who is turned on by feet or a pair of shoes is wrong. I do have a major problem with those who are into bondage because that is just sick."

—21-year-old female

"I really don't think that atypical sex exists. Everyone should find what feels good and natural for them; others' opinions and statistics shouldn't matter."

—20-year-old male

"From my point of view, fetishism misses the main point of sex: physical pleasure and emotional closeness. This sort of 'erotic communion' of sensation and emotion can be wholly fulfilling without the bells and whistles of whips, diapers, or anything else. To me, fetishism brings psychological incompleteness to the bedroom. It carries childhood problems, unresolved conflicts, and past trauma into an arena best suited for the psychologist's couch."

—23-year-old female

"My boyfriend always thought that having his feet licked would be weird and gross. I'd never tried it or had it done to me, but I'd heard a lot of people really love it, so on Valentine's day, I tried it. Now he likes it almost as much as oral sex. In fact, he gets excited when he hears me walking around barefoot!"

—20-year-old female

SEXUALITY CAN BE EXPRESSED in a variety of ways, some more common than others. Many of the less common behaviors have been negatively labeled by the public, often implying that the behavior is unnatural, pathological, or "perverted." In this chapter, we examine variations in sexual behavior that are not within the range of sexual expression in which people typically engage, including fetishism, exhibitionism, sexual masochism, and sexual sadism. We then turn to issues such as college students and voyeurism, sexual addiction, and BDSM, to name a few. We discuss these and other topics though a variety of perspectives with the intent distinguishing between the clinical, judgmental, or causal connotations of terms.

> There is hardly anyone whose sexual life, if it were broadcast, would not fill the world at large with surprise and horror.
>
> —Somerset Maugham
> (1874–1965)

● Sexual Variations and Paraphilic Behavior

The range of human sexual behavior is almost infinite. Yet most of our activities and fantasies, such as intercourse, oral-genital sex, and masturbation, cluster within the general range of our predominant cultural and social sexual norms. Those behaviors and fantasies that do not fall within this general range are considered variations. In this chapter and throughout the textbook, we use the term **sexual variations** to refer to those behaviors that are not *statistically* typical of American sexual behaviors or that occur in addition to the "mainstream" expression of sexuality.

What Are Sexual Variations?

"Sexual variation" is the most common term used, although terms like **atypical sexual behavior** or *kinky sex* are used. It is important to note, however, that atypical does not necessarily mean abnormal; it simply means that the majority of people do not engage in that behavior or that it occurs outside of the culturally sanctioned sexual behaviors. Even though today's society is less judgmental about sex, resulting in people who engage in sexual variations feeling less shame and guilt, some sexual variations are considered to be so extreme by the American Psychiatric Association (APA) that they are classified as mental

> It is very disturbing indeed when you can't think of any new perversions that you would like to practice.
>
> —James Pickey
> (1923–1997)

disorders. Classifying out-of-the-ordinary sexual behavior as deviant is not new. Psychiatry has long classified some sexual behaviors as mental disorders (De Block & Adriaens, 2013), and there continues to be debate among psychiatry and scientific communities about which sexual behaviors are and are not pathological (Belluck & Carey, 2013; Drescher, 2014; Voosen, 2013).

What Is Paraphilia?

The *Diagnostic and Statistical Manual of Mental Disorders, Fifth Edition (DSM-5)*, published by the American Psychiatric Association (APA, 2013), defines **paraphilia** as "any intense and persistent sexual interest other than sexual interest in genital stimulation or preparatory fondling with phenotypically normal, physically mature consenting human partners." The paraphilia is thus an out-of-the-ordinary sexual behavior that does not necessarily need psychiatric treatment. The *DSM-5* maintains the basic types of paraphilias from the prior edition but alters how they are diagnosed. *DSM-5* distinguishes between paraphilias, which are considered to be relatively harmless, and paraphilic disorders, which are considered harmful sexual behaviors. A **paraphilic disorder** is defined as "a paraphilia that is currently causing distress or impairment to the individual or a paraphilia whose satisfaction has entailed personal harm, or risk of harm, to others." Furthermore, in order to be considered paraphilic, the disorder needs to be recurrent, that is, occurring over a period of at least 6 months. The *DSM-5* notes that when an individual with a particular paraphilic impulse does not declare personal distress, has no impairment in functioning, and has no history of acting on the paraphilic urge, the person would be considered to have **paraphilic sexual interest** (e.g., fetishism sexual interest) but not a paraphilic disorder. For further discussion of the change of the views toward sexual variation and paraphilias, see the "Think About It" box. "Classifying Variant Sexual Behaviors as Paraphilia: The Changing Views of Psychology."

The distinction between a sexual interest, variation, or behavior that might be classified as a paraphilia as opposed to a paraphilic disorder is sometimes vague and often more a difference of degree than kind. For example, many men find that certain objects, such as black lingerie, intensify their sexual arousal; for other men, these objects are necessary for sexual arousal. In the first case, nothing is particularly unusual or harmful. But if the fetishistic fantasies, urges, or behaviors cause significant distress, lasts at least 6 months and is recurrent, the behavior would be considered a fetishistic disorder in the *DMS-5* (APA, 2013).

Table 1 lists eight of the most common, as well as six less common, paraphilias. To minimize the negative message of labeling and to recognize individuals' many components, it seems more appropriate to use the term "person with paraphilia" than "paraphiliac." This is the term we will use in this textbook.

For people with a paraphilia, the paraphilic behavior is the predominant sexual behavior, although they may participate in other sexual activities as well. They may engage in the paraphilic behavior every day or several times a day, or they may participate in two or more paraphilic behaviors (APA, 2013). Even though the behavior may lead to legal or interpersonal difficulties, it may be so rewarding and irresistible that they continue to practice it. Typically, persons with paraphilias feel that urges to participate in the behaviors are insistent, obsessional, or compulsory (Lehne, 2009). Mild versions of paraphilias may manifest only in disturbing fantasies, often occurring during masturbation. Severe versions can include sexual victimization of children and the use of threats or force with other adults (Seligman & Hardenberg, 2000).

TABLE 1 • Paraphilias

Most Common Paraphilias	Sexual Arousal Activity
Exhibitionism	Exposing one's genitals to an unsuspecting person
Fetishism	Using an inanimate object or focus on nongenital body parts
Frotteurism	Touching or rubbing sexually against a nonconsenting person in public places
Pedophilia	Having a sexual focus on a prepubescent child or children
Sexual masochism	Being humiliated, beaten, bound, or otherwise made to suffer
Sexual sadism	Inflicting psychological or physical suffering upon another person
Transvestism	Cross-dressing in clothing of the other sex
Voyeurism	Observing an unsuspecting person who is naked, disrobing, or having sex

Less Common Paraphilias	Sexual Arousal Activity
Coprophilia	Being sexually aroused from use of feces
Klismaphilia	Being sexual aroused from having enemas
Necrophilia	Having sexual activity with dead bodies
Telephone scatologia	Making sexual and obscene phone calls
Urophilia	Being sexually aroused from sight or thought of urine
Zoophilia	Having sexual activity with nonhuman animals (bestiality)

The overwhelming majority of people with paraphilic behaviors are males (Logan, 2008); they are most likely to engage in paraphilic activities between the ages of 15 and 25. Paraphilic disorders are diagnosed in all ethnic and socioeconomic groups and among all sexual orientations.

One important aspect of paraphilias is whether they involve coercion. **Noncoercive paraphilias** are regarded as relatively benign or harmless because they are victimless; that is, they involve only oneself or another consenting adult. Few noncoercive paraphilias are brought to public attention because of their private, victimless nature. Typically, domination and submission, fetishism, and transvestism are considered noncoercive paraphilias. Victimizing, or **coercive, paraphilias** represent nonconsensual sexual activity, such as voyeurism, exhibitionism, sexual masochism, sexual sadism, zoophilia, telephone scatologia, frotteurism, necrophilia, and pedophilia. These behaviors are a source of concern for society because of the harm they cause others.

It is also important to recognize that seemingly scientific or clinical terms may not be scientific at all. Instead, they may be pseudoscientific terms hiding moral judgments, as in the case of "nymphomania" and "satyriasis." **Nymphomania** is a pejorative term referring to "abnormal or excessive" sexual desire in a woman and is usually applied to sexually active single women. But what is "abnormal" or "excessive" is often defined moralistically rather than scientifically. Nymphomania is not recognized as a clinical condition by the APA (2013), as the term is based on prejudice, double standards, and male chauvinism (Kaplan & Krueger, 2010). Although the term "nymphomania" dates back

Of all the sexual aberrations, the most peculiar is chastity.

—Remy de Gourmont
(1858–1915)

think
about it

Classifying Variant Sexual Behaviors as Paraphilia: The Changing Views of Psychology

Over the past 150 years, American and European psychiatrists have conceptualized and categorized what they consider to be sexual deviance. Numerous sexual preferences, desires, and behaviors were pathologized and depathologized during that time, revealing psychiatry's constant and continuing challenge to distinguish out-of-the-ordinary sexual behavior from immoral, unethical, or illegal sexual behavior. This struggle is revealed in the works of nineteenth- and early twentieth-century psychiatrists and sexologists, as well as in more recent psychiatric textbooks and diagnostic manuals such as the *Diagnostic and Statistical Manual of Mental Disorders* (DSM) published by the American Psychiatric Association (De Block & Adriaens, 2013).

Since the APA began listing certain variant sexual behaviors as "paraphilia" in its 1980 edition of the DSM, the paraphilia construct has been widely critiqued. Critics of the DSM paraphilias contend that the listing of behaviors as paraphilic is merely an attempt to pathologize sexual behaviors not approved of by society. As noted previously, the most recent DSM version, *DSM-5* (APA, 2013), includes paraphilias but has changed how they are diagnosed. *DSM-5* distinguishes between relatively harmless and relatively harmful sexual behavior, resulting in two categories: paraphilia and paraphilic disorders.

Certain sexual behaviors were labeled mental disorders in earlier DSM editions but deleted in later editions (Byne, 2014; De Block & Adriaens, 2013; Drescher, 2014). A prime example of this involves the DSM's views on homosexuality. It was included in the DSM from the first edition until 1973, when it was removed as a mental disorder. A major change reflected in *DSM-5* is that the distinction between paraphilias and paraphilic disorders represents a greater acceptance of some unconventional sexual behaviors. For example, sexual masochism, sexual sadism, and fetishes are considered mental disorders only if they result in emotional distress and involve nonconsensual behaviors (Boskey, 2013).

Even though there has been increasing acceptance of certain sexual variant behaviors by the American Medical Association, the controversy over which behaviors represent mental disorders continues. Philosophy professors Andreas De Block and Pieter R. Adriaens (2013) state:

> The fact that the problem of distinguishing between sexual deviance and mental disorder keeps on haunting the literature has little to do with the scientific status of sexology, psychology, or psychiatry but rather with the hard-to-crack philosophical problem of defining (mental) disease and (mental health) (p. 294).

Think Critically

1. Do you believe that the DSM's classification of certain variant sexual behaviors as paraphilic disorders is "an attempt to pathologize sexual behaviors not approved by society" or a necessary way to address sexual behaviors that indeed represent mental illness and need medical or psychological/psychiatric treatment?

2. Where would you draw the line between out-of-the-ordinary sexual variation and sexual variation that is a mental disorder?

---

to the seventeenth century, it was popularized in the nineteenth century by Richard von Krafft-Ebing and others. Physicians and psychiatrists used the term to pathologize women's sexual behavior if it deviated from nineteenth-century moral standards.

American women with very strong sexual desire have been both largely ignored by researchers and stigmatized by society. However, an interview study of 44 highly sexual women aged 20–82 provided insights into their sexual lives and how their sexuality has affected them (Blumberg, 2003). "Highly sexual" was defined as a woman who either (1) typically desired sexual stimulation, usually to the point of orgasm, by herself or a partner six to seven times per week or more and acted upon the desire whenever possible or (2) thought of herself as a highly sexual person with sex often on her mind and considered her sexuality as an aspect that strongly and frequently affected her behavior, life choices, and quality of life satisfaction. The women reported that their lives had been strongly affected by their sexuality, that their sexual appetite was too intense to be ignored, and for some, it had a major impact on their time and energy. Many reported struggles and challenges in their lives because of their sexuality, including being labeled with historically pathologizing terms such as "nymphomaniac" and "sex addict," although the researcher conducting the interview concluded that neither the term "addiction" nor "compulsion" is applicable in describing these women. However, the women reported that their experiences as highly sexual women were filled with satisfactions and pleasure—in fact, each would not permanently change her sexuality if she had that option. The researcher also noted that many of the women indicated they wanted to participate in the study in hope that society would become more understanding and accepting of them and that other highly sexual women would become more accepting of themselves with less internal distress about their sexuality.

Satyriasis, referring to "abnormal" or "uncontrollable" sexual desire in men, is less commonly used than "nymphomania" because society has come to believe and expect men to be more sexual than women, resulting in less research interest in men's hypersexual behaviors and needs (Kelly, 2013). For this reason, definitions of satyriasis infrequently include the adjective "excessive." Instead, reflecting ideas of male sexuality as a powerful drive, "uncontrollable" becomes the significant adjective. Satyriasis is not recognized as a clinical condition by the APA (2013). Note that an alternative term more currently used than "nymphomania" or "satyriasis" is **hypersexuality,** meaning an excessive sex drive either in women or in men (Hyde & DeLamater, 2014). In recent years, some have labeled very highly sexual persons as being "sex addicts." To read a discussion about sex addiction, see the "Think About It" box "Sexual Addiction: Repressive Morality in a New Guise."

As you read this chapter, remember to distinguish clearly between the clinical, judgmental, or casual connotations of the various terms. It can be tempting to define a behavior you don't like or approve of as paraphilic. But, unless you are clinically trained, you cannot diagnose someone, including yourself, as having a mental disorder.

As touched on previously, the line between a sexual variation and a paraphilic disorder may not be exact and the "labeling" of specific behaviors as either may be open to debate and void of adequate scientific justification. Some mental health professionals believe that classifying some sexual behaviors as paraphilias is flawed and reflects a pseudoscientific attempt to control sexuality. However, for the sake of discussion, the presentation of sexual variation in this chapter is based on the paraphilias described in the *DSM-5*. Our discussion will first present an overview of each paraphilia, followed by the *DSM-5* criteria for paraphilic disorder.

● Types of Paraphilias

Fetishism

We attribute special or magical powers to many things: a lucky number, a saint's relic, an heirloom, a lock of hair, or an automobile. These objects possess a kind of symbolic magic. We will carry our boyfriend's or girlfriend's

> Through me forbidden voices.
> Voices of sexes and lusts . . .
> Voices veiled, and I remove the veil,
> Voices indecent by me clarified and transfigured.
>
> —Walt Whitman
> (1819–1892)

"Sexual Addiction": Repressive Morality in a New Guise?

Are you a sex addict? As you read descriptions of sexual addiction, you may begin to think that you are. But don't believe everything you read. Consider the following: "The moment comes for every addict," writes psychologist Patrick Carnes (1983, 1991), who developed and marketed the idea of sexual addiction, "when the consequences are so great or the pain so bad that the addict admits life is out of control because of his or her sexual behavior." Money is spent on pornography, affairs threaten a marriage, masturbation replaces jogging, and fantasies interrupt studying. Sex, sex, sex is on the addict's mind. And he or she has no choice but to engage in these activities.

According to Carnes, sex addicts cannot make a commitment; instead, they move from one hookup to another. Their addiction is rooted in deep-seated feelings of worthlessness, despair, anxiety, and loneliness. These feelings are temporarily allayed by the "high" obtained from sexual arousal and orgasm. According to Carnes, sexual addiction is viewed in the same light as alcoholism and drug addiction; it is an activity over which the addict has no control. And, as for alcoholism, a 12-step treatment program for sex addiction has been established by the National Council on Sexual Addiction/Compulsivity.

Are you wondering "Am I a sex addict?" Don't worry; you're probably not. The reason you might think you're suffering from sexual addiction is that its definition taps into many of the underlying anxieties and uncertainties we feel about sexuality in our culture. The problem lies not in you but in the concept of sexual addiction.

Although the idea of sexual addiction has found some adherents among clinical psychologists, they are clearly a minority. The influence of the sexual addiction concept is not the result of its impact on therapy, psychology, and social work. Its influence is due mainly to its popularity with the media, where talk-show hosts interview so-called sex addicts and advice columnists caution their readers about the signs of sexual addiction. The popularity of an idea is no guarantee of its validity, however. The sexual addiction concept lacks a scientific foundation and has been rejected by a number of sex researchers as nothing more than pop psychology. Sex addiction was not included in *DSM-5*, and it was noted that "at this time there is insufficient peer-reviewed evidence to establish the diagnostic criteria and course descriptions needed to identify these behaviors [e.g., sex addictions, exercise

addictions] as mental disorders" (APA, 2013). Some mental health professionals and sex researchers suggest that the idea of sexual addiction is really repressive morality in a new guise.

One problematic issue with the term "sex addiction" is that it does not fit the definition of addiction that alludes to physical and psychological dependence. Many behaviors associated with sex addiction are considered within the realm of sexual variation, although some may be extreme (Coleman, 1986; Levine & Troiden, 1988). A study of brain responses to visual images, including sexual ones, suggests that self-professed addicts may simply have a high sexual drive. The researchers analyzed brain responses of both men and women whose sexual behaviors were similar to people who typically sought treatment for sex addiction. The study participants were shown photographs chosen to evoke pleasant and unpleasant feelings. If a person were truly addicted to sex, images of sexual activity would result in a spike of brain activity similar to the way that images of cocaine have been shown to alter the brain activity of people addicted to the drug. However, the brain's responses to the sexual photographs were not predicted by measures of hypersexuality (e.g., difficulties resisting sexual behaviors despite exposure to risk), but related to the measure of sexual desire (e.g., desire for masturbation and sex with a partner) (Steele, Staley, Fong, & Prause, 2013; Preidt, 2013). Nicole Prause, study co-author and a researcher at UCLA, stated that the results show that hypersexuality does not appear to explain responses to sexual images more than just having a high libido.

Attempts to describe certain sexual behaviors by labeling them as sexual addictions continue to be problematic for the professional sexuality community. Different terms have been used in attempts to describe certain behavioral patterns. For example, Eli Coleman (1991, 1996; cited in Tepper & Owens, 2007), director of the human sexuality program at the University of Minnesota Medical School, favors "sexual compulsivity" over "sexual addiction" and goes further by distinguishing between compulsive and problematic sexual behavior:

> There has been a long tradition of pathologizing behavior which is not mainstream and which some might find distasteful. Behaviors which are in conflict with someone's value system may be problematic

but not obsessive-compulsive. Having sexual problems is common. Problems are caused by a number of nonpathological factors. . . . Some people will use sex as a coping mechanism similar to the use of alcohol, drugs, or eating. This pattern of sexual behavior is problematic. Problematic sexual behavior is often remedied by time, experience, education, or brief counseling (Coleman, 1991, p. 1).

Coleman and colleagues (1987; Coleman, Raymond, & McBean, 2003; Miner, Coleman, Center, Ross, & Simon Rosser, 2007) consider compulsive sexual behavior as a clinical syndrome in which the person experiences sexual urges, fantasies, and behaviors that are recurrent and intense and interfere with daily functioning.

The term "hypersexuality" has sometimes been used as a less pejorative term for sexual addiction, but it has not been accepted by the APA (Walters, Knight, & Langstrom, 2011). John Bancroft, senior research fellow and former director of The Kinsey Institute for Research in Sex, Gender, and Reproduction, and colleague Zoran Vukadinovic (2004) add even another perspective. After reviewing the concepts and theoretical bases of sexual addiction, sexual compulsivity, and sexual impulsivity (another labeling term), they concluded that it is premature to attempt an overriding definition. They continue by noting that until there is better understanding of this type of sexual expression, they prefer the general descriptive term "out-of-control sexual behavior" (Bancroft, 2009).

All of this discussion has challenged us to consider what is "excessive sexual behavior" and how culture shapes norms and our reactions and thoughts surrounding it. Certainly, it has caused mental health professionals to consider ways to address highly sexual persons.

If your sexual fantasies and activities are distressing to you, or your behaviors are emotionally or physically harmful to yourself or others, you should consult a therapist. The chances are, however, that your sexuality and your unique expression of it are healthy.

photograph, and sometimes talk to it or kiss it, ask for a keepsake if we part, and become nostalgic for a former love when we hear a particular song. All these behaviors are common, but they point to the symbolic power of objects, or fetishes.

Fetishism is sexual attraction to objects that become, for the person with the fetish, sexual symbols. The fetish is usually required or strongly preferred for sexual arousal because the person enjoys the way the object looks, tastes, smells, and/or feels (Kafka, 2010). Instead of relating to another individual, a person with fetishism gains sexual gratification from kissing a shoe, caressing a glove, drawing a lock of hair against his or her cheek, or masturbating with a piece of underwear. But the focus of a person with fetishism is not necessarily an inanimate object; he may be attracted to a woman's feet, ears, breasts, or legs, or he may have fetishes for both a body part and an inanimate object (Kafka, 2010). Commonly used fetish objects include rubber articles, leather clothing, and other wearing apparel. Exclusive attraction to body parts is known as **partialism.** However, using objects for sexual stimulation, such as vibrators, or using articles of female clothing for cross-dressing is not a sign of fetishism (APA, 2013). A study of the prevalence of fetishes involving Internet discussion groups representing at least 5,000 individuals found that the most common fetishes were for body parts or features (33%) and objects associated with the body (30%), such as panties and diapers. Feet and objects associated with feet, such as rubber, were the most frequently listed fetish targets (Scorolli, Ghirlanda, Enquist, Zattoni, & Jannini, 2007).

Some people sexualize inanimate objects or parts of the body, such as the foot.

© Fuse/Getty Images

Fetishistic behavior may be viewed as existing on a continuum, or existing in degrees, moving from a slight preference for an object, to a strong preference for it, to the necessity of the object for arousal, and finally to the object as a substitute for a sexual partner. Most people have slightly fetishistic traits. For example, some men describe themselves as "leg men" or "breast men"; they prefer dark-haired or light-haired partners. Some women are attracted to muscular men, others to hairy chests, and still others to shapely buttocks. However, to meet the *DMS-5* definition of fetishism disorder, the person must have a persistent and repetitive (for at least 6 months) use of or dependence on inanimate objects or a highly specific focus on a body part (typically not genital) as the primary factor needed for sexual arousal. Further, fetishistic disorder causes significant personal distress or impairment in social, occupational, or other important areas. Mental health clinicians report that it occurs nearly exclusively in males. Erectile difficulties are a typical outcome from the unavailability of the preferred body part or object during partner sex. Also, even when having a meaningful reciprocal and affectionate relationship, some persons with fetishistic disorder may prefer solitary sexual activity. Many persons who self-identify as fetish practitioners do not report clinical impairment and thus would not be diagnosed with a fetishistic disorder (APA, 2013).

Transvestism

Transvestism (*trans* means "cross," *vest* means "dress") is the wearing of clothing of the other sex for sexual arousal (Wheeler, Newring, & Draper, 2008). Many individuals with transvestism prefer to be labeled as **"cross-dressers"** instead of the more clinical label "transvestite," a term that some believe pathologizes cross-dressing behavior (Lehmiller, 2014). The literature indicates that cross-dressers are largely heterosexual males (Taylor & Rupp, 2004). However, there are studies of women who have erotic attachment to men's garments. The rarity of transvestism among women may have several reasons. One may be that our society is more accepting of women wearing "men's" clothing, such as pants and ties, than men wearing "women's" clothes. So women are not perceived as cross-dressing and men are less likely to report engaging in it because of negative social repercussions.

In a study of 1,032 cross-dressing men, excluding female impersonators and drag queens, 87% were heterosexual, 83% were currently married or had been previously, and 65% were college educated. Sixty percent reported that sexual excitement and orgasm often or almost always occurred with cross-dressing (Docter & Prince, 1997). **Female impersonators** are men who dress as women and **male impersonators** are women who dress as men, often as part of their job in entertainment. Gay men who cross-dress to entertain are often referred to as **drag queens.** Female and male impersonation and dressing in drag are not considered to be transvestism, in that those behaviors lack the components of sexual arousal and excitement.

Transvestism covers a broad range of behaviors. Some persons with transvestism prefer to wear only one article of clothing (usually a brassiere or panties) of the other sex in the privacy of their home; others choose to don an entire outfit in public. The frequency of cross-dressing ranges from a momentary activity that produces sexual excitement, usually through masturbation, to more

Cross-dressing may be a source of humor and parody, as the traditional boundaries of gender are explored and challenged.
© Mark Ralston/AFP/Getty Images

frequent and long-lasting behavior, depending on the individual, available opportunities, and mood or stressors.

The APA's *DMS-5* considers some cross-dressers as having transvestic disorder, a term that replaces transvestic fetishism which was used in prior editions. The transvestic fetishism label was too narrow in that even though for some cross-dressers this behavior is a form of fetishism, other cross-dressers become aroused by perceiving themselves as members of the other sex (labeled as autogynephilia) (Blanchard, 2010). The re-framing of transvestism in the *DSM-5* acknowledges cross-dressing is not inherently problematic even among those who do so habitually (APA, 2013; Boskey, 2013).

According to *DSM-5* (APA, 2013), **transvestic disorder** involves the recurrent and intense cross-dressing or thoughts of cross-dressing over at least 6 months accompanied with significant emotional distress that impairs social or interpersonal functioning. Transvestic disorder is nearly exclusively reported in males, the majority of which identify as heterosexual, and extremely rare in females. Less than 3% of males have reported even being sexually aroused by dressing in women's attire. In males, the initial indications of transvestic disorder may occur during childhood in the form of strong fascination with a particular women's clothing item which produces a generalized feeling of pleasurable excitement. In puberty, the cross-dressing begins to produce penile erection.

Men with transvestism are usually quite conventional in their masculine dress and attitudes. Dressed as women or wearing only one women's garment, they may become sexually aroused and masturbate or have sex with a woman. As time passes, however, the erotic element of the female garment may decrease and the comfort level increase. The majority of people with transvestism have

> *Those hot pants of hers were so damned tight, I could hardly breathe.*
>
> —Benny Hill
> (1924–1992)

> *I don't think painting my fingernails is a big deal. It's not like I'm sitting home by myself trying on lingerie. . . . When I cross-dress now, it's just another way I can show all the sides of Dennis Rodman.*
>
> —Dennis Rodman
> (1961–)

Actor James Franco appears in drag for a segment of the 83rd Academy Awards show. Franco, who has portrayed several gay or bisexual characters in movies and posed in drag for a magazine cover, has been frequently asked by the media if he is gay or bisexual himself. This skit at the Oscars seemed to be a way of thumbing his nose at all the speculation.

© Gabriel Bouys/AFP/Getty Images

❞ I don't mind drag—women have
   been female impersonators for
some time.

—Gloria Steinem
(1934–)

no desire to undergo a sex-change operation. If they do, there may be an accompanying diagnosis of gender dysphoria. Transvestism should not be confused with transsexualism. Most people with transvestism have no desire to change their anatomical sex, whereas transsexuals often do. "TV" is the acronym for "transvestism" and often appears in personal ads in underground newspapers and in Internet dating services.

Participating in cross-dressing can interfere with heterosexual relationships and be a major source of personal stress. Many people with transvestism marry or establish other committed relationships in hopes of "curing" their desire to cross-dress. Some men abate their cross-dressing when forming a new romantic relationship, but such abatement is usually temporary. Some voluntarily reveal their cross-dressing to a romantic partner or to their spouse after marriage, but for the majority, it is discovered. Invariably, the partners are distressed and blame themselves for somehow "emasculating" their partners. Some people with transvestism and their spouses and families are able to adjust to the cross-dressing. Data suggest, however, that women merely tolerate rather than support their partner's cross-dressing, and many feel betrayed, angry, and scared that outsiders will find out about their partner's behavior (Reynolds & Caron, 2000). Sometimes, however, the stress is too great, and separation follows soon after the transvestism is discovered.

Zoophilia

Zoophilia, sometimes referred to as "bestiality," involves deriving sexual pleasure from animals. True zoophilia occurs only when animals are the preferred sexual contact regardless of what other sexual outlets are available. Zoophilia is considered a coercive paraphilia based on the assumption that the animal is an unwilling participant. Few studies on the prevalence of zoophilia have been conducted. Alfred Kinsey and his colleagues reported that about 8% of the men and 4% of the women they surveyed had experienced at least one sexual contact with animals. Seventeen percent of the men who had been reared on farms had had such contact, but these activities accounted for less than 1% of their total sexual activity (Kinsey, Pomeroy, & Martin, 1948; Kinsey, Pomeroy, Martin, & Gebhard, 1953). A study of Native American adolescents found that 1% reported sexual contact with animals (Nagaraja, 1983). Crepault and Couture (1980) found that 5.3% of men had fantasized about having sex with an animal.

Among those who derive sexual pleasure from animals, the behavior usually begins in males during adolescence as a transitory phenomenon (Earls & Lalumière, 2009). Males are likely to have intercourse with the animal or to have their genitals licked by the animal. Females are more likely to have contact with a household pet, such as having intercourse, having the animal lick their genitals, or masturbating the animal. Despite earlier beliefs to the contrary, studies found that very few persons who had sex with animals considered the sex as a substitute for human sex; rather, for them it was just their preferred behavior (Beetz, 2004; Miletski, 2000, 2002).

A research study of 114 self-identified men with zoophilia examined sexual interest in animals. The participants were primarily acquired through the use of an online questionnaire, and those who volunteered were asked to refer others who had similar interests. More than 9 of every 10 men who self-identified as "zoophiles" indicated that they were concerned with the welfare of the animals. They emphasized the importance of consensual sexual activity with animals in contrast to persons they labeled as "**bestialists,**" those who have sex with animals but are not concerned with the animals' welfare. The men listed desire for affection and pleasurable sex as the most important reasons for sexual interest in animals.

Three study participants made these comments (Williams & Weinberg, 2003):

My relationship with animals is a loving one in which sex is an extension of that as it is with humans, and I do not have sex with a horse unless it consents (p. 526).

Although I do get an erection when interacting sexually with a stallion, my first priority is always the animal's pleasure, erection, and personal affection to me (p. 526).

Humans use sex to manipulate and control. Humans have trouble accepting who you are. They want to change you. Animals do not judge you. They just love and enjoy the pleasures of sex without all the politics (p. 527).

The most commonly reported animal partners were dogs (63%) and horses (29%); other partners were sheep, cats, cows, and chickens. Many of the men had not had sex with a human partner of either sex in the past year. The researchers suggest that sexual activity with animals is usually immediate, easy, and intense, thus reinforcing the behavior (Williams & Weinberg, 2003).

Voyeurism

Viewing sexual activities is a commonplace activity. Voyeuristic behaviors are the most frequently occurring of potentially law-breaking sexual behaviors (APA, 2013). Many individuals have used mirrors to view themselves during sexual behavior, watched their partners masturbate, videorecorded themselves and their partner having sex for later viewing, or watched others having intercourse. Americans' interest in viewing sexual activities has spawned a multibillion-dollar sex industry devoted to fulfilling those desires. Sexually explicit magazines, books, websites, and professionally produced X-rated videos are widely available. Topless bars, live sex clubs, strip and peep shows, reality

I have a mirrored ceiling over my bed because I like to know what I am doing.

—Mae West (1893–1980)

think
about it

Would You Watch? College Students and Voyeurism

Most research on voyeurism has focused on males in clinical and criminal settings. To investigate aspects of voyeurism in a relatively "normal" group of individuals, a sample of Canadian university students (232 women and 82 men) enrolled in a human sexuality class were asked to indicate whether they would watch an attractive person undressing or two attractive persons having sex in a hypothetical situation (Rye & Meaney, 2007). Students responded to the following scenario using a 0–100% scale, with 0% meaning "extremely unlikely to watch" to 100% being "extremely likely to watch." They were also asked if their responses would be different if there were a possibility of being caught and punished for their behavior. Students were presented with the following scenario:

You see someone whom you find *very* attractive. The person does not suspect that you can see him or her. He/she begins undressing.

Two questions were then posed:

1. If there were no chance of getting caught, how likely would it be that you would watch the person undressing?

2. He or she begins to have sex with another attractive person. How likely is it that you would watch the two people having sex?

Here is what the study found:

- With both men and women combined, the self-reported likelihood of watching an attractive person undress was significantly higher (67% on the 0 to 100% scale) than watching two attractive people having sex (45%).

- Men and women were not significantly different in their reported likelihood of watching an attractive person undress (73% men, 65% women).

- Men were significantly more likely than women (64% men, 39% women) to be willing to watch two attractive people having sex.

- When there was no possibility of being caught, men and women were much more likely to be willing to watch an attractive person undress.

- When there was no possibility of being caught, men and women were only slightly more likely to be willing to watch two attractive people having sex.

In discussing the results, the researchers noted that the students may have considered watching a couple having sex as more invasive than watching a person undress. They note that there are many more opportunities to observe others, covertly, in the different stages of undress (e.g., at the gym, at the beach) than seeing people having sex (usually limited to sex clubs or accidently walking in on a roommate or exhibitionistic, thrill-seeking couples in the college library stacks). The researchers also state that voyeuristic behavior may be acquired in several ways, such as evolutionary adaptations and social learning, then modified by social constraints, and that this perspective "fits well with Buss's (1998) sexual strategies theory. . . . Similarly, women may have less desire for sexual viewing, but may still engage in such behavior when social constraints are relaxed." The researchers also conclude that the study results support contentions that social constraints are a regulator of voyeurism.

Think Critically

1. How would you have answered the questions presented in this research study? Were there any responses that surprised you? Would the possibility of being caught alter your responses?

2. How would you feel if you found out you had been watched while undressing or having sex with someone?

3. If you have had sex, did you enjoy watching your partner undress? If so, what impact did this have on your sexual interaction?

SOURCE: Rye, B. J., & Meaney, G. J. (2007). Voyeurism: It is good as long as we do not get caught. *International Journal of Sexual Health, 19,* 47–56.

TV, sexting, and erotic dancing attest to the attraction of visual erotica. These activities are not considered **voyeurism** because the observed person is willing and these activities typically do not replace interpersonal sexuality. Hence, some degree of voyeurism appears to be socially acceptable (Lehmiller, 2014).

Very little research has been conducted on voyeurism, although a nationally representative study of 2,450 persons in Sweden examined the prevalence of voyeurism, as well as exhibitionism (discussed in the next section of this chapter). Twelve percent of males and 4% of females reported at least one incident of being sexually aroused by spying on others having sex (Langstrom & Seto, 2006). The researchers found that voyeurism and exhibitionism were associated with several variables; that is, those reporting voyeuristic and exhibitionistic behaviors were more likely to be male, to have more psychological problems, and to have lower life satisfaction. Further, they had greater odds of reporting other variant sexual behaviors, such as transvestism and sadomasochism. To learn what percentage of college students would watch a person undress or a couple have sex, see "Think About It" box "Would You Watch? College Students and Voyeurism."

According to the *DSM-5*, voyeuristic disorder involves recurring, intense sexual urges and fantasies related to secretly observing an unsuspecting person who is naked, disrobing, or engaging in sexual activity and that causes significant personal distress. The person with voyeuristic disorder has to be at least 18 years of age, as there is difficulty in differentiating it from age-appropriate puberty-related sexual curiosity and activity, and the disorder must occur over at least a 6-month period. Persons having this paraphilic impulse but declare no personal distress, have no impairment in functioning, and have no history of acting on these urges could be considered as having voyeuristic sexual interest rather than voyeuristic disorder (APA, 2013).

In order to become aroused, people with voyeurism must hide and remain unseen, and the person or couple being watched must be unaware of their presence. The excitement is intensified by the possibility of being discovered. Sometimes, the person with voyeurism will masturbate or imagine having sex with the observed person. People with voyeurism are sometimes called "peepers" or "peeping Toms" (Mann, Ainsworth, Al-Attar, & Davies, 2008). Watching others who know they are being observed, such as a sex partner, a stripper, or an actor in a sexually explicit film, is not classified as voyeurism. Voyeurism appeals primarily to heterosexual men (Seligman & Hardenburg, 2000), most of whom are content to keep their distance from their victim. Many lack social and sexual skills and may fear rejection.

In a more recent type of voyeurism, labeled "video voyeurism," video cameras are used to take pictures of persons in private places as they change their clothes, shower, or engage in sexual activities. For example, video cameras have been hidden in places that are considered private, such as in health clubs and gyms. In an effort to protect themselves, many voyeurism victims have sought legal recourse to halt the voyeurism. Nearly all states have legal prohibitions against video voyeurism. However, these laws have been difficult to enforce.

Exhibitionism

Also known as "indecent exposure," **exhibitionism** is the revealing of one's genitals to an unsuspecting person. The individual, almost always male and sometimes called a "flasher," may derive sexual gratification from the exposure of the genitals: A general population study in Sweden on voyeurism and exhibitionism found that 3.1% of the study participants (4.1% men, 2.1% women) reported at least one episode of being aroused by exposing their genitals to a stranger (Langstrom & Seto, 2006).

What is considered exhibitionism varies cross-culturally, but throughout most of the United States it is illegal to expose one's genitals or for a women to expose her nipples unless for a good reason such as breastfeeding. Exhibitionism is more often considered a problem and legally punishable when committed by a man, in contrast to such behavior by a woman. Because of the widespread incidence of exhibitionism, many women may have witnessed exhibitionism at least once in their lives. Between 40% and 60% of women college students have reported having had someone expose himself to them, commonly known as being flashed (Murphy & Page, 2008).

The *DSM-5* describes a person with exhibitionism disorder as one who experiences significant personal distress or social impairment for at least 6 months from the urges or one who exposes his or her genitals to a nonconsenting person. The nonconsenting person is considered a victim, as the experience can be very traumatizing. Persons having this paraphilic impulse but declare no personal distress, have no impairment in functioning, and have no history of acting on these urges could be considered having exhibitionism sexual interest but not exhibitionism disorder (APA, 2013). A person with exhibitionism often also has voyeuristic behaviors.

Genital exposure by a man is not a prelude or an invitation to intercourse. Instead, it is an escape from intercourse, for the man never exposes himself to a willing woman—only to strangers or near-strangers. Typically, he obtains sexual gratification after exposing himself as he fantasizes about the shock and horror he caused his victim. Other people with exhibitionism experience orgasm as they expose themselves; still others may masturbate during or after the exhibitionism. These men generally expose themselves to children, adolescents, and young women; they rarely expose themselves to older women. In those few instances in which a woman shows interest, the person with exhibitionism immediately flees. Usually, there is no physical contact. Exotic dancers and nude sunbathers are not considered people with exhibitionism because they typically do not derive sexual arousal from the behavior, nor do they expose themselves to unwilling people. Furthermore, stripping for a sex partner to arouse him or her involves willing participants.

Sometimes, the term "exhibitionist" is used in a pejorative way to describe a woman who dresses provocatively. These women, however, do not fit the American Psychiatric Association (2013) definition of exhibitionism. For example, they do not expose their genitals, nor does the provocative dressing cause marked distress or involve interpersonal behavior. Labeling women who dress provocatively as "exhibitionists" is more a case of a moral judgment than a scientific assessment. Actually, women in our culture have more socially acceptable ways of exposing their bodies than men. Showing breast cleavage, for example, is widely accepted in our culture (Carroll, 2010).

Men with exhibitionism often feel powerless, and their sexual relations with their wives or partners usually are poor. This sense of powerlessness gives rise to anger and hostility, which they direct toward other women by exhibiting themselves. However, they rarely are violent. If a person with exhibitionism confronts you, it is best to ignore and distance yourself from the person and then report the incident to the police. Reacting strongly, though a natural response, only reinforces the behavior.

Some people like to exhibit their bodies within public settings that are "legitimized," such as Mardi Gras. Such displays may be exhibitionistic, but they are not considered exhibitionism in the clinical sense.

© David McNew/Getty Images

Telephone Scatologia

Telephone scatologia—the making of obscene phone calls to unsuspecting people—is considered a paraphilia because the acts are compulsive and repetitive or because the associated fantasies cause distress to the individual.

Those who engage in this behavior typically get sexually aroused when their victim reacts in a shocked or horrified manner. Obscene phone calls are generally made randomly, by chance dialing. Some people with this paraphilia repeatedly make these calls.

The overwhelming majority of callers are male, but there are female obscene callers as well (Price, Kafka, Commons, Gutheil, & Simpson, 2002; Quayle, 2008). Male callers frequently make their female victims feel annoyed, frightened, anxious, upset, or angry, while the callers themselves often suffer from feelings of inadequacy and insecurity. They may use obscenities, breathe heavily into the phone, or say they are conducting sex research. Also, they usually masturbate during the call or immediately afterward. The victims of male callers often feel violated, but female callers have a different effect on male recipients, who generally do not feel violated or may find the call titillating (Matek, 1988).

If you receive a harassing or obscene phone call, the best thing to do is not to overreact and to quietly hang up the telephone. Don't engage in a conversation with the caller, such as trying to determine why the person is calling or why the person won't stop calling. Remember, the caller wants an audience. You should not give out personal information such as your name, e-mail address, or phone number to anyone who is a stranger or respond to any questions if you do not know the caller.

If the phone immediately rings again, don't answer it. If obscene calls are repeated, the telephone company suggests changing your number (many companies will do this at no charge), keeping a log of the calls, or, in more serious cases, working with law enforcement officials to trace the calls. Other solutions include screening calls with an answering service and obtaining caller ID. By the way, don't include your name, phone number, or other personal information, such as when you will be away and returning, in the outgoing message on your answering service. One final suggestion—be cautious in placing ads in newspapers or on electronic media or allowing strangers access to personal information on social networking sites. Use a post office number or e-mail address. If you feel you must give your phone number, don't give the address of your residence.

Frotteurism

Frotteurism (also known as "mashing," "groping," or "frottage") refers to the obtaining of sexual gratification by sexual pressing, rubbing, or touching against a nonconsenting person in a public location. It is not known how many people practice frotteurism, but 21% of college males in one study reported having engaged in at least one episode of frotteurism (Templeman & Stinnett, 1991). The APA (2013) says that frotteuristic behaviors may occur in nearly 30% of adult males in the general population.

The *DSM-5* describes a person with frotteuristic disorder as a person who experiences, for at least 6 months, significant personal distress or social impairment from recurrent and intense sexual arousal from rubbing or touching against a nonconsenting person. If this paraphilic impulse does not cause personal distress or impairment of other important areas of functioning and there is no acting on the urges, individuals are considered to have frotteuristic sexual interest, but not frotteuristic disorder (APA, 2013).

Froterurism, the rubbing or touching against a nonconsensual person, can occur in crowded public places such as at rock concerts.

© Robert Kohlhuber/Getty Images

The person with frotteurism, most often a male, usually carries out his touching or rubbing in crowded public places like subways or buses or at large sporting events or rock concerts (Lussier & Piché, 2008). When he enters a crowd, his initial rubbing can be disguised by the crush of people. He usually rubs his clothed penis against the fully clothed female's buttocks or thighs with his erect penis inside his pants. Less commonly, he may use his hands to rub a woman's buttocks, pubic region, thighs, or breasts. The type of contact may appear unintended, and a woman may not even notice the touch or pay heed to it, given the crowded situation. However, some women may feel victimized (Freund, Seto, & Kuban, 1997). If the woman discovers it, the man will usually run away. Hence, nearly all men with frotteurism are able to escape being caught. While mashing, the male may fantasize about having consensual sex with the women, and he may recall the mashing episode when masturbating in the future.

Frotteuristic disorder often occurs with other paraphilias, especially exhibitionism disorder and voyeuristic disorder (APA, 2013).

Necrophilia

> The dead person who loves will love forever and will never be weary of giving and receiving caresses.
>
> —Ernest Jones
> (1879–1958)

Necrophilia is sexual activity with a corpse. It is regarded as nonconsensual because a corpse is obviously unable to give consent. There are relatively few instances of necrophilia, largely because few people have access to cadavers, yet it retains a fascination in horror literature, especially vampire stories and legends, and in gothic novels. It is also associated with ritual cannibalism in other cultures. Within our own culture, *Sleeping Beauty* features a necrophilic theme, as does the crypt scene in Shakespeare's *Romeo and Juliet*. Most likely, necrophilia sexual behaviors are committed largely by those who work with corpses in mortuaries and morgues and who have become desensitized by them. Such behavior is illegal under laws regarding the handling of dead bodies (Kelly, 2013). However, the vast majority of persons working with corpses do not have urges to be sexual with a corpse.

In a review of 122 cases of supposed necrophilia or necrophilic fantasies, researchers found only 54 instances of true necrophilia (Rosman & Resnick, 1989).

The study found that neither sadism, psychosis, nor mental impairment was inherent in necrophilia. Instead, the most common motive for necrophilia was the possession of a partner who neither resisted nor rejected. Clearly, many people with necrophilia are severely mentally disturbed.

Pedophilia

Pedophilia is characterized by a sexual interest or focus on prepubescent children. The *DSM-5* defines pedophilic disorder as having "recurrent, for at least 6 months, intense sexual urges and sexually arousing fantasies involving sexual activity with a prepubescent child or children" that the individual has acted upon or finds distressing or that results in interpersonal difficulty (APA, 2013). A person with a sexual focus on prepubescent children who does not report feelings of shame, guilt, or anxiety about these impulses, is not functionally limited by these impulses, and never acted on these impulses is considered to have pedophilia sexual orientation but not pedophilic disorder. According to the APA, the children are aged 13 or younger and a person with pedophilic disorder must be at least 16 and at least 5 years older than the child. A late adolescent is not considered to have pedophilic disorder if he or she is involved in an ongoing sexual relationship with a 12-year-old or older child. The diagnostic criteria for this paraphilia did not change with the update to *DSM-5;* the only change was in renaming the diagnosis from pedophilia to pedophilic disorder. Almost all people with pedophilic disorder are males. Yet their sexual contacts with children are relatively rare, occurring probably in 3–5% of the male population (APA, 2013). Girls are about twice as likely to be the sexual objects of pedophilic behavior. The prevalence of pedophilic disorder among females is uncertain, but likely a fraction of the prevalence among males (APA, 2013; Seto, 2008).

In this section, we discuss only pedophilic disorder. Pedophilic disorder is different from "child sexual abuse," "child molestation," and "incest," although all denote sex with minors, which is a criminal action. Pedophilic disorder, as defined by the APA, is a psychiatric disorder. Not all of those who sexually abuse minors would be considered people with pedophilic disorder unless the APA criteria are met. Sexual contact with a minor is not, in itself, a determination of pedophilic disorder (Fagan, Wise, Schmidt, & Berlin, 2002). It is, however, illegal. Nonpedophilic disorder child sexual abuse and incest, their impact on the victims, and prevention of child sexual abuse are discussed later. Child sexual abuse is illegal in every state.

Some individuals with pedophilic disorder prefer only one sex, whereas others are aroused by both male and female children. Those attracted to females usually seek 8- to 10-year-olds, and those attracted to males usually seek slightly older children. Some people with pedophilic disorder are sexually attracted to children only, and some are aroused by both children and adults (APA, 2013).

Research has shown that many persons with pedophilic disorder have personality disorders, but why pedophilic disorder exists remains a puzzle (Madsen, Parsons, & Grubin, 2006; Seto, 2008). Pedophilic disorder seems to be a lifelong condition. Although it may fluctuate, increase or decrease with age, the use of pornography depicting prepubescent children is a helpful diagnostic indicator of pedophilic disorder. Many are fearful that their sexual abilities are decreasing or that they are unable to perform sexually with their partners (APA, 2013). Some adult males report that they were sexually abused as a child, although whether this correlation represents a causal influence of childhood sexual abuse on adult pedophilia remains unclear.

People with pedophilic disorder often use seduction and enticement to manipulate children—their own children, relatives, or children outside the family. The Internet provides a way for a person with pedophilic disorder to make contact with unsuspecting children. A man sometimes cruises chat rooms designed for children, and he may convince a girl to agree to e-mail, text, social media network, or telephone contact. He may befriend the girl, talking to her and giving her gifts.

Pedophilic behaviors rarely involve sexual intercourse. The person with pedophilic disorder usually seeks to fondle or touch the child, usually on the genitals, legs, and buttocks. Sometimes, he exposes himself and has the child touch his penis. He may masturbate in the presence of the child. Occasionally, oral or anal stimulation is involved.

BDSM, Sexual Masochism, and Sexual Sadism

Variations in sexual behavior are common, although the majority of people do not engage in these activities. One of the more widespread forms of sexual variation is **BDSM**—a term often used in popular culture for **b**ondage, **d**iscipline, **s**adism, and **m**asochism. BDSM is a favored term, as it represents a broad possibility of experiences in which sexual gratification is derived from being dominated, dominating another person, giving pain (sadism), or receiving pain (masochism) (Carroll, 2010; Kleinplatz & Moser, 2004; Krueger, 2010a, 2010b). Often, there is no clear dividing line between domination and submission and sexual sadism and sexual masochism, and the research literature has used all or only a few of the terms, as you will see in the studies cited in this section. The American Psychiatric Association (2013) does not list domination and submission as a paraphilic disorder, as it is considered consensual and does not result in psychological distress, but sexual sadism and sexual masochism, which can cause significant distress and involve a nonconsenting partner for sexual sadism, are listed as paraphilic disorders. Coercion separates sexual sadism from domination. But for consensual behaviors, there is no clear distinction. A rule of thumb for separating consensual sexual sadism and sexual masochism from domination and submission may be that sadism and masochism behaviors can be extreme, compulsive, and dangerous and are not commonly practiced. Sexual partners practicing sadism and masochism often make specific agreements ahead of time concerning the amount of pain and punishment that will occur during sexual activity. Nevertheless, the acting out of fantasies involves risk such as physical injury; thus, it is important that individuals communicate their preferences and limits before they engage in any new activity. The term "sadomasochism (S&M)" is also used by the general public to describe domination and submission, but it is no longer used as a clinical term in psychology and psychiatry to describe consensual domination and submission.

One misconception about BDSM is the stereotype that individuals who associate pain with sexual arousal are victims of childhood abuse who have developed psychological problems in adulthood (Lehmiller, 2014). However, persons who practice BSDM are no more likely to have psychological disorders than anyone else. A research study showed that BSDM is not linked to having experienced childhood sexual abuse, nor is it associated with greater levels of psychological distress in adulthood (Richters, de Visser, Rissel, Grulich, & Smith, 2008).

Domination and submission (D/S) are forms of fantasy sex, and the D/S behaviors are carefully controlled by elaborate shared scripts. The critical element is not pain but power. The dominant partner is perceived as all-powerful and the submissive partner as powerless. Significantly, the amount or degree of "pain," which is usually feigned or slight, is controlled by the submissive partner, typically by subtle nonverbal signals. As such, fantasy plays a central role, especially for the submissive person. As two people enact the agreed-upon master-slave script, the control is not complete. Rather, it is the *illusion* of total control that is fundamental to D/S (Hyde & DeLamater, 2014).

A large-scale study of a nonclinical population revealed that the majority of people who engage in domination and submission do so as "a form of sexual enhancement which they voluntarily and mutually choose to explore" (Weinberg, Williams, & Moser, 1984). As such, domination and submission are not a paraphilic disorder, since the behavior is consensual, does not cause psychological distress, and is without pain. To be considered paraphilic, such behavior requires that the suffering or humiliation of oneself or one's partner be real, not merely simulated (APA, 2013). (Sexual sadism and sexual masochism, which are considered coercive paraphilias, are discussed later.)

Domination and submission take many forms. The participants generally assume both dominant and submissive roles at different times; few are interested only in being on "top" or "bottom." Probably the most widely known form is **bondage and discipline (B&D).** B&D is a fairly common practice in which a person is bound with scarves, leather straps, underwear, handcuffs, chains, or other such devices while another simulates or engages in light-to-moderate discipline activities such as spanking or light flagellation (e.g., whipping or flogging). The bound person may be blindfolded or gagged. A woman specializing in disciplining a person is known as a **dominatrix,** and her submissive partner is called a slave. Bondage and discipline may take place in specialized settings called "dungeons" furnished with restraints, body suspension devices, racks, whips, and chains.

Janus and Janus (1993) reported that 11% of both men and women had experience with bondage. A more recent investigation of four "kinky" sexual behaviors—bondage or domination, sadomasochism, photo or video exhibitionism, and asphyxiation or breath play—among 347 lesbian and 58 bisexual women found that 32% and 41%, respectively, had ever participated in bondage/domination. The study also found that 40% reported ever engaging in at least one of the four behaviors and 25% reported engaging in multiple behaviors (Tomassilli, Golub, Bimbi, & Parsons, 2009).

Another common form of domination and submission is humiliation, in which the person is debased or degraded. Examples of humiliation include being verbally humiliated, receiving an enema ("water treatment"), being urinated on ("golden showers"), and being defecated on ("scat"). According to the *DSM-5,* sexual

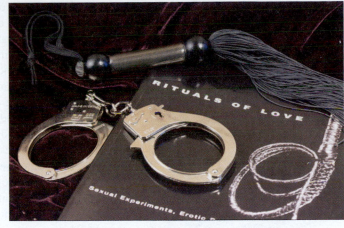

Bondage and discipline, or B&D, often involves leather straps, handcuffs, and other restraints as part of its scripting.

© Francis Hanna/Alamy

❝Ah beautiful, passionate body,
That never has ached with a heart!
On the mouth though the kisses are bloody,
Though they sting till it shudder and smart
More kind than the love we adore is
They hurt not the heart nor the brain
Oh bitter and tender Dolores Our Lady of Pain.

—Algernon Swinburne
(1837–1909)

❝It's been so long since I made love I can't even remember who gets tied up.

—Joan Rivers
(1933–2014)

Bettie Page, who has become a cult figure among those interested in domination and submission, was one of the most photographed women in the 1950s.

© Michael Ochs Archives/Getty Images

> Do not do unto others as you would that they should do unto you. Their tastes may not be the same.
>
> —George Bernard Shaw (1856–1950)

> I would love to be whipped by you, Nora, love!
>
> —James Joyce (1882–1941), from a love letter to his wife

pleasure derived from receiving enemas is known as **klismaphilia** (klis-muh-FIL-ee-uh), that derived from contact with urine is called **urophilia** (yore-oh-FIL-ee-uh), and that derived from contact with feces is called **coprophilia** (cop-ro-FIL-ee-uh). Humiliation activities may also include servilism, infantilism (also known as babyism), kennelism, and tongue-lashing. In servilism, the person desires to be treated as a servant or slave. In infantilism, the person acts in a babyish manner—using baby talk, wearing diapers, and being pampered, scolded, or spanked by his or her "mommy" or "daddy." "Kennelism" refers to being treated like a dog (wearing a studded dog collar and being tied to a leash) or ridden like a horse while the dominant partner applies whips or spurs. Tongue-lashing is verbal abuse by a dominant partner who uses language that humiliates and degrades the other person.

People engage in domination and submission in private or as part of an organized subculture complete with clubs and businesses catering to the acting out of D/S fantasies. This subculture is sometimes known as "the velvet underground." There are scores of noncommercial D/S clubs throughout the United States. The clubs are often specialized: lesbian S&M, dominant men/submissive women, submissive men/dominant women, gay men's S&M, and transvestite S&M. Leather sex bars are meeting places for gay men who are interested in domination and submission. The D/S subculture includes D/S videos, websites, books, social media networks, newspapers, and magazines.

A questionnaire study of 184 Finnish men and women who were members of two sadomasochistic-oriented clubs identified 29 sexual behaviors that were grouped in four different sexual scripts: hypermasculinity (e.g., using a dildo, an enema), administration and receipt of pain (e.g., hot wax, clothespins attached to nipples), physical restriction (e.g., using handcuffs), and psychological humiliation (e.g., face slapping and using knives to make surface wounds) (Alison, Santtila, Sandnabba, & Nordling, 2001; Santtila, Sandnabba, Alison, & Nordling, 2002). Research has shown that sadomasochistic behavior occurs among gay men, lesbian women, and heterosexual individuals (Sandnabba et al., 2002). Nineteen percent and 26% of lesbian and bisexual women, respectively, reported ever participating in sadomasochism (Tomassilli et al., 2009).

Sexual Sadism Disorder   According to the *DSM-5,* a person may be diagnosed with **sexual sadism** if, over a period of at least 6 months, she or he experiences intense, recurring sexual urges or fantasies involving real (not simulated) behaviors in which physical or psychological harm, including humiliation, is inflicted upon a victim for purposes of intense sexual arousal. The individual either has acted on these urges with a nonconsenting person or finds them extremely distressful (APA, 2013). Characteristic symptoms include violent sexual thoughts and fantasies involving a desire for power and control centering on a victim's physical suffering, which is sexually arousing (Kingston & Yates, 2008). The victim may be a consenting person with masochism or someone abducted by a person with sadism. The victim may be tortured, raped, mutilated, or killed; often, the victim is physically restrained and blindfolded or gagged. However, most rapes are not committed by sexual sadists.

Persons acknowledging sexual interest in physical and psychological suffering of others but declare no personal distress, have no impairment in functioning, and have no history of acting on these urges could be considered having sadistic sexual interest but would not meet the criteria for sadistic sexual disorder (APA, 2013). How often sexual sadism disorder occurs is unknown and is largely based on persons from forensic settings, nearly all males. *DSM-5* states that the prevalence varies widely, from 2% to 30%, depending on the criteria used.

Among individuals who have committed sexually motivated homicides, rates of sexual sadism disorder range from 37% to 75% (APA, 2013).

Sexual Masochism Disorder   According to the *DSM-5*, for a diagnosis of **sexual masochism disorder** to be made, a person must experience for a period of at least 6 months intense, recurring sexual urges or fantasies involving real (not simulated) behaviors of being "humiliated, beaten, bound, or otherwise made to suffer." These fantasies, sexual urges, or behaviors must result in significant distress or social impairment. A person who indicates no stress and the sexual masochism impulses do not impede personal goals is considered having masochistic sexual interest but not sexual masochistic disorder. Some individuals express the sexual urges by themselves (e.g., through self-mutilation or by binding themselves); others act with partners. Masochistic behaviors expressed with a partner may include being restrained, blindfolded, paddled, spanked, whipped, beaten, shocked, cut, "pinned and pierced," and humiliated (e.g., being urinated or defecated on or forced to crawl and bark like a dog). The individual may desire to be treated as an infant and be forced to wear diapers ("infantilism"). The degree of pain one must experience to achieve sexual arousal varies from symbolic gestures to severe mutilations. As noted previously, sexual masochism is the only paraphilia that occurs with some frequency in women (Hucker, 2008).

Autoerotic Asphyxia   A form of sexual masochism called **autoerotic asphyxia** (also called hypoxphilia, breath play, sexual asphyxia, or asphyxiphilia) links strangulation with masturbation. Those who participate in this activity seek to heighten their masturbatory arousal and orgasm by cutting off the oxygen supply to the brain. A person may engage in this practice either alone or with a partner. If death occurs, it is usually accidental. Autoerotic asphyxiation is an increasing phenomenon, with more than 1,000 fatalities in the United States per year and the ratio of male to female accidental deaths being more than 50 to 1 (Gosink & Jumbelic, 2000). Five percent of both lesbian and bisexual women reported ever having participated in asphyxiation (the limiting, restricting, or controlling of an individual's air supply) for the purposes of sexual arousal or to enhance orgasm (Tomassilli et al., 2009). Because of the secrecy and shame that accompany this and other masturbatory activities, it is difficult to know the exact number of individuals who find this practice arousing. Reports by participants are extremely rare or are masked by another cause of death.

Self-hanging is the most common method of autoerotic asphyxia, although some type of suffocation is frequently used (Hucker, 2011). Individuals often use ropes, cords, or chains along with padding around the neck to prevent telltale signs. Some devise hanging techniques that permit them to cut themselves loose just before losing consciousness. Others may place bags or blankets over their heads. Still others inhale asphyxiating gases such as aerosol sprays or amyl nitrate ("poppers"), a drug used to treat heart pain. The corpses are usually found either naked or partially clothed, often in women's clothing. Various forms of bondage have also been observed. A review of all published cases of autoerotic deaths from 1954 to 2004 found 408 deaths reported in 57 articles. The review revealed that autoerotic practitioners were predominantly White males ranging in age from 9 to 77 years. Most cases of asphyxia involved hanging, use of ligature, plastic bags, chemical substances, or a combination of these. Atypical methods accounted for about 10% of the cases and included electrocution, overdressing/body wrapping, foreign-body insertion, and chest compression (Sauvageau & Racette, 2006). Studies of survivors found that many of these individuals fantasized about masochistic scenarios during the autoerotic behavior (Hucker, 2011). The possibility of suicide should always be considered even in cases that initially appear to be accidental (Byard & Botterill, 1998).

Although researchers have some understanding of why people participate in this practice, it is more important that medical personnel, parents, and other adults recognize signs of it and respond with strategies commensurate with its seriousness. Those who engage in such sexual practices rarely realize the potential consequences of their behavior; therefore, parents and others must be alert to physical and other telltale signs. An unusual neck bruise; bloodshot eyes; disoriented behavior, especially after the person has been alone for a while; and unexplained possession of or fascination with ropes or chains are the key signs. Until we as a society can educate about, recognize, and respond to autoerotic asphyxia assertively and compassionately, we can expect to see more deaths as a result of this practice.

> One half the world cannot understand the pleasures of the other.
>
> —Jane Austin
> (1775–1817)

● Origins and Treatment of Paraphilias

How do people develop paraphilias? Research on the causes of paraphilias has been limited and difficult to conduct; hence, findings, though informative, are largely speculative (Laws & O'Donohue, 2008). As with many other behaviors, paraphilias probably result from some type of interaction among biology, sociocultural norms, and life experiences. Because most people with paraphilias are male, biological factors may be particularly significant. Some researchers have postulated that males with paraphilia may have higher testosterone levels than those without paraphilias, that they have had brain damage, or that the paraphilia may be inherited. Because the data are inconclusive, however, it has not been possible to identify a specific biological cause of paraphilia. People with paraphilia seem to have grown up in dysfunctional environments and to have had early experiences that limited their ability to be sexually stimulated by consensual sexual activity; as a result, they obtain arousal through varied means. They may have low self-esteem, poor social skills, and feelings of anger and loneliness; be self-critical; and lack a clear sense of self (Fisher & Howells, 1993; Goodman, 1993; Marshall, 1993; Ward & Beech, 2008). Another factor may be a limited ability to empathize with the victims of their behavior. The psychological outcomes of these behaviors direct sexual attraction and response away from intimate relationships in later life (Schwartz, 2000).

Therapists have found paraphilias to be difficult to treat (Laws & O'Donohue, 2008; McConaghy, 1998). Most people who are treated are convicted sex offenders, who have the most severe paraphilias, while those with milder paraphilias go untreated. Multifaceted treatments, such as psychodynamic therapy, aversive conditioning, cognitive-behavioral programs, relapse prevention, and medical intervention, have been tried to reduce or eliminate the symptoms of the paraphilia. Enhancing social and sexual skills, developing self-management plans, modifying sexual interests, and providing sexuality and relationship education may help people with paraphilia engage in more appropriate behavior (Marshall, Marshall, & Serran, 2006). However, even when the client desires to change, treatments may not be effective, and relapses often occur. A review of 80 studies found a 37% reduction in the re-offense rate among persons with paraphilia in contrast to those not receiving any treatment (Schmucker & Losel, 2008). Hence, some experts believe that prevention is the best approach, although prevention programs are currently very limited.

Final Thoughts

Studying variations in sexual behaviors reveals the variety and complexity of sexual behavior. It also underlines the limits of acceptance of sexual behavior outside of the predominant culture and social sexual norms. Mental health professionals and many others believe unconventional sexual behaviors, undertaken in private between consenting adults as the source of erotic pleasure, should be of concern only to the people involved. As long as physical or psychological harm is not done to oneself or others, is it anyone's place to judge? Coercive paraphilic behavior, however, may be injurious and should be treated.

Summary

Sexual Variations and Paraphilic Behavior

- *Sexual variation* is behavior in which less than the majority of individuals engage or that is outside of the "mainstream" of sexual behavior. Variant sexual behavior is not "abnormal" or "deviant" behavior, the definition of which varies from culture to culture and from one historical period to another.

- The American Psychiatric Association (APA) defines *paraphilia* as an intense and recurring sexual interest and impulse other than sexual interest in genital stimulation or preparatory fondling with a normal, physically mature adult.

- *The Diagnostic and Statistical Manual of Mental Disorders, Fifth Edition (DSM-5)*, a distinction was made between relatively harmless and relatively harmful sexual behaviors. *Paraphilia* is considered an out-of-the-ordinary sexual behavior that does not necessarily require psychiatric treatment; a *paraphilic disorder* is a persistent and recurring (for at least 6 months) sexual behavior that causes distress or social impairment and whose satisfaction entails personal harm, or risk of harm, to others. This distinction is a major change in the *DSM-5*, reflecting greater acceptance of some unconventional sexual behaviors.

- The distinction between sexual interests, variations, and behavior that might be classified as *paraphilic* or *paraphilic disorder* is often vague and often more a difference of degree than kind.

- *Paraphilic sexual interest disorder* describes a particular paraphilic impulse that does not cause personal distress nor impaired function and there is no history of the person acting on the impulse.

- Paraphilic behaviors may be noncoercive or coercive. *Noncoercive paraphilias*, such as *domination and submission*, *fetishism*, and *transvestism*, are considered relatively benign or harmless because they are victimless. *Coercive paraphilias* represent nonconsensual sexual activity with children and adults; examples include *voyeurism*, *sexual masochism*, *sexual sadism*, *frotteurism*, and *pedophilia*.

Types of Paraphilias

- *Fetishism* is sexual attraction to inanimate objects or nongenital body parts. The fetishism is usually required or strongly preferred for sexual arousal.

- *Transvestism* is the wearing of clothes of a member of the other sex, usually for sexual arousal, and is also called cross-dressing.

- *Zoophilia* involves animals as the preferred sexual outlet even when other outlets are available. It is also called bestiality.

- *Voyeurism* is the nonconsensual and secret observation of others who are naked, disrobing, or having sex for the purpose of sexual arousal.

- *Exhibitionism* is the exposure of the genitals to a nonconsenting stranger.

- *Telephone scatologia* is the nonconsensual telephoning of strangers and often involves the use of obscene language.

- *Frotteurism* involves touching or rubbing against a nonconsenting person for the purpose of sexual arousal.

- *Necrophilia* is sexual activity with a corpse.

- *Pedophilia* refers to sexual arousal and contact with children aged 13 or younger by adults. A person with pedophilia must be at least 16 and at least 5 years older than the child. Child sexual abuse is illegal in every state.

- *BDSM* is an acronym used to describe the combination of bondage, discipline, sadism, and masochism.

- *Domination and submission (D/S)* is a form of consensual fantasy sex involving no pain with perceived power as the central element.

- *Sexual sadism* refers to *disorder* sexual urges or fantasies of intentionally inflicting real physical or psychological pain or suffering on a person.

- *Sexual masochism disorder* is the recurring sexual urge or fantasy of being humiliated or made to suffer through real behaviors, not simulated ones.

- *Autoerotic asphyxia* is a form of sexual masochism linking strangulation with masturbatory activities.

Origins and Treatment of Paraphilias

- Paraphilias are likely the result of social/environmental, psychological, and biological factors.

- Paraphilic disorders are difficult to treat, and relapses often occur.

- Prevention programs may be the most effective way to address paraphilic disorders.

Questions for Discussion

- Are you comfortable with the term "sexual variations"? If yes, why is it a good term for you? If no, which term do you like to describe "unusual" sexual behavior? Explain.

- Do you consider certain sexual behaviors to be "deviant," "abnormal," or "perverted"? If so, how did you come to believe this?

- From the types of paraphilias discussed in this chapter, do you find any of them to be repulsive or even "pathological"?

- Do you agree with new *DSM-5* clarification of out-of-the-ordinary sexual behavior as paraphilia and paraphilic disorder? In your opinion, is this separation a progression of the APA toward a greater acceptance of sexual variation? Explain.

- Do you think that labeling certain sexual behaviors as paraphilic is a reflection of efforts to control and discourage behaviors that society does not want expressed? If yes, should any sexual behaviors, such as pedophilia, be controlled? If no, why do you think certain sexual behaviors are labeled paraphilias?

Sex and the Internet

Paraphilias

The web is one resource for locating information about paraphilias. Go to the Google website (http://www.google.com) and type "paraphilias" in the Google Search box. As you can see, there are a wide range of sites posted. Look over the posted sites and answer the following questions:

- What types of websites are listed?
- Are the sites primarily from medical and academic organizations, individuals, or commercial groups?
- Are there sites for specific paraphilias?
- Which sites provide the most valuable information to you? Why?
- Did you learn anything new about paraphilias from the websites? If so, what?
- Do you believe that any of the sites contain inaccurate or harmful information? Explain.

Suggested Websites

AllPsych Online

http://allpsych.com/disorders/paraphilias
Offers information on numerous psychiatric disorders, including symptoms, etiology, treatment, and prognosis for paraphilias and sexual disorders.

American Psychiatric Association

http://www.psych.org/home/search-results?k=paraphilias
Provides information on the APA's classification of paraphilias and paraphilic disorders with highlights of the changes in the latest version of the DSM.

WebMD

http://www.webmd.com/sexual_conditions/paraphilias
Describes common paraphilias and provides a search for paraphilia information.

Suggested Reading

Frances, A. (2013). *Saving normal: An insider's revolt against out-of-control psychiatric diagnosis, DSM-5, big pharma and the medicalization of ordinary life.* New York: William Morrow. The author presents a history of medical illness and an account of an explosion of psychiatric disorder in the United States. He cautions the mislabeling and diagnosis of normal daily issues as mental illness.

Greenberg, G. (2013). *The book of woe: The DSM and the unmaking of psychiatry.* London, UK: Penguin Books. Psychotherapist Gary Greenberg details a critical historical analysis of the APA's *Diagnostic and Statistical Manual of Mental Disorders* with interviews of persons on both sides of the treacheries and valuable strengths of the DSM.

Kleinplatz, P. J., & Moser, C. (2006). *Sadomasochism: Powerful pleasures.* Binghamton: NY: Harrington Park Press. Articles from leading experts discuss the results of research into practitioners' behaviors and perspectives and stresses greater tolerance and understanding of S&M.

Laws, D. R., & O'Donohue, W. (Eds.). (2008). *Sexual deviance: Theory, assessment and treatment* (2nd ed.). New York: Guilford Press. A collection of papers that examine the theories, assessment procedures, and treatment techniques for a spectrum of sexually variant behaviors.

Money, J. (1989). *Lovemaps.* Buffalo, NY: Prometheus Books. A description of variant and paraphilic behavior.

Tyler, A., & Bussel, R. K. (Eds.). (2006). *Caught looking: Erotic tales of voyeurs and exhibitionists.* San Francisco: Cleis Press. A collection of 20 short fiction stories with the theme being voyeurism and exhibitionism.

Valdez, N. (2010). *A little bit kinky: A couple's guide to rediscovering the thrill of sex.* New York: Broadway Books. This book, for both men and women, provides ideas for the "kinky" side of sex, from the little bit kinky to the kinkiest behaviors.

Contraception and Abortion

© Rafe Swan/Cultura/Getty Images

CHAPTER OUTLINE

Risk and Responsibility

Methods of Contraception

Abortion

Research Issues

"My parents and I never talked about sex until I had to ask them questions for one of my high school classes. They got so excited about the topic. I guess they were just waiting for me to ask. I remember my mom throwing a pack of condoms on the bed. She said, 'Just in case!' We just all laughed."

—20-year-old male

"During the summer before my sophomore year, things started to change. My father came into my room much as he had done the first time. It was 'The Talk, Part Two.' He asked me if I knew what a condom was and told me about abstinence. I told him I wasn't planning on having sex for a while, but I was lying; it was all I thought about. I felt awkward and embarrassed. Nevertheless, he made his point, and before he left he said, 'I love you.'"

—20-year-old male

"Mom gave me an important sense that my body was mine, that it was my responsibility and under my control. Birth control was always discussed whenever sex was mentioned, but when it was, it was treated like a joke. The message was that sex can be a magical thing as long as you are being responsible—responsible for not getting yourself or anyone else pregnant. Back then, sexually transmitted infections were not discussed, so it was the pill or a diaphragm for me and condoms for my brothers."

—26-year-old female

TODAY, MORE THAN EVER BEFORE, we are aware of the impact of fertility on our own lives, as well as on the world. Reproduction, once considered strictly a personal matter, is now a subject of open debate and political action. Yet, regardless of our public views, we must each confront fertility on a personal level. In taking charge of our reproductive potential, we must be informed about the availability and effectiveness of birth control methods, as well as ways to protect ourselves against sexually transmitted infections (STIs). But information is only part of the picture. We also need to understand our own personal needs, values, and habits, so that we can choose methods we will use consistently, thereby minimizing our risks.

In this chapter, we begin by examining the psychology of risk taking and the role of individual responsibility in contraception. We then describe in detail the numerous contraceptive devices and techniques that are used today: methods of use, effectiveness rates, advantages, and possible problems. Finally, we look at abortion, its effect on individuals and society, and research issues.

One year they asked me to be poster boy—for birth control.
—Rodney Dangerfield
(1921–2004)

Risk and Responsibility

A typical American woman who wants to have two children spends about 5 years pregnant, postpartum, or trying to become pregnant and 30 years trying to avoid pregnancy (Guttmacher Institute, 2015). Over the course of this time, her contraceptive needs will change; however, the most important factor in her choice of a method of contraception will often be its effectiveness.

In the United States, nearly half of all pregnancies and 82% of teen births each year are unintended and about 4 in 10 pregnancies are terminated by abortion (Guttmacher Institute, 2014.11a). Although on average a woman has only about a 2–4% chance of becoming pregnant during intercourse without contraception, age and timing affect the odds. For example, if intercourse occurs during ovulation, the chance of conception is about 25%. Over a period of a year, sexually active couples who do not use contraception have an 85% chance of conception.

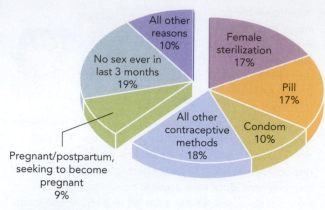

● FIGURE 1

Percentage of Women Aged 15–44, By Whether They Are Using Contraception and By Reason and Methods Used: United States, 2006–2012.

(*Source:* Jones, Mosher, & Daniels, 2012.)

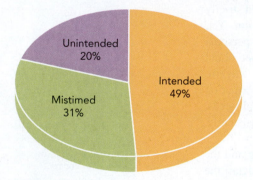

● FIGURE 2

Pregnancies, By Intention Status. Currently about half of the 6.6 million pregnancies in the United States each year are unintended. Most unintended pregnancies are attributable to nonuse, ambivalence, fear of side effects, inconsistent use, or incorrect use of contraceptives.

(*Source:* Guttmacher Institute, 2015.)

Because the gap between first sex and first birth is nearly 10 years (Guttmacher Institute, 2014.11b) and the potential for getting pregnant is so high for a sexually active, childbearing-age couple, it would seem reasonable that sexually active couples would use contraception to avoid unintended pregnancy. Unfortunately, all too often, this is not the case. In 2011–2013, approximately 62% of women aged 15–44 were using some type of contraceptive method, while 38% were sterile, pregnant, postpartum and breastfeeding, trying to become pregnant, or abstinent (Daniels, Daugherty, & Jones, 2014) (see Figure 1). Not surprisingly, the nonusers of contraception accounted for about half of unintended pregnancies; those who used contraception reported that the method either failed or was not used correctly or consistently (see Figure 2).

Numerous studies have indicated that the most consistent users of contraception are men and women who explicitly communicate about the subject. People at greatest risk for not using contraceptives are under age 20, are in casual dating relationships, and infrequently discuss contraception with their partners or others.

Women, Men, and Birth Control: Who Is Responsible?

If oral contraceptives for men became available, how many women would trust their partner to use them? Because women bear children and have most of the responsibility for raising them, women often have a greater interest than their partners in controlling their fertility. Also, it is generally easier to keep one egg from being fertilized once a month than to stop millions of sperm during each episode of intercourse. For these and other reasons, birth control has traditionally been seen as the woman's responsibility, but attitudes and practices are changing. The more education couples have, the more likely they are to talk about and utilize family planning (Jones et al., 2012). Education appears to instill confidence in both partners to discuss intended family size and birth control methods. Regardless of the motive or level of education, society no longer views the responsibility for birth control to lie solely with women. Rather, the majority of men as well as women perceive that there is gender equality in sexual decision making and equal responsibility for decisions about contraception. Male methods account for approximately 20% of all reversible contraceptive use (Guttmacher Institute, 2014.11c). These methods, the most common of which are the male condom and withdrawal, may be effective when used correctly and consistently. As opposed to an irreversible method, such as a vasectomy, reversible methods of birth control can be changed or stopped at any time. In fact, male methods of contraception predominate among couples 25–39 in all industrialized countries of the world except the United States. Although withdrawal, a common method in most countries, is not considered a reliable method of birth control, the condom is quite effective when used consistently and correctly, especially in combination with a spermicide.

When a partner becomes pregnant unexpectedly, the reactions and expectations of college men are often complex and multifaceted: ranging from ambivalent or avoidant to concerned and responsible. (Olmstead, Koon, Puhlman, Pasley, & Fincham, 2013). In a qualitative analysis, 148 college men were asked questions about an unplanned pregnancy, and three common responses emerged: They would expect to raise the child (87%), not raise the child (10%), or agree that their partner can decide (3%). Of those who expected to raise the child, most anticipated they would marry the child's mother. This research has significant implications for sexually active college men, particularly since they have been shown to engage in heavier drinking, which is linked to lower levels of condom use and other sexually risky behaviors (Cooper, 2002).

In addition to using a condom, a man can take contraceptive responsibility by: (1) exploring ways of being sexual without intercourse; (2) helping pay doctor or clinic bills and sharing the cost of pills, injections, or other birth control methods; (3) checking on supplies, helping keep track of his partner's menstrual cycle, and helping her with her part in the birth control routine; and (4) in certain circumstances like a long-term relationship, if no or no more children are planned, having a vasectomy.

When the history of our civilization is written, it will be a biological history, and Margaret Sanger will be its heroine.

—H. G. Wells
(1866–1946)

Navigating Reproductive Health

Reproductive health care reflects a deep commitment to supporting the family and makes a significant and necessary contribution to humankind. Margaret Sanger, widely regarded as the founder of the modern birth control movement, first acknowledged this when, in 1915, she opened an illegal clinic where women could obtain and learn to use the diaphragms she had shipped from Europe. Sanger believed that in order for women to lead healthier lives, they needed to be able to determine when to have children. Her advocacy also took the form of published birth control information, for which she was soon arraigned for violating the Comstock Laws, which made it a crime to sell or distribute materials that could be used for contraception or abortion. Later, in 1921, she founded the American Birth Control League, which we now know as Planned Parenthood Federation of America. It wasn't, however, until 1960 that the first birth control pills entered the U.S. marketplace. Fertility control, rather than abstinence, proved to be a major shift in the way women and some men regarded their sexuality and sexual expression.

Currently, the backbone of the nation's publicly funded family planning efforts is Title X, the Public Health Service Act, which makes effective contraceptive options accessible to all women, regardless of income. Clinical services for those who receive Title X support include a range of family planning and preventive health options that promote health and well-being among adolescents as well as adult men and women (see Figure 3 for recommended services).

The Title X package of care overlaps with services provided by the Affordable Care Act's (ACA) preventive services by expanding eligibility for private and public programs and guaranteeing contraceptive coverage

● **FIGURE 3**

Recommended Family Planning and Related Preventive Health Services.

(*Source:* Gavin, L., et al., 2014).

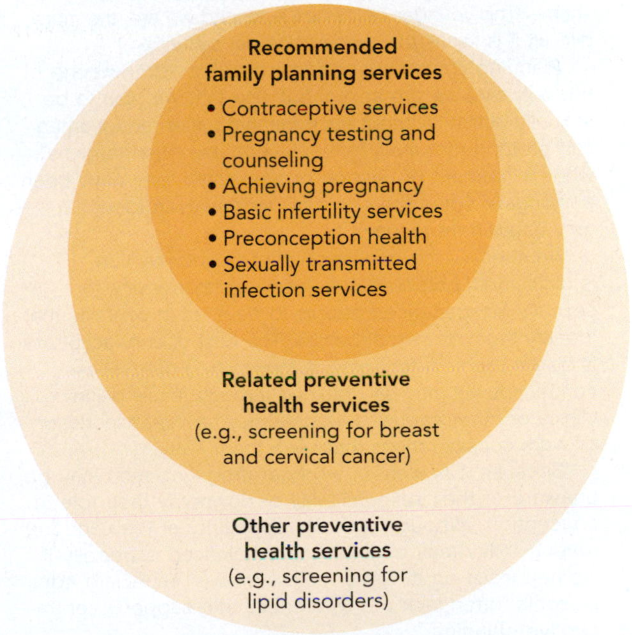

Recommended family planning services
- Contraceptive services
- Pregnancy testing and counseling
- Achieving pregnancy
- Basic infertility services
- Preconception health
- Sexually transmitted infection services

Related preventive health services
(e.g., screening for breast and cervical cancer)

Other preventive health services
(e.g., screening for lipid disorders)

think
about it

Risky Business: Why Couples Fail to Use Contraception

Most persons having sexual intercourse know they are taking a chance of getting pregnant when they don't use contraception. But the more frequently a person takes chances with unprotected intercourse without resultant pregnancy, the more likely he or she is to do so again. Eventually, the woman or couple will feel almost magically invulnerable to pregnancy. Each time they are lucky, their risk taking is reinforced.

The consequences of an unintended pregnancy—economic hardships, adoption, or abortion—may be overwhelming. So why do people take chances in the first place? Part of the reason is faulty knowledge. People often underestimate how easy it is to get pregnant, or they may not know how to use a contraceptive method correctly. Additionally, talking about or using some types of birth control can be uncomfortable and can interrupt spontaneity. But so can an unintended pregnancy.

Perceived Costs of Contraceptive Planning

One reason people avoid taking steps to prevent pregnancy is that they don't want to acknowledge their own sexuality. Acknowledging our sexuality is not necessarily easy, for it may be accompanied by feelings of guilt, conflict, and shame. The younger or less experienced we are, the more difficult it is for us to acknowledge our sexuality.

Planning contraception requires us to acknowledge not only that we are sexual but also that we plan to be sexually active. Without such planning, men and women can pretend that their sexual intercourse "just happens"—when a moment of passion occurs, when they have been drinking, or when there is a full moon—even though it may happen frequently.

Another reason people don't use contraception is difficulty in obtaining it. It is often embarrassing for sexually inexperienced people to be seen in contexts that identify them as sexual beings. The cost of contraceptives is also a problem for some. Although free or low-cost contraceptives may be obtained through family planning clinics or other agencies, people may have transportation or work considerations that keep them away.

Because it is women who get pregnant, men may be unaware of their responsibility or downplay their role in conception, although with the popularity of the condom, responsibility may become more balanced especially if women insist on it. Nevertheless, males, especially adolescents, often lack the awareness that supports contraceptive planning.

Many people, especially women using the pill, practice birth control consistently and effectively within an ongoing relationship but may give up their contraceptive practices if the relationship breaks up. They define themselves as sexual only within the context of a relationship. When men or women begin a new relationship, they may not use contraception because the relationship has not yet become established. They do not expect to have sexual intercourse or to have it often, so they are willing to take chances.

Using contraception such as a condom or spermicide may destroy the feeling of spontaneity in sex. For those who justify their sexual behavior by romantic impulsiveness, using these devices seems cold and mechanical.

Anticipated Benefits of Pregnancy

Ambivalence about pregnancy is a powerful incentive *not* to use contraception. For many people, being pregnant proves that a woman is indeed feminine on the most fundamental biological level. Getting a woman pregnant provides similar proof of masculinity for some men.

Pregnancy also proves beyond any doubt that a person is fertile. Many men and women have lingering doubts about whether they can have children. This is especially true for partners who have used contraception for a long time, but it is also true for those who take chances.

Another anticipated benefit of pregnancy is that it requires the partners to define their relationship and level of commitment to each other. It is a form of testing, albeit often an unconscious one. Many men and women unconsciously expect their partners to be pleased, but this is not always the reaction they get.

Finally, pregnancy involves not only two partners but possibly their parents as well, especially the woman's. Pregnancy may force a young person's parents to pay attention to and deal with him or her as an adult. Pregnancy may mean many things with regard to the parent-child relationship: a sign of rebellion, a form of punishment for a parental lack of caring, a plea for help and understanding, or an insistence on autonomy, independence, or adulthood.

Think Critically

1. If sexually active, do you take risks relative to not adequately protecting yourself or your partner from conception? If so, what kinds? Why?
2. When do you believe a person is more inclined to take risks?
3. What would you say to a sexual partner who hesitates in using a condom because he or she doesn't like the way it feels?

without copays (Guttmacher Institute, 2013). Those who have insurance through the ACA are now covered for their contraceptive methods and counseling, as prescribed by a health care provider. These plans cover the services without charging a copayment or coinsurance when they are provided by an in-network provider (HealthCare.gov, 2014). It is interesting to note that, for every $1.00 invested in helping women avoid unintended pregnancies, $5.68 is saved in Medicaid expenditures (Guttmacher Institute, 2013.11a). Additionally, the health law requires that preventive care services be provided by health plans to customers without cost. These services include annual well woman visits, depression screening, intimate partner violence screening and counseling, education about STIs, including HIV, and vaccines for flu, hepatitis, and HPV. Excluded are plans sponsored by certain exempt religious employers whose religious convictions do not cover certain types of contraceptive methods and counseling.

The ability of minors to consent to a range of health care services, including sexual and reproductive health care, has expanded dramatically in the last 30 years, with 26 states and the District of Columbia allowing those aged 12 and older to consent to contraceptive, prenatal, and STI services without parental involvement (Guttmacher Institute, 2014.11b). This trend reflects the recognition that many minors will remain sexually active and not seek services if they have to tell their parents beforehand. School districts are among those opting to provide birth control and condoms to their students. In spite of these efforts, many still need a place to go for contraceptive services, while others remain uninsured. Creative strategies aimed at both service providers and policymakers are needed to improve access to and use of contraceptives among women, especially those who are disadvantaged.

Adolescents and Contraception   In the United States, 614,000 teens became pregnant in 2010, with the overwhelming majority (82%) of those pregnancies being unintended (Guttmacher Institute, 2014.11c). Among these teens, the most cited reason for not using contraception was "I didn't think I could become pregnant" (Centers for Disease Control and Prevention, 2012). Eighteen percent of young men believed that having sex standing up helps prevent pregnancy (Kaye, Suellentrop, & Sloup, 2009). Despite the high levels of unplanned pregnancies, the overall teen pregnancy rate has actually declined since 1990, with effective use of contraception accounting for the decline. The majority of sexually experienced teens (78% of females and 85% of males) used contraceptives the first time they had sex, with condoms being their first method of choice (Martinez et al., 2011). Of the 2.7 million teenage women aged 15–19 who use contraceptives, 44% rely on the pill; 36% on the condom; 13% on other hormonal methods, such as the implant, injectable, patch, and ring; and 5% on other methods (Jones et al., 2012).

In 2014, the American Academy of Pediatrics (AAP) recommended that pediatricians consider **long-acting reversible contraceptive (LARC) methods**, namely, intrauterine devices (IUDs) and hormonal implants as "first-line contraceptive choices for adolescents." (Descriptions of these devices will follow in this chapter.) Also known as extended-use contraceptives, these options provide effective contraception for both adolescents and women for a prolonged period without requiring user action. As noted previously, the Affordable Care Act (ACA) provides funds for these and other contraceptives without out-of-pocket costs, which would otherwise be a critical barrier for use by teens.

The comedy *The To Do List* (2013), starring Aubrey Plaza, focuses on a set of teens who attempt to navigate their sexuality.

© Film Fanatic/Alamy

Planning contraception requires us to acknowledge our sexuality. One way a responsible couple can reduce the risk of unintended pregnancy is by visiting a family planning clinic—together.

© B. Boissonnet/BSIP/AGE Fotostock

● Methods of Contraception

The methods we use to prevent pregnancy or its progress vary widely. Thus, the best method of contraception is one that will be used consistently and correctly. Hopefully, this method is also one that is available and in harmony with one's preferences, fears, and expectations.

Contraception, or birth control, is the use of artificial methods or other techniques to prevent pregnancy. (Note that throughout this chapter we will be interchanging the terms "contraception" and "birth control.") This is done in a variety of ways, including: (1) barrier methods, such as condoms and diaphragms, which place a physical barrier between the sperm and the egg; (2) spermicides, which kill the sperm before they can get to the egg; (3) hormonal methods, such as the pill, the shot, the patch, the implant, and the ring, which inhibit the release of the oocyte from the ovary; and (4) intrauterine devices, which prevent the sperm from fertilizing the egg.

Choosing a Method

To be fully responsible in using birth control, individuals must know what options they have, how reliable these methods are, and what advantages and disadvantages including possible side effects each has. Thus, it is important to be aware of both personal health issues and the specifics of the methods themselves. (Table 1 shows the failure rates of contraceptives.)

Most women who are not currently using contraception go to a clinic or doctor's office knowing exactly what method they want. However, many of these women are not aware of other options available to them. In some instances, the method they think they want may not be medically appropriate or may not be one they will use correctly and consistently. Knowing the facts about the methods gives you a solid basis from which to make decisions, as well as more security once you reach a decision. (See Figure 4 for percentages of all women aged 15–44 who use contraceptives.)

To help you make an informed decision about which method of birth control is medically appropriate and will be used every time, consider these questions (Hatcher et al., 2011):

- Do you have any particular preferences or biases related to birth control?
- Do you know the advantages and disadvantages of each of the contraceptive methods?
- How convenient and easy is it to use this method?
- If you or your partner is at risk, does this method protect against STIs, including HIV?
- What are the effects of this method on menses?
- Is it important that you negotiate with your partner to help determine the method?
- What other influences (e.g., religion, privacy, past experience, friends' advice, and frequency of intercourse) might affect your decision?
- Have you discussed potential methods with your health care practitioner?

Knowledge and familiarity about contraceptive methods are strong determinants of use among young adults. Among unmarried women aged 18–29, for each correct response on a contraceptive knowledge scale, the odds of currently using a hormonal or long-acting reversible method increased by 17% and of using no method decreased by 17%. Other factors that increase the usage of a contraceptive method include having a higher income, being married, being religious, and cohabiting. The proportion of at-risk women who are not using a method is

TABLE 1 • Failure Rates and Relative Effectiveness of Contraceptives During First Year of Use

| Method | % of Women Experiencing an Unintended Pregnancy Within the First Year of Use | | % of Women Continuing Use at 1 Year | Relative Effectiveness |
	Typical Use (%)[a]	Perfect Use (%)[b]		
No method	85	85		Least effective: *18 or more* pregnancies per 100 women in a year
Spermicides (foams, creams, gels, suppositories, and film)	28	18	42	
Fertility awareness–based methods	24	12	47	
Withdrawal	22	4	46	
Sponge				
Parous women (given birth)	24	20	36	
Nulliparous women (never given birth)	12	9	—	
Condom				
Female	21	5	41	
Male	18	2	43	
Diaphragm	12	6	57	Effective: *6–12* pregnancies per 100 in a year
Combined pill and progestin-only pill	9	0.3	67	
Contraceptive patch	9	0.3	67	
Contraceptive ring	9	0.3	67	
DMPA contraceptive injection	6	0.2	56	
IUD				Most effective: *less than 1* pregnancy per 100 in a year
ParaGard	0.8	0.6	78	
Mirena and Skyla (Levonorgestrel)	0.2	0.2	80	
Single-rod contraceptive implant	0.05	0.05	84	
Female sterilization	0.5	0.5	100	
Male sterilization	0.15	0.10	100	

[a]The percentage of typical users who become pregnant within 1 year while using the method.
[b]The percentage of women who become pregnant within 1 year using the method *perfectly* every time.

SOURCE: Adapted from Hatcher, R. A., et al. (2011). *Contraceptive technology* (20th rev. ed.). New York: Reprinted by permission of Ardent Media.

highest among 15- to 19-year-olds (Guttmacher Institute, 2014.11a). Still, the pill remains one of the most popular methods of birth control for women, along with female sterilization and condoms (Daniels et al., 2014) (see Figure 4). Among the two thirds of women aged 15–44 who used birth control between 2011 and 2013, approximately 16% used the pill. Long-acting reversible contraceptives are becoming more popular, with their use nearly doubling over the past 5 years.

In the following discussion of method effectiveness, "perfect use" refers to the percentage of women who become pregnant during their first year of use

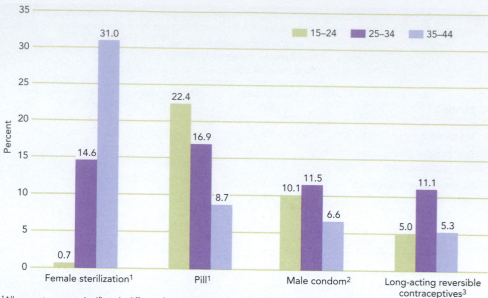

¹All percentages are significantly different from each other across age groups.
²Percentages for age group 15–24 and 25–34 are significantly different from age group 35–44.
³Percentages for age group 15–24 and 35–34 are significantly different from age group 25–34.

NOTES: For women using more than one method, categorized by the most effective method they were using. Long-acting reversible contraceptives include contraceptive implants and intrauterine devices. Access data table at: http://www.cdc. gov/nchs/ data/databriefs/ db173_table.pdf#1.

• FIGURE 4

Percentage of All Women Aged 15–44 Who Were Using Female Sterilization, the Pill, the Male Condom, and Long-Acting Reversible Contraceptives, by Age: United States, 2011–2013.

(*Source*: Daniels, K., Daugherty, J., & Jones, J., 2014).

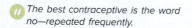 *The best contraceptive is the word no—repeated frequently.*

—Margaret Smith

when they use the method *correctly and consistently.* "Typical use" refers to the percentage of women who become pregnant during their first year of use; this number includes both couples who use the method correctly and consistently and those who do not (see Table 1). Thus, typical use is the more significant number to use when considering a method of contraception. Of those who use contraceptives consistently and correctly throughout the course of a year, only 5% become pregnant (Guttmacher Institute, 2014.11c).

Sexual Abstinence

Before we begin our discussion of devices and techniques for preventing conception, we must acknowledge the oldest and most reliable birth control method of all: abstinence. There is a wide variety of opinion about what constitutes sexual activity. However, from a family planning perspective, **abstinence** is the absence of genital contact that could lead to a pregnancy (i.e., penile penetration of the vagina). The term "celibacy" is sometimes used interchangeably with "abstinence." We prefer "abstinence" because "celibacy" often implies the avoidance of *all* forms of sexual activity and, often, a commitment to not marry or to maintain a nonsexual life.

Individuals who choose not to have intercourse are still free to express affection and to give and receive sexual pleasure if they so desire in a variety of ways, including talking, hugging, massaging, kissing, petting, and manually and orally stimulating the genitals. Those who choose abstinence from sexual intercourse as their method of birth control need to communicate this clearly to their partners. They should also be informed about other forms of contraception. And in the event that either partner experiences a change of mind, it can't hurt to have a condom handy. An advantage of abstinence is that refraining from sexual intercourse in a new relationship may allow two people to get to know and trust each other more before experiencing greater intimacy and it is 100% effective at preventing pregnancy.

Hormonal Methods

In addition to the tried-and-true birth control pill, several varieties of hormonal contraception are available. These include a pill that causes menstrual suppression, a birth control shot, a patch, a vaginal ring, and an implant.

The Pill **Oral contraceptives (OCs),** popularly called "the pill," are the most widely used form of reversible contraception in the United States, accounting for 17% of all contraceptives used (Guttmacher Institute, 2014.11c). The pill is actually a series of pills (various numbers to a package) containing synthetic estrogen and/or progesterone that regulate egg production and the menstrual cycle. When taken for birth control, oral contraceptives accomplish some or all of the following:

- Suppresses ovulation 90–95% of the time
- Thickens cervical mucus thereby preventing sperm penetration into the woman's upper genital tract
- Thins the lining of the uterus to inhibit implantation of the fertilized ovum
- Slows the rate of ovum transport
- Disrupts transport of the fertilized egg
- Inhibits capacitation of the sperm, which limits the sperm's ability to fertilize the egg

The pill produces basically the same chemical conditions that would exist in a woman's body if she were pregnant.

Types and Usage Oral contraceptives must be prescribed by a physician or family planning clinic. Most commonly prescribed are the combination pills, which contain a fairly standard amount of estrogen (usually about 35 micrograms) and different amounts of progestin, a synthetic form of progesterone, according to the pill type. In the triphasic pill, the amount of progestin is altered during the cycle, purportedly to approximate the normal hormonal pattern. Progestin-only pills (POPs), sometimes called "minipills," contain the hormone progestin. The minipill is considered slightly less effective than the combination pill, and it must be taken with precise, unfailing regularity to be effective. Taken at the same time each day, with no hormone-free days, the minipill provides an alternative to those who cannot safely take estrogen. These include women who are breastfeeding, have had weight loss (bariatric) surgery, have liver disease, or have had breast cancer.

A woman can begin taking oral contraceptives on the same day as she receives her prescription, providing she is not pregnant and not in need of emergency contraception. Women may prefer this "quick start" practice because other approaches generally leave a time gap between the time the pills are prescribed and the time one starts taking them. If a woman starts taking the pill within 5 days after starting her period, she is protected against pregnancy right away.

The pill is considered among the most effective birth control methods available when used correctly. But the pill is *not* effective when taken inconsistently. It must be taken every day, as close as possible to the same time each day. If one pill is missed, it should be taken as soon as the woman remembers, and the next one taken on schedule. If two pills are missed, the method cannot be relied on, and an additional form of contraception should be used for the rest of the cycle.

A shift to extended-use oral contraceptives acknowledges a little known fact: Women don't need to have monthly periods. Extended-cycle oral contraceptives

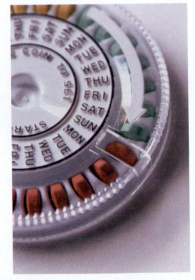

Although oral contraceptives are effective in preventing pregnancy, they do not provide protection against STIs, including HIV infection.

© Don Farrall/Getty Images

provide women with a safe, acceptable, and effective form of contraception (Planned Parenthood, 2014.11a). The use of these regimens provides women with more options and almost certainly improves the acceptability and efficacy of hormonal contraception.

Since none of the hormonal methods of birth control offer protection against STIs, women on the pill should consider the additional use of a condom, if she is not in a monogamous relationship or is unsure of her partner's STI status.

Effectiveness   Oral contraceptives are more than 99.7% effective if used correctly. The typical-use rate is 91%.

Advantages   The benefits of hormonal methods generally far outweigh any significant negative effects. Pills are easy to take. They are dependable. No applications or interruptions are necessary before or during intercourse. In fact, millions of women use the pill with moderate to high degrees of satisfaction. For many women, if personal health or family history does not contraindicate it, the pill is both effective and safe. Some women experience benefits such as more regular or reduced menstrual flow, less menstrual cramping, and some protection against pelvic inflammatory disease (PID) which often leads to infertility (Planned Parenthood, 2014.11b). The pill may offer some protection against bone thinning and ovarian and endometrial cancer, and may decrease the risk of benign breast conditions and iron deficiency anemia. In addition, evidence has revealed that women on the birth control pill are protected from ovarian cancer, even decades after they stop taking it.

Disadvantages   There are many possible side effects, which may or may not prevent the user from taking the pill. Those most often reported are spotting, breast tenderness, nausea or vomiting, and bleeding between periods (most often with progestin-only pills). Depending on the woman, hormones in the pills may increase or decrease a woman's sex drive.

These side effects can sometimes be eliminated by changing the prescription, but not always. Certain women react unfavorably to the pill because of existing health factors or extrasensitivity to female hormones. Women who are age 35 or over; have high cholesterol, certain inherited blood clotting disorders, or high blood pressure; need prolonged bed rest; smoke; or are prone to migraine headaches are usually considered poor candidates for the pill. Women have a higher risk of blood clots if they are obese. Certain medications may react differently or unfavorably with the pill, either diminishing in their therapeutic effect or interfering with oral contraceptive effectiveness. Thus, it is important to check with a doctor before starting any new prescriptions if a woman is taking the pill.

The pill also creates certain health risks, but to what extent is a matter of controversy. Though the pill has been studied extensively and is very safe, in rare instances hormonal methods can lead to serious problems. Some of the warning signs to look for spell out the word "ACHES." If a woman experiences any of these she needs to check with her clinician as soon as possible:

- **A**bdominal pain (severe)
- **C**hest pain
- **H**eadaches (severe)
- **E**ye problems (including blurred vision, spots, or a change in shape of the cornea)
- **S**welling and/or aching in the legs and thighs

Literature is mostly about sex and not much about having children and life is the other way round.

—David Lodge
(1921–2003)

A woman should also consult with her clinician if she develops severe mood swings or depression, becomes jaundiced (yellow-colored skin), misses two periods, or has signs of pregnancy.

Several brands of pills that have caught the attention of the public via a U.S. Food and Drug Administration (FDA) safety alert are Yaz, Gianvi, Yasmin, Ocella, Syeda, and Zarah. Compared to older forms of oral contraceptives, the newer type of progestin hormone in these pills may carry a higher risk of causing dangerous blood clots in the legs and lungs and other health problems (Planned Parenthood, 2014.11b).

The type of hormones and the stage of life when the pill is used may make them helpful at one point and harmful at another. The health risks for taking the pill are low for the young, but they increase with age. While no contraception is contraindicated based on age alone, estrogen-containing methods should be reserved for women without heart or blood-clotting risk factors (Baldwin & Jensen, 2013). The risk for side effects and complications also increase if a woman smokes, is overweight, has diabetes, or has high blood pressure. Pills are not recommended for those over the age of 35 and who smoke (Planned Parenthood, 2014.11b). Definite risks of cardiovascular complications and various forms of cancer exist because of the synergistic action of the ingredients in cigarettes and oral contraceptives. This caution should be separated from claims linking the pill to breast cancer. The most recent literature suggests that the pill has little, if any, effect on the risk of developing breast cancer (Planned Parenthood, 2014.11a).

Certain other factors may need to be taken into account in determining if oral contraceptives are appropriate for a woman. Since it is possible to get pregnant again shortly after a pregnancy or delivery, birth control needs to be considered. (For more information about birth control following delivery, see the section titled "Lactational Amenorrhea Method.")

Once a woman stops taking the pill, her menstrual cycle will usually resume within 2 months, though it may take several more months before it becomes regular. If a woman wants to become pregnant, it is recommended that she change to another method of contraception for 2–3 months after she stops taking the pill and then start efforts to conceive.

Birth Control Shot (Depo-Provera)   The **birth control shot,** known by the brand name Depo-Provera (DMPA), is an injection of the hormone progestin that is used to prevent pregnancy for 12 weeks. The progestin works by stopping ovulation and thickening the cervical mucus, which keeps sperm from reaching the eggs (Planned Parenthood, 2014.11c). A woman should get her first injection of DMPA within 7 days of the start of her menstrual period. The drug is effective immediately. If the shot is given within 5 days after a miscarriage or an abortion, or within 3 weeks after giving birth, a women is protected from pregnancy immediately. Most women can use the birth control shot safely; however, risks and side effects are similar to those of the pill. Irregular bleeding is the most common side effect, especially in the first 6–12 months of use. Additionally, after 1 year, half of those using the shot will stop having periods completely. This side effect is very common and may cause some women who are not having periods to worry that they are pregnant. When the shot is used correctly, it is very effective. There is no way to stop the side effects of Depo-Provera; they may continue for 12–14 weeks after the shot. Because it can take anywhere from 6 to 10 months to become pregnant following the last shot, Depo-Provera is not a good birth control method for those desiring an immediate pregnancy.

If a pregnancy does occur while a woman is on the shot, a rare occurrence, it is more likely to be an ectopic one, which can be life-threatening.

Effectiveness The perfect-use effectiveness rate is 99.8% while the typical-use rate is slightly less at 94%.

Advantages Because DMPA injections contain no estrogen, they do not appear to cause the rare but potentially serious problems associated with estrogen. Additionally, DMPA is highly effective for 3 months, causes women to have very light or missed periods (women vary in their reactions to this), decreased menstrual symptoms, and less pain from endometriosis. DMPA can also be a good choice for women who are breastfeeding.

Disadvantages Menstrual cycle disturbances may occur, including unpredictable or prolonged episodes of bleeding or spotting and temporary and reversible decrease in bone density.

Serious health problems are rarely associated with DMPA use; however, if a woman develops very painful headaches, heavy bleeding, serious depression, severe lower abdominal pain (may be a sign of pregnancy), or pus or pain at the site of the injection, she should see her physician. Because Depo-Provera lowers estrogen levels, it may cause women to lose calcium stored in their bones. Women who use the shot may also have temporary bone thinning, which will abate once a woman stops taking the shot. A women can protect her bones by exercising regularly and getting extra calcium and vitamin D either through diet or supplements.

Birth Control Patch The **birth control patch,** generic name xulane, is a thin, beige, plastic transdermal reversible method of birth control that releases synthetic estrogen and progestin to protect against pregnancy for 1 month (Planned Parenthood, 2014.11d). Each week for 3 consecutive weeks, one patch is removed and a new one is placed on the lower abdomen, buttocks, upper arm, or upper torso (excluding the breast). This is followed by a patch-free week, when menstruation occurs. The combination of hormones works the same way that oral contraceptives do. The patch is most effective when it is changed on the same day of the week for 3 consecutive weeks. Pregnancy can happen if an error is made in using the patch, especially if it becomes loose for longer than 24 hours or falls off or if the same patch is left on for more than 1 week.

If the patch has partially or completely detached for less than 24 hours, the woman should try to reapply it; however, if it does not stick well, a replacement should be applied. If a woman applies the patch late during week 1, she should apply a new patch as soon as she remembers. This becomes her new patch "change day." A backup method, such as a condom, should be used for 7 days after the patch is applied. If vaginal intercourse occurs without a backup method, emergency contraception should be used up to 5 days after unprotected intercourse.

Two groups of women that may need additional counseling about the use of the contraceptive patch are adolescents and women who are above 130% of ideal body weight. The latter group should be aware that they have a slightly increased risk of pregnancy due to lower levels of blood hormones.

Effectiveness Overall, contraceptive efficacy of the patch is similar to that of oral contraceptives; if used perfectly, the patch is more than 99% effective. Typical use results in a success rate of 91%.

The contraceptive patch, prescribed by a physician, protects against pregnancy for 1 month.

© Michael Keller/Corbis

Advantages   Like those who take OCs, many women who use the patch report the same benefits, including more-regular, lighter, and shorter periods. Furthermore, a woman's ability to become pregnant returns quickly when the patch is discontinued. The patch is safe, simple, and convenient, and it does not interfere with sex. Additionally, a woman does not have to remember to take a pill each day.

Disadvantages   The most common side effects reported by users of the patch include mild skin reactions, breast tenderness usually in the first one or two menstrual cycles following its first application, headaches, and nausea. The risk of stroke or heart attack is similar to that of combined oral contraceptives. The patch may cause more long-lasting side effects, including changing a women's sexual desire.

The Vaginal Ring (NuvaRing)

A **vaginal ring,** commonly referred to as NuvaRing, is a form of reversible, hormonal birth control (Planned Parenthood, 2014.11f). It is a small, flexible ring inserted high into the vagina once every 28 days (see Figure 5). The ring is kept in place for 21 days and removed for a 7-day break to allow a withdrawal bleed. The ring releases synthetic estrogen and progestin, preventing ovulation in a manner similar to that of other combined hormonal contraceptives. The vaginal ring is prescribed by a doctor and provides protection against pregnancy if implanted during the first 5 days of a woman's period.

Effectiveness   Like the other methods of hormonal contraception, if used perfectly, the vaginal ring is more than 99% effective. Typical use results in a success rate of 91%.

Advantages   The ring protects against pregnancy for 1 month and is easy to use. Many women who use the ring have more-regular, lighter, and shorter periods. A woman can stop using NuvaRing at any time, offering her more control over contraception than with some other hormonal methods of birth control. The

> *My best birth control now is to leave the lights on.*
>
> —Joan Rivers
> (1933–2014)

● **FIGURE 5**

The Vaginal Ring. Like a tampon, the ring can be placed anywhere in the vagina that is comfortable. There is no specific fit or need to check the position of the ring. If it causes pressure, the user may just push it farther into the vagina.

(first) © vario images GmbH & Co.KG/Alamy

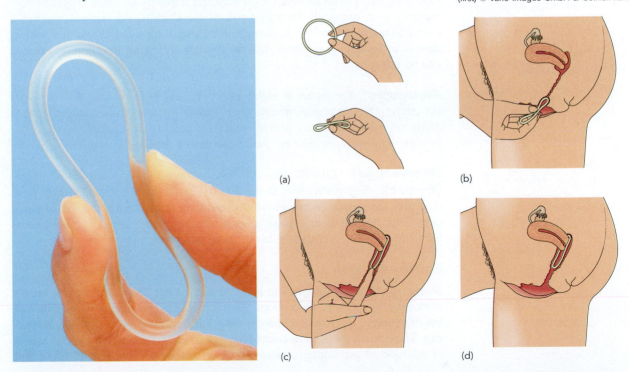

(a)

(b)

(c)

(d)

ring provides a consistent release of hormones, does not usually cause weight gain, and can be removed for up to 3 hours without compromising effectiveness.

Disadvantages   The side effects of the ring are similar to those associated with oral contraceptives. Additionally, there may be an increased risk of blood clots possibly due to the hormone desogesterel. Vaginal discharge, irritation, or infection; sensation of a foreign body; expulsion; and headaches may also occur. The ring should not be used by women who have weak pelvic floor muscles. Additionally, it may be less effective for women weighing more than 200 pounds. Regularly using oil-based medicines in the vagina for yeast infections while the ring is in place may increase the level of hormones released into the blood. This, however, will not reduce the effectiveness of the ring. The effect of using these types of yeast infection medications with long-term use of the vaginal ring is unknown.

Implants   The birth control **implant** is a thin, flexible, plastic rod about the size of a cardboard matchstick that is inserted under the skin of the upper arm and protects against pregnancy for up to 3 years (Planned Parenthood, 2014.11g). The implant is available under the brand names Implanon and Nexplanon. Like several other progestin-containing methods of birth control, implants prevent ovulation and fertilization and thicken the cervical mucus to block sperm.

Questions about the difference between the more widely used Implanon and the newer Nexplanon and Implanon NXT may arise. The later two implants are essentially identical to Implanon but have a small amount of a substance added to their core, so they are detectable by X-ray, which makes it easier to ensure they are in place. The newer implants also have a pre-loaded applicator for easier insertion.

Implants are among the most effective of the available contraceptives, similar in effectiveness to intrauterine devices (IUDs) and sterilization (see Table 1). Currently, there is no distinction between the implant and other progestin-only methods with respect to increased risk of blood clots. An implant requires a doctor to insert and remove it, along with the use of local anesthesia. If a woman desires to become pregnant within the 3 years following insertion, the device can be removed.

Advantages   The device is highly effective, easy to insert, and discrete; does not interrupt sex or require maintenance; has no estrogen-related side effects; is easily reversible; and may provide relief for pelvic pain due to endometriosis or other causes. It can also be used while breast feeding.

Disadvantages   Like all progestin-only methods, implants may cause unpredictable bleeding, particularly in the first 6–12 months of use, and weight gain; they may have insertion complications; and they may increase the risk of blood clots. The implant is also clinician-dependent, so once it is inserted, women have little control over their side effects or outcomes.

Barrier Methods

Barrier methods are designed to keep sperm and egg from uniting. The barrier device used by men is the condom. Barrier methods available to women include the diaphragm, the female condom, the contraceptive sponge, and the cervical cap. These methods of birth control have become increasingly popular because, in addition to preventing conception, they can reduce the risk of STIs. The effectiveness of all barrier methods is increased by use with spermicides, which are discussed later in this chapter.

The Condom A **condom** (**male condom**) is a thin, soft, flexible sheath of latex rubber, polyurethane, or processed animal tissue that fits over the erect penis to help prevent semen from being transmitted. Condoms prevent infections by covering the portals of entry and exit for many STI organisms (Planned Parenthood, 2014.11h).

Condoms are the third most widely used form of birth control in the United States after sterilization and the pill. Their use has increased significantly since the late 1980s, due in large part to their effectiveness in helping prevent the spread of STIs, including HIV, when they are used properly. Condoms are available in a wide variety of shapes, sizes, and colors. Some are dry, while others are lubricated.

A small proportion of condoms are made of polyurethane or other synthetic materials. These condoms are more resistant to deterioration than latex condoms, have a longer shelf life, and can provide an alternative if a person is allergic to latex. Unlike latex condoms, oil-based lubricants can be used with condoms made from synthetic materials.

Most condoms are very thin (but also strong), conduct heat well, and allow quite a bit of sensation to be experienced. While picking out condoms can be a fun experience, if a person needs them for protection, be sure to read the label to see if they are FDA-approved for use against unplanned pregnancy and STIs. Latex condoms should be used with water-based lubricants (like K-Y Jelly) or glycerine only because oil-based lubricants such as Vaseline can weaken the rubber. If a condom breaks, slips, or leaks, there are some things a person can do (see the section "Emergency Contraception" later in the chapter).

Women and Condom Use Today, a vast number of male condoms are purchased by women, and condom advertising and packaging increasingly reflect this trend. Several key points are relevant to the issue of women and condom use:

- Women experience more health consequences than men from STIs, including permanent infertility, for example. Condoms when used consistently and correctly are an effective means of reducing the risk of STI transmission and acquisition.

- Since women are far more likely to contract an STI from intercourse with a male partner than vice versa, it is in the woman's best interest to use or have her partner use a condom.

- Condoms help protect women against unplanned pregnancy, ectopic pregnancy, bacterial infections such as vaginitis and pelvic inflammatory disease (PID), viral infections such as herpes and HIV, cervical cancer, and infections that may harm a fetus or an infant during delivery.

- A woman can protect herself by insisting on condom use. Even if a woman regularly uses another form of birth control, such as the pill or an intrauterine device (IUD), she may want to have the added protection provided by a condom.

Male condoms come in a variety of sizes, colors, and textures; some are lubricated, and many have a reservoir tip designed to collect semen.

© Image Source/AP Images

Condom machines are often placed in bathrooms, subway stations, airports, and schools as a public health measure to promote safer sex. Rarely do these vending machines dispense female condoms.

© Sonda Dawes/The Image Works

practically
speaking

Tips for Effective Condom Use

Condoms can be very effective contraceptive devices when used properly. They also can reduce the risk of STIs, including HIV. Here are some tips for their use:

1. Use condoms every time you have vaginal, anal, or oral sex.

2. Check the expiration date on the package and press the container to make sure there is an air pocket.

3. Carefully open the condom package—teeth or fingernails can tear the condom.

4. If the penis is uncircumcised, pull back the foreskin before putting on the condom.

5. Use of a condom lubricated with nonoxynol-9 (N-9) is not recommended for vaginal or anal intercourse.

6. Put on the condom before it touches any part of a partner's body.

7. If you accidentally put the condom on wrong-side up, discard the condom and use another.

8. Leave about a half inch of space at the condom tip, and roll the condom all the way down the erect penis to the base. Push out any air bubbles.

9. Withdraw the penis soon after ejaculation. Make sure the male or his partner holds the base of the condom firmly against the penis as it is withdrawn.

10. After use, check the condom for possible tears. If you find a tear or hole, consider the use of emergency contraception (see the section "Emergency Contraception" later in the chapter). If torn condoms are a persistent problem, use a water-based lubricant such as K-Y Jelly.

11. Do not reuse a condom.

12. Keep condoms in a cool, dry, and convenient place.

13. To help protect against HIV and other STIs, always use a latex rubber or polyurethane condom, *not* one made of animal tissue.

14. Don't forget to incorporate sensual ways of placing the condom on the penis.

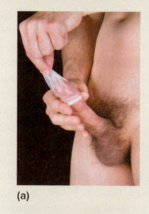
(a)

(b)

(c)

(d)

(a) Place the rolled condom on the erect penis, leaving about a half inch of space at the tip (first, squeeze any air out of the condom tip). (b) Roll the condom down, smoothing out any air bubbles. (c) Roll the condom to the base of the penis. (d) After ejaculation, hold the condom base while withdrawing the penis.

(a) © H.S. Photos/Alamy; (b) © H.S. Photos/Alamy; (c) © H.S. Photos/Alamy; (d) © H.S. Photos/Alamy

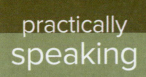

Correct Condom Use Self-Efficacy Scale

Correct and consistent condom use is one of the most effective methods for preventing the transmission of HIV, reducing the risk of other STIs, and lowering the risk of unplanned pregnancy. It is also known that young people aged 15–24 account for half of all STIs, even though they represent just 25% of the sexually active population (CDC, 2013.11a). Just what prevents individuals from making a decision to use condoms? The Condom Use Self-Efficacy Scale (CUSES) is designed to measure an individual's perception of the ease or difficult with which he or she can correctly apply and use a male condom. It measures an individual's perception of his or her ability to purchase condoms, apply and remove them, and negotiate their use with partners.

Directions

Circle the number that represents how easy or difficult it would be to do what each question asks.

1. How easy or difficult would it be for you to find condoms that fit you properly?

Very difficult				Very easy
1	2	3	4	5

2. How easy or difficult would it be for you to apply condoms correctly?

Very difficult				Very easy
1	2	3	4	5

3. How easy or difficult would it be for you to keep a condom from drying out during sex?

Very difficult				Very easy
1	2	3	4	5

4. How easy or difficult would it be for you to keep a condom from breaking during sex?

Very difficult				Very easy
1	2	3	4	5

5. How easy or difficult would it be for you to keep an erection while using a condom?

Very difficult				Very easy
1	2	3	4	5

6. How easy or difficult would it be for you to keep a condom on when withdrawing after sex?

Very difficult				Very easy
1	2	3	4	5

7. How easy or difficult would it be for you to wear a condom from start to finish of sex with your partner?

Very difficult				Very easy
1	2	3	4	5

Interpretation

A higher score indicates greater self-efficacy for correct use of male condoms.

SOURCE: Crosby, R. A., Graham, C. A., Milhausen, R. R., Sanders, S. A., & Yarber, W. L. (2011). In T. D. Fisher, C. M. Davis, W. L. Yarber, & S. L. Davis, (Eds.), *Handbook of sexuality-related measures* (3rd ed.). New York: Routledge.

Effectiveness   With perfect use, condoms are 98% effective in preventing conception, but user effectiveness is about 88%. Failures sometimes occur from using the condom incorrectly, but they are usually the result of not putting it on until after some semen has leaked into the vagina or simply not putting it on at all. When used in anal sex, a male condom is more likely to break and slip than when used for vaginal sex if adequate lubrication is not used.

Advantages   Condoms are easy to obtain and do not cause harmful side effects. They are simple to carry and are inexpensive or even free. Latex condoms help protect against STIs, including HIV infection, and lower the risk of unplanned pregnancy. Some men appreciate the slightly reduced sensitivity they experience when using a condom because it may help delay ejaculation.

It is now vitally important that we find a way of making the condom a cult object of youth.

—Germaine Greer
(1939–)

Possible Problems   Condoms can reduce but cannot eliminate the risks of STIs or unplanned pregnancy. The chief drawback of a condom is that it should be put on after the penis has become erect but before penetration. This interruption is a major reason users neglect to put condoms on. Some men and women complain that sensation is dulled, and very rarely cases of allergy to rubber are reported. Couples should try different types of condoms to see which one(s) they prefer.

The female condom

The **female condom** is a disposable, thin, loose-fitting sheath with a diaphragm-like ring at each end (Planned Parenthood, 2014.11i). One of the two rings is sealed shut inside the sheath and is used to insert and anchor the condom against the cervix. The open outer ring remains outside the vagina and acts as a barrier, protecting the vulva and the base of the penis (see Figure 6). The diaphragm is designed to line the entire inner wall of the vagina and to protect women against sperm. The pouch is lubricated both inside and outside with a non-spermicidal lubricant and is meant for one-time use. Some women use female condoms for anal sex; however, it is not known how effective they are in preventing STIs and HIV with this type of use (CDC, 2014.11a). If used correctly and consistently, the female condom reduces the risk of contracting many STIs, including HIV, and helps prevent pregnancy. Female and male condoms should not be used together because they can adhere to each other and cause one or both to slip out of position.

The female condom (brand names Reality, Femy, and Femidom) initially was made of polyurethane. Though safe and effective, polyurethane is a relatively expensive material to use, so the makers of the female condom released the FC2 version, which is made of nitrile, a cheaper material. New models of female condoms, such as Reddy condom and Cupid condom, which are made of latex, are currently being developed with the belief that a broader choice of contraception could lead to more consistent use of female condoms and result in fewer STIs and unplanned pregnancies ("Female condom," 2014).

Effectiveness   The perfect-use contraceptive effectiveness rate for female condoms is 95%, similar to that for other barrier methods in protecting against pregnancy. The typical-use effectiveness rate is 79%.

• **FIGURE 6**

The Female Condom in Position (left). The female condom is anchored around the cervix with a flexible ring much like a diaphragm. A larger ring secures the sheath outside the vagina and helps protect the vulva.

photo © McGraw-Hill Education/Jill Braaten, photographer

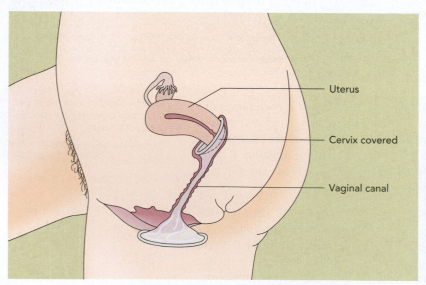

Uterus

Cervix covered

Vaginal canal

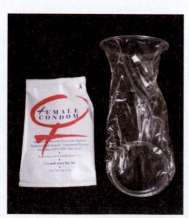

Advantages   One advantage of the female condom over the male condom is that it not only protects the vagina and cervix from sperm and microbes but also is designed so that the open end covers the woman's external genitals and the base of her partner's penis, thus offering both people excellent protection against infections. Because both polyurethane and nitrile are stronger than latex, the device is less likely than the male latex condom to break and can be used with both water- and oil-based lubricants. In addition, the condoms conduct heat well, so sensation is preserved. Female condoms may prove advantageous for women whose partners are reluctant to use a male condom, in part because they do not constrict the penis, as may male latex condoms. They also give women an additional way to control their fertility, do not require a prescription, and provide another means to help prevent STIs, including HIV.

Possible Problems   The female condom is relatively problem-free. The major complaint is aesthetic: Some women dislike the complete coverage of the female genitals provided by the condom (one of its chief health advantages) and don't want to use it for this reason. Sometimes, the female condom may slip into the vagina or anus during intercourse. It may also cause irritation of the vagina, vulva, penis, or anus. Noise made during intercourse may be distracting; however, additional lubricant can quiet this. Some women may find the female condom hard to insert or remove.

The Diaphragm

A **diaphragm** is a shallow, dome-shaped cup with a flexible rim that is placed deep inside the vagina, blocking the cervix, to prevent sperm from entering the uterus and fallopian tubes (Planned Parenthood, 2014.11j). In order to be as effective as possible, the diaphragm must be used with a spermicidal cream or jelly. Creams and jellies are considered more effective than foam for use with a diaphragm.

Once inserted, the diaphragm provides effective contraceptive protection for 6 hours. After intercourse, it should be left in place for at least 6 hours. A woman should not dislodge it or douche before it is time to remove it. If intercourse is repeated within 6 hours, the diaphragm should be left in place and more spermicide inserted with an applicator. To remove a diaphragm, the woman inserts a finger into her vagina and under the front of the diaphragm rim and then gently pulls it out. The diaphragm should be washed in mild soap and water and patted dry before being put away in its storage case. A diaphragm is available by prescription only and should be replaced about once a year. Diaphragms are available in different sizes, and a woman may need to be refitted for size after a pregnancy, a miscarriage, or an abortion; a 20% change in weight; or abdominal or pelvic surgery.

Effectiveness   Studies of diaphragm effectiveness have yielded varying results. Though the perfect-use effectiveness rate is quite high at 94%, the typical-use rate falls considerably, to 84%. Consistent, correct use is essential to achieve maximum effectiveness.

Advantages   The diaphragm is safe, is relatively inexpensive, has limited side effects, and can be discretely used.

Possible Problems   Some women dislike the process of inserting a diaphragm, or the mess or smell of the spermicide used with it. Some men complain of rubbing or other discomfort caused by the diaphragm. Some women are allergic to rubber. Some women have a slightly increased risk of repeated

When used correctly and consistently and with a spermicide, the diaphragm can be an effective method of contraception.

© McGraw-Hill Education/Jill Braaten, photographer

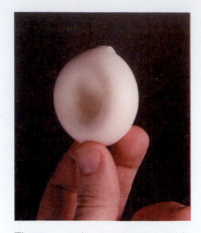

The sponge is easy to use and is relatively effective and safe, but it does not protect against HIV.

© McGraw-Hill Education/Jill Braaten, photographer

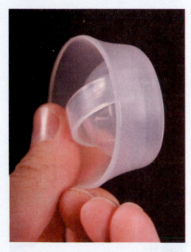

The cervical cap is smaller than a diaphragm and covers only the cervix.

© McGraw-Hill Education/Jill Braaten, photographer

Since if the parts be smooth conception is prevented, some anoint that part of the womb on which the seed falls with oil of cedar, or with ointment of lead or with frankincense, commingled with olive oil.

—Aristotle
(384–322 BCE)

urinary tract infections. Because there is a small risk of toxic shock syndrome associated with its use, a woman should not leave a diaphragm in her vagina for more than 24 hours. Diaphragms are generally used with the spermicide nonoxynol-9 (N-9), which can irritate tissues or increase the risk of contracting an STI, including HIV (CDC, 2014.11a).

The Sponge   The **sponge,** marketed in the United States as Today Sponge, is a round, plastic, foam shield that contains the spermicide N-9. The sponge measures about 2 inches in diameter and has a pouch in the center that fits over the cervix and a nylon loop attached to the bottom for removal (Planned Parenthood, 2014.11k). Because N-9 does not reduce the risk of HIV infection, women should always use a latex condom just as they should with all other contraceptive methods. The insertion and removal of the sponge are similar to that of the diaphragm and, with a little practice, is easy to do. An advantage of the sponge is that it can be left in place for up to 24 hours without reinsertion or the application of more spermicide. The sponge should not be left in place longer than 30 hours, because it can increase the risk of toxic shock syndrome. The perfect-use effectiveness rate varies, depending on whether a woman has had a baby, but averages 78% for typical use. The lowered effectiveness rate may be because the one size in which the sponge is available may not adequately cover the cervix that has been stretched during childbirth. Shelf life of the sponge is limited.

Cervical Cap   A **cervical cap** is a silicone, cup-shaped device that is inserted into the vagina to prevent pregnancy (Planned Parenthood, 2014.11l). Shaped like a sailor's cap, the cervical cap (brand name Fem Cap) comes in three sizes and must stay in place 6 hours after the last intercourse. It can also be worn for up to 48 hours, double the time recommended for similar birth control devices. The device is held in place by suction, must be used with a spermicide, and needs to be obtained through a health care provider. The perfect-use and typical-use effectiveness rates are similar to those of the diaphragm. It is more effective for women who have never given birth.

Advantages   The cervical cap may be more comfortable and convenient than the diaphragm for some women. Much less spermicide is used than with the diaphragm and spermicide need not be reapplied if intercourse is repeated. The cap can be inserted 15 minutes to several hours before intercourse and can be worn for as long as 48 hours. It does not interfere with the body physically or hormonally.

Possible Problems   Some users are bothered by an odor that may develop from the interaction of the cap's rubber with either vaginal secretions or the spermicide. There is some concern that the cap may contribute to erosion of the cervix. If a partner's penis touches the rim of the cap, it can become displaced during intercourse. Theoretically, the same risk of toxic shock syndrome exists for the cervical cap as for the diaphragm.

Spermicides

A **spermicide** is a substance that is toxic to sperm. The most commonly used spermicide in products sold in the United States is the chemical **nonoxynol-9 (N-9).** Though most women can use it safely, with repeated use for vaginal and anal intercourse, N-9 may irritate genital or rectal tissues and increase the risk of HIV (CDC, 2014.11a). Spermicidal preparations are available in a variety of forms—foam, film, cream, jelly, and suppository—and are considered most effective when used in combination with a barrier method of contraception such as the diaphragm, sponge, or cervical cap. Spermicides are sold in tubes, packets, or other containers that hold 12–20 applications. The perfect-use effectiveness is 82%, while the typical-use effectiveness is 72%.

Some people have allergic reactions to spermicides. Some women dislike the messiness or odor involved. Others experience irritation or inflammation, especially if they use any of the chemicals frequently.

Intrauterine Devices (IUDs)

An **intrauterine device (IUD)** is a long-acting, reversible contraceptive method that is inserted by a doctor into the uterus where it emits either copper or the hormone progestin, both of which are hostile to sperm (Planned Parenthood, 2014.11m). Three IUDs are available in the United States—ParaGard (sometimes called Copper-T) which is wrapped in copper coils and Mirena and the slightly smaller Skyla both of which contain progestin. ParaGard can remain in place for 12 years; Mirena for 5 years, and Skyla for 3 years (see Figure 7). All three types prevent fertilization. The copper IUD does so by slowly releasing

A variety of spermicides are among the birth control options available without a prescription.

© McGraw-Hill Education/Christopher Kerrigan, photographer

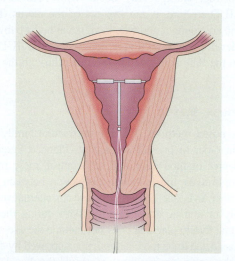

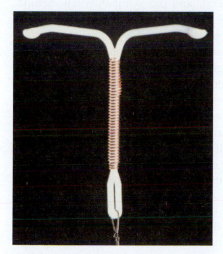

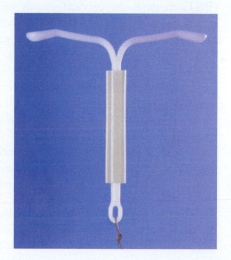

• **FIGURE 7**

Once the IUD is inserted, the threads attached to the IUD will extend into the vagina through the cervical opening. A copper-containing IUD (ParaGard) in position (left) and a progestin-releasing IUD (Mirena) (right).

(second) © Garry Watson/Science Source; (third) © Saturn Stills/Science Source copper into the uterine cavity, thereby stopping the sperm from reaching the egg. The hormone progestin causes the cervical mucus to thicken so the sperm cannot reach the egg and changes the lining of the uterus so implantation of a fertilized egg cannot occur.

Current evidence does not support the common belief that the IUD is an **abortifacient,** a device or substance that causes an abortion. Rather, it prevents fertilization.

Effectiveness   All IUDs are extremely effective. Once inserted, IUDs are 99% effective with perfect use; the typical-use effectiveness rate is 98%.

Advantages   Few methods of birth contol are as long-acting, convenient, effective, and economical as the IUD. Additionally, fertility rebounds quickly upon discontinuation. Once inserted, IUDs require little care and don't interfere with spontaneity during intercourse.

Disadvantages   Insertion may be uncomfortable and cramping or backache may persist for a few days. Spotting between periods may also occur in the first 3–6 months with Mirena or Skyla, along with irregular periods. Heavier periods and increased menstrual cramps may occur with ParaGard. Though serious problems with the IUD are-rare, it can slip out of the uterus. This is more likely to occur to those who are younger and who have never had a baby. In rare situations, a woman could develop an infection when using the IUD or in very rare circumstances when the IUD is inserted it can push through the wall of the uterus.

Fertility Awareness–Based Methods

Fertility awareness–based methods (FAMs) and natural family planning are ways to track ovulation in order to prevent pregnancy (Planned Parenthood, 2014.11n). Requiring a high degree of motivation and self-control, these methods are not for everyone. Some people make the following distinction between FAMs and natural family planning: With FAMs, the couple may use an alternative method such as a diaphragm with jelly or a male condom with foam during the fertile part of the woman's cycle. Natural family planning does not include the use of any contraceptive device and is thus considered to be more natural; it is approved by the Catholic Church.

FAMs include the calendar (rhythm) method, the basal body temperature (BBT) method, the cervical mucus method, and the symptothermal method, which combines all three methods. These methods are free and pose no health risks. If a woman wishes to become pregnant, awareness of her own fertility cycles is useful. But these methods are not suitable for women with irregular menstrual cycles or for couples not highly motivated to use them. Certain conditions or circumstances, such as recent menarche, approaching menopause, recent childbirth, breastfeeding, and recent discontinuation of hormonal contraceptives, make FAMs more difficult to use and require more extensive monitoring. Couples practicing abstinence during fertile periods may begin to take risks because their sexual desires may be unfulfilled. Among typical users of fertility awareness, about 24% of women experience unintended pregnancy during the first year of use if they don't use the method correctly or consistently.

The Calendar (Rhythm) Method   The **calendar** (**rhythm** or **standard days**) **method** is based on calculating "safer" days, which depends on knowing the range of a woman's longest and shortest menstrual cycles and abstaining from

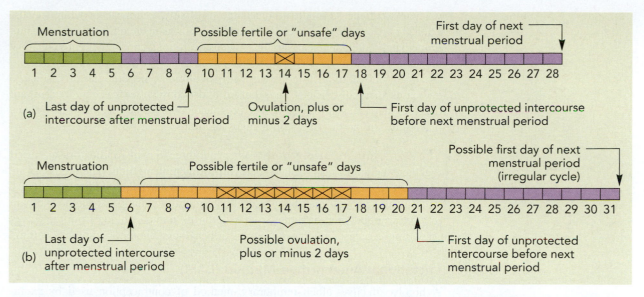

FIGURE 8

Fertility Awareness Calendar. To use the calendar method or other fertility awareness methods, a woman must keep track of her menstrual cycles. (a) This chart shows probable safe and unsafe days for a woman with a regular 28-day cycle. (b) This chart shows safe and unsafe days for a woman whose cycles range from 25 to 31 days. Note that the woman with an irregular cycle has significantly more unsafe days. The calendar method is most effective when combined with the basal body temperature (BBT) and cervical mucus methods.

unprotected vaginal intercourse during her peak fertile times. Because sperm generally live 2–4 days, the maximum period of time in which fertilization could be expected to occur may be calculated with the assistance of a calendar. To prevent pregnancy, a woman should not rely on this method alone. This method may not be practical or safe for women with irregular cycles.

Ovulation generally occurs 14 days (plus or minus 2 days) before a woman's menstrual period. However, ovulation can occur anytime during the cycle, including the menstrual period. Taking this into account, and charting her menstrual cycles for a minimum of 8 months to determine the longest and shortest cycles, a woman can determine her expected fertile period. (Figure 8 shows the interval of fertility calculated in this way.)

The Basal Body Temperature (BBT) Method

A woman's temperature tends to be slightly lower during the first part of her menstrual cycle and usually rises slightly during and after ovulation. It stays high until just before the next menstrual period. Changes will be in fractions of a degree from 1/10 to 1/2 a degree.

A woman practicing the **basal body temperature (BBT) method** must record her temperature every morning upon waking for 6–12 months to gain an accurate idea of her temperature pattern. This change can best be noted using a BBT thermometer before getting out of bed. Some BBT thermometers are meant to be used in the mouth, while others are designed for use in the rectum. When a woman can recognize the rise in her temperature and predict when in her cycle ovulation will occur, she can begin using the method. She should abstain from intercourse or use an alternative contraceptive method for 3–4 days before the expected rise in temperature and for 4 days after it has taken place.

Cervical Mucus Method

Women who use the **cervical mucus method** determine their stage in the menstrual cycle by examining the mucus secretions of the cervix. In many women, there is a noticeable change in the appearance and character of cervical mucus prior to ovulation. After menstruation, most

> *Women who miscalculate are called mothers.*
>
> —Abigail Van Buren (1918–2013)

women experience a moderate discharge of cloudy, yellowish or white mucus. Then, for a day or two, a clear, stretchy mucus is secreted. Ovulation occurs immediately after the clear, stretchy mucus secretions appear. The preovulatory mucus is elastic in consistency, rather like raw egg white, and a drop can be stretched into a thin strand. Following ovulation, the amount of discharge decreases markedly. The 4 days before and 4 days after these secretions are considered the unsafe days. Fewer pregnancies occur when intercourse takes place only on the dry days following ovulation.

The Symptothermal Method   When all three fertility indicators are used together, the approach is called the **symptothermal method.** The signs of one method can help confirm those of the others, which helps predict safer days. Additional signs that may be useful in determining ovulation are midcycle pain in the lower abdomen on either side, a slight discharge of blood from the cervix ("spotting"), breast tenderness, feelings of heaviness, and/or abdominal swelling.

Lactational Amenorrhea Method (LAM)

A highly effective, albeit temporary, method of contraception used by exclusively breastfeeding mothers is called the **lactational amenorrhea method,** or **LAM** (Planned Parenthood, 2014.11o). LAM relies on lactational infertility for protection from pregnancy. This method is more than 98% effective the first 6 months following a birth if the woman has not experienced her first postpartum menses and she is fully or nearly fully breastfeeding her child.

Breastfeeding women may start progestin-only methods at any time after delivery. Should a woman choose to use contraception, the implantable rod, the Depo-Provera shot, and some IUDs contain only the hormone progestin and are the methods of choice because they do not typically suppress milk production which may result in the discontinuation of breastfeeding or poor infant growth (Epsey, Ogburn, Leeman, Singh, & Schrader, 2012; Grimes, Lopez, O'Brien, & Raymond, 2013). While the literature is still unsettled concerning the potential impact of combined oral contraceptives on the suppression of milk production, similar concerns do not exist for these progestin-only contraceptives.

Sterilization

Sterilization involves surgical intervention that makes the reproductive organs incapable of producing or delivering viable gametes (sperm and eggs). Sterilization is the most widely used method of contraception in both developing and developed countries of the world (French National Institute, 2012). Of all women using a contraceptive in 2006–2010, 27% relied on female sterilization and 10% relied on male sterilization (Jones et al., 2012). Couples and individuals choose sterilization because they want to limit or end childbearing. All sterilization procedures are meant to be permanent (Planned Parenthood, 2014.11p). The sterilization procedure is simpler, safer, and cheaper when performed on men than when performed on women.

Sterilization for Women   Female sterilization is now a relatively safe, simple, and common procedure. Most female sterilizations are **tubal ligations,** familiarly known as "tying the tubes" (Figure 9). The fallopian tubes can also be sealed or closed with clips, clamps, or rings. Sometimes a small piece of the fallopian tube is also removed. Another method involves the insertion of tubes which completely

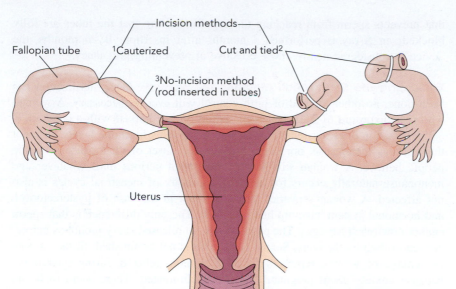

● **FIGURE 9**

Types of Female Sterilization.
A variety of techniques are used
to render a woman sterile.

Incision methods
¹Cauterized   Cut and tied²

Fallopian tube

³No-incision method
(rod inserted in tubes)

Uterus

block the fallopian tubes. The two most common operations are laparoscopy and mini-laparotomy. A mini-laparotomy is a procedure that can be done within 48 hours of childbirth. Generally, this surgery is not reversible; only women who are absolutely certain that they want no (or no more) children should choose this method.

Laparoscopy   A variety of techniques are used to sterilize women, and all seem to provide the same effectiveness. Sterilization by **laparoscopy** is one of the two most frequently used methods. This procedure is performed on an outpatient basis and takes 20–30 minutes. The woman's abdomen is inflated with gas to make the organs more visible. The surgeon inserts a rodlike instrument with a viewing lens (the laparoscope) through a small incision at the edge of the navel and locates the fallopian tubes. Through this incision or a second one, the surgeon inserts another instrument that closes the tubes, usually by electrocauterization (burning). Small forceps that carry an electric current clamp the tubes and cauterize them. The tubes may also be closed off or blocked with tiny rings, clips, or plugs; no stitches are required. There is a recovery period of up to a week. During this time, the woman will experience some tenderness, cramping, and vaginal bleeding. Rest is important. For every 1,000 women who have traditional incision methods, about 5 will become pregnant.

Transcervical Sterilization   A permanent method of birth control that does not require surgery is called **transcervical sterilization.** This method involves inserting a thin instrument through the cervix and uterus to reach the fallopian tubes, which are then blocked permanently with a micro-rod to prevent pregnancy. Currently, two methods are available in the United States, Essure and Adiana. Both are highly effective and convenient because insertion is usually done in an outpatient setting. During the first 3 months following insertion, the device will form a tissue barrier

Transcervical sterilization (Essure) involves inserting a micro-rod into each fallopian tube. Tissue growth (causing sterilization) takes about 12 weeks.

© Feature Photo Service/Newscom

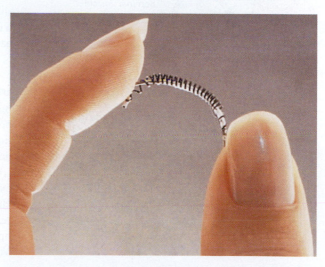

that prevents sperm from reaching the egg. To be sure that the tubes are fully blocked, an X-ray is performed 3 months after insertion. By 6 months, the device is considered nearly 100% effective at preventing pregnancy.

Evaluating the Sterilization Methods for Women   Once sterilization has been done, no other method of birth control will ever be necessary. A woman who risks exposure to STIs, however, should protect herself with a condom.

Sterilization does not reduce or change a woman's hormone levels. It is not the same as menopause, nor does it hasten the onset of menopause, as some people believe. A woman still has her menstrual periods until whatever age menopause naturally occurs for her. The regularity of menstrual cycles is also not affected. A woman's ovaries, uterus (except in the case of hysterectomy), and hormonal system have not been changed. The only difference is that sperm cannot now reach her eggs. The eggs, which are released every month as before, are reabsorbed by the body. Sexual enjoyment is not diminished. In fact, a high percentage of women report that they feel more relaxed during intercourse because anxiety about pregnancy has been eliminated. There seem to be no harmful side effects associated with female sterilization.

Sterilization for Men   A **vasectomy** is a permanent method of birth control in which each vas deferens is severed, thereby preventing sperm from entering the vas deferens and mixing with seminal fluids to form semen (Planned Parenthood, 2014.11q). Instead of being ejaculated with the semen, the sperm are absorbed by the body. A vasectomy takes approximately half an hour and can be done in a doctor's office or clinic. In this procedure, the physician makes a small incision (or two incisions) in the skin of the scrotum. Through the incision, each vas deferens is lifted, cut, tied, and often cauterized with electricity (Figure 10). With the "no-incision method," the skin of the scrotum is not cut. Rather, one puncture is made to reach both tubes, which are then tied off, cauterized, or blocked. After a brief rest, the man is able to walk out of the office; complete recuperation takes only a few days.

A man may retain some viable sperm in his system for days or weeks following a vasectomy. Because it takes about 3 months to use up these sperm, a couple should use other birth control until a semen analysis reveals no sperm are present in the semen.

Vasectomies are 99.9% effective. Regardless, the man may still need to use a condom to prevent acquiring or transmitting STIs. Sexual enjoyment will not be diminished; the man will still have erections and orgasms and ejaculate semen. A vasectomy is relatively inexpensive compared with female sterilization.

Relative to other birth control methods, the problems associated with a vasectomy, such as excessive pain, swelling, or infection are very low. Most problems occur when proper antiseptic measures are not taken during the operation or when the man exercises too strenuously in the few days after the vasectomy.

Men who equate fertility with virility and potency may experience psychological problems following a vasectomy. However, most men experience no adverse psychological reactions if they understand what to expect and have the opportunity to express their concerns and ask questions. Vasectomy should be considered permanent.

● **FIGURE** 10

Male Sterilization, or Vasectomy.
This is a relatively simple procedure that involves local anesthesia and results in permanent sterilization.

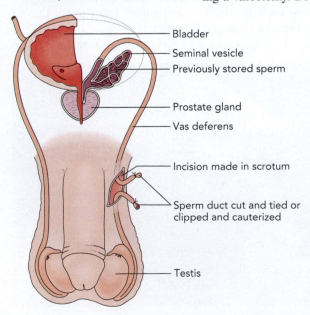

- Bladder
- Seminal vesicle
- Previously stored sperm
- Prostate gland
- Vas deferens
- Incision made in scrotum
- Sperm duct cut and tied or clipped and cauterized
- Testis

Emergency Contraception (EC)

No birth control device is 100% effective. Furthermore, intercourse sometimes occurs unexpectedly, and rape is, unfortunately, always a possibility. **Emergency contraception (EC),** also known as the "morning-after pill," and marketed as Plan B One-Step, Next Choice One Dose, or ella, is a safe and effective way to prevent pregnancy following unprotected intercourse (Planned Parenthood, 2014.11r). To be effective, these pills must be taken within 120 hours (up to 5 days) after unprotected intercourse. Plan B One-Step and Next Choice One Dose contain high levels of progestin, which is found in some types of daily-use oral contraceptive pills, while ella contains the ingredient ulipristal acetate. EC is not the "abortion pill" (RU-486) and it will not terminate an established pregnancy, in which the fertilized egg has already attached itself to the wall of the uterus, nor will it cause any harm to the developing fetus. Rather, EC inhibits ovulation and thickens cervical mucus, which prevents the sperm from joining the egg. With the exception of ella, which requires a prescription, most brand names of EC are available for anyone over the counter and without a prescription.

Progestin-only pills like Plan B One-Step and Next Choice One Dose are specially packaged as emergency contraception. They do not, however, have the same risks as taking hormonal contraceptives because the hormones do not stay in a woman's body as long as they do with ongoing birth control. Emergency contraception should not be used as a form of ongoing birth control because it is less effective. Though many women use EC with few or no problems, nausea and vomiting are among the most common side effects. Other side effects may include breast tenderness, irregular bleeding, dizziness, and headaches. Plan B One-Step and Next Choice One Dose are up to 89% effective when taken within 72 hours (3 days) after unprotected sex and continue to reduce the risk of pregnancy up to 120 hours after unprotected sex. Ella is 85% effective if taken within 120 hours (5 days) after unprotected sex. Both types of pills become less effective as time passes after sexual intercourse. Individuals who are obese (body mass index of at least 30) are not fully protected with the hormonal pills.

The ParaGard IUD can be used as EC when inserted by a health care practitioner within 120 hours (5 days) after unprotected sexual intercourse and then left in place to provide ongoing contraception for up to 12 years. The mechanism interferes with implantation and may act as a contraceptive if inserted prior to ovulation.

● Abortion

When most people hear the word "abortion," they think of a medical procedure. But **abortion,** or expulsion of the conceptus, can happen naturally or can be made to happen in one of several ways (Planned Parenthood, 2014.11s). Many abortions occur spontaneously—because a woman suffers a physical trauma, because the conceptus is not properly developed, or, more commonly, because physical conditions within the uterus break down and end the development of the conceptus. Approximately one third of all abortions reported annually in the United States are **spontaneous abortions** or death of a fetus before it can survive on its own, otherwise referred to as **miscarriage.** Abortions are very common in the United States, with 3 out of 10 women having an abortion by the time they are 45 years old. Over 90% of all abortions occur in the first 3 months of pregnancy, and 63% occur in the first 8 weeks (Mosher & Jones, 2010) (see Figure 11).

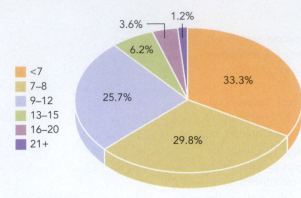

- <7
- 7–8
- 9–12
- 13–15
- 16–20
- 21+

33.3%

29.8%

25.7%

6.2%

3.6%

1.2%

● **FIGURE** 11

Weeks of Pregnancy When Women in the U.S. Have Abortions, 2010.*
One third of abortions occur at 6 weeks of pregnancy or earlier; 89% occur in the first 12 weeks.

*In weeks from the last menstrual period.

(*Source:* Guttmacher Institute. (2014). Fact sheet: Induced abortion in the United States. Available: http://www.guttmacher .org/pubs/fb_induced_abortion.html.)

Methods of Abortion

An abortion can be induced in several ways. Surgical methods are most common in this country, but the use of medications is also possible as is suction. Methods for early abortions (those performed in the first 3 months of pregnancy) differ from those for late abortions (those performed after the 3rd month).

Medication Abortion   After a decade of controversy, **medication abortion** (mifepristone, sold in the United States as Mifeprex, also known as RU-486) became available in the United States in 2000. Widely used in several European countries for over two decades, it has been shown to be safe, effective, and acceptable and has become an increasingly common alternative to surgical procedures (Planned Parenthood, 2014.11t). In fact, medication-induced abortions now account for 23% of all abortions (Jones & Jerman, 2014).

Doctors can now prescribe a number of regimens, though the two-drug regimen of mifepristone and misoprostol remains the most common. The first tablet, mifepristone, causes the placenta to separate from the endometrium, softens the cervix, and starts uterine contractions. The second tablet, misoprostol, can be taken by mouth or inserted into the vagina, usually within 48 hours of taking mifepristone. This drug causes uterine contractions so that the body passes the uterine contents. A medication abortion usually requires at least two visits to the doctor over several weeks and is only done in the first 9 weeks (63 days) after the first day of a woman's last period. A few states, however, have laws that limit the use of the abortion pill to 49 days. Some states also require those who are under 18 years to have one or both parents give permission for abortion. The effectiveness rate is about 97%. In the unlikely case that medication abortion does not work, a woman will need to have a surgical abortion.

Surgical Abortion   Surgical methods, also referred to as in-clinic abortions, include vacuum aspiration and dilation and evacuation (D&E) (Planned Parenthood, 2014.11u).

Vacuum Aspiration (First-Trimester Method)   **Vacuum aspiration** is the method used for nearly all first-trimester (up to 16 weeks) instrumental abortions. This safe and simple method is performed under local anesthesia. The first step involves the rinsing of the vagina with an antiseptic solution. Next, the cervix is dilated with a series of graduated rods. Then a small tube attached to a vacuum is inserted through the cervix. The uterus is gently vacuumed, removing the conceptus, placenta, and endometrial tissue (see Figure 12).

Dilation and Evacuation (D&E) (Second-Trimester Method)   **Dilation and evacuation (D&E)** is usually performed during the second trimester (later than 16 weeks) of pregnancy, and can be performed beyond week 24. Local or general anesthesia is used. The cervix is slowly dilated, and the fetus is removed by alternating use of a curette (a surgical instrument shaped like a spoon) with other procedures. Because it is a second-trimester procedure, a D&E is somewhat riskier and often more traumatic than a first-trimester abortion.

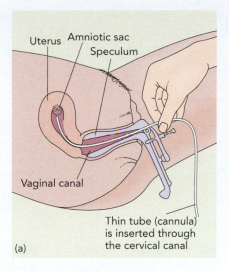

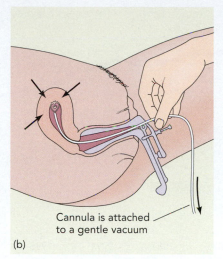

• **FIGURE 12**

Vacuum Aspiration. (a) A speculum is inserted into the vagina, local anesthesia is given for pain or sedation, the cervical canal is dilated, and a thin, hollow tube (cannula) is passed into the cervical canal. (b) The cannula is attached to a gentle vacuum, which draws out the tissue from the uterus.

In figure (a): Uterus, Amniotic sac, Speculum, Vaginal canal, Thin tube (cannula) is inserted through the cervical canal

In figure (b): Cannula is attached to a gentle vacuum

Second-Trimester Induction Abortions   In rare cases during the late part of the second trimester, abortion can be achieved by administering medications, such as misoprostol, that cause the uterus to contract and eventually expel the fetus and placenta. All second-trimester induced methods have side effects specific to the medications used.

Safety of Abortion

Abortions performed in the first trimester pose virtually no long-term physical or psychological complications (Guttmacher Institute, 2014.11d; Upadhyay et al., 2014). In fact, the risk of dying from a modern legal abortion is 1 in 1 million procedures if performed before 8 weeks. The single greatest factor influencing the safety of abortion is gestational age, with those performed in early pregnancy being the safest. Regardless of the method performed, however, almost all women have some bleeding after the procedure that lasts from several days to several weeks. For most women, transient feelings of loss, sadness, or stress that accompany the decision to have an abortion are often replaced with relief and satisfaction with their decision.

Women and Abortion

Many women are reluctant to talk openly about their abortion experiences, but accurate information about women who have abortions may help dispel their possible feelings of isolation or rejection.

A broad cross-section of U.S. women who have abortions (Guttmacher Institute, 2014.11d):

- 18% of women obtaining abortions are teenagers and 57% are in their 20s;
- 45% have never been married and are not cohabiting;
- 69% are economically disadvantaged;
- 36% are non-Hispanic White women, 30% are non-Hispanic Black women, 25% are Hispanic women, and 9% are women in other races;
- 65% report being Protestant or Catholic; and
- 61% have one or more children.

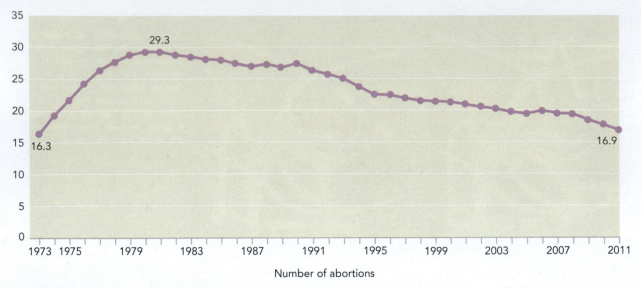

Number of abortions

• **FIGURE 13**

Number of Abortions per 1,000 Women Aged 15–44 by Year. In 2011, the U.S. abortion rate reached its lowest level since 1973.

(*Source:* Guttmacher Institute. (2014c). Fact sheet: Induced abortion in the United States. Available: http://www.guttmacher.org/pubs/fb_induced_abortion.html.)

With an estimated 1.1 million procedures performed in 2011, abortion is a common experience among women in the United States (Guttmacher Institute, 2014.11d). (See Figure 13.) In spite of this fact, abortion rates in the United States are at their lowest in 40 years. In 2011, the U.S. abortion rate was 16.9 per 1,000 women aged 15–44, the lowest it has been since abortion was legalized in 1973. It is important to remember that women who have abortions are as diverse as their reasons for doing so. The motives women have given for why they had an abortion underscore their understanding of the responsibilities of parenthood and family life. Three fourths of women cite concerns or responsibility for others; three fourths say they cannot afford a child; three fourths say that having a child would interfere with work, school, or the ability to care for dependents; and half say they do not want to be a single parent or are having problems with their husband or partner (Guttmacher Institute, 2014.11d).

Making a decision about abortion, regardless of the ultimate outcome, raises many emotional issues for women. There are few painless ways of dealing with an unintended pregnancy. For many women, such a decision requires a reevaluation of their relationships, an examination of their childbearing plans, a search to understand the role of sexuality in their lives, and an attempt to clarify their life goals. Clearly, women *and* men need accurate information about fertility cycles and the risk of pregnancy when a contraceptive is not used consistently or correctly, as well as access to contraceptive and abortion services.

Men and Abortion

In the abortion decision-making process, the vast majority of male partners know about and support the woman's decision (Guttmacher Institute, 2011). On the other hand, a sizable minority (12%) of U.S. women who obtained abortions were not in a relationship with the man who got them pregnant, and these women were unable, or saw little reason, to inform the biological father. Those who received the least amount of support (7%) were those who had experienced intimate partner violence. It's probably not surprising to know that the ability to rely on their partners for support vastly improves women's postabortion well-being and adjustment.

Still, there is the lure of fatherhood. A pregnancy forces a man to confront his own feelings about parenting. Parenthood for males, as for females, can be perceived as a profound right. For young men, there is a mixture of pride and fear about potential fatherhood and adulthood.

After an abortion, many men feel residual guilt, sadness, and remorse. It is also somewhat common for couples to split up after an abortion; the stress, conflict, and guilt can be overwhelming. Many clinics now provide counseling for men, as well as women, involved in an abortion.

The Abortion Debate

In the abortion debate, those who believe abortion should be prohibited generally identify themselves as "pro-life." Those who support a woman's right to choose for herself whether to have an abortion generally identify themselves as "pro-choice."

The Pro-Life Stance   For those who oppose abortion, there is a basic principle from which their stance follows: The moment an egg is fertilized, it becomes a human being with the full rights and dignity afforded other humans. An embryo is no less human than a fetus and a fetus is no less human than a baby. Morally, aborting an embryo is the equivalent of murder.

Even though the majority of those opposing abortion would consider rape and incest (and sometimes a defective embryo or fetus) to be exceptions, the pro-life leadership generally opposes any justification for an abortion other than to save the life of the pregnant woman. To abort the embryo of a rape or incest survivor, they reason, is still to take an innocent human life.

In addition, pro-life advocates argue that abortion is the first step toward a society that eliminates undesirable human beings. If we allow the elimination of embryos, they argue, what is to stop the killing of people who are disabled or elderly, or merely inconvenient? Finally, pro-life advocates argue that there are thousands of couples who want to adopt children but are unable to do so because so many pregnant women choose to abort rather than to give birth.

I have noticed that all the people who favor abortion have already been born.

—Ronald Reagan
(1911–2004)

The Pro-Choice Argument   Under safe, clean, and legal conditions, abortion is a very safe medical procedure. Self-administered or illegal, clandestine abortions, however, can be very dangerous. The continued availability of legal abortion is considered by most physicians, psychologists, and public health professionals to be critical to the public's physical and mental well-being. Those who believe that abortion should continue to be legal present a number of arguments. First, the fundamental issue is who decides whether a woman will bear children: the woman or the government? Because women continue to bear the primary responsibility for rearing children, pro-choice advocates believe that women should not be forced to give birth to unwanted children.

Second, in addition to supporting comprehensive sexuality education and contraception to eliminate much of the need for abortion, pro-choice advocates believe that abortion should continue to be available as birth control backup. Because no contraceptive method is 100% effective, unintended pregnancies occur even among the most conscientious contraceptive users.

There are few absolutes left in the age after Einstein, and the case of abortion, like almost everything else, is a case of relative goods and ills to be evaluated one against the other.

—Germaine Greer
(1939–)

Third, if abortion is made illegal, large numbers of women nevertheless will have illegal abortions, substantially increasing the likelihood of procedural complications, infections, and death. Those who are unable to have an abortion may be forced to give birth to and raise a child they did not want or cannot afford to raise.

Constitutional Issues In 1969 in Texas, 21-year-old Norma McCorvey, a single mother, discovered she was pregnant. In the hope of obtaining a legal abortion, she lied to her doctor, saying that she had been raped. Her physician informed her, however, that Texas prohibited all abortions except those to save the life of the mother. He suggested that she travel to California, where she could obtain a legal abortion, but she had no money. Two lawyers heard of her situation and took her case in order to challenge abortion restrictions as an unconstitutional invasion of the individual's right to privacy. For the case, McCorvey was given "Roe" as a pseudonym. Dallas County District Attorney Henry Wade was the defendant representing the State of Texas. In 1970, a court in Texas declared the law unconstitutional, but the state appealed the decision. Meanwhile, McCorvey had her baby and gave it up for adoption. Ultimately, the case reached the U.S. Supreme Court, which issued its famous *Roe v. Wade* decision in 1973. Under the 1973 *Roe* decision, a woman's right to abortion is guaranteed as a fundamental right, part of the constitutional right to privacy. At the time, only four states permitted abortion at the woman's discretion.

The *Roe* decision created a firestorm of opposition among political and religious conservatives and fueled a right-wing political resurgence. But because abortion was determined a fundamental right by the *Roe* decision, efforts by the states to stop it have thus far failed.

Since the 1973 Supreme Court decision in *Roe v. Wade,* states have been undergoing rigorous debate about how best to interpret, regulate, limit, and define under what circumstances a woman may obtain an abortion. Though a host of legislative challenges have occurred and a variety of abortion laws are on the books, many laws may not be enforced. A few highlights of the laws at the time of printing of this book include (Guttmacher Institute, 2014.11e):

- 39 states require an abortion to be performed only by a licensed physician;

- 42 states prohibit abortions after a specified point in pregnancy, most often after fetal viability is determined, except when necessary to protect the woman's life or health;

- 19 states prohibit "partial-birth" abortions, in spite of the fact that a definition for this term is not yet sufficiently precise or agreed upon;

- 26 states require a woman seeking an abortion to wait a specified period of time, usually 24 hours, between abortion counseling and the procedure; and

- 38 states require some type of parental involvement in a minor's decision to have an abortion.

At the writing of this book, federal contraceptive coverage under the Affordable Care Act (ACA) is heading for an important decision in 2015 (Guttmacher Institute, 2014.11f). The U.S. Supreme Court will hear arguments on a conflict between religiously motivated objections by employers and the rights, beliefs, and health care needs of employees and their dependents. In this case, the plaintiffs object to coverage of and counseling and education about specific methods they regard as methods of abortion: emergency contraceptive pills and IUDs. The ACA explicitly requires full coverage of contraceptive methods but does not require coverage of abortion. It's important to note that the scientific and legal definitions of abortion distinguish between contraception and abortion; however, those who challenge contraceptive coverage claim that certain methods of contraception are actually methods of abortion. Additionally, opponents argue that modern contraception has no legitimate health benefits and that it actually harms women, families, and society. These claims are countered by decades of scientific evidence and life experiences of millions of women.

The objective shared by the pro-life and pro-choice camps is the reduction in the number of abortions performed each year in this country. Research both in this country and abroad has demonstrated that education about effective and safe sexual choices and access to contraceptive services can decrease abortion rates (Pazol et al., 2011). While each state will continue to define and enforce laws according to the ideological standpoints of its leaders, the protection of legal abortion is in the hands of the Supreme Court. The votes of these justices are critical in influencing access to abortion in this country.

● Research Issues

Most users of contraception find some drawback to whatever method they choose. Hormonal methods may be costly or have undesirable side effects. Putting on a condom or inserting a sponge may seem to interrupt lovemaking. The inconveniences, the side effects, the lack of 100% effectiveness—all point to the need for more effective and more diverse forms of contraception than we have now.

High developmental costs, government regulations, social issues, political constraints, and marketing priorities all play a role in restricting contraceptive research. The biggest barrier to developing new contraceptive techniques may be the fear of lawsuits. Pharmaceutical manufacturers will not easily forget that the IUD market was virtually destroyed in the 1970s and 1980s by numerous costly lawsuits.

Another reason for limited contraceptive research is extensive government regulation, which requires exhaustive product testing. Although no one wants to be poisoned by medicines, perhaps it wouldn't hurt to take a closer look at the process by which new drugs become available to the public. Approval by the FDA takes an average of 7.5 years. Drug patents are in effect for only 17 years, so the pharmaceutical companies have less than 10 years to recover their developmental costs once a medication is approved for sale. Furthermore, pharmaceutical companies are not willing to expend millions in research only to have the FDA refuse to approve the marketing of new products. According to chemist Carl Djerassi (1981), the "father" of the birth control pill, safety is a relative, not an absolute, concept. We may need to reexamine the question "How safe is safe?" and weigh potential benefits along with possible problems.

Though research has investigated a number of contraceptives for men, none have been found to adequately eliminate sperm production while maintaining both the libido and physical health.

A lily pond, so the French riddle goes, contains a single leaf. Each day the number of leaves doubles—two leaves the second day, four the third, eight the fourth, and so on. Question: If the pond is completely full on the thirtieth day, when is it half full? Answer: On the twenty-ninth day. The global lily pond in which [six] billion of us live may already be half full.

—Lester Brown
(1934–)

Contraception helps us plan our lives. It also helps us to prosper and in some parts of the world survive. The topic of birth control provokes much emotional controversy. Individuals and institutions alike are inclined to believe in the moral rightness of their particular stance on the subject, whatever that stance may be. As each of us tries to find his or her own path through the quagmire of controversy, we can be guided by what we learn. We need to arm ourselves with knowledge—not only about the methods and mechanics of contraception but also about our own motivations, needs, weaknesses, and strengths.

Summary

Risk and Responsibility

- Over the period of 1 year, sexually active couples who do not use contraception have an 85% chance of getting pregnant. Not surprising, the nonusers of contraception account for about half of unintended pregnancies.

- Many people knowingly risk pregnancy by having unprotected intercourse. The more "successful" they are at risk taking, the more likely they are to take chances again. People also take risks because of faulty knowledge, denial of their sexuality, or a subconscious desire for a child.

- The backbone of the nation's publicly funded family planning efforts is Title X, which now overlaps with services provided by the Affordable Care Act (ACA).

Methods of Contraception

- *Long-acting, reversible contraceptive methods (LARCs)* are recommended as first-line contraceptive choices for adolescents and adult women. *Contraception* is birth control that works specifically by preventing the union of sperm and egg.

- The most reliable method of birth control is *abstinence*—refraining from sexual intercourse.

- *Oral contraceptives* are the most widely used form of reversible birth control in the United States. The majority of birth control pills contain synthetic hormones: progestin and usually estrogen. The pill is highly effective if taken regularly. There are side effects and possible problems for some users. The greatest risks are to smokers and women with certain

health disorders, such as cardiovascular problems. Other methods of hormonal contraception include the *birth control patch,* the *vaginal ring,* the *birth control shot,* and the *implant.*

- A *condom (male condom)* is a thin sheath of latex, rubber, polyurethane, or processed animal tissue that fits over the erect penis and prevents semen from being transmitted. It is the third most widely used contraceptive method in the United States. Condoms are very effective for contraception when used correctly. Latex and polyurethane condoms also help provide protection against STIs.

- The *female condom, diaphragm, sponge,* and *cervical cap* are barrier methods used by women. Each covers the cervical opening and is used with spermicidal jelly or cream. Female condoms, in addition to lining the vagina, cover much of the vulva (or anus, when used for anal sex), providing protection against disease organisms.

- *Spermicides* are chemicals that are toxic to sperm. Though *nonoxynol-9* is the most common ingredient in spermicides, it is no longer recommended for use on condoms. Spermicidal products include film, cream, jelly, and vaginal suppositories.

- An *intrauterine device (IUD)* is a small, flexible, plastic device that is inserted through the cervical opening into the uterus. It disrupts the fertilization and implantation processes.

- *Fertility awareness–based methods* (FAMs) involve a woman's awareness of her body's reproductive cycles. These include the *calendar (rhythm), basal body temperature (BBT), cervical mucus,* and *symptothermal methods.* These methods are suitable only for women with regular menstrual cycles and for couples with high motivation.

- The *lactational amenorrhea method (LAM)* is an effective, temporary method of contraception used by mothers who are exclusively breastfeeding their children.
- *Sterilization* is the most widely used method of contraception in the world. The most common form for women is *tubal ligation,* closing off the fallopian tubes. Another permanent method that does not require surgery is called *transcervical sterilization*. The surgical procedure that sterilizes men is a *vasectomy,* in which each vas deferens (sperm-carrying tube) is closed off. These methods of birth control are very effective.
- The use of *emergency contraception*, prevents pregnancy by keeping a fertilized egg from implanting into the uterus. When used within 3 days of unprotected intercourse, it can be quite effective. The ParaGard IUD can also be used as a post-coital form of birth control.

Abortion

- *Abortion,* the expulsion of the conceptus from the uterus, can be spontaneous or induced. *Medication abortion* is available in the United States to terminate early pregnancy. Surgical methods of abortion are *vacuum aspiration,* and *dilation and evacuation (D&E)*. Abortion is generally safe if done in the first trimester. Second-trimester abortions are riskier.
- In the United States, there are about 1.1 million abortions annually. The abortion rate has declined slightly in recent years.
- For women, the abortion decision is complex and raises many emotional issues. Though the majority of men support their partner's decision, many may still feel residual guilt and sadness following the abortion.
- In the abortion controversy, pro-life advocates argue that life begins at conception, that abortion leads to euthanasia, and that many who want to adopt are unable to because fewer babies are born as a result of abortion. Pro-choice advocates believe that women have the right to decide whether to continue a pregnancy, that abortion is needed as a birth control alternative because contraceptives are not 100% effective, and that if abortion is not legal, women will have unsafe illegal abortions. A key issue in the debate is when the embryo or fetus becomes human life.
- The current constitutional doctrine on abortion is evolving and dependent upon decisions of the U.S. Supreme Court and interpretations of state governments.

Research Issues

- High developmental costs, government regulations, political agendas, and marketing priorities all play a part in restricting contraceptive research. The biggest barrier, however, is the fear of lawsuits.

Questions for Discussion

- Who, in your opinion, should have access to contraception? Should the parent(s) of individuals younger than age 18 be informed that the child has obtained contraception? Why or why not?

- What considerations do you have before you would use a contraceptive? With whom would you discuss these? What sources of information might you use to verify your concerns or issues?

- If you or your partner experienced an unplanned pregnancy, what would you do? What resources do you have that would support your decision?

Sex and the Internet

Planned Parenthood

Most of us have heard about Planned Parenthood and the services it offers related to family planning. What we might not be aware of is the scope of the organization and the information it provides to aid us in our decisions. To learn more about Planned Parenthood or a specific topic related to its work, go to the group's website: http://www.plannedparenthood.org. Select a content area and answer the following:

- What topic did you choose? Why?
- What are five key points related to this topic?
- As a result of what you have learned, what opinions do you have or action would you take concerning this issue?
- Would you recommend this site to a person interested in learning more about family planning? Why or why not?

Suggested Websites

Association of Reproductive Health Professionals (ARHP)

http://www.arhp.org

A site for health care providers, as well as those interested in reproductive health news.

Bedsider

http://bedsider.org

Operated by The National Campaign to Prevent Teen and Unplanned Pregnancy, this site exclusively focuses on birth control with articles, interviews, resources, and reminders.

Centers for Disease Control and Prevention Reproductive Health Information Source

http://www.cdc.gov/reproductivehealth/index.htm

Provides information, research, and scientific reports on men's and women's reproductive health.

The Emergency Contraception Website

http://ec.princeton.edu

Operated by the Office of Population Research at Princeton University, this project is designed to provide accurate information about emergency contraception.

Men and Abortion

http://menandabortion.com/

For men and women, this site posts information that will be of use during counseling for, the procedure of, and recovery from abortion.

National Abortion and Reproductive Rights Action League

http://www.naral.org

Advocates for comprehensive reproductive health policies to secure reproductive *choice* for all Americans.

National Right to Life

http://www.nrlc.org

Its goal is to provide legal protection to human life.

Population Council

http://www.popcouncil.org

An international, nonprofit, nongovernmental organization that conducts biomedical, social science, and public health research on such topics as family planning, contraceptive development, and abortion.

Student Sex Life

http://www.studentsexlife.org

Developed by The National Campaign to Prevent Teen and Unplanned Pregnancy, the site is an educational resource for college students about birth control and healthy relationships.

United Nations Population Fund

http://www.unfpa.org

An international development agency that advocates for the rights of young people, including accurate information and services related to sexuality and reproductive health.

Suggested Reading

Browner, C. H., & Sargent, C. F. (Eds.). (2011). *Reproduction, globalization, and the state: New theoretical and ethnographic perspectives.* North Carolina: Duke University Press. Perspectives on how migration, communication, and technologies affect the reproductive lives of women and men in diverse societies.

Eig, J. (2014). *The birth of the pill.* New York: W. W. Norton. A fascinating look into the evolution of medical practices, funding, and ethics as well as a portrait of how women's reproductive lives are woven into our cultural history.

Everett, S. (2014). *Handbook of contraception and sexual health* (3rd ed.). New York: Routledge. Provides an integrated approach to sexual health and detailed information about contraceptive methods.

Hatcher, R. A., et al. (2011). *Contraceptive technology* (20th rev. ed.). New York: Ardent Media. Information on all methods of contraception, women's reproductive needs, and abortion.

Whitker, G., & Gilliam, M. (Eds.). (2014). *Contraception for adolescent and young adult women.* New York: Springer. Aimed primarily at health care practitioners, the text provides clinical recommendations regarding contraceptive care for adolescence and young women.

Conception, Pregnancy, and Childbirth

© ballyscanlon/Getty Images

CHAPTER OUTLINE

"When I was in my teens, I moved from my home [Guatemala] to the states and found things turned upside [down] from my traditional background. Take, for example, breastfeeding. In my country, it is a normal thing to breastfeed; you would not think twice about seeing a nurturing mother breastfeeding her child in public. Here, it seems to upset people's sensibilities when a nursing mother feeds her child in public. I wonder, that which is so natural and necessary, how can we debate whether a woman has a right to feed her child in public?"

—20-year-old female

"Pregnancy and childbirth have changed my life. As the mother of three young children, I look back at my pregnancies as probably three of the best periods of my life. Oh, sure, there were the days of exhaustion and nausea, pelvic heaviness, the large cumbersome breasts, and lost sleep, but in retrospect, they were overshadowed by the life growing inside of me. In giving life, I celebrate my womanhood."

—43-year-old female

"After getting married and having a daughter, things changed. While I was pregnant we, maybe, had sex 10 times. I was really sick during the first trimester and on bed rest during the second and third trimesters. At the time, it wasn't that big of a deal since we were so preoccupied with my health and our daughter. After she was born, it seemed that we were just out of practice and had a hard time initiating sex. When we did have sex we would both say, 'WOW, we should do this more often,' but then life would get in the way and 2 weeks would go by before we had sex again."

—28-year-old female

MANY PARENTS CONSIDER THE BIRTH of a child to be one of the happiest events of their lives. For most American women, pregnancy is relatively comfortable and the outcome predictably joyful. Yet, for increasing numbers of others, especially among the poor, the prospect of having children raises the specters of drugs, disease, malnutrition, and familial chaos. And there are those couples who have dreamed of and planned for families for years, only to find that they are unable to conceive.

In this chapter, we view pregnancy and childbirth from biological, social, and psychological perspectives. We consider pregnancy loss, infertility, and reproductive technology. And we look at the challenges of the transition to parenthood.

● Fertilization and Fetal Development

> *If your parents didn't have any children, there's a good chance that you won't have any.*
>
> —Clarence Day
> (1874–1935)

Once the **oocyte** (ovum, or unfertilized egg) has been released from the ovary, it drifts into the fallopian tube, where it may be fertilized if live sperm are present (see Figure 1). If the pregnancy proceeds without interruption, the birth will occur in approximately 266 days. Traditionally, physicians count the first day of the pregnancy as the day on which the woman began her last menstrual period; they calculate the due date to be 280 days, which is also 10 lunar months, from that day.

The Fertilization Process

The oocyte remains viable for 12–24 hours after ovulation; most sperm are viable in the female reproductive tract for 12–48 hours, although some may be viable for up to 5 days. Therefore, for fertilization to occur, intercourse must take place within 5 days before and 1 day after ovulation.

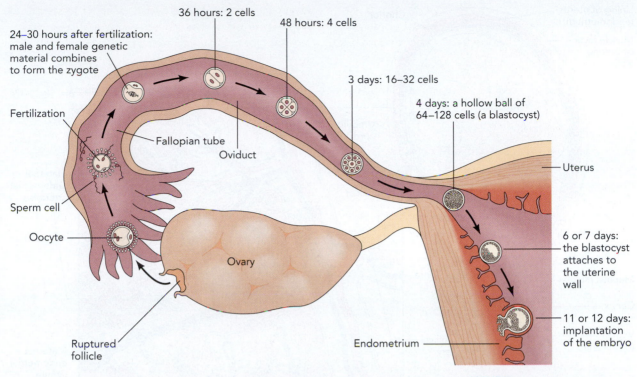

24–30 hours after fertilization: male and female genetic material combines to form the zygote

36 hours: 2 cells

48 hours: 4 cells

3 days: 16–32 cells

4 days: a hollow ball of 64–128 cells (a blastocyst)

Fertilization

Fallopian tube

Oviduct

Uterus

Sperm cell

Oocyte

Ovary

6 or 7 days: the blastocyst attaches to the uterine wall

Ruptured follicle

Endometrium

11 or 12 days: implantation of the embryo

● **FIGURE 1**

Ovulation, Fertilization, and Development of the Blastocyst. This drawing charts the progress of the released oocyte (unfertilized egg) through fertilization and pre-embryonic development.

Of the millions of sperm ejaculated into the vagina, only a few thousand (or even a few hundred) actually reach the fallopian tubes. The others leak from the vagina or are destroyed within its acidic environment. Those that make it into the cervix, which is easier during ovulation, when the cervical mucus becomes more fluid, may still be destroyed by white blood cells within the uterus. Furthermore, the sperm that actually reach the oocyte within a few minutes of ejaculation are not yet capable of getting through its outer layers. They must first undergo **capacitation,** the process by which their membranes become fragile enough to release the enzymes from their acrosomes, the helmetlike coverings of the sperm's nuclei. It takes 6–8 hours for this reaction to occur. It has been observed that sperm have receptor molecules that are attracted to a chemical released by the egg. Furthermore, the membrane of the sperm cell contains a chemical that helps the sperm adhere to, and eventually penetrate, the outer layer of the egg.

Once a single sperm is inside the oocyte cytoplasm, an electrical reaction occurs that prevents any other sperm from entering the oocyte. Immediately, the oocyte begins to swell, detaching the sperm that still cling to its outer layer. Next, it completes the final stage of cell division and becomes a mature ovum by forming the ovum nucleus. The nuclei of sperm and ovum then release their chromosomes, which combine to form the diploid zygote, containing 23 pairs of chromosomes. Each parent contributes one chromosome to each of the pairs. Fertilization is now complete, and pre-embryonic development begins. Within 9 months, this single cell, the zygote, may become the 600 trillion cells that constitute a human being.

> *Expectant parents who want a boy will get a girl, and vice versa; those who practice birth control will get twins.*
>
> —John Rush

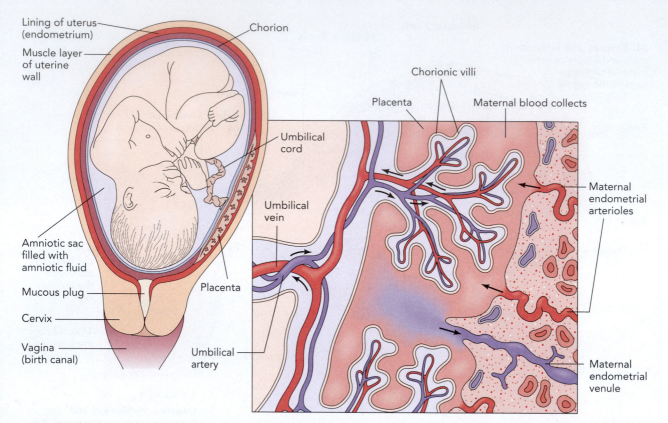

Lining of uterus (endometrium)

Muscle layer of uterine wall

Amniotic sac filled with amniotic fluid

Mucous plug

Cervix

Vagina (birth canal)

Chorion

Umbilical cord

Umbilical vein

Placenta

Umbilical artery

Chorionic villi

Placenta

Maternal blood collects

Maternal endometrial arterioles

Maternal endometrial venule

The Fetus in the Uterus and a Cross Section of the Placenta. The placenta is the organ of exchange between mother and fetus. Nutrients and oxygen pass from the mother to the fetus, and waste products pass from the fetus to the mother via blood vessels within the umbilical cord.

Development of the Conceptus

Following fertilization, the zygote undergoes a series of divisions, during which the cells replicate. After 4 or 5 days, there are about 100 cells, now called a **blastocyst.** On about the 5th day, the blastocyst arrives in the uterine cavity, where it floats for a day or two before implanting in the soft, blood-rich uterine lining (endometrium), which has spent the past 3 weeks preparing for its arrival. The process of **implantation** takes about 1 week. Human chorionic gonadotropin (HCG) secreted by the blastocyst maintains the uterine environment in an "embryo-friendly" condition and prevents the shedding of the endometrium, which would normally occur during menstruation.

The blastocyst, or pre-embryo, rapidly grows into an **embryo,** which will, in turn, be referred to as a **fetus** after the 8th week of **gestation** (pregnancy). During the first 2 or 3 weeks of development, the **embryonic membranes** are formed. These include the **amniotic sac** (also called the bag of water), a sac that holds the embryo (and later fetus). It consists of two membranes: The inner membrane, the **amnion,** contains the **amniotic fluid** and the fetus, while the outer membrane, the **chorion,** encloses the embryo and contributes to the development of the placenta (see Figure 2).

During the 3rd week, extensive cell migration occurs and the stage is set for the development of the organs. The first body segments and the brain begin to form. The digestive and circulatory systems begin to develop in the 4th week, and the heart begins to pump blood. By the end of the 4th week, the spinal cord and nervous system have also begun to develop. The 5th week sees the formation of arms and legs. In the 6th week, the eyes and ears form.

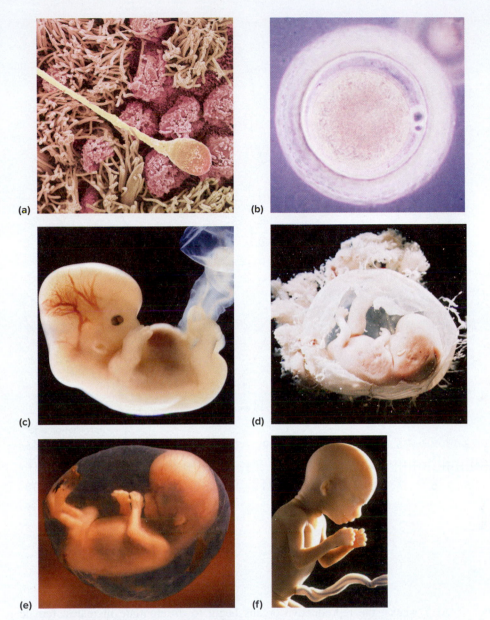

(a) After ejaculation, several million sperm move through the cervical mucus toward the fallopian tubes; an oocyte has moved into one of the tubes. On their way to the oocyte, millions of sperm are destroyed in the vagina, uterus, or fallopian tubes. Some go the wrong direction in the vagina, and others swim into the wrong tube. (b) The woman's and man's chromosomes have united, and the fertilized ovum has divided for the first time. After about 1 week, the blastocyst will implant itself in the uterine lining. (c) The embryo is 5 weeks old and is ⅖ of an inch long. It floats in the embryonic sac. The major divisions of the brain can be seen, as well as an eye, hands, arms, and a long tail. (d) The embryo is now 7 weeks old, is almost 1 inch long, and is connected to its umbilical cord. Its external and internal organs are developing. It has eyes, nose, mouth, lips, and tongue. (e) At 12 weeks, the fetus is over 3 inches long and weighs almost 1 ounce. (f) At 16 weeks, the fetus is more than 6 inches long and weighs about 7 ounces. All its organs have been formed. The time that follows is now one of simple growth.

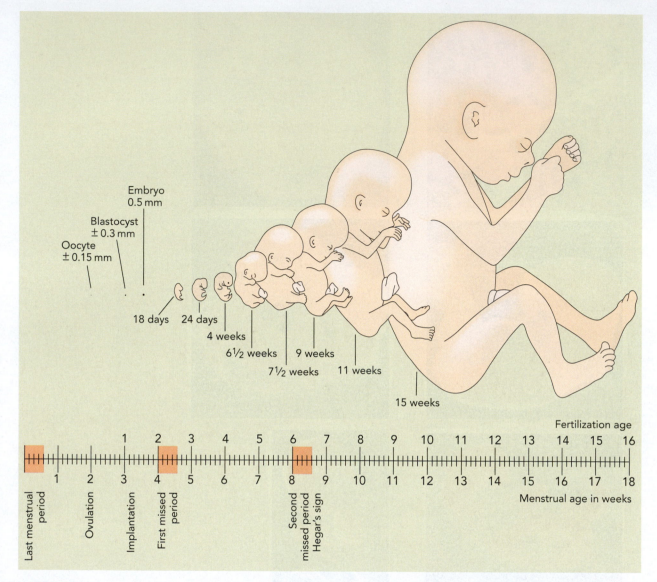

Embryo
0.5 mm

Blastocyst
± 0.3 mm

Oocyte
± 0.15 mm

18 days   24 days
4 weeks
6½ weeks   9 weeks
7½ weeks   11 weeks

15 weeks

Fertilization age

| 1 | 2 | 3 | 4 | 5 | 6 | 7 | 8 | 9 | 10 | 11 | 12 | 13 | 14 | 15 | 16 |

| 1 | 2 | 3 | 4 | 5 | 6 | 7 | 8 | 9 | 10 | 11 | 12 | 13 | 14 | 15 | 16 | 17 | 18 |

Menstrual age in weeks

Last menstrual period
Ovulation
Implantation
First missed period
Second missed period
Hegar's sign

• **FIGURE 3**

Growth of the Embryo and Fetus.
In this drawing, the actual sizes of the developing embryo and fetus are shown, from conception through the first 15 weeks.

What was your original face before you were born?

—Zen koan (riddle)

At 7 weeks, the reproductive organs begin to differentiate in males; female reproductive organs continue to develop. At 8 weeks, the fetus is about the size of a thumb although the head is nearly as large as the body. The brain begins to function to coordinate the development of the internal organs. Facial features begin to form and bones begin to develop. Arms, hands, fingers, legs, feet, toes, and eyes are almost fully developed at 12 weeks. At 15 weeks, the fetus has a strong heartbeat, some digestive functioning, and active muscles (see Figure 3). Most bones are developed by then and the eyebrows appear. At this stage, the fetus is covered with a fine, downy hair called **lanugo.**

Throughout its development, the fetus is nourished through the **placenta.** The placenta begins to develop from part of the blastocyst following implantation. It grows larger as the fetus does, passing nutrients from the mother's bloodstream to the fetus to which it is attached by the **umbilical cord.** The placenta serves as a biochemical barrier, allowing dissolved substances to pass to the fetus but blocking blood cells and large molecules.

think
about it

Child-Free: A Matter of Choice

Parenthood is now a matter of choice, thanks to the widespread use of contraception and changing perceptions of child-free couples. For the most part, women and men who want to have children can decide not only how many children they want but also when to have them. Among women aged 40–44, approximately 20% end their childbearing years without having had children (Livingston & Cohn, 2010). It appears that the most educated as well as White women are those groups who are most likely not to have borne a child. Among all women aged 40–44, the proportion that has never given birth has grown by 80% since 1976, when it was 10%. In the past, couples without children were referred to as "childless," conveying the sense that they were missing something they wanted or were supposed to have. But this term has been replaced with *child free*, as we have experienced a cultural shift and demographic trend in the direction of increasing numbers of women who expect and intend to remain nonparents. This trend is true for all racial and ethnic groups and most educational levels but has fallen significantly over the past decade among women with advanced degrees (Livingston & Cohn, 2010). In fact, children increasingly are seen as less central to a good marriage, with 41% of adults now saying that children are very important for a successful marriage, compared to 65% who agreed with that statement in 1990.

Even with less familial and social pressure to reproduce, the decision not to have children can be a difficult one. Factors that contribute to this decision include timing, divorce, ambivalence on the part of one partner, lack of desire to conceive or adopt a child when single, and career ambitions and promotions. Before they marry, couples usually have some idea that they will or will not have children. If the intent isn't clear from the start or if one partner's mind changes, the couple may have serious relationship problems ahead.

Think Critically

1. Do you want to have children? Why or why not?
2. What are your feelings about those who choose to remain child-free?
3. Do you believe that the government should provide tax incentives to couples who are child-free?

By 5 months, the fetus is 10–12 inches long and weighs between 1/2 and 1 pound. The internal organs are well developed, although the lungs cannot function well outside the uterus. At 6 months, the fetus is 11–14 inches long and weighs more than 1 pound. At 7 months, it is 13–17 inches long and weighs about 3 pounds. At this point, most healthy fetuses are viable; that is, capable of surviving outside the womb. Although some fetuses are viable at 5 or 6 months, they require specialized care to survive. The fetus spends the final 2 months of gestation growing rapidly. At term (9 months), it will be about 20 inches long and will weigh about 7 pounds. A full-term pregnancy lasts 40 weeks. Even though 37 weeks is also considered full term, studies show that babies born even a few weeks early are at greater risk for health problems than those who are born later (Boyle et al., 2012).

● Pregnancy

From the moment it is discovered, pregnancy affects people's feelings about themselves and their relationships with their partners, as well as the interrelationships of other family members. Pregnancy rates can also say something about society as a whole and can influence and be influenced by policy decisions. There were 3.9 million births in the United States in 2013, down less than 1% from 2012 and down 9% from 2007 (Martin, Hamilton, & Osterman, 2014). The 2013 fertility rate was at an all-time low: 62.5 per 1,000 women aged 15–44, with record lows among women under age 30. The birth rate for U.S. teenagers also fell 10% in 2013, to 26.5 per 1,000; the lowest ever recorded. The exact cause of these declines is uncertain, but it is known that when women become better educated and gain career opportunities, they postpone childbearing until they are older. Because not everyone chooses to be a parent, the term **child-free** is used to describe those who expect and intend to remain nonparents.

Preconception Care

The health of the mother before conception and early in pregnancy affects the health of the fetus. **Preconception care** comprises interventions that aim to identify and modify medical, behavioral, and social risks to a woman's health and pregnancy outcome through prevention and management. Preconception care can reduce the risk of problems during pregnancy and after the child's birth (National Institutes of Health, 2013). For example, increasing one's intake of folic acid, getting up-to-date on vaccines, discussing preexisting medical conditions, maintaining a healthy weight, and avoiding smoking, drinking, and taking drugs are among those behaviors that can reduce the risk of complications and improve the chances of a healthy pregnancy. It is extremely important that women and men who are sexually active and not consistently or effectively using contraception be mindful of the lifestyle choices they are making and seek medical attention before the woman attempts to become pregnant.

Pregnancy Detection

Chemical tests designed to detect the presence of **human chorionic gonadotropin (HCG),** which is produced immediately after a fertilized egg attaches to the uterus, can usually determine pregnancy approximately 1 week following a missed or spotty menstrual period. Pregnancy testing may be done in a doctor's office or family planning clinic, or at home with tests purchased from a drugstore or online. Such tests diagnose pregnancy within 7 days after conception with 98–99% accuracy.

A simple blood test can determine a baby's sex with 95% accuracy at 7 weeks and 99% accuracy at 20 weeks. If a Y chromosome is detected, the fetus is male; the absence of a Y chromosome means the fetus is female. The test is available to consumers online or at pharmacies; however, because it is not used for medical purposes, it is not yet regulated by the U.S. Food and Drug Administration. One potential concern about using such a test is that women might abort a fetus of an undesired sex. In fact, several companies do not sell such tests in China or India, where boys are prized over girls and fetuses found to be female are sometimes aborted (Devaney, Palomaki, Scott, & Bianchi, 2011).

The first reliable physical sign of pregnancy can be observed about 4 weeks after a woman misses her period. By this point, changes in her cervix and pelvis are apparent during a pelvic examination. At this stage, the woman is considered to be 8 weeks pregnant. Physicians calculate pregnancy as beginning at the time of the woman's last menstrual period rather than at the time of actual fertilization because that date is often difficult to determine. Another signal of pregnancy, called **Hegar's sign,** is a softening of the uterus just above the cervix, which can be felt during a vaginal examination. In addition, a slight purple hue colors the labia minora; the vagina and cervix also take on a purplish color rather than the usual pink.

Changes in Women During Pregnancy

A woman's early response to pregnancy will vary dramatically according to who she is, how she feels about pregnancy and motherhood, whether the pregnancy was planned, whether she has a secure home situation, and many other factors. Her feelings may be ambivalent and they will probably change over the course of the pregnancy.

A couple's relationship is likely to undergo changes during pregnancy. It can be a stressful time, especially if the pregnancy was unanticipated. On the other hand, women with supportive partners often have fewer health problems in pregnancy and more positive feelings about their changing bodies than those whose partners are not supportive ("Especially for fathers," n.d.). Communication is especially important during this period for many reasons, including the possibility that each partner may have preconceived ideas about what the other is feeling. Both partners may have fears about the baby's well-being, the approaching birth, their ability to parent, and the ways in which the baby will interfere with their own relationship. All of these concerns are normal. Sharing them, perhaps in the setting of a prenatal group, can strengthen the relationship. If the pregnant woman's partner is not supportive or if she does not have a partner, it is important that she find other sources of support—family, friends, women's groups—and that she not be reluctant to ask for help.

A pregnant woman's relationship with her own mother may also undergo changes. In a certain sense, becoming a mother makes a woman the equal of her own mother. She can now lay claim to co-equal status as an adult. Women who have depended on their mother tend to become more independent and assertive as their pregnancy progresses. Women who have been distant from, hostile to, or alienated from their mother may begin to identify with their mother's experience of pregnancy. Even women who have delayed childbearing until their 30s may be surprised to find their relationships with their mother changing and becoming more "adult." Working through these changing relationships is a kind of "psychological gestation" that accompanies the physiological gestation of the fetus.

The first trimester (3 months) of pregnancy may be difficult physically for the expectant mother. Approximately two thirds of women experience nausea, vomiting, fatigue, and painful swelling of the breasts. The nausea and vomiting that often occur during the first trimester of pregnancy usually subside with time. The pregnant woman may have fears that she will miscarry or that the child will not be normal. Her sexuality may undergo changes, resulting in unfamiliar needs for more, less, or differently expressed sexual behaviors, which may, in turn, cause anxiety. (Sexuality during pregnancy is discussed further in the "Think About It" box

Only through sexual union are new beings capable of existing. This union, therefore, represents a place between two worlds, a point of contact between being and nonbeing, where life manifests itself and incarnates the divine spirit.

—Alain Daniélou
(1907–1994)

The physical and psychological changes that accompany pregnancy can have a ripple effect on a woman's relationship with her partner and family.

© AGE Fotostock/SuperStock

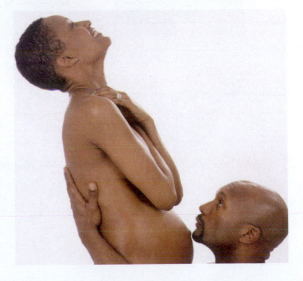

"Sexual Behavior During Pregnancy".) Education about the birth process and her own body's functioning and support from partner, friends, relatives, and health care professionals are the best antidotes to fear.

During the second trimester, most of the nausea and fatigue disappear, and the pregnant woman can feel the fetus move. Worries about miscarriage will probably begin to diminish, too, for the riskiest part of fetal development has passed. The pregnant woman may look and feel radiant. She will very likely be proud of her accomplishment and be delighted as her pregnancy begins to show. She may feel in harmony with life's natural rhythms. Some women, however, may be concerned about their increasing size, fearing that they are becoming unattractive. A partner's attention and reassurance may help ease these fears.

The third trimester may be the time of the greatest difficulties in daily living. The uterus, originally about the size of the woman's fist, enlarges to fill the pelvic cavity and pushes up into the abdominal cavity, exerting increasing pressure on the other internal organs (see Figure 4). Water retention (edema) is a fairly common problem during late pregnancy. It also tends to be worse at the end of the day and during the summer. Edema may cause swelling in the face, hands, ankles, and feet, but it can often be controlled by cutting down on the intake of salt, elevating the feet, eating healthy, and exercising. A women should call her physician if she notices swelling in her face, puffiness around her eyes, more than slight swelling in her hands, or excessive swelling of her feet or ankles. Her physical abilities also are limited by her size, and she may need to cut back her work hours or stop working.

In one study, physical activity during pregnancy resulted in babies with healthier hearts, even a full month after delivery (Reynolds, 2011). The effect was especially robust in the children whose mothers had exercised the most; these children showed slower heartbeats and presumably stronger hearts. It is unclear whether this training effect is a result of hormones released during exercise or a kind of "music" in the blood caused by gasping breaths and increased heartbeats. Exercise also helps improve circulation, which helps prevent constipation, varicose veins, leg cramps, and swelling of the ankles.

The woman and her partner may become increasingly concerned about the upcoming birth. Some women experience periods of antepartum depression, a mood disorder, preceding delivery. Untreated, it can lead to problems in both the women and baby. Others feel a sense of exhilaration and anticipation marked by bursts of industriousness. They feel that the fetus already is a member of the family. Both parents may begin talking to the fetus and "playing" with it by

• **FIGURE 4**

Mother and Fetus in Third Trimester of Pregnancy. The expanding uterus affects the mother's internal organs, causing feelings of pressure and possible discomfort.

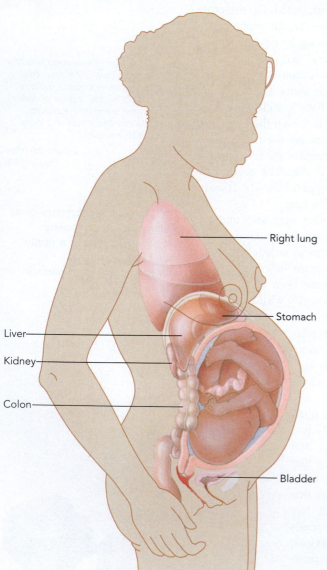

Right lung

Stomach

Liver

Kidney

Colon

Bladder

Sexual Behavior During Pregnancy

It is not unusual for a woman's sexual desires and behaviors to change during pregnancy, although there is great variation among women in these expressions of sexuality. Some women feel beautiful, energetic, and sensual and are very much interested in sex; others feel awkward and decidedly unsexy. It is also quite possible for a woman's sexual desires to fluctuate during this time. Men may also feel confusion or conflicts about sexual activity.

Although there are no "rules" governing sexual behavior during pregnancy, a few basic precautions should be observed:

- If the woman has had a prior miscarriage, she should check with her health care practitioner before having intercourse, masturbating, or engaging in other activities that might lead to orgasm. Powerful uterine contractions could induce a spontaneous abortion in some women, especially during the first trimester.
- If the woman has vaginal bleeding, she should refrain from all sexual activity and consult her physician or midwife at once.
- If the insertion of the penis or other object into the vagina causes pain that is not easily remedied by a change of position, the couple should refrain from penetration.
- Pressure on the woman's abdomen should be avoided, especially during the final months of pregnancy.
- Late in pregnancy, an orgasm is likely to induce uterine contractions. Generally, this is not considered harmful, but the pregnant woman may want to discuss it with her practitioner. Occasionally, labor begins when the waters break as the result of orgasmic contractions.

A couple may be uncertain as to how to express their sexual feelings, especially if it is their first pregnancy. The following guidelines may be helpful:

- Even during a normal pregnancy, sexual intercourse may be uncomfortable. The couple may want to try such positions as side by side or rear entry to avoid pressure on the woman's abdomen and to facilitate shallow penetration.
- Even if intercourse is not comfortable for the woman, orgasm may still be intensely pleasurable. She may wish to consider masturbating alone or with her partner or engaging in cunnilingus. It is important to note that air should *not* be blown into the vagina during cunnilingus.

Once the baby has been born, a couple can resume intercourse after the bleeding has stopped and the vaginal walls have healed. This may take anywhere from 4 to 8 weeks.

Think Critically

1. What are your views about having sex during pregnancy?
2. How comfortable would you be in discussing with your doctor the topic of sexuality during pregnancy?
3. What new information did you learn as a result of reading this box?

patting and rubbing the mother's belly. (The principal developmental tasks for the expectant mother and father are summarized in Table 1.)

Complications of Pregnancy and Dangers to the Fetus

Usually, pregnancy proceeds without major complications. Good nutrition, a moderate amount of exercise, and manageable levels of stress are among the most significant factors in a complication-free pregnancy. In addition, early and ongoing prenatal care is important.

Unfortunately, not all mothers have access to health care or live in a safe environment. This reality can be witnessed in the United States, which currently

TABLE 1 • Principal Tasks of Expectant Parents	
Mothers	**Fathers**
Development of an emotional attachment to the fetus	Acceptance of the pregnancy and attachment to the fetus
Differentiation of the self from the fetus	Acceptance and resolution of the relationship with his own father
Acceptance and resolution of the relationship with her own mother	Resolution of dependency issues involving parents or wife/partner
Resolution of dependency issues involving parents or husband/partner	Evaluation of practical and financial responsibilities
Evaluation of practical and financial responsibilities	

ranks 60th out of 180 countries in maternal deaths occurring during pregnancy. That is, for every 100,000 births in America in 2013, 18.5 women died. This compares with 8.2 women who died during pregnancy and birth in Canada, 6.1 in Britain, and only 2.4 in Iceland. Researchers are not sure why this is happening but are in almost unanimous agreement in pointing to a lack of access to health care, coupled with rising levels of poverty (Bhutta et al., 2014).

Effects of Teratogens   Substances other than nutrients may reach the developing embryo or fetus through the placenta. Although few extensive studies have been done on the subject, toxic substances in the environment can also affect the health of the fetus. Whatever a woman breathes, eats, or drinks is eventually received by the conceptus in some proportion. A fetus's blood-alcohol level, for example, is equal to that of the mother. **Teratogens** are substances or other factors that cause defects (e.g., brain damage or physical deformities) in developing embryos or fetuses. In fact, an estimated 10% of birth defects may be caused by teratogens in the environment (Farrer, 2010).

Chemicals and environmental pollutants are also potentially threatening. For example, pregnant women who live near fields and farms where pesticides are used have a significantly higher risk than other women of delivering children with autism or other developmental delays (Shelton et al., 2014). Continuous exposure to lead, most commonly in paint products or water from lead pipes, has been implicated in a variety of learning disorders. Mercury, from fish contaminated by industrial wastes, is a known cause of physical deformities. Solvents, pesticides, and certain chemical fertilizers should be avoided or used with extreme caution both at home and in the workplace. X-rays should also be avoided, if possible, during pregnancy.

Alcohol   There is no known safe amount of alcohol consumption during pregnancy or when trying to become pregnant (CDC, 2014.12a). Studies have linked heavy or chronic ingestion of alcohol during pregnancy to **fetal alcohol syndrome (FAS),** which can include unusual facial characteristics, small head and body size, congenital heart defects, defective joints, and intellectual and behavioral impairment. About half of all FAS children are developmentally disabled. Known prenatal consumption of alcohol without the associated facial features of FAS is linked to **fetal alcohol effect (FAE).** Children with FAE often have many of the same symptoms and issues as those with FAS, including intellectual and behavioral deficits.

Tobacco   Maternal cigarette smoking is associated with spontaneous abortion, persistent breathing problems, and a variety of complications during pregnancy and birth (CDC, 2014.12b). Smoking during pregnancy impairs placental development by reducing blood flow which can lead to a reduction of oxygen and micronutrients to the growing infant. Babies born to women who smoke during pregnancy may have low birth weight, suffer from fetal growth restriction, have a smaller head circumference, be born with cleft palate, and have a higher risk of sudden death syndrome.

Other Drugs   Mothers who regularly use opiates (heroin, morphine, codeine, and opium) are at greater risk for spontaneous abortion and are likely to have infants who are addicted to opiates at birth. In addition, these infants are at risk for neonatal intoxication, respiratory depression, low birth weight, heart defects, and learning and behavioral problems (March of Dimes, 2013).

Prescription drugs should be used during pregnancy only under careful medical supervision because some may cause serious harm to the fetus. Additionally, over-the-counter drugs, including vitamins and aspirin, as well as large quantities of caffeine-containing food and beverages, should be avoided or used only under medical supervision.

Infectious Diseases   Infectious diseases can also damage the fetus. For example, if a woman contracts German measles (rubella) during the first 3 months of pregnancy, her child may be born with physical or mental disabilities. Concerns about risks from inactivated virus or bacterial vaccinations during pregnancy are theoretical. No evidence exists of risk to the fetus from vaccinating pregnant women with inactivated virus or bacterial vaccines, and the benefits of vaccinating generally outweigh potential risks when the likelihood of disease exposure is high (CDC, 2014.12c). However, immunization against rubella, which is a live virus vaccine, should be done before the woman is pregnant; otherwise, the vaccine can pose a risk to the fetus. (For a list of general recommendations for use in pregnant women, see CDC's "Guidelines for Vaccinating Pregnant Women" [2014.12c].)

Sexually Transmitted Infections   STIs can complicate a pregnancy, be transmitted, and have serious effects on both a woman and her developing baby. The Centers for Disease Control and Prevention (CDC) recommends that all pregnant women be screened for chlamydia, gonorrhea, hepatitis B, HIV, and syphilis (CDC, 2013.12a). If a pregnant woman has contracted any of these or other STIs, she should discuss with her doctor potential effects on the baby, delivery procedures, treatment, and breastfeeding. The sooner a woman begins receiving medical care during pregnancy, the better the outcomes will be for both her and her unborn child.

Women who are pregnant can acquire an STI from their own risky behavior or from an infected partner. Because avoidance of STIs is critical throughout a woman's pregnancy, she may want to consider consistent and correct use of latex condoms for each episode of sexual intercourse.

Maternal Obesity   Obesity is a major public health and economic concern in the United States. Using data collected from 2011–2012, it is estimated that 35% of adults and 17% of children in the United States are obese (Ogden, Carroll, Kit, & Flegal, 2014). Maternal obesity, often defined as pre-pregnancy body mass index (BMI) of greater than 30, increases the risk of infertility, miscarriage, and adverse pregnancy outcomes, including higher risk of preterm birth, neural tube defects (including spina bifida), and death after birth (March of Dimes, 2011a; Jungheim, Traviseo, & Hopeman, 2013). In the mother, obesity increases the risk of gestational hypertension, preeclampsia, strokes, gestational diabetes, stillbirths, and cesarean section (CDC, 2014.12d).

With the increasing trend in childhood obesity, it is anticipated that as these children enter their childbearing age, the prevalence of maternal obesity during pregnancy will be even greater. Given that infant mortality in the United States is higher (at 5.9 per 1,000) than in at least 20 other developed countries (Kaiser Family Foundation, 2014), it is even more evident that obesity prevention should be practiced as a measure to reduce infant mortality. This includes seeking early and regular prenatal care, maintaining a healthy diet, and engaging in regular exercise.

Pregnancy After Age 35   Delaying pregnancy until after age 35 has become a common reality for many women, and most healthy women who get pregnant after age 35 and even into their 40s have healthy babies ("Pregnancy after 35," 2015). However, while men can father children late in life, the quality and quantity of a woman's eggs begin to decline in her late 20s and fall off rapidly after age 35, so that by age 40 her odds of conceiving have decreased and her risk of pregnancy-related complications and having a live baby with a chromosomal abnormality have increased. While the chromosomal abnormality Down syndrome affects 1 in 1,000 births at maternal age 30, the rate gradually increases to 1 in 30 births at maternal age 45 (March of Dimes, 2014). Paternal age also increases the likelihood of Down syndrome, but only if the mother is over 35. As women age, chronic illnesses such as high blood pressure and diabetes may also present pregnancy- and birth-related complications. Genetic counseling may help a woman and her partner assess their risks, make an informed choice about pregnancy, and decide whether or not to have testing for chromosomal abnormalities. The American College of Obstetricians and Gynecologists (2014) recommends that all pregnant women be offered a screening test for birth defects. Screening may include a blood test along with an ultrasound. If the screening test result shows increased risk of a birth defect or if a couple have risk factors for having a baby with certain birth defects, diagnostic tests are available. (These tests are discussed later in the chapter.)

Ectopic Pregnancy   In **ectopic pregnancy** (tubal pregnancy), which occurs in about 1 in 50 pregnancies, the fertilized egg grows outside the uterus, usually in a fallopian tube ("What to know about ectopic pregnancy," 2014). Any sexually active woman of childbearing age is at risk for ectopic pregnancy. Women who have abnormal fallopian tubes are at higher risk for ectopic pregnancy. Generally, this occurs because the tube is obstructed, most often as a result of pelvic inflammatory disease due to chlamydia and gonorrhea infections. Factors such as a previous ectopic pregnancy, treatment with assisted reproductive technology (discussed later in the chapter), and **endometriosis,** growth of tissue outside the uterus, can also increase the risk. The pregnancy will never come to term. The embryo may spontaneously abort, or the embryo and placenta will continue to expand until they rupture the fallopian tube. If the pregnancy is early and has not ruptured, drugs may be used instead of surgery to remove the conceptus. A ruptured ectopic pregnancy, however, is a medical emergency that can endanger the mother's life.

Pregnancy-Induced Hypertension   Previously referred to as toxemia or pre-eclampsia, **pregnancy-induced hypertension** is characterized by high blood pressure and edema, along with protein in the urine. It can occur after 20 weeks of pregnancy or shortly after delivery and affects 3–5% of all pregnancies in the United States ("Understanding preeclampsia," 2015). It can usually be treated by diet, bed rest, and medication. If untreated, it can progress to maternal convulsions and stroke, which pose a threat to mother and child. It is important for a pregnant woman to have her blood pressure checked regularly.

Preterm Births   Births that take place prior to 37 weeks of gestation are considered to be **preterm births.** About 11% of all pregnancies in the United States result in preterm births (Martin et al., 2014). A consequence of this is **low-birth-weight infants,** those who weigh less than 2,500 grams, or 5.5 pounds, at birth. About 35% of infant deaths in the United States are associated with preterm birth–related causes, more than any other single cause. The fundamental problem of prematurity is that many of the infant's vital organs are insufficiently developed. Most premature infants will grow normally, but many will experience long-term neurological disabilities, including breathing problems, feeding difficulties, cerebral palsy, and developmental delays. As premature infants get older, problems such as low intelligence, learning difficulties, poor hearing and vision, and physical awkwardness may become apparent. Nevertheless, the majority of preterm babies eventually catch up with their peers and thrive.

Preterm births are one of the greatest problems confronting obstetrics today; most of the cases are related to low or high maternal age, smoking, poor nutrition, and poor health in the mother. Prenatal care is extremely important as a means of preventing prematurity. We need to understand that if children's needs are not met today we will all face the consequences of their deprivation tomorrow. The social and economic costs are bound to be very high. (Table 2 lists various demographic facts of life for the United States and the rest of the world.)

Low birth weight affects about 8% of newborns in the United States. Adequate prenatal care significantly reduces the risk of low birth weight (Child Trends Databank, 2014).

© Peter Banos/Alamy

TABLE 2 • The Demographic Facts of Life		
	United States	**World**
Population	320 million	7.2 billion
Population density (people per square kilometer)	32	51
Median age	37	29
Population increase per year	2.7 million	78 million
Population growth rate	0.85%	1.1%
Population doubling time	82 years	64 years
Total fertility rate	2.1	2.5
Births per 1,000 women 15–19	27	52
Life expectancy	75 (male), 80 (female)	67 (male), 71 (female)
Births per year	4.4 million	135.8 million
Infant mortality rate (infant deaths per 1,000 live births)	6.5	42

SOURCES: Updated from The Demographic Facts of Life. Population Connection. Used by permission; U.S. Census Bureau (2014). Available at www.census.gov/popclock.

The pictures produced by ultrasound are called sonograms. They are used to determine fetal age, position of the fetus and placenta, and possible developmental problems.

© Blend Images/Alamy

Diagnosing Fetal Abnormalities

Both the desire to bear children and the wish to ensure that those children are healthy have encouraged the use of diagnostic technologies. Because of the number of screening tests available, guidelines discuss the advantages and disadvantages of each test and some of the factors that determine which screening test should be offered and when. The American College of Obstetricians and Gynecologists (2014) notes that the following prenatal tests are available to address concerns about birth defects:

- Carrier screening tests, which can be done before or during pregnancy, can show if a person carries a gene for an inherited disorder. Cystic fibrosis carrier screening is offered to all women of reproductive age because it is one of the most common genetic disorders.

- Screening tests assess the risk that a baby will have Down syndrome and other chromosome problems, as well as neural tube defects, but do not indicate whether the fetus actually has these disorders.

- Diagnostic tests can provide information about whether the fetus has a genetic condition and are most commonly done through ultrasound or on cells obtained through chorionic villus sampling or amniocentesis. **Chorionic villus sampling (CVS)** involves the removal of a small sample of cells taken from the placenta sometime between 10 and 13 weeks of gestation. **Amniocentesis** involves the withdrawal of a small amount of amniotic fluid from the uterus at 14–20 weeks of gestation (see Figure 5). The risk from loss from amniocentesis is 1%, while that for CVS is from .6% to 4.6% (Anderson & Brown, 2009).

- **Neural tube defect screening,** performed on the mother's blood to measure the level of alpha-fetoprotein, reveals possible defects of the spine, spinal cord, skull, and brain. This test should be offered during the second trimester to women who elect only first-trimester screening (CVS) for Down syndrome.

- Other tests can be performed to provide further information.

Regardless of the kind of prenatal diagnostic procedure done, there may be complications or risks for pregnancy loss associated with the tests, so the cost-benefit ratio of the procedure should be discussed with one's doctor.

● **FIGURE 5**

Diagnosing Fetal Abnormalities via (a) Amniocentesis and (b) Chorionic Villus Sampling.

Amniocentesis

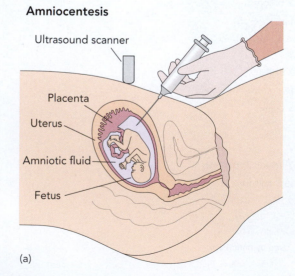

(a)

Chorionic villus sampling

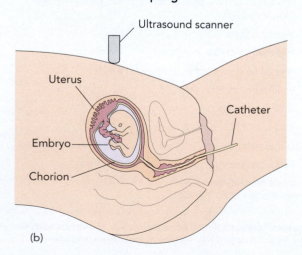

(b)

Pregnancy Loss

A normal pregnancy lasts about 40 weeks. The death of a fetus before 20 weeks is called early pregnancy loss. Often, the death is a miscarriage (spontaneous loss of a fetus before it can survive on its own), stillbirth, or death during early infancy—a devastating experience that has been largely ignored in our society. The death of a baby at any stage in the pregnancy is as emotional as it is physical. The statement "You can always have another one" may be meant as consolation, but it can be particularly chilling to a grieving mother or father.

Miscarriage Spontaneous abortion, or miscarriage, is a powerful natural selective force in bringing healthy babies into the world. About 10–15% of recognized pregnancies end before 20 weeks' gestation, but as many as half of all pregnancies may end in miscarriage because many losses occur before a women realizes she is pregnant (March of Dimes, 2012a). Many of these—more than 50%—happen because of chromosomal abnormalities. The first sign that a pregnant woman may miscarry is vaginal bleeding (spotting). If a woman's symptoms of pregnancy disappear and she develops pelvic cramps, she may be miscarrying; the fetus is usually expelled by uterine contractions. Most miscarriages occur in the first trimester (13 weeks) of pregnancy. Sometimes the embryos are healthy, but women miscarry for other reasons: for example, a misshapen or scarred uterus, insulin or hormonal imbalances, or chronic infections in the uterus. Women can take steps to lessen the likelihood of pregnancy loss, beginning with taking a multivitamin with folic acid, not smoking or using drugs (including the abuse of prescription drugs) reducing their intake of caffeine to no more than 200 mg (1 cup of coffee) per day, exercising, and maintaining a healthy weight.

Infant Mortality Because factors that affect the health of a population often impact infants, the infant mortality rate is often used as a barometer to measure the health and well-being of a nation (CDC, 2011.12a). The U.S. infant mortality rate, although at its lowest point in many decades, remains far higher than most of the developed world: an estimated 6.4 deaths for every 1,000 live births, or 37th worldwide in infant mortality (Geography IQ, 2014).

Although many infants die of poverty-related conditions, including lack of prenatal care, others die from congenital problems (conditions appearing at birth) or from infectious diseases, accidents, or other causes. Sometimes the causes of death are not apparent; more than 4,000 infant deaths per year are attributed to sudden unexpected infant death (SUID). The majority of these occur while the infant is sleeping in an unsafe environment (CDC, 2014.12e). **Sudden infant death syndrome (SIDS)** is one type of SUID whereby an infant of less than 1 year of age dies of an unexplained cause. SIDS is the third leading cause of infant death in the United States and the leading cause of death in infants 1 to 12 months. Unsafe sleep practices that can lead to accidental suffocation include soft bedding, rolling on top or against the infant while sleeping, wedging or entrapping an infant in a mattress, and strangulation by, for example, a crib railing. The American Academy of Pediatrics (2011) recommends that infants be breastfed and placed on their backs to sleep, and that parents not cover the heads of babies or overbundle them in clothing and blankets, not let them get too hot, not use soft bedding (including fluffy blankets, stuffed animals, and bumper rails), and keep the baby away from smoke.

Coping With Loss   The feelings of shock and grief felt by individuals whose child dies before, during, or after birth can be difficult to understand for those who have not had a similar experience. What they may not realize is that most women form a deep attachment to their children even before birth. At first, the attachment may be to a fantasy image of the unborn child. During the course of the pregnancy, the mother forms an acquaintance with her infant through the physical sensations she feels within her. Thus, the death of the fetus can also represent the loss of a dream and of a hope for the future. For both the mother and the father, this loss must be acknowledged and felt before psychological healing can take place.

Infertility

Some couples experience the pain of loss when they plan to have a child and then discover that they cannot get pregnant. **Infertility** is defined as the lack of pregnancy in the last 12 months despite having had unprotected sexual intercourse in each of those months with the same partner. Women who do not have regular menstrual cycles or are older than 35 years and have not conceived during a 6-month period of trying should consider seeing an infertility specialist. Fertility problems are equally likely to be caused by a disorder of the man (30%), disorder of the woman (30%), or both; in other cases, the cause is unexplained or attributable to both partners. In spite of the fact that Americans are waiting longer to get married, it appears that infertility numbers are declining, such that from 2006 to 2010, the percentage of married women aged 15–44 who were infertile was 6% (National Survey of Family Growth, 2013). For unmarried women living with a male partner, the data show 4.9% to be infertile.

The most common risk factors for infertility are advancing age, smoking, high or very low body weight, STIs, and consumption of alcohol (CDC, 2013.12b). The good news is that the majority of infertile couples can now be successfully treated using conventional fertility treatments, such as medications to trigger ovulation or surgical procedures to correct problems with the reproductive tract. For the remaining couples, assisted reproductive technologies offer the greatest possibility of pregnancy. In 2012, over 51,000 live births occurred as a result of these technologies (CDC, 2014.12f).

Female Infertility

About 11%, or 6.7 million, women aged 15–44 in the United States have difficulty getting or staying pregnant (CDC, 2014.12f). Most cases of infertility among women are due to physical factors. Hormones, stress, immunological factors, and environmental factors may also be involved.

Physical Causes   Most cases of female infertility are caused by problems with ovulation. Less commonly, blocked fallopian tubes, physical problems with the uterus, and uterine fibroids can contribute to infertility. In some of these cases, surgery can restore fertility. A number of factors can alter a woman's ability to become pregnant including age, smoking, alcohol use, stress, poor diet, athletic training, overweight or underweight, and STIs.

Many women are waiting until their 30s and 40s to have children. About one third of couples in which the woman is 35 or older have fertility problems, often caused by a variety of factors including ovaries that are less able to release eggs, a small number of eggs left, and eggs that are not healthy (CDC, 2013.12b). Additionally, some health problems can increase the risk of infertility in women including irregular, painful, or no menstrual periods, endometriosis, pelvic inflammatory disease, and having more than one miscarriage. It is a good idea for a woman to talk to a doctor before trying to get pregnant; a doctor can help her prepare her body for a baby and answer any questions she has about fertility.

Male Infertility

The primary causes of male infertility include having a **varicocele** (or varicose) vein above the testicle, low sperm count, decreased sperm motility, and poor sperm morphology (misshapen sperm) (CDC, 2013.12b). Sperm ducts may become blocked, or for some reason the male may not ejaculate. While sperm morphology is the best indicator of fertility, sperm counts are used instead because they are easier to perform.

Men are more at risk for infertility than women from environmental factors because they are constantly producing new sperm cells; for the same reason, men may also recover faster once the affecting factor has been removed. Toxic substances, such as lead and pesticides, are responsible for decreased number or poor health of sperm. Alcohol, tobacco, and marijuana use, as well as testosterone supplementation and anabolic steroid use, may also produce reduced sperm counts or abnormal sperm.

Emotional Responses to Infertility

By the time partners seek medical advice about their fertility problems they may have already experienced a crisis in confronting the possibility of not being able to become biological parents. Many such couples feel they have lost control over a major area of their lives. Coming to a joint decision with one's partner about goals, acceptable therapies, and an endpoint for therapy is important and advisable.

Infertility Treatment

Almost without exception, fertility problems are physical, not emotional, despite myths to the contrary. The two most popular myths are that anxiety over becoming pregnant leads to infertility and that if an infertile couple adopt a child the couple will then be able to conceive on their own. Neither has any basis in medical fact, although some presumably infertile couples have conceived following an adoption. This does not mean, however, that one should adopt a child to remedy infertility. In some cases, fertility is restored for no discernible reason; in others, the infertility remains a mystery. Treatment for a successful outcome, defined as delivering a child or achieving an ongoing pregnancy within 18 months, can be both emotionally and financially costly.

Enhancing Fertility   There are many ways that fertility can be enhanced, the most important of which involves the timing of coitus with respect to the woman's menstrual cycle. Because an ovum is viable for about 24 hours after ovulation, a pregnancy is most likely to occur when intercourse takes place at the same time as ovulation. If a man wears tight underwear, he might switch to boxer-type shorts to allow his testicles to descend from his body. However, for many couples, these techniques are not enough; they may seek medical intervention to diagnose and treat infertility.

Medical Intervention   Medical technology now offers more treatment options to men and to women trying to conceive a child. Prior to investing in any one of these, preventive steps such as avoiding alcohol, tobacco, and drugs; exercising; and eating a healthy diet should be taken to maximize the odds of becoming pregnant. The techniques and technologies developed to promote conception include the following:

- *Fertility medications.* A variety of medications can be used to treat infertility.

- *Surgery.* This is a treatment option for both male and female infertility. Used to correct a structural problem, surgery can often return normal fertility.

- *Artificial insemination.* Used if sperm numbers are too low, **artificial insemination (AI)** involves introducing sperm into the woman's vagina, cervix, or uterus (the latter is called intrauterine insemination). This procedure may be performed in conjunction with ovulation-stimulating medications.

- *Assisted reproductive technology (ART).* All fertility treatments in which both eggs and sperm are handled are known as **assisted reproductive technology (ART).** In general, ART procedures involve surgically removing eggs from a woman's ovaries, combining them with sperm in the laboratory, and returning them to the woman's body or donating them to another woman. The types of ART include the following (CDC, 2014.12f):

  - **IVF (in vitro fertilization).** This involves extracting a woman's eggs, fertilizing the eggs in the laboratory, and then transferring the resulting embryos into the woman's uterus through the cervix.

  - **Intracytoplasmic sperm injection (ICSI).** A single sperm is injected directly into a mature egg. The embryo is then transferred to the uterus or fallopian tube.

  - **GIFT (gamete intrafallopian transfer).** This involves the use of a fiber-optic instrument to guide the transfer of unfertilized eggs and sperm (gametes) into the woman's fallopian tubes through small incisions in her abdomen.

  - **ZIFT (zygote intrafallopian transfer)** and TET (tubal embryo transfer). A woman's eggs are fertilized in the laboratory with her partner's sperm and then transferred to her fallopian tube on day one (in ZIFT) or on day two (in TET).

ART is often categorized according to whether the procedure uses a woman's own eggs (nondonor) or eggs from another woman (donor) and according to whether the embryos used were newly fertilized (fresh) or previously fertilized, frozen, and then thawed (frozen). The success rates of ART vary and depend on many factors, including the age of the partners, the cause of infertility, the skill of the practitioner, the type of ART used, and whether the egg or the embryo is fresh or frozen. Nevertheless, the U.S. Department of Health & Human Services 2012.12a) reports that, depending on the age of the mother, between 11% and 39% of women are successful in birthing a child.

While ART can alleviate the burden of infertility on individuals and families, it can also present challenges, as evidenced by the high rates of multiple, preterm, and low-birth-weight

In vitro fertilization of an egg takes place by manually combining an egg and sperm in a laboratory dish and physically placing the embryo in the uterus.

© Medical RF/Phototake

deliveries. Although the large majority of births resulting from assisted technologies are free of birth defects, treatment with ART has been associated with an increased risk of birth defects, including cerebral palsy, as well as cardiovascular, musculoskeletal, urogenital, and gastrointestinal defects. The risk of birth defects associated with IVF, however, has not proven to be significant (Davies et al., 2012).

- **Surrogate motherhood.** In this case, one woman, a surrogate mother, agrees to become pregnant using the man's sperm and her own egg.

- **Gestational carrier.** A woman with ovaries but no uterus may use a gestational carrier whereby she uses her own egg, which is fertilized by the man's sperm. The embryo is then placed inside the carrier's uterus. In this case, the carrier will not be related to the baby.

When assisted reproductive technology is used to treat infertility, there is about a 1 in 2 chance of a multiple birth.

© Big Cheese Photo/JupiterImages

The most important factor for success of these procedures is the age of the woman. When a woman is using her own egg success rates decline as she ages and drop off even more dramatically after about age 37. Other factors to consider are whether the woman is using her own eggs and the number of embryos transferred. Still, thorny questions also plague the procedures: How much will a surrogate be paid? Are there additional costs for a cesarean section, multiple births, or loss of a surrogate's uterus? What if the intended parents change their mind or die during the pregnancy? If the surrogate needs bed rest, how much will the intended parents pay to replace her lost wages, child care, and housekeeping? What happens if the child has serious health problems? In spite of significant costs, risks, and uncertainty, it appears that patients are accepting these because the alternative is even more daunting: not having a child.

Sex selection, also marketed under the title "family balancing," is a technology that allows couples to choose whether to have a boy or a girl. It can be accomplished via both pre- and post-implantation of an embryo. By creating embryos outside the womb, then testing them for gender, pre-implantation genetic diagnosis can guarantee the sex of a baby. Price: about $18,000. Controversy arises, however, over potential sex imbalances in our population and cases in which the sex selection results do not match the parents' expectations.

Increasingly, gay and lesbian couples are creating families that are diverse along dimensions of social class, gender, and race.

© Bruce Rogovin/Getty Images

Each of these techniques creates new issues and dilemmas. For example, some lesbian women, especially those in committed relationships, are choosing to create families through artificial insemination. In part, the increasing acceptance of nontraditional families is providing this boom in biological parenthood. Many questions are raised when a lesbian couple contemplate having a baby in this way: Who will be the birth mother? What will the role status of the other mother be? Will the donor be known or unknown? If known, will the child have a relationship

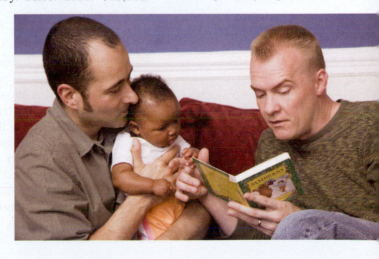

with him? Will the child have a relationship with the donor's parents? Who gets custody if the couple breaks up? Will there be a legal contract between the parenting parties? There are few precedents to learn from or role models to follow in these cases. Another issue such couples face is that the nonbiological parent may have no legal tie to the child. In fact, in some states, the nonbiological parent may adopt the child as a "second parent." Furthermore, society may not recognize a nonbiological parent as a "real" parent because children are expected to have only one "real" mother and one "real" father.

● Giving Birth

Throughout pregnancy, numerous physiological changes occur to prepare the woman's body for childbirth. Hormones secreted by the placenta regulate the growth of the fetus, stimulate maturation of the breasts for lactation, and ready the uterus and other parts of the body for labor. During the later months of pregnancy, the placenta produces the hormone **relaxin,** which increases flexibility in the ligaments and joints of the pelvic area. In the last trimester, most women occasionally feel uterine contractions that are strong but generally not painful. These **Braxton-Hicks contractions** exercise the uterus, preparing it for labor.

Labor and Delivery

During labor, contractions begin the **effacement** (thinning) and **dilation** (gradual opening) of the cervix. It is difficult to say exactly when labor starts, which helps explain the great differences reported in lengths of labor for different women. True labor begins when the uterine contractions are regularly spaced, effacement and dilation of the cervix occurs, and the fetus presents a part of itself into the vagina. During the contractions, the lengthwise muscles of the uterus involuntarily pull open the circular muscles around the cervix. This process generally takes 2–36 hours. Its duration depends on the size of the baby, the baby's position in the uterus, the size of the mother's pelvis, and the condition of the uterus. The length of labor tends to shorten after the first birth experience.

Labor can generally be divided into three stages. The first stage is usually the longest, lasting 4–16 hours or longer. An early sign of first-stage labor is the expulsion of a plug of slightly bloody mucus that has blocked the opening of the cervix during pregnancy. At the same time or later on, there is a second fluid discharge from the vagina. This discharge, often referred to as the "breaking of the waters," is the amniotic fluid, which comes from the ruptured amnion. Because the baby is subject to infection after the protective membrane breaks, the woman should receive medical attention soon thereafter, if she has not already.

The hormone oxytocin produced by the fetus, along with prostaglandins from the placenta, stimulate strong uterine contractions. At the end of the first stage of labor, which is called the **transition,** the contractions come more quickly and are much more intense than at the beginning of labor. Most women report that transition is the most difficult part of labor. During the last part of first-stage labor the baby's head enters the birth canal. This marks the shift from dilation of the cervix to expulsion of the infant. The cervical opening is now almost fully dilated about 10 centimeters (4 inches) in diameter, but the baby is not yet completely in position to be pushed out. Transition can take from a few minutes up to several hours.

Second-stage labor begins when the baby's head moves into the birth canal and ends when the baby is born. During this time, many women experience

If men had to have babies, they would only ever have one each.
—Princess Diana
(1961–1997)

a great force in their bodies. Some women find this the most difficult part of labor; others find that the contractions and bearing down bring a sense of euphoria.

The baby is usually born gradually. When the baby's head emerges and does not slip back in when a woman is pushing during birth this is known as crowning. With each of the final few contractions, a new part of the infant emerges (see Figure 6). The baby may even cry before he or she is completely born, especially if the mother did not have medication.

The baby will still be attached to the umbilical cord connected to the mother, which is not cut until it stops pulsating. He or she will appear wet and often be covered by a waxy substance called **vernix.** The head may look oddly shaped at first, from the molding of the soft plates of bone during birth. This shape is temporary; the baby's head usually achieves a normal appearance within 24 hours.

After the baby has been delivered, the uterus continues to contract, expelling the placenta, the remaining section of the umbilical cord, and the fetal membranes. Completing the third, and final, stage of labor, these tissues are

● **FIGURE 6**

The Birth Process: Labor and Delivery. (a) In the first stage, the cervix begins to efface (thin out) and dilate. (b) In the transition stage, the cervix dilates from 8 to 10 centimeters. (c) In the second stage, the infant is delivered. (d) In the third stage, the afterbirth (placenta) is delivered.

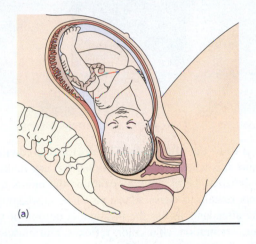

(a)

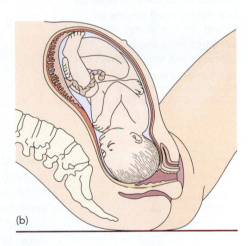

(b)

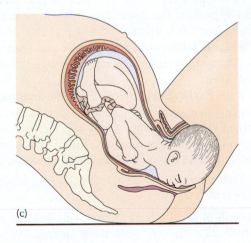

(c)

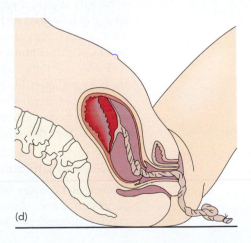

(d)

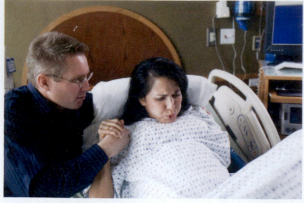

(a)

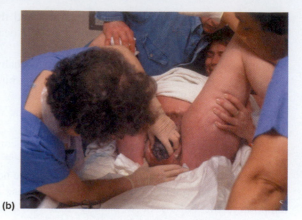

(b)

(a) During labor, uterine contractions cause the opening and thinning of the cervix. The length of labor varies from woman to woman and birth to birth. Encouragement from her partner can help the mother relax. (b) During transition, the mother is coached to push as the baby's head begins to crown. (c) The baby's head emerges from the womb. The placenta will soon follow.

(a) © RubberBall Productions/Getty Images;
(b) © Angela Hampton/Alamy;
(c) © Bubbles Photolibrary/Alamy

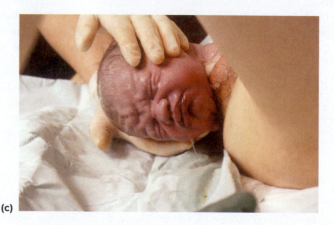

(c)

collectively referred to as the **afterbirth.** The doctor or midwife examines the placenta to make sure it is whole. If the practitioner has any doubt that the entire placenta has been expelled, he or she may examine the uterus to make sure no parts of the placenta remain to cause adhesions or hemorrhaging. Immediately following birth, the attendants assess the physical condition of the **neonate,** or newborn. Heart rate, respiration, skin color, reflexes, and muscle tone are individually rated with a score of 0 to 2. The total, called an **Apgar score,** will range between 7 and 10 if the baby is healthy. For a few days following labor, especially if it is a second or subsequent birth, the mother will probably feel strong contractions as the uterus begins to return to its prebirth size and shape. This process takes about 6 weeks. She will also have a bloody discharge called **lochia,** which continues for several weeks.

Following birth, and especially if the mother did not receive pain medication, the baby will probably be alert and ready to nurse. Breastfeeding (discussed later) provides benefits for both mother and child. If the infant is a boy, the parents will need to decide about circumcision, the surgical removal of the foreskin of the penis. (See the "Think About It" box "The Question of Male Circumcision.")

Choices in Childbirth

Women and couples planning the birth of a child have decisions to make in a variety of areas: place of birth, birth attendant(s), medications, preparedness classes, circumcision, breastfeeding, to name just a few. The "childbirth market"

The Question of Male Circumcision

Who shall decide when doctors disagree?

—Alexander Pope
(1688–1744)

In 1975, when about 93% of newborn boys were circumcised, the American Academy of Pediatrics and the American College of Obstetricians and Gynecologists issued a statement declaring that there is "no absolute medical indication" for routine circumcision. This procedure, which involves slicing and removing the sleeve of skin (foreskin) that covers the glans penis, has been performed routinely on newborn boys in the United States since the 1930s. Since that time, however, the national rates of newborn circumcision have fluctuated. From 1979 through 2010, there was an overall 10% decline, from 64.5% to 58.3% (Owings, Uddin, & Williams, 2013). These changes have most likely reflected the shifting guidance on routine newborn male circumcision.

In 1999, 2005, and most recently 2014, the American Academy of Pediatrics (AAP) changed from a neutral stance on circumcision to a recommendation that newborn male circumcision be available to families who desire it, as the benefits of the procedure outweigh the risks (AAP, 2014.12a). The American College of Obstetricians and Gynecologists has endorsed this recommendation, while the World Health Organization (WHO) and the Joint United Nations Program on HIV/AIDS (UNAIDS) have recommended that male circumcision be scaled up as an intervention for the prevention of heterosexually acquired HIV infections (WHO, 2014.12a). Following the release of AAP's stand, the Centers for Disease Control and Prevention (CDC) issued its own guidelines, which mirrored AAP's, and provided additional evidence to underscore the advantages of male circumcision (CDC, 2014.12g). The CDC stated that male circumcision reduces the risk of HIV and some STIs in heterosexual men. More specifically, male circumcision can:

- Cut a man's risk of getting HIV from an infected female partner by 50%–60%.
- Reduce their risk of genital herpes and certain strains of human papillomavirus (HPV) by 30% or more.
- Lower the odds of urinary tract infections during infancy as well as cancer of the penis in adulthood.

Because circumcision can be beneficial to older men as well, the CDC says information about the procedure also should be given to sexually active uncircumcised men, especially those considered to be at higher risk of contracting HIV.

Many parents choose to circumcise their sons because they feel it is more common or because they do not want their sons to feel different. Circumcision is a religious obligation for infant Jewish boys and a common procedure among Muslims, who account for the largest share of circumcised men worldwide.

At the same time, there are still reasons by parents who may choose not to circumcise, including fear of the risks of infection and other complications (though rare and usually minor), belief that the foreskin is needed to protect the tip of the penis, belief that a circumcised penis can decrease sexual pleasure in later life, and belief that proper hygiene can lower a boy's risk of getting infections, cancer of the penis, and STIs. For those whose boys are not circumcised, it is important to keep the penis clean. When the boy is old enough, he can learn how to manage this himself.

Though the wider U.S. population has adopted the practice of male circumcision, public awareness and opposition to circumcision have grown from those who underscore the pain, bleeding, and risk of infection to newborns. A growing number of people argue that circumcision violates a baby's human right because an infant can't consent and that it's akin to genital mutilation. Controversy has also surrounded a wave of state Medicaid programs that have stopped paying for newborn circumcision, which costs roughly $150 to $200. While the evidence continues to build on behalf of circumcision, so does the debate that surrounds this decision.

Think Critically

1. Given the evidence about circumcision, would you have your son circumcised? Why or why not?

2. How important would data be in deciding whether to have your son circumcised?

has responded to consumer concerns, so it's important for prospective consumers to fully understand their options.

Hospital Birth   Because of the traditional and seemingly impersonal care provided in some hospitals, many people in recent years have recognized the need for family-centered childbirth. Fathers and other relatives or close friends often participate today. Most hospitals permit while others require rooming-in, in which the baby stays with the mother rather than in the nursery, or a modified form of rooming-in.

Some form of pain relief is administered during most hospital deliveries, as are various hormones to intensify the contractions and to shrink the uterus after delivery. There are two types of pain-relieving drugs: analgesics, which provide pain relief without loss of feeling or muscle movement, and anesthetics, which block all feelings, including pain. The most common form of analgesic administration is the **epidural,** a regional anesthesia that is administered through a tiny catheter placed in the woman's lower back. When administered properly, an epidural diminishes the sensations of labor in the lower areas of the body. Drugs have been used successfully and safely during labor. However, the mother isn't the only recipient of the drug; it travels through the placenta to the baby, in whom it may reduce heart and respiration rates. The use of an epidural entails a slightly higher risk of vacuum or forceps delivery than does a drug-free birth.

Once a routine part of childbirth, **episiotomy** is an incision that enlarges the vaginal opening by cutting through the perineum toward the anus to assist in delivery of a baby. Contradicting the long-accepted rationale for the operation to make childbirth less damaging to the mother, a comprehensive analysis has concluded that having an episiotomy has no benefits and actually causes more complications than not having one (American College of Obstetricians and Gynecologists, 2006). As a result, a restrictive policy regarding episiotomy use has resulted in a decreased rate, from 60.9% in 1979 to 24.5% in 2004 (Franklin et al., 2009).

The baby is usually delivered on a table. If such factors as medication or exhaustion slow labor, he or she may be pulled from the womb with a vacuum extractor, which has a small suction cup that fits onto the baby's head, or forceps. In some cases of acute fetal distress, these instruments may be crucial in order to save the infant's life.

Elective Deliveries and Birth Rate   Statistics show that from 1990 to 2011, the percentage of women who chose **elective deliveries,** or those who scheduled a baby's birth prior to 39 weeks, are on the decline to a rate of 5% or less (March of Dimes, 2012b). As mentioned earlier, a full-term pregnancy lasts 40 weeks, but elective deliveries are often planned for 2 or 3 weeks earlier. And though 37 weeks is still considered full term, babies born even a few weeks early are at greater risk for health problems than those who are born later. The reasons for this are twofold: It's difficult to predict a woman's due date and the brain, heart, lungs, and immune system all mature at different rates. The March of Dimes stresses that some infants may indeed need a little more time in the womb than others to reach full maturity.

"Birth weight matters, and it matters for everyone," says David N. Figlio, a Northwestern University professor and researcher; however, it is not destiny (Figlio, Guryan, Karbownik, & Roth, 2014). Its effects are considerably smaller

> *Minor surgery is one that is performed on someone else.*
>
> —Eugene Robin, MD
> (1920–2000)

Childbirth classes enable both partners to understand and share the birth process.

© Brand X Pictures/Jupiterimages

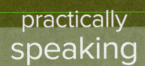

Making a Birth Plan

A good beginning makes a good ending.
—Anonymous (English proverb)

Prospective parents must make many important decisions. The more informed they are, the better able they will be to decide what is right for them. If you were planning a birth, how would you answer the following questions?

- Who will be the birth attendant—a physician or a nurse-midwife? Do you already have someone in mind? If not, what criteria are important to you in choosing a birth attendant? Have you considered hiring a labor assistant, sometimes called a *doula,* a professional childbirth companion employed to guide the mother during labor?

- Who will be present at the birth—your spouse or partner? Other relatives or friends? Children? How will these people participate?

- Where will the birth take place—in a hospital, in a birthing center, or at home? If in a hospital, is there a choice of rooms?

- What kind of environment will you create in terms of lighting, room furnishings, and sounds? Is there special music you would like to hear? Do you wish the birth to be recorded?

- What kinds of medication, if any, would you feel comfortable being given? Do you know what the options are for pain-reducing drugs? What about hormones to speed up or slow down labor? Under what conditions would they be acceptable?

- What about fetal monitoring? Will there be machines attached to the mother or the baby?

- What is your attendant's policy regarding food and drink during labor?

- What about freedom of movement during labor? Will you or your partner want the option of walking around during labor? Will there be a shower or bath available? Will the baby be delivered with the mother lying on her back with her feet in stirrups, or will she be free to choose her position, such as squatting or lying on her side?

- Under what conditions are an episiotomy or a cesarean section acceptable? Who will decide?

- Who will "catch" the baby as he or she is born? Who will cut the umbilical cord, and at what point will it be cut?

- What will be done with the baby immediately after birth? What kinds of tests will be done on the baby, and when? What other kinds of procedures, such as shots and medicated eyedrops, will be given, and when?

- Will the baby stay in the nursery, or is rooming-in available? Is there a visiting schedule?

- How will the baby be fed—by breast, bottle, or a combination of both? Will feeding be on a schedule or "on demand"? Is there someone with breastfeeding experience available to answer questions if necessary? Will the baby have a pacifier between feedings?

- If the baby is a boy, will he be circumcised? If so, when?

than those of social class, for example. However, birth weight has noticeable effects on, among other things, test scores: Among the top 5 percent of test scorers in elementary school, one in three weighed at least 8 pounds at birth, compared with only one in four of all babies. Though this may not be the definitive word on birth weight and timing, in 2011, the American Congress of Obstetricians and Gynecologists and other groups began pushing to eliminate induced labor before the 39th week of pregnancy if there was no clear medical reason (Reddy et al., 2011). It appears that conditions in the womb and infancy can cast a lifelong shadow, in that many forms of cancer and heart disease, among other conditions, may have their roots in the earliest stages of life (Barker, 2008). The best labor plan for women is to wait for delivery to begin on its own.

Cesarean Section

Cesarean section, or **C-section,** involves the delivery of a baby through an incision in the mother's abdominal wall and uterus. In 1970, 5.5% of American births were done by C-section. Although the World Health Organization (WHO) has long recommended that nations set a goal of no more than 15% of all births be by C-section (Gibbons et al., 2010), today about 33% of all births in the United States are done by C-section (Martin et al., 2014).

There are many medical reasons to deliver a baby by C-section, such as abnormalities of the placenta and umbilical cord and prolonged or ineffective labor. Although there is a lower mortality rate for infants born by C-section, the mother's mortality rate is higher. As with all major surgeries, there are possible complications, and recovery can be slow and difficult. Researchers from the Imperial College in London reviewed 35 studies that provided data on birth delivery characteristics and the long-term physical health of babies as they grew into adulthood (Darmasseelane, Hyde, Santhakumaran, Gale, & Modi, 2014). In comparison to vaginal deliveries, C-sections appeared to increase childhood risk of breathing problems, asthma, allergic reactivity, and other developmental issues, as well as raise the risk of obesity in adulthood by 26%.

The fact that a woman has had a previous cesarean delivery does not mean that subsequent deliveries must be C-sections. In fact, 60–80% of women who attempt a vaginal delivery after cesarean (VBAC) have successful vaginal deliveries (March of Dimes, 2011b). Many times the condition that made a C-section necessary in one birth will not exist in the next; thus, a VBAC is safer than a scheduled repeat C-section.

Prepared Childbirth

Increasingly, Americans are choosing from among such childbirth alternatives as prepared childbirth, rooming-in birthing centers, home birth, and midwifery.

Prepared childbirth or natural childbirth was popularized by English gynecologist Grantly Dick-Read (1972) who observed that fear causes muscles to tense, which in turn increases pain and stress during childbirth. He taught both partners about childbirth and gave them physical exercises to ease muscle tension. In the 1950s, French obstetrician Fernand Lamaze (1970) developed a method of prepared childbirth based on knowledge of conditioned reflexes. Women learn to mentally separate the physical stimulus of uterine contractions from the conditioned response of pain. With the help of a partner, women perform breathing and other exercises throughout labor and delivery. Prepared childbirth, then, is not so much a matter of controlling the birth process as of understanding it and having confidence in nature's plan. Prepared mothers, who usually attend classes with the father or another partner, handle pain better, use fewer pain-relieving drugs, express greater satisfaction with the childbirth process, and experience less postpartum depression than women who undergo routine hospital births.

Birthing Rooms and Centers

Birthing (maternity) centers, institutions of long standing in England and other European countries, are now integrated into many hospitals in the United States. Although they vary in size, organization, and orientation, birthing centers share the view that childbirth is a normal, healthy process that can be assisted by skilled practitioners (midwives or physicians) in a homelike setting. Some centers provide emergency care; all have procedures for transfer to a hospital if necessary.

Home Birth Home births have increased during the past three decades, although they still constitute a small fraction of total births. Careful medical screening and planning that eliminate all but the lowest-risk pregnancies can make this a viable alternative for some couples.

Midwifery and Doulas In most countries, midwives attend the majority of births. The United States has an increasing number of certified nurse-midwives who are registered nurses trained in obstetrical techniques. They are qualified for routine deliveries and minor medical emergencies. They also often operate as part of a medical team that includes a backup physician. Their fees are generally considerably less than a doctor's.

Unlike midwives, who are medical professionals, *doulas* do not make clinical decisions. Rather, they offer emotional support and manage pain using massage, acupressure, and birthing positions.

If a woman decides she wants to give birth with the aid of a midwife outside a hospital setting, she should have a thorough medical screening to make sure she and her infant will not be at risk during delivery. She should investigate the midwife's or doula's training and experience, the backup services available in the event of complications or emergencies, and the procedures for a transfer to a hospital if necessary.

Breastfeeding

About 3 days after childbirth, lactation—the production of milk—begins. Before lactation, sometimes as early as the second trimester, a yellowish liquid called **colostrum** is secreted by the nipples. It is what nourishes the newborn infant before the mother's milk comes in. Colostrum is high in protein and contains antibodies that help protect the baby from infectious diseases. Hormonal changes during labor trigger the changeover from colostrum to milk, but unless a mother nurses her child her breasts will soon stop producing milk. If she chooses not to breastfeed, she may be given an injection of estrogen soon after delivery to stop lactation. It is not certain, however, whether estrogen is actually effective; furthermore, it may increase the risk of blood clotting. (For more information about breastfeeding, see the "Practically Speaking" box "Breast Versus Bottle: Which is Better for You and Your Child?").

Breastfeeding provides the best nutrition for infants. It also helps protect against many infectious diseases, can lower breast cancer risk, especially if a woman breast-feeds longer than one year, and gives both mother and child a sense of well-being.

© Jose Luis Pelaez, Inc./Corbis

● Becoming a Parent

Men and women who become parents enter a new phase of their lives. Even more than marriage, parenthood signifies adulthood—the final, irreversible end of childhood. A person can become an ex-spouse but never an ex-parent. The irrevocable nature of parenthood may make the first-time parent doubtful and apprehensive, especially during the pregnancy. However, for the most part, parenthood has to be learned experientially, although ideas can modify practices. A person may receive assistance from more experienced parents, but ultimately each new parent has to learn on his or her own.

The time immediately following birth is a critical period for family adjustment. No amount of reading, classes, and expert advice can prepare expectant parents for the "real thing." The 3 months or so following childbirth (the "fourth trimester") constitute the **postpartum period.** This time is one of physical stabilization and emotional adjustment. The abrupt transition from being a

Before I got married, I had six theories about bringing up children. Now I have six children and no theories.

—John Wilmot, Earl of Rochester (1647–1680)

Breast Versus Bottle: Which Is Better for You and Your Child?

If you are a woman who plans to have children, you will have to decide whether to breastfeed or bottlefeed. Perhaps you already have an idea that breastfeeding is healthier for the baby but are not sure why.

The American Academy of Pediatrics (AAP) recommends exclusive breastfeeding for about 6 months, followed by continued breastfeeding as solid foods are introduced, with continuation for 1 year or longer as mother and baby desire (AAP, 2012.12a). In spite of these recommendations, only 18.8% of babies in the United States are exclusively breastfed through 6 months (CDC, 2014.12h). This is lower than the 25.5% goal in the U.S. government's "Healthy People 2020" objectives and significantly lower than the world's average of 38% (Bender, 2014).

Recognizing the health benefits of breastfeeding, the Affordable Care Act (ACA) of 2010 provides two major provisions to encourage mothers to breastfeed: (1) reasonable break time during working hours to express milk and (2) health insurance benefits to defray the costs associated with providing breast milk to infants, including coverage of breastfeeding pumps, education and counseling. The following list of many of the benefits and advantages should help you understand why mother's milk is the ideal food for most infants.

Physical Benefits of Breastfeeding

- Breast milk contains antibodies that protect the baby from many infectious diseases, including lower and upper respiratory tract infection, ear infections, diarrhea, and other maladies for at least 6 months.
- Breast milk forms softer curds in the infant's stomach, making digestion and elimination easier.
- Breast milk puts less stress on the infant's immature liver and kidneys because its total protein is lower than that of other mammalian milk.
- Breast milk is high in cholesterol which is needed for proper development of the nervous tissue.
- Breast milk causes fewer allergic reactions because of its concentration and type of protein.
- Breast milk is a better source of nutrition for low-birth-weight babies because nature adapts the content of the mother's milk to meet the infant's needs.
- Children who were breastfed have fewer problems with tooth decay.

- Breastfed babies are less likely to become obese.
- Breastfed babies have a lower risk of sudden infant death syndrome.
- For mothers, hormonal changes stimulated by breastfeeding cause the uterus to contract and return to its normal size.
- Breastfeeding mothers reduce their risk of ovarian and breast cancer, particularly if breastfeeding occurred for an extended period (at least one year).
- The longer a woman nurses, the lower her risk for developing types 1 and 2 diabetes.

Psychological Benefits of Breastfeeding

- The close physical contact of breastfeeding provides a sense of emotional well-being for mother and baby.
- Breastfeeding may help lower the risk of postpartum depression.

Health and Logistical Advantages of Breastfeeding

- Breastfeeding requires no buying, mixing, or preparing of formulas.
- Breast milk is not subject to incorrect mixing or spoilage.
- Breast milk is clean and is not easily contaminated.
- Breastfeeding provides some protection against pregnancy if the woman is breastfeeding exclusively.
- The breast is always available.
- Better infant health means fewer health insurance claims and less time off to care for sick children.

Bottlefeeding

For those women whose work schedules, health problems, or other demands prohibit them from breastfeeding, holding and cuddling the baby while bottlefeeding can contribute to the sense of emotional well-being that comes from a close parent-baby relationship. Bottlefeeding affords a greater opportunity for fathers to become involved in the feeding of the baby.

SOURCES: American Academy of Pediatrics (2014.12a); U.S. Department of Health & Human Services, Office on Women's Health (2014).

nonparent to being a parent may create considerable stress. Parents take on parental roles literally overnight, and the job goes on without relief around the clock. Many parents express concern about their ability to meet all the responsibilities of child rearing.

To support couples in the adjustment and care of their newborn child, the federal **Family and Medical Leave Act (FMLA)** assures eligible employees up to 12 weeks of unpaid, job-protected leave for specified family and medical reasons with continuation of group health insurance (U.S. Department of Labor, 2011). If the employee has to use some of that leave for another reason, including a difficult pregnancy, it may be counted as part of the 12-week FMLA leave entitlement.

The postpartum period may be a time of significant emotional upheaval. Even women who had easy and uneventful pregnancies may experience the "baby blues." New mothers often have irregular sleep patterns because of the needs of their newborn, the discomfort of childbirth, or the strangeness of the hospital environment. Some mothers may feel isolated from their familiar world. These are considered normal, self-limiting postpartum symptoms and generally go away within a week or two.

Postpartum depression, or moderate to severe depression in a woman after she has given birth, occurs in 8–19% of new mothers (CDC, 2013.12c). Like the blues, postpartum depression is thought to be related to hormonal changes brought on by sleep deprivation, weaning, and the resumption of the menstrual cycle. A prior history of depression also increases a woman's risk. It is common as well for anxiety disorders to arise or recur in the postpartum period, when some women feel hypervigilant about possible harm to their baby. The most serious and rarest postpartum mental illness is **postpartum psychosis.** Unlike the other disorders, postpartum psychosis is thought to be exclusively biologically based and related to hormonal changes. Affected women tend to have difficulty sleeping, be prone to agitation or hyperactivity, and intermittently experience delusions, hallucinations, and paranoia. This behavior represents a medical emergency and usually requires hospitalization. Depression rates, in comparison, vary from industrialized cultures (more) to nonindustrialized ones (less), suggesting that psychological, cultural, and social factors have a significant effect on whether a woman experiences postpartum depression.

As a result of rare but highly publicized instances in which infants have been abandoned and sometimes left to die, every state has enacted a provision to provide a safe and confidential means of relinquishing an unwanted infant (Guttmacher Institute, 2014.12a). Under certain circumstances and without the threat of prosecution for child abandonment, these policies, also called "safe haven" or "safe surrender," typically allow a parent or other specified person to relinquish an infant at specific locations or to personnel authorized to accept the child.

The sexual desire of women generally decreases during pregnancy and following delivery. By 12 weeks postpartum, the majority of women have resumed sexual intercourse; however, many experience sexual difficulties, particularly dyspareunia (genital pain) and lowered sexual desire. At 6 months postpartum, when the baby's presence and the demands of parenting often intrude on the sex lives of the parents, some women continue to report significantly lowered sexual desire. Depending on a couple's ability to adjust to the physical and psychological changes that occur during this time and the depth and range of their communication, most new parents experience a fulfilling sexual relationship. Information about what changes to expect may help new parents avoid making unfounded and harmful assumptions about their sexual relationship.

We learn from experience. A man never wakes up his second baby just to see it smile.

—Grace Williams

Cleaning and scrubbing can wait till tomorrow.
For babies grow up we've learned to our sorrow.
So quiet down cobwebs, dust go to sleep.
I'm rocking my baby and babies don't keep.

—Anonymous

For many people, the arrival of a child is one of life's most significant events. It signifies adulthood and conveys social status for those who are now parents. It creates the lifelong bonds of family. And it can fill the new parents with a deep sense of accomplishment and well-being.

Summary

Fertilization and Fetal Development

- Fertilization of the *oocyte* by a sperm usually takes place in the fallopian tube. The chromosomes of the oocyte combine with those of the sperm to form the diploid zygote; it divides many times to form a *blastocyst,* which *implants* itself in the uterine wall.

- The blastocyst becomes an *embryo* and then a *fetus,* which is nourished through the *placenta* via the *umbilical cord.*

- Pregnancy is now a matter of choice. Increasing numbers of individuals and couples are choosing to remain *child-free.*

Pregnancy

- *Preconception care* is aimed at interventions that help improve pregnancy outcomes.

- Tests designed to measure *human chorionic gonadotropin (HCG)* can determine pregnancy approximately 1 week following a missed period. *Hegar's sign* can be detected by a trained examiner. Pregnancy is confirmed by the detection of the fetal heartbeat and movements or through examination by ultrasound.

- A woman's feelings vary greatly during pregnancy. It is important for her to share her concerns and to have support from her partner, friends, relatives, and health care practitioners. Her feelings about sexuality are likely to change during pregnancy. Men may also have conflicting feelings. Sexual activity is generally safe unless there is pain, bleeding, or a history of miscarriage.

- Harmful substances may be passed to the embryo or fetus through the placenta. Substances or other factors that cause birth defects are called *teratogens;* these include alcohol, tobacco, certain drugs, and environmental pollutants. Infectious diseases such as rubella may damage the fetus. Sexually transmitted infections may be passed to the infant through the placenta or the birth canal during childbirth.

- *Ectopic pregnancy, pregnancy-induced hypertension,* and *preterm birth* are the most common complications of pregnancy.

- Abnormalities of the fetus may be diagnosed using *ultrasound, amniocentesis, chorionic villus sampling (CVS),* or *neural tube defect screening.*

- Some pregnancies end in miscarriage. Infant mortality rates in the United States are extremely high compared with those in other industrialized nations. Loss of a pregnancy or death of a young infant is a serious life event.

Infertility

- *Infertility* is the lack of pregnancy in the past 12 months despite having unprotected intercourse in each of those months with the same partner. Couples with fertility problems often feel they have lost control over an important area of their lives.

- Techniques for combating infertility include fertility medications, surgery, and *assisted reproductive technology. Surrogate motherhood* or relying on a *gestational carrier* may be options for childless couples.

Giving Birth

- In the last trimester of pregnancy, a woman feels *Braxton-Hicks contractions.* These contractions begin the *effacement* and *dilation* of the cervix to permit delivery.

- Labor can be divided into three stages. First-stage labor begins when uterine contractions become regular. When the cervix has dilated approximately 10 centimeters, the baby's head enters the birth canal; this is called *transition.* In second-stage labor, the baby emerges from the birth canal. In third-stage labor, the *afterbirth* is expelled.

- *Elective deliveries,* or those scheduled prior to a child's intended due date, consist of about 5% of all births.

- *Cesarean section,* or *C-section,* is the delivery of a baby through an incision in the mother's abdominal wall and uterus.

- *Prepared childbirth* encompasses a variety of methods that stress the importance of understanding the birth process, teaching the mother to relax, and giving her emotional support during childbirth.

- Birthing centers and birthing rooms in hospitals provide viable alternatives to traditional hospital birth settings for normal births. Instead of medical doctors, many women now choose trained nurse-midwives, while others have doulas as labor assistants.

- The American Academy of Pediatrics (AAP) now recommends newborn male *circumcision* be available to families who desire it. Reasons to choose circumcision include reduced risk for HIV and some STIs. Circumcision holds religious importance for Jews and Muslims.

- Mother's milk is more nutritious than formula or cow's milk and provides immunity to many diseases and conditions. Breastfeeding also offers benefits to mother, family, society, and the environment.

Becoming a Parent

- A critical adjustment period—the *postpartum period*—follows the birth of a child. The mother may experience feelings of depression (sometimes called "baby blues") that are a result of biological, psychological, and social factors. Though transient, the majority of women experience a decrease in sexual desire. Depending on a couple's ability to adjust to the physical and psychological changes that occur during this time, most new parents experience a fulfilling sexual relationship.

Questions for Discussion

- Most likely you have a strong opinion about pregnancy and how one would affect your life. If you or your partner became pregnant today, what would you do? Where would you go in order to receive support for your decision?

- If you or your partner were to have a child, where and how would you prefer to deliver the baby? Whom would you want present? What steps would you be willing to take in order to ensure that your wishes were granted?

- After trying but not being able to conceive for 1 year, you now realize that you or your partner may have a fertility problem. What measures would you consider in order to have a child? How much would you be willing to pay?

- Like many issues related to sexual orientation, adoption by same-sex couples is a controversial issue. What are your views on this, and do you feel that enacting laws is the best way to support your point of view?

Sex and the Internet

Pregnancy and Childbirth

Even though pregnancy is a natural and normal process, there are still myriad issues, questions, and concerns surrounding it. This is especially true when couples are considering pregnancy, are trying to become pregnant, or find out that the woman is pregnant. Fortunately, there is help and support on the Internet. One website aimed specifically at educating men and women about pregnancy is run by the Centers for Disease Control and Prevention (CDC): www.cdc.gov/pregnancy. Go to this site and select two topics you wish to learn more about. You might choose "Before Pregnancy" or "After the Baby

Arrives." After you have investigated the topics and perhaps linked them to another resource, answer these questions:

- What topics did you choose? Why?

- What three new facts did you learn about each topic?

- How might you integrate this information into your own choices and decisions around pregnancy or parenthood?

- What additional link did you follow, and what did you learn as a result?

Suggested Websites

Fatherhood.gov (National Responsible Fatherhood Clearinghouse)

www.fatherhood.gov
Established in 2005, provides tips and hints for dads and kids and a library for laypeople and professionals.

La Leche League International

http://www.llli.org
Provides advice and support for nursing mothers.

Population Connection

http://www.populationconnection.org/site/PageServer
Grassroots population organization that educates and advocates for action to stabilize world population.

Resolve: The National Infertility Association

http://www.resolve.org
Dedicated to providing education, advocacy, and support for men and women facing infertility.

Share: Pregnancy & Infant Loss Support

http://nationalshare.org
Serves those whose lives are touched by the death of a baby.

Society for Assisted Reproductive Technology

http://www.sart.org
Promotes and advances the standards for the practice of assisted reproductive technology.

Suggested Reading

For the most current research findings in obstetrics, see *Obstetrics and Gynecology, The New England Journal of Medicine,* and *JAMA: Journal of the American Medical Association.*

Brewer, S., Bhattacharya, S., Davies, J., Meredith, S., & Preston, P. (2011). *The pregnant body book.* New York: DK. A reference that looks at the nature of human pregnancy, including an exploration of the anatomy and physiology of the reproductive systems.

Brott, A. A., & Ash, J. (2010). *The expectant father* (3rd ed.). New York: Abbeville Press. A guide to the emotional, physical, and financial changes the father-to-be may experience during the course of his partner's pregnancy.

Jana, L. A., & Shu, J. (2011). *Heading home with your newborn* (2nd ed.). Elk Grove Village, IL: American Academy of Pediatrics. Offers parent-tested, pediatrician-approved advice.

Murkoff, H., & Mazel, S. (2008). *What to expect when you're expecting* (4th ed.). New York: Workman. Covers preconception care through postpartum.

Nilsson, L., & Hamburger, L. (2004). *A child is born* (4th ed.). New York: Delacourt/Seymour Lawrence. The study of birth, beginning with fertilization, told in stunning photographs with text.

Sawhill, I. V. (2014). *Generation unbound: Drifting into sex and parenthood without marriage.* Washington, DC: The Brookings Institute. Drawing on behavioral economics, the author offers recommendations for preventing unplanned pregnancy among young adults, especially the use of long-acting, reversible contraceptives.

Sher, G., Davis, V. M., & Stoess, J. (2013). *In vitro fertilization: The A.R.T. of making babies* (4th ed.). New York: Skyhorse. A comprehensive and accessible guide to the practice of in vitro fertilization.

Wiessinger, D., West, D., & Pittman, T. (2010). *The womanly art of breastfeeding* (8th ed.). New York: La Leche League International. A comprehensive and supportive guide to breastfeeding.

The Sexual Body in Health and Illness

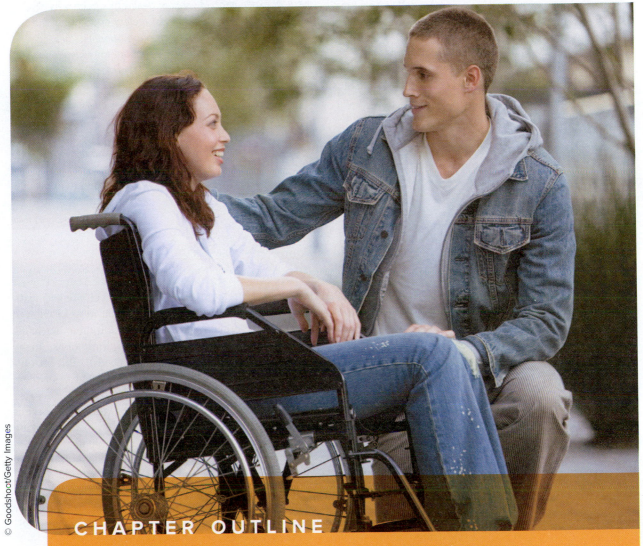

© Goodshoot/Getty Images

CHAPTER OUTLINE

Living in Our Bodies: The Quest for Physical Perfection

Alcohol, Drugs, and Sexuality

Sexuality and Disability

Sexuality and Cancer

Additional Sexual Health Issues

Sexual Orientation and Health

"I have learned not to take the media or anyone else's opinion as the gospel. Now when I look in the mirror, I see the strong, beautiful, Black woman that I am. I no longer see the woman who wanted breast implants and other superficial aspects of beauty. My beauty now flows from within, and all I had to acquire was love for myself and knowledge of myself, and it did not cost me anything."

—**21-year-old female**

"It was never about food; it was always about the way I felt inside. The day that changed my life forever was January 29, 2007. It was the mortifying reflection of myself off the porcelain toilet I hovered over that made me see the truth. At that moment, I knew I could no longer go on living or dying like a parched skeleton. I had to hit rock bottom before I realized that what I was doing was wrong. I feel that, even if twenty people had sat me down at that time and told me I had an eating disorder, I would have laughed. I was blind."

—**20-year-old female**

"Interestingly, I am writing this paper with a bald head. I used to have long, beautiful blonde hair. Chemotherapy took care of that little social/sexual status symbol. I was not at all prepared for losing my looks along with that much of my sexual identity. It has taken me by surprise to realize how much the way you look influences how people react to you, especially the opposite sex. The real lesson comes from the betrayal I feel from my body. I was healthy before, and now that I am sick, I feel as if my identity has changed. I always saw my body as sexual. Now after surgery, which left a large scar where my cleavage used to be, and with chemotherapy, which left me bald, I feel like my body is a medical experiment. My sexual desire has been very low, and I think it is all related to not feeling good about the way I look. Amazing how much of our identities are wrapped around the way we feel about the way we look. The good news for me is that my foundation is strong: I am not just what is on the outside."

—**26-year-old female**

"On the weekend, I like to go out with my friend. When I drink alcohol in excessive amounts, I never have any problems performing sexually. But when I smoke marijuana, I have a major problem performing up to my standards."

—**19-year-old male**

> *The essence of beauty is the unity of variety.*
>
> —William Somerset Maugham
> (1874–1965)

THE INTERRELATEDNESS OF OUR PHYSICAL HEALTH, our psychological well-being, and our sexuality is complex. It's not something that most of us even think about, especially as long as we remain in good health. On the other hand, we may encounter physical and emotional problems and limitations, many of which may profoundly influence our sexual lives. We need to inform ourselves about these problems so that we can help prevent or deal with them effectively.

In this chapter, we examine our attitudes and feelings about our bodies and look at specific health issues. We begin with a discussion of body image and its impact on sexuality. Next we look at the relationship between alcohol and other drugs and our sexuality. Then we turn to issues of sexuality and disability. We also discuss the physical and emotional effects of specific diseases such as diabetes, heart disease, arthritis, and cancer as they influence our sexual functioning. Finally, we address other issues specific to women or men and look at the impact that sexual orientation has on health and well-being.

As we grow emotionally and physically, we may also develop new perceptions of what it means to be healthy. We may discover new dimensions in ourselves to lead us to a more fulfilled and healthier sex life.

● Living in Our Bodies: The Quest for Physical Perfection

Health is more than the absence of disease and sexual health is more than the presence of healthy sexual parts. According to the World Health Organization (2006):

> **Sexual health** is a state of physical, emotional, mental and social well-being related to sexuality; it is not merely the absence of disease, dysfunction or infirmity. Sexual health requires a positive and respectful approach to sexuality and sexual relationships, as well as the possibility of having pleasurable and safe sexual experiences, free of coercion, discrimination and violence. For sexual health to be attained and maintained, the sexual rights of all persons must be respected, protected and fulfilled.

Sexual health has to do with how we function biologically, but it is also a function of our behavior and our awareness and acceptance of our bodies. In terms of sexuality, good health requires us to know and understand our bodies, to feel comfortable with them. It requires a woman to feel at ease with the sight, feel, and smell of her vulva, and to be comfortable with and aware of her breasts—their shape, size, and contours. Sexual health requires a man to accept his body, including his genitals, and to be aware of physical sensations such as lower back pain or a feeling of congestion in his bladder. A sexually healthy man abandons the idea that masculinity means he should ignore his body's pains, endure stress, and suffer in silence.

Our general health affects our sexual functioning. Fatigue, stress, and minor ailments all affect our sexual interactions. If we ignore these aspects of our health, we are likely to experience a decline in our sexual desires, as well as suffer physical and psychological distress. A person who always feels tired or stressed or who is constantly ill or debilitated is likely to feel less sexual than a healthy, rested person. Health and sexuality are gifts we must nurture and respect, not use and abuse.

Contrary to popular stereotypes, people of all shapes, sizes, and ages can lead healthy and happy sexual lives.

© Image Source/Getty Images

> *I wouldn't sue anyone for saying I had a big prick. No man would. In fact, I might pay them to do it.*
>
> —Joe Orton
> (1933–1967)

Eating Disorders

Many of us are willing to pay high costs—physical, emotional, and financial—to meet the expectations of our culture and to feel worthy, lovable, and sexually attractive. Although having these desires is clearly a normal human characteristic, the means by which we try to fulfill them can be extreme and even self-destructive. Many American women and some men try to control their weight by dieting, but some people's fear and loathing of fat often combined with fear or disgust regarding sexual functions impels them to extreme eating behaviors. Compulsive overeating (binge eating) and compulsive overdieting (which may include self-starvation and binge eating and purging)—and combinations thereof—are the behaviors classified as **eating disorders.**

Most people with eating disorders have certain traits, such as low self-esteem, perfectionism, difficulty dealing with emotions, unreasonable demands for self-control, negative perceptions of self in relation to others, and, of course, a fear of becoming fat. Often, the person lacks adequate skills for dealing with stress.

> *Muscles I don't care about—my husband likes me to be squishy when he hugs me.*
>
> —Dixie Carter
> (1939–2010)

Body Image and Sexuality: Are They One and the Same?

O, that this too too solid flesh would melt;
Thaw and resolve itself into a dew!

—William Shakespeare, *Hamlet* (1564–1616)

Most Americans would agree that the way one feels about one's body has a powerful effect on self-esteem and the ability to enjoy life, including one's sex life. Researchers have confirmed this by associating positive body image with a pleasurable sex life (Satinsky, Reece, Dennis, Sanders, & Bardzell, 2012). Others have associated body image with several aspects of better overall adjustment, functioning, and well-being, including higher self-esteem and optimism, more proactive coping styles, higher levels of attractiveness, higher educational achievement, fewer disordered eating patterns, and more negative attitudes toward cosmetic surgery (Swami, 2009; Swami, Hadji-Michael, & Furnham, 2008; Woertman & van den Brink, 2012; Wood-Barcalow, Tylka, & Augustus-Horvath, 2010). Contrary to this, body dissatisfaction has been linked to eating disorders, sexual aversion, sexual avoidance, risky sexual behavior, and sexual problems (Reissing, Laliberte, & Davis, 2005).

Just why does body image have such a significant effect on individuals' attitudes and behaviors? From what experiences or images do negative feelings about our body arise? Evolutionary theorists report that women's physical attractiveness is important because it gives male sexual partners information about their health and potential reproductive success (Buss & Schmitt, 2011). In Western cultures, this often translates to a woman's appeal as a sexual partner being dependent on her visual appearance. Men, on the other hand, may use age preference as a marker for reproductive success, with women in their mid-20s being most desirable ("Evolutionary psychology," 2014). Two authors (Bancroft & Graham, 2011) have postulated that a man's experience is dominated by the pursuit of sexual pleasure, whereas a woman's is dominated by a sense of being desired and of emotional intimacy. Desirable body image may be one component of this pursuit.

Media images of women's bodies often present an ideal that is not representative of most women: tall, slim-hipped, long-legged, large-breasted, and many pounds lighter. Men, on the other hand, are presented as tall, buff, hairless, and angular. Because we know that sexual attraction and desire are influenced by complex individual, bio-

logical, behavioral, and social factors, it's difficult to determine exactly how the media influence attitudes or behaviors. Additionally, because there is no universally objective, ideal body shape, size, or look, just as there is no "right" way a body should move or respond, body image is inseparable from a particular society's understanding of the social constructs of beauty, including gender, age, and race. While none of us are born evaluating our bodies, we soon learn to, which in turn will often determine the way in which we interpret what we see in the mirror and how we regard a potential partner. As a result, the beauty ideal established and reinforced by the media often leads both men and women to feel not only bad about themselves but often critical when their beloved does not measure up. The internal clashes between the idealized and the real may bring repressive or destructive behaviors into the bedroom and relationship.

The literature underscores just how closely body image and sexuality are related. In a review of 57 studies of evidence regarding the association between sexuality and body image among healthy women, the overall finding was that body image issues can affect all domains of sexual functioning, including sexual desire, arousal, orgasm, and satisfaction (Woertman & van den Brink, 2012). Particularly salient in this review was the impact of awareness and self-consciousness or negative body evaluations on the individual: during sexual activity, they interfered with both sexual responses and experiences.

With so much research dedicated to negative body image, it's interesting to note the results of findings when body image is examined in the context of sexual health among young women. A group of researchers in the Neatherlands explored the sexual health of university women, aged 18–35, who had been or were sexually active, in order to assess whether positive body esteem impacts a woman's sexuality. Their online survey provided questions about body image, its affect during sexual activity, sexual frequency, and levels of sexual self-esteem (van den Brink, Smeets, Hessen, Talens, & Woertman, 2013). Data from 319 participants revealed some interesting findings:

■ Overall, the women's level of body dissatisfaction was minimal. Instead, the majority reported neutral or mildly positive body evaluations with 30% of the sample clearly reporting positive evaluations.

- Those who were body-satisfied had lower body mass indexes (BMIs) and reported less body image investment, less overweight preoccupation, and less body self-consciousness during sexual activity.
- With regard to sexual health, body-satisfied women reported better sexual functioning, higher sexual self-esteem, and higher frequency of sexual activity with a partner.

In this case, we may need to determine which cultural factors (having American versus Dutch parents, sexuality education, conservative versus sex-positive views, etc.) contribute to body satisfaction and sexual health.

One outcome of body image is its relationship to sexual desire. It may be interesting to note that problems with sexual desire are among the most common sexual difficulties presented in therapy (Hock 2007). Although there are still limited data, the overall findings indicate that positive body image experiences are associated with higher levels of sexual desire (Woertman & van den Brink, 2012).

While research will continue to explore the connections between body image, well-being, and sexuality, clinicians who work with individuals with distorted body image and often-associated eating disorders must take into consideration the complexity of the issues and be able to provide individualized, prolonged treatment. What we can most likely anticipate is that as long as an overly thin woman or extremely buff man represents the American ideal, there will continue to be negative consequences in the bedroom. The impact of these will depend in part on the ability of men and women to detach from defining themselves or others by their bodies and to avoid or limit contact with sources that perpetuate false or unrealistic ideals.

Think Critically

1. How would you evaluate your body image? From what sources have you drawn your ideals?
2. Which gender do you feel is most impacted by issues related to body image? Why do you think this is true?
3. What influence does body image have on sexual self-esteem? Sexual health? Sexual functioning? What measures might you take to begin to improve those areas of your body image where you personally feel uncomfortable?

The American Psychiatric Association (2013) states that a primary goal for those experiencing eating disorders is to have an accurate diagnosis which can help define a treatment plan. Eating disorders are frequently present with other psychiatric disorders, such as depression, substance abuse, and anxiety disorders (National Institute of Mental Health [NIMH], 2010).

Although many studies of eating disorders have singled out White middle-class and upper-class women, these problems transcend ethnic, socioeconomic, gender, and age boundaries. The median age for the onset of eating disorders is about 12 to 13 years old (Swanson, Crow, LeGrange, Swendsen, & Merikangas, 2011). Most research suggests that eating disorders are equally common among White females and Latinas, more frequent among American Indian females, and not as common among African American and Asian American females. Among minority racial/ethnic groups, the females who are younger, have more body weight, are better educated, and identify with middle-class values are at higher risk for eating disorders than their peers (Insel & Roth, 2010).

While body image and eating disorders have been discussed extensively in the heterosexual population, until recently little has been known about how prevalent these are in gay men, lesbian women, and transsexual people. Findings from a study of over 56,000 heterosexual, gay, and lesbian individuals revealed that all women, regardless of sexual orientation, are similar in their level of body satisfaction; that is, they adhere to cultural ideals of attractiveness, including a high preoccupation with their weight, low evaluation of their appearance, and the experience of negative effects of their body image on their quality of life and sex life (Peplau et al., 2009). In contrast, the majority of men, both gay and heterosexual, reported being satisfied with their bodies. Nonetheless, a greater

The doll, Lammily, has replaced Barbie as the 'new normal.' With brown hair, shorter legs, thicker waist, and less makeup, kids can appreciate her for her positive body image.

© Nickolay Lamm/Rex Features/AP Images

percentage of gay men than heterosexual men were dissatisfied. Among those with gender dysphoria, those transitioning from male to female (MtF) reported to be at an enhanced risk of developing eating disorders and body image dissatisfaction (Vocks, Stahn, Loenser, & Legenbauer, 2009).

● Alcohol, Drugs, and Sexuality

In the minds of many Americans, sex and alcohol or sex and "recreational" drugs go together. Although experience shows us that sexual performance and enjoyment generally decrease as alcohol or drug consumption levels increase, many people cling to the age-old myths.

Alcohol Use and Sexuality

The belief that alcohol and sex go together, although not new, is certainly reinforced by popular culture. Alcohol advertising often features beautiful, scantily clad women. Beer drinkers are portrayed as young, healthy, and fun-loving. Wine drinkers are romantics, surrounded by candlelight and roses. Those who choose Scotch are the epitome of sophistication. These images reinforce long-held cultural myths associating alcohol with social prestige and sexual enhancement.

It is well known that alcohol use among college students is very common. Of those college students who drink alcohol, 43% reported binge drinking (five or more drinks) the last time they "partied" or socialized (American College Health Association, 2014.13a). Drinking is associated with sexual risks. In fact, most risky first-time sexual encounters involve being inebriated (George et al., 2009). In highly charged sexual situations, intoxication has been reported to increase drinkers' willingness to engage in unprotected intercourse by fostering their belief that they are aroused.

Because of the ambivalence we often have about sex—"It's good but it's bad"—many people feel more comfortable about initiating or participating in sexual activities if they have had a drink or two. This phenomenon of activating behaviors that would normally be suppressed is known as **disinhibition.** Although a small amount of alcohol may have a small disinhibiting, or relaxing, effect, greater quantities can result in aggression, loss of judgment, poor coordination, and loss of consciousness.

Alcohol affects the ability of both men and women to become sexually aroused. Men may have difficulty getting or maintaining an erection, and women may not experience vaginal lubrication. Physical sensations are likely to be dulled. Chronic users of alcohol typically experience desire and arousal difficulties. Researchers have determined that drinking a six-pack of beer in less than 2 hours can affect testosterone and sperm production for up to 12 hours. This does not mean, however, that no sperm are present; production is slowed, but most men will remain fertile when drinking alcohol.

Researchers are not sure if alcohol use causes risky sexual behavior, but it is possibly part of a risky health behavior problem.

© PNC/Getty Images

However, ingestion of large amounts of alcohol by both men and women can contribute to infertility and birth defects.

Alcohol use has also been found to be associated with numerous dangerous consequences such as unwanted sexual intercourse and sexual violence. The disinhibiting effect of alcohol allows some men to justify various types of sexual violence they would not otherwise commit. Men may expect that alcohol will make them sexually aggressive and act accordingly. In drinking situations, women are viewed as more sexually available when impaired. Thus, males may participate in drinking situations expecting to find a sexual partner. Additionally, a woman who has been drinking may have difficulty in sending and receiving cues about expected behavior and in resisting assault. Alcohol use is often a significant factor in sexual violence of all types. Studies of college students have shown that alcohol consumption by either the perpetrator or the person raped, or both, increases the chance of sexual assault. They also show that the higher the amount of alcohol consumption by either person up to a point when alcohol impairs performance in men, the more likely the sexual victimization to the woman will be severe. This is particularly true for intoxicated men who have hostile attitudes toward women (Abbey, 2012).

Drinking alcohol has long been known to be associated with sexual risk taking. For example, when college students were asked if, within the past 12 months, they experienced unprotected sex while drinking alcohol, 16% reported they had (American College Health Association, 2014). However, alcohol use among young people is just one component of an overall risk behavior pattern and not the cause of sexual risk behavior. Additionally, impulsivity/sensation seeking, sociability, and usual drinking pattern provide a broader explanation for sexual risk taking than acute alcohol effects (Velez-Blasini, 2008).

Other Drug Use and Sexuality

Substances that purport to increase sexual desire or improve sexual function are called **aphrodisiacs.** In addition to drugs, aphrodisiacs can include perfumes and certain foods, particularly those that resemble genitals, such as bananas and oysters. Ground rhinoceros horn has been considered an aphrodisiac in Asia, possibly giving rise to the term "horny" (Taberner, 1985). Research, both personal and professional, inevitably leads to the same conclusion: One's inner fantasy life and a positive image of the sexual self, coupled with an interested and involved responsive partner, are the most powerful aphrodisiacs. Nevertheless, the search continues for this elusive magic potion, and many people take a variety of drugs in an attempt to enhance their sexual experiences.

Studies have examined the prevalence of the use of drugs as an aphrodisiac. A sample of 1,114 sexually experienced individuals aged 18–39 years was studied to determine if the participants had ever used a drug to enhance their sexual experience. Among the 28% who reported ever using a drug to improve sexual functioning, several drugs were commonly cited (see Figure 1). When considering this self-report, it is important to realize that the "placebo effect" of aphrodisiacs has been estimated at 33% (American Cancer Society, 2014.13a).

Most recreational drugs, although perceived as increasing sexual enjoyment, actually have the opposite effect. Many prescribed medications have negative effects on sexual desire and functioning as well, and users should read the information accompanying the prescription or ask the pharmacist about any sexual side effects. Although some recreational drugs may reduce inhibitions

Most Commonly Cited Drugs Used
by a Sample of 18- to 39-Year-Olds
Who Reported Ever Using a Drug to
Improve Sexual Functioning.

(*Source*: Foxman, Sevgi, & Holmes, 2006.)

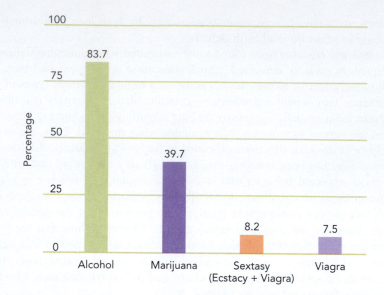

and appear to enhance the sexual experience, many also cause problems with fertility and sexual desire and functioning. They can also interfere with fertility and have a serious impact on overall health and well-being.

Marijuana users often report that its use during sexual encounters increases stimulation and sensations. The effects of marijuana, however, are in large part influenced by the expectations of its users; therefore, no definitive statement can be made about how marijuana affects sexual encounters. Specific information about its effects in a relationship can be found by looking at the role it plays in a couple's life. In some cases, marijuana or any drug can become either an aid or a crutch to help people deal with situations or behaviors they find uncomfortable. Long-term marijuana use can also cause or contribute to low motivation to achieve and to low sex drive.

The substance amyl nitrate, also known as "poppers," is a fast-acting muscle relaxant and coronary vasodilator, meaning it expands the blood vessels around the heart. Medically, it is used to relieve attacks of angina. Some people attempt to intensify their orgasms by "popping" an amyl nitrate vial and inhaling the vapor. The drug causes engorgement of the blood vessels in the penis, vagina, and anus. It also causes a drop in blood pressure, which may result in feelings of dizziness and giddiness. The most common side effects are severe headaches and fainting, and, if allowed to touch the skin, the drug can cause burns.

Another drug widely considered to be an aphrodisiac is cantharides, or "Spanish fly." This substance is produced by drying and heating certain beetles' bodies until they disintegrate into a powder. There have not yet been controlled studies to confirm its aphrodisiac effect. Taken internally, the substance causes acute irritation and inflammation of the genitourinary tract, including the kidneys, bladder, and urethra, and it can result in permanent tissue damage and death. This substance is banned in the United States.

LSD and other psychedelic drugs (including mescaline and psilocybin) have no positive effects on sexual response. They may actually cause constant and painful erections, a condition called priapism.

Cocaine, a central nervous system stimulant, reduces inhibitions and enhances feelings of well-being. But regular use nearly always leads to sexual function difficulties in both men and women, as well as an inability to have a erection or orgasm. Male cocaine users also have a lower sperm count, less active sperm, and more abnormal sperm than nonusers. The same levels of sexual impairment occur among those who snort the drug and those who smoke or "freebase" it. Those who inject cocaine experience the greatest sexual function difficulties.

MDMA (Ecstasy or Molly) is a hallucinogenic amphetamine that produces heightened arousal, a mellowing effect, and an enhanced sense of self, as well as distortions in sensory and time perception. It is an illegal drug with no legitimate use. Many of these tablets also contain a number of other drugs or drug combinations that can be harmful. In spite of this, 7% of college students report using it (American College Health Association, 2014). The drug has been associated with dehydration due to physical exertion without breaks for water; heavy use has been linked to paranoia, liver damage, and heart attacks. Because users feel increased empathy, ecstasy can lower sexual inhibitions. However, men generally cannot get erections when they are high but are often very sexual when the effects of the drug begin to fade.

The use of methamphetamine, often referred to as "crystal," "Christina," or "Tina," is increasingly becoming associated with casual sex. Prized as an aphrodisiac and stimulant used to prolong sexual arousal without orgasm, methamphetamine can be snorted, inhaled, swallowed, or injected. The sharp increase in sexual interest caused by crystal use can lead to dangerous behavior. And methamphetamine use may increase the user's susceptibility to HIV infection and progression through the use of contaminated needles, increased risky sexual behaviors, and poor medication adherence ("NIDA topics in brief," 2011). Some men, in an attempt to enhance sexual functioning, mix recreational drugs such as methamphetamine, amyl nitrate, and ecstasy with Viagra or other prescription drugs used for erectile problems. The combination of methamphetamine or amyl nitrate and erection-enhancing prescription drugs such as Viagra and Cialis has sometimes resulted in a phenomenon known as a "sexual marathon," during which sexual activity can be prolonged over hours or even days.

Aside from the adverse physical effects of recreational drugs themselves, their use is associated with greater risk for acquiring STIs, including HIV infection ("Lancet HIV," 2014). Addiction to cocaine, especially crack cocaine, has led to the widespread bartering of sex for cocaine. This practice, as well as the injection of cocaine or heroin, combined with the low rate of condom use, has led to epidemics of STIs, including AIDS, in many urban areas.

Current interest in nutrition, natural healing, and nutritional supplements, coupled with the accessibility of the Internet, has helped fuel an industry that is selling products to stimulate or improve sexuality. Such herbs as avena sativa, cayenne, yohimbe, and damiana are claimed to increase sexual stamina, performance, and/or sensation. Additionally, lotions such as Zestra, a blend of botanical oils and extracts that promises to enhance sexual arousal for women, are available. There is no current evidence to support any of these medicinal aids as effective at improving sexual functioning. However, if some individuals do benefit, it may be because they *believe* that the products work. It is important to be aware that many of the herbs mentioned previously can have side effects ranging from mild to severe.

The use of recreational drugs has become an all too common part of the party scene.

© John Stanmeyer/VII/AP Images

● Sexuality and Disability

A wide range of disabilities and physically limiting conditions affect human sexuality, yet the sexual needs and desires of those with disabilities have generally been overlooked and ignored. Nearly 20% of people in the U.S. have a disability, with more than half of them reporting it severe enough to impose a limitation on their life (U.S. Census Bureau, 2012.13a). Certainly, a disability or chronic condition does not inevitably mean the end of a person's sexual life. In 1987, Ellen Stohl, a young woman who uses a wheelchair, created a controversy by posing seminude in an eight-page layout in *Playboy*. Some people (including some editors at *Playboy*) felt that the feature could be construed as exploitive of people with disabilities. Others, Stohl among them, believed that it would help normalize society's perception of individuals who have disabilities. She said, "I realized I was still a woman. But the world didn't accept me as that. Here I am a senior in college [with] a 3.5 average, and people treat me like I'm a 3-year-old" (quoted in Cummings, 1987). Though Stohl's layout in *Playboy* occurred almost three decades ago, even today we rarely see media depictions of people living with disabilities or chronic illness as having sex lives.

Among the most significant issues facing those with disabilities as well as those who care for them is the belief that people with disabilities are less sexual than those without disabilities. In fact, sexual expression is a component of personality, which is separate from erectile function or fertility status. Other common myths about disability and sexuality include (Klein & Meier, 2013):

- Sex means sexual intercourse.
- Among those who have disabilities, talking about sex is not natural, proper, or necessary.
- Sex is for younger people who are able-bodied.
- Sex should be spontaneous.
- A firm penis and an orgasm are requirements for satisfying sex.

Because of the complexity of physical, psychological, and emotional changes that may occur as a result of a disability, it's important to educate the person with a disability about sexuality, as well as to involve and communicate with those who support him or her. Issues related to desires, needs, and sexual function should be explored and addressed in a comfortable and nonjudgmental setting.

Physical Limitations and Changing Expectations

Many people are subject to sexually limiting conditions for some or all of their lives. These conditions may be congenital, appearing at birth, such as cerebral palsy (a neuromuscular disorder) and Down syndrome (a developmentally disabling condition). They may be caused by a disease such as diabetes, arthritis, or cancer or be the result of an accident, as in the case of spinal cord injuries.

In cases in which the spinal cord is completely severed, for example, there is no feeling in the genitals, but that does not eliminate sexual desires or exclude other possible sexual behaviors. Many men with spinal cord damage are able to have full or partial erections; some may ejaculate.

However, the effects on sexual response are generally associated with the degree and location of the injury. Nearly 40% of quadriplegic men are able to experience orgasm and ejaculation (Ducharme & Gill, 1997). Those who are not

Though media may be portraying more disabilities in movies, such as *The Theory of Everything*, people with disabilities still remain neglected, and if they are seen, misrepresented.

© Pictorial Press Ltd/Alamy

I get the feeling people think that because I am in a chair there is just a blank space down there.

—Anonymous quote in the book *The Ultimate Guide to Sex and Disability* capable of ejaculation may be able to father a child through electroejaculation sperm retrieval and intrauterine insemination of the man's partner. In this procedure, the prostate gland is electrically stimulated through the rectum, causing erection and ejaculation. Many women with spinal cord damage injuries are able to have painless childbirth, although forceps delivery, vacuum extraction, or cesarean section may be necessary. Since sexuality is still a relatively new target of pharmacological research, little is known about the impact of these kinds of treatments on sexuality-related outcomes. Research from clinical reports and practice finds that medication or treatments for neurological diseases, including spinal cord injuries, have varied effects on both sexual functioning and sexual well-being (Verschuren, Enzlin, Dijkstra, Geertzen, & Dekker, 2010).

All individuals, including those with physical and mental limitations, have a need for touch and intimacy.
© P. Broze/Getty Images

Women with spinal cord injuries experience many of the same sexual responses as other women, including (in about 50% of women with such injuries) the capacity to experience an orgasm (Sipiski, Alexander, Gómez-Marín, & Spalding, 2007). People with spinal cord injuries (and anyone else, for that matter) may engage in oral or manual sex—anything, in fact, they and their partners find pleasurable and acceptable. They may discover a wide variety of erogenous areas, such as their breasts, thighs, necks, ears, or underarms.

To establish sexual health, people with disabilities must overcome previous sexual function expectations and realign them with their actual sexual capacities. A major problem for many people with disabilities is overcoming the anger or disappointment they feel because their bodies don't meet the cultural "ideal." They often live in dread of rejection, which may or may not be realistic, depending on whom they seek as partners. Many people with disabilities have rich fantasy lives. This is fortuitous because imagination is a key ingredient in developing a full sex life. Robert Lenz, a consultant in the field of sexuality and disability, received a quadriplegic (paralyzed from the neck down) spinal cord injury when he was 16 (Lenz & Chaves, 1981). In the film *Active Partners,* he says:

> One thing I do know is that I'm a much better lover now than I ever was before.
> There are a lot of reasons for that, but one of the biggest is that I'm more relaxed.
> I don't have a list of do's and don'ts, a timetable or a proper sequence of moves
> to follow, or the need to "give" my partner an orgasm every time we make love.
> Sex isn't just orgasm for me; it's pleasuring, playing, laughing, and sharing.

Educating people with physical limitations about their sexuality and using a holistic approach that includes counseling to build self-esteem and combat negative stereotypes are increasingly being recognized as crucial issues by the medical community. Important tasks of therapists working with people who have disabilities are to give their clients "permission" to engage in sexual activities that are appropriate to their capacities and to suggest new activities or techniques. Researchers suggest that nonpenetrative sexual behaviors should be affirmed as valid and healthy expressions of the individual's or couple's sexuality. Clients should also be advised about the use of vibrators, artificial penises and vaginas, and other aids to sexual enhancement. Certainly, with proper and adequate support, people with disabilities can have full and satisfying sex lives.

Vision and Hearing Impairment

Loss of sight or hearing, especially if it is total and has existed from infancy, presents many difficulties in both the theoretical and the practical understanding of sexuality. A young person who has been blind from birth is unlikely to know what a person of the other sex actually "looks" (or feels) like. Children who are deaf often do not have parents who communicate well in sign language; as a result, they may not receive much instruction about sexuality at home, nor are they likely to understand abstract concepts such as "intimacy." Older individuals who experience significant losses of sight or hearing may become depressed, develop low self-esteem, and withdraw from contact with others. Because they don't receive the visual or auditory cues that most of us take for granted, people with hearing or vision impairments may have communication difficulties within their sexual relationships. These difficulties often can be overcome with education or counseling, depending on the circumstances. Schools and programs for children who are sight- and hearing-impaired offer specially designed curricula for teaching about sexuality.

Chronic Illness

Diabetes, cardiovascular disease, and arthritis are three of the most prevalent diseases in America. Although these conditions are not always described as disabilities, they may require considerable adjustments in a person's sexuality because they, or the medications or treatments given to control them, may affect libido, sexual capability or responsiveness, and body image. It is important to acknowledge that the partner's sexuality may also be affected by chronic illness. Additionally, many older partners find themselves dealing with issues of disease and disability as well as those of aging.

There may be other disabling conditions, too numerous to discuss here, that affect our lives or those of people we know. Some of the information presented here may be applicable to conditions not specifically dealt with, such as multiple sclerosis or post-polio syndrome. We encourage readers with specific questions regarding sexuality and chronic diseases to seek out networks, organizations, and self-help groups that specialize in those issues.

Diabetes **Diabetes mellitus,** commonly referred to simply as diabetes, is a chronic disease characterized by an excess of sugar in the blood and urine, due to a deficiency of insulin, a protein hormone. About 29 million people in the United States, or 9.3% of the population, have diabetes (Centers for Disease Control and Prevention (CDC), 2014.13a); of these, nearly 28% are undiagnosed. Nerve damage or circulatory problems caused by diabetes can cause sexual problems. Men with diabetes are often more affected sexually by the disease than are women. Estimates of the prevalence of erectile dysfunction vary widely, ranging from 20% to 75% (National Diabetes Information Clearinghouse [NDIC], 2012). Some men with diabetes experience problems with sexual desire, difficulty getting an erection, and not experiencing orgasm. Heavy alcohol use, obesity, age, smoking, and poor blood-sugar control also increase the risk of erectile problems.

Diabetes can affect a woman's sexuality as well. Female sexual function difficulties have been found to occur in 18–42% of sexually active women with diabetes (NDIC, 2012). Some women with diabetes may have less interest in being sexual because of frequent yeast infections. High blood-sugar levels can make some women feel tired or irritable, resulting in reduced sexual interest. Also, intercourse may be painful because of vaginal dryness.

Problems with sexual functioning in men and women with diabetes are also associated with fear of failure, reduced self-esteem, and problems with acceptance of the disease. While it may be difficult to discuss these feelings with a partner, it's important not to give up. Finding someone on your health care team to talk with may also be helpful.

Cardiovascular Disease

Obviously, a heart attack or stroke is a major event in a person's life, affecting important aspects of daily living. Following an attack, a person often enters a period of depression in which the appetite declines, sleep habits change, and there is fatigue and a loss of libido. There is often an overwhelming fear of sex based on the belief that sexual activity might provoke another heart attack or stroke. Sexual function difficulties are common in cardiac patients and, in men, may precede cardiac symptoms; over 50% of men with coronary artery disease have erectile problems (Jackson, 2009). The partners of male heart attack patients also express great concern about sexuality. They are fearful of the risks, concerned over sexual function difficulties, and apprehensive about the possibility of another attack during intercourse. Most people can start sexual activity again 3 to 6 weeks after their condition becomes stable following an attack if the physician agrees (National Institute on Aging, 2008). In general, the chance of a person with a prior heart attack having another one during sex is no greater than that of anyone else.

LAMENT OF A CORONARY
*My doctor has made a prognosis
That intercourse fosters thrombosis,
But I'd rather expire fulfilling desire
Than abstain, and suffer neurosis.*

—Anonymous

Arthritis

About one in five Americans has some type of arthritis, most of them older women, but the disease may afflict and disable children and adolescents as well (CDC, 2013.13a). Arthritis is a painful inflammation and swelling of the joints, usually of the knees, hips, and lower back, which may lead to disfigurement of the limbs. Sometimes, the joints can be moved only with great difficulty and pain; sometimes, they cannot be moved at all. Arthritis is a leading cause of disability in Americans and a major cause of work limitation in the United States. The cause of arthritis is not known.

Sexual intimacy may be difficult for people with arthritis because of the pain and stiffening that accompanies it. Oral sex, general pleasuring of the body, and creative sexual positioning have definite advantages for those with arthritis. Applying moist heat to the joints or sharing a shower or bath with a partner prior to sexual activity can help.

Developmental Disabilities

Developmental disabilities are a diverse group of severe, lifelong, chronic conditions attributable to mental and/or physical impairments that begin during the developmental period and result in major lifestyle limitations. People with developmental disabilities most often have problems with major life activities such

Though most people support the right of consenting adults to have access to sexuality education and a sexual life, few acknowledge the needs and rights of those with disabilities to have the same.

© Realistic Reflections

as language, mobility, learning, self-help, and independent living. The sexuality of those who have developmental disabilities has only recently been widely acknowledged by those who work with them. The capabilities of individuals with developmental disabilities vary widely. People with mild or moderate disabilities may be able to learn to behave appropriately, protect themselves from abuse, and understand the basics of reproduction. Some manage to marry, work, and raise families with little assistance.

Sexuality education is extremely important for adolescents who have developmental disabilities. Some parents may fear that this will "put ideas into their heads," but it is more likely given the combination of explicit media and Internet images and the effects of increased hormonal output, that the ideas are already there. It may be difficult or impossible to teach more severely affected people how to engage in safer sexual behaviors. There is ongoing debate about the ethics of mandatory birth control or sterilization for those who have developmental disabilities. These issues are especially salient in cases in which there is a chance of passing the disability to a child.

The Sexual Rights of People With Disabilities

Although many of the concerns of people with disabilities are becoming more visible through the courageous efforts of certain groups and individuals, much of their lives still remains hidden. By refusing to recognize the existence and concerns of those with physical and developmental limitations, the rest of us do a profound disservice to our fellow human beings and, ultimately, to ourselves. The United Nations General Assembly (1993) noted that states "should promote their [persons' with disabilities] rights to personal integrity and ensure that laws do not discriminate against persons with disabilities with respect to sexual relationships, marriage, and parenthood." The federal Developmental Disabilities Assistance and Bill of Rights Act of 2000 explicitly states that individuals with intellectual disability have the fundamental right to engage in meaningful relationships with others (U.S. Department of Health and Human Services, 2000).

The sexual rights of persons with disabilities should be the same as those for persons without disabilities and include the following:

- The right to sexual expression.
- The right to privacy.
- The right to be informed about and have access to needed services, such as contraceptive counseling, medical care, genetic counseling, and sex counseling.
- The right to choose one's marital status.
- The right to have or not have children.
- The right to make one's own decisions and develop to one's full potential.

● Sexuality and Cancer

Cancer is not a single disease; it is more than 300 distinct illnesses that can affect any organ of the body. These various cancers grow at different speeds and have different treatment success and failure rates. Most cancers, but not all (e.g., leukemia), form solid tumors.

All cancers have one thing in common: They are the result of the aberrant behavior of cells. Cancer-causing agents (carcinogens) are believed to scramble the messages of the DNA within cells, causing the cell to abandon its normal functions. Tumors are either benign or malignant. **Benign tumors** usually are slow growing and remain localized. **Malignant tumors,** however, are cancerous. Instead of remaining localized, they invade nearby tissues and disrupt the normal functioning of vital organs. The process by which the disease spreads from one part of the body to another, unrelated part is called **metastasis.** This metastatic process, not the original tumor, accounts for the vast majority of cancer deaths.

Women and Cancer

Because of their fear of breast cancer and cancer of the reproductive organs, some women avoid having regular breast examinations or Pap tests. If a woman feels a lump in her breast or her doctor tells her she has a growth in her uterus, she may plunge into despair or panic. These reactions are understandable, but they are also counterproductive. Most lumps and bumps are benign conditions, such as uterine fibroids, ovarian cysts, and fibroadenomas of the breast.

Breast Cancer   Excluding cancer of the skin, breast cancer is the most common cancer in women and the second leading cause of cancer deaths in women (American Cancer Society, 2014.13b). It is predicted that in 2015 about 231,840 new cases of invasive breast cancer will be diagnosed, with about 40,300 women dying from the disease (American Cancer Society, 2014.13c). Experts estimate that in the United States about one of every eight women (12.4%) born today will be diagnosed with breast cancer at some time during her life (American Cancer Society, 2014.13c). In spite of these staggering numbers, the incidence of female breast cancer actually declined in 2000, then dropped by about 7% from 2002 to 2003. This was thought to be due to the decrease in use of hormone therapy during and following menopause. Death rates have also been falling since 1989, especially among women younger than 50, with the decreases believed to be the result of earlier screening, increased awareness, and improved treatment.

The most significant risk factor for breast cancer is age. Other factors that increase a woman's risk of developing breast cancer include inherited changes in certain genes, personal or family history of breast cancer, dense breasts, beginning to menstruate before age 12 or starting menopause after age 55, a first full-term pregnancy after age 30, never having been pregnant, obesity after menopause, race and ethnicity, and alcohol use. Studies have shown that using combined hormone therapy (progestin and estrogen) after menopause also increases the risk of acquiring and dying from breast cancer. While much research has looked for links between breast cancer and other factors, including diet and vitamin intake, chemicals in the environment, tobacco smoke, night work, and breast implants, the results of these studies still prove to be inconclusive (American Cancer Society, 2014.13b).

The 5-year survival rate from breast cancer varies greatly, depending on many factors, including the grade of the cancer and the presence of hormone receptors on the cancer cells. Those who are diagnosed in the earliest stages (1 and 2) have a 93–100% survival rate; however, these rates drop for each stage of diagnosis (American Cancer Society, 2014.13d).

Studies have found that lesbian and bisexual women have higher rates of breast cancer than heterosexual women (American Cancer Society, 2014.13e). Factors more likely to affect lesbian and bisexual women include not having had children and not having breastfed, not having used oral contraceptives, and being older when they first give birth. At the same time, bisexual and lesbian women also tend to get less routine health care than other women, including colon, breast, and cervical cancer screening. Additionally, they have lower rates of health insurance, may fear discrimination, and may have had negative experiences with health care providers. Missing routine cancer screenings, for example, can lead to cancer being diagnosed at a later stage when it is harder to treat. It is especially important for lesbian and bisexual women to find providers who are accepting and culturally and medically competent.

Detection **Breast self-exam (BSE),** a method of checking one's own breasts for lumps or suspicious changes, has been widely advocated as a technique that can help women find early variations in their breasts. This implies that finding a lump early will save lives; however, no study to date has found that BSE reduces breast cancer deaths (National Cancer Institute, 2014a). As a result of earlier data, in 2003 the American Cancer Society revised its breast cancer screening guidelines to suggest that BSE be optional; however, the technique can be used to help a woman become familiar with the way her breasts normally look and feel. The screening guidelines from the American Cancer Society and the National Cancer Institute are listed in Table 1.

Another test that has widely been used to detect breast cancer is **mammography,** or the use of X-rays to detect breast tumors before they can be seen or felt. The American Cancer Society (2014.13f) recommends that women aged 40 and older have a mammogram each year and continue to do so even if they are in good health. They suggest that women at increased risk (e.g., having family history, genetic tendency, past breast cancer) should talk with their doctors about the benefits and limitations of mammography screening as well as other detection tests (e.g., magnetic resonance imagining, or MRI) or of having more frequent exams. At the same time, it's important to note that a committee convened by the National Institutes of Health has declined to recommend universal screening with mammography for women; however, the agency did acknowledge that screening mammography may lead to a decrease in breast cancer mortality (National Cancer Institute, 2014a). Helping guide this recommendation were results from one of the largest and longest-running studies of mammograms ever conducted, the Canadian National Breast Cancer Screening Study (Miller, Wall, Baines, Sun, To, & Narod, 2014), which reported that the screening tests do not improve a woman's chances for surviving breast cancer. More specifically, "annual mammography in women aged 40–59 does not reduce mortality from breast cancer beyond that of physical examination or usual care when adjuvant therapy for breast cancer is freely available." The researchers also found that only 20% of cancers detected via mammography and treated with often-dangerous chemotherapy, surgery, or radiation therapies actually posed a threat to the women's health. With this much controversy, the American College of Physicians recommends that women consult with their doctors before undergoing routine mammography as the risk of false-positives and other issues can cause anxiety and possible harm.

TABLE 1 • Screening Guidelines for the Early Detection of Breast Cancer: American Cancer Society and U.S. Preventive Services Task Force

American Cancer Society	U.S. Preventive Services Task Force
Self-Breast Exam (BSE)	
Women in their 20s—optional	Recommends against teaching BSE
Clinical Breast Exam	
Women in their 20s and 30s—periodic/regular health exam, preferably every 3 years	Insufficient evidence to assess benefits and harms
Starting at age 40—yearly exam by health professional	
Mammogram	
Ages 40 and over—yearly and continued testing as long as a woman is in good health	Ages 40–49: Individual choice
	Ages 50–74: Screening mammography recommended every 2 years
	Ages 75 and older: Insufficient evidence to assess benefits and harms*
MRI	
Not recommended if lifetime risk of breast cancer is less than 15% (based on risk assessment tools)	Insufficient evidence to assess balance of benefits and harms*
Insufficient evidence for yearly MRI if lifetime risk is between 15–20%	
Mammogram and MRI	
Yearly only for women who are at high risk for breast cancer based on certain risk factors	Insufficient evidence to assess balance of benefits and harms*

SOURCES: American Cancer Society. (2014.13f). American Cancer Society recommendations for early breast cancer detection in women without breast symptoms. Available: http://www.cancer.org/cancer/breastcancer/moreinformation/breastcancerearlydetection/breast-cancer-early-detection-acs-recs; U.S. Preventive Services Task Force. (2009). Breast cancer screening. Available: http://www.uspreventiveservicestaskforce.org/Page/Topic/recommendation-summary/breast-cancer-screening?ds=1&s=breast%20cancer (Last visited 5/7/15).

*U.S. Preventive Services Task Force. (2015). Breast cancer screening draft recommendations. Available: http://screeningforbreastcancer.org/?ds=1&s=breast%2520cancer%2520screening (Last visited 5/7/15).

Early detection is an important part of preventive care. The earlier breast cancer is found, the better the chances that treatment will be effective and the breast can be saved. The goal is to discover cancer prior to symptoms appearing. Most physicians believe that early detection of breast cancer saves thousands of lives each year.

It is important to recognize that most breast lumps—75–80%—are *not* cancerous. Many disappear on their own. Of lumps that are surgically removed for diagnostic purposes (biopsied), 80% prove to be benign. Most are related to **fibrocystic disease,** a common and generally harmless breast condition, not really a disease at all, or they are fibroadenomas, round, movable growths, also harmless, that occur in young women. Because some benign breast lumps can increase a woman's chance of developing breast cancer, it is important that any breast lumps be checked by a health care provider.

Treatment Most women with breast cancer undergo some type of surgery to remove the primary tumor. Other reasons for surgery include finding out whether the cancer has spread to the lymph nodes under the arm, restoring the breast's appearance, and relieving symptoms of advanced cancer. Common breast cancer surgeries described by the American Cancer Society (2014.13g) include the following (see Figure 2):

- *Lumpectomy*. This procedure involves the removal of only the breast lump and some normal tissue around it.
- *Partial (segmental)* **mastectomy**. This surgery involves the removal of more of the breast tissue than with a lumpectomy.
- *Simple, or total, mastectomy*. This operation involves the removal of the entire breast, but not the lymph nodes from under the arm or muscle tissue from beneath the breast.
- *Modified radical mastectomy*. This surgery involves the removal of the entire breast and some of the lymph nodes under the arm. This is the most common breast cancer surgery.
- *Radical mastectomy*. This operation involves the removal of the entire breast, lymph nodes, and chest wall muscles under the breast. Because the modified radical mastectomy has proved to be just as effective, with less disfigurement and fewer side effects, radical mastectomy is rarely done now.

Surgery may also be combined with other treatments such as chemotherapy, hormone therapy, or radiation therapy.

Additional treatments for cancer are external radiation and chemotherapy. The female hormone, estrogen, promotes the growth of breast cancer cells in some women. For these women, several methods, including the use of the drug tamoxifen, can block the effects of estrogen or lower its levels (American Cancer Society, 2014.13g).

Angelina Jolie's announcement in 2013 that she had a preventive double mastectomy raised awareness and controversy about breast cancer and the issues around genetic testing, risk, prophylactic surgery, and body image. Preventive mastectomy should only be considered after a woman has received genetic and psychological counseling.

• **FIGURE 2**

Types of Surgical Treatment for Breast Cancer.

(*Source:* Reprinted by the permission of the American Cancer Society, Inc. from www.cancer.org. All rights reserved.)

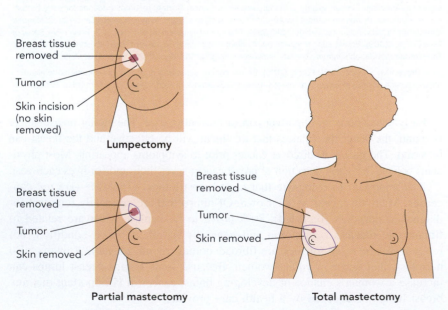

Sexual Well-Being and Adjustment After Treatment   Sexuality is one aspect of life that may be profoundly altered by cancer. In fact, it is widely recognized that changes to sexual well-being following diagnosis and treatment of breast cancer can be one of the most problematic aspects of life with the impact lasting for many years following successful treatment. The largest study of sexual well-being in the context of breast cancer published to date found that 33% of women report a negative impact on their sexuality. In spite of this significant number, the authors speculate this to be a "significant underestimate" of women's actual experience. Still, only 25% of breast cancer patients reported that they had discussed sexual well-being with a health professional (Ussher, Perz, & Gilbert, 2012).

For most women, there is little preparation for the many distressing changes that may occur as a result of breast cancer diagnosis and treatment, including decreases in the frequency of sex, sexual arousal, interest, and desire, as well as in sexual pleasure, satisfaction, and intimacy. These may be due to a range of factors, including tiredness and pain, psychological distress and body image, and medically induced menopausal changes, such as vaginal dryness and hot flashes. While these changes are not inevitable, worries about the impact on the body and concern about body image are quite common (Fobair et al., 2006).

Relationship context and partner reaction, along with the complexity of the woman with breast cancer's own responses, are matters to be addressed both personally and in a health care setting. Psychologically, the loss of a breast may symbolize for a woman the loss of sexuality; she may feel scarred and be fearful of rejection. However, even when a partner is supportive, that validation does not always alleviate the negative feelings that a survivor may

Surviving cancer can deepen one's appreciation of life. Notice the tattoo along this woman's mastectomy scars.

© Steve Wisbauer/Photographer's Choice/ Getty Images

have about herself and her sexuality. While both negative and positive accounts of the impact of cancer on sexual relationships have been reported, in a meta-analysis of distress in couples coping with cancer, one researcher summed up the literature by concluding that further research is needed on "just how much cancer intrudes upon and organizes the daily lives of couples" (Hagedoorn et al., 2008, p. 24).

Many women with breast cancer have adjusted well. However, there is still a need to not only understand how various cancer treatments affect sexuality but also to provide support to those with cancer-related sexual function problems. Realizing that there are alternative ways of expressing one's sexuality can be valuable. The woman and her partner can decide what is satisfying and pleasurable. And, of course, being comfortable with her own sexuality can enhance a woman's self-esteem and make coping with cancer easier.

Cervical Cancer and Cervical Dysplasia **Cervical dysplasia,** also called **cervical intraepithelial neoplasia (CIN),** is a condition of the cervical epithelium (covering membrane of cervix). Although this is not cancer, it is considered a precancerous condition. Most cases occur in women aged 25–35, although it can develop at any age ("Cervical Dysplasia," 2014). Most often cervical dysplasia is caused by the human papillomavirus (HPV), a common virus that is spread through sexual contact. There are several factors that may increase a woman's risk of cervical dysplasia including having sexual intercourse before age 18, giving birth before age 16, having multiple sexual partners, having another illness, using medications that suppress the immune system, and smoking. Most of the time there are no symptoms. Without treatment many cases of severe cervical dysplasia lead to invasive cancer; the risk of cancer is lower for mild dysplasia. Early diagnosis and prompt treatment cure nearly all cases of cervical dysplasia; however, the conditions may return.

It may take 10 or more years for cervical dysplasia to develop into cancer. The more advanced and dangerous malignancy is invasive cancer of the cervix (ICC), also called **cervical cancer.** The American Cancer Society (2014.13i) estimates about 12,900 new cases of invasive cervical cancer will occur in 2015 and that 4,100 women will die from this disease. As previously stated, the most important risk factor for cervical cancer is infection by the sexually transmitted human papillomavirus (HPV). It's important to note, however, that most women with HPV do not get cervical cancer because the infection usually goes away on its own, without treatment. Additional risk factors include age (most newly diagnosed cases are found in women under 50), HIV infection, which makes women more vulnerable to HPV, chlamydia infection, poor diet, many sexual partners, a mother who was given diethylstilbestrol (DES) during pregnancy, having sexual intercourse at an early age, long-term use of oral contraceptives, being overweight, having a compromised immune system, cigarette smoking, family history, and low socioeconomic status. When detected and treated in its early stages, the disease is both prevented from spreading to other organs and cured. Unusual discharge, bleeding, spotting, or pain or bleeding during sex may be signs of cervical cancer (American Cancer Society, 2014.13i).

In June 2006, the U.S. Food and Drug Administration approved a vaccine, called Gardasil, that would protect thousands of women each year from cervical cancer. Later, in 2014, the FDA also approved Gardasil 9, which protects against additional HPV strains. The vaccine, the world's first cancer vaccine and a major medical advance, works to prevent against the strains of HPV most likely to cause cancer.

Detection   The most reliable means of early detection of cervical cancer is the **Pap test** (or Pap smear). This is a simple procedure that can not only detect cancer but also reveal changes in cells that make them precancerous. A Pap test can warn against cancer even before it begins, and the use of the Pap test has resulted in dramatic decreases in cervical cancer deaths in the United States. Newer, liquid-based Pap tests do not find more cancers or precancers than conventional tests but do lower the chance that the test will need to be repeated and have the benefit that the same sample can be used for HPV testing.

The Pap test is usually done during a pelvic exam and takes about a minute. Cell samples and mucus are lightly scraped from the cervix and examined under a microscope. If anything unusual is found, the physician will do further tests. Unfortunately, the test is not as effective in detecting cancer in the body of the uterus, which occurs in women most frequently during or after menopause.

The American Cancer Society (2014.13i) offers the following guidelines for early detection of precancerous changes of the cervix:

- *Cervical cancer screening (testing) should begin at age 21.* Women under age 21 should *not* be tested.

- *Women between ages 21 and 29* should have a Pap test every 3 years. HPV testing should *not* be used in this age group unless it is needed after an abnormal Pap test result.

- *Women over age 65* who have had regular screenings in the previous 10 years should stop cervical cancer screening as long as they haven't had any serious precancers found in the last 20 years. Women with a history of precancers should continue to have testing for at least 20 years after the abnormality was found.

- *A woman who has had a total hysterectomy* (removal of the uterus and cervix) should stop cervical screening unless the hysterectomy was done as a treatment for cervical precancer or cancer. Women who have had a hysterectomy without removal of the cervix should continue cervical cancer screening according to the preceding guidelines.

- *Women of any age* should *not* be screened every year by any screening method.

- *Women who have been vaccinated against HPV* should follow the preceding guidelines.

Some women—because of their history—may need to have a different screening schedule for cervical cancer.

To make the Pap test more accurate, women should not schedule the appointment during their menstrual period. Additionally, for 48 hours prior to the test, they should not have intercourse, douche, or use tampons, birth control foams, jellies, or other vaginal creams or vaginal medications. Coverage for cervical cancer screening is mandated by the Affordable Care Act.

Diagnosis and Treatment   If a woman has certain symptoms that suggest cancer or if the Pap test shows abnormal cells she will have a test called a colposcopy. This test itself causes no more discomfort than any other speculum exam, has no side effects, and can be done safely even if a woman is pregnant. If an

think
about it

Female Genital Cutting: Mutilation or Important Custom?

In African countries, some parts of Asia, and the Middle East, and among certain immigrant communities in North America and Europe, female infants, girls, or young women may undergo female genital mutilation/cutting (FGM/C). An estimated 100 to 140 million girls and women worldwide have undergone FGM/C and more than 3 million girls are at risk each year on the African continent alone (Population Reference Bureau, 2014). FGM/C is often performed on girls between ages 4 and 12, however in some cultures it is practiced as early as a few days after birth or as late as just prior to marriage. In the late 1970s, several international organizations, including the World Health Organization, began using the term "female genital mutilation" to refer to this procedure emphasizing that the act violates girls' and women's human rights, alters or causes injury to the female genital organs, and has no health benefits. The United Nations Children's Fund and the United Nations Population Fund use the less judgmental expression "female genital mutilation/cutting" (World Health Organization, 2014.13a). For the sake of this discussion, we will use the less judgmental "female genital cutting" as well.

One type of FGC is clitoridectomy, or female circumcision: having their clitoris slit or cut out entirely and all or part of their labia sliced off. The sides of their vulvas or their vaginal openings may be stitched together—a process called infibulation—leaving only a tiny opening for the passage of urine and menstrual blood. These surgeries are generally performed in unsanitary conditions, with a knife, a razor, or even a tin can lid or piece of broken glass, without medical anesthesia; antiseptic powder or concocted pastes may be applied. FGC has no known health benefits. On the contrary, the effects of the devastatingly painful operations include bleeding, infections, infertility, scarring, the inability to enjoy sex, and, not uncommonly, death. Upon marriage, a young woman may experience considerable pain and bleeding as the entry to the vagina is reopened by tearing her flesh. In childbirth, the old wounds must be reopened surgically, or tearing will result. Women who have undergone FGC and their babies are more likely to die during childbirth (World Health Organization, 2014.13a).

This ancient custom, practiced mainly in Africa, is difficult for outsiders to understand. Why would loving parents allow this to be done to their defenseless daughter, and even hold her down during the procedure? As with many other practices, including male circumcision in our own culture, the answer is "tradition." Persons who

Female genital mutilation/cutting is common in many African and Middle Eastern countries.

© Safin Hamed/AFP/Getty Images

conduct circumcisions and contribute to childbirth needs in communities mostly carry out the practice. However, health care providers perform more than 18% of all FGC, with an increasing trend toward medicalization in many countries (WHO, 2014.13a). Beyond tradition, the surgery is practiced for several reasons, including as a way of controlling women's sexuality, often resulting in impaired sexual enjoyment.

Though progress has been made in curtailing FGC through international responses and resolutions, research shows that if practicing communities themselves decide to abandon FGC, the practice could be eliminated very rapidly (WHO, 2014.13a). However, strongly held customs are hard to change, and there are still many places where it continues.

Think Critically

1. Which is the better term: *female genital cutting* or *female genital mutilation*? Why?
2. Should female genital cutting be eliminated worldwide or should it be permitted in countries where it is an important custom?
3. Does FGC violate the human rights of girls and women? If so, in what ways? If not, why?

abnormal area is seen on the cervix, a **biopsy,** or a surgical remove of the tissue for diagnosis, will be done. A biopsy is the only way to tell for certain if abnormal cells are precancer, true cancer, or neither. Several types of biopsies are used.

Treating women with abnormal test results can prevent cervical cancer from developing. Thus, if a doctor sees an abnormal area during the colposcopy, he or she will be able to remove it with any one of a variety of procedures. A woman will need follow-up exams to make sure that the abnormality does not return; however, if it does, the treatments can be repeated. Rarely will surgery be required to remove the cervix. The varieties of treatments available are almost always effective in destroying precancers and preventing them from developing into true cancer (American Cancer Society, 2014.13i).

The patient must combat the disease along with the physician.

—Hippocrates, Aphorisms (460–370 BCE)

Ovarian Cancer

Ovarian cancer is the fifth-ranked cause of cancer death in women. The American Cancer Society (2014.13j) estimates that there will be about 21,290 new cases of ovarian cancer in the United States in 2015 and that about 14,180 women will die from the disease. The odds of a woman getting ovarian cancer during her lifetime are about 1 in 73. The risk of getting ovarian cancer and dying is 1 in 100. Evidence links pregnancy, breastfeeding, tubal ligation or hysterectomy, and use of oral contraceptives or the birth control shot with a lower risk of ovarian cancer, perhaps because each gives the woman a rest from ovulation and eases the hormonal fluctuations that occur within the ovaries.

Factors that increase risk include age (about half of all ovarian cancers are found in women over 63), use of the fertility drug clomiphene citrate, more monthly periods, a family history of ovarian cancer, not having children, estrogen replacement therapy, smoking and alcohol use, breast cancer, obesity, and poor diet. Ovarian cancer is hard to diagnose because there are no symptoms in the early stages; it is not usually detectable by a Pap test. Diagnosis is done by pelvic examination and needle aspiration (removal of fluid) or biopsy. Treatment involves surgical removal of the tumor and ovary, often followed by radiation or chemotherapy. Follow-up care is especially important. If ovarian cancer is found early, the chances of survival are much greater. Though 94% of women will survive at least 5 years if the cancer is found and treated before it has spread outside the ovary, only 20% of ovarian cancers are found at this stage (American Cancer Society, 2014.13j).

Uterine (Endometrial) Cancer

Nearly 53,000 new cases of cancers of the uterus were estimated for 2014, with 8,000 women in the United States dying from uterine cancer (American Cancer Society, 2014.13k). More than 95% of cancers of the uterus involve the endometrium, the lining of the uterus. Certain women appear more at risk for developing endometrial cancer than others, including those who are over age 55, are obese, have used estrogen therapy or the drug tamoxifen, have a history of infertility, are diabetic, have menstruated before age 12, or experienced menopause after age 52 (American Cancer Society, 2014.13k).

Hysterectomy

The surgical removal of the uterus and ligaments in order to treat some cancers or severe gynecological problems is called a **radical hysterectomy.** The cervix and an inch or two of the deep vagina around the cervix are also removed. If a woman is under the age of 40, the surgeon will often try to leave an ovary or part of one. If a woman is between 40 and 50 when she has surgery, doctors weigh the benefits of removing both ovaries to prevent ovarian cancer against the costs of causing sudden early menopause. A somewhat less complicated procedure is a hysterectomy, which involves the removal of the upper part of the uterus and cervix. This is most often used to treat endometrial cancer. The ovaries and fallopian tubes are not removed unless there is some other reason to do so (American Cancer Society, 2013.13a).

Certain conditions make a hysterectomy necessary: (1) when a cancerous or precancerous growth cannot be treated otherwise, (2) when noncancerous growths on the uterus become so large that they interfere with other organs, such as when they hinder bladder or bowel functions, or cause pain or pressure, (3) when bleeding is so heavy that it cannot be controlled or when it leads to anemia, and/or (4) when severe infection cannot be controlled in any other way. If a woman's physician recommends a hysterectomy, she should have the opinion confirmed by a second physician.

Removal of the ovaries can result in lowered libido because testosterone, the sex-drive hormone, is mainly produced there. Furthermore, the absence of ovarian estrogen can cause menopausal symptoms such as vaginal dryness and thinning of the vaginal walls. A hysterectomy alone is unlikely to cause sexual function problems. In fact, a radical hysterectomy does not alter a woman's ability to feel sexual pleasure. A woman does not need a uterus or cervix to have an orgasm. Getting educated and participating in therapy or self-help groups can be very useful for post-hysterectomy women who wish to improve the quality of their sexual lives and relationships.

Vaginal Cancer   Vaginal cancer is rare. The American Cancer Society (2014.13l) estimated that there were about 3,170 new cases of vaginal cancer in the United States in 2014, with about 880 women dying from this cancer. Although the exact cause of most vaginal cancers is not known, established risk factors include age (almost half of cases occur in women who are 70 and older), mother's use of DES when pregnant, HPV infection, previous cervical cancer, and smoking. Symptoms include abnormal vaginal bleeding, vaginal discharge, a mass that can be felt, and pain during intercourse. Treatment options, based on the type of cancer and the stage of the disease when diagnosed, are surgery, radiation, and chemotherapy in combination with radiation for advanced disease.

Men and Cancer

Generally, men are less likely than women to get regular checkups and to seek help at the onset of symptoms. This tendency can have unfortunate consequences where reproductive cancers are concerned, because early detection can often mean the difference between life and death. Men should pay attention to what goes on in their genital and urinary organs, as well as in the rest of their bodies.

Prostate Cancer   Prostate cancer is the most common form of cancer, excluding skin cancer, among American men; it causes the second highest number of deaths among men diagnosed with cancer (lung cancer is first). The American Cancer Society (2014.13m) estimates that there will be about 220,800 new cases of prostate cancer in the United States in 2015, with about 27,540 deaths. One man in 7 will get prostate cancer during his lifetime, but only 1 man in 38 will die from this disease.

Risk factors for prostate cancer include aging, a family history, being African American, a high-fat diet, and obesity. Prostate cancer is more common in North America and northwestern Europe than in Asia, Africa, Central America, and South America. For reasons still unknown, African American men are more likely to have prostate cancer, to have a more advanced disease when it is found, and to die from it than men of other races. Prostate cancer occurs less frequently in Asian American and Hispanic/Latino men than in non-Hispanic White men. About two thirds of prostate cancers are found in men over age 65.

Researchers have tried to determine if there is an association between risk for prostate cancer and ejaculation frequency. A longitudinal study of 29,342 men from the National Cancer Institute revealed that high ejaculations frequency—21 or more ejaculations per month—had a decreased risk of prostate cancer compared with men who reported 4 to 7 ejaculations a month throughout their lifetimes (Leitzmann, Platz, Stampfer, Willet, & Giovannucci, 2004). In theory, high ejaculation frequency may decrease the concentration of potentially irritating or harmful substances in the prostate. Further study is needed to investigate possible protection mechanisms.

Detection   Various symptoms may point to prostate cancer, a slow-growing disease, but often there are no symptoms or symptoms may not appear for many years. Although the symptoms in the following list are more likely to indicate prostatic enlargement or benign tumors than cancer, they should never be ignored. By the time signs do occur, the cancer may have spread beyond the prostate. When symptoms do occur, they may include:

- Urine flow that is not easily stopped, weak urinary stream, or the need to urinate more frequently
- Difficulty in getting an erection
- Blood in urine or semen
- Continuing pain in the lower back, pelvis, hips, or other areas from cancer that has spread to bones
- Weakness or numbness in the legs or feet, or loss of bladder control from cancer pressing on the spinal cord

It is important to be aware that other diseases or problems can cause these symptoms.

Like breast cancer screening, guidelines for the detection of prostate cancer are somewhat controversial (see Table 2). With organizations such as the U.S. Preventive Services Task Force (2012) and the American Urological Association (2013), each having slightly different recommendations, it may be difficult for men and their health care providers to decide if prostate screening testing is needed and if so which tests will be conducted. According to evidence reviewed by the National Cancer Institute (2014b), screening with digital rectal exam (DRE) or with prostatic-specific antigen (PSA) will detect some prostate cancer that would have caused problems. However, the organization acknowledges that it is not clear whether early detection and treatment lead to any change in the natural history and outcome of the disease. Based on solid evidence, screening leads to some degree of overtreatment, including radical prostatectomy (removal of the prostate gland) and radiation therapy, both of which can result in permanent side effects in many men.

Updated guidelines from the American Cancer Society (2014.13m) recommend a more individual approach, suggesting that men have a chance to make

TABLE 2 • Screening Guidelines for the Early Detection of Prostate Cancer: American Cancer Society and U.S. Preventive Services Task Force

American Cancer Society	U.S. Preventive Services Task Force
Following a discussion with their doctor, men should make an informed decision about screening. This discussion should take place: ■ at age 50 with average risk; ■ age 45 at high risk; ■ age 40 for highest risk	There is evidence that PSA-based screening programs result in cases of asymptomatic prostate cancer and that these cases will either have a tumor that will not progress or will progress so slowly that it would have remained asymptomatic for the man's lifetime.
Digital Rectal Exam (DRE)	
Can be done as a part of screening	No recommendation
Prostate-Specific Antigen (PSA)	
For men who wish to be screened	Not recommended for any age; screening results in overdiagnosis
Men who do not have a 10-year life expectancy	
No testing	No recommendation

SOURCES: American Cancer Society. (2014). American Cancer Society recommendations for prostate cancer early detection. Available: http://www.cancer.org/cancer/prostatecancer/moreinformation/prostatecancerearlydetection/prostate-cancer-early-detection-acs-recommendations; U.S. Preventive Services Task Force. (2012). Final recommendation statement: Prostate cancer screening. Available: http://www.uspreventiveservicestaskforce.org/Page/Document/RecommendationStatementFinal/prostate-cancer-screening (Last visited 5/7/15).

an informed decision with their health care provider. It also recommends that doctors stop giving the digital rectal exam (DRE) because it has not clearly shown a benefit, though it can remain an option.

A blood test, called the **prostate-specific antigen (PSA) test,** can be used to help diagnose prostate cancer. At the same time, research shows that PSA poses dilemmas, particularly because levels of PSA can be elevated in men with a benign condition called **prostatic hyperplasia,** when the prostate gland enlarges and blocks the flow of urine. Additionally, the test cannot distinguish between aggressive and mild forms of the disease.

Some research has shown that many, and probably most, tumors discovered during the screenings are so small and slow growing that they are unlikely to do any harm to patients. Prostate cancer develops slowly over many years and most cases are not life-threatening. Other research has shown that when dangerous tumors are found, the mortality rates are usually the same among men who had regular screenings and those who did not see a physician until they developed symptoms. However, if a young man gets prostate cancer it will probably shorten his life if it is not caught early. For an older man or one in poor health, prostate cancer may never become a major problem because it often grows so slowly.

Detection Depending on the stage of the cancer and age of the man, treatment may include surgery, androgen deprivation therapy, radiation therapy, chemotherapy, or a combination of any of these. Some men may simply undergo active surveillance. If the cancer has not spread beyond the prostate gland, all or part of the gland may be removed by surgery. Radical surgery has a high cure rate,

Oh, to be seventy again [at the age of 91, upon seeing a young woman].

—Oliver Wendell Holmes, Sr. (1809–1894)

Testicular Self-Examination

Most doctors agree that a man increases the chances of early cancer detection by performing a monthly testicular self-exam. However, doctors still debate whether a man should perform this exam. What they do agree upon is that it is important for a man to know what his own testicles feel like normally so that he will recognize any changes. The best time to perform the examination is after a warm shower or bath, when the scrotum is relaxed.

1. Stand in front of a mirror and look for any swelling on the scrotum.

2. Hold the penis out of the way and examine each testicle separately. With your thumb on top of the testicle and two fingers underneath, gently roll the testicle to check for lumps or areas of particular firmness. A normal testicle is smooth, oval, and uniformly firm to the touch. Don't worry if your testicles differ slightly in size; this is common. And don't mistake the epididymis, the sperm-carrying tube at the rear of the testicle, for an abnormality.

3. If you find any hard lumps or nodules, or if there has been any change in shape, size, or texture of the testicles, a sudden collection of fluid in the scrotum, a dull ache in the lower back or pain in a testicle or the scrotum, consult a physician. These signs may not indicate a malignancy, but only your physician can make a diagnosis.

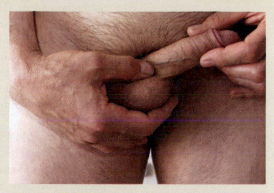

Most testicular cancers can be found at an early stage.

© John Henderson/Alamy

SOURCE: American Cancer Society. (2015.13a). Testicular self-exam. Available: http://www.cancer.org/cancer/testicularcancer/moreinformation/doihavetesticularcancer/do-i-have-testicular-cancer-self-exam (Last visited 5/7/15).

but it often results in incontinence and erectile difficulties. Because prostate cancer often spreads slowly, some men may never need treatment. The premise of watchful-waiting is that cases of localized cancer may advance so slowly that they are unlikely to cause men, especially older men, any health problems during their lifetime.

Sex counseling should be an integral part of treatment for men who have had prostate cancer surgery. The American Cancer Society (2014.13m) also suggests several options for erection-enhancing drugs—Viagra, Levitra, Stendra, or Cialis—for those who experience erection difficulties after surgery. These drugs will not work, however, if important nerves are removed or damaged during surgery.

Since the exact cause of prostate cancer is unknown, it is not possible to prevent most cases of the disease. But many risk factors can be controlled. The American Cancer Society (2014.13m) suggests eating less red meat and fat and eating more vegetables, fruits, and whole grains, which may also lower one's risk for some other types of cancer and diseases. Some evidence shows that taking the drug Proscar or Avodart might help reduce the risk of prostate cancer, but it's not clear if the benefits outweigh the risks. The American Cancer Society (2014.13m) recommends that men thinking about taking these drugs to reduce their risk of prostate cancer discuss it with their doctors.

Testicular Cancer   According to the American Cancer Society (2013.13b), about 8,820 new cases of testicular cancer were estimated to be diagnosed in 2014, with an estimated 380 deaths. The chance of a man developing testicular cancer in his lifetime is 1 in about 270. Because treatment is very successful, the risk of dying from this cancer is 1 in 5,000. The exact cause of most cases of testicular cancer is unknown, but risk factors include age (the average age at the time of diagnosis is about 33), undescended testicle(s), a family history of testicular cancer, HIV infection, cancer of the other testicle, and race and ethnicity. A man who has had cancer in one testicle has about a 3% chance of developing cancer in the other testicle. This is usually a new cancer. The risk of developing testicular cancer in the United States is about 4 to 5 times greater for White men than for African American men and more than 3 times that for Asian American men. The risk for Hispanics is between the risks for Asians and non-Hispanic Whites (American Cancer Society, 2013.13b).

Detection   Most cases of testicular cancer can be found as a result of signs or symptoms. The first sign of testicular cancer is usually a painless lump or slight enlargement and a change in the consistency of the testicle or the testicle becomes swollen or large. Some types of testicular cancers have no symptoms until the advanced stage. Although the tumors that grow on the testes are generally painless, there may be low back pain. If the tumor is growing rapidly, there may be severe pain in the testicles. Because of the lack of symptoms and pain in the early stage, men often do not go to a doctor for several months after discovering a slightly enlarged testicle.

The examination of a man's testicles is a valuable part of a general physical examination and the American Cancer Society includes testicular examination in its recommendations for routine cancer-related checkups. Whether a man should perform a regular testicular self-examination is debated, though. The American Cancer Society (2013.13b) believes that it is important to make men aware of testicular cancer and to remind them that any testicular mass should be immediately evaluated by a physician. Some doctors recommend monthly testicular self-examination by all men after puberty. The American Cancer Society (2013.13b) believes that for men with average testicular cancer risk there is no medical evidence to suggest that monthly examination is any more effective than simple awareness and prompt medical attention. However, whether to perform this examination is a decision best made by each man. Men with certain risk factors, such as previous testicular cancer or a family history should consider monthly self-examinations and discuss the issue with their doctors. Most often ultrasound and blood tests are used as diagnostic tools for testicular cancer.

Treatment   Testicular cancer is a highly treatable form of cancer. The three main methods of treatment are surgery, radiation therapy, and chemotherapy. After the affected testicle is removed, an artificial one may be inserted in the scrotal sac. Radiation treatment or chemotherapy may follow.

Although the cure rate for all types of testicular cancer is very high, provided the disease has not widely metastasized, the man's fertility is often a major concern. Since boys and men usually develop cancer in only one testicle, the remaining testicle usually can make enough testosterone to keep a man healthy and able to reproduce. If the other testicle needs to be removed because the cancer is in both testicles or if it has spread, the man will need to take some form of testosterone therapy for the rest of his life. However, testicular cancer or its treatment can make a man infertile. Thus, before treatment starts, men who might wish to father children may choose to store sperm in a sperm bank for later use. Advances in assisted reproductive methods such as in vitro fertilization have also made fatherhood possible, even if a man's sperm counts are extremely low. In some cases, if one testicle is left, fertility returns after the testicular cancer has been treated. This typically occurs at about 2 years after chemotherapy has stopped (American Cancer Society, 2013.13b).

Penile Cancer   Cancer of the penis affects only 1 out of every 100,000 men and accounts for less than 1% of cancers in men in the United States. The American Cancer Society (2013.13b) estimated that about 1,640 new cases of penile cancer were diagnosed in 2014, with an estimated 320 deaths from it. Although it is very rare in North America and Europe, it is more common in parts of Africa and South America, where it accounts for up to 10% of cancers in men. Risk factors include HPV infection, smoking, having AIDS, being treated for psoriasis with ultraviolet light and a drug called psoralen, and age. Nearly two thirds of cases are diagnosed in men over 65. For reasons not entirely clear, men who are circumcised as babies have less than half the chance of getting cancer of the penis than those who are not.

Many cases of penile cancer can be detected early on. Men should be alert to any unusual growths on or other abnormalities of the penis. If such changes occur, men should promptly consult a physician. Treatment options include surgery, radiation, and chemotherapy. Most early-stage penile cancers can be completely cured by fairly minor surgery with little or no damage to the penis. Removal of all or part of the penis is rare except for late-stage cancer. Adult men can lower their risk of penile cancer by avoiding the things that are known to increase the risk.

Breast Cancer in Men   Breast cancer is about 100 times less common among men than among women. The lifetime risk of a man getting breast cancer is 1 in 1,000. However, an estimated 2,350 new cases of breast cancer are estimated to occur in 2015 in men in the United States, with about 440 deaths (American Cancer Society, 2014.13n). As is the case for women, most breast disorders in men are benign. Known risk factors include aging (the average age is about 68 at diagnosis), family history of breast cancer for both male and female blood relatives, heavy alcohol use, inherited gene mutation (responsible for some breast cancers in women), Klinefelter syndrome, radiation exposure, liver disease, physical inactivity and obesity, and estrogen treatment (for prostate cancer, for example). Symptoms of possible breast cancer include a lump or swelling of the breast, skin dimpling or puckering, nipple retraction (turning inward), redness or scaling of the nipple or breast skin, and discharge from the nipple. Diagnosis involves clinical breast examination, mammography, ultrasound, nipple discharge examination, and biopsy. Male breast cancer is treated with surgery, radiation therapy, and chemotherapy. The survival rate is very high following early-stage detection and are about the same for both men and women when looking at each stage of breast cancer (American Cancer Society, 2014.13n).

Anal Cancer in Men and Women

Anal cancer is fairly uncommon, although the number of cases has been increasing for many years. The American Cancer Society (2014.13o) estimated that about 7,270 new cases of anal cancer will be diagnosed in 2015, with about 1,010 deaths. Women get anal cancer slightly more often than men. Most anal cancer may be due to high prevalence of HPV infection. In fact, women with a history of cervical or precervical cancer have an increased risk of anal cancer. Additionally, risk factors include having numerous lifetime sex partners, history of receptive anal intercourse particularly under age 30, HIV infection, anal warts, and smoking. Pain in the anal area, change in the diameter of the stool, abnormal discharge from the anus, and swollen lymph glands in the anal or groin areas are the major symptoms of anal cancer. Bleeding occurs in more than half of the cases of anal cancer and is usually the first sign of the disease. The digital rectal examination for prostate cancer will find some cases of rectal cancer. Like many other cancers, surgery, radiation therapy, and chemotherapy are the major treatments for anal cancer (American Cancer Society, 2014.13o). Because the majority of anal cancers are linked to HPV and HIV, condoms will provide some protection against the virus. As previously discussed, vaccines are available to protect against certain HPV infections as well as help prevent anal cancers and precancers in both men and women.

● Additional Sexual Health Issues

In this section, we discuss two disorders of the female reproductive system, toxic shock syndrome and endometriosis, as well as some other sexual health issues.

Toxic Shock Syndrome

Toxic shock syndrome (TSS) is caused by the *Staphylococcus aureus* bacterium, a common agent of infection. This organism is normally present in the body and usually does not pose a threat. Although the earliest cases of TSS involved women who were using tampons, today less than half of the cases are associated with their use. Toxic shock syndrome can also occur with skin infections, burns, and after surgery and can affect children, postmenopausal women, and men ("Toxic shock syndrome," 2012). Women of all ages can get TSS, but those under age 30 are at higher risk because they may not have developed antibodies to the disease. TSS can occur in men—for example, from skin wounds and surgery—but it is uncommon.

It is recommended that all women who use tampons reduce the already low risk by carefully following the directions for insertion, choosing the lowest-absorbing one for their flow, changing the tampon more frequently, and using tampons less regularly ("Toxic shock syndrome," 2012).

TSS can be treated effectively if it is detected. The warning signs are sudden fever (102°F or higher), diarrhea, low blood pressure, a rash that peels after 1–2 weeks, and problems with the function of at least three organs. Additionally, there may be vomiting, fainting or nearly fainting, and muscle aches and headaches. Early detection is critical; otherwise, TSS can be fatal. Women should talk with their health care provider about any new information regarding prevention.

Vulvodynia

One condition that has received little attention from the general public is **vulvodynia,** defined as chronic vulvar pain or discomfort of the vulva ("Vulvodynia," 2013). The specific cause of the pain is unknown; however, it tends to be diagnosed when other causes of vulvar pain, such as infections or skin diseases, are ruled out. Additionally, the condition may be associated with any number of factors, including injury or irritation of the nerves in the pelvic region, elevated levels of inflammatory substances in the vulvar tissue, or pelvic floor muscle weakness or spasm. Though the exact number of women with vulvodynia is unknown, it is estimated that 9–18% of women between the ages of 18 and 64 may experience vulvar pain during their lifetimes (Arnold, Bachmann, Rosen, & Rhoads, 2007). Because many women either do not seek help or are unable to receive answers from their doctors, many are without treatment. However, once diagnosed, a variety of treatment options are available, including topical medications; drug treatments, including pain relievers, antidepressants, or anticonvulsants; biofeedback therapy; physical therapy to strengthen pelvic floor muscles; and surgery to remove the affected skin and tissue in localized vulvodynia.

Endometriosis

Endometriosis is a disease in which tissue that normally grows inside the uterus instead grows outside the uterus ("Endometriosis," 2013). It is one of the most common gynecological diseases, with its primary symptoms including pain and infertility. Most lesions or patches of endometriosis occur in the pelvic cavity, either on or under the ovaries, on the fallopian tubes, behind the uterus, or on the bowels or bladder. Interestingly, the size and location of the lesions are not related to the severity of the pain or its location. Because some women have endometriosis but may not have symptoms or have it diagnosed, it's difficult to know how many actually have the condition. Estimates suggest that 6–10% of women of reproductive age, or 5 million women in the United States, have the disease. Factors that may increase the risk of endometriosis include a relative who has had the disease, menstrual periods that started before age 11, shorter monthly cycles (less than 27 days), and menstrual cycles that are heavy and last more than 7 days.

Symptoms of endometriosis include pain (usually pelvic pain, which can be very intense), very painful cramps or periods, heavy periods, intestinal pain, pain during or after sex, and infertility. Some women do not have symptoms and may not find out they have the disease until they have trouble getting pregnant. It is usually diagnosed by imaging tests (e.g., ultrasound); however, surgery is the only way to be sure of the diagnosis. There is currently no cure for endometriosis, but there are ways to minimize the symptoms caused by the condition, and endometriosis-related fertility often can be treated successfully using hormones and surgery ("Endometriosis," 2013).

Prostatitis

Prostatitis is a frequently painful condition that involves inflammation of the prostate and sometimes the area around the prostate ("Prostatitis," 2014). It is the most common urinary tract problem for men younger than age 50 and the third most common among men older than age 50. There are currently four types of prostatitis, one of which is chronic, two are bacterial, and one is asymptomatic and inflammatory. The factors that affect a man's chance of developing prostatitis differ depending on the type; however, men with nerve damage in the lower urinary tract due to surgery or trauma and men with a history of lower urinary tract infections are more vulnerable to this problem.

Symptoms of prostatitis vary and depend on the cause, but many include frequent and urgent need to urinate and pain or burning when urinating, often accompanied by pelvic, groin, or low-back pain. Prostatitis can be difficult to diagnose because the symptoms often are similar to those of other medical conditions such as bladder infections, bladder cancer, or prostate enlargement. Digital rectal exam and urine, semen, and blood tests are used to diagnose prostatitis. A biopsy may also be taken. Treatment depends on the type of prostatitis and can include anti-inflammatory drugs, antibiotics, and/or pain medications.

A man does not necessarily need to avoid sexual intercourse if he has prostatitis. Prostatitis is usually not made worse by sexual activity, although sometimes men with prostatitis will experience pain during ejaculation or sexual intercourse. If sex is too painful, a man may consider abstaining from sexual activity until the prostatitis symptoms improve (Mayo Clinic, 2014.13a).

● Sexual Orientation and Health

Research specifically focused on sexual orientation did not begin until the 1950s. Then the origins of sexual orientation and the psychological functioning of gay, lesbian, bisexual, and transgendered (GLBT) individuals were the focus of inquiry. During the 1970s, studies of GLBT people as psychologically healthy individuals emerged, and some of the research of the 1980s examined issues related to the development of GLBT individuals across their life span. With the advent of HIV/AIDS occurring in the United States in the 1980s, research priorities shifted to the biology of the disease and preventive means to stop it. Even as this continues, it is apparent that the study of sexual orientations and sexual well-being is relatively new and still emerging.

As discussed elsewhere, the inclusion of sexual orientation in CDC survey data collection finally allows evidence to be submitted that might influence research decisions and funding about special and unique health needs of sexual minorities (Ward, Dahlhamer, Galinsky, & Joestl, 2014). Data reveal significant differences in health-related behaviors, health status, and health care access and utilization among U.S. adults aged 18–64 who identified as straight, gay, lesbian, or bisexual (GLB). Specific health behaviors that show disparities between those who identified as GLB as compared with those who identified as straight included a higher incidence of smoking and alcohol consumption among the GLB population. Additionally, a higher percentage of those who identified as bisexual experienced serious psychological distress in the past 30 days compared with their straight counterparts, while a higher percentage of bisexual women were obese. Regarding health care access, a higher percentage of those who identified as lesbian and bisexual indicated they did not have a usual place to go for medical care, with bisexual adults having the highest rates of failure to obtain needed medical care in the past year due to cost (Ward et al., 2014).

Among these disparities, discrimination causes many GLBT people to avoid seeking medical care, and when they do get treatment, evidence shows that GLBT people are often not treated with the respect or cultural competence that other patients receive and deserve (Human Rights Campaign, 2015). For example, 56% of GLB people and 70% of transgender and gender nonconforming people had at least one of the following experiences when attempting to access health care: being refused needed care; health care professionals refusing to touch them or using excessive precautions; health care professionals using harsh or abusive language; being blamed for their health status; or health care professionals being physically rough or abusive (Lambda Legal, 2010). Among those diagnosed or living with HIV, it is estimated that in 2015 half of all Americans living with HIV will be over the age of 50, yet one of every six new HIV diagnoses is in a person over age 50. In addition to suffering other medical ailments, only half of those older Americans who have HIV are in care, and only a third of them have suppressed viral loads (SAGE, 2013).

Seeking to address these and previously reported disparities between the GLBT and straight populations, the U.S. Department of Health and Human Services' *Healthy People 2020* initiative now includes the goal of improving the health, safety, and well-being of gay, lesbian, bisexual, and transgendered persons. In the meantime, there are still enormous challenges that remain for LBGT communities in accessing quality, nondiscriminatory health care services. These barriers often result in poorer health outcomes and have serious and even catastrophic consequences to both individuals and society.

Final Thoughts

In this chapter, we've explored issues of self-image and body image as they interact with our society's ideas about beauty and sexuality. We've considered the effects of alcohol and certain drugs on our sexuality. We've looked at physical limitations and disabilities and cancer and other health issues. Our intent is to provide you with information in order to help assist you in identifying potential problems and making responsible decisions around your own health and well-being as well as to stimulate your thinking about how society deals with certain aspects of sexual health. We encourage you to learn more about your own body and your own sexual functioning. If things don't seem to work right, if you don't feel well, or if you have questions, consult your physician or other health care practitioner. If you're not satisfied, get a second opinion. Read about health issues that apply to you and the people you're close to. Because we live in our bodies, we need to appreciate and respect them. By taking care of ourselves physically and mentally, we can maximize our pleasures in sexuality and in life.

Summary

Living in Our Bodies: The Quest for Physical Perfection

- *Sexual health* is a state of physical, emotional, mental, and social well-being related to sexuality. As such, it requires us to know, understand, and feel comfortable with our bodies.

- Our society is preoccupied with bodily perfection. As a result, *eating disorders* have become common, especially among young women. Eating disorders reduce a person's health and vigor; are carried out in secrecy; are accompanied by obsessions, depression, anxiety, and guilt; lead to self-absorption and emotional instability; and are characterized by a lack of control.

Alcohol, Drugs, and Sexuality

- Drugs and alcohol are commonly perceived as enhancers of sexuality, although in reality this is rarely the case.

- Researchers are beginning to believe that alcohol use among young people is just one component of an overall risky health behavior pattern—not the cause of sexual risk behavior—and that other factors are powerful causes of risk.

- Some people use alcohol to give themselves permission to be sexual. Some men may use alcohol to justify sexual violence. People under the influence of alcohol or drugs tend to place themselves in risky sexual situations, such as exposing themselves to sexually transmitted infections.

- Substances that purport to increase sexual desire or improve sexual performance are called *aphrodisiacs.* It's important to note that the placebo effect may account for approximately 33% of reported response to an aphrodisiac.

Sexuality and Disability

- A wide range of disabilities and physical limitations can affect sexuality. People with these limitations need support and education so that they can enjoy their full sexual potential. Society as a whole needs to be aware of the concerns of people with disabilities and to allow them the same sexual rights as others have.

- Chronic illnesses such as diabetes, cardiovascular disease, and arthritis pose special problems with regard to sexuality. People with these diseases and their partners can learn what to expect of themselves sexually and how to best cope with their particular conditions.

Sexuality and Cancer

- Cancer in its many forms occurs when cells begin to grow aberrantly. Most cancers form tumors. *Benign tumors* grow slowly and remain localized. *Malignant tumors* can spread throughout the body. When malignant cells are released into the blood or lymph system, they begin to grow away from the original tumor; this process is called *metastasis.*

- Other than cancers of the skin, breast cancer is the most common cancer among women. Although the survival rate is improving, those who survive it may still suffer psychologically. *Mammograms* (low-dose X-ray screenings) are the principal method of detection, though some are challenging its risks versus benefits. Surgical removal of the breast is called *mastectomy;* surgery that removes only the tumor and surrounding lymph nodes is called *lumpectomy.* Radiation and chemotherapy are also used to fight breast cancer.

- *Cervical dysplasia,* or *cervical intraepithelial neoplasia (CIN),* the appearance of certain abnormal cells on the cervix, can be diagnosed by a *Pap test.* It may then be treated by *biopsy,* cauterization, cryosurgery, or other surgery. If untreated, CIN may lead to cervical cancer.

- New cases of ovarian cancer have been slowly decreasing since 1991. Pregnancy, breastfeeding, birth control, tubal ligation, and hysterectomy are considered factors that lower the risk of ovarian cancer.

- Several vaccinations, the most common one known as Gardasil and Gardasil 9, guards against strains of the STI human papillomavirus (HPV) that cause cervical cancer and genital warts and are available for males and females.

- Nearly all cancers of the uterus involve the endometrium, the lining of the uterus. Uterine cancer is treated with surgery (hysterectomy), radiation, or both.

- A *radical hysterectomy* is the surgical removal of the uterus and its ligaments in order to treat some cancers or severe gynecological problems. A hysterectomy is required when cancerous or precancerous growths cannot be treated with less invasive procedures, when noncancerous growths interfere with other organs, when heavy bleeding or severe infection cannot be otherwise controlled, and when severe infection cannot be otherwise controlled.

- Prostate cancer is the most common form of cancer among men, excluding skin cancer. If detected early, it has a high cure rate. It is recommended that men discuss with their doctor the risks and benefits of prostate cancer screening. Surgery, radiation, hormone therapy, and chemotherapy are possible treatments.

- Testicular cancer affects relatively young men with the average age of diagnosis being 33. If caught early, it is curable. Self-examination is recommended by some doctors for early detection.

- Penile cancer affects only 1 in 100,000 men in the United States, with most early-stage cancers being completely cured. Men can develop breast cancer, but this cancer is 100 times more common among women.

- Anal cancer is uncommon, although it has been increasing in both men and women in recent years.

Additional Sexual Health Issues

- *Toxic shock syndrome (TSS)* is a potentially fatal disease caused by the *Staphylococcus aureus* bacterium. The disease is easily cured with antibiotics if caught early.

- *Vulvodynia* is a chronic vulvar pain or discomfort of the vulva. At this time, there is no cure for vulvodynia.

- *Endometriosis* is a disease in which tissue that normally grows inside the uterus instead grows outside the uterus. It is a major cause of infertility. Symptoms include intense pelvic pain and abnormal menstrual bleeding. Treatment depends on a number of factors. Various hormone treatments and types of surgery are employed.

- *Prostatitis* is the inflammation of the prostate gland. Antibiotics and pain medications are the primary treatment for prostatitis. No evidence has been found that prostatitis increases the risk of prostate cancer.

Sexual Orientation and Health

- The inclusion of sexual orientation in CDC survey data collection finally allows evidence to be submitted that might influence research decisions and funding about special health needs of sexual minorities.

- Discrimination causes many LGBT people to avoid seeking medical care, and when they do many are often not treated with respect or cultural competence.

Questions for Discussion

- Is there too much emphasis on body perfection in our society? Have you had friends who took extreme measures to make their body fit the cultural ideal? How have you dealt with pressure to have a certain body?

- How comfortable are you in discussing your sexual and reproductive health with your doctor? If you feel uncomfortable, why do you think you feel that way?

- Do many of your peers use alcohol as a "sexual lubricant," hoping that its use will lead to sexual activity? Do you know of individuals who regret being sexual while under the influence of alcohol? What, in your opinion, is the role of alcohol in dating?

Sex and the Internet

Cancer and Sexuality

The American Cancer Society (ACS) has an extensive website that provides detailed information on prevention of and risk factors for, detection and symptoms of, and treatment for the various cancers, including those of the reproductive system. The impact of cancer of the reproductive structures on sexuality also is discussed. Go to the ACS website (http://www.cancer.org) to research this issue. After getting on the website, select a specific type of cancer, and answer the following questions:

- What are the risk factors for the cancer?

- How can that type of cancer be prevented?

- What are some of the methods used to treat this form of cancer?

- What are the sexuality-related outcomes of the cancer and its treatment?

Suggested Websites

National Breast Cancer Foundation

http://www.nationalbreastcancer.org/

Aims to help women by providing information and help and inspiring hope to those affected by breast cancer.

National Cancer Institute

http://www.cancer.gov/

Supports and disseminates research and information that help expand our understanding of cancer: its screening, causes, treatments, and prevention.

National Coalition for Sexual Health

http://nationalcoalitionforsexualhealth.org/

Aims to improve sexual health and well-being by encouraging conversations about sexual health and promoting high quality sexual health information and health services.

National Eating Disorders Association

http://www.nationaleatingdisorders.org/

Dedicated to providing education, resources, and support to those affected by eating disorders.

Services and Advocacy for Gay, Lesbian, Bisexual, and Transgender Elders (SAGE)

http://sageusa.org/

The country's largest and oldest organization dedicated to improving the lives of lesbian, gay, bisexual, and transgender (LGBT) older adults, including quality-of-life issues related to health and wellness.

Testicular Cancer Resource Center (TCRC)

tcrc.acor.org

Devoted to helping people understand testicular and extragonadal germ cell tumors.

Zero—The End of Prostate Cancer

www.zerocancer.org

Contains information on prostate cancer, outreach, and advocacy.

Suggested Reading

Aggleton, P., & Parker, R. (eds.). (2012). *Routledge Handbook of Sexuality, Health and Rights*. New York: Routledge. Provides an overview of emerging and controversial issues in the field of human sexuality, including sexual health and human rights.

Cash, T. F., & Smolak, L. (eds.). (2011). *Body Image: A Handbook of Science, Practice and Prevention*. New York: Guilford Press. A comprehensive volume of specific topics that address the complexity of body image experiences.

Committee on Lesbian, Gay, Bisexual, and Transgender Health Issues and Research Gaps and Opportunities; Board on the Health of Select Populations. (2011). *The health of lesbian, gay, bisexual, and transgender people: Building a foundation for better understanding*. Washington, DC: Institute of Medicine. Assesses the state of science on the health status of the LGBT populations, identifies research gaps and opportunities, and outlines a research agenda for the National Cancer Institute.

Katz, A. (2009). *Woman, cancer, sex*. Also: *Man, cancer, sex*. (2009). Pittsburgh: Hygenia Press. Both books explain the changes that many women and men with cancer experience and offer practical and compassionate advice on how to handle these changes.

McRuer, R., & Mollow, A. (eds.). (2012). *Sex and Disability*. Durham, NC: Duke University Press. This collection of essays considers how sex and disability come together and how disabled people negotiate sex and sexual identities in an ableist and heteronormative culture.

© Radius Images/Alamy

CHAPTER OUTLINE

"Sometimes my sexual desire gets so low that I will not be intimate with my girlfriend for a few weeks. And then there are times when sexual desire is so high that I can't control myself. Why is this?"

—**19-year-old male**

"My friend has a problem that seems to occur once every few months. He suddenly becomes not able to get erect. It seems like it happens very suddenly."

—**18-year-old male**

"I have not experienced any sexual function difficulties. On the other hand, I have been with my boyfriend for 3 years and I only had two orgasms. I enjoy having sex with him even though I don't have an orgasm every time. Sometimes I'm really into it, but sometimes I'm not. I do sometimes feel like something is wrong, but I do feel it is normal and okay as long as I enjoy it. I guess I may be thinking about it too hard, but like I said, I enjoy it either way."

—**21-year-old female**

"When having a sexual experience with a new partner, I sometimes have a sense of guilt about past relationships. This can make performing in the new situation really difficult."

—**21-year-old male**

"I always had a really low sex drive with past boyfriends. I never understood why until I started dating my current boyfriend. The key is communication! We're open with each other and honest about what we like and dislike. Now my sex drive is through the roof!"

—**20-year-old female**

When sex is good, it's 10% of the relationship. When it is bad, it's 90%.
—Charles Muir

When our innermost desires are revealed and are met by our own loved one with acceptance and validation, the shame dissolves.
—Esther Pevel
(1958–)

THE QUALITY OF OUR SEXUALITY is intimately connected to the quality of our lives and relationships. Because our sexuality is an integral part of ourselves, it reflects our excitement and boredom, intimacy and distance, emotional well-being and distress, and health and illness. As a consequence, our sexual desires and activities ebb and flow. Sometimes, they are highly erotic; other times, they may be boring. Furthermore, many of us who are sexually active may sometimes experience sexual function difficulties or problems, often resulting in disappointment in ourselves, our partners, or both. Studies indicate that many men and women report occasional or frequent lack of desire, problems in arousal or orgasm, and pain during intercourse or noncoital sex. Here are the "real-life" facts that illustrate that not all couple sex matches media portrayals of couples always having great sex (McCarthy & McCarthy, 2003, 2009):

- Less than 50% of happy, sexually satisfied couples described having similar desire, arousal, orgasm, and pleasure during a particular sexual episode.

- For about 25% of the sexual experiences, one partner described the sex as positive, whereas the other considered it as "OK." However, these experiences were good for nourishing the intimacy of the relationship. Sometimes one partner "went along for the ride."

- Fifteen percent of sexual experiences were considered unremarkable even though there were no sexual function problems. If the couple had to do it over again, they probably would have chosen something else to do.

- Five to 15 percent of the sexual experiences were dissatisfying or represented a sexual function problem.

Later in this chapter, we discuss the prevalence and predictions of sexual function difficulties found in five nationally representative studies to illustrate the commonality of sexual problems. The widespread variability in our sexual functioning suggests how "normal" at least occasional sexual difficulties are. Sex therapist Bernie Zilbergeld (1999) writes:

> Sex problems are normal and typical. I know, I know, all of your buddies are functioning perfectly and never have a problem. If you really believe that, I have a nice piece of oceanfront property in Kansas I'd like to talk to you about.

In this chapter, we look at several common sexual function difficulties, their causes, and ways to enhance your sexuality to bring greater pleasure and intimacy.

● Sexual Function Difficulties: Definitions, Types, and Prevalence

Most of the literature concerning sexual difficulties or problems with sexual functioning deals with heterosexual couples; thus, most of the discussion in this chapter reflects that bias. Unfortunately, too little research has been done on the sexual function difficulties of gay, lesbian, bisexual, or transgender individuals and couples (Institute of Medicine, 2011). In general, heterosexual individuals, gay men, and lesbian women seemingly experience similar kinds of sexual function problems, yet further research is needed on sexual function difficulties among varied populations.

Defining Sexual Function Difficulties: Different Perspectives

The line between "normal" sexual functioning and a sexual difficulty or problem is not always clear. Enormous variation exists in levels of sexual desire and forms of expression, and these differences do not necessarily indicate any sexual function difficulty. It can be challenging to determine exactly when something is a sexual function problem, and so we must be careful in defining a particular sexual function difficulty as a problem. Some people have rigid and possibly unrealistic expectations for their own or their partner's sexual expression and may perceive something wrong with their behavior that need not be considered a "sexual function problem." Still, people sometimes experience difficulties in sexual function that are so persistent that they would benefit from sex therapy (Strassburg & Mackaronis, 2014).

Health care providers, including sex therapists, need to be aware of different types of sexual function difficulties that can interfere with sexual satisfaction and intimacy. Therefore, a structure to diagnose and address difficulties can be valuable. However, there has been some debate among sexuality and mental health professionals about which terms accurately describe sexual function problems and how to classify these difficulties (West, Vinikoor, & Zolnoun, 2004). Though categories such as "dysfunction," "disorder," "difficulty," and "problems" have been used, this chapter presents alternate classification models.

The standard medical diagnostic classification of sexual function difficulties is found in the American Psychiatric Association's *Diagnostic and Statistical Manual of Mental Disorders, Fifth Edition* (APA, 2013), which uses the terms "dysfunction" and "disorders." Because the *DSM*'s is the most widely used classification system, the discussion of various sexual function difficulties in the professional literature is largely based on the *DSM* and uses the terms "sexual dysfunction" and "sexual disorders." Thus, the *DSM* terminology is quoted often in this chapter, particularly in the context of the *DSM* categories of sexual dysfunction.

Most of sex is psychological—most of it is between our ears and not between our legs.

—Joy Browne
(1944–)

Couples can experience sexual function difficulties that may lead to dissatisfaction, as well as frustration, with their sex lives.

© KG-Photography/Corbis

An alternative term to "sexual dysfunction" is **sexual function dissatisfaction.** Sexual dissatisfaction is a common outcome of a difficulty in sexual functioning. In contrast to the broad medical focus of the *DSM* term, this term reflects an individual perception. That is, a person or couple can experience some of the *DSM* dysfunctions yet be satisfied with their sex lives. The difficulty in functioning might be considered a "dysfunction" only when the two people are dissatisfied and decide they may have a problem. The "dissatisfaction" concept is a fundamental tenet of the classification system for women's sexual problems of the Working Group for a New View of Women's Sexual Problems (2001). The system begins with a woman-centered definition of sexual function problems as "discontent or dissatisfaction with any emotional, physical, or relational aspects of sexual experience"—a definition that could also be applied to men. Furthermore, according to the World Health Organization's (2010.14a) International Classification of Diseases and Related Health Problems (ICD-10), "sexual dysfunction" includes "the various ways in which an individual is unable to participate in a sexual relationship as he or she would wish."

An advantage of the term "sexual function dissatisfaction" is that it acknowledges sexual scripts as individual and avoids an overarching definition of what is "normal" versus what is dysfunctional (i.e., pathological). Adopting this subjective and personal view might help people be more comfortable with their own sexuality and less likely to feel "sexually flawed." We favor the terms "sexual function difficulties" and "sexual function dissatisfaction" and use them in this chapter whenever possible. However, in citing reports or research related to sexual difficulties, we often utilize the terms used therein.

Two alternate classifications of sexual function difficulties and dissatisfaction, based on medical and feminist models, illustrate different perspectives on the origins and causes of sexual problems: the *DSM-5* and the Working Group for a New View of Women's Sexual Problems.

The *Diagnostic and Statistical Manual of Mental Disorders*

The fifth edition of the APA's *Diagnostic and Statistical Manual of Mental Disorders* (*DSM-5*) (2013) labels sexual function difficulties as disorders and characterizes them according to the four phases of Masters and Johnson's sexual response cycle. The *DSM-5* defines **sexual dysfunction** as "a clinically significant disturbance in a person's ability to respond sexually or to experience sexual pleasure." The *DSM-5* sexual dysfunctions/disorders are presented in Table 1. More specific diagnostic criteria are presented in the discussion of each dysfunction/disorder. Several changes in the categories of sexual dysfunctions were made in the *DSM-5* from the prior edition. Some existing categories were combined and new, gender-specific diagnoses were added. All dysfunctions require the symptoms to be present for at least 6 months (except for dysfunctions caused by substance or medication use) and cause significant distress to the individual. The disorders could occur at any time during sexual activity, meaning that the person could have more than one disorder, as often occurs.

The *DSM-5* states that "sexual response has a requisite biological underpinning, yet it is usually experienced in an intrapersonal, interpersonal, and cultural context." That is, sexual response and function occur as an interaction of

TABLE 1 ● *DSM-5* Sexual Dysfunction/Disorders

Female sexual interest/arousal disorder	Absent/reduced sexual thoughts, fantasies, initiation and receptivity and absent/reduced arousal and pleasure during sexual activity
Male hypoactive sexual desire disorder	Persistence or absence of sexual thoughts, fantasies, and desire for sexual activity
Erectile disorders	Difficulty with erections during partnered sexual activity
Female orgasmic disorders	Difficulty in experiencing orgasms or reduced intensity of orgasms during sexual activity
Premature (early) ejaculation	Experiencing "early" ejaculation following vaginal penetration
Delayed ejaculation	Marked delay in or inability to ejaculate usually during partnered sexual activity
Genito-pelvic pain/penetration disorder	Difficulties related to genital and pelvic pain and vaginal penetration during intercourse
Substance/medication-induced sexual dysfunction	A specific substance presumed to cause the sexual dysfunction

SOURCE: *Diagnostic and Statistical Manual of Mental Disorder, Fifth Edition: (DSM-5).* Arlington, VA: American Psychiatric Association.

biological, sociocultural, and psychological factors, including those related to the sexual partner; the relationship; individual vulnerability, psychological problems, or stressors; culture or religion; and medical issues.

For each sexual dysfunction, the *DSM-5* has subtypes based on the onset of the dysfunction and the context in which it occurs. Lifelong dysfunctions are those sexual problems present from the first sexual experience; acquired patterns develop only after a period of relatively normal functioning. A *generalized pattern of dysfunction* refers to sexual problems that are not limited to certain types of situations, stimulation, or partners. A situational sexual dysfunction is one that occurs only with certain types of situations, stimulation, or partners. In most instances, the dysfunction, whether generalized or situational, occurs during sexual activity with a partner. Acquired and situational dysfunctions typically are more successfully addressed in sex therapy (APA, 2013).

Although the *DSM-5* is the most widely used categorization of sexual disorders, it largely reflects a psychiatric medical model and has been criticized. It generally presents problems only in the heterosexual context, and it focuses on genital events in a linear sequence of desire, arousal, orgasm, and so on (Basson, Wierman, van Lankveld, & Brotto, 2010).

A New View of Women's Sexual Problems   In recent years, more attention has been directed to increasing our understanding of female sexual desire and function difficulties (Basson et al., 2010; Katz-Wise & Hyde, 2014; Wood, Koch, & Mansfield, 2006). The Working Group for a New View of Women's Sexual Problems (2001), a group of clinicians and social scientists, offers a classification system called A New View of Women's Sexual Problems. This system classifies women's sexual function difficulties based on women's needs and sexual realities. The Working Group contends that the widely utilized *DSM* framework for sexual dysfunctions does not adequately address the totality of factors impacting female sexuality—specifically, situational factors. This contention was based on the fourth edition of the *DSM* (APA, 2000). The more recently published *DSM-5* (APA, 2013) stresses that five factors—sexual partner factors; relationship factors; individual vulnerability factors, psychological problems, or stresses; culture and religion factors; and medical factors—must be considered in the assessment and diagnosis of sexual function problems in that they may be relevant to the cause of the problem and/or the treatment of the dysfunction. These factors are nearly similar to the four categories of possible underlying factors of female sexual dissatisfaction identified by the Working Group. Even though the *DSM-5* now addresses nonphysiological aspects of female sexuality and this "new" Working Group perspective was published over a decade ago, the Working Group's contribution remains an important addition to our understanding of female sexual response and pleasure.

The Working Group claims that a physiological framework for sexual dysfunction has shortcomings as applied to women:

- *A false notion of sexual equivalency between men and women.* Early researchers emphasized similarities in men's and women's physiological responses during sexual activities and concluded that their sexual problems must also be similar. The few studies that asked women to describe their own experiences found significant differences.

- *The unacknowledged role of relationships in sexuality.* The Working Group states that the relational aspects of women's sexuality, which are often fundamental to sexual function satisfaction and problems, have not been adequately addressed. It contends that the reduction of "normal sexual functioning" to physiology implies, incorrectly, that sexual dissatisfaction can be treated without considering the relationship in which sex occurs.

- *The leveling of differences among women.* The Working Group contends that women are dissimilar and the varied components of their sexuality do not fit neatly into the categories of desire, arousal, orgasm, and pain.

The Working Group suggests a women-centered definition of sexual function problems "as discontent or dissatisfaction with any emotional, physical, or relational aspect of sexual experience," which may arise in one or more of four categories underlying the dissatisfaction:

- *Sociocultural, political, or economic factors.* These include inadequate sexuality education, lack of access to health services, a perceived inability to meet cultural norms regarding correct or ideal sexuality, inhibitions due to conflict between the sexual norms of the subculture or culture of origin and those of the dominant culture, and a lack of interest, time, or energy due to family and work obligations.

- *Partner and relationship problems.* These include discrepancies in desire for sexual activity or in preferences for various sexual activities, inhibitions about communicating preferences, loss of interest due to conflicts over commonplace issues, and inhibitions due to a partner's health status or sexual problems.

- *Psychological problems.* These include past abuse; problems with attachment, rejection, cooperation, or entitlement; fear of pregnancy and sexually transmitted infections (STIs); and loss of partner or good sexual reputation.

- *Medical factors.* These include numerous local or systemic medical conditions, pregnancy, STIs, and side effects of drugs, medications, and medical treatments, including surgery.

Prevalence and Cofactors

National studies have been conducted on the prevalence of sexual function difficulties and factors related to them. We will briefly describe the major findings of five such studies conducted in Britain, Denmark, Portugal, and the United States.

Looking at the results of these studies will provide an overview of how common and universal certain sexual function difficulties are and the factors related to the problems. The prevalence of sexual function difficulties and their cofactors are generally in the same range from study to study. Differences in prevalence may reflect varied study methodologies, such as how sexual function problems are defined or perceived by the respondent, and variations in the period of time assessed (e.g., the problem may have occurred in the past year, in the past month, or at the last sexual event), which may make it difficult to compare the data from one study to the other. Note that the following studies are cross-sectional, which means it is not possible to determine causality—some of the factors identified in the studies (e.g., sociodemographic factors, relationship difficulties) may have caused the sexual function problems and dissatisfaction, whereas other factors may be a consequence of sexual function problems.

From a nationally representative study, called the third National Survey of Sexual Attitudes and Lifestyle (Natsal-3), 4,913 men and 6,777 women aged 16–74 years who lived in Britain (England, Scotland, and Wales) and who were sexually active in the past year were interviewed concerning their sexual function (Mitchell et al., 2013). "Sexually active" was defined as vaginal, oral, or anal intercourse with an other-sex or same-sex partner or partners. A major strength of this study was that it defined partners as either other-sex or same-sex and its assessment of factors related to sexual problems. Figure 1 presents the percentage of individual sexual function problems and dissatisfaction lasting 3 months or more in the past year by gender and age group. Sexual response problems persisting at least 3 months in the preceding year were common, even among the younger study participants. More than 40% of men and 50% of women reported one or more problems. For men, the most frequently reported problems were lack of interest in sex (15%), reaching climax more quickly than desired (15%), and difficulty in getting or keeping an erection (13%). For women, the most commonly reported problems were lack of interest in sex (34%), difficulty in reaching climax (16%), an uncomfortably dry vagina (13%), and lack of enjoyment (12%). As shown in Figure 1, for the youngest participants (16–24 years) the most commonly reported problem for men was reaching climax too soon (17%) and for women it was lacking sex interest (25%) and difficulty reaching climax (21%). Despite these difficulties, only 10% of both men and women reported distress about their sex lives (defined as sexual thoughts, sexual feelings, sexual activity, and sexual relationships). The most frequently reported issue within relationships was an imbalance in level of sexual interest between partners. The study found that low sexual function was associated with several factors:

- Increased age
- Depression
- Self-reported poor health status
- Experiencing the end of a relationship
- Inability to talk easily about sex with a partner
- Not being happy in the relationship
- Engaging in fewer than four sexual episodes in the past 4 weeks
- Having had same-sex partners
- Paying for sex (men only)
- Higher number of lifetime sexual partners (women only)
- Negative sexual health outcomes such as experience of nonvoluntary sex

• FIGURE 1

Percentage of Sexually Active Men and Women in Britain, Aged 16–74; Reporting Selected Sexual Problems Lasting 3 Months or More in the Past Year.

(*Source:* Adapted from Mitchell et al., 2013.)

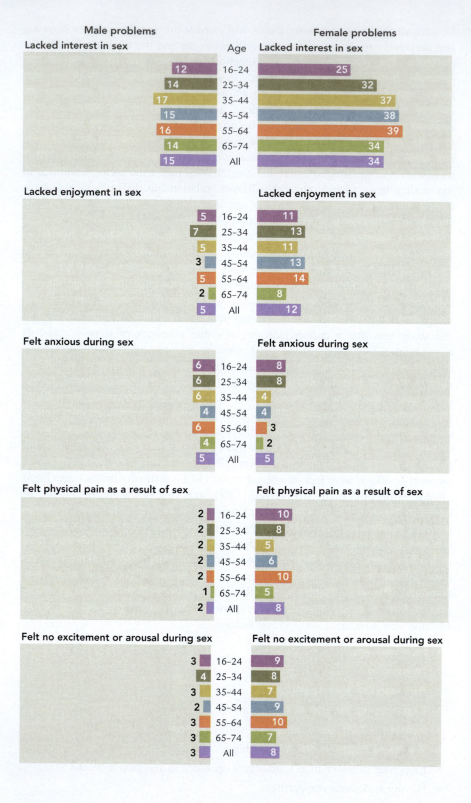

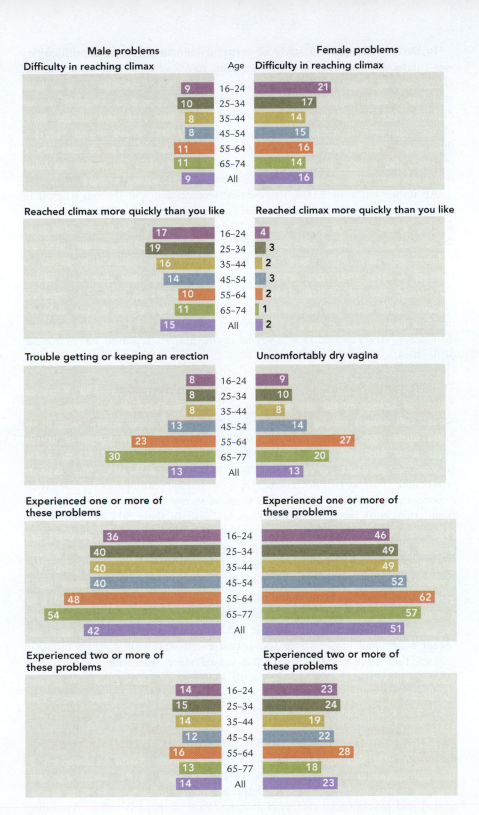

Male problems

Difficulty in reaching climax

Age	
16–24	9
25–34	10
35–44	8
45–54	8
55–64	11
65–74	11
All	9

Reached climax more quickly than you like

Age	
16–24	17
25–34	19
35–44	16
45–54	14
55–64	10
65–74	11
All	15

Trouble getting or keeping an erection

Age	
16–24	8
25–34	8
35–44	8
45–54	13
55–64	23
65–77	30
All	13

Experienced one or more of these problems

Age	
16–24	36
25–34	40
35–44	40
45–54	40
55–64	48
65–77	54
All	42

Experienced two or more of these problems

Age	
16–24	14
25–34	15
35–44	14
45–54	12
55–64	16
65–77	13
All	14

Female problems

Difficulty in reaching climax

Age	
16–24	21
25–34	17
35–44	14
45–54	15
55–64	16
65–74	14
All	16

Reached climax more quickly than you like

Age	
16–24	4
25–34	3
35–44	2
45–54	3
55–64	2
65–74	1
All	2

Uncomfortably dry vagina

Age	
16–24	9
25–34	10
35–44	8
45–54	14
55–64	27
65–77	20
All	13

Experienced one or more of these problems

Age	
16–24	46
25–34	49
35–44	49
45–54	52
55–64	62
65–77	57
All	51

Experienced two or more of these problems

Age	
16–24	23
25–34	24
35–44	19
45–54	22
55–64	28
65–77	18
All	23

In Denmark in 2005, a study of sexual dysfunction and sexual difficulties was conducted examining 4,415 Danes aged 16–95 years as part of the Danish Health and Morbidity Program (Christensen et al., 2011). Overall, 11% of both men and women reported at least one sexual dysfunction (a frequent sexual difficulty that was perceived as a problem) in the past year, and another 68% of men and 69% of women reported infrequent or less severe sexual function difficulties. The highest prevalence of sexual dysfunctions was in men above 60 years and women below 30 years or above 50. Further, economic hardship was associated with sexual dysfunctions, particularly among women.

An online study of 1,009 heterosexual women and 390 lesbian women in Portugal assessed self-perceived sexual function problems and their associated distress levels over the past 6 months (Peixoto & Nobre, 2014). To determine the prevalence of sexual difficulties and dissatisfaction, the researchers selected a novel approach: They chose only those women who reported moderate to extreme distress from their sexual problem. Using this data analysis control, they found that for lesbian women, 10% reported sexual pain, 7% reported orgasmic difficulties and lack of desire, and 6% reported sexual arousal difficulties. For heterosexual women, 13% reported sexual pain, 12% reported orgasmic difficulties, 10% reported lack of sexual desire, and 9% reported sexual arousal difficulties.

The National Survey of Sexual Health and Behavior The National Survey of Sexual Health and Behavior (NSSHB) assessed several measures of sexual functioning among a random sample in the United States. Data from 3,900 adults aged 18–59 years who reported about their last partnered sexual event were analyzed. Participants were asked to evaluate that sexual event relative to pleasure, arousal, erection/lubrication difficulty, and orgasm (Herbenick et al., 2010.14a). The degree to which the participants reported their experiences for each of the five measures is shown in Figure 2. The NSSHB found that most men and women—even those in their 50s—evaluated the experience of their last sexual event as high on a scale measuring pleasure and arousal. For men, age was associated with greater erection difficulties, greater pain during sexual activity, and less likelihood of experiencing orgasm. For women, older age was associated with more problems with lubrication and a greater likelihood of experiencing orgasm. The study also found that men with a relationship partner reported greater arousal, greater pleasure, more frequent orgasm, fewer problems with erectile function, and less pain during their last sexual event than those whose last sexual event was with a nonrelationship partner. For women, those whose last sexual event was with a relationship partner reported greater problems with arousal and lubrication yet greater likelihood of their partner experiencing orgasm than women whose last sexual event was with a nonrelationship partner.

The National Health and Social Life Survey: Sexual Dysfunction Findings The National Health and Social Life Survey (NHSLS), using a U.S. national sample of 1,749 women and 1,410 men aged 18–59, found that self-reported sexual dysfunctions are widespread and are influenced by both health-related and psychosocial factors (Laumann, Paik, & Rosen, 1999). According to the NHSLS, sexual dysfunctions were more prevalent among women (43%) than men (31%) and were generally most common among young women and older men (Figure 3). Sexual dysfunctions were associated with poor quality of

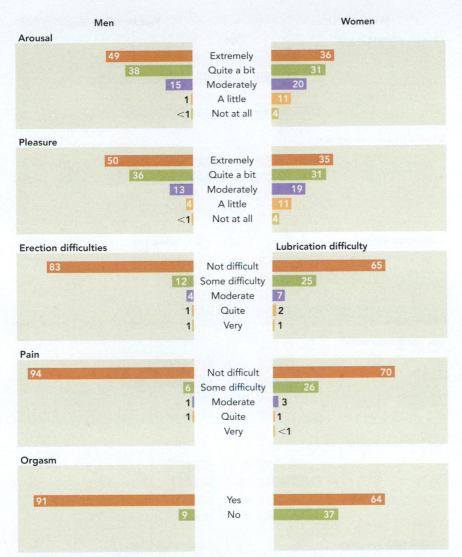

Men | | Women
Arousal

49	Extremely	36
38	Quite a bit	31
15	Moderately	20
1	A little	11
<1	Not at all	4

Pleasure

50	Extremely	35
36	Quite a bit	31
13	Moderately	19
4	A little	11
<1	Not at all	4

Erection difficulties | | Lubrication difficulty

83	Not difficult	65
12	Some difficulty	25
4	Moderate	7
1	Quite	2
1	Very	1

Pain | |

94	Not difficult	70
6	Some difficulty	26
1	Moderate	3
1	Quite	1
	Very	<1

Orgasm

91	Yes	64
9	No	37

Note: Percents are rounded; hence, the total may exceed 100%.

• FIGURE 2

Percentage of Self-Reported Sexual Functioning at Most Recent Partnered Sexual Event Among U.S. Adults Aged 18–59, 2009.

(*Source:* Adapted from Herbenick et al., 2010.14a.)

life (i.e., lower emotional satisfaction and happiness), although females appeared to be impacted by this factor more than males. Those who experienced emotional or stress-related problems had more difficulties.

Disorders of Sexual Desire

The number-one sexual function problem of American couples is inhibited sexual desire. Discrepancies in sexual desire, discussed in the "Practically Speaking" box "Sexual Desire: When Appetites Differ" is the most common complaint that leads couples to sex therapy. More than one half of married couples experience inhibited sexual desire or desire discrepancy at some time in their marriage. Inhibited sexual desire causes more stress in a marriage than any other sexual function problem (McCarthy & McCarthy, 2003; Northrup, Schwartz, & Witte, 2012).

Defining low desire is tricky, often subjective, as there is no norm level of sexual desire; further, any such definition is often based on an assumption that there is an optimal level of sexual desire (Hall, 2004; van Lankveld, 2013).

Sexual desire is a fragile, mysterious appetite.

—Michael Castleman
(1950–)

• FIGURE 3

Percentage of Self-Reported Sexual Function Difficulties in the Past 12 Months Among U.S. Adults Aged 18–59, by Gender and Age.

(*Source:* Adapted from Laumann et al., 1999.)

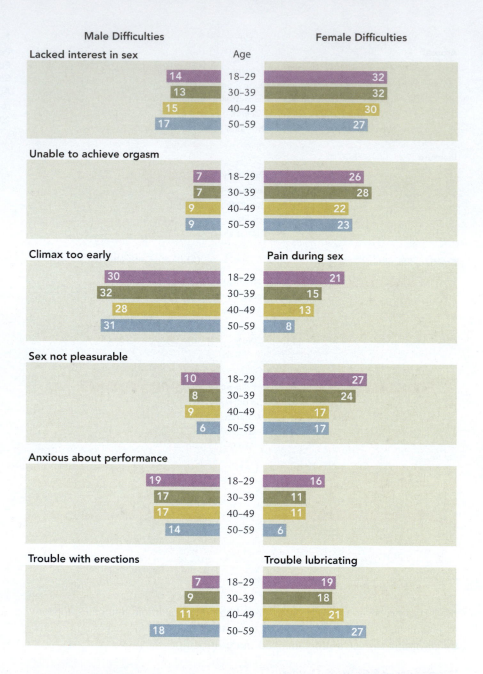

Male Difficulties / **Female Difficulties**

Lacked interest in sex

		Male	Age	Female
		14	18–29	32
		13	30–39	32
		15	40–49	30
		17	50–59	27

Unable to achieve orgasm

Male	Age	Female
7	18–29	26
7	30–39	28
9	40–49	22
9	50–59	23

Climax too early / Pain during sex

Male	Age	Female
30	18–29	21
32	30–39	15
28	40–49	13
31	50–59	8

Sex not pleasurable

Male	Age	Female
10	18–29	27
8	30–39	24
9	40–49	17
6	50–59	17

Anxious about performance

Male	Age	Female
19	18–29	16
17	30–39	11
17	40–49	11
14	50–59	6

Trouble with erections / Trouble lubricating

Male	Age	Female
7	18–29	19
9	30–39	18
11	40–49	21
18	50–59	27

If you have a comfortable compatible love without sexual sparks, you don't have enough. If you have sexual heat but not friendship, you don't have enough. Neither lust nor love by itself is enough. You have to have passion.

—Carol Cassell
(1936–)

Certainly, sexually "normal" people vary considerably in their sexual interests, fantasies, and desires and occasionally experience a lack of desire (see Figures 1 and 3). Research has found that men reported more sexual desire than women. Persons in a same-sex relationship reported a slightly higher sexual desire than those in other-sex relationships (Holmberg & Blair, 2009; Laumann, Paik, & Rosen, 1999; Michell et al., 2013). Low sexual desire is most often acquired; that is, the person felt sexual previously but no longer experiences desire. The good news: It is often transitory. People with lower sexual desire often reluctantly participate in sex when it is initiated by a partner. A study of 63 persons aged 18–24 in a committed heterosexual relationship found that 17% of all sexual activity was rated as compliant/obliging with no difference between men and women being compliant (Vannier & O'Sullivan, 2010). Most often, lower sexual desire develops in adulthood in association with psychological distress resulting from depression, stressful life events, or interpersonal difficulties. The loss of desire, whether ongoing or situational, can negatively affect a relationship (APA, 2013; Brotto & Smith, 2014). Anger within a relationship can also diminish sexual desire. Over time, if the anger is not resolved, it may develop into resentment or hatred that colors every aspect of the relationship. Most people cannot experience sexual desire for someone with whom they are angry or whom they deeply resent. Drugs, hormone deficiency, and illness can also decrease desire.

One should note that beyond any individual, situational, or relationship factors that can result in low sexual desire, sexual desire declines for most people through time. For example, a Finnish study of 2,650 adults found that feelings of sexual desire decreased as the individual aged (Figure 4) and as a relationship continued through the years (Figure 5) (Kontula, 2009; Kontula & Haavio-Mannila, 2009).

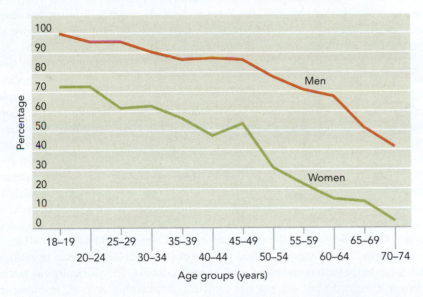

● **FIGURE 4**

Percentage of Finnish Adults Who Indicated That They Feel Sexual Desire at Least a Few Times a Week.

(*Source:* Kontula, 2009.)

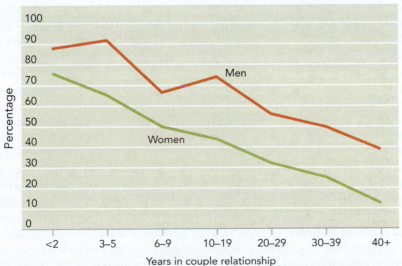

● **FIGURE 5**

Percentage of Finnish Adults Who Indicated That If They Could Choose Freely They Would Like to Have Intercourse at Least Twice a Week.

(*Source:* Kontula, 2009.)

Gay men and lesbian women may experience lower sexual desire for a number of reasons, one of which could be that they are having difficulty with their sexual orientation (Margolies, Becher, & Jackson-Brewer, 1988; Reece, 1988).

Two female sexual function disorders listed in prior *DSM* editions—hyposexual desire disorder and female sexual arousal disorder—were combined in the *DSM-5* into a single diagnosis, **female sexual interest/arousal disorder** (APA, 2013). For a diagnosis of this disorder, at least half of six disorders must occur that deal with absent/reduced interest in sexual activity, sexual/erotic thoughts or fantasies, sexual excitement/pleasure during sexual activity (75–100% of the times), sexual interest/arousal in response to sexual cues, and genital or body sensations during sexual activity (75–100% of the times) and no/reduced initiation of sexual activity or being unreceptive of partner's initiation. Further, the indicators must occur for at least 6 months and cause significant individual distress. The *DSM-5* states that sexual desire and arousal frequently coexist and often simultaneously characterize the complaints of women experiencing this disorder. Desire discrepancy within a partner relationship in which a women has a lower sexual desire does not meet the criteria for this disorder, nor does common short-term changes in sexual interest or arousal that may be adaptive to events in a woman's life, such as having a child or the stress of unpaid bills.

The lack of sexual pleasure is a common complaint of women with low sexual desire. This disorder is frequently associated with problems experiencing orgasm, pain during sexual activity, low frequency of sexual activity, and couple discrepancies in desire. Unrealistic expectations and norms regarding the "normal or appropriate" level of sexual interest or arousal, poor sexual techniques, relationship problems, lack of accurate information, and mood disorders are also associated with this disorder (APA, 2013). A study of 741 women of mean age 48 years verified many of these associations. This study found that sexual desire was lower among older, postmenopausal women; those being in the current relationship for a long time; and those whose partner experienced a sexual dysfunction, suggesting that a sexual difficulty in one partner is likely associated with sexual difficulties in the other partner (McCabe & Goldhammer, 2012).

The term "frigid" was once used to describe this problem, but this pejorative and value-laden term is no longer used by professionals. This difficulty can occur when a woman desires sex but has difficulty maintaining arousal, resulting in vaginal dryness and tightness and subsequent discomfort if intercourse is attempted. Thirty-five percent of women in the NSSHB reported at least some difficulty with lubrication (see Figure 2), a problem shown to increase with age (see Figure 3). Female sexual arousal disorders are often accompanied by sexual desire and orgasm disorders, as well as sexual avoidance and stress in sexual relationships. If there are no physiological or substance use reasons for poor lubrication, this disorder is diagnosed as psychological in origin (APA, 2000). However, the lack of vaginal lubrication may be misleading, as some women reporting dryness indicate the presence of sexual excitement and arousal. These women often use supplemental lubricants. Further, some women report their clitoris engorged and their vagina lubricated but they did not feel psychologically aroused. Given these experiences, many sex therapists believe that sexual arousal is much more of a psychological process in women than in men (Keesling, 2006).

Also new to the *DSM-5* is a separate disorder for men, **male hypoactive sexual desire disorder,** defined as both low/absent desire for sexual activity and deficient/absent sex-related thoughts or fantasies that persist for a minimum duration of 6 months and cause significant individual distress (APA, 2013). Male hypoactive sexual desire disorder may be associated with erectile and/or ejaculatory difficulties. Men with this disorder may not initiate partnered sexual activity and are minimally responsive to partner initiation of sex. Desire discrepancy within a partner relationship in which the man has a lower sexual desire does not meet the criteria for this disorder. The *DSM-5* states that there is a normative decline in sexual desire as men age and that mental health, alcohol use, self-directed homophobia in gay men, interpersonal and relational problems, lack of healthy attitudes and lack of accurate knowledge, and trauma from early life experiences may account for low desire.

The repeated inability to obtain and maintain erections during partnered sexual activities is called **erectile disorder** by the *DSM-5* (APA, 2013). The problem must have been present for at least 6 months, must occur in the majority of occasions, and must cause significant personal distress (i.e., at least 75% of the time). Many men experiencing erection difficulties may have low self-esteem, low self-confidence, decreased sexual satisfaction, reduced sexual desire, and a decreased sense of masculinity. Acquired erectile disorder is likely to continue in most men. According to the *DSM-5*, about 20% of men fear erection difficulties on their first sexual episode, with about 8% reporting problems that hindered penetration during their first sexual episode.

At one time, this disorder was called "impotence," but like "frigid," this value-laden and pejorative term is no longer used. This very common male sexual difficulty was treated primarily by therapists before the introduction of Viagra and other prescription erection-enhancing drugs. Sexual anxiety, fear of failure, high performance standards, concerns about sexual performance, and low sexual desire and excitement, as well as specific medical conditions and medications, are often associated with erectile disorder (APA, 2000, 2013; Hall, Shackelton, Rosen, & Araujo, 2010).

Eighteen percent of the men in the NSSHB reported at least some difficulty with erections during their most recent partnered sexual event (see Figure 3). The prevalence of erectile disorder increases with age, with more than twice as many men 50–59 reporting problems with erections as men 18–29 in the NHSLS (see Figure 3) and with nearly four times as many men aged 65–77 reporting problems with erection as men aged 16–44 in the Natsal-3 (see Figure 1). However, it is important to note that, like female arousal disorders, male erectile disorders are not an inevitable consequence of aging. But the health problems that often accompany aging increase the disorder's prevalence. The prevalence of erectile difficulty has been directly correlated with certain diseases, such as hypertension, diabetes mellitus, and heart disease; certain medications, such as cardiac drugs and antihypertensives; cigarette smoking in association with treated heart disease and treated hypertension; excessive alcohol consumption; suppression and expression of anger; obesity; and depression (Bancroft, 2009; Nusbaum, 2002).

The diagnosis of erectile disorder is usually psychologically based. Men who have erections while sleeping or masturbating obviously are physically able to have erections, meaning that an erectile disorder during two-person sexual activity has a psychological origin. As with the other sexual dysfunctions, erectile disorder is a diagnosable problem in the *DSM-5* only when the man or his partner is dissatisfied and distressed by the occurrence (Schwartz, 2000).

Sex therapist and author Barbara Keesling (2006) gives some cautions relative to expectations of erections. She notes that men's concept of an adequate erection varies considerably from person to person, and that a man does not necessarily have an erection problem if he doesn't have reflex or spontaneous

Thou treacherous, base deserter of my flame,
False to my passion, fatal to my fame,
Through what mistaken magic dost thou prove
So true to lewdness, so untrue to love?

—John Wilmot, Earl of Rochester
(1647–1680)

Sexual Desire: When Appetites Differ

Surprising how the most common sexual problem is not low libido, rapid ejaculation, or difficulty with orgasm: it is that people are not prepared for the extent of individual differences in human sexuality.

—Sandra Pertot
(1950–)

How much sexual desire is "normal" and what can couples do when one partner has more—or less—desire than the other? Sex therapist and clinical psychologist David Schnarch (2002) observes:

> Couples frequently argue about low desire, but their real issue is *difference* in desires. Neither partner's desire need be particularly low or high. Disparity in sexual desire is couples' most common sexual complaint.

For most long-term relationships, sexual passion subsides, but not always at the same rate for each partner. Differences in sexual desire may impact the couple relationship. For example, one study of 1,054 married couples found that higher individual sexual desire discrepancies among married persons may erode the well-being of the relationship. In this study, husbands were more likely than wives to report large discrepancies between desired and actual frequency of sexual contact with their spouse (Willoughby, Farero, & Busby, 2014). Most sex therapists believe that differences arise because, for example, one or both partners may be fatigued, ill, under the influence of alcohol or other drugs, or consumed with the tasks of daily living. Or there may be problems with the sexual relationship of the couple, such as anger or imbalance of power between the partners.

Clinical psychologist and sex therapist Sandra Pertot, in her book *When Your Sex Drives Don't Match* (2007), presents another perspective on why couples experience variation in sexual desire. She contends that the sexual issues, including very common desire discrepancies, typically do not represent individual pathology or relationship problems but, instead, reflect the fact that there are different sexual types, which she labels "libido types," such as sensual, erotic, stressed, detached, and disinterested. Interestingly, she states that "people are different just because they are, not because there is anything wrong with them" and encourages an acceptance of different libido types as one way to minimize misinterpreting each other's sexuality.

Michael Castleman (2004), an award-winning medical writer, notes in his book *Great Sex: A Man's Guide to the Secret Principles of Total-Body Sex* that the partner who desires more sex often may experience an array of feelings; such as rejection, confusion, and anger, may feel unloved and unattractive; and may be labeled a "sex fiend." The person who wants more sex may stop initiating sex just to see how long it will take his or her partner to ask for it; often this takes a long time, making the high-desire partner even more frustrated or angry. The partner with the lower-desire may feel guilty, confused, and resentful of perceived constant demands for sex and may believe that the other partner doesn't love him or her but just wants sex. Castleman notes that "as goodwill erodes, it becomes harder to ask about sex. Couples often slip into two modes: bickering and silence." He continues by noting that both partners may have more power than they realize—the power to drive each other crazy. Another unfortunate outcome of persistent desire differences may be the decline in nonsexual affection: Holding hands, hugging, or cuddling on the sofa, for example, often becomes more infrequent.

Castleman notes that there is no magic formula for resolving sexual desire differences, but here are some suggestions he offers for dealing with libido differences in couples:

- *Count your blessings.* The higher-desire partner may want sex more often than the lower-desire partner. But at least the lower-desire person wants sex sometimes. Isn't some sex better than none? Because differences in sexual desire occur in most long-term relationships, adapting to the change is the key.

- *Don't try to change your partner's libido.* In a couple with desire differences, each partner may hope that the other person will change and acquire a compatible level of desire. But it is difficult for a person to do that. Sexual desire can change, but this must come from within the person.

- *Consider your choices and negotiate.* A couple having chronic difficulties with sexual desire has three choices: (1) break up, (2) do nothing and live in misery, or (3) negotiate a mutually agreed compromise. Couples wanting to live comfortably with each other have no choice other than to compromise by being flexible, showing good faith, and being willing to invest in the happiness of the relationship.

- *Schedule sex dates.* Certainly there is some excitement when sex occurs spontaneously. But scheduling has an advantage of eliminating sexual uncertainty for couples facing major desire differences. Both partners know when sex will occur: The higher-desire person then may not make as many sexual advances, and the lower-desire person will not have to experience repeated requests.

- *Cultivate nonsexual affection.* Once sex dates are scheduled, nonsexual affection has less chance of being misconstrued as having sexual expectations. Being held and touched is one of the most important ways to nurture a relationship, and knowing that it has no sexual connotations may provide a great relief.

- *Savor your solution.* Once a couple negotiates a mutual compromise, the relationship often improves and resentments slowly fade. The lower-desire person may become more comfortable, which often improves that person's responsiveness. There may still be some desire differences; the ability to compromise means that the couple has found a workable solution for their relationship.

Because fluctuations in individual sexual desire are a normal part of life, as are differences in desire between partners, individuals may choose masturbation as an acceptable and pleasurable outlet for sexual desire. As is true for all areas of sexual functioning, the important thing to remember, when sexual appetites differ, is that communicating openly and honestly and appreciating what a person brings to the relationship pave the way to resolution and fulfillment. Cultivating sexuality by planning for sex, using one's imagination, learning to be playful, recognizing your partner's mystery, and respecting his or her privacy can all increase desire. If given sufficient attention, desire often returns (Perel, 2006; Pertot, 2007).

erections from viewing a partner's body, for example. Many men, even young men, almost always need direct stimulation to have an erection. Also, she says that "it's probably also unrealistic to expect that your erection will maintain the same level of rigidity throughout the course of a sexual encounter." During any particular sexual encounter, a man's erection can vacillate between several levels of rigidity depending on the amount of stimulation.

Another sexual function difficulty related to desire is called **sexual aversion disorder,** the aversion to any form of partnered sexual activity. This problem is considered to be uncommon and was dropped from the *DSM-5,* since clinicians rarely used this diagnostic category (Brotto, 2010; Lehmiller, 2014). However, we have chosen to include a discussion of this problem, given that this type of behavior does occur and represents a serious issue to those who experience it.

For those experiencing sexual aversion, the possibility of sexual contact may cause anxiety, disgust, or fear, and some sufferers create covert strategies (e.g., traveling, sleeping, or being heavily involved with work) to avoid sex (APA, 2000). A mere kiss, touch, or caress may cause a phobic response out of fear that it might lead to something sexual. Sometimes, these responses are internalized; other times, they can lead to panic attacks and physiological responses such as sweating, nausea, vomiting, and diarrhea. For people with this disorder, the frequency of sexual contact with a partner is rare and can lead to severe relationship stress. Sexual aversion often results from severely negative parental attitudes during childhood; sexual trauma, such as rape or sexual abuse, especially in women; consistent sexual pressure from a long-term partner; a history of erectile difficulties in men; and/or gender identity confusion.

Barry McCarthy and Emily McCarthy, in their book *Rekindling Desire: A Step-by-Step Program to Help Low-Sex and No-Sex Marriages* (2003), write about what they call "no-sex marriages," the extreme of desire problems that they define as having sex less than 10 times a year. They state that couples in a no-sex marriage experience a cycle of anticipatory anxiety, negative experiences, and eventually avoidance of sex—a cycle that they did not plan for in their marriage. According to the McCarthys, about one in five marriages is a no-sex marriage. The longer the couple avoids sexual contact, the more difficult it is to

Is Intercourse Enough? The Big "O" and Sexual Behaviors

Many of us measure both our sexuality and ourselves in terms of orgasm: Did we have one? Did our partner have one? If so, was it good? Did we have simultaneous orgasms? Did it occur through oral sex, vaginal or anal intercourse, or a combination of these and other means? The questions go on. It's obvious to most people that orgasms are an erotic and intimate component of most relationships.

As we look at our sexuality, we can see some pressure to be successful lovers. Men talk of performance anxiety. Both men and women tend to evaluate a woman's sexual self-worth in terms of her being orgasmic. For men, the significant question about women's sexuality has shifted from "Is she a virgin?" to "Is she orgasmic?" While these questions will continue to trouble some, a more significant question arises between men and women: In sexual encounters, is penile-vaginal intercourse sufficient to stimulate orgasm? Scholars are quick to acknowledge, "That depends." Personal and relationship factors, anxiety and shame about one's sexuality, trust, sleep, stress, comfort with one's body, and the type of sexual stimulation received, to name a few, all play important roles in sexual satisfaction, including orgasm.

Because male orgasm is closely tied to reproduction, evolutionary scientists have never had difficulty explaining it; it ensures reproduction. In the same vein, scientists have for decades searched for an evolutionary function for female orgasm but have not been as successful. Possibly, one effect of orgasm is to increase a suction in the uterus to draw up ejaculated semen, thereby increasing the retention of sperm (Komisaruk, Whipple, Nasserzadeh, & Beyer-Flores, 2010). Since women can have sexual intercourse and become pregnant without experiencing orgasm, perhaps there is no evolutionary function for orgasm (Lloyd, 2005). However, as philosopher and professor Elisabeth Lloyd acknowledges, evolution does not dictate what is culturally important.

Data from a national study help answer the question of whether one aspect, vaginal intercourse between heterosexual couples, is enough or if other sexual behaviors are necessary for men and women to experience orgasm during partnered sex. The National Survey of Sexual Health and Behavior (NSSHB) assessed sexual behaviors during the most recent partnered event of a probability sample of 3,990 U.S. adults aged 18–59

(Herbenick et al., 2010.14a). The NSSHB found that during the most recent sexual event:

- A wide variety of sexual behaviors occur during any sexual behavior. Of these, 33% of men and 39% of women reported having engaged solely in penile-vaginal intercourse.

- Men reported that they had an orgasm more frequently if the sexual event included penile-vaginal intercourse.

- Women reported that they were more likely to have had an orgasm if they gave or received oral sex, had penile-vaginal sex, or received anal sex.

- Both men and women were more likely to experience orgasm if they engaged in a wider array of sexual behaviors.

Another study, the Australian Study of Health and Relationships, also assessed behaviors during the participants' most recent sexual encounter (Richters, de Visser, Rissel, & Smith, 2006). In a representative sample of 5,111 Australians aged 15–59, the researchers found that of the 95% of men and women reporting having vaginal intercourse:

- About 8 in 10 reported manual stimulation of the woman by the man.

- About 7 in 10 reported manual stimulation of the man by the woman.

- About one quarter reported cunnilingus and fellatio.

- Less than 1 in 10 reported anal intercourse.

- Almost all men (95%) experienced orgasm in encounters that included vaginal intercourse, whereas orgasm for women was less likely (50%) among those who reported having only vaginal intercourse.

- For women, the rate of orgasm (70%) was higher among those reporting intercourse plus receiving manual stimulation or intercourse plus cunnilingus, although orgasm did not necessarily occur during these practices. Orgasm was even more likely for those who had vaginal intercourse and had received both manual and oral stimulation.

The researchers cautioned that we should not assume that everyone having a sexual encounter wants to experience an orgasm; that is, not everyone needs to have an orgasm to be physically and emotionally satisfied. They note that a woman may have an intercourse-only encounter (a "quickie" or "freebie") with her male partner to oblige the man. Further, some nonintercourse events may be a man obliging the woman; that is, the man might provide manual and oral stimulation of the woman, although he is not interested in experiencing orgasm himself. Likewise, for some, tenderness, intimacy, and affection may be more important determinants of intimacy and gratification than having an orgasm.

While the question "Was it good for you?" may initiate a dialogue, the statement "Orgasm is good for us" acknowledges a fact. Though it's apparent that orgasm feels good, some of us may not recognize that orgasm is indeed good *for* our health. Sexual activity not only burns quite a few calories and boosts the metabolism but also improves immune function, helps you sleep better, and relieves menstrual cramps and stress. In fact, substantial connections between women's sexual satisfaction and all three aspects of their well-being (relational, mental, and physical) have been reported (Holmberg, Blair, & Phillips, 2010).

The idea that women fake orgasm is familiar, probably because there is considerable pressure on them to do so. What is less well known is that some men also pretend orgasm. Research on pretending orgasm can provide interesting insights into sexual scripts and their functions and meanings for both sexes. Professor Sandra Caron (2013) found that 28% of college men and 69% of college women at one U.S. university reported faking orgasm, saying they weren't just doing it—they were performing it. Frequently reported reasons for pretending orgasm (reported by both sexes) were that orgasm was

unlikely, they wanted sexual activity to end, and they wanted to avoid negative consequences (hurting their partner's feelings) and obtain positive ones (pleasuring their partners) (Muehlenhard & Shippee, 2009).

When we measure our sexuality by orgasm only, we discount activities that do not necessarily lead to orgasm such as touching, caressing, and kissing. In other words, we may ignore erotic pleasure as an end in itself. Still, the question about intercourse—"Is it enough?"—troubles many. Part of the joy of sexuality is to listen, learn, and acknowledge the multitude of factors that contribute to fun and meaningful sexual expression, which may or may not include orgasm.

Think Critically

1. How important is experiencing orgasm? Does this vary by sex? age?
2. Are you interested in providing sexual stimulation other than intercourse? Are you (or would you be) comfortable and willing to request or introduce a variety of sexual behaviors into your relationship?
3. Can a person experience physical satisfaction and not experience an orgasm during sex? Do women and men feel the same way about this?
4. If you are sexually active, have you ever faked an orgasm? Why or why not?

break the cycle and the more they blame each other. Further, the more shameful they feel, the harder it is to break the cycle. The McCarthys note, however, that motivated couples can reestablish desire through self-help and therapy.

As with heterosexuals, gay men and lesbian women may enjoy certain activities, such as kissing or mutual masturbation, but feel aversion to other activities. For gay men, sexual aversion often focuses on issues of anal eroticism (Reece, 1988; Sandfort & de Keizer, 2001). For lesbian women, it may focus on cunnilingus (Nichols, 1987), which is often their preferred activity for reaching orgasm.

Interestingly, the *DSM-5* does not include a "hyperactive sexual desire disorder," implying that its authors, mental health professionals, do not believe that high sexual desire is a mental disorder. This is contrary to the view of the general public and some professionals who espouse the concept of sexual addiction. Sexual desire exists on a continuum, with some people having very low desire and others having very high desire. Most people seem to be somewhere in the middle, however.

Orgasmic Disorders

According to the *DSM-5*, a difficulty experiencing orgasm and/or markedly reduced intensity of orgasmic sensations in women is called **female orgasmic disorder.** For a diagnosis, these symptoms must occur on almost or all (about 75–100%) occasions during sexual activity with a minimal duration of about 6 months. The experience of an orgasm via clitoral stimulation not during intercourse does not meet the criteria for a clinical diagnosis of female orgasmic disorder (APA, 2013). Orgasmic difficulties are the second most common sexual function difficulty (after low sexual desire) treated by therapists (Keesling, 2006). The most common sexual functioning problems of women in the Natsal-3 study (see Figure 1) were lacking interest in sex (34%) and difficulty experiencing orgasm (16%) (Mitchell et al., 2013). Female orgasmic disorder has also been called anorgasmia, inorgasmia, pre-orgasmia, inhibited female orgasm, and the pejorative "frigidity." Most female orgasmic disorders are lifelong rather than acquired problems; once a woman learns how to have an orgasm, it is uncommon for her to lose that capacity (APA, 2000).

Female orgasm is not universal; a slight minority never or rarely have them. The NSSHB found that 37% of women reported not having an orgasm at their most recent partnered sexual event (see Figure 2). About 10% of women do not experience orgasm throughout their lifetime (APA, 2013). No relationships were found between certain personality traits or psychopathology and orgasm among women in the NHSLS study (Laumann et al., 1999).

Women use a wide variability in the type and intensity of stimulation that results in orgasm. Clitoral stimulation is required by many to experience orgasm, and a relatively small proportion of women indicate that they always experience orgasm during penile-vaginal intercourse. The age of first orgasm for women is more variable than for men—it may occur anytime from the prepubertal period to well into adulthood. Women's reports of having experienced orgasm increase with age, as shown in the Natsal-3 data (see Figure 1) and the NHSLS data (see Figure 3). Many women learn to experience orgasm as they try a wide array of stimulation and become more knowledgeable about their bodies. Orgasm consistency (i.e., usually or always) among women is higher during masturbation than during partnered sexual behavior (APA, 2013).

Some women who enjoy sexual activity with partners have difficulty experiencing orgasm with them, thereby sometimes causing dissatisfaction or distress within the relationship. Many women with female orgasmic disorder have negative or guilty attitudes about their sexuality, relationship difficulties, and physical and mental health problems and are influenced by sociocultural factors such as gender role expectations, and religion. Inadequate sexual stimulation is also a factor in this disorder (APA, 2000, 2013). Keesling (2006) states that "the number-one reason why some women have difficulty with orgasm is lack of experience with self-touch." As described in the "Think About It" box "Is Intercourse Enough? The Big 'O' and Sexual Behaviors," studies have found that women were more likely to experience orgasm during partnered sex that included a wider variety of sexual behaviors than intercourse.

Women differ on their views of how important orgasm is to their feeling satisfied during partnered sex. Some women have wondered "Why all this fuss about having orgasm during sex?" and have questioned whether women need to have orgasms during partnered sex to feel sexually satisfied. Overall, satisfaction with sexual activity in women is not strongly correlated with experiencing an orgasm. Many women report high levels of satisfaction during sexual activity despite never or rarely ever experiencing orgasm (APA, 2013).

A recurring and continuing (for at least 6 months) pattern of ejaculation during partnered sexual activity within about 1 minute following vaginal penetration and before the individual desires, and that causes interpersonal distress, is called **premature (early) ejaculation** in the *DSM-5* (APA, 2013). Even though premature (early) ejaculation may occur in nonvaginal sexual activities, a specific time duration criterion has not been created for those activities. Studies have shown that premature ejaculation is one of the most common sexual function difficulties in the male general population. The prevalence of men who experienced premature ejaculation reported in studies varies: Men in the Natsal-3 study reported between 10% and 17% reached climax more quickly than desired (see Figure 1), and the NHSLS found between 30% and 32% men reported climaxing earlier than desired (see Figure 3). Using the *DSM-5* criteria of early ejaculation being within about 1 minute of vaginal penetration, only 1–3% of men would be diagnosed with this disorder (APA, 2013; Rowland, 2012a).

As with many sexual difficulties, there is a problem with definitions: What is premature ejaculation? The definition may vary among individuals, populations, and cultures. Some sex therapists have defined it according to how long intercourse lasts, how many pelvic thrusts there are, and how often the woman experiences orgasm. Therapist Helen Singer Kaplan (1974) suggested that the absence of voluntary control at orgasm is the key to defining premature ejaculation. Actually, many males with premature ejaculation report a lack of control over the moment of ejaculation (APA, 2013). Some sex therapists suggest that the term "involuntary ejaculation" is the more accurate term, given that the treatment focuses on acquiring voluntary control over something that has been involuntary (Castleman, 2004). Early ejaculation is a problem when the man or his partner is dissatisfied by the amount of time it takes him to ejaculate. Some couples want intercourse to last a long time, but others are not concerned about that.

Couples often are confused, bewildered, and unhappy when the man consistently ejaculates too early, although women seem to be increasingly more disturbed by the disorder than men are. The woman may be sexually dissatisfied, while her partner may feel that she is too demanding. He may also feel considerable guilt and anxiety. They may begin to avoid sexual contact with each other. The man may experience erectile problems because of his anxieties over early ejaculation, and he may withdraw from sexual activity completely. Other factors may contribute to early or involuntary ejaculation in men, such as inexperience in negotiating with a sexual partner, inadequate understanding of sexual response in both women and men, unwittingly training themselves to ejaculate quickly during masturbation, inability to relax deeply during sexual intercourse, nonsensual lovemaking, and a narrow focus on the penis and a partner's genitals during sex (Castleman, 2004; Rowland, 2012b).

Most men with early or involuntary ejaculation can delay ejaculation during self-masturbation for a longer period of time than during coitus. With sexual experience and aging, many males learn to delay ejaculation, but others continue to ejaculate early and may seek professional help (APA, 2000, 2013). This disorder often occurs in young and sexually inexperienced males, especially those who have primarily been in situations in which speed of ejaculation was important so as for example, to avoid being discovered. It is the number-one sexual function complaint of young men.

What about premature, or early, orgasm among women? This phenomenon is not typically considered a sexual function difficulty by women or their partners and is not listed as a sexual dysfunction disorder in the *DSM-5*. The prevalence of early orgasm is rarely reported by women: Between 1% and 4% of women in the Natsal-3 study (see Figure 1) indicated that they reached climax more quickly than they liked (Mitchell et al., 2013). Some women who have orgasms very quickly may not be interested in continuing sexual activity; others, however, are open to continued stimulation and may have repeated orgasms.

The persistence and recurrent (at least for 6 months) marked delay or inability to ejaculate that causes personal distress is identified in the *DSM-5* as **delayed ejaculation.** The inability or difficulty in ejaculating occurs despite adequate sexual stimulation and the desire to experience ejaculation. The diagnostic criteria state that this difficulty must be experienced during nearly all occasions (about 75–100%). The complaint from the man or his partner usually comes from this problem occurring during partnered sexual activity. Prolonged thrusting to experience orgasm to the point of exhaustion or genital discomfort often occurs, resulting in the couple ceasing attempts. Some men report that they began to avoid partnered sexual activity because of repeated difficulties in ejaculating. Ejaculation and orgasm are two separate events that usually occur at the same time, but not always. Given this, a man experiencing delayed ejaculation may have an orgasm (full body experience) but is unable to ejaculate at all or have delayed ejaculation. In the most common form of delayed ejaculation, the man cannot ejaculate during intercourse but can from a partner's manual or oral stimulation.

How often delayed ejaculation occurs is difficult to ascertain because there is no consensus as to what constitutes a reasonable time or number of penile thrusts to experience ejaculation or what is unreasonably long for most men and their partners. Clinicians report that it is the least commonly reported sexual function complaint. Only 75% of men report always ejaculating during sexual activity; of the remainder, less than 1% complain of difficulty in ejaculating that lasts more than 3 months. Around 1 in 10 men of the Natsal-3, HSSHB, and NHSLS studies reported difficulties with experiencing orgasm (see Figures 1–3). The *DSM-5* states that men in their 80s report twice as much difficulty in ejaculating than men younger than 50 years. Age-related decreases in fast-conducting peripheral sensory nerves and in sex steroid secretion may be related to increased occurrence of delayed ejaculation in men older than 50 years.

As with other sexual function disorders, delayed ejaculation may occur as an interaction of biological, sociocultural, and psychological factors, including those related to the sexual partner; the relationship; individual vulnerability, psychological problems, or stressors; culture or religion; and medical issues. Anxiety-provoking sexual situations can interfere with a man experiencing an orgasm, or a man may not be able to have an ejaculation in situations in which he feels guilty or conflicted. Often, the individual can overcome this disorder when he and his partner are able to comfortably discuss the issue, when the situation or partner changes, or when he engages in a fantasy or receives additional stimulation (APA, 2013).

Sexual Pain Disorders

The *DSM-5* combined the conditions **vaginismus** (muscle spasms around the vagina) and **dyspareunia** (painful intercourse) from the *DSM-IV-TR* into one category, **genital-pelvic pain/penetration disorder,** with four diagnostic categories: (1) marked difficulty having vaginal intercourse/penetration, (2) marked vaginal or pelvic pain during a vaginal intercourse or penetration attempt, (3) marked fear or anxiety about vaginal or pelvic pain in anticipation of, during, or as a result of vaginal penetration, and (4) marked tensing or tightening of the pelvic floor muscles during attempted vaginal penetration. Diagnosis of genital-pelvic pain/penetration disorder is based on persistent and recurrent difficulty with any one of the four symptoms and the fact that the symptoms cause significant interpersonal distress. These issues may occur in conjunction with other sexual function difficulties, such as low sexual desire, and partner difficulties, such as problems with erections and ejaculation. Like most sexual function difficulties, factors related to the partner, the relationship, individual vulnerability, religion/culture, and medical issues may be relevant to experiencing genital-pelvic pain/penetration disorder.

The diagnostic vaginal intercourse/penetration category of the genital-pelvic pain/penetration disorder represents a range from a total inability to experience vaginal penetration in any circumstance (e.g., intercourse, gynecological examinations, tampon insertion) to an ability to easily experience penetration in one situation but not another. Women experiencing the marked vaginal or pelvic pain report mild to severe pain associated with intercourse that can be characterized as burning, cutting, shooting, or throbbing, for example. The pain may continue after intercourse and may occur during urination. Many women experience pain occasionally during intercourse, but much fewer men report pain (see Figures 1–3). Persistent pain among women may indicate difficulties that need to be addressed. Marked anxiety about genital or pelvic pain in association with intercourse is frequently reported by women who have regularly experienced pain during intercourse. This reaction may result in avoidance of intercourse or vaginal penetration.

The tensing or tightening of pelvic muscles represents an involuntary spasm of the outer third of the vagina (the pubococcygeus muscle); that is, the muscles around the vaginal opening go into involuntary spasmodic contractions, preventing the insertion of a penis, finger, tampon, or speculum. The most frequent clinical issue is when a woman is not able to experience intercourse or vaginal penetration with a partner, although this disorder may also occur during gynecological examinations. This difficulty is found more often in younger women than older women (APA, 2000, 2013).

Another type of pain associated with sex that is not included in the *DSM-5* is **anodyspareunia,** pain occurring during anal intercourse. Gay men sometimes experience this, often due to lack of adequate lubrication. The depth of penile penetration into the anus, the rate of thrusting, and anxiety or embarrassment about the situation often are associated with anodyspareunia (Rosser, Short, Thurmes, & Coleman, 1998). A study of 404 men who have sex with men found that 55 (14%) experienced anodyspareunia; these men reported their pain as lifelong, experienced psychological distress as a result, and avoided anal sex for periods of time (Damon & Rosser, 2005). Among heterosexual women, a substantial proportion experience pain at initial and subsequent anal intercourse (Stulhofer & Ajdukovic, 2011). A study of 1,265 women, aged 18–30, who reported two or more episodes of anal intercourse, found that nearly one half (49%) had discontinued their first episode because of pain or discomfort, although a majority of women subsequently continued anal sex. Of the 505 women who reported two or more anal intercourse episodes in the past year, nearly 1 in 10 reported severe pain. More than two thirds of these women reported that their pain level remained unchanged from their first anal intercourse experience. The researchers hypothesized that the inability to relax was the major cause of the pain.

Discussing sexuality and becoming educated about one's sexual functioning with a qualified health care professional can sometimes help resolve questions, issues, or problems.

© Jose Luis Pelaez, Inc./Blend Images/ Corbis

Substance/Medication-Induced Sexual Dysfunction

The *DSM-5* added a category of sexual disorder, called **substance/medication-induced sexual dysfunction.** Sexual dysfunction can occur with intoxication use of numerous drugs such as alcohol, opioids, sedatives, antidepressants, hypnotics, antipsychotics, stimulants, hormonal contraceptives, illicit/recreational drugs, and other unknown substances. The prevalence of substance/medication-induced sexual dysfunction is not known, although some research has been conducted. For example, studies have shown that 25–80% of persons taking certain antidepressants report sexual side effects. About one half of persons taking antipsychotic medications report experiencing sexual side effects, including difficulties with sexual desire, erection, lubrication, ejaculation, and orgasm. Difficulties with sexual functioning appear greater in persons abusing heroin (about 60–70%) than in individuals who abuse amphetamines and ecstasy (APA, 2013). Many persons using prescription medications do not realize that the drug may impair sexual functioning. One should inquire about this possibility from a health care provider or pharmacist.

Other Disorders

Two other disorders not mentioned in the *DSM-5* because they are based on physical conditions are Peyronie's disease and priapism. These conditions can also cause other difficulties in sexual functioning.

Peyronie's Disease   A condition in which calcium deposits and tough fibrous tissue develop in the corpora cavernosa within the penis is known as **Peyronie's disease.** This problem occurs primarily in older men (usually for no apparent reason) and can be quite painful. The disease results in a curvature of the penis, which, in severe cases, interferes with erection and intercourse. Medical treatments can alleviate the source of discomfort, and sometimes the condition disappears without treatment. A study involving 4,432 men in Germany found the prevalence of Peyronie's disease was 3.2% (Schwarzer et al., 2001). For the record, rarely are penises perfectly straight; most curve to one side.

Priapism   Prolonged and painful erection, occurring when blood is unable to drain from the penis, is called **priapism.** Lasting from several hours to a few days, this problem is not associated with sexual thoughts or activities. Rather, it results from certain medications, including some antidepressants, erectile dysfunction medications, and excessive doses of penile injections for producing an erection. Medical conditions such as sickle-cell disease and leukemia may also cause priapism.

● Physical Causes of Sexual Function Difficulties and Dissatisfaction

Until recently, researchers believed that most sexual function difficulties and dissatisfaction were almost exclusively psychological in origin. Current research challenges this view as more is learned about the intricacies of sexual physiology, such as the subtle influences of hormones. Our vascular, neurological, and endocrine systems are sensitive to changes and disruptions. As a result, various illnesses and disturbances to these systems may have an adverse effect on our sexual functioning. Some prescription drugs, such as medication for hypertension or for depression, may affect sexual responsiveness. Chemotherapy and radiation treatment for cancer, and pain from cancer, can affect sexual desire and responsiveness (American Cancer Society, 2015.14a).

Physical Causes in Men

Diabetes and alcoholism are leading causes of male erectile difficulties; together, they account for several million cases. Diabetes damages blood vessels and nerves, including those within the penis. Other causes of sexual function difficulties include lumbar disc disease and multiple sclerosis, which interfere with the nerve impulses regulating erection. In addition, atherosclerosis causes blockage of the arteries, including the blood flow necessary for erection. Spinal cord injuries and prostate-cancer treatment may affect erectile abilities as well. Alcoholism and drug use are widely associated with sexual difficulties. Smoking may also contribute to erection difficulties (Gades et al., 2005; Rowland, 2012a). One study found that men who are heavy smokers are 50% more likely to experience erectile problems than nonsmokers (National Center for Environmental Health, 1995). Bicycle-induced sexual difficulties can occur as a result of a flattening of the main penile artery, thereby temporarily blocking the blood flow required for erections. Diseases of the heart and circulatory system may be associated with erectile difficulty. A four-country study of 2,400 men found that "erectile dysfunction was associated with diabetes, heart disease, lower urinary tract symptoms, heavy smoking and depression and increased by 10 percent per year of age" (Nicolosi, Moreiba, Shirai, Bin Mohd Tambi, & Glasser, 2003).

Physical Causes in Women

Organic causes of female orgasmic disorder include medical conditions such as diabetes and heart disease, hormone deficiencies, and neurological disorders, as well as general poor health, extreme fatigue, drug use, and alcoholism. Spinal cord injuries may affect sexual responsiveness. Multiple sclerosis can decrease vaginal lubrication and sexual response.

Genital pain during intercourse may result from an obstructed or thickened hymen, clitoral adhesions, infections, painful scars, a constrictive clitoral hood, vulvodynia, or a weak **pubococcygeus** (pew-bo-kawk-SEE-gee-us) (PC) muscle, the pelvic floor muscle surrounding the urethra and the vagina. Antihistamines used to treat colds and allergies can reduce vaginal lubrication, as can marijuana. Endometriosis and ovarian and uterine tumors and cysts may affect a woman's sexual response.

The skin covering the clitoris can become infected. Women who masturbate too vigorously can irritate their clitoris, making sexual interactions painful. A partner can also stimulate a woman too roughly, causing soreness in the vagina, urethra, or clitoral area. And unclean hands may cause a vaginal or urinary tract infection.

● Psychological Causes of Sexual Function Difficulties and Dissatisfaction

Sexual function difficulties and dissatisfaction may have their origin in any number of psychological causes. Some difficulties and dissatisfaction originate from immediate causes, others from conflict within the self, and still others from a particular sexual relationship.

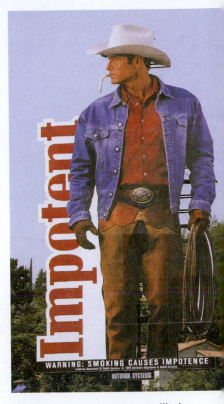

Men who smoke are more likely to experience erection problems ("impotence") than men who do not smoke.

© Jerzy Dabrowski/picture-alliance/dpa/AP Images

Immediate Causes

The immediate causes of sexual function difficulties and dissatisfaction include fatigue, stress, ineffective sexual behavior, and sexual anxieties.

Fatigue and Stress   Many sexual function difficulties and dissatisfaction have fairly simple causes. Individuals may find themselves physically exhausted from the demands of daily life. They may bring their fatigue into the bedroom in the form of sexual apathy or disinterest. "I'm too tired to make love tonight" can be a truthful description of a person's feelings. What these couples may need is not therapy or counseling but temporary relief from their daily routines.

Long-term stress can also contribute to lowered sexual drive and reduced responsiveness. A person preoccupied with making financial ends meet, raising children, or coping with prolonged illness, for example, can temporarily lose sexual desire.

Ineffective Sexual Behavior   Ignorance, ineffective sexual communication, and misinformation prevent partners from being effectively sexual with each other. Ineffective sexual stimulation is especially relevant in explaining why some women do not experience orgasm in sexual interactions, as discussed earlier and in the box "Is Intercourse Enough? The Big 'O' and Sexual Behaviors."

Some individuals have not learned effective sexual stimulation behaviors because they are inexperienced. They may have grown up without easily accessible sexual information or positive role models.

Sexual Anxieties   A number of anxieties, such as performance anxiety, can lead to sexual function difficulties and dissatisfaction (Bancroft, 2009). If a man fails to experience an erection or a woman is not orgasmic, he or she may feel anxious and fearful. And the anxiety may block the very response desired.

Performance anxieties may give rise to **spectatoring,** in which a person becomes a spectator of her or his own sexual behaviors (Masters & Johnson, 1970). When people become spectators of their sexual activities, they critically evaluate and judge whether they are "performing" well or whether they are doing everything "right." Some sex therapists suggest that spectatoring is involved in most orgasmic difficulties.

Performance anxiety may be even more widespread among gay men (Sandfort & de Keizer, 2001). Sex researcher Rex Reece (1988) writes: "Many gay men move in a social, sexual milieu where sexual arousal is expected immediately or soon after meeting someone. If response is not rapidly forthcoming, rejection is very likely."

Excessive Need to Please a Partner   Another source of anxiety is an excessive need to please a partner. A man who feels this need, sometimes labeled as trying to be the "delivery boy," may want a speedy erection to please or impress his partner. He may feel that he must "give her orgasms" through his expert lovemaking or always delay his orgasm until after his partner's orgasm. A woman who experiences this anxiety may want to have an orgasm quickly to please her partner (Castleman, 2004; Salisbury &

The demands of work and child rearing may create fatigue and stress which can create sexual apathy for one or both partners.

© Altrendo Images/Getty Images

Fisher, 2013). She may worry that she is not sufficiently attractive to her partner or that she is sexually inadequate.

One result of the need to please is that men and women may pretend to have orgasms. (Meg Ryan famously demonstrated faking an orgasm in a deli in the film *When Harry Met Sally.*) Women fake orgasm most often to retain their mate (Kaighobadi, Shackeford, & Welling, 2012) or to avoid disappointing their partner or hurting his feelings. According to sex therapist Kathryn Hall (2004), these women "are buying into the myth that men are really concerned only with satisfying their own ego." Both men and women also fake orgasm to present a false image of their sexual performance. Unfortunately, faking orgasm miscommunicates to the partner that a person is equally satisfied. Because the orgasmic problem is not addressed, negative emotions may simmer. The wisest decision is never to pretend to experience feelings, interests, or pleasures that do not happen (Hall, 2004).

> *In the 1990s a feminist joke asked, "Why do women fake orgasm?" and answered "Because men fake foreplay." In the masculinist version, the question was "Why do women fake orgasm?" and the answer, "Because they think men care."*
>
> —Angus McLaren

Conflict Within the Self

Negative parental attitudes toward sex are frequently associated with subsequent sexual function difficulties and dissatisfaction. Much of the process of growing up is a casting off of the sexual guilt and negativity instilled in childhood. Some people fear becoming emotionally intimate with another person. They may enjoy the sex but fear the accompanying feelings of vulnerability and, so, withdraw from the sexual relationship before they become emotionally close to their partner (Hyde & DeLamater, 2014). And among gay men, lesbian women, and bisexual individuals, internalized homophobia—self-hatred because of one's homosexuality—is a major source of conflict that can be traced to a number of factors, including conservative religious upbringing (Frost & Meyer, 2009).

Sources of severe sexual function difficulties include childhood sexual abuse, adult sexual assault, and rape. Guilt and conflict do not usually eliminate a person's sex drive; rather, they inhibit the drive and alienate the individual from his or her sexuality. He or she may come to see sexuality as something bad or "dirty," rather than something to happily affirm.

Therapists Robert Firestone, Lisa Firestone, and Joyce Catlett (2006) provide an alternative perspective on the decline of sexual passion in long-term relationships and marriage. They believe that the decline cannot be attributed to the reasons usually given, such as familiarity, gender differences, economic hardships, and other stressors, but rather to changes in the relationship dynamics, the emergence of painful feelings from childhood, and fears of rejection that cause partners to retreat to a more defended posture. Many men and women have difficulty in maintaining sexually satisfying relationships "because in their earlier relationships, hurt and frustration caused them to turn away from love and closeness and to become suspicious and self-protective." In advising couples in longer-term relationships, the therapists note:

> To sustain a loving sexual relationship, individuals must be willing to face the threats to the defense system that loving another person and being loved for oneself evoke. To be able to accept genuine affection, tenderness, love, and fulfilling sexual experiences as part of an ongoing relationship, they must be willing to challenge their negative voices, modify the image of themselves formed in the family, and give up well-entrenched defenses, which would cause them a great deal of anxiety.

> *Pleasure is the object, duty, and the goal of all rational creatures.*
>
> —Voltaire
> (1694–1770)

Relationship Causes

Sexual function difficulties do not exist in a vacuum, but usually within the context of a relationship. All couples at some point experience difficulties in their sexual relationship. Sex therapist David Schnarch (2002) writes that "sexual problems are common among healthy couples who are normal in every other way—so common, in fact, that they are arguably a sign of normality." Most frequently, married couples go into therapy because they have a greater investment in the relationship than couples who are dating or cohabiting. Sexual function difficulties in a dating or cohabiting relationship often do not surface; it is sometimes easier for couples to break up than to change the behaviors that contribute to their sexual function problems.

Sex therapist Esther Perel, in her book *Mating in Captivity* (2006), presents a provocative view of desire difficulties in marriage, one that is counter to often-held perspectives among sex therapists. She contends that eroticism thrives on the unpredictable and that increased intimacy often leads to a decrease in sexual desire. Perel states that love is fed by knowing everything about one's partner, while desire needs mystery, and that love wants to shrink the distance between the two people, while desire is energized by it. She continues by declaring that "as an expression of longing, desire requires elusiveness." Perel contends that couples may be more successful in maintaining and cultivating sexual desire by enriching their separate lives instead of always striving for closeness. The challenge for many couples is balancing separateness with togetherness, as both are important components of a loving relationship.

If sexual function problems are left unresolved, disappointment, rage, anger, resentment, power conflicts, and hostility often become a permanent part of couple interaction.

> As with singers in a harmony, a harmonious sex life is not necessarily one in which you are both wanting and doing exactly the same things in the same way, but one that is characterized by blending the strengths that you each have to create an agreeable and pleasant sex life.
>
> —Sandra Pertot
> (1950–)

Sexual Function Enhancement

Improving the quality of a sexual relationship is referred to as **sexual function enhancement.** There are several sexual function–enhancement programs for people who function well sexually but who nevertheless want to improve the quality of their sexual interactions and relationships. The programs generally seek to provide accurate information about sexuality, develop communication skills, foster positive attitudes, provide sexual homework for practicing techniques discussed in therapy, and increase self-awareness (Castleman, 2004).

Developing Self-Awareness

Being aware of our own sexual needs is often critical to enhancing our sexual functioning.

What Is Good Sex?   Sexual stereotypes present us with images of how we are supposed to behave sexually. Images of the "sexually in charge" man and the "sexual but not too sexual" woman may interfere with our ability to express our own sexual feelings, needs, and desires. We follow the scripts and stereotypes we have been socialized to accept, rather than our own unique responses. Following these cultural images may impede our ability to have what therapist Carol Ellison calls "good sex." In an essay about intimacy-based sex therapy, Ellison (1985) writes that we will know we are having good sex if we feel good about ourselves, our partners, our relationships, and our sexual behaviors. Further, we will feel good about sex before, during, and after being sexual with our partners (Hall, 2004). Good sex does not necessarily include orgasm or intercourse. It can be kissing, cuddling, masturbating, performing oral or anal sex, and so on. Sex therapist and clinical psychologist Marty Klein (2012) states that culture dictates a hierarchy of sexual behaviors, with some activities being superior to others. In Western culture the pinnacle of heterosexual sexual behavior is intercourse; it is considered to be the most enjoyable, natural, and intimate sexual behavior. Below intercourse in the hierarchy are other forms of genital sex (touching of the genitals) with a partner, such as oral sex, anal sex, and hand jobs, then followed by masturbation and intimate behaviors not involving touching the genitals, such as touching of the breasts. Kissing is the ultimate expression of intimacy for some people; for others, it is considered boring or a turnoff. One limitation of the concept of sexual hierarchy is that it can minimize the intimacy and pleasure of behaviors "lower" on the hierarchy, and it implies that intercourse must occur in order to have successful sex. With an emphasis on and even a frequent expectation for good sex, one might ask if there is a cost to this approach to couple sex. See the "Think About It" box "Good Enough Sex: The Way to Lifetime Couple Satisfaction" for an alternative model to good or "perfect" partnered sex.

Good sex involves the ability to communicate well nonverbally—through laughter and positive body language and facial expressions—as well as verbally.

© Jonnie Miles/Getty Images

Discovering Your Conditions for Good Sex

Zilbergeld (1999) has suggested that to fully enjoy our sexuality we need to explore our "conditions for good sex." There is nothing unusual about requiring conditions for any activity. Of conditions for good sex, Zilbergeld (1999) writes:

> In a sexual situation, a condition is anything that makes you more relaxed, more comfortable, more confident, more excited, more open to your experience. Put differently, a condition is something that clears your nervous system of unnecessary clutter, leaving it open to receive and transmit sexual messages in ways that will result in a good time for you.

Each individual has his or her own unique conditions for good sex. This might include factors such as feeling intimate and emotionally close with one's partner, feeling trust toward one's partner, being physically and mentally alert, and embracing one's own sexual desire and eroticism (Ogden, 2008; Zilbergeld, 1999). If you are or have been sexually active, to discover your conditions for good sex, think about the last few times you were sexual and were highly aroused. Then compare those times with other times when you were much less aroused. Identify the needs that underlie these factors and communicate these needs to your partner.

When adults experience passions, it's usually not in response to incredible sex or the perfect body—it's in response to giving themselves permission to let go emotionally.

—Marty Klein
(1950–)

Doing Homework Exercises

Sexual function–enhancement programs often specify exercises for couples to undertake in private. Such "homework" exercises require individuals to make a time commitment to themselves or their partner. Typical assignments include the following exercises:

- *Mirror examination.* Use a full-length mirror to examine your nude body. Use a hand mirror to view your genitals. Look at all your features in an uncritical manner; view yourself with acceptance.

"Good Enough Sex": The Way to Lifetime Couple Satisfaction

Sex provides a buffet of experiences: at times, sex is enthusiastic, cheerful, erotic, gratifying and at other times uninspiring.

—Metz and McCarthy
(2011)

Renowned sex therapists and authors Michael Metz and Barry McCarthy, in their book *Enduring Desire: Your Guide to Lifetime Intimacy* (2011), challenge the current cultural models of "perfect sex" and "perfect intercourse" with an alternative concept for long-term, committed couples, the "Good Enough Sex" (GES) model. They contend that prevailing beliefs that sex should always be perfect are toxic and can lead to disappointment and disillusionment. Unrealistic expectations about sex precipitate a sense of failure as "great sex" in committed relationships, particularly, is uneven and variable. Metz and McCarthy state that the GES model with its physical, psychological, and interpersonal dimensions is not a cop-out that leads to mediocre, boring, or mechanical sex but rather a "roadmap to a lifetime of terrific, meaningful sex, a guide to help you feel sexually satisfied, not in a fantasy world but in real life." They note that research suggests that regular, variable, and flexible couple sex that is fully integrated into real life is the best couple sex. The GES model does not lead to disappointing compromise or feelings of "selling out" but rather to feelings of relief, affirmation, and inspiration; it seeks *realistically great sex* grounded on a realistic appreciation that variations in couple sex over time are both healthy and necessary.

The GES approach works best when one develops realistic, flexible, accurate, and positive beliefs about GES's three dimensions, what great sex is and is not, and what sex can be for "oneself". GES partners embrace concepts such as:

- Sexual satisfaction varies from one experience to the next.
- Achieving high-quality sex is a lifelong process.
- Sexual function difficulties are opportunities for increased cooperation and intimacy.
- Satisfied couples cooperate as an intimate team.
- Quality sex is flexible: You adapt to the inevitable variability and difficulties.

- Sex fits real life, and real life should be brought into the sexual relationship.
- The best sex involves being intimate and erotic partners.
- Quality sex is cooperative relationship sex.

There are numerous benefits of "Good Enough Sex." One feels self-assured and proud of being a sexual person knowing that positive, realistic expectations decrease embarrassment and shame about one's body and sexuality. A person will view sex as a normal, real, and positive part of an honest and genuine life. One adopts beliefs that sex is "decent" and wild and that passionate couple sex is "good." One accepts that sex is variable and creates flexible ways to integrate variability into the couple's life situation to enhance mutual pleasure. Partners form an intimate team to discover the meanings of sexuality and to balance eroticism and intimacy. Metz and McCarthy state that "no longer bound by shame, no longer having to be different than who you are, no longer anxiously fearing failure, and no longer pursuing perfection, you feel self assured, confident, and content."

Think Critically

1. In what ways does society stress "perfect sex"?
2. Do you think by adopting the "Good Enough Sex" approach one would be settling for mediocre and boring sex? Explain your response.
3. Is the "Good Enough Sex" approach realistic for college-age students? Why or why not?
4. If you have been in a sexual relationship, have you experienced "great sex" and "uninspiring sex"? If so, how did you deal with that? Is the "Good Enough Sex" approach a good way to deal with the variability of sex?

SOURCE: Metz, M. E., & McCarthy, B. W. (2011). *Enduring desire: Your guide to lifelong intimacy.* New York: Routledge.

- *Body relaxation and exploration.* Take 30–60 minutes to fully relax. Begin with a leisurely shower or bath; then, remaining nude, find a comfortable place to touch and explore your body and genitals.

- *Masturbation.* In a relaxed situation, with body oils or lotions to enhance your sensations, explore ways of touching your body and genitals that bring you pleasure. Do this exercise for several sessions without having an orgasm; experiencing erotic pleasure without orgasm is the goal. If you are about to have an orgasm, decrease stimulation. After several sessions without having an orgasm, continue pleasuring yourself until you have an orgasm.

- *Sexual voice.* Each person has his or her own erotic "sexual voice," which is enhanced by discovering, nurturing, and integrating into the couple's sexual style. Traditionally, many women have been dependent on the male partner's eroticism and his sexual lead; the woman was not supposed to have her own erotic voice (McCarthy & McCarthy, 2009). Women who develop their own sexual voice open themselves up to a more satisfying and rewarding sexual experience with a partner.

- *Kegel exercises for women and men.* Originally developed to help women with controlling urination, Kegel exercises involve exercising a muscle in the pelvic floor called the pubococcygeus (P.C.) muscle. The Kegel exercises basically involve tightening the P.C. muscle as one does to stop the flow of urine. These exercises can aid in increasing one's sexual awareness and functioning. (See the "Practically Speaking" box "Kegel Exercises for Men and Women" to learn about why and how to do these exercises.)

- *Erotic aids.* Products designed to enhance erotic responsiveness, such as vibrators, dildos, G-spot stimulators, artificial vaginas and mouths, clitoral stimulators, vibrating nipple clips, explicit videos, oils, lubricants, and lotions, are referred to as **erotic aids.** They are also called **sex toys,** emphasizing their playful quality. Vibrators and dildos seem to be the most common sex toys and are usually considered "women's toys." But, of course, they can be for either gender and can be used alone or with a partner. Two national studies of men and women in the U.S., aged 18 to 60, assessed lifetime use of vibrators: 44.8% of men had incorporated a vibrator into their sexual activities during their lives and 52.5% of women had ever used a vibrator (Herbenick, Reece, Sanders, Ghassemi, & Fortenberry, 2009; Reece et al., 2009). You may wish to try using a sex toy or shower massage as you masturbate with your partner or by yourself. You may also want to view erotic DVDs, go online to find sexually explicit images, or read erotic poetry or stories to yourself or your partner.

Intensifying Erotic Pleasure

One of the most significant elements of enhancing our physical experience of sex is intensifying arousal. In intensifying arousal, the focus is on erotic pleasure rather than on sexual functioning. This can be done in a number of ways.

A vibrator can be a valuable aid in increasing sexual arousal and experiencing an orgasm.

© H.S. Photos/Alamy

Kegel Exercises for Women and Men

Kegel exercises were originally developed by gynecologist Arnold Kegel (KAY-gul) to help women with problems controlling urination. They were designed to strengthen and give women voluntary control of a muscle called the pubococcygeus, or P.C. for short. The P.C. muscle is part of the sling of muscle stretching from the pubic bone in front to the tailbone in back, also called the pelvic floor. Because the muscle encircles not only the urinary opening but also the outside of the vagina, some of Kegel's patients discovered a pleasant side effect—increased sexual awareness. Many report that the sensations are similar for men and women. If you are a man, the exercises can be valuable to you for improving erectile function and learning ejaculatory control. In fact, a British study found that erection function improved significantly in men after 3 months of Kegel exercises (Dorey, Speakman, Feneley, Swinkels, & Dunn, 2005). So, men, when reading the directions, just substitute your genitals in places where the directions talk about "vagina" and so on.

Why Do Kegel Exercises?

- They can help you be more aware of feelings in your genital area.
- They can increase circulation in the genital area.
- They may help increase sexual arousal started by other kinds of stimulation.
- They can be useful during childbirth to help control the strength and duration of pushing.
- They can be helpful after childbirth to restore muscle tone in the vagina.
- They can help men improve erection function and control the timing of ejaculation.
- If urinary incontinence is a problem, strengthening these muscles may improve urinary control.

Identifying Your P.C. Muscle

Sit on the toilet. Spread your legs apart. See if you can stop and start the flow of urine without moving your legs. That's your P.C. muscle, the one that turns the flow on and off. If you don't find it the first time, don't give up; try again the next time you have to urinate. (For the British

study cited previously, the researchers instructed the men to tighten their pelvic floor as if they were trying to prevent intestinal gas from escaping or to try retracting the penis and lifting the scrotum and testicles.)

How to Do the Exercises

- *Slow Kegels:* Tighten the P.C. muscle as you did to stop the urine. Hold it for a slow count of three. Relax it.
- Quick *Kegels:* Tighten and relax the P.C. muscle as rapidly as you can.
- *Pull in–push out:* Pull up the entire pelvic floor as though trying to suck water into your vagina. Then push or bear down as if trying to push the imaginary water out. (This exercise will use a number of stomach or abdominal muscles as well as the P.C. muscle.)

At first, do 10 of each of these three exercises (one set) five times every day. Each week, increase the number of times you do each exercise by five (15, 20, 25, etc.). Keep doing five "sets" each day.

Exercise Guidelines

- You can do these exercises anytime during daily activities that don't require a lot of moving around—for example, while driving your car, watching television, sitting in school or at your computer, or lying in bed.
- When you start, you will probably notice that the muscle doesn't want to stay "contracted" during "slow Kegels" and that you can't do "quick Kegels" very rapidly or evenly. Keep at it. In a week or two, you will probably notice that you can control the muscle quite well.
- Sometimes, the muscle will start to feel a little tired. This is not surprising—you probably haven't used it very much before. Take a few seconds' rest and start again.
- A good way to check on how you are doing is to insert one or two lubricated fingers into your vagina. Men can place a finger into their rectum to feel the anus contract. Because it may be a month or so before you notice results, be patient.

Finally, always remember to keep breathing naturally and evenly while doing your Kegels.

Developing Bridges to Desire Sex therapist Barry McCarthy and author Emily McCarthy (2009) state that sexual desire is the core element of a healthy sexuality and that developing and maintaining sexual desire is important to a satisfying couple sexual style. Couples prefer to experience the fun and energizing effect of spontaneous sex that is common in the romantic/passionate sex/idealization phase of a new sexual relationship in which sex occurs nearly every time the couple get together. But for couples past the 6-month to 2-year passionate sex phase, especially those with demanding jobs, kids, mortgages, and so on, most sexual encounters are planned and many couples begin to experience lower sexual desire. This occurs because couples are not able to transfer from the passionate sex stage to an enduring intimate and erotic couple sexual style. The key is to integrate intimacy and eroticism by "building bridges to desire."

The McCarthys state that "bridges to desire require ways of thinking, anticipating, and experiencing a sexual encounter that makes sex inviting." The most important bridge to desire involves couples anticipating a sexual encounter in which the partner is involved, giving, and aroused. Each partner and the couple should be creative in developing and maintaining bridges to desire. Even though individual bridges are important, discovering unique, mutual bridges can be a valuable couple resource. The more varied the bridges, the easier it is to maintain desire. Further, the more bridges to desire, the more ways to connect and reconnect through touch. One way to develop a bridge to desire is for each partner to inform the other partner what his or her two favorite ways to initiate a sexual encounter are and two favorite ways to be invited for a sexual encounter. Revealing your thoughts on how your partner can be a better lover may enhance sexual pleasure for both of you. (See the "Think About It" box "My Partner Could Be a Better Lover If . . . : What Men and Women Want from Their Sexual Partners" which lists the top things both men and women want from their partners.)

Some individuals and couples use erotic aids such as vibrators, dildos, videos, oils, lubricants, and lotions to enhance their sexual pleasure and responsiveness.

© Rachel Torres/Alamy

Sexual Arousal Sexual arousal refers to the physiological responses, fantasies, and desires associated with sexual anticipation and activity. We have different levels of arousal, and they are not necessarily associated with particular types of sexual activities. Sometimes, we feel more sexually aroused when we kiss or masturbate than when we have sexual intercourse or oral sex.

The first element in increasing sexual arousal is having your conditions for good sex met. If you need privacy, find a place to be alone; if you need a romantic setting, go for a relaxing walk or listen to music by candlelight; if you want limits on your sexual activities, tell your partner; if you need a certain kind of physical stimulation, show or tell your partner what you like.

A second element in increasing arousal is focusing on the sensations you are experiencing. Once you begin an erotic activity such as massaging or kissing, do not let yourself be distracted. When you're kissing, don't think about what you're going to do next or about an upcoming test. Instead, focus on the sensual experience of your lips and heart.

Alternatives to Intercourse Waiting, delaying, and facing obstacles may intensify arousal. This is one of the pleasures of sexual abstinence that may be forgotten soon after you begin intercourse. Renowned sex therapist and author Lonnie Barbach (2001) suggests that sexually active people may intensify

> ❝ The best aphrodisiac is an involved, aroused partner.
>
> McCarthy and McCarthy
> (2009)

> ❝ License my roving hands, and let them go,
> Behind, before, above, between, below.
>
> —John Donne
> (1572–1631)

My Partner Could Be a Better Lover If . . . : What Men and Women Want from Their Sexual Partners

Most desire is unspoken.

—Northrup, Schwartz, and Witte (2012)

"I wish my partner was a better lover." How often have you thought that? Most of us have wished that at one time or another, but we have been afraid to tell our partners. We are afraid to make a request, fearing that our partner will interpret the request as an attack on his or her sexual skills, which may result in anger and even more sexual and emotional problems. So many people remain silent. Actually, for many people their sexual needs and desires are hidden and are unspoken. This can leave them frustrated, and disappointed, feeling "short-changed" and resentful.

After seeing this box title, you may be curious: What do men and women want from their sexual partners? Research has addressed that. An Internet study of over 77,000 individuals around the world asked respondents to select from a long list of choices the top two things they feel that are missing from the sexual relationship (Northrup et al., 2012). Here are the top three choices of what a partner could do to be a better lover:

What Men Want from Their Partners

1. *Sexual diversity (30%).* Even though these men were not necessarily unhappy, many complained that sex with their partners was always predictable. They wanted to mix things up a little bit with new foreplay behaviors and intercourse positions or their partner initiating sex more frequently.
2. *Less passivity (22%).* These men wanted their partners to express more passion. They wanted to expand their usual bounds of sexual excitement.
3. *Sexual noises (16%).* More partner feedback, positive reinforcement, and encouragement were desired by these men. They would like more sexual noises from their partners, like those that let them know that their partners are experiencing enjoyment during sex.

What Women Want from Their Partners

1. *Foreplay (25%).* These women stated that they do not get enough foreplay. They want to be touched more often and for longer periods of time.
2. *Romance (20%).* More romance and loving passion were desired by these women.
3. *Less predictability (19%).* These women wanted less predictability and more diversity in sexual behaviors. They wanted more spontaneous and fun sex.

The researchers note that "it is amazing how constrained sexual intimacy can be, even when we have the security of a truly loving relationship." Even couples who have been together long-term may be hesitant and embarrassed to ask for and explain what they desire and want. Unfortunately, culture has taught many of us that "wild abandon sex" is shameful and even wrong. The researchers conclude by noting that "if you keep your intimate sexual thoughts a secret, your sexual relationship has no chance to improve." In a novel way, the researchers continue by proclaiming that squeamishness and prudishness make chilling bedfellows. So be brave and tell your sex partner what you are thinking, and welcome your partner declaring his or her desires.

Think Critically

1. Are the results of this study surprising or what you thought? Explain.
2. Will the findings help you be a better lover? If so, in what way?
3. Do you believe you could tell a partner what would make him or her a better lover? If not, why? If so, how would you do this?
4. What are your thoughts about the idea that "wild abandon sex" is shameful?

SOURCES: Northrup, C., Schwartz, P., & Witte, J. (2012). *The normal bar: The surprising secrets of happy couples and what they reveal about creating a new normal in your relationship.* New York: Harmony.

arousal by placing a ban on partnered sexual activity for a period of time. During this time, explore other ways of being erotic or sexual, such as showering together, giving or receiving an erotic massage without genital stimulation, sharing one's sexual fantasies, or dancing together sexually.

Changing a Sexual Relationship and Managing Sexual Difficulties

In his book *Resurrecting Sex* (2002), David Schnarch, a prominent sex therapist and clinical psychologist, discusses common sexual function difficulties of couples and provides practical suggestions for addressing them. Schnarch says that every couple has sexual function problems at some point, although most couples do not anticipate that they will end up experiencing sexual dissatisfaction. In a statement that might seem surprising, he notes, "If your sexual relationship stays the same, you are more likely to have sexual dysfunctions (and be bored to death)." Schnarch declares that changing the sexual relationship is necessary for couples having sexual function problems and suggests 22 ways to "resurrect sex." His concepts and strategies for resolving sexual function difficulties include the following:

1. Put some effort into the nonsexual aspects of the relationship. Focus on the tasks of daily living that you share.
2. Expand your repertoire of sexual behaviors, "tones," styles, and meanings. Push yourself to try sexual behaviors that might seem to be a stretch. Resurrecting sex means doing things differently.
3. Address any issues you and your partner have swept under the carpet. Trying to be intimate and sexual when you are angry, frustrated, or resentful often does not work.
4. Deal with unresolved personal issues. They can hinder your arousal and make you vulnerable to sexual difficulties.
5. Do not become overly concerned with possible unconscious meanings of your sexual problems, and don't get sidetracked playing amateur psychoanalyst. No personality traits or life experiences invariably result in sexual function difficulties. Pay attention to your specific situation, and focus on what is actually happening to you.
6. Recognize that changing a sexual relationship typically involves embracing a deeper connection. Given that many couples do not achieve much emotional connection through sex, this can be a challenge. Intimate, deep connection during sex requires a sensory and emotional bond with your partner.

Schnarch guarantees one thing: To resurrect or improve an intimate relationship, you have to change the current relationship. He notes that this is no small task. Rather, it involves, for example, raising your level of stimulation, accepting new truths about you and your partner, becoming closer, and changing yourself in the process. Resurrecting sex requires being able to make positive changes without taking out frustrations on your partner, even if you think he or she deserves it.

Biomedical and behavioral interventions are effective for treating some individuals experiencing sexual function difficulties. However, sometimes treatment

think
about it

Sexual Turn-Ons and Turn-Offs:
What College Students Report

What turns college men and women on and off sexually? Are there gender differences and similarities? Sex researcher Robin R. Milhausen conducted an online study of 822 heterosexual students (440 women and 382 men) aged 18–37 from Indiana University who were randomly selected to participate. She contends that a greater understanding of factors that turn on and turn off men and women can be valuable in increasing sexual well-being and improving sexual relationships. Here are the study's major findings.

Some Important Factors Men and Women Agreed On

Factors that *enhance sexual arousal* for both men and women were:

- A good sense of humor, self-confidence, and intelligence
- Feeling desired as a partner
- Spontaneous and varied sex (e.g., not the same activities every time, having sex in a different setting)
- Fantasizing about and anticipating a sexual encounter
- Doing something fun together

Turn-offs for both men and women were:

- A lack of balance in giving and receiving during sex
- A partner who is self-conscious about his or her body
- Worrying about getting a bad sexual reputation
- Worrying about STIs
- Using condoms

Some Important Factors Men and Women Disagreed On

- Women were more concerned about their sexual functioning (e.g., being a good lover, worrying about taking too long to become aroused, feeling shy or self-conscious).
- Being in a relationship characterized by trust and emotional safety was considered more important to sexual arousal for women than for men.

- More women than men indicated that "feeling used" was a big turn-off.
- Men more often considered a variety of sexual stimuli (e.g., thinking about someone they find sexually attractive, "talking dirty," thinking and talking about sex, being physically close to a partner) as enhancers to sexual arousal.
- Women more often considered partner characteristics and behaviors (e.g., partner showing talent, interacting well with others, doing chores) as enhancers to sexual arousal.
- Women more often considered elements of the sexual setting (e.g., a setting where they might be seen or heard while having sex) as inhibitors to sexual arousal.
- Women were more aware of the role of hormones in sexual arousal.
- Women more often considered elements of the sexual interaction (e.g., partner not sensitive to the signals being given and received during sex, being uncertain how her partner feels) as inhibitors of sexual arousal.
- More men than women *disagreed* that "going right to the genitals" during sex would be a turn-off during sex.

Think Critically

1. Were you surprised by any of the findings? Which one and why?
2. Are some of the results similar to what you would consider sexual turn-ons and turn-offs?
3. Have you learned anything from this study that you might use in your future sexual encounters?
4. Do you think the results would be similar for gay and lesbian couples?

SOURCES: Milhausen, R. R. (2004). *Factors that inhibit and enhance sexual arousal in college men and women.* Doctoral dissertation. Indiana University, Bloomington, IN; Milhausen, R. R., Yarber, W., Sanders, S., & Graham, C. (2004, Nov.). *Factors that inhibit and enhance sexual arousal in college men and women.* Paper presented at the annual meeting of the Society for the Scientific Study of Sexuality, Orlando, FL.

TABLE 2 • Strategies to Cope With Sexual Difficulties

Coping Category	Examples of Strategies from the Data
Changing circumstances to fit goals	
Seek to alter circumstances	■ Seek to solve the problem medically (e.g., with Viagra) or psychologically ■ Close down a relationship and begin a new one
Changing goals to fit circumstances	
Engage flexible stance toward the importance of sex	■ Relegate sex in relation to other priorities ■ Focus on other aspects of the relationship ■ Focus on other priorities
Lower expectations	■ Accept a trade-off between being with someone you love and having the perfect physical sexual experience ■ Expect to have "good" sex less often
Engage flexible definitions of "good-enough" sex	■ Shift from viewing excitement as most important to viewing intimacy as most important
Living with a gap between goals and circumstances	
Normalization	■ Come to see your experience as normal ■ Compare your experience favorably with others
Avoidance	■ Avoid sexual activity ■ Avoid initiating sexual relationships ■ Avoid thinking about the problem

SOURCE: From Mitchell, R., King, M., Nazareth, I., & Wellings, K. (2001). Managing sexual difficulties: A qualitative investigation of coping strategies. *The Journal of Sex Research, 48,* 325–333. Reprinted by permission of The Society for the Scientific Study of Sexuality.

fails, resulting in individuals having to find ways to cope with and adjust to the difficulties. Little research has been conducted on how to do this. An interview study of 32 individuals living in Portugal and who experienced varied sexual function difficulties was conducted to identify the range of coping responses to their sexual problems (Mitchell, King, Nazareth, & Wellings, 2001). Three broad coping approaches, along with strategies, were identified (see Table 2): changing circumstances to fit goals, changing goals to fit circumstances, and living with a gap between goal and circumstances either by normalizing one's experience or by avoiding the problem. The findings revealed that the participants negotiated the meaning and significance of sexual experience within themselves and in response to outside factors, notably their sexual partner. The third approach, of living with a gap between goals and circumstances by normalizing one's situation or by avoiding the problem, may seem too unlikely to result in a mutually successful resolution, although in certain circumstances it may be effective. In commenting about the study results, the researchers stated:

> Where treatment fails or is not possible, adaptation will be much more likely where patients are encouraged toward more flexible definitions of good-enough sex and flexible prioritization of sex. Our use of the concept of good-enough sex was validated by participant descriptions of normality less than perfect. (p. 332)

• Treating Sexual Function Difficulties

There are several psychologically based approaches to sex therapy, the most important ones being behavior modification and psychosexual therapy. A systematic and meta-analysis review of available studies of psychological interventions for sexual dysfunctions from 1980 to 2009 found that they are effective options for treating sexual dysfunctions. Evidence varies across the different sexual function difficulties but good efficacy exists for female sexual interest/arousal disorder (Fruhauf, Gerger, Schmidt, Munder, & Barth, 2013). William Masters and Virginia Johnson were the pioneers in the cognitive-behavioral approach; one of the most influential psychosexual therapists is Helen Singer Kaplan. Medical approaches may also be effective with some sexual function problems.

Masters and Johnson: A Cognitive-Behavioral Approach

The program developed by Masters and Johnson for the treatment of sexual function difficulties was the starting point for contemporary sex therapy. They not only rejected the Freudian approach of tracing sexual function problems to childhood; they also relabeled sexual function problems as sexual dysfunctions rather than aspects of neuroses. Masters and Johnson (1970) argue that the majority of sexual function problems are the result of sexual ignorance, faulty techniques, or relationship problems. They treated difficulties using a combination of cognitive and behavioral techniques, and they treated couples rather than individuals.

Couples With Difficulties   Cognitive-behavioral therapists approach the problems of erectile and orgasmic difficulties by counseling the couple rather than the individual. They regard sexuality as an interpersonal phenomenon rather than an individual one. In fact, they tell their clients that there are no individuals with sexual function difficulties, only couples with sexual function difficulties. Sex therapist Sandra Pertot (2007) states that "even people with secure, happy personal histories can end up with unsatisfying sexual relationships, because it is how your individual sexuality interacts with your partner's that defines what is a problem and what isn't." In this model, neither individual is to blame for any sexual dissatisfaction; rather, it is their mutual interaction that sustains a difficulty or resolves a problem. Masters and Johnson called this principle "neutrality and mutuality" (Masters & Johnson, 1974).

Sensate Focus   A common therapeutic method is **sensate focus,** the focusing on touch and the giving and receiving of pleasure (see Figure 6). The other senses—smell, sight, hearing, and taste—are worked on indirectly as a means of reinforcing the touch experience. To increase their sensate focus, the couple is given "homework" assignments. In the privacy of their own home, the partners are to take off their clothes so that nothing will restrict their sensations. One partner must give pleasure and the other receive it. The giver touches, caresses, massages, and strokes his or her partner's body everywhere except the genitals and breasts. The purpose is not sexual arousal but simply sense awareness.

Specific Treatment Techniques   Sex therapy utilizes different techniques for treating specific problems. Treatment techniques for four major problems are briefly described in this section.

Full nakedness! All joys are due to thee,
As souls unbodied, bodies unclothed must be,
To taste whole joys.

—John Donne
(1572–1631)

Female Orgasmic Disorder   After doing sensate focus, the woman's partner begins to touch and caress her vulva; she guides the partner's hand to show what she likes. The partner is told, however, not to stimulate the clitoris directly because it may be extremely sensitive and stimulation may cause pain rather than pleasure. Instead, the partner caresses and stimulates the area around the clitoris, the labia, and the upper thighs. During this time, the partners are told not to attempt to have an orgasm because it would place undue performance pressure on the woman. They are simply to explore the woman's erotic potential and discover what brings her the greatest pleasure.

Here is a special message to partners of women who have difficulty experiencing orgasm during sex: Support her to have an orgasm any way it happens for her. Sexual partners do not give each other orgasms—lovers are traveling companions experiencing their own erotic journey (Castleman, 2004). Sex therapist and author Marty Klein, speaking to partners of women with orgasmic difficulties, states that "you can create the environment in which your lover feels relaxed enough and turned on enough to have one [orgasm]. But, she creates her own orgasm. You don't *give* it to her" (quoted in Castleman, 2004). In support of Klein's contention that a woman creates her own orgasm, a study of 2,371 women revealed that many women do things during sex beyond getting specific physical stimulation to aid them in experiencing orgasm (Ellison, 2000). The most frequent activities of these women are shown in Table 3. For example, 9 in 10 women indicated that they positioned their body in a way to get the stimulation they needed.

Erection Difficulties   When the problem is erection difficulties, the couple is taught that fears and anxieties are largely responsible and that the removal of these fears is the first step in therapy. Once these are removed, the man is less likely to be an observer of his sexuality; he can become a participant rather than a spectator or judge.

After integrating sensate focus into the couple's behavior, the partners are told to play with each other's genitals, but not to attempt an erection. Often, erections may occur because there is no demand on the man; however, he is encouraged to let his penis become flaccid again, then erect, then flaccid, as reassurance that he can successfully have erections. This builds his confidence, as well as his partner's, by letting him know that the partner can excite him.

Therapists also try to dispel many of the erection myths. Although the majority of difficulties with erections are caused by a combination of factors, such as

 The penis, far from being an impenetrable knight in armor, in fact bears its heart on its sleeve.

—Susan Bordo
(1947–)

TABLE 3 • Women's Most Frequent Activities to Facilitate Orgasm During Intercourse[a]

Activity	Percentage
Positioned my body to get the stimulation I needed	90
Paid attention to my physical sensations	83
Tightened and released my pelvic muscles	75
Synchronized the rhythm of my movements to my partner's	75
Asked or encouraged my partner to do what I needed	74
Got myself in a sexy mood beforehand	71
Focused on my partner's pleasure	68
Felt/thought how much I love my partner	65
Engaged in a fantasy of my own	56

[a]From a list of 14 possible answers, the answers that were chosen by at least one half of the women who responded to the sentence "In addition to getting specific physical stimulation, I often have done the following to help me reach orgasm during sex with a partner."

SOURCE: C.R. Ellison, Women's Sexualities: Generations of Women Share Intimate Secrets of Sexual Self-Acceptance. Read File Publications, 2006. Copyright © 2006 by Carol Ellison. All rights reserved. Used with permission.

relationship difficulties, cardiovascular problems, and depression, becoming more knowledgeable and realistic about erections is an important step to overcoming difficulties (Rosen, Miner, & Wincze, 2014). Common erection myths include the following (Castleman, 2004):

- *Erection is something that is achieved.* Penises don't become erect through work, but from just the opposite. The more sensual the lovemaking, the more likely an erection will occur.

- *Men are sex machines, always ready, always hard.* A man can really enjoy sex, but if certain conditions are not met, his penis might not become aroused. Instead of thinking of sex as performance, think about it as play that occurs best when both partners are able to relax.

- *During a sexual encounter, you get only one shot at an erection.* Erection changes during a sexual encounter are very common. If an erection subsides during sex, the man shouldn't tense up and decide it is over but instead breathe deeply, keep the faith, and ask the partner to provide stimulation that is sensual.

- *I blew it last time; I will never get it up again.* It's a mistake to overgeneralize from a single sexual episode to a lifetime of erection difficulties. Overgeneralizing can cause stress, sometimes resulting in a self-fulfilling prophecy.

- *If I can't have an erection, my partner can't be sexually satisfied.* Certainly there are numerous ways of providing sexual stimulation to a partner without an erection. How many people who care about their partners would leave him if he has erection problems? Most would want to help him resolve them.

Early Ejaculation Cognitive-behavioral therapists treat early or rapid ejaculation by using initially the same pattern as in treating erection difficulties. They concentrate especially on reducing fears and anxieties and increasing sensate focus and communication. Then they use a simple exercise called the **squeeze technique**

(see Figure 7). The penis is brought manually to a full erection and stimulation continues. Just before he is about to ejaculate, his partner squeezes his penis with thumb and forefinger just below the corona. After 30 seconds of inactivity, the partner arouses him again and, just prior to ejaculation, squeezes again. Using this technique, the couple can continue for 15–20 minutes before the man ejaculates.

Some sex therapists suggest that a man can learn ejaculatory control by increasing his ability to extend the plateau phase of his sexual response cycle, largely through learning to delay ejaculation during masturbation. They encourage men to learn their plateau phase well and, when the "point of no return" is reached during masturbation, the man should stop stroking his penis but not cease caressing completely. This "start-stop" technique can be done by the man himself or by a sexual partner. He should also strengthen his P.C. muscle, so that he can squeeze it to delay ejaculation at the point of no return. Then he returns to masturbation and repeats the cycle several times. For a man to learn ejaculatory control, sex therapists recommend masturbation several times a week for about 30–60 minutes per session. After several weeks, many men are able to hold themselves in the plateau phase for as long as they want. Further, if a man can learn to last 15 minutes, he can probably last as long as he'd like (Castleman, 2004; Keesling, 2006).

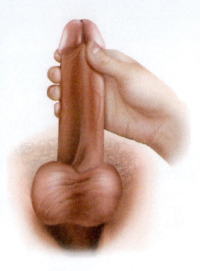

• FIGURE 7
Squeeze Technique

Delayed Ejaculation   One way in which delayed ejaculation is treated is by having the man's partner manipulate his penis. The partner asks for verbal and physical directions to bring him the most pleasure possible. It may take a few sessions before the man has his first ejaculation. The idea is to identify his partner with sexual pleasure and desire. He is encouraged to relax to keep the P.C. muscle from tightening and to feel stimulated, not only by his partner but also by the partner's erotic responses to him. After the man has experienced orgasm through manual stimulation, he can then proceed to vaginal or anal intercourse. With further instruction and feedback, the man should be able to function sexually without fear of delayed ejaculation.

Sex therapist Barbara Keesling (2006) states, "Ejaculation will happen when it happens," and it will happen when the man focuses on the sensations that allow ejaculation to occur rather than trying to make it happen.

Kaplan: Psychosexual Therapy

Helen Singer Kaplan (1974, 1979, 1983) modified Masters and Johnson's behavioral treatment program to include psychosexual therapy. The cognitive-behavioral approach works well for arousal and orgasmic difficulties resulting from mild to midlevel sexual anxieties. Such severe anxieties may manifest themselves in female sexual interest/arousal disorder, male hypoactive sexual desire disorder and sexual aversion disorder.

Other Nonmedical Approaches

Both cognitive-behavioral and psychosexual therapy are expensive and take a considerable amount of time. In response to these limitations, "brief" sex therapy and self-help and group therapy have developed.

PLISSIT Model of Therapy   One of the most common approaches used by sex therapists is based on the **PLISSIT model** (Annon, 1974, 1976). "PLISSIT" is an acronym for the four progressive levels of sex therapy: **p**ermission, **l**imited information, specific suggestions, and intensive therapy. About 90% of sexual function difficulties can be successfully addressed in the first three levels; only about 10% of patients require extensive therapy.

The first level in the PLISSIT model involves giving permission. At one time or another, most sexual behaviors were prohibited by important figures in our lives. Because desires and activities such as fantasies or masturbation were not validated, we often question their "normality" or "morality." We shroud them in secrecy or drape them with shame. Without permission to be sexual, we may experience sexual difficulties and dissatisfaction. Sex therapists act as "permission givers" for us to be sexual.

The second level involves giving limited information. This information is restricted to the specific area of sexual function difficulties. If a woman has an orgasmic disorder, for example, the therapist might explain that not all women are orgasmic in coitus without additional manual stimulation before, during, or after penetration.

The third level involves making specific suggestions. If permission giving and limited information are not sufficient, the therapist next suggests specific "homework" exercises. For example, if a man experiences early or involuntary ejaculation, the therapist may suggest that he and his partner try the squeeze technique. A woman with orgasmic disorder might be instructed to masturbate with or without her partner to discover the best way for her partner to assist her in experiencing orgasm.

The fourth level involves undergoing intensive therapy. If the individual continues to experience a sexual function problem, he or she will need to enter intensive therapy, such as psychosexual therapy.

Self-Help and Group Therapy The PLISSIT model provides a sound basis for understanding how partners, friends, books, sexuality education films, self-help exercises, and group therapy can be useful in helping us deal with the first three levels of therapy: permission, limited information, and specific suggestions. Partners, friends, books, sexuality education films, and group therapy sessions under a therapist's guidance, for example, may provide "permission" for us to engage in sexual exploration and discovery. From these sources, we may learn that many of our sexual fantasies and behaviors are very common.

The first step in dealing with a sexual function difficulty can be to tap your own immediate resources. Begin by discussing the problem with your partner; find out what he or she thinks. Discuss specific strategies that might be useful. Sometimes, simply communicating your feelings and thoughts will resolve the dissatisfaction. Seek out friends with whom you can share your feelings and anxieties. Find out what they think; ask them whether they have had similar experiences and, if so, how they handled them. Try to keep your perspective—and your sense of humor.

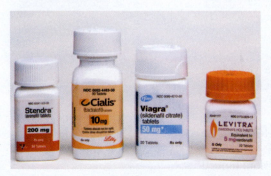

Four prescription drugs—Viagra, Cialis, Stendra, Levitra—have revolutionized the treatment of male erection difficulties.

© Studio Works/Alamy

Medical Approaches

Sexual function difficulties are often a combination of physical and psychological problems. Even people whose difficulties are physical may develop psychological or relationship problems as they try to cope with their difficulties. Thus, treatment for organically based problems may need to include psychological counseling. The combined medical and psychological intervention has several advantages, such as greater treatment efficacy and patient satisfaction (Althof, 2010).

Vaginal pain caused by inadequate lubrication and thinning vaginal walls often occurs as a result of the decreased estrogen associated with menopause. A lubricating jelly or estrogen therapy may help. Vaginitis, endometriosis, and pelvic inflammatory disease may also make intercourse painful. Lubricants or short-term menopausal hormone therapy often resolves difficulties. Loss of sex drive and function, low energy and strength, depressed mood, and low self-esteem may sometimes occur from testosterone deficiency. The sex lives of people with significant testosterone deficiencies may be helped by testosterone supplements.

Most medical and surgical treatments for men have centered on erection difficulties. Such approaches include microsurgery to improve a blood flow problem, suction devices to induce and maintain an erection, a prosthesis implanted in the penis and abdomen, and drugs injected into the penis. Because these methods are not practical or pleasant, they became virtually obsolete with the introduction of an erection-enhancing drug, Viagra, in 1998 by Pfizer. Viagra, the trade name for sildenafil citrate, is the first effective and safe oral drug for the treatment of male erection difficulty, whether caused by psychological or medical conditions.

Viagra revolutionized the treatment of erection difficulties, representing the beginning of a pharmacological approach to treating sexual difficulties. Medical literature shows that Viagra is effective and well tolerated, even for men who have taken the drug for a long period of time, and can improve the sexual satisfaction of both the man and his partner in couples with male erection difficulties (Heiman et al., 2007; Padma-Nathan, Eardley, Kloner, Laties, & Montorsi, 2002). In 2003, two other drugs were approved by the FDA for the treatment of erection problems: GlaxoSmithKline and Bayer's Levitra (vardenafil HCI) and Eli Lilly's Cialis (tadalafil). These three drugs are one of the most popular groups of drugs in pharmaceutical industry history. In April 2012, the U.S. Food and Drug Administration approved another erection-enhancing drug, Stendra (avanafil). About 100 million men globally have sought medical help for erectile dysfunction and the drugs are now commonly used as first-time therapy for ED (Rosen et al., 2014). The National Survey of Sexual Health and Behavior found that 3% of U.S. men aged 18–59 had used an erection medication the last time they had sex. Use was greater for men in the 50–59 age group (8%) than the younger age groups (e.g., 18–24, <1%) (Herbenick et al., 2010.14a). Viagra and Levitra are effective for a few hours, whereas Cialis is effective for 24 to 36 hours. Among the several benefits of the erection-enhancing drugs is that they are often effective in treating erection difficulties that occur as a result of prostate-cancer treatment and surgery, including complete removal of the prostate (American Cancer Society, 2015).

Erection-enhancing drugs allow the muscles in the penis to relax and penile arteries to dilate, thus expanding the erectile tissues that squeeze shut the veins in the penis. They are taken before sex; the amount of time the effects last varies depending on the drug. The drugs do not increase sexual desire, nor do they produce an erection itself; there still must be sexual stimulation. After sex is over, the erection goes away. The primary psychological role of the erection drugs is to eliminate the anticipatory and performance anxiety surrounding intercourse, which will usually, in itself, result in erections and increased confidence. Some men take the drugs as a "quick fix" for a temporary problem or as "insurance," even though they may not really need them. Because Viagra increases pelvic blood flow, many women began using it when it was first released in hopes of increasing sensation and orgasm. These experiences, and the results of medical research,

The penis used to have a mind of its own. Not anymore. The erection industry has reconfigured the organ, replacing the finicky original with a more reliable model.

—David Friedman
(1949–)

though, have yielded mixed results as insufficient vasocongestion probably does not solely account for orgasm difficulties in women. Efforts to create an effective drug (e.g., Flibanserin) for female sexual difficulties, particularly low sexual desire, continue but to no avail (Angier, 2007; Bancroft, 2009; Landau, 2014).

The U.S. Food and Drug Administration notes that these drugs are safe for most men if used according to the directions, except for men taking nitrates (often prescribed for chest pain) and those having poor cardiovascular health. Headaches, visual disturbances, and flushing sometimes occur, and in rare cases extended and painful erections occur (Ashton, 2007; Reitman, 2004). Some men are using the erection drugs casually, as party drugs or as insurance against the effects of alcohol and for a desired increase in "prowess" (Harte & Meston, 2011). The mixing of street drugs and an erection-enhancing drug is dangerous. And people should never use someone else's erection-enhancing drug; they should always get their own prescription from a doctor.

Some experts caution people not to over-rely on medical approaches to solve sexual function difficulties (see the "Think About It" box "The Medicalization of Sexual Function Problems"). Sex therapist and clinical psychologist Julian Slow-inski (2007) states that "a man's sexual functioning is determined and affected by the health of his body and lifestyle, his personal emotional state, the quality of his relationship, and the influence of life and environmental stress." Most sexual function difficulties can be resolved through individual and couple therapy. The optimal approach in the use of drugs is in concert with psychotherapy.

Numerous homeopathic products, often known as "natural sexual enhancers," are being sold on the Internet and at health-food stores, convenience stores, and drugstores, promising to "spice up your sex life," "rekindle desire," and "improve sexual performance." Supported by unsubstantiated claims and personal testimonials, these capsules, herbal erection creams, sprays, lubricants, gels, and tonics promise greater sexual arousal and rock-hard erections. These products are not regulated by the U.S. Food and Drug Administration, may or may not contain ingredients listed on the label, and instead may contain ingredients that could be harmful to people, especially those with medical conditions. Conclusive evidence of the effectiveness of the natural sexual enhancers treating male and female sexual function problems has not been established. In short, there aren't any natural "magic bullets" that turn you into an instant, perfect love machine. As suggested throughout this book, enhancing your emotional and physical health, as well as your relationship with your partner, is usually the best path to sexual fulfillment.

Gay, Lesbian, and Bisexual Sex Therapy

Until recently, sex therapists treated sexual function difficulties as implicitly heterosexual. The model for sexual functioning, in fact, was generally orgasmic heterosexual intercourse. There was virtually no mention of gay, lesbian, bisexual, or transgender sexual concerns.

For gay men, lesbian women, and bisexual individuals, sexual issues differ from those of heterosexuals in several ways. First, although gay men and lesbian women may have arousal, desire, erectile, or orgasmic difficulties, the context in which they occur may differ significantly from that of heterosexual individuals (Institute of Medicine, 2011). Problems among heterosexuals most often focus on sexual intercourse, whereas the sexual dissatisfaction of gay men, lesbian women, and bisexual people focuses on other behaviors. Gay men in sex therapy,

think
about it

The Medicalization of Sexual Function Problems

Since the early 1980s, a number of pharmacological therapies have been introduced for treatment of men's sexual function problems. The erection-enhancing drugs—Viagra, Levitra, Cialis, and Stendra—enable some men suffering from hypertension, diabetes, and prostate problems to get an erection by increasing the flow of blood to the penis, provided there is sexual stimulation. However, the pills do not cure fractured relationships, make people more sensual lovers, enlarge penises, end age-related sexual limits, or address the complexity of all sexual problems (Marshall, 2012; Moynihan & Mintzes, 2010; Reitman, 2004; Slowinski, 2007). One problem with the erection-enhancing drugs is that they reinforce the widespread, but mistaken, belief that an erection equals a satisfying sexual experience for both men and women. It perpetuates the notion, fed by many erotic videos, that sticking an erection into an erotic opening is the only thing sex is about (Castleman, 2004). Sex therapist Marty Klein says that "it's possible to have a rock-hard erection and still have lousy sex" (quoted in Castleman, 2004). The pills often help individuals postpone or avoid self and couple analysis. Some experts contend that the erection-enhancing pills have, thus, medicalized sexual problems, resulting in the prevailing medical model that promotes a specific norm of sexual functioning: correct genital performance (Tiefer, 2001). The medical solution would be to take a pill for an erection problem, thus taking the focus off the individual and the dynamics of the relationship (Bancroft, 2009; Tiefer, 2001, 2004). However, the best use of Viagra (and Levitra, Cialis, and Stendra) is in the context of a comprehensive assessment and intervention by a sex therapist that focuses on the physical, emotional, and relational aspects of the male (McCarthy, 1998; Slowinski, 2007).

The "Viagra phenomenon," the most recent event in the medicalization of male sexuality, has both positive and negative consequences: It enables millions of men to have reliable erections, but it also calls for a similar pill that would increase female sexual response. John Bancroft, senior research fellow at The Kinsey Institute, in speaking about pharmacological approaches to female sexual function problems, contends that the term "sexual dysfunction" commonly used in medicine is misleading and dangerous; portraying sexual difficulties as dysfunctions "encourages physicians to prescribe drugs to change sexual function when the attention should be paid to other aspects of the woman's life" (quoted in Moynihan, 2002). Bancroft (2002, 2009) stated that a

Viagra-type drug might influence female sexual response and enjoyment but treatment should not separate sexual expression from other factors that influence sexual functioning in women, such as fatigue, stress, or threatening behavior from their partners.

Leonore Tiefer (2004), a sex therapist and psychiatry faculty member at New York University School of Medicine, says that innumerable professional and scientific conferences have been held on female sexual dysfunction, enthusiastically backed by drug companies. She contends that this is an effort to sell female sexual function problems as a new medical disorder solvable by medical treatments. In response to this, she and other experts developed a perspective of female sexuality, The New View of Women's Sexual Problems, described earlier in this chapter, to challenge the medicalization of women's sexuality.

Tiefer (2012) states that with increasing emphasis on the search for sexual desire and orgasm, satisfaction may become more elusive; sexual discontent will become universal and therapies infinite. In looking ahead to the future of medicalization of sexual function problems, she contends that the marketplace is always at work for new solutions. She notes that:

> However, as the growth of alternative sexualities expands, the paradigm of problems and therapies may shift away from medicalization and biomedicalization toward a multisexualities diversity model. Society and people will continue to need various kinds of help, but perhaps in the next era they won't turn—or first turn—to medicine or a model centered on health or illness to lead the way. (p. 317)

Think Critically

1. Do you think that the sexuality of men and women is being medicalized?
2. Do you think it would be easier to take an erection-enhancing drug than seek therapy for erection difficulties?
3. Should a drug like Viagra be developed for women?
4. Are people over-relying on drugs to solve their sexual function problems?

practically speaking

Seeking Professional Assistance

Just because something is not "functioning" according to a therapist's model does not necessarily mean that something is wrong. You need to evaluate your sexuality in terms of your own and your partner's satisfaction and the meanings you give to your sexuality. If, after doing this, you are unable to resolve your sexual function difficulties yourself, seek professional assistance. It is important to realize that seeking such assistance is not a sign of personal weakness or failure. Rather, it is a sign of strength, for it demonstrates an ability to reach out and a willingness to change. It is a sign that you care for your partner, your relationship, and yourself. As you think about therapy, consider the following:

- What are your goals in therapy? Are you willing to make changes in your relationship to achieve your goals?

- Do you want individual, couple, or group therapy? If you are in a relationship, is your partner willing to participate in therapy?

- What characteristics are important for you in a therapist? Do you prefer a female or a male therapist? Is the therapist's age, religion, or ethnic background important to you?

- What are the therapist's professional qualifications? There are few certified sex therapy programs; most therapists who treat sexual function difficulties come from various professional backgrounds, such as psychiatry, clinical psychology, psychoanalysis, marriage and family counseling, and social work. The American Association of Sexuality Educators, Counselors, and Therapists certifies sex therapists and has a list of

certified persons with contact information, by state and country, on its website (http://www.aasect.org). Because there is no licensing in the field of sex therapy, it is important to seek out those trained therapists who have licenses in their generalized field.

- What is the therapist's approach? Is it behavioral, psychosexual, psychoanalytic, medical, religious, spiritual, feminist, or something else? Do you feel comfortable with the approach?

- If necessary, does the therapist offer a sliding-scale fee, based on your level of income?

- If you are a lesbian, gay, or bisexual person, does the therapist affirm your sexual orientation? Does the therapist understand the special problems gay men, bisexual individuals, and lesbian women face?

- After a session or two with the therapist, do you have confidence in him or her? If not, discuss your feelings with the therapist. If you believe your dissatisfaction is not a defense mechanism, change therapists.

Most sex therapists believe that their work results in considerable success. Not all problems can be resolved completely, but some—and often great—improvement usually occurs. Short-term therapy of 10 or fewer sessions helps some people, although most require therapy for 4 months or longer (McCarthy & McCarthy, 2009). Much of therapy's success depends on a person's willingness to confront painful feelings and to change. This entails time, effort, and often considerable amounts of money. But ultimately, the difficult work may reward partners with greater satisfaction and a deeper relationship.

---

for example, most often experience aversion toward anal eroticism (Reece, 1988; Sandfort & de Keizer, 2001). Lesbian women in sex therapy frequently complain about aversive feelings toward cunnilingus. Female orgasmic difficulty, however, is not frequently viewed as a problem (Margolies et al., 1988). Heterosexual women, in contrast, frequently complain about lack of orgasm.

Second, lesbian women, gay men, and bisexual individuals must deal with both societal homophobia and internalized homophobia. Fear of violence makes it difficult for gay men, bisexual individuals, and lesbian women to openly express their affection in the same manner as heterosexuals. As a consequence, lesbian women, bisexual individuals, and gay men learn to repress their expressions of feelings in public; this repression may carry over into the private realm

Impulse arrested spills over, and the flood is feeling, the flood is passion, the flood is even madness: It depends on the force of the current, the height and strength of the barrier. . . . Feeling lurks in that interval of time between desire and its consummation.

—Aldous Huxley
(1894–1963)

It is important for gay, lesbian, and bisexual people with sexual difficulties to choose a therapist who affirms their orientation and understands the special issues confronting them.

© Beau Lark/Corbis

as well. Internalized homophobia may result in diminished sexual desire, creating sexual aversion and fostering guilt and negative feelings about sexual activity.

Third, gay men must deal with the association between sex and HIV infection that has cut a deadly swath through the gay community. The death of friends, lovers, and partners has left many depressed, which, in turn, affects sexual desire and creates high levels of sexual anxiety. Many gay men are fearful of contracting HIV even if they practice safer sex. And HIV-positive men, even if they are practicing safer sex, are often afraid of transmitting the infection to their loved ones.

These unique lesbian, bisexual, and gay individuals' concerns along with those who identify as gender non-conforming or transsexual require that sex therapists expand their understanding and treatment of sexual function problems. For example, if the therapist is heterosexual, he or she needs to have a thorough knowledge of sexual orientation issues and the special needs of gay, lesbian, bisexual, and gender non-conforming individuals. Therapists further need to be aware of their own assumptions and feelings about varied sexual orientations and gender identities.

Final Thoughts

As we consider our sexuality, it is important to realize that sexual function difficulties and dissatisfaction are commonplace. But sex is more than orgasms or certain kinds of activities. Even if we have function difficulties in some areas, there are other areas in which we may be fully sexual. If we have erection or orgasmic problems, we can use our imagination to expand our repertoire of erotic activities. We can touch each other sensually, masturbate alone or with our partner, and caress, kiss, eroticize, and explore our bodies with fingers and tongues. We can enhance our sexuality if we look at sex as the mutual giving and receiving of erotic pleasure, rather than a command performance. By paying attention to our conditions for good sex, maintaining intimacy, and focusing on our own erotic sensations and those of our partner, we can transform our sexual relationships.

Summary

Sexual Function Difficulties: Definitions, Types, and Prevalence

- The line between "normal" sexual functioning and a sexual function difficulty is often not definitive.
- Difficulties in sexual functioning are often called sexual problems, sexual disorders, or *sexual dysfunctions*.
- The *Diagnostic and Statistical Manual of Mental Disorders, Fifth Edition* (*DSM-5*) classifies four types of sexual dysfunctions: sexual desire problems, orgasmic disorders, sexual pain disorders, and substance/medication-induced sexual dysfunction. According to a woman-centered classification system, sexual function difficulties arise from cultural and relational factors, as well as psychological and medical problems.
- A sexual function difficulty can be defined as a disappointment on the part of one or both partners.
- Several national studies show that many men and women experience, on occasion, sexual function difficulties. Numerous factors, such as personal and relationship problems, aging, personal health, socioeconomic issues, unrealistic expectations, and attitudes toward sexuality, impact sexual functioning.
- *Female sexual interest/arousal disorder* is the absent/reduced sexual thoughts, fantasies, initiation and receptivity and absent/reduced arousal and pleasure during sexual activity. This disorder is frequently associated with problems of experiencing orgasm, pain during sexual activity, low frequency of sexual activity, poor sexual techniques, and relationship problems. Lack of sexual interest is the most common female sexual function difficulty.
- *Male hypoactive sexual desire disorder* is the persistence or absence of sexual thoughts, fantasies, and desire for sexual activity. This disorder may be associated with erectile and/or ejaculatory difficulties.
- *Erectile disorder* is the difficulty with erections during partnered sexual activity. Many men experiencing erection difficulties may have low self-esteem, low self-confidence, decreased sexual satisfaction, reduced sexual desire, and a decreased sense of masculinity.
- *Sexual aversion disorder* is a consistently phobic response to sexual activities or the idea of such activities.
- *Female orgasmic disorder* is the difficulty in experiencing orgasms or reduced intensity of orgasms during sexual activity. Orgasmic difficulties are the second most common female problem treated by therapists.
- *Delayed ejaculation* is inability or difficulty in ejaculating despite adequate sexual stimulation or desire to experience ejaculation.
- *Premature (early) ejaculation* is, according to the *DSM-5*, a pattern of early ejaculation during partnered sexual activity within 1 minute following vaginal penetration and before the individual desires. Some debate exists on how long intercourse should take place to be classified as having premature/early ejaculation. Early ejaculation is fairly common in the general population.
- *Genito-pelvic/penetration disorder* is difficulty related to genital and pelvic pain and vaginal penetration during intercourse. The category represents a total inability to experience vaginal penetration in any circumstance (e.g., intercourse, gynecological examination, tampon insertion), to being able to easily experience penetration in one situation but not another.
- *Substance/medication-induced sexual dysfunction* is the difficulty in sexual functioning that can occur with intoxication or soon after or during withdrawal of numerous drugs including prescription and illicit/recreational drugs.

Physical Causes of Sexual Function Difficulties and Dissatisfaction

- Health problems such as diabetes and alcoholism can cause erectile difficulties. Some prescription drugs affect sexual responsiveness.
- Coital pain caused by inadequate lubrication and thinning vaginal walls often occurs as a result of decreased estrogen associated with menopause. Lubricants can resolve the difficulties.

Psychological Causes of Sexual Function Difficulties and Dissatisfaction

- Sexual function difficulties may have their origin in any number of psychological causes. The immediate causes of these difficulties lie in the current situation, including fatigue and stress, ineffective sexual behavior, sexual anxieties, and an excessive need to please a partner. Internal conflict caused by religious teachings, guilt, negative learning, and internalized homophobia can contribute to dissatisfaction, as can relationship conflicts.

Sexual Function Enhancement

- Many people and all couples experience sexual function difficulties and dissatisfaction at one time or another. Differences in sexual desire are the most common complaint among couples. The widespread variability of sexual functioning suggests the "normality" of at least occasional sexual function difficulties.

- *Sexual function enhancement* refers to improving the quality of one's sexual relationship. Sexual function–enhancement programs generally provide accurate information about sexuality, develop communication skills, foster positive attitudes, and increase self-awareness. Awareness of your own sexual needs is often critical to enhancing your sexuality. Enhancement of sex includes the intensification of arousal.

- There has been a dramatic increase in over-the-counter, natural sexual enhancers, but none have been scientifically shown to be effective.

Treating Sexual Function Difficulties

- Masters and Johnson developed a cognitive-behavioral approach to sexual function difficulties. They relabeled sexual problems as dysfunctions rather than neuroses or diseases, used direct behavior modification practices, and treated couples rather than individuals. Treatment includes *sensate focus* without intercourse, "homework" activities, and, finally, "permission" to engage in sexual intercourse. Kaplan's psychosexual therapy program combines behavioral activities with insight therapy.

- The *PLISSIT model* of sex therapy refers to four progressive levels: *p*ermission, *l*imited *i*nformation, *s*pecific *s*uggestions, and *i*ntensive *t*herapy. Individuals and couples can often resolve their sexual function difficulties by talking them over with their partners or friends, reading self-help books, and attending sex therapy groups. If they are unable to resolve their difficulties in these ways, they should consider intensive sex therapy.

- Viagra was introduced in the United States in 1998 and was the first effective and safe oral drug for treatment of male erection difficulty. Subsequently, three other prescription drugs, Levitra, Cialis, and Stendra, have been approved by the U.S. Food and Drug Administration. These drugs do not increase sexual excitement but rather facilitate blood engorgement in the penis.

- Some sexuality professionals claim that drug companies have exaggerated and "medicalized" sexual function difficulties to promote sales.

- There are three significant concerns for gay men, bisexual individuals, and lesbian women in sex therapy. First, the context in which problems occur may differ significantly from that of a heterosexual person; there may be issues revolving around anal eroticism and cunnilingus. Second, they must deal with both societal homophobia and internalized homophobia. Third, gay men must deal with the association between sex and HIV/AIDS and other sexually transmitted infections.

- In seeking professional assistance for a sexual problem, it is important to realize that seeking help is not a sign of personal weakness or failure but rather a sign of strength.

Questions for Discussion

- Do you think that sexual function difficulties should be determined by a medical group such as the American Psychiatric Association or by what the individual and/or couple decides is dissatisfying?

- If you have been sexual with another person, have you ever experienced sexual function dissatisfaction or difficulty? After reading this chapter, do you think that this experience is actually a "sexual dysfunction" or possibly a dissatisfaction based on an unrealistic expectation of what sex should be like? Did you talk to your partner about the disappointment?

- What do you consider to be a satisfying sexual experience with a partner? Did the information in this chapter cause you to reevaluate what you consider "good sex" for you and a partner?

- If you had a sexual function difficulty, how comfortable would you be in seeking help from a sex therapist?

- If you or your male partner were having difficulties with erections, would you seek prescription drugs (Viagra, Levitra, Cialis, or Stendra) to deal with the problem? Is it possible for a man and his partner to have good sex without an erection?

Suggested Websites

American Family Physician

http://www.aafp.org

Provides information about both female and male sexual function difficulties.

New View Campaign

http://www.newviewcampaign.org

Promotes an alternative view of female sexual function difficulties, challenges the pharmaceutical industry, and calls for further research on these difficulties.

Cleveland Clinic

http://my.clevelandclinic.org/disorders/sexual_dysfunction/hic_sexual_dysfunction_in_males.aspx

Provides an overview of sexual dysfunction in both men and women and a discussion of diseases and medications that affect sexual function.

Women's Sexual Health

http://www.womenssexualhealth.com

Addresses the questions and concerns of women and their partners concerning female sexual function difficulties and includes a "Physician Locator" to help them find local physicians who treat these difficulties.

Suggested Reading

Binik, Y. M., & Hall, K. S. K. (2014). *Principles and practice of sex therapy* (5th ed.). New York: Guilford Press. A multidisciplinary perspective on the causes and treatment of sexual dysfunctions that integrates current research with clinical practice. All chapters are authored by internationally recognized experts.

Cassell, C. (2008). *Put passion first: Why sexual chemistry is the key to finding and keeping lasting love.* New York: McGraw-Hill. Written for women (but can be valuable to men, too), this book helps the reader understand the significance and role of sexual passion within a relationship with emphasis on increasing couple intimacy.

Castleman, M. (2004). *Great sex: A man's guide to the secret principles of total-body sex.* New York: Rodale. An exceptionally easy-to-read and practical book for men in which the author quotes well-respected sex therapists throughout the book to show therapists' suggestions for various sexual function problems.

Keesling, B. (2006). *Sexual healing: The complete guide to overcoming common sexual problems* (3rd ed.). Alameda, CA: Hunter House. A greatly expanded edition of the classic book on the healing power of sex that offers more than 125 exercises that help with a wide range of sexual function difficulties.

Klein, M. (2012). *Sexual intelligence: What we really want from sex—and how to get it.* New York: HarperOne. Presents a very sex-positive, realistic, and healthy perspective on enhancing sexual pleasure for individuals and couples.

McCarthy, B. W., & McCarthy, E. (2009). *Discovering your couple sexual style.* New York: Routledge. Focuses on helping couples enhance intimacy and sexual satisfaction by providing relevant sexual information, exercises, and practical tools.

Metz, M. E., & McCarthy, B. W. (2011). *Enduring desire: Your guide to lifelong intimacy.* New York: Routledge. A superb guide on creating and maintaining a satisfying sex life across ages of a long-term relationship.

Moynihan, R., & Mintzes, B. (2010). *Sex, lies & pharmaceuticals.* Vancouver, British Columbia: Greystone Books. Explores the causes of women's sexual dissatisfaction and the global efforts of drug companies to medicalize women's sexual problems.

Ogden, G. (2008). *The return of desire: A guide to discovering your sexual passions.* Boston: Trumpeter. Written by an experienced sex therapist, this book is a wise guide that focuses on women and enhancing their sexual desire and passion.

Perel, E. (2006). *Mating in captivity.* New York: Harper. Presents a provocative perspective on intimacy and sex in exploring the paradoxical union of domesticity and sexual desire.

Pertot, S. (2007). *When sex drives don't match.* New York: Marlow & Company. Presents 10 libido types and how they affect a couple along with rational ways for couples to work through differing sex drives.

Schnarch, D. (2002). *Resurrecting sex.* New York: HarperCollins. Deals with the sexual problems of couples and offers frank talk about sex, intimacy, and relationships.

Sexually Transmitted Infections

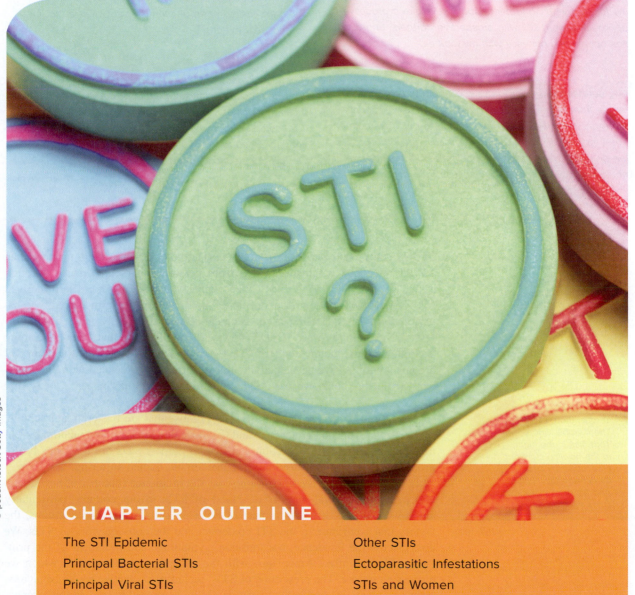

© pederk/iStock/Getty Images

CHAPTER OUTLINE

The STI Epidemic

Principal Bacterial STIs

Principal Viral STIs

Vaginal Infections

Other STIs

Ectoparasitic Infestations

STIs and Women

Preventing STIs

"Up to this date, I have slept with about thirteen men. My most recent 'wake-up call' was from a threat from a prospective partner and from a human sexuality course. I took a test for HIV; the result was negative. However, I did get infected and passed on genital warts to my ex-boyfriend. I simply pretended that I had never slept with anyone else and that if anyone had cheated it was him. It never fazed me that I was at such a risk for contracting HIV. My new resolutions are to educate my family, friends, and peers about sex, take a proactive approach toward sex with prospective partners, and discuss sex openly and honestly with my mother."

—**23-year-old female**

"My partner and I want to use a condom to protect ourselves from STIs. But I feel inadequate when we are intimate and he cannot keep an erection to put a condom on. I feel too embarrassed for him to discuss the situation. So, we both walk away a bit disappointed—him because he could not stay erect and me because I did not take the time or have the courage to help him. I think if he masturbated with a condom on it would help him with his performance anxiety problem."

—**22-year-old female**

"STIs and HIV are precisely the reason I exercise caution when engaging in sexual activity. I don't want to ever get an STI, and I'd rather never have sex again than have HIV."

—**24-year-old male**

"Why do males often convince women to have sex without proper protection? I don't understand this because there is always a risk of getting an STI. I know that women think about this just as often as men do, but why is it that men do not seem to care?"

—**21-year-old female**

"I am usually very careful when it comes to my sexual relations and protecting myself from STIs, but there have been a couple of times when I've drunk a lot and have not practiced safe sex. It scares me that I have done things like that and have tried to make sure it doesn't happen again. STIs are just a very uncomfortable subject."

—**27-year-old male**

O rose, thou art sick!
The invisible worm
That flies in the night,
In the howling storm,
Has found thy bed
Of crimson joy,
And his dark secret love
Does thy life destroy.

—William Blake
(1757–1827)

THE TERM "SEXUALLY TRANSMITTED INFECTIONS" (STIs) refers to more than 25 infectious organisms passed from person to person primarily through sexual contact. STIs were once called venereal diseases (VDs), a term derived from Venus, the Roman goddess of love. More recently, the term "sexually transmitted diseases" (STDs) replaced "venereal diseases." Actually, many health professionals continue to use "STD." However, some believe that "STI" is a more accurate and less judgmental term. That is, a person can be infected with an STI organism but not have developed the illness or disease associated with the organism. So in this book, we use "STI," although "STD" may appear when other sources are cited.

There are two general types of STIs: (1) those that are bacterial and curable, such as chlamydia and gonorrhea, and (2) those that are viral and incurable—but treatable—such as HIV infection and genital herpes. STIs are a serious health problem in our country, resulting in considerable human suffering.

In this chapter and the next, we discuss the **incidence** (number of new cases) and **prevalence** (total number of cases) of STIs in our country, particularly among youth, the disparate impact of STIs on certain population groups, the factors that contribute to the STI epidemic, and the consequences of STIs. We also discuss the incidence, transmission, symptoms, and treatment of the principal STIs that affect Americans, with the exception of HIV/AIDS, which we discuss elsewhere. The prevention of STIs, including protective health behaviors, safer sex practices, and communication skills, is also addressed in this chapter.

The STI Epidemic

The federal Institute of Medicine (IOM) characterizes STIs as "hidden epidemics of tremendous health and economic consequences in the United States," adding that "STDs represent a growing threat to the nation's health and national action is urgently needed." The IOM notes that STIs are a challenging public health problem because of their "hidden" nature. The IOM adds that "the sociocultural taboos related to sexuality are a barrier to STD prevention" (Eng & Butler, 1997). The "silent" infections of STIs make them a serious public threat requiring greater personal attention and increased health care resources.

STIs: The Most Common Reportable Infectious Diseases

STIs are common in the United States, but identifying exactly how many cases there are is impossible, and even estimating the total number is difficult. Often, an STI is "silent"—that is, it goes undiagnosed because it has no early symptoms or the symptoms are ignored and untreated, especially among people with limited access to health care. Asymptomatic infections can be diagnosed through testing, but routine screening programs are not widespread, and social stigmas and the lack of public awareness about STIs may result in no testing during visits to health care professionals. And even when STIs are diagnosed, reporting regulations vary. Only a few STIs—gonorrhea, syphilis, chlamydia, hepatitis A and B, HIV/AIDS, and chancroid—must be reported by health care providers to local or state health departments and to the federal Centers for Disease Control and Prevention (CDC). But no such reporting requirement exists for other common STIs, such as genital herpes, human papillomavirus (HPV), and trichomoniasis. In addition, the reporting of STI diagnoses is inconsistent. For example, some private physicians do not report STI cases to their state health departments (American Social Health Association [ASHA], 2006; CDC, 2014.15a). In spite of the underreporting and undiagnosed cases, several significant indicators illustrate the STI problem in the United States:

- STIs are the most commonly reported infectious diseases in the United States. In 2012, STIs represented four of the six most frequently reported infectious diseases (CDC, 2014.15a) (see Figure 1).

- An estimated 20 million new STI cases occur each year (CDC, 2013.15a).

- STIs impact the lives of more than 110 million men and women across the United States, costing the American health care system nearly $17 billion yearly in direct medical costs alone (CDC, 2013.15a).

- By age 25, one in two young persons will acquire an STI (Cates, Herndon, Schulz, & Darroch, 2004).

- More than one half of sexually active men and women will become infected with an STI at some point in their lives (CDC, 2011.15a).

- One in five sexually active adolescent females have an STI, such as chlamydia and human papillomavirus (HPV) (Forhan et al., 2009).

Who Is Affected: Disparities Among Groups

Anyone, regardless of gender, race/ethnicity, social status, or sexual orientation, can get an STI. What people do—not who they are—exposes them to the organisms that cause STIs. Nevertheless, some population groups are

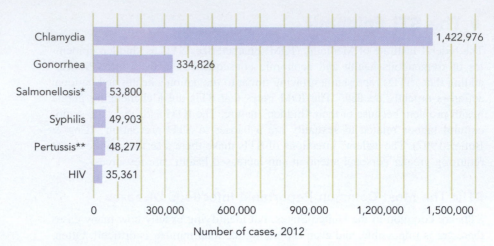

Number of cases, 2012

*Infection with the *Salmonella* bacterium that causes diarrheal illness.
** Whooping cough.

disproportionately affected by STIs; this disparity reflects gender, age, and racial and ethnic differences (CDC, 2014.15b).

Gender Disparities   Overall, the consequences of STIs for women often are more serious than those for men. Generally, women contract STIs more easily than men and suffer greater damage to their health and reproductive functioning. STIs often are transmitted more easily from a man to a woman than vice versa. Women's increased likelihood of having an asymptomatic infection results in a delay in diagnosis and treatment (ASHA, 1998a; CDC, 2014.15c).

A kind of "biological sexism" means that women are biologically more susceptible to infection than men when exposed to an STI organism (Hatcher et al., 2007). A woman's anatomy may increase her susceptibility to STIs. The warm, moist interior of the vagina and uterus is an ideal environment for many organisms. The thin, sensitive skin inside the labia and the mucous membranes lining the vagina may also be more receptive to infectious organisms than the skin covering a man's genitals. The symptoms of STIs in women are often very mild or absent, and STIs are more difficult to diagnose in women due to the physiology of the female reproductive system. The long-term effects of STIs for women may include pelvic inflammatory disease (PID), ectopic pregnancy, infertility, cervical cancer, and chronic pelvic pain, as well as possible severe damage to a fetus or newborn, including spontaneous abortion, stillbirth, low birth weight, neurological damage, and death (CDC, 2014.15c).

Lesbian and bisexual women may also be at risk for STIs. A nationally representative study found the rates of self-reported genital herpes and genital warts to be 15–17% among self-identified bisexual women and 2–7% among self-identified lesbian women (Tao, 2008), both groups aged 15–44. According to a study conducted in Sydney, Australia, women who had sex with other women had a higher rate of bacterial vaginosis (BV) than heterosexual women. Among the women who had sex with other women, 93% reported previous sexual contact with men; they had a median (the numerical value in the middle of the upper half and lower half of a group of numbers) of 12 lifetime male sexual partners, compared with 6 lifetime partners for the heterosexual women. Thus, lesbian women may not be free of STI risk because many women who have sex with other women and self-identify as lesbian also have sex with men during their lifetime (Fetters, Marks, Mindel, & Estcourt, 2000).

A nationally representative study of 7,296 women, aged 24–32, found that more than 9 in 10 women reporting having had one or more female partners also reported having had penile-vaginal sex with a man (Lindley, Walsemann, & Carter, 2013). A study of 35 lesbian and bisexual women aged 16–35 found that BV was associated with reporting a partner with BV, vaginal lubricant use, and the sharing of sex toys (Marrazzo, Thomas, Agnew, & Ringwood, 2010). Studies have found that women who had sex with both men and women had greater odds of having acquired a bacterial STI and had more HIV/STI behavioral risk factors than women who had sex only with men or women (Bauer, Jairam, & Baidoobonso, 2010; Kaestle & Waller, 2011; Lindley et al., 2013; Mercer et al., 2007; Scheer et al., 2002). A case study found that female-to-female transmission of syphilis occurred through oral sex (Campos-Outcalt & Hurwitz, 2002).

Surveillance data on several STIs suggest that an increasing number of men who have sex with men (MSM) are acquiring STIs. For example, in recent years, MSM have accounted for an increasing number of estimated syphilis cases in the United States. In 2013, 75% of syphilis cases were among MSM (CDC, 2014.15c).

Age Disparities

Compared to older adults, sexually active young adolescents 12 to 19 years old, and young adults 20 to 24 years of age, are at higher risk for acquiring an STI. About one half of new STI cases are among individuals aged 15–24, although they comprise only about one quarter of the sexually active population (CDC, 2014.15c; Satterwhite et al., 2013; Weinstock, Berman, & Cates, 2004). Young people are at greater risk because they are, for example, more likely to have multiple sexual partners, to engage in risky behavior, to select higher-risk partners, and to face barriers to accessing quality STI prevention products and services (CDC, 2007.15a, 2014.15c).

Racial and Ethnic Disparities

Race and ethnicity in the United States are STI risk markers that correlate with other basic determinants of health status, such as poverty, access to quality health care, health care–seeking behavior, illegal drug use, and communities with high prevalence of STIs. STI rates are higher among racial and ethnic minorities. (See Figures 2 and 3 for rates of two STIs—chlamydia and gonorrhea—by race/ethnicity, 2012.) Social factors, such as poverty and lack of access to health care, in contrast to inherent factors, account for this discrepancy.

Factors Contributing to the Spread of STIs

According to the Institute of Medicine, "STDs are behavioral-linked diseases that result from unprotected sex," and behavioral, social, and biological factors contribute to their spread (Eng & Butler, 1997). These factors are obstacles to the control of STIs in the United States.

Behavioral Factors

Early Initiation of Intimate Sexual Activity People who are sexually active at an early age are at greater risk for STIs because this early initiation increases the total time they are sexually active and because they are more likely to have nonvoluntary intercourse, to have a greater number of sexual partners, and to

• **FIGURE** 2

Rates of Chlamydia by Race/Ethnicity and Sex, United States, 2012.

(*Source*: CDC, 2014.15d.)

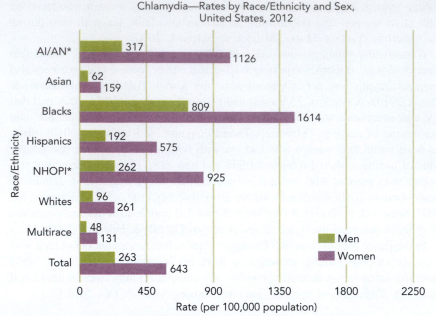

Chlamydia—Rates by Race/Ethnicity and Sex, United States, 2012

*AI/AN = American Indians/Alaska Natives; NHOPI = Native Hawaiian and Other Pacific Islanders.
NOTE: Includes 47 states and the District of Columbia reporting race/ethnicity data.

• **FIGURE** 3

Rates of Gonorrhea by Race/Ethnicity and Sex, United States, 2012.

(*Source*: CDC, 2014.15d.)

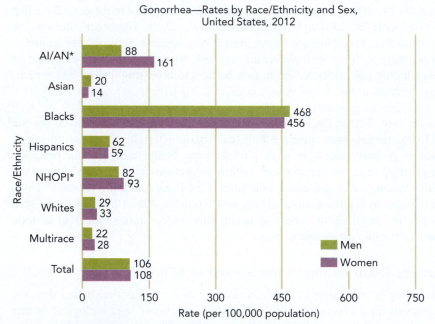

Gonorrhea—Rates by Race/Ethnicity and Sex, United States, 2012

*AI/AN = American Indians/Alaska Natives; NHOPI = Native Hawaiian and Other Pacific Islanders.
NOTE: Includes 47 states and the District of Columbia reporting race/ethnicity data.

use condoms less consistently (Manlove, Ryan, & Franzetta, 2003). For example, a nationally representative sample of 9,844 respondents found that the odds of contracting an STI for an 18-year-old who first had intercourse at age 13 were more than twice those of an 18-year-old who first had intercourse at age 17 (Kaestle, Halpern, Miller, & Ford, 2005).

Sequential Sexual Relationships The more exclusive sexual partners an individual has over a period of time (called **serial monogamy**), the greater the chance of acquiring an STI. For example, according to one national study, 1% of respondents with 1 sexual partner within the past year, 4.5% of those with 2–4 partners, and 5.9% of those with 5 or more partners reported that they had become infected with an STI. In addition, the more sexual partners respondents had, the more likely it was that each of those partners was unfamiliar and nonexclusive. Being unfamiliar with partners, especially knowing the person for less than 1 month before first having sex, and having nonexclusive partners were both strongly associated with higher STI incidence (Laumann, Gagnon, Michael, & Michaels, 1994). Data from the National Survey of Men and the National Survey of Women discovered that the likelihood of contracting an STI increased with an increase in the number of lifetime sexual partners: Compared to persons with 1 partner, those reporting 2 or 3 partners have 5 times the likelihood of having an STI, and the odds are as high as 31 to 1 for those reporting 16 or more lifetime partners (Tanfer, Cubbins, & Billy, 1995). A nationally representative study of women of varied sexual orientations found that women who had 1–5 five sexual partners were less likely to report being diagnosed with an STI than those who had 10 or more sexual partners (Lindley et al., 2013).

Concurrent Sexual Relationships Having **concurrent sexual relationships**—overlapping sexual partnerships—facilitates the spread of STIs. Research has shown that sexual concurrency, along with short gaps between partners, is associated with individual STI risk (Manhart, Aral, Holmes, & Foxman, 2002). This risk is especially true during acute HIV infection when transmission is greatest. A nationally representative study of men found that 11% reported concurrent sexual relationships in the past year, mostly involving women. These men were less likely to use a condom during their last sexual encounter; were less likely than those not reporting concurrent sexual partners to be married; and were more likely to report several risk factors, including drug or alcohol intoxication during sexual intercourse, nonmonogamous female and male partners, and sexual intercourse with men (Adimora & Schoenbach, 2007; Doherty, Schoenbach, & Adimora, 2009). Among women in a nationally representative study, the prevalence of reported concurrent sexual relationships was 12%, with lowest concurrency being among those currently married (Adimora et al., 2002). A study of STI clinic patients—one half reporting concurrent sexual partners in the past 3 months—found that both men and women believed that having concurrent partners was normal. They thought that no one was exclusive and that, based on previous relationships with nonexclusive partners, they found it difficult to trust their partners and be emotionally invested in the relationship. Most of the study participants, particularly the women, were looking for exclusive sexual relationships (Senn, Scott-Sheldon, Seward, Wright, & Carey, 2011).

High-Risk Sexual Partners Having sexual intercourse with a person who has had many partners increases the risk of acquiring an STI. One example of this is a female who has a bisexual male partner. Often, the female does not know that her male partner also has sex with men. Another example is when an older, sexually experienced person has sex with a younger and less experienced partner (Boyer et al., 2000; Thurman, Holden, Shain, & Perdue, 2009). Also, a survey of 1,515 men aged 18–35 attending health centers found that those who had purchased sex were twice as likely to be infected with an STI than those who had not purchased sex (Decker, Raj, Gupta, & Silverman, 2008). People often select new sexual partners from their social network. If a person acquires an STI, then the social network could be considered a high-prevalence group, thus increasing a person's chance of future STI infections. Research has shown that selecting new partners from outside one's social network is associated with reduced risk for repeat STIs (Ellen et al., 2006).

High-Risk Sexual Behavior   Certain sexual behaviors with a partner put individuals at higher risk for acquiring an STI than other behaviors. For example, a study of 1,084 heterosexual men and women patients at an STI clinic found that individuals who had ever engaged in anal intercourse were more likely to report a history of having had an STI (Gorbach et al., 2009). A study of women in the rural southern United States found that those who reported engaging in more high-risk behaviors in the past 12 months were more likely to report having an STI during the same time (Yarber, Crosby, & Sanders, 2000).

Inconsistent and Incorrect Condom Use   Correctly using a latex male condom during each sexual encounter and at any time the penis comes into contact with the partner significantly reduces the risk of STIs. Several studies have shown that both correct and consistent condom use are associated with lower STI rates in both men and women and lower rates of pelvic inflammatory disease (PID) outcomes in women (Crosby & Bounse, 2012; Hutchinson, Kip, & Ness, 2007; Nielson et al., 2010; Wald et al., 2005).

Substance Abuse   The abuse of alcohol and drugs is associated with high-risk sexual behavior, although researchers are not certain if there is a cause-and-effect relationship between alcohol/drug use and risky sexual behavior. Substances may affect cognitive and negotiating skills before and during sex, lowering the likelihood that partners will protect themselves from STIs and pregnancy (U.S. Department of Health and Human Services, 2011.15a). A review of 11 studies of problem drinking and STIs showed an overall association between problematic alcohol use and STI infection (Cook & Clark, 2005).

Sexual Coercion   Not all people enter sexual relationships as willing partners, particularly women. The 2013 Youth Risk Behavior Survey (CDC, 2014.15e) revealed that 7% of the adolescents (grades 9–12) surveyed had experienced forced sexual intercourse, with a greater percentage of females (11%) being coerced than males (4%). Individuals experiencing sexual violence are less able to protect themselves from STIs.

Lack of Knowledge of and Concern About STIs   It is important for persons who are sexually active with partners to have knowledge about the wide range of STIs and the ways they are transmitted and prevented. With increased STI information on the Internet and in school health classes, most persons have some fundamental knowledge of STIs and the potential for acquiring an STI through risk behavior. However, there are gaps in knowledge among some persons. A study of 300 sexually active adolescent females, some of whom had received an STI diagnosis and were recruited from health care sites, concluded that they knew more about their previous STI than about other STIs, including ones they had unknowingly contracted. That is, they appeared to learn about STIs mainly after an STI diagnosis, too late for effective prevention behavior,

practically speaking

Preventing STIs: The Role of Male Condoms and Female Condoms

For decades, the male condom has been promoted by public health officials as an important STI prevention device for sexually active individuals. However, there has been much discussion about how effective condoms really are in preventing HIV and other STIs. Some skeptics argue that condoms fail too often and that claims of condom effectiveness are misleading and exaggerated. Interestingly, despite these claims and denunciations by skeptics, a random telephone survey of 517 Indiana residents found that nearly 92% considered condoms at least somewhat effective in preventing HIV and STIs (Yarber, Milhausen, Crosby, & Torabi, 2005).

The Centers for Disease Control and Prevention (CDC) has issued statements and recommendations on male condoms, female condoms, and STI prevention for public health personnel.

Male Condoms

The CDC's (2007.15b, 2009.15a, 2014.15f) recommendations about the male latex condom and the prevention of STIs, including HIV, are based on information about the ways the various STIs are transmitted, the physical nature of condoms, the coverage or protection that condoms provide, and epidemiological studies of condom use and STIs. About STI prevention and condoms, the CDC has this to say:

> For persons whose sexual behaviors place them at risk for STDs, correct and consistent use of the male latex condom can reduce the risk of STD transmission. However, no protective method is 100 percent effective, and condom use cannot guarantee absolute protection against any STD. Furthermore, condoms lubricated with spermicides are no more effective than other lubricated condoms in protecting against the transmission of HIV and other STDs. In order to achieve the protective effect of condoms, they must be used correctly and consistently. Incorrect use can lead to condom slippage or breakage, thus diminishing their protective effect. Inconsistent use (e.g., failure to use condoms with every act of intercourse) can lead to STD transmission because transmission can occur with a single act of intercourse.

In addressing specific STIs, the CDC has stated that latex condoms, when used consistently and correctly, are highly effective in preventing the sexual transmission of HIV and reduce the risk of transmission of gonorrhea, chlamydia, and trichomoniasis. Correct and consistent use of latex condoms reduces the risk of genital herpes, syphilis, and chancroid only when the infected area or site of potential exposure is protected. Genital ulcer diseases and human papillomavirus (HPV) infections can occur in both male and female genital areas that are covered or protected by a latex condom, as well as areas that are not covered. Condom use may reduce the risk for HPV infection and HPV-associated diseases such as genital warts and cervical cancer. Three other nonlatex condoms are available. Polyurethane (plastic) or polyisoprene (synthetic rubber) condoms provide protection against STIs and are good options for people with latex allergies. The other type is natural membrane condoms, which are not recommended for protection against STIs (CDC, 2011.15a, 2011.15b, 2014.15f).

Female Condoms

Female condoms are thin pouches made of a synthetic latex product called nitrile. When worn in the vagina, female condoms are just as effective as male condoms at preventing STIs, HIV, and pregnancy. Some people use female condoms for anal sex, but it is not known how well they prevent STIs and HIV when used this way. Research has shown that HIV cannot travel through the nitrile barrier. It is safe to use any kind of lubricant with nitrile female condoms (CDC, 2014.15f).

SOURCES: Centers for Disease Control and Prevention. (2014.15f). HIV prevention. Available: http://www.cdc.gov/hiv/basics/prevention.html (Last visited 12/8/14); Centers for Disease Control and Prevention. (2007). Male latex condoms and sexually transmitted diseases. Available: http://www.cdc.gov/condomeffectivness/latex.htm (Last visited 10/12/08); Centers for Disease Control and Prevention. (2010). Sexually transmitted diseases treatment guidelines, 2010. *Morbidity and Mortality Weekly Report, 59* (No. RR-12); Yarber, W. L., Milhausen, R. R., Crosby, R. A., & Torabi, M. R. (2005). Public opinion about condoms for HIV and STD prevention: A midwestern state telephone survey. *Perspectives on Sexual and Reproductive Health, 37,* 148–154; Centers for Disease Control and Prevention. (2011). Condoms and STDs: Fact sheet for public health personnel. Available: http://www.cdc.gov/condomeffectiveness/latex.htm (Last visited 11/16/11).

early medical detection, or prompt disease treatment (Downs, de Bruin, Murray, & Fischhoff, 2006). Focus groups of lesbian and bisexual women revealed that the knowledge of the potential for STI transmission between women and of bacterial vaginosis was limited (Marrazzo, Coffey, & Bingham, 2005). A study of 1,101 women aged 18–25 found that 75% believed they were at low risk of acquiring an STI in the next year even though most were having unprotected sex. Some of the women did not perceive STIs as a "big deal" and were desensitized to the risk of contracting STIs (Yarnall et al., 2003). Last, a review of 55 research articles published since 2009 focusing on barriers to HPV vaccination initiation and completion among U.S. adolescents found that some underserved and disadvantaged youth had limited knowledge about HPV and HPV vaccination. The researchers concluded that their limited knowledge is an impediment to more adolescents taking advantage of the HPV vaccination (Holman et al., 2014).

Erroneous Perception of Partner's STI Status   People also often do not have an adequate perception of whether or not their sexual partner has been diagnosed with an STI. In one study of STI clinic patients in Southern California, participants indicated that they did not use condoms when they perceived new sexual partners to be STI-free. Instead of directly discussing their partners' sexual history, they relied on both visual and verbal cues to judge whether their partners were disease-free. This assessment reflected serious error in judgment because most of the study participants had, in fact, contracted an STI (Hoffman & Cohen, 1999). A study of heterosexual couples attending outpatient clinics found that 10% of women and 12% of men were unaware that their partner had recently received an STI diagnosis. Two percent of women and 4% of men were unaware that their partner was HIV-positive (Witte, El-Bassel, Gilbert, Wu, & Chang, 2010). This kind of information underscores the need for communication and honesty as part of STI prevention.

Social Factors

Poverty and Marginalization   Individuals in lower socioeconomic groups and those in social networks in which high-risk behavior is common and access to health care is limited are disproportionately affected by STIs. These groups include sex workers (people who exchange sex for money, drugs, or other goods), adolescents, persons living in poverty, migrant workers, and incarcerated individuals. STIs, substance abuse, and sex work are closely connected (Eng & Butler, 1997). Analysis of nationally representative data of adults aged 18–27 found that contextual conditions were associated with prevalence and recent contraction of STIs. As the number of contextual conditions increased, STI prevalence similarly increased. Conditions associated with STIs included housing insecurity, exposure to crime, having been arrested, gang participation, childhood sexual abuse, frequent alcohol use, and depression (Buffardi, Thomas, Holmes, & Manhart, 2008).

Access to Health Care   Access to high-quality and culturally sensitive health care is imperative for early detection, treatment, and prevention counseling for STIs. Unfortunately, health services for STIs are limited in many low-income areas where STIs are common, and funds for public health programs are scarce. Without such programs, many people in high-risk social networks have no access to STI care.

It is important for persons who are sexually active to have knowledge about the wide range of STIs and the ways they are transmitted and prevented.

© BananaStock/PunchStock

Secrecy and Moral Conflict About Sexuality   One factor that separates the United States from other countries with lower rates of STIs is the cultural stigma associated with STIs and our general discomfort with sexuality issues. Historically, a moralistic, judgmental stance on STIs has hindered public health efforts to control STIs. For example, significant funding for AIDS research did not begin until it was clear that heterosexual individuals as well as gay men were threatened (Altman, 1985; Shilts, 1987).

Biological Factors

Asymptomatic Nature of STIs   Most STIs either do not produce any symptoms or cause symptoms so mild that they go unnoticed or disregarded. A long time lag—sometimes years—often exists between the contracting of an STI and the onset of significant health problems. During the time in which the STI is asymptomatic, a person can unknowingly infect others. The individual may not seek treatment, allowing the STI to damage the reproductive system.

Resistance to Treatment or Lack of a Cure   Because resistant strains of viruses, bacteria, and other pathogens are continually developing, antibiotics that have worked in the past may no longer be effective in treating STIs. Infected people may continue to transmit the STI, either because they believe they have been cured or because they currently show no symptoms. And some STIs, such as genital herpes, genital warts, and HIV, cannot be cured but can be treated. The individual who has any of these viruses is always theoretically able to transmit them to others.

Susceptibility in Women   Adolescent women are highly susceptible to acquiring chlamydia and gonorrhea because of an immature cervix (ASHA, 1998b). Women who practice vaginal douching are also at greater risk for PID and STIs (CDC, 2014.15g; National Women's Health Information Center, 2002).

Uncircumcised Penis   Research on the impact of male circumcision in stopping the spread of HIV infection and other STIs has been conducted for over a decade in Africa, and the medical evidence of its value has become more clear. Both the American Academy of Pediatrics (AAP) and the Centers for Disease Control and Prevention (CDC) state that newborn male circumcision has medical benefits and that these benefits outweigh the risks. Strong evidence indicates that male circumcision can (American Academy of Pediatrics, 2014.15a; CDC, 2014.15h; "CDC draft guidelines: Circumcision benefits outweigh risks," 2014):

- Decrease a man's risk of acquiring HIV from an infected female partner by 50–60%.
- Reduce the risk of genital herpes and certain strains of HPV by at least 30%.
- Significantly reduce the risk of acquiring syphilis.
- Lower the risk of urinary tract infections during infancy and cancer of the penis during adulthood.

However, research has not shown that circumcision reduces an HIV-infected man's chances of transmitting HIV to women or to another man during same-sex behavior. The AAP and CDC do not recommend routine circumcision of newborn infants, although the rate of infant male circumcision has been dropping in the United States, but they state that decision is best made by parents

practically speaking

STI Attitude Scale

What one believes about STIs, how one feels about STIs, and one's intention to behave in a particular way influence STI risk-related behavior. The STI Attitude Scale was developed to measure the attitudes of young adults to determine whether they may be predisposed to high or low risk for contracting a sexually transmitted infection. The scale presented here is an updated version of the originally published scale. Follow the directions, and mark your responses to the statements below. Then calculate your risk as indicated.

Directions

Read each statement carefully. Indicate your first reaction by writing the abbreviation that corresponds to your answer.

Key

SA = Strongly agree
A = Agree
U = Undecided
D = Disagree
SD = Strongly disagree

1. How I express my sexuality has nothing to do with STIs.
2. It is easy to use the prevention methods that reduce my chances of getting an STI.
3. Responsible sex is one of the best ways of reducing the risk of STIs.
4. Getting early medical care is the main key to preventing the harmful effects of STIs.
5. Choosing the right sexual partner is important in reducing my risk of getting an STI.
6. A high prevalence of STIs should be a concern for all people.
7. If I have an STI, I have a duty to get my sexual partners to seek medical treatment.
8. The best way to get my sexual partner to STI treatment is to take him or her to the doctor with me.
9. Changing my sexual behaviors is necessary once the presence of an STI is known.
10. I would dislike having to follow the medical steps for treating an STI.
11. If I were sexually active, I would feel uneasy doing things before and after sex to prevent getting an STI.
12. If I were sexually active, it would be insulting if a sexual partner suggested we use a condom to avoid getting an STI.
13. I dislike talking about STIs with my peers.

14. I would be uncertain about going to the doctor unless I was sure I really had an STI.
15. I would feel that I should take my sexual partner with me to a clinic if I thought I had an STI.
16. It would be embarrassing to discuss STIs with my sexual partner if I were sexually active.
17. If I were to have sex, the chance of getting an STI makes me uneasy about having sex with more than one partner.
18. I like the idea of sexual abstinence (not having sex) as the best way of avoiding STIs.
19. If I had an STI, I would cooperate with public health workers to find the source of my infection.
20. If I had an STI, I would avoid exposing others while I was being treated.
21. I would have regular STI checkups if I were having sex with more than one partner.
22. I intend to look for STI signs before deciding to have sex with anyone.
23. I will limit my sexual activity to just one partner because of the chances of getting an STI.
24. I will avoid sexual contact anytime I think there is even a slight chance of getting an STI.
25. The chance of getting an STI will not stop me from having sex.
26. If I had a chance, I would support community efforts to control STIs.
27. I would be willing to work with others to make people aware of STI problems in my town.

Scoring

Calculate points as follows:

Items 1, 10–14, 16, and 25: Strongly agree = 5, Agree = 4, Undecided = 3, Disagree = 2, Strongly disagree = 1
Items 2–9, 15, 17–24, 26, and 27: Strongly Agree = 1, Agree = 2, Undecided = 3, Disagree = 4, Strongly disagree = 5

The higher the score, the stronger the attitude that may predispose a person toward risky sexual behaviors. You may also calculate your points within three subscales: Items 1–9 represent the "belief subscale," items 10–18 the "feeling subscale," and items 19–27 the "intention to act" subscale.

SOURCE: Yarber, W. L., Torabi, M. R., & Veenker, H. C. (1989). Development of a three-component sexually transmitted diseases attitude scale. *Journal of Sex Education and Therapy, 15*, 36–49.

in consultation with their physician and accounting for what is medically best for their child and their religious and cultural preferences and ethnic traditions.

Consequences of STIs

The list of problems caused by STIs seems almost endless. Women and infants suffer more serious health damage than men from all STIs. Without medical attention, some STIs can lead to blindness, cancer, heart disease, infertility, ectopic pregnancy, miscarriage, and even death (CDC, 2007.15a, 2014.15c; Yarber, 2003).

A serious outcome of STI infection is that the presence of other STIs increases the likelihood of both transmitting and acquiring HIV. When someone who is infected with another STI is exposed to HIV through sexual contact, the likelihood of acquiring HIV infection through sexual contact is at least 2–5 times higher than when he or she is not infected with an STI. Research has also shown that if an HIV-infected individual is also infected with another STI, that person is more likely to transmit HIV through sexual contact than HIV-infected persons not infected with another STI (CDC, 2010.15b).

Besides having human costs, the estimated cost of STI treatment within the U.S. health care system is almost $17 billion every year. This cost does not include indirect, nonmedical costs such as lost wages and productivity due to illness, out-of-pocket expenses, and costs related to STI transmission to infants (CDC, 2014.15i; Chesson et al., 2011).

● Principal Bacterial STIs

In this section we discuss chlamydia, gonorrhea, urinary tract infections, and syphilis, the major bacterial STIs. As indicated earlier, bacterial STIs are curable. Table 1 summarizes information about all of the principal STIs, including bacterial STIs, viral STIs, vaginal infections, other STIs, and **ectoparasitic infestations** (parasites that live on the outer skin surfaces).

Chlamydia

The most common bacterial STI and most commonly reported infectious disease (see Figure 1) in the United States is caused by an organism called *Chlamydia trachomatis,* commonly known as **chlamydia.** In 2013, 1,401,906 cases of chlamydia were reported to the CDC. During 1993–2011, the rate of reported chlamydial infection increased from 188 to 453 cases per 100,000 population. During 2012–2013, the rate decreased to 447 cases per 100,000 (see Figure 4).

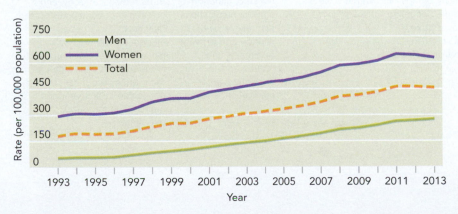

● **FIGURE 4**

Rates of Chlamydia by Sex, United States, 1993–2013.

(*Source:* CDC, 2014.15c.)

TABLE 1 • **Principal Sexually Transmitted Infections**

STI and Infecting Organism	Symptoms	Time from Exposure to Occurrence	Medical Treatment	Comments
Bacterial STIs				
Chlamydia (*Chlamydia trachomatis*)	*Women:* 75% asymptomatic; others may have abnormal vaginal discharge or pain with urination. *Men:* About one half asymptomatic; others may have discharge from penis, burning or itching around urethral opening, or persistent low fever.	7–21 days.	Antibiotics	If untreated, may lead to pelvic inflammatory disease (PID) and subsequent infertility in women. Sexually active females aged 25 and younger need testing every year.
Gonorrhea (*Neisseria gonorrhoeae*)	*Women:* Up to 80% asymptomatic; others may have symptoms similar to those of chlamydia. *Men:* Some asymptomatic; others may have itching, burning or pain with, urination discharge from penis ("drip").	*Women:* Often no noticeable symptoms. *Men:* Usually 2–5 days, but possibly 30 days or more.	Antibiotics	If untreated, may lead to pelvic inflammatory disease (PID) and subsequent infertility in women. People with gonorrhea can more easily contract HIV.
Urethritis (various organisms)	Painful and/or frequent urination; discharge from penis; women may be asymptomatic. Can have discharge from vagina and painful urination.	1–3 weeks.	Antibiotics	Laboratory testing is important to determine appropriate treatment.
Syphilis (*Treponema pallidum*)	*Stage 1:* Red, painless sore (chancre) at bacterium's point of entry. *Stage 2:* Skin rash over body, including palms of hands and soles of feet.	*Stage 1:* 10–90 days (average 21 days). *Stage 2:* 6 weeks after chancre appears.	Antibiotics	Easily cured, but untreated syphilis can lead to damage of internal organs. There is a two- to fivefold increase of acquiring HIV when already infected with syphilis.
Viral STIs				
HIV infection and AIDS (human immunodeficiency virus)	Possible flulike symptoms but often no symptoms during early phase. Variety of later symptoms, including weight loss, persistent fever, night sweats, diarrhea, swollen lymph nodes, bruise-like rash, persistent cough.	Several months to several years.	No cure available, although new treatment drugs have improved the health and lengthened the lives of many HIV-infected individuals.	HIV infection is usually diagnosed by tests for antibodies against HIV. One in seven people living with HIV are unaware of their infections.
Genital herpes (herpes simplex virus)	Small sore or itchy bumps on genitals or rectum, becoming blisters that may rupture, forming painful sores; flulike symptoms with first outbreak.	Within 2 weeks.	No cure, although antiviral medications can relieve pain, shorten and prevent outbreaks, and reduce transmission to partners when medication is taken.	Virus remains in body, and outbreaks of contagious sores may recur. Most people diagnosed with first episode have four to five symptomatic recurrences a year, although recurrences are most noticeable in first year and decrease in frequency over time.

STI and Infecting Organism	Symptoms	Time from Exposure to Occurrence	Medical Treatment	Comments
Genital human papillomavirus infection (group of viruses)	Over 40 HPV sexually transmitted types, including genital warts, infect the genitals, rectum, mouth, and throat.	Most people with genital HPV infection do not know they are infected; some get visible genital warts. In 90% of cases, the body clears HPV naturally within 2 years.	Visible genital warts can be removed by patient or health care provider with prescribed medication.	Some HPV types can cause cervical cancer. HPV usually disappears on its own without causing health problems. Most people who have sex acquire HPV at some time in their lifetime. Vaccines protect girls and women against genital warts and cervical, anal, vaginal, and vulvar cancers and boys and men against genital warts and anal cancers.
Viral hepatitis (hepatitis A or B virus)	Fatigue, diarrhea, nausea, abdominal pain, jaundice, darkened urine due to impaired liver function.	1–4 months.	No medical treatment available; rest and fluids are prescribed until disease runs its course.	Hepatitis B is more commonly spread through sexual contact. Both A and B can be prevented by vaccinations.
Vaginal Infections				
Vaginitis (*Gardnerella vaginalis*, *Trichomonas vaginalis*, or *Candida albicans*)	Intense itching of vagina and/or vulva, unusual discharge with foul or fishy odor, painful intercourse. Men who carry organisms may be asymptomatic.	Within a few days up to 4 weeks.	Depends on organism; oral, topical, and vaginal medications are available.	Not always acquired sexually. Other causes include stress, birth control pills, pregnancy, tight pants or underwear, antibiotics, douching, vaginal products, and poor diet.
Ectoparasitic Infestations				
Pubic lice, crabs (*Pediculosis pubis*)	Itching, blue and gray spots, and insects or nits (eggs) in pubic area; some people may have no symptoms.	Hatching of eggs in 6–10 days.	Creams, lotions, or shampoos—both over-the-counter and prescription.	Avoid sexual contact with people having unusual spots or insects or nits in the genital area. Also avoid contaminated clothing, sheets, and towels.

However, the number of reported cases of chlamydia remains high among age groups, geographical regions, and both sexes. For example, 949,270 cases of chlamydial infection were reported in 2013 among persons aged 15–24, representing 68% of all reported chlamydia cases. Racial differences also persist; reported case rates and prevalence estimates among Blacks continue to be substantially higher than among other racial/ethnic groups (see Figure 2) (CDC, 2014.15c).

Chlamydia is so common in young women that, by age 30, 50% of sexually experienced women show evidence that they had chlamydia sometime during their lives (CDC, 2001). Women who develop the infection 3 or more times have as great as a 75% chance of becoming infertile. Pelvic inflammatory disease (PID) occurs in 10–15% of women with untreated chlamydia. Also, research shows that women infected with chlamydia have a 5 times greater chance of acquiring HIV if exposed (CDC, 2011.15c). Untreated chlamydia can be quite painful and can lead to conditions requiring hospitalization, including acute arthritis. Infants of mothers infected with chlamydia may develop dangerous eye, ear, and lung infections.

Any sexually active person can become infected with chlamydia. This is particularly true for adolescent girls and young women since their cervix is not fully matured and is probably more susceptible to infection. Chlamydia can be transmitted during unprotected vaginal, anal, or oral sex from someone who has chlamydia and from an infected mother to her baby during vaginal childbirth. Men who have sex with men are at risk for chlamydial infections, since chlamydia can be transmitted during oral or anal sex. If the sex partner is male, one can still get chlamydia even if he does not ejaculate. Chlamydia is known as a "silent" disease; about three fourths of infected women and about one half of infected men have no symptoms. If symptoms do occur, they usually appear within 1–3 weeks after exposure.

When early symptoms occur in women, they are likely to include unusual vaginal discharge, a burning sensation when urinating and frequent urination, and unexplained vaginal bleeding between menstrual periods. Later symptoms, when the infection spreads from the cervix to the fallopian tubes, are low abdominal pain, lower back pain, bleeding between menstrual periods, a low-grade fever, and pain during intercourse. One third to one half of men are asymptomatic when first infected. Men's symptoms may include unusual discharge from the penis, a burning sensation when urinating, itching and burning around the urethral opening (urethritis), pain and swelling of the testicles, and a low-grade fever. The last two symptoms may indicate the presence of chlamydia-related **epididymitis,** inflammation of the epididymis. Untreated epididymitis can lead to infertility. Rectal pain, discharge, or bleeding may occur in men or women who acquired chlamydia during receptive anal intercourse. Chlamydia can be cured with the correct treatment. A study of 3,076 men who have sex with men that was conducted in London HIV clinics found that the prevalence of chlamydia in the rectum was 8% and in the urethra 5%. HIV and rectal chlamydia coinfection was 38%. Most of the rectal infections (69%) were asymptomatic and would not have been found if screening had not been conducted (Annan et al., 2009). Chlamydia can also be found in the throats of men and women engaging in oral sex with an infected person (CDC, 2011.15a, 2011.15c, 2014.15j).

The CDC recommends yearly chlamydia testing for all sexually active women aged 25 and younger, older women with risk factors (new sex partner or multiple sex partners), and all pregnant women. The CDC reports that only 38% of sexually active young women aged 15–25 were screened for chlamydia in the previous year (CDC, 2012.15b). Repeat infection with chlamydia is common. One should be tested 3 months after treatment, even if the sexual partner was treated (CDC, 2014.15j). Two types of laboratory tests can be used to detect chlamydia. One kind tests a urine sample; another tests fluid from a man's penis or a woman's cervix. A Pap smear does not test for chlamydia (CDC, 2011.15c).

Gonorrhea

Gonorrhea is the second most commonly reported notifiable disease in the United States (see Figure 1), where the highest reported rates of infection are among sexually active young people aged 15–24 and in some geographical areas

African Americans. It is estimated that more than 700,000 persons in the United States become infected with gonorrhea each year, and less than half of these infections are reported to the CDC. In 2013, 333,004 cases of gonorrhea in the United States were reported to the CDC, a rate of 106 per 100,000 (CDC, 2011.15c, 2011.15d, 2014.15c). Popularly referred to as "the clap" or "the drip," gonorrhea is caused by the *Neisseria gonorrhoeae* bacterium. The organism thrives in the warm, moist environment provided by the mucous membranes lining the mouth, throat, vagina, cervix, urethra, and rectum. Gonorrhea is transmitted during vaginal, anal, or oral sex with an infected person. Ejaculation does not have to occur for gonorrhea to be transmitted or acquired.

Men tend to experience the symptoms of gonorrhea more readily than women, notably as a watery discharge ("drip") from the penis, the first sign of urethritis. (*Gonorrhea* is from the Greek, meaning "flow of seed.") Some men infected with gonorrhea may have no symptoms at all. Other men have signs and symptoms that appear 2–5 days after infection. But symptoms can take as long as 30 days to appear (CDC, 2011.15d). Besides a watery discharge, symptoms in men may include itching or burning at the urethral opening and pain when urinating. If untreated, the disease soon produces other symptoms, such as thick yellow or greenish discharge, increasing discomfort or pain with urination, and painful or swollen testicles.

Up to 80% of women with gonorrhea show no symptoms or very mild symptoms, which they tend to ignore. Because untreated gonorrhea, like untreated chlamydia, can lead to PID, it is important for women to be on guard for symptoms and to be treated if they think they may have been exposed to gonorrhea (e.g., if they have had numerous sexual partners). Symptoms a woman may experience include thick yellow or white vaginal discharge that might be bloody, a burning sensation when urinating, unusual pain during menstruation, and severe lower abdominal pain. Both females and males may have mucous discharge from the anus, blood and pus in feces, irritation of the anus, and mild sore throat.

Gonorrhea is curable with several antibiotics. However, drug-resistant strains of gonorrhea are increasing in many parts of the United States and the world, making successful treatment more difficult. Persons with gonorrhea should be tested for other STIs. Untreated gonorrhea can cause sterility in both sexes, ectopic pregnancy, prostate damage, epididymitis, scarring of the urethra in men, and testicular pain. Gonorrhea may be passed to an infant during childbirth, causing conjunctivitis (an eye infection) and even blindness if not treated. People with gonorrhea can more easily contract HIV. People with HIV infection and gonorrhea are more likely than people with HIV infection alone to transmit HIV to others (CDC, 2008.15a, 2011.15d, 2014.15k).

Urinary Tract Infections

Urethritis, the inflammation of the urethra, can result from sexual exposure and noninfectious conditions. Among the several organisms that cause these infections, the most common and most serious is chlamydia. Urinary tract infections are sometimes referred to as **nongonococcal urethritis (NGU).** The diagnosis of NGU occurs more frequently in men, largely due to their anatomy. In men, urethritis may produce a burning sensation when urinating, burning or itching around the opening of the penis, white or yellowish discharge from the penis, and underwear stain. Women are likely to be asymptomatic. They may not

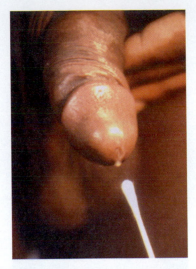

Gonorrhea infection in men is often characterized by a discharge from the penis. The discharge is gathered for medical examination by a cotton swab.

Renelle Woodall/CDC

*I had the honor
    To receive, worse luck!
From a certain empress
A boiling hot piss.*

—Frederick the Great
(1712–1786)

realize they are infected until a male partner is diagnosed. If a woman does have symptoms, they are likely to include itching or burning while urinating and unusual vaginal discharge.

It is important to have a laboratory test for an unusual discharge from the penis or vagina so that the appropriate antibiotic can be prescribed. Antibiotics are usually effective against NGU. Untreated NGU may result in permanent damage to the reproductive organs of both men and women and problems in pregnancy. The organisms that cause NGU in men may cause other infections in women, such as cervicitis, which is discussed later in this chapter (ASHA, 2008, 2011a; CDC, 2011.15a, 2014.15l). The most common urinary tract infection among women, cystitis, is briefly discussed later in this chapter.

Syphilis

Syphilis, a genital ulcerative disease, is caused by the bacterium *Treponema pallidum.* In the United States, health officials reported 56,471 cases of syphilis in 2013, including 17,375 cases of primary and secondary syphilis (see below for explanation of primary and secondary syphilis). Total syphilis case counts and rates in 2013 were the highest recorded since 1996. The highest ratio of syphilis in 2013 occurred in individuals aged 20–29. Syphilis continues to be a serious problem in the South and in urban areas in other parts of the United States and among MSM (CDC, 2011.15a, 2014.15c; Su, Beltrami, Zaidi, & Weinstock, 2011). In 2013, 75% of the reported primary and secondary (P&S) syphilis cases were among MSM, largely because of high rates of HIV coinfection and high-risk sexual behavior.

Treponema pallidum is a spiral-shaped bacterium (a spirochete) that requires a warm, moist environment such as the genitals or the mucous membranes inside the mouth to survive. It is spread by direct contact with a syphilis sore during vaginal, anal, and oral sexual behavior. Syphilis cannot be spread through contact with toilet seats, doorknobs, swimming pools, hot tubs, bathtubs, shared clothing, or eating utensils. The syphilis bacterium of an infected mother can infect the baby during the pregnancy. Depending on how long the woman has been infected, she may have a high risk of having a stillborn baby or giving birth to a baby who dies soon after birth. An infected baby may be born and not have any signs or symptoms, but if not treated immediately the baby may develop serious health problems within a few weeks. Untreated infants may become developmentally delayed, have seizures, or die. Untreated syphilis in adults may lead to brain damage, heart disease, blindness, and death.

Syphilis has often been called "the great imitator," since many of its signs and symptoms are indistinguishable from those of other diseases. However, many people infected with syphilis do not have any symptoms for years but remain at risk for complications if they are not treated. Although transmission can more easily occur from individuals with sores who are in the primary and secondary stages, many of these sores are unrecognized or hidden. Thus, transmission may occur from people who are unaware of their infection. Syphilis progresses through three discrete stages, although it is most often treated during the first two:

■ *Stage 1: Primary syphilis.* The first symptom of syphilis appears from 10 to 90 days (average 21 days) after contact with an infected partner. It is a small, red, pea-sized bump that soon develops into a round, painless sore

And he died in the year fourteen-twenty. Of the syphilis, which he had a-plenty.

—François Rabelais (1490–1553)

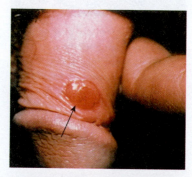

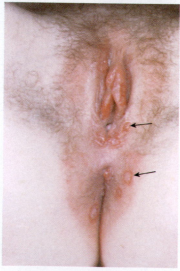

The first symptom of syphilis is a red, pea-sized bump called a chancre at the site where the bacterium originally entered the body as shown by the arrows above.

(first) © Collection CNRI/Phototake; (second) CDC

called a **chancre** (SHANK-er). The person's lymph nodes may also be swollen. The chancre may appear on the labia, the shaft of the penis, the testicles, or the rectum; within the vagina; within the mouth; or on the lips. Unless it is in a visible area, it may not be noticed. Without treatment, it will disappear in 3–6 weeks, but the bacterium remains in the body and the person is still highly contagious.

- *Stage 2: Secondary syphilis.* Untreated primary syphilis develops into secondary syphilis about 6 weeks after the chancre has disappeared. The principal symptom at this stage is a skin rash that neither itches nor hurts. The rash is likely to occur on the palms of the hands and the soles of the feet, as well as on other areas of the body. The individual may also experience fever, swollen lymph nodes, patchy hair loss, headaches, weight loss, muscle aches, and fatigue. The rash or other symptoms may be very mild or may pass unnoticed. The person is still contagious.

- *Stage 3: Latency.* If secondary syphilis is not treated, the symptoms disappear within 2–6 weeks and the latent stage begins. The infected person may experience no further symptoms for years or perhaps never. After about a year, the bacterium can no longer be spread to sex partners, although a pregnant woman can still transmit the disease to her fetus. The late stages of syphilis can develop in about 15% of people who have not been treated for syphilis and can appear 10–30 years after infection was acquired. In the late stages, damage may occur many years later in internal organs, such as the brain, nerves, eyes, heart, blood vessels, liver, bones, and joints. Damage could also include difficulty coordinating muscle movements, paralysis, numbness, gradual blindness, dementia, and even death.

In the primary, secondary, and early latent stages, syphilis can be successfully treated with antibiotics. There is an estimated two- to fivefold increase in the chances of acquiring HIV if exposed to that infection when syphilis is present (CDC, 2014.15c, 2014.15m).

Skin rash is a common symptom of untreated syphilis that appears about 6 weeks once the chancre has disappeared.

© Science Photo Library/Corbis

● Principal Viral STIs

Four principal viral STIs—HIV and AIDS, genital herpes, genital human papillomavirus infection, and hepatitis—are discussed here. Recall that diseases caused by viruses are treatable but not curable.

HIV and AIDS

On June 5, 1981, the U.S. government published a report warning about a rare disease, eventually named acquired immunodeficiency syndrome, or AIDS (CDC, 1981.15a). Since that time, this disease has become an enormous public health challenge nationally and globally. Human immunodeficiency virus (HIV)—the virus that causes AIDS—and AIDS have claimed millions of lives worldwide, becoming one of the deadliest epidemics in human history. Despite advances in medical testing and treatment and prevention efforts HIV/AIDS remains a significant public health problem. Because of its major global impact and continued medical and prevention challenge, we have decided to devote an entire chapter to HIV and AIDS.

The Tuskegee Syphilis Study: A Tragedy of Race and Medicine

In 1932 in Macon County, Alabama, the U.S. Public Health Service, with the assistance of the Tuskegee Institute, a prestigious Black college, recruited 600 African American men to participate in an experiment involving the effects of untreated syphilis on Blacks. Of this group, 399 men had been diagnosed with syphilis and 201 were controls. The study was originally meant to last 6–9 months, but "the drive to satisfy scientific curiosity resulted in a 40-year experiment that followed the men to 'end point' (autopsy)" (Thomas & Quinn, 1991). The history of this experiment—the racial biases that created it, the cynicism that fueled it, and the callousness that allowed it to continue—is chillingly chronicled by James Jones (1993) in *Bad Blood: The Tuskegee Syphilis Experiment* and Susan Reverby (2009) in *Examining Tuskegee: The Infamous Syphilis Study and Its Legacy.*

The purpose of the study was to determine if there were racial differences in the developmental course of syphilis. The racial prejudice behind this motivation may seem hard to fathom today, yet, as we shall see, the repercussions still reverberate strongly through African American communities (Ross, Essien, & Torres, 2006).

Much of the original funding for the study came from the Julius Rosenwald Foundation (a philanthropic organization dedicated to improving conditions within African American communities), with the understanding that treatment was to be a part of the study. Although Alabama law required prompt treatment of diagnosed venereal diseases, the state Public Health Service managed to ensure that treatment was withheld from the participants. Even after 1951, when penicillin became the standard treatment for syphilis, the Public Health Service refused to treat the Tuskegee "subjects" on the grounds that the experiment was a "never-again-to-be-repeated opportunity" (Jones, 1993).

The Tuskegee participants were never informed that they had syphilis. The Public Health Service, assuming they would not understand medical terminology, referred to it as "bad blood," a term used to describe a variety of ailments in the rural South. The participants were not told their disease was sexually transmitted, nor were they told it could be passed from mother to fetus.

It was not until 1966 that anyone within the public health system expressed any moral concern over the study. A congressional subcommittee headed by Senator Edward Kennedy began hearings in 1973. The results included the rewriting of the Department of Health,

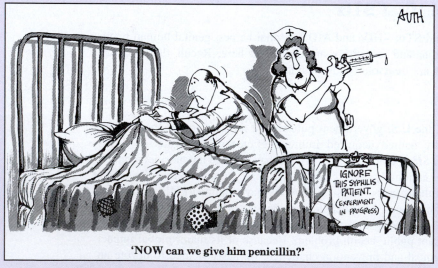

'NOW can we give him penicillin?'

Education, and Welfare's regulations on the use of human subjects in scientific experiments. A $1.8-billion class-action suit was filed on behalf of the Tuskegee participants and their heirs. A settlement of $10 million was reached out of court. Each survivor received $37,500 in damages, and the heirs of the deceased each received $15,000. Also, a congressionally mandated program, the Tuskegee Health Benefit Program, provides comprehensive lifetime medical benefits to the affected widows and offspring of participants in the Tuskegee syphilis study (Reverby, 2009).

Current public health efforts to control the spread of HIV infection, AIDS, and other STIs raise the specter of genocide and beliefs of conspiracy among many members of the African American community. Research on African American people living in the United States has found that a significant proportion of respondents endorsed HIV/AIDS conspiracy beliefs; that is, HIV/AIDS was created by the federal government to kill and wipe out African Americans. Among African American men, stronger conspiracy beliefs were significantly associated with negative attitudes about condoms and lower likelihood of condom use (Bogart, Galvan, Wagner, & Klein, 2011; Bogart & Thornton, 2005; Hutchinson et al., 2007; Ross et al., 2006).

Many of the current beliefs of African American people about HIV/AIDS as a form of genocide are attributed to the Tuskegee syphilis study. On both physiological and psychological levels, there is much healing to be done. Even though it is unthinkable that such a study would be done today, efforts must still be made to ensure that all people are protected against such tragedies.

For reflections on the legacy of the Tuskegee study, see Caplan, 1992; Jones, 1993; King, 1992; and Reverby, 2009. Several Internet sites provide further information about this terrible experiment, including the transcript of President Clinton's 1997 formal apology to study participants.

Think Critically

1. Is it possible for another medical experiment like the Tuskegee syphilis study to happen in America today? Explain your view.

2. What can be done to prevent another Tuskegee syphilis study?

3. What can the medical and scientific community do to gain the trust of all Americans?

Genital Herpes

Genital herpes is an STI caused by the **herpes simplex virus (HSV)** type 1 (HSV-1) and type 2 (HSV-2). Most genital herpes is caused by HSV-2. Nationally representative data show that genital herpes infection occurs commonly in the United States, with 16.2% of people aged 14–49, or about 1 in 6 persons in that age group, having a genital HSV-2 infection (CDC, 2014.15o). Genital HSV-2 infection is more common in women (about 1 in 5 women aged 14–49) than men (about 1 in 9 men aged 14–49). This may be due to male-to-female transmission being more likely than female-to-male transmission. Herpes can make people more susceptible to HIV infection, and it can make HIV-infected individuals more infectious (CDC, 2010.15c). Actually, many HIV-infected persons are coinfected with HSV-2 (Romanowski et al., 2009).

HSV-1 and HSV-2 can be found and released from the sores that the viruses cause, but it also can be released between outbreaks from skin that does not appear to be broken or have a sore (Tronstein, 2011). Generally, a person can get HSV-2 infection only during sexual contact with someone who has a genital HSV-2 infection. It is important to know that transmission can occur from an infected partner who does not have a visible sore and may not know that he or she is infected. HSV-1 can cause genital herpes, but it more often causes infections of the mouth and lips, so-called fever blisters. HSV-1 infection of the genitals can be caused by oral-genital or genital-genital contact with a person infected with HSV-1. Genital HSV-1 outbreaks recur less regularly than genital HSV-2 outbreaks.

Most infected people have no or minimal signs or symptoms from HSV-1 and HSV-2 infection. When signs appear, they typically occur within 2 weeks

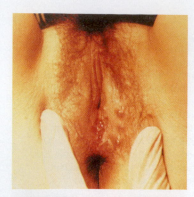

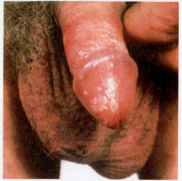

Herpes lesions may develop on the penis, perineum, anus, or vulva or within the vagina.

(first) © Luis M. de la Maza, Ph.D. M.D./
Phototake; (second) © Wellcome Image
Library/Custom Medical Stock Photo

after the virus is transmitted and appear as one or more blisters on or around the genitals or rectum. These symptoms are sometimes called "having an outbreak." The blister breaks, leaving tender ulcers (sores) that may take 2–4 weeks to heal the first time they occur. Most people diagnosed with a first episode of genital herpes can expect to have several (typically four or five) outbreaks within a year, but they are almost always less severe and shorter than the first outbreak. Even though the infection can stay in the body indefinitely, the number of outbreaks tends to decrease over a period of years (CDC, 2008.15b, 2010.15c).

Managing HSV There is no cure for herpes, but there are medications that can help keep the virus in check (Handsfield, Warren, Werner, & Phillips, 2007). Antiviral medications can relieve pain, shorten the duration of sores, prevent bacterial infections at the open sores, and prevent outbreaks while the person is taking the medications. To avoid spreading herpes to another part of the body, such as the eyes, infected persons should not touch the sores or fluids. Other actions that may be useful in preventing, shortening the duration of, or lessening the severity of recurrent outbreaks include getting plenty of rest, maintaining a balanced diet, avoiding tight clothes, keeping the area cool and dry, taking aspirin or other painkillers, and reducing stress.

Individuals with herpes should inform their partners and together decide what precautions are right for them. Because having sex during a recognized outbreak or when other symptoms are present (e.g., flulike symptoms, swollen glands, fever) puts an uninfected partner at risk, people should abstain from sex when signs and symptoms of either oral or genital herpes are present. The male latex condom can help prevent infections, but only when the condom covers the ulcer. However, outbreaks can also occur in areas that are not covered by a condom, so condoms may not fully protect someone from getting herpes. Condoms should be used between outbreaks of the ulcers because even if someone does not have symptoms, that person can still infect sexual partners. Also, daily suppressive therapy for symptomatic herpes can reduce transmission to partners. Pregnant women or their partners who have HSV should be sure to discuss precautionary procedures with their medical practitioners.

Genital Human Papillomavirus Infection

Genital human papillomavirus infection, or **genital HPV,** is a group of viruses that includes more than 100 different strains; over 40 are sexually transmitted and can infect the genitals, rectum, mouth, and throat. Currently, about 79 million people in the United States are infected with HPV, with 14 million new infections reported each year, accounting for one third of all new STIs. HPV is the most common STI among young, sexually active people, particularly women. HPV is so common that nearly all sexually active men and women get it at some point in their lives. By age 50, at least 80% of women will have acquired genital HPV infection (ASHA, 2011b; CDC, 2011.15f, 2014.15n).

You can get HPV by having oral, vaginal, or anal sex with someone who has the virus. It is most commonly spread during vaginal or anal sex. HPV can be passed even when an infected person has no signs or symptoms. In rare instances, a pregnant woman can pass HPV to her baby during vaginal delivery. The incubation period—the period between the time a person is first exposed to a disease and the time the symptoms appear—is usually 6 weeks to 8 months. You cannot see HPV. Most people who have a genital HPV infection do not know they are infected. Also, you can develop symptoms years after you have sex with someone who is infected, making it difficult to know when you first became infected.

Sometimes, certain types of HPV can cause **genital warts** in men and women. Other HPV types can cause cervical cancer and less common cancers of the vulva, vagina, anus, and penis. The types of HPV that can cause genital warts are not the same as the types that can cause cancer. HPV types are referred to as "low risk" (wart causing) or "high risk" (cancer causing). In 90% of the cases, the body's immune system clears the HPV—both high-risk and low-risk types—naturally within 2 years. If a high-risk HPV infection is not cleared by the immune system, it can linger for many years and turn abnormal cells into cancer over time. About 10% of women with high-risk HPV on their cervix will develop long-lasting HPV infections that will put them at risk for cervical cancer (CDC, 2008.15c, 2011.15f).

The Pap test can identify abnormal or precancerous tissue in the cervix so that it can be removed before cancer develops. Abnormal changes on the cervix are likely caused by HPV. An HPV DNA test, which can find high-risk HPV on a women's cervix, may also be used with a Pap test in certain cases. There is no general test for men and women to check one's overall "HPV status," nor is there an approved HPV test to find HPV on the genitals or in the mouth or throat. HPV usually goes away on its own, without causing health problems. So an HPV infection that is found today will most likely not be there a year or two from now. Hence, there is no reason to be tested just to find out if you have HPV now. But you should get tested for signs of diseases that HPV can cause, such as cervical cancer (CDC, 2008.15c, 2011.15f, 2013.15b).

The genital-wart history of a national sample of 8,849 men and women found that 7% of women and 4% of men reported ever being diagnosed with genital warts (Dinh, Sternberg, Dunne, & Markowitz, 2008). About 1% of sexually active adults in the United States have genital warts at some point in their lives, and about 360,000 people get genital warts each year (CDC, 2014.15n). Research has shown that being infected with genital warts can be a psychological burden, with adverse effects resulting in a decreased quality of life. These findings reveal the need for greater community efforts for HPV vaccination of both females and males (Senecal et al., 2011).

Genital warts usually appear as soft, moist, pink or flesh-colored swellings, usually in the genital area. They can also be flat, single or multiple, small or large, and sometimes cauliflower shaped. They can appear on the penis or scrotum, in or around the vagina or anus, on the cervix, or on the groin or thigh. Visible genital warts can be removed by the patient him- or herself with prescribed medications or treated by a health care provider. Some people choose not to treat warts but see if they disappear on their own. No one treatment is better than another. If the warts cause discomfort or problems such as interfering with urination, they can be removed by cryosurgery (freezing) or laser surgery. Removal of the warts does not eliminate HPV from the person's system. Because the virus can lie dormant in the cells, in some cases warts can return months or even years after treatment. The extent to which a person can still transmit HPV after the visible warts have been removed is unknown.

In recent years, a major medical breakthrough has occurred in protecting thousands of females and males against the health-impairing outcomes of HPV infection. HPV vaccines have been developed, and the U.S. Department of Health and Human Services highly recommends their use. In June 2006, the U.S. Food and Drug Administration (FDA) approved the HPV vaccine Gardasil (Merck) for use by females aged 9–26; in October 2009, this vaccine was

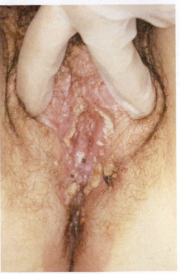

Genital warts appear in a variety of forms.

(first) © Dr. Hercules Robinson/Phototake; (second) © Bart's Medical Library/Phototake

also licensed for use in males aged 9–26. Gardasil protects against HPV types 6 and 11 (the cause of 90% of genital warts) and types 16 and 18 (the cause of 70% of cervical cancer). Gardasil also prevents HPV associated with anal, vulvar, and vaginal cancers. In 2009, another HPV vaccine, Cervarix (Glaxo-SmithKline), was approved for types 16 and 18. Both of these vaccines are given in three shots over 6 months (ASHA, 2011a; CDC, 2011.15a, 2011.15g). In December 2014, the FDA approved Gardasil 9 for the protection against nine HPV types, five more than Gardasil. Gardasil 9, approved for both males and females ages 9–26, has the potential to prevent about 90% of cervical, vulvar, vaginal, and anal cancers caused by HPV types 16, 18, 31, 45, and 52 as well as to prevent genital warts caused by types 6 and 11 (U.S. Food and Drug Administration, 2014). Like the original Gardasil, Gardasil 9 is to be administered as three separate injections over 6 months. All types of HPV vaccination are most effective if they are provided before a person ever has sex with another individual.

Research has shown that HPV vaccination has helped decrease the number of new HPV infections. For example, data from the National Health and Nutrition Examination Survey revealed that HPV infections fell 56% in adolescent females aged 14–19 in the vaccine era (2007–2010) compared with the prevaccine era (2003–2006). (Markowitz et al., 2013). One study found that since the Gardasil HPV vaccination began in 2007 in Australia, the number of women seeking treatment for genital warts decreased 59% (Donovan et al., 2011).

Despite its significant health value, the effort to vaccinate all young people has faced difficulties. For example, nationally representative data have shown that only one third of girls aged 13–17 have been vaccinated (Pruitt & Schootman, 2010). Studies have shown that some girls taking the HPV vaccine did not complete the vaccine series in the 6-month time period or did not complete the series (Widdice, Bernstein, Leonard, Marsolo, & Kahn, 2011) or would not take the vaccine even if it was free (Crosby, Casey, Vanderpool, Collins, & Moore, 2011). In addition, parental acceptance of the HPV vaccine has been mixed (Dempsey, Butchart, Singer, Clark, & Davis, 2011; Milhausen, Crosby, & Yarber, 2008). Although many parents accept HPV vaccination, some parents believe that vaccinating girls against HPV condones premarital/teen sex (Darden et al., 2013; Holman et al., 2014). However, research has shown that HPV vaccination does not increase sexual behavior among teens. For example, in a Canadian study, 128,712 girls in grades 8 and 9 who received the HPV vaccination were followed to grades 10 to 12; results found that the vaccination did not have any significant effect on increased risk of pregnancy or non-HPV-related STIs (Smith, Kaufman, Strumpf, & Lévesque, 2014). Further, a study of 1,398 HPV-vaccinated girls, ages 11 and 12, who were followed for four years showed that HPV vaccination in the recommended ages was not associated with increased sexual activity-related risk (Bednarczyk, Davis, Ault, Orenstein, & Omer, 2012). Further educational efforts to promote the value of HPV vaccines, particularly to parents, need to occur.

If you have HPV, don't blame your current sexual partner or assume that your partner is not sexually exclusive with you. Remember, most people who have sex will have HPV at some time in their lives, and they may have HPV for a very long time before it is detected. Most people do not realize they are infected or that they are passing on the virus to a sexual partner. Sexual partners usually share HPV, particularly those who are together for a long time. There should be no shame or blame involved with having genital HPV; the virus is very common.

Viral Hepatitis

Hepatitis is a viral disease meaning inflammation of the liver. The most common types of the virus that can be sexually transmitted are hepatitis A and hepatitis B. A third type, hepatitis C, is a common virus passed on primarily through contact with infected blood; risk of transmittal from sexual partners or from mothers to newborns during birth is low. Of people with HIV infection, 10% also have hepatitis B and 25% also have hepatitis C (CDC, 2013.15c).

Hepatitis A is usually spread when a person ingests fecal matter—even in microscopic amounts—from contact with objects, food, or fluids contaminated by feces from an infected person. In the United States, there are an estimated 20,000 new hepatitis A infections each year, a decrease from 56,000 estimated new infections in 2004. A highly effective vaccine, which is routinely given to all children, travelers to certain countries, and persons at risk for the disease, can prevent hepatitis A. Although the symptoms of hepatitis A are similar to those of hepatitis B, the disease is not considered as dangerous. People can spread hepatitis A even if they don't look or feel sick. Individuals infected with hepatitis A usually experience short-term illness, recover completely, and develop immunity against reinfection (CDC, 2009.15b, 2011.15h, 2012.15a).

Hepatitis B is 50–100 times more infectious than HIV. It is commonly and most easily spread through sexual contact, in blood, semen, saliva, vaginal secretions, and urine. In the United States, two thirds of acute hepatitis cases resulted from sexual contact with the virus. It can also be contracted by using contaminated needles and syringes, including those used in ear piercing, acupuncture, and tattooing, and by sharing the toothbrush or razor of an infected person. Unlike hepatitis A, hepatitis B is not spread routinely through food or water. It is not spread by sharing eating utensils, breastfeeding, hugging, kissing, holding hands, coughing, sneezing, or by contaminated water. An estimated 1.2 million Americans are chronically infected with hepatitis B. The number of new infections per year has declined dramatically from an average of 260,000 per year in the 1980s to about 40,000 a year currently (CDC, 2009.15c, 2011.15h, 2013.15d). Anyone can get hepatitis B, but individuals in their teens and twenties are at greater risk. Because hepatitis B spreads "silently"—that is, without easily noticeable symptoms—many people are not aware it is in their communities. Chronic hepatitis B is a serious disease that can result in long-term health problems in about 15%–25% of those infected and even death. About 3,000 people die every year from hepatitis B–related liver disease (CDC, 2009.15c).

Hepatitis B can be prevented by a simple, widely available vaccine. The CDC (2009.15c) recommends routine vaccination for those most at risk, including sexually active people not in a long-term, exclusive relationship, men who have sex with men, people who share drug-injection equipment, people whose sexual partner has hepatitis B, and people with HIV. Screening for hepatitis B is also recommended for pregnant women so that their newborns can be immediately vaccinated if necessary. Usually given as three shots over a 6-month period, the vaccine is safe and effective and provides lasting protection. Tattoos and body piercings should be done at parlors that thoroughly sterilize the instruments used to penetrate the skin.

In 2009, there were an estimated 16,000 new hepatitis C virus infections in the United States. An estimated 3.2 million individuals in the U.S. have chronic hepatitis C, and about 75–85% of people who become infected with hepatitis C will develop a chronic infection. About 8,000 to 10,000 people die every year from hepatitis C–related liver disease. Risk of infection from sexual activity is low unless it involves blood contact; numerous sexual partners, failure to use condoms, a history of STIs, and sexual activities involving trauma (e.g., "rough" sex) increase the risk. About 50–90% of HIV-infected persons who use injection drugs are also infected with hepatitis C. Most cases of hepatitis C can be traced to blood transfusions before 1992, the sharing of needles during injection drug use, and accidental needle-sticks. Known as the "silent epidemic," hepatitis C damages the liver over the course of many years, and even decades, before symptoms appear.

The symptoms of all forms of hepatitis include fatigue, diarrhea, nausea, abdominal pain, jaundice, darkened urine, and an enlarged liver. About 15–25% of people who get hepatitis C will clear the virus from their bodies without treatment and will not get a chronic infection. There is no medical treatment nor vaccine for hepatitis C. Occasionally, serious liver damage or death results (CDC, 2009.15d, 2011.15h).

● Vaginal Infections

Vaginal infections, or **vaginitis,** affect most women at least once in their lives. These infections are often, though not always, sexually transmitted. They may also be induced by an upset in the normal balance of vaginal organisms by such things as stress, birth control pills, antibiotics, tight pants, wet underwear, and douching. The three principal types of vaginitis are bacterial vaginosis, candidiasis, and trichomoniasis.

Bacterial Vaginosis

Bacterial vaginal infections, referred to as **bacterial vaginosis (BV),** may be caused by a number of different organisms, most commonly *Gardnerella vaginalis,* often a normal inhabitant of the healthy vagina. An overabundance of *Gardnerella,* however, can result in vaginal discharge, odor, pain, itching, or burning. Bacterial vaginosis is the most common vaginal infection in women of childbearing age and, in the United States, is common among pregnant women. An estimated 29% of American women (21 million) aged 14–49 have BV now, but the vast majority do not report symptoms to their health care provider (CDC, 2008.15d, 2010.15d; Koumans et al., 2007). Not much is known about how women get bacterial vaginosis, and there are many unanswered questions about the role that harmful bacteria play in causing it and what role sexual activity plays in its development. The CDC does not consider BV an STI. Any woman can get BV, although some activities can upset the normal balance of bacteria in the vagina and put women at risk, including having a new sexual partner or numerous partners and douching. Research has shown that douching at least once a month is associated with BV but that most female hygienic behaviors, such as type of underwear, menstrual protection, or hygienic spray or towelettes, were found not to be related to BV (Hutchinson, Kip, & Ness, 2007; Klebanoff et al., 2010). Bacterial vaginosis may also be spread between female sex partners (Bailey, Farquhar, & Owen, 2004). Women who have never had sexual intercourse may get BV (Tabrizi, Fairley, Bradshaw, & Garland, 2006). Most often this infection causes no complications, although having it can increase a woman's susceptibility to HIV infection and other STIs, such as chlamydia and gonorrhea, and can increase the chances that an HIV-infected woman can pass HIV to her sexual partner (Cohen et al., 2012). BV may also put a woman at increased risk for some complications during pregnancy (CDC, 2014.15g).

Even though bacterial vaginosis sometimes clears up without treatment, all women with symptoms of BV should be treated with antibiotics, so that the bacteria that cause BV do not infect the uterus and fallopian tubes. Male partners generally do not need to be treated (CDC, 2010.15d). A study of women at high risk for STIs found that consistent condom users had a 45% decreased risk for BV than women not using condoms consistently (Hutchinson et al., 2007).

Genital Candidiasis

Genital candidiasis, also known as a "yeast infection," is a common fungal infection that occurs when there is an overgrowth of the fungus *Candida albicans. Candida* is always present in the body (e.g., vagina, mouth, gastrointestinal tract) in a small amount; however, when an imbalance occurs, such as when the normal acidity of the vagina changes or when hormonal balance changes, *Candida* can multiply. Women with a vaginal yeast infection usually experience itching or burning, with or without a "cottage cheese–like" vaginal discharge. Males with genital candidiasis, which occurs on rare occasions, may have an itchy rash on the penis. Nearly 75% of all adult women have had at least one vaginal yeast infection in their lifetime. While most cases are caused by the person's own *Candida* organisms, the use of birth control pills or antibiotics, frequent douching, pregnancy, and diabetes can promote yeast infections. Less commonly, *Candida* infections are transmitted from person to person through sexual intercourse. Genital candidiasis occurs more often and with more severe symptoms in people with weakened immune systems.

Antifungal drugs, taken orally, applied directly to the affected area, or used vaginally, are the drug of choice for vaginal yeast infections and are effective 80–90% of the time. Because over-the-counter (OTC) treatments are becoming more available, more women are diagnosing themselves with vaginal yeast infections and using one of a family of drugs called "azoles" for therapy. However, personal misdiagnosis is common, and studies show that as many as two thirds of OTC drugs sold to treat vaginal yeast infections are used by women *without* the disease, which may lead to resistant infections. Resistant infections are very difficult to treat with currently available medications. Therefore, it is important to be sure of the diagnosis before treating with OTC or other antifungal medications (CDC, 2010.15e, 2014.15p).

> Sex is a pleasurable exercise in plumbing, but be careful or you'll get yeast in your drainpipe.
>
> —Rita Mae Brown
> (1944–)

Trichomoniasis

Trichomoniasis is an STI caused by a single-celled protozoan parasite, *Trichomonas vaginalis.* Trichomoniasis is the most common curable STI in young, sexually active women. In the United States, an estimated 3.7 million people have the infection, but only 30% develop any symptoms of trichomoniasis. In one study of 1,209 women attending three STI clinics, trichomoniasis, unlike other STIs, was found more often in older compared to younger women (Helms et al., 2008). In women, the vagina is the most common site of infection; in men, it is the urethra. The parasite is sexually transmitted during penile-vaginal intercourse or vulva-to-vulva contact with an infected person. Women can acquire the disease from infected men or women, but men usually contract it only from infected women. Trichomoniasis can increase the risk of getting or spreading other STIs, such as HIV. Symptoms are more common in women than men. It is unclear why some people with the infection get symptoms, while others do not. Some women have signs and symptoms within 5–28 days after exposure, which include frothy, yellow-green vaginal discharge with a strong odor. The infection may also cause discomfort during intercourse and urination, as well as itching and irritation of the female genital area and, rarely, lower abdominal pain. Some men may temporarily have an irritation inside the penis, mild discharge, or slight burning after urination or ejaculation. For both women and men, a physical examination and a laboratory test are used to diagnose trichomoniasis, although it is harder to detect in men (CDC, 2007.15d, 2013.15e).

Prescription drugs are effective in treating trichomoniasis. To prevent reinfection, both partners must be treated, even if the partner is asymptomatic.

● Other STIs

A number of other STIs appear in the United States, but with less frequency than they do in some developing countries. Among these other STIs are the following:

- Chancroid is a painful sore or group of sores on the penis, caused by the bacterium *Hemophilus ducreyi.* Women may carry the bacterium but are generally asymptomatic for chancroid.

- Cytomegalovirus (CMV) is a virus of the herpes group that affects people with depressed immune systems. A fetus may be infected with CMV in the uterus.

- Enteric infections are intestinal infections caused by bacteria, viruses, protozoans, or other organisms that are normally carried in the intestinal tract. Amebiasis, giardiasis, and shigellosis are typical enteric infections. They often result from anal sex or oral-anal contact.

- Granuloma inguinale appears as single or multiple nodules, usually on the genitals, that become lumpy but painless ulcers that bleed on contact.

- Lymphogranuloma venereum (LGV) begins as a small, painless lesion at the site of infection and then develops into a painful abscess, accompanied by pain and swelling in the groin.

- Molluscum contagiosum, caused by a virus, is characterized by smooth, round, shiny lesions that appear on the trunk, on the genitals, or around the anus.

● Ectoparasitic Infestations

Although they are not infections per se, parasites such as scabies and pubic lice can be spread by sexual contact. Scabies and pubic lice are considered ecto-parasitic parasites or infestations, since they live on the outer surfaces of the skin.

Scabies

The red, intensely itchy rash caused by the barely visible mite *Sarcoptes scabiei* is called **scabies.** It usually appears on the genitals, buttocks, feet, wrists, knuckles, abdomen, armpits, or scalp as a result of the mites' tunneling beneath the skin to lay their eggs and the baby mites' making their way back to the surface. Typically, fewer than 15 mites can be present on the entire body of an infested person. On a person, scabie mites can live as long as 1–2 months, but off a person they usually do not survive more than 48–72 hours. When a person is infected with scabie mites for the first time, symptoms usually do not appear for up to 2 months; an infected person still can spread scabies during this time, even though he or she does not have symptoms. It is highly contagious and spreads quickly among people who have close contact, both sexual and non-sexual. The mites can also be transferred during prolonged contact with infested linens, furniture, or clothing. Scabies is usually treated with a prescribed lotion, applied at bedtime and washed off in the morning. Clothing, towels, and bedding of people who have scabies should be disinfected by washing in hot water and drying in high heat or by dry cleaning (CDC, 2010.15f).

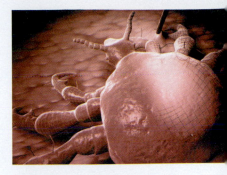

Pubic lice, or "crabs," are easily spread during intimate contact; they can also be transmitted via bedding, towels, or underwear.

© MedicalRF.com

Pubic Lice

The tiny *Phthirus pubis,* commonly known as a "crab," moves easily from the hair of one person to that of another (probably along with several of its relatives). **Pubic lice** usually are found in the genital area on pubic hair, although they can be found on other coarse body hair such as hair on the legs, armpits, mustache, and beard. To live, lice must feed on blood. When pubic lice mate, the male and female grasp adjacent hairs; the female soon begins producing eggs (nits), which she attaches to the hairs at the rate of about three eggs a day for 7–10 days. The nits hatch within 6–10 days and begin reproducing in about 2–3 weeks, creating a very ticklish (or itchy) situation. Although pubic lice and nits can be large enough to be seen with the naked eye, a magnifying lens may be necessary to find lice or eggs.

Pubic lice can be transmitted during sexual contact with a person who has crabs, moving from the pubic hair of one person to the pubic hair of another. Contact generally must be prolonged; a quick handshake or hug, for example, will usually not spread pubic lice. They may fall into underwear, sheets, or towels, where they can survive up to a day *and* lay eggs, which hatch in about a week. Thus, it is possible to get crabs simply by sleeping in an infected person's bed, wearing his or her clothes, or sharing a towel. A common misconception is that pubic lice can be spread easily by sitting on a toilet seat. This would be extremely rare, because lice cannot live long away from a warm body and they do not have feet designed to hold on to or walk on smooth surfaces such as toilet seats. Also, animals do not spread pubic lice.

People can usually tell when they have pubic lice. There is intense itching, and upon inspection, they discover a tiny, pale, crablike louse or its minuscule, pearly nits attached near the base of a pubic hair. There are both prescription and over-the-counter treatments for pubic lice. An infested person does not have to shave off his or her pubic hair to get rid of crabs. In addition to killing all the lice and nits on the body, infested individuals must wash all linen and clothing in hot water and dry it in high heat, or the crabs may survive (ASHA, 2011c; CDC, 2010.15l, 2013.15f).

● STIs and Women

In addition to the direct effects that STIs have on the body, women are vulnerable to complications from STIs that threaten their fertility. These are related to the biological factors, discussed earlier, that make women more susceptible to STIs and make STIs more difficult to detect in women.

Pelvic Inflammatory Disease (PID)

Pelvic inflammatory disease (PID), also known as salpingitis, is one of the leading causes of female infertility. Up to 750,000 women experience an episode of acute PID annually, resulting in 10–15% of these women becoming infertile each year due to the consequences of PID. Based on a nationally represented sample from 2006 to 2010, about 4.2% of U.S. women have reported being treated for PID in their lifetime (CDC, 2011.15i, 2014.15g).

PID occurs when bacteria move upward from a woman's vagina or cervix into her uterus, fallopian tubes, and other reproductive organs. Several organisms can cause PID, but many cases are associated with gonorrhea and chlamydia. An estimated 10–20% of women with chlamydia or gonorrhea may develop PID if they do not receive adequate treatment (CDC, 2014.15c; Paavonen, Westrom, & Eschenback, 2008). A prior episode of PID increases the risk of another episode because the reproductive organs may have been damaged during the initial episode. Sexually active women in their childbearing years are at most risk, and those under age 25 are more likely to develop PID than those older than 25. Because the cervix of teenage girls and young women is not fully mature, their susceptibility to the STIs that are linked to PID is increased. Women with repeated episodes of PID are more likely to suffer infertility, ectopic pregnancy, or chronic pelvic pain than those who have had just one episode. Risk behaviors for PID include having numerous sex partners, having a partner who has more than one sex partner, and douching.

Symptoms of PID vary from none, to subtle and mild, to severe. PID is difficult to diagnose because of the absent or mild symptoms, and many episodes go undetected. PID goes unrecognized by women and their health care providers about two thirds of the time. Because there is no precise test for PID, a diagnosis is usually based on clinical findings. Symptoms of PID include lower abdominal pain, fever, unusual vaginal discharge that may have a foul odor, painful intercourse, painful urination, irregular menstrual bleeding, and, rarely, pain in the upper right abdomen. PID can be cured with several types of antibiotics. Additionally, a woman's sex partner(s) should be treated to decrease the risk of reinfection, even if the partner(s) has no symptoms (CDC, 2010.15a, 2014.15q).

Cervicitis

Cervicitis is an inflammation of the cervix, the lower end of the uterus. Cervicitis might be a sign of upper genital infection, most often caused by a sexually transmitted infection such as gonorrhea or chlamydia. Frequently there are no signs of cervicitis, but some women complain of abnormal vaginal discharge, painful urination, and vaginal bleeding between menstrual periods, such as after sexual intercourse. A woman is at greater risk for cervicitis associated with STIs if she engages in high-risk sexual behavior, such as not using condoms or having sex with numerous partners, and if she began having sex at an early age. Having a history of STIs is also a risk factor. Since the signs of cervicitis are not often noticed, the infection may be discovered only in the course of a medical test. This is one important reason to have regular pelvic exams. A woman may not need treatment for cervicitis if it is not caused by an STI. If it is caused by an STI, both the woman and her partner are likely to need treatment. Prescription medications often are effective in clearing up the inflammation of cervicitis (CDC, 2007.15c, 2011.15a, 2014.15l; Mayo Clinic, 2014.15a).

Cystitis

A bladder infection that affects mainly women, **cystitis** is often related to sexual activity, although it is not transmitted from one partner to another. Cystitis is an infection of the bladder characterized by painful, burning urination and a nearly constant need to urinate.

Cystitis occurs when a bacterium such as *Escherichia coli,* normally present in the lower intestine and in fecal material, is introduced into the urinary tract. This can occur when continuous friction (from intercourse or manual stimulation) in the area of the urethra traumatizes the tissue and allows nearby bacteria to enter the urinary tract. It often occurs at the beginning of a sexual relationship, when sexual activity is high (hence the nickname "honeymoon cystitis"). Cystitis resulting from a bacterial infection is generally treated by antibiotics (Mayo Clinic, 2012). If cystitis is not treated promptly with antibiotics, more serious symptoms such as lower abdominal pain, fever, and kidney pain will occur. Damage to the kidneys may occur if treatment is delayed.

● Preventing STIs

It seems that STIs should be easy to prevent, at least in theory. But in reality, STI prevention involves a subtle interplay of knowledge, psychological factors, couple dynamics, and behaviors.

Avoiding STIs

STIs can be transmitted by sexual contact with an infected partner, by infected blood in injection-drug equipment, and from an infected mother to her child. Because we know that STIs are transmitted by certain behaviors, we know exactly how to keep from getting them. Those behaviors are particularly important because research has shown, for example, that many people underestimate their risk of becoming infected with an STI and the risk behavior of potential sexual partners, and in one study most heterosexual dating couples with a sexual relationship had not done anything in the past 4 weeks to avoid STIs (Billy, Grady, & Sill, 2009; Masaro, Dahinten, Johnson, Ogilvie, & Patrick, 2008). In a survey of 1,497 women and men at 75 clinics and physician offices across California, a considerable proportion of study participants said that they would have unprotected sex, even when they were recently counseled about birth control and had access to subsidized contraceptive services. In response to whether they would have sex without contraception, 30% said a definite "yes," and 20% indicated "sometimes" or "maybe" (Foster, Higgins, Biggs, McCain, Holtby, & Brindis, 2012). This kind of thinking is contributing significantly to the rise in incidence and outcomes associated with STIs. Here is how to avoid STIs:

1. *Practice abstinence.* The closest thing to a foolproof method of STI prevention is abstaining from intimate sexual contact, especially penile-vaginal intercourse, anal intercourse, and oral sex. Hugging, kissing, caressing, and mutual masturbation are all ways of sharing intimacy that are extremely unlikely to transmit STIs. Freely adopted, abstinence is a legitimate personal choice regarding sexuality. If you wish to remain abstinent, you need to communicate your preferences clearly to your dates or partners.

An important part of controlling the spread of STIs is having free access to condoms and relevant information.

© IDREAMSTOCK/Alamy

2. *Practice sexual exclusivity.* **Sexual exclusivity** means that you agree to be sexually active with only one person, who has agreed to be sexually active only with you. Partners who practice sexual exclusivity will not contract an STI through sexual contact unless one partner had an STI when he or she started having sexual contact. Being in a long-term, mutually exclusive relationship with an uninfected partner is one of the most reliable ways to avoid STIs. Certainly, it is not always possible to know if someone is infected or if he or she is exclusive. This is one reason it is wise to refrain from sexual activity until you can form a trusting relationship with a partner.

3. *Reduce risk during sexual intimacy.* Unless you are certain that your partner is not infected, you should not allow his or her blood, semen, or vaginal fluids to touch your genitals, mouth, or anus. One of the best ways to prevent these fluids from entering your body is to properly use the male latex condom (or polyurethane or polyisoprene condom if allergic to latex). Studies have shown that some couples who use condoms at the beginning of their sexual relationship often stop using them and turn to hormonal contraception. Certainly, the lack of condom use for these couples makes them vulnerable to STI transmission if one of the partners is not sexually exclusive. Douching, washing, and urinating after sex have been suggested as possible ways of reducing STI risk, but their effectiveness has not been proved.

4. *Select partners carefully.* Knowing whether a partner might be infected with an STI can be tricky. Thus, this strategy is often not reliable. Certainly, you should avoid sexual contact with someone at high risk for having an STI, such as an individual who has had numerous or has concurrent partners and/or who injects drugs. A person may not be honest about his or her sexual partners or drug use. As shown in studies, it is usually impossible to determine who is infected by merely looking at the person or by his or her reputation. One research project showed that the most attractive persons were perceived to be at least risk for STI/HIV (Hennessy, Fishbein, Curtis, & Barrett, 2007). According to another study, the participants had used visual and verbal cues to judge if their partners were disease-free. But in this case, their judgment was wrong, as most of their partners had contracted an STI (Hoffman & Cohen, 1999). A study of STI clinic patients found that many used partner attributes and relationship characteristics (family, trust, knowledge of partner's sexual history) as an index in evaluating partner safety; their assessments were inaccurate when compared to their partner's self-reported risk (Masaro et al., 2008). If you do not know each other well, you would be wise to exchange contact information in the event of an STI infection or other problem or, better yet, wait until you know each other better before initiating sexual activity.

5. *Avoid numerous partners.* As noted in this chapter, having numerous sexual partners (concurrent or sequential sexual relationships) increases the risk for STIs.

6. *Avoid injection and other drugs.* Another way to avoid HIV and hepatitis B is to not inject drugs and to not share needles and syringes if drugs are injected. Certainly, the drug equipment should be cleaned if sharing occurs. Not only can drugs harm your health, but they can also alter your judgment.

7. *Get tested.* Since many STIs don't have early symptoms in most infected persons, getting tested for STIs before having sex with someone is a critical step in stopping the transmission and acquisition of STIs. If you are infected, then you can take steps to protect yourself and your partner. When seeing a health care provider, ask specifically for STI tests. It is important that one's sexual partner be tested also. Many couples go for STI testing together prior to beginning a sexual relationship. If either you or your partner is infected, both of you need to receive treatment at the same time to avoid getting reinfected. Some STI testing and prevention counseling is covered under the Affordable Care Act.

8. *Get vaccinated.* Vaccines are a safe, effective, and recommended method to prevent hepatitis A, hepatitis B, and HPV.

9. *Protect babies.* Most STIs can be transmitted from mother to child during pregnancy or childbirth. Most often, proper medical treatment can protect the baby from permanent damage. HIV-infected mothers should not breast-feed their babies. A woman who has an STI and becomes pregnant should inform her doctor, and all pregnant women should be checked for STIs.

10. *Be a good communicator.* Acquiring an STI requires that you have been sexually intimate with another person. Avoiding an STI demands even more intimacy because it frequently means having to talk. You need to learn how best to discuss prevention with potential sexual partners and to communicate your thoughts, feelings, values, needs, and sexual boundaries. Ideally, discussing one's past sexual experiences can be helpful in revealing vital health-related information, such as possible risk of STI infection. However, research has found that both male and female college students are reluctant to reveal past partnered sexual experiences (Anderson, Kunkel, & Dennis, 2011). Good communicators are less likely to do things against their values or beliefs. And you should never have sex with someone who will not talk about STI prevention.

Treating STIs

If you contract an STI, you can infect others. Practicing health-promoting behaviors will prevent others from acquiring an STI.

1. *Recognize STI symptoms.* People who practice risky sexual behaviors or inject drugs should be alert to possible STI symptoms, especially if they have sex with partners at risk for STIs. To help avoid STIs, you should know what symptoms to look for, in yourself and others. Changes in the genitals may indicate an infection, although symptoms of some STIs can appear anywhere, and some changes may indicate a health problem other than an STI. If you suspect an infection, you should not try to diagnose the condition yourself but should consult a physician or health care provider. In general, the symptoms of STIs are genital or rectal discharge, abdominal pain, painful urination, skin changes, genital itching, and flulike conditions. However, some STIs do not have any symptoms until the disease is well advanced, symptoms often disappear and then come back, and most STIs can still be passed on to someone even when the symptoms are not visible, are absent, or disappear. Actually, most people who are infected with an STI have no noticeable symptoms. Males are likely to notice symptoms earlier and more frequently

practically speaking

Safer and Unsafe Sex Practices

Safer sex practices are an integral part of good health practices. Many people prefer the term "safer sex" to "safe sex" because all sexual contact carries at least a slight risk—a condom breaking, perhaps—no matter how careful we try to be.

Safer Practices

- Hugging
- Kissing (but possibly not deep, French kissing)
- Massaging
- Petting
- Masturbation (solo or mutual, unless there are sores or abrasions on the genitals or hands)
- Erotic videos, books, and so on

Possibly Safe Practices

- Deep, French kissing, unless there are sores in the mouth
- Vaginal intercourse with a latex condom (or polyurethane or polyisoprene condom if allergic to latex)

- Fellatio with a latex condom
- Cunnilingus, if the woman is not menstruating or does not have a vaginal infection (a latex dental dam provides extra protection)
- Anal intercourse with a latex condom (experts disagree about whether this should be considered "possibly safe" even with a condom because it is the riskiest sexual behavior without one)

Unsafe Practices

- Vaginal or anal intercourse without a latex condom
- Fellatio without a latex condom
- Cunnilingus, if the woman is menstruating or has a vaginal infection and a dental dam is not used
- Oral-anal contact without a dental dam
- Contact with blood, including menstrual blood
- Semen in the mouth
- Use of vibrators, dildos, and other "toys" without washing them between uses

---

than females. If you suspect an infection, you should stop having sex, stop injecting drugs, promptly see a health care provider, and have sexual partners go to a doctor or clinic.

2. *Seek treatment.* If you suspect that you have an STI, you should seek medical care immediately. Knowing your STI status is a critical step in stopping STI transmission. Public STI and HIV/AIDS clinics, private doctors, family planning clinics, and hospitals are all places to get treatment. Do not use home remedies, products bought in the mail or online, or drugs obtained from friends.

3. *Get partners to treatment.* People who get treatment for an STI are doing the right thing, but they also need to encourage sexual partners and injection-drug-use partners to seek professional care immediately. This helps prevent serious illness in the partner, prevents reinfection, and helps control the STI epidemic. Because the first sign that a woman has an STI is often when her male partner shows symptoms, female partners especially should be advised. And even if a partner has no symptoms of an STI, he or she should still see a health care provider.

We kill our selves, to propagate our kinde.

—John Donne
(1572–1631)

A national panel of public health officials and youth, in its 2004 report addressing the STI problem among youth aged 15–24, *Our Voices, Our Lives, Our Futures: Youth and Sexually Transmitted Diseases* (Cates, Herndon, Schulz, & Darroch, 2004), emphasized in the conclusion the importance and role of youth in stemming the STI problem in America. Still pertinent today, the report stated:

> In conclusion, young people need to participate in protecting their health, talking with their partners and others about sexual issues, pursuing how and when to get medical testing, and making wise choices as they grow up. It is the responsibility of the larger community to support young people with adequate and easy access to STD information and services. Young people are not mere statistical victims of this country's STD epidemic, and they are not unique in acquiring sexually transmitted infections. They have a crucial role to play in designing, running, and evaluating programs aimed at protecting youth from STDs. In partnership with parents, policy makers, health-care providers, religious leaders, educators, and others, youth hold the key to conquering this epidemic in American society. When youth are able to prevent STDs and make healthy choices for themselves, the results benefit not only youth, but society at large and potentially future generations.

Summary

The STI Epidemic

- STIs are a "hidden" epidemic in the United States, representing four of the six most frequently reported infectious diseases. STIs negatively affect more than 110 million Americans. Women, teens and young adults, and minority racial and ethnic groups are disproportionately affected by STIs.
- STIs are behavior-linked diseases resulting largely from unprotected sexual contact. Behavioral, social, and biological factors contribute to the spread of STIs. The behavioral risk factors include early initiation of intimate sexual activity, sequential sexual relationships, concurrent sexual relationships, high-risk sexual partners, high-risk sexual behavior, inconsistent and incorrect condom use, substance abuse, sexual coercion, lack of personal knowledge and concern about STIs, and erroneous perception of partner's risk. Social risk factors include poverty and marginalization, lack of access to health care, and secrecy and moral conflict about sexuality. Biological factors include the asymptomatic nature of STIs, resistance to treatment, and lack of cures.

- Without medical attention, STIs can lead to serious health problems, including sterility, cancer, heart disease, blindness, ectopic pregnancy, miscarriage, and death. The presence of an STI increases the risk of acquiring an HIV infection if exposed. The direct cost of STIs is almost $16 billion annually.

Principal Bacterial STIs

- Bacterial STIs are curable and include chlamydia, gonorrhea, urinary tract infections (NGU), and syphilis.
- *Chlamydia* is the most common bacterial STI in the United States and very common in young women, in whom repeated chlamydial infections can lead to infertility.
- *Gonorrhea* is the second most commonly notifiable disease in the United States. Men tend to experience the symptoms of gonorrhea more readily than women. Untreated gonorrhea can lead to pelvic inflammatory disease.
- *Urinary tract infections* can occur in both men and women and are sometimes referred to as

nongonococcal urethritis. Untreated NGU can lead to damage of the reproductive organs of both men and women.

- *Syphilis,* a genital ulcerative disease, increases by two- to fivefold the chances of an infected person acquiring HIV if exposed to an HIV-infected person.

Principal Viral STIs

- Viral STIs are incurable, but treatable, and include HIV and AIDS, genital human papillomavirus infection, genital herpes, and hepatitis.
- *HIV and AIDS* has become one of the deadliest epidemics in human history.
- *Genital human papillomavirus* infection, or HPV, is the most common STI among sexually active young people, particularly women. Some people infected with HPV get genital warts. Persistent HPV infection is a key risk factor for cervical cancer. Vaccines have been approved for both males and females that protect against HPV strains that can result in cervical and anal cancer and genital warts.
- One in five women and one in nine men aged 14–49 are infected with genital herpes. Genital herpes can make people more susceptible to HIV infection, and it can make HIV-infected individuals more infectious.
- *Hepatitis* is a viral disease affecting the liver. The most common types that can be sexually transmitted are hepatitis A and hepatitis B.

Vaginal Infections

- Vaginal infections, or *vaginitis,* are often, though not always, sexually transmitted and include bacterial vaginosis, candidiasis, and trichomoniasis.
- *Bacterial vaginosis (BV)* is the most common vaginal infection in women of childbearing age. Any woman can get BV, even women who never have had sexual intercourse.
- *Candidiasis,* also known as a "yeast infection," is an overgrowth of a normally present fungus in the body. Nearly 75% of all adult women have at least one vaginal yeast infection in their lifetime.
- *Trichomoniasis* is the most common curable STI in young, sexually active women. An estimated 3.7 million people in the United States have the infection, yet only 30% develop any symptoms of trichomoniasis.

Other STIs

- Several STIs that do not appear in the United States as often as in developing countries are chancroid, cytomegalovirus, enteric infections, granuloma inguinale, lymphogranuloma, and molluscum contagiosum.

Ectoparasitic Infestations

- Ectoparasitic infestations are parasites that live on the outer surface of the skin and can be spread sexually. They include scabies and pubic lice.
- *Scabies* is caused by a barely visible mite and is highly contagious. It spreads quickly among people who have close contact, sexually or nonsexually (e.g., prolonged contact with infested bedding).
- *Pubic lice,* commonly known as "crabs," can move easily from the pubic hair of one person to that of another.

STIs and Women

- Women tend to be more susceptible than men to STIs and to experience graver consequences, such as pelvic inflammatory disease (PID), an infection of the fallopian tubes that can lead to infertility, and ectopic pregnancy. *Cervicitis* is the inflammation of the cervix, most commonly caused by an STI. Intense stimulation of the vulva can irritate the urethra, leading to *cystitis* (bladder infection).

Preventing STIs

- STI prevention involves the interaction of knowledge, psychological factors, couple dynamics, and risk-avoiding behaviors. Ways to avoid STIs include abstinence, sexual exclusivity, careful partner selection, condom use, and avoidance of numerous partners and injection drugs. People practicing risky behavior should be alert to possible STI symptoms, seek treatment promptly if an STI is suspected, and inform partners of a known or suspected STI.

Questions for Discussion

- Given that condoms are one of the most important measures for reducing the risk of STI transmission and that many young people do not like condoms, what can be done to make condom use more appealing?

- What would be your most important concern if you just learned you had an STI? Who would you tell? What resources would you need? And where could you go to get help?

- Would it be difficult for you to inform a past sexual partner that you have an STI and that he or she might have it too? What would be your "opening line" to get the discussion started?

Sex and the Internet

The American Sexual Health Association

The American Sexual Health Association (ASHA), founded in 1914, is a nonprofit organization focusing on STI prevention. ASHA publishes a variety of educational materials, provides direct patient support through a national STI hotline and resource centers, and advocates increased funding for STI programs and sound public policies on STI control. ASHA also operates a website: http://www.ashastd.org. Go to it and then answer the following questions:

- What programs does ASHA offer?
- What services are provided on its website?
- What are the current ASHA headlines?
- What links are available at the ASHA website?

If you were diagnosed with an STI, would you seek more information from this site? Why or why not?

Suggested Websites

Centers for Disease Control and Prevention

http://www.cdc.gov/hiv
Provides information on HIV/AIDS.
http://www.cdc.gov/std
Provides information on STIs.

Joint United Nations Programme on HIV/AIDS

http://www.unaids.org
Contains epidemiological information on HIV/AIDS worldwide, as well as perspectives on HIV/AIDS-related issues.

Kaiser Family Foundation

http://www.kff.org
Offers fact sheets and news releases on STI and HIV/AIDS.

Rural Center for AIDS/STD Prevention

http://www.indiana.edu/~aids
Provides information about issues related to HIV/STI prevention in rural communities.

World Health Organization

http://www.who.int/topics/sexually_transmittedinfections/en
Provides STI fact sheets and publications as well as information on related topics.

Suggested Reading

Brandt, A. M. (1987). *No magic bullet: A social history of venereal disease in the United States since 1880.* New York: Oxford University Press. An informative and highly readable history of the social and political aspects of STIs.

Dizon, D. S., & Krychman, M. L. (2011). *Questions and answers about human papillomavirus (HPV).* Burlington, MA: Jones & Bartlett. Written by two medical doctors, this book provides authoritative answers to the most commonly asked questions about HPV.

Hayden, D. (2003). *Pox: Genius, madness, and the mysteries of syphilis.* Boulder, CO: Basic Books. From Beethoven to Oscar Wilde, from Van Gogh to Hitler, this book describes the effects of syphilis on the lives and works of seminal figures from the fifteenth to twentieth centuries.

Lowry, T. P. (2005). *Venereal disease and the Lewis and Clark expedition.* Lincoln: University of Nebraska Press. Describes how sex and venereal disease affected the men and mission of the Lewis and Clark expedition.

Reverby, S. M. (2009). *Examining Tuskegee: The infamous syphilis study and its legacy.* Chapel Hill: University of North Carolina Press. An analysis of the 40-year syphilis experiment by the U.S. Public Health Service involving hundreds of African American men.

Wilton, L., Palmer, R. T., & Maramba, D. C. (Eds.). (2014). *Understanding HIV and STI prevention for college students.* New York: Routledge. This edited volume explores HIV/STI related topics of interest to college students such as the hooking-up culture, sexual violence, LGBT, and students of color, as well as HIV/STIs in community colleges, rural colleges, and minority-serving institutes.

HIV and AIDS

© Mandel Ngan/AFP/Getty Images

CHAPTER OUTLINE

"I am aware of HIV and STDs, and they are not something I take lightly. In my relationship, trust and honesty are key points, and we discussed our histories ahead of time. We then made educated decisions."

—20-year-old female

"I no longer hate you or feel angry with you [AIDS]. I realize now that you have become a positive force in my life. You are a messenger who has brought me a new understanding of my life and myself. So for that I thank you, forgive you, and release you. Because of you I have learned to love myself."

—21-year-old male

"My father had AIDS. When he found out, I was only four years old. My parents chose to keep it a secret from me and my brothers. I lived with my dad then. Though he felt sick sometimes, we did the normal things that a family would do throughout the rest of my childhood. When I turned twelve Dad became very sick and was hospitalized. I went to live with my mother. When Dad came out of the hospital, he went to live with my grandparents. Still, no one told me what was wrong with him. Two years later, my mom finally told me that Dad had AIDS and was going to die soon. I was shocked and mad at both of my parents for not telling me earlier. My mom wouldn't let me go see Dad because he looked really bad and was in a lot of pain. I didn't get to see him or talk to him before he died. If I had known he was going to die so soon, I would have found a way to see him."

—19-year-old female

"You have to deal not only with the illness [AIDS] but with the prejudices that you encounter every day."

—26-year-old male

"I think HIV and STDs are the biggest reasons why I'm not promiscuous. I'd love to have sex with multiple partners and experiment, but even if I used a condom every time, I would still feel very much at risk. That is why I am monogamous in my relationship."

—20-year-old female

FEW PHENOMENA HAVE CHANGED the face of sexuality as dramatically as the appearance over 30 years ago of the microscopic virus known as **HIV,** or **human immunodeficiency virus.** In the early 1980s, physicians in San Francisco, New York, and Los Angeles began noticing repeated occurrences of formerly rare diseases among young and relatively healthy men. Kaposi's sarcoma, a cancer of the blood vessels, and *Pneumocystis carinii* pneumonia, a lung infection that is usually not dangerous, had become killer diseases because of the breakdown of the immune system of the men in whom these diseases were being seen (Centers for Disease Control and Prevention [CDC], 1981.16a). Even before the virus responsible for the immune system breakdown was discovered, the disease was given a name: acquired immunodeficiency syndrome, or AIDS. In the mid-1980s, the causative agent of AIDS, HIV, was discovered.

At first, AIDS within the United States seemed to be confined principally to three groups: gay men, Haitians, and people with hemophilia. Soon, however, it became apparent that AIDS was not confined to just a few groups; the disease spread into communities with high rates of injection drug use and into the general population, including heterosexual men and women (and their children) at all socioeconomic levels. The far-reaching consequences of the AIDS epidemic, in addition to the pain and loss directly caused by the illness, have included widespread fear, superstition, stigmatization, prejudice, and hatred. Ignorance of its modes of transmission has fueled the flames of homophobia among some people. Among others, it has kindled a general fear of sexual expression.

> AIDS has changed us forever. It has brought out the best of us, and the worst.
>
> —Michael Gottlieb, MD
> (1948–)

By now, most of us know how HIV is spread. And yet, for a variety of reasons, people continue to engage in behaviors that put them at risk. We hope that the material in this chapter will help you make healthy, informed choices for yourself and become an advocate for education and positive change in the community. Because of the tremendous amount of AIDS research being conducted, some of the information presented here, particularly HIV/AIDS incidence and prevalence, could be outdated by the time this book appears in print. For updates on HIV/AIDS research findings and news, contact the U.S. Centers for Disease Control and Prevention (CDC) (the web address is given in the "Sex and the Internet" section) or one of the agencies or websites listed at the end of this chapter.

We begin the chapter by describing the biology of the disease and the immune system. We next discuss the epidemiology and transmission of HIV and the demographic aspects of the epidemic—that is, the effect of HIV/AIDS on various groups and communities. Then we address HIV prevention, testing, and current treatment. Finally, we discuss living with HIV or AIDS.

● What Is AIDS?

AIDS is an acronym for **acquired immunodeficiency syndrome.** This medical condition was so named because HIV is acquired (not inherited) and subsequently affects the body's immune system to the point where it often becomes deficient in combating disease-causing organisms, resulting in a group of symptoms that collectively indicate or characterize a disease or syndrome.

To monitor the spread of AIDS through a national surveillance system, the CDC has established a definition of AIDS. To receive an AIDS diagnosis under the CDC's classification system a person must, in most cases, have a positive blood test indicating the presence of HIV antibodies and a CD4 (also called T lymphocyte or T cell) count (discussed later) below 200. AIDS can still be diagnosed if the person has one or more of the diseases or conditions associated with AIDS (discussed shortly, regardless of the CD4 count). If a person has HIV antibodies, as measured by a blood test, but does not meet the other criteria, he or she is said to "have HIV," "be HIV-positive," "be HIV-infected," or "be living with HIV." Infection with HIV produces a spectrum of diseases that progress from an asymptomatic state to AIDS, the final stage of HIV infection. The rate of this progression varies (CDC, 1992, 2007.16a, 2014.16a).

In 1993, the CD4 count, along with cervical cancer/cervical intraepithelial neoplasia (CIN), pulmonary tuberculosis, and recurrent bacterial pneumonia, was added to the CDC definition of AIDS (CDC, 1992). These additions led to a dramatic increase in the number of people who "officially" have AIDS.

Conditions Associated With AIDS

The CDC lists over 20 clinical conditions to be used in diagnosing AIDS along with HIV-positive status (CDC, 1996, 2014.16b; U.S. Department of Health and Human Services, 2010). These conditions fall into several categories: opportunistic infections, cancers, conditions associated specifically with AIDS, and conditions that *may* be diagnosed as AIDS under certain circumstances. A person cannot rely on symptoms to establish that he or she has AIDS. Each symptom can be related to other illnesses. Remember, AIDS is a medical diagnosis made by a physician using the specific CDC criteria.

think
about it

The Stigmatization of HIV and Other STIs

The fear of stigma leads to silence, and when it comes to fighting AIDS, silence is death.

—Kofi Annan, former secretary general, United Nations (1938–)

The deep ambivalence our society feels about sexuality is clearly brought to light by the way in which we deal with HIV and other STIs. If we think we have strep throat, we waste no time getting ourselves to a health center or doctor to obtain the appropriate medication. But let's say we're experiencing some discomfort when we urinate, and there's an unusual discharge. We may disregard the symptoms at first. Soon, we're feeling some pain, and we know something is definitely not right. With fear and trepidation, we slink into the clinic or doctor's office, hoping we don't see anyone we know so we won't have to explain why we're there. When we pick up our prescription, we can't look the pharmacist in the eye. And then there's the whole problem of telling our partner—or, worse yet, partners—about our predicament.

Why all this emotion over an STI but not over strep throat? Where does all the fear, denial, embarrassment, guilt, shame, and humiliation come from? Why are STIs the only class of illnesses we categorize by their *mode of transmission* rather than by the type of organism that causes them? All these questions stem from a common source: the stigmatization of persons who contract HIV or another STI. The Joint United Nations Programme on HIV/AIDS (UNAIDS) (2005) describes the origin of HIV stigmatization and some of its negative outcomes:

> HIV stigma stems from fear as well as associations of AIDS with sex, disease and death, and with behaviours that may be illegal, forbidden or taboo, such as pre- and extramarital sex, sex work, sex between men, and injecting drug use. Stigma also stems from lack of awareness and knowledge about HIV. Such stigma can fuel the urge to make scapegoats of, and blame and punish, certain people or groups. Stigma taps into existing prejudices and patterns of exclusion and further marginalizes people who might already be more vulnerable to HIV infection.

Fear of stigmatization and feelings of shame are among the principal factors contributing to the spread of HIV and other STIs (Mahajan et al., 2008). For example, in a sample of clinic patients and others at high risk for gonorrhea and HIV in seven cities, both shame and stigma were related to seeking STI-related care, but stigma may have been a more powerful barrier to obtaining such care (Fortenberry et al., 2002). A telephone survey in Alabama found that STIs are shrouded in secrecy and shame and that infected women are more stigmatized than infected men, although men are held responsible for spreading STIs (Lichtenstein, Hook, & Sharma, 2005). A study of 40 African American men who have sex with men (MSM) found that 88% experienced HIV stigma, 90% experienced sexual minority stigma, and 78% experienced both. Men with high HIV stigma were significantly more likely to engage in unprotected sex while high or intoxicated. Those endorsing more HIV stigma reported more receptive anal intercourse (Radcliffe et al., 2010). HIV-infected patients in the Netherlands were assessed to determine if HIV stigma was related to their taking of HIV medications: Those with the higher HIV stigma had greater nonadherence to the daily taking of all of the HIV medications (Sumari-de Boer, Sprangers, Prins, & Nieuwkerk, 2012).

The UNAIDS (2008, 2010) says that stigma and other societal causes of HIV risk and vulnerability are roadblocks to HIV prevention worldwide and need to be addressed as a "rights-based" response to the epidemic. The organization states that "long-term success in responding to the epidemic will require sustained progress in reducing human rights violations associated with it, including gender inequality, stigma and discrimination."

Think Critically

1. How have you observed HIV/STI stigma among your friends or others in our society? How were these stigmas demonstrated?

2. In your view, what can be done to eliminate the cultural stigma of HIV/STI?

3. If you became infected with HIV or another STI, would stigma and shame be an issue for you? If so, how would you deal with it? From what resources would you seek help and support?

Opportunistic Infections Diseases that take advantage of a weakened immune system are known as **opportunistic infections (OIs).** Normally, these infections do not develop in healthy people or are not life-threatening. In general, people with CD4 counts greater than 500 are not at risk for OIs. For people with CD4 counts around 500, however, the daily fluctuations in CD4 cell counts can leave them vulnerable to minor infections; candidiasis (thrush), a fungus infection that affects the respiratory system and vagina; and yeast infections (U.S. Department of Health and Human Services, 2010). Common OIs associated with HIV include certain types of tuberculosis, a parasitic disease of the brain and central nervous system, and certain types of pneumonia, including *Pneumocystis carinii* **pneumonia (PCP),** caused by a common organism (probably a protozoan or fungus) that is not usually harmful. Once someone has a dangerous opportunistic illness, life expectancy without treatment falls to about one year (CDC, 2014.16a).

Cancers Certain types of cancer are commonly associated with AIDS, including cancer of the lymphatic system, invasive cervical cancer, and a cancer of the blood vessels called **Kaposi's sarcoma.** Cervical cancer and CIN are more common in women who are HIV-positive than in women who are not. Kaposi's sarcoma, rare in healthy people, causes red or purple blotches to appear under the skin.

Clinical Conditions Conditions specifically linked to AIDS include wasting syndrome, symptoms of which include severe weight loss with weakness and persistent diarrhea, and AIDS dementia, characterized by impairment of mental and physical functioning and changes in mood and behavior.

Other Infections Infections that may lead to an AIDS diagnosis under certain circumstances include candidiasis; genital herpes; and cytomegalovirus, a virus of the herpes family that is often sexually transmitted.

Because the immune systems of people with HIV may not be functioning well (and those of people with advanced AIDS certainly are not), these individuals may be subject to numerous other infections that would not normally be much of a problem, such as colds, the flu, and intestinal infections. Health precautions for people living with HIV are discussed later in the chapter.

Symptoms of HIV Infection and AIDS

Within 2–4 weeks of becoming infected with HIV, some people develop flulike symptoms (often described as "the worst flu ever") that may last for a few days or several weeks, but others have no symptoms. Persons living with HIV may appear and feel healthy for 10 years or more after becoming infected. But even if they feel healthy, HIV is still affecting their bodies. Further, during this time, HIV infection may not show up on an HIV test, but persons having the infection are highly contagious and can spread the infection to others. Early diagnosis can be very valuable to effective HIV treatment, as we discuss later (CDC, 2014.16a).

Understanding AIDS: The Immune System and HIV

The principal components of blood are plasma (the fluid base), red blood cells, white blood cells, and platelets.

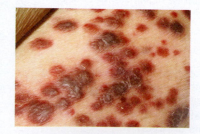

Kaposi's sarcoma is a cancer of the blood vessels commonly associated with AIDS. It causes red or purple blotches to appear under the skin.

National Cancer Institute (NCI)

Leukocytes   There are several kinds of **leukocytes,** or white blood cells, all of which play major roles in defending the body against invading organisms and mutant (cancerous) cells. Because HIV invades and eventually kills some kinds of leukocytes, it impairs the body's ability to ward off infections and other harmful conditions that ordinarily would not be threatening. The principal type of leukocyte we discuss is the lymphocyte.

Macrophages, Antigens, and Antibodies   White blood cells called **macrophages** engulf foreign particles and display the invader's antigen (*anti*body *gen*erator) like a signal flag on their own surfaces. **Antigens** are large molecules that are capable of stimulating the immune system and then reacting with the antibodies that are released to fight them. **Antibodies** bind to antigens, inactivate them, and mark them for destruction by killer cells. If the body has been previously exposed to the organism (by fighting it off or being vaccinated), the response is much quicker because memory cells are already biochemically programmed to respond.

B Cells and T Cells   The **lymphocytes** (a type of leukocyte) crucial to the immune system's functioning are **B cells** and several types of **T cells.** Like macrophages, **helper T cells** (also called CD4T or CD4 cells) are programmed to "read" the antigens and then begin directing the immune system's response. They send chemical signals to B cells, which begin making antibodies specific to the presented antigen. Helper T cells also stimulate the proliferation of B cells and T cells (which are genetically programmed to replicate, or make copies of themselves) and activate both macrophages and **killer T cells,** transforming them into agents of destruction whose only purpose is to attack and obliterate the enemy. Helper T cells display CD4, a type of protein receptor. The number of helper T cells (CD4 cells) in an individual's body is an important indicator of how well the immune system is functioning, as we discuss later.

The Virus

A **virus** is a protein-coated package of genes that invades a cell and alters the way in which the cell reproduces itself. Viruses can't propel themselves independently, and they can't reproduce unless they are inside a host cell. It would take 16,000 human immunodeficiency viruses to cover the head of a pin in a single layer. Under strong magnification, HIV resembles a spherical pin cushion, bristling with tiny, pinheadlike knobs (see Figure 1). These knobs are the antigens, which contain a protein called GP 120; the CD4 receptors on a helper T cell are attracted (fatally, as it turns out) to GP 120. Within the virus's protein core is the genetic material (RNA) that carries the information the virus needs to replicate itself. Also in the core is an enzyme called **reverse transcriptase,** which enables the virus to "write" its RNA (the genetic software or program) into a cell's DNA. In the normal genetic writing process, RNA is transcribed from DNA. Viruses with the ability to reverse the normal genetic writing process are known as **retroviruses.** There are numerous variant strains of HIV as a result of mutations. The virus begins undergoing genetic variation as soon as it has infected a person, even before antibodies develop. This tendency to mutate is one factor that makes HIV difficult to destroy.

Effect on T Cells   When HIV enters the bloodstream, helper T cells rush to the invading viruses, as if they were specifically designed for them. Normally at this stage, a T cell reads the antigen, stimulating antibody production in the

A T cell infected with HIV begins to replicate the virus, which buds from the cell wall, eventually killing the host cell.

© MedicalRF.com

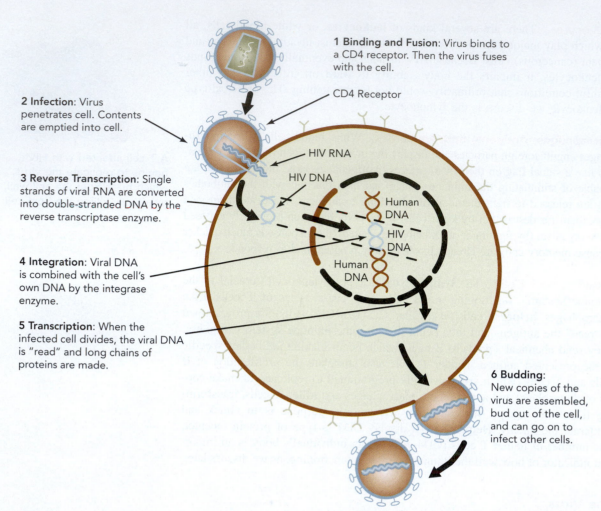

1 Binding and Fusion: Virus binds to a CD4 receptor. Then the virus fuses with the cell.

CD4 Receptor

2 Infection: Virus penetrates cell. Contents are emptied into cell.

HIV RNA

HIV DNA

3 Reverse Transcription: Single strands of viral RNA are converted into double-stranded DNA by the reverse transcriptase enzyme.

Human DNA

HIV DNA

Human DNA

4 Integration: Viral DNA is combined with the cell's own DNA by the integrase enzyme.

5 Transcription: When the infected cell divides, the viral DNA is "read" and long chains of proteins are made.

6 Budding: New copies of the virus are assembled, bud out of the cell, and can go on to infect other cells.

• FIGURE 1

The Infection of a CD4 Cell by HIV.

(*Source:* Adapted from *HIV Lifecycle.* Fact Sheet 106. University of New Mexico, Health Sciences Center, April 18, 2008. www.aidsinfonet.org/fact_sheets/view/106. Used with permission.)

B cells and beginning the process of eliminating the invading organism. In the case of HIV, however, although antibody production does begin, the immune process starts to break down almost at once. HIV injects its contents into the host T cell and copies its own genetic code into the cell's genetic material (DNA). As a result, when the immune system is activated, the T cell begins producing HIV instead of replicating itself. The T cell is killed in the process. HIV also targets other types of cells, including macrophages, dendritic cells (leukocytes found in the skin, lymph nodes, and intestinal mucous membranes), and brain cells.

HIV-1 and HIV-2   Almost all cases of HIV in the United States involve the type of the virus known as HIV-1. Another type, HIV-2, has been found to exist mainly in West Africa. Both HIV-1 and HIV-2 have the same mode of transmission and are associated with similar OIs and AIDS, although HIV-2 is less infectious than HIV-1.

AIDS Pathogenesis: How the Disease Progresses

As discussed earlier, when viruses are introduced into the body, they are immediately taken up by helper T cells and quickly moved to the lymph nodes. HIV

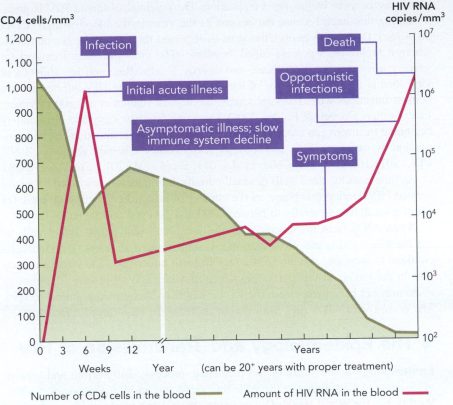

CD4 cells/mm³

1,200
1,100
1,000
900
800
700
600
500
400
300
200
100
0

Infection

Initial acute illness

Asymptomatic illness; slow immune system decline

Death

Opportunistic infections

Symptoms

HIV RNA copies/mm³

10⁷
10⁶
10⁵
10⁴
10³
10²

0   3   6   9   12   1   Years

Weeks   Year   (can be 20⁺ years with proper treatment)

Number of CD4 cells in the blood   Amount of HIV RNA in the blood

● **FIGURE 2**

The General Pattern of HIV Infection.

During the initial acute illness, CD4 levels (green line) fall sharply and HIV RNA levels (red line) increase; many infected people experience flulike symptoms during this period. Antibodies to HIV usually appear 3–8 weeks after the initial infection. During the asymptomatic phase that follows, CD4 levels (a marker for the status of the immune system) gradually decline, and HIV RNA levels again increase. Due to declines in immunity, infected individuals eventually begin to experience symptoms; when CD4 levels drop very low, people become vulnerable to serious opportunistic infections characteristic of AIDS. Modern treatment delays or slows the decline of the CD4 level. Chronic or recurrent illnesses continue until the immune system fails and death results.

(*Source:* Adapted from Fauci, A. S., et al. [1996]. Immunopathogenic mechanisms of HIV infection. *Annals of Internal Medicine, 124,* 654–663. Copyright © 1996 by American College of Physicians—Journals. Reproduced with permission of American College of Physicians.)

begins replication right away within the host cells. Most people will develop detectable antibodies to HIV within 3–8 weeks after exposure. The process by which a person develops antibodies is called **seroconversion.** A person's **serostatus** is HIV-negative if antibodies to HIV are not detected and HIV-positive if antibodies are detected.

T-Cell (CD4) Count   *T-cell count*—also called CD4 count—refers to the number of helper T cells that are present in a cubic millimeter of blood. A healthy person's CD4 count averages about 1,000, but it can range from 500 to 1,600, depending on a person's general health and whether he or she is fighting off an illness.

Phases of Infection   The pace of disease progression is variable, with the time between infection with HIV and development of AIDS ranging from a few months to many years, depending on several factors, including treatment regimens and the person's genetic makeup and health status (see Figure 2). Fortunately, people with HIV who are taking proper medication can live a long time before their immune system is damaged enough for AIDS to develop. When a person is first infected with HIV, he or she may experience severe flulike symptoms as the immune system goes into high gear to fight off the invader. These symptoms usually disappear within a week to a month and are often mistaken for those of another viral infection. More persistent and severe symptoms may not appear for 10 years or more after HIV first enters the body in adults. His or her CD4 count may temporarily plunge as the virus begins rapid replication. The potential to spread HIV is greatest during this stage because the amount of the virus in the blood is high (CDC, 2014.16a). During this period, the virus is dispersed throughout the lymph nodes, where it replicates, a process called "seeding." The virus may stay localized for years, but it continues to replicate and destroy T cells. Research has shown that viral load is the chief predictor of transmission of HIV; the HIV-infected person is most infectious when the viral load is the highest (Quinn et al., 2000; Wilson, Law, Grulich, Cooper, & Kaldor, 2008). Detecting infection early and immediately beginning treatment can reduce the viral load, reduce the likelihood of sexual transmission by well over 90%, and boost longevity (Cates, Chesney, & Cohen, 1997; CDC, 2011.16a, 2014.16c; Cohen et al., 2011; Samji et al., 2013; Sternberg, 2008).

As time goes by, the T cells gradually diminish in number, destroyed by newly created HIV. During this phase, as the number of infected cells goes up, the CD4 count goes down, generally to between 200 and 500 per millimeter of blood.

When AIDS is in the advanced phase, the T cells and other fighter cells of the immune system are no longer able to trap foreign invaders. Infected cells continue to increase, and the CD4 count drops to under 200. The virus is detectable in the blood. At this point, the person may be fairly ill to very ill, although some may not have symptoms. The CD4 count may continue to plummet to zero. The person with AIDS dies from one or more of the opportunistic infections.

● The Epidemiology and Transmission of HIV

Epidemiology is the study of the incidence, process, distribution, and control of diseases. An **epidemic** is the wide and rapid spread of a contagious disease. Worldwide, the World Health Organization (WHO) and the Joint United Nations Programme on HIV/AIDS (UNAIDS) report that about 35 million people are living with HIV and more than 39 million people have died from AIDS, making this epidemic one of the most destructive in recorded history. As shown in Figure 3, the prevalence of HIV infection is by far the greatest in Africa. In 2013, an estimated 1.5 million people died from AIDS and an estimated

● **FIGURE** 3

Percentage of Adults (Prevalence %) by Region Worldwide Who Were Living With HIV in 2013.

(*Source:* Adapted from World Health Organization. Global Health Observatory Map Gallery, 2014.16a.)

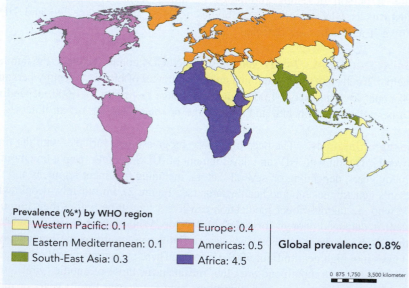

Prevalence (%*) by WHO region

Western Pacific: 0.1

Eastern Mediterranean: 0.1

South-East Asia: 0.3

Europe: 0.4

Americas: 0.5

Africa: 4.5

Global prevalence: 0.8%

0 875 1,750 3,500 kilometer

*Estimated number of adults aged 15–49 years living with HIV in 2013 divided by the 2013 population aged 15–49

2.1 million individuals were newly infected with HIV. Over 5,000 new infections occur globally each day (World Health Organization, 2014.16b).

The WHO/UNAIDS states that the rates of new HIV infections are going down all over the world, resulting from the massive expansion of HIV interventions worldwide. WHO/UNAIDS believes that the HIV epidemic can be ended. HIV intervention efforts such as improved and greater availability of prevention and health care services, an expanding array of effective medical interventions, and the development and implementation of effective behavioral change programs have transformed the HIV epidemic. Substantial—and in some instances, remarkable—progress has been made in the past three to four years: Significant reductions in new HIV infections among adults and children have occurred, from 2.5 million acquiring HIV in 2009 to 2.1 million in 2013. However, WHO/UNAIDS states that much remains to be done, particularly in reaching key and marginalized populations such as men who have sex with men (MSM), sex workers, injection drug users, adolescents and young people, transgender individuals, and persons in prisons (World Health Organization, 2014.16c).

The Epidemiology of HIV/AIDS in the United States

In the United States, since the diagnosis of the first AIDS case over three decades ago, the number of persons living with HIV has grown from a few dozen to an estimated 880,442 persons in 2011. However, the acquisition of HIV is showing encouraging declines, yet disparities continued in some population groups as discussed below. Even though from 2008 through 2012 the annual estimated number of diagnoses of HIV infection in the U.S. remained relatively stable (between about 42,000–49,000) the estimated annual rate of HIV diagnoses decreased 5.6 percent from 16.2 per 100,000 in 2008 to 15.1 in 2012 (CDC, 2014.16d). Actually, the annual diagnosis of HIV decreased more than 30% the past decade or so (Johnson et al., 2014).

An estimated 47,989 persons were diagnosed with HIV infection in 2012. The proportion of HIV cases differs by sex: In 2012, males accounted for 80% of diagnosed HIV cases. The transmission category for each sex also varies (see Figure 4). Eighty percent of the adult and adolescent male HIV/AIDS cases

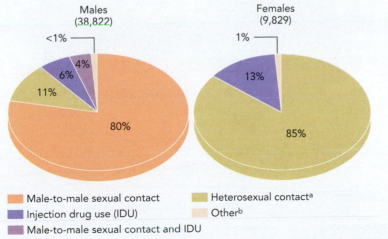

Males (38,822)
<1%
4%
6%
11%
80%

Females (9,829)
1%
13%
85%

- ■ Male-to-male sexual contact
- ■ Injection drug use (IDU)
- ■ Male-to-male sexual contact and IDU
- ■ Heterosexual contact[a]
- ■ Other[b]

Note. Data include persons with a diagnosis of HIV infection regardless of stage of disease at diagnosis. Percentage may not be 100% because of rounding.
[a]Heterosexual contact with a person known to have, or to be at high risk for, HIV infection.
[b]Includes hemophilia, blood transfusion, perinatal exposure, and risk factor not reported or not identified.

● **FIGURE** 4

Proportion of HIV Diagnoses Among U.S. Adults and Adolescents by Sex and Transmission Category, 2012.

(*Source:* CDC, 2014.16e.)

• FIGURE 5

Change in U.S. Adult and Adolescent AIDS Cases by Transmission Category and Year of Diagnosis, 1985–2012.

(*Source:* CDC, 2014.16e.)

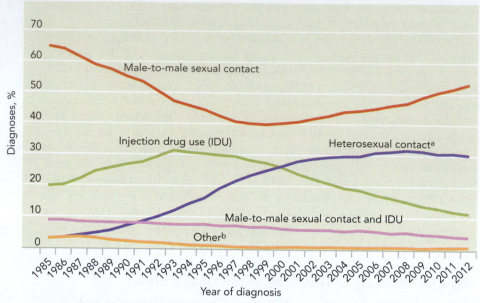

aHeterosexual contact with a person known to have, or to be at high risk for, HIV infection.
bIncludes hemophilia, blood transfusion, perinatal exposure, and risk factor not reported or not identified.

were attributed to male-to-male sexual contact, and 85% of the adult and adolescent female HIV/AIDS cases were attributed to high-risk heterosexual contact (CDC, 2014.16e).

The proportional distribution of AIDS cases by transmission category has shifted since the beginning of the epidemic (see Figure 5), with the percentage of cases for male-to-male sexual contact decreasing, then rising to 53% of all AIDS diagnoses in 2012 and the percentage for high-risk heterosexual contact increasing and then leveling off. The proportional distribution of AIDS diagnosis among races/ethnicities has changed since the beginning of the epidemic (see Figure 6). The proportion of AIDS diagnoses among Whites has decreased; the

• FIGURE 6

Change in U.S. AIDS Cases by Race/Ethnicity and Year of Diagnosis, 1985–2012.

(*Source:* CDC, 2014.16e.)

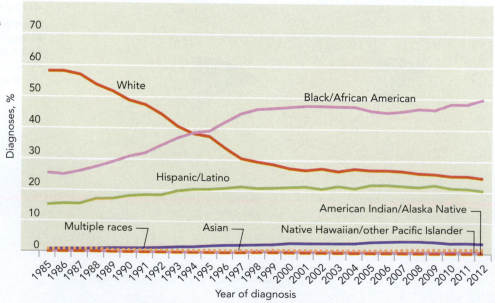

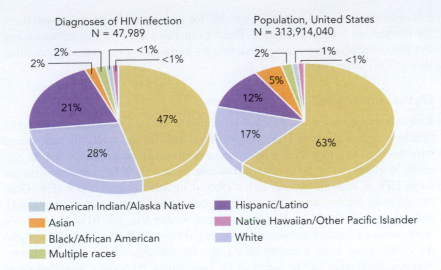

Diagnoses of HIV infection
N = 47,989

2% 2% <1% <1%
21%
47%
28%

Population, United States
N = 313,914,040

2% 1% <1%
5%
12%
17%
63%

■ American Indian/Alaska Native
■ Asian
■ Black/African American
■ Multiple races

■ Hispanic/Latino
■ Native Hawaiian/Other Pacific Islander
■ White

● **FIGURE 7**

Proportion of Diagnoses of HIV Infection and Population by Race/Ethnicity, 2012, United States.

(*Source:* CDC, 2011.16c.)

proportions among African Americans have increased (CDC, 2011.16b). The pie charts in Figure 7 illustrate the distribution of HIV diagnoses reported during 2012 among races/ethnicities and the racial/ethnic distribution in the United States. African Americans and Hispanics are disproportionately affected by the AIDS epidemic in comparison to their proportional distribution in the general population (CDC, 2014.16f).

Using HIV surveillance data and vital statistics from the 37 states in the United States and Puerto Rico, the Centers for Disease Control and Prevention analyzed the estimated lifetime risk of being diagnosed with HIV (see Table 1). Lifetime risk estimates are often reported in the popular press and in scientific literature for cancer and other diseases, but until recently no such estimates have been generated for HIV. **Lifetime risk** is typically considered to be the number of people who would need to be followed throughout their lives to observe one occurrence of the disease. As shown in Table 1, in 2007, the estimated lifetime

TABLE 1 ● **Estimated Lifetime Risk for HIV Diagnosis, by Race/Ethnicity, 33 States and Puerto Rico, 2007.[a]**

Race/Ethnicity	Male	Female	Total
All combined	2.0% (1 in 50)	0.7 (1 in 143)	1.4 (1 in 71)
American Indian/Alaska Native	1.0% (1 in 100)	0.5 (1 in 200)	0.8 (1 in 125)
Asian	0.7% (1 in 142)	0.2 (1 in 500)	0.5 (1 in 200)
Black/African American	6.3% (1 in 16)	3.1 (1 in 32)	4.7 (1 in 21)
Hispanic/Latino	2.8% (1 in 36)	0.9 (1 in 111)	1.9 (1 in 53)
Native Hawaiian/other Pacific Islander	3.1% (1 in 32)	0.6 (1 in 166)	1.9 (1 in 53)
White	1.0% (1 in 100)	0.2 (1 in 500)	0.6 (1 in 167)

[a]Based on HIV surveillance data and vital statistics in 37 states in the United States and Puerto Rico.

SOURCE: Adapted from Centers for Disease Control and Prevention (CDC). (2010.16a). Estimated lifetime risk for diagnosis of HIV infection among Hispanics/Latinos—37 states and Puerto Rico, 2007. *Morbidity and Mortality Weekly Report, 59* (40), 1297–1301.

risk of being diagnosed with HIV was 2% for males, or 1 in 50 males, and 0.7% for females, or 1 in 143 females. These estimates varied by race/ethnicity and can help strengthen prevention education by highlighting the risk of contracting HIV (CDC, 2010.16a).

Myths and Modes of Transmission

Research has revealed a great deal of valuable medical, scientific, and public health information about HIV transmission, and the ways HIV is transmitted have been clearly identified. However, false information not supported by scientific findings is still being shared. Because of this, the CDC has described the ways HIV is transmitted and has corrected misconceptions about HIV. Only certain body fluids—blood, semen, pre-seminal fluid (pre-cum), vaginal fluids, and breast milk—from an HIV-infected person can transmit HIV. These fluids must contact a mucous membrane or damaged tissue or be directly injected into the bloodstream from a needle or syringe for transmission to possibly occur. Mucous membranes can be found inside the rectum, the vagina, the opening of the penis, and the mouth. The CDC (2014.16g) states that in the United States HIV is spread mainly by: (1) having anal or vaginal sex with someone who has HIV, (2) having multiple sex partners or having other STIs, which can increase risk of HIV infection through sex, and (3) sharing injection drug equipment such as needles with someone who is infected with HIV. The CDC also says that babies born to HIV-infected women may become infected before or during birth or through breastfeeding after birth. (A more detailed description of these transmission routes is presented later in this chapter.)

By now, most people have a more accurate understanding of HIV/AIDS and know the difference between actual transmission routes and transmission myths. But just to briefly review: Scientific and epidemiological evidence shows that the chances are essentially zero of acquiring HIV from an environmental surface (e.g., toilet seat), from nonsexual household or other-settings contact with an HIV-infected person, from typical social contact (e.g., hugging, shaking hands), from food-serving establishments, from closed-mouth or social kissing, from insect (e.g., mosquito) bites, from sport-participation accidents involving blood, or from donating blood. Contact with the saliva (e.g., being spit on by an HIV-infected person), tears, or sweat from an HIV-infected person has never been shown to result in transmission of the virus. The CDC knows of no instances of HIV being transmitted through tattooing or body piercing, although hepatitis B virus has been transmitted during some of these procedures. Also, being bitten by an HIV-infected person is not a common method of transmitting HIV. Of the few reports in the medical literature in which HIV appeared to be transmitted by a bite, severe trauma with extensive tissue tearing and damage and the presence of blood were reported (CDC, 2010.16b, 2011.16d). There is no risk of transmission if the skin is not broken. Also, reports are extremely rare of HIV transmission from contact between broken skin, wounds, or mucus and HIV-infected blood or blood-contaminated body fluids.

Some people have been concerned about the possibility of acquiring HIV from a blood transfusion and organ donations. Contaminated donated blood, plasma, body organs, and semen are all capable of sustaining HIV. Because of this, medical procedures in the United States involving these materials now include screening for HIV or destroying the virus, and the chance of acquiring

HIV from these procedures is extremely low. To be absolutely safe, some people who know they will have surgery donate their own blood a few weeks before the operation so that it will be available during surgery if needed. Donated organs are screened for HIV, and there are guidelines regarding semen donation for artificial insemination.

Eating food that has been chewed by an HIV-infected person, such as an infected mother pre-chewing food that is fed to her baby, could theoretically be a way of transmitting HIV. However, the contamination, which is very rare, occurs when infected blood from the chewer's mouth mixes with food while chewing. Being struck with an HIV-contaminated needle or other sharp objects—a risk mainly for health care workers—is a less common way of spreading HIV (CDC, 2010.16b, 2011.16d, 2014.16g).

Sexual Transmission

Recall that HIV can be found in the semen, pre-seminal fluid, vaginal fluid, or blood of a person infected with the virus. Latex barriers, condoms, dental dams, and surgical gloves, if used properly, can provide good protection against the transmission of HIV.

Anal Intercourse   Unprotected anal sex (no condom use) is considered to be the most risky sexual behavior, and either sexual partner can become infected with HIV during anal sex (CDC, 2014.16g). In general, however, the partner receiving the semen is at greater risk of getting HIV because the lining of the rectum is thin and may allow the virus to enter the body. However, a person who inserts his penis into an infected partner is also at risk, since HIV can enter through the urethra or through small cuts, abrasions, or open sores on the penis. Some people mistakenly believe that only men who have sex with men are at risk of HIV through anal sex. However, a national study of men and women aged 15–44 from the 2006–2008 National Survey of Family Growth found that 36% of females and 44% of males ever had anal sex with an other-sex partner (National Center for Health Statistics, 2011). Further, the National College Health assessment found that during spring semester in 2014, 7% and 4% of college men and women reported anal intercourse in the past 30 days (American College Health Association, 2014.16a). Research has shown that heterosexual intercourse among men and women is often unprotected (i.e., no condom is used) and has been associated with other HIV/STI risk behavior and with STI diagnosis (Javanbakht et al., 2010; Jenness et al., 2011).

Vaginal Intercourse   Vaginal-penile sex is the second highest sexual risk behavior. It is possible for either partner to become infected with HIV this way, although women have a much higher risk for getting HIV during vaginal sex without a condom than men do. In women, the lining of the vagina can tear and allow HIV to enter the body. HIV can also be directly absorbed through the mucous membranes that line the vagina and cervix. In men, HIV can enter the body through the urethra or small cuts or open sores on the penis. Men who are not circumcised are at greater risk of HIV infection through vaginal sex than are circumcised men (CDC, 2014.16g). Adolescent females are biologically more susceptible to HIV than older women because their immature cervixes may be more easily infected (Braverman & Strasburger, 1994). However, the virus can enter the bloodstream through the urethra or through small cuts or

> *Wake up. Don't let someone feed you a line and don't be afraid to ask questions. Find out yourself.*
>
> —Ryan White
> (1971–1990)

open sores on the penis. Menstrual blood containing HIV can also facilitate transmission of the virus to a sexual partner.

Oral Sex   HIV may be transmitted during fellatio, cunnilingus, or analingus (oral–anal contact), although evidence suggests that the risk is much less than that from unprotected anal or vaginal sex. There have been a few cases of HIV transmission from performing oral sex on a person infected with HIV (CDC, 2010.16b). However, receiving fellatio, giving or receiving cunnilingus, and giving or receiving analingus carry little or no risk. The highest oral sex risk is to individuals with ejaculation in the mouth on an HIV-infected man. The risk of HIV transmission increases if the person performing oral sex has cuts or sores around or in the mouth or throat, if the male receiving oral sex ejaculates in the mouth of the person performing oral sex, or if the person receiving oral sex has another STI. If the person performing oral sex has HIV, blood from the mouth may enter the body of the person receiving oral sex through the lining of the urethra, vagina, cervix, or anus or directly into the body through small cuts or open sores. If the person receiving oral sex has HIV, the blood, semen, pre-seminal fluid, or vaginal fluid may contain the virus. Cells lining the mouth of the person performing oral sex may allow HIV to enter the body. The exact risk of HIV transmission is difficult to measure because people who participate in oral sex may also participate in other sexual behaviors. When HIV transmission occurs, it may be the result of oral sex or other, riskier sexual activities such as anal or vaginal sex (CDC, 2014.16h).

Kissing   Kissing, because it involves saliva, is frequently a concern among those who are unsure how HIV is transmitted. As we said, HIV is not transmitted casually, so kissing on the cheek is very safe. Transmission through kissing alone is extremely rare. There are extremely rare cases of HIV being transmitted via deep "French" kissing, but in each case infected blood was exchanged due to bleeding gums or sores in the mouth. Prolonged open-mouth kissing could damage the mouth or lips and allow HIV to pass from an infected person to a partner and then enter the body through cuts or sores in the mouth (CDC, 2010.16b, 2014.16g). Because of this possible risk, the CDC (2010.16b) recommends against open-mouth kissing with an infected partner.

Sex Toys   Although unlikely, HIV can be transmitted in vaginal secretions on such objects as dildos and vibrators; therefore, it is very important that these objects not be shared or that they be washed thoroughly before use.

Injection Drug and Substance Use

Sharing needles or other paraphernalia used to inject drugs provides an ideal pathway for HIV. An injection drug user (IDU) may have an immune system that has already been weakened by poor health, poor nutrition, or an STI. IDUs who become infected often pass the virus sexually to their partners.

At the beginning of every drug injection, blood is introduced into the needle and syringe. The reuse of a blood-contaminated needle or syringe by another drug injector (sometimes called "direct syringe sharing") is a high risk of HIV transmission because infected blood can be injected directly into the bloodstream. Infected blood can be introduced into drug solutions by using blood-contaminated syringes to prepare the drugs, reusing water, and reusing bottle caps, spoons, or other containers ("spoons" and "cookers") used to dissolve drugs in water and to heat drug solutions. Also, infected blood can be introduced by reusing pieces of cotton filters ("cottons") used to filter out small particles that could block the needle. "Street sellers" of syringes may repackage used syringes and sell them as sterile needles. For this reason, people who continue to inject drugs should obtain syringes from reliable sources of sterile syringes, such as pharmacies or needle exchange programs. Sharing a needle or syringe for any use, including skin popping and injecting steroids, can put one at risk for HIV and other blood-borne infections.

When we think of injection drug use, we usually think in terms of psychotropic (mind-affecting) drugs such as heroin or cocaine. We may conjure up images of run-down tenement rooms or "shooting galleries," where needles are passed around. But these are not the only settings for sharing drugs. HIV transmission in connection with the recreational use of injection drugs also occurs among people from the middle or upper class. Moreover, injection drug use exists among athletes and bodybuilders, who may share needles to inject steroids. HIV can be transmitted just as easily in a brightly lit locker room or upscale living room as in a dark alley.

Although injection drug use is a direct route of HIV transmission, drinking, smoking, ingesting or inhaling drugs such as alcohol, crack cocaine, methamphetamine ("meth"), and amyl nitrite ("poppers") are also associated with increased risk for HIV infection. Excessive alcohol consumption, particularly binge drinking, is an important risk factor for HIV infection, since it is linked to less frequent use of condoms and numerous sex partners. Crack cocaine's short-lived high and addictiveness can create a compulsive cycle in which users quickly exhaust their resources and turn to other ways to get the drug, including trading sex for drugs or money, thus increasing risk for HIV infection. Methamphetamine has long been associated with increased HIV risk, as it is associated with high-risk sexual behavior with non-steady sexual partners. The use of amyl nitrite has also been linked to risky behaviors, illegal drug use, and STIs among gay and bisexual men and recently to adolescents in part because it increases sexual pleasure (CDC, 2014.16i).

Mother-to-Child Transmission

Women infected with HIV can transmit HIV to their babies during pregnancy, labor and delivery, and breastfeeding. Called **perinatal HIV transmission (mother-to-child),** this mode of transmission is the most common route of HIV infection in children and is the source of almost all the AIDS cases of children in the United States. Most of the children with AIDS are members of minority races/ethnicities. About one quarter to one third of all untreated pregnant women infected with HIV will pass the infection to their babies. HIV can also be transmitted to babies via an HIV-infected caregiver who gives the infant pre-chewed food. When HIV is diagnosed before or during pregnancy, HIV transmission to the baby or child can be reduced to less than 1% if appropriate medical treatment is given, the virus becomes undetectable, and the mother does not breastfeed. HIV infection of newborns has been almost eradicated in the United States because of voluntary prenatal HIV testing and medical treatment, yet about 200 infants are still infected with HIV annually. Many of these infections involve women who were not tested early enough in pregnancy or who did not receive prevention services (CDC, 2007.16b, 2011.16d, 2014.16j).

Factors Contributing to Infection

Researchers have found that certain physiological or behavioral factors increase one's risk of contracting HIV. For people of both sexes, these include behaviors already discussed, such as anal intercourse, numerous sexual partners, and injection drug use. There is considerable biological evidence that the presence of other STIs increases the likelihood of both transmitting and acquiring HIV (Fleming & Wasserheit, 1999). This is true whether the STI causes open sores (e.g., syphilis, herpes) or does not cause breaks in the skin (e.g., chlamydia, gonorrhea). People are 2–5 times more likely to become infected with HIV when they have other STIs. There are two ways that having an STI can increase the probability of acquiring HIV. If the STI causes irritation of the skin (e.g., from syphilis, herpes, or HPV), breaks in the skin or open sores may make it easier for HIV to enter the body during sexual contact. Even STIs that do not cause breaks or open sores (e.g., chlamydia, gonorrhea, trichomoniasis) can increase the risk by causing inflammation that increases the number of cells that can serve as targets of HIV. In addition, an HIV-infected person also infected with an STI is 3–5 times more likely than other HIV-infected people to transmit HIV through sexual contact. This appears to happen because there is an increase in concentration of HIV in the semen and genital fluids of HIV-positive people who are also infected with an STI. Although HIV can be transmitted in a single encounter, it usually takes several exposures for a person to contract the virus. Moreover, the probability of HIV transmission is greater when the viral load is the highest, particularly in the early stage of the infection (Cates et al., 1997; CDC, 2010.16b; Gray et al., 2001; Keele et al., 2008).

● AIDS Demographics

The statistical characteristics of populations are called **demographics.** Public health researchers often look at groups of people in terms of age, socioeconomic status, living area, ethnicity, sex, and so on in order to understand the dynamics of disease transmission and prevention. When STIs are involved, they naturally look at sexual behaviors as well. No one is exempt from HIV exposure by virtue of belonging or not belonging to a specific group. But certain groups appear *as a whole* to be at greater risk than others because they have unique challenges in the prevention, diagnosis, and treatment of HIV/AIDS. Many individuals within these groups may not be at risk, however, because they do not engage in risky behaviors.

Minority Races/Ethnicities and HIV

In the early 1980s in the United States, HIV/AIDS was primarily considered a gay, White disease. Today, however, the epidemic has expanded, and the proportional distribution of AIDS cases among minority racial and ethnic groups has shifted and, as mentioned earlier, Blacks and Hispanics are disproportionately affected (see Figure 7). Being of a minority race/ethnic group is not, in itself, a risk factor for HIV infection and other STIs. However, race/ethnicity in the United States is a risk marker that correlates with other, more fundamental determinants of health status, such as poverty, homelessness, lack of access to quality health care, avoiding seeking health care, substance abuse, stigma and discrimination, and residence in communities with a high prevalence of HIV and other STIs.

Although poverty itself is not a risk factor, studies have found a direct relationship between higher AIDS incidence and lower income. A study of a diverse sample of women from urban health clinics found that socioeconomic status, not race/ethnicity, had both direct and indirect associations with HIV risk behaviors; the women with lower income had riskier sexual behaviors (Ickovics et al., 2002). Several socioeconomic problems associated with poverty (e.g., housing insecurity and limited access to health care) directly or indirectly raise HIV risk (Buffardi, Thomas, Holmes, & Manhart, 2008). Some minority race/ethnic communities are reluctant to acknowledge sensitive issues such as homosexuality and substance use.

African Americans Of all racial and ethnic groups in the United States, African Americans have been impacted most severely by HIV and AIDS (see Figure 7). In the United States HIV/AIDS is a health crisis for African Americans. Young Black gay and bisexual man are especially at risk. At all stages of HIV/AIDS—from infection with HIV to death from AIDS—Blacks are disproportionately affected compared to other racial/ethnic groups. The reasons for this are not directly related to race or ethnicity but, rather, to the barriers faced by many African Americans, including poverty, high incidence of another STI, limited HIV prevention education, and the stigma of HIV/AIDS. Another barrier to HIV prevention is homophobia and concealment of male-to-male behavior. Homophobia and stigmatization can cause some African American men who have sex with men to identify themselves as heterosexual or not to disclose their same-sex behaviors. Black men are more likely than other MSM not to identify themselves as gay men. This absence of disclosure of self-identification may make it more difficult to present appropriate HIV prevention education. Other factors that contribute to higher risk among African Americans include higher rates of STIs than other racial/ethnic groups in the United States, lack of awareness of HIV status, and the tendency to have sex with partners of the same race/ethnicity, resulting in their facing a greater risk of HIV infection with each new sexual encounter (CDC, 2011.16e).

Compared to other races/ethnicities, African Americans accounted for more new diagnoses of HIV infection in 2012—47%—than all racial/ethnic groups in the United States, yet they represent only 12% of the U.S. population (CDC, 2014.16f) (see Figure 7). Further, Blacks account for a high proportion of those living with HIV and those ever diagnosed with AIDs. Blacks living with HIV/AIDS often do not live as long and die more frequently. The rate of new HIV infection in African Americans, based on population size, is 8 times that of whites. Blacks have a much greater lifetime estimated risk of being diagnosed with HIV than Whites and Hispanics: 6.2%, or 1 in 16, for Black males and 0.9%, or 1 in 32, for Black females (see Table 1). In 2012, Black men accounted for 71% of the estimated new HIV infections among all African Americans. Black men who have sex with men (MSM) have been particularly impacted: They account for the vast majority of new HIV infections among all African American men and the highest number of new HIV infections among all gay and bisexual men. In 2012, Black women accounted for 6,299 (28%) of the estimated new HIV infections among all adult and adolescent

The HIV epidemic has dramatically and disproportionly affected African Americans. The disease poses a serious threat to the future health and well-being of many African American communities.

© Bill Aron/PhotoEdit

African Americans. Most new infections among African American women (88%) are attributed to heterosexual contact. The estimated rate of new HIV infections in Black women was 20 times that of white women and almost 5 times that of Hispanic/Latino women (CDC, 2011.16c, 2014.16f, 2014.16k).

Hispanics/Latinos The Hispanic/Latino community, which includes a diverse mixture of ethnic groups and cultures, is the fastest growing and largest ethnic group in the United States, and the HIV/AIDS epidemic is a serious threat to that community. Injection drug use, STIs, poverty, education, and cultural beliefs are some of the HIV prevention challenges that face them.

In 2012, Hispanics/Latinos accounted for 21% of new diagnoses of HIV infection (CDC, 2014.16f) (see Figure 7). In 2010, the rate of new infections among Hispanics/Latinos was three times that of Whites (CDC, 2014.16l). The relatively high rates among Latino women may be due to the emphasis of male dominated gender roles which may not allow some women to insist on the use of a condom. The estimated lifetime risk of a HIV diagnosis for Hispanic males is 2.8% or 1 in 36; for females, 0.9%, or 1 in 111 (see Table 1). In 2012, Latino men accounted for 81% of new HIV infections among all Latinos. Latino MSM accounted for 87% of new HIV infections among all Latino men and 20% of all MSM in 2010. Among Latino MSM, 67% of new HIV infections occurred in men under age 35 and Latina women accounted for 14% of new HIV infections among Latinos in 2010 (CDC, 2014.16l). Given the growth of the Hispanic/Latino community in the United States, the prevalence of HIV/AIDS among this group will increasingly affect the health status of the nation. Prevention programs must give special attention to the cultural diversity that exists within this and other diverse communities.

Asian Americans Despite the growth of the Asian population in the United States, the number of HIV diagnoses among Asian Americans has remained stable and represented only 2% of new HIV infections in 2012 in the U.S. and dependent areas (CDC, 2014.16e) (see Figure 7). In 2011, of the estimated 982 new HIV infections among adult and adolescent Asian Americans, 84% (821) were men and 16% (153) were women. Eighty-six percent (705) of the estimated 821 HIV diagnoses among Asian American men in 2011 were attributed to male-to-male sexual contact, and 92% (141) of the estimated 153 HIV diagnoses among Asian American women were attributed to heterosexual contact. Only about four out of ten Asian Americans have ever been tested for HIV. More than one-third of Asian Americans develop AIDS within a relatively short time after being diagnosed which may indicate that they are not receiving adequate care and treatment in time to prevent them from developing AIDS. Some Asian Americans may avoid seeking testing, counseling, or treatment because of language barriers or fear of discrimination, the stigma of homosexuality, immigration issues, or fear of bringing shame to their families. Traditional Asian cultures may emphasize male-dominated gender roles that empower men and deprive women of sexual negotiating power, which may affect the rate of heterosexual HIV transmission of Asian American women (CDC, 2014.16m).

Native Hawaiians and Other Pacific Islanders National HIV estimates show that Native Hawaiians and Other Pacific Islanders (NHOPI) in the United States represent a very small proportion of HIV infections: In 2012, less than 1% of new HIV diagnoses were among NHOPI (CDC, 2014.16e) (see Figure 7).

In 2011, 70 and 10 of the HIV diagnoses among NHOPI were men and women, respectively: Sixty-one of the men diagnoses were attributed to male-to-male sexual contact and 8 diagnoses among women were attributed to heterosexual contact. In 2011, the rate of HIV diagnoses in NHOPI was more than twice as high as rates among whites. One in four NHOPI living with HIV are unaware of their infection. Socioeconomic factors such as poverty, inadequate or no health coverage, language barriers, and lower educational attainment among NHOPI may contribute to lack of awareness about HIV risk and higher-risk behaviors. Further, NHOPI customs, such as those that prioritize obligations to family and taboos on intergenerational sexual topics and sexual health discussion, may stigmatize sexuality in general and homosexuality specifically, as well as interfere with HIV risk-reduction such as condom use (CDC, 2014.16n).

American Indians and Alaska Natives

Among American Indians and Alaska Natives, HIV/AIDS is not always apparent because of their small population size. The number of new diagnoses of HIV infection for this population group was less than 1% of the total number of new HIV diagnoses reported in the United States in 2012 (CDC, 2014.16.e) (see Figure 7). The largest transmission category for men was male-to-male sexual contact and high-risk sexual behavior for women. Twenty-one percent of American Indians and Alaska Natives infected with HIV are unaware of their infection. Poverty, lower levels of education and higher levels of unemployment, and less access to health care coexist as risk factors for HIV infection among American Indians and Alaska Natives. Alcohol and illicit drug use are higher among American Indians and Alaska Natives than among people of other races or ethnicities. American Indian and Alaska Native gay and bisexual men may face culturally-based stigma and confidentiality concerns that limit opportunities for education and HIV testing, especially among those living in rural communities or on reservations. These indicators increase the vulnerability of American Indians and Alaska Natives to additional health stress, including HIV infection.

To be effective, HIV/AIDS prevention education must account for the numerous populations of American Indians and Alaska Natives by tailoring programs to individual tribal cultures and beliefs. The American Indian and Alaska Native population makes up over 560 federally recognized tribes plus at least 50 state-recognized tribes whose members speak over 170 languages. Because each tribe has its own culture, beliefs, and practices and these tribes may be subdivided into language groups, it can be challenging to create effective programs for each group (CDC, 2008.16a, 2014.16o).

The Gay Community

"AIDS has given a human face to an invisible minority," says Robert Bray of the National Gay and Lesbian Task Force. From the beginning of the HIV/AIDS epidemic in the United States, the most disproportionate impact has been among the MSM group. Although epidemiologists do not know for certain how HIV first arrived in the gay community, they do know that it spread like wildfire, mainly because anal sex is such an efficient mode of transmission. Furthermore, initial research, education, and prevention efforts were severely hampered by a lack of government and public interest in what was perceived to be a "gay disease" (Shilts, 1987). Now, over 30 years after the virus first appeared, the gay community continues to reel from the repeated blows dealt by AIDS and to represent the largest HIV transmission category.

Male-to-male sexual contact is a behavioral description of a diverse population, many of whom identify themselves either privately or publicly as a gay man or bisexual person. Others may engage in sex with men but not think of themselves as a gay man or bisexual person. Even though the numbers of AIDS cases for MSM decreased during the 1980s and 1990s, recent surveillance data show an increase in HIV diagnoses for this group representing 64% of the diagnosis of HIV infection among adults and adolescents in the United States and 6 geographic dependent areas in 2012 (see Figures 4 and 5). MSM still represent the largest transmission category, accounting for 53% of the AIDS cases among adult and adolescent persons diagnosed with HIV infection in 2012 (CDC, 2014.16c).

As previously stated, HIV/AIDS has dramatically impacted African American MSM. Among gay and bisexual men in 2012 in the United States, African Americans accounted for the largest estimated number and percentage of diagnoses of HIV infection (11,957, 39%), followed by Whites (10,069, 33%), and Hispanics/Latinos (7,057, 23%). Among gay and bisexual men in 2012, African Americans accounted for the highest estimated number and percentage of persons with diagnosed HIV infection ever classified as having AIDS (6,010, 40%), followed by Whites (4,734, 32%) and Hispanics/Latinos (3,289, 22%). Young African American gay and bisexual men aged 13–24 years are especially affected by HIV, having dramatic increases in HIV infection diagnosis in contrast to other racial/ethnic groups (see Figure 8) (CDC, 2014.16f, 2014.16p).

Sexual risk behaviors account for most HIV infections in MSM. Anal sex without a condom continues to be a major health threat to MSM, particularly having unprotected anal sex ("barebacking") with casual partners. The reasons for unprotected sex are not completely understood, but research points to several factors, including optimism about improved HIV treatment, substance use, being unsure of their HIV serostatus, complex sexual decision making, and seeking partners on the Internet (CDC, 2010.16c, 2014.16q; Wolitski, 2005). Some of these men may be **serosorting,** or having sex or unprotected sex with a partner whose HIV serostatus, they believe, is the same as their own. For

I think God did send AIDS for a reason. It was to show how mean and sinful a healthy man can be toward a sick man.

—Joe Bob Briggs
(1953–)

● FIGURE 8

Diagnoses of HIV Infection Among Men Who Have Sex with Men Aged 13–24 Years, by Race/Ethnicity, 2008–2011, United States and 6 Dependent Areas.

(*Source*: Centers for Disease Control and Prevention, 2014.16g.)

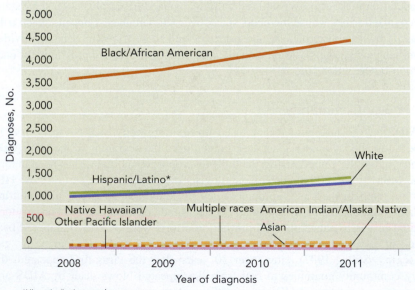

*Hispanics/Latinos can be any race.

men with casual partners, serosorting alone is likely to be less effective than always and correctly using condoms, in part because some men do not know or disclose their HIV serostatus (Golden, Stekler, Hughes, & Wood, 2008; Golden, Dombrowski, Kerani, & Stekler, 2012; Truong et al., 2006). Actually, a study using mathematical modeling found that serosorting is unlikely to be beneficial to many MSM populations and could more than double the risk of acquiring HIV in settings with low HIV testing (Wilson et al., 2010).

Over three decades into the HIV epidemic, evidence points to an underestimation of risk and difficulty in maintaining safer sex practices among gay and bisexual men. The success of newer medical treatments may have had the unintended consequence of increasing risk behaviors among MSM, because some gay men seem to have abandoned safer sex practices.

Activism continues to focus public attention on the need for greater resources to control the HIV/AIDS epidemic.

© Jes Aznar/AFP/Getty Images

Other than sexual risk behavior, factors that increase HIV risk among MSM are high rates of other STIs, social discrimination, poverty, lack of access to health care, stigmatization, concurrent psychosocial problems, lack of risk assessment, being unaware of infection, childhood sexual abuse, alcohol and illicit drug use, homophobia, complacency about HIV, and partner violence. Because of the severity of the HIV/AIDS problem among MSM, the U.S. government has placed major emphasis on combating the devastating impact of HIV/AIDS in this population. For example, the CDC has allocated a significant portion of its budget toward providing support to state and local health departments and community-based organizations for prevention services for MSM, including those in minority ethnic/racial groups. The CDC (2010.16c, 2014.16q) also supports biomedical approaches to HIV prevention such as taking antiviral medication prior to becoming exposed to HIV and training and technical assistance for several HIV prevention interventions that focus on MSM.

Women and HIV/AIDS

Early in the epidemic, HIV infection and AIDS were diagnosed for relatively few women and female adolescents. Now, we know that many women were infected with HIV resulting from injection drug use but their infections were not diagnosed. In 2012 in the United States women accounted for 20% (9,829) of new HIV diagnoses. One in four people living with HIV infection in the U.S. are women. Women account for 20% of the cumulative AIDS diagnoses in the U.S. since the beginning of the epidemic. High-risk heterosexual contact was the source of 85% of these newly diagnosed infections. At some point, an estimated 1 in 143 women will be diagnosed with HIV infection. When comparing groups by race/ethnicity, gender and transmission category, the fourth largest number of all new HIV infections in the U.S. in 2010 occurred among African American women with heterosexual contact. Of the total number of new HIV infection diagnoses among adult and adolescent women in 2012, 64% were among black/African American women, 16% among White women, and 16% among Hispanic/Latino women. At some point in their lifetimes, an estimated 1 in 32 African American women will be diagnosed with HIV infection (CDC, 2010.16a, 2014.16e, 2014.16r).

Several factors place women at ever greater risk for HIV infection. Both unprotected vaginal and anal intercourse pose a risk for transmission, but unprotected anal sex presents a greater risk. Some women may be unaware of their male partner's risk factors for HIV infection, such as unprotected sex with numerous and concurrent partners, sex with men, and injection drug use, as well as an HIV and other STI diagnosis (CDC, 2014.16r; Montgomery, Mokotoff, Gentry, & Blair, 2003; Witte, El-Bassel, Gilbert, Wu, & Chang, 2010). Other risk factors include having experienced sexual abuse, injection drug and other substance use, intimate partner violence, the presence of some STIs, poverty, limited access to high-quality health care, and the exchange of sex for money or to meet other needs (CDC, 2011.16f; Hess et al., 2012). Some women infected with HIV report more than one risk factor such as those cited here plus inequity in relationships, socioeconomic stresses, and psychological distress. For example, a study of Black women from North Carolina who were infected with HIV found that their most commonly cited reasons for risky behavior were financial dependence on male partners, feeling invincible, low self-esteem coupled with the need to feel loved by a male figure, and alcohol and drug use (CDC, 2004).

An HIV diagnosis can have a dramatic negative impact on a woman's sexual interest and activity, sense of sexual attractiveness, and appeal to a sexual partner. In a sample of HIV-infected women, many reported that sex had become too plagued with anxiety, worry, danger, and stress to still be enjoyable. The loss of their sense of themselves as desirable, attractive, and enticing women was very painful for the women. Many would have liked the companionship of men rather than a sexual relationship (Siegel & Scrimshaw, 2006).

Female-to-female transmission of HIV appears to be a rare occurrence, but there are case reports of it. The well-documented risk of female-to-female transmission of HIV shows that vaginal secretions and menstrual blood may contain the virus and that mucous membrane (e.g., oral, vaginal) exposure to these secretions has the potential to lead to HIV infection. To reduce the risk of HIV transmission, women who have sex with women should avoid exposure of a mucous membrane, such as the mouth, to vaginal secretions and menstrual blood. Condoms should be used correctly and consistently for each sexual contact or when using sex toys, and sex toys should not be shared. Also, natural rubber latex sheets, dental dams, cut open condoms, latex gloves, or plastic wrap may provide some protection from contact with body fluids during oral sex and possibly reduce the risk of HIV transmission (CDC, 2010.16b).

Transgender People and HIV

Transgender communities in the United States are among the groups at highest risk for HIV infection. Transgender women are particularly at high risk: In New York City, from 2007 to 2010, there were 191 new diagnoses of HIV infection among transgender people, 99% of which were among transgender women. About 90% of these women were Blacks/African Americans and over half (52%) were in their 20s. A review of studies of HIV in countries with data available for transgender people estimated that HIV prevalence for transgender women was nearly 50 times as high as for other adults of reproductive age.

Many cultural, socioeconomic, and health-related factors contribute to the HIV epidemic and prevention challenges in U.S. transgender communities. Discrimination and stigma can hinder access to education, employment, and housing opportunities and may help explain why transgender people who experience significant economic difficulties often pursue high-risk activities, including sex work, to meet their basic survival needs. Lack of family support, limited health care access, and negative health care encounters also contribute to high risk of HIV infection (CDC, 2013.16a).

Children and HIV/AIDS

As noted previously, perinatal transmission (HIV transmission from mother to child during pregnancy, labor and delivery, or breastfeeding) is the most common route of HIV infection in children. In 2012, an estimated 242 children aged less than 13 years were diagnosed with HIV infection: 176 were Black/African American, 33 White, 12 Asian, 33 multiple races, 1 Native Hawaiian/Other Pacific Islander, and 0 American Indian/Alaska Native. Since the mid-1990s, HIV testing and preventive interventions have resulted in more than a 90% decline in the number of children perinatally infected with HIV in the United States (CDC, 2014.16j). From the beginning of the HIV/AIDS epidemic, 9,802 children have been diagnosed with AIDS, with only 11 children diagnosed in 2012, down from 948 in 1992 (CDC, 2014.16d).

The incidence of AIDS among children has been dramatically reduced by CDC recommendations for routine counseling and voluntary prenatal HIV testing for women and the use of medical treatment to prevent perinatal transmission.

HIV/AIDS Among Youth

Far too many young people in the United States are at risk for HIV infection. In 2011, youth aged 15–24 accounted for 21% (10,294 cases) of the total 49,274 HIV diagnoses in the United States and dependent areas (CDC, 2013.16c) (Figure 9). Almost 60% of youth with HIV in the United States do not know

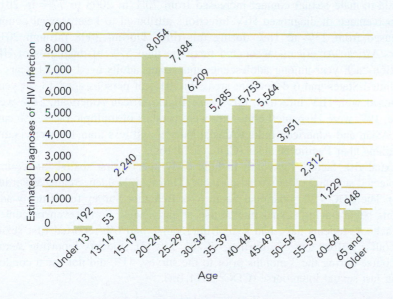

• FIGURE 9

Estimated Diagnoses of HIV Infection in the United States, 2011, by Age.

(*Source:* CDC, 2013.16b.)

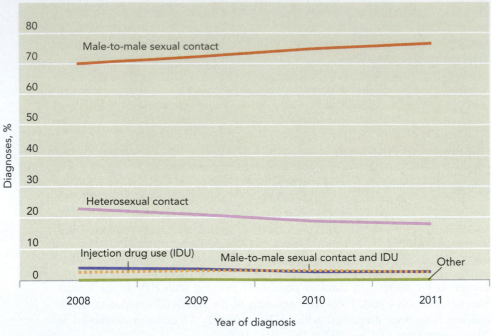

• **FIGURE** 10

Diagnoses of HIV Infection Among Adolescents and Youth Adults Aged 13–24 Years, by Transmission Category 2008–2011, United States and 6 Dependent Areas.

(*Source*: CDC, 2014.16e.)

> *I have never shared needles. And obviously I'm not a gay man. The only thing I did was something every single one of you has already done or will do.*
>
> —Krista Blake, infected with HIV as a teenager

they are infected. Gay, bisexual, and other men who have sex with men account for most of the new HIV infections. Figure 10 presents the percentage distribution of diagnoses of HIV infection by transmission category for adolescents and young adults 13–24 years of age diagnosed from 2008 through 2011 in the United States and 6 dependent areas (CDC, 2013.16c). Among adolescents and young adults, the estimated percentage of diagnosed HIV infections attributed to male-to-male sexual contact increased from 70% in 2008 to 77% in 2011. The percentage of diagnosed HIV infections attributed to heterosexual contact decreased from 23% to 18% during this time. During 2008 through 2011, Blacks/African Americans accounted for more than 55% of diagnoses of HIV infection each year among adolescents and young adults aged 13–24 years in the United States and 6 dependent areas. In 2011, of persons aged 13–24 years diagnosed with HIV infection, 60% were Black/African American, 18% were White, 19% were Hispanic/Latino, 2% were persons of multiple races, 1% each were Asian and American Indian/Alaska Native, and less than 1% were Native Hawaiian/Other Pacific Islander (CDC, 2014.16s).

Sexual risk factors for youth include early age of first sexual intercourse, unprotected sex, and older sexual partners (Thurman, Holden, Shain, & Perdue, 2009). The CDC's 2014 national Youth Risk Behavior Survey found many adolescents begin having sexual intercourse at early ages: Forty-seven percent of high school students have had sexual intercourse and 6% reported first sexual intercourse before age 13. Further, of the 34% of students reporting sexual intercourse during the 3 months prior to the survey, 41% did not use a condom during last sexual intercourse (CDC, 2014.16t).

A CDC study showed that young MSM and minority MSM were more likely unaware of their HIV infection. Young MSM may be at risk, since they have not been reached by effective HIV interventions or prevention education, especially because many sexuality education programs do not include information about sexual orientation. Other HIV risk factors for HIV infection include having experienced sexual abuse, the presence of another STI, and high usage rates of alcohol and other drugs. Runaways, homeless youth, and young persons dependent on drugs are at high risk for HIV if they exchange sex for drugs, money, or shelter. Also, many youth are not concerned about becoming infected with HIV, which often results in their not taking measures to protect themselves from HIV (CDC, 2011.16g).

Older Adults and HIV/AIDS

A growing number of people aged 50 and older in the United States are living with HIV infection and many have the same HIV risk factors as younger Americans. In 2011, 8,440 cases of new HIV infections were diagnosed among adults aged 50 and older, representing over 17% of the total new HIV diagnoses (see Figure 9). Compared to the early days of the epidemic, when most cases among older adults were contracted through a blood transfusion, more cases are now the result of unprotected sex and injection drug use. In 2010, 60% of the newly diagnosed HIV infections for males were male-to-male sexual contact; for women 82% of new HIV infections were from heterosexual contact. Contributing to the higher rates among both older men and older women are the similarity of symptoms of AIDS with other age-related diseases, increasing population of sexually active divorced singles, a lack of awareness on the part of physicians, hesitancy to discuss their sexual behavior and drug use with physicians, and a sense among older people that they are not vulnerable to AIDS. Because of an increasingly aging society and the recent availability of sexual performance enhancement prescription drugs (e.g., Viagra), focus on the prevention of HIV and other STIs among older adults has increased (Lovejoy et al., 2008). Older Americans are more likely than younger Americas to be diagnosed with HIV infection later in the course of their disease (CDC, 2008.16a, 2013.16c).

Geographic Region and HIV

The majority of U.S. adults and adolescents diagnosed with HIV infection in 2011 resided in metropolitan areas with populations of 500,000 or more. Blacks/African Americans accounted for the largest percentage of diagnoses of HIV infection regardless of the population of the area of residence at diagnosis. The South had the largest number of HIV diagnoses. The distribution of HIV diagnoses in the South shows larger percentages in smaller metropolitan (50,000–499,999) and nonmetropolitan areas compared to other regions of the United States. In each of the population categories in the United States, at least 73% of diagnoses of HIV infection among males during 2011 were among those with infections attributed to male-to-male sexual contact (CDC, 2011.16h, 2014.16u). Several factors may contribute to AIDS cases in rural communities: lack of availability of and access to health care services, lack of HIV testing, poverty, sexual risk behavior, injection drug use, political barriers, and stigmatization. These barriers are particularly difficult to overcome in the rural areas (Ohl & Perencevich, 2011; Rural HIV/STD Prevention Work Group, 2009; Sarnquist et al., 2011; Yarber & Crosby, 2011).

Health Protective Sexual Communication Scale

The Health Protective Sexual Communication Scale (HPSCS) assesses how often people discuss health protection, safer sex, sexual histories, and condom/contraception use with a first-time partner. High scores on the HPSCS are strongly linked to high-risk sexual behaviors, including multiple partners, incorrect or inconsistent condom use, and alcohol use before sex. An adapted form of the HPSCS follows.

The HPSCS is designed for individuals who have had a new sexual partner in the past 12 months. If this is not the case for you, it might be in the future. The scale can alert you to health protection issues that are important to discuss, so go ahead and look at the questions.

Directions

Read each question carefully, and record your immediate reaction by writing the number that best applies.

Key

1 = Always
2 = Almost always
3 = Sometimes
4 = Never
5 = Don't know
6 = Decline to answer

Note: Questions 9 and 10 are excluded for gay men and lesbian women.

How often in the past 12 months have you:

1. Asked a new sex partner how he/she felt about using condoms before you had intercourse?

2. Asked a new sex partner about the number of past sexual partners he/she had?

3. Told a new sexual partner about the number of sexual partners you have had?

4. Told a new sexual partner that you won't have sex unless a condom is used?

5. Discussed with a new sexual partner the need for both of you to get tested for HIV before having sex?

6. Talked with a new sexual partner about not having sex until you have known each other longer?

7. Asked a new sexual partner if he/she has ever had some type of STD, such as genital herpes, genital warts, syphilis, chlamydia, or gonorrhea?

8. Asked a new sexual partner if he/she has ever shot drugs such as heroin, cocaine, or speed?

9. Talked about whether you or a new sexual partner has ever had homosexual experiences?

10. Talked with a new sexual partner about birth control before having sex for the first time?

Scoring

To obtain your score, add up the points for all items. The lower your score, the more health protective sexual communication occurred with a new partner.

SOURCE: Catania, J. A. (2011). Health Protective Sexual Communication Scale. In Fisher, T. D., Davis, C. M., Yarber, W. L., & Davis, S. L. (Eds.)., *Handbook of sexuality-related measures*. (3rd ed.). New York, NY: Routledge, pp. 591–594.

Few studies have compared the sexual risk behavior of rural and urban residents. Analysis of national probability data indicates that rural residents are at greater risk for health problems compared to residents of metropolitan areas (Auchincloss & Hadden, 2002). However, because rural areas often have more conservative values, rural residence has been viewed as protective of sexual risk that might lead to HIV/STIs in contrast to urban areas. Data from a nationally representative survey of adults in the United States were analyzed

to compare coital risk behaviors of single, young adult rural men and women to those of their nonrural counterparts. No significant differences were found between rural and nonrural men and women relative to lifetime number of penile-vaginal intercourse partners, number of penile-vaginal intercourse partners in the past 3 months, frequency of unprotected sex during the previous 4 weeks, condom use at last sexual contact, ever having had an HIV test, and discussing correct condom use with a health professional during the last HIV test. This suggests that effective HIV prevention education must be provided in rural as well as urban areas of the United States (Yarber, Milhausen, Huang, & Crosby, 2008).

● Prevention and Treatment

As a whole, many segments of our society remain ambivalent about the realities of HIV risk. Actually, the percentage of Americans who believe that HIV/AIDS is among the most urgent health problems facing the nation has dropped in recent years. Many people assume that their partners are not HIV-infected because they look healthy, "clean," and/or attractive. In addition, some believe that the federal government has failed to provide enough resources to combat the HIV/AIDS problem. With tens of thousands of Americans—many of them young adults—becoming infected with HIV each year, inactivity and apathy become enemies in the fight against this disease. Today, an increasing number of ways to prevent HIV transmission and acquisition are available. In this section, we discuss these methods.

Protecting Ourselves

To protect ourselves and those we care about from HIV infection, there are some things we should know in addition to the basic facts about transmission and prevention. To protect ourselves, we need to honestly assess our risks and act to avoid acquiring HIV. We need to develop our communication skills so that we can discuss risks and prevention with our partner or potential partner. (To assess how often you discuss health protective concerns related to safer sex, sexual histories, and condom or contraception use with a new partner, see the "Practically Speaking" box "Health Protective Sexual Communication Scale.") If we want our partner to disclose information about past high-risk behavior, we have to be willing to do the same.

Disclosure of HIV-positive status is critical, as research has shown that people make poor judgments about their sexual partner's HIV status (Niccolai, Farley, Ayoub, Magnus, & Kissinger, 2002). One study of female patients at a clinic and their regular male partners revealed that 2% of women and 4% of men were unaware whether their partner was HIV-positive (Witte et al., 2010). A study found that attractive romantic sexual partners are perceived as less likely to have HIV/AIDS or another STI (Hennessy, Fishbein, Curtis, & Barrett, 2007). Studies have shown that many people engage in risky sexual behavior with partners perceived to be "safe" but have "safer" sex with those judged to be riskier (Hennessy et al., 2007). Another study showed that many people are relying on partner attributes and relationship characteristics when assessing the HIV/STI status of a sexual partner. Partners who were known well and trusted were evaluated as safe, yet these assessments of partners'

sexual risk were shown to be inaccurate when compared to partners' self-reported risk. The researchers concluded that when trust has been "established" in a relationship, some people assume their partner is safe even when there is evidence of risky sexual behavior (Masaro, Dahinten, Johnson, Ogilvie, & Patrick, 2008).

We may need to have information on HIV testing. If we have engaged in high-risk behavior, we may want to be tested for our own peace of mind and that of our partner. If we test positive for HIV, we need to make important decisions regarding our health, sexual behavior, and lifestyle. Actually, research has shown that people living with HIV who know of their infection, in contrast to those living with HIV who don't know they are infected, are more likely to take precautions to prevent HIV transmission (Pinkerton, Holtgrave, & Galletly, 2008).

If we are sexually active with more than one long-term, exclusive partner, we need to start using condoms correctly and consistently. Many people remain unconvinced regarding either their own vulnerability to HIV or the usefulness of condoms in preventing its transmission. Male latex, polyurethane, polyisoprene, and female condoms, when used consistently and correctly, can greatly reduce the risk of HIV and other STIs. (See the "Think About It" box "'Do You Know What You Are Doing?'" to learn about common condom-use mistakes by college students.) But the effectiveness of condoms has been disputed lately.

Representing a major breakthrough in HIV prevention, the U.S. Food and Drug Administration approved in July, 2012 the first drug shown to reduce the risk of acquiring HIV infection. The drug Trauvada has shown to be safe and helpful in blocking HIV; that is, if taken daily, the drug's presence in the bloodstream can often stop HIV from taking hold and spreading in the body. This HIV prevention method is called **pre-exposure prophylaxis,** or **PrEP.** The word "prophylaxis" means to prevent the spread or control the spread of an infection or a disease. PrEP is meant to be used consistently, as a pill taken every day, and to be used with other prevention options such as condoms. Several studies of PrEP have shown that if taken regularly it can reduce the risk of acquiring HIV by more than 90%. CDC recommends that PrEP be considered for people who are HIV-negative and who are at substantial risk for HIV infection. PrEP should also be considered if you are HIV-negative and in an ongoing sexual relationship with an HIV-positive partner. PrEP should be considered for people who inject drugs, including those who have injected illicit drugs in the past 6 months and who have shared injection equipment or been in drug treatment for injection drug use in the past 6 months. Also, PrEP should be considered if you are not in an exclusive relationship with a recently tested, HIV-negative partner and are a:

- gay or bisexual man who has had anal sex without a condom or been diagnosed with an STI in the past 6 months or
- heterosexual man or woman who does not regularly use condoms during sex with partners of unknown HIV status who are a substantial risk for HIV infection such as people who inject drugs or have bisexual partners.

If you think you may be at substantial risk for HIV, talk to a health care provider about PrEP (CDC, 2014.16v, 2014.16w). Studies have shown that its use does not result in substantial increased sexual risk-taking among HIV-negative MSM

and HIV-negative persons in heterosexual couples in which the other person is HIV positive (Liu et al., 2013; Mugwanya et al., 2013a, 2013b).

For people who need to prevent HIV infection after a single high-risk event of potential HIV exposure—such as sex without a condom, needle-sharing injection drug use, or sexual assault—there is another option called **post-exposure prophylaxis, or PEP.** PEP involves taking antiretroviral medicines as soon as possible after possible exposure, but no more 72 hours (3 days) after you may have been exposed to HIV to try to reduce the chance of being HIV-positive. Two or three drugs are usually prescribed and must be taken daily for 28 days. These medicines keep HIV from making copies of itself and spreading throughout the body. PEP is not the correct choice for people who may be exposed to HIV frequently. As stated previously, PEP should be used right after an uncommon situation with potential HIV exposure. It is not a substitute for regular use of other proven HIV prevention methods such as PrEP, correct and consistent condom use, and use of sterile injection equipment. Remember, if you are at ongoing risk for HIV, speak to a physician about PrEP. Places that you can seek treatment with PEP include a physician's office, emergency rooms, urgent care clinics, or a local HIV clinic (CDC, 2014.16x).

Saving Lives Through Prevention

Factors Showing Prevention Efficacy   The Centers for Disease Control and Prevention states that research clearly indicates that HIV prevention works and saves lives. HIV incidence has been reduced by more than two-thirds since the height of the U.S. HIV epidemic. Despite continued increases in numbers of people living with HIV, new infections have remained at about 50,000 new infections per year since the 1990s, indicating that HIV testing, prevention, and treatment programs are effectively reducing the rate of HIV transmission. As a result, hundreds of thousands of new HIV infections and billions of dollars for medical costs have been averted (CDC, 2012.16a).

Using national estimates of selected HIV risk behaviors, researchers have found that fewer persons are now engaging in HIV risk behaviors. About 10% of men and 8% of women in 2006–2010 reported at least one HIV risk–related behavior. In 2002, 13% of men and 11% of women reported one or more risk behaviors (Chandra, Billioux, Copen, & Sionean, 2012).

A review of 18 meta-analyses of sexual risk reduction interventions found significant increases in condom use and reductions in unprotected sex (Noar, 2008). Another meta-analytic review of HIV prevention interventions was conducted to see if they not only decreased sexual risk behavior but also may have inadvertently increased sexual behavior. This analysis of 174 studies of HIV risk reduction interventions showed that HIV prevention programs did not increase the frequency of sexual activity. Some studies that were behavioral theory–based showed that HIV prevention interventions reduced the frequency of sexual activity and the number of sexual partners (Smoak, Scott-Sheldon, Johnson, Carey, & SHARP Research Team, 2006). Also, a review of 29 couple-based HIV prevention interventions revealed that the programs increased condom use with main partners and

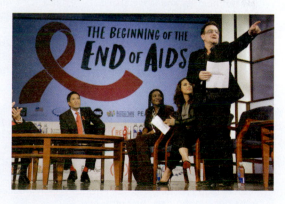

Bono, lead singer of the Irish rock band U2, is in the company of other public figures who have established charities that help fight HIV/AIDS.

© Chip Somodevilla/Getty Images

think
about it

"Do You Know What You Are Doing?" Common Condom-Use Mistakes Among College Students

For those wanting to prevent STIs and pregnancy, condom use is necessary for *all* sexual episodes. But consistent use is only part of the answer—the condom must be used correctly if it is to be effective.

Very little research has been conducted on correct condom use, but the first comprehensive study of college male students produced some startling and alarming results. Researchers at The Kinsey Institute for Research in Sex, Gender, and Reproduction and the Rural Center for HIV/STD Prevention at Indiana University determined the prevalence of male condom–use errors and problems among samples of undergraduate, single, self-identified heterosexual men (N = 158) who applied the condom to themselves and single, self-identified heterosexual women (N = 102) who applied a condom to their male partner. These studies were conducted at a large, Midwestern university. Participants were asked to indicate if the error or problem occurred at least once during the past 3 months during sex, defined as when the male put his penis in a partner's mouth, vagina, or rectum. The percentage of the errors and problems that occurred at least once in the past 3 months were remarkably similar, whether or not the male applied the condom to himself or whether his female partner applied the condom to him. The table indicates some of the most important errors and problems.

A subsequent focus group study of undergraduates who reported male condom use for other-sex behavior in the previous month found that they had concerns about male condoms, including mistrust of each gender in supplying and properly using condoms, inadequate lubrication during condom use, condoms partially or fully slipping off during sex, "losing" part or all of the condom in the vagina, delayed applications, and irritation and reduced sensation (Yarber et al., 2007). An Internet study of men examined another aspect of condom-use problems: ill-fitting condoms. Men reporting ill-fitting condoms were more likely to report breakage and slippage as well as incomplete condom use (late application and/or early removal of the condom). Interestingly, the study also found that ill-fitting condoms diminished sexual functioning and pleasure during penile-vaginal intercourse for both men and women (Crosby, Yarber, Graham, & Sanders, 2010).

The researchers concluded that the condom-use errors and problems reported in these studies indicate a possible high risk of exposure of the participants to HIV/STIs and unintended pregnancy. They also stated that the effectiveness of condom use against HIV/STIs and unintended pregnancy is contingent upon correct condom use.

Error/Problem	Male Appliers	Female Appliers
Put condom on after starting sex	43%*	51%*
Did not hold tip and leave space	40%	46%
Put condom on the wrong side up (had to flip it over)	30%	30%
Used condom without lubricant	19%	26%
Took condom off before sex was over	15%	15%
Did not change to new condoms when switching between vaginal, oral, and anal sex (for those switching)	81%	75%
Condom broke	29%	19%
Condom slipped off during sex	13%	19%
Lost erection before condom was put on	22%	14%
Lost erection after condom was on and sex had begun	20%	20%

*Percentage reporting that the error or problem occurred at least once in the past 3 months.

Think Critically

1. Did the types and frequency of condom-use errors and problems found in these studies surprise you? Explain.
2. Why do you think these errors and problems occurred?
3. Is it really that difficult to use condoms correctly? Why or why not?
4. What can be done to promote correct condom use?

SOURCES: Crosby, R. A., Sanders, S. A., Yarber, W. L., Graham, C. A., & Dodge, B. (2002). Condom use errors and problems among college men. *Sexually Transmitted Diseases, 29,* 552–557; Crosby, R. A., Yarber, W. L., Graham, C. A., & Sanders, S. A. (2010). Does it fit okay? Problems with condom use as function of self-reported fit. *Sexually Transmitted Infections, 86,* 36–38; Sanders, S. A., Graham, C. A., Yarber, W. L., & Crosby, R. A. (2003). Condom use errors and problems among young women who put condoms on their male partners. *Journal of the American Medical Women's Association, 58,* 95–98; Yarber, W. L., Graham, C. A., Sanders, S. A., Crosby, R. A., Butler, S. M., & Hartzell, R. M. (2007). "Do you know what you are doing?" College students' experiences with male condoms. *American Journal of Health Education, 39,* 322–331.

decreased concurrent sexual partnerships. Given these findings and the small number of available couple-based HIV interventions, the researchers suggest that an increased targeting of HIV prevention should be directed toward couples (LaCroix, Pellowski, Lennon, & Johnson, 2013).

Syringe Exchange Programs Syringe exchange programs (SEPs), especially those that provide information about risks and HIV prevention, also play an important role. Multiple literature reviews have concluded that SEPs clearly improve the health outcomes of injection drug users by reducing the transmission of blood-borne diseases like HIV and lowering high-risk injecting behaviors (Institute of Medicine, 2006; Nacopoulos, Lewtas, & Ousterhout, 2010; Palmateer et al., 2010). However, these programs are controversial because some people believe that they endorse or encourage drug use. Others feel that because the drug use already exists, saving lives should be the first priority. Actually, several studies have shown that exchange programs can reduce injection drug risk behavior, such as syringe sharing.

Although syringe exchange programs are illegal in some areas, they are often allowed to continue as long as the workers keep a low profile. Syringe exchange activists believe that high priority should be given to legalizing and expanding these programs, which are cost-effective and have the potential to save thousands of lives.

HIV Testing

HIV testing is available in many areas, including local health departments, clinics, substance abuse programs, offices of private physicians, hospitals, and sites specifically set up for that purpose. For information on where to find an HIV testing site, visit the National HIV Testing Resources website at http://www. hivtest.org and enter your zip code, call CDC-INFO (800-232-4636), or text your zip code to KNOWIT (566948) and you will receive a text back with a testing site near you. All of these resources are confidential.

Community outreach programs provide information about the types of prevention and assistance available to those at high risk for HIV.

© Jeff Greenberg/Alamy

Ignorance breeds passivity, pessimism, resignation, or a sense that AIDS is someone else's problem.

—Paul Farmer, MD
(1959–)

Sharing needles and other injection drug equipment is a common mode of HIV transmission via infected blood. For ejection drugs users, some organizations provide clean needles or exchange clean ones for used ones.

© Brennan Linsley/AP Images

Who Should Get Tested?   Screening for HIV infection is a major HIV control strategy. The CDC has promoted HIV testing, and the number of people who have had one HIV screening test in their lifetime has increased. However, an estimated one in six individuals living with HIV is unaware of his or her infection and may be unknowingly transmitting the virus to others. Knowing one's HIV status can reduce the number of new infections. The CDC recommends that health care providers test everyone between ages 13 and 64 at least once a year as part of routine health care. Research shows that the majority of people who know they are infected take steps to prevent the transmission of HIV to others (Marks, Crepaz, & Janssen, 2006).

If you participate in any of the following behaviors, you should definitely get an HIV test. If you continue with any of these behaviors, you should get tested at least once a year. Sexually active gay and bisexual men may benefit from more frequent testing (e.g., every 3 to 6 months).

- Have had sex with someone who is HIV-positive or whose status you didn't know since your last HIV test
- Have injected drugs (including steroids, hormones, or silicone) and shared equipment (or works, such as needles and syringes) with others
- Have exchanged sex for drugs or money
- Have been diagnosed with or sought treatment for an STI
- Have been diagnosed with or sought treatment for hepatitis or tuberculosis
- Have been sexually assaulted
- Are planning to get pregnant or are already pregnant
- Have had sex with someone who could answer yes to any of the preceding risk behaviors, has had numerous partners, or whose history you do not know

If you have been in a long-term sexual relationship with one person, you should find out for sure whether you or your partner has HIV. If you are both HIV-negative, and you both are sexually exclusive and do not have other risks for HIV infection, then you probably won't need another HIV test unless your situation changes.

When Should One Get Tested?   The immune system usually takes 3–8 weeks to produce antibodies to fight against HIV, but tests differ in how soon they are able to detect antibodies. Nearly all the HIV tests look for the antibodies, but some look for the virus itself. The time period following infection but prior to a positive result is called the **window period.** Hence, deciding when to get tested depends on when you may have been exposed and which test is used. One should ask the health care provider about the window period for the HIV test one is taking. If a home HIV test is used, that information can be found in the materials included in the packaging of the test. A few people will have a longer window period, so if a person gets a negative antibody test result in the first 3 months after possible exposure, a repeat test should be taken after 3 months. Ninety-seven percent of people will develop antibodies in the first 3 months after they are infected. In rare instances, it can take up to 6 months to develop antibodies to HIV.

What Kinds of Tests Are Available?   The most common HIV test is the **antibody screening test,** a test for detecting the antibodies that the body makes against HIV. The test may be conducted in a lab or as a **rapid test** at the testing site and may be performed on blood or oral fluid (not saliva). Because the level of antibody in oral fluid is lower than it is in blood, blood tests tend to find infection sooner after exposure than do rapid HIV tests.

Several tests are now being used more frequently to detect both antibodies and antigens (part of the virus itself). These tests can identify recent infection earlier—as soon as 3 weeks after exposure to HIV—than tests that detect only antibodies. These tests require blood testing, not oral fluid testing. The rapid test, which uses blood or oral fluid, is used for screening, producing quick results in 30 minutes or less. If this test is conducted during the window period, it may not locate antibodies and may give false-negative results. All positive rapid tests require a follow-up test to confirm the result. **RNA tests** detect the virus directly instead of the antibodies to HIV; thus, they are able to detect HIV as soon as it appears in the bloodstream—at about 10 days after infection—but before antibodies develop. RNA tests cost more than antibody tests and are not typically used for screening, although a physician may order one as a follow-up to a positive antibody test.

Follow-up diagnostic testing is performed if the first antibody test result is positive. This is done to determine if the initial test result is accurate. If the first test is a rapid test and is positive, follow-up testing is done at a medical setting. If the first test is a lab test and is positive, the lab will use the same blood specimen as the first test to conduct a follow-up test.

Currently, there are two home-based HIV tests: the Home Access HIV-1 Test System and the OraQuick In-Home HIV test. Anyone buying a home test online should make sure it is approved by the U.S. Food and Drug Administration (FDA). The **Home Access HIV-1 Test System** is a home collection kit involving pricking your finger to collect a blood sample, sending the sample to a licensed laboratory, then calling in for results as early as the next business day. The test is anonymous. If the results are positive, a follow-up test is performed right away. The home test manufacturer provides confidential counseling and referral for treatment. The tests conducted on the blood sample collected at home find infection later after infection than most lab-based tests using blood from a vein but earlier than tests conducted with oral fluid. The **OraQuick In-Home HIV Test** provides rapid results in the home. The testing procedure involves swabbing the mouth for an oral fluid sample and using a kit to test it, with the results available in 20 minutes. If the results are positive, a follow-up test is required. The test manufacturer provides confidential counseling and referral to follow-up testing sites. Because the level of antibody in oral fluid is lower than it is in blood, oral fluid tests find infection later after exposure than do blood tests. Up to 1 in 12 people may test false-negative with this test.

What Does a Negative or Positive HIV Test Mean?   A negative test does not necessarily mean that you do not have HIV. Testing may have been conducted during the window period. Ask your healthcare provider if and when you need to get tested again. Your HIV test result reveals only your HIV status, not that of your partner. HIV is not transmitted every time you have sex, so taking a HIV test is not a way to find out if your partner is infected. If screening and follow-up tests are positive, you are considered HIV-positive. As explained earlier, that does not mean you have AIDS, the most advanced stage of HIV disease. If you are diagnosed as HIV-positive, you should see a licensed health care provider to begin treatment, even if you do not feel sick. It is important to get screened for STIs and to have a TB (tuberculosis) test. Getting professional help if you smoke cigarettes, drink too much alcohol, or use illegal drugs, is advised since these behaviors can weaken the immune system.

You should inform your partner or partners about your HIV status before having any sexual contact with them; use condoms and/or dental dams with every sexual contact; and do not share needles, syringes, or other drug paraphernalia. If you have a steady, HIV-negative partner, discuss whether he or she should consider PrEP.

If you test positive for HIV, your sexual or drug-using partners may also be infected and should get tested. If you are nervous about disclosing your test results because you fear being threatened or injured by a partner, ask your health care provider to tell him or her that he or she might have been exposed to HIV. Health departments do not reveal your name to your partners; they only inform them that they may have been exposed to HIV and should get tested. Most states have laws that require an HIV-positive person to inform his or her sexual partners if the person is HIV-positive before having oral, vaginal, or anal sex or before sharing drugs. You can be charged with a crime if you don't inform your partner, even if the partner doesn't become infected. In most cases, your family or friends will not know your test results or HIV status unless you inform them yourself. Telling your family may seem difficult, but studies have shown that people who disclose their HIV status respond better to treatment than those who don't (CDC, 2014.16c).

Treatments

When AIDS first surfaced in the United States in the early 1980s, there were no drugs to combat the underlying immune deficiency and few treatments for the opportunistic diseases that resulted. People with AIDS were not likely to live longer than a few years. Researchers, however, have developed drugs to fight both HIV infection and its associated infections and cancers. HIV treatment is the use of anti-HIV medications to keep an HIV-infected person healthy. Treatment can help people at all stages of HIV disease. Although anti-HIV medications can treat HIV infection, they cannot cure it.

The advent in 1996 of potent combination antiretroviral therapy (ART), sometimes called highly active antiretroviral therapy (HAART) or combination antiretroviral therapy (cART)) changed the course of the HIV epidemic. These "cocktails" of three or more antiretroviral drugs used in combination (called an HIV regimen) have given patients and their doctors new optimism in fighting the epidemic and have significantly improved life expectancy to decades instead of years. ART is recommended for all people infected with HIV and involves taking the medicines every day. There are more than 20 HIV medicines available to make up the HIV regimen. A person's initial HIV regimen usually includes three or more HIV medicines. As mentioned previously, HIV attacks destroy the infection-fighting CD4 cells of the immune system. Loss of CD4 cells makes it hard for the body to fight off infections. HIV medicines prevent HIV from replicating, which reduces the amount of HIV in the body and gives the immune system a chance to recover. Even though there is still some HIV in the body, the immune system is strong enough to fight off infections and cancers. ART works best when the doctor finds a combination of drugs and a treatment plan that keep HIV in check with the least side effects. Despite the fact that many persons on ART are living longer and are healthier than without ART, ART does not cure HIV but, rather, works to keep it from damaging the immune system. And the HIV-infected person can still transmit the virus to others.

ART should start immediately after an HIV-positive test because evidence shows that ART can help the person live longer, can lower the risk of developing non-HIV-related illnesses (e.g., heart disease, diabetes), and reduces the chances of HIV transmission to others. Hence, early treatment of HIV-infected persons dramatically reduces the rates of new infection. However, this "treatment as prevention" method, as the CDC calls it, is not 100% effective, as there has been at least one report of HIV transmission from a person with suppressed viral load to an uninfected sexual partner. One study of **serodiscordant** heterosexual couples (one HIV-positive, the other HIV-negative) found that ART use by the infected person reduced HIV transmission risk to the uninfected partner by 92% (Donnell et al., 2010).

Treatment for HIV infection should not be started until the person is ready, since a lot of commitment is needed to follow a demanding drug regimen and, in most cases, the treatment will have to be taken for life. Once HIV treatment begins, it is possible to have an undetectable viral load within 3 to 6 months, but the person will not be considered cured because there still will be some HIV in the body. However, an undetectable viral load indicates that the anti-HIV medications are working effectively to keep the person healthy and reduce the risk of HIV transmission to others (CDC, 2013.16d; National Institutes of Health, 2015).

Unfortunately, ART does not work for everyone: Some people respond very well but others do not. Sometimes when HIV has been exposed to a medication for a long time, the virus is not affected by it. In this case, the health care provider will change the medication to one that does affect the virus (U.S. Department of Health and Human Services, 2011.16a).

The search for a cure for AIDS continues. Learning more about the genetics of the small number of HIV-infected individuals who remain healthy may lead to new therapies that can help others. Gene therapy, in which the immune system is reconstructed with genetically altered resistant cells, is one promising approach. For HIV/STI prevention, researchers are working on topical microbicides, chemical or biological substances that can kill or neutralize viruses and bacteria present in semen or cervical or vaginal secretions. The goal is to develop a microbicidal gel, cream, film, or suppository that individuals can apply to the vagina prior to intercourse. A major value of microbicides is that women can have much more control of HIV/STI prevention, particularly when they have limited ability to get their male partners to use condoms. Recently, trials of an antiretroviral gel have shown that microbicide can be effective, although there are many obstacles to overcome prior to its availability to the general public (Shattock & Rosenberg, 2012). A rectal HIV microbicide is also currently in development. However, it will be many years before a single agent is approved for consumer use, in part because of scientific challenges related to the biology of the rectum and cultural reluctance to address anal sex. As a cream or gel, or maybe a douche or an enema, a rectal microbicide could offer protection when condoms are used and back-up protection in the event of condom breakage or slippage. Also, the rectal microbicide could be a safe and effective alternative for couples who are unwilling or unable to use condoms (International Rectal Microbicide Advocates, 2011; Microbicide Trials Network, 2014). According to

The Names Project Foundation created the AIDS Memorial Quilt as a poignant and powerful tool in preventing HIV infection. Each square has been lovingly created by friends and families of people who have died of AIDS. The quilt now contains more than 48,000 panels.

© Hisham Ibrahim/Corbis

the International AIDS Vaccine Initiative (2011), an AIDS vaccine with 50% efficacy given to 30% of the population would avert 5.6 million new infections in low- and middle-income countries from 2015 to 2030. Work has also begun to develop an STI microbicide that would be topically used for penile cleaning before and after sex.

Development of an effective and safe vaccine for HIV is the ultimate goal, but many biological and social challenges have to be overcome. Vaccines tested have failed to achieve expectations. HIV is one of the most changeable viruses identified to date and there are many different strains. Creating a vaccine that can inactivate all HIV strains remains a major obstacle (HIV Vaccine Trials Network, 2015). While some progress has been achieved, it will still be many years before an HIV vaccine is licensed and widely available. Microbicides and a vaccine would provide another barrier to HIV transmission, but individual practice of safe sex would remain paramount.

● Living With HIV or AIDS

People infected with HIV or diagnosed with AIDS have the same needs as everyone else—and a few more. If you are HIV-positive, in addition to dealing with psychological and social issues you need to pay special attention to maintaining good health. If you are caring for someone with HIV or AIDS, you also have special needs.

If You Are HIV-Positive

A positive antibody test is scary to just about anyone. However, a positive test result is valuable news: It is news that may make it possible to save your life. If you don't learn about your status in this way, you probably will not know until a serious opportunistic infection announces the presence of HIV. At that point, many of your best medical options have been lost, and you might have spread the virus to others who would not otherwise have been exposed. But remember, although HIV infection is serious, people with HIV are living longer, healthier lives than ever before, thanks to new and effective treatments.

Staying Healthy Longer   It is important to find a physician who has experience working with HIV and AIDS, and—even more important, perhaps—who is sensitive to the issues confronted by individuals infected with HIV. Begin treatment promptly once your doctor tells you to. Keep your appointments and follow the doctor's instructions. If your doctor prescribes medicine for you, take the medicine exactly the way he or she tells you, since taking only some of your medicine gives your HIV infection more chance to fight back. Taking ART medications on schedule increases their effectiveness. If you get sick from your medicine, call your doctor for advice; don't make changes to what your doctor has prescribed on your own or because of advice from friends. In addition to appropriate medical treatment, factors that can help promote your continuing good health include good nutrition, plenty of rest, exercise, limited (or no) alcohol use, and stress reduction. You should also stop smoking tobacco because it increases susceptibility to pneumonia. And you should get immunizations to prevent infections such as pneumonia and flu.

In addition, if you decide to have sexual contact with another person, it means practicing safer sex, even if your partner is also HIV-positive. Researchers caution that one can become reinfected with different HIV strains. Moreover, STIs of all kinds can be much worse for people with an impaired immune system. HIV doesn't mean an end to being sexual, but it does suggest that different ways of expressing love and sexual desire may need to be explored. If you are living with HIV or AIDS, you may need many kinds of support: medical, emotional, psychological, and financial. Your doctor, your local health department and social services departments, local AIDS service organizations, and the Internet can help you find all kinds of help.

Addressing Your Other Needs   The stigma and fear surrounding HIV and AIDS often make it difficult to get on with the business of living. Among gay and bisexual men, social support is generally better for Whites than for Blacks; in Black communities, there tends to be less affirmation from primary social support networks and less openness about sexual orientation. Women, who often concern themselves with caring for others, may not be inclined to seek out support groups and networks. But people who live with HIV and AIDS say that it's important not to feel isolated. If you are HIV-positive, we encourage you to seek support from AIDS organizations in your area.

Partner Notification   Both current and past partners should be notified so that they can be tested and receive counseling. In many states, HIV-infected people are required by law to notify current and recent sexual and needle-sharing partners. AIDS counselors and health care practitioners encourage those with HIV to make all possible efforts to contact past and current partners. In some cases, counselors try to make such contacts, with their clients' permission.

> The evidence demonstrates that we are not powerless against the epidemic, but our response is still a fraction of what it needs to be.
>
> —Peter Piot, MD
> (1949–)

As we have seen, HIV/AIDS remains a major public health challenge. HIV continues to take a severe toll on many communities in the United States, with gay and bisexual men of all races, African Americans, and Latinos bearing the heaviest burden. Not only is HIV/AIDS a medical problem, but barriers such as stigmatization, discrimination, limited health care and prevention education messages, and gender inequity impede progress in controlling the epidemic. We must do more—as individuals, in our communities, and as a nation—to expand our prevention efforts to people at risk and stop the spread of HIV. As we know, HIV can be avoided. We hope that this chapter has provided you with the information and motivation that will serve as your vaccine against HIV/AIDS.

Summary

What Is AIDS?

- *AIDS* is an acronym for *acquired immunodeficiency syndrome.* For a person to receive an AIDS diagnosis, he or she must have a positive blood test indicating the presence of *HIV (human immunodeficiency virus)* antibodies and have a T-cell count below 200; if the T-cell count is higher, the person must have 1 or more of over 20 diseases or conditions associated with AIDS to be diagnosed with the disease.

- A host of symptoms are associated with HIV/AIDS. Because these symptoms may indicate many other diseases and conditions, HIV and AIDS cannot be self-diagnosed; diagnosis by a clinician or physician is necessary.

- *Leukocytes,* or white blood cells, play a major role in defending the body against invading organisms and cancerous cells. One type, the *macrophage,* engulfs foreign particles and displays the invader's *antigen* on its own surface. *Antibodies* bind to antigens, inactivate them, and mark them for destruction by *killer T cells.* Other white blood cells called *lymphocytes* include *helper T cells* (also called CD4T or CD4 cells), which are programmed to "read" the antigens and then begin directing the immune system's response. The number of helper T cells in an individual's body is an important indicator of how well the immune system is functioning.

- *Viruses* are primitive entities; they can't propel themselves independently, and they can't reproduce unless they are inside a host cell. Within the HIV's protein core is the genetic material (RNA) that carries the information the virus needs to replicate itself. A *retrovirus* can "write" its RNA (the genetic program) into a host cell's DNA.

- Although HIV begins replication right away within the host cells, it is not detectable in the blood for some time—often years. HIV antibodies, however, are generally detectable in the blood within 3–8 weeks. A person's *serostatus* is HIV-negative if antibodies are not present and HIV-positive if antibodies are detected. "T-cell count," or "CD4 count," refers to the number of helper T cells that are present in a cubic millimeter of blood.

- When a person is first infected with HIV, he or she may experience severe flulike symptoms. During this period, the virus is dispersed throughout the lymph nodes and other tissues. The virus may stay localized in these areas for years, but it continues to replicate and to destroy T cells. As the number of infected cells goes up, the number of T cells goes down. In advanced AIDS, the T-cell count drops to under 200, and the virus itself is detectable in the blood.

The Epidemiology and Transmission of HIV

- The number of adults and adolescents living with HIV in the United States has grown to over 800,000. Worldwide, about 35 million people are now living with HIV. Rates of new infections are the highest in sub-Saharan Africa.

- Rates of new HIV infection are decreasing all over the globe—the annual diagnosis of HIV in the United States has decreased more than 30% in the past decade or so.

- HIV is not transmitted by casual contact.

- Activities or situations that may promote HIV transmission include sexual transmission through vaginal or anal intercourse without a condom; fellatio without a condom; cunnilingus without a latex or other barrier; the sharing of needles and syringes contaminated with infected blood; in-utero infection from mother to fetus, from blood during delivery, from pre-chewed baby food, or in breast milk; the sharing of sex toys without disinfecting them; accidental contamination when infected blood enters the body through mucous membranes (eyes or mouth) or cuts, abrasions, or punctures in the skin (relatively rare); and blood transfusions (very rare).

- Certain physiological or behavioral factors increase the risk of contracting HIV. In addition to anal intercourse, numerous sexual partners, and injection drug use, these factors include having an STI (especially if genital lesions are present) and multiple exposures to HIV.

AIDS Demographics

- HIV/AIDS is often linked with poverty, which has roots in racism and discrimination. In the United States, African Americans and Latinos have been disproportionately affected by HIV and STIs in comparison to other racial/ethnic groups.

- Certain groups have been particularly impacted by the AIDS epidemic in the United States: racial/ethnic minorities (particularly African Americans), men who have sex with men, women, and young adults.

- Because young people often have a sense of invulnerability, they may put themselves at great risk without understanding the consequences of their sexual behavior.

Prevention and Treatment

- To protect ourselves and those we care about from HIV, we need to be fully knowledgeable of what constitutes risky behaviors and how to avoid them, develop communication skills so that we can talk with our partners, and get information on HIV testing. If we are sexually active with more than one long-term, exclusive partner, we need to use condoms correctly and consistently.

- Free or low-cost HIV testing is available in many areas.

- Antiretroviral medications—the combination of drugs is called antiretroviral therapy (ART)—are available for treatment of HIV/AIDS. Many people on the ART regimen have an increase in quality of life and longevity.

Living With HIV or AIDS

- An HIV or AIDS diagnosis may be a cause for sadness and grief, but it also can be a time for reevaluation and growth. Those whose friends or family members are living with HIV, or who are themselves HIV-positive, need information and practical and emotional support.

- Early detection of HIV can greatly enhance both the quality and the longevity of life. Appropriate medical treatment and a healthy lifestyle are important. People with HIV or AIDS also need to practice safer sex and consider seeking support from AIDS organizations.

Questions for Discussion

- What behaviors or measures have you taken or will you take to prevent yourself from contracting HIV?

- Despite the seriousness of the HIV/AIDS epidemic, some people continue to practice risky sexual behaviors and injection drug use; many of them are not receptive to HIV prevention messages. What do you suggest as strategies to reach these individuals?

- Individuals who are diagnosed with an HIV infection react in many ways. How do you think you would react?

- What would be your most important concern if you just learned that you had been infected with HIV?

Suggested Websites

Centers for Disease Control and Prevention

http://www.cdc.gov/hiv/
Provides information on HIV/AIDS.
http://www.cdc.gov/std/
Provides information on STIs.

Joint United Nations Programme on HIV/AIDS

http://www.unaids.org
Contains epidemiological information on HIV/AIDS worldwide, as well as perspectives on HIV/AIDS–related issues.

Kaiser Family Foundation

http://www.kff.org
Offers fact sheets and new releases on STIs and HIV/AIDS.

National Institutes of Health

http://www.nih.gov
Provides current information about HIV/AIDS.

Rural Center for AIDS/STD Prevention

http://www.indiana.edu/~aids
Provides information about issues related to HIV/STI prevention in rural communities in the United States.

U.S. Government

http://aids.gov
The federal government's Internet source for HIV prevention and treatment.

Suggested Reading

Halkitis, P. (2014). *The AIDS generation: Stories of survival and resilience.* Oxford, United Kingdom: University of Oxford Press. Stories of pain, suffering, hope, survival, and resilience of a generation of gay men in the midst of the AIDS epidemic.

Harden, V. A., & Fauci, A. S. (2012). *AIDS at 30: A history.* Lincoln, NE: Potomac Books. A history of HIV/AIDS written for a general audience that emphasizes the medical response to the epidemic.

Pepin, J. (2011). *The origins of AIDS.* Cambridge, United Kingdom: Cambridge University Press. The author looks back to the early-twentieth-century events in Africa that triggered the emergence of HIV/AIDS and traces its subsequent development into the most dramatic and destructive epidemic of modern times.

Pisani, E. (2008). *The wisdom of whores: Bureaucrats, brothels, and the business of AIDS.* New York: W. W. Norton. A "flame-throwing" epidemiologist talks about sex, drugs, mistakes, ideologies, and hopes of international AIDS prevention.

Quammen, D. (2015). *The chimp and the river: How AIDS emerged from an African forest.* New York: W. W. Norton. The real story of how AIDS originated from a virus in a chimpanzee, jumped to one human, and then infected 60 million people.

Shilts, R. (1987). *And the band played on: People, politics, and the AIDS epidemic.* New York: St. Martin's Press. The fascinating story behind the "discovery" of AIDS, complete with real heroes and, unfortunately, real villains.

chapter

17

Sexual Coercion

© Socialstock/Superstock

CHAPTER OUTLINE

Sexual Harassment

Harassment and Discrimination Against Gay, Lesbian, Bisexual, and Transgender People

Sexual Violence

Child Sexual Abuse

557

"I was sexually harassed at work, but I stood my ground. I told the guy to knock it off or I'd sue him. It worked—he quit 3 weeks later."

—20-year-old female

"At a very young age, I remember being sexually molested by two neighbors who were a couple years older than I. They did not insert anything in me. I was not physically hurt, but I remember losing my voice and the will to defend myself. I remember my father calling my name from the back porch and I could not answer him. I felt I had lost all power to speak or move. The regret of allowing this to happen to me still lingers in my feelings toward others and myself. I believe this event has contributed to shaping some deep paranoia and mistrust toward my peers, and I have carried this for a long time."

—22-year-old female

"When I reached the first grade, my mother's boyfriend moved in with us. Living with him was the biggest nightmare of my life. One night I was asleep and was awakened by

something. It was my mother's boyfriend, and what woke me up was his hand. He was touching me in my sleep while he watched television. He did not touch me under my clothes and he did not caress me, but he would place his hand on my private parts and that made me feel very uncomfortable. I used to move and roll around a lot so he would move his hand. I became afraid to sleep at night because I thought he would be there. These events affected me emotionally and psychologically."

—20-year-old male

"I was sexually abused when I was about eight years old. My cousin and uncle molested me several times. They abused me for as long as 3 years. After this time, I decided to run away because I did not have a father, and I knew that my mother would not believe what happened to me. I tried to tell people what had happened to me, but everyone would call me a liar or crazy. In my town, people believed that if a woman was sexually abused it was her fault because she provoked the men. This includes child abuse. In my home, my family never talked about sex or sexuality, and I think that is one of the reasons I did not know that what happened to me wasn't my fault."

—21-year-old female

> *Being forced is poison for the soul.*
> —Ludwig Borne
> (1786–1837)

ALTHOUGH SEXUALITY PERMITS US to form and sustain deep bonds and intimate relationships, it has a darker side. For some people, sex is linked with coercion, degradation, aggression, and abuse. In these cases, sex becomes a weapon—a means to exploit, humiliate, or harm others. In this chapter, we first examine the various aspects of sexual harassment, including the distinction between flirting and harassment and the sexual harassment that occurs in schools, colleges, and the workplace. Next, we look at harassment, prejudice, and discrimination directed against gay men, lesbian women, and bisexual and transgender persons. Then we examine sexual violence, including date rape and stranger rape, the motivations for rape, and the consequences of rape. Finally, we discuss child sexual abuse, examining the factors contributing to abuse, the types of abuse and their consequences, and programs for preventing it.

● Sexual Harassment

Sexual harassment refers to two distinct types of behavior: (1) the abuse of power for sexual ends and (2) the creation of a hostile environment. In terms of abuse of power, sexual harassment consists of unwelcomed sexual advances, requests for sexual favors, or other verbal or physical conduct of a sexual nature as a condition of instruction or employment. Refusal to comply may result in reprisals. Only a person with power over another can commit the first kind of harassment. When someone acts in sexual ways that interfere with another person's performance at school or in the workplace, he or she is creating a **hostile environment.** Such harassment is illegal.

What Is Sexual Harassment?

Title VII of the Civil Rights Act of 1964 first made various kinds of discrimination, including sexual harassment, illegal in the workplace. Title VII applies to employers with 15 or more employees, including local, state, and federal employees, employment agencies, and labor organizations. In 1980, the U.S. Office of Equal Employment Opportunity Commission (EEOC) issued guidelines regarding both verbal and physical harassment in the work and education environments. The EEOC defined sexual harassment as unwelcome sexual advances, requests for sexual favors, and other verbal or physical conduct of a sexual nature when this conduct: (1) explicitly or implicitly affects an individual's employment, (2) unreasonably interferes with an individual's work performance, or (3) creates an intimidating, hostile, or offensive work environment. A major component of the EEOC guidelines is that the behavior is unwanted and unwelcome and might affect employment conditions. The sexual aggression does not have to be explicit, and even the creation of a hostile environment that can affect work performance constitutes sexual harassment. The victim as well as the harasser may be a man or a woman. Also, it is unlawful for an employer to retaliate against an individual for filing a discrimination charge or opposing employment practices that discriminate based on sex (U.S. Equal Employment Opportunity Commission, 2009; U.S. Merit Systems Protection Board, 1995). Further, the victim does not have to be the person harassed but could be anyone affected by the conduct. In fiscal year 2011, 11,364 sexual harassment charges were filed with the EEOC, down from a high of 15,889 in fiscal year 1997 (U.S. Equal Employment Opportunity Commission, n.d.).

Sexual harassment is a mixture of sex and power; however, power is often the dominant element. In school and the workplace, men and women are devalued by calling attention to their sexuality. For women especially, sexual harassment may be a way to keep them "in their place" and make them feel vulnerable.

There are other forms of behavior that, although not illegal, are considered by many to be sexual harassment. These include unwanted sexual jokes and innuendos and unwelcome whistles, taunts, and obscenities directed, for example, from a man or group of men to a woman walking past them. As with all forms of harassment, these apply to male-female, male-male, and female-female interactions. They also include a man "talking to" a woman's breasts or body during conversation or persistently giving her the "once-over" as she walks past him, sits down, or enters or leaves a room. It may also be a suggestive comment or unsolicited photograph sent via e-mail or social media. Clinical psychologist Elizabeth Powell (1996) lists the following as examples of sexual harassment:

- Verbally harassing or abusing someone
- Exerting subtle pressure for sexual activity
- Making remarks about a person's clothing, body, or sexual activities
- Leering at or ogling a person's body

Sexual harassment, particularly in the workplace, creates a stressful and hostile environment for the victim.

© Digital Vision

- Engaging in unwelcome touching, patting, or pinching
- Brushing against a person's body
- Making demands for sexual favors accompanied by implied or overt threats concerning one's job or student status
- Physically assaulting someone

Such incidents may make a person feel uncomfortable and vulnerable. They have been described, in fact, as "little rapes." The cumulative effect of these behaviors is to lead women to limit their activities, to avoid walking past groups of men, and to stay away from beaches, concerts, parties, and sports events unless they are accompanied by others. Sometimes, charges of sexual harassment are ignored or trivialized, and blame often falls on the victim. Sexual harassment more commonly occurs in school or the workplace, as well as in other settings, such as between patients and doctors or mental health and sex therapists.

One type of harassment that may not involve sexual harassment, per se, is **stalking.** The CDC's National Intimate Partner and Sexual Violence Survey (NISVS), an ongoing, nationally representative telephone survey of the U.S. population of persons 18 years or older, assesses the prevalence and characteristics of stalking, as well as sexual violence and intimate partner violence. Respondents are classified as experienced being stalked if they report: (1) having experienced multiple stalking tactics or a single tactic numerous times from the same perpetrator and (2) having felt very fearful or believed that they or someone close to them would be harmed or killed as a result of a perpetrator's stalking behavior. Examples of stalking behaviors measured by the NISVS included receiving unwanted e-mail messages, instant messages, sexting, or messages through social media; being watched or followed; having someone approach or show up in the victim's home, workplace, or school when unwanted; and posting information or spreading rumors about the victim on the Internet, in a public place, or by word of mouth.

The NISVS report using 2011 data (Breiding et al., 2014) found that in the U.S. an estimated 15.2% of women (18.3 million) had experienced stalking during their lifetime. Further, an estimated 4.2% of women (about 5.1 million) were stalked in the 12 months prior to taking the survey. Nationally, an estimated 7.5% of men (nearly 6.5 million) have experienced being stalked during their lifetime, while an estimated 2.1% (2.4 million) were stalked in the 12 months prior to taking the survey. A variety of tactics were used to stalk persons (Figure 1). As shown, there are both some similarities and differences in tactics used against men and women. Both women and men who experienced stalking in their lifetime identified their stalkers as persons whom they knew or with whom they had an intimate relationship (see Figure 2). An intimate partner was the most commonly identified stalker. Among persons reporting being stalked in their lifetime, females were stalked an estimated 88.3% by only male perpetrators and 7.1% had only female perpetrators. Among males, almost one half (an estimated 48%) were stalked by only male perpetrators, while a nearly identical proportion (an estimated 44.6%) were stalked only by female perpetrators.

Persons who are stalked sometimes fear that the behavior will never stop and that they will be physically harmed. They may wonder what will happen next and experience negative psychological outcomes, such as anxiety, depression, and insomnia. Most college campuses provide educational and support services for persons who experience being stalked. Stalking is a crime in all 50 states, the District of Columbia, and the U.S. Territories, which allows the police to arrest a person who continually stalks.

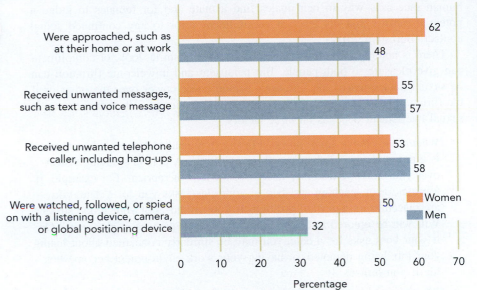

• **FIGURE 1**

Type and Percentage of Most Common Stalking Tactics Used Against Women and Men Who Reported Being Stalked in Their Lifetime.

(*Source:* Breiding, M. J., et al. (2014). Prevalence and characteristics of sexual violence, stalking, and intimate partner violence victimization—National Intimate Partner and Sexual Violence Survey, United States, 2011. *Morbidity and Mortality Weekly Report, 63*(8), 1–18.)

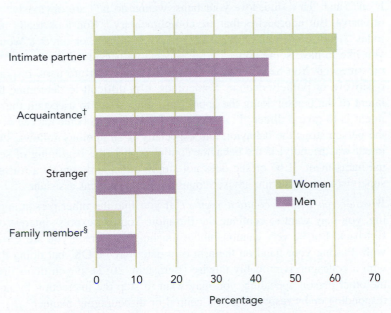

• **FIGURE 2**

Lifetime Reports of Stalking Among Female and Male Victims, by Type of Perpetrator.*

(*Source:* Breiding, M. J., et al. (2014). Prevalence and characteristics of sexual violence, stalking, and intimate partner violence victimization—National Intimate Partner and Sexual Violence Survey, United States, 2011. *Morbidity and Mortality Weekly Report, 63*(8), 1–18.)

*Relationship is based on victims' reports of their relationship at the time the perpetrator first committed any violence against them. Due to the possibility of multiple perpetrators, the combined percentages exceed 100%.

†Includes friends, neighbors, family friends, first date, someone briefly known, and persons not known well.

§Includes immediate and extended family members.

Flirtation Versus Harassment

Flirting is an ambiguous, goal-oriented behavior with potential sexual or romantic overtones. That is, we flirt with a purpose, but since we are "testing the waters," we try not to reveal what the purpose might be. Scientists believe, from an evolutionary mating perspective, that flirting was developed to advance the human race as a way to help males find a mate and for females to judge a potential partner and his level of commitment prior to any continued social contact (Bernstein, 2012).

There is nothing wrong with flirtation, per se. A smile, look, or compliment can give pleasure to both people. But persistent and unwelcome flirtation can be sexual harassment if the flirtatious person holds power over the other or if the flirtation creates a hostile school or work environment. Whether flirtation is sexual harassment depends on three factors:

- *Whether you have equal power.* Flirting may lead to trouble when there is a power difference between the two people. A person's having power over you limits your ability to refuse, for fear of reprisal. For example, if a professor or teaching assistant in your class asks you for a date, you are placed in an awkward position. If you say no, will your grade suffer? Will you be ignored in class? What other consequences might occur? Or if your boss asks for a date, you may be similarly concerned about losing your job, being demoted, or having your work environment become hostile if you refuse.

- *Whether you are approached appropriately.* "Hi babe, nice tits, wanna get it on?" and "Hey stud, love your buns, wanna do it?" are obviously offensive. But approaches that are complimentary ("You look really nice today"), indirect ("What do you think of the class?"), or direct ("Would you like to have some coffee?") are acceptable because they do not pressure you. You have the opportunity to let the overture pass, respond positively, or politely decline. Sometimes, it is difficult to determine the intent of the person doing the approaching. One way to ascertain the intent is to give a direct "I" message and ask that the behavior cease. If the person stops the behavior, and especially if an apology follows, the intent was friendly; if the behavior continues, it is the beginning of sexual harassment. If he or she does not stop, you should contact a trusted supervisor, an academic advisor/counselor, or a resident assistant.

- *Whether you wish to continue contact.* If you find the other person appealing, you may want to continue the flirtation. You can express interest or flirt back. But be very cautious about touching the person you are flirting with. Placing your hand on the arm of a date may be OK, but doing that with a colleague is probably unwise (Bernstein, 2012). If you don't find the other person appealing, you may want to stop the interaction by not responding or by responding in a neutral or discouraging manner.

The issue is complicated by several factors related to culture and gender. Differing cultural expectations may lead to misinterpretation. For example, when a Latino, whose culture encourages mutual flirting, says "*muy guapa*" ("good looking") to a Latina walking by, the words may be meant *and* received as a compliment. But when a Latino says the same thing to a non-Latina, he may be dismayed at her negative reaction. He perceives her as uptight, and she perceives him as rude, but each is misinterpreting the other because of cultural differences.

Three significant gender differences may contribute to sexual harassment. First, men are generally less likely to perceive activities as harassing than are women. The difference in perception often is for the more subtle forms of harassment, as both men and women believe that overt activities such as deliberate touching constitute sexual harassment. Second, men tend to misperceive women's friendliness as sexual interest (La France, Henningsen, Oates, & Shaw, 2009). Third, men are more likely than women to perceive male-female relationships as adversarial. A study involving undergraduate students found that when women flirt in a sexually suggestive way men perceive them to be more attractive, but when men flirt this way women view them as pushy and less attractive (Frisby, Dillow, Gaughan, & Nordlund, 2011). Given all this, not surprisingly, 84% of the harassment claims filed in 2010 were by women. Interestingly, the percentage of males filing sexual harassment claims increased from 9.1% in 1992 to 16.4% in 2010 (U.S. Equal Employment Opportunity Commission, n.d.).

Power differences also affect perception. Personal questions asked by an instructor or a supervisor, for example, are more likely to be perceived as sexual harassment than they would be if a student or co-worker asked them. What needs to be clarified is the basis of the relationship: Is it educational, business, or professional? Is it romantic or sexual? Flirtatious or sexual ways of relating are inappropriate in the first three contexts.

Harassment in School and College

Sexual harassment in various forms is widespread. It does not necessarily begin in adulthood; it may begin as early as middle childhood.

Harassment in Elementary and High School

It's a "time-honored" practice for boys to "tease" girls: calling them names, spreading sexual gossip, and so on. If such behavior is defined as teasing, its impact is discounted; it is just "fun." But if the behavior is thought of as sexual harassment, then the behaviors may be viewed in a new light.

According to a 2011 nationally representative survey of sexual harassment among 1,965 students in grades 7–12, 56% of the girls and 40% of the boys reported some form of sexual harassment in the 2010–2011 school year, the vast majority being peer-to-peer harassment (Hill & Kearl, 2011). Most of the incidents were verbal harassment, such as unwelcome sexual comments, jokes, or gestures. Nearly one third (30%) indicated that they were sexually harassed by text, e-mail, Facebook, or other electronic means; many of these students were also sexually harassed in person. Girls were more likely to be sexually harassed in person than boys (52% vs. 35%) and by text, e-mail, Facebook, or other electronic means (36% vs. 24%). An equal percentage of boys and girls (18%) reported being called gay or lesbian. The vast majority of students (87%) said they were negatively affected by the harassment, with girls reporting more negative outcomes than boys. Negative effects included trouble sleeping, not wanting to go to school, and changing the way they went to and came home from school. One half of the students who were sexually harassed said they did nothing afterward in response to the episode. Eighteen percent of the boys and 14% of the girls indicated that they sexually harassed other students; 44% of those students did not think the harassment was "a big deal" and 39% said they were trying to be funny. Of those students who harassed other students, 92% of the girls and 80% of the boys reported that they had been the target of sexual harassment themselves. To address sexual harassment in schools, students suggested that the school designate a person to talk to, provide online resources, and hold in-class discussions. However, the most common recommendations were allowing students to report problems anonymously, enforcing sexual harassment policies, and punishing harassers.

Among middle and secondary school students, sexual harassment occurs most often when boys are in groups. Their motives may be designed to heighten their group status by denigrating girls—rather than based on any specific animosity toward a particular girl. Harassment is usually either ignored by adults or regarded as normal or typical behavior among boys—"boys will be boys."

Greater attention is being given to alerting the public about the harassment problem in schools. For example, to help decrease harassment in elementary and secondary schools, the U.S. Department of Health & Human Services has created a helpful website, www.stopbullying.gov. This website provides valuable information such as state laws and policies, how to prevent and respond to bullying, and a special feature called "Get Help Now," which lists various problems associated with bullying and then gives suggestions on how to deal with them.

Harassment in College   Sexual harassment on college and university campuses has become a major concern. In 2005, the American Association of University Women (AAUW) (2006) conducted the most comprehensive survey to date of sexual harassment on college campuses. The online survey of 2,036 undergraduates aged 18–24 included students enrolled in public and private two-year and four-year colleges. Sixty-two percent of female students and 61% of male students reported that they had been verbally or physically sexually harassed while in college. The students reported several types of harassment (see Figure 3); sexual comments and jokes were the most common. Among female students who experienced sexual harassment, one third said they felt afraid and one fifth indicated they were disappointed in their college experience because of the sexual harassment. Although more than two thirds of the female students and more than one third of the male students who had experienced sexual harassment felt very

• **FIGURE 3**

Types of Sexual Harassment Experienced by College Students. The figures are based on a 2005 survey of college undergraduates in the United States.

(*Source:* From Hill, C., & Silva, E. *Drawing the Line: Sexual Harassment on Campus.* Copyright © 2005 by American Association of University Women. Reprinted by permission.)

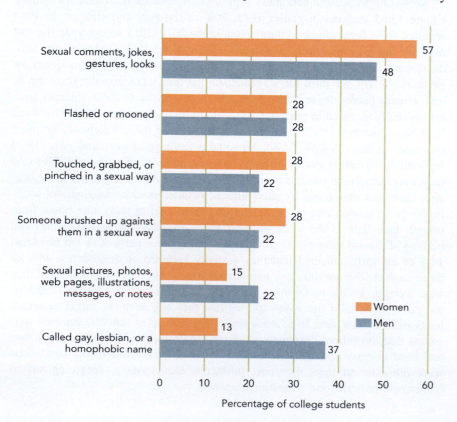

or somewhat upset by it, only 7% reported the incident to a faculty member or other college employee. Slightly more than one half of the men surveyed and about one third of the women reported they had sexually harassed someone, largely because they thought it was funny. Lesbian, gay, bisexual, and transgender (LGBT) students (73%) experienced more sexual harassment than heterosexual students (61%) and were harassed more often (18% vs. 7%).

Two major problems in dealing with issues of sexual harassment in college are gender differences in levels of tolerance and attribution of blame. Women are often blamed for not taking a "compliment" and for provoking unwanted sexual attention by what they wear or how they look. These attitudes are widely held, especially among men.

Because of sexual harassment, many students, especially women students, find it difficult to study; others worry about their grades. If the harasser is an instructor controlling grades or a coach providing team leadership, students fear reporting the harassment. They may use strategies such as avoiding courses or sports taught by the harasser or choosing another advisor. In extreme cases, the emotional consequences may be as severe as for rape victims. However, many students, particularly women, view the dating of students by professors as unethical behavior rather than harassment.

Most universities and colleges have developed sexual harassment policies, most of which prohibit romantic/sexual relationships between students and professors. A fundamental principle of these policies is that the student-professor relationship cannot be truly consensual, given the professor's considerable power over the student's academic standing and career plans.

Harassment in the Workplace

Issues of sexual harassment are complicated in the workplace because the work setting, like college, is one of the most important places where adults meet potential partners. As a consequence, sexual undercurrents or interactions often take place. Flirtations, romances, and "affairs" are common in the work environment. The line between flirtation and harassment can be problematic—especially for men. Many women do not realize they are being harassed until much later. When they identify the behavior, they report feeling naïve or gullible, as well as guilty and ashamed. As they learn more about sexual harassment, they are able to identify their experiences for what they are—harassment.

Sexual harassment in the workplace is a serious problem affecting tens of thousands of both men and women. The results of an AOL Jobs Survey reported in 2011 indicated that one in six persons has been sexually harassed at work, with 43% and 51% of those harassed stating that they were harassed by a supervisor or a peer, respectively. Of the 35% reporting the harassment to authorities, 47% were women and 21% were men. In a 2008 telephone poll of 782 U.S. workers conducted by Louis Harris and Associates, 31% and 7% of female and male workers, respectively, reported being sexually harassed at work. All of the women and 59% of the men reported that the harasser was a person of the other sex (Mahabeer, 2011). An Employment Law Alliance survey of 826 employees found that 7% indicated they had been involved in a romantic relationship with a supervisor or a subordinate, and 43% noted they believed the relationship has hurt productivity (Hirschfeld, 2004). Romantic relationships at work can become a sexual harassment issue as well as lead to perceived favoritism and low morale.

Sexual harassment tends to be most pervasive in formerly all-male occupations, in which it is a means of exerting control over women and asserting male dominance. Such male bastions as the technology sector, building trades, the trucking industry, law enforcement, and the military have been especially resistant to the presence of women. For example, a 2013 U.S. Department of Veterans Affairs anonymous survey of more than 1,100 women who served in Afghanistan and Iraq found that nearly half had been sexually harassed, and about one quarter said they had been sexually assaulted. In 2011, about one in five women in the military said that they had experienced unwanted sexual contact by another service member since joining the military. Female soldiers are 180 times more likely to be sexually assaulted by a colleague solider than killed by the enemy. As a result, military sexual trauma is the major cause of posttraumatic stress disorder among U.S. military women ("Sexual assault in the military," 2013; Zoroya, 2013). The Pentagon believes that the number of sexual assaults are going down, citing its estimate that 19,000 men and women were assaulted in 2014, although the number of reported cases were 5,400 in fiscal year 2014 versus 5,061 cases in fiscal year 2013 (Cooper, 2014). Even though the focus of sexual assault in the military has largely been on women, of the estimated 26,000 service members experiencing unwanted sexual trauma in 2012, 53% involved attacks on men. However, given the much larger number of male service members than women, the ratio of military women being sexually assaulted compared to men is much higher (Dao, 2013).

Some veterans who are survivors of rape claim that investigations of alleged rape are mishandled (Hefling, 2011). The reported rates of sexual trauma in the military probably underrepresent the actual amount, as many abused persons have been reluctant to report abuse, given that doing so will harm their careers or that nothing will be done to stop the abuse or punish the abuser. An anonymous survey found that 62% of women who indicated that they had reported a sexual assault also stated that they had experienced some form of retaliation socially, professionally, or both (Hilad, 2014). Given the greater public attention to sexual trauma in the U.S. military, the Department of Defense has increased its efforts to adequately respond and prevent sexual harassment and abuse in the military (U.S. Department of Defense, 2013).

Although most sexual harassment situations involve men harassing women, men can be the victims of harassment, from either a woman or a man. The U.S. Supreme Court has ruled that a man can file legal action against a man for sexual harassment (Solomon, 1998).

Sexual harassment can have a variety of consequences for the victim, including depression, anxiety, shame, humiliation, and anger, as will be discussed later in the chapter.

Harassment in Public Spaces

Sexual harassment in public places, also called **street harassment,** is a common occurrence experienced by many people, often with profound consequences. The organization Stop Street Harassment (Kearl, 2014) describes street harassment as "unwanted interactions in public places between strangers that are motivated by a person's actual or perceived gender, sexual orientation, or gender expression and make the harassed feel annoyed, angry, humiliated, or scared." Street harassment can occur not only on the streets but also in stores, on public transportation, in parks, and at beaches and includes the following:

- Calling out offensive comments
- Honking, whistling, and making vulgar gestures

- Making sexually explicit comments or demands and sexist comments
- Stating homophobic or transphobic slurs
- Following someone
- Flashing or masturbating in public
- Grabbing or rubbing against someone
- Sexually assaulting someone

Most women in the United States across all ages, races, income levels, sexual orientations, and geographical areas experience street harassment. Some men, especially those who self-identify as gay, bisexual, queer, or transgendered, also experience street harassment. Persons of color and those who identify as LGBT are disproportionately impacted by street harassment. Street harassment is unique from sexual harassment in school and the workplace or dating or domestic violence because it occurs between strangers in public places, making any legal recourse very difficult.

Stop Street Harassment commissioned a national study of street harassment of 2,000 people in the United States in early 2014 (see Figure 4) (Kearl, 2014). Major findings included:

- Sixty-five percent of women reported that they have experienced street harassment in their lifetime: 57% experienced verbal harassment, 41% physical aggression, including sexual touching (23%), following (20%), flashing (14%), and being forced to do something sexual (9%).
- One quarter of men reported experiencing street harassment, including 18% experiencing verbal harassment and 16% experiencing physically aggressive forms (see Figure 4).
- Eighty-six percent of women and 79% percent of men reported experiencing street harassment more than once. Women more often than men indicated that the harassment happened sometimes, often, or daily.
- Men were overwhelmingly the harassers of both men and women, although 20% of men said their harasser was a lone woman.
- As a result of street harassment, most harassed persons changed their lives in some way, such as constantly assessing their surroundings, going places with others, and, to a more extreme end, quitting a job or moving to a different neighborhood.
- About one half said they did something proactive about the harassment, such as telling the harasser to stop or back off.

Stop Street Harassment declares that harassment in public places is a human rights violation and a form of gender violence, resulting in many harassed persons, especially women, to feel less safe in public places and to limit their time there. This type of harassment can cause emotional and physical harm. Stop Street Harassment states that "everyone deserves to be safe and free from harassment as they go about their day."

• **FIGURE 4**

Percentage of Women and Men Experiencing Forms of Sexual Harassment in Public Spaces in Their Lifetime.

(*Source:* Kearl, M. (2014). *Unsafe and harassed in public spaces: A national street harassment report.* Reston, VA: Stop Street Harassment.)

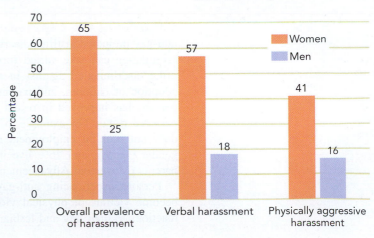

● Harassment and Discrimination Against Gay, Lesbian, Bisexual, and Transgender People

Researchers have identified two forms of discrimination, or bias, based on sexual orientation: heterosexual bias and anti-gay prejudice.

Heterosexual Bias

Heterosexual bias, also known as **heterosexism** or **heterocentric behavior,** and widely (and silently) accepted in society, media, and the family, involves the tendency to see the world in heterosexual terms and to ignore or devalue homosexuality (Griffin, 1998; Walls, 2008). Heterosexual bias may take many forms. Examples of this type of bias include the following:

- *Ignoring the existence of lesbian, gay, bisexual, and transgender people.* Discussions of various aspects of human sexuality may ignore gay, lesbian, bisexual, and transgender people, assuming that such individuals do not exist, are not significant, or are not worthy of inclusion. Without such inclusion, discussions of human sexuality are really discussions of *heterosexual* sexuality.

- *Segregating gay, lesbian, bisexual, and transgender people from heterosexual people.* When sexual orientation is irrelevant, separating certain groups from others is a form of segregation, as in efforts to not permit gay persons to openly date or bring a same-sex partner to a social work event or a school event such as a prom.

- *Subsuming gay, lesbian, bisexual, and transgender people into a larger category.* Sometimes, it is appropriate to make sexual orientation a category in data analysis, as in studies of adolescent suicide rates. If orientation is not included, findings may be distorted.

Prejudice, Discrimination, and Violence

Anti-gay prejudice is a strong dislike, fear, or hatred of gay, lesbian, bisexual, and transgender people because of their sexual orientation. Homophobia is an irrational or phobic fear of gay, lesbian, bisexual, and transgender people. Not all anti-gay feelings are phobic in the clinical sense of being excessive and irrational, but they may be unreasonable or biased. The feelings may, however, be within the norms of a biased culture.

Outcomes of Anti-Gay Prejudice and Discrimination As a belief system, anti-gay prejudice justifies discrimination based on sexual orientation. This discrimination can take varied forms: Gay, lesbian, and transgender people are often discriminated against in access to housing, employment opportunities, adoption of children, and parental rights. Even though the climate for LGBT persons has improved in recent years, these individuals still face obstacles to personal rights. For example, 52% of LGBT individuals reside in a state that does not prohibit employment discrimination based on sexual orientation or gender identity, and 76% live in states that are silent on fostering by LGBT parents (Movement Advancement Project, 2014a, 2014b).

Persons experiencing anti-gay prejudice may be harassed and bullied and become victims of physical violence. Anti-gay prejudice influences parents' reactions to their gay and lesbian children, often leading to estrangement. As a result, many gay, lesbian, bisexual, and transgender persons suffer various negative outcomes, including these:

- More gay men and lesbian women live in poverty compared to heterosexual individuals (Mushovic, 2011).

- Data from the Massachusetts Youth Risk Behavior Survey revealed that sexual minority teenagers are more likely to be unaccompanied (without their parents or guardians) and homeless (Corliss, Goodenow, Nichols, & Austin, 2011).

- Analysis of Youth Risk Behavior Survey data from seven states and six large urban school districts from 2001 to 2009 found that sexual minority students, particularly gay, lesbian, and bisexual students, had more sexual contact with both sexes and were more likely to engage in other health risk behaviors, such as behaviors related to attempted suicide, than other students (CDC, 2011.17a).

- A study in the medical journal *Pediatrics* reported that gay, lesbian, and bisexual youth in Oregon were five times more likely to attempt suicide than their heterosexual counterparts (Hatzenbuehler, 2011). When suicide occurs among gay teens, it is often attributed to unsupportive environments.

- Another study published in *Pediatrics* found that students who identify as lesbian, gay, and bisexual tend to face greater rates of being bullied in school than their heterosexual peers, although the bullying declined as they got older. Data collected from 4,135 teens and young adults in England over 7 years revealed that 57% and 52% of gay and bisexual girls and boys, respectively, aged 13–14 years, reported being bullied in school. However, 49% and 38% of heterosexual girls and boys, respectively, of the same age were bullied. Fortunately, the bullying declined as the youth got older: At ages 18–20, only 6% of the girls and 9% of the boys reported being bullied (Robinson, Espelage, & Rivers, 2013).

- The 2009 National School Climate Survey of middle and high school students found that nearly 9 in 10 lesbian, gay, bisexual, and transgender youth experienced harassment at school in the past year, and about two thirds felt unsafe at school because of their sexual orientation. Many of those bullied experienced depression and anxiety, and almost one third skipped school in the past month because of fear for their safety (Gay, Lesbian, and Straight Education Network, 2010).

- In a national online poll of 1,197 LGBT individuals, 39% indicated that at some point in their lives a family member or close friend rejected them because of their sexual orientation or gender identity. Thirty percent said that they had been physically attacked, 29% indicated that they had been made to feel unwelcomed in a place of worship, and 21% indicated that they had been treated unfairly by an employer. Fifty-eight percent said they had been a target of slurs or jokes (Pew Research Center's Social and Demographic Trends, 2013).

Violence Against Gay Men and Lesbian Women   Violence against gay men and lesbian women has a long history. At times, such violence has been sanctioned by religious institutions. During the Middle Ages, leaders of the religious court called the Inquisition condemned "sodomites" to death by burning. In the sixteenth century, England's King Henry VIII made sodomy punishable by death. In our own times, homosexual individuals were among the first victims of the Nazis, who killed 50,000 in concentration camps. Because of worldwide violence and persecution against lesbian women and gay men, in 1992 the Netherlands, Germany, and Canada granted asylum to men and women based on their homosexuality (Farnsworth, 1992).

Today, gay men, lesbian women, and other sexual minorities are frequent targets of violence. In 2013, 2,001 hate violence incidents involving lesbian, gay, bisexual, transgender, queer, and HIV-affected (LGBTQH) communities were reported. Hate violence is a pervasive and persistent issue for all lesbian, gay, bisexual, transgender, queer (LGBTQ), and HIV-affected people, disproportionately impacting transgender persons, particularly transgender women and people of color. White gay men represent the largest group (50%) of hate violence survivors. Hate violence includes several types of incidents, such as sexual assault/rape, robbery, vandalism, homicide, assault/attempted assault, intimidation, verbal harassment, incidents with police, and even murder. Unfortunately, only one half of these hate crimes are reported to police (National Coalition of Anti-Violence Programs, 2013). A review of 75 studies that examined the prevalence of sexual assault victimization against people who identify as gay or bisexual men (GB men) and as lesbian or bisexual women (LB women) in the United States found the mean estimate of lifetime sexual assault to be 30% for GB men and 43% for LB women (Rothman, Exner, & Baughman, 2011).

The brutal murder of Matthew Shepard, a gay University of Wyoming student, in 1998; the dragging death of a 34-year-old African American man, James Byrd, Jr., in 1998; the beating and strangulation of Gwen Araujo, a 17-year-old transsexual female, in 2002; and the fatal classroom shooting of 15-year-old Lawrence King, who identified as gay, in 2008, are four murders that have received national media attention. After more than a decade of advocacy, the Matthew Shepard and James Byrd, Jr. Hate Crimes Prevention Act was signed into law by President Obama on October 28, 2009. This law gives the Department of Justice the power to investigate and prosecute, as a federal crime, bias-motivated violence against an individual because of the person's actual or perceived sexual orientation, gender identity, color, religion, national origin, or disability.

Ending Anti-Gay Prejudice and Enactment of Antidiscrimination Laws

As mentioned, gay, lesbian, bisexual, and transgender people are discriminated against in many ways that harm their self-esteem and mental health. Education and positive social advocacy and interactions are important ways to combat anti-gay prejudice. Another way is to create legislation to guarantee gay, lesbian, bisexual, and transgender individuals' equal protection under the law.

The Movement Advancement Project (MAP), an independent think tank focusing on expediting equality for lesbian, gay, bisexual, and transgender people, states it "works to uncover how inequitable and prejudiced laws have a negative effect on LGBT lives—and what needs to happen to make things better" (Movement Advancement Project, 2015). MAP has created equality maps that summarize laws that affect LGBT Americans on a state-by-state and issue-by-issue basis. Figure 5 shows which states provide law and policy protection from hate crimes related to sexual orientation and gender equality. MAP states that 35% of the LGBT population live in states that have laws covering sexual orientation and gender identity, 71% live in states that have hate crime laws covering sexual orientation, 16% live in states with laws that do not cover either

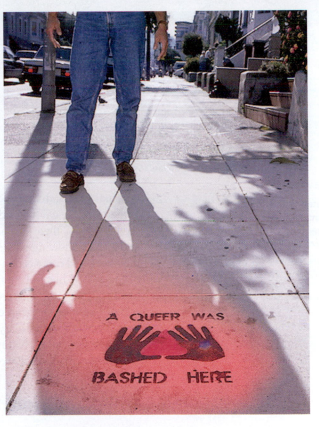

During the Middle Ages, gay men (called sodomites) were burned at the stake as heretics (above left). In Germany in 1933, the Nazis burned the library of sex reformer Magnus Hirschfeld and forced him to flee the country (above right). (See Chapter 2 to learn of Hirschfeld's sexual reform efforts.) Gay men and lesbian women were among the first Germans the Nazis forced into concentration camps, where over 50,000 of them were killed. Today, violence against gay men and lesbian women, known as gay-bashing, continues (right). The pink triangle recalls the symbol the Nazis required lesbian women and gay men to wear, just as they required Jews to wear the Star of David.

(first) © Art Reserve/Alamy; (second) © Bettmann/Corbis; (third) © Woodfin Camp and Associates

sexual orientation or gender equality, and 11% live in states with no hate crime laws (Movement Advancement Project, 2014c).

Certainly, one of the most significant recent legal advances in gay rights was the lifting of the U.S. military's "Don't Ask, Don't Tell" (DADT) policy, which banned openly gay service members. In all, 14,326 military gay, lesbian, and

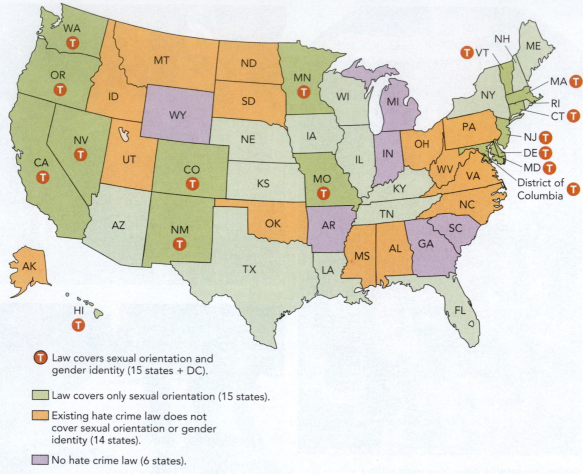

• **FIGURE 5**

States With Hate Crime Laws Protecting People Based on Sexual Orientation and Gender Equality, September 2014.

(*Source:* www.lgbtmap.org/equality-maps/legal_equality_by_state. Copyright © 2014 www: Hate crimes. Movement Advancement Project. Reprinted by permission.)

bisexual men and women were discharged under this policy, introduced in 1993. Under DADT, gay individuals were free to serve in the military as long as they didn't discuss their sexual orientation and no one else accused them of homosexuality. Following congressional action, educational sessions of current service members, and certification from the President, Secretary of Defense, and Chairman of the Joint Chiefs of Staff that the repeal of the policy would not harm military readiness, DADT was ended on September 20, 2011. Now, the military can accept applications from openly gay recruits. Other changes include eliminating references in their military records of being banned from the military because of their homosexuality, halting pending investigations and discharges, and allowing service members discharged under DADT to re-enlist (Barnes, 2011).

• Sexual Violence

In recent years, we have increasingly expanded our knowledge about sexually violent behavior and its consequences. Earlier, researchers had focused primarily on **rape,** usually defined as penile-vaginal penetration performed against a *woman's* will through the use or threat of force. In the 1970s, feminists challenged the belief that rape is a form of harmful sexual disorder. Instead, they argued, rape is an act of violence and aggression against women, and the principal motive is power, not sexual gratification. As a result of feminist influence, the focus of research shifted.

Contemporary research now focuses on a broad range of sexual-related behavior against another person and utilizes varied terms. In the reports, terms such as "sexual violence," "sexual aggression," "sexual assault," and "sexual coercion" are used, sometimes interchangeably and without clear definition, leading to possible confusion for the reader. Because of this, one should attempt to ascertain exactly what behaviors are studied when interpreting the findings. This textbook uses the term **sexual violence** whenever possible, following the vocabulary used by the CDC's National Intimate Partner and Sexual Violence Survey, United States, 2011 (NISVS) (Breiding et al., 2014). However, other terms are also used in the discussion, since the results of research studies have utilized varied terms. The NISVS research focused on sexual violent behaviors, as stated in its latest report:

> The specific types of sexual violence assessed included rape (completed or attempted forced penetration or alcohol- or drug-facilitated penetration) and sexual violence other than rape, including being made to penetrate a perpetrator, sexual coercion (nonphysically pressured unwanted penetration), unwanted sexual contact (e.g., kissing or fondling), and noncontact unwanted sexual experiences (e.g., being flashed or forced to view sexually explicit media). (p. 3)

The NISVS reported the occurrence of these behaviors of men and women in the United States, as shown in Figure 6. The NISVS also assessed sexual stalking and intimate partner violence (a person being slapped, shoved, hit, or slammed against something or insulting or humiliating an intimate partner). Both men and women are the victims of sexual violence. Gay men, lesbian women, and bisexual and transgender individuals have an equal or higher prevalence of experiencing sexual violence compared to heterosexuals.

Sexual coercion is a broader term than "rape" or "sexual aggression." It includes arguing, pleading, and cajoling, as well as force and the threat of force. **Sexual assault** is a term used by the criminal justice system to describe forced sexual contact that does not necessarily include penile-vaginal intercourse and so does not meet the legal definition of rape. Thus, for example, individuals could be prosecuted for engaging in forced anal intercourse or for forcing an object into the anus. Both "survivor" and "victim" are used to describe persons who have experienced sexual violence. Many agencies and individuals prefer the term "survivor," believing that term is more empowering. The term "victim" is still used in some research studies and in the criminal

• **FIGURE 6**

Percentage of Women and Men Having Experienced in Their Lifetime Various Sexual Violence Tactics Against Them.

(*Source:* Breiding, M. J., Smith, S. G., Basile, K. C., Walters, M. L., Chen, J., & Merrick, M. T. (2014). Prevalence and characteristics of sexual violence, stalking, and intimate partner violence victimization—National Intimate Partner and Sexual Violence Survey, United States, 2011. *Morbidity and Mortality Weekly Report, 63*(8), 1–18.)

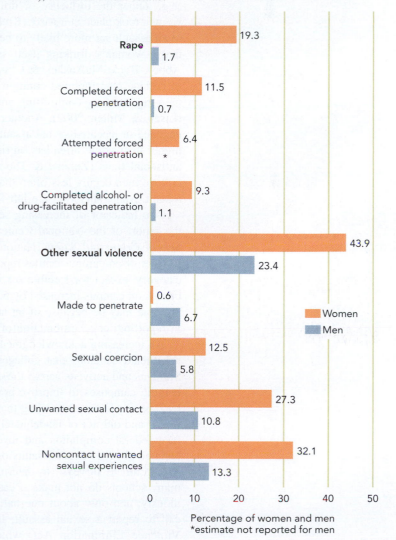

Percentage of women and men
*estimate not reported for men

justice context (The White House Council on Women and Girls, 2014). In this book we generally use the term "survivor"; however, we also use the terms utilized in the cited research studies and reports.

Campus Sexual Violence

Sexual violence is a serious problem on many college campuses. For example, one in five women report being sexually assaulted while in college, most often during their freshman or sophomore year (Krebs, Lindquist, Warner, Fisher, & Martin, 2009). Reported rapes on campus are very low; that is, many more rapes occur than are reported. The college culture appears to fuel the problem: Many survivors are abused while they are drunk, under the influence of drugs, passed out, or incapacitated in some other way. "Perpetrators" often "prey" on those they perceive to be vulnerable, and sometimes surreptitiously provide their victims with drugs or alcohol. The majority of college rape survivors are assaulted at parties by someone they know, such as a classmate, friend, or date. A 2007 study found that 58% of rapes were against women who were incapacitated (e.g., under the influence of drugs/alcohol) and 28% of forced rapes against women took place at a party (Krebs et al., 2009). "Perpetrators" who drink prior to an assault are more likely to believe that alcohol increases their sex drive and that a woman's drinking itself signals that she is interested in sex (Zawacki, Abbey, Buck, McAuslan, & Clinton-Sherrod, 2003). One study found that 7% of college men reported committing rape or attempted rape, and 63% of these men reported to committing multiple offenses, on average six rapes each (Lisak & Miller, 2002). Another study, of 238 college men, found that 68% engaged in repeated sexual assault and coercion and that these offenders scored higher than single offenders on risky behaviors, sexually aggressive beliefs, and antisocial traits (Zinzow & Thompson, 2014). Although sexual assault among college men occurs less often than among women, men also experience sexual assault. Many survivors are left feeling isolated, ashamed, or to blame.

One indicator of increasing sexual assault on college campuses is found in the report of the National Center for Education Statistics called *Indicators of School Crime and Safety* (National Center for Education Statistics, 2014). The number of on-campus crimes reported in 2011 was lower than in 2001 for every category, except for forcible sex offenses. The number of reported forcible sex crimes on campus increased by 52%, from 2,200 in 2001 to 3,300 in 2011. This increase may be because of an actual increase in sexual assault or an increase in reporting, or a combination of both.

An increasing acknowledgment of the college student sexual assault problem has fueled demands that colleges and universities make their campuses safer. Students and activists across the country have formed national movements challenging campuses to improve how they handle rape. Lawsuits have been filed by rape survivors, contending that their campus has a "sexually hostile environment" and did not or inadequately responded to rape cases. Dozens of colleges face federal complaints and investigations under Title IX on how they have handled alleged sexual assaults on campus. Only about one in six colleges conduct "climate surveys" to determine the prevalence of campus sexual assault; many schools do not make it easy for assault victims to report attacks anonymously; and only about one half of campuses have a hotline that victims can call to report a sexual assault. In 2013, Congress passed the Campus Sexual Violence Elimination Act, which mandates that colleges offer prevention programs (Marklein & Shesgreen, 2014; Sander, 2013). In 2014, President Obama created the Task Force to Protect Students from Sexual Assault (White House Task Force to Protect Students from Sexual Harassment, 2014). The Task Force created a website—NotAlone.gov— to tell sexual assault survivors that they are not alone by helping them locate a crises service center, teaching them their rights, and assisting them in filing a complaint. The task force presented a set of action steps and recommendations in its report, *Not Alone: The First Report of the White House Task Force to Protect Students from Sexual Assault* (White House Task Force to Protect Students from Sexual Assault, 2014):

- *Identify the problem.* A toolkit for determining the extent of sexual assault will be provided to colleges.

- *Prevent sexual assault and engaging men.* Promising prevention strategies will be identified. The task force is researching new ideas and solutions and advocating finding ways to empower men to become an important part of the solution. Men should be engaged as allies to prevent sexual assault.

- *Effectively respond when a student is sexually assaulted.* When students are sexually assaulted, a school needs a plan that should include (1) someone a survivor can talk to in confidence: (2) a comprehensive sexual misconduct policy; (3) trauma-informed training for school officials; (4) better school disciplinary systems; and (5) partnerships with the community.

- *Increase transparency and improving enforcement.* The federal government is committed to making enforcement efforts more efficient. More resources for both students and colleges will be provided. For example, the task force website—NotAlone.gov—will include information for sexual assault survivors on their legal rights, definitions of legal terms, and their state's privacy laws. Information on colleges' legal obligations to protect students from sexual assault is provided.

Also in 2014, the U.S. Department of Education issued rules designed to make college campuses safer from sexual violence. These new regulations, considered a significant step by many advocates and higher education officials, come as colleges are struggling with their legal responsibility in responding to students' allegations of being sexually assaulted. Two major rules are:

- Colleges are required to train faculty, staff, and students on preventing sexual assault, dating violence, domestic violence, and stalking.

- Alleged survivors and accused perpetrators can choose an advocate such as a lawyer, campus official, or family member to appear with them throughout the disciplinary proceedings.

To the disappointment of some advocates, the new regulations do not provide a standard of evidence that should be used to decide if sexual assault has occurred and how students determined to have been responsible for sexual assault should be penalized by the college. Further, the rules do not define sexual consent (Lewontin, 2014).

The Nature and Incidence of Rape

Rape is a means of achieving power or expressing anger and hatred. Rape *forces* its survivor into an intimate physical encounter with the rapist against his or her will. The survivor does not experience pleasure; he or she experiences terror. In most cases, the survivor is a woman; sometimes, the survivor is a man. In most cases, however, the assailant is a man. The weapon in rape is the penis (which may be supplemented by a knife or a gun); the penis is used to attack, subordinate, and humiliate the survivor. History reveals that rape occurs more frequently when women are devalued and the negative outcomes of rape are perceived to be low by the assailant (Lalumière, Harris, Quinsey, & Rice, 2005).

Rape is not only a specific behavior but also a threat. Girls are warned against talking to or getting into cars with strangers; women are warned against walking alone down dark streets and leaving doors and windows unlocked. Men may fear assault, but women fear assault *and* rape. As a result, many women live with the possibility of being raped as a part of their consciousness. Rape and the fear of rape are facts of life for women; this is not true for most men.

The actual prevalence rates of rape in the United States are unknown because most survivors do not report the crime. According to the Rape, Abuse & Incest National Network (2009a), someone in the United States is sexually assaulted every 2 minutes. The 2011 National Intimate Partner and Sexual Violence Survey found that nearly 1 in 5 women (19%) and 1 in 50 men (2%) in the United States have been raped at some time in their lives; nearly 1 in 2 women and 1 in 5 men have experienced sexual violence and victimization other than rape at some point in their lives (Breiding et al., 2014). The U.S. Department of Justice's National Crime Victimization Survey (NCVS) (2013) states that the total number of reported rapes/sexual assaults of persons aged 12 and older was 346,000 in 2012. The 2009 NCVS reported that 80% of female survivors knew their assailant (see Figure 7), whereas 26% of the male survivors knew their assailant.

National data also show that adolescents experience sexual coercion. The Centers for Disease Control and Prevention (CDC) found that nationwide 11% of female students and 5% of male students in grades 9–12 had been forced to have sexual intercourse when they did not want to (CDC, 2010.17a).

Myths About Rape

Our society has a number of myths about rape, which encourage rather than discourage it. According to one myth, women are to blame for their own rapes, as if they somehow "deserved" them or were responsible for them. Often, women who were raped worried that they might be blamed for their assaults.

Erroneous rape beliefs, such as "If I only wore different clothes" or "I must have led him on" can influence sexual scripts that, in turn, impact one's attitudes about sexuality and sexual behavior. Recall that sexual scripts are culturally determined patterns of sexual expression that inform desire and actual behavior. Research shows that many individuals still have erroneous rape scripts. This may be a barrier preventing persons who have been raped from acknowledging the assault as well as allowing persons who rape to engage in sexual violence while denying it is rape (Edwards, Turchik, Dardis, Reynolds, & Gidycz, 2011; Ryan, 2011). Belief in rape myths is also part of a larger belief structure that includes gender-role stereotypes, sexual conservatism, acceptance of interpersonal violence, and the belief that men are different from women. Men

• **FIGURE 7**

Type of Relationship With Offender of Female Survivors of Rape and Sexual Assault.

(*Source:* Data from U.S. Department of Justice, 2010.)

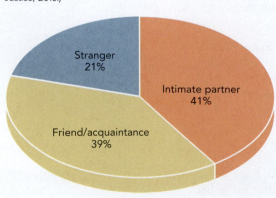

Note: Total percent is greater than 100% because of rounding.

practically speaking

Preventing Sexual Assault

There are no guaranteed ways to prevent sexual assault or coercion. Each situation, assailant, and targeted woman or man is different. But rape education courses may be effective in reducing the rape myths that provide support for sexual aggression.

To reduce the risk of date rape, consider these guidelines:

1. When dating someone for the first time, even if you have established a relationship over the Internet, go to a public place such as a restaurant, movie, or sports event.

2. Share expenses. A common scenario is a date expecting you to exchange sex for his or her paying for dinner, the movie, drinks, and so on.

3. Avoid using drugs or alcohol if you do not want to be sexual with your date. Such use is associated with date rape.

4. Avoid ambiguous verbal or nonverbal behavior, particularly any behavior that might be interpreted as "teasing." Make sure your verbal and nonverbal messages are identical. If you want to only cuddle or kiss, for example, tell your date that those are your limits. Tell him or her that if you say no you mean no. Don't feel obligated to do anything you don't want to do. If necessary, reinforce your statement emphatically, both verbally and physically (by pushing the person away).

5. If your date becomes sexually coercive despite your direct communication, consider physical denials such as pushing, slapping, and kicking. Make up a reason to leave even if it's a lie, such as you're not feeling well.

To reduce the risk of stranger rape, consider the following guidelines. But try to avoid becoming overly vigilant; use reasonable judgment. Do not let fear control your life.

1. Do not identify yourself as a person living alone, especially if you are a woman. Use initials on the mailbox and in the telephone directory.

2. Don't open your door to strangers; keep your house and car doors locked. Have your keys ready when you approach your car or house. Look in the back seat before getting into your car. Don't isolate yourself with someone you don't trust or know.

3. Avoid dark and isolated areas. Be aware of your surroundings and walk with a purpose. Trust your instincts. Don't put music headphones in both ears that lessen your awareness of the surroundings. Carry a whistle or airhorn, and take a cell phone when you are out by yourself. Let people know where you are going and what time you expect to get home.

4. If someone approaches you threateningly, turn and run. If you can't run, resist. Studies indicate that resisting an attack by shouting, causing a scene, or fighting back can deter the assailant. Fighting and screaming may reduce the level of the abuse without increasing the level of physical injury. Many women who are injured during a rape appear to have been injured *before* resisting. Trust your intuitions, whatever approach you take.

5. Be sure your cell phone is with you and you have taxi money, or bus fare.

6. Be alert to possible ways to escape. Talking with an assailant may give you time to find an escape route.

7. Take self-defense training. It will raise your level of confidence and your fighting abilities. You may be able to scare off the assailant, or you may create an opportunity to escape. Many women take self-defense training following an incidence of sexual aggression to reaffirm their sense of control.

8. Do not post personal data or contact information on social networking sites.

If you are sexually assaulted (or the survivor of an attempted assault), report the assault as soon as possible. You are probably not the assailant's first victim. As much as you might want to, do not change clothes or shower. Semen and hair or other materials on your body or clothing may be very important in arresting and convicting a rapist. You may also want to contact a rape crisis center; its staff members are knowledgeable about dealing with the police and the traumatic aftermath of rape. But most importantly, remember that you are not at fault. The rapist is the only one to blame.

SOURCE: Rape, Abuse & Incest National Network. (2009b). *Ways to reduce sexual assault.* Washington, DC.

are more likely than women to believe rape myths. The following list of 13 common rape myths can clarify misunderstandings about rape:

- *Myth 1: Rape is a crime of passion.* Rape is an act of violence and aggression and is often a life-threatening experience. While sexual attraction may be one component, power, anger, and control are the dominant factors resulting in gratification. Actually, most rapists have access to other, willing sexual partners but choose to rape.

- *Myth 2: Women want to be raped.* It is popularly believed that women have an unconscious wish to be raped. Also, some people believe that many women mean "yes" when they say "no." This myth supports the misconception that a woman enjoys being raped because she sexually "surrenders," and it perpetuates the belief that rape is a sexual behavior rather than a violent one.

- *Myth 3: "But she wanted sex."* This myth contends that some rape survivors wanted to have sex. That is, they had desire and so the forced sex cannot be rape. Of course, it is possible to want to have sex but decide not to consent to sex. It is rape if the victim did not consent to sex even if the survivor wanted sex. Peterson and Muehlenhard (2007) stated that "rape is about the absence of consent, not the absence of desire."

- *Myth 4: Women ask for it.* Many people believe that women "ask for it" by their behavior. One study found that provocative dress on the part of the survivor of a date rape resulted in a greater perception that the survivor was responsible and that the rape was justified (Cassidy & Hurrell, 1995). Despite some attempts to reform rape laws, women continue to bear the burden of proof in these cases. No one, female or male, ever deserves to be raped, and regardless of what a person says, does (such as flirting), or wears, she or he does not cause the rape. Actually, most rapes are premeditated and planned by the perpetrator. Opportunity is the critical factor in determining when a rapist will rape.

- *Myth 5: The woman did not fight back or scream, so it wasn't rape.* Women may be scared of being hurt or losing their lives; they are paralyzed with fear even if there is no weapon or obvious physical force used. Rape is rape whether or not there is a struggle (Stop Violence Against Women, 2014).

- *Myth 6: Women are raped only by strangers.* Women are warned to avoid or distrust strangers as a way to avoid rape; such advice, however, isolates them from normal social interactions. Furthermore, studies indicate that 80% of all rapes of women are committed by nonstrangers such as acquaintances, friends, dates, partners, husbands, or relatives (U.S. Department of Justice, 2010).

- *Myth 7: Women could avoid rape if they really wanted to.* This myth reinforces the stereotype that women "really" want to be raped or that they should curtail their activities. Women are often warned not to be out after dark alone. Approximately two thirds of rapes/sexual assaults occur between 6 P.M. and 6 A.M., but nearly 6 in 10 occur at the victim's home or the home of a friend, relative, or neighbor (Greenfeld, 1997; McCabe & Wauchope, 2005a). Women are also approached at work, on their way to or from work, or at their place of worship or are kidnapped from shopping centers or parking lots at midday. Restricting women's activities does not seem to have an appreciable impact on rape. Men are often

Just because a woman is dressed provocatively does not mean she is inviting rape.

physically larger and stronger than women, making it difficult for women to resist. Sometimes, weapons are used and physical violence occurs or is threatened. And assailants catch their victims "off guard" because they choose the time and place of attack.

- *Myth 8: Women cry rape for revenge.* This myth suggests that women who are "dumped" by men accuse them of rape as a means of revenge. Actually, the prevalence of false rape accusations is very low. False reporting is unlikely because of the many obstacles women face before an assailant is brought to trial and convicted.

- *Myth 9: Rapists are crazy or psychotic.* Very few men who rape are clinically psychotic; they are usually "ordinary" men. The vast majority are psychologically indistinguishable from other men, except that rapists appear to have more difficulty handling feelings of hostility and are more likely to express their anger through violence. Studies on date rape find that rapists differ from nonrapists primarily in a greater hostility toward women, acceptance of traditional gender roles, and greater willingness to use force.

- *Myth 10: Most rapists are a different race/ethnicity than their victims.* Most rapists and their victims are members of the same racial/ethnic group.

- *Myth 11: Men cannot control their sexual urges.* This myth is based on the belief that men, when subjected to sexual stimuli, cannot control their sexual feelings. This also implies that women have some responsibility for rape by provoking this "uncontrollable" sexuality of men through their attire or appearance. Men, like women, can learn to appropriately and responsibly express their sexuality.

- *Myth 12: Rape is "no big deal."* About one in three women who are injured during rape or physical assault require medical care. Rape survivors can also experience negative mental health outcomes and are more likely to engage in harmful behaviors to cope with the trauma, such as drinking, smoking, or using drugs.

- *Myth 13: Men cannot be raped.* Men can be victims of sexual violence from either men or women. This issue is discussed in more detail later in this section.

Forms of Rape

Persons who rape may be dates, acquaintances, partners, husbands, fathers, or other family members, as well as strangers.

Date Rape   The most common form of rape is sexual intercourse with a dating partner that occurs against the victim's will, with force or the threat of force. It is known as **date rape.** Sometimes, the term **acquaintance rape** has been used interchangeably with the term "date rape." However, Rana Sampson (2003), an expert on crime control, says that they are different. That is, most acquaintance rapes do not happen during a date; they occur when two people just happen to be in the same place. Because some of the rape literature uses the terms "date rape" and "acquaintance rape" interchangeably, the discussion often does not differentiate these two types of rape and may actually be talking about one or both. Actually, some of the following discussion about date rape may also be applicable to acquaintance rape; however, we discuss some of the specific aspects of acquaintance rape among college students in a later section.

11 *Undismayed, he plucks the rose*
In the hedgerow blooming.
Vainly she laments her woes,
Vainly doth her thorns oppose,
Gone her sweet perfuming.

—German art song

Alcohol and/or drugs are often involved in date rapes (see the "Think About It" box "Date/Acquaintance Rape Drugs: An Increasing Threat"). Men who believe in rape myths are more likely to see alcohol consumption in women as a sign that they are sexually available.

Incidence   Lifetime experience of date rape ranges from 13% to 27% for women, according to various studies (Rickert & Wiemann, 1998). If the definition is expanded to include attempted intercourse as a result of verbal pressure or the misuse of authority, then women's lifetime incidence increases significantly. Among college students, the most likely assailant is a peer.

Acquaintance Rape   Sampson (2003) notes that acquaintance rape accounts for the vast majority of college rapes and that there are various types of acquaintance rape, such as party rape (can also include gang rapes), rape in a nonparty and nondate situation (e.g., while studying together), and rape by a former sexual partner. Environmental factors that may contribute to the possibility of acquaintance rape include alcohol and drugs, availability of a private room in a fraternity or off-campus house, loud music that can drown out a person's calls for help, and a cover-up by the house's residents. By contrast, date rape usually occurs as the two people are getting to know each other and the rape may occur in a car or residence after the date. Stranger rape, which is much less common than acquaintance rape on college campuses, usually occurs in isolated parts of campus, such as campus garages; in these cases, the victim may not have consumed any alcohol and no prior relationship (or even acquaintance) exists between the survivor and the rapist.

Sampson (2003) outlines several factors found in research of acquaintance rape that might increase a woman's vulnerability. Noting that a woman's condition or behavior does not cause rape, these factors include frequently drinking enough to get drunk, drinking so much that she cannot resist forceful sexual advances, using drugs, having previously been a survivor of sexual assault, being single, participating in social activities with sexually predatory men, being in an isolated site, miscommunicating about sex, and holding less conservative attitudes about sexual behavior. According to the Rape, Abuse & Incest National Network (2009c), a person is more vulnerable to acquaintance rape when, over time, he or she becomes used to or more comfortable with the offender's intrusion into his or her personal space. Consequently, the victim may no longer consider the intrusive behavior threatening or may suppress feelings of fear. The offender then uses the victim's trust to isolate the victim from others. The Network advises that a person finding himself or herself in a threatening situation should listen to his or her instinctual sense of fear and discomfort and leave the situation.

Confusion Over Consent   Sexual consent is difficult to define. As we have previously discussed, much sexual communication is nonverbal and ambiguous. The fact that we don't usually give verbal consent to sexual activity indicates the significance of nonverbal clues. Nonverbal communication is imprecise, however, and can be misinterpreted easily if not reinforced verbally. For example, men frequently mistake a woman's friendliness for sexual interest. They often misinterpret a woman's cuddling, kissing, and fondling as a desire to engage in sexual intercourse (Fisher & Walters, 2003; Gillen & Muncer, 1995; Henningsen, Henningsen, & Valde, 2006).

think
about it

Date/Acquaintance Rape Drugs:
An Increasing Threat

So-called date rape drugs have become an increasing threat, particularly for young people. These drugs are placed in beverages so that the person consuming the drink will be incapacitated, thus compromising his or her ability to give consent and increasing the person's vulnerability to sexual contact. They also can minimize the resistance and memory of the victim. Although described commonly as "date rape" drugs, the drugs are used not only during dates but also by acquaintances; hence, the more accurate term is "date/acquaintance rape drugs." The drugs are also sometimes used during gang rapes.

Drugging an unwilling or unknowing person is a crime. In 1996, the Drug-Induced Rape Prevention and Punishment Act was passed, making it a felony to distribute controlled substances, such as those classified as date/acquaintance rape drugs, to someone without that person's knowledge and with the intent to commit violence, including rape, against that person (Woodworth, 1996).

Briefly, here are some of the major date/acquaintance rape drugs (Womenshealth.gov, 2014):

- *Alcohol.* Although many people may not think of alcohol as a date/acquaintance drug, alcohol is the most frequently used substance in drug-facilitated assault. Certainly it is easily accessible in many social situations and very common on college campuses. In most cases, the person consumes the alcohol voluntarily. Often he or she is encouraged to drink enough to lose inhibition or consciousness.

- *Rohypnol.* Also known as "roofies," "roach," "forget pill," "Mexican valium," and "mind erasers," Rohypnol is not approved for medical use in the United States and is not available legally but is becoming an increasingly popular street drug. This small, white tablet quickly dissolves in liquid. Alcohol increases the effects of Rohypnol.

- *GHB.* Also known as "grievous bodily harm," "easy lay," "liquid ecstasy," and "bedtime scoop," GHB has not been approved for sale by the FDA since 1990. GHB is sold on the street as a clear, odorless liquid and a white, crystalline powder, but since it is made in home labs its effects can be unpredictable. Alcohol increases the effects of GHB.

- *Benzodiazepines.* These drugs are legal forms of Rohypnol that are prescribed as anti-anxiety and sleeping medications in the United States. Put into a drink in powder or liquid form, they markedly impair or eliminate functions that typically allow a person to resist an assault. Alcohol increases the effects of benzodiazepines.

- *Ketamine.* Also known as "Special K," "Vitamin K," and "K," ketamine is an anesthetic typically used by veterinarians. A fast-acting liquid, ketamine causes individuals to feel detached from their bodies and unable to fight back or remember what happened.

- *Ecstasy.* Also known as "X-TC," "X," and "E," ecstasy is the most common club drug. Illegal in the United States, ecstasy is a hallucinogenic and stimulant with psychedelic effects. Available in powder or liquid form, ecstasy causes people to feel extreme relaxation, sensitivity to touch, and a lowered ability to perceive danger.

To protect yourself from date/acquaintance rape drugs, it is essential that you watch what you drink at parties or on dates. Do not take any drinks (soda, coffee, or alcohol) from someone you do not know well and trust, and refuse open-container beverages. Don't share drinks or drink from punch bowls or other common containers. If someone offers to get you a drink from a bar or at a party, go with that person to order your drink. Never leave your drink unattended, and go to parties with a friend and leave with a friend. If you think you've been drugged, call 9-1-1 or get to an emergency room. If possible, keep a sample of the beverage. If you are a victim of drug-facilitated assault, do not blame yourself. The sexual assault was not your fault; the offender is solely to blame and is the one who took advantage of your diminished capacity (Ellis, 2002; MedicineNet.com, 2014; Office of Women's Health, 2008, 2012; Rape, Abuse & Incest National Network, 2009d).

Think Critically

1. How common is the use of rape/acquaintance rape drugs on your campus? In what type of situations does it occur?

2. What can a person do to avoid being vulnerable to date/acquaintance rape?

Confusion over whether consent for sex has been given may lead to a strong disagreement between partners.

© Stockbyte/Getty Images

A woman must make her boundaries clear verbally, and men need to avoid misinterpreting clues. One study of young heterosexual adults found that women with intercourse experience, more often than men and more often than women without intercourse experience, emphasized the value of consent and preferred explicit verbal communication to obtain it (Humphreys, 2004). In an effort to assure that verbal consent to sex would occur, the California legislature in September 2014 passed a bill that would require California colleges receiving state-financed student aid to change their definition of consent in their state's sexual assault policies. The traditional "no means no" standard has been replaced with an **affirmative consent,** also known as a "yes means yes." The bill defined consent as "affirmative, conscious, and voluntary agreement to engage in sexual activity." The affirmative consent need not be spoken, although the underlying message of the new definition is that silence does not necessarily mean consent. Further, lack of protest or resistance does not mean consent. The affirmative consent must be ongoing throughout the sexual activity and can be withdrawn at any time. Intoxication cannot be used as an alibi for thinking that there was consent. The burden for obtaining consent would rest on the student initiating sex to obtain a "yes" instead of the intended partner to state a "no." Proponents understand that the new policy has limitations but also believe that it is worth trying. Opponents feel that it is vague, impractical, difficult to prove legally (e.g., who would corroborate that the person said "yes"?), represents an effort to micromanage sex, and does not eliminate the "he said, she said" quandary. Some question what happens if a "yes" is not obtained. Sex researcher Kathleen Bogle (2014) states that a person cannot consent to sex when he or she is intoxicated and contends that rape "perpetrators" do not care if the person consents. Bogle points out another flaw in the "yes means yes" law:

> The California legislation implies that sexual assaults occur due to misunderstandings and that the word "yes" will clarify things and thereby prevent sexual assaults. Are we to believe the problem stems from perpetrators—usually men—who mistakenly think women are consenting when they are not? (p. A35)

Sex researchers Kristen Jozkowski and Zoe Peterson (2013) state:

> An important question to consider is this: If a man goes ahead with a sexual encounter without affording his female partner the opportunity to provide an affirmation agreement or a refusal, does this fit a legal or perhaps an ethical definition of sexual assault or rape? Such sexual activity seems to fall into a gray space between consensual and nonconsensual sex. (p. 522)

Some opponents to the "yes" consent standard point out that nonverbal cues can accurately indicate consent (Vendituoli, 2014; "When yes means yes," 2014). The results of studies by New Zealand sex researcher Melanie Beres (2010, 2014) suggest that men and women are easily able to identify a casual partner's willingness to have sex and that there is little miscommunication between them. (To read more about the results of this research, see the "Think About It" box "Can Men and Women Accurately Judge a Partner's Willingness to Have Casual Sex?") In 2003, Illinois became the first state to pass a law explicitly stating that people have a right to withdraw their consent to sexual activity at any time. The law specified that, no matter how far the sexual interaction has progressed, a "no" means no when someone wants to stop (Parsons, 2003).

Our sexual scripts often assume "yes" unless a "no" is directly stated (Muehlenhard, Ponch, Phelps, & Giusti, 1992). This makes individuals "fair

think
about it

Can Men and Women Accurately Judge a Partner's Willingness to Have Casual Sex?

Popular belief suggests that miscommunication, assumptions, and an inability to read a partner's willingness to have casual sex (that is, sex with a partner not known well) can lead to undesired sex. Sexual coercion and violence, including rape, are often attributed to a misunderstanding between men and women. Men overestimating women's interest in sex and women displaying "token resistance" to sex (saying "no" when she means "yes") are among the major forms of miscommunication and misunderstanding between the sexes. Rape prevention programs have thus responded to these assumptions by educating women to communicate more clearly their sexual boundaries to their dates and partners, as well as educating men toward greater acceptance of "no means no" and their partner's wishes and desires (Beres, 2010; Beres, Senn, & McCaw, 2014; Fisher & Walters, 2003; Henningsen et al., 2006).

New Zealand sex researcher Melanie Beres and colleagues explored issues related to the communication of desire and willingness/nonwillingness for sex among two nonrandom samples of heterosexual college students from both New Zealand and Canada and heterosexual Canadian young adults (aged 19 to 30). The results are summarized as follows.

College Student Study (Beres et al., 2014)

Men and women students were asked to imagine themselves in a particular heterosexual dating situation and write what they think happened between the beginning, when sex was refused by one partner, and the end when sex happened. That is, the study examined how the students made sense of sexual interactions and how miscommunication factors in when a man makes a move for sex but the woman partner refuses.

- The data revealed no evidence for miscommunication between the partners when there were differences in desire for sex.
- Ambivalence about sex was frequently identified by both men and women and was most often resolved to the satisfaction of both partners.
- Coercion by men was present in a minority of narratives even when there was clear understanding of the women's refusals.
- The study concluded that there was minimal widespread miscommunication within the heterosexual stories.

Young Adults (Beres, 2010)

Young adult men and women were interviewed to explore the different ways they reported communicating with their heterosexual casual sex partners and how they understand their own and their partners' expressions of willingness to have sex.

- Both women and men described similar communication patterns even when acceptance or rejection of a sexual invitation occurred.
- Both men and women utilized a combination of three themes when describing their communication with casual sex partners:

  1. *Tacit Knowing*
     Almost all said it is easy to determine when someone was interested in casual sex—"you just know."

  2. *Refusing Sex*
     Some men mentioned nonverbal indications of refusal or discomfort as an indicator that a women did not want to continue with the sexual activity. Women also mentioned signs of disinterest as a way they conveyed no interest in sex.

  3. *Active Participation*
     Active participation, e.g., pulling their partner closer or pushing away, sighing, breathing heavily and moaning, and becoming irritated were all indicators of whether the person is willing to continue sexual contact.

- The study concluded that the men and women were easily able to identify a potential partner's willingness to have sex through refusals and active participation and even via subtle forms of nonverbal refusals.

Summary of the Two Studies

These two studies suggest that there is little miscommunication between sexual partners when there is a disparity in desire for sex and that both men and women are easily capable of reading their partner's willingness/nonwillingness to participate in sexual activity. The researchers state that rape prevention programs based on sexual communication are not adequately addressing the issue of consent and that they should teach persons to expect to be literate in the ways of communicating willingness/nonwillingness to have sex and that they, themselves, are equipped to read this form of communication.

Think Critically

1. Do you believe the study finding that both young adult men and women can easily read their partner's willingness/nonwillingness to have sex? Explain.

2. If you have had sex with a partner, was it easy or difficult to assess whether or not your partner was willing to have sex? Was this assessment based on verbal communication, tacit knowledge, refusing sex, and/or active participation?

3. What do you think should be the focus of rape prevention programs?

SOURCES: Beres, M. (2010). Sexual miscommunication? Untangling assumptions about sexual communication between casual sex partners. *Culture, Health & Sexuality: An International Journal for Sex Research, Intervention and Care, 12,* 1–4; Beres, M. A., Senn, C. Y., & McCaw, J. (2014). Navigating ambivalence: How heterosexual young adults make sense of desire differences. *Journal of Sex Research, 5,* 765–776; Fisher, T. D., & Walters, A. S. (2003). Variables in addition to gender that help to explain differences in perceived sexual interest. *Psychology of Men and Masculinity, 4,* 154–162; Henningsen, D. D., Henningsen, M. L. M., & Valde, K. S. (2006). Gender differences in perception of women's sexual interest during cross-sex interactions: An application and extension of cognitive valence theory. *Sex Roles, 54,* 821–829.

game" unless they explicitly say "no." But the assumption of consent puts women at a disadvantage. Because men traditionally initiate sex, a man can initiate sex whenever he desires without the woman explicitly consenting. Actually, some men feel that the best way to get sex with a women, whether she is willing or not, is to simply engage in the desired behavior and then pretend that the behavior was unintentional or occurred because of a misunderstanding. A woman's refusal of sex can be considered "insincere" because consent is always assumed. Such thinking reinforces a common sexual script in which men initiate and women refuse so as not to appear "promiscuous." A research study of 185 college men suggested that men are conceptualized as the gender that initiates sex and that women are the gatekeepers whose sexual pleasure is secondary to that of the male partner. These scripts may contribute to an environment in which women may be reluctant to initiate sex or to say yes to sex too quickly out of fear of being labeled negatively (Jozkowski & Peterson, 2013). In this script, the man continues, believing that the woman's refusal is "token." Some common reasons for offering "token" refusals include a desire not to appear "loose," not being sure how the partner feels, inappropriate surroundings, and game playing, which few women (and men) actually engage in. Because some women sometimes say "no" when they mean "coax me," male-female communication may be especially unclear regarding consent. Studies of college students found that more women than men reported sexual teasing, a form of provocation implying a promise of sexual contact but followed with refusal, and that they were more likely to agree that various forms of sexual violence are justified in situations in which the woman is perceived as "leading a man on" or "giving mixed signals" (Locke & Mahalik, 2005; Meston & O'Sullivan, 2007). However, contemporary beliefs of most people and the law say that if a rape survivor did not explicitly consent to sex, it is rape, even though the survivor flirted with the perpetrator, had been drinking, or experienced sexual arousal or orgasm during the incident (Peterson & Muehlenhard, 2007). (To learn one study's findings of how college men and women define, communicate, and interpret sexual consent and nonconsent see the "Think About It" box "How College Students Indicate and Interpret Consent to Have Sex.")

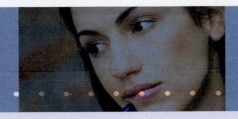

think
about it

How College Students Indicate and Interpret Consent to Have Sex

Sexual assault is often defined by the lack of consent for sex. The absence of sexual consent is frequently the major component of research and legal definitions of sexual violence, including rape. Indicating or saying "yes" is typically considered consent, yet the exact definition of consent in the literature is often lacking (Beres, 2007). This lack of specificity may lead to some confusion about how to express consent and whether consent was given in any one particular couple sexual situation. It is important to know how individuals communicate and interpret consent and nonconsent, particularly as it relates to possible sexual assault. More research is needed on how individuals conceptualize, give, and get sexual consent. Sex researcher Kristen Jozkowski and colleagues (2013, 2014) examined how Midwestern U.S. college men and women (N=185) define, communicate, and interpret sexual consent and nonconsent. Here is what the researchers found:

- There was no difference by gender regarding how consent was defined. Most participants stated that consent is defined as either an agreement to have sex or two people willing to have sex with each other. About 16% of students defined consent as "saying yes to sex."

- Overall, participants were more likely to endorse verbal cues than nonverbal indicators of consent, yet men were more likely than women to use nonverbal cues to express consent.

- Women were more likely than men to indicate consent via verbal cues and a combination of both verbal and nonverbal cues.

- Relative to verbal cues, men (27%) often reported telling their partner that they were "going to engage in sexual activity with them," and women frequently reported just allowing the sexual activity to happen or not saying no to the sexual activity. About one in five men (22%) said they ask the women if she wants to have sex.

- Participants were more likely to use nonverbal than verbal cues to interpret their partner's consent. This was the strategy most reported by men. However, women were more likely to rely on verbal cues for the partner's consent.

- Men, more than women, interpreted consent from their partners when they asked for sex and were told "yes." Women interpreted that their partner was consenting to sex when he was asking for it. Actually, about one-half of the women (47%) said they gave consent only after being asked by the man.

- Verbal communication or a combination of verbal and nonverbal cues were more often reported for the more intimate sexual behaviors such as penile-vaginal and penile-anal sex, whereas nonverbal communication was frequently reported for less intimate behaviors such as "fooling around/intimate touching."

- Some men (27%), in comparison to no women, utilized aggressive deceptive tactics to get sex.

- A few men (13%) pretended that intercourse occurred because of a mistake.

The researchers concluded that the gender differences found in this study "may help explain some misunderstandings or misinterpretations of consent or agreement to engage in sexual activity, which could possibly contribute to the occurrence of acquaintance rape." From the study findings, a greater attention to components of consent would appear to be an important addition to campus sexual assault prevention initiatives.

Think Critically

1. Do the study findings surprise you? If so, in what way? If not, why do you feel this way?
2. Which of the cues would you find most easy or difficult to do?
3. From the study's results would you likely change your method of getting sexual consent from a partner? If so, in what way?
4. What traditional sexual scripts were revealed in these studies?

SOURCE: Jozkowski, K. N., Peterson, Z. D., Sanders, S. A., Dennis, B., & Reece, M. (2014). Gender differences in heterosexual college students' conceptualization and indicators of sexual consent: Implications for contemporary sexual assault prevention education. *Journal of Sex Research, 51,* 904–915; Jozkowski, K. N., & Peterson, Z. D. (2013). College students and sexual consent: Unique insights. *Journal of Sex Research, 50,* 517–523.

Postrefusal Sexual Persistence   Men are more likely than women to think of male-female relationships as a "battle of the sexes." They believe that because relationships are conflictual, refusals are to be expected as part of the battle. A man may feel he should persist because his role is to conquer, even if he's not interested in sex. Researcher Cindy Struckman-Johnson and her colleagues (Struckman-Johnson, Struckman-Johnson, & Anderson, 2003) investigated college students' pursuit of sexual contact with a person after he or she has refused an initial advance, a behavior they call **postrefusal sexual persistence.** They believe that all postrefusal behaviors are sexually coercive, in that the other person has already communicated that he or she does not consent to the sexual behavior. The researchers examined tactics in four areas: (1) sexual arousal (e.g., kissing and touching, taking off clothes), (2) emotional manipulation and deception (e.g., repeatedly asking, telling lies), (3) exploitation of the intoxicated (e.g., taking advantage of and purposely getting a target drunk), and (4) physical force (e.g., blocking a target's retreat, using physical restraint) (see Figure 8). The researchers found that postrefusal sexual persistence was fairly common: Nearly 70% of the students had been subjected to at least one tactic of postrefusal sexual persistence since the age of 16, and one third indicated that they had used a tactic. More women (78%) than men (58%) reported having been subjected to such tactics since age 16, and more men (40%) than women (26%) reported having used such tactics.

Stranger Rape   As mentioned previously, NCVS reports that in 21% of cases involving women and 74% of cases involving men who were raped or sexually assaulted, the rape was committed by a stranger (U.S. Department of Justice, 2010). A typical stranger-rape scenario does not necessarily involve an unknown assailant hiding in the bushes or a stairwell on a dark night. Rather, it is likely to involve a chance meeting with a person who seems friendly and congenial. For example, a woman relaxes her guard because the man seems nice and even protective. He casually maneuvers her to an isolated place—an alley, a park, an apartment, or a house—where he quickly and brutally assaults her.

Marital Rape   By 1993, marital rape had become a crime in all 50 states, although the majority still have exceptions, usually with regard to the use of

• **FIGURE 8**

Percentage of College Men and Women Experiencing Postrefusal Sexual Persistence Tactics.

(*Source:* Adapted from Struckman-Johnson, Struckman-Johnson, & Anderson, 2003.)

Experienced the tactic

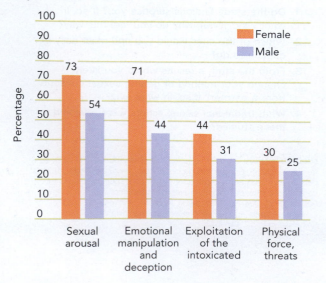

Perpetrated the tactic

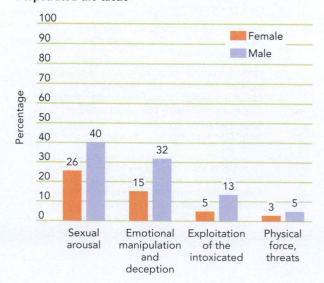

force. Laws against marital rape, however, have not traditionally been widely enforced. A review of marital rape literature found that marital rape is experienced by 10–14% of all married women and 40–50% of battered married women (Martin, Taft, & Resick, 2007).

Many people discount rape in marriage as a "marital tiff" that has little relation to "real" rape. Women are more likely than men to believe that a husband would use force to have sexual intercourse with his wife. When college students were asked to describe marital rape, they created "sanitized" images: "He wants to and she doesn't, so he does anyway," or "They are separated, but he really loves her, so when he comes back to visit, he forces her because he misses her." The realities are very different.

Marital rape survivors experience feelings of betrayal, anger, humiliation, and guilt. Following their rape, many wives feel intense anger toward their husbands; others experience constant terror because they are living with their assailant. A minority feel guilt and blame themselves for not being better wives. Others develop negative self-images and view their lack of sexual desire as a reflection of their own inadequacies rather than as a consequence of abuse. Many do not report rape, thinking that no one will believe them. Some do not even recognize that they have been legally raped. It's important to note that many of these responses to rape are experienced by both heterosexual and same-sex couples.

Gang Rape   Among adults, gang rape disproportionately occurs in close-knit groups such as fraternities, athletic teams, street gangs, prison groups, and military units. Gang rape may be perpetrated by strangers or acquaintances. It may be motivated not only by the desire to wield power but also by male-bonding factors. It is a common form of adolescent rape, most often occurring with strangers. When gang rape takes place on campus, the attackers may know the woman, who may have been invited to a party or an apartment, and alcohol is often involved (Sampson, 2003). The assailants demonstrate their masculinity and "share" a sexual experience with their friends. Gang sexual assaults are typically more violent than rapes committed individually. Hence, the victims of gang rape are more likely to suffer traumatic outcomes, such as posttraumatic stress syndrome and suicide attempts, than victims of a single rapist. Persons gang-raped report the rape to police and health care professionals more frequently than victims of a single offender do but they receive more negative social reactions from those they tell about their assaults than victims of a single offender (Gidycz & Koss, 1990; Ullman, 2007).

Statutory Rape   Consensual sexual contact with a person younger than a state's **age of consent**—the age at which a person is legally deemed capable of giving informed consent—is termed **statutory rape.** The laws rarely are limited to sexual intercourse but, instead, include any type of sexual contact. The age of consent varies from age 16 to 18 in most states. This means that individuals below the age of consent cannot legally consent to sex, and anyone having sex with them is, by definition, in violation of the law. In some states, factors such as age differences between partners, the age of the survivor, and the age of the defendant are considered (Glosser, Gardiner, & Fishman, 2004). To address situations in which both sexual partners are below the age of consent or the offender is near the age of the minor, some states have created "Romeo and Juliet laws." In some states a defense for no criminal charges is allowed. Other states have reduced punishment for statutory rape, such as imposing only a fine or probation eliminating the requirement to register as a sex offender ("Ask a

The husband cannot be guilty of rape committed by himself upon his lawful wife, for by their mutual matrimonial consent and contract, the wife gives herself in kind unto the husband which she cannot retract.

—Sir Matthew Hale
(1609–1676)

criminal lawyer," 2014). The enforcement of statutory rape laws, however, is generally sporadic or arbitrary. (To learn the age of consent law in a particular state, check the website http://www.sexlaws.org.)

Male Rape   Sexual assaults against males may be perpetrated by other men or by women. Most rapes of men are by other men. In some states, the word "rape" is used only to define forced vaginal sexual intercourse, whereas forced anal intercourse is termed "sodomy." More recently, states have started using gender-neutral terms such as "sexual assault" or "criminal sexual conduct," regardless of whether the victim is a man or a woman. To be specific, we have chosen the term "male rape."

Surveys reveal that men experience sexual victimization, although not at the same levels as women (Stemple & Meyer, 2014). For example, the National Intimate Partner and Sexual Violence Survey (Breiding et al., 2014) found that an estimated 1.7% of men (about 2 million men) were raped in their lifetimes and about one in five experienced other sexual violence (see Figure 6). Experts, however, believe that the statistics vastly underrepresent the actual number of males who are raped. Though society is becoming increasingly aware of male rape, the lack of complete tracking of sexual crimes against men and the lack of research about their effects on survivors are indicative of the attitude held by society at large—that although male rape occurs, the topic is not taken seriously. Although many people believe that the majority of male rape incidents occur in prison, research suggests that the conditions for male rape are not unique to prison. Rather, all men, regardless of who or where they are, should be regarded as potential victims.

There are also many reasons male victims do not come forward and report being raped. Perhaps the main reason is the fear of many that they will be perceived as being homosexual. Male sexual assault has nothing to do with the sexual orientation of the attacker or the survivor, just as a sexual assault does not make the victim gay, bisexual, or heterosexual. Male rape is a violent crime that affects heterosexual men as often as gay men (Men Can Stop Rape, 2007). Furthermore, the sexual orientation of the survivor does not appear to be of significance to half of the offenders, and most assailants in male rape are heterosexual.

In the aftermath of an assault, many men blame themselves, believing that they in some way granted permission to the rapist. One study of 358 men who had been sexually assaulted by another male found that those exposed to nonconsensual sex were about three times more likely to abuse alcohol and have attempted suicide than those who had not been victimized (Ratner et al., 2003). Male rape survivors suffer from fears similar to those felt by female rape victims, including the belief that they actually enjoyed or somehow contributed or consented to the rape. Heterosexual male survivors sometimes worry that they may have given off "gay vibes" that the rapist picked up and then acted on (Men Can Stop Rape, 2007). Some men may suffer additional guilt because they became sexually aroused and even ejaculated during the rape. These men, and our culture, may assume that if the man had an erection he must have wanted the sexual contact (Rosin, 2014). However, these are normal, involuntary, physiological reactions connected to the parasympathetic fear response and do not imply consent or enjoyment. Another concern for male rape survivors is society's belief that men should be able to protect themselves and that the rape was somehow their own fault.

Although they are uncommon, there are some instances of women sexually assaulting men. Despite being threatened with knives and guns, the men are able to have erections. No matter whether the male was sexually assaulted by a female or a male, many of these survivors may believe that the rape threatens the very essence of their masculinity and manhood (Ellis, 2002).

Sexual and Physical Violence Among Gay and Lesbian Individuals

Like mixed-sex couples, there is considerable sexual violence in gay and lesbian relationships. Forty-four percent of lesbian women and 61% of bisexual women, in contrast to 35% of heterosexual women, have experienced rape, physical violence, and/or stalking in their lifetime by an intimate partner. Twenty-six percent of gay men and 37% of bisexual men, in contrast to 29% of heterosexual men, have experienced rape, physical violence, and/or stalking in their lifetime by an intimate partner (Walters, Chen, & Breiding, 2013).

Characteristics of Rapists   A review of research (Baumeister, Catanese, & Wallace, 2002; Hanson & Morton-Bourgon, 2005; Hoertel, Strat, Schuster, & Limosin, 2012; Malamuth, Sockloskie, Koss, & Tanaka, 1991; Muehlenhard & Linton, 1987) found that sexually coercive men, in contrast to noncoercive ones, tend to share several characteristics:

- They hold traditional beliefs about women and women's roles.
- They grew up in a violent home environment.
- They have an antisocial orientation.
- They display hostility toward women.
- They believe in rape-supportive myths.
- They accept general physical violence.
- They express anger and dominance sexually.
- They report high levels of sexual activity.
- They use exploitative techniques.
- They report alcohol and drug use.
- They report early sexual experiences.
- They tend to be narcissistic, having low empathy and a sense of entitlement.
- They have significantly lower education.
- They are more likely to report having a wide range of antisocial behavior.

One study examined the patterns of sexually coercive behavior among samples of 266 Asian American men and 299 European American men for over one year. Men were classified into various groups, including sexually coercive and noncoercive, based on their sexual history. The researchers found that the strongest predictor of sexual coercive behavior was past sexual coercion. Also, the men who were persistently sexually coercive were higher than the other groups in delinquency and hostile masculinity (Hall, DeGarmo, Eap, Teten, & Sue, 2006).

Motivations for Rape

Most stranger rapes and some acquaintance or marital rapes can be characterized as anger rapes, power rapes, or sadistic rapes (Groth, Burgess, & Holmstrom, 1977; McCabe & Wauchope, 2005a, 2005b).

Anger Rape   Anger rapists are physically violent, displaying anger overtly such as by using a knife or force, and their victims often require hospitalization (McCabe & Wauchope, 2005b). For the rapist, rape is the ultimate method of expressing their anger. Sex is a weapon for humiliating and degrading the survivor. Victims are often forced to perform certain sexual behaviors, such as fellatio, on the assailant. Clinical psychologist Nicholas Groth (1979) describes anger rape in this way:

> The assault is characterized by physical brutality. Far more actual force is used . . . than would be necessary if the intent were simply to overpower the victim and achieve sexual penetration. . . . His aim is to hurt and debase his victim, and he expresses contempt for her through abusive and profane language.

Power Rape   Power rapes are acts of dominance and control. Typically, the rapist wishes not to hurt the victim but, rather, to dominate him or her sexually. The rape may be triggered by what the rapist regards as a slight to his or her gender identity. The rapist attempts to restore his or her sense of power, control, and identity by raping. He or she uses sex to compensate for a sense of sexual inadequacy, applying only as much force as is necessary to rape the victim (McCabe & Wauchope, 2005b). The rapist may believe that the victim may end up enjoying the rape even though there was initial resistance.

Sadistic Rape   A violent fusion of sex and aggression, sadistic rapes are by far the most brutal. A sadistic rapist finds "intentional maltreatment of his/her victim intensely gratifying and takes pleasure in her/his torment, anguish, distress, helplessness and suffering" (Groth & Birnbaum, 1978). The sexual assaults of the rapist are deliberate, calculated, and preplanned (Groth & Birnbaum, 1979). Bondage is often involved, and the rape may have a ritualistic quality. The victim is often severely injured and may not survive the attack. Although sadistic rapes are overwhelmingly the most brutal, they are also by far the least frequent.

The Aftermath of Rape

Rape crisis centers help sexual assault survivors cope with the effects of rape trauma.

© SCPhotos/Alamy

Most rape survivors report being roughed up by the rapist, and about 90% report some physical injury (Rape Network, 2000), although the vast majority do not sustain serious physical harm. Other effects of sexual assault can include substance abuse, self-harm, the Stockholm Syndrome (emotional bonding with the abuser), sleep disorders, depression, and **posttraumatic stress disorder (PTSD),** a group of characteristic symptoms that follow an intensely distressing event outside of a person's normal life experience (Rape, Abuse & Incest National Network, 2009e).

It is important that rape survivors gain a sense of control over their lives to counteract the feelings of helplessness they experienced during their rape. They need to cope with the depression and other symptoms resulting from their trauma.

Rape Trauma Syndrome   Rape is a traumatic event, to which the survivor may have a number of responses, and each survivor's response will vary depending on the situation (Rape, Abuse & Incest National Network, 2009e). The emotional changes undergone as a result of rape are collectively known as **rape trauma syndrome.** Rape survivors are likely to experience depression, anxiety, restlessness, and guilt. These responses are consistent with posttraumatic stress disorder (PTSD), an official diagnostic category of the American Psychiatric Association (2013). Anyone who has been raped can develop PTSD. The following description of the aftermath of rape is presented in the context of outcomes for women. In general, the impact of rape on male victims has been underestimated and overlooked in research. However, male rape survivors often experience significant physical and psychological trauma from the assault, including long-term effects of anxiety, depression, self-blame, loss of self-image, emotional distancing, feelings of anger and vulnerability, and self-harming behaviors (Ellis, 2002; Men Can Stop Rape, 2007; Walker, Archer, & Davies, 2005).

Rape trauma syndrome consists of two phases: an acute phase and a long-term reorganization phase. The acute phase begins immediately following the rape and may last for several weeks or more. In the first few hours after a rape, the person's responses are characterized by feelings of self-blame and fear. A woman may believe that she was somehow responsible for the rape: She was wearing something provocative, she should have kept her doors locked, she should have been suspicious of her attacker, and so on. Self-blame, however, only leads to depression. Following the acute phase, the rape survivor enters the long-term reorganization phase. The rape is a crisis in a person's life and relationships. In a nationally representative sample of 4,451 Australian women, aged 16–85 years, those who had been the survivor of rape, sexual assault, stalking, or intimate partner violence (27%) were drastically more likely to develop a mental disorder at some point in their lives. Fifty-seven percent reporting a history of sexual abuse also experienced depression, bipolar disorder, posttraumatic stress syndrome, substance abuse, or anxiety versus 28% of the women who had not experienced sexual violence. Nearly 9 of 10 (89%) of women who had been exposed to at least three different types of violence experienced mental illness or substance abuse. Episodes of the violence often occur early in life but the mental disorders may not emerge until years later. Given that the rates of sexual violence are nearly comparable in the United States and Australia, it has been hypothesized that a similar study conducted in the United States would reveal comparable findings (Rees et al., 2011).

A person who has been raped may be wracked by fears that the attacker will return, that he or she may be killed, that others will react negatively. There are often signs of tension, such as difficulty concentrating, hypervigilance, nausea, gastrointestinal problems, headaches, irritability, sleeplessness, restlessness, and jumpiness (Krakow et al., 2000). The rape survivor may also feel humiliated, angry, embarrassed, and vengeful. In general, women are more likely than men to display these varied symptoms following rape (Fergusson, Swain-Campbell, & Horwood, 2002; Sorenson & Siegel, 1992).

Long-term stress reactions are often exacerbated by the very social support systems and staff designed to assist people. These systems and individuals have sometimes proved to be more psychologically damaging to survivors than the rape itself, a phenomenon known as secondary victimization. Examples of these support systems and individuals include the criminal justice system, the media, emergency and hospital room personnel, social workers, family and friends, employers, and clergy. Nevertheless, the most important thing you can do to help someone you care about who suffers from symptoms of PTSD is to help him or her get professional help.

Lara Logan, a South African journalist and CBS correspondent, broke a month's-long silence when she revealed that she was sexually assaulted by a mob in Cairo's Tahrir Square just as the dictatorship of Hosni Mubarak was falling.

© Chris Hondros/Getty Images

Effects on Sexuality   Typically, both men and women find that their sexuality is severely affected for at least a short time after a rape. A review of numerous studies on the impact of sexual assault and sexual functioning clearly showed several serious outcomes:

- The frequency of sexual contact decreases after sexual assault.
- Avoidance of sexual contact appears to be related to sexual function difficulties.
- Sexual pleasure and satisfaction seem to diminish for a considerable group of victims for at least 1 year after the assault.

Supporting Someone Who Has Been Raped

The mission of the organization Men Can Stop Rape is to mobilize men to use their strength for creating cultures free from violence, especially men's violence against women. One of its fact sheets provides suggestions on helping people who say they were raped:

Supporting survivors: When someone says, "I was raped":

1. *Believe the person.* It is not your role to question whether a rape occurred but to be there to ease the pain.

2. *Help the person explore the options.* Don't take charge of the situation and pressure rape survivors to do what you think they should do. That's what the rapist did. Give them the freedom to choose a path of recovery that is comfortable for them, even if you'd do it differently. Remember, there is no one right way for a survivor to respond after being assaulted.

3. *Listen to the person.* It is critical that you let survivors know that they can talk to you about their experience when they are ready. Some may not wish to speak with you immediately, but at some point during the healing process, it is likely that they will come to you for support. When that happens, don't interrupt, or yell, or inject your feelings. Your caring but silent attention will be invaluable.

4. *Ask before you touch.* Don't assume that physical contact, even in a form of a gentle hug, will be comforting to survivors. Many survivors, especially within the first few weeks after assault, prefer to avoid sex or simple touching even with those they love and trust. One way to signal to survivors that you are ready to offer physical comfort is to sit with an open posture and a hand, palm up, nearby.

5. *Recognize that you have been assaulted, too.* We can't help but be hurt when someone we love is made to suffer. Don't blame yourself for the many feelings you will likely have in response to learning that someone close to you has been raped. Sadness, confusion, anger, helplessness, fear, guilt, disappointment, shock, anxiety, desperation, compassion—all are common reactions for survivors and their significant others.

6. *Never blame them for being assaulted.* No one ever deserves to be raped—no matter what they wore, how many times they had sex before, if they were walking alone at night, if they got drunk, if they were married, or if they went to the perpetrator's room. Even if survivors feel responsible, say clearly and caringly that being raped wasn't their fault.

7. *Get help for yourself.* Whether you reach out to a friend, family member, counselor, religious official, or whomever, make sure you don't go through the experience alone. Most rape crisis centers offer counseling for significant others and family members because they realize that the impact of rape extends far beyond the survivors. Keeping your feelings inside will only make you less able to be there for the survivors. Remember, getting help when needed is a sign of strength, not weakness.

- Some victims develop sexual function problems, such as fear and arousal and desire dysfunctions, which reoccur for years after the assault.

- Factors such as young age, a known offender, and penetration during the assault are related to sexual function difficulties.

- Emotions felt during and immediately after the assault, such as anger toward self, shame, and guilt, may predict sexual function problems.

- Sexual function problems are related to other psychological problems, including PTSD symptoms and depression.

- Some women perceive that their "mate value" has been diminished. In other words, some survivors perceive themselves to be less desirable following being raped.

The studies also revealed that a loving and understanding partner seems to be a protective factor in minimizing the negative outcomes of the sexual assault. Engaging in pleasurable, consensual sexual activities appears to help alleviate aversion feelings related to sexuality (Jozkowski & Sanders, 2012; Perilloux, Duntley, & Buss, 2012; van Berlo & Ensink, 2000).

● Child Sexual Abuse

Child sexual abuse is any sexual-related activity between an adult and a child. Child sexual abuse is not limited to penetration, force and pain, or touching but involves an adult engaging in any sexual behavior (e.g., looking, showing, or touching) with a child to meet the adult's interest or sexual needs. Abusive physical contact or touching includes: (1) an adult touching the child's genitals; (2) forcing a child to touch someone else's genitals or play sexual games; (3) putting a foreign object inside a child's vagina or anus; and (4) oral sex and vaginal or anal penetration by any body part of the adult. Non-contact sexual abuse includes: (1) showing sexually explicit images to a child; (2) deliberately exposing an adult's genitals to a child; (3) photographing a child in sexual poses; (4) encouraging a child to witness sexual behaviors; and (5) inappropriately viewing a child undress or use the bathroom. A growing and serious type of child sexual abuse is the making and downloading of sexual images of children on the Internet. A person who views sexually abusive images of children on the Internet is also considered to be participating in the abuse. In a broad sense, sexual touching between children can be considered child sexual abuse. This type of abuse is usually defined as when there is a significant age gap between the children (usually 3 or more years) or if the children are very different in terms of their development or size ("What is considered child sexual abuse?", 2014).

It does not matter whether the adult perceives the child to be engaging in the sexual activity voluntarily. Because of the child's age, he or she cannot give informed consent; the activity can only be considered as self-serving to the adult. The topic of child sexual abuse has received increased national attention due to the widespread allegations and verifications of child molestation against clergy in the Catholic Church. The revelation of widespread child sexual abuse by priests, bishops, and cardinals has rocked the nation and world, resulting in resignations, lawsuits, imprisonments, and even deaths, including those caused by suicide.

There are no reliable annual surveys of sexual assaults on children. The U.S. Department of Justice's annual National Crime Victimization Survey does not include victims aged 12 and younger. It is also difficult to know how many children are sexually abused because many cases are not reported. Further, because of the stigma of sexual abuse and the enormous emotional distress caused by abuse, many survivors keep the abuse a secret. One research study found that the amount of time between the end of sexual abuse and the survivor revealing the abuse averaged 14 years (Roesler, 2000). Twelve percent of men and 17% of women who participated in the National Health and Social Life Survey (Laumann, Gagnon, Michael, & Michaels, 1994) reported that they had been sexually touched when they were children. According to the congressionally mandated Fourth National Incidence Study of Child Abuse and Neglect (Sedlak et al., 2010), girls are sexually abused more often than boys. A 10-year review of published research on child sexual abuse found that the prevalence rate of being sexually abused as a child was 17% for adult women and 8% for adult men (Putnam, 2003). Worldwide, sexual contact between an adult and a child has been reported by about 20% of women and 8% of men (Pereda, Guilera, Forns, & Gomez-Benito, 2009). Most child sexual abuse is committed by men (Murray, 2000). In a nationally representative study, of the 1 in 15 U.S. adults who reported having been forced to have sex, 26% of women and 41% of men indicated that they were under 12 years of age at the time of the abuse. Thirty-five percent of women and 28% of men were between 12 and 17 years old (Basile et al., 2007).

Child sexual abuse is generally classified into two categories. **Intrafamilial child sexual abuse** is sexual abuse by biologically related people (parents and an older sibling) and is referred to as **incest. Extrafamilial child sexual abuse** is sexual abuse by acquaintances and strangers. (Figure 9 shows the type of relationship between the child survivor and the perpetrator in one study.) As shown, nonparent relatives were the most common offenders (30%) and parents were the least common (3%) (Snyder & Sickmund, 2006). Pedophilic disorder is classified by the American Psychiatric Association (2013) as recurrent (for at least 6 months), intense sexual urges with a prepubescent child or children that the individual has acted upon or finds distressing or that results in interpersonal difficulty. Sometimes the terms "child sexual abuse" and "pedophilia" are used interchangeably, and the line between them may be muddled, but the APA definition of pedophilic disorder is a more stringent definition than child sexual abuse. Most occurrences of child sexual abuse are attributed to pedophilic disorder (Murray, 2000). Child sexual abuse that does not meet the criteria for pedophilic disorder is an adult's sexual interaction with a child that is not necessary sexually motivated but may have other nonsexual motivations, such as anger, power, and aggression.

One cannot determine who is a child molester from appearance—child molesters look like ordinary people. But research has shown that child molesters, in general, differ from nonmolesters. They are usually heterosexual males (Valente, 2005) and often have, for example, lower intelligence, more-difficult family histories, less-developed social skills, lower self-esteem, and lower life satisfaction than nonmolesters (Finkelhor, 1990; Hunter, Figueredo, & Malamuth, 2003).

The victimization may involve force or the threat of force, pressure, or manipulation. Genital fondling and touching are the most common forms of child sexual abuse (Haugaard & Reppucci, 1998). The most serious or harmful

● **FIGURE 9**

Relationship Between the Child Survivor and the Perpetrator of Sexual Abuse.

(*Source:* Snyder, H. N., & Sickmund, M. [2006]. *Juvenile offenders and victims: 2006 national report.* Washington, DC: U.S. Department of Justice.)

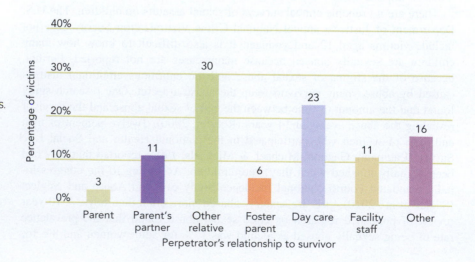

forms of child sexual abuse include actual or attempted penile-vaginal penetration, fellatio, cunnilingus, and anilingus (oral stimulation of the anus), with or without the use of force. Other serious forms of abuse range from forced digital penetration of the vagina to fondling of the breasts (unclothed) or simulated intercourse without force.

Effects of Child Sexual Abuse

Until recently, much of the literature on child sexual abuse was anecdotal, case studies, or small-scale surveys of nonrepresentative groups. Nevertheless, numerous well-documented consequences of child sexual abuse hold true for both intrafamilial and extrafamilial abuse. These include both initial and long-term consequences. Many child sexual abuse survivors experience symptoms of posttraumatic stress disorder (Day, Thurlow, & Wolliscroft, 2003; Paolucci, Genuis, & Violato, 2001).

In recent years, some women and men have stated that they were sexually abused during childhood but had repressed their memories of it. They later recovered the memory of it, often with the help of therapists. When these recovered memories surfaced, those accused often expressed shock and denied the abuse ever happened. Instead they insisted that those memories were figments of the imagination. The question of whom to believe has given rise to a vitriolic "memory war": recovered memories versus false memories. Each side has its proponents, and the fierce controversy about the nature of recovered memories of child sexual abuse continues today.

Initial Effects   The initial consequences of sexual abuse occur within the first couple of years or so and appear in many of the children survivors. Typical effects include the following (Calam, Horne, Glasgow, & Cox, 1998; Carlson, McNutt, & Choi, 2003; Wonderlich et al., 2000):

- *Emotional disturbances,* including fear, sadness, self-hatred, anger, temper tantrums, depression, hostility, guilt, and shame
- *Physical consequences,* including difficulty in sleeping, changes in eating patterns, and headaches
- *Sexual disturbances,* including significantly higher rates of open masturbation, sexual preoccupation, exposure of the genitals, and indiscriminate and frequent sexual behaviors that might lead to pregnancy and STIs
- *Social disturbances,* including difficulties at school, truancy, running away from home, and early marriages by abused adolescents. In fact, a large proportion of homeless youths are fleeing parental sexual abuse.

Long-Term Effects   Although there can be some healing of the initial effects, child sexual abuse may leave lasting scars on the adult survivor. These adults often have significantly higher incidences of psychological, physical, and sexual problems than the general population. Abuse may, for example, predispose some women to sexually abusive dating relationships.

Long-term effects of child sexual abuse include the following (Chen et al., 2010; Najman, Dunne, Purdie, Boyle, & Coxeter, 2005; Roller, Martsolf, Draucker, & Ross, 2009; Sachs-Ericsson et al., 2005):

- *Depression,* the symptom most frequently reported by adults sexually abused as children
- *Self-destructive tendencies,* including suicide attempts and thoughts of suicide

- *Somatic disturbances and dissociation,* including anxiety and nervousness, insomnia, chronic pain, eating disorders (anorexia and bulimia), irritable bowel syndrome, feelings of "spaciness," out-of-body experiences, and feelings that things are "unreal"
- *Health risk behaviors,* including tobacco use, alcoholism, obesity, and unsafe sexual behaviors that may result in STIs and unintended pregnancy
- *Negative self-concept,* including feelings of low self-esteem, isolation, and alienation
- *Interpersonal relationship difficulties,* including problems in relating to both sexes and to parents, in responding to their own children, and in trusting others
- *Revictimization,* in which women abused as children are more vulnerable to rape and marital violence
- *Sexual function difficulties,* in which survivors find it difficult to relax and enjoy sexual activities or in which they avoid sex and experience hypoactive (inhibited) sexual desire and lack of orgasm

A study of 534 women and 643 men attending a public STI clinic examined whether the severity of sexual abuse in childhood impacted sexual risk behavior in adulthood. The study found that penetration either by itself (i.e., without force) or with force was associated with greater sexual risk behavior. Specifically, those reporting childhood sexual abuse involving penetration and/or force also reported more lifetime sexual partners and more previous STI diagnoses. Also, men experiencing sexual abuse with force and penetration reported a greater number of episodes of sex trading (exchanging sex for money, drugs, etc.), and women who were abused with penetration, regardless of whether force was involved, reported the most episodes of sex trading. Hence, the more severe childhood sexual abuse was associated with riskier adult sexual behavior (Senn, Carey, Vanable, Coury-Doniger, & Urban, 2007).

Treatment Programs

As stated earlier in this section, survivors of childhood sexual abuse often suffer both immediate and long-term negative outcomes. It is vital that they receive adequate support and therapy involving both cognitive and behavioral approaches. Therapy should be available and considered for the child following the sexual abuse, as well as when the child becomes an adolescent and then an adult (McDonald et al., 2005). It is common now to deal with child sexual abuse by offering therapy programs that function in conjunction with the judicial system, particularly when the offender is an immediate family member, such as a father. Sex abusers also need treatment. This is important not only to assist these individuals in developing healthier child and adult relationships but also to avoid any future abuse episodes.

Preventing Child Sexual Abuse

Programs focusing on preventing child sexual abuse have been developed; however, they have been hindered by several factors. In confronting these problems, child abuse prevention (CAP) programs have been very creative. Most programs include group instruction in schools, either as a component of regular classroom instruction or as an after-school program. These programs typically address three audiences: children, parents, and professionals. CAP programs aimed at children use plays, puppet shows, films, visual media, books, and comic books to teach children that they have rights: to control their own bodies (including their genitals), to feel "safe," and to not be touched in ways that feel confusing or wrong. The CAP programs stress that children are not at fault when such abuse does occur. These programs generally teach children three strategies: (1) to say "no," (2) to get away from the assailant or situation, and (3) to tell a trusted adult about what happened and to keep telling until they are believed.

Other programs focus on educating parents, who, it is hoped, will in turn educate their children. These programs seek to help parents discover abuse or abusers by identifying warning signs. Parents seem reluctant in general to deal with sexual abuse issues with their children. Many do not feel that their children are at risk, are fearful of unnecessarily frightening their children, and may also feel uncomfortable talking with their children about sex in general, much less about such taboo subjects as incest. In addition, parents may not believe their own children's reports of abuse or may feel uncomfortable confronting a suspected abuser, who may be a partner, an uncle, a friend, or a neighbor.

CAP programs also seek to educate professionals, especially teachers, physicians, mental health workers, and police officers. Because of their close contact with children and their role in teaching children about the world, teachers are especially important. Professionals are encouraged to watch for signs of sexual abuse and, depending on their role, to report or investigate children's accounts of such abuse. Signs that may indicate the presence of child sexual abuse are nightmares or other sleep problems, depression or withdrawal from family or friends, statements from the child that there is something wrong with him or her in the genital area, unusual interest in or avoidance of all things related to sexuality, refusal to talk about a secret shared with an adult or older child, suddenly having money or other gifts without reason, and refusal to go to school (American Academy of Child and Adolescent Psychiatry, 2008; StopItNow, 2014).

In 1997, the U.S. Supreme Court ruled in favor of what is now referred to as Megan's Law. Enacted in 1995, the law requires law enforcement authorities to make information about registered sex offenders available to the public. That is, the law calls for schools, day-care centers, and youth groups to be notified about moderate-risk sex offenders in the community. For high-risk offenders, the law requires that the police go door-to-door, notifying neighborhood residents. It also requires sex offenders who have been paroled or recently released from prison to register with local authorities when moving to a community. The law is named for Megan Kanka, a 7-year-old who was raped and murdered by a twice-convicted sex offender who lived across the street from her. Although parts of the law have been challenged, the Supreme Court has rejected objections (Carelli, 1998). The Court ruled in 2003 that photos of convicted offenders may be posted on the Internet (CNN.com/Law Center, 2003). Most communities see the law as a welcome victory for their children.

In efforts to further prevent child sexual abuse, most states and many communities have enacted laws directed toward sex offenders to, for example, extend prison sentences, require offenders to register with the police, restrict where they can live (not near schools or playgrounds), improve public notification of their whereabouts, and order electronic monitoring (Koch, 2006). All states have Internet registries of sex offenders. For many of the legal attempts to make identity of sex offenders easily accessible to the public, constitutional and safety issues relative to the rights of the offender have been raised. For example, a man who shot two sex offenders to death in April 2006 indicated that he had gotten their names from the state's online sex offender registry ("Maine killer's use of sex-offender list," 2006). Human

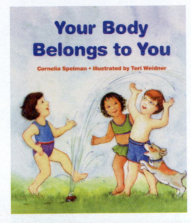

One objective of child sexual abuse prevention programs is to teach children the difference between "good" touching and "bad" touching.

"Your Body Belongs to You" by Cornelia Spelman and illustrated by Teri Weigner. Albert Whitman & Company publisher.

Rights Watch, in its report *No Easy Answers* (2007), states that state and federal laws designed to monitor released offenders and protect the public may be counterproductive—they may actually cause more harm than good. The report notes that laws restricting where sex offenders can live and requiring public notification of their crimes have not been shown to reduce sex crimes. Further, no other country in the world governs where sex offenders can live. Human Rights Watch says that, according to the U.S. Department of Justice, only 5.3% of sex offenders re-offend in 3 years (Human Rights Watch, 2007; Rozas, 2007). As you can see, efforts to protect children from sexual abuse can involve several components, not all of which are compatible and some of which are controversial.

Final Thoughts

Sexual harassment, anti-gay harassment and discrimination, sexual violence, and sexual abuse of children represent the darker side of human sexuality. Their common thread is the humiliation, subordination, or victimization of others. But we need not be victims. We can educate ourselves and others about these activities, and we can work toward changing attitudes and institutions that support these destructive and dehumanizing behaviors.

Summary

Sexual Harassment

- *Sexual harassment* includes two distinct types of illegal harassment: the abuse of power for sexual ends and the creation of a *hostile environment*. Sexual harassment may begin as early as middle childhood. In college, 6 in every 10 female students and male students have experienced some form of sexual harassment (verbal or physical) from other students, faculty members, or administrators.

- About 15% and 8% of men and women, respectively, have experienced being stalked in their lifetime.

- In the workplace, both fellow employees and supervisors may engage in sexual harassment. In many instances, harassment does not represent sexual attraction as much as an exercise of power.

Harassment and Discrimination Against Gay, Lesbian, Bisexual, and Transgender People

- Researchers have identified two forms of discrimination or bias against gay, lesbian, bisexual, and transgender people: heterosexual bias and anti-gay prejudice.

- *Heterosexual bias* includes ignoring, segregating, and submerging gay, lesbian, bisexual, and transgender people into larger categories that make them invisible.

- *Anti-gay prejudice* is a strong dislike, fear, or hatred of gay, lesbian, bisexual, and transgender people. It is acted out through offensive language, discrimination, and violence. Anti-gay prejudice is derived from a deeply rooted insecurity concerning a person's own sexuality and gender identity, a strong fundamentalist religious orientation, or simple ignorance.

Sexual Violence

- *Rape* is typically defined as penile-vaginal penetration performed against a woman's will through the use or threat of force. Males can be raped; most rapes of men are by other men. *Sexual violence* refers to any sexual activity against a person's will through the use of force, argument, pressure, alcohol/drugs, or authority. *Sexual coercion,* a broader term than "rape" or "sexual aggression," includes arguing, pleading, and cajoling, as well as force or the threat of force. *Sexual assault* is the term used by the legal system for criminal sexual contact that does not meet the legal definition of rape.

- Myths about rape encourage rape by blaming women. Men are more likely than women to believe rape myths.

- Nearly 1 in 5 women and 1 in 50 men have been raped sometime in their lives.

- Sexual violence on many college campuses is a serious problem, with one in five women reporting being sexually assaulted while in college. An increasing acknowledgment of the extent of student sexual assault has fueled demands that colleges and universities make their campuses safer.

- Sexual consent is often difficult to determine, given that we usually don't give verbal consent to sexual activity.

- *Date rape* and *acquaintance rape* are common forms of rape. Alcohol or drugs are often involved. There is also considerable sexual coercion in gay relationships; there is less coercion in lesbian relationships.

- The majority of reported rapes are by strangers. Stranger rapes are more likely to involve guns or knives than date or acquaintance rapes.

- Gang rape may be perpetrated by strangers or acquaintances. It may be motivated by a desire for power and by male-bonding factors.

- Most male rape survivors have been raped by other men. Because the motive in sexual assaults is power and domination, sexual orientation is often irrelevant.

- Most stranger rapes (and some acquaintance and marital rapes) can be characterized as anger rapes, power rapes, or sadistic rapes.

- The emotional changes undergone as a result of rape are collectively known as *rape trauma syndrome*. These survivors may experience depression, anxiety, restlessness, and guilt. The symptoms following rape are consistent with *posttraumatic stress disorder (PTSD)*. Rape trauma syndrome consists of an acute phase and a long-term reorganization phase. Women find their sexuality severely affected for at least a short time after being raped.

Child Sexual Abuse

- *Child sexual abuse* is any sexual interaction between an adult and a child. *Incest* is sexual contact between individuals too closely related to legally marry.

- The initial effects of abuse include physical consequences and emotional, social, and sexual disturbances. Child sexual abuse may leave lasting scars on the adult survivor.

- *Sexual abuse trauma* includes traumatic sexualization, betrayal, powerlessness, and stigmatization. Treatment programs use both cognitive and behavioral psychotherapy to assist the survivor.

- Child abuse prevention (CAP) programs that focus on skills training, such as self-protective behaviors, appear to be the most effective. CAP programs generally teach children to say "no," to get away from the assailant or situation, and to tell a trusted adult about what happened.

Questions for Discussion

- How common is sexual harassment on your campus? What makes it sometimes difficult to determine the difference between flirting and sexual harassment?

- What are your reactions to the California "Yes means yes" law requiring both participants of a sexual encounter to say "yes" prior to and ongoing throughout the encounter?

- Why do you think people rape? Are they mainly motivated by need for sexual gratification, by need for power and control, or by other reasons?

- What do you think you could do to help someone who has been raped? What resources or organizations would you recommend?

- Have you observed anti-gay prejudice? If so, what could have been done to prevent it, if anything?

- What do you think can be done to prevent child sexual abuse?

Sex and the Internet

Not Alone

NotAlone.gov is a website of the White House Task Force to Protect Students from Sexual Assault. Its purpose is convey to students that they are not alone and to help schools live up to their obligation to protect students from sexual violence. The site provides information for students, schools, and anyone interested in finding resources on how to respond to and prevent sexual assault on college and university campuses and in our schools. Click on various resources and answer these questions:

- What type of reports, documents, and resources does the site provide?

- What are the resources in your area to get support if you are in a crisis situation?

- What are your rights under federal law and your school's responsibility to respond to sexual violence?

- How can one file a sexual assault complaint with one's school or university and what happens after the complaint is filled?

- What hotlines and other resources that deal with sexual violence are available?

Suggested Websites

Feminist Majority Foundation

http://www.feminist.org

Discusses its latest projects and gives information about feminist issues.

Human Rights Campaign

http://www.hrc.org

Offers the latest information on political issues affecting lesbian, gay, bisexual, and transgender Americans.

Movement Advancement Project

http://www.lgbtmap.org

An independent think tank that provides research, insight, and analyses that help expedite equality for lesbian, gay, bisexual, and transgender people.

National Coalition of Anti-Violence Programs

http://www.avp.org

The only national coalition dedicated to reducing violence among lesbian, gay, bisexual, and transgender individuals.

National Sexual Violence Resource Center

http://www.nsvrc.org

A project of the Pennsylvania Coalition Against Rape; a resource for information about rape and links to other sites.

Stop It Now

http://www.stopitnow.org

Provides support, information, and resources to help keep children safe.

Stop Street Harassment

http://www.stopstreetharassment.org

A nonprofit organization dedicated to documenting and ending gender-based street harassment worldwide.

Stop Violence Against Women

http://www.stopvaw.org

A forum for information, advocacy, and change in promoting women's human rights worldwide.

U.S. Equal Employment Opportunity Commission

http://www.eeoc.gov

Provides information on federal laws prohibiting job discrimination and gives directions for filing a charge.

Suggested Reading

Bass, E., & Davis, L. (2008). *The courage to heal* (4th ed.). New York: HarperCollins. A comprehensive guide that weaves together personal experience and professional knowledge to assist survivors of sexual abuse.

Cook, P. W., & Hodo, T. L. (2013). *When women sexually abuse men: The hidden side of rape, stalking, harassment, and sexual assault.* Westport, CT. Addresses an overlooked aspect of sexual violence: male rape by females. Beyond rape, the text also examines sexual harassment, stalking, and sexual assault of men by women.

Fetner, T. (2008). *How the religious right shaped lesbian and gay activism.* Minneapolis: University of Minnesota Press. Descriptions of the two movements are significantly shaped by their rivals.

Real, A. K., & Evans, P. (2014). *Living through this: Listening to the stories of sexual violence survivors.* Boston: Beacon Press. Rape and sexual violence survivors describing how their lives have been shaped, but not redefined, by their sexual violence.

Reddington, F. P., & Kreisel, B. W. (2009). *Sexual assault: The victims, the perpetrators, and the criminal justice system.* Durham, NC: Carolina Academic Press. A discussion of the legal aspects of victimization and other topics such as rape myths, male victims, and perpetrators. Great reference for clinics, survivors, and families.

Richards, T. N., & Marcum, C. D. (2014). *Sexual victimization: Then and now.* Thousand Oaks, CA: Sage. Examines the continuum of sex crimes and the perception of survivors and society.

Sandy, P. R. (2007). *Fraternity gang rape: Sex, brotherhood, and privilege on campus.* New York: New York University Press. Discusses the nature of fraternity gang rape and how Greek life in general contributes to a culture that promotes the exploitation of women on college campuses.

Temkin, J., & Krahe, B. (2008). *How ignorance perpetuates sexual assault myths, abuse, and injustice.* Portland, OR: Hart. A concise and detailed discussion of the justice gap, the gap between the number of offenses recorded by the police and the number of convictions.

Sexually Explicit Materials, Prostitution, and Sex Laws

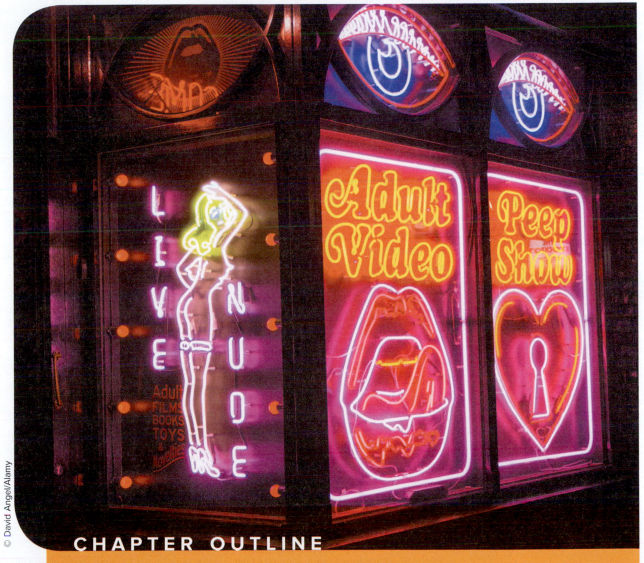

© David Angel/Alamy

"My boyfriend and I sometimes use X-rated movies while we have sex. We have learned some new techniques from them, and they really help us get turned on. Some of our friends had recommended that we get them. At first, we were a little hesitant to use them, but now watching the movies has become a regular part of our sex. But I wonder if something is wrong with us having to use the movies. And, at times, I still feel uncomfortable using them. I sure haven't told any of my friends about them."

—21-year-old female

"I was only sixteen when I traveled to Peru with Carlos, who was twenty-nine. We were in Lima for two days, and while we were there, Carlos took me to a hotel so we could both have sex with prostitutes. At the time, I did not really understand what was happening until after it occurred. Carlos knew that I was a virgin and thought this would be a fantastic way for me to become a 'man.' I felt embarrassed, dirty, and ashamed of myself."

—24-year-old male

"She (my aunt) actually started molesting me when I was six. She would come home late at night, drunk, and carry me into her bed so that she could perform oral sex on me. She molested me until I was twelve years old. She was a prostitute, so later in my molestation she tried to include her tricks, but I cried my way out of it every time."

—26-year-old female

MONEY AND SEX are bound together in the production and sale of sexually explicit material and in prostitution. Money is exchanged for sexual images or descriptions contained in films, electronic media, magazines, books, music, and photographs that depict people in explicit or suggestive sexual activities. Money is also exchanged for sexual services provided by streetwalkers, call girls, escorts, massage parlor workers, and other sex workers. The sex industry is a multibillion-dollar enterprise with countless millions of consumers and customers. As a nation, however, we feel ambivalent about sexually explicit material and prostitution. Many people condemn it as harmful, immoral, and exploitative and wish to censor or eliminate it. Others see it as a harmless and even beneficial activity, an erotic diversion, or an aspect of society that cannot or should not be regulated; they believe censorship and police action do greater harm than good.

In this chapter, we examine sexually explicit material, including depictions of sex in popular culture, the role of technology in the distribution of sexually explicit material, the effects of sexually explicit material, and censorship issues. We then examine prostitution, focusing on females and males working in the sex industry, the legal issues involved, and the impact of HIV and other STIs. We then discuss current laws dealing with private, consensual sexual behavior among adults and end the chapter with legal issues related to gay marriage.

> *Since the human body is perfect in all forms, we cannot see it often enough.*
>
> —Kenneth Clark
> (1903–1983)

> *Obscenity is best left to the minds of man. What's obscene to one may not offend another.*
>
> —William O. Douglas
> (1898–1980)

● Sexually Explicit Material in Contemporary America

Studying sexually explicit material objectively is difficult because such material often triggers deep and conflicting feelings we have about sexuality. Many people enjoy sexually explicit material, others find it degrading, and still others may simultaneously feel aroused and guilty.

Pornography or Erotica: Which Is It?

As sexual themes, ideas, images, and music increasingly appear in art, literature, and popular culture, the boundaries blur between what is socially acceptable and what is considered erotic or obscene. Much of the discussion about sexually explicit material concerns the question of whether such material is, in fact, erotic or pornographic—that is, whether viewing it causes positive or harmful outcomes. Unfortunately, there is a lack of agreement about what constitutes erotica or pornography. Part of the problem is that "erotica" and "pornography" are subjective terms, and the line separating them can be blurred. **Erotica** describes sexually explicit material that can be evaluated positively. (The word "erotica" is derived from the Greek *erotikos,* meaning "a love poem.") It often involves mutuality, respect, affection, and a balance of power and may even be considered to have artistic value. **Pornography** represents sexually explicit material that may be evaluated negatively and might include anything that depicts sexuality and causes sexual arousal in the viewer. ("Pornography" is a nineteenth-century word derived from the Greek *porne,* meaning "prostitute," and *graphos,* meaning "depicting.") Webster's *New World Collegiate Dictionary* defines pornography as "writing, pictures, etc. intended to arouse sexual desire."

Sexually explicit materials are legal in the United States; however, materials that are considered to be obscene are not. Although the legal definition of **obscenity** varies, the term generally implies a personal or societal judgment that something is offensive; it comes from the Latin word for "filth." Often, material depicting the use of violence and aggression or degrading and dehumanizing situations is deemed obscene. Because such a determination involves a judgment, critics often point to the subjective nature of this definition. (Obscenity and the law are discussed in detail later in the section.)

The same sexually explicit material may evoke a variety of responses in different people. "What I like is erotica, but what you like is pornography" may be a facetious statement, but it's not entirely untrue. It has been found that people view others as more adversely affected than themselves by sexually explicit material. Judgments about sexually explicit material tend to be relative.

Because of the tendency to use "erotica" as a positive term and "pornography" as a negative term, we will use the neutral term "sexually explicit material" whenever possible. **Sexually explicit material (SEM)** is material such as photographs, videos, films, magazines, and books whose primary themes, topics, or depictions involve sexuality that may cause sexual arousal; the genitals or intimate sexual behaviors typically are shown. Sometimes, however, the context of studies we are citing may require us to use either "erotica" or "pornography" rather than "sexually explicit material." This is especially true if the studies use those terms or are clearly making a positive or negative evaluation.

Sexually Explicit Material and Popular Culture

In the nineteenth century, technology transformed the production of sexually explicit material. Cheap paper and large-scale printing, combined with mass literacy, created an enormous market for books and drawings, including sexually explicit material. Today, technology is once again extending the forms in which this material is conveyed.

In recent decades, sexually explicit material, especially soft-core (material that portrays sexual behaviors in a highly suggestive rather than an explicit way), has become an integral part of popular culture. Until the advent and expansion

> *How can you accuse me of liking pornography when I don't even have a pornograph?*
> —Groucho Marx (1890–1977)

> *The difference between pornography and erotica is lighting.*
> —Gloria Leonard (1940–2014)

> *Obscenity is whatever happens to shock some elderly and ignorant magistrate.*
> —Bertrand Russell (1872–1970)

The touching of one's genitals by music performers sends a strong sexually explicit message.

© Mat Hayward/Getty Images

The *Fifty Shades of Grey* novels and the movie have been polarizing: Some believe they depict a romantic and erotic story that encourages women to explore their sexuality whereas others think that they glorify abusive intimate relationships.

© Guy Corbishley/Alamy

of the Internet, *Playboy, Penthouse,* and *Hustler* were among the most widely circulated magazines in America. The depiction of sexual activities is not restricted to online and print material, however. Various establishments offer live entertainment. Bars, for example, feature nude dancers. Some clubs or adult entertainment establishments employ erotic dancers who expose themselves and simulate sexual behaviors before their audience, and some even have "live sex shows." The Internet, cable and satellite television sex channels, and DVD revolutions have been so great that homes have largely supplanted adult theaters or "porno" movie houses as sites for viewing sexually explicit films. The sexually explicit material industry is big business in the United States, with an estimated revenue of several billion dollars annually (Dines, 2010).

The availability of in-home media such as sexually explicit films and downloadable clips and films on the Internet has had a profound effect on *who* views erotic films. In the past, adult movie houses were the domain of men; relatively few women entered them. Most explicit DVDs or films, as well as books and magazines, have been marketed to heterosexual men. However, in part because of the success of shows like *Sex and the City* and books and films like *Fifty Shades of Grey,* women are becoming the fastest-growing consumers of adult entertainment and erotica, including sexually explicit materials and sex toys (Comella, 2008). But with erotic films available for viewing in the privacy of the home, women and couples have become consumers of sexually explicit material. The inclusion of women in the audience has led to the production of **femme porn,** sexually explicit material catering to women and heterosexual couples. Compared to other types of porn, femme porn typically involves women in its production and has story lines that depict emotional intimacy and greater equality between the sexes, is less male centered, avoids violence, and is more sensitive to women's erotic fantasies (Milne, 2005).

The Consumption of Sexually Explicit Materials

Studies have been conducted to assess public consumption of sexually explicit materials (SEM), why people use online erotic material, and their preferences for visual sexual stimuli. Many people use SEM. For example, national random sampling surveys of adults 18 or older found that 25–35% and 15–20% of men and women, respectively, report having viewed a sexually explicit video in the last year (Buzzell, 2005). The General Social Survey, a national random personal-interview survey, revealed that in 1970 26% of adult men had seen sexually explicit videos and 34% had viewed them in 2010 (Wright, 2013). With the dramatic increase in computer availability and use on college campuses, college students have ample access to sexually explicit websites. In general, male students have greater consumption and acceptance of sexually explicit videos than female students (Willoughby, Carroll, Nelson, & Padilla-Walker, 2014). For example, a study of college students from the northwestern United States found that 92% of men and 50% of women reported having used SEM in their lifetime (Morgan, 2011). Finally, an examination of 969 college students in the southeastern United States found that 33% reported viewing sexually explicit video in the past 30 days: Among these students, 35% reported viewing the videos once, 31% a few times a month, 10% about weekly, 14% a few times a week, 6% daily, 2% a few times a day, and 2% several times a day (Braithwaite, Coulson, Keddington, & Fincham, 2015). (For more information about the findings of these three studies, see the "Think About It" box "College Students and the Viewing of Sexually Explicit Materials".)

The reason people utilize online pornography has been understudied. A study of 321 undergraduate male and female students assessed specific motivations for Internet pornography use and how gender and erotophilia/erotophobia are associated with motivations (Paul & Shim, 2008). Four motivations for online viewing of erotic material were found: (1) to build or maintain a relationship; (2) for mood management, such as to increase arousal or for entertainment; (3) out of habit; and (4) for the purpose of sexual fantasy—to feel as if they themselves were interacting with the actors in the sexual scenes. Males showed stronger motivations for viewing the pornography than females for all four of the motivations. Last, the more erotophilic students (those who had more positive sexual attitudes) were more likely than the more erotophobic students to be motivated to use Internet pornography for all four motivations.

Fifteen men and 30 women (15 using oral contraception), heterosexual and aged 23–45, were shown 216 sexual pictures to determine whether men and women had preferences for certain types of visual sexual stimuli. Men and women did not differ in their overall interest in the photos, as indicated by equal subjective ratings and the amount of time viewing the pictures. The researchers note that this finding is counter to commonly held assumptions that men find visual sexual stimulation more interesting and arousing than do women. The study also found that both genders rated pictures of the other sex receiving oral sex as least sexually attractive. Participants looked longer at photos of intercourse in which they could more clearly see the female's body. Women rated pictures showing an indirect female gaze more attractive, but the males did not indicate any difference in preference. Also, participants did not look as long at close-up genital images, and women using oral contraceptives and men found these images as less sexually attractive as photos less focused on the genitals. These findings show overall comparable interest in the sexual photos between men and women, although there were some sex-specific differences (Rupp & Wallen, 2009).

Themes, Content, and Actors of Sexually Explicit Videos

Many of the themes found in sexually explicit material are also found in the mainstream media. Music videos, TV shows, and movies, for example, often contain sexual scenes and innuendos and images of the subordination of women. They differ primarily in their levels of explicitness.

Many "mainstream" sexually explicit videos target a male, heterosexual audience and portray stereotypes of male sexuality: dominant men with huge, erect penises, able to "last long" and satisfy eager and acquiescent women who are driven mad by their sexual prowess. The major theme of the films is "cookbook" sex; they show fellatio, cunnilingus, vaginal and anal sex, climax with the man ejaculating on the woman's body or face (called "the cum shot"), and the woman often faking an orgasm. The focus is typically on the physical beauty of the woman "star," with threesomes (two women and one man) or group sex sometimes featured. The male actors may not even be "good-looking" (Cassell, 2008; Paul, 2006).

Studies assessing the impact of viewing Internet sexually explicit videos have been increasing, but little research on the content of the videos has been conducted. One major contentious issue of these videos is whether or not they depict gender

> Perversity is the muse of modern literature.
>
> —Susan Sontag (1933–2004)

> The older one grows, the more one likes indecency.
>
> —Virginia Woolf (1882–1941)

think
about it

College Students and the Viewing of Sexually Explicit Materials

Accessibility to and acceptability of sexually explicit materials (SEM) are becoming more widespread in our increasingly technological world. In contrast to the 1980s, when one would have to go to a store and ask for "porn" magazines (often located behind the counter) or visit an adult theater (located in a "seedy" part of town), young people today can easily access SEM on the Internet or on satellite television. Given the easy access to SEM, it is important to examine the prevalence, acceptance, and associations of SEM among young people. The major findings of four studies of SEM and college students are presented here.

Researchers at Indiana University used a study group of 245 college students to assess the effects of pornography from their perspective (Weinberg, Williams, Kleiner, & Irizarry, 2010). The study focused on determining if viewing pornography appeared to expand sexual horizons through normalization as well as enhance willingness to try new sexual behaviors and relationships through empowerment. The qualitative data found that viewing pornography can expand the appeal and expression of a variety of sexual behaviors. That is, pornography's profusion and dissemination of sexual scripts seem to have, for some people, a liberating impact. For example, there was an association between the frequency of viewing pornography among heterosexual men and the appeal of vibrator use as sometimes depicted in pornography. The researchers noted, however, that this normalization did not necessarily lead to desire or empowerment to engage in sex with partners outside the relationship.

Family life researcher Jason Carroll of Brigham Young University and his colleagues assessed pornography use among 813 men and women college students from six college sites across the United States (Carroll et al., 2008). Pornography was defined as media (such as Internet, movies, and/or magazines) portraying nudity and sexual behaviors used to increase or intended to increase sexual arousal. Here are some of their major findings:

- About two thirds of the men and one half of the women agreed that viewing pornography is an acceptable way to express one's sexuality.
- Nearly 9 in 10 of the men and nearly one third of the women reported using pornography. Nearly half of the men and only 3% of the women reported pornography use weekly or more often.

- For men, significant associations were found between use of pornography and greater number of lifetime sexual partners and higher acceptance of premarital, casual, and extramarital behaviors.
- For women, higher acceptance and use of pornography were significantly related to higher acceptance of casual sexual behavior, greater number of sexual partners in the past 12 months and lifetime, and alcohol use, binge drinking, and cigarette use.

Psychology researcher Elizabeth Morgan of Boise State University examined how levels of SEM use during adolescence and young adulthood are related to sexual preferences, sexual behaviors, and sexual and relationship satisfaction among 782 college men and women from the northwestern region of the United States (Morgan, 2011). Viewing pornography was defined as intentionally looking at pictures of nude individuals, movies in which there are nude individuals, pictures or movies of people having sex, written or audio material that describes people having sex, or real-life nude individuals. Sex was defined as vaginal, anal, or oral penetration. Major findings included the following:

- Slightly over 9 in 10 young men and one half of young women reported ever having used various types of SEM.
- Men participants were more likely to have used all types of SEM than women except sexually explicit books.
- Women users were more likely to report viewing SEM with a dating partner, whereas men users were more likely to report viewing SEM alone, when not in a relationship, and when masturbating.
- Higher frequency of SEM use and consumption of a greater number of SEM types were found to have significant association with more sexual experience (i.e., higher number of sexual intercourse partners, higher number of casual partners, and lower age of first intercourse).
- The frequency of SEM use and number of types of SEM viewed were both associated with stronger sexual preferences for the types of sexual behaviors typically presented in the SEM.

A study involving undergraduate students from a public university in the southeastern United States examined whether an association exists between viewing sexually explicit videos and hooking up (Braithwaite et al., 2015). The findings revealed that more frequent viewing of the videos was associated with higher incidence of hooking up and a higher number of unique hooking-up partners. Not only was this association for kissing and intimate touching but it also was for more risky sexual behaviors such as oral sex and sexual intercourse. Finally, the study found that more frequent viewing of the videos was associated with having had more previous sexual partners of all types, more one-occasion sexual partners ("one-night stands"), plans to have a higher number of sexual partners in the future, and more permissive sexual scripts.

These studies were exploratory in nature. Given the relatively high prevalence of SEM use among college students, further studies of SEM use, such as longitudinal and experimental research, should be conducted. For example, does the viewing of SEM among young people for long periods of time cultivate unrealistic expectations in their own sexual expression with a partner that could lead to pervasive dissatisfaction, or do most young adults recognize the difference between some SEM and real-life experiences? Further, the studies reported here examined the association of SEM use with other variables such as frequency of sexual behaviors; cause and effect was not established. Exploring whether the sex-related attitudes, behaviors, and feelings precede or follow SEM use would be beneficial (Morgan, 2011).

Think Critically

1. Do any of the findings surprise you? If so, which ones and why are they surprising?

2. After reading the findings, do you feel more or less accepting of SEM as a positive way of expressing your sexuality?

3. Do you believe that SEM use impacts college students' sexual attitudes and behavior negatively (e.g., leads to unrealistic expectations) or positively (e.g., is a healthy way for a couple to learn new sex techniques that improve their relationship)? If no, why? If yes, why and how?

4. If you were presenting a lecture on SEM to college students, what are the most important messages you would convey?

SOURCES: Braithwaite, S. R., Coulson, G., Keddington, K., & Fincham, F. D. (2015). The influence of pornography on sexual scripts and hooking up among emerging adults in college. *Archives of Sexual Behaviors, 44,* 111–123; Carroll, J. S., Padilla-Walker, L. M., Nelson, L. J., Olson, C. D., Barry, C. M., & Madsen, S. D. (2008). Pornography acceptance and use among emerging adults. *Journal of Adolescent Health, 23,* 6–30; Morgan, E. M. (2011). Associations between young adults' use of sexually explicit materials and their sexual preferences, behaviors, and satisfaction. *Journal of Sex Research, 48,* 520–530; Weinberg, M. S., Williams, C. J., Kleiner, S., & Irizarry, Y. (2010). Pornography, normalization, and empowerment. *Archives of Sexual Behavior, 39,* 138–141.

equality (e.g., women are generally objectified). Researchers from the University of Amsterdam conducted a content analysis of 400 sexually mainstream explicit Internet videos (both professional and amateur produced) from four of the most visited "porn" websites (Pornhub, RedTube, YouPorn, and xHamster) (Klaassen & Peter, 2014). These websites are mainly aimed for the heterosexual audience. The analysis focused on three main dimensions of gender equality: objectification, power, and violence. The objectification dimension was defined as instrumentality (a female or male body used for another person's sexual gratification and an emphasis of the body or body parts of one actor while the other actor gained sexual pleasure) and dehumanization (whether the actor was depicted as having feelings and thoughts and as making his or her own choices). Power was defined as depicted dominance/submission power differences independent of sexual activity (e.g., boss, doctor, secretary, student, social roles) and power differences in the context of sex. Violence was defined as physically violent acts and response and coerced sex. The researchers concluded, from the study findings, that "the vast majority of sexual activities in these videos were depicted as consensual" (p. 10). Here are detailed findings of the study that lead to the researchers' conclusions:

- *Objectification.* The women actors, in contrast to the men actors, were more likely to be instrumentalized. Close-ups of women's body parts (61% of sex scenes) included close-ups of their genitals, buttocks, and/or breasts; close-ups of men's genitals, buttocks, and/or chest (19%) occurred less frequently. Men actors (69%) were more often manually stimulated than women (59%). Oral stimulation of men (81%) was more often depicted than women (48%) being stimulated orally. Men (76%) were more likely to experience orgasm than were women (17%). Relative to dehumanization, no evidence was found of a general dehumanization of women. But men were more likely dehumanized than women. About an equal proportion of the sex scenes showed men (36%) initiating sex and women (32%) initiating sex. Men actors (94%) were slightly more likely to be depicted as having sex for their own enjoyment and pleasure than were women actors (85%). However, more scenes showed women's faces in close-ups (59%) than the faces of men (12%).

- *Power.* The depiction of power independent of sexual activity between the men actors and women actors was nearly equal. However, power differences in the sexual activities more likely depicted men as dominant and women as submissive, although over 4 of 10 scenes (46%) showed equal dominance/submission.

- *Violence.* When violent behaviors were shown, women (37%) were more likely than men (3%) to be the recipients. The violent behaviors toward women were typically spanking (in 27% of scenes) and inserting penis very far into a woman's mouth (19%). More violent behaviors were rarely depicted. In response to these violent behaviors, women responded neutrally (61%), positively (12%), or first appearing to be in displeasure then switching to expressing pleasure (20%). Relative to depiction of coerced sex, 6% of both men and women were depicted as not initially wanting to engage in sexual activity. Less than 1% of the scenes depicted both men and women actors as intoxicated. Although scenes of being manipulated were rare, women (5%) were depicted as being manipulated more frequently than men (1%).

One criticism of most sexually explicit films is that they do not represent the unique individuality of sexual expression or how women experience erotic fulfillment. Very little focus is on relationships, emotional intimacy, nonsexual aspects of life, or the woman's sexual satisfaction. Rarely are lovers shown massaging each other's shoulders or whispering "I love you." Nor do lovers ask each other questions such as "Is this OK?" or "What can I do to help you feel more pleasure?" (Castleman, 2004). Some sex therapists criticize these films as reinforcing an unhealthy and unrealistic image of sexuality: That men are all-powerful and that women are submissive objects, deriving all sexual satisfaction from male domination. Further, the films can also give a false impression of how sex should be experienced and how bodies should look. They can give an impression that all men have large penises and that women derive more pleasure from large penises despite that research shows that most women indicate that a larger penis does not increase their ability to experience an orgasm (Costa, Miller, & Brody, 2012). Other myths portrayed by the videos are that all women remove their hair in the genital and anal area and that women can experience orgasm easily and from almost any intercourse position (Lehmiller, 2014).

Gay and lesbian sexually explicit films differ somewhat from heterosexual-focused films. Gay porn typically features attractive, young, muscular, "well-hung" men and focuses on the eroticism of the male body. Lesbian-explicit films usually depict realistic sexual interactions with a range of body types and both butch (notably masculine in manner or appearance) and femme styles. Sex between men is rarely shown in heterosexual films, presumably because it would make heterosexual men uncomfortable. But heterosexual-focused films may sometimes portray sex between women because many heterosexual men find such depictions sexually arousing.

Beyond any negative or positive attitudes toward sexually explicit videos, many people wonder what type of a person chooses to be a "porn star." In general, actresses in the adult video entertainment industry are viewed more negatively than typical women (Polk & Cowan, 1996). This stereotyped perception of adult video performers and sex workers, in general, is called the "damaged goods" hypothesis. This hypothesis has not been based on scientific studies but comes from public perception. It contends, for example, that actresses in the sexually explicit video industry have come from extremely bad backgrounds, are less psychologically healthy than nonperformer women, are drug abusers, and were abused as children. However, these perceptions lack scientific support. To address this void, a study was conducted to compare the self-reports of 177 "porn actresses" to a matched sample of woman based on age, ethnicity, and marital status (Griffith, Mitchell, Hart, Adams, & Gu, 2012). The study found that the actresses were more likely to consider themselves bisexual, had first sex at an earlier age, had more sexual partners, were more concerned about contracting an STI, and enjoyed sex more than the matched sample. However, there was no difference in child sexual abuse. Porn actresses had higher levels of self-esteem, positive feelings, social support, sexual satisfaction, and spirituality than the matched group. However, women performers were more likely to have ever used 10 different types of drugs than the comparison group. The researchers concluded by declaring that the findings did not support the "damaged goods" hypothesis. They state that "the majority of indicators of recent functioning suggested that porn actresses are not impaired compared to the matched sample with regard to CSA [child sexual abuse] rates, quality of life, self-esteem, and recent drug use, and that they appear more similar to women not employed as porn actresses than previously thought" (p. 11).

Another study of 134 women adult film performers found several differences when comparing women performers to a matched group of women (Grudzen et al., 2011). The actresses initiated sex 3 years earlier, had seven more personal sexual partners, and were more likely to use condoms consistently in their personal lives than the matched women. The researchers concluded that the women adult film performers we more likely to engage in HIV/STI risk behaviors when compared to the matched group of women.

Little is known about the characteristics of men adult film performers. A study was conducted to compare the self-reports of 105 porn actors to a sample of matched men based on age, ethnicity, and marital status (Griffith et al., 2012). The findings indicated that the actor's first sex was at an earlier age, they had more sexual partners and a higher enjoyment of sex, they were more concerned about contracting an STI, and they were less likely to use a condom during a first-time sexual encounter in comparison to the matched sample of men. The actors also had higher levels of self-esteem and quality-of-life indicators, were more likely to have used five different types of drugs, and were more likely to have used marijuana in the past 6 months than the matched group. There was no difference in the self-report of childhood sexual abuse between the two groups. The researchers concluded that the findings indicate a mixed support for negative stereotypes of men adult film performers.

The Effects of Sexually Explicit Material

There are a number of concerns about the effects of sexually explicit material. Beyond what was discussed in the prior section on the Internet and SEM, researchers have questions such as: Does SEM cause people to engage in "deviant" behavior? Is it a form of sex discrimination against women? And, finally, does it cause violence against women?

Western man, especially the Western critic, still finds it very hard to go into print and say: "I recommend you go and see this because it gave me an erection."

—Kenneth Tynan
(1927–1980)

Sexual Expression People who read or view sexually explicit material usually recognize it as fantasy; they use it as a release from their everyday lives. Exposure to such material temporarily encourages sexual expression and may activate a person's *typical* sexual behavior pattern or enhance experimentation. A study of 4,600 young people, aged 15–25, living in the Netherlands found that there was a direct association between watching sexually explicit media and a variety of sexual behaviors—in particular, adventurous behaviors—but the association was small (Hald, Kuyper, Adam, & de Wit, 2013). Given this, the researchers concluded that the "data suggest that other factors such as personal disposition—especially sexual sensation seeking—rather than consumption of sexually explicit material may play a more important role in a range of sexual behaviors of adolescents and young adults" (quoted in Molnar, 2013). Researchers from the University of Zagreb (Croatia) used data from a population-based sample of 1,005 Croatian adults aged 18–25 to assess if use of pornography and sexual sensation was related to risky sexual behavior (Sinkovic, Stulhofer, & Bozic, 2013). The researchers concluded that "overall, the findings do not support the notion that pornography use is substantially associated with sexual risk taking among young adults, but suggest that early exposure to sexually explicit material and high sexual sensation seeking are additive risk factors for sexual risk taking."

Sexually explicit material deals with fantasy sex, not sex as we know it in the context of human relationships. This sex usually takes place in a world in which people and situations are defined in exclusively sexual terms. People are stripped of their nonsexual connections. They are interested in sexually explicit material for a number of reasons. First, they enjoy the sexual sensations erotica arouses; it can be a source of intense pleasure. Masturbation or other sexual activities, pleasurable in themselves, may accompany the use of SEM or follow it. Second, since the nineteenth century, SEM has been a source of sexual information and knowledge. Eroticism generally is hidden from view and discussion. Because the erotic aspects of sexuality are rarely talked about, SEM can fill the void. Third, sexually explicit material, like fantasy, may provide an opportunity for people to rehearse sexual activities. Fourth, reading or viewing SEM to obtain pleasure or to enhance one's fantasies or masturbatory experiences may be regarded as safer sex.

Sex therapist Barbara Keesling (2006) states that she often recommends the use of sexually explicit materials to women who experience low sexual desire and sexual arousal problems. She notes that "women can sometimes learn to become more aroused by retraining themselves in the ability to feel physical arousal at the sight of sexually explicit images." Keesling also states that since some women may "shut down" because of their belief that some sexually explicit material may be disgusting, they should try to find material that is both acceptable and arousing to them. Men are cautioned that sexually explicit materials are typically all-genital and that such focus can cause problems in sexual expression with others; they should not buy into the idea that sex should occur as it does in most adult films. Medical writer Michael Castleman (2004) suggests the following for men, although his advice could also apply to women:

> Stop trying to imitate what you see in pornography—the rushed, mechanical sex that's entirely focused on the genitals. Instead, cultivate the opposite of porn: leisurely, playful, creative, whole-body, massage-based lovemaking that includes the genitals, but is not obsessed with them.

The only thing pornography has been known to cause is solitary masturbation.

—Gore Vidal
(1925–2012)

Whatever you choose, however many roads you travel, I hope that you choose not to be a lady. I hope you will find some way to break the rules and make a little trouble out there. And I also hope that you will choose to make some of that trouble on behalf of women.

—Nora Ephron
(1941–2012)

Among some romantic couples, the use of sexually explicit videos occurs by individual partners or with both partners jointly. Studies have been conducted on the relationship of video use in couples and components of the romantic relationship such as sexual and relationship satisfaction. (To find out what the studies found, see the "Think About It" box "College Students and the Viewing of Sexually Explicit Materials.")

With the increasing availability of sexual videos, a new label for high-frequency use has emerged in the popular media and clinical practice: porn addiction. Related to the term "sex addiction," proponents who espouse this label believe that it is "excessive use" of porn that leads directly to individual breakdown such as job loss and divorce. Rarely is this label used by scientists who study high-frequency sexual behavior and many actually reject the label. The new edition of the *Diagnostic and Statistical Manual* (*DSM*) does not include sex addition, illustrating the contention that it may not even exist. Clinical psychologist David Ley and colleagues (Ley, Prause, & Finn, 2014) examined the scientific literature dealing with pornography use, concluding that there is insufficient scientific evidence to support this model. Simply because someone frequently repeats a behavior does not mean it is a problem and certainly not an addiction. Whenever negative outcomes follow such behaviors, the impact of other factors such as relationship status and culture must first be examined. Persons using visual sexual stimuli (VSS) report being more aroused by VSS as well as reporting greater sexual desire. They also are more aroused by VSS use. Ley and colleagues state that

> the ability to label VSS use as addictive appears to serve sociocultural functions. The label supports moralistic judgments, the stigmatization of sexual minorities, and suppression of certain sexual expressions and behaviors. The concept of porn addiction is one mechanism to exert social control over sexuality as expressed or experienced through modern technological means. (p. 101)

Sexual Aggression   In 1970, the President's Commission on Pornography and Obscenity concluded that pornography did not cause harm or violence. It recommended that all legislation restricting adult access to it be repealed as inconsistent with the First Amendment.

In the 1980s, President Ronald Reagan established a new pornography commission under Attorney General Edwin Meese. In 1986, the Attorney General's Commission on Pornography stated that "the most prevalent forms of pornography" were violent; it offered no evidence, however, to substantiate its assertion (U.S. Attorney General's Commission on Pornography [AGCOP], 1986). There is, in fact, no evidence that the majority of sexually explicit material is violent; actually, very little contains aggression, physical violence, or rape, as shown in the Klaassen & Peter (2014) study cited earlier.

In the 1970s, feminists and others working to increase rape awareness began to call attention to the violence against women portrayed in the media. They found rape themes in sexually explicit material especially disturbing, arguing that those images reinforced rape myths. Again, however, there is no evidence that nonviolent sexually explicit material is associated with actual sexual aggression against women. Even the conservative commission on pornography agreed that nonviolent sexually explicit material had no such effect (AGCOP, 1986). It did assert that "some forms of sexually explicit

Some contemporary video games have strong, suggestive sexual messages.

© Paul Sakuma/AP Images

think
about it

Sexually Explicit Material Use in Romantic Couples: Beneficial or Harmful?

The impact of using sexually explicit materials (SEM) by individuals has been widely studied. However, what about couples? Viewing SEM may have an effect on a person, but is SEM related to couple sexual and relationship quality? To any extent that SEM can influence individual sexual expression and pleasure, the overall couple relationship may also be influenced. As we know, there is a strong correlation between a couple's sexual satisfaction and the relationship satisfaction. Often, couples or one couple partner wonders if the use of SEM is beneficial or harmful to the relationship quality. Unfortunately, the use of SEM as related to relationship quality has received limited research attention.

This box highlights the major findings of recent studies of SEM and couples, followed by a brief summary of a sample of other reports. As varied terms are used in these studies, we use the terms used in the specific study. An association between two study variables, such as pornography use and relationship commitment, does not show cause and effect. For example, use of SEM may contribute to less relationship commitment or a weaker relationship commitment may lead to more SEM use.

Four hundred four primarily heterosexual students (largely undergraduate) from a large southeastern U.S. university were assessed to determine their expectations for pornography use while in a committed relationship or while married (Olmstead, Negash, Pasley, & Fincham, 2013). Students completed online surveys that included open-ended questions in which they provided written comments. Here are the major findings, followed by a few of the student comments:

- Seventy percent of men and 46% of women reported circumstances (alone or with a partner) in which pornography use was acceptable.

- About one quarter of men and women viewed pornography use unacceptable because they were in a committed relationship.

- Five percent and 13% of men and women, respectively, reported that pornography use was unacceptable in any situation.

- The acceptance was more conditional for women than men: Women were less accepting if pornography use became habitual and "addictive" and wanted to

protect the quality of their partner's continued love, respect, and commitment them.

- Many believed watching pornography alone or together would enhance the relationship.

- Among those accepting pornography, many comments focused on viewing pornography to improve the quality of their sexual relationship and add "spice" to the sexual and couple relationship.

- Among those not accepting pornography, comments largely focused on a belief that pornography was not necessary since they had a partner to fulfil their sexual needs and that their partner used pornography because of deficits in the partner or the relationship.

"My expectation is for each of us to use proper discretion. Yes, I think it is okay for each of us to view them while we are alone or together. I think it is completely normal for someone to be turned on or sexually attracted to the way someone else looks. I admit that I am at times. But at the same time there is a bold line of discretion when a harmless couple minutes turns into a couple hours habit."

—18-year-old woman (p. 631)

"Viewing these materials could help the relationship. A circumstance in which you can view these alone is if you want to surprise your loved one with a new move that you couldn't think of. To watch it together can help you think of another way to have sex, like coming up with different positions.

—18-year-old man (p. 630)

"Viewing porn can be potentially dangerous to a relationship. If viewed alone, without a partner knowing it can create secrets in the relationship and could be their first step to cheating. It could, however, be used as a way to spice up things in the bedroom if viewed together."

—22-year-old man (p. 628)

"Personally, I don't believe it's bad or it's good. Sexually explicit material simply shows human sexuality put into action. One partner or the other can view it as long as both consent to the sexually explicit material. However, it should not take away from the overall passion of the relationship, and if it does then it has become excessive."

—20-year-old woman (p. 630)

"Sexually explicit material should not be in a marriage or a relationship. That adds additional stress to be perfect or compare yourself to the people that your partner is fantasizing about. You shouldn't view them even together, because sometime down the road it will cause problems whether it be addiction, jealousy, or infidelity."

—18-year-old man (p. 631)

A study of 617 couples who were married or cohabiting examined the associations among pornography use and relationship satisfaction and sexual quality (Poulsen, Busby, & Galovan, 2013). Use of pornography by males was associated with lower sexuality quality (satisfaction with physical intimacy experienced in their relationship and how often problems occurred) for both men and women. However, female use of pornography was associated with greater female sexual quality. A Norwegian national representative study of 398 heterosexual couples found that couples who used pornography together to enhance their sexual relationship (15% of the sample) had an open erotic climate relative to talking about sexual desires and fantasies, less male erection problems, and less negative views of self for the female (Daneback, Traeen, & Mansson, 2009).

Higher pornography consumption was related to lower relationship commitment among a sample of 367 college undergraduates (Lambert, Negash, Stillman, Olmstead, & Fincham, 2012). Higher frequencies of SEM use were related to less sexual and relationship satisfaction among a sample of 782 college students (Morgan, 2011). A Canadian study of 340 women found that those women who believed that their partners were honest about their pornography use reported higher levels of relationship satisfaction. Mutual pornography use was not associated with higher levels of relationship satisfaction (Resch & Alderson, 2013). Finally, an Internet study of 217 heterosexual couples revealed that men's use of sexual media (e.g., written stories, videos, telephone sex, and Internet erotic chatting) was associated with less couple satisfaction for both men and women. Women's use of sexual media was related to greater relationship satisfaction for the men, but the sexual media use was not related to the women's relationship satisfaction. In contrast to solitary sexual media use, shared use was related to greater relationship satisfaction. Further, no relationship between sexual functioning and sexual use has been found for both men and women (Bridges & Morokoff, 2011).

Think Critically

1. Did any of the study findings concur with or dispute your beliefs about SEM? Explain.

2. If you are in relationship (or imagine you are), how would you feel about using SEM alone, or with your partner? If your partner used SEM?

3. In your view, does the use of SEM among couples have more positive or negative outcomes? Explain.

SOURCES: Bridges, A. J., & Morokoff, P. J. (2011). Sexual media use and relational satisfaction in heterosexual couples. *Personal Relationships, 18,* 562–585; Daneback, K., Treen, B., & Mansson, S. (2009). Use of pornography in a random sample of Norwegian heterosexual couples. *Archives of Sexual Behavior, 38,* 746–753; Lambert, N. M., Stillman, T. F., Olmstead, S. B., & Fincham, F. D. (2012). A love that doesn't last: Pornography consumption and weakened commitment to one's romantic partner. *Journal of Social and Clinical Psychology, 31,* 41–438; Morgan, E. M. (2011). Associations between young "adults" use of sexually explicit materials and their sexual preferences, behaviors, and satisfaction. *Journal of Sex Research, 48,* 520–530; Olmstead, S. B., Negash, S., Pasley, K., & Fincham, F. D. (2013). Emerging adults' expectations for pornography use in the context of future committed relationships: A qualitative study. *Archives of Sexual Behavior, 42,* 625–635; Poulsen, F. O., Busby, D. M., & Galovan, A. M. (2013). Pornography use: Who uses it and how it is associated with couple outcomes. *Journal of Sex Research, 50,* 72–83; Resch, M., & Alderson, K. (2013). Female partners of men who use pornography: Are honesty and mutual use associated with relationship satisfaction? *Journal of Sex & Marital Therapy.* doi: 10.1080/00926623X.2012.751077.

materials bear a causal relationship . . . to sexual violence," but it presented no scientific proof.

A review of research studies and violent crime data was conducted to determine any influence of pornography on sexual aggression (Ferguson & Hartley, 2009). The review found that evidence for a causal relationship between exposure to pornography and sexual aggression was slim and inconsistent. Further, at the time of the study, the United States rate for rape was decreasing and the availability and consumption of pornography was increasing, as also occurred in most industrial countries. From the review, the researchers concluded that "Considered altogether, the available data about pornography consumption and rape rates in the United States seem to rule out a causal relationship, at least with respect to pornography availability causing an increase in the incidence of rape." The researchers suggested that the available research and official statistics might actually provide evidence of a catharsis effect of pornography; that is, the use of pornography might actually be a way of alleviating sexual aggression. However, they point out that the data

My reaction to porno films is as follows: After the first ten minutes, I want to go home and screw. After the first twenty minutes, I never want to screw anything as long as I live.

—Erica Jong
(1942–)

cannot scientifically be used to determine that pornography has a cathartic effect on rape behavior. Recall, we have noted in this book that a correlation between two variables does not show cause and effect.

Contact with sexually explicit material is a self-regulated choice, and research on factors related to such self-directed behavior is very limited: "Existing findings by and large fail to confirm fears of strong antisocial effects of self-directed exposure to sexually explicit media" (Fisher & Barak, 2001). Despite some of these more recent findings, whether violent sexually explicit material causes sexual aggression toward women remains a fractious issue.

Sex Discrimination   Since the 1980s, feminists have been divided over the issue of sexually explicit material. One segment of the feminist movement, which identifies itself as antipornography, views sexually explicit material as inherently degrading and dehumanizing to women. Many in this group believe that sexually explicit material provides the basis for women's subordination by turning them into sex objects. They argue that SEM inhibits women's attainment of equal rights by encouraging the exploitation and subordination of women.

Feminist and other critics of this approach point out that it has an antisexual bias that associates sex with exploitation. Sexually explicit images, rather than specifically sexist images, are singled out. Furthermore, discrimination against and the subordination of women in Western culture have existed since ancient times, long before the rise of sexually explicit material. The roots of subordination lie far deeper. The elimination of sexual depictions of women would not alter discrimination against women significantly, if at all. Sex researchers William Fisher and Clive Davis, in their review of research on the impact of sexually explicit materials, state that sexual scientists are against any anti-woman attitudes and aggression that some people fear would result from experience with pornography. They suggest that remedies for such attitudes and behavior linked to pornography could be achieved through education, policies and laws, and social change, for example (Fisher & Davis, 2007). However, they also state:

> The inconsistent evidence connecting pornography with harm would indicate that efforts to fight pornography as a way of combating anti-woman attitudes and anti-woman aggression would not effectively bring about the sought-after result.

Leonore Tiefer (2004), clinical associate professor of psychiatry at the New York University School of Medicine and sex therapist who is a primary spokesperson for newer views of women's sexuality, states that sexually explicit materials can contribute to women's sexual power. She notes that empowerment, not protection, is the path to sexual growth in women. Tiefer states that

> if we accept that women's sexuality has been shaped by ignorance and shame and is just beginning to find new opportunities and voices for expression, then now is exactly the wrong time to even think about campaigns of suppression. Suppressing pornography will harm women struggling to develop their own sexualities.

Child Pornography   Child pornography is a form of child sexual exploitation. Children used for the production of sexually explicit materials, who are usually between the ages of 6 and 16, are motivated by friendship, interest in sexuality, offers of money, or threats. Younger children may be unaware that their photographs are being used sexually. A number of these children are related to the photographer. Many children who have been exploited in this way exhibit distress and poor adjustment; they may suffer from depression, anxiety, and guilt. Others engage in destructive and antisocial behavior.

Digital cameras and smartphones with cameras, plus the ability to download photographs onto computers, have made this into what some call the "golden age of child pornography." Children and teenagers have been reported taking pictures of each other and posting them on the Internet or sending them to each other, a practice called "sexting." The fact that the possession of such images is a crime does not deter people from placing or viewing them on the Internet. Laws governing obscenity and child pornography already exist and, for the most part, can be applied to cases involving the Internet to adequately protect minors. Unlike some sexually explicit material, child pornography has been found to be patently offensive and therefore not within the zone of protected free speech. Internet child pornography is common.

Censorship, Sexually Explicit Material, and the Law

To censor means to examine in order to suppress or delete anything considered objectionable. **Censorship** occurs when the government, private groups, or individuals impose their moral or political values on others by suppressing words, ideas, or images they deem offensive. Obscenity, as noted previously, is the state of being contrary to generally accepted standards of decency or morality. During the first half of the twentieth century, under American obscenity laws, James Joyce's *Ulysses* and the works of D. H. Lawrence were prohibited, Havelock Ellis's *Studies in the Psychology of Sex* was banned, nude paintings were removed from gallery and museum walls, and everything but chaste kisses was banned from the movies for years.

U.S. Supreme Court decisions in the 1950s and 1960s eliminated much of the legal framework supporting literary censorship on the national level. But censorship continues to flourish on the state and local levels, especially among schools and libraries. The women's health book *The New Our Bodies, Ourselves* has been a frequent object of attack because of its feminist perspective and descriptions of lesbian sexuality. Two children's books have been added to the list of most censored books: Lesléa Newman's *Heather Has Two Mommies* and Michael Willhoite's *Daddy's Roommate*. Both books have come under attack because they describe children in healthy lesbian couple and gay couple families. Judy Blume's books for teenagers, J. D. Salinger's *The Catcher in the Rye,* and the *Sports Illustrated* swimsuit issue are regular items on banned-publications lists. And exhibits of the photographs taken by the late Robert Mapplethorpe have been strenuously attacked by the more conservative groups for "promoting" homoeroticism.

Obscenity Laws Sexually explicit material itself is not illegal, but materials defined as legally obscene are. It is difficult to arrive at a legal definition of obscenity for determining whether a specific illustration, photograph, novel, or film is obscene. Traditionally, U.S. courts have considered material obscene if it tended to corrupt or deprave its user. Over the years, the law has

> **"** A dirty book is seldom a dusty one.
> —Anonymous

> **"** If a man is pictured chopping off a woman's breast, it only gets an "R" rating; but if, God forbid, a man is pictured kissing a woman's breast, it gets an "X" rating. Why is violence more acceptable than tenderness?
> —Sally Struthers (1948–)

Two of the most heavily censored books in America are Lesléa Newman's *Heather Has Two Mommies* and Michael Willhoite's *Daddy's Roommate* (shown here). These books are opposed because they depict a lesbian couple family and a gay couple family, respectively.

© Michael Willhoite from *Daddy's Roommate,* Alyson Books, 1991

been debated in a number of court cases. This process has resulted in a set of criteria for determining what is obscene:

- The dominant theme of the work must appeal to prurient sexual interests and portray sexual conduct in a patently offensive way.
- Taken as a whole, the work must be without serious literary, artistic, political, or scientific value.
- A "reasonable" person must find the work, when taken as a whole, to possess no social value.

The problem with these criteria, as well as the earlier standards, is that they are highly subjective. For example, who is a reasonable person? Most of us would probably find that a reasonable person has opinions regarding obscenity that closely resemble our own. Otherwise, we would think that he or she was unreasonable. However, there are many instances in which "reasonable people" disagree about whether material has social value. In 1969, the U.S. Supreme Court ruled, in *Stanley v. Georgia,* that private possession of obscene material in one's home is not illegal (Sears, 1989). This does not, however, apply to child pornography.

As we saw earlier, our evaluation of sexually explicit material is closely related to how we feel about such material. Our judgments are based not on reason but on emotion. Justice Potter Stewart's exasperation in *Jacobelis v. Ohio* (1965) reveals a reasonable person's frustration in trying to define pornography: "But I know it when I see it."

The Issue of Child Protection

In 1988, the United States passed the Child Protection and Obscenity Enforcement Act, which supports stiff penalties for individuals involved in the production, distribution, and possession of child pornography. Since then, the development and distribution of child pornography, as well as minors' access to online pornography, have been the focus of the U.S. Congress, resulting in the passing of numerous legislative acts. As you can see in Table 1, the bills have most often been turned down by the courts, usually based on protection of free speech; however, there have been a few instances of the courts upholding the law.

The Communications and Decency Act of 1996 tried to address the problem of sexual exploitation of children and teens over the Internet by making it a crime to send obscene or indecent messages to minors via e-mail, chat rooms, and websites (Biskupic, 2004). In 1997, the U.S. Supreme Court ruled that the statute was not constitutional because it violated the First Amendment's guarantee of free speech. In two subsequent rulings, the Court rejected the law that made it a crime to send an indecent message online to a person under age 18 and rejected the ban on computer-generated "virtual" child pornography and other fake images of sex, saying that the law could have banned works of art (Biskupic, 2002, 2003a, 2004). However, in 2008, the U.S. Supreme Court upheld the Child Obscenity and Pornography Act of 2003, a law that made it a crime to produce or possess sexually explicit images of children as well as to "pander" to willing audiences through advertising, presenting, distributing, or soliciting such material. The 2003 law applies even if the material consists solely of computer-generated images or digitally altered photographs of adults, and even if the offer of material is fraudulent (e.g., the material does not exist) (Greenhouse, 2008; Mears, 2008). Justice Antonin Scalia, writing for the majority, noted, "Offers to provide and obtain child pornography are categorically

TABLE 1 • Congressional Efforts to Protect Children From Online Pornography and Court Rulings

1996	The Communications Decency Act is passed by Congress, banning the posting or sending of obscene or indecent messages on the Internet to persons under age 18.
1998	The Child Online Protection Act (COPA) is passed by Congress, targeting material "harmful to minors" only on commercial websites. The age of those protected is lowered to under 17. COPA is challenged by the American Civil Liberties Union and online publishers on the grounds that it violates free-speech rights.
1999	The Communications Decency Act is rejected by the U.S. Supreme Court, calling it too vague and broad.
2000	COPA is struck down by a U.S. appeals court citing the statute's attempt to set "community standards" for the Internet. COPA defined materials that should be banned as those that "the average person, applying contemporary community standards, would find . . . designed to appeal to . . . the prurient interest."
2002	The Supreme Court rules that the use of community standards does not, by itself, make COPA too broad.
2003	A U.S. appeals court again rejects COPA, saying that the law is not the least restrictive way the government can shield minors from online porn.
2004	COPA is not permitted to take effect by ruling of the U.S. Supreme Court. The justices suggest that the law is likely unconstitutional and that computer software filters may be a less restrictive way to screen sexually explicit materials. The statute is sent back to a lower court.
2007	U.S. district court judge issues a permanent injunction against COPA, stating that it violates the First and Fifth Amendments of the U.S. Constitution. The federal government appeals the ruling.
2009	COPA ends as the U.S. Supreme Court turns away the government's final attempt to revive the law.

SOURCE: Adapted from "Congress' Attempts at Limits Have Faced Several Obstacles," *USA Today,* June 30, 2004, p. 6A (Years 1996–2004). Reprinted with permission.

excluded from the First Amendment" (quoted in Greenhouse, 2008). Free-speech proponents question whether mainstream movies or innocent photographs of babies and young children, for example, might now be subject to prosecution.

Another law intended to keep adult material away from Net-surfing children is the Child Online Protection Act (COPA). Passed in 1998, it sought to require Internet users to give an adult ID before accessing a commercial site containing "adult" materials (Miller, 2000). The law has been blocked twice by the U.S. Supreme Court. Table 1 provides a summary of congressional efforts to protect children from online pornography and subsequent court rulings. In its 2004 ruling, the U.S. Supreme Court stated that the use of filtering software on home computers might be the best method of shielding children from pornography while preserving the rights of adults. Justice Kennedy wrote for the majority, stating that the Court presumes that any government attempts to limit explicit materials on the web are unconstitutional (Biskupic, 2004). In 2007, COPA was again struck down. A U.S. district court judge ruled that the defendant (the federal government) had failed to show that COPA is the least restrictive, most effective alternative in achieving the goal of shielding minors from online pornography and that COPA is impermissibly vague and overbroad. The judge also noted that "perhaps we do the minors harm if First Amendment protections, which they will inherit fully, are chipped away in the name of their protection" (U.S. District Court, Eastern District of Pennsylvania, 2007). In January 2009, COPA ended more than a decade after Congress had approved it. The U.S. Supreme Court rejected the government's final effort to revive the law by turning away the appeal without comment ("Internet pornography law dies quietly in Supreme Court," 2009).

With millions of children accessing the Internet from home, serious questions must be asked about their access to certain kinds of information, pictures, graphics, videos, animation, and interactive experiences. Government censorship,

> To slurp or not to slurp at the fountain of filth is a decision to which each of us is entitled.
>
> —Stephen Kessler

> Murder is a crime. Describing murder is not. Sex is not a crime. Describing sex is.
>
> —Bill Margold (1943–)

academic freedom, constitutionally protected speech, child safety concerns, public health dilemmas—these and other troublesome issues are at the core of the Internet–free-speech debate.

Our inability to find criteria for objectively defining obscenity makes it potentially dangerous to censor such material. We may end up using our own personal standards to restrict speech otherwise guaranteed by the First Amendment. By enforcing our own biases, we could endanger the freedom of others.

● Prostitution

The exchange of sexual behaviors such as intercourse, fellatio, anal intercourse, discipline and bondage, and obscene insults for money and/or goods is called **prostitution.** More recently, instead of the term "prostitute," the terms "sex worker" and "commercial sex worker" have often been used, particularly by prostitutes, to identify themselves and other work in the "sex industry" such as phone sex, exotic dancing, Internet sex, and acting in sexually explicit films. Many individuals who enter prostitution do so for monetary gains; hence, prostitution can represent a form of work (Cobbina & Oselin, 2011). However, given that some research shows negative aspects of prostitution and that some prostitutes are coerced by a third party, some feminists are uncomfortable with connoting prostitution as a type of sex work and are hesitant to "celebrate the existence of a market for commoditized sex" (Davidson, 2002). We have decided to use the term "prostitution/prostitute," to distinguish it from other types of "sex work." However, we recognize that "sex work" is a term preferred by many prostitutes and is becoming more frequently used to describe prostitution.

Boys and girls as well as men and women, including cross-dressers, transgender persons, and transsexual persons work as prostitutes. By far the most common form of prostitution is women selling sex to men. The second most common is male prostitutes making themselves available to men. Less common is males selling sex to females. Prostitution between two women is rare. A growing international market of child and teenager sex slaves has fueled the economies of developing countries and spawned a multibillion-dollar industry commonly referred to as "sex trafficking" (see the "Think About It" box "Sex Trafficking: A Modern-Day Slavery").

Male customers of female prostitutes, called "johns," represent a wide range of occupations, ethnicities, ages, and marital statuses. Although the seeking of prostitution is often considered a natural part of the masculine sexual experience, research has shown that most men do not seek prostitutes and very few are regular customers (Monto, 2004). Men go to prostitutes for many reasons. Some want to experience a certain sexual behavior that their partner is unwilling to try, or they may not have a regular partner. Some desire to have sex with someone having a certain image, such as sexy or very athletic looking, and some customers find that the illicit nature of being with a prostitute is attractive. Some like the anonymity of being sexual with a prostitute: No courting is required, there are no postsex expectations, and it is less entangling than having extrarelational/extramarital sex. Some men with very active sex lives simply want more sexual partners. Nonsexual reasons, such as companionship, sympathy, and friendship, can also be motives for seeking prostitutes. Finally, some young men go to a prostitute as their first sexual experience (Bernstein, 2001; Brents, Jackson, & Hausbeck, 2010). Curiously, a study of 140 men from large cities in the Midwest and on the West Coast who have used prostitutes found that 6 in 10 men were currently in a sexual relationship, only one third reported that they enjoyed sex with a female prostitute, and 57% reported that they had tried to stop using prostitutes. The study also found that the common impression that men seek prostitutes when sexually dissatisfied with marital sex was only mildly supported, and the data did not support the notion that men seek "unusual" sexual behaviors such as bondage with a female prostitute. Nearly 30% indicated that they had used alcohol prior to visiting a prostitute (Sawyer, Metz, Hinds, & Brucker, 2001–2002; Weitzer, 2005).

Females Working in Prostitution

Determining the number of women who are prostitutes is difficult for many reasons, including different definitions of prostitution as well as the secrecy often involved with the accepting of money for sex. Further, the prevalence of female prostitution varies widely internationally. A study in the Netherlands found that 3% of women (and 3% of men) in the adult population aged 19–69 reported ever having received money for sex. In other countries, the prevalence is around 1% (Bakker & Vanwesenbeeck, 2006; Vanwesenbeeck, 2013). Some studies can also give us an idea of the prevalence of men purchasing sex from female prostitutes, although the numbers may not reflect the true prevalence because the stigma associated with prostitution may result in underreporting. A study of a representative sample of men from around the world found that, on average, about 9–10% of the men had purchased sex from a female prostitute in the past 12 months (Carael, Slaymaker, Lyerla, & Sarkar, 2006). And in a national study of 4,545 Norwegian men, 13% reported ever paying for sex (Schei & Stigum, 2010).

Sex as Work   Many women who accept money or drugs for sexual activities do not consider themselves prostitutes. Prostitutes often identify themselves as "working girls" or "sex workers," probably an accurate description of how they perceive themselves in relation to sex. Common, but more pejorative, terms are "whore" and "hooker." They are usually sex workers not because they like anonymous sex and different partners, per se, but because they perceive it as good-paying work. Many prostitutes, particularly younger ones, can earn more money from their sex work than other types of work. The financial draw is greater for women, as the demand for them by men is much greater than the demand for male prostitutes. Large groups of female prostitutes, and to a much lesser degree male prostitutes, often "follow the money" and travel or migrate to where large groups of men with money are located. That is, where there is money, there is prostitution (Vanwesenbeeck, 2013). They generally do not expect to enjoy sex with their customers and avoid emotional intimacy by drawing boundaries around their emotional selves, thereby dissociating their physical sexuality from their inner selves. Many separate sex as a physical expression for which they are paid from sex as an expression of intimacy and pleasure (Brents et al., 2010). Two prostitutes who work in Nevada's legal brothels (see discussion of Nevada's brothels in a following section) talk about the difference between sex at work and sex at home (quoted in Brents et al., 2010). Many prostitutes don't kiss their clients; one said, "You don't get personal. Kissing is personal and romantic." In contrast to clients, sex with husbands or boyfriends is where "I really put my feelings into it, and I give him all my love, you know, I'm giving him me."

Entrance Into Prostitution   Many women begin working as prostitutes in their younger years, even in their early teens (Dittman, 2004). Analysis of the National Longitudinal Study of Adolescent Health, a nationally representative sample of 13,294 U.S. adolescents in grades 7 through 12 found that 3.5% of

Identifying women as sexual beings whose responsibility is the sexual service of men is the social base for gender specific slavery.

—Kathleen Berry

think
about it

Sex Trafficking: A Modern-Day Slavery

An estimated 4.5 million persons globally are trapped in forced sexual exploitation. Sex trafficking, a form of human trafficking, is being call a "modern-day slavery" that exists throughout the world, including the United States. Women, men, and children are being forced to perform commercial sex against their will. In 2014, the National Human Trafficking Resource Center (NHTRC) hotline received reports of 3,840 cases of sex trafficking within the United States (Bello, 2015). The NHTRC had more than 72,000 interactions (phone calls, e-mails, and online tip forms) between 2007 and 2012: 41% of the sex trafficking cases were women, representing 85% of all sex trafficking cases. According to federal law, minors under the age of 18 induced into commercial sex are considered victims of sex trafficking (Polaris Project, 2015a, 2015b). U.S. Immigration and Custom Enforcement authorities report that the number of sex trafficking cases in the United States increased from 615 in fiscal year 2010 to 987 in fiscal year 2014 (Bello, 2015). According to the United Nations International Children's Emergency Fund (UNICEF), as many as 2 million children are forced into prostitution in the global commercial sex trade (U.S. Department of State, 2010). With profits soaring and prosecution difficult, this pathological phenomenon shows no signs of abating.

To lure persons into prostitution, sex traffickers use many methods, such as violence, lies, coercion, debt bondage, and a promise of a high-paying job. Some may promise a romantic relationship, during which they may initially establish a period of false love. During this period, they promise a better life, give gifts, and share sexual and physical intimacy. However, eventually, to keep the person in commercial sex, the trafficker often resorts to various control tactics, including physical and emotional abuse, confiscation of identification and money, and isolation.

Many types of persons can be forced into prostitution: U.S. citizens, foreign nationals, children, teens, adult men and women, and LGBT individuals. Traffickers often target homeless and runaway youth—survivors of parental and domestic abuse and sexual abuse, for example. Sex trafficking exists in various venues, such as in fake massage businesses, online escort services, and residential brothels; on streets; and at truck stops, hotels, motels, and strip clubs. In street-based sex trafficking, the prostitutes are expected to have enough clients to earn a nightly quota of $500 or more (Polaris Project, 2015a).

Sex trafficking among children and teens is particularly disturbing. Families may sometimes feel they have little choice but to send their children into deplorable situations because, for example, they are simply too poor to feed their children. Increased trade across borders, lack of education (including sexuality education) of children and their parents, inadequate legislation, lack of or poor law enforcement, the eroticization of children by the media—all have contributed to commercial sexual exploitation of children (Chelala, 2000). In eastern and southern Africa, children who are orphaned as a result of AIDS may lack the support they need from other family members. Children from industrialized countries may be fleeing abusive homes. In Southeast Asia, attitudes and practices perpetuate the low status of girls (Sternberg, 2005).

Sex trafficking of children and young teens is not limited to countries other than the United States. Nearly 300,000 American children and teens, most of them young girls, are at risk for sex trafficking (Polaris Project, 2010; The Advocates for Human Rights, 2009; U.S. Department of State, 2010). The National Center for Missing & Exploited Children estimated that, in 2014, one in six endangered runaways reported to the center was probably a victim of sex trafficking (National Center for Missing & Exploited Children, 2015). Most of those trafficked into the United States are from Latin America, Southeast Asia, and Eastern Europe. The Federal Bureau of Investigation (FBI) estimates that tens of thousands of children and young women have been trafficked into the United States. These victims, both girls and boys, range in age from 9 to 19, with the average being 11. Many of these children and young teens are runaways or kids who have been abandoned, whereas others are from "good families" or have been lured or coerced by skillful predators who promise jobs, money, clothing, and modeling careers. Pimps move these young people from state to state, which makes this a federal matter. In 2003, the FBI initiated a project called Lost Innocence, which specializes in child and teen sex trafficking (Fang, 2005; FBI, 2010; "Teen girls tell their stories," 2006). This project has successfully rescued more than 3,400 children and has resulted in the conviction of over 1,500 pimps and madams (FBI, 2015).

Children who enter sexual servitude at an early age suffer profound physical and psychological consequences. They can become malnourished, be at an increased risk for STIs (including HIV/AIDS), and suffer feelings of guilt and inadequacy, to name just a few of the effects.

In the United States, the Trafficking Victims Protection Act (TVPA) of 2000 made human trafficking within the United States a federal crime. The TVPA defines sex trafficking as "the recruitment, harboring, transportation, provision, or obtaining of a person for the purposes of a commercial sex act, in which the commercial sex act is induced by force, fraud, or coercion, or which the person induced to perform such an act has not attained 18 years of age." The term "commercial sex act" is defined as any sexual behavior from which anything of value is given to or received by any persons (National Human Trafficking Resource Center, 2015). Further, the law allows women trafficked into the United States to receive permanent residence status after 3 years from the issuance of a temporary residence visa (Victims of Trafficking and Violence Protection Act of 2000, 2000). Also, according to U.S. law, Americans caught paying children for sex while in foreign countries can be prosecuted in the United States (National Center for Missing & Exploited Children, 2011). Education, social mobilization and awareness building, legal support, social services, psychosocial counseling, and prosecution of perpetrators are but a few of the strategies that have been used to address this problem. Much more must be done to protect the endangered lives and well-being of the world's children.

Think Critically

1. What, in your opinion, contributes to the demand for child sex workers?

2. What more do you think could be done to address sex trafficking worldwide?

3. What, if any, additional laws should the United States enact to prevent the trafficking of children and young women into the United States?

these adolescents (32.1% of whom were girls) had ever exchanged sex for drugs or money (Edwards, Iritani, & Hallfors, 2006).

Childhood victimization—sexual molestations, incest, and physical abuse—is often discussed as a background factor in both adolescent girls' and boys' entrance into prostitution (Cobbina & Oselin, 2011; Widom & Kuhns, 1996). Sexual abuse increases the likelihood that a preadolescent or an adolescent will become involved in deviant street culture and activities. Physically and sexually abused youths are more likely to be rejected by their conventional peers and to become involved in delinquent activities. One major reason young people flee home is parental abuse—generally sexual abuse for girls and physical abuse for boys.

Girls usually are introduced into prostitution by pimps, men upon whom prostitutes are emotionally and financially dependent. Prostitutes give their pimps the money they earn; in turn, pimps provide housing, buy them clothes and jewelry, and offer them protection on the streets. Many girls and young women are "sweet-talked" into prostitution by promises of money, protection, and companionship. Adolescent prostitutes are more likely than adults to have pimps.

Once involved with pimps, women are frequently abused by them. The women also run the risk of abuse and violence from their customers. Prostitutes who solicit customers on the streets (called **streetwalkers**) are especially vulnerable.

Personal Background and Motivation   Many adult prostitutes are women who were targets of early male sexual aggression, had extensive sexual experience in adolescence, were rejected by peers because of sexual activities, and were not given adequate emotional support by their parents. There are high rates of physical and sexual abuse (including intrafamilial abuse) and neglect in their childhoods (Widom & Kuhns, 1996). Often, their parents failed to provide them with a model of affectionate interaction. As a result, as the girls grew up, they tended to be anxious, to feel lonely and isolated, and to be unsure of their own identity. Another common thread running through the lives of most prostitutes is an economically disadvantaged background. However, there is a wide range of motivations and backgrounds among those who enter this "oldest profession." As one ex-prostitute notes (quoted in Queen, 2000):

> When I began sex work, I did not expect the range of education and life experience I found in my colleagues. Like many people, I believed prostitution was mainly engaged in by women who have no options. But I ended up working with women who were saving to buy houses, put kids through school, put themselves through school, start businesses. (p. 4)

Research has shown that adolescent prostitutes describe their general psychological state of mind as very negative, depressed, unhappy, or insecure at the time they first entered prostitution. Many had run away from home and engaged in sexual risk behaviors. There were high levels of drug use, including alcohol, methamphetamines, marijuana, cocaine, and heroin, and many of those who became drug addicts later turned to prostitution to support their drug habit (Edwards et al., 2006). Their emotional state made them particularly vulnerable to pimps.

No single motive seems to explain why someone becomes a prostitute. It is probably a combination of environmental, social, financial, and personal factors that leads a woman to this profession. When prostitutes describe the most attractive things about life in the prostitution subculture, they describe them in monetary and material terms. One woman prostitute notes, "I said to myself how can I do these horrible things and I said money, money, money" (quoted in Weisberg, 1990). Compared with a minimum-wage job, which may be the only alternative, prostitution appears to be an economically rational decision.

Prostitutes are aware of the psychological and physical costs. A 15-year longitudinal study of 130 sex workers found that sex work was associated with higher incidences of illness—including STIs, mental health problems, and substance abuse—and death (Ward & Day, 2006). Prostitutes fear physical and sexual abuse, AIDS and other STIs, harassment, jail, and legal expenses. They are aware as well of the damage done to their self-esteem from stigmatization and rejection by family and society, negative feelings toward men and sex, bad working conditions, lack of a future, and control by pimps. Many do not enjoy being a prostitute, and one international study found that nearly 90% wanted out of prostitution (Farley et al., 2003).

In many countries, the availability of prostitutes has become part of the tourist economy, with the money paid to prostitutes an important part of the national income (Baker, 1995; Sternberg, 2005). In developing countries such as India, Thailand, and the Philippines, where social and economic conditions combine with a dominant male hierarchy and acceptance of a sexual double standard, many people in those countries see prostitution as a necessary and accepted occupation.

> ❚❚ *Prostitutes are degraded and punished by society; it is their humiliation through their bodies—as much as their bodies—which is being purchased.*
> —Phyllis Chester
> (1940–)

Forms of Female Prostitution   Female prostitutes work as streetwalkers, in brothels and massage parlors, and for escort services that advertise through newspapers and the web. Some academics believe that the great majority of prostitutes in the United States live indoor and, for the most part, unnoticed lives.

Streetwalkers   Estimates vary, but approximately 10% of American prostitutes are streetwalkers (Queen, 2000). Streetwalking is usually the first type of prostitution in which adolescents become involved; it is also the type they prefer, despite its being at the bottom of the hierarchy of prostitution and having the greatest cultural stigma. Many advertise by dressing provocatively and hanging out at locales noted for prostitution. Women working as streetwalkers are often high school dropouts or runaways who fled abusive homes and went into prostitution simply to survive. An interview study of 40 female street prostitutes from five U.S. cities showed that adolescent and adult women had different pathways into prostitution (Cobbina & Oselin, 2011). For adolescents, many ran away from home to escape childhood victimization, including physical abuse, sexual molestation, and incest. They subsequently became a street prostitute to reclaim control over their sexuality. Ironically, those adolescents who were encouraged to become a prostitute by male figures began early to feel disempowered because their work was "managed" by others. Adolescent women who had regular contact with prostitutes viewed this type of work as acceptable and glamorous, and they embraced the lifestyle at an early age. The first pathway for the adult-onset streetworkers was to support a drug addiction. These women claimed they were morally opposed to becoming a prostitute and reluctant to do so, yet their drug addiction was so powerful that it overrode these beliefs, as they needed money to support their habit. The last pathway among the adult-onset prostitutes was fueled by financial instability.

Because of their inability to screen clients or control their working conditions, streetwalkers are the most likely of prostitutes to be victimized.

© McGraw-Hill Education/Christopher Kerrigan, photographer

Not all streetwalkers come out of desperate situations, however; some are married and have satisfactory sexual relationships in their private lives. Because streetwalkers make their contacts through public solicitation, they are more visible and more likely to be arrested. Without the ability to easily screen their customers, streetwalkers are more likely to be beaten, robbed, or raped. One study found that more than 95% of street prostitutes had been sexually assaulted and 75% had been raped (Farley, 2003). The study also found that people often consider prostitutes to be "unrapable" or even deserving of being raped. Streetwalkers are also susceptible to severe mental health problems. A qualitative study of 29 street youths engaged in the sex trade found that they had a high rate of attempted suicide (Kidd & Kral, 2002). Further, most women interviewed in a study of streetwalkers in Scotland indicated that their work had a profoundly negative impact on their self-esteem and their life with family, friends, and partners (McKeganey, 2006).

Streetwalkers suffer more occupational hazards such as assault, kidnapping, threats by a weapon, robbery, and rape than the so-called indoor prostitutes of the brothels, massage parlors, and escort services or independent call girls, or Internet purveyors. They have less control over working conditions such as freedom to refuse clients and particular sexual behaviors, are more likely to have been coercively trafficked into prostitution, have less access to protective services, and depend more on pimps than indoor workers do (Weitzer, 2005).

In contrast to other types of prostitutes, streetwalkers' sexual activity with clients typically is less varied and shorter (Hock, 2007). Fellatio is their most common activity; less than one quarter of their contacts involve sexual intercourse. In a study of men arrested for soliciting female prostitutes in three western U.S. cities, fellatio was the most common behavior experienced in prior contact with a prostitute (Monto, 2001).

Brothels   Brothels, also called "houses of prostitution," "whorehouses," and "houses of ill repute," can be found in most large cities but, in the United States, are legal only in 10 rural counties in Nevada. A study of women working as prostitutes at the Nevada brothels found that, prior to entering the brothels, they had worked as illegal prostitutes and wanted relief from the stress of such work, had been working in other legal sex work such as stripping or in adult movies, and had worked in low-paying, service-industry jobs and needed a better-paying job to survive (Brents et al., 2010). Prostitution in brothels has higher status than streetwalking, and it is safer. Indeed, protection from violence is a major advantage of Nevada's legal brothels; they are the safest of all environments in which women sell consensual sex for money

Prostitution is legal and subject to government regulation in 10 rural counties in Nevada.

© K.M. Cannon/AP Images

(Brents & Hausbeck, 2005). Several safety precautions, such as panic buttons, listening devices, and management surveillance, are used in Nevada brothels (Weitzer, 2005). Further, the Nevada brothel prostitutes are required to have regular medical and STI exams, one outcome of which is less STI transmission. Also, to help prevent STIs, men who pay for services must submit to inspection of their genitals by the prostitutes. A major attraction of brothels is their comfortable and friendly atmosphere. In brothels, men can have a cup of coffee or a drink, watch television, or casually converse with the women. Many customers are regulars. Sometimes, they go to the brothel simply to talk or relax rather than to engage in sex: There are relatively few brothels today; most have been replaced by massage parlors.

Researchers from the University of Nevada, Las Vegas, conducted an in-depth peer-reviewed study of the women who are prostitutes in the Nevada brothels. The findings on the nearly 40 women who were interviewed were published in the 2010 book *The State of Sex* (Brents et al., 2010). From the findings, the researchers concluded that "we do not believe that selling sex itself is inherently harmful to women." And they found no evidence of trafficking or women working against their will. They concluded that Nevada's legal brothels are preferable to criminalization of prostitution and that they prevent violence, STIs, and severe exploitation but that improved labor practices are needed. The findings fueled the debate on prostitution among those who were critical of the study and believed that prostitution exploits women and should be ended (Schmidt, 2011).

Male brothels, often called "stables," are common in Southeast Asia and in some large cities in the United States. These stables are where male prostitutes are available for sex with male customers, although there are also some male brothels for female customers, called "stud farms."

Masseuses   There are relatively few brothels today; most have been replaced by massage parlors. The major difference between brothels and massage parlors is that brothels present themselves as places specifically dedicated to prostitution, whereas massage parlors try to disguise their intent. Most massage parlors provide only massages. However, some massage parlors are fronts to prostitution and offer customers any type of sexual service they wish for a fee, which is negotiated with the masseuses. But most are "massage and masturbation only" parlors. These so-called M-and-M parlors are probably the most widespread; their primary service is the "local," "hand finishing," or "relief" massage in which there is only masturbation. By limiting sex to masturbation, these parlors are able to avoid legal difficulties, because most criminal sex statutes require genital penetration, oral sex, discussion of fees, and explicit solicitation for criminal prosecution. Women who work M-and-M parlors are frequently referred to as "hand whores"; these women, however, often do not consider themselves prostitutes, although they may go into prostitution later. Many masseuses run newspaper and website ads for their services and work on an out-call basis, meeting customers at their hotel rooms or homes.

Call Girls   Call girls have the highest status among prostitutes, experience less social stigma than other prostitutes, and have among the safest working environments, as they can experience more control over their working conditions and whom they have as customers than streetwalkers. They are usually better educated than other prostitutes, often come from a middle-class background, and dress fashionably. A call girl's fee is high—much higher than those of a streetwalker or masseuse. She operates through contacts and referrals; instead of the street, she takes to the telephone or computer and arranges to meet her customers at the customer's residence or at his hotel room or hers. The call girl is the one, not the agency, who arranges for the sex, thus providing the agency some protection from prosecution. Another major difference between call girls and streetwalkers is that streetwalkers usually have fleeting interactions with customers, whereas call girls are much more likely to provide "emotional work," such as counseling and befriending their customers (Lever & Dolnick, 2000; Lucas, 1998). Further, call girls often have interactions that resemble a dating experience involving conversation and receiving gifts, hugs, kisses, massages, and oral sex from the clients (Weitzer, 2005).

Call girls often work for escort services that advertise through newspapers and the web. Escort agencies supply attractive escorts for social occasions and never advertise that they provide sexual services, although most do. Agencies usually specialize in one type of sex, that is, female-for-male, male-for-male, female-for-female, or male-for-female. Some offer transgender prostitutes. Not all escorts work through an agency; some are independent and communicate with clients themselves ("Prostitution," n.d.).

Males Working in Prostitution

Although there has been extensive research into prostitution, most of it concerns female prostitution. Most research on male prostitution focuses on street hustlers, the male equivalent of streetwalkers. There are other kinds of male prostitutes, such as call boys, rent boys, masseurs, and prostitutes who work out of gay bars, who have not been extensively investigated. Male sex workers (MSWs) represent varied backgrounds ranging from those with few literacy skills to middle-class and wealthy men working in varied conditions such as the street, clubs, and escort agencies. Increasingly, they are utilizing escort agencies and making their availability known through the Internet (Minichiello, Marino, & Browne, 2000). A minority of males who work as prostitutes are gigolos—heterosexual men providing sexual services for women in exchange for money. Their customers are usually wealthy, middle-aged women who seek sex, a social "companion," or a young man. The gigolo phenomenon illustrates that women, like men, will pay for sex. Another type of male prostitute is kept boys—young men financially supported for sexual services by an older "sugar daddy." The overwhelming majority of male prostitutes sell their sexual services to other males and one study of 38 MSWs from a single escort service found that most identified as gay or bisexual (Smith, Grov, Seal, & McCall, 2013). Young male prostitutes are called "chickens," and the customers who are attracted to them are known as "chickenhawks."

Historical beliefs that male sex work is clandestine and violent have not been shown in empirical studies conducted since the 1990s. A broad overview of the literature on MSWs found that "MSWs should not be necessarily thought of as psychologically unstable, desperate, or destitute, with many making an occupational choice to engage in sex work as the outcome of a rational economic decision" (Minichiello, Scott, & Callander, 2013). (The same could be said about many female sex workers.) The study of 38 MSWs from a single escort service cited earlier found that even though earning an income was the primary incentive for the sex work, there were also downsides (Smith et al., 2013). Many of the MSWs stated that selling sex was personally offensive and inconsistent with their personal moral beliefs and they would not want others to know about their work. The researchers suggested that MSWs must overcome social stigma, issues dealing with self-concept, and attraction to customers to become MSWs. Renowned sex researcher Ian Vanswesenbeeck of Utrecht University in the Netherlands states that the stigma of male sex work is less than for female sex work (Vanwesenbeeck, 2013). That is, women in sex work are more frequently the object of political concerns and interventions.

Street hustlers, like female prostitutes, are often young adults with drug, alcohol, and health issues.

© Chris Schmidt/Vetta/Getty Images

MSWs appear to have better options to be left alone to do their work. Vanwesen-beeck states that MSWs "may be somewhat more likely to experience self-determination, autonomy, and control over their work and thus be somewhat less likely to have their health and well-being seriously threatened, but they too experience stigma and its vast social consequences." The most common types of sexual behaviors male prostitutes engage in are fellatio and anal sex. Male sex workers are usually expected to ejaculate during the sexual encounters. Because of the refractory period, the number of clients seen by male sex workers in a short period of time is limited, in contrast to female sex workers. Women usually do not have orgasms during sex with a client; further, women do not have a refractory period.

Most males are introduced to prostitution through the influence of their peers. A typical male begins when a friend suggests that he can make "easy money" on the streets. Hustlers sometimes live alone or with roommates, whereas female streetwalkers usually live with their pimps. However, one interview study of 90 street-based male sex workers (mean age 32 years) found that they had high levels of homelessness. These men also had contact with the criminal justice system for drug and property offenses, as well as a high rate of attempted suicide (Kidd & Kral, 2002; Ross, Timpson, Williams, Amos, & Bowen, 2007).

Male prostitution is shaped by three subcultures: the peer delinquent subculture, the gay subculture, and the transvestite subculture. The **peer delinquent subculture,** an antisocial street subculture, is characterized by male and female prostitution, drug dealing, panhandling, theft, and violence. Young people in this culture sell sex for the same reason they sell drugs or stolen goods—to make money. Teenage hustlers may not consider themselves gay, because they are selling sex rather than seeking erotic gratification. Instead, they may identify themselves as a bisexual or heterosexual person. They may find their customers in urban "sex zones"—adult bookstores, topless bars, and adult movie houses—which cater to the sexual interests of people of all sexual orientations. And they are more likely to work the street than bars. Recall that 3.5% of 13,294 adolescents of a nationally representative study reported that they had exchanged sex for drugs or money. Two thirds of these youth (68%) were boys. For both genders, the odds of having exchanged sex for money or drugs were higher for those who had used drugs, had run away from home, and were depressed (Edwards et al., 2006).

In contrast to male delinquent prostitutes, gay male prostitutes engage in prostitution as a means of expressing their sexuality *and* making money. They identify themselves as gay and work primarily in gay neighborhoods or gay bars. Many are "pushed-away" children who fled their homes when their parents and peers rejected them because of their sexual orientation. The three most important reasons they give for engaging in prostitution are money, sex, and fun/adventure. Sex work appears to be accepted more in the gay community, as well as less stigmatized (Koken, Bimbi, Parsons, & Halkitis, 2004).

Few studies have been published that examine clients who pay for sex with male escorts. In 2012, an online survey was conducted about male clients' most recent hire for sexual purposes (Grov, Wolff, Smith, Koken, & Parsons, 2014). The survey found that:

- Eighty-nine percent of the clients were White/Caucasian.
- Ninety percent of the clients were HIV negative.
- Three quarters of the clients identified as gay, 18% bisexual, and 4% heterosexual.
- The mean rate paid to escorts was $250 per hour, with most appointments lasting 1 to 2 hours.

- Oral sex behavior was common (80% gave, 69% received), 30% reported anal insertive sex, and 34% reported anal receptive sex.
- Only 12% reported unprotected anal sex.
- The clients reported high satisfaction with the encounters.
- Clients having receptive anal intercourse (whether protected or not) reported greater satisfaction.

A major finding of the study is that the male clients and MSWs engaged in relatively high rates of protected anal sex. Hence, the clients appear to be keenly aware of the need for protection from HIV/STI during anal sex and the MSWs are insisting on condom use.

Very little is known about male transvestite prostitutes. They are a diverse group, distinct from other male and female prostitutes, and they can be found in most major cities. Their clients are heterosexual, bisexual, and gay men. Many of their heterosexual clients believe that the transvestites are women, but others are aware that the prostitutes are transvestites.

Another type of male prostitute is the **she-male,** also referred to as shemale, a male who has undergone breast augmentation. The she-male's client may mistakenly believe that the he is a she. Often, the client is another she-male or a male who knows that the prostitute is genitally a male (Blanchard, 1993).

Prostitution and the Law

Arrests for prostitution and calls for cleanups seem to be a communal ritual practiced by influential segments of the population to reassert their moral, political, and economic dominance. The arrests are symbolic of community disapproval, but they are often selective and ineffective at ending prostitution.

Female prostitution is the only sexual offense for which women are extensively prosecuted; the male patron is seldom arrested. Prostitutes are subject to arrest for various activities, including vagrancy and loitering, but the most common charge is for solicitation. **Solicitation**—a word, a gesture, or an action that implies an offer of sex for sale—is defined vaguely enough that women, and men, who are not prostitutes occasionally are arrested on the charge because they act "suspiciously." It is usually difficult to witness a direct transaction in which money passes hands, and such arrests are also complicated by involving the patron.

There are periodic attempts to repeal laws criminalizing prostitution because it is perceived as a victimless crime: Both the prostitute and the customer engage in it voluntarily. Other people, especially feminists, want to repeal such laws because they view prostitutes as being victimized by their pimps, their customers, the law enforcement system, and social stigmas (Valera, Sawyer, & Schiraldi, 2001; Weitzer, 2010).

Reformers propose that prostitution be either legalized or decriminalized. In recent years, there has been a shift throughout the world from prohibition of prostitution to legalization, reflecting new sexual norms and a new economic climate. As of 2014, 49% of 100 countries had legalized prostitution; 12% had limited legality, and 39% prohibit prosecution (ProCon.org, 2014). The United States still lags behind in changing prohibitionist policies (Brents et al., 2010).

Those who support legalizing prostitution want to subject it to licensing and registration by police and health departments, as in Nevada and parts of Europe. Those who propose decriminalization want to remove criminal penalties for engaging in prostitution; prostitutes would be neither licensed nor registered. Many reformers believe that prostitutes should be accorded the same political

> I regret to say that we of the FBI are powerless to act in cases of oral-genital intimacy, unless it has in some way obstructed interstate commerce.
>
> —J. Edgar Hoover
> (1895–1972)

> Driven underground, prostitution became integrated into the underworld of crime. Like the prohibition of liquor, the criminalization of prostitution became a self-fulfilling prophecy. Like the birth control movement—which also began with the aim of elevating women's status—the antiprostitution movement resulted in the professional and official victimization of poor women.
>
> —Ruth Rosen
> (1945–)

and legal protections and rights as all citizens (Davidson, 2002). Some prostitutes have organized groups, such as the North American Task Force on Prostitution (NTFP), Prostitutes' Education Network, and COYOTE (Call Off Your Old Tired Ethics) to push for decriminalization and support. NTFP's goals include repealing existing prostitution laws, ensuring the rights of prostitutes and other sex workers, promoting the development of social support services for sex workers, and ending the public stigma associated with sex work.

Whatever one's opinion about decriminalizing adult prostitution, the criminalization of adolescent prostitution needs to be reevaluated. Treating juvenile prostitutes as delinquents overlooks the fact that in many ways adolescent prostitutes are more victims than criminals. As researchers and concerned others examine such social problems as the sexual and physical abuse of children, running away, and adolescent prostitution, they are discovering a disturbing interrelationship. The law, nevertheless, does not view adolescent prostitution as a response to victimization and an attempt to survive on the streets. Instead, it treats it as a criminal behavior and applies legal sanctions. A more appropriate response might be to offer counseling, halfway houses, alternative schooling, and job training.

The Impact of HIV/AIDS and Other STIs on Prostitution

Prostitution has received increased attention as a result of the HIV/AIDS epidemic. Numerous studies have documented a high frequency of many STIs, including HIV, among female, male, and male-to-female transgender prostitutes (e.g., Cohan et al., 2006; Edwards et al., 2006; Jin et al., 2010; van Veen, Gotz, van Leeuwen, Prins, & van de Laar, 2010). There are several reasons female and male prostitutes are at higher risk than the general population. First, many prostitutes are injection drug users, and injection drug use is one of the primary ways of transmitting HIV infection. Prostitutes exchanging sex for crack in crack houses are also at high risk for HIV infection as well as other STIs. Second, prostitutes are at higher risk for STI/HIV infection because they have numerous partners. Third, prostitutes do not always require their customers to use condoms. Male prostitutes are at even greater risk than female prostitutes because of their high-risk sexual practices, especially anal intercourse, and their high-risk gay/bisexual clientele. What can we learn from all of the above? That clients of prostitutes are putting themselves, *as well as their partners,* at high risk for HIV and other STIs if they do not use condoms.

● Sexuality and the Law

A basic tenet of our society is that all Americans are equal under the law. But state laws relating to sexuality vary from one state to another, with people having widely differing rights and privileges. Though most Americans don't give much thought to the government's decision making concerning their sexual lives, they generally agree that sexual behavior is private and that what occurs in their bedrooms is their own business. They may even think that sexuality-related laws are for other people, not themselves. As a result, most Americans don't think about how their lives can be impacted by the law depending on where they live or visit.

Laws related to various aspects of human sexuality, such as HIV/AIDS, child sexual abuse, prostitution, and hate crimes based on sexual orientation and gender identity, have been discussed throughout the book. In this section, we discuss laws related to two specific sexuality-related areas: private, consensual sexual behavior between adults and same-sex marriage.

Legalizing Private, Consensual Sexual Behavior

Historically, the United States has enacted laws that criminalize certain sex-related behaviors, such as sexual harassment, rape, incest, sexual assault, exhibitionism, and prostitution. For the most part, there has been a strong consensus among Americans as to the need for and value of such laws. However, one area of sexual behavior, referred to as **sodomy,** has provoked considerable debate. Sodomy has had several definitions, including any sexual behaviors between members of the other or the same sex that cannot result in procreation (some of which were considered "crimes against nature") and sexual behaviors considered to be "homosexual acts." Oral and anal sex are the behaviors typically considered to be sodomy. Rooted in sixteenth-century English laws prohibiting nonprocreative sex, the first American antisodomy law was passed in 1610 in colonial Virginia; the penalty was death. In 1873, South Carolina became the last state to repeal capital punishment for sodomy. Sodomy laws were used to target individuals participating in same-sex behaviors (Greenberg, 2003; "Social evolution changed," 2003).

Every state had laws banning sodomy until 1961, when Illinois repealed its sodomy ban. By mid-2003, only 13 states had sodomy laws, of which 9 states had laws prohibiting sodomy between both same-sex and other-sex partners, and 4 states outlawed sodomy between same-sex partners only. Civil rights activists and the gay community protested that the laws violated individual rights, were rarely enforced, and provided grounds for other types of discrimination based on sexual orientation. Other groups, particularly those that believe homosexuality is immoral, fought to retain the laws.

On June 26, 2003, in *Lawrence et al. v. Texas,* the U.S. Supreme Court struck down, by a decisive 6–3 vote, the Texas law that banned sex between people of the same gender. Considered by many as a "watershed moment" in advancing sexual rights in America, the verdict reversed the Supreme Court's 1986 ruling in *Bowers v. Hardwick* that upheld a state's right (Georgia) to criminalize sodomy. The Court said that the *Bowers* ruling was incorrect then and is incorrect today. This landmark ruling also invalidated the antisodomy laws in the 13 remaining states that had them. Thereafter, the sexual behaviors of consenting adults in private—no matter the gender of the partners—was legal in every state.

The Texas case originated in 1998 when John Geddes Lawrence and Tyron Garner were discovered having sex by a Harris County sheriff's officer who had entered Lawrence's residence while responding to a false report about an armed intruder. They were fined $200 each (Biskupic, 2003b) for violating state law prohibiting oral and anal sex between same-sex partners. In writing for the majority, Justice Anthony Kennedy (Supreme Court of the United States, 2003) stated that

> the case does involve two adults who, with full and mutual consent from each other, engaged in sexual practices common to a homosexual lifestyle. The petitioners [Lawrence and Garner] are entitled to respect for their private lives. The State cannot demean their existence or control their destiny by making their private sexual conduct a crime. The right to liberty under the Due Process Clause gives them the full right to engage in their conduct without intervention of the government.

The *Lawrence et al. v. Texas* ruling by the U.S. Supreme Court is considered a milestone ruling for gay rights advocates. For gay men in particular, not only did the decriminalization of same-sex behavior bring relief but it also helped validate them as human beings and reduced some of the stigma they face. In recent years there have been several court rulings significant to gay rights issues. Gay men and lesbian women can be fired from their jobs, denied the opportunity to

I would rather be exposed to the inconveniences attending too much liberty than to those attending too small a degree of it.

—Thomas Jefferson
(1743–1826)

In considering deviant behavior, it is wise to remember that it is not the prevalence of deviance that triggers social reforms, but rather what deviance symbolizes.

—Ruth Rosen

adopt children, denied custody of their own children, and denied housing because of their sexual orientation. To keep current on legal issues related to gay men and lesbian women, go to the Human Rights Campaign website: http://www.hrc.org.

Same-Sex Marriage

The right for same-sex couples to legally marry has been a major social and political issue in the United States. Concerned that some states might legalize gay marriages, Congress in 1996 passed the Defense of Marriage Act (DOMA), which defined marriage as a union between one man and one woman and that states do not have to recognize same-sex marriages from other states. By mid-2011, 12 states had created their own version.

On June 26, 2013, the U.S. Supreme Court struck down the federal Defense of Marriage Act (DOMA), prompting federal judges throughout the country to eliminate states' bans on same-sex marriage. The 5–4 ruling of *United States v. Edith Windsor* forced the federal government to legally recognize married gay men and lesbian women by lifting the ban on over 1,000 federal benefits such as family medical leave, tax benefits, Social Security benefits, and veterans' benefits. At the time of the ruling, 13 states permitted same-sex marriage; the total rapidly increased to 37 states in early 2015. Further, for the first time the majority (53%) of Americans supported gay marriage to be legal in 2011, and in 2014 56% (78% of 18- to 29-year-olds) supported same-sex marriage (Gallup, 2014). Only 27% supported gay marriage in 1997. This rapid acceptance and legal rulings for a major social issue had little precedence. Richard Wolf, writer for *USA Today,* captured the essence of this swift change by stating that since the DOMA ruling, gay marriage "moved from seemingly incredible to inevitable" (Wolf, 2014b). Inevitable it was and on June 26, 2015, in a 5–4 decision of *Obergefell v. Hodges*, the U.S. Supreme Court legalized same-sex marriage in all 50 states, ruling that states cannot withhold from gay men and lesbian women the same marital rights as those enjoyed by heterosexual couples for thousands of years. This milestone decision resolves one of the most significant civil rights issues of the 21 century by declaring that the 14th Amendment of the U.S. Constitution provides a fundamental right, regardless of sex, for individuals to marry (Wolf and Heath, 2015a, 2015b). In writing for the majority, Justice Anthony Kennedy, stated that "Same-sex couples seek in marriage the same legal treatments as opposite-sex couples, and it would disparage their choices and diminish their personhood to deny them this right" (Wolf and Heath, 2015b).

By mid-2015, 22 countries had legally approved the freedom to marry for same-sex couples nationwide (year of approval in parenthesis): Netherlands (2001), Belgium (2003), Spain (2005), Canada (2005), South Africa (2006), Norway (2009), Sweden (2009), Portugal (2010), Iceland (2010), Argentina (2010), Denmark (2012), France (2013), Brazil (2013), Uruguay (2013), New Zealand (2013), Britain (2014), Luxembourg (2014), Finland (2014), Scotland (2014), Ireland (2015), Greenland (2015), and the United States (2015). Regional or court-ordered provisions for gay marriage occur in Mexico. Many other countries worldwide offer some protections for same-sex couples (Freedom to Marry, 2015a, 2015b, 2015c).

Advocating Sexual Rights

Policymakers and advocates of free speech continue to scrutinize states' sexuality laws and enforcement practices and to monitor and report on them. One such

> *Whether and to whom to marry, how to express sexual intimacy, and whether and how to establish a family—these are among the most basic of every individual's liberty and due process rights.*
>
> —Margaret Marshall, chief justice of the Massachusetts Supreme Court (1944–)

On the night of June 26, 2015, the date the U.S. Supreme Court legalized same-sex marriage, the White House was lit up in the gay pride, rainbow-flag colors in celebration of the landmark victory for marriage equality.

© Bloomberg/Getty

advocacy group is the Sexuality Information and Education Council of the United States (SIECUS), which states:

> Sexual rights are human rights, and they are based on the inherent freedom, dignity, and equality of all human beings. Sexual rights include the right to bodily integrity, sexual safety, sexual privacy, sexual pleasure, and sexual healthcare; the right to make free and informed sexual and reproductive choices; and the right to have access to sexual information based on sound scientific evidence.

In many ways, sexuality-related laws reflect an ambivalence about sexuality in America's culture. For some sexuality-related issues, there is not a consensus, although laws have been enacted. This is particularly evident with issues relating to sexuality education and abortion. Although some laws seem to be based on sexuality as something from which we must be protected, in other cases, the absence of laws speaks loudly. For example, many states have yet to protect against sexual harassment and discrimination based on sexual orientation, and every state has work to do in developing laws that support sexual rights and sexual health. Recall the World Association for Sexual Health's Declaration of Sexual Rights, which identifies 16 sexual rights. The expression of many of these rights has been hampered by laws and social restriction. Further legal protection of fundamental sexual rights is needed for people to fully attain individual sexual health.

Final Thoughts

The world of commercial sex is one our society approaches with ambivalence. Society simultaneously condemns sexually explicit material and prostitution yet provides both to customers. Because of conflicting attitudes and behaviors, our society rarely approaches the issues surrounding sexually explicit material and prostitution with disinterested objectivity. Now, in every state, adults can legally participate in private consensual sexual behavior with other adults and get married, no matter what their sexual orientation is, but other fundamental sexual rights remain hampered by laws or social restriction.

Summary

Sexually Explicit Material in Contemporary America

- There is a lack of agreement about what constitutes *erotica, pornography,* and *obscenity* because they are subjective terms. The term *sexually explicit material* is a more neutral term.
- The viewing of sexually explicit materials is becoming more common. One study of college students revealed that 33% reported viewing sexually explicit videos in the past 30 days.
- The increasing availability of erotic films in the privacy of the home via DVDs, pay-for-view television, and the Internet has led to an increase in viewers. The inclusion of women in the audience has led to *femme porn.*

- The legal guidelines for determining whether a work is obscene are that the dominant theme of the work must appeal to prurient sexual interests and portray sexual conduct in a patently offensive way; taken as a whole, the work must be without serious literary, artistic, political, or scientific value; and a reasonable person must find the work, when taken as a whole, to possess no social value. Obscene material is not protected by law.
- People who read or view sexually explicit material usually recognize it as fantasy. They use it as a release from their everyday lives. Sexually explicit material temporarily encourages sexual expression, activating a person's typical sexual behavior pattern. People are interested in sexually explicit material because they enjoy sexual sensations. It is a source

of sexual information and knowledge, it enables people to rehearse sexual activities, and it is safer sex.

- Child pornography is a form of sexual exploitation that, because of the Internet, has become a worldwide problem. U.S. courts have prohibited its production, sale, and possession.

- Some feminists believe that sexually explicit material represents a form of sex discrimination against women because it places them in what they believe to be a degrading and dehumanizing context. Other feminists believe that opponents of sexually explicit material have an antisex bias.

- In 1970, the President's Commission on Pornography and Obscenity concluded that pornography does not cause harm or violence. Over the years, there has been a heated debate over the effects of sexually explicit material. There is no definitive evidence, however, that nonviolent sexually explicit material is associated with sexual aggression against women, nor is there evidence that sexually violent material produces lasting changes in attitudes or behaviors.

Prostitution

- *Prostitution,* also called sex work, is the exchange of sexual behaviors for money and/or goods. Both men and women work as prostitutes. Women are generally introduced into this type of sex work by pimps.

- Adolescent prostitutes describe their psychological state as negative when they first enter prostitution. Streetwalkers run the risk of abuse and violence from their customers. Prostitutes report various motives for entering prostitution, including quick and easy money, the prostitution subculture, and the excitement of "the life." Fellatio is the most common sexual behavior of streetwalkers.

- Prostitutes solicit on streets and work in brothels and massage parlors. Some masseuses have intercourse with clients, but most provide only masturbation. Call girls (escorts) have the highest status among prostitutes.

- Most research on male prostitution focuses on street hustlers. Male prostitution is shaped by the *peer delinquent,* gay male, and transvestite subcultures. The three most important reasons given for engaging in prostitution are money, sex, and fun/adventure.

- Prostitution is legal in the United States in 10 rural counties in Nevada. A study of these brothels concluded that they are a good alternative to criminalization of prostitution.

- Arrests for prostitution are symbols of community disapproval; they are not effective in curbing prostitution. Female prostitution is the only sexual offense for which women are extensively prosecuted; the male patron is seldom arrested. Decriminalization of prostitution is often urged because it is a victimless crime or because prostitutes are victimized by their pimps, customers, police, and the legal system. Some people advocate regulation by police and health departments.

- Prostitutes are at higher risk for HIV/AIDS than the general population because some are injection drug users, have multiple partners, and do not always require their customers to use condoms. Female and male prostitutes and their customers may provide a pathway for HIV and other STIs into the general heterosexual community.

Sexuality and the Law

- In 2003, the U.S. Supreme Court overturned state anti*sodomy* laws in the 13 remaining states that had them, making it legal for consenting adult gay men and lesbian women, as well as heterosexual individuals, to have sex in private in all states.

- In June 2013 the U.S. Supreme Court struck down the federal Defense of Marriage Act (DOMA), which defined marriage as a union between one man and one woman. Subsequently, the number of states legalizing same-sex marriage rapidly increased to 37 states in early 2015. On June 26, 2015, the U.S. Supreme Court by a 5–4 ruling legalized gay marriage in all 50 states.

- By mid-2015, 22 countries worldwide legally permitted same-sex marriage.

Questions for Discussion

- Imagine that you were assigned to argue that the federal government should regulate sexually explicit material. What would you say? Imagine the converse: that sexually explicit material should be available freely to adults in the marketplace. How would you advocate that position?

- Do you think that sexually explicit materials are helpful, harmful, or neutral? What place, if any, do they have in a society? Explain your position on this issue.

- Do you think that prostitution should be legalized/regulated (i.e., licensed and/or registered by health and police departments) or decriminalized (i.e., no criminal penalties and no licensing or registration) or neither? Defend your stance.

- Do you agree or disagree with the U.S. Supreme Court ruling legalizing gay marriage in all 50 states? Why or why not?

Sex and the Internet

American Civil Liberties Union

Protection of our First Amendment rights is part of the mission of the American Civil Liberties Union (ACLU). But what exactly is this organization, what does it do, and how can it help you? To find out, click to the ACLU's home page (http://www.aclu.org) and find one topic related to this chapter or text that interests you. This could include Internet issues, free speech, HIV/AIDS, lesbian and gay rights, privacy, reproductive rights, or women's rights. After reading information related to this topic, answer the following:

- What new information or news release did you find related to this topic?

- What is the history or background of laws related to it?

- What is the ACLU's stance?

- What is your position, and why?

Suggested Websites

Human Rights Campaign

http://www.hrc.org
The HRC advocates for equal rights for LGBT individuals.

National Center for Missing & Exploited Children

http://www.missingkids.com
Serves as a resource on the issues of missing and sexually exploited children.

National Coalition Against Censorship

http://www.ncac.org
Provides action alerts, censorship news, and frequently asked questions about censorship.

Polaris Project

http://www.polarisproject.org
Named after the North Star, which guided slaves toward freedom along the Underground Railroad, Polaris Project provides a comprehensive approach to combating human trafficking and modern-day slavery.

Prostitutes' Education Network

http://www.bayswan.org
Provides information and resources related to prostitution.

Prostitution Research and Education

www.prostitutionresearch.com
Advocates for alternatives to prostitution, including emotional and physical health care for sex workers.

U.S. Supreme Court

http://www.supremecourtus.gov
Lists U.S. Supreme Court decisions by year and volume. Type in "sodomy" in the search box to locate the Court's ruling on the *Lawrence et al. v. Texas* case.

Suggested Reading

Angell, J. (2004). *Call girl.* Sag Harbor, NY: Permanent Press. A revealing memoir of a university professor who is also a call girl.

Brents, B. G., Jackson, C. A., & Hausbeck, K. (2010). *The state of sex: Tourism, sex, and sin in the New American heartland.* New York: Routledge. A decade-long multimethod study of Nevada's legal brothels that captures the voices of the brothels' sex workers.

Coleman, L. (2014). *The philosophy of pornography: Contemporary perspectives.* Lanham, MD: Rowman & Littlefield. A balanced perspective of both the pro- and anti-porn view of pornography in modern society.

Rosen, R. (2012). *Beaver street: A history of modern pornography.* London: United Kingdom: Headpress. An electrifying account of porn's golden age by an author who worked behind the x-rated scenes of porn magazines.

Sanger, W. (2014). *The history of prostitution—Illustrated edition.* Heritage Illustrated Publishing. A detailed, objective study of prostitution in New York City illustrated with paintings by renowned artists.

Smith, T. (2012). *Whore stories: A revealing history of the world's oldest profession.* Fort Collins, OH: Adams Media. Sheds light on one of our more stigmatized icons—prostitution—by a wistful review of the cultural history of prostitution.

Spector, J. (Ed.). (2006). *Prostitution and pornography: Philosophical debate about the sex industry.* Stanford, CA: Stanford University Press. This anthology examines the debates about the sex industry, discussing the ways prostitution, pornography, and other forms of commercial sex are made subject to legislation.

Weitzer, R. (Ed.). (2010). *Sex for sale: Prostitution, pornography, and the sex industry* (2nd ed). New York: Routledge. Examines sex work and the sex industry.

Glossary

abortifacient A device or substance that causes an abortion.

abortion The expulsion of the conceptus, either spontaneously or by induction.

abstinence Refraining from sexual intercourse.

acculturation The process of adaptation by an ethnic group to the attitudes, behaviors, and values of the dominant culture.

acquaintance rape A nonconsensual sexual encounter by two people who just happen to be in the same place and know each other.

acquired immunodeficiency syndrome (AIDS) A chronic disease caused by the human immunodeficiency virus (HIV), in which the immune system is weakened and unable to fight opportunistic infections such as *Pneumocystis carinii* pneumonia (PCP) and Kaposi's sarcoma.

adolescence The social and psychological state that occurs between the beginning of puberty and full adulthood.

affirmative consent Explicitly saying yes to any sexual behavior with another person.

afterbirth The placenta, the remaining section of the umbilical cord, and the fetal membranes.

agape In John Lee's typology of love, altruistic love.

age of consent The age at which a person is legally deemed capable of giving consent.

alveoli (singular, *alveolus*) Small glands within the female breast that begin producing milk following childbirth.

amenorrhea The absence of menstruation, unrelated to aging.

amniocentesis A process in which amniotic fluid is withdrawn by needle from the uterus and then examined for evidence of possible birth defects.

amniotic fluid The fluid within the amniotic sac that surrounds the embryo or fetus.

amniotic sac A sac that holds the embryo (and later fetus). Also called the bag of water.

anal eroticism Sexual activities involving the anus.

anal intercourse The insertion of the erect penis into the partner's anus.

anal stage In Freudian theory, the period from age 1 to 3, during which the child's erotic activities center on the anus.

analingus The licking of the anal region.

anatomical sex Identification as male or female based on physical sex characteristics such as gonads, uterus, vulva, vagina, and penis.

androgen Any of the male hormones, including testosterone.

androgen insensitivity syndrome (AIS) A condition whereby a genetic male (XY) is unable to respond to male hormones or androgens. As a result, the person has some or all of the physical characteristics of a woman.

androgyny The combination of both traditional masculine and feminine qualities.

anodyspareunia Pain occurring during anal intercourse.

antibody A cell that binds to the antigen of an invading cell, inactivating it and marking it for destruction by killer cells.

antibody screening test A test for detecting the antibodies that the body makes against HIV.

anti-gay prejudice A strong dislike, fear, or hatred of gay men and lesbian women because of their same-sex behavior.

antigen A molecular structure on the wall of a cell capable of stimulating the immune system and then reacting with the antibodies that are released to fight it.

anus The opening of the rectum, consisting of two sphincters, circular muscles that open and close like valves.

anxious/ambivalent attachment A style of infant attachment characterized by separation anxiety and insecurity in relation to the primary caregiver.

Apgar score The cumulative rating of the newborn's heart rate, respiration, color, reflexes, and muscle tone.

aphrodisiac A substance that supposedly increases sexual desire or improves sexual function.

areola A ring of darkened skin around the nipple of the breast.

artificial insemination (AI) Involves introducing sperm into the woman's vagina, cervix, or uterus (the latter is called intrauterine insemination). This procedure may be performed in conjunction with ovulation-stimulating medications.

asexuality A state of having no sexual attraction to anyone or low or absent interest in sexual activity.

assigned gender The gender ascribed by others, usually at birth.

assisted reproductive technology (ART) A procedure in which a woman's ovaries are stimulated and her eggs surgically removed, combined with sperm, and returned to her body. Commonly referred to as artificial insemination.

attachment The emotional tie between an infant and his or her primary caregiver.

atypical sexual behavior Sexual activity that is not statistically typical of usual sexual behavior.

autoerotic asphyxia A form of sexual masochism linking strangulation with masturbation.

autoeroticism Sexual self-stimulation or behavior involving only the self; includes masturbation, sexual fantasies, and erotic dreams.

autofellatio Oral stimulation of the penis by oneself.

avoidant attachment A style of infant attachment characterized by avoidance of the primary caregiver as a defense against rejection.

bacterial vaginosis (BV) A vaginal infection commonly caused by the bacterium *Gardnerella vaginalis.*

Bartholin's gland One of two small ducts on either side of the vaginal opening that secrete a small amount of moisture during sexual arousal.

basal body temperature (BBT) method A contraceptive method based on a woman's temperature in the morning upon waking; when her temperature rises, she is fertile.

B cell A type of lymphocyte involved in antibody production.

BDSM An acronym used to describe the variant sexual behaviors that combine bondage, discipline, sadism, and masochism.

benign prostatic hyperplasia (BPH) Enlargement of the prostate gland, affecting many men over age 50.

benign tumor A nonmalignant (noncancerous) tumor that grows slowly and remains localized.

bestialists People who have sexual contact with animals but are not concerned with the animals' welfare.

bias A personal leaning or inclination.

biased sample A nonrepresentative sample.

biopsy Surgical removal of tissue for diagnosis.

birth canal The passageway through which an infant is born; the vagina.

birth control patch A transdermal reversible method of birth control that releases synthetic estrogen and progestin to protect against pregnancy for 1 month.

birth control shot An injectable, hormonal method of birth control that is used to prevent pregnancy for 12 weeks.

bisexuality An emotional and sexual attraction to members of both sexes.

blastocyst A collection of about 100 human cells that develops from the zygote.

bondage and discipline (B&D) Sexual activities in which one person is bound while another simulates or engages in light or moderate "disciplinary" activities such as spanking and whipping.

Braxton-Hicks contractions Uterine contractions during the last trimester of pregnancy that exercise the uterus, preparing it for labor.

breast self-examination (BSE) A method of checking one's own breasts for lumps or suspicious changes.

calendar (rhythm or standard days) methods Methods based on calculating "safer" days, which depend on the range of a woman's longest and shortest menstrual cycles and absteinance from unprotected vaginal intercourse during her peak fertile times.

capacitation The process by which a sperm's membranes become fragile enough to release the enzymes from its acrosomes.

caring Making another's needs as important as one's own.

castration anxiety In Freudian theory, the belief that the father will cut off the child's penis because of competition for the mother/wife.

celibacy Not engaging in any kind of sexual activity.

censorship The suppression of words, ideas, or images by governments, private groups, or individuals based on their political or moral values.

cervical cancer Invasive cancer of the cervix (ICC).

cervical cap A silicon, cup-shaped device that is inserted into the vagina to prevent pregnancy.

cervical dysplasia or **cervical intraepithelial neoplasia (CIN)** A condition of the cervical epithelium (covering membrane) that may lead to cancer if not treated.

cervical mucus method A contraceptive method using a woman's cervical mucus to determine ovulation.

cervicitis The swelling (inflammation) of the cervix, usually the result of an infection.

cervix The end of the uterus, opening toward the vagina.

cesarean section (C-section) The delivery of a baby through an incision in the mother's abdominal and uterine walls.

chancre A round, pea-sized, painless sore symptomatic of the first stage of syphilis.

child-free Individuals or couples who choose not to have children.

child sexual abuse Any sexual interaction (including fondling, erotic kissing, oral sex, and genital penetration) between an adult and a child.

chlamydia An STI caused by the *Chlamydia trachomatis* organism. Also known as chlamydial infection.

chorion The embryo's outermost membrane.

chorionic villus sampling (CVS) A procedure in which tiny pieces of the membrane that encases the embryo are removed and examined for evidence of possible birth defects.

cilia Tiny, hairlike tissues on the fimbriae that become active during ovulation, moving the oocyte into the fallopian tube.

circumcision The surgical removal of the foreskin which covers the glans penis.

cisgender People whose sex assignment at birth corresponds to their gender identity and expression. *See also* gender normative.

clinical research The in-depth examination of an individual or a group by a clinician who assists with psychological or medical problems.

clitoral hood A fold of skin covering the glans of the clitoris.

clitoris (plural, *clitorides*) An external sexual structure that is the center of arousal in the female; located above the vagina at the meeting of the labia minora.

coercive paraphilia Sexual behavior involving victimization and causing harm to others.

cognitive development theory A child development theory that views growth as the mastery of specific ways of perceiving, thinking, and doing that occurs at discrete stages.

cognitive social learning theory A child development theory that emphasizes the learning of behavior from others, based on the belief that consequences control behavior.

cohabitation   The practice of living together and having a sexual relationship.

coitus   Penile-vaginal sex.

colostrum   A yellowish substance containing nutrients and antibodies that is secreted by the breasts 2–3 days prior to actual milk production.

come out   To publicly acknowledge one's sexual orientation, such as gay, lesbian, or bisexual.

commitment   A determination, based on conscious choice, to continue a relationship or a marriage.

communication   A transactional process in which symbols, such as words, gestures, and movements, are used to establish human contact, exchange information, and reinforce or change attitudes and behaviors.

concurrent sexual relationships   Overlapping sexual relationships with more than one partner.

condom or **male condom**   A thin, soft, flexible sheath of latex rubber, polyurethane, or processed animal tissue that fits over the erect penis to prevent semen from being transmitted and to help protect against STIs. *See also* female condom.

conflict   A communication process in which people perceive incompatible goals and interference from others in achieving their goals.

congenital adrenal hyperplasia   A group of inherited disorders of the adrenal gland whereby individuals born with this condition lack an enzyme needed by the adrenal gland to make the hormones cortisol and aldosterone.

contraception   The prevention of conception or impregnation.

control group   A group that is not being treated in an experiment.

coprophilia   A paraphilia in which a person gets sexual pleasure from contact with feces.

corona   The rim of tissue between the glans and the penile shaft.

corpora cavernosa   The hollow chambers in the shaft of the clitoris or penis that fill with blood and swell during arousal.

corpus luteum   The tissue formed from a ruptured ovarian follicle that produces important hormones after the oocyte emerges.

corpus spongiosum   A column of erectile tissue within the penis enclosing the urethra.

correlational study   The measurement of two or more naturally occurring variables to determine their relationship to each other.

Cowper's gland or **bulbourethral gland**   One of two small structures below the prostate gland that secrete a clear mucus into the urethra prior to ejaculation.

cross-dresser   Wearing of clothing of the other sex for sexual arousal.

cross-dressing   Wearing the clothing of a member of the other sex.

crura (singular, *crus*)   The internal branches of the clitoral or penile shaft.

cryptorchidism   A condition that occurs in a minority of infants whereby one or both of the testes fail to descend. Also known as undescended testis.

cultural equivalency perspective   The view that attitudes, behaviors, and values of diverse ethnic groups are basically similar, with differences resulting from adaptation to historical and social forces such as slavery, discrimination, or poverty.

cunnilingus   Oral stimulation of the female genitals.

cystitis   A bladder infection, affecting mainly women, that is often related to sexual activity, although it is not transmitted from one partner to another.

date rape   Sexual penetration with a dating partner that occurs against the victim's will, with force or the threat of force.

delayed ejaculation   A marked delay in or inability to ejaculate, usually during partnered sexual activity.

demographics   The statistical characteristics of human populations.

dependent variable   In an experiment, a factor that is likely to be affected by changes in the independent variable.

diabetes mellitus   A chronic disease characterized by excess sugar in the blood and urine due to a deficiency of insulin.

diaphragm   A cup with a flexible rim that is placed deep inside the vagina, blocking the cervix, to prevent sperm from entering the uterus.

dilation   Gradual opening of the cervix.

dilation and evacuation (D&E)   A second-trimester abortion method in which the cervix is slowly dilated and the fetus removed by alternating curettage with other instruments and suction.

disinhibition   The phenomenon of activating behaviors that would normally be suppressed.

disorders of sex development (DSD)   Variations in congenital sex anatomy that are considered atypical for females or males. Also called intersex.

domestic partnership   A legal category granting some rights ordinarily reserved to married couples to committed, cohabiting heterosexual, gay men, and lesbian women couples.

dominatrix   In bondage and discipline, a woman who specializes in "disciplining" a submissive partner.

drag queens   Gay men who cross-dress to entertain.

DSM-5   *The Diagnostic and Statistical Manual of Mental Disorders*, the 2013 update of the mental disorders classification and diagnostic tool published by the American Psychiatric Association. The *DSM-5* addresses sexual function difficulties and paraphilias.

dual control model   A theoretical perspective of sexual response based on brain function and the interaction between sexual excitation and sexual inhibition.

dysmenorrhea   Pelvic cramping and pain experienced by some women during menstruation.

dyspareunia   A female sexual functioning difficulty characterized by painful intercourse.

eating disorder   Eating and weight management practices that endanger a person's physical and emotional health.

ectoparasitic infestation   Parasitic organisms that live on the outer skin surfaces, not inside the body.

ectopic pregnancy   A pregnancy in which the fertilized ovum is implanted in any tissue other than the uterine wall. Most ectopic pregnancies occur in the fallopian tubes. Also known as a tubal pregnancy.

effacement   Thinning of the cervix during labor.

egocentric fallacy   An erroneous belief that one's own personal experiences and values are held by others in general.

EIA (enzyme immunoassay)   A test used to detect antigen-soliciting molecules specifically related to autoimmune disorders and cancer.

ejaculation   The process by which semen is forcefully expelled from the penis.

ejaculatory duct   One of two structures within the prostate gland connecting with the vasa deferentia.

ejaculatory inevitability   The point at which ejaculation is imminent in the male.

elective deliveries   Those who schedule a baby's birth prior to 39 weeks.

Electra complex   In Freudian theory, the female child's erotic desire for the father and simultaneous fear of the mother.

embryonic membranes   The embryo's membranes include the amnion, amniotic fluid, yolk sac, chorion, and allantois.

embryo   The early form of life in the uterus between the stages of blastocyst and fetus.

emergency contraception (EC)   The use of hormones or a copper IUD to prevent a pregnancy from occurring.

emission   The first stage of ejaculation, in which sperm and semen are propelled into the urethral bulb.

endometriosis   A disease in which tissue that normally grows inside the uterus instead grows outside the uterus.

endometrium   The inner lining of the uterine walls.

epidemic   A wide and rapid spread of a contagious disease.

epidemiology   The study of the causes and control of disease epidemics.

epididymis   The coiled tube, formed by the merging of the seminiferous tubules, where sperm mature.

epididymitis   Inflammation of the epididymis.

epidural   A method of anesthetic delivery during childbirth in which a painkilling drug is continuously administered through a catheter in the woman's lower back.

episiotomy   An incision that enlarges the vaginal opening by cutting through the perineum toward the anus to assist in the delivery of a baby.

erectile disorders   Difficulty with erections during partnered sexual activity.

erection   The process of the penis becoming rigid through vasocongestion; an erect penis.

erogenous zone   Any area of the body that is highly sensitive to touch and associated with sexual arousal.

eros   In John Lee's typology of love, the love of beauty.

erotic aid or **sex toy**   A device, such as a vibrator or dildo, or a product, such as oils or lotions, designed to enhance erotic responsiveness.

erotica   Sexually explicit material that is evaluated positively.

erotophilia   A positive emotional response to sexuality.

erotophobia   A negative emotional response to sexuality.

estrogen   The principal female hormone, regulating reproductive functions and the development of secondary sex characteristics.

ethnocentric fallacy or **ethnocentrism**   The belief that one's own ethnic group, nation, or culture is innately superior to others.

exhibitionism   Exposing one's genitals to an unsuspecting person.

experimental research   The systematic manipulation of an individual or the environment to learn the effect of such manipulation on behavior.

expressiveness   Revealing or demonstrating one's emotions.

expulsion   The second stage of ejaculation, characterized by rapid, rhythmic contraction of the urethra, prostate, and muscles at the base of the penis, causing semen to spurt from the urethral opening.

extradyadic involvement   Sexual or romantic relationships outside of a primary marital or dating dyad.

extrafamilial child sexual abuse   Child sexual abuse by someone unrelated to the child.

fallacy   An error in reasoning that affects one's understanding of a subject.

fallopian tube   One of two uterine tubes extending toward an ovary.

familismo   Emphasis on family among Hispanics/Latinos.

Family and Medical Leave Act (FMLA)   A law that allows an employee to take unpaid leave for the birth and care of a newborn child, during his or her own illness, or to care for a sick family member.

feedback   The ongoing process in which participants and their messages create a given result and are subsequently modified by that result.

fellatio   Oral stimulation of the penis.

female condom   A soft, loose-fitting, disposable polyurethane sheath with a diaphragm-like ring at each end that covers the cervix, vaginal walls, and part of the external genitals to prevent conception and to help protect against sexually transmitted infections.

female impersonators   Men who dress as women.

female orgasmic disorders   Difficulty in experiencing orgasms or reduced intensity of orgasms during sexual activity.

female sexual interest/arousal disorder   Absent/reduced sexual thoughts, fantasies, initiation, and receptivity and arousal and pleasure during sexual activity.

feminism   Efforts by both men and women to achieve greater equality for women.

femme porn   Sexually explicit material catering to women and heterosexual couples.

fertility awareness-based methods (FAMS)   Sometimes referred to as "natural family planning"; ways to track ovulation in order to prevent pregnancy.

fetal alcohol effect (FAE)   Moderate alcohol consumption by pregnant women, resulting in some intellectual and behavior deficits.

fetal alcohol syndrome (FAS)   Chronic ingestion of alcohol by pregnant women, resulting in unusual facial features, congenital heart defects, defective joints, and behavioral and intellectual impairment in children.

fetishism   Using an inanimate object or focus on nongenital body parts.

fetus   The stage of life from 8 weeks of gestation to birth.

fibrocystic disease   A common and generally harmless breast condition in which fibrous tissue and benign cysts develop in the breast.

fimbriae   Fingerlike tissues that drape over the ovaries, but without necessarily touching them.

5-alpha reductase deficiency   A condition whereby a genetic male (XY) does not produce enough of a hormone called dihydrotestosterone (DHT), a shortage of which will disrupt the formation of the external sex organs, causing individuals to be born with external genitalia that appear female.

flirting   Coy behaviors used to indicate romantic or sexual interest in another person.

follicle-stimulating hormone (FSH)   A hormone that regulates ovulation.

follicular phase   The phase of the ovarian cycle during which a follicle matures.

foreskin   The portion of the sleevelike skin covering the shaft of the penis that extends over the glans penis. Also known as prepuce.

frenulum   The triangular area of sensitive skin on the underside of the penis, attaching the glans to the foreskin.

friends with benefits   An uncommitted, non-long-term casual sexual relationship between acquaintances.

frotteurism   Touching or rubbing sexually against a nonconsenting person in public places.

gamete   A sex cell containing the genetic material necessary for reproduction; an oocyte (ovum) or sperm.

gay   Emotional and sexual attraction between persons of the same sex. *See also* homosexual.

gender   The socially constructed roles, behaviors, activities, and attributers that a society considers appropriate for men and women.

gender dysphoria   A new diagnosis in the *Diagnostic and Statistical Manual-5 (DSM-5)* that emphasizes the individual's felt sense of "incongruence" with natal gender, rather than cross-gender behavior.

gender identity   A person's internal sense of being male or female.

gender normative   People whose sex assignment at birth corresponds to their gender identity and expression. *See also* cisgender.

gender role   The attitudes, behaviors, rights, and responsibilities that society associates with each sex.

gender-role stereotype   A rigidly held, oversimplified, and overgeneralized belief about how each gender should behave.

gender schema   A set of interrelated ideas used to organize information about the world on the basis of gender.

gender variance   A nonpathologizing alternative to psychiatric diagnoses that acknowledges a person's unwillingness or desire to conform to societal gender norms.

gender variant   Individuals who cannot or choose not to conform to societal gender norms associated with their biological sex.

gender variation   A person's inability or unwillingness to conform to societal gender norms associated with his or her biological sex.

genetic sex   Identification as male or female based on chromosomal and hormonal sex characteristics.

genital candidiasis   A yeast infection caused by an overgrowth of *Candida albicans*, which is always present in the body.

genital human papillomavirus infection or **genital HPV**   Viruses, many of which are sexually transmitted, that infect the genital and rectal areas of both females and males. Certain types of human papillomavirus infection (HPV) can cause genital warts in men and women.

genitals   The reproductive and sexual organs of males and females. Also known as genitalia.

genital stage   In Freudian theory, the period in which adolescents become interested in genital sexual activities, especially sexual intercourse.

genital warts   An STI caused by the human papillomavirus (HPV).

genito-pelvic pain/penetration disorder   Difficulties related to genital and pelvic pain and vaginal penetration during intercourse.

gestation   Pregnancy.

gestational carrier   A carrier who is not related to the fetus. In this case, a woman with ovaries but no uterus uses her own egg and the man's sperm to create the embryo, which is then placed within the carrier's uterus.

GIFT (gamete intrafallopian transfer)   An ART procedure that transfers gametes into the woman's fallopian tubes through small incisions in her abdomen.

glans clitoris   The erotically sensitive tip of the clitoris.

glans penis   The head of the penile shaft.

gonad   An organ (ovary or testis) that produces gametes.

gonadotropin   A hormone that acts directly on the gonads.

gonadotropin-releasing hormone (GnRH)   A hormone that stimulates the pituitary gland to release follicle-stimulating hormone (FSH) and luteinizing hormone (LH), initiating the follicular phase of the ovarian cycle.

gonorrhea   An STI caused by the *Neisseria gonorrhoeae* bacterium.

Grafenberg spot (G-spot)   According to some researchers, an erotically sensitive area on the upper front wall of the vagina midway between the introitus and the cervix.

gynecomastia   Swelling or enlargement of the male breast.

halo effect   The assumption that attractive or charismatic people possess more desirable social characteristics than are actually present.

Hegar's sign   The softening of the uterus above the cervix, indicating pregnancy.

helper T cell   A lymphocyte that "reads" antigens and directs the immune system's response.

hepatitis   A viral disease affecting the liver; several types of the virus can be sexually transmitted.

herpes simplex virus (HSV)   The virus that causes genital herpes.

heteronormativity   Any set of norms that hold that people fall into distinct genders, with natural roles, and are presumed to be heterosexual.

heterosexual bias or **heterosexism** or **heterocentric behavior**   The tendency to see the world in heterosexual terms and to ignore or devalue homosexuality.

heterosexuality   Emotional and sexual attraction between members of the other sex.

HIV   *See* human immunodeficiency virus.

Home Access HIV-1 Test A home collection kit involving drawing blood from the finger, sending the samples to a licensed laboratory and then calling in for the results the next day.

homoeroticism Sexual attraction, desire, or impulses directed toward members of the same sex; homosexuality.

homologous structure A similarity in structures that perform the same function.

homophobia An irrational or phobic fear of gay men and lesbian women. *See also* anti-gay prejudice, heterosexual bias.

homosexuality Emotional and sexual attraction between members of the same sex. *See also* gay.

hooking up Sexual encounters with a nonromantic partner, often a friend.

hormone A chemical substance that acts as a messenger within the body, regulating various functions.

hostile environment As related to sexuality, a work or educational setting that interferes with a person's performance because of sexual harassment.

hot flash An effect of menopause consisting of a period of intense warmth, flushing, and perspiration, typically lasting 1–2 minutes.

human chorionic gonadotropin (HCG) A hormone produced right after a fertilized egg attaches to the uterus; its function is to promote the maintenance of the corpus luteum.

human immunodeficiency virus (HIV) The virus that causes AIDS.

hymen A thin membrane partially covering the introitus prior to first intercourse or other breakage.

hypospadias A hormonal condition in which the opening of the penis, rather than being at the tip, is located somewhere on the underside, glans, or shaft or at the junction of the scrotum and penis.

implant A contraceptive device inserted under the skin that protects against pregnancy for up to 3 years. Implanon is the most common among them.

implantation The process by which a blastocyst becomes embedded in the uterine wall.

incest Sexual intercourse between individuals too closely related to legally marry, usually interpreted to mean father-daughter, mother-son, or brother-sister activity.

incidence The number of new cases of a disease within a specified time, usually 1 year.

independent variable In an experiment, a factor that can be manipulated or changed.

induction A type of reasoning in which arguments are formed from a premise to provide support for its conclusion.

infertility The lack of pregnancy in the last 12 months despite having had unprotected sexual intercourse in each of those months with the same partner.

informed consent Assent given by a mentally competent individual at least 18 years old with full knowledge of the purpose and potential risks and benefits of participation.

infundibulum The tube-shaped end of each fallopian tube.

instrumentality Being oriented toward tasks and problem solving.

interfemoral intercourse Movement of the penis between the partner's thighs.

internalized homophobia Negative attitudes and affects toward homosexuality in other persons and toward same-sex attraction in oneself.

intimate love Love based on commitment, caring, and self-disclosure.

intracytoplasmic sperm injection (ICSI) An ART procedure that involves injecting a single sperm directly into a mature egg; the embryo is then transferred to the uterus or fallopian tube.

intrafamilial child sexual abuse Child sexual abuse by biologically and step-related individuals.

intrauterine device (IUD) A long-acting, reversible contraceptive method that involves the placement of a small, flexible, plastic device into the uterus to prevent sperm from fertilizing the egg.

interview A formal meeting in which one or more persons ask a person questions about a specific topic.

introitus The opening of the vagina.

in vitro fertilization (IVF) An ART procedure that combines sperm and oocyte in a laboratory dish and transfers the blastocyst to the mother's uterus.

jealousy An aversive response that occurs because of a partner's real, imagined, or likely involvement with a third person.

Kaplan's tri-phasic model of sexual response A model that divides sexual response into three phases: desire, excitement, and orgasm.

Kaposi's sarcoma A rare cancer of the blood vessels that is common among people with AIDS.

Kegel exercises A set of exercises for women designed to strengthen and give voluntary control over the pubococcygeus and to increase sexual pleasure and awareness. For males, the exercises can be valuable in improving erectile function and learning ejaculatory control.

killer T cell A lymphocyte that attacks foreign cells.

Klinefelter syndrome A condition in which a male has one or more extra X chromosomes, causing the development of female secondary sex characteristics.

klismaphilia A paraphilia in which a person gets sexual pleasure from receiving enemas.

labia majora (singular, *labium majus*) Two folds of spongy flesh extending from the mons pubis and enclosing the labia minora, clitoris, urethral opening, and vaginal entrance. Also known as outer lips.

labia minora (singular, *labium minus*) Two small folds of skin within the labia majora that meet above the clitoris to form the clitoral hood. Also known as inner lips.

lactation The production of milk in the breasts (mammary glands).

lactational amenorrhea method (LAM) A highly effective, temporary method of contraception used by exclusively breastfeeding mothers.

lanugo The fine, downy hair covering the fetus.

laparoscopy A form of tubal ligation using a viewing lens (the laparoscope) to locate the fallopian tubes and another instrument to cut or block and close them.

latency stage   In Freudian theory, the period from age 6 to puberty, in which sexual impulses are no longer active.

leukocyte   White blood cell.

Leydig cell   Cell within the testes that secretes androgens. Also known as an interstitial cell.

libido   The sex drive.

lifetime risk   The risk within one's lifetime of a disease.

limbic system   A group of structures in the brain associated with emotions and feelings; involved with producing sexual arousal.

lochia   A bloody vaginal discharge following childbirth.

long-acting reversible contraceptive (LARC) methods   Birth control methods that provide effective contraception for an extended period without requiring user action. They include IUDs and hormonal implants.

Loulan's sexual response model   A model that incorporates both the biological and the affective components into a six-stage cycle.

low-birth-weight infants   Those born weighing less than 2,500 grams, or 5.5 pounds.

ludus   In John Lee's typology of love, playful love.

lumpectomy   Breast surgery that removes only the malignant tumor and surrounding lymph nodes.

luteal phase   The phase of the ovarian cycle during which a follicle becomes a corpus luteum and then degenerates.

luteinizing hormone (LH)   A hormone involved in ovulation.

lymphocyte   A type of leukocyte active in the immune response.

machismo   In Latino culture, highly prized masculine traits.

macrophage   A type of white blood cell that destroys foreign cells.

male hypoactive sexual desire disorder   Persistence or absence of sexual thoughts, fantasies, and desire for sexual activity.

male impersonators   Women who dress as men.

malignant tumor   A cancerous tumor that invades nearby tissues and disrupts the normal functioning of vital organs.

mammary gland   A mature female breast.

mammography   The use of X-rays to detect breast tumors before they can be seen or felt.

mania   In John Lee's typology of love, obsessive love.

mastectomy   The surgical removal of part or all of the breast.

Masters and Johnson's four-phase model of sexual response   A model that divides sexual response into four phases: excitement, plateau, orgasm, and resolution.

masturbation   Stimulation of the genitals for pleasure.

mate poaching   A deliberate effort to lure a person who is already in a relationship to a brief or long-term relationship with oneself.

medication abortion   A two-drug regimen used to terminate early pregnancy. Previously known as RU-486.

menarche   The onset of menstruation.

menopausal hormone therapy (MHT)   The administration of estrogen (often along with progestin) to relieve the symptoms of menopause. Also known as hormone replacement therapy (HRT).

menopause   The complete cessation of menstruation.

menorrhagia   Heavy or prolonged bleeding that may occur during a woman's menstrual cycle.

menses   The menstrual flow, in which the endometrium is discharged.

menstrual cycle   The more-or-less monthly process during which the uterus is readied for implantation of a fertilized ovum. Also known as uterine cycle.

menstrual phase   The shedding of the endometrium during the menstrual cycle.

menstrual synchrony   Simultaneous menstrual cycles that occur among women who work or live together.

metastasis   The process by which cancer spreads from one part of the body to an unrelated part via the bloodstream or lymphatic system.

miscarriage   The spontaneous expulsion of the fetus from the uterus. Also called spontaneous abortion.

misogyny   The hatred of or disdain for women.

Mittelschmerz   A sharp twinge that may occur on one side of the lower abdomen during ovulation.

mons pubis   In the female, the mound of fatty tissue covering the pubic bone; the pubic mound. Also known as mons veneris.

mons veneris   The pubic mound; literally, "mountain of Venus." Also known as mons pubis.

myotonia   Increased muscle tension.

necrophilia   A paraphilia involving recurrent, intense urges to engage in sexual activities with a corpse.

neonate   A newborn.

neural tube defect screening   A test on a pregnant woman's blood during the second trimester to measure the level of alpha-fetoprotein; test results reveal possible defects of the spine, spinal cord, skull, and brain.

neurosis   A psychological disorder characterized by anxiety or tension.

nocturnal orgasm or emission   Orgasm and, in males, ejaculation while sleeping; usually accompanied by erotic dreams. Also known as wet dream.

noncoercive paraphilia   Harmless and victimless paraphilia sexual behavior.

nongonococcal urethritis (NGU)   Urethral inflammation caused by something other than the gonococcus bacterium.

nonoxynol-9 (N-9)   The sperm-killing chemical in spermicide.

normal sexual behavior   Behavior that conforms to a group's typical patterns of behavior.

nymphomania   A pseudoscientific term referring to "abnormally high" or "excessive" sexual desire in a woman.

objectivity   The observation of things as they exist in reality as opposed to one's feelings or beliefs about them.

obscenity   That which is deemed offensive to "accepted" standards of decency or morality.

observational research   Studies in which the researcher unobtrusively observes people's behavior and records the findings.

Oedipal complex   In Freudian theory, the male child's erotic desire for his mother and simultaneous fear of his father.

oocyte   The female gamete, referred to as an egg or ovum.

oogenesis   The production of oocytes; the ovarian cycle.

open marriage   A marriage in which both partners agree to allow each other to have openly acknowledged and independent relationships with others, including sexual ones.

opinion   An unsubstantiated belief in or conclusion about what seems to be true according to an individual's personal thoughts.

opportunistic infection (OI)   An infection that normally does not occur or is not life-threatening but that takes advantage of a weakened immune system.

oral contraceptive (OC)   A series of pills containing synthetic estrogen and/or progesterone that regulate egg production and the menstrual cycle. Commonly known as "the pill."

oral-genital sex   The touching of a partner's genitals with the mouth or tongue.

oral stage   In Freudian theory, the period lasting from birth to age 1, in which infant eroticism is focused on the mouth.

OraQuick in-house HIV test   A testing procedure involving swabbing the mouth for an oral fluid sample and using a kit to test it with the results being available in 20 minutes.

orgasm   The climax of sexual excitement, including rhythmic contractions of muscles in the genital area and intensely pleasurable sensations; usually accompanied by ejaculation in males beginning in puberty.

orgasmic platform   A portion of the vagina that undergoes vasocongestion during sexual arousal.

os   The cervical opening.

ovarian cycle   The more-or-less monthly process during which oocytes are produced.

ovarian follicle   A saclike structure in which an oocyte develops.

ovary   One of a pair of organs that produce oocytes.

ovulation   The release of an oocyte from the ovary during the ovarian cycle.

ovulatory phase   The phase of the ovarian cycle during which ovulation occurs.

ovum (plural, **ova**)   An egg; an oocyte; the female gamete.

oxytocin   A hormone that stimulates uterine contractions during birth and possibly orgasm. Known as the "love hormone," oxytocin has a major role in pair bonding.

pansexual   An individual or group who is sexually interested in and open to other people regardless of gender.

Pap test   A method of testing for cervical cancer by scraping cell samples from the cervix and examining them under a microscope.

paraphilia   Any intense and persistent sexual interest other than sexual interest in genital stimulation or preparatory fondling with phenotypically normal, physically mature consenting human partners.

paraphilic disorder   A paraphilia that is currently causing distress or impairment to the individual or a paraphilia whose satisfaction has entailed personal harm, or risk of harm, to others.

paraphilic sexual interest   The American Psychiatric Association classification of persons with paraphilic interest but who are not impaired by the interest and who do not declare distress about the paraphilic impulses.

partialism   A paraphilia in which a person is sexually attracted to a specific body part.

participant observation   A method of observational research in which the researcher participates in the behaviors being studied.

pathological behavior   Behavior deemed unhealthy or diseased by current medical standards.

pedophilia   Having a sexual focus on a prepubescent child or children.

peer delinquent subculture   An antisocial youth subculture.

pelvic floor   The underside of the pelvic area, extending from the top of the pubic bone to the anus.

pelvic inflammatory disease (PID)   An infection of the fallopian tube (or tubes), caused by an organism such as *C. trachomatis* or *N. gonorrhoeae,* in which scar tissue may form within the tubes and block the passage of eggs or cause an ectopic pregnancy; a leading cause of female infertility. Also called salpingitis.

penis   The male organ through which semen and urine pass.

penis envy   In Freudian theory, a female desire to have a penis.

perimenopause   A period of gradual changes and adjustments a woman's body goes through prior to menopause, before menstruation stops completely.

perinatal HIV transmission (mother to child)   Women transmit HIV to their babies during pregnancy or labor and delivery.

perineum   An area of soft tissue between the genitals and the anus that covers the muscles and ligaments of the pelvic floor.

Peyronie's disease   A painful male sexual disorder, resulting in curvature of the penis, that is caused by fibrous tissue and calcium deposits developing in the corpora cavernosa of the penis.

phallic stage   In Freudian theory, the period from age 3 through 5, during which both male and female children exhibit interest in the genitals.

pheromone   A sexually arousing chemical substance secreted into the air by many kinds of animals.

placenta   The organ of exchange between mother and fetus.

pleasuring   Erotic, nongenital touching.

plethysmograph   A device attached to the genitals to measure physiological response.

PLISSIT model   A model for sex therapy consisting of four progressive levels: **p**ermission, **l**imited **i**nformation, **s**pecific **s**uggestions, and **i**ntensive **t**herapy.

***Pneumocystis carinii* pneumonia (PCP)x**   An opportunistic lung infection caused by a common, usually harmless organism, frequently occurring among people with AIDS.

polyamory   Involves a lifestyle of being open to having more than one loving intimate relationship at a time, with the full knowledge and consent of all partners involved.

pornography   Sexually explicit material that is generally evaluated negatively.

post-exposure prophylaxis (PEP)   HIV-negative persons taking antiretroviral medicine to help prevent HIV infection as soon as possible after possible exposure to HIV.

postpartum depression   A form of depression thought to be related to hormonal changes following the delivery of a child.

postpartum period   The period (about 3 months) following childbirth, characterized by physical stabilization and emotional adjustment.

postpartum psychosis A serious and rare postpartum mental illness thought to be biologically based and related to hormonal changes.

postrefusal sexual persistence Continued requests for sexual contact after being refused.

posttraumatic stress disorder (PTSD) A group of characteristic symptoms, such as depression, that follow an intensely distressing event outside a person's normal life experience.

pragma In John Lee's typology of love, practical love.

precocious puberty The appearance of physical and hormonal signs of pubertal development at an earlier age than is considered normal.

preconception care Interventions that aim to identify and modify medical, behavioral, and social risks to a woman's health or pregnancy outcome through prevention and management.

pre-exposure prophylaxis (PrEP) HIV-negative persons at substantial risk for HIV taking antiretroviral medicine every day to help prevent becoming infected with HIV.

pregnancy-induced hypertension Condition characterized by high blood pressure, edema, and protein in the urine.

premature (early) ejaculation "Early" ejaculation following vaginal penetration.

premenstrual dysphoric disorder Severe premenstrual symptoms, sufficient enough to disrupt a woman's functioning.

premenstrual syndrome (PMS) A set of severe symptoms associated with menstruation.

prepared childbirth Based on knowledge of conditioned reflexes, women learn to mentally separate the physical stimulus of uterine contractions from the conditioned response of pain.

preterm birth Birth that takes place prior to 37 weeks of gestation.

prevalence Overall occurrence; the total number of cases of a disease, for example.

priapism Prolonged and painful erection due to the inability of blood to drain from the penis.

progesterone A female hormone that helps regulate the menstrual cycle and sustain pregnancy.

proliferative phase The buildup of the endometrium in response to increased estrogen during the menstrual cycle.

prostaglandins Natural substances made by the cells in the endometrium and other parts of the body. High levels in women can cause dysmenorrhea.

prostate gland A muscular gland encircling the urethra that produces about one third of the seminal fluid.

prostate-specific antigen (PSA) test A blood test used to help diagnose prostate cancer.

prostatic hyperplasia A benign condition in which the prostate gland enlarges and blocks the flow of urine.

prostatitis A frequently painful condition that involves inflammation of the prostate and sometimes the areas around the prostate.

prostitution The exchange of sex for money and/or goods.

protection from harm A basic entitlement of all participants in research studies, including the right to confidentiality and anonymity.

proximity Nearness in physical space and time.

psychoanalysis A psychological system developed by Sigmund Freud that traces behavior to unconscious motivations.

psychosexual development Development of the psychological components of sexuality.

puberty The stage of human development when the body becomes capable of reproduction.

pubic lice *Phthirus pubis,* colloquially known as crabs; tiny lice that infest the pubic hair.

pubococcygeus A part of the muscular sling stretching from the pubic bone in front to the tailbone in back.

queer A reclaimed, self-affirming umbrella term used by some gay men, lesbian women and transgendered person.

queer theory Identifies sexuality as a system that cannot be understood as gender neutral or by the actions of heterosexual males and females. It proposes that one's sexual identity and one's gender identity are partly or wholly socially constructed.

radical hysterectomy The surgical removal of the uterus and ligaments in order to treat some cancers or severe gynecological problems.

random sample A portion of a larger group collected in an unbiased way.

rape Sexual penetration against a person's will through the use or threat of force.

rape trauma syndrome The emotional changes an individual undergoes as a result of rape.

rapid test An HIV test which uses blood or oral fluid that produces results in 30 minutes or less.

rebound sex Sexual experiences in the aftermath of a romantic relationship breakup.

refractory period For men, a period following ejaculation during which they are not capable of having ejaculation again.

relaxin A hormone produced by the placenta in the later months of pregnancy that increases flexibility in the ligaments and joints of the pelvic area. In men, relaxin is contained in semen, where it assists in sperm motility.

representative sample A small group representing a larger group in terms of age, sex, ethnicity, socioeconomic status, orientation, and so on.

repression A psychological mechanism that keeps people from becoming aware of hidden memories and motives because they arouse guilt or pain.

reproduction The biological process by which individuals are produced.

retrograde ejaculation The backward expulsion of semen into the bladder rather than out of the urethral opening.

retrovirus A virus capable of reversing the normal genetic writing process, causing the host cell to replicate the virus instead of itself.

reverse transcriptase An enzyme in the core of a retrovirus, enabling it to write its own genetic program into a host cell's DNA.

RNA tests Detects HIV directly instead of the antibodies to HIV.

root The portion of the penis attached to the pelvic cavity.

satyriasis An excessive, uncontrollable sexual desire in a man.

scabies A red, intensely itchy rash appearing on the genitals, buttocks, feet, wrists, knuckles, abdomen, armpits, or scalp, caused by the barely visible mite *Sarcoptes scabiei*.

schema A set of interrelated ideas that helps individuals process information by organizing it in useful ways.

scientific method A systematic approach to acquiring knowledge by collecting data, forming a hypothesis, testing it empirically, and observing the results.

script In sociology, the acts, rules, and expectations associated with a particular role.

scrotum A pouch of skin that holds the two testes.

secondary sex characteristics The physical changes that occur as a result of increased amounts of hormones targeting other areas of the body.

secretory phase The phase of the menstrual cycle during which the endometrium begins to prepare for the arrival of a fertilized ovum; without fertilization, the corpus luteum begins to degenerate.

secure attachment A style of infant attachment characterized by feelings of security and confidence in relation to the primary caregiver.

self-disclosure The revelation of personal information that others would not ordinarily know because of its riskiness.

semen or **seminal fluid** The ejaculated fluid containing sperm.

seminal vesicle One of two glands at the back of the bladder that secrete about 60% of the seminal fluid.

seminiferous tubules Tiny, tightly compressed tubes in which spermatogenesis takes place.

sensate focus The focusing on touch and the giving and receiving of pleasure as part of the treatment of sexual difficulties.

serial monogamy A succession of monogamous (exclusive) marriages or relationships.

seroconversion The process by which a person develops antibodies.

serodiscordant A couple in which one person is HIV-positive and the other is HIV-negative.

serosorting Having sex with a partner one believes has the same HIV status (negative or positive) as one's own HIV status.

serostatus The absence or presence of antibodies for a particular antigen.

sex flush A darkening of the skin or a rash that temporarily appears as a result of blood rushing to the skin's surface during sexual excitation.

sex information/advice genre A media genre that transmits information and norms about sexuality to a mass audience.

sexologist A specialist in the study of human sexuality. Also called sex researcher.

sex reassignment surgery (SRS) A process that brings a person's genitals in line with his or her gender identity and diminishes the serious suffering the person experiences.

sex selection Pre- and post-implantation methods that allow couples to choose whether to have a boy or a girl. (Also marketed as "family balancing.")

sexism Discrimination against people based on their sex rather than their individual merits.

sexting The creating, sharing, and forwarding of sexually suggestive text and nude or nearly nude images.

sexual assault A legal term for forced sexual contact that does not necessarily include penile-vaginal intercourse.

sexual aversion disorder A sexual function disorder characterized by a consistently phobic response to sexual activities or the idea of such activities.

sexual coercion Any kind of sexual activity initiated with another person through the use of argument, pressure, pleading, or cajoling, as well as force, pressure, alcohol or drugs, or authority.

sexual debut Penile-vaginal or anal intercourse that occurs for the first time in a person's life; it is often considered a milestone for many adolescents.

sexual diary The personal notes a study participant makes of his or her sexual activity and then reports to a researcher.

sexual dysfunction A clinically significant disturbance in a person's ability to respond sexually or to experience sexual pleasure.

sexual exclusivity Sexual partners who have sex only with each other.

sexual function dissatisfaction A condition in which an individual or a couple, not based on a medical diagnosis, decide they are unhappy with their sexual relationship and that they have a problem. Also known as sexual function difficulties or sexual dysfunction.

sexual function enhancement Improvement in the quality of one's sexual function.

sexual harassment The abuse of power for sexual ends; the creation of a hostile work or educational environment because of unwelcomed conduct or conditions of a sexual nature.

sexual health Physical, mental, and social well-being related to sexuality.

sexual identity One's self-label or self-identification as a heterosexual, homosexual, or bisexual person.

sexual intercourse The movement of bodies while the penis is in the vagina. Sometimes also called vaginal intercourse or penile-vaginal intercourse.

sexual interest An inclination to behave sexually.

sexually explicit material (SEM) Material such as photographs, films, magazines, books, or Internet sites, whose primary themes, topics, or depictions involve sexuality or cause sexual arousal.

sexual masochism Being humiliated, beaten, bound, or otherwise made to suffer.

sexual orientation The pattern of sexual and emotional attraction based on the gender of one's partner.

sexual response cycle A sequence of changes and patterns that take place in the genitals and body during sexual arousal.

sexual sadism A paraphilia characterized by recurrent, intense urges to engage in real (not fantasy) sexual behaviors in which the person inflicts physical or psychological harm on a victim.

sexual scripts Sexual behaviors and interactions learned from one's culture.

sexual strategies theory The theory that men and women have different short-term and long-term mating strategies.

sexual variation Sexual variety and diversity in terms of sexual orientation, attitudes, behaviors, desires, fantasies, and so on; sexual activity not statistically typical of usual sexual behavior.

sexual violence A broad term for rape, including extreme behaviors such as forced penetration.

sexualize (sexualization) Occurs when a person's value comes only from his or her sexual appeal or behavior, to the exclusion of other characteristics, and when a person is sexually objectified.

shaft The body of the penis.

she-male A male who has undergone breast augmentation.

smegma A cheesy substance produced by several small glands beneath the foreskin of the penis and hood of the clitoris.

social construction The development by society of social categories, such as masculinity, femininity, heterosexuality, and homosexuality.

social construction theory Views gender as a set of practices and performances that occur through language and a political system.

socioeconomic status Ranking in society based on a combination of occupational, educational, and income levels.

sodomy Term used in the law to define sexual behaviors other than penile-vaginal intercourse, such as anal sex and oral sex.

solicitation In terms of prostitution, a word, gesture, or action that implies an offer of sex for sale.

spectatoring The process in which a person becomes a spectator of his or her sexual activities, thereby causing sexual function difficulties.

sperm The male gametes.

spermarche In boys the development of sperm in the testicles.

spermatic cord A tube suspending the testis within the scrotal sac, containing nerves, blood vessels, and a vas deferens.

spermatogenesis The process by which a sperm develops from a spermatid.

spermicide A substance that is toxic to sperm.

sponge (Today sponge) A round, plastic foam birth control device that contains spermicide.

spontaneous abortion The natural expulsion of the conceptus, commonly referred to as miscarriage.

squeeze technique A technique for the treatment of early or involuntary ejaculation in which the partner squeezes the erect penis below the glans immediately prior to ejaculation.

stalking A course of action that would cause a reasonable person to feel fear.

status An individual's position or ranking in a group.

statutory rape Consensual sexual intercourse with a female under the age of consent.

stereotype A set of simplistic, rigidly held, overgeneralized beliefs about a particular type of individual or group of people, an idea, and so on.

sterilization A surgical procedure that makes the reproductive organs incapable of producing or "delivering" viable gametes (sperm and eggs).

storge In John Lee's typology of love, companionate love.

strain gauge A device resembling a rubber band that is placed over the penis to measure physiological response.

street harassment Unwelcomed sexual advances.

streetwalker A prostitute who solicits on the streets.

substance/medication-induced sexual dysfunction A specific substance presuming causing the sexual dysfunction.

sudden infant death syndrome (SIDS) One type of sudden unexplained infant death whereby an infant of less than 1 year of age dies of an unexplained cause.

surrogate motherhood An approach to infertility in which one woman bears a child for another.

survey research A method of gathering information from a small group to make inferences about a larger group.

sweating The moistening of the vagina by secretions from its walls. Also called vaginal transudation.

swinging A wide range of sexual activities conducted between three or more people. Typically, swinging activities occur when a married or otherwise committed couple engages with another couple, multiple couples, or a single individual.

symptothermal method A fertility awareness method combining the three fertility indicators.

syphilis An STI caused by the *Treponema pallidum* bacterium.

tantric sex A sexual technique based on Eastern religions in which a couple shares "energy" during sexual intercourse.

T cell Any of several types of lymphocytes involved in the immune response.

telephone scatologia A paraphilia involving recurrent, intense urges to make obscene telephone calls.

tenting The expansion of the inner two thirds of the vagina during sexual arousal.

teratogens Substances or other factors that cause defects in developing embryos or fetuses.

testicles or **testes** (singular, testis) The paired male gonads inside the scrotum.

testosterone A steroid hormone associated with sperm production, the development of secondary sex characteristics in males, and the sex drive in both males and females.

testosterone replacement therapy Treatment that is indicated when both clinical symptoms and signs suggestive of androgen deficiency and decreased testosterone levels are present.

Title IX An education amendment that protects people from discrimination based on sex in education programs or activities that receive federal financial assistance.

toxic shock syndrome (TSS) A potentially life-threatening condition caused by the *Staphylococcus aureus* bacterium and linked to the use of superabsorbent tampons and other devices that block the vagina or cervix during menstruation.

transcervical sterilization A permanent method of birth control that does not require surgery.

transgender An umbrella term for those whose gender expression or identity is not congruent with the sex assigned at birth and whose gender is not validated by the dominant culture.

transition The end of the first stage of labor, when the infant's head enters the birth canal.

transsexuality A phenomenon in which a person is intent to live through actions, dress, hormone therapy, and/or surgery as a gender other than that assigned at birth. Most (but not all) transsexuals engage in some process of altering either primary or secondary sexual characteristics through hormone treatment or surgery or both.

transvestic disorder The recurrence and intense cross-dressing or thoughts of cross-dressing over at least 6 months accompanied with significant emotional distress that impairs social or interpersonal functioning.

transvestism Cross-dressing in clothing of the other sex.

triangular theory of love A theory developed by Robert Sternberg emphasizing the dynamic quality of love as expressed by the interrelationship of three elements: intimacy, passion, and commitment.

tribidism A behavior in which one partner lies on top of the other and moves rhythmically for genital stimulation.

trichomoniasis A vaginal infection caused by *Trichomonas vaginalis*. Also known as trich.

trust Belief in the reliability and integrity of another person, process, thing, or institution.

tubal ligation The cutting and tying off (or other method of closure) of the fallopian tubes so that ova cannot be fertilized.

Turner syndrome (45,XO) A chromosomal condition in which a female does not have the usual pair of X chromosomes.

two-spirit In many cultures, a male who assumes female dress, gender role, and status.

twerk To dance in a sexually provocative manner.

umbilical cord The cord connecting the placenta and fetus, through which nutrients pass.

unrequited love Love that is one-sided or not openly reciprocated or understood.

urethra The tube through which urine (and, in men, semen) passes.

urethral opening In females, the opening in the urethra, through which urine is expelled. In males, the opening in the urethra, through which semen is ejaculated and urine is excreted.

urethritis Inflammation of the urethra.

urophilia A paraphilia in which a person gets sexual pleasure from contact with urine.

uterus A hollow, thick-walled, muscular organ held in the pelvic cavity by flexible ligaments and supported by several muscles. Also known as womb.

vacuum aspiration A first-trimester form of abortion using vacuum suction to remove the conceptus and other tissue from the uterus.

vagina In females, a flexible, muscular organ that begins between the legs and extends diagonally toward the small of the back. It encompasses the penis during sexual intercourse and is the pathway (birth canal) through which an infant is born.

vaginal ring A vaginal form of reversible, hormonal birth control. Commonly referred to as NuvaRing.

vaginismus A sexual function difficulty characterized by muscle spasms around the vaginal entrance, preventing the insertion of a penis.

vaginitis Any of several kinds of vaginal infection.

value judgment An evaluation as "good" or "bad" based on moral or ethical standards rather than objective ones.

variable An aspect or factor that can be manipulated in an experiment.

varicocele A varicose vein above the testicle that may cause lowered fertility in men.

vas deferens (plural, *vasa deferentia*) One of two tubes that transport sperm from the epididymis to the ejaculatory duct within the prostate gland.

vasectomy A permanent method of birth control in which each vas deferens is severed, thereby preventing sperm from entering the vas deferens and mixing with seminal fluids to form semen.

vasocongestion Blood engorgement of body tissues.

vernix The waxy substance that sometimes covers an infant at birth.

vestibule The area enclosed by the labia minora.

virus A protein-coated package of genes that invades a cell and alters the way in which the cell reproduces itself.

voyeurism Observing an unsuspecting person who is naked, disrobing, or having sex.

vulva The collective term for the external female genitals.

vulvodynia Chronic vulvar pain or discomfort of the vulva.

window period The variable amount of time it takes for the immune system to produce enough antibodies to be detected by an antibody test.

ZIFT (zygote intrafallopian transfer) An ART procedure whereby a woman's eggs are fertilized in the laboratory and then transferred to her fallopian tubes.

zoophilia A paraphilia involving recurrent, intense urges to engage in sexual activities with animals. Also referred to as bestiality.

References

Abbey, A. (2012). Alcohol's role in sexual violence perpetration: Theoretical explanations, existing evidence, and future directions. *Alcohol and Drug Review, 30*(5), 481–489. Available: http://www.ncbi.nlm.nih.gov/pmc/articles/PMC3177166/ (Last visited 1/2/15).

Abramson, P. R., & Mosher, D. L. (1975). Development of a measure of negative attitudes toward masturbation. *Journal of Consulting and Clinical Psychology, 43,* 485–490.

Accord Alliance. (2011). Clinical guidelines for the management of disorders of sex development in childhood. Available: http://www.accordalliance.org (Last visited 6/9/11).

ACT for Youth Center of Excellence. (2009). Proceedings of the Adolescent Sexual Health Symposium. Available: http://ecommons.cornell.edu/bitstream/1813/19158/2/ASHS_Proceedings.pdf (Last visited 8/19/14).

ACT for Youth Center of Excellence. (2014). What is sexual health? Available: http://www.actforyouth.net/health_sexuality/sexual_health/ (Last visited 8/19/14). Used with permission.

Adimora, A. A., Schoenbach, V. J., Bonas, M., Martinson, F. E. A., Donaldson, R. H., & Stancil, T. R. (2002). Concurrent sexual partnerships among women in the United States. *Epidemiology, 13,* 320–327.

Adimora, A. A., Schoenbach, V. J., & Doherty, I. A. (2007). Concurrent sexual partnerships among men in the United States. *American Journal of Public Health, 97,* 2230–2237.

Ahrold, T. K., & Meston, C. M. (2010). Ethnic differences in sexual attitudes of U.S. college students: Gender, acculturation, and religiosity factors. *Archives of Sexual Behavior, 39,* 190–202.

Ahrons, C. (2004). *We're still family.* New York: HarperCollins.

Ainsworth, M., et al. (1978). *Patterns of attachment: A psychological study of the strange situation.* Hillsdale, NJ: Erlbaum.

Albert, B. (2012). With one voice 2012: America's adults and teens sound off about teen pregnancy. Available: http://thenationalcampaign.org/resource/one-voice-2012 (Last visited 7/28/14).

Alcott, W. (1868). *The physiology of marriage.* Boston: Jewett.

Alison, L., Santtila, P., Sandnabba, N. K., & Nordling, N. (2001). Sadomasochistically oriented behavior: Diversity in practice and meaning. *Archives of Sexual Behavior, 30,* 1–12.

Allen, E. S., Atkins, D., Baucom, D. H., Snyder, D., et al. (2005). Intrapersonal, interpersonal, and contextual factors in engaging in and responding to extramarital involvement. *Clinical Psychology: Science and Practice, 12,* 101–130.

Allen, K. R., & Goldberg, A. E. (2009). Sexual activity during menstruation: A qualitative study. *Journal of Sex Research, 46*(6), 535–545.

Althof, S. E. (2010). What's new in sex therapy. *Journal of Sexual Medicine, 7,* 5–13.

Altman, D. (1985). *AIDS in the mind of America.* Garden City, NY: Doubleday.

Amaro, H., Raj, A., & Reed, E. (2001). Women's sexual health: The need for feminist analyses in public health in the decade of behavior. *Psychology of Women Quarterly, 25,* 324–334.

Amato, P. R. (2000). The consequences of divorce for adults and children. *Journal of Marriage and Family, 62,* 1269–1287.

Amato, P. R. (2003). Reconciling divergent perspectives: Judith Wallerstein, quantitative family research & children of divorce. *Family Relations, 52*(4), 332–339.

Amato, P. R. (2010). Research on divorce: Continuing trends and new developments. *Journal of Marriage and Family, 72,* 650–666.

Amato, P. R., Kane, J. B., & James, S. (2011). Reconsidering the good divorce. *Family Relations, 60*(5), 511–524. Available: http://www.ncbi.nlm.nih.gov/pmc/articles/PMC3223936/ (Last viewed 9/30/14).

American Academy of Child and Adolescent Psychiatry. (2008). Facts for families: Child sexual abuse. Available: http://www.aacp.org/cs/roots/facts_for_families/child_sexual_abuse (Last visited 10/7/08).

American Academy of Pediatrics. (2010). AAP updates guidelines to help families make positive media choices. Available: https://www.aap.org/en-us/about-the-aap/aap-press-room/Pages/AAP-Updates-Guidance-to-Help-Families-Make-Positive-Media-Choices.aspx

American Academy of Pediatrics. (2011). SIDS and other sleep-related infant deaths: Expansion of recommendations for a safe infant sleeping environment. Available: http://pediatrics.aappublications.org/content/early/2011/10/12/peds.2011-2284 (Last visited 10/30/11).

American Academy of Pediatrics. (2014.1a). Teen magazines and their effect on girls. Available: http://www.healthychildren.org/English/family-life/Media/pages/Teen-Magazines-and-Their-Effect-on-Girls.aspx (Last visited 3/17/14).

American Academy of Pediatrics. (2014.11a). Contraception for adolescents. *Pediatrics, 134*(4), 1244–1256.

American Academy of Pediatrics. (2014.12a). Policy statement: Breastfeeding and the use of human milk. *Pediatrics, 129*(3), 827–841. Available: http://pediatrics.aappublications.org/content/129/3/e827.full#content-block (Last visited 12/18/14).

American Academy of Pediatrics. (2014.15a). Where we stand on circumcision. Available: http://www.healthychildren.org/English/ages-sages/prenatal/decisions-to-make/Pages/Circumcision.html (Last visited 12/10/14).

American Association of Retired Persons (AARP). (2010). Sex, romance and relationships: AARP survey of midlife and older adults. Washington, DC: Author.

American Association of University Women (AAUW). (2006). Drawing the line: Sexual harassment on campus. Available: http://www.aauw.org/newsroom/presskits/DTL_Press_Conf_060124/DTL_012406.cfm (Last visited 1/10/06).

American Cancer Society. (2013.13a). Radical hysterectomy. Available: http://www.cancer.org/treatment/treatmentsandsideeffects/physicalsideeffects/sexualsideeffectsinwomen/sexualityforthewoman/sexuality-for-women-with-cancer-rad-hysterectomy (Last visited 1/7/15).

American Cancer Society. (2013.13b). Testicular cancer. Available: http://www.cancer.org/cancer/testicularcancer/detailedguide/index (Last visited 1/8/15).

American Cancer Society. (2014.13a). Placebo effect. Available: http://www.cancer.org/treatment/treatmentsandsideeffects/treatmenttypes/placebo-effect (Last visited 1/2/15).

American Cancer Society. (2014.13b). What are the key statistics about breast cancer? Available: http://www.cancer.org/cancer/breastcancer/detailedguide/breast-cancer-key-statistics (Last visited 1/5/15).

American Cancer Society. (2014.13c). What are the risk factors for breast cancer? Available: http://www.cancer.org/cancer/breastcancer/detailedguide/breast-cancer-risk-factors (Last visited 1/5/15).

American Cancer Society. (2014.13d). Breast cancer survival rates by stage. Available: http://www.cancer.org/cancer/breastcancer/detailedguide/breast-cancer-survival-by-stage (Last visited 1/5/15).

American Cancer Society. (2014.13e). Cancer facts for lesbians and bisexual women. Available: http://www.cancer.org/healthy/find-cancerearly/womenshealth/cancer-facts-for-lesbians-and-bisexual-women (Last visited 1/5/15).

American Cancer Society. (2014.13f). American Cancer Society recommendations for early breast cancer detection in women without breast symptoms. Available: http://www.cancer.org/cancer/breastcancer/moreinformation/breastcancerearlydetection/breast-cancer-early-detection-acs-recs (Last visited 1/5/15).

American Cancer Society. (2014.13g). How is breast cancer treated? Available: http://www.cancer.org/cancer/breastcancer/detailedguide/breast-cancer-treating-general-info (Last visited 1/6/15).

American Cancer Society. (2014.13i). What is cervical cancer? Available: http://www.cancer.org/cancer/cervicalcancer/detailedguide/cervical-cancer-what-is-cervical-cancer (Last visited 1/7/15).

American Cancer Society. (2014.13j). Ovarian cancer. Available: http://www.cancer.org/cancer/ovariancancer/detailedguide/index (Last visited1/7/15).

American Cancer Society. (2014.13k). What is endometrial cancer? Available: http://www.cancer.org/cancer/endometrialcancer/detailedguide/endometrial-uterine-cancer-what-is-cancer (Last visited 1/7/15).

American Cancer Society. (2014.13l). Vaginal cancer. Available: http://www.cancer.org/cancer/vaginalcancer/detailedguide/index (Last visited 1/7/15).

American Cancer Society. (2014.13m). Prostate cancer. What is prostate cancer? Available: http://www.cancer.org/cancer/prostatecancer/detailedguide/prostate-cancer-what-is-prostate-cancer (Last visited 1/8/15).

American Cancer Society. (2014.13n). Breast cancer in men. Available: http://www.cancer.org/cancer/breastcancerinmen/detailedguide/breast-cancer-in-men-what-is-breast-cancer-in-men (Last visited 1/13/15).

American Cancer Society. (2014.13o). Anal cancer. Available: http://www.cancer.org/cancer/analcancer/detailedguide/anal-cancer-what-is-anal-cancer (Last visited 1/13/15).

American Cancer Society. (2015.13a). Testicular self-exam. Available: http://www.cancer.org/cancer/testicularcancer/moreinformation/doihavetesticularcancer/do-i-have-testicular-cancer-self-exam (Last visited 5/7/15).

American Cancer Society. (2015.14a). Cancer, sex, and sexuality. Retrived February 10, 2015 from: http://www.cancer.org/treatment/treatmentand side effects/physicalsideeffects/sexual.

American College Health Association (ACHA). (2011, Dec.). Position statement on preventing sexual violence on college and university campuses. Available: http://www.acha.org/Publications/docs/ACHA_Statement_Preventing_Sexual_Violence_Dec2011.pdf (Last visited 6/23/14).

American College Health Association. (2014.13a). Spring 2014 reference group data report. Available: http://www.acha-ncha.org/docs/ACHA-NCHA-II_ReferenceGroup_DataReport_Spring2014.pdf (Last visited 1/2/15).

American College Health Association. (2014.16a). *American College Health Association—National College Health Assessment II: Undergraduate Students Reference Group Executive Summary Spring 2014.* Hanover, MD: American College Health Association.

American College of Obstetricians and Gynecologists (ACOG). (2006). ACOG recommends restricted use of episiotomies: News release. Available: http://www.acog.org/from_home/publications/press_releases/nr03-31-06-2.cfm (Last visited 11/24/08).

American College of Obstetricians and Gynecologists (ACOG). (2007). New recommendations for Down syndrome: Screening should be offered to all pregnant women. Available: http://www.acog.org/from_home/publications/press_releases/nr01-02-07.cfm (Last visited 10/14/08).

American College of Obstetricians and Gynecologists (ACOG). (2014). Diagnostic tests for birth defects. Available: https://www.acog.org/Patients/FAQs/Diagnostic-Tests-for-Birth-Defects#what (Last visited 12/15/14).

American Community Survey. (2013). Selected social characteristics in the United States: 2009–2013. *United States Census Bureau.* Available: http://factfinder.census.gov/faces/tableservices/jsf/pages/productview.xhtml?pid=ACS_13_5YR_DP02&prodType=table (Last visited 1/27/15).

American Psychiatric Association (APA). (2000). *Diagnostic and statistical manual of mental disorders* (4th ed., text revision). Washington, DC: Author.

American Psychiatric Association (APA). (2012a). Position statement on access to care for transgender and gender variant individuals. Washington, DC: Author.

American Psychiatric Association (APA). (2012b). Position statement on discrimination against transgender and gender variant individuals. Washington, DC: Author.

American Psychiatric Association. (2013). *Diagnostic and statistical manual of mental disorders* (5th ed.). Arlington, VA: Author.

American Psychiatric Association (APA). (2013). *Diagnostic and statistical manual for mental disorders,* (5th ed.). Arlington, VA: Author.

American Psychiatric Association (APA). (2013.13a). Feeding and eating disorders. Available: http://www.dsm5.org/Documents/Eating%20Disorders%20Fact%20Sheet.pdf (Last visited 1/2/15).

American Psychological Association, Task force on the sexualization of girls. (2007). *Report of the APA Task Force on the Sexualization of Girls.* Available: http://www.apa.org/pi/women/programs/girls/report.aspx (Last visited 1/21/11).

American Psychological Association, Task force on the sexualization of girls. (2010). *Report of the APA task force on the sexualization of girls*. Available: http://www.apa.org/pi/women/programs/girls/report-full.pdf (Last visited 7/25/14).

American Psychological Association (APA). (2011). Hormones and desire. Available: https://www.apa.org/monitor/2011/03/hormones.aspx (Last visited 6/13/14).

American Social Health Association (ASHA). (1998a). STD statistics. Available: http://www.ashastd.org/std/stats/html (Last visited 12/5/00).

American Social Health Association (ASHA). (1998b). Chlamydia: What you should know. Available: http://sunsite.unc.edu/ASHA/std/chlam.html#intro (Last visited 2/14/98).

American Social Health Association (ASHA). (2006). STD/STI statistics. Available: http://www.ashastd.org/learn/learn_statisticss.cfm (Last visited 10/14/08).

American Social Health Association (ASHA). (2008). NGU (nongonococcal urethritis). Available: http://www.ashastad.org/learn/learn_ngu.cfm (Last visited 10/22/08).

American Social Health Association (ASHA). (2011a). NGU (non-gonococcal urethritis). Available: http://www.ashastd.org/learn/learn_ngu.cfm (Last visited 11/14/11).

American Social Health Association (ASHA). (2011b). Learn about HPV. Available: http://www.ashastd.org/hpv_learn_fastfacts.cfm (Last visited 11/14/11).

American Social Health Association (ASHA). (2011c). Crabs. Available: http://www.ashastgd.org/learn/learn_crabs_facts.cfm (Last visited 11/14/11).

American Society of Aesthetic Plastic Surgery. (2013). Cosmetic surgery national data bank. Available: http://www.surgery.org/sites/default/files/Stats2013_3.pdf (Last visited 6/14/14).

American Society of Plastic Surgeons. (2014). Plastic surgery procedures continue steady growth in U.S. Available: http://www.plasticsurgery.org/news/past-press-releases/2014-archives/plastic-surgery-procedures-continue-steady-growth-in-us.html (Last visited 6/13/14).

American Urological Association. (2013). Early detection of prostate cancer: AUA guidelines. Available: http://www.auanet.org/education/guidelines/prostate-cancer-detection.cfm (Last visited 1/8/15).

Anderson, C. L., & Brown, C. E. L. (2009, January 15). Fetal chromosomal abnormalities: Antenatal screening and diagnosis. *American Family Physician, 79*(2), 117–123.

Anderson, M., Kunkel, A., & Dennis, M. R. (2011). "Let's (not) talk about that": Bridging the past sexual experiences taboo to build healthy romantic relationships. *Journal of Sex Research, 48,* 381–391.

Androgen insensitivity syndrome. (2014). Genetics home reference. Available: http://ghr.nlm.nih.gov/condition/androgen-insensitivity-syndrome (Last visited 7/11/14).

Angier, N. (2007, April 10). Search for the female equivalent of Viagra is helping to keep lab rats smiling. *New York Times,* p. D4.

Annan, N. T., et al. (2009). Rectal chlamydia—A reservoir of undiagnosed infection in men who have sex with men. *Sexually Transmitted Infections, 85,* 176–179.

Annon, J. (1974). *The behavioral treatment of sexual problems.* Honolulu: Enabling Systems.

Annon, J. (1976). *Behavioral treatment of sexual problems: Brief therapy.* New York: Harper & Row.

Armstrong, N. R., & Wilson, J. D. (2006). Did the "Brazilian" kill the pubic louse? *Sexually Transmitted Infections, 82,* 265–266.

Arnold, L. D., Bachmann, G. A., Rosen, R., & Rhoads, G. G. (2007). Assessment of vulvodynia symptoms in a sample of U.S. women: A prevalence survey with a nest case control study. *American Journal of Obstetrics and Gynecology, 196*(2), 128e1–128e6.

Ashton, A. K. (2007). The new sexual pharmacology: A guide for the clinician. In S. Leiblum (Ed.), *Principles and practice of sex therapy* (4th ed., pp. 509–542). New York: Guilford Press.

Ask a criminal lawyer. (2014). Statutory rape. Available: http://criminal.findlaw.com/criminal-charges/statutory-rape.html?DCMP-GOO-CRIM (Last visited 9/28/14).

Attridge, M. (2013). Jealousy and relationship closeness: Exploring the good (reactive) and bad (suspicious) sides of romantic jealousy. *Sage Open, 3*(1). Available: http://classic.sgo.sagepub.com/content/3/1/2158244013476054.full (Last visited 10/24/14).

Auchincloss, A. H., & Hadden, W. (2002). The health effects of rural-urban residence and concentrated poverty. *Journal of Rural Health, 18,* 319–336.

Aughinbaugh, A., Robles, O., & Sun, H. (2013). Marriage and divorce: Patterns by gender, race and educational attainment. U.S. Bureau of Labor Statistics, *Monthly Labor Review.* Available: http://www.bls.gov/opub/mlr/2013/article/marriage-and-divorce-patterns-by-gender-race-and-educational-attainment-1.htm (Last visited 9/30/14).

Avis, N. E., Crawford, S. L., Greendale, G., Bromberger, J. T., et al. (2015, Jan. 16). Duration of menopausal vasomotor symptoms over the menopause transition. *JAMA Internal Medicine.* Available: http://archinte.jamanetwork.com/article.aspx?articleid=2110996 (Last visited 3/15/15).

Backstrom, L., Armstrong, E. A., & Puentes, J. (2012). Women's negotiation of cunnilingus in college hookups and relationships. *Journal of Sex Research, 49,* 1–2.

Bailey, J., Dunne, M., & Martin, N. (2000). Genetic and environmental influences on sexual orientation and its correlates in an Australian twin sample. *Journal of Personality and Social Psychology, 78,* 524–536.

Bailey, J. M., Pillard, R. C., Neale, M. C., & Agyei, Y. (1993). Heritable factors influence sexual orientation in women. *Archives of General Psychiatry, 50*(3), 217–223.

Bailey, J. V., Farquhar, C., & Owen, C. (2004). Bacterial vaginosis in lesbians and bisexual women. *Sexually Transmitted Diseases, 31*(11), 691–694.

Baird, J. (2014, April 6). Neither female nor male. *New York Times,* opinion pages.

Baker, C. P. (1995). Child chattel: Future tourists for sex. *Insight on the News, 11,* 11.

Bakker, F., & Vanwesenbeeck, I. (Eds.). (2006). *Seksuele gezondheid in Nederland 2006.* [Sexual health in the Netherlands 2006]. [RNG-studies nr.9]. Delft: Eburon.

Baldwin, M. K., & Jensen, J. T. (2013). Contraception during the perimenopause. *Maturitas, 76*(3), 235–242.

Ball, A. L. (2014, April 4). Who are you on Facebook now? *New York Times,* Fashion & Style.

Bancroft, J. (2002). The medicalization of female sexual dysfunction: The need for caution. *Archives of Sexual Behavior, 31,* 451–455.

Bancroft, J. (2009). *Human sexuality and its problems* (3rd ed.). Edinburgh, Scotland: Elsevier.

Bancroft, J., & Graham, C. A. (2011). The varied nature of women's sexuality: Unresolved issues and a theoretical approach. *Hormones and Behavior, 59*(5), 717–729.

Bancroft, J., Graham, C. A., Janssen, E., & Sanders, S. A. (2009). The dual control model: Current status and future directions. *Journal of Sex Research, 46*(2–3), 121–142.

Bancroft, J., & Vukadinovic, Z. (2004). Sexual addiction, sexual compulsivity, sexual impulsivity, or what? *Journal of Sex Research, 41,* 225–234.

Bandura, A. (1977). *Social learning theory.* Englewood Cliffs, NJ: Prentice Hall.

Barbach, L. (2001). *For each other: Sharing sexual intimacy* (Rev. ed.). Garden City, NY: Doubleday.

Barber, L. L., & Cooper, M. L. (2014). Rebound sex: Sexual motives and behaviors following a relationship breakup. *Archives of Sexual Behavior, 43*(2), 251–265.

Barker, D. J. (2008). *Nutrition in the womb.* Available: http://www.barker.org/ (Last visited 12/20/14).

Barnes, J. E. (2011, June 20). "Don't ask" policy draws to a close. *Wall Street Journal,* p. A5.

Bartky, S. L. (1990). *Femininity and domination: Studies in the phenomenology of oppression.* New York: Routledge.

Basile, K. C., Chen, J., Black, M. C., & Saltzman, L. E. (2007). Prevalence and characteristics of sexual violence victimization among U.S. adults, 2001–2003. *Violence and Victims, 22,* 437–448.

Basson, R., Wierman, M. E., van Lankveld, J., & Brotto, L. (2010). Summary of the recommendations on sexual dysfunctions for women. *Journal of Sexual Medicine, 7,* 14–326.

Bauer, G. R., Jairam, J. A., & Baidoobonso, S. M. (2010). Sexual health, risk behaviors, and substance use in heterosexual-identified women with female sex partners: 2002 U.S. National Survey of Family Growth. *Sexually Transmitted Diseases, 37,* 531–537.

Baumeister, R. (2011). *Sexual economics: A research-based theory of sexual interactions, or why the man buys dinner.* Paper presented at the annual meeting of the American Psychological Association, District of Columbia.

Baumeister, R. F. (2000). Gender differences in erotic plasticity: The female sex drive as socially flexible and responsive. *Psychological Bulletin, 126*(3), 347–374.

Baumeister, R. F., Catanese, K. R., & Wallace, H. M. (2002). Conquest by force: A narcissistic reactance theory of rape and sexual coercion. *Review of General Psychology, 6,* 92–135.

Bednarczyk, R. A., Davis, R., Ault, K., Orenstein, W. S., & Omer, S. B. (2012). Sexual activity-related outcomes after human papillomavirus vaccination of 11- to 12-year olds. *Pediatrics, 130,* 798–805.

Beemyn, G. (2015) Best practices to support trans and non-binary gender students. *Campus Pride. Available:* http://www.campuspride.org/tools/best-practices-to-support-transgender-and-other-gender-nonconforming-students/ (Last visited 6/2/15). Used with permission.

Beetz, A. M. (2004). Bestiality/zoophilia: A scarcely investigated phenomenon between crime, paraphilia and love. *Journal of Forensic Psychology Practice, 4,* 1–36.

Bell, A., Weinberg, M., & Hammersmith, S. (1981). *Sexual preference: Its development in men and women.* Bloomington: Indiana University Press.

Bello, M. (2015). Sex traffic ring on ICE's most wanted. *USA Today,* p. 3A.

Belluck, P., & Carey, B. (2013, May 7). Psychiatry's new guide falls short, experts say. *New York Times,* p. A12.

Bem, D. J. (1996). Exotic becomes erotic: A developmental theory of sexual orientation. *Psychological Review, 103,* 320–335.

Bem, D. J. (2000). Exotic becomes erotic: Integrating biological and experiential antecedents of sexual orientation. In A. R. D'Augelli & C. L. Patterson (Eds.), *Lesbian, gay, and bisexual identities and youth: Psychological perspectives* (pp. 52–68). New York: Oxford University Press.

Bem, S. L. (1983). Gender schema theory and its implications for child development: Raising gender-aschematic children in a gender-schematic society. *Signs, 8*(4), 598–616.

Bender, R. (2014, March 19). China needs milk and France has it. *Wall Street Journal,* p. B-1.

Beres, M. (2010). Sexual miscommunication? Untangling assumptions about sexual communication between casual sex partners. *Culture, Health & Sexuality, 12,* 1–14.

Beres, M. A., Senn, C. Y., & McCaw, J. (2014). Navigating ambivalence: How heterosexual young adults make sense of desire differences. *Journal of Sex Research, 51,* 765–776.

Bernstein, E. (2001). The meaning of purchase: Desire, demand and the commerce of sex. *Ethnography, 2,* 389–420.

Bernstein, E. (2012, November 13). The new rules of flirting. *Wall Street Journal,* pp. D1–D2.

Bersamin, M. M., Zamboanga, B. L., Schwartz, S. J., Donellan, M. B., Hudson, M., Weisskirch, R. S., et al. (2014). Risky business: Is there an association between casual sex and mental health among emerging adults? *Journal of Sex Research, 51,* 43–51.

Best, K. (2007, December 17). Kiss and tell: Smooches make or break a relationship. *Indianapolis Star,* p. E1.

Bhutta, Z. A., Das, J. K., Bahl, R., Lawn, J. E., Salam, R. A., Paul, V. K., Sankar, M. J., Blencowe, H., Rizvi, A., Chou, V. B., & Walker, N. (2014). Can available interventions end preventable deaths in mothers, newborn babies, and stillbirths, and at what cost? *The Lancet, 384*(9940), 347–370.

Billy, J. O. G., Grady, W. R., & Sill, M. E. (2009). Sexual risk-taking among adult dating couples in the United States. *Perspectives on Sexual and Reproductive Health, 41,* 74–83.

Biro, F. M., Greenspan, L. C., & Galvez, M. P. (2012). Puberty in girls of the 21st century. *Journal of Pediatric Adolescent Gynecology, 25*(5), 289–294. Available: http://www.ncbi.nlm.nih.gov/pmc/articles/PMC3613238/ (Last visited 11/12/14).

Biro, F. M., Greenspan, L. C., Galvez, M. P., et al. (2013). Onset of breast development in a longitudinal cohort. *Pediatrics, 132:* 1019-1027. Available: http://pediatrics.aappublications.org/content/132/6/1019.full.pdf+html (Last visited 7/25/14).

Biskupic, J. (2002, April 17). "Virtual" porn ruling hinged on threat to art. *USA Today,* p. A3.

Biskupic, J. (2003a, March 4). Case tests Congress's ability to make libraries block porn. *USA Today,* p. A3.

Biskupic, J. (2003b, June 27). Gay sex ban struck down. *USA Today,* p. A1.

Biskupic, J. (2004, June 30). It may be up to parents to block web porn. *New York Times,* p. 6A.

Blackless, M., Charuvastra, A., Derryck, A., Fausto-Sterling, A., Lauzanne, K., & Lee, E. (2000). How sexually dimorphic are we? Review and synthesis. *American Journal of Human Biology, 12*(2), 151–166.

Blackwood, E. (1984). Sexuality and gender in certain Native American tribes: The case of cross-gender females. *Signs, 10,* 27–42.

Blanchard, R. (1993, Mar.). The she-male phenomena and the concept of partial autogynephilia. *Journal of Sex and Marital Therapy, 19*(1), 69–76.

Blanchard, R. (2010). The DSM diagnostic criteria for transvestic fetishism. *Archives of Sexual Behavior, 39,* 363–372.

Blanchard, R., & Bogaert, A. F. (2004). Proportion of homosexual men who owe their sexual orientation to fraternal birth order: An estimate based on two national probability samples. *American Journal of Human Biology, 16,* 151–157.

Blanchard, R., Cantor, J., Bogaert, A., Breedlove, S., & Ellis, L. (2006). Interaction of fraternal birth order and handedness in the development of male homosexuality. *Hormones and Behavior, 49,* 405–414.

Blank, H. (2012). *Straight: The surprisingly short history of heterosexuality.* Boston: Beacon Press.

Blechman, E. A. (1990). *Emotions and the family: For better or for worse.* Hillsdale, NJ: Erlbaum.

Blum, D. (1997). *Sex on the brain.* New York: Viking Press.

Blumberg, E. S. (2003). The lives and voices of highly sexual women. *Journal of Sex Research, 40,* 146–157.

Blumstein, P., & Schwartz, P. (1983). *American couples.* New York: McGraw-Hill.

Bogaert, A., Friesen, C., & Klentrou, P. (2002). Age of puberty and sexual orientation in a national probability sample. *Archives of Sexual Behavior, 31,* 73–81.

Bogart, L., & Thornton, S. (2005). Are HIV/AIDS conspiracy beliefs a barrier to HIV prevention among African Americans? *Journal of Acquired Immune Deficiency Syndromes, 38*(2), 213–218.

Bogart, L. M., Galvan, F. H., Wagner, G. J., & Klein, D. J. (2011). Longitudinal association of HIV conspiracy beliefs with sexual risk among Black males living with HIV. *AIDS and Behavior, 15,* 1180–1186.

Bogle, K. A. (2014, October 31). "Yes means yes" isn't the answer. *Chronicle of Higher Education,* pp. A35–36.

Bonilla, L., & Porter, J. (1990). A comparison of Latino, Black, and non-Hispanic attitudes toward homosexuality. *Hispanic Journal of Homosexuality, 12,* 439–452.

Borneman, E. (1983). Progress in empirical research on children's sexuality. *SIECUS Report,* 1–5.

Borrello, G., & Thompson, B. (1990). A note regarding the validity of Lee's typology of love. *Journal of Psychology, 124*(6), 639–644.

Boskey, E. (2013). Sexuality in the *DSM 5*: Research, relevance, and reaction. *Contemporary Sexuality, 47,* 1, 305.

Bostwick, H. (1860). *A treatise on the nature and treatment of seminal disease, impotency, and other kindred afflictions* (12th ed.). New York: Burgess, Stringer.

Bourdeau, B., Thomas, V. K., & Long, J. K. (2008). Latino sexual styles: Developing a nuanced understanding of risk. *Journal of Sex Research, 45*(1), 71–81.

Bowleg, L., Teti, M., Massie, J. S., Patel, A., Malebranche, D. J., & Tschann, J. M. (2011). What does it take to be a man? What is a real man? Ideologies of masculinity and HIV sexual risk among Black heterosexual men. *Culture, Health & Sexuality, 13*(5), 545–559.

Boyer, C. B., Shafer, M., Wibbelsman, C. J., Seeberg, D., Teitle, E., & Lovell, N. (2000). Associations of sociodemographic, psychosocial, and behavioral factors with sexual risk and sexually transmitted diseases in teen clinic patients. *Journal of Adolescent Health, 27,* 102–111.

Boyle, E. M., Poulsen, G., Field, D. J., Kurinczuk, J. J., Wolke, D., Alfirevic, Z., & Quigley, M. A. (2012). Effects of gestational age at birth on health outcomes at 3 and 5 years of age: Population based cohort study. *British Medical Journal, 344,* e896.

Bradbury, T. (n.d.). Which conflicts consume couples the most? *PBS: This emotional life.* Available: http://www.pbs.org/thisemotionallife/blogs/which-conflicts-consume-couples-most (Last visited 11/3/14).

Bradshaw, C., Kahn, A. S., & Saville, B. K. (2010). To hook up or date: Which gender benefits? *Sex Roles, 62,* 661–669.

Braithwaite, S. R., Coulson, G., Keddington, K., & Fincham, F. D. (2015). The influence of pornography on sexual scripts and hooking up among emerging adults in college. *Archives of Sexual Behavior, 44,* 111–123.

Brambilla, D. J., Matsumoto, A. M., Araujo, A. M., & McKinlay, J. E. (2013). The effect of diurnal variation on clinical measurement of serum testosterone and other sex hormone levels. *Journal of Clinical Endocrinology & Metabolism, 94*(3). Available: http://press.endocrine.org/doi/abs/10.1210/jc.2008–1902 (Last visited 7/2/14).

Braverman, E. R. (2011). *Younger (sexier) you.* New York: Rodale.

Braverman, P., & Strasburger, V. (1994, Jan.). Sexually transmitted diseases. *Clinical Pediatrics,* 26–37.

Breiding, M. J., Smith, S. G., Basile, K. C., Walters, M. L., Chen, J., & Merrick, M. T. (2014). Prevalence and characteristics of sexual violence, stalking, and intimate partner violence victimization—National Intimate Partner and Sexual Violence Survey, United States, 2011. *Morbidity and Mortality Weekly Report, 63*(8), 1–18.

Brelsford, G. M., Luquis, R., & Murray-Swank, N. A. (2011). College students' permissive sexual attitudes: Links to religiousness and spirituality. *International Journal for the Psychology of Religion, 21,* 127–136.

Brents, B., & Hausbeck, K. (2005). Violence and legalized brothel prostitution in Nevada. *Journal of Interpersonal Violence, 20,* 270–295.

Brents, B. G., Jackson, C. A., & Hausbeck, K. (2010). *The state of sex: Tourism, sex, and sin in the new American heartland.* New York: Routledge.

Bridges, A. J., & Morokoff, P. J. (2011). Sexual media use and relational satisfaction in heterosexual couples. *Personal Relationships, 18,* 562–585.

Brizendine, L. (2010). *The male brain.* New York: Crown.

Brody, S. (2010). The relative health benefits of different sexual activities. *Journal of Sexual Medicine, 7,* 1336–1361.

Brotto, L. A. (2010). The DSM diagnostic criteria for sexual aversion disorder. *Archives of Sexual Behavior, 39,* 271–277.

Brotto, L. A., & Smith, K. B. (2014). Sexual desire and pleasure. In D. L. Tolman & L. M. Diamond (Eds.), *APA handbook of sexuality and psychology* (pp. 205–244). Washington, DC: American Psychiatric Association.

Brotto, L. A., Chik, H. M., Ryder, A. G., Gorzalka, B. G., & Seal, B. N. (2005). Acculturation and sexual function in Asian women. *Archives of Sexual Behavior, 6,* 613–626.

Broussard, M. (2014). Dating stats you should know. Match.com. Available: http://www.match.com/cp.aspx?cpp=/cppp/magazine/article0.html&articleid=4671 (Last accessed 9/27/14).

Brown, P. L. (2006, December 2). Supporting boys or girls when the line isn't clear. *New York Times,* p. A1.

Buffardi, A. L., Thomas, K. K., Holmes, K. K., & Manhart, L. E. (2008). Moving upstream: Ecosocial and psychosocial correlates of sexually transmitted infections among young adults in the United States. *American Journal of Public Health, 98,* 1128–1136.

Bullough, V. (1991). Transvestism: A reexamination. *Journal of Psychology and Human Sexuality, 4*(2), 53–67.

Bullough, V. L. (1994). *Science in the bedroom: A history of sex research.* New York: Basic Books.

Bullough, V. L. (2004). Sex will never be the same: The contributions of Alfred C. Kinsey. *Archives of Sexual Behavior, 33,* 277–286.

Buss, D. (2003). *The evolution of desire: Strategies of human mating* (Rev. ed.). New York: Basic Books.

Buss, D. (2006). Strategies for human mating. *Psychological Topics, 15,* 239–260.

Buss, D. M. (1994). *The evolution of desire: Strategies of human mating.* New York: Basic Books.

Buss, D. M. (1998). Sexual strategies theory: Historical origins and current status. *Journal of Sex Research, 35,* 19–31.

Buss, D. M. (1999). *Evolutionary psychology: The new science of the mind.* Boston: Allyn & Bacon.

Buss, D. M. (2000). *Dangerous passion: Why jealousy is as necessary as love and sex.* New York: Simon & Schuster.

Buss, D. M. (2003). Sexual strategies: A journey into controversy. *Psychological Inquiry, 14,* 219–226.

Buss, D. M., & Schmitt, D. P. (1993). Sexual strategies theory: An evolutionary perspective on human mating. *Psychological Review, 100*(2), 204–232.

Buss, D. M., & Schmitt, D. P. (2011). Evolutionary psychology and feminism. *Sex Roles, 64,* 768–787.

Buss, D. M., Larsen, R. J., Westen, D., & Semmelroth, J. (1992). Sex differences in jealousy: Evolution, physiology, and psychology. *Psychological Science, 3,* 251–255.

Bussey, K., & Bandura, A. (1999). Social cognitive theory of gender development and differentiation. *Psychological Review, 106,* 676–713.

Butler, J. (1993). *Bodies that matter: On the discursive limits of sex.* New York: Routledge.

Buzzell, T. (2005). Demographic characteristics of persons using pornography in three technological contexts. *Sexuality and Culture, 9,* 28–48.

Byard, R. W., & Botterill, P. M. B. (1998). Autoerotic asphyxial death—Accident or suicide? *American Journal of Forensic Medicine and Pathology, 19,* 377–380.

Byers, E. S. (2005). Relationship satisfaction and sexual satisfaction: A longitudinal study of individuals in long-term relationships. *Journal of Sex Research, 42*(2), 113–118.

Byers, F. S., Henderson, J., & Hobson, K. M. (2009). University students' definitions of sexual abstinence and having sex. *Archives of Sexual Behavior, 38,* 665–674.

Byne, W. (2014). Forty years after the removal of homosexuality from the DSM: Well on the way but not there yet. *LGBT Health, 1,* 1–3.

Byne, W., Bradley, S. J., Coleman, E., Eyler, A. E., Green, R., Menvielle, E. J., Meyer-Bahlburg, H. F. L., Pleak, R. R., & Tompkins, D. A. (2012). Report of the American Psychiatric Association Task Force on treatment of gender identity disorder. *Archives of Sexual Behavior, 41,* 759–796.

Calam, R., Horne, L., Glasgow, D., & Cox, A. (1998). Psychological disturbance and child sexual abuse: A follow-up study. *Child Abuse and Neglect, 22,* 901–913.

Calderone, M. S. (1983). Childhood sexuality: Approaching the prevention of sexual disease. In G. Albee et al. (Eds.), *Promoting sexual responsibility and preventing sexual problems.* Hanover, NH: University Press of New England.

Calzo, J. P. (2013). Hookup versus romantic relationship sex in college: Why do we care and what do we do? *Journal of Adolescent Health, 52,* 515–516.

Campos-Outcalt, D., & Hurwitz, S. (2002). Female-to-female transmission of syphilis: A case report. *Sexually Transmitted Diseases, 29,* 119–120.

Cann, A., Mangum, J. L., & Wells, M. (2001). Distress in response to relationship infidelity: The roles of gender and attitudes about relationships. *Journal of Sex Research, 38*(3), 185–190.

Cantor, J. M., Blanchard, R., Paterson, A. D., & Bogaert, A. F. (2002). How many gay men owe their sexual orientation to fraternal birth order? *Archives of Sexual Behavior, 3,* 63–71.

Caplan, A. L. (1992). Twenty years after: The legacy of the Tuskegee syphilis study. When evil intrudes. *Hastings Center Report, 22*(6), 29–32.

Capshew, J. H. (2012). *Herman B. Wells: The promise of the American university.* Bloomington: Indiana University Press.

Carael, M., Slaymaker, E., Lyerla, R., & Sarkar, S. (2006). Clients of sex workers in different regions of the world: Hard to count. *Sexually Transmitted Infections, 82*(Suppl–3), iii26–iii33.

Carelli, R. (1998, February 24). High Court turns down Megan's Law challenges. *San Francisco Chronicle,* p. A1.

Carlson, B. E., McNutt, L., & Choi, D. Y. (2003). Childhood and adult abuse among women in primary health care: Effects on mental health. *Journal of Interpersonal Violence, 18,* 924–941.

Carnes, P. (1983). *Out of shadows.* Minneapolis: CompCare.

Carnes, P. (1991). Progress in sex addiction: An addiction perspective. In R. T. Francoeur (Ed.), *Taking sides: Clashing views on controversial issues in human sexuality* (3rd ed.). Guilford, CT: Dushkin.

Caron, S. (2013). *The sex lives of college students: Two decades of attitudes and behaviors.* Orono, ME: Maine College Press.

Carpenter, L. M. (2001). The ambiguity of "having sex": The subjective experiences of virginity loss in the United States. *Journal of Sex Research, 38,* 138–139.

Carpenter, L. M. (2002). Gender and the meaning and experience of virginity loss in contemporary United States. *Gender & Society, 16,* 345–365.

Carpenter, L. M. (2005). *Virginity lost: An intimate portrait of first sexual experiences.* New York: New York University Press.

Carpenter, L. M., & DeLamater, J. (2012). Studying gendered sexualities over the life course. In L. M. Carpenter & J. DeLamater (Eds.), *Sex for life.* New York: New York University Press.

Carroll, J. L. (2010). *Sexuality now: Embracing diversity.* Belmont, CA: Wadsworth.

Carroll, J. S., Padilla-Walker, L. M., Nelson, L. J., Olson, C. D., Barry, C. M., & Madsen, S. D. (2008). Pornography acceptance and use among emerging adults. *Journal of Adolescent Research, 23,* 6–30.

Cassell, C. (2008). *Put passion first: Why sexual chemistry is the key to finding and keeping lasting love.* New York: McGraw-Hill.

Cassidy, L., & Hurrell, R. M. (1995). The influence of victim's attire on adolescents' judgments of date rape. *Adolescence, 30*(118), 319–404.

Castleman, M. (2004). *Great sex: A man's guide to the secret principles of total-body sex.* New York: Rodale Books.

Catania, J. A. (2011). Health Protective Sexual Communication Scale. In Fisher, T. D., Davis, C. M., Yarber, W. L., & Davis, S. L. (Eds.)., *Handbook of sexuality-related measures.* (3rd ed.). New York, NY: Routledge, pp. 591–594.

Cate, R. M., & Lloyd, S. A. (1992). *Courtship.* Newbury Park, CA: Sage.

Cates, J. R., Herndon, N. L., Schulz, S. L., & Darroch, J. E. (2004). *Our voices, our lives, our futures: Youth and sexually transmitted diseases.* Chapel Hill: School of Journalism and Mass Communication, University of North Carolina at Chapel Hill.

Cates, W., Chesney, M. A., & Cohen, M. S. (1997). Primary HIV infection—A public health opportunity. *American Journal of Public Health, 87*(12), 1928–1930.

CDC draft guidelines: Circumcision benefits outweigh risks. (2014, December 7). *Hoosier Times,* p. E7.

Centers for Disease Control and Prevention (CDC). (1981.15a, 1981.16a). Pneumocystis pneumonia—Los Angeles. *Morbidity and Mortality Weekly Report, 30,* 250–252.

Centers for Disease Control and Prevention (CDC). (1992). 1993 revised classification system for HIV infection and expanded surveillance case definition for AIDS among adolescents and adults. *Morbidity and Mortality Weekly Report, 41,* 961–962.

Centers for Disease Control and Prevention (CDC). (1996). Surveillance report: U.S. AIDS cases reported through December 1995. *HIV/AIDS Surveillance Report, 7*(2), 1–10.

Centers for Disease Control and Prevention (CDC). (2001). Chlamydia disease information. Available: http://www.cdc.gov/nchstp/dstd/Fact_Sheets/Factschlamydiainfo.htm (Last visited 12/12/01).

Centers for Disease Control and Prevention (CDC). (2004). HIV transmission among Black women—North Carolina, 2004. *Morbidity and Mortality Weekly Report, 54,* 217–222.

Centers for Disease Control and Prevention (CDC). (2007.15a). Sexually transmitted disease surveillance. Available: http://www.cdc.gov/std/stats/toc2006.htm (Last visited 10/15/08).

Centers for Disease Control and Prevention (CDC). (2007.15b). Male latex condoms and sexually transmitted diseases. Available: http://www.cdc.gov/condomeffectiveness/latex.htm (Last visited 10/12/08).

Centers for Disease Control and Prevention (CDC). (2007.15c). Sexually transmitted diseases treatment guidelines, 2006. Available: http://www.cdc.gov/std/treatment/2006/clinical.htm (Last visited 10/20/08).

Centers for Disease Control and Prevention (CDC). (2007.15d). Trichomoniasis. Available: http://www.cdc.gov/std/trichomonas/STYDFact-Trichomoniasis.htm (Last visited 10/13/08).

Centers for Disease Control and Prevention (CDC). (2007.16a). Living with HIV/AIDS. Available: http://www.cdc.gov/hiv/resources/brochures/livingwithhim.htm (Last visited 11/14/08).

Centers for Disease Control and Prevention (CDC). (2007.16b). Mother-to-child (perinatal) HIV transmission and prevention. Available: http://www.cdc.gov/topics/perinatal/resources/factsheets/perinatal.htm (Last visited 11/4/08).

Centers for Disease Control and Prevention (CDC). (2008.15a). Gonorrhea. Available: http://www.cdc.gov/std/Gonorrhea/STDFact-gonorrhea.htm (Last visited 10/13/08).

Centers for Disease Control and Prevention (CDC). (2008.15b). Genital herpes. Available: http://www.cdc.gov/std/Herpes/STDFact-Herpes.htm (Last visited 10/13/08).

Centers for Disease Control and Prevention (CDC). (2008.15c). Genital HPV infection. Available: http://www.cdc.gov/std/HPV/STDFact -HPV.htm (Last visited 10/13/08).

Centers for Disease Control and Prevention (CDC). (2008.15d). Bacterial vaginosis. Available: http://www.cdc.gov/std/by/STDFact-Bacterial-Vaginosis.htm (Last visited 10/13/08).

Centers for Disease Control and Prevention (CDC). (2008.16a). HIV/AIDS among American Indians and Alaska Natives. Available: http://www.cdc.gov/resources/factsheets/aian.htm (Last visited 11/4/08).

Centers for Disease Control and Prevention (CDC). (2009.15a). Condoms and STDs: Fact sheet for public health personnel. Available: http://www.cdc.gov/condom effectiveness/latex.htm (Last visited 4/14/09).

Centers for Disease Control and Prevention (CDC). (2009.15b). Hepatitis A FAQs for the public. Available: http://www.cdc.gov/hepatitis/A/aFAQ.htm (Last visited 12/2/11).

Centers for Disease Control and Prevention (CDC). (2009.15c). Hepatitis B FAQs for the public. Available: http://www.cdc.gov/hepatitis/B/BFAQ.htm (Last visited 12/2/11).

Centers for Disease Control and Prevention (CDC). (2009.15d). Hepatitis C FAQs for the public. Available: http://www.cdc/gov/hepatitis/C/CFAQ.htm (Last visited 12/2//11).

Centers for Disease Control and Prevention (CDC). (2010.15a). 2009 sexually transmitted diseases surveillance slides. Available: www.cdc.gov/std/stats09/slides.htm (Last visited 11/29/11).

Centers for Disease Control and Prevention (CDC). (2010.15b). The role of STD detection and treatment in HIV prevention—CDC fact sheet. Available: http://www.gov/std/STDFact-STD-HIV.htm (Last visited 11/23/11).

Centers for Disease Control and Prevention (CDC). (2010.15c). Genital herpes—CDC fact sheet. Available: http://www.cdc.gov/std/Herpes/STDFact-Herpes.htm (Last visited 11/10/11).

Centers for Disease Control and Prevention (CDC). (2010.15d). Bacterial vaginosis—CDC fact sheet. Available: http://www.cdc.gov/std/BV/STDFact-Bacterial-Vaginosis.htm (Last visited 11/10/11).

Centers for Disease Control and Prevention (CDC). (2010.15e). Candidiasis. Available: http://www.cdc.gov/cxzved/divisions/dfbmd/diseases/candidiasis/index.htm (Last visited 12/5/11).

Centers for Disease Control and Prevention (CDC). (2010.15f). Scabies frequently asked questions. Available: http://www.cdc.gov/parasites/scabies/gen_info/faqs.html (Last visited 12/5/11).

Centers for Disease Control and Prevention (CDC). (2010.151). Crabs—frequently asked questions. Available: http://www.cdc.gov/parasites/lice/pubic/gen_info/faqs.html (Last visited 12/5/11).

Centers for Disease Control and Prevention (CDC). (2010.16a). Estimated lifetime risk for diagnosis of HIV infection among Hispanics/Latinos—37 States and Puerto Rico, 2007. *Mortality and Morbidity Weekly Report, 59,* 1297–1301.

Centers for Disease Control and Prevention (CDC). (2010.16b). HIV transmission. Available: http://www.cdc.gov/hiv/resources/qa/transmission.htm (Last visited 12/13/11).

Centers for Disease Control and Prevention (CDC). (2010.16c). HIV among gay, bisexual and other men who have sex with men. Available: http://wwwl.cdc.gov/hiv/topics/msm/index.htm (Last visited 12/8/11).

Centers for Disease Control and Prevention (CDC). (2010.17a). Youth risk behavior surveillance—United States, 2009. *Morbidity and Mortality Weekly Report, 59, 1–142.* Available: http://www.cdc.gov/mmwr/pdf/ss5905.pdf (Last visited 6/28/11).

Centers for Disease Control and Prevention (CDC). (2011.12a). CDC health disparities and inequalities report—United States, 2011. *Morbidity and Mortality Weekly Report, 60,* 1–116.

Centers for Disease Control and Prevention (CDC). (2011.12a). Infant mortality. Available: http://www.cdc.gov/reproductivehe-alth/MaternalInfantHealth/InfantMortality.htm (Last visited 12/16/14).

Centers for Disease Control and Prevention (CDC). (2011.15a). *Sexually transmitted disease surveillance 2010*. Atlanta, GA: U.S. Department of Health and Human Services.

Centers for Disease Control and Prevention (CDC). (2011.15b). Condoms and STDs: Fact sheet for public health officials. Available: http://www.cdc/gov/condomeff ectiveness/latex.htm (Last visited 12/6/11).

Centers for Disease Control and Prevention (CDC). (2011.15c). Chlamydia—CDC fact sheet. Available: http://www.cdc.gov/std/chlamydia/STDFact-Chlamyhdia.htm (Last visited 11/10/11).

Centers for Disease Control and Prevention (CDC). (2011.15d). Gonorrhea—CDC fact sheet. Available: http://www.cdc.gov/std/Gonorrhea/STDFact-gonorrhea.htm (Last visited 11/10/11).

Centers for Disease Control and Prevention (CDC). (2011.15e). CDC health disparities and inequalities report—United States, 2011. *Morbidity and Mortality Weekly Report, 60*, 1–116.

Centers for Disease Control and Prevention (CDC). (2011.15f). Genital HPV infection—CDC fact sheet. Available: http://www .gov/std/HPV/STDFact-HPV.htm (Last visited 11/28/11).

Centers for Disease Control and Prevention (CDC). (2011.15g). HPV vaccine information for young women—CDC fact sheet. Available: http://www.cdc.gov/HPV/STDFact-HPV-vaccine-young-women.htm (Last visited 11/10/11).

Centers for Disease Control and Prevention (CDC). (2011.15h). Viral hepatitis surveillance—United States, 2009. Available: http://www.cdc.gov/hepatitis/Statistics/2009Surveillance/ Commentary.htm (Last visited 12/2/11).

Centers for Disease Control and Prevention (CDC). (2011.15i). Infertility FAQs. Available: http://www.cdc.gov/reproductivehealth/ Infertility/ (Last visited 10/25/11).

Centers for Disease Control and Prevention (CDC). (2011.16a). *Sexually transmitted disease surveillance 2010.* Atlanta: U.S. Department of Health and Human Services.

Centers for Disease Control and Prevention (CDC). (2011.16b). HIV surveillance—Epidemiology of HIV infection (through 2009): Slide set. Available: http://www.cdc.gov/hiv/topics/ surveillance/resources/slides/general/index.htm (Last visited 12/09/11).

Centers for Disease Control and Prevention (CDC). (2011.16c). HIV surveillance by race/ethnicity (through 2009). Available: http://www.cdc.gov/hiv/topics/surveillance/resources/slides/race-ethnicity (Last visited 12/14/11).

Centers for Disease Control and Prevention (CDC). (2011.16d). Basic information about HIV and AIDS. Available: http://www .cdc.gov/hiv/topics/basic/index.htm (Last visited 12/8/11).

Centers for Disease Control and Prevention (CDC). (2011.16e). HIV among African Americans. Available: http://www.cdc.gov/ hiv/topics/aa/index.htm (Last visited 12/8/11).

Centers for Disease Control and Prevention (CDC). (2011.16f). HIV among women. Available: http://cdc.gov/hiv/topics/women/ index.htm (Last visited 12/8/11).

Centers for Disease Control and Prevention (CDC). (2011.16g). HIV among youth. Available: http://www.cdc.gov/hiv/youth/ index.htm (Last visited 12/8/11).

Centers for Disease Control and Prevention (CDC). (2011.16h). HIV surveillance in urban and nonurban areas: Slide set. Available: http://www.cdc.gov/hiv/topics/surveillance/resources/ slides/urban-nonurban/index.htm (Last visited 12/19/11).

Centers for Disease Control and Prevention (CDC). (2011.17a). Sexual identity, sex of sexual contacts, and health-risk behaviors among students in grades 9–12—Youth risk behavior surveillance, selected sites, United States. *Morbidity and Mortality Weekly Report, 60*(SS07), 1–133.

Centers for Disease Control and Prevention (CDC). (2012, January 20). Prepregnancy contraceptive use among teens with unintended pregnancies resulting in live births—Pregnancy risk assessment monitoring system (PRAMS), 2004–2008. *Morbidity and Mortality Weekly Report, 61*(2), 25–29. Available: http:// www.cdc.gov/mmwr/preview/mmwrhtml/mm6102a1.htm?s_ cid=mm6102a1_w (Last visited 12/7/14).

Centers for Disease Control and Prevention (CDC). (2012.15a). Hepatitis B. Atlanta: U.S. Department of Health and Human Services.

Centers for Disease Control and Prevention (CDC). (2012.15b). Press release: National estimate shows not enough young women tested for chlamydia. Available: http://www.cdc.gov/ nchhstp/newsroom/2012/stdconference2012pressrelease.html (Last visited 12/11/14).

Centers for Disease Control and Prevention (CDC). (2012.16a). Driving down new HIV infections: CDC's high-impact prevention approach. Atlanta, GA: CDC.

Centers for Disease Control and Prevention (CDC). (2013.6a). Teen pregnancy prevention 2010–2015. Available: http://www. cdc.gov/teenpregnancy/preventteenpreg.htm (Last visited 8/15/14).

Centers for Disease Control and Prevention (CDC). (2013.11a). CDC fact sheet: Incidence, prevalence, and costs of sexually transmitted infections. Available: http://www.cdc.gov/std/stats/ sti-estimates-fact-sheet-feb-2013.pdf (Last visited 12/4/14).

Centers for Disease Control and Prevention (CDC). (2013.12a). STDs & pregnancy – CDC fact sheet. Available: http://www. cdc.gov/std/pregnancy/stdfact-pregnancy.htm (Last visited 12/15/14).

Centers for Disease Control and Prevention (CDC). (2013.12b). Infertility FAQs. Available: http://www.cdc.gov/reproductivehe-alth/Infertility/ (Last visited 12/16/14).

Centers for Disease Control and Prevention (CDC). (2013.12c). Depression among women of reproductive age. Available: http:// www.cdc.gov/reproductivehealth/Depression/ (Last visited 12/18/14).

Centers for Disease Control and Prevention (CDC). (2013.13a). Prevalence of doctor-diagnosed arthritis and arthritis-attributable activity limitation—United States, 2010–2012. *Morbidity and Mortality Weekly Report, 64*(44), 869–873. Available: http:// www.cdc.gov/mmwr/preview/mmwrhtml/mm6244a1.htm?s_ cid=mm6244a1_w (Last visited 1/4/15).

Centers for Disease Control and Prevention (CDC). (2013.15a). Incidence, prevalence, and cost of sexually transmitted infections in the United States. Available: www.cdc.gov/std/stats/ sti-estimates-fact-sheet-feb-2013.pdf (Last visited 12/3/14).

Centers for Disease Control and Prevention (CDC). (2013.15b). Cervical cancer screening with the HPV test and the Pap test in women ages 30 and older. Available: http://www.cdc. gov/cancer/ hpv/basic_info/screening/pap_test_result.htm (Last visited 12/12/14).

Centers for Disease Control and Prevention (CDC). (2013.15c). Viral hepatitis: Information for gay and bisexual men. Atlanta: U.S. Department of Health and Human Services.

Centers for Disease Control and Prevention (CDC). (2013.15d). Hepatitis and sexual health. Atlanta: U.S. Department of Health and Human Services.

Centers for Disease Control and Prevention (CDC). (2013.15e). Trichomoniasis—CDC fact sheet. Atlanta: U.S. Department of Health and Human Services.

Centers for Disease Control and Prevention (CDC). (2013.15f). Parasites—Lice—Pubic "crabs" live. Available: http://www .cdc.gov/parasites/lice/pubic/gen_info/faqs.html (Last visited 12/2/14).

Centers for Disease Control and Prevention (CDC). (2013.16a). HIV among transgendered people. Available: http://www.cdc. gov/hiv/risk/transgender (Last visited 1/5/14).

Centers for Disease Control and Prevention (CDC). (2013.16b). Diagnoses of HIV infection in the United States and dependent areas, 2011. *HIV Surveillance Report, 23.*

Centers for Disease Control and Prevention (CDC). (2013.16c). HIV among older Americans. Available: http://www.cdc.gov/hiv/risk/age/olderamericans/index.html (Last visited 12/26/14).

Centers for Disease Control and Prevention (CDC). (2013.16d). Prevention benefits of HIV treatment. Available: http://www.cdc.gov/hiv/prevention/research/tap (Last visited 1/12/15).

Centers for Disease Control and Prevention (CDC). (2014.2a). HIV among African Americans. Available: http://www.cdc.gov/hiv/risk/racialethnic/aa/facts/index.html (Last visited 11/11/14).

Centers for Disease Control and Prevention (CDC). (2014.2b). Youth risk behavior surveillance—United States, 2013. *Mortality and Morbidity Report, 63*(4), 1–168.

Centers for Disease Control and Prevention (CDC). (2014.6a). Teen pregnancy: The importance of prevention. Available: http://www.cdc.gov/teenpregnancy/ (Last visited 8/15/14).

Centers for Disease Control and Prevention (CDC). (2014.6b, July 18). QuickStats: Birth rates for females aged 15-19 years, by race/ethnicity – National Vital Statistics System, United States, 1991-2013. *Morbidity and Mortality Weekly Report (MMWR), 63*(28), 609. Available: http://www.cdc.gov/mmwr/preview/mmwrhtml/mm6328a6.htm (Last accessed 8/13/14).

Centers for Disease Control and Prevention (CDC). (2014.11a). HIV prevention. Available: http://www.cdc.gov/hiv/basics/prevention.html (Last visited 12/29/14).

Centers for Disease Control and Prevention (CDC). (2014.12a). Fetal alcohol spectrum disorders (FASDs). Available: http://www.cdc.gov/ncbddd/fasd/facts.html (Last accessed 12/11/14).

Centers for Disease Control and Prevention (CDC). (2014.12b). Pregnant? Don't smoke! Available: http://www.cdc.gov/features/pregnantdontsmoke/index.html (Last visited 12/11/14).

Centers for Disease Control and Prevention (CDC). (2014.12c). Guidelines for vaccinating pregnant women. Available: http://www.cdc.gov/vaccines/pubs/preg-guide.htm (Last visited 12/14/14).

Centers for Disease Control and Prevention (CDC). (2014.12d). Pregnancy complications. Available: http://www.cdc.gov/reproductivehealth/MaternalInfantHealth/PregComplications.htm (Last visited 12/15/14).

Centers for Disease Control and Prevention (CDC). (2014.12e). About SUID and SIDS. Available: http://www.cdc.gov/sids/aboutsuidandsids.htm (Last visited 12/16/14).

Centers for Disease Control and Prevention (CDC). (2014.12f). Infertility. Available: http://www.cdc.gov/nchs/fastats/infertility.htm (Last visited 12/16/14).

Centers for Disease Control and Prevention (CDC). (2014.12g). Sexually transmitted diseases treatment guidelines, 2014. Available: http://www.cdc.gov/std/treatment/2014/2014-std-guidelines-peer-reviewers-08-20-2014.pdf (Last visited 12/18/14).

Centers for Disease Control and Prevention (CDC). (2014.12h). Breastfeeding report card, United States, 2014. Available: http://www.cdc.gov/breastfeeding/pdf/2014breastfeedingreportcard.pdf (Last visited 12/20/14).

Centers for Disease Control and Prevention (CDC). (2014.13a). National diabetes statistics report, 2014. Available: http://www.cdc.gov/diabetes/pubs/statsreport14/national-diabetes-report-web.pdf (Last visited 1/4/15).

Centers for Disease Control and Prevention (CDC). (2014.15a). Summary of notifiable diseases—United States 2012. *Mortality and Morbidity Report, 61*(53), 1–122.

Centers for Disease Control and Prevention (CDC). (2014.15b). STD health equity. Available: http://www.cdc.gov/std/health-disparities/default.htm (Last visited 12/2/14).

Centers for Disease Control and Prevention (CDC). (2014.15c). *Sexually transmitted disease surveillance 2013*. Atlanta: U.S. Department of Health and Human Services.

Centers for Disease Control and Prevention (CDC). (2014.15d). Slide set: STDs in racial and ethnic minorities. Available: http://www.cdc.gov/std/stats12/slides.htm (Last visited 12/3/14).

Centers for Disease Control and Prevention (CDC). (2014.15e). Youth risk behavior surveillance—United States, 2013. *Mortality and Morbidity Report, 63*(4), 1–168.

Centers for Disease Control and Prevention (CDC). (2014.15f). HIV prevention. Available: http://www.cdc.gov/hiv/basics/prevention.html (Last visited 12/8/14).

Centers for Disease Control and Prevention (CDC). (2014.15g). Bacterial vaginosis—CDC fact sheet. Atlanta: U.S. Department of Health and Human Services.

Centers for Disease Control and Prevention (CDC). (2014.15h). HIV prevention. Available: http://www.cdc.gov/hiv/basics/prevention.html (Last visited 12/8/14).

Centers for Disease Control and Prevention (CDC). (2014.15i). Reported STDs in the United States—CDC fact sheet. Atlanta: U.S. Department of Health and Human Services.

Centers for Disease Control and Prevention (CDC). (2014.15j). Chlamydia—CDC fact sheet. Atlanta: U.S. Department of Health and Human Services.

Centers for Disease Control and Prevention (CDC). (2014.15k). Gonorrhea—CDC fact sheet. Atlanta: U.S. Department of Health and Human Services.

Centers for Disease Control and Prevention (CDC). (2014.15l). Diseases characterized by urethritis and cervicitis. Available: http://www.cdc.gov/std/treatment/2010/urethritis-and-cervicitis.htm (Last visited 12/11/14).

Centers for Disease Control and Prevention (CDC). (2014.15m). Syphilis—CDC fact sheet. Atlanta: U.S. Department of Health and Human Services.

Centers for Disease Control and Prevention (CDC). (2014.15n). Genital HPV infection—CDC fact sheet. Atlanta: U.S. Department of Health and Human Services.

Centers for Disease Control and Prevention (CDC). (2014.15o). Genital herpes—CDC fact sheet. Atlanta: U.S. Department of Health and Human Services.

Centers for Disease Control and Prevention (CDC). (2014.15p). Genital/vulvovaginal candidiasis (VVC). Available: http://www.cdc.gov/fungal/diseases/candidasis/genital/index.html (Last visited 12/16/14).

Centers for Disease Control and Prevention (CDC). (2014.15q). Pelvic inflammatory disease (PID). Available: http://www.cdc.gov/std/pid/stdfact-pid-detailed.htm (Last visited 12/16/14).

Centers for Disease Control and Prevention (CDC). (2014.16a). About HIV/AIDS. Available: http://cdc.gov/his/basics/whatishiv.html (Last visited 12/16/14).

Centers for Disease Control and Prevention (CDC). (2014.16b). Opportunistic infections. Available: http://cdc.gov/hiv/living/opportunisticinfections.html (Last visited 12/29/14).

Centers for Disease Control and Prevention (CDC). (2014.16c). Testing. Available: http://www.cdc.gov/hiv/basics/testing.html (Last visited 12/29/14).

Centers for Disease Control and Prevention (CDC). (2014.16d). Diagnoses of HIV infection in the United States and dependent areas, 2012. Atlanta: CDC.

Centers for Disease Control and Prevention (CDC). (2014.16e). HIV surveillance—Epidemiology of HIV infection (through

2012): Slide set. Available: http://www.cdc.gov/hiv/library/slideSets/index.html (Last visited 12/26/14).

Centers for Disease Control and Prevention (CDC). (2014.16f). HIV surveillance by race/ethnicity (through 2012): Slide set. Available: http://www.cdc.gov/hiv/library/slideSets/index.html (Last visited 12/26/14).

Centers for Disease Control and Prevention (CDC). (2014.16g). HIV transmission. Available: http://cdc.gov/hiv/basics/transmission.html (Last visited 12/29/14).

Centers for Disease Control and Prevention (CDC). (2014.16h). Oral sex and HIV risk. Available: http://www.cdc.gov/hiv/behavior/oralsex.html (Last visited 12/26/14).

Centers for Disease Control and Prevention (CDC). (2014.16i). HIV and substance abuse in the United States. Available: http://www.cdc/gov/hiv/risk/behavor/substanceuse.html (Last visited 12/26/14).

Centers for Disease Control and Prevention (CDC). (2014.16j). HIV among pregnant women, infants, and children. Available: http://www.cdc.gov/hiv/risk/gender/pregnantwomen/facts/index/html (Last visited 12/26/14).

Centers for Disease Control and Prevention (CDC). (2014.16k). HIV among African Americans. Available: http://www.cdc.gov/hiv/risk/racialethnic/aa/facts/index.index.html (Last visited 12/26/14).

Centers for Disease Control and Prevention (CDC). (2014.16l). HIV among Hispanics. Available: http://www.cdc.gov/risk/racialethnic/hispaniclatinos/facts/index.html (Last visited 12/26/14).

Centers for Disease Control and Prevention (CDC). (2014.16m). HIV infection among Asians in the United States and dependent areas. Available: http://www.cdc.gov/his/risk/racialethnic/asians/index.html (Last visited 12/26/14).

Centers for Disease Control and Prevention (CDC). (2014.16n). HIV among African American gay and bisexual men. Available: http://www.cdc.gov/hiv/risk/racialethnic/bmsm/facts/index.html (Last visited 12/26/14).

Centers for Disease Control and Prevention (CDC). (2014.16o). HIV/AIDS among American Indians and Alaska Natives. Available: http://www.cdc.gov/hiv/risk/racialEthnic/aian/index.html (Last visited 12/26/14).

Centers for Disease Control and Prevention (CDC). (2014.16p). HIV among African American gay and bisexual men. Available: http://www.cdc.gov/hiv/risk/racialethnic/bmsm/facts/index.html (Last visited 12/26/14).

Centers for Disease Control and Prevention (CDC). (2014.16q). HIV among gay and bisexual men. Available: http://www.cdc.gov/hiv/risk/gender/msm/facts/index.html (Last visited 1/6/15).

Centers for Disease Control and Prevention (CDC). (2014.16r). HIV among women. Available: http://www.cdc.gov/hiv/risk/gender/women/facts/index.html (Last visited 12/26/14).

Centers for Disease Control and Prevention (CDC). (2014.16s). HIV surveillance in adolescents and young adults: Slide set. Available: http://www.cdc.gov/library/slideSets/index.html (Last visited 1/6/14).

Centers for Disease Control and Prevention (CDC). (2014.16t). Youth risk behavior surveillance—United States, 2013. *Mortality and Morbidity Report, 63*(4), 1–168.

Centers for Disease Control and Prevention (CDC). (2014.16u). HIV surveillance in urban and nonurban areas: Slide set. Available: http://www.cdc.gov/library/slideSets/index.html (Last visited 1/7/14).

Centers for Disease Control and Prevention (CDC). (2014.16v). HIV prevention. Available: http://www.cdc.gov/hiv/basics/prevention.html (Last visited 12/26/14).

Centers for Disease Control and Prevention (CDC). (2014.16w). PrEP 101. Available: http://www.cdc.gov/hiv/basics/prep.html (Last visited 12/26/14).

Centers for Disease Control and Prevention (CDC). (2014.16x). PEP 101. Available: http://www.cdc.gov/hiv/basics/pep.html (Last visited 12/26/14).

Cervical dysplasia. (2014). *MedlinePlus*. Available: http://www.nlm.nih.gov/medlineplus/ency/article/001491.htm (Last visited 1/7/15).

Cespedes, Y., & Huey, S. (2008). Depression in Latino adolescents: A cultural discrepancy perspective. *Culture Diversity and Ethnic Minority Psychology, 14,* 168–172.

Chae, D. H., & Ayala, G. (2010). Sexual orientation and sexual behavior among Latino and Asian Americans: Implications for unfair treatment and psychological distress. *Journal of Sex Research, 47*(5), 451–549.

Chalabi, M. (2014). Why we don't know the size of the transgender population. *HuffPost Gay voices*. Available: http://fivethirtyeight.com/features/why-we-dont-know-the-size-of-the-transgender-population/ (Last visited 1/25/15).

Chambers, W. C. (2007). Oral sex: Varied behaviors and perceptions in a college population. *Journal of Sex Research, 44,* 28–42.

Chandra, A., Billioux, V. G., Copen, C. E., & Sionean, C. (2012). HIV risk-related behaviors in the United States household population aged 15–44 years: Data from the National Survey of Family Growth, 2002 and 2006–2010. *National Health Statistics Report, 46*. Available: http://www.cdc.gov/nchs/data/nhsr/nhsr046.pdf (Last visited 4/18/12).

Chandra, A., Mosher, W. D., Copen, C., & Sionean, C. (2011). Sexual behavior, sexual attraction, and sexual identity in the United States: Data from the 2006–2008 National Survey of Family Growth. *National Health Statistics Report, 36*. Available: http://www.cdc.gov/nchs/data/nhsr/nhsr036.pdf (Last visited 6/29/11).

Chelala, C. (2000, November 28). The unrelenting scourge of child prostitution. *San Francisco Chronicle,* p. A27.

Chen, L. P., et al. (2010). Sexual abuse and lifetime diagnosis of psychiatric disorders: Systematic review and meta-analysis. *Mayo Clinic Proceedings, 85,* 618–629.

Chesson, H. W., et al. (2011). A brief review of the estimated economic burden of sexually transmitted diseases in the United States: Inflation-adjusted updates of previously published cost studies. *Sexually Transmitted Infections, 38,* 880–891.

Chia, M., & Abrams, R. C. (2005). *The multi-orgasmic woman: Sexual secrets every woman should know*. London: Rodale International.

Child Trends Data Bank. (2014). Low and very low birth weight infants. Available: http://www.childtrends.org/wpcontent/uploads/2014/01/57_Low_Birth_Weight.pdf (Last visited 12/15/14).

Chivers, M., Suschinsky, K. D., Timmers, A. D., & Bossio, J. A. (2014). Experimental, neuroimaging, and psychophysiological methods in sexuality research. In D. L. Tolman & L. M. Diamond (Eds.), *APA Handbook of sexuality and psychology* (pp. 81–98). Washington, DC: American Psychological Association.

Chivers, M. L., Seto, M. C., Lalumière, M. L., & Grimbos, T. (2010). Agreement of self-reported and genital measures of sexual arousal in men and women: A meta-analysis. *Archives of Sexual Behavior, 39,* 5–56. Available: http://www.springerlink.com/content/f8162672t32hu531/fulltext.pdf (Last visited: 8/12/10).

Choi, K. H., Han, C., Paul, J., & Ayala, G. (2011). Strategies of managing racism and homophobia among US ethnic and racial minority men who have sex with men. *AIDS Education and Prevention, 23*(2), 145–158. Available: http://www.ncbi.nlm.nih.gov/pmc/articles/PMC3083124/ (Last visited 9/27/14).

Christensen, B. S., Gronback, M., Osler, M., Pedersen, B., Graugaard, C., & Frisch, M. (2011). Sexual dysfunctions and difficulties in Denmark: Prevalence and associated sociodemographic factors. *Archives of Sexual Behavior, 40,* 121–132.

Christopher, F. S., & Sprecher, S. (2000). Sexuality in marriage, dating, and other relationships: A decade review. *Journal of Marriage and Family, 62,* 999–1017.

Clark, T. D. (1977). *Indiana University: Midwestern pioneer: Vol. 3. Years of fulfillment.* Bloomington: Indiana University Press.

CNN.com/Law Center. (2003, March 5). Supreme Court upholds sex offender registration laws. Available: http://www.cnn.com/2003/law/03/05/scotus.sex.offenders.ap/index (Last visited 3/5/03).

Cobbina, J. E., & Oselin, S. S. (2011). It's not only the money: An analysis of adolescent versus adult entry into street prostitution. *Sociological Inquiry, 81,* 310–332.

Cohan, D., Lutnick, A., Davidson, P., Cloniger, C., Herlyn, A., Breyer, J., et al. (2006). Sex worker health: San Francisco style. *Sexually Transmitted Infections, 82,* 418–422.

Cohen, C. R., Lingappa, J. R., Baeten, J. M., Ngayo, M. O., Spiegel, C. A., Hong, T., et al. (2012). Bacterial vaginosis associated with increased risk of female-to-male HIV-1 transmission: A prospective cohort analysis among African couples. *PloS Medicine.* doi: 10.1371/journal.pmed.1001251.

Cohen, E. (2010). New Year's resolution: Have more sex. Available: http://com.site.printthis.clickability.como/pt/cpt?/action5cpt&title5New1Year$27s1resolution (Last visited 1/7/10).

Cohen, M. S., Chen, Y. Q., McCauley, M., Gamble, T., Hosseinpour, M. C., Kumarasamy, N., et al. (2011). Prevention of HIV-1 infection with early antiretroviral therapy. *New England Journal of Medicine, 365,* 493–505.

Cohn, D. (2013). Love and marriage. Pew Research Social and Demographic Trends. Available: http://www.pewsocialtrends.org/2013/02/13/love-and-marriage/

Coleman, E. (1986, July). Sexual compulsion vs. sexual addiction: The debate continues. *SIECUS Report, 14*(6), 7–11.

Coleman, E. (1987). Sexual compulsivity: Definition, etiology, and treatment considerations. *Journal of Chemical Dependency Treatment, 1,* 189–204.

Coleman, E. (1991). Compulsive sexual behavior: New concepts and treatments. *Journal of Psychology and Human Sexuality, 4,* 37–52.

Coleman, E. (1996). *What sexual scientists know about compulsive sexual behavior.* Allentown, PA: Society for the Scientific Study of Sexuality.

Coleman, E., Bockting, W., Botzer, M., Cohen-Kettnis, P., et al. (2011). Standards of care for the health of transsexual, transgender, and gender-non-conforming people, version 7. *International Journal of Transgenderism, 13,* 165–232. Available: http://www.wpath.org/uploaded_files/140/files/IJT%20SOC,%20V7.pdf (Last visited 7/8/14).

Coleman, E., Raymond, N., & McBean, A. (2003). Assessment and treatment of compulsive sexual behavior. *Minnesota Medicine, 86*(7), 42–47.

Coleman, L. M. (2001). *Young people, "risk" and sexual behavior: A literature review.* Report prepared for the Health Development Agency and the Teenage Pregnancy Unit. Brighton, England: Trust for the Study of Adolescence.

Coleman, L. M., & Cater, S. M. (2005). A qualitative study of the relationship between alcohol consumption and risky sex in adolescents. *Archives of Sexual Behavior, 34,* 649–661.

Comella, L. (2008). It's sexy: It's big business. And it's not just for men. *Contexts, 7,* 61–63.

Congenital adrenal hyperplasia. (2014). MedlinePlus. Available: http://www.nlm.nih.gov/medlineplus/ency/article/000411.htm (Last visited 7/11/14).

Connell, R. W. (1995). *Masculinities.* Berkeley: University of California Press.

Cook, R. L., & Clark, D. B. (2005). Is there an association between alcohol consumption and sexually transmitted diseases? A systematic review. *Sexually Transmitted Diseases, 32,* 156–164.

Cooley, P. C., Rogers, S. M., Turner, C. F., Al-Tayyib, A., Willis, G., & Ganapathi, L. (2001). Using touch screen audio-CASI to obtain data on sensitive topics. *Computers in Human Behavior, 17,* 285–293.

Cooper, H. (2014, December 3). Reports of sexual assaults in military on rise. *New York Times.* Available: http://www.nytimes.com/2014/12/04/us/reports-of-sexual-assaults-in-military-on-rise.html (Last visited 12/12/14).

Cooper, M. L. (2002). Alcohol use and risky sexual behavior among college students and youth: Evaluating the evidence. *Journal of Studies on Alcohol, Suppl. 14,* 101–117.

Cooper, M. L. (2006). Does drinking promote risky sexual behavior? A complex answer to a simple question. *Current Directions, 15,* 19–23.

Copen, C., Daniels, K., & Mosher, W. D. (2013). First premarital cohabitation in the United States: 2006–2010. National Survey of Family Growth. *National Health Statistics Reports, 64.* Available: http://www.cdc.gov/nchs/data/nhsr/nhsr064.pdf (Last visited 9/27/14).

Corliss, H. L., Goodenow, C. S., Nichols, L., & Austin, S. B. (2011). High burden of homelessness among sexual-minority adolescents: Findings from a representative Massachusetts high school sample. *American Journal of Public Health, 101,* 1683–1689.

Costa, R., Miller, G. F., & Brody, S. (2012). Women who prefer longer penises are more likely to have vaginal orgasms (but not clitoral orgasms): Implications for an evolutionary theory of vaginal orgasm. *Journal of Sexual Medicine.* doi: 10.1111/j.1743-6109.2012.02917.x.

Couper, M. P., Tourangeau, R., & Marvin, T. (2009). Taking the audio out of audio-CASI. *Public Opinion Quarterly, 73,* 281–303.

Crepault, C., & Couture, M. (1980). Men's erotic fantasies. *Archives of Sexual Behavior, 9,* 565–581.

Crooks, R., & Baur, K. (2005). *Our Sexuality* (9th ed.). Belmont, CA: Thomas Wadsorth.

Crosby, R. A., & Bounse, S. (2012). Condom effectiveness: Where we are now? *Sexual Health, 9,* 10–17.

Crosby, R. A., Casey, B. R., Vanderpool, R., Collins, T., & Moore, G. R. (2011). Uptake of free HPV vaccination among young women: A comparison of rural versus urban rates. *Journal of Rural Health, 27,* 380–384.

Crosby, R. A., DiClemente, R. J., & Salazar, L. F. (2006). *Research methods in health promotion.* San Francisco: Jossey-Bass.

Crosby, R. A., Yarber, W. L., Graham, C. A., & Sanders, S. A. (2010). Does it fit okay? Problems with condom use as a function of self-reported fit. *Sexually Transmitted Infections, 86,* 36–38.

Crouch, S. R., Waters, E., McNair, R., Power, J., & Davis, E. (2014). Parent-reported measures of child health and wellbeing in same-sex parent families: A cross-section survey. *BMC Public Health, 14,* 635.

Cummings, J. (1987, June 8). Disabled model defies sexual stereotypes. *New York Times,* p. 17.

Cupach, W. R., & Comstock, J. (1990). Satisfaction with sexual communication in marriage. *Journal of Social and Personal Relationships, 7,* 179–186.

Cutler, W. (1999). Human sex-attractant pheromones: Discovery, research, development, and application in sex therapy. *Psychiatric Annals, 29,* 54–59.

Damon, W., & Rosser, B. R. S. (2005). Anodyspareunia in men who have sex with men. *Journal of Sex and Marital Therapy, 31,* 129–141.

Daneback, K., Traeen, B., & Mansson, S. (2009). Use of pornography in a random sample of Norwegian heterosexual couples. *Archives of Sexual Behavior, 38,* 746–753.

Daniels, K., Daugherty, J., & Jones, J. (2014). Current contraceptive status among women aged 15–44: United States, 2011–2013. *NCHS Data Brief, 173.* Available: http://www.cdc.gov/nchs/data/databriefs/db173.htm (Last visited 5/3/15).

Dao, J. (2013, June 23). When victims of military sex assaults are men. *New York Times,* pp. A1, A12.

Darden, P. M., Thompson, D. M., Roberts, J. R., Hale, J. J., Pope, C., Naifeh, M., et al. (2013). Reasons for not vaccinating adolescents: National Immunization Survey of Teens, 2008–2010. *Pediatrics, 131,* 645–651.

Darmasseelane, K., Hyde, M. J., Santhakumaran, S., Gale, C., & Modi, N. (2014). Mode of delivery and offspring body mass index, overweight and obesity in adult life: A systematic review and meta-Analysism. *PLoS ONE.* Available: http://siecus.org/index.cfm?fuseaction=Feature.showFeature&featureid=2375&pageid=682&parentid=478 (Last visited 12/10/14).

Das, A., Waite, L. J., & Laumann, E. O. (2012). Sexual expression over the life course. In L. M. Carpenter & J. DeLamater (Eds.), *Sex for life.* New York: New York University Press.

Davidson, J. K., & Darling, C. A. (1986). The impact of college-level sex education on sexual knowledge, attitudes, and practices: The knowledge/sexual experimentation myth revisited. *Deviant Behavior, 7,* 13–30.

Davidson, J. O. (2002). The rights and wrongs of prostitution. *Hypatia, 17,* 84–98.

Davies, M. J., Moore, V. M., Willson, K. J., Van Essen, P., Priest, K., Scott, H., Haan, E. A., & Chan, A. (2012). Reproductive technologies and the risk of birth defects. *New England Journal of Medicine, 366,* 1803–1813. Available: http://www.nejm.org/doi/full/10.1056/NEJMoa1008095#t=articleTop (Last viewed 12/16/14).

Davis, K. E., & Todd, M. J. (1985). Assessing friendship: Prototypes, paradigm cases and relationship description. In S. Duck & D. Perlman (Eds.), *Understanding personal relationships: An interdisciplinary approach.* Newbury Park, CA: Sage.

Davis, S. R., Davison, S. L., Donath, S., & Bell, R. J. (2005). Circulating androgen levels and self-reported sexual fluctuation in women. *Journal of the American Medical Association, 294*(17), 2167–2168.

Dawood, K., Kirk, K. M., Bailey, J. M., Andrews, P. W., & Martin, N. G. (2005). Genetic and environmental influences on the frequency of female orgasm. *Twin Research and Human Genetics, 8,* 27–33

Day, A., Thurlow, K., & Wolliscroft, J. (2003). Working with childhood sexual abuse: A survey of mental health professionals. *Child Abuse and Neglect, 27,* 191–198.

De Block, A., & Adriaens, P. R. (2013). Pathologizing sexual deviance: A history. *Journal of Sex Research, 50,* 276–298.

De Cuypere, G., T'Sjoen, G., Beerten, R., Selvaggi, G., De Sutter, P., Hoebeke, P., et al. (2005). Sexual and physical health after sex reassignment surgery. *Archives of Sexual Behavior, 34,* 679–690.

Decker, M. R., Raj, A., Gupta, J., & Silverman, J. G. (2008). Sex purchasing and associations with HIV/STI among a clinic-based sample of U.S. men. *Journal of Acquired Immune Deficiency Syndromes, 48,* 355–365.

DeLamater, J., & Friedrich, W. (2002). Human sexual development. *Journal of Sex Research, 38,* 10–14.

DeLamater, J. D., & Sill, M. (2005). Sexual desire in later life. *Journal of Sex Research, 42*(2), 138–149.

Dempsey, A. F., Butchart, A., Singer, D., Clark, S., & Davis, M. (2011). Factors associated with parental intentions for male human papillomavirus vaccination: Results of a national survey. *Sexually Transmitted Diseases, 38,* 769–776.

Denny, D. (1997). Transgender: Some historical, cross-cultural, and contemporary models and methods of coping and treatment. In B. Bullough, V. L. Bullough, & J. Elias (Eds.), *Gender blending.* New York: Prometheus Books.

Des Jarlais, D. C., Paone, D., Milliken, J., Turner, C. F., Miller, H., Gribble, J., et al. (1999). Audio-computer interviewing to measure risk behavior for HIV among injecting drug users: A quasi-randomized trial. *The Lancet, 353,* 1657–1661.

Devaney, S., Palomaki, G., Scott, J. A., & Bianchi, D. W. (2011). Noninvasive fetal sex determination using cell-free fetal DNA. *Journal of the American Medical Association, 306*(6), 627–636.

di Mauro, D. (1995). Executive summary. Sexuality research in the United States: An assessment of the social and behavioral sciences. Social Science Research Council. Available: http://www.kinseyinstitute.org/resources/sexrealn.html (Last visited 8/1/06).

Diamond, L. (2008). *Sexual fluidity: Understanding women's love and desire.* Cambridge, MA: Harvard University Press.

Diamond, L. (2013, Oct. 5). Just how different are female and sexual male sexual orientation? New York: Cornell University Lecture Series. Available: http://www.cornell.edu/video/lisa-diamond-on-sexual-fluidity-of-men-and-women (Last visited 6/4/14).

Diamond, M. (1996). Prenatal predisposition and the clinical management of some pediatric conditions. *Journal of Sex and Marital Therapy, 22*(3), 139–147.

Diamond, M., & Sigmundson, H. K. (1997). Management of intersexuality: Guidelines for dealing with individuals with ambiguous genitalia. *Archives of Pediatrics and Adolescent Medicine, 151,* 1046–1050.

Diaz, R. M. (1998). *Latino gay men and HIV: Culture, sexuality and risk behavior.* New York: Routledge.

Dick-Read, G. (1972). *Childbirth without fear* (4th ed.). New York: Harper & Row.

Dindia, K. (1992). Sex differences in self-disclosure: A meta-analysis. *Psychological Bulletin, 112,* 1069–124.

Dindia, K. (1994). The intrapersonal-interpersonal dialectical process of self-disclosure. In S. Duck (Ed.), *Understanding relationship processes IV: The dynamics of relationships* (pp. 27–57). Mahwah, NJ: Lawrence Erlbaum Associates, Inc.

Dines, G. (2010). *Pornland: How porn has hijacked sexuality.* Boston: Beacon Press.

Dinh, T., Sternberg, M., Dunne, E. F., & Markowitz, L. E. (2008). Genital warts among 18- to 59-year-olds in the United States, National Health and Nutrition Examination Study, 1999–2004. *Sexually Transmitted Diseases, 35,* 357–360.

"Disorders of Sex Development, (2014)" *Medscape.* Available: http://emedicine.medscape.com/article/1015520-overview (Last visited 1/25/15).

Dittman, M. (2004). Getting prostitutes off the street. *Monitor on Psychology, 35*(9), 71.

Dixson, B. J., Dixson, A. F., Bishop, P. J., & Parish, A. (2010). Human physique and attractiveness in men and women: A New Zealand—U.S. Comparative Study. *Archives of Sexual Behavior, 39,* 798–806.

Djerassi, C. (1981). *The politics of contraception.* New York: Freeman.

Docter, R. F., & Prince, V. (1997). Transvestism: A survey of 1032 cross-dressers. *Archives of Sexual Behavior, 26,* 589–606.

Dodge, B., Reece, M., Herbenick, D., Schick, V., Sanders, S. A., & Fortenberry, J. D. (2010). Sexual health among U.S. Black and Hispanic men and women: A national representative study. *Journal of Sexual Medicine, 7,* 330–345.

Doherty, I. A., Schoenbach, V. J., & Adimora, A. A. (2009). Condom use and duration of concurrent partnerships among men in the United States. *Sexually Transmitted Infections, 36,* 265–272.

Donnell, D., et al. (2010). Heterosexual HIV-1 transmission after initiation of antiretroviral therapy: A prospective cohort analysis. *The Lancet, 375,* 2092–2098.

Donovan, B., et al. (2011). Quadrivalent human papillomavirus vaccination and trends in genital warts in Australia: Analysis of national sentinel surveillance data. *The Lancet Infectious Diseases, 11,* 39–44.

Dorey, G., Speakman, M. J., Feneley, R. C. L., Swinkels, A., & Dunn, C. D. R. (2005). Pelvic floor exercises for erectile dysfunction. *British Journal of Urology, 96,* 595–597.

Downs, J. S., de Bruin, W. B., Murray, P. J., & Fischhoff, B. (2006). Specific STI knowledge may be acquired too late. *Journal of Adolescent Health, 38,* 65–67.

Dowshen, S. (2012). Precocious puberty. Kids Health. Available: http://kidshealth.org/parent/medical/sexual/precocious.html# (Last visited 11/13/14).

Drescher, J. (2014). Controversies in gender diagnoses. *LGBT Health, 1*(1), 10–14.

Drigotas, S., Rusbult, C., & Verette, J. (1999). Level of commitment, mutuality of commitment, and couple well-being. *Personal Relationships, 6,* 389–409.

Drucker, D. J. (2014). *The classification of sex: Alfred Kinsey and the organization of knowledge.* Pittsburgh: University of Pittsburgh Press.

Ducharme, S. H., & Gill, K. M. (1997). *Sexuality after spinal cord injury: Answers to your questions.* Baltimore: Brookes.

Dworkin, S. L., & O'Sullivan, L. (2005). Actual versus desired initiation patterns among a sample of college men: Tapping disjunctures within traditional male sexual scripts. *Journal of Sex Research, 42,* 150–158.

Eagly, A. (1987). *Sex differences in social behavior: A social role interpretation.* Hillsdale, NJ: Erlbaum.

Earls, C. M., & Lalumière, M. L. (2009). A case study of preferred bestiality. *Archives of Sexual Behavior, 38,* 605–609.

"Early puberty: Causes and consequences." (2014). WebMD. Available: http://www.webmd.com/children/guide/causes-symptoms (Last visited 7/29/14).

Easton, J. A., & Shackelford, T. K. (2009). Morbid jealousy and sex differences in partner-directed violence. *Human Nature, 30,* 342–350.

Ebadi, S., & Moaveni, A. (2006). *Iran awakening: A memoir of revolution and hope.* New York: Random House.

Edozien, F. (2003, July 8). Fighting AIDS face to face. *The Advocate,* 46–49.

Edwards, J. M., Iritani, B. J., & Hallfors, D. D. (2006). Prevalence and correlates of exchanging sex for drugs or money among adolescents in the United States. *Sexually Transmitted Infections, 82,* 354–358.

Edwards, K. M., Turchik, J. A., Dardis, C. M., Reynolds, N., & Gidycz, C. A. (2011). Rape myths: History, individual and institutional-level presence, and implications for change. *Sex Roles, 65,* 761–773.

Ellen, J. M., et al. (2006). Sex partner selection, social networks, and repeat sexually transmitted infections in young men: A preliminary report. *Sexually Transmitted Diseases, 33,* 18–21.

Elliott, L., & Brantley, C. (1997). *Sex on campus: The naked truth about the real sex lives of college students.* New York: Random House.

Ellis, C. D. (2002). Male rape—The silent victims. *Collegian, 9,* 34–39.

Ellis, L. (1996). Theories of homosexuality. In R. C. Savin-Williams & K. M. Cohen (Eds.), *The lives of lesbians, gays and bisexuals.* Fort Worth, TX: Harcourt Brace.

Ellison, C. (1985). Intimacy-based sex therapy. In W. Eicher & G. Kockott (Eds.), *Sexology.* New York: Springer-Verlag.

Ellison, C. (2000). *Women's sexualities.* Oakland, CA: New Harbinger.

eMarketer. (2013). Digital set to surpass TV in time spent with US media. Available: http://www.emarketer.com/Article/Digital-Set-Surpass-TV-Time-Spent-with-US-Media/1010096 (Last visited 3/27/14).

Endometriosis. (2013). National Institutes of Health. Available: http://www.nichd.nih.gov/health/topics/endometri/Pages/default.aspx (Last visited 1/14/15).

Eng, T. R., & Butler, W. T. (Eds.). (1997). *The hidden epidemic: Confronting sexually transmitted diseases.* Washington, DC: National Academies Press.

Epsey, E., Ogburn, T., Leeman, L., Singh, R., & Schrader, R. (2012). Effect of progestin vs. combined oral contraceptive pills on lactation: A double-blind randomized controlled study. *Obstetrics & Gynecology, 119*(1), 5–13. Available: http://www.ncbi.nlm.nih.gov/pmc/articles/PMC3586805/ (Last visited 12/2/14).

Epstein, A. (1997, June 10). Justices will rule on issue of same-sex harassment. *The Oregonian,* p. A1.

Especially for fathers. (n.d.). American College of Obstetricians and Gynecologists. Education Pamphlet AP032.

Evolutionary psychology: Why women like older men and men like younger women. (2014). *Science 2.0.* Available: http://www.science20.com/news_articles/evolutionary_psychology_why_women_like_older_men_and_men_like_younger_women-145652 (Last visited 1/15/15).

Facts about hypospadias. (2013). Centers for Disease Control and Prevention. Available: http://www.cdc.gov/ncbddd/birthdefects/Hypospadias.html (Last visited 7/1/14).

Fagan, P. J., Wise, T. N., Schmidt, C. W., & Berlin, F. S. (2002). Pedophilia. *Journal of the American Medical Association, 288,* 2458–2465.

Fagin, D. (1995, February 1). DES moms, gay or bisexual daughters: Study links exposure to sexual orientation. *San Francisco Chronicle.*

Fang, B. (2005, October 24). Why more kids are getting into the sex trade—And how the feds are fighting back. *U.S. News and World Report,* pp. 30–34.

Farley, M., Cotton, A., Lynne, J., et al. (2003). Prostitution and trafficking in nine countries: An update on violence and posttraumatic stress disorder. In M. Farley (Ed.), *Prostitution, trafficking and traumatic stress* (pp. 33–74). Binghamton, NY: Haworth Press.

Farnsworth, C. H. (1992, January 14). Homosexual is granted refugee status in Canada. *New York Times,* p. A5.

Farrer, F. (2010, Aug.). Contraception for teratogenic medications. *SA Pharmaceutical Journal,* 28–31.

Federal Bureau of Investigation (FBI). (2010). Innocence lost. Available: http://www.fbi/about-us/investigate/vc_majorthefts/cac/innocencelost (Last visited 10/14/11).

Federal Bureau of Investigation. (2014). A parents' guide to Internet safety. Available: http://www.fbi.gov/stats-services/publications/parent-guide (Last visited 4/2/14).

Federal Bureau of Investigation. (2015). Violent Crimes Against Children. Available: http://www.fbi.org.gov/about-us/investigate/vc_majorthefts/cac/innocentlost.

Feinberg, L. (1996). *Transgender warriors: Making history from Joan of Arc to Rupaul.* Boston: Beacon Press.

Female condom. (2014). Avert. Available: http://www.avert.org/female-condom.htm (Last visited 12/4/14).

Fenigstein, A., & Preston, M. (2007). The desired number of sexual partners as a function of gender, sexual risks, and the meaning of "ideal." *Journal of Sex Research, 44,* 879–895.

Feray, J. C., & Herzer, M. (1990). Homosexual studies and politics in the 19th century: Karl Maria Kertbeny. *Journal of Homosexuality, 19*(1), 23–47.

Ferguson, C. J., & Hartley, R. D. (2009). The pleasure is momentary . . . the expense damnable? The influence of pornography on rape and sexual assault. *Aggression and Violent Behavior, 14,* 323–329.

Fergusson, D. M., Swain-Campbell, N. R., & Horwood, L. J. (2002). Does sexual violence contribute to elevated rates of anxiety and depression in females? *Psychological Medicine, 32,* 991–996.

Fetters, K., Marks, C., Mindel, A., & Estcourt, C. S. (2000). Sexually transmitted infections and risk behaviors in women who have sex with women. *Sexually Transmitted Infections, 76,* 345–349.

Fielder, R. L., & Carey, M. P. (2010). Predictors and consequences of sexual "hookups" among college students: A short-term prospective study. *Archives of Sexual Behavior, 39,* 1105–1119.

Fielder, R. L., Carey, K. B., & Carey, M. P. (2013). Are hookups replacing romantic relationships? A longitudinal study of first-year female college students. *Journal of Adolescent Health, 52,* 657–659.

Fielder, R. L., Walsh, J. L., Carey, K. B., & Carey, M. P. (2014). Sexual hookups and adverse health outcomes: A longitudinal study of first-year college women. *Journal of Sex Research, 51,* 131–144.

Figlio, D., Guryan, J., Karbownik, K., & Roth, J. (2014). The effects of poor neonatal health on children's cognitive development. Available: http://www.ipr.northwestern.edu/publications/docs/workingpapers/2013/IPR-WP-13-08.pdf (Last visited 12/18/14).

Finer, L. B., & Philbin, J. M. (2014). Trends in ages at key reproductive transitions in the United States, 1951–2010. *Women's Health Issues, 23*(3), e-1- e-9. Available: http://www.guttmacher.org/pubs/journals/j.whi.2014.02.002.pdf (Last visited 9/2/14).

Finkelhor, D. (1990). Early and long-term effects of child sexual abuse: An update. *Professional Psychology: Research and Practice, 21,* 325–330.

Firestone, R. W., Firestone, L. A., & Catlett, J. (2006). *Sex and love in intimate relationships.* Washington, DC: American Psychological Association.

Fisher, D., & Howells, K. (1993). Social relationships in sexual offenders. *Sexual and Marital Therapy, 8,* 123–136.

Fisher, H. (2004). *Why we love: The nature and chemistry of romantic love.* New York: Henry Holt and Company.

Fisher, H. (2009). *Why him? Why her?* New York: Henry Holt and Company.

Fisher, M. L., Worth, K., Garcia, J. R., & Meredith, T. (2012). Feelings of regret following uncommitted sexual encounters in Canadian university students. *Culture, Health & Sexuality, 14,* 45–57.

Fisher, T. D., & Walters, A. S. (2003). Variables in addition to gender that help to explain differences in perceived sexual interest. *Psychology of Men and Masculinity, 4,* 154–162.

Fisher, W. (1986). A psychological approach to human sexuality. In D. Byrne & K. K. Kelley (Eds.), *Alternative approaches to human sexuality.* Hillsdale, NJ: Erlbaum.

Fisher, W. (1998). The Sexual Opinion Survey. In C. M. Davis, W. L. Yarber, R. Bauserman, G. Schreer, & S. L. Davis (Eds.), *Handbook of sexuality-related measures.* Thousand Oaks, CA: Sage.

Fisher, W. A., & Barak, A. (2001). Internet pornography: A social psychological perspective on Internet sexuality. *Journal of Sex Research, 38,* 312–323.

Fisher, W. A., & Davis, C. M. (2007). *What sexual scientists know about pornography.* Allentown, PA: Society for the Scientific Study of Sexuality.

5-alpha reductase deficiency. (2014). Genetics home reference. Available: http://ghr.nlm.nih.gov/condition/5-alpha-reductase-deficiency (Last visited 7/11/14).

Fleming, D. T., & Wasserheit, J. N. (1999). From epidemiological synergy to public health policy and practice: The contribution of other sexually transmitted diseases to sexual transmission of HIV infection. *Sexually Transmitted Diseases, 75,* 3–17.

Fobair, P., Stewart, S. L., Chang, S., et al. (2006). Body image and sexual problems in young women with breast cancer. *Psychooncology, 15,* 579–594.

Foldes, P., & Buisson, O. (2009). The clitoral complex: A dynamic sonographic study. *Journal of Sexual Medicine, 6,* 1223–1231.

Ford, C., & Beach, F. (1951). *Patterns of sexual behavior.* New York: Harper & Row.

Forhan, S. E., Gottlieb, S. L., Sternberg, M. R., Xu, F., Datta, D., McQuillan, G. M., et al. (2009). Prevalence of sexually transmitted infections among female adolescents aged 14 to 19 in the United States. *Pediatrics, 124,* 1505–1512.

Fortenberry, J. D., Cecil, H., Zimet, G. D., & Orr, D. P. (1997). Concordance between self-report questionnaires and coital diaries for sexual behaviors of adolescent women with sexually transmitted infections. In J. Bancroft (Ed.), *Researching sexual behavior.* Bloomington: Indiana University Press.

Fortenberry, J. D., McFarlane, M., Bleakley, A., Bull, S., Fishbein, M., Grimley, D., et al. (2002). Relationship of stigma and shame to gonorrhea and HIV screening. *American Journal of Public Health, 92,* 378–381.

Foster, D. G., Higgins, J. A., Biggs, M. A., McCain, C., Holtby, S., & Brindis, C. D. (2012). Willingness to have unprotected sex. *Journal of Sex Research, 49,* 61–68.

Foucault, M. (1978). *The history of sexuality: Vol. 1.* New York: Pantheon.

Foxman, B., Sevgi, A., & Holmes, K. (2006). Common use in the general population of sexual enhancement aids and drugs to enhance sexual experience. *Sexually Transmitted Diseases, 33,* 156–162.

Franklin, E. A., Wang, L., Bunker, C. H., et al. (2009). Episiotomy in the United States: Has anything changed? *American Journal of Obstetrics & Gynecology, 200,* 1e1–1e6.

Frederick, D. A., & Haselton, M. G. (2007). Why is masculinity sexy? Tests of the fitness indicator hypothesis. *Personality and Social Psychology Bulletin, 33,* 1167–1183.

Freedom to Marry. (2015a). The freedom to marry internationally. Available: http://www.fredomtomarry.org/landscape/entry/c/international (Last visited 2/17/15).

Freedom to Marry. (2015b). Historic victory: Ireland votes Yes on the freedom to marry. Available: http://www.freedomtomarry.org/blog/entry/the-freedom-to-marry-comes-to-Ireland (Last visited: 6/2/15).

Freedom to Marry. (2015c). Greenland approves the freedom to marry for same-sex couples. Avaiable: http://www.freedomtomarry.org/blog/entry/greenland-approves-the-freedom-to-marry-for-same-sex-couples (Last visited: 6/2/15)

French National Institute for Demographic Studies. (2012). What are the most widely used contraceptive methods across the world? Available: http://www.ined.fr/en/everything_about_population/demographic-facts-sheets/faq/most-widely-used-contraceptive-methods-world/ (Last visited 12/7/14).

Freud, S. (1938). Three contributions to the theory of sex. In A. A. Brill (Ed.), *The basic writings of Sigmund Freud.* New York: Modern Library.

Freund, K., Seto, M., & Kuban, M. (1997). Frotteurism and the theory of courtship disorder. In D. Laws & W. O'Donohue (Eds.), *Sexual deviance: Theory, assessment, and treatment.* New York: Guilford Press.

Friedman, M. R., Dodge, B., Schick, V., Herbenick, D., Hubach, R., Bowling, J., Goncalves, G., Krier, S., & Reece, M. (2014, April 21). From bias to bisexual health disparities: Attitudes toward bisexual men and women in the United States. *GLBT Health.* Available: http://online.liebertpub.com/doi/abs/10.1089/lgbt.2014.0005 (Last visited 9/4/14).

Friedrich, W., Fisher, J., Broughton, D., Houston, M., & Shafran, C. (1998). Normative sexual behavior in children: A contemporary sample. *Pediatrics, 101,* e9.

Frisby, B. N., Dillow, M. R., Gaughan, S., & Nordlund, J. (2011). Flirtatious communication: An experimental examination of perceptions of social-sexual communication motivated by evolutionary forces. *Sex Roles, 64,* 682–694.

Frost, D. M., & Meyer, I. H. (2009). Internalized homophobia and relationship quality among lesbians, gay men, and bisexuals. *Journal of Counseling Psychology, 56,* 97–109.

Fruhauf, S., Gerger, H., Schmidt, H. M., Munder, T., & Barth, J. (2013). Efficacy of psychological interventions for sexual dysfunction: A systematic review and meta-analysis. *Archives of Sexual Behavior, 42,* 915–933.

Gades, N. M., et al. (2005). Association between smoking and erectile dysfunction: A population-based study. *American Journal of Epidemiology, 161,* 346–351.

Gagnon, J. H. (1975). Sex research and social change. *Archives of Sexual Behavior, 4,* 112–141.

Gagnon, J. H., & Simon, W. (1973). *Sexual conduct: The origins of human sexuality.* Chicago: Aldine.

Gale, J., & Pettypiece, S. (2013, Jan. 13). Brazilian bikini waxes make crab lice endangered species. Bloomberg News. Available: http://www.bloomberg.com/news/2013-01-13/brazilian-bikini-waxes-make-crab-lice-endangered-species-health.html (Last visited 6/3/14).

Galinsky, A., & Sonenstein, F. L. (2013). Relationship commitment, perceived equity, and sexual enjoyment among young adults in the United States. *Archives of Sexual Behavior, 42,* 93–104.

Galinsky, A. M. (2012). Sexual touching and difficulties with sexual arousal and orgasm among U.S. older adults. *Archives of Sexual Behavior, 41,* 875–890.

Gallup, Inc. (2014). Same-sex marriage support reaches new high at 55%. Available: http://www.gallup.com/poll/169640/sex-marriage-support-reaches-new-high.aspx (Last visited 2/17/15).

Garcia, J. R., & Fisher, H. E. (in press). Why we hook up: Searching for sex or looking for love? *Culture, Health and Sexuality.*

Garcia, J. R., Massey, S. G., Merriwether, A. M., & Seibold-Simpson, S. M. (2013, Aug.). *Orgasm experiences among emerging adult men and women: Gender, relationship context, and attitudes toward casual sex.* Poster presented at the annual meeting of the International Academy of Sex Research, Chicago, Illinois.

Garcia, J. R., Reiber, C., Massey, S. G., & Merriwether, A. M. (2012). Sexual hookup culture: A review. *Review of General Psychology, 16,* 161–176.

Garcia, J. R., Reiber, C., Merriwether, A. M., Heywood, L. L., & Fisher, H. E. (2010, Mar.). *Touch me in the morning: Intimately affiliative gestures in uncommitted and romantic relationships.* Paper presented at the Annual Conference of the North Eastern Evolutionary Psychology Society, New Paltz, New York.

Gatzeva, M., & Paik, A. (2011). Emotional and physical satisfaction in noncohabiting, cohabiting, and marital relationships: The importance of jealous conflict. *Journal of Sex Research, 48*(1), 29–42.

Gavin, L., Moskosky, S., Carter, M., Glass, E., et al. (2014). Providing quality family planning services: Recommendations of CDC and the U.S. Office of Population Affairs. *Morbidity and Mortality Weekly Report, 63*(RR-4):1–54. Available: http://www.cdc.gov/mmwr/pdf/rr/rr6304.pdf (Last visited 11/19/14).

Gay & Lesbian Alliance Against Defamation (GLAAD). (2014). Tips for allies of transgender people. Available: http://www.glaad.org/transgender/allies

Gay, Lesbian, and Straight Education Network. (2010). 2009 National School Climate Survey: Nearly 9 out of 10 LGBT students experience harassment in school. Available: http://www.glsen.org/cgi-bin/iowa/all/news/record/2624.html (Last visited 9/1/11).

Gay, P. (1986). *The bourgeois experience: The tender passion.* New York: Oxford University Press.

Geary, D. C., Vigil, J., & Byrd-Craven, J. (2004). Evolution of human mate choice. *Journal of Sex Research, 41,* 27–42.

Geography IQ. (2014). Available: http://www.geographyiq.com/ranking/ranking_Infant_Mortality_Rate_aall.htm (Last visited 12/16/14).

George, W. H., Davis, K. C., Norris, J., Heiman, J. R., Stoner, S. A., Schact, R. L., Herndershot, C. S., & Kajumulo, K. F. (2009). Indirect effects of acute alcohol intoxication on sexual risk-taking: The roles of subjective and physiological sexual arousal. *Archives of Sexual Behavior, 38,* 498–513.

Gergen, K. J. (1985). The social constructionist movement in modern psychology. *American Psychologist, 40,* 266–275.

Gerressu, M., Mercer, C. H., Graham, C. A., Wellings, K., & Johnson, A. M. (2008). Prevalence of masturbation and associated factors in a British national probability survey. *Archives of Sexual Behavior, 37,* 266–278.

Gibbons, L., Belizán, J. M., Lauer, J. A., Betrán, A. P., Merialdi, M., & Althabe, F. (2010). The global numbers and costs of additionally needed and unnecessary caesarean sections performed per year. World Health Report. Available: http://www.who.int/healthsystems/topics/financing/healthreport/30C-sectioncosts.pdf (Last visited 12/10/14).

Gidycz, C. A., & Koss, M. P. (1990). A comparison of group and individual sexual assault victims. *Psychology of Women Quarterly, 14,* 325–342.

Giles, L. C., Glonek, G. F. V., Luszca, M. A., & Andrew, G. R. (2005). Effect of social networks on 10-year survival in very old Australians: The Australian Longitudinal Study of Aging. *Journal of Epidemiology and Community Health, 59,* 574–579.

Gillen, K., & Muncer, S. J. (1995). Sex differences in the perceived causal structure of date rape: A preliminary report. *Aggressive Behavior, 21*(2), 101–112.

Gilmore, M. R., Gaylord, J., Hatway, J., Hoppe, M. J., Morrison, D. M., Leigh, B. C., et al. (2001). Daily data collection of sexual and other health-related behaviors. *Journal of Sex Research, 38,* 35–42.

Girl Scout Research Institute. (2011, Oct.). Real to me: Girls and reality TV. Author.

Glassenberg, A. N., Feinberg, D. R., Jones, B. C., Little, A. C., & DeBruine, L. M. (2010). Sex-dimorphic face shape preference in heterosexual and homosexual men and women. *Archives of Sexual Behavior, 39,* 1289–1296.

Glauber, R. (2008). Race and gender in families and at work: The fatherhood wage premium. *Gender & Society, 22,* 8–30.

Glosser, A., Gardiner, K., & Fishman, M. (2004). Statutory rape: A guide to state laws and reporting requirements. Available: http://www.lewin.com/Lewin_Publications/Human_Services/StateLawsReport.htm (Last visited 3/26/06).

Golden, M. R., Dombrowski, J. C., Kerani, R. P., & Stekler, J. D. (2012). Failure of serosorting to protect African American men who have sex with men from HIV infection. *Sexually Transmitted Infections, 39,* 659–664.

Golden, M. R., Stekler, J., Hughes, J. P., & Wood, R. W. (2008). HIV serosorting in men who have sex with men: Is it safer? *Journal of Acquired Immune Deficiency Syndromes, 49,* 212–218.

Gomez, A. M., Beougher, S. C., Chakravarty, D., Neilands, T. B., Mandic, C. G., Darbes, L. A., & Hoff, C. C. (2012). Relationship factors as predictors of broken agreements about outside sexual partners: Implications for HIV prevention among gay couples. *AIDS & Behavior 16*(2), 1584–1588. Available: http://cregs.sfsu.edu/wp-content/uploads/2012/08/breaks_authorversion.pdf (Last visited 10/15/14).

Gonzalez-Lopez, G., & Vival-Ortiz, S. (2008). Latinas and Latinos, sexuality and society: A cultural sociological perspective. In H. Rodriguez, R. Saenz, and C. Menjivar (Eds.), *Latinas/os in the United States: Changing the face of America.* New York: Springer.

Goodman, A. (1993). Diagnosis and treatment of sexual addiction. *Journal of Sex and Marital Therapy, 19,* 225–251.

Gorbach, P. M., et al. (2009). Anal intercourse among young heterosexuals in three sexually transmitted disease clinics in the United States. *Sexually Transmitted Diseases, 36,* 193–198.

Gosink, P. D., & Jumbelic, M. I. (2000). Autoerotic asphyxiation in a female. *American Journal of Forensic Medicine and Pathology, 21,* 114–118.

Gottman, J., & Carrere, S. (2000, Oct.). Welcome to the love lab. *Psychology Today,* pp. 42–47.

Gottman, J. M., Levenson, R. W., Gross, J., Frederickson, B. L., McCoy, K., et al. (2003). Correlates of gay and lesbian couples, relationship satisfaction and relational dissolution. *Journal of Homosexuality, 45*(1), 23–43.

Graham, C. A., & Bancroft, J. (1997). A comparison of retrospective interview assessment versus daily ratings of sexual interest and activity in women. In J. Bancroft (Ed.), *Researching sexual behavior.* Bloomington: Indiana University Press.

Gray, P. B., & Garcia, J. R. (2013). *Evolution and human sexual behavior.* Cambridge, MA: Harvard University Press.

Gray, R. H., Wawer, M. J., Brookmeyer, R., Sewankambo, N. K., Serwadda, D., Wabwire-Mangen, F., Lutalo, T., Li, X., van Cott, T., Quinn, T. C., & Rakai Project Team. (2001). Probability of HIV-1 transmission per coital act in monogamous, heterosexual, HIV-1-discordant couples in Rakai, Uganda. *The Lancet, 357,* 1149–1153.

Greenberg, J. C. (2003, June 27). Supreme Court strikes down laws against homosexual sex. *Chicago Tribune,* sec. 1, pp. 1, 4.

Greenfeld, L. (1997). *Sex offenses and offenders: An analysis of data on rape and sexual assault.* Washington, DC: U.S. Department of Justice, Bureau of Justice Statistics.

Greenhouse, L. (2008, May 20). Court upholds child pornography law, despite free speech concerns. *New York Times,* p. A17.

Gregor, T. (1985). *Anxious pleasures.* Chicago: University of Chicago Press.

Grello, C., Welsh, D. P., & Harper, M. S. (2006). No strings attached: The nature of casual sex in college students. *Journal of Sex Research, 43*(3), 255–267.

Griffin, G. (1998). Understanding heterosexism—The subtle continuum of homophobia. *Women and Language, 21,* 11–21.

Griffith, J. D., Mitchell, S., Hammond, B., Gu, L. L., & Hart, C. L. (2012). A comparison of sexual behaviors and attitudes, self-esteem, quality of life, and drug use among pornography actors and a matched sample. *International Journal of Sexual Health, 24,* 254–266.

Griffith, J. D., Mitchell, S., Hart, C. L., Adams, L. T., & Gu, L. L. (2012). Pornography actresses: An assessment of the damaged goods hypothesis. *Journal of Sex Research.* doi: 10.1080/00224499.2012.719168.

Grimes, D. A., Lopez, L. M., O'Brien, P. A., & Raymond, E. G. (2013). Progestin-only pills for contraception. *The Cochrane Collaboration.* Available: http://onlinelibrary.wiley.com/doi/10.1002/14651858.CD007541.pub3/pdf/standard (Last visited 12/2/14).

Grossman, J. M., Tracy, A. J., Charmaraman, L., Ceder, I., & Erkut, S. (2014). Protective effects of middle school comprehensive sex education with family involvement. *Journal of School Health, 84,* 739–747.

Groth, A. N., & Birnbaum, H. J. (1978). Adult sexual orientation and attraction to underage persons. *Archives of Sexual Behavior, 7,* 175–181.

Groth, A. N., & Birnbaum, H. J. (1979). *Men who rape: The psychology of the offender.* New York: Plenum Press.

Groth, A. N., Burgess, A. W., & Holmstrom, L. L. (1977). Rape: Power, anger, and sexuality. *American Journal of Psychiatry, 104*(11), 1239–1243.

Grov, C., Parsons, J. T., & Bimbi, D. S. (2010). The association between penis size and sexual health among men who have sex with men. *Archives of Sexual Behavior, 39,* 788–797.

Grov, C., Wolff, M., Smith, M. D., Koken, J., & Parsons, J. T. (2014). Male clients of male escorts: Satisfaction, sexual behavior, and demographic characterisitcs. *Journal of Sex Research, 51,* 827–837.

Grudzen, C. R., Meeker, D., Torres, J., Du, Q., Anderson, R. M., & Gelberg, L. (2011). HIV and STI risk behaviors, knowledge, and testing among female adult film performers as compared to other Calfornia women. *AIDS and Behavior.* DOI. 10.1007/s10461-011-0090-0.

Grulich, A. E., de Visser, R. O., Smith, A. M. A., Rissel, C. E., & Richters, J. (2003). Sex in Australia: Homosexual experience and recent homosexual encounters. *Australian and New Zealand Journal of Public Health, 27,* 155–163.

Guttmacher Institute. (2008.4a). In brief: Improving contraceptive use in the United States, 2008 Series, No. 1.

Guttmacher Institute. (2011). Most women obtaining abortions report their partners know of and support their decision. Available: https://guttmacher.org/media/nr/2011/02/01/index.html (Last visited 12/9/14).

Guttmacher Institute. (2013.11a). Title X: An essential investment, now more than ever. Available: http://www.guttmacher.org/pubs/gpr/16/3/gpr160314.html#chart1 (Last visited 11/16/14).

Guttmacher Institute. (2014.6a, May). American teens' sexual and reproductive health. Fact sheet. Available: http://www.guttmacher.org/pubs/FB-ATSRH.html (Last visited 7/29/14).

Guttmacher Institute. (2014.11a). Contraception drives decline in teen pregnancy–and expanded access to LARC methods could accelerate this trend. Available: http://www.guttmacher.org/media/inthenews/2014/10/07/index.html (Last visited 12/7/14).

Guttmacher Institute. (2014.11b). Growing gap between first sex and first birth means women face longer period of risk for unintended pregnancy. Available: https://guttmacher.org/media/nr/2014/04/10/index.html (Last visited 12/3/14).

Guttmacher Institute. (2014.11c). Contraceptive use in the United States. Available: http://www.guttmacher.org/pubs/fb_contr_use.html (Last visited 11/15/14).

Guttmacher Institute. (2014.11d). Fact sheet: Induced abortion in the United States. Available: http://www.guttmacher.org/pubs/fb_induced_abortion.html (Last visited 12/8/14).

Guttmacher Institute. (2014.11e). An overview of abortion laws. Available: http://www.guttmacher.org/statecenter/spibs/spib_OAL.pdf (Last visited 12/9/14).

Guttmacher Institute. (2014.11f). *Guttmacher Policy Review, 17*(1). Contraceptive coverage at the U.S. Supreme Court: Countering the rhetoric with evidence. Available: http://www.guttmacher.org/pubs/gpr/17/1/gpr170102.html (Last visited 12/9/14).

Guttmacher Institute. (2014.12a). Infant abandonment. Available: http://www.guttmacher.org/statecenter/spibs/spib_IA.pdf (Last visited 12/18/14).

Guttmacher Institute. (2015). Unintended pregnancy in the United States. Available: http://www.guttmacher.org/pubs/FB-Unintended-Pregnancy-US.html (Last visited 11/15/15).

Ha, T., van den Berg, J. E. M., Engels, R. C. M. E., & Lichtwarck-Aschoff, A. (2012). Effects of attractiveness and status in dating desire in homosexual and heterosexual men and women. *Archives of Sexual Behavior, 41,* 673–682.

Hagedoorn, M., Sanderman, R., Bolks, H. N., et al. (2008). Distress in couples coping with cancer: A meta-analysis and critical review of role and gender effects. *Psychological Bulletin, 134*(1), 1–30.

Hald, G. M., Kuyper, L., Adam, P., & de Wit, J. (2013). Does viewing explain doing? Assessing the association between sexually explicit materials use and sexual behaviors in a large sample of Dutch adolescents and young adults. *Journal of Sexual Medicine, 10,* 2986–2995.

Hall, G. C. N., DeGarmo, D. S., Eap, S., Teten, A. L., & Sue, S. (2006). Initiation, desistance, and persistence of men's sexual coercion. *Journal of Counseling and Clinical Psychology, 74,* 732–742.

Hall, K. (2004). *Reclaiming your sexual self: How you can bring desire back into your life.* Hoboken, NJ: Wiley.

Hall, P. C., West, J. H., & Hill, S. (2011). Sexualization in lyrics of popular music from 1959 to 2009: Implications for sexuality educators. *Sexuality and Culture.* Available: http://link.springer.com.library2.csumb.edu:2048/article/10.1007/s12119-011-9103-4#page-1 (Last visited 3/27/14).

Hall, S. A., Shackelton, R., Rosen, R., & Araujo, A. B. (2010). Risk factors for incident erectile dysfuncton among community-dwelling men. *Journal of Sexual Medicine, 7,* 712–722.

Halpern-Felsher, B. L., & Reznik, Y. (2009). Adolescent sexual attitudes and behaviors: A developmental perspective. *The Prevention Researcher, 16*(4), 3–6.

Hamilton, B. E., Martin, J. A., Osterman, M. J. K., & Curtin, S. C. (2014, May 29). Births: Preliminary data for 2013. *CDC/NCHS, National Vital Statistics Reports, 63*(2). Available: http://www.cdc.gov/nchs/data/nvsr/nvsr63/nvsr63_02.pdf (Last accessed 8/13/14).

Hamilton, D. T., & Morris, M. (2010). Consistency of self-reported sexual behavior in surveys. *Archives of Sexual Behavior, 39,* 842–860.

Handsfield, H. H., Warren, T., Werner, M., & Phillips, J. A. (2007). Suppressive therapy with valacyclovir in early genital herpes: A pilot study of clinical efficacy and herpes-related quality of life. *Sexually Transmitted Diseases, 34,* 339–343.

Hanson, R. K., & Morton-Bourgon, K. E. (2005). The characteristics of persistent sexual offenders: A meta-analysis of recidivism studies. *Journal of Counseling and Clinical Psychology, 73,* 1154–1163.

Harding, S., & Norberg, K. (2005). New feminist approaches to social science methodologies: An introduction. *Signs: Journal of Women in Culture and Society, 30,* 2009–2015.

Harte, C. B., & Meston, C. M. (2011). Recreational use of erectile dysfunction medications in undergraduate men in the United States: Characteristics and associated risk factors. *Archives of Sexual Behavior, 40,* 597–606.

Harvard Men's Health Watch. (2014). Is testosterone replacement therapy safe? Available: http://www.health.harvard.edu/press_releases/is-testosterone-replacement-therapy-safe (Last visited 6/13/14).

Harvey, J. H., Wenzel, A., & Sprecher, S. (2004). *The handbook of sexuality in close relationships.* Mahwah, NJ: Erlbaum.

Hatcher, R. A., Trussell, J., Nelson, A. L., Cates, W., Kowal, D., & Policar, M. S. (2011). *Contraceptive technology* (20th rev. ed.). New York: Ardent Media.

Hatcher, R. A., Trussell, J., Stewart, F., Nelson, A. L., Cates, W., Guest, F., et al. (2007). *Contraceptive technology* (19th ed.). New York: Ardent Media.

Hatfield, E., & Walster, G. W. (1978). *A new look at love.* Lanham, MD: University Press of America.

Hatzenbuehler, M. L. (2011). The social environment and suicide attempts in lesbian, gay, and bisexual youth. *Pediatrics, 127,* 896–903.

Haugaard, J. J., & Reppucci, N. D. (1998). *The sexual abuse of children: A comprehensive guide to current knowledge and intervention strategies.* San Francisco: Jossey-Bass.

Haverluck, M. F. (2014, Sept. 19). Unprecedented: Singles outnumber marrieds in U.S…. where are they? *OnenewsNow.com.* Available: http://www.ncbi.nlm.nih.gov/pmc/articles/PMC3083124/ (Last accessed 9/27/14).

Hazan, C., & Shaver, P. (1987). Romantic love conceptualized as an attachment process. *Journal of Personality and Social Psychology, 52*(3), 511–524.

HealthCare.gov. (2014). Birth control benefits. Available: https://www.healthcare.gov/coverage/birth-control-benefits/ (Last visited 11/19/14).

Hefling, K. (2011, February 15). Veterans say rape cases mishandled. Available: http://s.apnews.com/db_16026/contentdetail.htm?contentguid9hSlzmhM (Last visited 2/15/11).

Heiman, J. R., Talley, D. R., Bailen, J. L., Oskin, T. A., Rosenberg, S. J., Pace, C. R., Creanga, D. L., & Bavendam, T. (2007). Sexual function and satisfaction in heterosexual couples when men are administered sildenafil citrate (Viagra) for erectile dysfunction: A multicentre, randomised, double-blind, placebo-controlled trial. *BJOG: An International Journal of Obstetrics and Gynaecology, 114,* 437–447.

Heiss, G., et al. (2008). Health risks and benefits 3 years after stopping randomized treatment with estrogen and progestin. *Journal of the American Medical Association, 299*(9), 1036–1045.

Helms, D. J., et al. (2008). Risk factors for prevalent and incident trichomonas vaginalis among women attending three sexually transmitted disease clinics. *Sexually Transmitted Diseases, 35,* 484–488.

Hennessy, M., Fishbein, M., Curtis, B., & Barrett, D. W. (2007). Evaluating the risk and attractiveness of romantic partners when confronted with contradictory cues. *AIDS and Behavior, 11,* 479–490.

Henningsen, D. D., Henningsen, M. L. M., & Valde, K. S. (2006). Gender differences in perception of women's sexual interest during cross-sex interactions: An application and extension of cognitive valence theory. *Sex Roles, 54,* 821–829.

Herbenick, D., Reece, M., Hensel, D., Sanders, S., Jozkowski, K., & Fortenberry, J. D. (2011). Association of lubricant use with women's sexual pleasure, sexual satisfaction, and genital symptoms: A prospective daily diary study. *Journal of Sexual Medicine, 8,* 202–212.

Herbenick, D., Reece, M., Sanders, S., Ghassemi, A., & Fortenberry, J. D. (2009). Prevalence and characteristics of vibrator use by women in the United States: Results from a nationally representative study. *Journal of Sexual Medicine, 6,* 1857–1866.

Herbenick, D., Reece, M., Schick, V., & Sanders, S. A. (2013). Erect penis length and circumference dimensions of 1,661 sexually active men in the United States. *Journal of Sexual Medicine, 11,* 93–101.

Herbenick, D., Reece, M., Schick, V., Sanders, S. A., Dodge, B., & Fortenberry, J. D. (2010.2a). Sexual behavior in the United States: Results from a national probability sample of men and women ages 14–94. *Journal of Sexual Medicine, 7,* 255–265.

Herbenick, D., Reece, M., Schick, V., Sanders, S. A., Dodge, B., & Fortenberry, J. D. (2010.2b). Sexual behaviors, relationships, and perceived health status among adult women in the United States: Results from a national probability sample of men and women. *Journal of Sexual Medicine, 7,* 277–290.

Herbenick, D., Reece, M., Schick, V., Sanders, S. A., Dodge, B., & Fortenberry, J. D. (2010.2c). An event-level analysis of the sexual characteristics and composition among adults ages 18–59: Results from a national probability sample of men and women. *Journal of Sexual Medicine, 7,* 346–361.

Herbenick, D., Reece, M., Schick, V., Sanders, S. A., Dodge, B., & Fortenberry, J. D. (2010.9a). Sexual behavior in the United States: Results from a national probability sample of men and women ages 14–94. *Journal of Sexual Medicine, 7,* 255–265.

Herbenick, D., Reece, M., Schick, V., Sanders, S. A., Dodge, B., & Fortenberry, J. D. (2010.14a). An event-level analysis of the sexual characteristics and composition among adults ages 18–59: Results from a national probability sample of men and women. *Journal of Sexual Medicine, 7,* 346–361.

Herbenick, D., Schick, V., Reece, M., Sanders, S., & Fortenberry, J. D. (2010.7a). Pubic hair removal among women in the United States: Prevalence, methods, and characteristics. *Journal of Sexual Medicine, 7*(3), 3322–3330.

Herdt, G., & McClintock, M. (2000). The magical age of 10. *Archives of Sexual Behavior, 29*(6), 587–606.

Herz, R. (2007). *The scent of desire: Discovering our enigmatic sense of smell.* New York: William Morrow.

Herzer, M. (1985). Kertbeny and the nameless love. *Journal of Homosexuality, 12,* 1–26.

Hess, J. A., & Coffelt, T. A. (2012). Verbal communication about sex in marriage: Patterns of language use and its connection with relational outcomes. *Journal of Sex Research, 49*(6), 603–612.

Hess, K. L., Javanbakht, M., Brown, J. M., Weiss, R. E., Hsu, P., & Gorbach, P. M. (2012). Intimate partner violence and sexually transmitted infections among young adult women. *Sexually Transmitted Diseases, 39,* 366–371.

Hicks, T. V., & Leitenberg, H. (2001). Sexual fantasies about one's partner versus someone else: Gender differences in incidence and frequency. *Journal of Sex Research, 38,* 43–50.

Higginbotham, E. B. (1992). African-American women's history and the metalanguage of race. *Journal of Women in Culture and Society, 17,* 251–274.

Hilad, J. (2014, December 5). Retaliation still a major issue for troops who report sexual assault, study finds. *Stars and Stripes.* Available: http://www.strips.com/news/retaliaton-still-a-majr-issue-for-trops-who-report-sexual-assaults.html (Last visited 12/19/14).

Hill, C., & Kearl, H. (2011). *Crossing the line: Sexual harassment at school.* Washington, DC: American Association of University Women.

Hill, S. A (2002). Teaching and doing gender. *Sex Roles, 47,* 493–504.

Hine, D. C. (1989). Rape and the inner lives of Black women in the Middle West: Preliminary thoughts on the culture of dissemblance. *Signs, 14,* 915.

Hinkley, D. (2014, March 5). Average American watches 5 hours of TV per day, report shows. *New York Daily News.* Available: http://www.nydailynews.com/life-style/average-american-watches-5-hours-tv-day-article-1.1711954 (Last visited 7/28/14).

Hirschfeld, M. (1991). *Transvestites: The erotic drive to cross dress.* Buffalo: Prometheus Books.

Hirschfeld, S. (2004). Sex in the workplace: Employment Law Alliance Poll finds 24% involved in sexually-explicit computing. Available: http://www.employmentlawalliance.com/en/node/1324 (Last visited 5/26/09).

HIV Vaccine Trials Network. (2015). HIV is one of the most changeable viruses discovered to date. Available: http://www.hvtn.org/en/science/science-feature-story.html (Last visited 1/13/15).

Hock, R. R. (2007). *Human sexuality.* Upper Saddle River, NJ: Pearson Education.

Hoebeke, P., Selvaggi, G., Ceulemans, P., De Cuypere, G., T'Sjoen, G., Weyers, S., Decaestecker, K., & Monstrey, S. (2005). Impact of sex reassignment surgery on lower urinary tract function. *European Urology, 47*(3), 398-402.

Hoertel, N., Strat, Y. L., Schuster, J., & Limosin, F. (2012). Sexual assaulters in the United States: Prevalence and psychiatric correlates in a national sample. *Archives of Sexual Behavior, 41,* 1379–1387.

Hoffman, V., & Cohen, D. (1999). A night with Venus: Partner assessments and high-risk encounters. *AIDS Care, 11,* 555–566.

Holman, D. M., Benard, V., Roland, K. B., Watson, M., Liddon, N., & Stokely, S. (2014). Barriers to human papillomavirus vaccination among US adolescents: A systematic review of the literature. *JAMA Pediatrics, 168,* 76–82.

Holmberg, D., & Blair, K. L. (2009). Sexual desire: Communication, satisfaction, and preferences of men and women in same-sex versus mixed-sex relationships. *Journal of Sex Research, 46,* 57–66.

Holmberg, D., Blair, K. L., & Phillips, M. (2010). Women's sexual satisfaction as a predictor of well-being in same-sex versus mixed-sex relationships. *Journal of Sex Research, 47*(1), 1–11.

Holstege, G., Georgiadis, J. R., Paans, A. M., Meiners, L. C., van der Graff, F. H., & Reinders, A. A. (2003). Brain activation during human male ejaculation. *Journal of Neuroscience, 34,* 9185–9193.

Hooker, E. (1957). The adjustment of the overt male homosexual. *Journal of Projective Psychology, 21,* 18–31.

Hucker, S. J. (2008). Sexual masochism: Psychopathology and theory. In D. R. Laws & W. T. O'Donohue (Eds.), *Sexual deviance: Theory, assessment, and treatment* (2nd ed.). New York: Guilford Press.

Hucker, S. J. (2011). Hypoxyphilia. *Archives of Sexual Behavior, 40,* 1323–1326.

Hughes, A., Houk, C., Ahmed, S. F., Lee, P. A., & LWPES/ESE Consensus Group. (2006). Consensus statement on management of intersex disorders. *Archives of Disease in Childhood, 91,* 554–562.

Hughes, S. M., & Kruger, D. J. (2011). Sex differences in post-coital behaviors in long- and short-term mating: An evolutionary perspective. *Journal of Sex Research, 48,* 496–505.

Hughes, S. M., Harrison, M. A., & Gallup, G. G. (2007). Sex differences in romantic kissing among college students: An evolutionary perspective. *Evolutionary Psychology, 5,* 612–663.

Human Rights Campaign. (2014.5a). Corporate equality index 2014. Available: http://www.hrc.org/campaigns/corporate-equality-index (Last visited 6/24/14).

Human Rights Campaign. (2014.8a). Marriage equality polling. Available: http://www.hrc.org/resources/entry/marriage-equality-polling (Last visited 11/17/14).

Human Rights Campaign. (2015). Health and aging. Available: http://www.hrc.org/topics/health-and-aging (Last visited 1/15/15).

Human Rights Watch. (2007). No easy answers. Available: http://www.hrw.reports/2007/us0907 (Last visited 8/17/08).

Humphreys, L. (1975). *Tearoom trade: Impersonal sex in public places.* Chicago: Aldine.

Humphreys, T. P. (2004). Understanding sexual consent: An empirical investigation of the normative script for young heterosexual adults. In M. Cowling & P. Reynolds (Eds.), *Making sense of sexual consent.* Aldershot, England: Ashgate.

Humphreys, T. P. (2013). Cognitive frameworks of virginity and first intercourse. *Journal of Sex Research, 50*(7), 664–675.

Hunter, J. A., Figueredo, A. J., & Malamuth, N. M. (2003). Juvenile sex offenders: Toward the development of a typology. *Sexual Abuse: Journal of Research and Treatment, 15,* 27–48.

Hutchinson, A., Begley, E. B., Sullivan, P., Clark, H. A., Boyett, B. C., & Kellerman, S. E. (2007). Conspiracy beliefs and trust in information about HIV/AIDS among minority men who have sex with men. *Journal of Acquired Immune Deficiency Syndromes, 45,* 503–506.

Hutchinson, K. B., Kip, K. E., & Ness, R. B. (2007). Condom use and its association with bacterial vaginosis and bacterial vaginosis-associated vaginal microflora. *Epidemiology, 18,* 702–708.

Hyde, J. S., & DeLamater, J. D. (2008). *Understanding human sexuality* (10th ed). New York: McGraw-Hill.

Hyde, J. S., & DeLamater, J. D. (2011). *Understanding human sexuality* (11th ed.). New York: McGraw-Hill.

Hyde, J. S., & DeLamater, J. D. (2014). *Understanding Human Sexuality* (12th ed.). New York: McGraw-Hill Education.

Hymowitz, K. S. (2014). How single motherhood hurts kids. *New York Times,* p. SR6.

Ickovics, J. R., Beren, S. E., Grigorenko, E. L., Morrill, A. C., Druley, J. A., & Rodin, J. (2002). Pathways of risk: Race, social class, stress, and coping as factors predicting heterosexual risk behaviors for HIV among women. *AIDS and Behavior, 6,* 339–350.

Ijams, K., & Miller, L. D. (2000). Perceptions of dream-disclosure: An exploratory study. *Communication Studies, 51,* 135–148.

Infographic: An inside look at the sex lives of parents. (2014). YourTango.com. Available: http://www.yourtango.com/2014219533/parents-check-out-infographic-your-sex-lives#.VCdPjeee8SQ (Last visited 9/27/14).

Ins and outs of menstrual cups: How do they differ from tampons? (2012, June 27). *Go Ask Alice.* Available: http://goaskalice.columbia.edu/ins-and-outs-menstrual-cups-151-how-do-they-differ-tampons-and-pads (Last visited 6/4/14).

Insel, P. M., & Roth, W. T. (2010). *Core concepts in health* (11th ed., brief). New York: McGraw-Hill.

Institute of Medicine. (2006). *Preventing HIV infection among injecting drug users in high risk countries: A comprehensive approach.* Washington, DC: National Academies Press.

Institute of Medicine. (2011). *The health of lesbian, gay, bisexual, and transgendered people.* Washington, DC: National Academies Press.

IntelHealth. (2013). Health A to Z: Premenstrual syndrome (PMS). Available: http://www.intelihealth.com/article/premenstrual-syndrome-pms (Last visited 6/4/14).

International AIDS Vaccine Initiative. (2011). Antibody discoveries reveal new targets. Available: http://www.iaiv.org/Pages/home.aspx? (Last visited 12/21/11).

International Rectal Microbicide Advocates. (2011). What is a rectal microbicide? Available: http://www.rectalmicrobicides.org (Last visited 12/21/11).

Internet pornography law dies quietly in Supreme Court. (2009, January 22). *Herald Times*, p. E3.

Intersex. (2014). MedlinePlus. Available: http://www.nlm.nih.gov/medlineplus/ency/article/001669.htm (Last visited 7/2/14).

Ionannidis, J. P. (2005). Contradicted and initially stronger effects in highly cited clinical research. *Journal of the American Medical Association, 294,* 218–228.

Ishii-Kuntz, M. (1997). Chinese American families. In M. K. DeGenova (Ed.), *Families in cultural context.* Mountain View, CA: Mayfield.

Jackson, G. (2009). Sexual response in cardiovascular disease. *Journal of Sex Research 46*(2–3), 233–236.

Jadva, V., Hines, M., & Golombok, S. (2008). Infants' preferences for toys, colors, and shapes: Sex differences and similarities. *Archives of Sexual Behavior, 39,* 1261–1273.

Jannini, E. A., Fisher, W. A., Bitzer, J., & McMahon, C. G. (2009). Is sex just fun? How sexual activity improves health. *Journal of Sexual Medicine, 6,* 2640–2648.

Janus, S., & Janus, C. (1993). *The Janus report on sexual behavior.* New York: Wiley.

Jasienska, S., Lipson, P., Thune, I., & Ziomkiewicz, A. (2006). Symmetrical women have higher potential fertility. *Evolution and Human Behavior, 27,* 390–400.

Javanbakht, M., et al. (2010). Prevalence and correlates of heterosexual anal intercourse among clients attending public sexually transmitted disease clinics in Los Angeles County. *Sexually Transmitted Diseases, 37,* 369–376.

Jayson, S. (2007, July 9). Charles Atlas was right: Brawny guys get the girls. *USA Today,* p. D6.

Jenness, S. M., et al. (2011). Unprotected anal intercourse and sexually transmitted diseases in high-risk heterosexual women. *American Journal of Public Health, 101,* 745–750.

Jin, X., et al. (2010). HIV prevalence and risk behaviors among male clients of female sex workers in Yunnan, China. *Journal of Acquired Immune Deficiency Syndromes, 53,* 124–130.

Johnson, A. S., Hall, H. I., Hu, X., Lansky, A., Holtgrave, D. R., & Mermin, J. (2014). Trends in diagnosis of HIV infection in the United States, 2002–2011. *Journal of the American Medical Association, 312,* 332–334.

Joint United Nations Programme on AIDS and World Health Organization. (2005). AIDS epidemic update: December 2005. Available: http://www.unaids.org/Epi2005/doc/report.html (Last visited 11/22/05).

Joint United Nations Programme on HIV/AIDS. (2008). 08 report on the global AIDS epidemic. Available: http:www//unaids/org/en/KnowledgeCentre/HIVData/GlobalReport/2008/2008_Global_report.asp (Last visited 11/17/08).

Jonason, P. K., Li, N. P., & Cason, M. J. (2009). The "booty call": A compromise between men's and women's ideal mating strategies. *Journal of Sex Research, 46,* 460–470.

Jones, A. (2014, Jan. 22). Sex and the single tween. *Newsweek.*

Jones, J., Mosher, W., & Daniels, K. (2012). Current contraceptive use in the United States, 2006–2010, and changes in patterns of use since 1995. *National Health Statistics Reports, 60.* Available: http://www.cdc.gov/nchs/data/nhsr/nhsr060.pdf (Last visited 12/7/14).

Jones, J. H. (1993). *Bad blood: The Tuskegee syphilis experiment* (Rev. ed.). New York: Free Press.

Jones, R. K., & Jerman, J. (2014). Abortion incidence and service availability in the United States, 2011. *Perspectives on Sexual and Reproductive Health, 46*(1), 3–14.

Jozkowski, K. N., & Peterson, Z. D. (2013). College students and sexual consent: Unique insights. *Journal of Sex Research, 50,* 517–523.

Jozkowski, K. N., & Sanders, S. A. (2012). Health and sexual outcomes of women who have experienced forced or coercive sex. *Women and Health, 52,* 101–118.

Jozkowski, K. N., Peterson, Z. D., Sanders, S. A., Dennis, B., & Reece, M. (2014). Gender differences in heterosexual college students' conceptualizations and indicators of sexual consent: Implications for contemporary sexual assault prevention education. *Journal of Sex Research, 51,* 904–916.

Jungheim, E. S., Traviseo, J. L., & Hopeman, M. M. (2013). Weighing the impact of obesity on female reproductive function and fertility. *Nutritional Review, 71,* 1. Available: http://www.ncbi.nlm.nih.gov/pmc/articles/PMC3813308/#R1 (Last visited 12/15/14).

Kaestle, C. E., & Halpern, T. (2007). What's love got to do with it? Sexual behaviors of opposite-sex couples through emerging adulthood. *Perspectives on Sexual and Reproductive Health, 39*(3), 134–200.

Kaestle, C. E., & Waller, M. W. (2011). Bacterial STDs and perceived risk among minority young adults. *Perspectives on Sexual and Reproductive Health, 43,* 158–163.

Kaestle, C. E., Halpern, C. T., Miller, W. C., & Ford, C. A. (2005). Young age at first intercourse and sexually transmitted infections in adolescents and young adults. *American Journal of Epidemiology, 161,* 774–778.

Kaestle, E., & Ivory, A. H. (2012). A forgotten sexuality: Content analysis of bisexuality in the medical literature over two decades. *Journal of Bisexuality, 12*(1), 35–48. Available: http://www.tandfonline.com/doi/full/10.1080/15299716.2012.645701#.VAZAckie8SQ (Last visited 9/2/14).

Kafka, M. P. (2010). The DSM diagnostic criteria for fetishism. *Archives of Sexual Behavior, 26,* 357–362.

Kaighobadi, F., Shackeford, T. K., & Welling, L. L. M. (2012). Do women pretend orgasm to retain mate? *Archives of Sexual Behavior, 41,* 1121–1106.

Kaiser Family Foundation. (2014). Infant mortality rate (total deaths per 1,000 births). Available: http://kff.org/global-indicator/infant-mortality-rate/ (Last visited 12/15/14).

Kaplan, A. (1979). Clarifying the concept of androgyny: Implications for therapy. *Psychology of Women, 3,* 223–230.

Kaplan, H. S. (1974). *The new sex therapy.* New York: Brunner/Mazel.

Kaplan, H. S. (1979). *Disorders of desire.* New York: Brunner/Mazel.

Kaplan, H. S., & Horwith, M. (1983). *The evaluation of sexual disorders: Psychological and medical aspects.* New York: Brunner/Mazel.

Kaplan, M. S., & Krueger, R. B. (2010). Diagnosis, assessment, and treatment of hypersexuality. *Journal of Sex Research, 47,* 181–198.

Katz-Wise, S. L., & Hyde, J. S. (2014). Sexuality and gender: The interplay. In *APA handbook of sexuality and psychology* (pp. 29–62). Washington, DC: American Psychological Association.

Kaye, K., Suellentrop, K., & Sloup, C. (2009). *The fog zone: How misperceptions, magical thinking, and ambivalence put young adults at risk for unplanned pregnancy*. Washington, DC: The National Campaign to Prevent Teen and Unplanned Pregnancy. Available: http://thenationalcampaign.org/resource/fog-zone (Last visited 12/7/14).

Kearl, H. (2014). *Unsafe and harassed in public places: A national street harassment report*. Reston, VA: Stop Street Harassment.

Keele, B. F., et al. (2008). Identification and characterization of transmitted and early founder virus envelopes in primary HIV-1 infection. *Proceedings of the National Academy of Sciences, 105,* 7552–7557.

Keesling, B. (2006). *Sexual healing: The complete guide to overcoming common sexual problems* (3rd ed.). Alameda, CA: Hunter House.

Kellogg, N. (2009). Clinical report: The evaluation of sexual behaviors in children. *Pediatrics, 124*(3), 992–998.

Kelly, G. F. (2013). *Sexuality today*. New York: McGraw-Hill.

Kelly, M. P., Strassberg, D. S., & Kircher, J. R. (1990). Attitudinal and experiential correlates of anorgasmia. *Archives of Sexual Behavior, 19*(2), 165–167.

Kennedy, H. (1988). *The life and works of Karl Heinrich Ulrichs: Pioneer of the modern gay movement*. Boston: Alyson.

Keuls, E. (1985). *Reign of the phallus: Sexual politics in ancient Athens*. Berkeley: University of California Press.

Khan, A., & Khanum, P. A. (2000). Influence of son preferences on contraceptive use in Bangladesh. *Asia-Pacific Population Journal, 15*(3), 43–56.

Kidd, S. A., & Kral, M. J. (2002). Suicide and prostitution among street youth: A qualitative analysis. *Adolescence, 37,* 411–431.

Kilchevsky, A., Vardi, Y., Lowenstein, L., & Gruenwald, I. (2012). Is the female G-spot truly a distinct anatomic entity? *Journal of Sexual Medicine, 9*(3), 719–726.

Kim, J., & Iglesia, C. B. (2013, Jan. 28). Designer genitalia: Fad, benefit, or mutilation? Available: www.medscape.com/viewarticle778067_print (Last visited 7/2/14).

Kim, J. L. (2009). Asian American women's retrospective reports of their sexual socialization. *Psychology of Women Quarterly, 33*(3), 334–350.

King, P. A. (1992). Twenty years after. The legacy of the Tuskegee syphilis study. The dangers of difference. *Hastings Center Report, 22*(6), 35–38.

Kingston, D. A., & Yates, P. M. (2008). Sexual sadism: Assessment and treatment. In D. R. Laws & W. T. O'Donohue (Eds.), *Sexual deviance: Theory, assessment, and treatment* (2nd ed.). New York: Guilford Press.

Kinsey, A., Pomeroy, W., & Martin, C. (1948). *Sexual behavior in the human male*. Philadelphia: Saunders.

Kinsey, A., Pomeroy, W., Martin, C., & Gebhard, P. (1953). *Sexual behavior in the human female*. Philadelphia: Saunders.

Kirby, D. (2007). Emerging answers, 2007. Research findings on programs to reduce teen pregnancy and sexually transmitted diseases. Scotts Valley, CA: The National Campaign to Prevent Teen and Unplanned Pregnancy.

Kirby, D. (2008). The impact of abstinence and comprehensive sex and STD/HIV education programs on adolescent sexual behavior. *Sexuality Research and Policy, 5*(3), 18–27.

Kirshenbaum, S. (2011). *The science of kissing*. New York: Grand Central.

Klaassen, M. J. F., & Peter, J. (2014). Gender (In) equality in Internet pornography: A content analysis of popular pornographic Internet videos. *Journal of Sex Research*. doi: 10.1080/00224499.2014.976782.

Klebanoff, M. A., et al. (2010). Personal hygienic behaviors and bacterial vaginosis. *Sexually Transmitted Diseases, 37,* 94–99.

Klein, M. (2012). *Sexual intelligence: What we really want to know from sex—and how to get it*. New York; Harper One.

Klein, M. J., & Meier, R. H. (2013). Sexuality and disability. *Medscape*. Available: http://emedicine.medscape.com/article/319119-overview (Last visited 1/4/15).

Kleinplatz, P., & Moser, C. (2004). Toward clinical guidelines for working with BDSM clients. *Contemporary Sexuality, 38,* 1, 4.

Klinefelter syndrome. (2014a). Genetics home reference. Available: http://ghr.nlm.nih.gov/condition/klinefelter-syndrome (Last visited 7/11/14).

Klinefelter syndrome. (2014b). MedlinePlus. Available: http://www.nlm.nih.gov/medlineplus/ency/article/000382.htm (Last visited 7/11/14).

Koch, W. (2006, May 24). States get tougher with sex offenders. *USA Today*, p. A1.

Kohlberg, L. (1966). A cognitive-developmental analysis of children's sex-role concepts and attitudes. In E. E. Maccoby (Ed.), *The development of sex differences*. Palo Alto, CA: Stanford University Press.

Koken, J. A., Bimbi, D. S., Parsons, J. T., & Halkitis, P. N. (2004). The experience of stigma in the lives of male Internet escorts. *Journal of Psychology and Human Sexuality, 16,* 13–32.

Komisaruk, B. R., Whipple, B., Nasserzadeh, S., & Beyer-Flores, C. (2010). *The orgasm answer guide*. Baltimore: Johns Hopkins University Press.

Kontula, O. (2009). *Between sexual desire and reality: The evolution of sex in Finland*. Helsinki, Finland: Vaestoliitto.

Kontula, O., & Haavio-Mannila, E. (2009). The impact of aging on human sexual activity and sexual desire. *Journal of Sex Research, 46,* 46–56.

Koumans, E. H., et al. (2007). The prevalence of bacterial vaginosis in the United States, 2001–2004; Associations with symptomatic, sexual behaviors, and reproductive health. *Sexually Transmitted Diseases, 34,* 864–869.

Krakow, B., Germain, A., Tandberg, D., Koss, M., Schrader, R., Hollifield, M., et al. (2000). Sleep breathing and sleep movement disorders masquerading as insomnia in sexual-assault survivors. *Comprehensive Psychiatry, 41,* 49–56.

Kramer, A. (2014). *Virgin territory: What young adults say about sex, love, relationships, and the first time*. Washington, DC: The National Campaign to Prevent Teen and Unplanned Pregnancy. Available: http://tnc.ikshare.com/sites/default/files/resource-primary-download/virgin-territory-final.pdf (Last visited 8/14/14).

Krebs, C. P., Lindquist, C. H., Warner, T. D., Fisher, B. S., & Martin, S. L. (2009). College women's experiences with physically forced, alcohol- or other drug-enabled, and drug-facilitated sexual assault before and since entering college. *Journal of American College Health, 57,* 639–647.

Krivickas, K. M., & Lofquist, D. (2010). Demographics of same-sex couple households with children. Washington, DC: U.S. Census Bureau. Available: http://www.census.gov/population/www/socdemo/Krivickas-Lofquist%20PAA%202011.pdf (Last visited 8/10/11).

Krueger, R. B. (2010a). The DSM diagnostic criteria for exhibitionism, voyeurism, and frotteurism. *Archives of Sexual Behavior, 39,* 325–345.

Krueger, R. B. (2010b). The DSM diagnostic criteria for sexual masochism. *Archives of Sexual Behavior, 39,* 346–356.

Kuehnle, K., & Drozd, L. (2012). *Parenting plan evaluations: Applied research for the family court.* Cambridge, MA: Oxford University Press.

Kuper, L. E., Nussbaum, R., & Mustanski, B. (2012). Exploring the diversity of gender and sexual orientation identities in an online sample of transgender individuals. *Journal of Sex Research, 49*(2–3), 244–254.

La France, B. H., Henningsen, D. D., Oates, A., & Shaw, C. M. (2009). Social-sexual interactions: Meta-analysis of sex differences in perceptions of flirtatiousness, seductiveness, and promiscuousness. *Communication Monographs, 76,* 263–268.

Lacey, R. S., Reifman, A., Scott, J. P., Harris, S. M., & Fitzpatrick, J. H. (2004). Sexual-moral attitudes, love styles and mate selection. *Journal of Sex Research, 41*(2), 121–128.

LaCroix, J. M., Pellowski, J. A., Lennon, C. A., & Johnson, B. T. (2013). Behavioral interventions to reduce sexual risk for HIV in heterosexual couples; A meta-analysis. *Sexually Transmitted Infections, 89,* 60–627.

Ladas, A., Whipple, B., & Perry, J. (1982). *The G spot.* New York: Holt, Rinehart & Winston.

Laframboise, S., & Anhorn, M. (2008). The way of the two spirited people. Available: http://www.dancingtoeaglespiritsociety.org/twospirit.php (Last visited 7/19/14).

Lalumière, M., Blanchard, R., & Zucker, K. (2000). Sexual orientation and handedness in men and women: A meta-analysis. *Psychological Bulletin, 126,* 575–592.

Lalumière, M. L., Harris, G. T., Quinsey, V. L., & Rice, M. E. (2005). *The causes of rape.* Washington, DC: American Psychological Association.

Lamaze, F. (1970). *Painless childbirth* (Rev. ed.). Chicago: Regnery. (1st ed., 1956).

Lambda Legal. (2010). When health care isn't caring: Lambda Legal's survey of discrimination against LGBT people and people living with HIV. New York: Lambda Legal. Available: www.lambdalegal.org/health-care-report (Last visited 1/15/15).

Lambert, N. M., Negash, S., Stillman, T. F., Olmstead, S. B., & Fincham, F. D. (2012). A love that doesn't last: Pornography consumption and weakened commitment to one's romantic partner. *Journal of Social and Clinical Psychology, 31,* 41–438.

Lancet HIV: High rates of recreational drug use among HIV-positive gay and bisexual men in UK strongly linked with condomless sex. (2014). Available: http://www.eurekalert.org/pub_releases/2014-09/tl-tlh090414.php (Last visited 1/2/15).

Landau, E. (2014, January 11). *Where's the sex drive drug for women?* CNN Health. Available: http://www.cnn.com/2014/01/11/health/female-sex-drive-drug/index.html?iref=allsearch (Last visited 3/28/14).

Langstrom, N., & Seto, M. (2006). Exhibitionistic and voyeuristic behavior in a Swedish national population study. *Archives of Sexual Behavior, 35,* 427–435.

Langstrom, N., Rahman, Q., Carlstrom, E., & Lichtenstein, P. (2010). Genetic and environmental effects on same-sex sexual behavior: A population study of twins in Sweden. *Archives of Sexual Behavior, 39,* 75–80.

Laumann, E., Gagnon, J., Michael, R., & Michaels, S. (1994). *The social organization of sexuality.* Chicago: University of Chicago Press.

Laumann, E. O., Paik, A., & Rosen, R. C. (1999). Sexual dysfunction in the United States: Prevalence and predictors. *Journal of the American Medical Association, 281,* 537–544.

Law, B. M. (2011). Hormones and desire. *American Psychological Association, 42*(3), 4. Available: http://www.apa.org/monitor/2011/03/hormones.aspx (Last visited 1/25/15).

Laws, D. R., & O'Donohue, W. T. (2008). Introduction. In D. R. Laws & W. T. O'Donohue (Eds.), *Sexual deviance: Theory, assessment, and treatment* (2nd ed.). New York: Guilford Press.

Lee, J. A. (1973). *The color of love.* Toronto: New Press.

Lee, J. A. (1988). Love styles. In R. Sternberg & M. Barnes (Eds.), *The psychology of love.* New Haven, CT: Yale University Press.

Lee, P. A., Houk, C. P., Ahmed, S. F., Ieuan, A., & Hughes, I. A. (2006). Consensus statement on management of intersex disorders. *Pediatrics, 118*(2), 488–500.

Lefkowitz, E. S., Gillen, M. M., Shearer, C. L., & Boone, T. L. (2004). Religiosity, sexual behaviors, and sexual attitudes during emerging adulthood. *Journal of Sex Research, 41*(2), 150–159.

Lehmiller, J. J. (2014). *The psychology of human sexuality.* West Sussex, UK: John Wiley & Sons.

Lehne, G. K. (2009). Phenomenology of paraphilia: Lovemap theory. In F. M. Saleh et al. (Eds.), *Sex offenders: Identification, risk assessment, treatment, and legal issues.* New York: Oxford University Press.

Leitenberg, H., & Henning, K. (1995). Sexual fantasy. *Psychological Bulletin, 117*(3), 469–496.

Leitzmann, M. F., Platz, E. A., Stampfer, M. J., Willet, W. C., & Giovannucci, E. (2004). Ejaculation frequency and subsequent risk of prostate cancer. *Journal of the American Medical Association, 291,* 1578–1586.

Lenhart, A. (2012). Teenagers, smartphones & texting. Washington, DC: Pew Research Center's Internet & American Life Project. Available: www.pewinternet.org/~/media//Files/Reports/2012/PIP_Teenagers_Smartphones_and_Texting.pdf (Last visited 7/1/14).

Lenhart, A. (2014). Teens & technology: Understanding the digital landscape. Available: http://www.pewinternet.org/2014/02/25/teens-technology-understanding-the-digital-landscape/ (Last visited 7/19/14).

Lenz, R., & Chaves, B. (1981). Becoming active partners: A couple's perspective. In D. Bullard & S. Knight (Eds.), *Sexuality and disability: Personal perspectives.* St. Louis: Mosby.

Letherby, G. (2003). *Feminist research in theory and practice.* Buckingham, United Kingdom: Open University Press.

Lever, J. (1995, August 22). Lesbian sex survey. *The Advocate,* pp. 23–30.

Lever, J., & Dolnick, D. (2000). Clients and call girls: Seeking sex and intimacy. In R. Weitzer (Ed.), *Sex for sale: Prostitution and the sex industry.* New York: Routledge.

Lever, J., Frederick, D. A., & Peplau, L. A. (2006). Does size matter? Men's and women's views on penis size across the lifespan. *Psychology of Men & Masculinity, 7*(3), 129–143.

Levine, M. P., & Troiden, R. (1988). The myth of sexual compulsivity. *Journal of Sex Research, 25*(3), 347–363.

Lewontin, M. (2014, October 31). Final federal rules on sexual violence emphasize training. *Chronicle of Higher Education,* p. A4.

Ley, D., Prause, N., & Finn, P. (2014). The emperor has no clothes: A review of the 'Pornography Addiction' model. *Current Sexual Health Reports.* DOI: 10.1007/s11930-014-0016-8.

Lichtenstein, B., Hook, E. W., III, & Sharma, A. K. (2005). Public tolerance, private pain: Stigma and sexually transmitted infections in the American Deep South. *Culture, Health & Sexuality, 7,* 43–57.

Lindau, S. T., & Gavrilova, N. (2010). Sex, health, and years of sexually active life gained due to good health: Evidence from two U.S. population based cross sectional surveys of aging. *British Medical Journal, 340,* c810. Available: http://www.ncbi.nlm.nih.gov/pmc/articles/PMC2835854/ (Last visited 6/1/11).

Linden, D. J. (2011). *The compass of pleasure: How our brains make fatty foods, orgasm, exercise, marijuana, generosity, vodka, learning, and gambling feel so good.* New York: Penguin.

Lindley, L. L., Walsemann, K. M., & Carter, J. W. (2013). Invisible and at risk: STDs among young adult sexual minority women in the United States. *Perspectives on Sexual and Reproductive Health, 45,* 66–73.

Lips, H. (2007). *Sex and gender* (6th ed.). New York: McGraw-Hill.

Lips, H. (2014). *Gender: The basics.* New York: Routledge.

Lisak, D., & Miller, P. M. (2002). Repeat rape and multiple offending among undetected rapists. *Violence and Victims, 17,* 73–84.

Little, A. C., Apicella, C. L., & Marlowe, F. W. (2007). Preferences for symmetry in human faces in two cultures: Data from the UK and Hadza, an isolated group of hunter-gathers. *Proceedings of the Royal Society, 274,* 3113–3117.

Liu, A. Y., Vittinghoff, E., Chillag, K., Mayer, K., Thompson, M., Groshskopf, L., et al. (2013). Sexual risk behavior among HIV-uninfected men who have sex with men participating in a Tenofovir preexposure prophylaxis randomized trial in the United States. *Epidemiology and Prevention, 64,* 87–94.

Livingston, G., & Cohn, D. (2010). Childless up among all women; down among women with advanced degrees. Pew Research Center. Available: http://www.pewsocialtrends.org/2010/06/25/childlessness-up-among-all-women-down-among-women-with-advanced-degrees/ (Last visited 12/11/14).

Lloyd, E. (2005). *The case of the female orgasm.* Cambridge, MA: Harvard University Press.

Locke, B. D., & Mahalik, J. R. (2005). Examining masculinity norms, problem drinking, and athletic involvement as predictors of sexual aggression in college men. *Journal of Counseling Psychology, 52,* 279–283.

Lofgren-Martenson, L., & Mansson, S. (2010). Lust, love, and life: A qualitative study of Swedish adolescents' perceptions and experiences with pornography. *Journal of Sex Research, 47,* 568–579.

Logan, C. (2008). Sexual deviance in females. In D. R. Laws & W. T. O'Donohue (Eds.), *Sexual deviance: Theory, assessment, and treatment* (2nd ed.). New York: Guilford Press.

Lovejoy, T. J., et al. (2008). Patterns and correlates of sexual activity and condom use behavior in persons 50-plus years of age living with HIV/AIDS. *AIDS and Behavior, 6,* 943–956.

Lucas, A. (1998). *The disease of being a woman: Rethinking prostitution and subordination.* Doctoral dissertation, University of California.

Lussier, P., & Piché, L. (2008). Frotteurism: Psychopathology and theory. In D. R. Laws & W. T. O'Donohue (Eds.), *Sexual deviance: Theory, assessment, and treatment* (2nd ed.). New York: Guilford Press.

Lyubomirsky, S. (2013). *The myths of happiness.* New York: Penguin.

Mackey, R. A., & O'Brien, B. A. (1999). Adaptation in lasting marriages. *Families in Society: The Journal of Contemporary Human Services, 80*(6), 587–602.

MacNeil, S., & Byers, E. S. (2009). Role of sexual self-disclosure in the sexual satisfaction of long-term heterosexual couples. *Journal of Sex Research, 46*(1), 3–14.

Madsen, L., Parsons, S., & Grubin, D. (2006). The relationship between the five-factor model and *DSM* personality disorder in a sample of child molesters. *Personality and Individual Differences, 40,* 227–236.

Mah, K., & Binik, Y. M. (2002). Do all orgasms feel alike? Evaluating a two-dimensional model of the orgasm experience across gender and sexual context. *Journal of Sex Research, 39*(2), 104–113.

Mahabeer, P. (2011). Sexual harassment still pervasive in the workplace. *AOL Jobs Week 2001.* Available: http://jobs.aol.com/articles/2011/01/28/sexual-harassment-in-the-workplace/ (Last visited 8/30/11).

Mahajan, A. P., et al. (2008). Stigma in the HIV/AIDS epidemic: A review of the literature and recommendations for the way forward. *AIDS, 22*(Suppl. 2), S67–S79.

Mahay, J., Laumann, E., & Michaels, S. (2001). Race, gender, and class in sexual scripts. In E. Laumann & R. Michael (Eds.), *Sex, love and health in America* (pp. 197–238). Oxford, UK: Oxford University Press.

Maier, T. (2009). *Masters of sex.* New York: Basic Books.

Maine killer's use of sex-offender list. (2006, April 18). *New York Times,* p. A19.

Malamuth, N. M., Sockloskie, R. J., Koss, M. P., & Tanaka, J. S. (1991). Characteristics of aggressors against women: Testing a model using a national sample of college students. *Journal of Consulting and Clinical Psychology, 59,* 670–781.

Male and female orgasm—different? (2013). *Go Ask Alice.* Available: http://goaskalice.columbia.edu/male-and-female-orgasm-different (Last visited 6/13/14).

Mandara, J., Murray, C. B., Telesford, J. M., Varner, F. A., & Richman, S. B. (2012, Feb.). Observed gender differences in African-American mother-child relationships and child behavior. *Family Relations, 61,* 129–141.

Manhart, L. E., Aral, S. O., Holmes, K. K., & Foxman, B. (2002). Sex partner concurrency: Measurement, prevalence, and correlates among urban 18–39-year-olds. *Sexually Transmitted Diseases, 29,* 133–143.

Manlove, J., Ryan, S., & Franzetta, K. (2003). Patterns of contraceptive use within teenagers' first sexual relationship. *Perspectives on Sexual and Reproductive Health, 35,* 246–255.

Mann, R. E., Ainsworth, F., Al-Attar, Z., & Davies, M. (2008). In D. R. Laws & W. T. O'Donohue (Eds.), *Sexual deviance: Theory, assessment, and treatment* (2nd ed.). New York: Guilford Press.

March of Dimes. (2011a). Overweight and obesity during pregnancy. Available: http://www.marchofdimes.org/pregnancy/overweight-and-obesity-during-pregnancy.aspx# (Last visited 12/15/14).

March of Dimes. (2011b). Vaginal birth after cesarean. Available: http://www.marchofdimes.com/pregnancy/vaginalbirth_vbac.html (Last visited 10/29/11).

March of Dimes. (2012a). Pregnancy loss. Available: http://www.marchofdimes.org/loss/miscarriage.aspx# (Last visited 12/16/14).

March of Dimes. (2012b). Medically unnecessary early deliveries declining. Available: http://www.marchofdimes.org/news/medically-unnecessary-early-deliveries-declining.aspx# (Last visited 12/18/14).

March of Dimes. (2013). Smoking, alcohol, and drugs. Available: http://www.marchofdimes.org/pregnancy/illicit-drug-use-during-pregnancy.aspx (Last visited 12/11/14).

March of Dimes. (2014). Down syndrome. Available: http://www.marchofdimes.org/baby/down-syndrome.aspx (Last visited 12/15/14).

Margolies, L., Becher, M., & Jackson-Brewer, K. (1988). Internalized homophobia: Identifying and treating the oppressor within. In Boston Lesbian Psychologies Collective (Eds.), *Lesbian psychologies.* Urbana: University of Illinois Press.

Mark, K. P., Janssen, E., & Milhausen, R. R. (2011). Infidelity in heterosexual couples: Demographic, interpersonal and personality-related predictors of extradyadic sex. *Archives of Sex Behavior.* Available: http://www.kinseyinstitute.org/publications/PDF/Infidelity%20in%20hetero%20couples.pdf (Last visited 10/24/14).

Marklein, M. B., & Shesgreen, D. (2014, July 10). Colleges ignoring sexual assault, senator charges. *USA Today,* p. 3A.

Markowitz, L. E., Harin, S., Lin, C., Dunne, E. F., Steinau, M., McQuillan, G., et al. (2013). Reduction in human papillomavirus (HPV) prevalence among women following HPV vaccination introduction in the United States, National Health and Nutrition Examination Surveys, 2003–2010. *Journal of Infectious Diseases, 208,* 385–393.

Marks, G., Crepaz, N., & Janssen, R. (2006). Estimating sexual transmission of HIV from persons aware and unaware that they are infected with the virus in the USA. *AIDS, 20,* 1447–1450.

Marrazzo, J. M., Coffey, P., & Bingham, A. (2005). Sexual practices, risk perception, and knowledge of sexually transmitted disease risk among lesbian and bisexual women. *Perspectives on Sexual and Reproductive Health, 37*(1), 6–12.

Marrazzo, J. M., Thomas, K. K., Agnew, K., & Ringwood, K. (2010). Prevalence and risks for bacterial vaginosis in women who have sex with women. *Sexually Transmitted Infections, 37,* 335–339.

Marshall, B. L. (2012). Medicalization and the refashioning of age-related limits on sexuality. *Journal of Sex Research, 49,* 337–343.

Marshall, D. (1971). Sexual behavior on Mangaia. In D. Marshall & R. Suggs (Eds.), *Human sexual behavior.* New York: Basic Books.

Marshall, W. L. (1993). The role of attachments, intimacy, and loneliness in the etiology and maintenance of sexual offending. *Sexual and Marital Therapy, 8,* 109–121.

Marshall, W. L., Marshall, L. E., & Serran, G. A. (2006). Strategies in the treatment of paraphilias: A critical review. *Annual Review of Sex Research, 17,* 162–182.

Martin, E. K., Taft, T. T., & Resick, P. A. (2007). A review of marital rape. *Aggression and Violent Behavior, 12,* 3329–3347.

Martin, J. A., Hamilton, B. E., & Osterman, M. J. K. (2014). Births in the United States, 2013. *NCHS Data Brief, 175.* Available: http://www.cdc.gov/nchs/data/databriefs/db175.htm (Last visited 12/21/14).

Martinez, G., Copen, C. E., & Abma, J. C. (2011). Teenagers in the United States: Sexual activity, contraceptive use, and childbearing, 2006–2010 National Survey of Family Growth. *Vital and Health Statistics,* 2011, Series 23, No. 31. Available: http://www.cdc.gov/nchs/data/series/sr_23/sr23_031.pdf (Last visited 1/27/15).

Martins, Y., Preti, G., Crabtree, C. R., Runyan, T., Vainius, A. A., & Wysocki, C. J. (2005). Preference for human body odors is influenced by gender and sexual orientation. *Psychological Science, 16,* 694–701.

Masaro, C. L., Dahinten, V. S., Johnson, J., Ogilvie, G., & Patrick, D. M. (2008). Perceptions of sexual partner safety. *Sexually Transmitted Infections, 35,* 566–571.

Masters, N. T., Casey, E., Wells, E. A., & Morrison, D. M. (2013). Sexual scripts among young heterosexually active men and women: Continuity and change. *Journal of Sex Research, 50*(5), 409–420.

Masters, W. H., & Johnson, V. E. (1966). *Human sexual response.* Boston: Little, Brown.

Masters, W. H., & Johnson, V. E. (1970). *Human sexual inadequacy.* Boston: Little, Brown.

Masters, W. H., & Johnson, V. E. (1974). *The pleasure bond.* Boston: Little, Brown.

Matek, O. (1988). Obscene phone callers. In D. Dailey (Ed.), *The sexually unusual.* New York: Harrington Park Press.

Mayo Clinic. (2012). Cystitis. Available: http://www.mayoclinic.org/diseases-conditions/cystitis/basics/defintion/con-2002404076 (Last visited 12/16/14).

Mayo Clinic. (2014.13a). Prostatitis. Available: http://www.mayoclinic.org/diseases-conditions/prostatitis/expert-answers/prostatitis/FAQ-20058150 (Last visited 114/15).

Mayo Clinic. (2014.15a). Cervicitis. Available: http://www.mayoclinic.org/diseases-conditions/cervicitis/basics/definition-2026738 (Last visited 12/16/14).

McAuliffe, T. L., DiFrancesico, W., & Reed, B. R. (2007). Effects of question format and collection mode on the accuracy of retrospective surveys of health risk behavior: A comparison with daily sexual activity diaries. *Health Psychology, 26,* 60–67.

McCabe, M. P., & Goldhammer, D. L. (2012). Demographic and psychological factors related to sexual desire among heterosexual women in a relationship. *Journal of Sex Research, 49,* 78–87.

McCabe, M. P., & Wauchope, M. (2005a). Behavioral characteristics of men accused of rape: Evidence for different types of rapists. *Archives of Sexual Behavior, 34,* 241–253.

McCabe, M. P., & Wauchope, M. (2005b). Behavioral characteristics of rapists. *Journal of Sexual Aggression, 11,* 235–249.

McCallum, E. B., & Peterson, Z. D. (2012). Investigating the impact of inquiry mode on self-reported sexual behavior: Theoretical considerations and review of the literature. *Journal of Sex Research, 49,* 212–226.

McCarthy, B. W. (1998). Integrating Viagra into cognitive-behavioral couples sex therapy. *Journal of Sex Education and Therapy, 23,* 302–308.

McCarthy, B. W., & McCarthy, E. (2003). *Rekindling desire: A step-by-step program to help low-sex and no-sex marriages.* New York: Brunner/Routledge.

McCarthy, B. W., & McCarthy, E. (2009). *Discovering your couple sexual style.* New York: Routledge.

McConaghy, N. (1998). Pedophilia: A review of the evidence. *Australian and New Zealand Journal of Psychiatry, 32,* 252–265.

McCormick, N. (1996). Our feminist future: Women affirming sexuality research in the late twentieth century. *Journal of Sex Research, 33*(2), 99–102.

McDonald, A., et al. (2005). Randomized trial of cognitive-behavioral therapy for chronic posttraumatic stress disorder in adult female survivors of childhood sexual abuse. *Journal of Clinical and Consulting Psychology, 73,* 515–524.

McKeganey, N. (2006). Street prostitution in Scotland: The views of working women. *Drugs, Education, Prevention and Policy, 13*, 151–166.

McWhirter, D. (1990). Prologue. In D. McWhirter, S. A. Sanders, & J. M. Reinisch (Eds.), *Homosexuality/heterosexuality: Concepts of sexual orientation.* New York: Oxford University Press. p. 48.

Mead, M. (1975). *Male and female.* New York: Morrow.

Meana, M. (2010). Elucidating women's (hetero) sexual desire: Definitional challenges and content expansion. *Journal of Sex Research, 47*(2), 104–122.

Mears, B. (2008). Justices: Child porn is not protected speech. Available: http://site.printthis.clickability.com/pt/cpt?action5cpt&title5Justices%3A1Child1porn (Last visited 5/19/08).

MedicineNet.com. (2014). Date rape drugs. Available: http://www.medicinenet.com/date_rape_drugs/article.htm (Last visited 9/23/14).

Men Can Stop Rape. (2007). Men who have been sexually assaulted. Available: http://www.mencanstoprape.org/Table/Handouts (Last visited 9/19/11).

Mercer, C. H., et al. (2007). Women who report having sex with women: British national probability data on prevalence, sexual behaviors, and health outcomes. *American Journal of Public Health, 97*, 1126–1133.

Mercer, C. H., Fenton, K. A., Copes, A. J., Wellings, K., Erens, B., McManus, S., et al. (2004). Increasing prevalence of male homosexual partnerships and practices in Britain, 1990–2000: Evidence from national probability surveys. *AIDS, 18*, 1453–1458.

Meston, C., & Buss, D. (2007). Why humans have sex. *Archives of Sexual Behavior, 22*, 477–507.

Meston, C. M., & Buss, D. M. (2009). *Why women have sex.* New York: Henry Holt.

Meston, C. M., & O'Sullivan, L. F. (2007). Such a tease: Intentional sexual provocation within heterosexual interactions. *Archives of Sexual Behavior, 36*, 531–542.

Metz, M. E., & McCarthy, B. W. (2011). *Enduring desire: Your guide to lifelong intimacy.* New York: Routledge.

Meyer-Bahlburg, H. F. L. (2009). Variants of gender differentiation in somatic disorders of sex development: Recommendations for Version 7 of the World Professional Association for Transgender Health's *Standards of Care. International Journal of Transgenderism, 11*(4), 2226–237.

Michael, R. T., Gagnon, J. H., Laumann, E. O., & Kolata, G. (1994). *Sex in America: A definitive study.* Boston: Little Brown.

Microbicide Trials Network. (2014). Rectal microbicides fact sheet. Available: http://www.mtnstopshiv.org/node/2864 (Last visited 1/13/15).

Miletski, H. (2000). Bestiality/zoophilia: An exploratory study. *Scandinavian Journal of Sexology, 3*, 149–150.

Miletski, H. (2002). *Understanding bestiality and zoophilia.* Germantown, MD: Ima Tek Inc.

Milhausen, R. R., Crosby, R. A., & Yarber, W. L. (2008). Public opinion in Indiana regarding the vaccination of middle school students for HPV. *The Health Education Monograph, 25*(2), 21–27.

Miller, A. B., Wall, C., Baines, C. J., Sun, P., To, T., & Narod, S. A. (2014). Twenty five year follow-up for breast cancer incidence and mortality of the Canadian National Breast Screening Study: Randomized screening. *British Medical Journal, 348.* g366.Available: http://www.bmj.com/content/348/bmj.g366 (Last visited 1/6/15).

Miller, C. C. (2014, Dec. 2). The divorce surge is over, but the myth lives on. *New York Times.* Available: html?hp&action=click&pgtype=Homepage&module=photo-spot-region&region=top-news&WT.nav=top-news&abt=0002&abg=0&_r=1 (Last visited 12/2/14).

Miller, L. (2000, October 17). Panel agrees: Rethink new porn laws. *USA Today*, p. D3.

Milne, C. (2005). *Naked ambition: Women pornographers and how they are changing the sex industry.* Berkeley, CA: Pub Group West.

Miner, M. H., Coleman, E., Center, B., Ross, M., & Simon Rosser, B. (2007). The compulsive sexual behavior inventory: Psychometric properties. *Archives of Sexual Behavior, 36*, 579–587.

Minichiello, V., Marino, R., & Browne, J. (2000). Commercial sex between men: A prospective diary-based study. *Journal of Sex Research, 37*, 151–160.

Minichiello, V., Scott, J., & Callander, D. (2013). New pleasures and old dangers: Reinventing male sex work. *Journal of Sex Research, 50*, 263–275.

Mitchell, K. R., Mercer, C. H., Plaubidis, G. B., Jones, K. G., Datta, J., Field, N., et al. (2013). Sexual function in Britain: Findings from the third National Survey of Sexual Attitudes and Lifestyles (Natsal-3). *The Lancet, 382*, 1817–1829.

Mitchell, R., King, M., Nazareth, I., & Wellings, K. (2001). Managing sexual difficulties: A qualitative investigation of coping strategies. *The Journal of Sex Research, 48*, 325–333.

Moalem, S. (2009). *How sex works.* New York: HarperCollins.

Mock, S. E., & Eiback, R. P. (2012). Stability and change in sexual orientation identity over a 10-year period in adulthood. *Archives of Sexual Behavior, 41*, 641–648.

Molnar, A. (2013). Sexually explicit material affects behavior in young people less than thought. Available from: http://www.eurekalert.org/pub_releases/2013-04/w-sem041813.php (Last visited: 4/25/13).

Montagu, A. (1986). *Touching* (3rd ed.). New York: Columbia University Press.

Montgomery, J. P., Mokotoff, E. D., Gentry, A. C., & Blair, J. M. (2003). The extent of bisexual behavior in HIV-infected men and implications for transmission to their female partners. *AIDS Care, 15*, 829–837.

Monto, M. A. (2001). Prostitution and fellatio. *Journal of Sex Research, 38*, 140–145.

Monto, M. A. (2004). Female prostitution, customers, and violence. *Violence Against Women, 10*, 160–188.

Moran, M. (2013, April 5). New gender dysphoria criteria replace GID. *Psychiatric News, 48*(7), 9–14.

Morgan, E. M. (2011). Associations between young adult's use of sexually explicit materials and their sexual preferences, behaviors, and satisfaction. *Journal of Sex Research, 48*, 520–530.

Mosher, W. D., & Jones, J. (2010). Use of contraception in the United States: 1982–2008. National Center for Health Statistics. *Vital Health Statistics, 23*(29). Available: http://www.cdc.gov/nchs/data/series/sr_23/sr23_029.pdf (Last visited 11/11/11).

Motluk, A. (2003). The big brother effect: The more older brothers you have, the more likely you are to be gay. What's going on? *New Scientist, 177*, 44–47.

Movement Advancement Project. (2014a). Foster and adoption laws. Available: http://www.lgbtmap.org/equality-maps/foster_and_adoption_laws (Last visited 9/11/14).

Movement Advancement Project. (2014b). Non-discrimination laws. Available: http://www.lgbtmap.org/equality-maps/non_discrimination_laws (Last visited 9/11/14).

Movement Advancement Project. (2014c). Hate crime laws. Available: http://www.lgbtmap.org/equality-maps/hate_crime_laws. (Last visited 9/11/14).

Movement Advancement Project. (2015). Policy and issue analysis. Available: http://www.lgbtmap.org/policy-and-issue-analysis (Last visited: 7/9/15).

Moynihan, R. (2002). The making of a disease: Female sexual dysfunction. *British Medical Journal, 326,* 45–47.

Moynihan, R., & Mintzes, B. (2010). *Sex, lies & pharmaceuticals.* Vancouver, British Columbia: Greystone Books.

Muehlenhard, C. L. (2011). Examining stereotypes about token resistance to sex. *Psychology of Women Quarterly, 35,* 676–683.

Muehlenhard, C. L., & Linton, M. A. (1987). Date rape and sexual aggression in dating situations: Incidence and risk factors. *Journal of Consulting Psychology, 34,* 186–196.

Muehlenhard, C. L., & Peterson, Z. D. (2005). Wanting and not wanting sex: The missing discourse of ambivalence. *Feminism & Psychology, 15,* 15–20.

Muehlenhard, C. L., & Shippee, S. K. (2009). Men's and women's reports of pretending orgasm. *Journal of Sex Research, 46,* 1–16.

Muehlenhard, C. L., Ponch, I. G., Phelps, J. L., & Giusti, L. M. (1992). Definitions of rape: Scientific and political implications. *Journal of Social Issues, 48*(1), 23–44.

Mugwanya, K. K., Donnell, D., Celum, C., Thomas, K., Ndase, P., Mugo, N., et al. (2013a). Sexual behaviour of heterosexual men and women receiving antiretroviral pre-exposure prophylaxis for HIV prevention: a longitudinal analysis. *The Lancet Infectious Diseases, 13,* 1021–1028.

Mugwanya, K. K., Donnell, D., Mugo, N., Thomas, K. K., Ngure, K., Katabira, E., et al. (2013b). Sexual behavior of heterosexual men and women receiving antiretroviral pre-exposure prophylaxis for HIV prevention: Post-unblinding analysis of the partners PrEP study. *Sexually Transmitted Infections.* DOI: 10.1136/sextrans-2013-051184.0144.

Murphy, W., & Page, J. (2008). Psychological profile of pedophiles and child molesters. *Journal of Psychology, 134,* 211–224.

Murray, J. B. (2000). Psychological profile of pedophiles and child molesters. *The Journal of Pscyhology: Interdisciplinary and Applied, 134,* 211–224.

Mushovic, I. (2011, September 1). Progress obscures gay inequality. *USA Today,* p. 7A.

Mustanski, B., & Liu, R. T. (2013). A longitudinal study of predictors of suicide attempts among lesbian, gay, bisexual and transgender youth. *Archives of Sexual Behavior, 42,* 437–448.

Nacopoulos, A. G., Lewtas, A. J., & Ousterhout, M. M. (2010). Syringe exchange programs: Impact on injection drug users and the role of the pharmacist from a U.S. perspective. *Journal of the American Pharmacists Association, 50,* 148–157.

Nagaraja, J. (1983). Sexual problems in adolescents. *Child Psychiatry Quarterly, 16,* 9–18.

Nagel, J. (2003). *Race, ethnicity, and sexuality: Intimate intersection frontiers.* New York: Oxford University Press.

Najman, J. M., Dunne, M. P., Purdie, D. M., Boyle, F. M., & Coxeter, P. D. (2005). Sexual abuse in childhood and sexual dysfunction in adulthood: An Australian population-based study. *Archives of Sexual Behavior, 34,* 517–526.

Nakano, M. (1990). *Japanese American women: Three generations, 1890–1990.* Berkeley, CA: Mina Press.

Nanda, S. (1990). *Neither man nor woman: The Hijras of India.* Belmont, CA: Wadsworth.

The National Campaign to Prevent Teen and Unplanned Pregnancy. (2012). Teen childbearing, single parents and father involvement. Available: https://thenationalcampaign.org/sites/default/files/resource-primary-download/childbearing-singleparenthood-fatherinvolvement.pdf (Last visited 11/14/14).

The National Campaign to Prevent Teen and Unplanned Pregnancy. (2014). Teen pregnancy. Available: https://thenationalcampaign.org/why-it-matters/teen-pregnancy (Last visited 8/13/14).

National Cancer Institute. (2014a). Breast cancer screening. Available: http://www.cancer.gov/cancertopics/pdq/screening/breast/HealthProfessional/page1 (Last visited 1/6/15).

National Cancer Institute. (2014b). Prostate cancer screening. Available: http://www.cancer.gov/cancertopics/pdq/screening/prostate/HealthProfessional (Last visited 1/8/15).

National Center for Education Statistics. (2014). *Indicators of school crime and safety: 2013.* Available: http://nces.ed.gov/programs/crimeindicators/crimeindicators2013/ind_22asp (Last visited 10/1/14).

National Center for Environmental Health. (1995). Smoking men at risk for erectile dysfunction. *Contemporary Sexuality, 29*(2), 8.

National Center for Health Statistics. (2011). Sexual behavior, sexual attraction, and sexual identity in the United States: Data from the 2006–2008 National Survey of Family Growth. Available: http://www.cdc.gov/nchs/data/nhsr08.pdf (Last visited 5/10/11).

National Center for Missing & Exploited Children. (2011). What is sex tourism involving children? Available: http://www.missingkids.com/missingkids/servlet/PageServlet?LanguageCountry1en_US (Last visited 10/14/11).

National Center for Missing & Exploited Children. (2015). Child sex trafficking. Available: http://www.missingkids.com/1in6 (Last visited 2/11/15).

National Coalition of Anti-Violence Programs. (2013). *Lesbian, gay, bisexual, transgendered, queer, and HIV-affected hate violence in 2013.* New York: New York City Gay and Lesbian Anti-Violence Project, Inc.

National Diabetes Information Clearinghouse (NDIC). (2012). Sexual and urological problems of diabetes. Available: http://www.diabetes.niddk.nih.gov/dm/pubs/sup/ (Last visited 1/4/15).

National Health and Nutrition Examination Survey (2011). Data documentation, codebook and frequency. Available: http://www.cdc.gov/nchs/nhanes/limited_access/RHQ_F_R.htm (Last visited 10/1/14).

National Human Trafficking Resource Center. (2015). Sex trafficking. Available: http://www.traffickingresourcecenter.org/type-trafficking/sex-trafficking (Last visited 2/3/15).

National Institute of Mental Health. (2010). Eating disorders. Available: http://www.nimh.nih.gov/health/topics/eating-disorders/index.shtml (Last visited 1/15/11).

National Institute on Aging. (2008). Can we prevent aging? Available: http://www.nia.nih.gov/HealthInformation/Publications/preventaging.htm (Last visited 7/8/08).

National Institute on Aging. (2010). Can we prevent aging? Available: http://www.nia.nih.gov/healthinformation/publications/preventaging.htm (Last visited 7/28/11).

National Institute on Aging. (2012). Hormones and menopause: Tips from the National Institute on Aging. Available: http://www.nia.nih.gov/sites/default/files/hormones_and_menopause_0.pdf (Last visited 10/1/14).

National Institute on Aging. (2014). Sexuality in later life. Available: http://www.nia.nih.gov/health/publication/sexuality-later-life (Last visited 6/13/14).

National Institutes of Health. (2013). What can a woman do to promote a healthy pregnancy before she gets pregnant? Available: http://www.nichd.nih.gov/health/topics/preconceptioncare/conditioninfo/pages/before-pregnancy.aspx (Last visited 12/11/14).

National Institutes of Health. (2015). HIV treatment: The basics. Available: http://www.aidsinfo.nih.gov/education-materials/fact-sheets/21/51/hiv-treatment-the-basics (Last visited 1/12/15).

"National sexuality education standards: Core content and skills, K–12." (2012). *Journal of School Health*. Available: http://www.futureofsexed.org/documents/josh-fose-standards-web.pdf (Last visited 8/19/14).

National Survey of Family Growth. (2013). Infertility. Available: http://www.cdc.gov/nchs/nsfg/key_statistics/i.htm#infertility (Last visited 12/20/14).

National Women's Health Information Center. (2002). Douching. Available: http://www.4woman.gov/faq/douching (Last visited 11/4/05).

Nelson, H. D., Walker, M., Zakher, B., & Mitchell, J. (2012). Menopausal hormone therapy for the primary prevention of chronic conditions: A systematic review to update the U.S. Preventive Services Task Force recommendations. *Annals of Internal Medicine, 157*(2), 104.

Niccolai, L. M., Farley, T. A., Ayoub, M. A., Magnus, M. K., & Kissinger, P. J. (2002). HIV-infected persons' knowledge of their sexual partners' HIV status. *AIDS Education and Prevention, 14,* 183–189.

Nichols, M. (1987). Lesbian sexuality: Issues and developing theory. In Boston Lesbian Psychologies Collective (Ed.), *Lesbian psychologies: Explorations and challenges*. Urbana: University of Illinois Press.

Nicolosi, A., Moreiba, E., Shirai, J., Bin Mohd Tambi, M., & Glasser, D. (2003). Epidemiology of erectile dysfunction in four countries: Cross-national study of the prevalence and correlates of erectile dysfunction. *Urology, 61,* 201–206.

NIDA topics in brief: Methamphetamine addiction: Progress, but need to remain vigilant. (2011). Available: http://www.drugabuse.gov/publications/topics-in-brief/methamphetamine-addiction-progress-need-to-remain-vigilant.htm (Last visited 5/9/12).

Nielson, C. M., et al. (2010). Consistent condom use is associated with lower prevalence of human papillomavirus infection in men. *Journal of Infectious Diseases, 202,* 445–451.

Noar, S. (2008). Behavioral interventions to reduce HIV-related sexual risk behavior: Review and synthesis of meta-analytic evidence. *AIDS and Behavior, 3,* 335–353.

North American Menopause Society. (2012). Smoking makes menopause misery. Available: http://www.menopause.org/for-women/menopause-take-time-to-think-about-it/consumers/2012/09/19/smoking-makes-menopause-misery (Last visited 10/1/14).

North American Menopause Society. (2014). Androgens, antidepressants and other drugs on which the jury's still out. Available: http://www.menopause.org/for-women/sexual-health-menopause-online/effective-treatments-for-sexual-problems/androgens-antidepressants-and-other-drugs-on-which-the-jury-s-still-out (Last visited 6/8/14).

Northrup, C., Schwartz, P., & Witte, J. (2012). *The normal bar.* New York: Harmony.

Northrup, C., Schwartz, P., & Witte, J. (2014). *The normal bar.* New York: Crown.

Northrup, T. (2013). Examining the relationship between media use and aggression, sexuality, and body image. *Journal of Applied Research on Children: Informing Policy for Children at Risk, 4*(1), Article 3. Available: http://digitalcommons.library.tmc.edu/childrenatrisk/vol4/iss1/3 (Last visited 4/2/14).

Nusbaum, M. R. (2002). Erectile dysfunction: Prevalence, etiology, and major risk factors. *Journal of the American Osteopathic Association, 102*(Suppl. 4), S1–S56.

Oakley, A. (1985). *Sex, gender, and society* (Rev. ed.). New York: Harper & Row.

Office of Adolescent Health. (2013). November 2013: Teen media use part 1—Increasing and on the move. Available: http://www.hhs.gov/ash/oah/news/e-updates/eupdate-nov-2013.html (Last visited 3/27/14).

Office on Women's Health. (2008). *Date rape drugs.* Washington, DC: U.S. Department of Health and Human Services.

Office on Women's Health. (2012). What are date rape drugs? Available: http://www.womenshealth.gov/publications/our-publications/fact-sheet/date-rape-drugs.html (Last visited 9/22/14).

Ogden, C., Carroll, M. D., Kit, B. K., & Flegal, K. M. (2014). Prevalence of childhood and adult obesity in the United States, 2011–2012. *Journal of the American Medical Association, 311*(8), 806–814.

Ogden, G. (2008). *The return of desire: A guide to rediscovering your sexual passion.* Boston: Trumpeter.

Ohl, M. E., & Perencevich, E. (2011). Frequency of human immunodeficiency virus (HIV) testing in urban vs. rural areas of the United States: Results from a nationally-representative sample. *BMC Public Health, 11,* 681.

Okazaki, S. (2002). Influences of culture on Asian Americans' sexuality. *Journal of Sex Research, 39*(1), 34–41.

Olmstead, S. B., Koon, J. T., Puhlman, D. J., Pasley, K., & Fincham, F. D. (2013). College men, unplanned pregnancy, and marriage: What do they expect? *Journal of Sex Research, 50*(8), 808–819.

Olmstead, S. B., Negash, S., Pasley, K., & Fincham, F. D. (2013). Emerging adults' expectations for pornography use in the context of future committed relationships: A qualitative study. *Archives of Sexual Behavior, 42,* 625–635.

Orr, A. (2014). Title IX Protection of Transgender and Gender Nonconforming Students. National Center for Lesbian Rights. Available: http://www.nclrights.org/title-ix-protection-of-transgender-and-gender-nonconforming-students/ (Last visited 9/12/14).

Owen, J., & Fincham, F. D. (2011). Young adults' emotional reactions after hooking-up encounters. *Archives of Sexual Behavior, 40,* 321–330.

Owen, J. J., Rhoades, G. K., Stanley, S. M., & Fincham, F. D. (2010). "Hooking up" among college students: Demographic and psychosocial correlates. *Archives of Sexual Behavior, 39,* 653–663.

Owens, E. W., Behun, R. J., Manning, J. C., & Reid, R. C. (2012). The impact of Internet pornography on adolescents: A review of the research. *Sexual Addiction & Compulsivity, 19,* 99–122.

Owings, M., Uddin, S., & Williams, S. (2013). Trends in circumcision for male newborns in U.S. hospitals: 1979–2010. Available: http://www.cdc.gov/nchs/data/hestat/circumcision_2013/Circumcision_2013.pdf (Last visited 12/18/14).

Paavonen, J., Westrom, L., & Eschenback, N. (2008). Pelvic inflammatory disease. In K. Holmes, P. Sparling, W. Stamm, P. Piot, J. Wasserheit, L. Corey, et al. (Eds.), *Sexually transmitted diseases* (4th ed., pp. 1017–1050). New York: McGraw-Hill.

Padma-Nathan, H., Eardley, I., Kloner, R. A., Laties, A. M., & Montorsi, F. (2002). A 4-year update on the safety of sildenafil citrate (Viagra). *Urology, 60*(S2), 67–90.

Paik, A. (2010). "Hookups," dating, and relationship quality: Does the type of sexual involvement matter? *Social Science Research, 39,* 739–753.

Palmateer, N., et al. (2010). Evidence for effectiveness of sterile injecting equipment provision in preventing hepatitis C and human immunodeficiency virus transmission among injecting drug users: A review of review. *Addiction, 105,* 844–859.

Paolucci, E. O., Genuis, M. L., & Violato, C. (2001). A meta-analysis of the published research on the effects of child sexual abuse. *Journal of Psychology, 135,* 17–36.

Papp, L. M., Cummings, E. M., & Goeke-Morey, M. C. (2009). For richer, for poorer: Money as a topic of marital conflict in the home. *Family Relations, 58,* 91–103.

Parker, R., & Gagnon, J. (Eds.). (1995). *Conceiving sexuality: Approaches to sex research in a post-modern world.* New York: Routledge.

Parrinder, G. (1980). *Sex in the world's religions.* New York: Oxford University Press.

Parsons, C. (2003, July 29). Sexual consent measure is signed. *Chicago Tribune,* pp. 1, 7.

Paul, B., & Shim, J. W. (2008). Gender, sexual affect, and motivations for Internet pornography use. *International Journal of Sexual Health, 20,* 187–199.

Paul, E. L., McManus, B., & Hayes, A. (2000). "Hookups": Characteristics and correlates of college students' spontaneous and anonymous sexual experiences. *Journal of Sex Research, 37*(1), 76–88.

Paul, P. (2006). *Pornified: How pornography is transforming our lives, our relationships, and our families.* New York: Times Books.

Pawlowski, D. R. (1998). Dialectical tensions in marital partners' accounts of their relationships. *Communication Quarterly, 46,* 369–412.

Pazol, K., Zane, S. B., Parker, W. Y., Hall, L. R., Berg, C., & Cook, D. A. (2011). Abortion surveillance—United States, 2008. *Morbidity and Mortality Weekly Report 60*(15), 1–41.

Peixoto, M. M., & Nobre, P. (2014). Prevalence of sexual problems and associated distress among lesbian and heterosexual women. *Journal of Sex & Marital Therapy.* doi: 10.1080/009263X.2014.918066.

Peloquin, K., Brassard, A., Lafontaine, M. F., & Shaver, P. R. (2014). Sexuality examined through the lens of attachment theory: Attachment, caregiving, and sexual satisfaction. *Journal of Sex Research, 51*(5), 561–576.

Peplau, L. A., Fingerhut, A., & Beals, K. P. (2004). Sexuality in the relationships of lesbians and gay men. In J. Harvey, A. Wenzel, & S. Sprecher (Eds.), *The handbook of sexuality in close relationships* (pp. 349–269). Mahwah, NJ: Erlbaum.

Peplau, L. A., Frederick, D. A., Yee, C., Maisel, N., Lever, J., & Ghavami, N. (2009). Body image satisfaction in heterosexual, gay and lesbian adults. *Archives of Sexual Behavior, 38,* 713–725.

Pereda, N., Guilera, G., Forns, M., & Gomez-Benito, J. (2009). The prevalence of child sexual abuse in community and student samples: A meta-analysis. *Clinical Psychology Review, 29,* 328–338.

Perel, E. (2006). *Mating in captivity.* New York: Harper.

Perilloux, C., Duntley, J. D., & Buss, D. M. (2012). The costs of rape. *Archives of Sexual Behavior, 41,* 1099–1106.

Perrin, E. C., Siegel, B. S., & the Committee on Psychological Aspects of Child and Family Health. (2013). Promoting the well-being of children whose parents are gay or lesbian. *Pediatrics, 131*(4), 1374–1383.

Perrin, P. B., Heesacker, M., Tiegs, T. J., Swan, A. W., et al. (2011). Aligning Mars and Venus: The social construction and instability of gender differences in romantic relationships. *Sex Roles, 64*(9–10), 613–628.

Perry, J. D., & Whipple, B. (1981). Pelvic muscle strength of female ejaculators: Evidence in support of a new theory of orgasm. *Journal of Sex Research, 17*(1), 22–39.

Pertot, S. (2007). *When your sex drives don't match.* New York: Marlowe & Company.

Peterson, Z. D., & Muehlenhard, C. L. (2007). Conceptualizing the "wantedness" of women's consensual and nonconsensual sexual experiences: Implications for how women label their experiences with rape. *Journal of Sex Research, 44,* 72–88.

Pew Research Center's Social and Demographic Trends. (2013). A survey of LGBT Americans: Attitudes, experiences and values in changing times. Available: http://www.pewsocialtrends.org/2013/06/12/a-survey-of-lgbt-americans (Last visited 9/11/14).

Pew Research Internet Project. (2013, Oct. 21). Online dating and relationships. Available: http://www.pewinternet.org/2013/10/21/online-dating-relationships/ (Last visited 4/2/14).

Pew Research Internet Project. (2014, Feb. 11). Couples, the Internet, and social media. Available: http://www.pewinternet.org/2014/02/11/couples-the-internet-and-social-media/ (Last visited 3/27/14).

Pinkerton, S. D., Bogart, L. M., Cecil, H., & Abramson, P. R. (2002). Factors associated with masturbation in a collegiate sample. *Journal of Psychology and Human Sexuality, 14,* 103–121.

Pinkerton, S. D., Holtgrave, D. R., & Galletly, C. L. (2008). Infections prevented by increasing HIV serostatus awareness in the United States, 2001 to 2004. *Journal of Acquired Immune Deficiency Syndromes, 47,* 354–357.

Pistole, M. C. (1995). College students' ended love relationships: Attachment style and emotion. *Journal of College Student Development, 36*(1), 53–60.

Planned Parenthood. (2012). Let's talk: Parents and teens talk about sexuality: A national poll. Available: http://www.plannedparenthood.org/files/8313/9610/5916/LT_2012_Poll_Fact_Sheet_final_2.pdf (Last visited 7/28/14).

Planned Parenthood. (2014.4a). Men's sexual health. Available: http://www.plannedparenthood.org/health-info/men/ (Last visited 6/14/14).

Planned Parenthood. (2014.11a). Q & A with Dr. Cullins: Birth Control. Available: http://www.plannedparenthood.org/health-info/ask-dr-cullins/birth-control-qa (Last accessed 12/2/14).

Planned Parenthood. (2014.11b). Birth control pills. Available: http://www.plannedparenthood.org/health-info/birth-control/birth-control-pill (Last visited 12/2/14).

Planned Parenthood. (2014.11c). Birth control shot at a glance. Available: http://www.plannedparenthood.org/health-info/birth-control/birth-control-shot-depo-provera (Last visited 12/2/14).

Planned Parenthood. (2014.11d). Birth control patch (Ortho Evra). Available: http://www.plannedparenthood.org/health-info/birth-control/birth-control-patch-ortho-evra (Last visited 12/2/14).

Planned Parenthood. (2014.11f). Birth control vaginal ring (Nuva Ring). Available: http://www.plannedparenthood.org/health-info/birth-control/birth-control-vaginal-ring-nuvaring (Last visited 12/3/14).

Planned Parenthood. (2014.11g). Birth control implant (Implanon and Nexplanon). Available: http://www.plannedparenthood.org/health-info/birth-control/birth-control-implant-implanon (Last visited 12/3/14).

Planned Parenthood. (2014.11h). Condom. Available: http://www.plannedparenthood.org/health-info/birth-control/condom (Last visited 12/3/14).

Planned Parenthood. (2014.11i). Female condom. Available: http://www.plannedparenthood.org/health-info/birth-control/female-condom (Last visited 23/4/14).

Planned Parenthood. (2014.11j). Diaphragm. Available: http://www.plannedparenthood.org/health-info/birth-control/diaphragm (Last visited 12/4/14).

Planned Parenthood. (2014.11k). Birth control sponge (Today Sponge). Available: http://www.plannedparenthood.org/health-info/birth-control/birth-control-sponge-today-sponge (Last visited 12/4/14).

Planned Parenthood. (2014.11l). Cervical cap (FemCap). Available: http://www.plannedparenthood.org/health-info/birth-control/cervical-cap (Last visited 12/4/14).

Planned Parenthood. (2014.11m). IUD. Available: http://www.plannedparenthood.org/health-info/birth-control/iud (Last visited 12/6/14).

Planned Parenthood. (2014.11n). Fertility awareness-based methods (FAMs). Available: http://www.plannedparenthood.org/health-info/birth-control/fertility-awareness (Last visited 12/6/14).

Planned Parenthood. (2014.11o). Breastfeeding as birth control. Available: http://www.plannedparenthood.org/health-info/birth-control/breastfeeding (Last visited 12/7/14).

Planned Parenthood. (2014.11p). Sterilization for women (tubal ligation). Available: http://www.plannedparenthood.org/health-info/birth-control/sterilization-women (Last visited 12/7/14).

Planned Parenthood. (2014.11q). Vasectomy. Available: http://www.plannedparenthood.org/health-info/birth-control/vasectomy (Last visited 12/8/14).

Planned Parenthood. (2014.11r). Morning-after pill (Emergency contraception). Available: http://www.plannedparenthood.org/health-info/morning-after-pill-emergency-contraception (Last visited 12/8/14).

Planned Parenthood. (2014.11s). Abortion. Available: http://www.plannedparenthood.org/health-info/abortion (Last visited 12/8/14).

Planned Parenthood. (2014.11t). The abortion pill. Available: http://www.plannedparenthood.org/health-info/abortion/the-abortion-pill (Last visited 12/8/14).

Planned Parenthood. (2014.11u). In-clinic abortion procedures. Available: http://www.plannedparenthood.org/health-info/abortion/in-clinic-abortion-procedures (Last visited 12/8/14).

Pogrebin, L. C. (1983). *Family politics.* New York: McGraw-Hill.

Polaris Project. (2010). International trafficking. Available: http://www.polarisproject.org/human-trafficking/international-trafficking (Last visited 10/14/11).

Polaris Project. (2015a). Sex trafficking in the U.S. Available: http://www.polarisproject.org/human-trafficking/sex-trafficking-in-the-us (Last visited 2/3/15).

Polaris Project. (2015b). Human trafficking trends in the United States. Available: http://www.polarisproject.org/humn-trafficking/overview/human-trafficking-trends (Last visited 2/3/15).

Polk, R. K., & Cowan, G. (1996). Perceptions of female pornography stars. *Canadian Journal of Human Sexuality, 5,* 221–229.

Population Reference Bureau. (2014). Female genital mutilation/cutting: Data and trends. Available: http://www.prb.org/pdf14/fgm-wallchart2014.pdf (Last visited 5/6/15).

Poston, D. L., & Baumle, A. K. (2010). Patterns of asexuality in the United States. *Demographic Research, 23,* Article 18, 509–530. Available: http://www.demographic-research.org/volumes/vol23/18/23-18.pdf (Last visited 10/15/14).

Potdar, R., & Koenig, M. A. (2005). Does audio-CASI improve reports of risky behavior? Evidence from a randomized field trial among young urban men in India. *Studies in Family Planning, 36,* 107–116.

Potts, M., & Short, R. V. (1999). *Ever since Adam and Eve: The evolution of human sexuality.* Cambridge, MA: Cambridge University Press.

Poulsen, F. O., Busby, D. M., & Galovan, A. M. (2013). Pornography use: Who uses it and how it is associated with couple outcomes. *Journal of Sex Research, 50,* 72–83.

Powell, E. (1996). *Sex on your own terms.* Minneapolis: CompCare.

Pregnancy after 35. (2015). WebMD. Available: http://www.webmd.com/baby/guide/pregnancy-after-35 (Last visited 5/5/15).

Preidt, R. (2013). Is *'sex addiction' for real? Study says maybe not.* Retrieved August 5, 2013, from *Web*MD website:http://www.webmd.com/sex/news/20130723/is-sex-addiction-for-real-says-maybe-not.

Premenstrual dysphoric disorder. (2012). *MedlinePlus.* Available: http://www.nlm.nih.gov/medlineplus/ency/article/007193.htm (Last visited 8/3/14).

Price, M., Kafka, M., Commons, M. L., Gutheil, T. G., & Simpson, W. (2002). Telephone scatologia—comorbidity with other paraphilias and paraphilia-related disorders. *International Journal of Law and Psychiatry, 25,* 37–49.

ProCon.org. (2014). 100 countries and their prostitution policies. Retrieved February 12, 2015 from http://prostitution.procon.org/view.resource.php?resourceID=000772.

Prostatitis. (2014). U.S. Dept. of Health and Human Services, National Kidney and Urologic Diseases Information Clearinghouse. Available: http://kidney.niddk.nih.gov/kudiseases/pubs/prostatitis/ (Last visited 1/14/15).

Prostitution. (n.d.). *Wikipedia.* Available: http://en.wikipedia/org/wiki/ Prostitution (Last visited 4/7/06).

Pruitt, S. L., & Schootman, M. (2010). Geographic disparity, area poverty, and human papillomavirus vaccination. *American Journal of Preventive Medicine, 38,* 525–533.

Putnam, F. W. (2003). Ten-year research update review: Child sexual abuse. *Journal of the American Academy of Child and Adolescent Psychiatry, 42,* 269–278.

Quayle, E. (2008). Online sex offending: Psychopathology and theory. In D. R. Laws & W. T. O'Donohue (Eds.), *Sexual deviance: Theory, assessment, and treatment* (2nd ed.). New York: Guilford Press.

Queen, C. (2000, November 19). Sex in the city. *San Francisco Chronicle,* pp. 1, 4.

Quinn, T. C., Wawer, M. J., Sewankambo, N., Serwadda, D., Chuanjun, L., Wabwire-Mangen, F., et al. (2000). Viral load and heterosexual transmission of human immunodeficiency virus type 1. *New England Journal of Medicine, 342,* 921–929.

Quist, M. C., Watkins, C. D., Smith, F. G., Little, A. C., DeBruine, L. M., & Jones, B. C. (2012). Sociosexuality predicts women's preferences for symmetry in men's faces. *Archives of Sexual Behavior, 41,* 1415–1421.

Radcliffe, J., Doty, N., Hawkins, L. A., Gaskins, C. S., Beidas, R., & Rudy, B. J. (2010). *AIDS Patient Care and STDs, 24,* 493–499.

Raffaelli, M., & Ontai, L. L. (2004). Gender socialization in Latino/a families: Results from two retrospective studies. *Sex Roles, 50,* 287–299.

Randall, H. E., & Byers, E. S. (2003). What is sex? Students' definitions of having sex, sexual partner, and unfaithful sexual behavior. *Canadian Journal of Human Sexuality, 12,* 87–96.

Rape, Abuse, and Incest National Network. (2009a). How often does sexual assault occur? Available: http://www.rainn.org/get-information/statistics/frequency-of-sexual-assault (Last visited 9/15/11).

Rape, Abuse & Incest National Network. (2009b). Ways to reduce your risk of sexual assault. Available: http://rainn.org/get-information/sexual-assault-prevention (Last visited 9/18/14).

Rape, Abuse, and Incest National Network. (2009c). Acquaintance rape. Available: http://www.rainn.org/get-information/types-of-sexual-assault/acquaintance-rape (Last visited 9/15/11).

Rape, Abuse, and Incest National Network. (2009d). Who are the victims? Available: http://www.rainn.org/get-information/statistics/sexual-assault-victims (Last visited 9/17/11).

Rape, Abuse and Incest National Network. (2009e). Effects of sexual abuse. Available: http://www.rainn.org/get-information/effects-of-sexual-assault (Last visited 9/19/11).

Rape Network. (2000). Rape is a crime of silence. Available: http://www.rapenetwork.com/whatisrape.html (Last visited 11/16/00).

Rashidian, A. (2010). *Understanding the sexual-selves of Iranian-American women: A qualitative study* (unpublished doctoral dissertation). University of New England, Armidale, New South Wales, Australia.

Rathus, S. A., Nevid, J. S., & Fichner-Rathus, L. (2002). *Human sexuality: A world of diversity*. Boston: Allyn & Bacon.

Rathus, S. A., Nevid, J. S., & Fichner-Rathus, L. (2005). *Human sexuality in a world of diversity* (6th ed.). Boston: Allyn & Bacon.

Ratner, P. A., Johnson, J. L., Shoveller, J. A., Chan, K., Martindale, S. L., Schilder, A. J., et al. (2003). Nonconsensual sex experienced by men who have sex with men: Prevalence and association with mental health. *Patient Education and Counseling, 49,* 67–74.

Reddy, U. M., Bettegowda, V., Dias, T., Yamada-Kushnir, T., Do, C. W., & Willinger, M. (2011). Term pregnancy: A period of heterogeneous risk for infant mortality. *Obstetrics & Gynecology, 117*(6), 1279–1287.

Reece, M., Herbenick, D., Sanders, S. A., Dodge, B., Ghassemi, A., & Fortenberry, J. D. (2009). Prevalence and characteristics of vibrator use by men in the United States. *Journal of Sexual Medicine, 6,* 1867–1874.

Reece, M., Herbenick, D., Schick, V., Sanders, S. A., Dodge, B., & Fortenberry, J. D. (2010.2a). Condom use rates in a national probability sample of males and females ages 14 to 94 in the United States. *Journal of Sexual Medicine, 7,* 266–276.

Reece, M., Herbenick, D., Schick, V., Sanders, S. A., Dodge, B., & Fortenberry, J. D. (2010.2b). Sexual behaviors, relationships, and perceived health status among adult men in the United States: Results from a national probability sample. *Journal of Sexual Medicine, 7,* 291–204.

Reece, M., Herbenick, D., Schick, V., Sanders, S. A., Dodge, B., & Fortenberry, J. D. (2010.9a). Findings from the National Survey of Sexual Health and Behavior (NSSHB). *Journal of Sexual Medicine, 7*(Suppl. 5), 243–373.

Reece, R. (1988). Special issues in the etiologies and treatments of sexual problems among gay men. *Journal of Homosexuality, 15,* 43–57.

Rees, S., Silove, D., Chey, T., Steel, Z., Creamer, M., Teesson, M., et al. (2011). Lifetime prevalence of gender-based violence in women and the relationship with mental disorders and psychological function. *Journal of the American Medical Association, 306,* 513–521.

Regan, P. C., Shen, W., De La Pena, E., & Gosset, E. (2007). "Fireworks exploded in my mouth": Affective responses before, during, and after the very first kiss. *International Journal of Sexual Health, 19*(2), 1–16.

Reiber, C., & Garcia, J. R. (2010). Hooking up: Gender differences, evolution, and pluralistic ignorance. *Evolutionary Psychology, 8,* 390–404.

Reimers, S. (2007). The BBC Internet study: General methodology. *Archives of Sexual Behavior, 36,* 147–161.

Reiss, I. (1980). A multivariate model of the determinants of extramarital sexual permissiveness. *Journal of Marriage and Family, 42,* 395–411.

Reiss, I. (1989). Society and sexuality: A sociological explanation. In K. McKinney & S. Sprecher (Eds.), *Human sexuality: The societal and interpersonal context*. Norwood, NJ: Ablex.

Reissing, E. D., Laliberte, G. M., & Davis, H. J. (2005). Young women's sexual adjustment: The role of sexual self-schema, sexual self-efficacy, sexual aversion, and body attitudes. *Canadian Journal of Human Sexuality, 14,* 77–85.

Reitman, V. (2004, September 12). Viagra users are getting younger and younger. *Indianapolis Star,* pp. J1, J4.

Resch, M., & Alderson, K. (2013). Female partners of men who use pornography: Are honesty and mutual use associated with relationship satisfaction? *Journal of Sex & Marital Therapy.* DOI: 10.1080/00926623X.2012.751077.

Reverby, S. M. (2009). *Examining Tuskegee: The infamous syphilis study and its legacy*. Chapel Hill: University of North Carolina Press.

Reynolds, A., & Caron, S. L. (2000). How intimate relationships are impacted when heterosexual men crossdress. *Journal of Psychology and Human Sexuality, 12,* 63–77.

Reynolds, G. (2011, April 13). Exercising for two. *New York Times.* Available: http://well.blogs.nytimes.com/2011/14/13/exercising-for-two/ (Last visited: 5/5/15).

Rice, E., Rhoades, H., Winetrobe, H., Sanchez, M., Montoya, J., Plant, A., & Kordic, A. (2014). Sexually explicit cell phone messaging associated with sexual risk among adolescents. *Pediatrics, 133*(2), 276–282. Available: http://pediatrics.aappublications.org/content/133/2/e276.full.html (Last visited 6/30/14).

Richards, K. (1997). What is a transgenderist? In B. Bullough, V. L. Bullough, & J. Elias (Eds.), *Gender blending*. New York: Prometheus Books.

Richters, J., de Visser, R., Rissel, C., & Smith, A. (2006). Sexual practices at last heterosexual encounter and occurrence of orgasm in a national survey. *Journal of Sex Research, 48*(3), 217–226.

Richters, J., de Visser, R. O., Rissel, C. E., Grulich, A. E., & Smith, A. A. (2008). Demographic and psychological features of participants in bondage and discipline, "sadomasochism" or dominance and submission (BDSM): Data from a national survey. *Journal of Sexual Medicine, 5,* 1600–1668.

Rickert, V. I., & Wiemann, C. M. (1998). Date rape among adolescents and young adults. *Journal of Pediatric and Adolescent Gynecology, 11,* 167–175.

Robbins, C. L., Schick, V., Reece, M., Herbenick, D., Sanders, S. A., Dodge, B., & Fortenberry, J. D. (2011). Prevalence, frequency and associations of masturbation with partnered sexual behaviors among US adolescents. *Archives of Pediatric Medicine, 165*(12), 1087–1093.

Roberts, D. F., Foehr, U. G., & Rideout, V. (2010). *Generation M2: Media in the lives of 8- to 18-year-olds.* Menlo Park, CA: Henry J. Kaiser Foundation.

Robinson, J. P., & Lubienski, S. T. (2011). The development of gender achievement gaps in mathematics and reading during elementary and middle school: Examining direct cognitive assessments and teacher ratings. *American Educational Research Journal, 48*(2), 268–302.

Robinson, J. P., Espelage, D. L., & Rivers, I. (2013). Developmental trends in peer victimization and emotional distress in LGB and heterosexual youth. *Pediatrics.* doi: 10.1542/peds.2012-2595.

Robinson, P. (1976). *The modernization of sex.* New York: Harper & Row.

Robles, T. F., Trombello, J. M., Slatcher, R. B., & McGinn, M. M. (2013). Marital quality and health: A meta-analytic review. American Psychological Association: *Psychological Bulletin.* Available: http://richslatcher.com/papers/RoblesEtal_PsychBull_2013.pdf (Last visited 11/3/14).

Rodriguez, M. (2012). CDC releases 2011 YRBS data: Fewer youth receiving information about HIV and AIDS. *SIECUS News Release.* Available: http://www.siecus.org/index.cfm?fuseaction=Feature.showFeature&featureid=2171&pageid=611&parentid=479 (Last visited 8/14/14).

Roesler, T. A. (2000, Oct.). Adult's reaction to child's disclosure of abuse will influence degree of permanent damage. *Boston University Child and Adolescent Behavior Newsletter,* pp. 1–2.

Roisman, G. I., Clausell, E., Holland, A., Fortuna, K., & Elieff, C. (2008). Adult romantic relationships as contexts of human development: A multimethod comparison of same-sex couples with opposite-sex dating, engaged, and married dyads. *Developmental Psychology, 44*(1), 91–101.

Roller, C., Martsolf, D. S., Draucker, C. B., & Ross, R. (2009). The sexuality of childhood sexual abuse survivors. *International Journal of Sexual Health, 21,* 49–60.

Romanowski, B., et al. (2009). Seroprevalence and risk factors for herpes simplex virus infection in a population of HIV-infected patients in Canada. *Sexually Transmitted Diseases, 36,* 165–169.

Rosario, M., Scrimshaw, E. W., & Hunter, J. (2011). Different patterns of sexual identity development over time: Implications for the psychological adjustment of lesbian, gay and bisexual youths. *Journal of Sex Research, 48*(1), 3–15.

Roscoe, W. (1991). *The Zuni man/woman.* Albuquerque: University of New Mexico Press.

Rose, T. (2004). *Longing to tell: Black women talk about sexuality and intimacy.* New York: Macmillan.

Rosen, R. C., Miner, M. M., & Wincze, J. P. (2014). Erectile dysfunction: Integration of medical and psychological approaches. In Y. M. Binik & K. S. K. Hall (Eds.), *Principles and practices of sex therapy* (5th ed., pp. 61–81). New York: Guilford Press.

Rosin, H. (2014, April 29). When men are raped. Available: http://www.slate.com/articles/double_x/doublex?2014/male_rape_in_america_a_new_study (Last visited 9/29/14).

Rosman, J., & Resnick, P. J. (1989). Sexual attraction to corpses: A psychiatric review of necrophilia. *Journal of the American Academy of Psychiatry and the Law, 17*(2), 153–163.

Ross, M. W., Essien, E. J., & Torres, I. (2006). Conspiracy beliefs about the origin of HIV/AIDS in four racial/ethnic groups. *Journal of Acquired Immune Deficiency Syndromes, 41,* 342–344.

Ross, M. W., Timpson, S. C., Williams, M. L., Amos, C., & Bowen, A. (2007). Stigma consciousness concerns related to drug use and sexuality in a sample of street-based male sex workers. *International Journal of Sexual Health, 19,* 57–65.

Rosser, S., Short, B. J., Thurmes, P. J., & Coleman, E. (1998). Anodyspareunia, the unacknowledged sexual dysfunction: A validation study of painful receptive anal intercourse and its psychosexual concomitants in homosexual men. *Journal of Sex and Marital Therapy, 24,* 281–292.

Rothman, E. F., Exner, D., & Baughman, A. L. (2011). The prevalence of sexual assault against people who identify as gay, lesbian, or bisexual in the United States: A systematic review. *Trauma, Violence, & Abuse, 12,* 56–66.

Rowland, D. L. (2012a). *Sexual dysfunction in men.* Cambridge, MA: Hogrefe Publishing.

Rowland, D. L. (2012b). *Sexual dysfunction in women.* Cambridge, MA: Hogrefe Publishing.

Rozas, A. (2007, September 13). U.S. sex-offender laws are called ineffective. *Chicago Tribune,* p. 3.

Rupp, H. A., & Wallen, K. (2009). Sex-specific content preferences for visual sexual stimuli. *Archives of Sexual Behavior, 38,* 417–426.

Rural HIV/STD Prevention Work Group. (2009). *Tearing down fences: HIV/STD prevention in rural America.* Bloomington, IN: Rural Center for AIDS/STD Prevention.

Russell, S. T., Van Campen, K. S., & Muraco, J. A. (2012). Sexuality development in adolescence. In L. M. Carpenter & J. DeLamater (Eds.), *Sex for life.* New York: New York University Press.

Ryan, K. M. (2011). The relationship between rape myths and sexual scripts: The social construction of rape. *Sex Roles, 65,* 774–782.

Rye, B. J., & Meaney, G. J. (2007). Voyeurism: Is it good as long as we do not get caught? *International Journal of Sexual Health, 19,* 47–56.

Sachs-Ericsson, N., et al. (2005). Childhood sexual and physical abuse and the 1-year prevalence of medical problems in the National Comorbidity Survey. *Health Psychology, 24,* 32–40.

Sadker, D., & Zittleman, K. (2005). Gender bias lives, for both sexes. *Education Digest, 70*(8), 27–30.

SAGE. (2013). Older Americans: The changing face of HIV/AIDS and aging in America. Available: http://www.sageusa.org/files/SenatehearingFactSheet_HIVandOlderAdults.pdf#__utma=149406063.286063367.1421348768.1421348768.1421348768.1&__utmb=149406063.9.10.1421348768&__utmc=149406063&__utmx=-&__utmz=149406063.142134876 8.1.1.utmcsr=yahoolutmccn=%28organic%29lutmcmd=organiclutmctr=%28not%20provided%29&__utmv=-&__utmk=29266364 (Last visited 1/15/15).

Sakaluk, J. K., Todd, L. M., Milhausen, R., Lachowsky, N. J., & Undergraduate Research Group in Sexuality. (2014). Dominant heterosexual sexual scripts in emerging adulthood: Conceptualizations and measurement. *Journal of Sex Research, 51,* 516–531.

Salisbury, C. M. A., & Fisher, W. A. (2013). "Did you come": A qualitative exploration of gender differences in belief, experiences, and concerns regarding female orgasm occurrence during heterosexual interactions. *Journal of Sex Research.* doi: 10.1080/00224499.2013.838934.

Salisbury, C. M. A., & Fisher, W. A. (2014). "Did you come?" A qualitative exploration of differences in beliefs, experiences, and concerns regarding female orgasm occurrence during heterosexual sexual interactions. *Journal of Sex Research, 51*(6), 616–631.

Samji, H., Cescon, A., Hogg, R. S., Modur, S. P., Althoff, K. N., Buchacz, A. N., et al. (2013). Closing the gap: Increases in life expectancy among treated HIV-positive individuals in the United States and Canada. *Plos One.* DOI: 10.1371/journal.pone.0081365.

Sampson, R. (2003). *Acquaintance rape of college students.* Washington, DC: U.S. Department of Justice.

Sanchez, Y. M. (1997). Families of Mexican origin. In M. K. DeGenova (Ed.), *Families in cultural context: Strengths and challenges in diversity.* Mountain View, CA: Mayfield.

Sander, L. (2013, August 16). Quiet no longer, rape survivors put pressure on colleges. *Chronicle of Higher Education,* pp. A20–A21.

Sanders, S., & Reinisch, J. (1999). Would you say you "had sex" if . . . ? *Journal of the American Medical Association, 281,* 275–277.

Sanders, S. A., Hill, B. J., Yarber, W. L., Graham, C. A., Crosby, R. A., & Milhausen, R. R. (2010). Misclassification bias: Diversity in conceptualisations about having "had sex." *Sexual Health, 7,* 31–34.

Sanders, S. A., Reece, M., Herbenick, D., Schick, V., Dodge, B., & Fortenberry, J. D. (2010). Condom use during most recent vaginal intercourse event among a probability sample of adults in the United States. *Journal of Sexual Medicine, 7,* 362–373.

Sanders, S. A., Reinisch, J. M., & McWhirter, D. P. (1990). Homosexuality/heterosexuality: An overview. In D. P. McWhirter, S. A. Sanders, & J. M. Reinisch (Eds.), *Homosexuality/heterosexuality: Concepts of sexual orientation.* New York: Oxford University Press.

Sandfort, T. G., & de Keizer, M. (2001). Sexual problems in gay men: An overview of empirical research. *Annual Review of Sex Research, 12,* 93–120.

Sandnabba, N., Santtila, P., Alison, L., & Nordling, N. (2002). Demographics, sexual behavior, family background and abuse experiences of practitioners of sadomasochistic sex: A review of recent research. *Sexual and Relationship Theory, 17,* 39–55.

Santtila, P., Sandnabba, N. K., Alison, L., & Nordling, N. (2002). Investigating the underlying structure of sadomasochistically oriented behavior. *Archives of Sexual Behavior, 31,* 185–196.

Sarnquist, C. C., et al. (2011). Rural HIV-infected women's access to medical care: Ongoing needs in California. *AIDS Care, 23,* 792–796.

Sarpolis, K. (2011). First menstruation: Average age and physical signs. *ObGyn.net.* Available: http://www.obgyn.net/young-women/first-menstruation-average-age-and-physical-signs (Last visited 11/19/14).

Satinsky, S., Reece, M., Dennis, B., Sanders, S., & Bardzell, S. (2012). An assessment of body appreciation and its relationship to sexual function in women. *Body Image, 9,* 137–144.

Satterwhite, C. L., Torrone, E., Meites, E., Dunne, E. F., Mahajan, R., Ocfemia, M. C., et al. (2013). Sexually transmitted infections among US women and men: Prevalence and incidence estimates. *Sexually Transmitted Diseases, 40,* 187–193.

Sauvageau, A., & Racette, S. (2006). Autoerotic deaths in the literature from 1954 to 2004: A review. *Journal of Forensic Sciences, 51,* 140–146.

Savic, I., & Lindstrom, P. (2008). PET and MRI show differences in cerebral asymmetry and functional connectivity between homosexual and heterosexual subjects. *Proceedings from the National Academy of Sciences, 105*(27), 9403–9408. Available: http://www.pnas.org/content/105/27/9403.full?sid586495aa4-b272-49f2-82c5-eadb15b678ff (Last visited 6/29/11).

Savin-Williams, R., & Ream, G. L. (2007). Prevalence and stability of sexual orientation components during adolescence and young adulthood. *Archives of Sexual Behavior, 36,* 385–394.

Savin-Williams, R. C. (2005). The new gay teen: Shunning labels. *The Gay and Lesbian Review Worldwide.* Available: http://glreview.com/12.6-williams.php (Last visited 1/17/06).

Savin-Williams, R. C. (2014). An exploratory study of the categorical versus spectrum nature of sexual orientation. *Journal of Sex Research, 51*(4), 446–453.

Sawyer, S., Metz, M. E., Hinds, J. D., & Brucker, R. A. (2001–2002). Attitudes toward prostitution among males: A "Consumers' Report." *Current Psychology, 20,* 363–376.

Schecter, E. (2009). Sexual fluidity: The new sexuality paradigm. Available: http://www.goodtherapy.org/blog/sexual-fluidity/ (Last visited 3/23/11).

Scheer, S., Peterson, I., Page-Shafer, K., Delgado, V., Gleghorn, A., Ruiz, J., Molitor, F., McFarland, W., Klausner, J., & Young Women's Survey Team. (2002). Sexual and drug use behavior among women who have sex with both women and men: Results of a population-based survey. *American Journal of Public Health, 92,* 1110–1112.

Schei, B., & Stigum, H. (2010). A study of men who pay for sex, based on the Norwegian National Sex Surveys. *Scandinavian Journal of Public Health, 38,* 135–140.

Schick, V., Calabrese, S. K., & Herbenick, D. (2014). Survey methods in sexuality research. In D. L. Tolman & L. M. Diamond (Eds.), *APA handbook of sexuality and psychology* (pp. 81–98). Washington, DC: American Psychological Association.

Schmidt, P. (2011, September 18). Scholars of legal brothels offer a new take on the "oldest profession." *Chronicle of Higher Education.* Available: http://chronicle.com/article/Scholars-of-Brothels/ 129047 (Last visited 10/3/11).

Schmitt, D. P. (2003). Universal sex differences in the desire for sexual variety: Tests from 52 nations, 6 continents, and 13 islands. *Journal of Personality and Social Psychology, 85,* 85–104.

Schmitt, D. P., & Buss, D. M. (2001). Human mate poaching: Tactics and temptations for infiltrating existing partnerships. *Journal of Personality and Social Psychology, 80,* 894–917.

Schmucker, M., & Losel, F. (2008). Does sexual offender treatment work? A systematic review of outcome evaluations. *Psicothema, 20,* 10–19.

Schnarch, D. (2002). *Resurrecting sex.* New York: HarperCollins.

Schwartz, J. (2007, January 27). Of gay sheep, modern science and the perils of bad publicity. *New York Times,* pp. A1, A16.

Schwartz, S. (2000). *Abnormal psychology: A discovery approach.* Mountain View, CA: Mayfield.

Schwarzer, U., Sommer, F., Klotz, T., Braun, M., Reifenrath, B., & Engelmann, U. (2001). The prevalence of Peyronie's disease: Results of a large survey. *BJU International, 88,* 727–730.

Schwimmer, B. (1997). The Dani of New Guinea. Available: http://www.umanitoba.ca/faculties/arts/anthropology/tutor/case_studies/dani/ (Last visited 11/3/05).

Scorolli, C., Ghirlanda, S., Enquist, M., Zattoni, S., & Jannini, E. A. (2007). Relative prevalence of different fetishes. *International Journal of Impotence, 19,* 432–437.

Scott, D. (2010). *Extravagant abjection: Blackness, power, and sexuality in the African American literary imagination (sexual cultures)*. New York: New York University Press.

Sears, A. E. (1989). The legal case for restricting pornography. In D. Zillman & J. Bryant (Eds.), *Pornography: Research advances and policy considerations*. Hillsdale, NJ: Erlbaum.

Sedlak, A. J., Mettenburg, J., Basena, M., Petta, I., McPherson, K., Greene, A., et al. (2010). *Fourth National Incident Study of Child Abuse and Neglect (NIS-4): Report to Congress*. Washington, DC: U.S. Department of Health and Human Services, Administration for Children and Families.

Seligman, L., & Hardenberg, S. A. (2000). Assessment and treatment of paraphilias. *Journal of Counseling and Development, 78,* 107–113.

Senecal, M., Brisson, M., Maunsell, E., Ferenczy, A., Franco, E. L., Ratman, S., et al. (2011). Loss of quality of life associated with genital warts: Baseline analyses from a prospective study. *Sexually Transmitted Infections, 87,* 209–215.

Senn, T. E., Carey, M. P., Vanable, P. A., Coury-Doniger, P., & Urban, M. (2007). Characteristics of sexual abuse in childhood and adolescence influence sexual risk behavior in adulthood. *Archives of Sexual Behavior, 36,* 637–645.

Senn, T. E., Scott-Sheldon, A. J., Seward, D. X., Wright, E. M., & Carey, M. P. (2011). Sexual partner concurrency of urban male and female STD clinic patients: A qualitative study. *Archives of Sexual Behavior, 40,* 775–784.

Seto, M. (2008). Pedophilia: Psychopathology and theory. In D. R. Laws & W. T. O'Donohue (Eds.), *Sexual deviance: Theory, assessment, and treatment* (2nd ed.). New York: Guilford Press.

Sexual assault in the military. (April 5, 2013). *The Week,* p. 11.

Sexuality Information and Education Council of the United States (SIECUS). (2004). *Guidelines for comprehensive sexuality education* (3rd ed.). New York: Author.

Sexuality Information and Education Council of the United States (SIECUS). (2009). Fact sheet: What the research says … comprehensive sex education. Available: http://www.siecus.org (Last visited 8/17/10).

Shackelford, T. K., Goetz, A. T., LaMunyon, C. W., Quintus, B. J., & Weekes-Shackelford, V. A. (2004). Sex differences in sexual psychology produce sex-similar preferences for a short-term mate. *Archives of Sexual Behavior, 33,* 405–412.

Shattock, R. J., & Rosenberg, Z. (2012). Microbicides: Topical prevention against HIV. *Cold Harbor Perspectives in Medicine.* DOI: 10.110.cshperspect.a007385.

Shaver, P. (1984). *Emotions, relationships, and health*. Newbury Park, CA: Sage.

Shaver, P., Hazan, C., & Bradshaw, D. (1988). Love as attachment: The integration of three behavioral systems. In R. Sternberg & M. Barnes (Eds.), *The psychology of love*. New Haven, CT: Yale University Press.

Shelton, J. F., Geraghty, E. M., Tancredi, D. J., Delwiche, L. D., Schmidt, R. J., Ritz, B., Hansen, R., & Hertz-Picciotto, I. (2014). Neurodevelopmental disorders and prenatal residential proximity to agricultural pesticides: The CHARGE study. *Environmental Health Perspectives, 122*(10). Available: http://ehp.niehs.nih.gov/1307044/ (Last visited 12/20/14).

Shilts, R. (1987). *And the band played on: Politics, people, and the AIDS epidemic*. New York: St. Martin's Press.

Siegel, K., & Scrimshaw, E. W. (2006). Diminished sexual activity, interest, and feelings of attractiveness among HIV-infected women in two eras of the AIDS epidemic. *Archives of Sexual Behavior, 35,* 437–449.

Simon, W., & Gagnon, J. H. (1987). A sexual scripts approach. In W. T. O'Donohue (Ed.), *Theories of human sexuality*. New York: Plenum Press.

Singh, D., Deogracias, J. J., Johnson, L. L., Bradley, S. J., Kibblewhite, S. J., Owen-Anderson, A., Peterson-Badali, M., Meyer-Bahlburg, H. F. L., & Zucker, K. J. (2010). The gender identity/gender dysphoria questionnaire for adolescents and adults: Further validity evidence. *Journal of Sex Research, 47*(1), 49–58.

Sinkovic, M., Stulhofer, A., & Bozic, J. (2013). Revisiting the association between pornography use and risky sexual behaviors: The role of early exposure to pornography and sexual sensation seeking. *Journal of Sex Research, 50,* 633–641.

Sipiski, M. L., Alexander, C. J., Gómez-Marín, O., & Spalding, J. (2007). The impact of spinal cord injury on psychogenic sexual arousal in males. *Journal of Urology, 177,* 247–251.

Slater, D. (2013, January 13). Darwin was wrong about dating. *New York Times,* pp. SR 7, 11.

Slowinski, J. (2007). Sexual problems and dysfunctions of men. In A. Owens & M. Tepper (Eds.), *Sexual health: State-of-the art treatments and research*. Westport, CT: Praeger.

Smith, A., & Dugga, M. (2013). Online dating and relationships. *Pew Research Internet Project.* Available: http://www.pewinternet.org/2013/10/21/online-dating-relationships/ (Last visited 9/30/14).

Smith, A. M. A., Rissel, C. E., Richters, J., Grulich, A. E., & de Visser, R. O. (2003). Sex in Australia: Sexual identity, sexual attraction and sexual experience among a representative sample of adults. *Australian and New Zealand Journal of Public Health, 2,* 138–145.

Smith, L. M., Kaufman, J. S., Strumpf, E. C., & Lévesque, L. E. (2014). Effect of human papillomavirus (HPV) vaccination on clinical indicators of sexual behavior among adolescent girls: The Ontario Grade 8 HPV Vaccine Cohort Study. *Canadian Medical Association Journal.* doi: 10.1503/cmaj.140900.

Smith, M. D., Grov, C., Seal, D. W., & McCall, P. (2013). A social-cognitive analysis of how young men become involved in male escorting. *Journal of Sex Research, 50,* 1–10.

Smoak, N. D., Scott-Sheldon, L. A. J., Johnson, B. T., Carey, M. P., & SHARP Research Team. (2006). Sexual risk reduction interventions do not inadvertently increase the overall frequency of sexual behavior: A meta-analysis of 174 studies with 116,735 participants. *Journal of Acquired Immune Deficiency Syndromes, 41,* 374–384.

Smolak, L., & Murnen, S. K. (2011). Gender, self-objectification and pubic hair removal. *Sex Roles, 65*(7–8), 506–517.

Snyder, H. N., & Sickmund, M. (2006). *Juvenile offenders and victims: 2006 national report*. Washington, DC: U.S. Department of Justice.

Snyder, P. J. (2014). Male reproductive aging. In J. Strauss & R. L. Iarbieri (Eds.), *Yen & Jaffe reproductive endocrinology* (pp. 340–351). Philadelphia: Elsevier.

So, H., & Cheung, F. M. (2005). Review of Chinese sex attitudes and applicability of sex therapy for Chinese couples with sexual dysfunction. *Journal of Sex Research, 42*(2), 93–101.

Social, Digital and Mobile Around the World. (2014). Active users by social platform. Available: http://www.slideshare.net/wearesocialsg/social-digital-mobile-around-the-world-january-2014 (Last visited 4/2/14).

Social evolution changed nature of sodomy. (2003, June 27). *Chicago Tribune,* p. A4.

Solomon, J. (1998, March 16). An insurance policy with sex appeal. *Newsweek*, p. 44.

Solomon, S. E., Rothblum, E. D., & Balsam, K. F. (2005). Money, housework, sex, and conflict: Same-sex couples in civil unions, those not in civil unions, and heterosexual married siblings. *Sex Roles, 52*, 561–575.

Sorenson, S. B., & Siegel, J. M. (1992). Gender, ethnicity, and sexual assault: Findings from a Los Angeles study. *Journal of Social Issues, 48*(1), 93–104.

Spector, D. (2013, Feb. 12). The *Sports Illustrated* swimsuit issue: A $1 billion empire. *Business Insider.* Available: http://www.businessinsider.com/business-facts-about-the-sports-illustrated-swimsuit-issue-2013-2 (Last visited 6/30/14).

Sprecher, S. (1994). Two sides to the breakup of dating relationships. *Personal Relationships, 1,* 199–222.

Sprecher, S. (2002). Sexual satisfaction in premarital relationships: Associations with satisfaction, love, commitment, and stability. *Journal of Sex Research, 39*(3), 190–196.

Sprecher, S., & McKinney, K. (1993). *Sexuality.* Newbury Park, CA: Sage.

Sprecher, S., & Toro-Morn, M. (2002). A study of men and women from different sides of earth to determine if men are from Mars and women are from Venus in their beliefs about love and romantic relationships. *Sex Roles, 46*(5–6), 131–147.

Stanger-Hall, K. F., & Hall, D. W. (2011). Abstinence-only education and teen pregnancy rates: Why we need comprehensive sex education in the U.S. *PLos ONE, 6*(10). doi: 10.1371/journal.pone.0024658.

Staples, R. (1991). The sexual revolution and the Black middle class. In R. Staples (Ed.), *The Black family* (4th ed.). Belmont, CA: Wadsworth.

Staples, R. (2006). *Exploring Black sexuality.* Boulder, CO: Rowman & Littlefield.

Staples, R., & Johnson, L. B. (1993). *Black families at the crossroads: Challenges and prospects.* San Francisco: Jossey-Bass.

Steele, V. R., Staley, C., Fong, T., & Prause, N. (2013). Sexual desire, not hypersexuality, is related to neurophysiological responses elicited by sexual images. *Socioaffective Neuroscience & Psychology, 3,* 20770.

Stemple, L., & Meyer, I. H. (2014). The sexual victimization of men in America: New data challenge old assumptions. *American Journal of Public Health, 104,* e19–e26.

Sternberg, R. (1986). A triangular theory of love. *Psychological Review, 93,* 119–135.

Sternberg, R., & Grajek, S. (1984). The nature of love. *Journal of Personality and Social Psychology, 47,* 312–327.

Sternberg, R. J. (1988). *The triangle of love: Intimacy, passion, commitment.* New York: Basic Books, 1988.

Sternberg, R. J., & Barnes, M. L. (1989). *The psychology of love.* New Haven, CT: Yale University Press.

Sternberg, S. (2005, February 24). In India, sex trade fuels HIV's spread. *USA Today,* pp. D1–D2.

Sternberg, S. (2008, October 27). Early HIV treatment radically boosts survival. *USA Today,* p. D7.

StopItNow. (2014). What is considered child sexual abuse. Available: http://www.stopitnow.org/warning_signs_csa_defintion. (Last visited: 10/2/14).

Stop Violence Against Women. (2014). Myths & facts about date rape. Available: http://www.domesticviolenceinfo.ca/article/myths-and-facts-about-date-rape-236-asp (Last visited 9/18/14).

Storms, M. D. (1980). Theories of sexual orientation. *Journal of Personality and Social Psychology, 38,* 783–792.

Storms, M. D. (1981). A theory of erotic orientation development. *Psychological Review, 88,* 340–353.

Strasburger, V. C., Jordan, A. B., & Donnerstein, E. (2010). Health effects of media on children and adolescents. *Pediatrics, 125,* 756–767.

Strassberg, D. S., & Lowe, K. (1995). Volunteer bias in sex research. *Archives of Sexual Behavior, 24*(4), 369–382.

Strassburg, D. S., & Mackaronis, J. E. (2014). Sexuality and psychotherapy. In D. L. Tolman & L. M. Diamond (Eds.), *APA handbook of sexuality and psychology* (pp. 105–135). Washington, DC: American Psychological Association.

Struckman-Johnson, C., Struckman-Johnson, D., & Anderson, P. B. (2003). Tactics of sexual coercion: When men and women won't take no for an answer. *Journal of Sex Research, 40,* 76–86.

Stulhofer, A., & Ajdukovic, D. (2011). Should we take **anodyspareunia** seriously? A descriptive analysis of pain during receptive anal intercourse in young heterosexual women. *Journal of Sex & Marital Therapy, 37,* 346–358.

Su, J. R., Beltrami, J. F., Zaidi, A. A., & Weinstock, A. A. (2011). Primary and secondary syphilis among Black and Hispanic men who have sex with men: Case report data from 27 states. *Annals of Internal Medicine, 155,* 145–151.

Sumari-de Boer, I. M., Sprangers, M. A., Prins, J. M, & Nieuwkerk, P. T. (2012). HIV stigma and depressive symptoms are related to adherence and virological response to antiretroviral treatment among immigrant and indigenous HIV infected patients. *AIDS and Behavior, 16,* 1681–1689.

Supreme Court of the United States. (2003, June 26). John Geddes Lawrence and Tyron Garner, Petitioners *v.* Texas. Majority opinion.

Svoboda, E. (2008). Scents and sensibility. *Psychology Today,* January-February.

Swami, V. (2009). Body appreciation, media influence, and weight status predict consideration of cosmetic surgery among female undergraduates. *Body Image, 6,* 315–317.

Swami, V., & Tovee, M. J. (2013). Men's oppressive beliefs predict their breast size preferences in women. *Archives of Sexual Behavior, 42,* 1199–1207.

Swami, V., Hadji-Michael, M., & Furnham, A. (2008). Personality and individual difference correlates of positive body image. *Body Image, 5,* 322–325.

Swanson, S., Crow, S., LeGrange, D., Swendsen, J., & Merikangas, K. (2011). Prevalence and correlates of eating disorders in adolescents. *Archives of General Psychology.* Available: www.nationaleatingdisorders.org/prevalence-and-correlates-eating-disorders-adolescents (Last visited 1/2/15).

Taberner, P. V. (1985). *Aphrodisiacs: The science and the myth.* Philadelphia: University of Pennsylvania Press.

Tabrizi, S. N., Fairley, C. K., Bradshaw, C. S., & Garland, S. M. (2006). *Gardnerella vaginosis* and *Atopobium vaginae* in virginal women. *Sexually Transmitted Diseases, 33,* 663–665.

Tanfer, K., Cubbins, L. A., & Billy, J. O. G. (1995). Gender, race, class and self-reported sexually transmitted disease incidence. *Family Planning Perspectives, 27,* 196–202.

Tannen, D. (2001). Sex, lies and conversation: Why is it so hard for men and women to talk to each other? In E. Ksenych & D. Liu (Eds.). *Conflict, Order and Action: Readings in Sociology.* Toronto, Ontario: Canadian Scholars' Press.

Tanner, L. (2005, July 17). Latest research findings: Research is often wrong. *Indianapolis Star,* p. A23.

Tao, G. (2008). Sexual orientation and related viral sexually transmitted disease rates among U.S. women aged 15 to 44 years. *American Journal of Public Health, 98,* 1007–1009.

Tashiro, T., & Frazier, P. (2003). "I'll never be in a relationship like that again": Personal growth following romantic relationship breakups. *Personal Relationships, 10,* 113–128.

Taylor, V., & Rupp, L. J. (2004). Chicks with dicks, men in dresses: What it means to be a drag queen. *Journal of Homosexuality, 46,* 113–133.

Teen girls tell their stories of sex trafficking and exploitation in U.S. (2006, February 9). ABC News. Available: http://abcnews. go.com/Primetime/story?id515967788page51 (Last visited 3/30/06).

"Teen health and the media." (2014). Fast facts: Television is a major part of daily life. Available: http://depts.washington.edu/thmedia/view.cgi?section=medialiteracy&page=fastfacts (Last visited 11/19/14).

Templeman, T., & Stinnett, R. (1991). Patterns of sexual arousal and history in a "normal" sample of young men. *Archives of Sexual Behavior, 20*(2), 137–150.

Tepper, M. S., & Owens, A. F. (2007). Current controversies in sexual health: Sexual addiction and compulsion. In A. F. Owens & M. S. Tepper (Eds.), *Sexual health: State-of-the-art treatments and research.* Westport, CT: Praeger.

Thables, V. (1997). A survey analysis of women's long-term post-divorce adjustment. *Journal of Divorce and Remarriage, 27*(3–4), 163–175.

Thayer, L. (1986). *On communication.* Norwood, NJ: Ablex.

The Advocates for Human Rights. (2009). *The facts: Sex trafficking.* Minneapolis: Author.

The National Campaign to Prevent Teen and Unplanned Pregnancy. (2009). Sex and tech: Results from a survey of teens and young adults. Available: https://thenationalcampaign.org/resource/sex-and-tech (Last visited 5/27/15).

The White House Council on Women and Girls. (2014). *Rape and sexual assault: A renewed call to action.* Washington, DC: The White House.

Thigpen, J. W. (2009). Early sexual behavior in a sample of low-income, African-American children. *Journal of Sex Research, 46,* 67–69.

Thigpen, J. W. (2012). Childhood sexuality. In L. M. Carpenter & J. DeLamater (Eds.), *Sex for life.* New York: New York University Press.

Thomas, D., Flaherty, T. D., & Binns, H. (2004). Parent expectations and comfort with discussion of normal childhood sexuality and sexual abuse prevention during office visits. *Ambulatory Pediatrics, 4*(3), 232–236.

Thomas, S. B., & Quinn, S. C. (1991). The Tuskegee syphilis study, 1932 to 1972: Implications for HIV education and AIDS risk education programs in the Black community. *American Journal of Public Health, 81*(11), 1498–1504.

Thurman, A. R., Holden, A. E. C., Shain, R. N., & Perdue, S. T. (2009). The male sexual partners of adult versus teen women with sexually transmitted infections. *Sexually Transmitted Diseases, 36,* 768–774.

Tiefer, L. (2001). A new view of women's sexual problems: Why new? Why now? *Journal of Sex Research, 38*(2), 89–110.

Tiefer, L. (2004). *Sex is not a natural act and other essays* (2nd ed.). Boulder, CO: Westview Press.

Tiefer, L. (2012). Medicalizations and demedicalization of sexuality therapies. *Journal of Sex Research, 49,* 311–318.

Tiggemann, M. (2005). Television and adolescent body image: The role of program content and viewing motivation. *Journal of Social and Clinical Psychology, 24*(30), 361–381.

Tomassilli, J. C., Golub, S. A., Bimbi, D. S., & Parsons, J. T. (2009). Behind closed doors: An exploration of kinky sexual behaviors in urban lesbian and bisexual women. *Journal of Sex Research, 46,* 438–445.

Tovee, J., Tasker, K., & Benson, P. J. (2000). Is symmetry a visual cue to attractiveness in the human female body? *Evolution and Human Behavior, 21,* 191–200.

Toxic shock syndrome. (2012). *MedlinePlus.* Available: http://www.nlm.nih.gov/medlineplus/ency/article/000653.htm (Last visited 1/13/15).

Treas, J., & Giesen, D. (2000). Sexual infidelity among married and cohabiting Americans. *Journal of Marriage and Family, 62,* 48–60.

Tronstein, E. (2011). Genital shedding of herpes simplex virus among symptomatic and asymptomatic persons with HSV-2 infection. *Journal of the American Medical Association, 305,* 1411–1449.

Trujillo, C. M. (1997). Sexual identity and the discontents of difference. In B. Greene (Ed.), *Ethnic and cultural diversity among lesbians and gay men.* Thousand Oaks, CA: Sage.

Truong, H. M., et al. (2006). Increases in sexually transmitted infections and sexual risk behavior without a concurrent increase in HIV incidence among men who have sex with men in San Francisco: A suggestion of HIV serosorting? *Sexually Transmitted Infections, 82,* 461–466.

Turner syndrome. (2014). Genetics home reference. Available: http://ghr.nlm.nih.gov/condition/turner-syndrome (Last visited 7/11/14).

2011 National School Climate Survey (2012). *GLSEN.* Available: http://www.glsen.org/sites/default/files/2011%20National%20School%20Climate%20Survey%20Full%20Report.pdf (Last visited 1/26/15).

U.S. Attorney General's Commission on Pornography (AGCOP). (1986). *Final report.* Washington, DC: U.S. Government Printing Office.

U.S. Census Bureau. (2012.7a). America's families and living arrangements: 2012. Available: http://www.census.gov/prod/2013pubs/p20-570.pdf (Last viewed 9/16/14).

U.S. Census Bureau. (2012.13a). Nearly 1 in 5 people have a disability in the United States, Census Bureau Reports. Available: https://www.census.gov/newsroom/releases/archives/miscellaneous/cb12-134.html (Last visited 5/6/15).

U.S. Census Bureau. (2013.7a). Household relationship and living arrangements of children under 18 years, by age and sex: 2013. Available: http://www.census.gov/hhes/families/data/cps2013C.html) (Last visited 9/30/14).

U.S. Census Bureau. (2013.7b). National marriage and divorce rate trends. Available: http://www.cdc.gov/nchs/nvss/marriage_divorce_tables.htm (Last visited 9/27/14).

U.S. Census Bureau. (2014.7a). American's families and living arrangements: 2013. Available: http://www.census.gov/newsroom/releases/pdf/cb14ff-21_unmarried.pdf (Last visited 9/4/14).

U.S. Census Bureau. (2014.7b). Characteristics of same-sex couple households: 2013. Available: http://www.census.gov/hhes/samesex/ (Last viewed 9/27/14).

U.S. Department of Defense. (2013). Department of Defense annual report on sexual assault in the military: Fiscal year 2012. Washington, DC.

U.S. Department of Health and Human Services, Office on Women's Health. (2014). Breastfeeding. Available: http://www.womenshealth.gov/publications/our-publications/fact-sheet/Breastfeeding.pdf (Last visited 12/18/14).

U.S. Department of Health and Human Services. (2000). The Development Disabilities Assistance and Bill of Rights Act of 2000. Available: http://www.acf.hhs.gov/programs/add/ddact/DDACT2.html (Last visited 9/17/08).

U.S. Department of Health and Human Services. (2010). Opportunistic infections and their relationship to HIV/AIDS. Available: http://www.aid-basics/staying-healthy-with-hiv-aids/potential-related-health (Last visited 12/29/14).

U.S. Department of Health and Human Services. (2011.15a). Healthy people, 2020: Lesbian, gay, bisexual and transgender health. Available: http://www.healthypeople.gov/2020/topicsobjectives2020/overview.aspx?topicid525 (Last visited 7/27/11).

U.S. Department of Health and Human Services. (2011.16a). HIV/AIDS overview: Treatment. Available: http://www.aids.gov/hiv-aids-basics/hiv-aids-101/overview/treatment (Last visited 12/21/11).

U.S. Department of Health and Human Services. (2012.7a). Lesbian, gay, and transgender health. Available: http://www.healthypeople.gov/2020/topics-objectives/topic/lesbian-gay-bisexual-and-transgender-health (Last visited 12/2/14).

U.S. Department of Health and Human Services. (2012.12a). Infertility fact sheet. Available: http://www.womenshealth.gov/publications/our-publications/fact-sheet/infertility.html#b (Last visited 12/16/14).

U.S. Department of Justice. (2010). *Criminal victimization, 2009.* Washington, DC: Bureau of Justice Statistics.

U.S. Department of Justice. (2013). *National Crime Victimization Survey.* Washington, DC: Bureau of Justice Statistics.

U.S. Department of Labor. (2011). Family and Medical Leave Act, 2011. Available: http://www.dol.gov/whd/fmla/ (Last visited 10/30/11).

U.S. Department of State. (2010). *The 2010 trafficking in persons report.* Washington, DC: Author.

U.S. District Court, Eastern District of Pennsylvania. (2007). Attorney General of the United States: Final adjudication Lowell A. Reed, Jr., March 22, 2007. Available: http://www.paed.uscourts.gov (Last visited 6/12/08).

U.S. Equal Employment Opportunity Commission. (2009). Facts about sexual harassment FSE/4. Available: http://www.eeoc.gov/facts/fs-sex.html (Last visited 8/29/11).

U.S. Equal Employment Opportunity Commission. (n.d.). Sexual harassment charges EEOC & FEPAs combined: FY 1997–FY 2011.

U.S. Food and Drug Administration. (2014, December 10). FDA press release: FDA approves Gardasil 9 for prevention of certain types of cancers caused by five additional types of HPV. Available: http://www.fda/gov/NewsEvents/Newsroom/PressAnnouncements/ucm42645.htm (Last visited 12/14/14).

U.S. Merit Systems Protection Board. (1995). *Sexual harassment in the federal workplace: Trends, progress, continuing challenges.* Washington, DC: Author.

U.S. Preventive Services Task Force. (2012). Final recommendation statement: Prostate cancer screening. Available: http://www.uspreventiveservicestaskforce.org/Page/Document/RecommendationStatementFinal/prostate-cancer-screening (Last visited 1/8/15).

U.S. Preventive Services Task Force. (2015). Breast cancer screening draft recommendations. Available: http://screeningforbreastcancer.org/?ds=1&s=breast%2520cancer%2520screening (Last visited 5/7/15).

Ullman, S. E. (2007). Comparing gang and individual rapes in a community sample of urban women. *Violence and Victims, 22,* 43–51.

Understanding preeclampsia and eclampsia–The basics. (2015). *WedMD.* Available: http://www.webmd.com/hypertension-high-blood-pressure/guide/understanding-preeclampsia-eclampsia-basic-information (Last visited 5/4/15).

United Nations Development Programme. (2014). Human development report. Available: http://hdr.undp.org/en/content/table-4-gender-inequality-index (Last visited 10/15/14).

United Nations General Assembly. (1993). Standard rules on the equalization of opportunities for persons with disabilities. Available: http://www.un.org/esa/socdev/enable/rights/wgrefa14.html (Last visited 1/10/06).

Upadhyay, U. D., Desai, S., Zildar, V., Weitz, T. A., Grossman, D., Anderson, P., & Taylor, D. (2014, December 5). Incidence of emergency department visits and complications after abortions. *Obstetrics & Gynecology* (Published ahead of print).

Ussher, J. M., Perz, J., & Gilbert, E. (2012). Changes to sexual well-being and intimacy after breast cancer. *Cancer Nursing, 35*(6), 456–465.

Valente, S. M. (2005). Sexual abuse of boys. *Journal of Child and Adolescent Psychiatric Nursing, 18,* 10–16.

Valera, R., Sawyer, R., & Schiraldi, G. (2001). Perceived health needs of inner-city street prostitutes: A preliminary study. *American Journal of Health and Behavior, 25,* 50–59.

van Anders, S. (2012). Testosterone and sexual desire in healthy women and men. *Archives of Sexual Behavior, 41,* 1471–1484. Available: http://www.academia.edu/1454716/Testosterone_and_Sexual_Desire_in_Healthy_Women_and_Men (Last visited 7/2/14).

van Berlo, W., & Ensink, B. (2000). Problems with sexuality after sexual assault. *Annual Review of Sex Research, 11,* 235–257.

van den Brink, F., Smeets, M. A. M., Hesssen, D. J., Talens, J. G., & Woertman, L. (2013). Body satisfaction and sexual health in Dutch female university students. *Journal of Sex Research, 50*(8), 786–794.

van Lankveld, J. (2013). Does "normal" sexual functioning exist? *Journal of Sex Research, 50*(3–4), 205–206.

Vannier, S. A., & O'Sullivan, L. F. (2010). Sex without desire: Characteristics of occasions of sexual compliance in young committed relationships. *Journal of Sex Research, 47,* 429–439.

van Veen, M. G., Gotz, H. M., van Leeuwen, P. A., Prins, M., & van de Laar, M. J. W. (2010). HIV and sexual risk behavior among commercial sex workers in the Netherlands. *Archives of Sexual Behavior, 39,* 714–723.

Vanwesenbeeck, I. (2013). Prostitution push and pull: Male and female perspectives. *Journal of Sex Research,* 50, 11–16.

Velez-Blasini, C. J. (2008). Evidence against alcohol as a proximal cause of sexual risk taking among college students. *Journal of Sex Research, 45,* 118–128.

Vendituoli, M. (2014, July 4). In sexual-misconduct policies, difficulty arises in defining "yes." *Chronicle of Higher Education,* p. A10.

Verschuren, J. E. A., Enzlin, P., Dijkstra, P. U., Geertzen, J. H. B., & Dekker, R. (2010). Chronic disease and sexuality: A generic conceptual framework. *Journal of Sex Research 47*(2), 153–170.

Victims of Trafficking and Violence Protection Act of 2000. (2000). Available: http://www.state.gov/documents/organization/10492.pdf (Last visited 6/16/08).

Vocks, S., Stahn, C. A., Loenser, K., & Legenbauer, T. (2009). Eating and body image disturbances in male-to-female and female-to-male transsexuals. *Archives of Sexual Behavior, 38,* 364–377.

Voosen, P. (2013, Sept. 13). Inside a revolution in mental health. *The Chronicle Review,* B6–B9.

Vulvodynia. (2013). National Institutes of Health. Available: http://www.nichd.nih.gov/health/topics/vulvodynia/Pages/default.aspx (Last visited 1/14/15).

Wade, L. D., Kremer, E. C., & Brown, J. (2005). The incidental orgasm: The presence of clitoral knowledge and the absence of orgasm for women. *Women & Health, 41*(1), 117–138.

Wald, A., et al. (2005). The relationship between condom use and herpes simplex virus acquisition. *Annals of Internal Medicine, 143,* 707–713.

Walker, J., Archer, J., & Davies, M. (2005). Effects of rape on men: A descriptive analysis. *Archives of Sexual Behavior, 34,* 69–80.

Walls, N. E. (2008). Toward a multidimensional understanding of heterosexism: The changing nature of prejudice. *Journal of Homosexuality, 55,* 20–70.

Walter, C. (2008, Feb.–Mar.). Affairs of the lips. *Scientific American Mind,* pp. 24–29. Available: http://www.sciAmMind.com (Last visited 7/25/08).

Walters, G. D., Knight, R. A., & Langstrom, N. (2011). Is hypersexuality dimensional? Evidence for the *DSM-5* from general population and clinical samples. *Archives of Sexual Behavior, 40,* 1309–1321.

Walters, M. L., Chen, J., & Breiding, M. J. (2013). *National Intimate Partner and Sexual Violence Survey (NISVS): Victimization by sexual orientation.* Atlanta: Centers for Disease Control and Prevention.

Ward, B. W., Dahlhamer, J. M., Galinsky, A. M., & Joestl, S. S. (2014, July 15). Sexual orientation and health among U.S. adults: National Health Interview Survey, 2013. *National Health Statistics Reports, 77.* Available: http://www.cdc.gov/nchs/data/nhsr/nhsr077.pdf (Last visited 1/14/15).

Ward, H., & Day, S. (2006). What happens to women who sell sex? Report of a unique occupational cohort. *Sexually Transmitted Infections, 82,* 413–417.

Ward, T., & Beech, A. R. (2008). An integrated theory of sex offending. In D. R. Laws & W. T. O'Donohue (Eds.), *Sexual deviance: Theory, assessment, and treatment* (2nd ed.). New York: Guilford Press.

Webb, P. (1983). *The erotic arts.* New York: Farrar, Straus & Giroux.

Weeks, J. (1986). *Sexuality.* New York: Tavistock/Ellis Horwood.

Weinberg, M. S., Williams, C. J., & Moser, C. (1984). The social constituents of sadomasochism. *Social Problems, 31,* 379–389.

Weinberg, M. S., Williams, C. J., Kleiner, S., & Irizarry, Y. (2010). Pornography, normalization, and empowerment. *Archives of Sexual Behavior, 39,* 1389–1401.

Weinstock, H., Berman, S., & Cates, W. (2004). Sexually transmitted diseases among American youth: Incidence and prevalence estimates, 2000. *Perspectives on Sexual and Reproductive Health, 36*(1), 6–10.

Weis, D. L. (2002). The need to integrate sexual theory and research. In M. W. Wiederman & B. Whitley, Jr. (Eds.), *Handbook for conducting research on human sexuality.* Mahwah, NJ: Erlbaum.

Weisberg, D. K. (1990). *Children of the night.* New York: Free Press.

Weitzer, R. (2005). New directions in research in prostitution. *Crime, Law and Social Change, 43,* 211–235.

Weitzer, R. (2010). The mythology of prostitution: Advocacy research and public policy. *Sex Research and Social Policy, 7,* 15–29.

Wells, B. (1986). Predictors of female nocturnal orgasm. *Journal of Sex Research, 23,* 421–427.

Wells, H. B. (1980). *Being lucky.* Bloomington: Indiana University Press.

Wells, T., Baguley, T., Sergeant, M., & Dunn, A. (2013). Perceptions of human attractiveness comprising face and voice cues. *Archives of Sexual Behavior, 42,* 805–811.

West, S. L., Vinikoor, L. C., & Zolnoun, D. (2004). A systematic review of the literature on female sexual dysfunction prevalence and predictors. *Annual Review of Sex Research, 15,* 40–172.

What is considered child sexual abuse? (2014). StopItNow. Available: http://.stopitnow.org/warning_signs_csa_defintion (Last visited 10/8/14).

What to know about ectopic pregnancy. (2014). *WebMD.* Available: http://www.webmd.com/baby/guide/pregnancy-ectopic-pregnancy?page=2 (Last visited 12/15/14).

Wheeler, J., Newring, K. A. B., & Draper, C. (2008). Transvestic fetishism: Psychopathology and theory. In D. R. Laws & W. T. O'Donohue (Eds.), *Sexual deviance: Theory, assessment, and treatment* (2nd ed.). New York: Guilford Press.

When yes means yes. (2014, September 9). *New York Times,* p. A26.

Where we stand: Gay and lesbian parents. (2014). Healthychildren.org Available: http://www.healthychildren.org/English/family-life/family-dynamics/types-of-families/Pages/Where-We-Stand-Gay-and-Lesbian-Parents.aspx (Last visited 9/27/14).

Whipple, B. (2002). Review of Milan Zaviacic's book: *The human female prostate: From vestigial Skene paraurethral glands and ducts to woman's functional prostate. Archives of Sexual Behavior, 31,* 457–458.

Whipple, B., & Komisaruk, B. (1999). Beyond the G spot: Recent research on female sexuality. *Psychiatric Annals, 29,* 34–37.

Whipple, B., Knowles, J., & Davis, J. (2007). The health benefits of sexual expression. In M. S. Tepper & A. F. Owens (Eds.), *Sexual health: Vol. 1. Psychological foundations.* Westport, CT: Praeger.

Whipple, B., Ogden, G., & Komisaruk, B. R. (1992). Physiological correlates of imagery-induced orgasm in women. *Archives of Sexual Behavior, 21*(2), 121–133.

Whitehead, M., & Holland, P. (2003). What puts children of lone parents at a health disadvantage?. *Lancet, 361*(9354), 271–271.

White House Task Force to Protect Students from Sexual Harassment. (2014). *Not alone: The first report of the White House Task Force to protect students from sexual assault.* Washington, DC: The White House.

Widdice, L. E., Bernstein, D. J., Leonard, A. C., Marsolo, K. A., & Kahn, J. A. (2011). Adherence to the HPV vaccine dosing intervals and factors associated with completion of 3 doses. *Pediatrics, 127,* 77–84.

Widom, C. S., & Kuhns, J. B. (1996). Childhood victimization and subsequent risk for promiscuity, prostitution, and teenage pregnancy: A prospective study. *American Journal of Public Health, 86*(11), 1607–1612.

Wiederman, M. W. (1999). Volunteer bias in sexuality research using college student participation. *Journal of Sex Research, 36,* 59–66.

Wiederman, M. W. (2005). The gendered nature of sexual scripts. *The Family Journal, 13,* 496–502.

Williams, C. J., & Weinberg, M. S. (2003). Zoophilia in men: A study of sexual interest in animals. *Archives of Sexual Behavior, 32,* 523–535.

Williams, T., Pepitone, M., Christensen, S., & Cooke, B. (2000, March 30). Finger-length ratios and sexual orientation. *Nature, 404,* 455–456.

Willoughby, B. J., Carroll, J. S., Nelson, L. J., & Padilla-Walker, L. M. (2014). Associations between relational sexual behavior, pornography use, and pornography acceptance among US college students. *Culture, Health & Sexuality: An International Journal of Research, Intervention and Care.* doi: 10.1080/13691058.2014.927075.

Willoughby, J. B., Farero, A.M., & Busby, D. M. (2014). Exploring the effects of sexual desire discrepancy among married couples. *Archives of Sexual Behavior, 43,* 551–562.

Wilson, D. P., et al. (2010). Serosorting may increase the risk of HIV acquisition among men who have sex with men. *Sexually Transmitted Diseases, 37,* 13–17.

Wilson, D. P., Law, M. G., Grulich, A. E., Cooper, D. A., & Kaldor, J. M. (2008). Relation between HIV viral load and infectiousness: A model-based analysis. *The Lancet, 372,* 314–320.

Wingood, G. M., DiClemente, R. J., Bernhardt, J. M., Harrington, K., Davies, S. L., Robillard, A., et al. (2002). A prospective study of exposure to rap music videos and African American female adolescents' health. *American Journal of Public Health, 93,* 437–439.

Winters, J., Christoff, K., & Gorzalka, B. B. (2009). Conscious regulation of sexual arousal in men. *Journal of Sex Research, 46*(4), 330–343.

Witte, S. S., El-Bassel, N., Gilbert, L., Wu, E., & Chang, M. (2010). Lack of awareness of partner STD risk among heterosexual couples. *Perspectives on Sexual and Reproductive Health, 42,* 49–55.

Wlodarski, R., & Dunbar, R. I. M. (2013). Examining the possible functions of kissing in romantic relationships. *Archives of Sexual Behavior.* doi: 10.1007/s10508-013-0190-1.

Woertman, L., & van den Brink, F. (2012). Body image and female sexual functioning and behavior: A review. *Journal of Sex Research, 49*(2–3), 184–211.

Wolf, R. (2014a, June 25). Year after gay marriage ruling, a changed land. *USA Today,* p. 1A.

Wolf, R. (2014b, December 29, 2014). Heroine of gay-marriage movement feels pride in progress. *Indianapolis Star,* p.4B.

Wolf, R., & Heath, B. (2015a, June 28, 2015). History made in 33 pages. *USA Today,* p. B1, B3.

Wolf, R., & Heath, B. (2015b, June 27, 2015). Marriage for all. *USA Today,* p. B1

Wolitski, R. (2005). The emergence of barebacking among gay men in the United States: A public health perspective. *Journal of Gay and Lesbian Psychotherapy, 9,* 13–38.

Womenshealth.gov. (2014). Date rape drugs fact sheet. Available: http://www.womenshealth.gov/publications/our-publications/fact-sheet/date-rape-drugs-html. (Last visited: 9/22/2014).

Wonderlich, S. A., et al. (2000). Relationship of childhood sexual abuse and eating disturbances in children. *Journal of the American Academy of Child & Adolescent Psychiatry, 39,* 1277–1283.

Wood, J. M., Koch, P. B., & Mansfield, P. K. (2006). Women's sexual desire: A feminist critique. *Journal of Sex Research, 43,* 236–244.

Wood, M. L., & Price, P. (1997). Machismo and marianismo: Implications for HIV/AIDS risk reduction and education. *American Journal of Health Sciences, 13*(1), 44–52.

Wood-Barcalow, N. L., Tylka, T. L., & Augustus-Horvath, C. L. (2010). "But I like my body": Positive body image characteristics and a holistic model for young-adult women. *Body Image, 7,* 106–116.

Woodworth, T. W. (1996). DEA congressional testimony. Available: http://www.usdoj.gov/dea/ (Last visited 2/6/97).

Working Group for a New View of Women's Sexual Problems. (2001). A new view of women's sexual problems. In E. Kaschak & L. Tiefer (Eds.), *A new view of women's sexual problems.* New York: Haworth Press.

World Health Organization (WHO). (2006). Defining sexual health. Available: http://www.who.int/reproductive-health/publications/sexualhealth (Last visited 9/10/08).

World Health Organization (WHO). (2010.6a). Developing sexual health programmes: A framework for action. Available: http://whqlibdoc.who.int/hq/2010/WHO_RHR_HRP_10.22_eng.pdf (Last visited 7/6/11).

World Health Organization (WHO). (2010.14a). *International statistical classification of diseases and related health problems.* Available: http://www.who.int/classifications/icd/en (Last visited 4/4/12).

World Health Organization (WHO). (2011). Genomic Resource Center. Available: http://www.who.int/genomics/en (Last visited 6/7/11).

World Health Organization (WHO). (2014.12a). Male circumcision for HIV prevention. Available: http://www.who.int/hiv/topics/malecircumcision/en/

World Health Organization (WHO). (2014.13a). Female genital mutilation. Available: http://www.who.int/mediacentre/factsheets/fs241/en/ (Last visited 1/15/15).

World Health Organization (WHO). (2014.16a). Global Health Observatory Map Gallery: World: Adult HIV prevalence (15–49 years), 2013—By WHO region. Available: http:gamapserver.who.int/mapLibary/app/searchResults.aspx (Last visited 12/27/14).

World Health Organization (WHO). (2014.16b). Fact sheet: HIV/AIDS. Available: http://www.who.int/mediacentre/factsheets/fs360 (Last visited 12/27/14).

World Health Organization (WHO). (2014.16c). Global update on the health sector response to HIV, 2014. Geneva, Switzerland: WHO.

World Professional Association for Transgender Health. (2012). Version 7. *Standards of care for the health of transsexual, transgender, and gender-non-conforming people.* Available:

http://www.wpath.org/uploaded_files/140/files/Standards%20of%20Care,%20V7%20Full%20Book.pdf (Last visited 6/12/15).

Wortman, L., & van den Brink, F. (2012). Body image and female sexual functioning and behavior: A review. *Journal of Sex Research, 49*(2), 184–211.

Wright, P. J. (2013). U.S. males and pornography, 1973–2010: Consumption, predictors, correlates. *Journal of Sex Research, 50,* 60–71.

Wyatt, G. E., Williams, J. K., & Myers, H. F. (2008). African-American sexuality and HIV/AIDS: Recommendations for future research. *Journal of the National American Medical Association, 100,* 50–51.

Yarber, W. L. (1992). While we stood by . . . the limiting of sexual information to our youth. *Journal of Health Education, 23,* 326–335.

Yarber, W. L. (2003). *STDs and HIV: A guide for today's teens.* Reston, VA: American Association for Health Education.

Yarber, W. L., & Crosby, R. A. (2011). Rural and non-rural Indiana residents' opinion about condoms for HIV/STD prevention. *Health Education Monograph, 28*(2), 46–53.

Yarber, W. L., & Sayad, B. W. (2010). Sexuality education for youth in the United States: Conflict, content, research and recommendations. *Kwartalnik Pedagogiczny, 2*(216), 147–164.

Yarber, W. L., Crosby, R. A., & Sanders, S. A. (2000). Understudied HIV/STD risk behaviors among a sample of rural South Carolina women: A descriptive pilot study. *Health Education Monograph Series, 18,* 1–5.

Yarber, W. L., Graham, C. A., Sanders, S. A., Crosby, R. A., Butler, S. M., & Hartzell, R. M. (2007). "Do you know what you're doing?" College students' experiences with male condoms. *American Journal of Health Education, 38,* 322–331.

Yarber, W. L., Milhausen, R. R., Crosby, R. A., & Torabi, M. R. (2005). Public opinion about condoms for HIV and STD prevention: A midwestern telephone survey. *Perspectives on Sexual and Reproductive Health, 37*(3), 148–154.

Yarber, W. L., Milhausen, R. R., Huang, B., & Crosby, R. A. (2008). Do rural and non-rural single, young adults differ in their risk and protective HIV/STD behaviors? Results from a national survey. *Health Education Monograph, 25,* 7–12.

Yarber, W. L., Torabi, M. R., & Veenker, H. C. (1989). Development of a three-component sexually transmitted diseases attitude scale. *Journal of Sex Education and Therapy, 15,* 36–49.

Yarnall, K. S. H., McBride, C. M., Lyna, P., Fish, L. J., Civic, D., Grothaus, L., et al. (2003). Factors associated with condom use among at-risk women students and nonstudents seen in managed care. *Preventive Medicine, 37,* 163–170.

Ying, Y., & Han, M. (2008). Cultural orientation in Southeast Asian American young adults. *Cultural Diversity and Ethnic Minorities Psychology, 14*(1), 29–37.

Younger, J., Aron, A., Parke, S., Chatterjee, N., & Mackey, S. (2010). Viewing pictures of a romantic partner reduces experimental pain: Involvement of neural reward systems. *PloS One.* Available: http://www.plosone.org/article/info%3Adoi%2F10.1371%2Fjournal.pone.0013309 (Last visited 3/22/11).

Youth Risk Behavior Survey, 2013. (2014). Centers for Disease Control and Prevention, *Morbidity and Mortality Weekly Report.* Available: http://www.cdc.gov/mmwr/pdf/ss/ss6304.pdf (Last visited 1/26/15).

Zawacki, T., Abbey, A., Buck, P. O., McAuslan, P., & Clinton-Sherrod, A. M. (2003). Perpetrators of alcohol-involved assaults: How do they differ from other sexual assault perpetrators and nonperpetrators? *Aggressive Behavior, 29,* 366–380.

Zilbergeld, B. (1992). *The new male sexuality.* New York: Bantam Books.

Zilbergeld, B. (1999). *Male sexuality* (Rev. ed.). Boston: Little, Brown.

Zinzow, H. M., & Thompson, M. (2014). A longitudinal study of risk factors for repeated sexual coercion and assault in U.S. college men. *Archives of Sexual Behavior.* doi: 1007/s10508-013-0243-5.

Zivony, A., & Lobel, T. (2014). The invisible stereotypes of bisexual men. *Archives of Sexual Behavior, 43,* 1165–1176.

Zoroya, G. (2013, April 23). Survey: More women in military report sex abuse. *USA Today,* p. 3A.

Zurbriggen, E. L., & Yost, M. R. (2004). Power, desire, and pleasure in sexual fantasies. *Journal of Sex Research, 41,* 288–300.

Name Index

Subject Index

Note: Page references followed by italicized "*f*" or "*t*" refer to figures or tables, respectively.